# Volkswagen

## Beetle
## Karmann Ghia

## Official Service Manual Type 1

## 1966, 1967, 1968, 1969

# Volkswagen
## Service Manuals from Robert Bentley, Inc.

Volkswagen
Beetle and Karmann Ghia Official Service Manual, Type 1
Model Years 1966, 1967, 1968, 1969

Volkswagen
Beetle, Super Beetle and Karmann Ghia Official Service Manual, Type 1
Model Years 1970, 1971, 1972, 1973, 1974, 1975, 1976

Volkswagen
Station Wagon/Bus Official Service Manual, Type 2
Model Years 1968, 1969, 1970, 1971, 1972, 1973, 1974, 1975, 1976

Volkswagen
Fastback and Squareback Official Service Manual, Type 3
Model Years 1968, 1969, 1970, 1971, 1972, 1973

# Beetle
# Karmann Ghia

## Official Service Manual Type 1
## 1966, 1967, 1968, 1969



Volkswagen of America, Inc.

Published and distributed by:

ROBERT BENTLEY, INC.
872 Massachusetts Avenue
Cambridge, Massachusetts 02139

This manual may be purchased at authorized Volkswagen dealers, at selected bookstores and automotive accessories and parts dealers or directly by mail from the Publisher, Robert Bentley, Inc. at the above address.

NOTE TO USERS OF THIS MANUAL

The Publisher encourages comments from readers of this Manual. Such communications have been and will be carefully considered in preparation of further editions of this and other VW Manuals. Please write to Robert Bentley, Inc., at the address on this page.

Library of Congress Catalog Card No. 70-189047
ISBN 0-8376-0416-8



42-01-1192-1

Manufactured in the United States of America

Getting Started 1
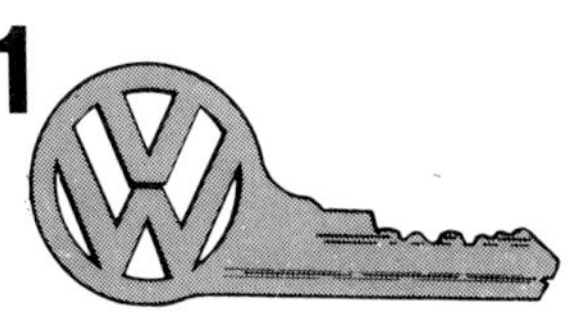

Engine 2
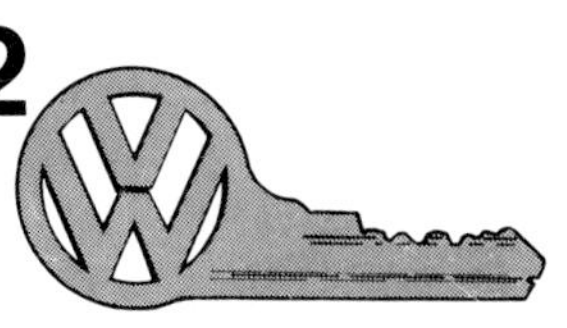

Fuel System 3

Front Axle 4
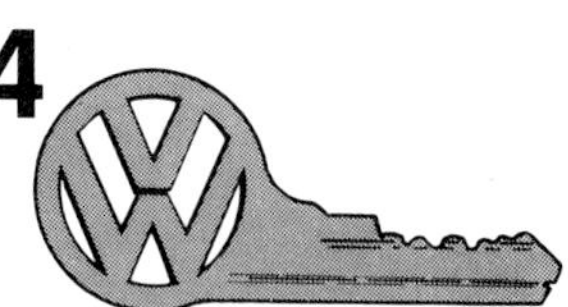

Transmission and Rear Axle 5
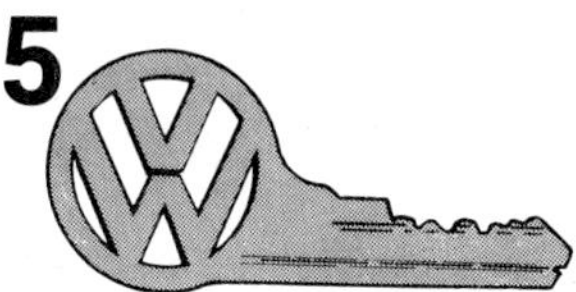

Automatic Stick Shift 6
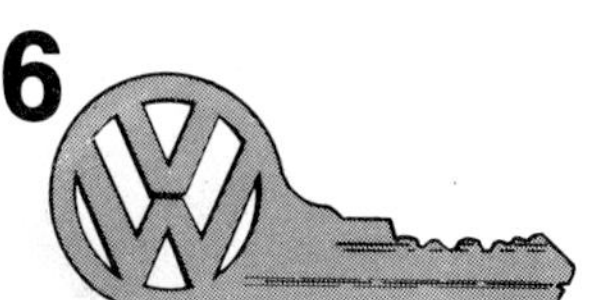

Brakes 7

Lubrication and Maintenance 8
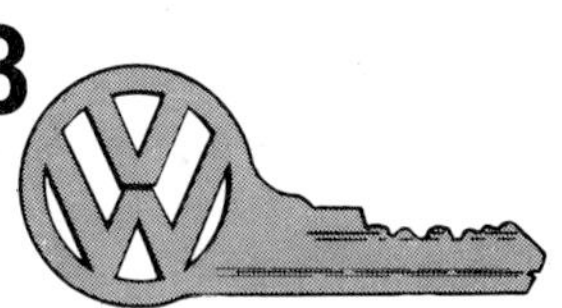

Body and Frame 9
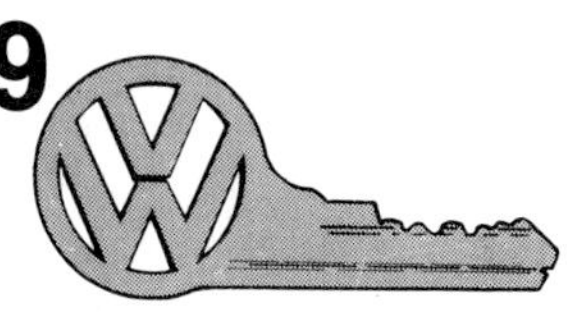

Electrical System 10
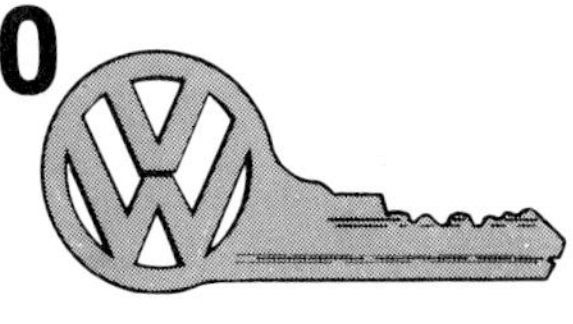

# GETTING STARTED

## Contents

**1. Notes, Cautions and Warnings** . . . . . . . . . . 3

**2. Safety Rules** . . . . . . . . . . . . . . . . . . . . . 3

**3. Use of Manual** . . . . . . . . . . . . . . . . . . . . 3

**4. VW Dealer Diagnosis and Maintenance** . . . . . 4

**5. Scope of Manual** . . . . . . . . . . . . . . . . . . 4

**6. Tools** . . . . . . . . . . . . . . . . . . . . . . . . . 5

**7. Parts** . . . . . . . . . . . . . . . . . . . . . . . . . 6

**8. Taking Care of Your Car** . . . . . . . . . . . . . 6
- 8.1 Care of the Chassis . . . . . . . . . . . . . . 6
  - Washing . . . . . . . . . . . . . . . . . . . . . 7
- 8.2 Care of the Paint . . . . . . . . . . . . . . . 7
  - Washing . . . . . . . . . . . . . . . . . . . . . 7
  - Waxing . . . . . . . . . . . . . . . . . . . . . . 8
  - Polishing . . . . . . . . . . . . . . . . . . . . . 8
  - Removing Tar Spots . . . . . . . . . . . . . 8
  - Removing Insects . . . . . . . . . . . . . . . 8
  - Removing Tree Sap . . . . . . . . . . . . . . 8
  - Touch-up Paint . . . . . . . . . . . . . . . . 8
- 8.3 Caring for Chrome . . . . . . . . . . . . . . 8
- 8.4 Cleaning Windows . . . . . . . . . . . . . . 8
  - Caring for Windshield Wiper Blades . . . . 8
  - Caring for Door and Window Strips . . . . 8
  - Airing the Car . . . . . . . . . . . . . . . . . 8
- 8.5 Cleaning Cloth Upholstery . . . . . . . . . 8
- 8.6 Cleaning Leatherette . . . . . . . . . . . . 8
- 8.7 Seats . . . . . . . . . . . . . . . . . . . . . . . 9
  - Sedan and Convertible . . . . . . . . . . . 9
  - Karmann Ghia Models . . . . . . . . . . . 9
  - Cleaning Safety Belts . . . . . . . . . . . . 9
- 8.8 Caring for Convertible Tops . . . . . . . . 9

**9. Lifting the Car** . . . . . . . . . . . . . . . . . . . 9
- 9.1 Jacking and Supporting . . . . . . . . . . . 9

**10. Production Survey** . . . . . . . . . . . . . . . . 11

**TABLES**

a. Removal of Stains . . . . . . . . . . . . . . . . . 7

b. Production Survey . . . . . . . . . . . . . . . . . 11

# Getting Started

This Manual covers the VW Beetles, convertibles and Karmann Ghia models that were produced for the American market in the years 1966 through 1969. In the Volkswagen classification, these are Type 1 cars.

The period 1966–69 was an interesting one in the development of VW cars. Performance was stepped up. Several major components and systems were redesigned. It was a time of transition. Step by step, the changes carried VW from the early basic Beetle of the 1200 cc engine to the Super Beetle and other advanced cars of the 1970s. Reflecting this trend of change and improvement, the Manual deals with both the 1300 cc and 1500 cc engines, both the swing and double-joint rear axles, both manual and Automatic Stick Shift transmissions. If you master the material in this book, you will not only understand the mechanism of the pre-1966 Beetles but also will have established a groundwork for understanding the more sophisticated mechanisms of the post-1969 cars. Meanwhile, of course, you will be learning how to disassemble, assemble and repair the 1966–1969 Type 1.

A Manual dealing with subject matter of this kind must be written for an audience that represents a wide range of mechanical know-how and experience, from a little to a lot. The Beetle seems to invite tinkering, and the beginner is almost as eager as the expert to accept the invitation. Drivers who have never touched a spark plug seem to feel the itch to grab a wrench and get to work.

But as everyone knows, when you go to work on any car, the Beetle included, safety is of the utmost importance. And it is not just your safety but the other fellow's too.

The detailed and explicit instructions we give in this book are the procedures the VW factory has prepared for VW mechanics and Authorized VW Dealer workshops. But in outlining for you these approved methods of working on VW cars, the point we try to emphasize above all is that work on any car calls for caution. The experienced mechanic has one rule that he applies to every job he does. It is an excellent rule for you if you are going to work on your VW. This basic guiding principle is: DON'T FORCE IT.

1

## 1. NOTES, CAUTIONS AND WARNINGS

Throughout this Manual you will come on a good many indented passages headed **NOTE** or ***CAUTION*** or ***WARNING.*** These headings have different meanings. A **NOTE** contains information you will need to keep in mind while you are performing the specific task under discussion. A ***CAUTION*** is stronger. ***CAUTION*** calls attention to information you need to keep from damaging your car when you do the job under discussion. ***WARNING,*** strongest of the three, advises of the possibility of injury.

Read all the **NOTEs,** ***CAUTIONs*** and ***WARNINGs.*** You will find some ***CAUTIONs*** and ***WARNINGs*** repeated. Read them all. Never skip over a ***CAUTION*** or a ***WARNING.*** Even if you do not intend to work on your car, you will profit from these ***CAUTIONs*** and ***WARNINGs.*** The information in them is valuable to anyone who has anything to do with cars.

## 2. SAFETY RULES

***WARNING —***

- Never work under a lifted car unless it is solidly supported on stands intended for the purpose. Do not support a car on cinder blocks or hollow tile or props of any material that might crumble under continuous load.
- If you are going to work under a car on the ground, make sure that the ground is level. Block the wheels to keep the car from rolling. Disconnect the battery ground strap to keep someone from carelessly or inadvertently starting the engine.
- Keep on your toes when you work around a running engine. Alertness will save you a mangled hand or even worse.
- Never run an engine in an inadequately ventilated place. Carbon monoxide kills.
- Tie long hair behind your head. Snagging your hair in the fan belt could break your neck.
- Never wear a necktie or necklace or loose clothing when you work on your car. Take off all jewelry.
- Never smoke when you are near fuel or fuel containers (including the fuel tank of your car). Clear the area of everything that might ignite the fuel. Get approved fire extinguishers and always keep one or more within reach.
- Never store fuel, brake fluid, oil or cleaning solvents in any food or drink container. Someone might by mistake take a drink from it. Do not use containers that might lead you to intermix any of these fluids.
- Always disconnect the battery before you start work on fuel system or electrical system of your car.

***CAUTION —***

- Use only replacement parts that meet VW specifications.
- Use tools appropriate to the work at hand.
- Use pneumatic tools only to loosen fasteners or attachments. Never use a pneumatic tool to tighten a fastener.
- If you lack the proper tools or have doubts of your ability to do the job correctly, take your car to your local Authorized VW Dealer.
- Before you start a job, be sure that you have the recommended tools and all the parts you will need.
- Read the instructions thoroughly and follow them carefully. Don't attempt shortcuts.
- Light your working area adequately. Have a portable safety light for working inside the car.
- Always have a container at hand to catch fuel, oil or other fluid you are draining from the car. When the fluid has been drained, remove it to a safe place, away from fire hazards. Spilled gas and oil damage asphalt and create fire hazards. Wipe up spills at once. But don't store oily rags—they can burn spontaneously.
- Be mindful of the environment and ecology. Before you drain the crankcase, find out the proper way to dispose of the oil. Do not pour oil on the ground, down a drain or in a stream, pond or lake. Consult the local ordinances on disposal of wastes.

Carelessness can lead to damage to your car, destruction of other property, injury to yourself or others. Incorrect servicing or sloppy adjustments can change the performance of your car. Improper tuning can reduce the effectiveness of the emission control system. Shortcuts or other careless workmanship may impair the dependability and even the safety of your Volkswagen.

If you are going to work on a car, keep one rule uppermost in your mind at all times:

SAFETY FIRST!

## 3. USE OF MANUAL

The do-it-yourself mechanic usually expects to save some money in repairs while he is having the fun and satisfaction of working on his own car. For him this Manual offers VW-recommended maintenance and repair procedures. But the ordinary driver, who may never venture beyond a simple tune-up or even attempt tinkering at all, also can profit from the theory and practical instruction in this book. He can learn to recognize when his car needs attention. He can learn how the car works.

This knowledge should increase the fun he finds in driving and certainly will help him to avoid trouble. He will be in a better position to have repairs made before damage has been caused. Furthermore, when he does take his car to one of the many Authorized VW Dealers, he will have the satisfaction of being able to understand what has been done to his car and why.

## 4. VW Dealer Diagnosis and Maintenance

The Authorized VW Dealer is the man best equipped to handle any problems you may have with your car. Even if you feel capable of doing the work yourself, you can use the VW Diagnosis and Maintenance System to tell you what probably is wrong with the car or to corroborate your own diagnosis. Every VW owner is invited to make use of the service. The great advantage if you are a do-it-yourselfer is that the diagnostic data can help you to fix the right things and not waste your time, money or effort replacing parts that do not need replacement.

The Authorized VW Dealer has, of course, a complex battery of diagnostic instruments which not many do-it-yourselfers (if any) are likely to have. New developments are adding to this diagnostic capability all the time, but the needs of the man who owns an older car are not being neglected. Even the latest diagnostic equipment for the advanced VW cars of the 1970s has an interface for the older cars.

There is another aspect of the home repair job in which the cooperation of your VW Dealer is essential. If you are going to do the job right and obtain a safe result, you must install the right parts to the correct specifications. Your VW Dealer is the authority here.

> ***WARNING —***
> *Never alter an adjustment on your car or install a replacement part unless you have received assurance from an Authorized VW Dealer that the proposed re-adjustment or the proposed replacement part is both appropriate and safe for your car. The chassis number and engine number of the particular car are needed when this decision is made. Always give the dealer these numbers when you order a part.*

## 5. Scope of Manual

The instructions in this Manual apply only to Type 1 cars of 1966-69 manufactured for the American market. Earlier and later Type 1 cars and the European and other export versions may differ in certain details but not enough to make the Manual altogether useless for owners of those models. All the general descriptions and the discussions of theory in the book will be appropriate, as will many of the procedures for disassembly, assembly and repair. The owner of such a car should, however, be especially careful about proceeding with any specific task on the basis of the information in this Manual. He may want to check with the local Authorized VW Dealer to find out whether the instructions apply to his car.

The VWs of these years that are found in Canada include the same models (with certain modifications) built for export to the United States and also 1966, 1967 and 1968 models with 1200 cc engines. The only significant difference in cars with 1300 and 1500 engines is that the Canadian models have different heaters. Obviously, the Canadian owner of a 1300 or 1500 VW of the years 1966–69 can use this Manual for his guide.

The quickest overall view of the cars covered in this Manual can be obtained by noting the differences that have appeared in the models, year by year. The following is a brief listing of the improvements introduced from 1966 through 1969. Chassis numbers of each model year are given. Engine numbers are distinguished by the serial letter appearing before the digits. The letter "F" precedes the engine numbers for the 50-horsepower 1300 engines on 1966 cars. The letter "H" designates engine numbers on the 53-horsepower 1500 engines powering all the other cars covered in this Manual.

> **NOTE —**
> Engine numbers appear on the flange of the generator support in the rear engine compartment. Chassis numbers are found on the frame tunnel under the rear seat and on the identification plate near the spare tire in the front compartment. In VW nomenclature all the Type 1 cars are Series 100 vehicles and have model numbers beginning with the numeral 1 (113, 114, etc.).

The changes by model year:

**1966** (Chassis numbers 116 000 001 to 116 1 021 298)

© 1972 VWoA—962

1 

1. Increased horsepower (from 40 to 50) and displacement (from 1200 to 1300 cc). Number 1300 on rear lid.
2. Ventilating slots in wheels. Flat hub caps.
3. Emergency flasher switch.
4. Headlight dimmer switch mounted on turn signal lever.
5. Defroster outlet at center of dash.
6. Semi-circular horn ring.

**1967** (Chassis numbers 117 000 001 to 117 844 892)

© 1972 VWoA—963

1. Increased horsepower (from 50 to 53) and displacement (from 1300 to 1500 cc).
2. Single-unit headlights with chrome rims installed in fender recesses.
3. Dual-circuit brake system, with independent operation of front and rear brakes.
4. Back-up lights.
5. Parking light incorporated in front turn signals.
6. Locking buttons on doors.
7. 12-volt electrical system (36-amp battery).
8. VOLKSWAGEN nameplate on engine lid.

**1968** (Chassis numbers 118 000 000 to 118 1 016 098)

© 1972 VWoA—964

1. One-piece bumpers (bows and overriders eliminated, bumper height raised).
2. Head restraints built into front seat backrests.
3. Automatic Stick Shift (option).
4. Fuel tank filler neck outside car (spring-loaded flap).
5. Push-button catch on front hood, louver on front hood air intake.
6. Fresh air ventilating system.
7. Energy-absorbing collapsible steering column.
8. Exhaust emission control system.
9. Flat door handles with built-in trigger release.
10. Back-up and brake lights and rear turn signals combined in single housing.
11. Sticker on door post certifying compliance with all federal safety standards.

**1969** (Chassis numbers 119 000 001 to 119 1 093 704)

© 1972 VWoA—965

1. Rear window defogger and defroster (electric heating wires on inner surface of glass).
2. Double-joint rear axle for better ride and handling.
3. Warning lights on speedometer face identified by letters or other symbols.
4. Ignition lock combined with steering wheel locking device.
5. Lock on fuel tank filler neck flap (release under dash panel on right side).
6. The front hood release was moved to the glove compartment.
7. Day/night rear view mirror.
8. Warm air outlets along floor moved to rear (remote control knobs on door columns).

## 6. TOOLS

Volkswagen relies on an assortment of special tools designed for specific operations on VW cars. Some of these tools duplicate work that can also be done with common tools. The difference is that the special VW tools do the job more easily and with a precision that eliminates tedious repetition of measurement. Other VW tools designed for very precise and specialized measurements or adjustments of VW components are, of course, unique and not adapted to other work.

You will see some of these tools in the illustrations in this Manual. A number of tool companies make them. If you are interested in obtaining any of them, get in touch with any leading manufacturer of tools. If he cannot supply you with VW tools, he should be able to tell you where to get them. VW does not endorse products by brand name but can only recommend a class of product that meets specified requirements.

For the beginner or the home mechanic with only modest experience, a good rule of thumb regarding tools is the following: If the tool shown in an illustration here is more elaborate than the ones you already have and know how to use, take your car to the Authorized VW Dealer and let him do the work this time. Then if you want to pursue the subject, get the specialized tool and by study and practice make sure that you know how to use it.

Minimum equipment for getting a start in the simpler maintenance and repair procedures required to keep your VW in tune would include at least the following tools:

**Tool List**

1. Open end wrenches: 8 mm, 10 mm, 13 mm (2), 17 mm, 19 mm
2. Offset box wrenches: 10 mm, 13 mm
3. Box wrenches: 7 mm, 10 mm, 13 mm, 19 mm, 21 mm
4. a. Sockets: 10 mm, 15 mm, 17 mm, 19 mm, 21 mm, 13/16 inch (12 point spark plug socket, 3/8 inch drive)
   b. Extensions 2½ and 6 inches, 3/8 inch drive
   c. Sliding T-handle (8 inches long maximum), 3/8 inch drive
   d. Ratchet, 3/8 inch drive
5. Torque wrench: 0 to 150 foot-pounds, 3/8 inch drive
6. Phillip's screwdrivers: No. 1 (with magnetic tip), No. 2, No. 3
7. Screwdrivers (flat blade type): 1/8 inch, 3/16 inch, 3/8 inch
8. Pliers, insulated handles
9. Tire pressure gauge
10. Wire type thickness gauge with bending lever, 0.020, 0.024, 0.028 inch
11. Flat type feeler gauge, 0.006, 0.016 inch
12. Hex head wrench: 17 mm
13. Combination instrument or dwell meter, tachometer, and stroboscopic timing light
14. Hand oil can
15. Hand grease gun
16. Oil can opener/spout
17. Support stands, 11 inches high when lowered (2)
18. Drift pin 1/4 inch
19. Funnel, plastic
20. Offset screwdriver (flat blade type)
21. Clamp, fuel line
22. Rubber mallet

The open end and regular and offset box wrenches are sold in size combinations, such as 8 mm on one end and 10 mm on the other end.

As you progress, you no doubt will acquire other tools. Among the possibilities will be a voltmeter, ammeter and ohmmeter, hydrometer, compression gauge, vacuum gauge, and fuel pressure gauge. The use of these is described in appropriate places in this Manual.

## 7. PARTS

VW cars can be counted on to perform satisfactorily only when parts meeting VW specifications have been properly installed in them. This statement assumes that a replacement part meeting VW specifications will be selected by matching its parts number against the chassis number and engine number of the car it is to be installed in.

The owners of cars manufactured in the years covered by this Manual may find that some replacement parts obtained from Authorized VW Dealers are different from the original parts in the car. This situation arises because an improved modified part has been developed as a substitute and the stock of original parts has been allowed to run out. In these instances it is better to accept the modified part. Even if some minor reworking is necessary to obtain a fit, you will find the new part worth the trouble.

With all these preliminaries digested and the cautions and warnings observed, you are now ready to get started. The obvious place to begin, and the one where the least technical skill is required, is on the outside of the car.

## 8. TAKING CARE OF YOUR CAR

Keeping up the appearance of your Volkswagen need not be a burdensome task, but it will require some work on your part and some interest in the properties of paint, enamel, wax, cleaning preparations and so forth.

### 8.1 Care of the Chassis

The factory gave your car a coat of wax-based undersealer to protect the floor plates, axles and undersides of fenders from corrosion. This coat gave good protection for the first six months, but beyond that point mechanical damage from stones, sand and other debris began to leave portions of the chassis exposed. The wax film now should be repaired with one of the commercially available undercoatings. As the need arises, follow up this treatment by having the wheel housings and adjacent parts of the chassis sprayed.

### Washing

The best time to wash the underside of the car is just after it has been driven in the rain. If you use a brush, take care when you are scrubbing near the speedometer cable in the left front wheel and around the hydraulic brake hoses at all the wheels.

## 8.2 Care of the Paint

Even the finest paint needs a certain amount of care. The paint on your car is under constant attack from sunlight, rain, hail, industrial fumes, soot, dirt, rocks, pebbles, and dust. Winter conditions are worst of all. The salts spread on roads to melt snow and ice damage the paint and corrode the metal. Your car needs regular washing and waxing the year around, but in winter it needs this protection more often.

The items listed below have been made especially for your VW and will help you to preserve the beauty of its finish. All these items are available at your local Authorized Volkswagen Dealer. Detailed instructions on how to use them are printed on the containers.

| Application | Volkswagen Product |
|---|---|
| Cleaning car, convertible top, upholstery, whitewall tires | All Purpose Cleaner—ZVW 243 101 |
| Cleaning chrome | Chrome Cleaner and Protection—000 096 061 |
| Cleaning windshield | Windshield Washer Anti-Freeze and Solvent—ZVW 241 101 |
| Polishing paint | Combination Car Cleaner and Wax—ZVW 241 109<br>Paint Polish—000 096 001 |
| Waxing paint | Classic Car Wax—ZVW 246 101 |
| Preserving chrome | Chrome Preservative—000 096 067 |
| Touch-up paint | Touch-up Paint. All Colors |

For instructions on removal of stains see **Table a.**

### Washing

Wash your car with a sponge and clear water. To avoid scratching the paint, rinse the sponge frequently. Do not wash the car in direct sunshine.

### Table a. Removal of Stains

| Stain | Removal of new stains | Removal of old stains |
|---|---|---|
| Oil or grease | Remove with dry, soft cloth, turning cloth several times. Do not make the stain larger by rubbing. Dab discoloration on the surface with a rag moistened with benzine. Rub dry with a soft cloth | Moisten clean, soft cloth with benzine or alcohol and rub spot carefully. Rub dry. Turn cloth several times to avoid spreading stain. |
| Shoe polish | The same treatment as for oil or grease. Turpentine may be used as well as benzine or alcohol | |
| Tar | Remove with VW Combination Car Cleaner or commercially available tar remover. There is no need to wash car after use of VW cleaner, but it may be necessary to wash off solvent in other cleaners. Follow manufacturer's directions | |
| Synthetic resin, cellulose or oil paints | Remove with dry, soft cloth as with oil and grease. Rub remaining stains with rag moistened in water or with a piece of rubber | Moisten cloth with synthetic resin or cellulose thinner, turpentine or benzine and rub spot carefully until dry. For synthetic resin stains use synthetic resin thinner, for cellulose stains cellulose thinner and for oil stains turpentine or benzine. |
| Blood | Moisten a cloth in cold or lukewarm water and dab the stain off. Do not make it worse by rubbing | |
| Rust | Moisten a soft rag with solution of 1 part hydrochloric acid to 9 parts of water and dab rust spots carefully. Do not spread them by rubbing. Do not allow solution to soak into crevices, corners or seams, as more rust will be created. After this treatment wipe off with a rag moistened with clean water to remove all traces of the solution. The rags should be destroyed. | |

If clear water alone is not enough to remove the dirt, use the All Purpose Cleaner with water. After washing, use clear water to rinse away all traces of the All Purpose Cleaner. To avoid spotting, be careful to wipe the car dry.

#### Waxing

Wax your car whenever the finish seems to need it. If water clings in patches instead of rolling off the paint in beads, your car needs to be washed and waxed. When you use Combination Car Cleaner and Wax on your car, you do not need to go through a separate waxing operation afterward.

#### Polishing

When the shine on the paint has dulled and you cannot bring it back with waxing, your car needs polishing. Follow the directions on the manufacturer's label. After polishing, wax the car.

#### Removing Tar Spots

The chemical action of road tar will damage paint. Use a recommended tar remover to remove the tar as soon as possible. Wash away all traces of the remover with a solution of soap powder and water, then rinse.

#### Removing Insects

Use a lukewarm mild solution of soap powder and water to remove dried-on insect remains. Rinse thoroughly.

#### Removing Tree Sap

Certain trees drip in summer and cover parked cars with sticky spots. Wash off the spots with a solution of powdered soap and water. Afterward wax the car.

#### Touch-up Paint

Minor paint damage, such as small scratches and chipping, can be touched up with a paint applicator, available at your Authorized VW Dealer. In the spare wheel compartment you will find a sticker with a number. This number is the code for the paint color on your car, and the paint applicator to match carries the same code number.

### 8.3 Caring for Chrome

Use the recommended chrome-cleaner and polish to clean the chrome parts on your car. For protection, especially in winter, coat the chrome with Volkswagen's Chrome Cleaner and Protection.

### 8.4 Cleaning Windows

Use a sponge with warm water to wash the windows on your car and a chamois to dry them, but be careful not to use the same chamois on the paint. Paint cleaners and polishes are likely to contain silicones, which will cause streaking on the windows. A good windshield cleaner will remove the streaking.

#### Caring for Windshield Wiper Blades

In dry periods windshield wiper blades pick up tar, oil, grease and insects. From time to time take off the blades and scrub them with a hard brush and alcohol or a detergent solution. If the blades still do not clean the windshield properly, replace them (see **ELECTRICAL SYSTEM**).

#### Caring for Door and Window Strips

Weatherstrips seal properly only as long as they remain flexible and undamaged. From time to time coat them with talcum powder or spray them with a silicone preparation.

#### Airing the Car

If your car must remain in a closed garage for any length of time, air the garage occasionally and open the car for an airing of the interior. Regular airing should prevent formation of mold or damp stains.

### 8.5 Cleaning Cloth Upholstery

Use a vacuum cleaner or a fairly stiff brush to clean the cloth upholstery in your car. Remove ordinary spots with a lukewarm solution of soap and water. Treat grease and oil spots with spot remover. Do not pour the cleaner directly on the upholstery but apply with a cloth to avoid leaving rings. Rub spot with a circular motion, working from outside in to center of spot.

> ***WARNING —***
> *Combustible cleaning fluids should be used in well-ventilated places only. Read the container labels carefully and observe all the warnings.*

### 8.6 Cleaning Leatherette

Clean the leatherette parts of the headlining, side trim panels and seats with a soft cloth or brush. If the leatherette is very dirty, use Volkswagen's All Purpose Cleaner. Use dry foam cleaner only on the seats and back rests. Liquid cleaners will penetrate the fabric. Whenever possible, wipe off grease or paint spots before they have a chance to dry. If they have dried, take them off with All Purpose Cleaner. Use turpentine to remove stains from shoe polish, but be careful. If left on too long, turpentine can damage the dust-repellent surface of the leatherette. It will only soak into the material to collect dust and soil your clothes.

## 8.7 Seats

### Sedan and Convertible

To remove the front seats, lift the lever on the right-hand side of the seat and slide seat forward until the spring on the left side of the seat frame can be unhooked. Then slide the seat forward until it stops. Depressing leaf spring on track will then allow seat to slide forward and out. Clean the runners and grease them lightly before re-installing the seat.

To remove the rear seat cushion, push it towards the luggage compartment and then lift it and take it out diagonally. Loosen backrest screws and take out back seat.

To re-install the seat, push it to the rear until the lower seat frame engages behind the edge of the support and then press down. Take care not to damage the seat material.

### Karmann Ghia Models

To remove the front seat of the Ghia coupe, move the locking lever towards the frame tunnel and push the seat forward out of the runners. Clean runners and grease them lightly before putting the seat back.

### Cleaning Safety Belts

Keep safety belts clean. If cleaning is necessary, wash them with a mild soap solution, without removing them from the car.

Do not bleach or dye safety belts. Do not use any other cleaning agents. They may weaken the webbing.

Check that buckles and retractors work smoothly. Check belt webbings and bindings for damage. The belts should always be kept on top of the seat for ready use. Do not permit them to get caught under the seat.

## 8.8 Caring for Convertible Tops

The top cover does not require special care, but you should clean the plastic material of the top regularly. If the top is very dirty, clean it with Volkswagen All Purpose Cleaner or a solution of soap powder in water. You can use a stiff brush on dirt in the grained surface of the material, but be careful not to scratch the paint. After washing the top, rinse the entire car with clear water. Never use paint-thinner, a chlorine-based spot remover or similar preparations on spots in the top material. Such chemicals will damage it. Wipe stubborn spots with a cloth moistened with an appropriate cleaner and then wash well with lukewarm soap solution.

Occasionally clean the pivot points of the top linkage with a dry cloth. Apply a few drops of oil to the pivot points, holding a cloth underneath to catch any drippings. Wipe the points dry.

Squeaks from friction between the rubber weatherstrips and the window frames of the convertible can be stopped by rubbing the strips with talcum powder or spraying with a silicone preparation.

## 9. LIFTING THE CAR

If you are going to do much work on your Volkswagen, you sooner or later will find it necessary to raise the car off the ground. Even if changing a tire at the roadside is the limit of your career as a mechanic, you have to jack up the car. In the interest of safety any lifting procedure, even the simplest one, calls for caution and good equipment.

Lifting the car to a height that allows you to stand up while working underneath requires expensive equipment. To protect yourself from injury and the car from damage, you must be careful at all times when using a lift and observe without fail one particular precaution:

> ***WARNING—***
> *Never attempt to loosen or tighten a wheel bolt or axle bolt when the car is on a lift. The torque you must exert on the bolt may topple the car off the lift. Always have the car on the ground when you loosen or tighten the wheel or axle bolts.*

## 9.1 Jacking and Supporting

Your Volkswagen weighs only two-thirds as much as the average American car but requires the same care in jacking. For jacking it up and supporting it you will need the following equipment:

- Jack (comes with car)
- Long breaker bar (for operating lever-type jack)
- 2 support stands
- 2 wood blocks

The jack (Fig. 1) will be of a type operated by a lever (the breaker bar). Never use a jack that was not designed specifically for the Volkswagen.

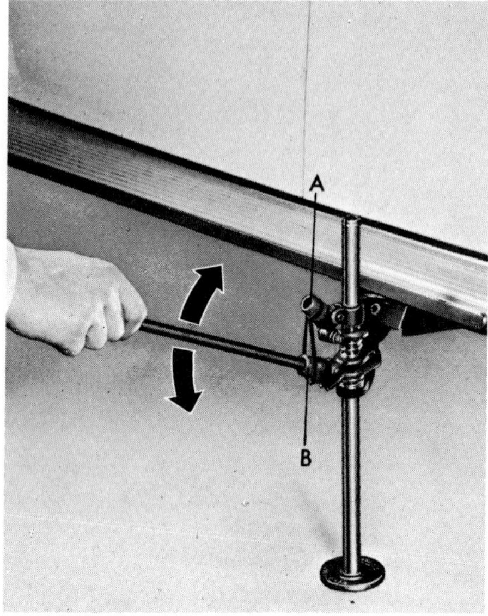


**Fig. 1.** Breaker bar used as lever for jack fits in upper link (A) to raise car, lower link (B) to lower car.

***CAUTION —***
*Because of the VW body construction, bumper jacks and scissor jacks are unsuitable for lifting the cars covered in this Manual.*

Under the running board in front of each rear fender you will find a reinforced socket. These sockets are built into the car to receive the lifting arm of the jack. The sockets are precisely located. When the jacking force is applied at the socket, the front wheel and the rear wheel on that side of the car are lifted off the ground together.

***WARNING —***
*Jacking the car at any point other than the sockets provided for that purpose may damage the car and could lead to an accident resulting in injury.*

The surface on which you rest the jack should be firm and flat. If the car cannot be moved, you may have to clear and level a base for the jack. To spread the load on a soft surface, rest the jack on a 2 x 8 x 8 inches or larger wooden block. Never use concrete or cinder blocks, rocks or tile. These materials may crumble under continuous load.

Before you lift the car, take precautions to prevent it from rolling. Set the parking brake. Use the wooden blocks to block the front and rear wheels (Fig. 2) that will remain on the ground. When you are going to work under the car, disconnect the battery ground strap to prevent accidental starting of the engine.

**Fig. 2.** Wooden blocks against wheels remaining on ground prevent supported car from rolling off stands.

Use the jack only to lift the car. Except in the emergency of a roadside tire change, never rely on the jack to support the car. Never get under the car to work unless it is supported solidly on commercial stands built for the purpose. Do not use concrete blocks, stacked wood or other makeshifts.

The car should always have two wheels on the ground and be supported on two stands (Fig. 3). Lay out your work to fit this position of the car. Most tasks require only one end or one side of the car to be off the ground. If the whole car must be raised, go to your Authorized VW Dealer or to another shop or service station equipped with a lift.

**Fig. 3.** Support stands in place as seen here hold car off ground on one side.

Raising the right or left side of the car enables you to get at both wheels, heater control cable, valve cover and shock absorber.

**To raise left or right side of vehicle:**

1. Drive car to firm, level surface.
2. Set parking brake.
3. Place a block in front and behind each wheel on the side opposite the one to be lifted.
4. Insert jack in socket and lift side of car until it is approximately 1½ inches higher than the top of the support stand on which it will rest.
5. Place support stands under front and rear support points (Fig. 4). Lower car onto stands.

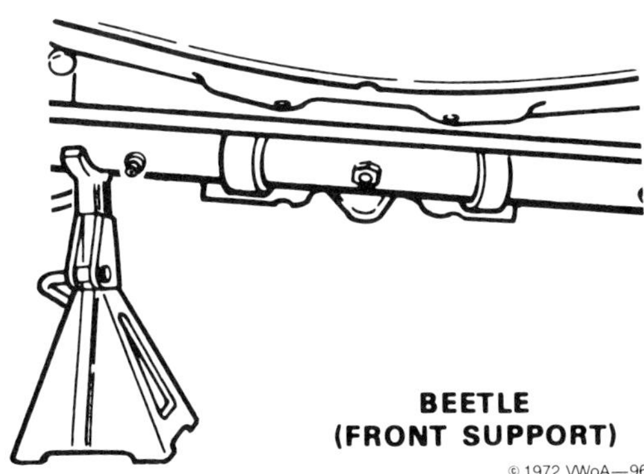


**Fig. 4.** Support point at left front of Beetle is seen here with support stand in place.

6. Check position of stands to be sure that they remain vertical under weight of the car.
7. When work is completed, raise car with jack until it is clear of stands. Remove stands. Lower car to ground.

1

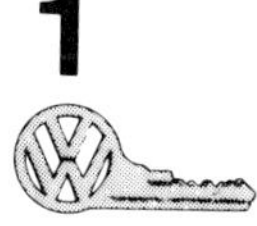

***CAUTION —***
*Always jack car higher than the support stands and then lower car onto stands. This precaution assures you that you will be able to get the car off the stands with the jack when your work is done.*

**To raise front or rear end of vehicle:**

1. Jack up one side of car as in previous procedure.
2. Place support stand under front (rear) support point on that side of car.
3. Lower car onto support stand. Remove jack.
4. Jack up other side of car. Place support stand under front (rear) support point on that side of car.
5. Lower car onto support stand.
6. Place wood blocks in front and behind the rear (front) wheels to prevent car from rolling.

## 10. PRODUCTION SURVEY

Table b gives the chassis numbers and the engine numbers for the cars produced in the Model Years covered in this Manual.

### Table b. Production Survey

| Year | Beetle chassis number | Karmann Ghia chassis number | 1300 cc engine 40 b.h.p. = 50 b.h.p. (DIN) (SAE) | 1500 cc engine 44 b.h.p. = 53 b.h.p. (DIN) (SAE) | 1500 cc engine (M 157)* 44 b.h.p. = 53 b.h.p. (DIN) (SAE) |
|---|---|---|---|---|---|
| August 1965 | 116 000 001 | 146 000 001 | F 0 000 001 | | |
| December 1965 | 116 463 103 | 146 463 103 | F 0 442 242 | | |
| July 1966 | 116 1021 300 | 146 1021 300 | F 0 940 716 | | |
| August 1966 | 117 000 001 | 147 000 001 | | H 0 204 001 | |
| December 1966 | 117 442 503 | 147 442 503 | | H 0 576 613 | |
| July 1967 | 117 999 000 | 147 999 000 | | H 0 874 199 | |
| August 1967 | 118 000 001 | 148 000 001 | | | H 5 000 001 |
| December 1967 | 118 431 603 | 148 398 736 | | | H 5 173 897 |
| July 1968 | 118 1016 100 | 148 999 000 | | | H 5 414 585 |
| August 1968 | 119 000 001 | 149 000 001 | | | H 5 414 586 |
| December 1968 | 119 474 780 | 149 474 780 | | | H 5 648 888 |
| July 1969 | 119 1200 000 | 149 1200 000 | | | H 5 900 000 |

***Engines with Exhaust Emission Control**

# Section 2

# ENGINE

2

## Contents


1. **General Description** . . . . . 5
   - Engine Mounting . . . . . 5
   - Crankcase . . . . . 5
   - Crankshaft . . . . . 5
   - Connecting Rods . . . . . 5
   - Pistons . . . . . 5
   - Cylinders . . . . . 5
   - Cylinder Heads . . . . . 5
   - Camshaft and Valve Gear . . . . . 5
   - Cooling System . . . . . 5
   - Engine Lubrication System . . . . . 5
   - Ignition . . . . . 6
   - Clutch . . . . . 6
   - Automatic Stick Shift . . . . . 6

2. **Removing and Installing Engine** . . . . . 7
   - 2.1 Removing and Installing Engine (manual transmission) . . . . . 7
   - 2.2 Removing and Installing Engine (Automatic Stick Shift) . . . . . 9

3. **Dissassembling and Assembling Engine** . . . . . 10
   - 3.1 Removing and Installing Cover Plates . . . . . 10
   - 3.2 Removing and Installing Engine Rear Cover Plate . . . . . 11
   - 3.3 Removing and Installing Fan Housing . . . . . 12
   - 3.4 Removing and Installing Fan . . . . . 13

4. **Cooling System** . . . . . 13
   - 4.1 Removing and Installing Air Control Flaps 14
   - 4.2 Adjusting Thermostat . . . . . 14

5. **Fan Belt** . . . . . 14
   - 5.1 Checking Fan Belt Tension . . . . . 14
   - 5.2 Adjusting Fan Belt Tension . . . . . 14
   - 5.3 Removing and Installing Fan Belt . . . . . 15
   - 5.4 Removing and Installing Crankshaft Pulley . . . . . 16

6. **Intake Manifold** . . . . . 16
   - 6.1 Removing and Installing Intake Manifold with Preheater Pipe . . . . . 16

7. **Exhaust System** . . . . . 17
   - 7.1 Removing and Installing Muffler . . . . . 17
   - 7.2 Removing and Installing Tail Pipes . . . . . 18
   - 7.3 Removing and Installing Heat Exchangers . . . . . 18

8. **Valve Gear and Cylinder Heads** . . . . . 20
   - 8.1 Removing and Installing Valve Rocker Mechanism . . . . . 20
   - 8.2 Disassembling and Assembling Rocker Arms . . . . . 20
   - 8.3 Removing and Installing Cylinder Heads . 21

9. **Valves** . . . . . 22
   - 9.1 Removing and Installing Valves . . . . . 22
   - 9.2 Reconditioning Valve Stems and Keepers 23
   - 9.3 Replacing Valve Guides . . . . . 23
   - 9.4 Refacing Valve Seats . . . . . 23
   - 9.5 Fitting Valves . . . . . 24
   - 9.6 Refacing Valves . . . . . 25
   - 9.7 Grinding Valves . . . . . 25
   - 9.8 Valve Clearance . . . . . 26
   - 9.9 Adjusting Valves . . . . . 26

10. **Cylinders** . . . . . 27
    - 10.1 Removing and Installing Cylinder . . . . . 27

11. **Pistons and Piston Rings** . . . . . 28
    - 11.1 Piston Rings . . . . . 28
    - 11.2 Removing and Installing Pistons . . . . . 29
    - 11.3 Piston Clearance . . . . . 31

# 2 Engine


**12. Flywheel/Crankcase Assembly** . . . . . . . . . . 32
12.1 Removing and Installing Flywheel . . . . 33
12.2 VW Automatic Stick Shift Drive Plate . . . 34
12.3 Removing and Installing Crankshaft Oil Seal (engine assembled) . . . . . . . . . 34
12.4 Crankshaft End Play . . . . . . . . . . . . 35

**13. Crankcase** . . . . . . . . . . . . . . . . . . . . . 35
13.1 Disassembling and Assembling Crankcase . . . . . . . . . . . . . . . . . 36

**14. Camshaft** . . . . . . . . . . . . . . . . . . . . . 38
14.1 Removing and Installing Camshaft . . . . 38

**15. Crankshaft** . . . . . . . . . . . . . . . . . . . . 40
15.1 Disassembling and Assembling Crankshaft . . . . . . . . . . . . . . . . . 41
15.2 Grinding Crankshaft . . . . . . . . . . . . 42

**16. Connecting Rods** . . . . . . . . . . . . . . . . 43
16.1 Checking and Installing Connecting Rods 43
16.2 Repairing Connecting Rods . . . . . . . 44

**17. Engine Lubrication System** . . . . . . . . . . . 47
17.1 General Description . . . . . . . . . . . . 47
Cold Engine . . . . . . . . . . . . . . . . 47
Warming Engine . . . . . . . . . . . . . . 48
Hot Engine . . . . . . . . . . . . . . . . . 48
17.2 Crankcase Ventilation . . . . . . . . . . . 48
17.3 Removing and Installing Oil Filler and Breather . . . . . . . . . . . . . . . . . 48
17.4 Removing and Installing Oil Strainer (no oil in engine) . . . . . . . . . . . . . 49
17.5 Removing and Installing Oil Pressure Relief Valve . . . . . . . . . . . . . . . . . 50
17.6 Removing and Installing Oil Cooler . . . 50
17.7 Removing and Installing Oil Pump (single and double pump) . . . . . . . . . 51
17.8 Double Oil Pump (Automatic Stick Shift engine) . . . . . . 52

**18. Ignition System** . . . . . . . . . . . . . . . . . 53
18.1 General Description . . . . . . . . . . . . 54
18.2 Ignition Coil . . . . . . . . . . . . . . . . 54
Maintenance of Coil . . . . . . . . . . . . 54
Inspection of Coil . . . . . . . . . . . . . 54
18.3 Distributor . . . . . . . . . . . . . . . . . 54
Vacuum Advance . . . . . . . . . . . . . 55
Centrifugal Advance . . . . . . . . . . . . 55
Spark Advance Malfunctions . . . . . . . 56
18.4 Condenser . . . . . . . . . . . . . . . . . 57
18.5 Maintenance of Distributor . . . . . . . . 57
18.6 Adjusting Contact Breaker Points . . . . 57
18.7 Dwell Angle . . . . . . . . . . . . . . . . 58
18.8 Replacing Breaker Points . . . . . . . . . 58
18.9 Static Ignition Timing (engine not running) 58
18.10 Ignition Timing (engine running) . . . . . 59
18.11 Testing Condenser . . . . . . . . . . . . 59
18.12 Removing and Installing Condenser . . . 60
18.13 VW Distributor . . . . . . . . . . . . . . 60
18.14 Maintenance of VW Distributor . . . . . . 61
18.15 Removing and Installing Distributor . . . 61
18.16 Removing and Installing Distributor Drive Shaft . . . . . . . . . . . . . . . . . . . 62
18.17 Disassembling and Assembling Distributor . . . . . . . . . . . . . . . . . 63
18.18 Checking Distributor on Test Stand . . . 64
18.19 Spark Plugs . . . . . . . . . . . . . . . . 64
Types . . . . . . . . . . . . . . . . . . . 64
Maintenance and Inspection . . . . . . . 65

**19. Clutch** . . . . . . . . . . . . . . . . . . . . . . 65
19.1 Operation . . . . . . . . . . . . . . . . . 66
19.2 Adjustments . . . . . . . . . . . . . . . . 66
19.3 Removing and Installing Clutch . . . . . 66
19.4 Clutch Release Bearing . . . . . . . . . . 67
19.5 Disassembling and Overhauling Clutch (coil spring type) . . . . . . . . . . . . . 69
19.6 Troubleshooting the Clutch . . . . . . . . 70
19.7 Assembling and Adjusting Clutch . . . . 70

**20. Repairing Tapped Holes** . . . . . . . . . . . . 72

**21. Bench Testing Engine** . . . . . . . . . . . . . 72
21.1 Preparation for Testing . . . . . . . . . . 72
21.2 Starting Engine . . . . . . . . . . . . . . 73
21.3 Bench Procedure . . . . . . . . . . . . . 73
21.4 Checks on Bench . . . . . . . . . . . . . 73
21.5 Final Inspection . . . . . . . . . . . . . . 73
Checking for Oil Leaks . . . . . . . . . . 73
Re-check . . . . . . . . . . . . . . . . . 73
21.6 Partly Reconditioned Engines . . . . . . 73
21.7 Storage of Engines . . . . . . . . . . . . 73
21.8 Testing Engines with Automatic Stick Shift . . . . . . . . . . . . . . . . . . . . 73
21.9 Fuel Consumption Tests on Dynamometer . . . . . . . . . . . . . . . 74

**22. Engine Technical Data** . . . . . . . . . . . . . 75
I. General Description . . . . . . . . . . . . 75
II. Introduction Dates of Engine Modifications . . . . . . . . . . . . . . . . 76
III. Tolerances and Wear Limits . . . . . . . . 77
IV. Performance Data . . . . . . . . . . . . . 81
V. Tightening Torques . . . . . . . . . . . . 81


**TABLES**


a. Specifications for Regrinding Valves . . . . . . . 25
b. Specifications for Regrinding Crankshaft . . . . . 42
c. Distributor Specifications . . . . . . . . . . . . . 55
d. Clutch Troubleshooting . . . . . . . . . . . . . . 71

# Engine

2

The four-cycle engine in the VW cars covered in this Manual is air-cooled and rear-mounted and has two pairs of opposed cylinders with overhead valves. Two models of this engine, the 1300 and the 1500, power the Beetles and Karmann Ghias produced through the years 1966–1969. Though the two engines differ in displacement and performance, they have the same design and except to a trained eye look alike. Fig. 1 gives two cutaway views of the 1500 engine.

The actual specifications of the two engines in displacement and brake horsepower are, respectively:

1285 cc (78.3 cubic inches) 50 SAE bhp
1493 cc (91.1 cubic inches) 53 SAE bhp

The 1300 engine dates from August 1965, and the 1500 from August 1966. It should be noted that cars equipped with Automatic Stick Shift have engines that differ in some respects from the standard 1500 engine. These differences are illustrated and described in appropriate sections of the Manual.

The similarities in design of the 1300 and 1500 engines lead to similarities in the procedures for removal and installation, assembly and disassembly and repair. Where differences exist, they will be pointed out. But for all the improvements that have been made over the years, the design of the engine remains basically the same, and the person who understands one version of it will have no difficulty understanding later models.

Some of the procedures outlined in this section on the Beetle engine will be beyond the capability of the average car owner because he will not have the required equipment. The subsection "Bench Testing Engine" is an example. Only the experienced mechanic in a well-equipped shop can make immediate use of this kind of information, but we hope that the enthusiastic car owner will find something of interest, too. Anything that enlarges his knowledge of the car will increase the pleasure he finds in driving.

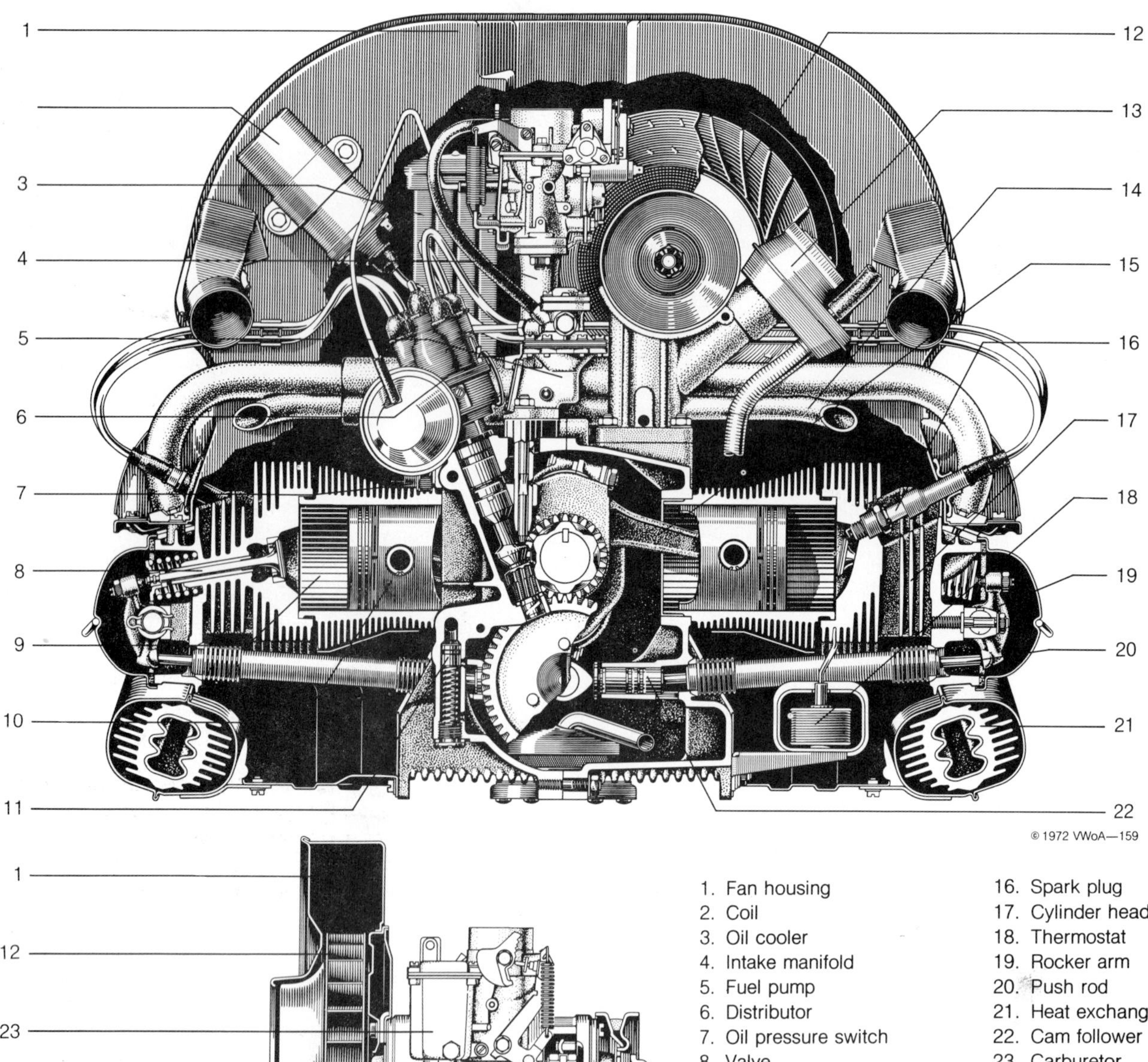


1. Fan housing
2. Coil
3. Oil cooler
4. Intake manifold
5. Fuel pump
6. Distributor
7. Oil pressure switch
8. Valve
9. Cylinder
10. Piston
11. Oil pressure relief valve
12. Fan
13. Oil filler
14. Pre-heating pipe
15. Connecting rod
16. Spark plug
17. Cylinder head
18. Thermostat
19. Rocker arm
20. Push rod
21. Heat exchanger
22. Cam follower
23. Carburetor
24. Generator
25. Flywheel
26. Crankshaft
27. Oil pump
28. Camshaft
29. Oil strainer
30. Clutch

**Fig. 1.** The 1500 engine, which powers 1967–69 cars covered in this Manual, is shown here as seen from the rear of the car (above) and from the left side (below). Comparable views of the earlier 1300 engine would show a voltage regulator attached to the generator but few other noticeable differences. The regulator for the 1500 engine is installed elsewhere in the car, depending on the model.

## 1. GENERAL DESCRIPTION

To give you a quick overview of the VW engine and its operation before you tackle any of the adjustment or repair procedures, we will devote a few paragraphs to a brief description of the major engine components and systems. In this discussion we will go from one component or system to the next in an order that seems to give the clearest and most easily understood picture of the engine. We will not, however, attempt to preserve this same order through the **ENGINE** section. Actual workshop procedures often will dictate quite different sequences, and, of course, we must follow those procedures.

### Engine Mounting

Two studs and two bolts attach the engine to the transmission case at the rear of the car.

### Crankcase

The split crankcase is a pressure die casting of lightweight magnesium alloy. For close fit the halves are machined together. Replacements must be made in these machined pairs. Single halves are not available as replacement parts.

### Crankshaft

The forged crankshaft, which is heat-treated at all bearing journals, turns in four lead-coated aluminum alloy bearings. The No. 1 bearing (counted from the clutch end) takes up the crankshaft end-thrust. The No. 2 bearing is a split shell.

The flywheel carries the starter ring gear. A gland nut and four dowel pins in the crankshaft hold the flywheel and fix its position. A Woodruff key in a slot in the crankshaft secures the timing gear and distributor drive gear. Another Woodruff key fixes the position of the crankshaft pulley on the shaft, and a bolt secures it.

The clutch end of the crankshaft has an oil seal. The pulley end has an oil thrower and an oil return thread.

### Connecting Rods

The four H-section connecting rods are steel forgings. The rod bearings on the crankshaft are three-layer shells. The bearings on the piston pins at the other ends of the rods are steel bushings with lead-bronze coating.

### Pistons

The aluminum alloy pistons have three rings. The upper two are compression rings. The bottom one is the oil scraper ring. The piston pins are full-floating. A circlip at each end of a pin secures it laterally in the bore.



### Cylinders

The four cast iron cylinders are identical. Any cylinder in the engine can be replaced with a new cylinder and matching piston assembly. It is not necessary to replace cylinders in sets or pairs.

The cylinders have large fins for cooling.

### Cylinder Heads

Each pair of cylinders has a cast aluminum alloy cylinder head. These castings also have fins for cooling. Valve seat inserts are shrunk into place in cylinder head. No gasket is used between cylinder and cylinder head.

### Camshaft and Valve Gear

The camshaft runs in three split, steel-backed aluminum alloy bearings, driven from the crankshaft by helical gearing. The No. 3 bearing has a shoulder to take up the thrust. The camshaft gear is riveted to the shaft. Lobes on the camshaft drive the cam followers, push rods and rocker arms to operate the valves. Each lobe operates one valve in each cylinder of an opposed pair.

### Cooling System

A radial fan turning with the generator on the armature shaft draws cool air into the engine compartment. Power for the fan (and the generator) comes from the crankshaft by means of an adjustable V-belt. The fan spins at approximately twice engine speed.

The fresh air drawn in by the fan comes through an opening in the fan housing. Deflector plates in the fan housing and around the cylinders direct this air stream past the large cylinder fins to bleed off cylinder heat. A thermostat controlling four air flaps regulates the volume of air flow into the cylinder ducting. The flaps close for cold engine starts and open as the engine warms up to operating temperature.

### Engine Lubrication System

A pressure feed system with an oil cooler in the circuit lubricates the VW engine.

The camshaft drives the oil pump, which is of the gear type and is installed in the crankcase at the end of the camshaft. The pump draws oil from the lowest part of crankcase and forces it through the cooler into the oil passages. Some oil goes through the crankshaft main bearings into drillings in crankshaft itself to lubricate the connecting rod bearings. Another flow lubricates the camshaft bearings. Oil also is fed through the hollow push rods to lubricate the rocker arms and valve stems. Cylinder walls, pistons and piston pins are splash-lubricated.

The oil cooler is installed in the fan housing, where it is exposed to the air flow from the fan. When the engine is at operating temperature, all oil from the pump must pass through the cooler before it reaches the various bearings. Even at high engine speeds and high outside temperatures, the cooler keeps the oil temperature low enough to maintain its lubricating properties.

When the oil is cold and thick, the oil pressure relief valve opens to allow some oil to by-pass the cooler and flow directly to the engine.

The automatic oil pressure switch in the line between oil pump and oil cooler operates warning light on driver's instrument panel (Fig. 2). At an oil pressure of 2.1 to 3.6 psi the switch breaks circuit to warning light. Light is on when ignition is on and oil pressure is too low to move a diaphragm and thus break the circuit.

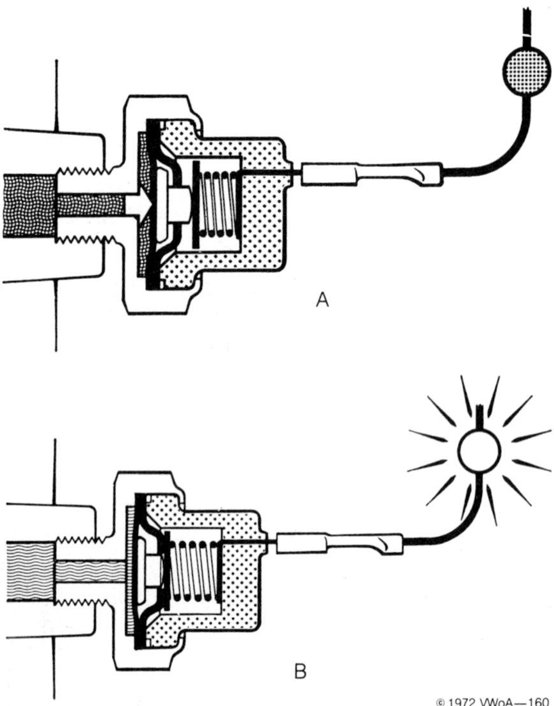


**Fig. 2.** Green or red light glows on the speedometer dial when oil pressure is low. At (A) build up of pressure in oil line at left of oil pressure switch is forcing diaphragm to move (white arrow) to right, breaking circuit. Light goes off. In (B) decrease of pressure allows diaphragm to move to left and close the circuit. Light goes on.

### Ignition

The ignition system consists of the ignition coil, the distributor with condenser and the spark plugs. The coil steps up battery voltage to produce a hot spark at the plug. The distributor directs the flow of electric current to each spark plug in turn and controls the timing of combustion in the individual cylinders for smoothest and most efficient production of power.

### Clutch

A single-plate disk clutch fitted in the flywheel transfers engine power to the transmission. The driven plate is free to slide axially on the splined transmission drive shaft. The clutch cover, the pressure plate and the springs are bolted concentrically to the flywheel face.

### Automatic Stick Shift

VW cars with the Automatic Stick Shift were introduced in 1967, beginning with chassis No. 118 071 448 and engine No. H 0 879 927. The 1500 engine for this transmission has the following modifications:

1. Drive plate instead of flywheel
2. Gland nut without needle bearing or felt ring
3. Double instead of single oil pump
4. Intake manifold with vacuum connection (11.5 mm in diameter) for control valve of the shift clutch servo mechanism
5. Carburetor with vacuum connection (4 mm in diameter) for control valve
6. Rear engine cover plate with hole for oil line
7. Engine secured with four M 10 bolts. Heli-Coil thread inserts in crankcase instead of the two studs of the standard engine
8. Ignition timing at 0 degrees (Top Dead Center).

The drive plate, which takes the place of a flywheel, is attached to the crankshaft with a gland nut (tightening torque 216 ft. lbs.). The torque coverter is secured to the drive plate with four socket head M 8 bolts. These bolts must be removed when engine is taken out of car.

When the gland nut is loosened or tightened, the drive plate is held with a special tool called a retaining ring. A special bracket is attached (Fig. 3) to hold the converter when the Automatic Stick Shift engine is removed from the car.

The double oil pump, like the standard single pump, is driven from the camshaft. In addition to supplying oil to engine, it must also supply oil to torque converter in a circuit separate from the engine circuit. The two pumps are fitted one behind the other, separated by a plate with two oil seals. Oil pump cover houses two connections for converter oil lines and a pressure relief valve. Pressure relief valve prevents converter circuit pressure from rising above 35 to 54 psi (2.5 to 3.8 kg/cm$^2$).

© 1972 VWoA—161

**Fig. 3.** Converter of Automatic Stick Shift engine must be held in place with special bracket when engine is removed from car. Bracket is attached at center of converter and at a bolt, as here.

## 2. Removing and Installing Engine

The car must be raised about 3 feet for removal of the engine. This operation calls for the use of good jacks. A lift will make the job much easier. Some steps of the procedure will be difficult for a man working alone.

> **NOTE—**
> With exceptions to be noted later, instructions for removing Automatic Stick Shift engine follow procedure for standard engine.

In all the instructions that follow, "front of the engine" will mean toward the front of the car. "Rear of the engine" will mean part closest to you when you open the lid of the engine compartment.

### 2.1 Removing and Installing Engine
(manual transmission)

Changes in the cooling system for the 1500 engine and installation of additional components on cars with Emission Control Systems introduced some differences in procedures between the earliest cars covered in this Manual and the later models. Differences will be noted where they occur. Most of them will be self-evident.

**To remove:**

> ***WARNING—***
> *Before you do anything else, disconnect the battery ground strap to prevent arcing at the starter (hot) leads.*

1. On 1500 engines disconnect the carburetor preheating air control cable (Bowden cable).
2. Remove hoses to air cleaner.
3. Remove air cleaner.
4. On models with Emission Control Systems remove throttle positioner.
5. Disconnect cables from generator, coil, oil pressure switch and carburetor. Disconnect back-up light cables at right side of engine.
6. Disconnect accelerator cable from carburetor. Pull accelerator cable guide tube out of fan housing as far as it will go. Pull out exposed portion of accelerator cable behind fan housing.
7. Take off the two air hoses that extend from fan housing to muffler connection on rear cover plate.
8. Remove both intake manifold preheater pipe sealing plates.
9. Remove rear cover plate and heat exchanger inlet stub pipes.
10. Lift vehicle.
11. Pull fuel hose from metal tube on body frame (forward of engine). Plug ends of hose and tube.
12. Disconnect both heater flap cables. On 1966–67 cars be sure to note positions of cables and flaps for correct re-installation.
13. Detach flexible heater ducts from engine and swing them out of the way. On 1968–69 cars be careful not to uncoil the spring-like metal ducts.
14. Remove nuts from the two lower engine mounting studs/bolts (depending on model). See Fig. 4.

2

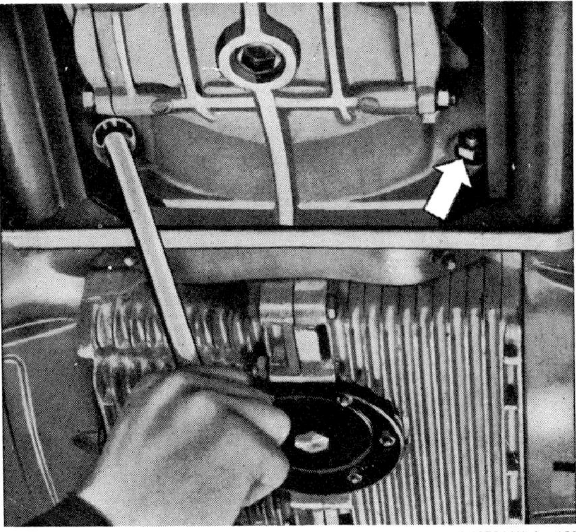
© 1972 VWoA—162

**Fig. 4.** Lower mounting of engine is on two studs/bolts (depending on model). Arrow points to one. Wrench is on nut of other.

15. Lower car until it is about 3 feet from ground. Slide jack under engine.
16. Bring jack up snugly against oil strainer cover.

***WARNING—***
*Jack must be in position before you begin to remove nuts.*

17. Remove nuts from two upper engine mounting bolts (see Fig. 5).

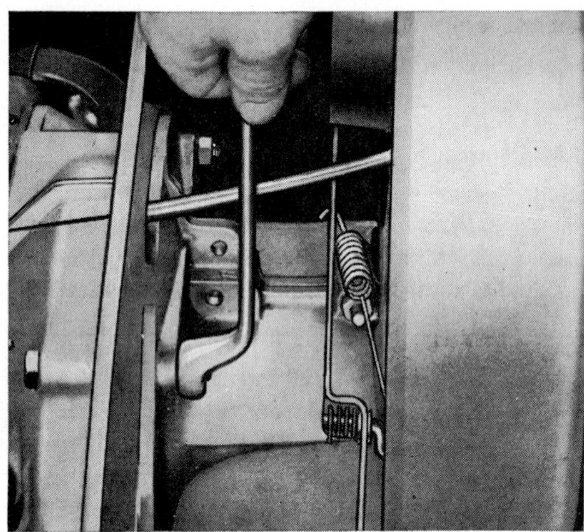

© 1972 VWoA—163

**Fig. 5.** Upper mounting of engine consists of two bolts. Removing nuts is a two-man job on early versions.

**NOTE—**
If you cannot get at the 17 mm securing nuts with the hinged engine hood (lid) in place, you will have to remove the hood. But first try to reach the nuts with a flat ratchet wrench. On 1966–67 cars you will need an assistant to hold the bolts from in front of the engine while you are unscrewing the nuts.

18. Pull engine to the rear until the clutch release plate clears the transmission drive shaft. (The crankshaft pulley will be almost touching the rear cross member.)

***CAUTION—***
*It may be necessary to rock the engine gently to free it from the transmission case, but be careful not to pull the engine too far to the side or too far up or down. You could bend or otherwise damage the drive shaft.*

19. Carefully lower jack and at the same time, pull engine out of car (see Fig. 6).

© 1972 VWoA—164

**Fig. 6.** Suitable jack is required to lower engine from raised car.

**NOTE—**
Before disassembling engine make sure that you clean it thoroughly to avoid damage from dirt deposits.

The installation procedure is basically the reverse of removal, but several additional steps are required.

**To install:**

1. Check clutch release bearing for wear (see **19.3 Removing and Installing Clutch**) and replace if necessary. Spray bearing with molybdenum disulfide lubricant (Moly-Kote®). If old bearing is to be used again, roughen the plastic thrust surface a little with sandpaper and coat with molybdenum disulfide powder.
2. With a clean cloth rub molybdenum disulfide powder lightly on drive shaft splines.
3. Lubricate starter bushing lightly with multi-purpose grease.
4. Clean transmission case and engine flange faces. Check condition of gland nut needle bearing.
5. When inserting engine and guiding it over drive shaft, be careful of the shaft, the clutch disk gland nut needle bearing and the release bearing. The job will be easier if you engage a gear and turn the crankshaft pulley back and forth.
6. To make sure that the splines of the main drive shaft will engage with the splines of the clutch

driven plate, you will have to center the driven plate on the flywheel. The best tool for this task is a pilot made from an old main drive shaft. With pilot inserted through the driven plate, the correct location can be obtained.

7. Position engine over lower studs in the transmission flange. Press engine firmly against flange. Tighten nuts uniformly, starting with upper ones.
8. Adjust clutch pedal for free play (see **19.5 Disassembling and Overhauling Clutch**).
9. Make sure engine seal completely seals rear engine cover plate.
10. Adjust accelerator cable at full throttle.
11. If distributor housing was rotated, adjust timing (see **18.9 Static Ignition Timing** and **18.10 Ignition Timing**).

## 2.2 Removing and Installing Engine
(Automatic Stick Shift)

Several additional procedures are necessary when removing and installing this engine.

**To remove:**

1. Disconnect cable from control valve.
2. Take vacuum hoses off carburetor and intake manifold.
3. Loosen union nut on ATF pressure line to converter and position line to keep ATF from running out.
4. Loosen union nut on ATF suction line and seal line with soldered-up M 16 x 1.5 union nut (see Fig. 7).

© 1972 VWoA—165

**Fig. 7.** Union nut (arrow) on oil suction line must be taken off and line sealed when Automatic Stick Shift engine is removed from car. See text.

5. Remove the four M 8 bolts from drive plate through hole in transmission case. Turn engine with pulley to bring bolts into line with hole.

**NOTE —**
For removal of converter/drive plate bolts engine must be turned to line the bolts up with access hole in transmission case. If this cannot be done it will be necessary to remove engine with converter after first taking off rear engine cover plate. If you follow this procedure, remember to replace the converter oil seal (Fig. 8).

2

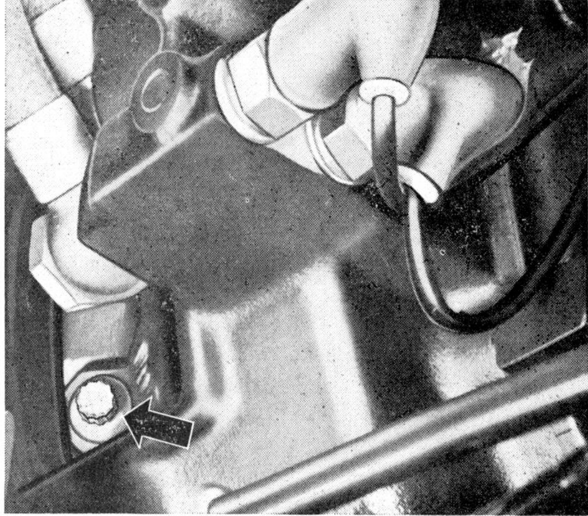

© 1972 VWoA—166

**Fig. 8.** Drive plate bolt (arrow) on Automatic Stick Shift engine must be removed through hole in transmission case.

***WARNING —***
*Before loosening engine bolts, support engine with floor jack and adapter.*

6. When engine has been removed, hold converter with a bracket.

**To install:**

1. Remove bracket before installing engine.
2. Insert upper engine bolts first and tighten nuts lightly. Then tighten lower bolts. Take care not to damage Heli-Coil threaded inserts.
3. When installing converter/drive plate bolts, be careful not to drop a bolt into the transmission case. If you do, you will have to remove the engine again to retrieve it.

4. Tighten bolts to 22 ft.lbs. (3 mkg).
5. Check ATF level of ATF tank and top up if necessary (see **22. Engine Technical Data**).

## 3. DISASSEMBLING AND ASSEMBLING ENGINE

With exception of steps 1, 7 and 10, this procedure can be completed with engine in the car.

### 3.1 Removing and Installing Cover Plates

**To remove:**

1. Remove engine front cover plate (see Fig. 9).
2. Take off air hoses between fan housing and heat exchangers.
3. Remove hose between warm air adapter and air cleaner.
4. Remove crankshaft pulley cover.
5. Remove preheater duct sealing plate.

**Fig. 9.** Cover plates and housings in the engine assembly are indicated here. In disassembly of engine, plates and housings must be removed in sequence given in text. Engine shown is the 1300 of 1966 car.

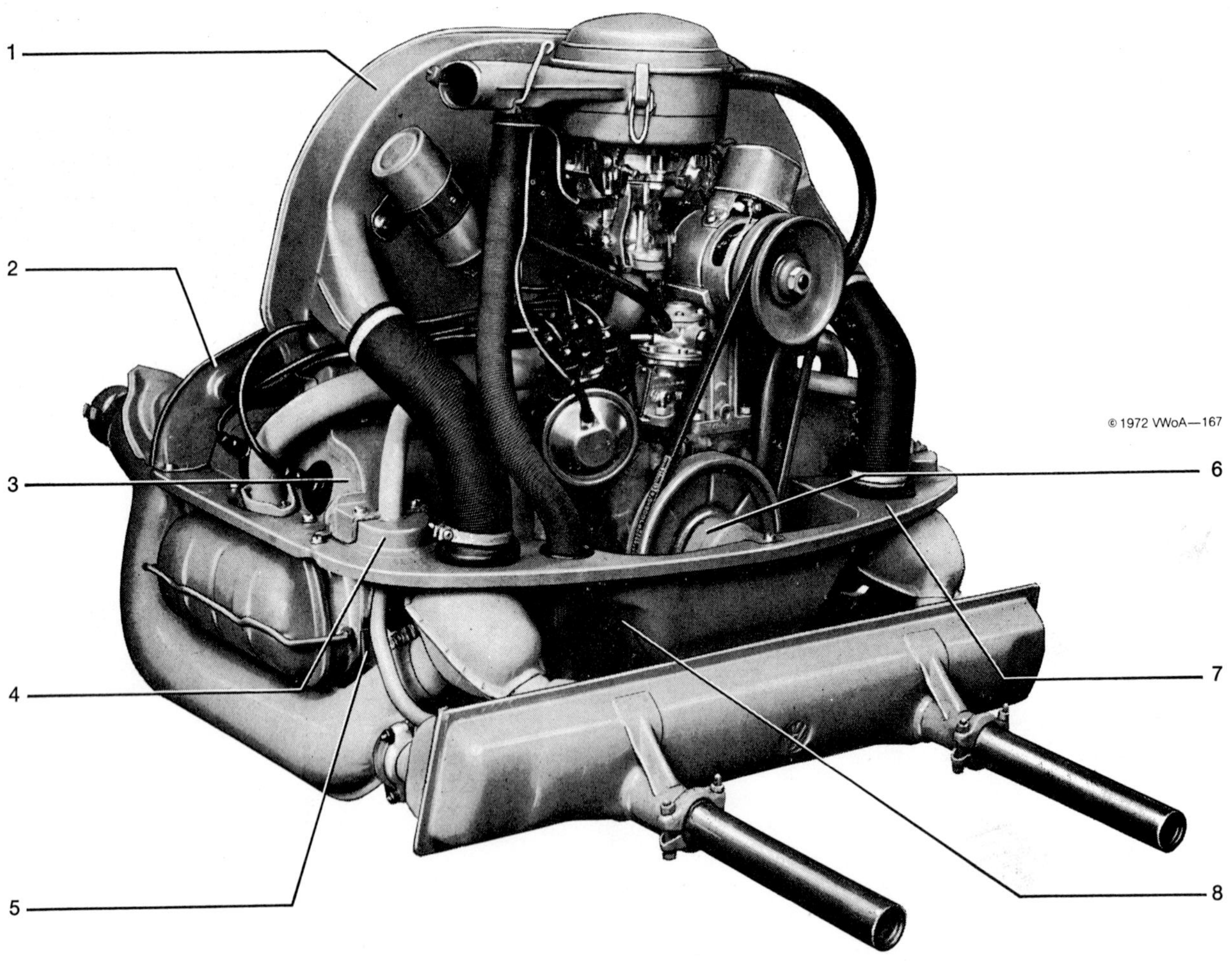


1. Fan housing
2. Front engine cover plate
3. Cylinder cover plate
4. Pre-heater pipe sealing plate
5. Air deflector plate
6. Crankshaft pulley cover
7. Rear engine cover plate
8. Crankshaft pulley lower plate

6. Remove engine rear cover plate.
7. Remove generator and fan housing as unit and air control flaps.
8. Remove intake manifold with preheater pipe.
9. Remove rear air deflector plate and lower part of warm air duct.
10. Lift off cylinder cover plates.
11. Remove plate underneath crankshaft pulley after taking the pulley off.

**To install:**

1. When replacing cylinder cover plates, check the condition and sealing of spark plug rubber caps. Replace caps that are broken or no longer flexible (Fig. 10).

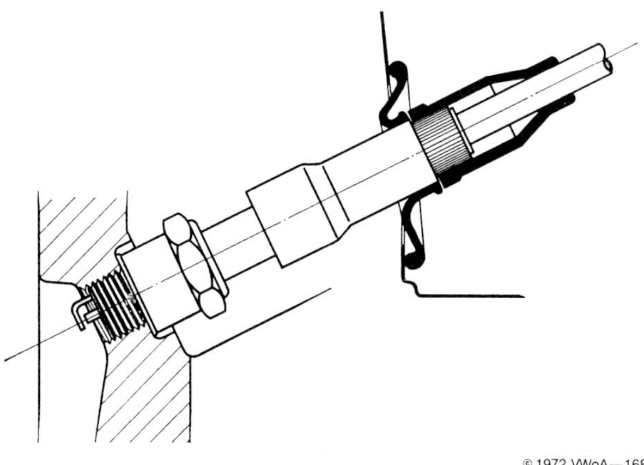


**Fig. 10.** Rubber caps on spark plugs provide tight seals on cylinder cover plates.

2. Make sure that the cylinder cover plates fit snugly on outside of fan housing to prevent loss of cooling air.

## 3.2 Removing and Installing Engine Rear Cover Plate

**To remove:**

1. Take off hoses between fan housing and heat exchangers.
2. Remove carburetor pre-heater hose (or hoses).
3. Remove crankshaft pulley cover.
4. Remove manifold pre-heater pipe sealing plates (Fig. 11).

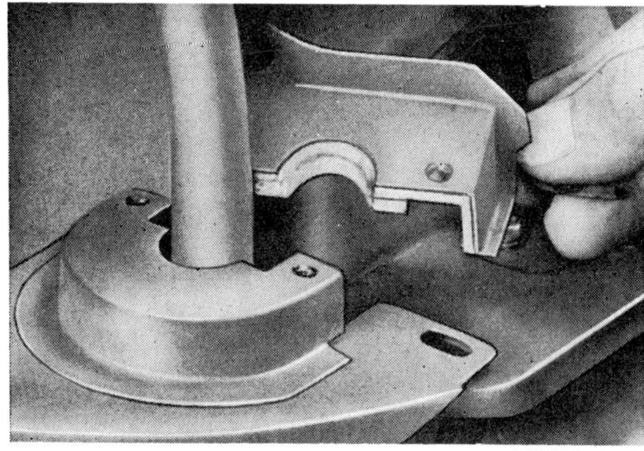


2

**Fig. 11.** Sealing plate for manifold pre-heater pipe has asbestos seal, which can be seen at lower edge of semi-circular opening in the held part.

5. Remove rear engine cover plate (Fig. 12).

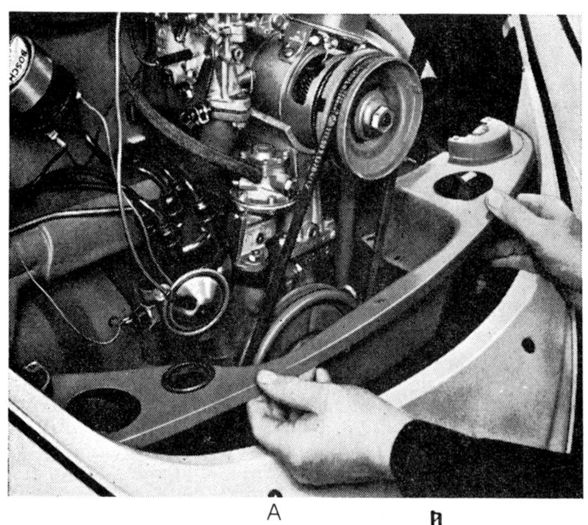


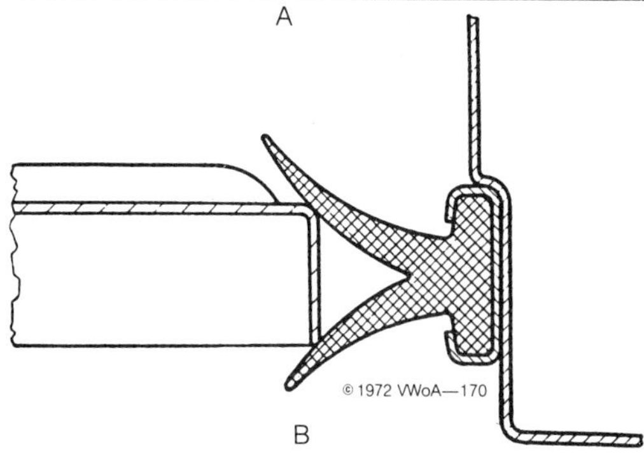


**Fig. 12.** Rubber seal for rear engine cover plate (A) should fit on plate as shown in (B), with one lip over upper edge of plate and other lip below.

**To install:**

1. Check asbestos seal in cover plate and in manifold pre-heater pipe sealing plate.
2. Make sure that cover plate does not touch connections on heat exchangers.

3. Make sure that flat sides of the two rubber grommets are on engine cover plate (see Fig. 13).

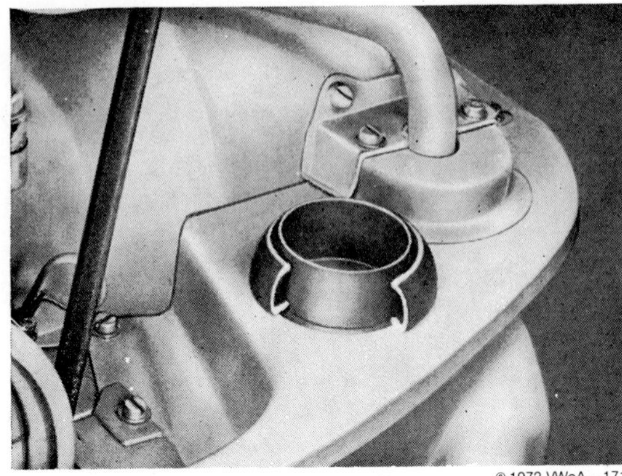


**Fig. 13.** Rubber grommets are installed around hose openings in rear engine cover plate.

4. When engine cover plate is installed, make sure that upper lip of rubber seal is over cover plate and lower lip on lower edge (Fig. 12).

## 3.3 Removing and Installing Fan Housing

**NOTE ——**
Unless specified, all procedures apply only to engine removed from car.

**To remove:**

1. Remove hoses that carry fresh air to heat exchangers.
2. Take off fan belt.
3. Loosen bolt on generator strap. Slide strap forward. If voltage regulator is mounted integrally with generator, pull cable off regulator.
4. Take distributor cap off and pull spark plug connectors off at plugs.
5. Remove screws from both sides of fan housing.
6. On later model cars remove right rear part of lower cooling air duct (flat cover).
7. Insert socket through hole in air deflector plate and disconnect thermostat.
8. After chalking location marks for thermostat bracket to give you the correct position for reinstallation, remove the bracket retaining nut.
9. Unscrew thermostat from connecting rod and remove.
10. Lift off fan housing with generator.

***CAUTION ——***
*Before installing repaired or re-assembled generator, polarize it to give pole shoes residual magnetism of correct polarity. See **ELECTRICAL SYSTEM** for instructions.*

**To install fan housing:**

1. Check housing for damage or loosening of air deflector plates. Replace damaged parts.
2. If you removed the flaps from the fan housing in the previous procedure, re-install them. Check for smooth operation.
3. Insert thermostat connecting rod in hole in cylinder head and lower fan housing.
4. The fan housing must fit closely on the cylinder cover plates to prevent loss of cooling air. If necessary for fit, bend cover plates slightly.
5. Push generator strap onto generator support.
6. Fasten screws on both sides of fan housing and tighten generator strap.
7. Screw thermostat on connecting rod and secure thermostat to bracket with M 8 x 15 bolt (Fig. 14).

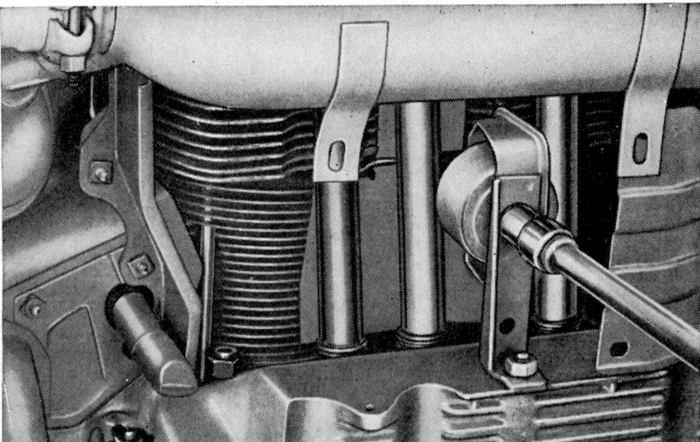


**Fig. 14.** Thermostat, seen here from below, is the cup-like part on a bracket just to right of center of picture. Socket is on bolt that fastens thermostat to lower arm of bracket.

8. Align bracket with the location marks you chalked and tighten securing nut.
9. Install right rear part of lower cooling air duct.

## 3.4 Removing and Installing Fan

The special importance of the fan in the VW cooling system requires precision in all procedures dealing with this component.

**To remove:**

1. Take out the four fan cover bolts with a T-wrench.
2. Remove generator and fan.
3. While someone holds fan, unscrew nut.
4. Remove fan, spacer washers and hub.

**To install:**

1. Place hub on generator shaft. Make sure Woodruff key is properly seated.
2. Insert spacer washers.
3. Place fan in position.
4. Use torque wrench to tighten special nut, 40 to 47 ft. lbs. (5.5 to 6.5 mkg).
5. Check distance from fan to cover. In Fig. 15 clearance "a" = 0.08 inch (2.0 mm). Insert spacer washers between hub and thrust washer to obtain this measurement. Used spacer washers should be placed between thrust washer and fan.

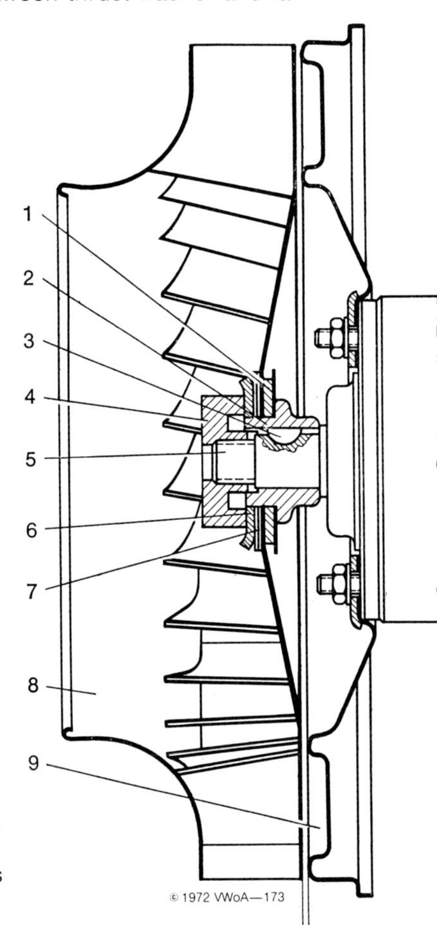


1. Thrust washer
2. Fan hub
3. Woodruff key
4. Special nut
5. Generator shaft
6. Lock washer
7. Spacer washers
8. Fan
9. Fan cover

**Fig. 15.** Fan assembly is shown in this cutaway diagram. The clearance labeled "a" between the fan and the fan cover should be 0.08 inch (2.0 mm).

6. Insert generator in fan housing.
7. Tighten the four cover bolts.

**NOTE —**
The generator with a diameter of 105 mm, which has a separate regulator (see **ELECTRICAL SYSTEM**), must be installed as a unit with the fan cover. Be sure to position the assembly with air slots down.



## 4. COOLING SYSTEM

Cooling system of VW engine is designed to provide maximum flow of cool air around cylinders as soon as engine has warmed up. Key components in this design (Fig. 16) are cooling air flaps and engine thermostat.

The thermostat connecting rod, which you see as part 8 in Fig. 16, ties the flaps and thermostat together. The flaps are spring-loaded to stay open. The thermostat expands or contracts, depending on temperature. When the engine is cold, contraction of the thermostat pulls the flaps shut. When the engine warms up, the thermostat expands. As expansion relaxes the pull of the thermostat, the spring-loading returns the flaps to the normal open position. With the flaps open, air rushes in to cool the engine.

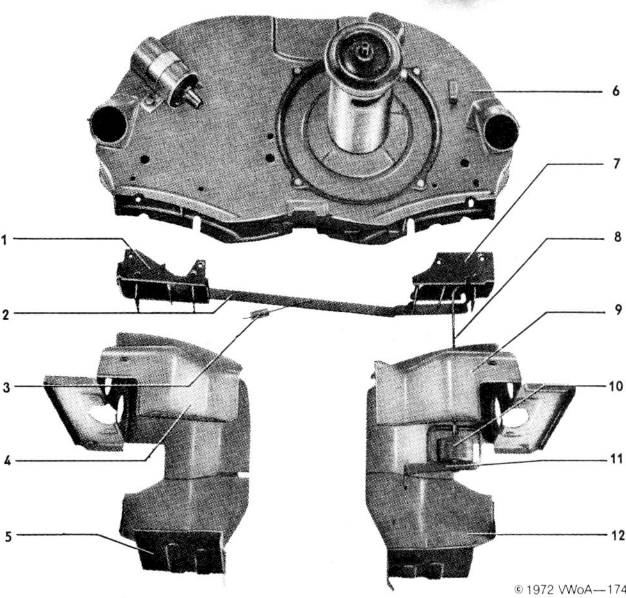


1. Control flaps, left
2. Connecting link
3. Return spring for link
4. Cylinder cover plate, left
5. Air duct, lower part, left
6. Fan housing
7. Control flaps, right
8. Thermostat rod
9. Cylinder cover plate, right
10. Thermostat
11. Thermostat bracket
12. Air duct, lower part, right

**Fig. 16.** Cooling system for the engine includes components shown here, plus the fan.

### 4.1 Removing and Installing Air Control Flaps

Reference to Fig. 16 will help you to follow the procedures for removing and adjusting the flaps.

**To remove:**

1. Unhook connecting link return spring.
2. Remove the eight screws securing control flaps.
3. Remove the two flap housings.

**To install:**

This procedure is the reverse of removal. Make sure that the rubber stop is inserted in the right flap housing.

### 4.2 Adjusting Thermostat

For this procedure the lower air deflector plate (see Fig. 9) is removed.

**To adjust:**

1. Screw thermostat on connecting rod.
2. Loosen mounting nut on thermostat bracket.
3. Press air flaps open. Move thermostat bracket down in its slot until upper arm of bracket is touching top of thermostat. The flaps and thermostat are now in a simulated warm air engine position. Fig. 17 shows the position.
4. Tighten the bracket nut.
5. Move thermostat up, down to test flap operation.
6. Pulling flaps shut, tighten bolt that fastens thermostat to lower arm of bracket.

**Fig. 17.** Thermostat bracket moves (arrows) in slot for adjustment of thermostat and air flaps. Position shown simulates hot engine, with flaps open. Pulling thermostat down to lower arm of bracket closes flaps. See text.

## 5. FAN BELT

The fan belt, powered by the crankshaft pulley, drives the generator and the cooling fan. The belt is under continuous heavy stress, especially at high engine speeds, and is subject to stretching as well as wear. Though the life expectancy of the VW fan belt is very high, you should always carry a spare in your car.

The tension of the fan belt is important. The belt should not be too tight on the two pulleys or too slack. If too slack, it will slip and cause overheating of the engine. If too tight, it may break under the severe stresses. A new belt may stretch slightly in the first 500 or 600 miles. The tension should be checked.

### 5.1 Checking Fan Belt Tension

With your thumb, press the belt at a point midway between the two pulleys. If under correct tension, the belt will give approximately ⅝ inch (15 mm). See Fig. 18.

**Fig. 18.** Fan belt in good condition and correct adjustment gives about ⅝ inch (15 mm) when pressed with thumb.

In general, a cracked, frayed or oil-soaked fan belt is to be considered unserviceable and should be replaced.

### 5.2 Adjusting Fan Belt Tension

The generator pulley consists of separate halves (plates) with spacer washers between them. A Woodruff key fixes the position of the front half of the pulley on the shaft. The retaining nut on the end of the shaft secures the assembly. Extra washers are kept on the shaft between the rear half of the pulley and the retaining nut.

The number of washers between the pulley halves determines belt tension because it sets the separation between the halves. When the pulley halves are close together, the belt rides high, without slack. When the pulley halves are farther apart, the belt tension slackens.

***WARNING —***
*Before beginning any work on the V-belt, make sure that the ignition is off and the gearshift in neutral. Set the parking brake. Do not wear a necktie or loose clothing that in case of accidental starting of the engine could be snagged in the V-belt or pulleys.*

**To adjust:**

1. Insert blade of screwdriver through cutout in front half of generator pulley and brace it against generator housing bolt to keep pulley from turning when you apply force to a wrench on the pulley nut (see Fig. 19).

© 1972 VWoA—177

**Fig. 19.** Screwdriver in slot of generator/fan pulley braces pulley against torque of wrench when nut is loosened.

2. Remove pulley nut as shown and take off outer half of pulley.

3. Adjust belt tension by changing the number of washers between pulley halves. Taking washers out increases tension. Putting washers in decreases tension. (Keep extra washers on shaft between outer half of pulley and the pulley nut.) See Fig. 20.

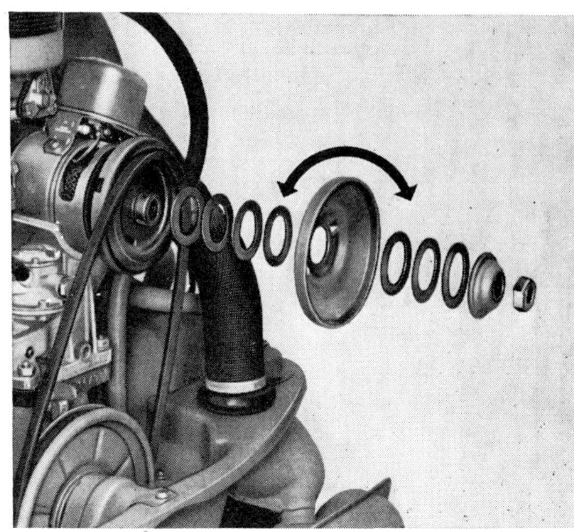

© 1972 VWoA—178

**Fig. 20.** Spacer washers between halves of fan belt pulley adjust tension on fan belt. Spares are carried on pulley shaft between pulley and nut. See text for adjustment.

4. Check tension by pressing belt with thumb as in Fig. 18. Belt should yield about ⅝ inch.

**NOTE —**
Belt slackness is taken up by removing washers. If belt is too tight, washers should be added.

When it has become necessary to remove all the washers from the pulley halves to obtain proper tension, the belt is too stretched or worn to be kept in service. Even if the adjustment seems to be correct, a belt in this condition should be replaced. And always keep a new replacement in the car.

## 5.3 Removing and Installing Fan Belt

Procedures for removal and installation will be found on the following page. However, it will be helpful to study Fig. 20 before proceeding.

**To remove:**

1. Remove crankshaft pulley cover plate (see Fig. 9).

2. Take off outer half of generator pulley as in procedure for adjusting belt tension.

3. Remove belt.

2

**To install:**

1. Loop new belt over crankshaft pulley.
2. Position belt on inner half of generator pulley and attach outer half.
3. Tighten pulley nut just enough to hold outer half of pulley in place. Insert screwdriver in pulley slot (fig. 19) and tighten pulley nut with wrench. Remove screwdriver from slot.
4. Turn pulley with wrench until belt rides up between pulley halves.
5. Insert screwdriver in slot again to hold pulley and use torque wrench to tighten pulley nut to 40 to 47 ft. lbs. Recheck belt adjustment.

### 5.4 Removing and Installing Crankshaft Pulley

**To remove:**

1. Take off fan belt.
2. Unscrew securing bolt and take off pulley (Fig. 21). If engine is in car, the rear cover plate must be removed first.

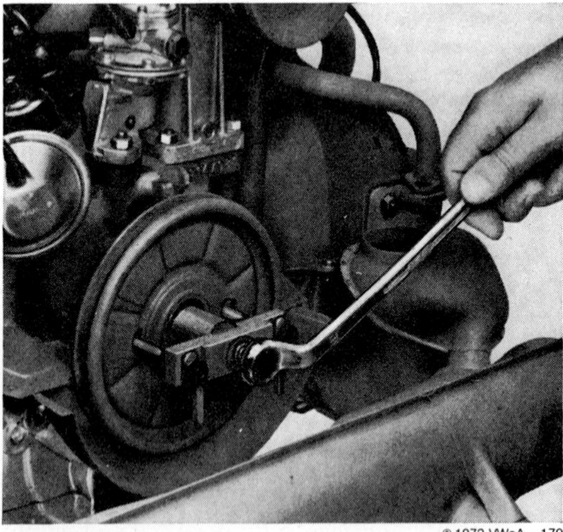



**Fig. 21.** Extractor is used in removal of crankshaft pulley.

When a disassembled engine is being re-assembled, installation of the crankshaft pulley (Fig. 22) follows installation of the oil pump and of the pulley lower plate, in that order.

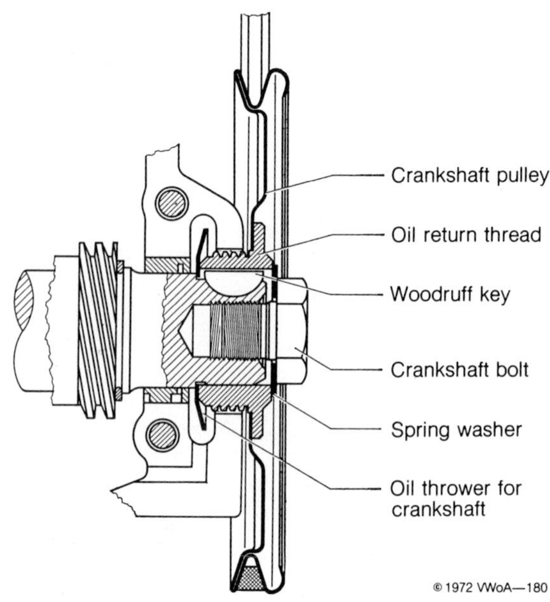




**Fig. 22.** Crankshaft pulley assembly is shown here in cross-section.

**To install:**

1. Before installation, check crankshaft pulley for proper seating. Inspect surface on which the belt runs. Clean and lubricate the oil return thread, using oil with molybdenum disulfide additive.
2. Make sure that crankshaft pulley turns on shaft without run-out.

## 6. INTAKE MANIFOLD

Some differences will be found in the intake manifolds on the cars covered in this Manual. On cars with Emission Control Systems hoses run from the intake manifold to the throttle positioner or altitude corrector. Cars with Automatic Stick Shift have vacuum lines running from the intake manifold to the shift clutch servo. None of these variations, however, requires substantial change in the basic instructions that follow.

### 6.1 Removing and Installing Intake Manifold with Preheater Pipe

The installation procedure requires a whole new set of gaskets. Before you start your work, be sure that you have at hand all the specified sizes.

**To remove manifold:**

1. Remove generator and attached fan as unit.
2. Remove nuts on cylinder heads and bolts on exhaust flanges.

3. Disconnect accelerator cable and choke wire at the carburetor. Disconnect wire from the electromagnetic pilot jet.

**NOTE** —
On engines with Automatic Stick Shift disconnect vacuum lines.

4. Lift off intake manifold with carburetor.
5. Using screwdriver, carefully pry out copper sealing ring. See Fig. 23.

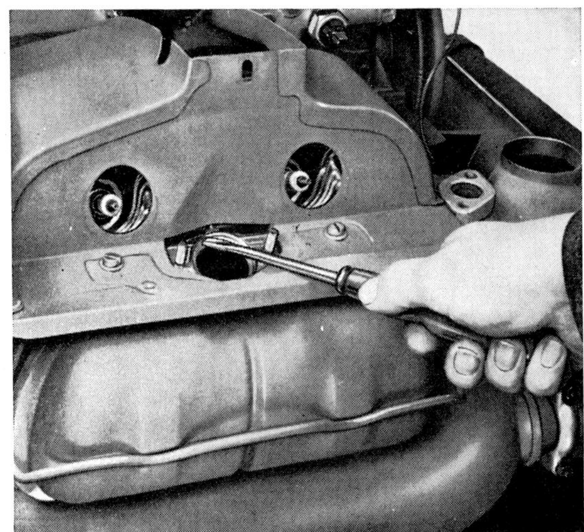

© 1972 VWoA—181

**Fig. 23.** Copper sealing rings at cylinder head are pried out with screwdriver when intake manifold with preheating pipe is removed.

**To install:**

1. Check that intake manifold and preheating pipe flanges are flat and undamaged. Inspect for leakage (cracks). See Fig. 24.

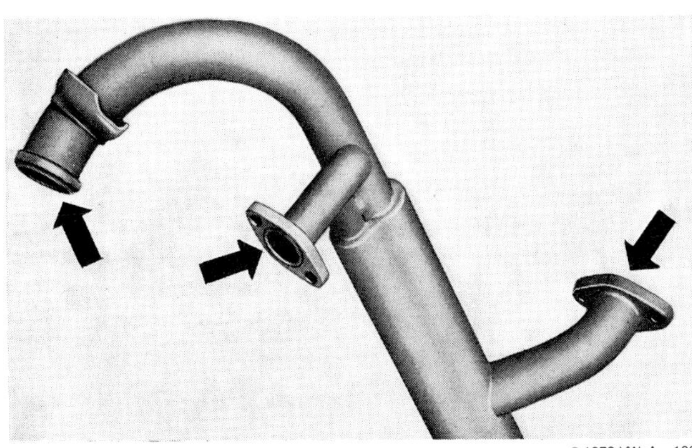

© 1972 VWoA—182

**Fig. 24.** Intake manifold flanges (arrows) should be checked for cracks or other damage.

2. Use new gaskets in cylinder heads and at flanges. The preheater gasket with the smaller opening goes on the left side.
3. When manifold is installed, all flange holes must align with studs and threaded holes.
4. Tighten nuts and bolts uniformly.

2

## 7. Exhaust System

On VW cars the exhaust system includes the muffler, tail pipes, heat exchangers and various couplings and connections.

### 7.1 Removing and Installing Muffler

New gaskets will be required for this procedure. Before starting work, obtain the correct sizes.

**To remove:**

1. Take off heat exchanger clamps.
2. Take off clamps connecting warm air channels (fig. 27, part 17).
3. Remove muffler flange nuts (see Fig. 25). Take off preheater adapter pipe.

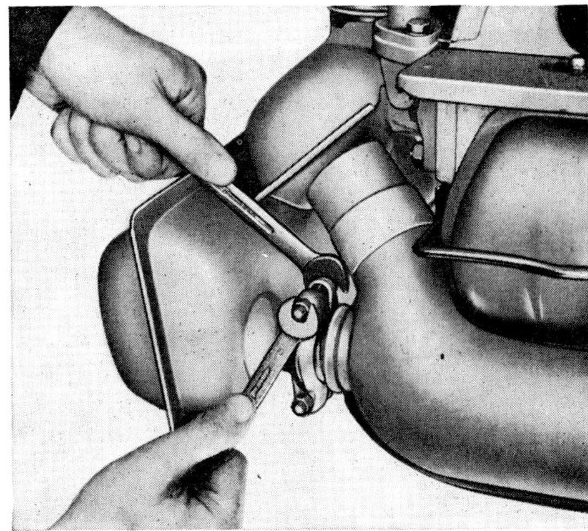

© 1972 VWoA—183

**Fig. 25.** Two wrenches are used as here to remove bolts from muffler flange clamps.

4. Remove the four bolts retaining the manifold preheater pipe.

5. Take off muffler and gaskets between cylinder head flanges and muffler.

**NOTE —**
If muffler sticks, tap along it with rubber mallet until you can pull it clear. If you install new muffler, use new tail pipes with it.

**To install:**

1. Check muffler and exhaust pipes for leaks or damage. If necessary, straighten pipes. The cone-shaped sealing surfaces must not be damaged. See Fig. 26.

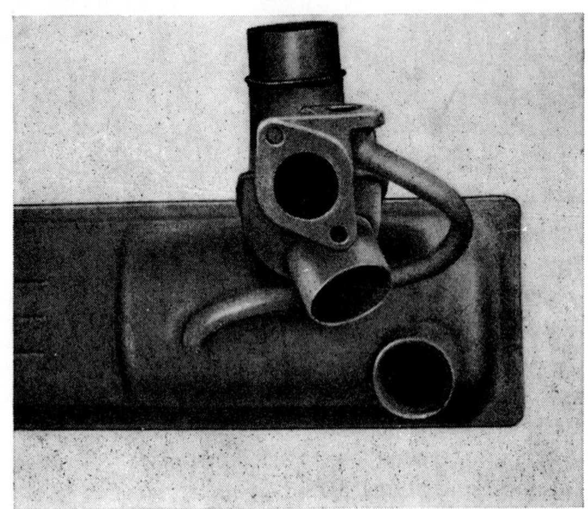

© 1972 VWoA—184

**Fig. 26.** Exhaust pipe sealing surfaces at the muffler should be checked for leaks before installation. Conical seals must be undamaged. Installation of seals requires care.

2. Use new gaskets.
3. Go through removal procedure in reverse order.

## 7.2 Removing and Installing Tail Pipes

Kits containing new clamps and gaskets for this job are available. On an older car you may find it necessary to heat the tail pipe before you can pull it out. A very stubborn pipe usually will yield if you hit it with a hammer while it is hot. Use heavy pliers, not your fingers, to hold a heated pipe.

**To remove:**

1. Take off tail pipe clamps (Fig. 25 suggests a method).
2. Remove all old gasket material from muffler flanges.

***WARNING —***
*If you are going to apply heat to the tail pipe, make sure that you have a fire extinguisher at hand.*

3. Pull out tail pipe.

**To install:**

1. Put gasket on muffler end of tail pipe and insert pipe into muffler.

**NOTE —**
On 1966-67 cars the tail pipes should not enter muffler more than 1.8 inches. On 1968-69 models 3.4 inches is the limit. Obtain these fittings by first measuring total length of pipe and then subtracting the length protruding after insertion.

2. Put clamps around gasket and muffler flange. Tighten snugly with fingers.
3. Tighten clamp bolts, working first on one and then the other, until tail pipe is secured. You should not be able to rotate the pipe or pull it loose.

## 7.3 Removing and Installing Heat Exchangers

This procedure calls for new gaskets all around. Check on sizes before starting the work. Fig. 27 shows the parts of this assembly and gives their names.

**To remove:**

1. Take off hoses between fan housing and heat exchangers.
2. Remove engine rear cover plate.
3. Remove nuts on front of cylinder head and connecting clamps on warm air pipe (Fig. 28).
4. Remove screws in cover plate below fan pulley (Fig. 29).
5. Remove exhaust pipe clamps.
6. Take a good hold on heat exchanger (it is heavy), push forward and remove.

**To install:**

1. Carefully check outer shell and exhaust pipe for damage.

***WARNING —***
*If the heat exchangers leak, poisonous exhaust gases can enter the heating system.*

**Fig. 27.** Exhaust system consists of the components shown in this exploded view.

© 1972 VWoA—187

1. Tail pipe (2)
2. Retaining ring, 35 mm diameter (4)
3. Seal, 35 mm diameter (2)
4. M 6 nut, self-locking (8)
5. Clamp (8)
6. M 6 x 43 bolt (8)
7. Muffler
8. Seal, 35 mm diameter, for heat exchanger (2)
9. Heater hose (2)
10. Hose clamp, 9 mm wide (4)
11. Heater hose grommet (2)
12. Connecting pipe (2)
13. Preheating pipe gasket (left)
14. Preheating pipe gasket (right)
15. Exhaust pipe flange gasket (4)
16. M 8 nut, self-locking (8)
17. Clamp, 25 mm wide (2)
18. Heat exchanger (2)
19. M 5 x 10 bolt (2)
20. Pin (2)
21. C-washer (4)
22. Link (2)
23. Pin (2)
24. Clamp washer (2)
25. Heater flap lever (2)
26. Return spring (2)

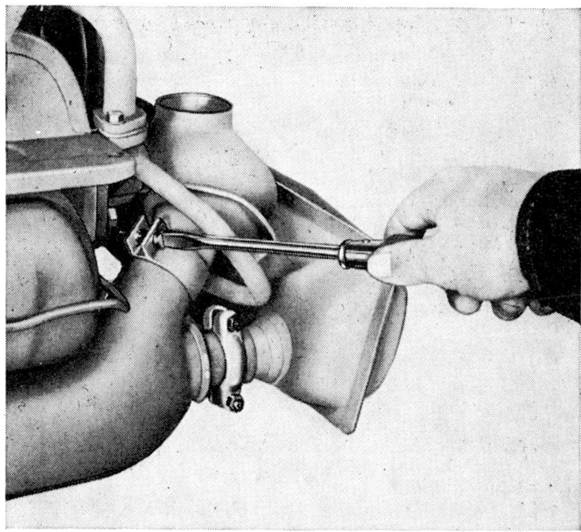

© 1972 VWoA—185

**Fig. 28.** Connecting clamps are loosened and moved along heat exchanger.

© 1972 VWoA—186

**Fig. 29.** Screws shown here secure heat exchanger to lower cover plate.

2. The flange sealing surfaces must be clean and smooth. Flanges which have been distorted by excessive tightening should be straightened or machined. Use new gaskets.
3. Follow steps of removal procedure in reverse order.

## 8. Valve Gear and Cylinder Heads

Before removing cylinder head cover to get at valve operating mechanism, be sure to clean off encrusted road dirt on the cylinder heads and engine cover plates.

### 8.1 Removing and Installing Valve Rocker Mechanism

After working on the rocker arms, clean all exposed parts of the valve gear before you replace the cylinder head cover.

**To remove:**

1. Take off valve cover.
2. Remove rocker shaft retaining nuts (Fig. 30). Loosen them a little at a time, working alternately from one nut to the other.

**Fig. 30.** Rocker arms are exposed when cylinder head cover has been removed. Wrench here is loosening securing nut for removal of rocker arms and shaft.

3. Take off rocker shaft with rocker arms.
4. Remove stud seals.

**To install:**

1. Install new stud seals.
2. Install rocker shaft. Make sure that chamfered edges of the supports face outward (Fig. 31) and the slots upward.

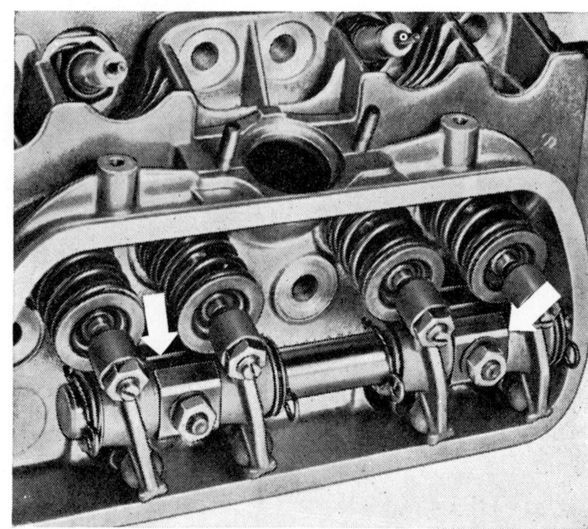



**Fig. 31.** Rocker shaft must be installed with chamfered edges of supports (right arrow) facing outward from cylinder and with slots (left arrow) upward.

3. Using torque wrench, tighten nuts on rocker shaft studs to 18 ft. lbs. (2.5 mkg).

**NOTE —**
If valve stem ends are in good condition but valves are noisy, the rocker arms may be binding. Check thrust side of the rocker shaft and the rocker arm bushings for scoring. Smooth rough surfaces with fine emery cloth. Use only copper-plated retaining nuts.

4. Adjust valves.
5. Fit new valve cover gaskets.

**NOTE —**
Carefully clean away old gasket material and clean inside of cover before fitting new gaskets.

6. Attach valve covers.
7. After test-running engine, check valve covers for leakage.

### 8.2 Disassembling and Assembling Rocker Arms

Fig. 32 shows the rocker assembly for cylinders on one side of crankshaft. The illustration makes clear the correct positions of parts in relation to each other.

**Fig. 32.** Rocker assembly is shown in exploded view, with one pair of arms in place on shaft and other pair disassembled. Support is the metal block between each pair of arms. Chamfered edges and slot mentioned in Fig. 31 caption are visible here.

**To disassemble:**

1. Remove spring clips from rocker arm shaft.
2. Remove washers, rocker arms and bearing supports.

**To assemble:**

1. Check rocker arm shaft for wear.
2. Look closely for signs of wear in seats and ball sockets of rocker arm. Inspect valve adjusting screws.
3. Follow, in reverse order, the two steps of procedure for disassembly.

## 8.3 Removing and Installing Cylinder Heads

Careful fitting of these assemblies is important.

**To remove:**

1. Take off cylinder head nuts.
2. Lift off cylinder head.

**To install:**

1. Check cylinder head for cracks in combustion chamber and exhaust ports. Cracked cylinder heads must be replaced.
2. Check studs for tight fit. If necessary use Heli-Coil threaded inserts.
3. Note that between cylinder and cylinder head there is no sealing ring or gasket (see Fig. 33).

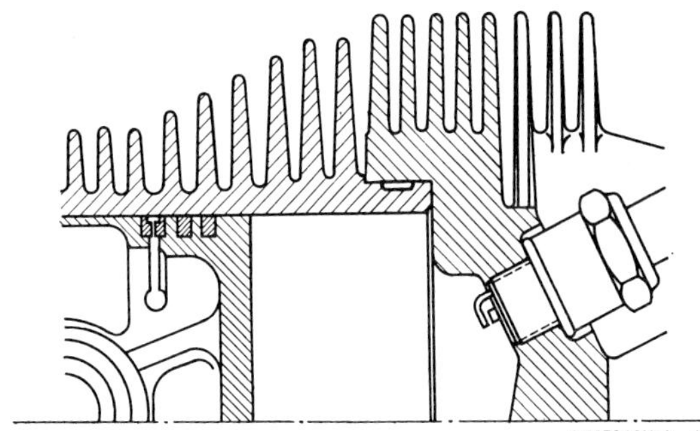


**Fig. 33.** Cylinder head fit is very important in VW engine assembly. As shown here, there is no sealing ring between cylinder and cylinder head. Cracked cylinder heads must be replaced.

4. When installing cylinder head, make sure that oil seals at ends of push rod tubes are properly seated (see Fig. 34).

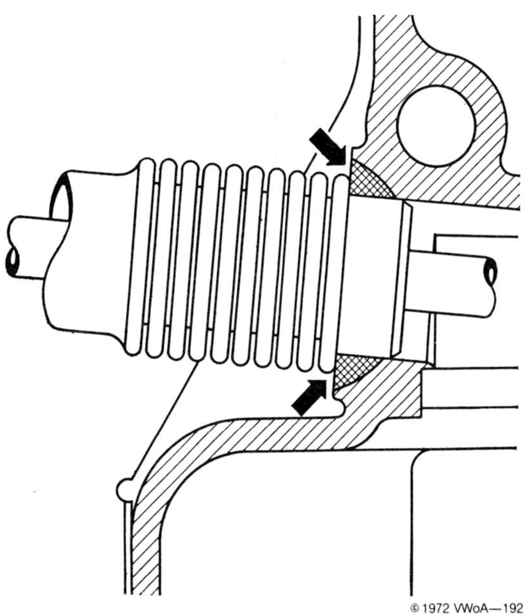


**Fig. 34.** Oil seal (arrows) at rocker arm end of push rod tube is seated as shown here.

2

5. Position push rod tubes with seams upward. For perfect sealing, stretch used tubes to correct length before installation (Fig. 35). Work carefully to avoid cracking tubes.

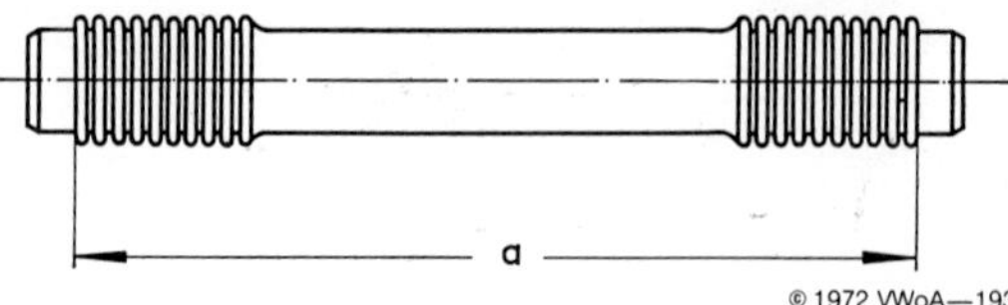


**Fig. 35.** Push rod tube is seated with seam upward and for perfect sealing must be stretched (if necessary) to specified length. Dimension "a" is specified at 7.48 to 7.52 inches (190 to 191 mm).

6. Install cylinder head washers.
7. In order shown in Fig. 36, torque nuts to a first tightening of 7 ft. lbs. (1 mkg).

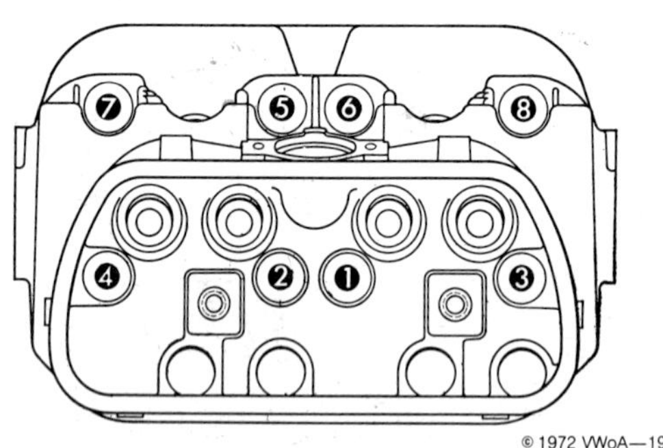


**Fig. 36.** First tightening of cylinder head nuts follows sequence given by numbers on this diagram. See text for torque specifications.

8. Then, in the order shown in Fig. 37, fully tighten nuts to 22 to 23 ft. lbs. (3 to 3.2 mkg).

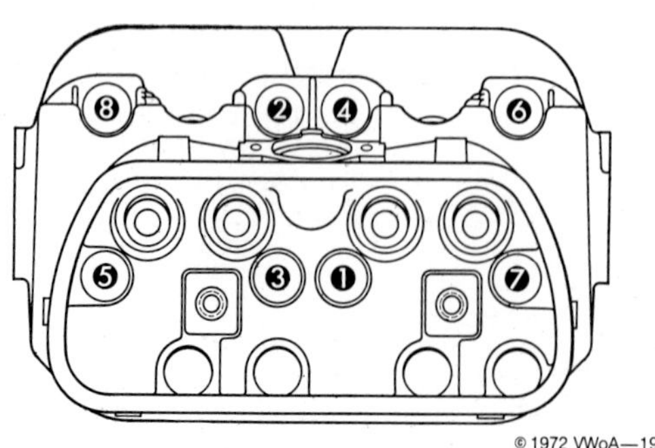


**Fig. 37.** Final tightening of cylinder head nuts follows sequence given by numbers on this diagram. See text for torque specifications.

## 9. VALVES

Repair work of some kind on the valve assembly (Fig. 38) or on the valves themselves is usually the purpose for undertaking the following removal and disassembly procedures.

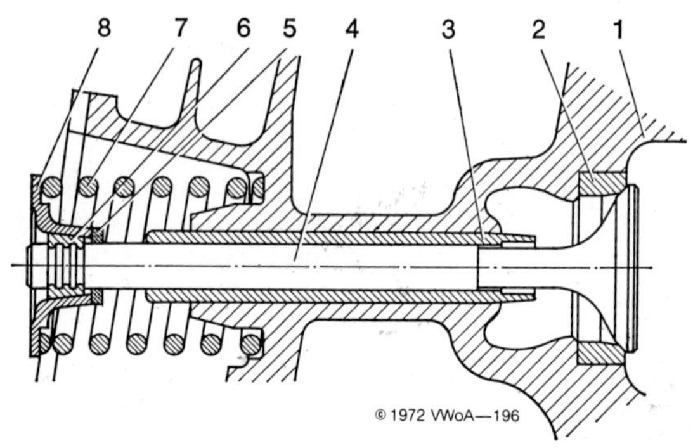


1. Cylinder head
2. Valve seat insert
3. Valve guide
4. Valve
5. Oil deflector ring
6. Valve keeper
7. Valve spring
8. Valve spring cap

**Fig. 38.** Valve assembly is shown here in cross-section.

### 9.1 Removing and Installing Valves

A special tool is required to compress valve springs.

**To remove:**

1. Take off cylinder head.
2. Press valve spring cap down until keeper (split cotter) can be removed from valve stem. Then remove cap, valve spring and oil deflector ring. Use special tool to compress spring (see Fig. 39).

**Fig. 39.** Special tool shown here compresses valve springs for removal of valves. Cylinder head must be in this position.

3. Remove valve.
4. Follow same sequence for each valve.

In 1966-67 cars slight burring may be found on the valve stem where the keeper seats (arrows in Fig. 40). Before the valve can be pulled from the guide, it will be necessary to remove this burr with a fine-toothed file.

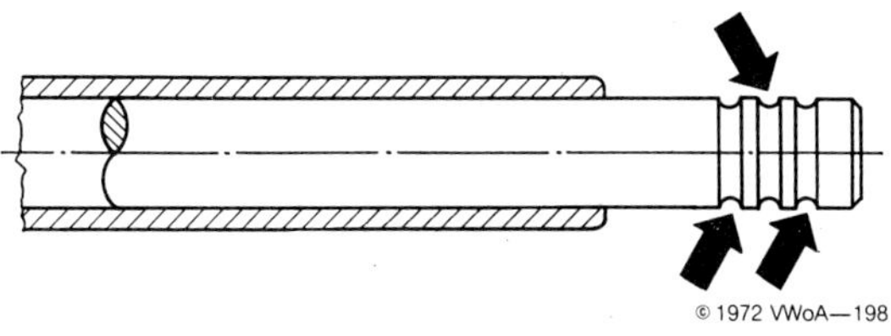


**Fig. 40.** Burring on valve stem is likely to occur under keeper at points indicated by arrows. Burrs must be removed before valve can be withdrawn from guide.

**To install:**

1. Check valve springs. A standard length under a specified load is required of VW valve springs. The specifications are:

| | |
|---|---|
| Loaded length | 1.22 inches (31 mm) |
| Load | 117.2 to 134.8 lbs. (53 to 61 kg) |

2. Check valve keepers before installation.

## 9.2 Reconditioning Valve Stems and Keepers

New or worn keepers may require some careful grinding of the inside surfaces. Keepers should fit evenly around the valve stem but not interfere with rotation of the valve. Reconditioning of stems and keepers reduces valve noise.

**To recondition valve stems and keepers:**

1. Check valve stem for run-out.
2. Check valve guide for wear.
3. Check valve for wear and leakage. Carefully polish rough valve stems with emery cloth.
4. Coat valve stem with molybdenum disulfide paste and insert valve into guide.
5. Fit oil deflector ring on valve stem with a sleeve.
6. Install valve spring with the more tightly wound end toward cylinder head.
7. Follow this procedure for the remaining valves.

## 9.3 Replacing Valve Guides

Valve guides can be replaced only in a repair shop which has special tools. Carbon deposits in guides can be removed with a reamer or broach.

2

## 9.4 Refacing Valve Seats

The valve seat inserts are shrunk into the cylinder heads, and replacing them may be difficult in the typical repair shop. It is possible, however, to reface a burned or otherwise damaged valve seat, and as long as sufficient material remains for another cut, this reconditioning procedure can be repeated. There must be enough material for the tool to cut a 15-degree chamfer without cutting beyond the boundary of the insert. If the 15-degree cut extends to the edge of the insert, the cylinder head must be replaced.

The width of the valve seat is shown as measurement (a) in Fig. 41. On the intake valve this measurement is

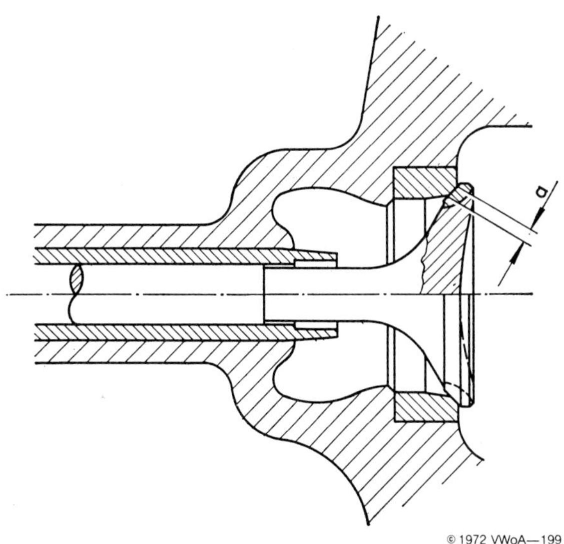


**Fig. 41.** Valve seating is illustrated in this cutaway drawing. Seat width is measurement labeled "a". It is specified for intake valves as 0.05 to 0.06 inch (1.3 to 1.6 mm) and for exhaust valves as 0.07 to 0.08 inch (1.7 to 2.0 mm).

0.05 to 0.06 inch (1.3 to 1.6 mm). On the exhaust valve it is 0.06 to 0.08 inch (1.7 to 2.0 mm). Refacing of the seat is done with a special tool (See Fig. 42). Three faces are cut at angles of (respectively) 75 degrees, 45 degrees and 15 degrees to the plane of the valve seat. The 75-degree chamfer is at the stem end, the 15-degree chamfer at the cylinder end and the 45-degree cut in the middle (see Fig. 42).

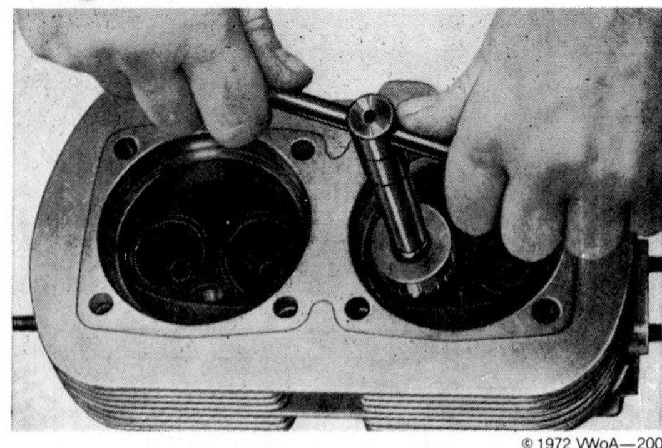


**Fig. 42.** Seat refacing is done with special cutting tool.

**To resurface valves:**

1. Cut 45-degree face. Cut carefully to obtain a concentric seating surface but take off the minimum of metal. Otherwise, the service life of the seat will be reduced. As soon as the entire surface has been faced, stop cutting. See Fig. 43.

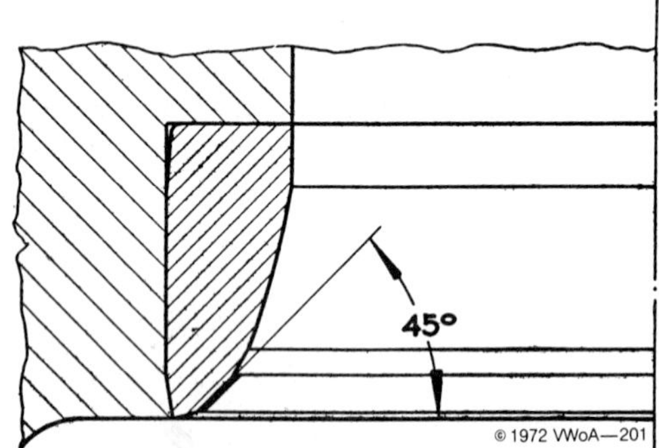


**Fig. 43.** Middle face of valve seat is cut at angle of 45 degrees.

2. Cut 75-degree face. This cut is no more than a slight chamfer of inner edge of seat (Fig. 44).

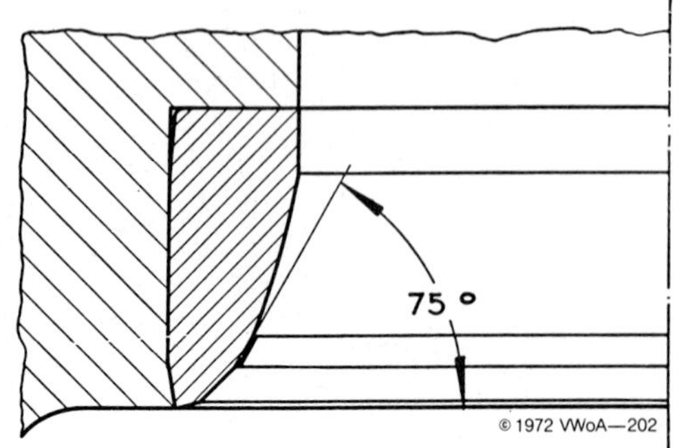


**Fig. 44.** Inner face of valve seat is cut at angle of 75 degrees.

3. Cut 15-degree face (Fig. 45). Chamfer outer edge of seat until correct width for seat is obtained, measurement "a" in Fig. 41.

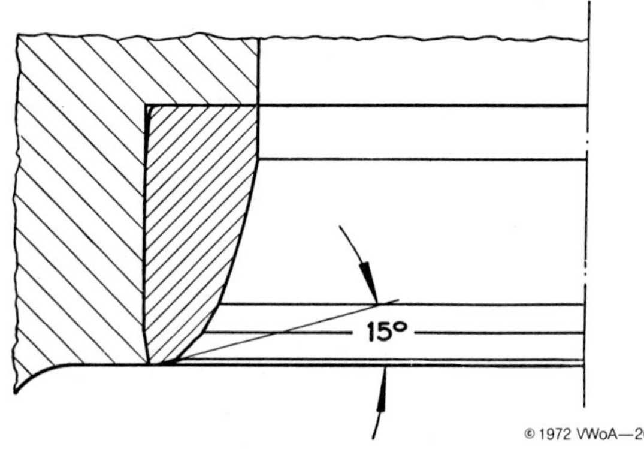


**Fig. 45.** Outer face of valve seat (the critical one) is cut at an angle of 15 degrees. See text.

## 9.5 Fitting Valves

The fitting of valves, whether new or used, must be precise. While a new valve may not require grinding, the contact pattern on the valve seat should be checked before you proceed to install the valve. A used valve almost always requires refacing and grinding. There are standard procedures for checking valves and valve seats and for reconditioning valves.

**To check valve:**

1. With wire brush scrub valve head until every trace of carbon deposit has been removed.
2. Examine valve closely for burns and signs of wear. Reface valve if necessary (see Fig. 46 and **Table a**). If valve face is badly burned or pitted, replace valve.

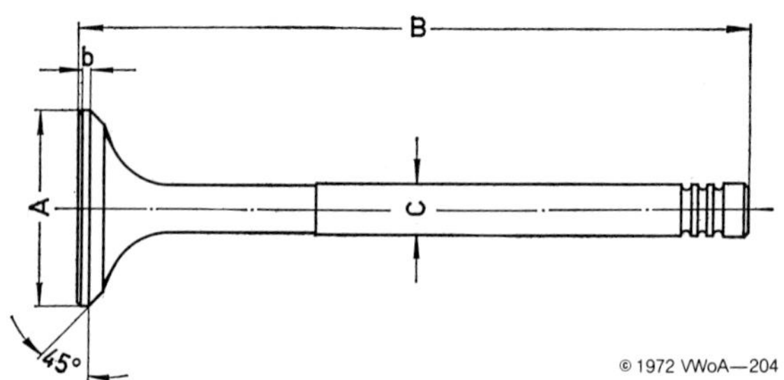


A. Valve face diameter
B. Valve length
C. Valve stem diameter
b. Valve head margin

**Fig. 46.** Valve dimensions are specified to thousands of an inch (hundredths of a millimeter). See table in text for measurements labeled in this drawing.

**Table a. Specifications for Regrinding Valves**

| | Intake Valve | Exhaust Valve |
|---|---|---|
| A* | 1.294-1.303 in. (32.9-33.1 mm)** | 1.177-1.185 in. (29.7-30.1 mm)** |
| B | 4.386-4.417 in. (110.7-111.6 mm) | 4.394-4.425 in. (110.7-112.0 mm) |
| C | 0.3126-0.3130 in. (7.94-7.95 mm) | 0.3114-0.3118 in. (7.91-7.92 mm) |
| b | 0.031-0.059 in. (0.8-1.5 mm) | 0.039-0.067 in. (1.00-1.70 mm) |
| Face angle | 44 degrees | 45 degrees |

***The identifying labels A, B, C and b refer to measurements shown in Fig. 46.**
****Specifications for valve diameters in 53 SAE bhp engine are different Intake Valve = 1.396 in. (35.5 mm) Exhaust Valve = 1.259 in. (32.0 mm)**

2

3. Discard any valve with warped stem or damaged keeper seat, or one that shows signs of seizure. Do not attempt to straighten or grind a valve stem.
4. Small caps are available for valves with damaged stem ends. Fit cap on end of stem (see Fig. 47) before installing rocker arm.

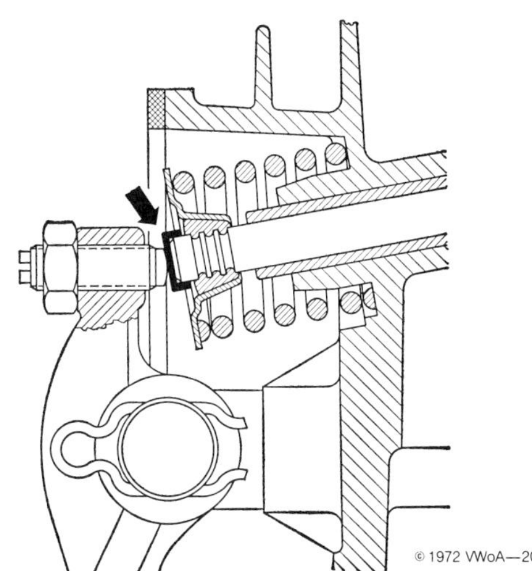


**Fig. 47.** Valve cap (arrow) on damaged end of valve stem restores valve to usefulness.

**To check valve seating:**

1. Coat face of valve lightly with prussian blue.
2. Insert coated valve into valve seat. Applying light pressure, rotate valve a quarter turn.
3. Lift valve off seat and examine contact pattern left on seat face. If valve is seating correctly, it transfers an even coating of blue to the seat face. There should be no bare spot on the face. Color of pattern should be uniform.

## 9.6 Refacing Valves

Refacing valves on a valve-turning or grinding machine calls for precision. Exhaust valves especially are subjected to high thermal stress, and certain specifications must be maintained. Allowable limits for the dimensions shown in Fig. 46 are given in **Table a.** It is highly important to preserve dimension "b" when refacing exhaust valves. Never grind or attempt to straighten valve stems.

## 9.7 Grinding Valves

This lapping procedure requires a valve grinding tool, which is in effect a straight handle with a rubber vacuum cup on the end (Fig. 48). The cup holds the valve while you are turning it on the valve seat.

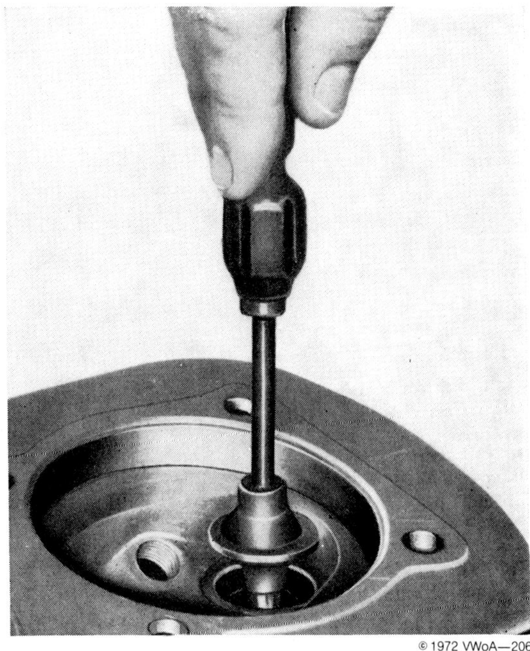


**Fig. 48.** Valve grinding is done with tool shown here, a sort of miniature "plumber's friend." See text.

**To top valve:**

1. Coat valve seat with valve grinding compound and insert valve in guide.
2. Holding tool as you would a screwdriver, apply suction cup to valve face and rotate valve on valve seat.
3. Lift valve off seat from time to time to inspect your work. Each time shift position of valve slightly to keep from cutting grooves in seat.

**NOTE —**
After grinding, clean valve and valve seat thoroughly. Make sure every trace of grinding compound has been removed.

4. Check valve seating, as before.

### 9.8 Valve Clearance

Valve clearance refers to the gap between the valve stem end and the adjusting screw in the rocker arm. Engine performance and the durability of valves and valve seats depend to some extent on proper clearance, which should be checked and corrected regularly and carefully. The engine must be cold when valve clearance is checked or adjusted. Valve clearance specifications are:

Intake valve: 0.006 inch (0.15 mm)
Exhaust valve: 0.006 inch (0.15 mm)

Clearance increases when the engine first warms up but returns to the original measurement when the engine becomes hot. When clearance is insufficient, it can cause the following damage or malfunctions:

Burning of valves and valve seats
Distortion of valves
Reduced compression
Uneven engine running
Alteration of valve timing.

The following faults can be attributed to excessive clearance:

Altered valve timing with noise
Uneven engine running
Poor performance from insufficient cylinder charge.

### 9.9 Adjusting Valves

Valve clearance must be adjusted in a definite sequence: cylinders No. 1, No. 2, No. 3, No. 4. The ignition must be OFF, of course, and for checking and adjusting valve clearance the engine must be cold. Both valves of the cylinder being adjusted must be closed; that is, the piston of the cylinder must be at Top Dead Center, in firing position.

**The procedure:**

1. Remove cylinder head cover.
2. By turning the generator/fan pulley, rotate engine until the distributor rotor arm is pointing toward the No. 1 cylinder mark on rim of the distributor housing (see Fig. 49). This is a small notch in the rim at about the five o'clock position. Check position of the TDC timing notch in the crankshaft pulley. It must be lined up with the split in the crankcase. This alignment shows that the No. 1 cylinder is in firing position.

**Fig. 49.** Rotor arm alignment in distributor for adjustment of valves is shown by slanting line across distributor. Arm must point to No. 1 cylinder mark on distributor rim. Piston then is at TDC.

3. Use 0.006-inch feeler gauge (0.15 mm) to check valve clearance. Clearance is correct when you can just push the gauge through gap between valve stem end and adjusting screw in the rocker arm (see Fig. 50).
4. If clearance is not correct, loosen adjusting screw lock nut.
5. Turn adjusting screw until feeler gauge can be pushed through gap quickly. It must not be necessary to use force.
6. Holding adjusting screw, tighten lock nut.
7. Repeat procedure with other valve.

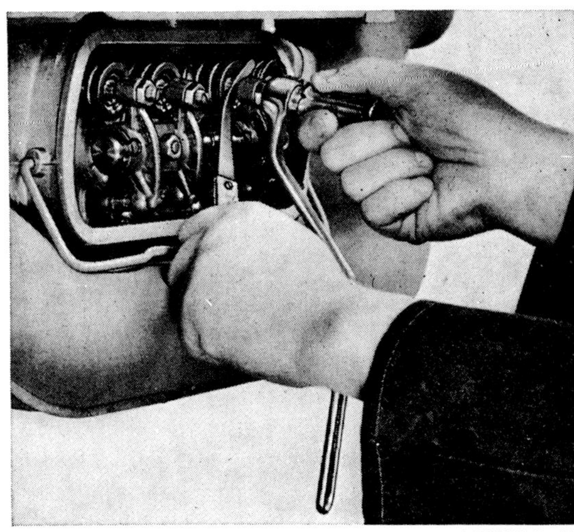



**Fig. 50.** Clearance between valve stem and rocker arm adjusting screw is checked with feeler gauge. See text.

8. After both of the lock nuts have been tightened, recheck adjustment.
9. Turn crankshaft counter-clockwise 180 degrees. (The distributor rotor will turn 90 degrees.) Repeat adjustment procedure for cylinder No. 2, and proceed through same steps to adjust valves of remaining cylinders. Engine must be turned another 180 degrees counter-clockwise for each succeeding cylinder.
10. Fit new gaskets on cylinder head covers and put covers back on engine.

## 10. CYLINDERS

You can replace any of the four cylinders of the VW engine without having to replace any of the others, but you must make sure that each cylinder and its piston are a matching fit.

### 10.1 Removing and Installing Cylinder

This procedure calls for scrupulous cleanliness.

**To remove:**

1. Remove deflector plate below cylinder.
2. Take cylinder off.

**To install:**

1. Check cylinder for wear. If necessary, replace it with matched cylinder and piston of same size.
2. Carefully inspect cylinder seating surface on the crankcase. Inspect cylinder shoulder and gasket. Dirt on any of these surfaces (see Fig. 51) can cause distortion of cylinder. The surfaces must be perfectly clean.

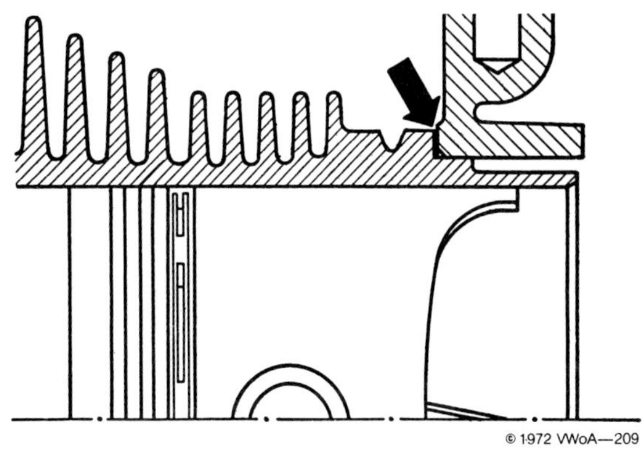



**Fig. 51.** Cylinder seat on crankcase must be perfectly clean at point indicated by arrow. Foreign matter here will distort hot cylinder.

3. Put a new gasket between cylinder and crankcase.
4. Put oil on piston and piston pin.
5. Compress piston rings with compressing tool and make sure that ring gaps are offset.
6. Oil the cylinder wall and slide cylinder over piston. Crankcase studs (see Fig. 52) must not touch cylinder cooling fins.

**Fig. 52.** Crankcase studs must hold cylinders without touching cylinder fins.

2

7. Install deflector plates, making sure to seat them correctly, as in Fig. 53. If necessary, bend plates until they press against cylinder head studs. Otherwise, the plates may work loose and rattle.

**Fig. 53.** Deflector plates, which direct cooling air flow around cylinders, must bear tightly on studs to prevent rattling.

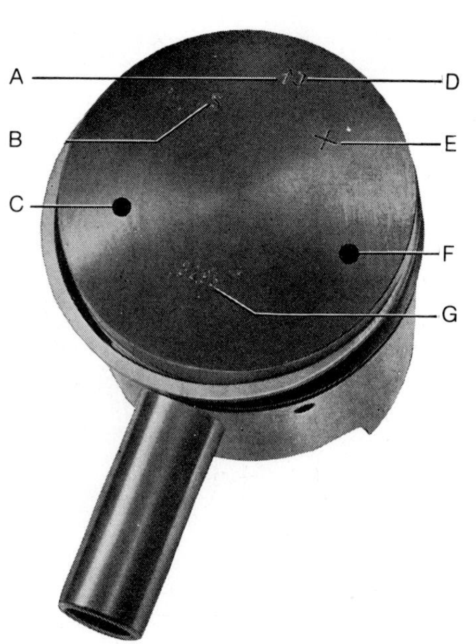




**Fig. 54.** Piston markings identify pistons as to diameter and weight and give coded directions regarding installation. See text.

## 11. PISTONS AND PISTON RINGS

The top surface (head or crown) of a VW piston carries marking coded to indicate the size and weight in comparison with standard piston size and weight. Some of the markings are stamped in the metal. Others are spots of colored paint.

In Fig. 54 the coding on the crown of the piston contains the following instructions:

A. Arrow (indented or stamped) points toward flywheel when piston is installed correctly.

B. Indented or stamped symbols give details of piston bore size (s means "black" and w means "white").

C. Paint spot (blue, pink, green) indicates matching size.

D. Letter near arrow corresponds to index of part number of the piston. It serves as an identification mark.

E. Indented or stamped symbol gives details of weight grading (+ or −).

F. Paint spot indicates weight grading (brown means slightly under standard weight; grey means slightly over standard weight).

G. Number gives piston size in millimeters.

### 11.1 Piston Rings

A new crankshaft with "X" oil holes requires special piston rings in all 1300 engines from chassis No. 117 560 696 and engine No. F1 081 423 and in all 1500 engines from chassis No. 117 811 587 and engine H0 823 800. A stepped piston ring is substituted for the previously standard bottom compression ring, and there is a new oil control ring with a spiral expander.

The standard VW method of measuring piston ring gap is illustrated in Fig. 55. Using the matching piston as a pusher to prevent tilt, you push the ring into the cylinder for about a quarter of an inch (5 mm). Then use a feeler gauge to measure ring gap, as shown in Fig. 55.

The limits specified for ring gap measurement on all engines are:

For compression rings . . . . . . . . 0.012 to 0.018 inch (0.30 to 0.45 mm)

For oil scraper rings . . . . . . . . . 0.010 to 0.016 inch (0.25 to 0.40 mm)

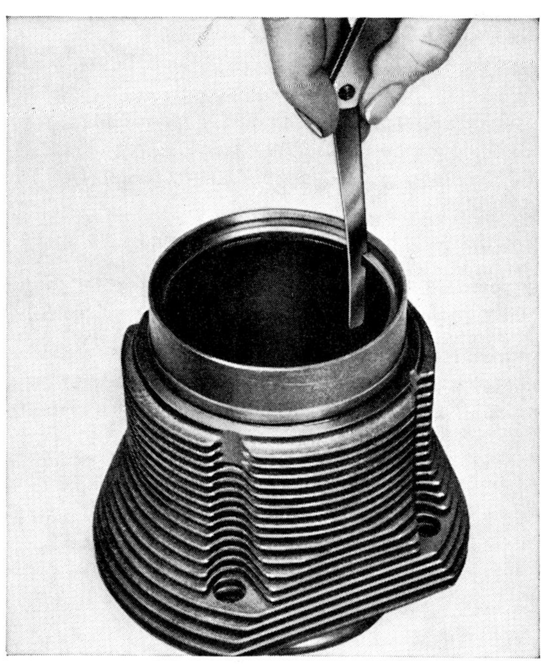
© 1972 VWoA—213

**Fig. 55.** Ring gap is measured with piston ring inside cylinder. Feeler gauge is used as shown here. See text for specifications.

The wear limits specified are:

For compression rings . . . . . . . 0.035 inch (0.90 mm)

For oil scraper rings . . . . . . . . 0.037 inch (0.95 mm)

The standard VW method of measuring side clearance in the piston ring grooves is illustrated in Fig. 56.

© 1972 VWoA—214

**Fig. 56.** Ring clearance in groove in piston is measured with feeler gauge as shown here. See text for specifications.

Use a feeler gauge, pushing it into the gap between ring and side of ring groove in the piston.

The limits specified for side clearance measurement are:

For top compression rings . . . . 0.0027 to 0.0035 inch (0.07 to 0.09 mm)

For lower compression rings . . . 0.0019 to 0.0027 inch (0.05 to 0.07 mm)

For oil rings . . . . . . . . . . . . . . . 0.001 to 0.002 inch (0.03 to 0.05 mm)

2

The wear limits specified are:

For top compression rings . . . . 0.0047 inch (0.12 mm)

For lower compression rings . . . 0.004 inch (0.10 mm)

For oil rings . . . . . . . . . . . . . . 0.004 inch (0.10 mm)

## 11.2 Removing and Installing Pistons

**To remove:**

1. Remove cylinder.
2. Put matching marks on piston and cylinder to enable you to return piston to original position (see Fig. 57).

© 1972 VWoA—215

**Fig. 57.** Matching marks on pistons and cylinders ensure re-installation of pistons in correct positions.

3. Using circlip pliers, remove piston pin circlip.
4. Remove piston pin and take out piston.

5. To avoid damage, keep rings on piston if possible, but if they must be removed, use piston ring tool (Fig. 58).

© 1972 VWoA—216

**Fig. 58.** Piston ring tool should always be used for removal or installation of rings.

**To install:**

1. Clean piston. Remove carbon from top and grooves of piston, being careful not to damage surfaces. If you find an uneven wear pattern and uneven deposits of carbon, check connecting rod. A distorted rod can cause uneven wear.
2. If wear requires replacement of piston, select another piston of corresponding size. The difference in weight between pistons in an engine must not exceed 10 grams.
3. Select piston rings of proper size. Insert ring in cylinder and use piston to push ring squarely in, as described above. Then measure ring gap with feeler gauge, as in Fig. 55.
4. Using piston ring tool to avoid damage, insert rings in proper grooves. Make sure that compression rings are installed right side up. The side on which you find the English word **top** (or the German word **oben**) goes toward top of piston (Fig. 59). Be sure to stagger ring gaps.
5. A circlip goes in the piston pin hole at each side of the piston. Insert first the one that goes in the side

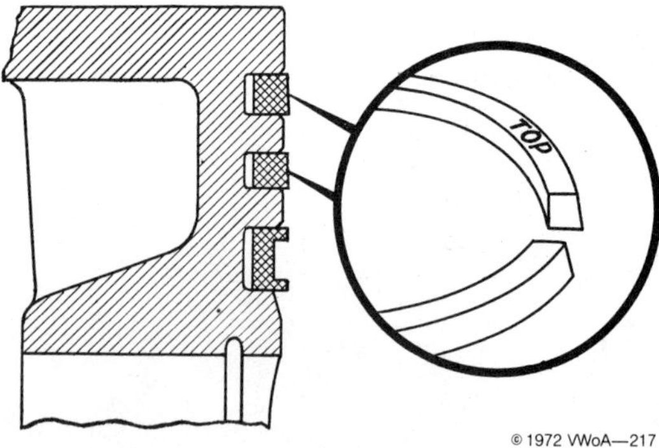


© 1972 VWoA—217

**Fig. 59.** Compression ring has the word **top** (or the German word **oben**) on side that goes toward top of piston when ring is installed.

toward flywheel (Fig. 60). It is important to have arrow (or the German word **vorn**) pointing toward flywheel when you install the piston.

© 1972 VWoA—218

**Fig. 60.** Circlip (lock ring) goes in piston pin hole at each side. Insert the one toward the flywheel first.

Because the piston pin is offset from the center line of the assembly, the bearing of piston on cylinder wall changes as the piston approaches TDC. At this point combustion has not yet occurred. Side thrust is relatively small. The arrangement of the assembly causes the piston to tilt gently toward the opposite side of the cylinder wall. Pistons usually slap here, especially if clearance between piston and cylinder wall is excessive, but the VW configuration avoids this noise. Fig. 61 illustrates the change in thrust as engine goes through the four cycles of its operation.

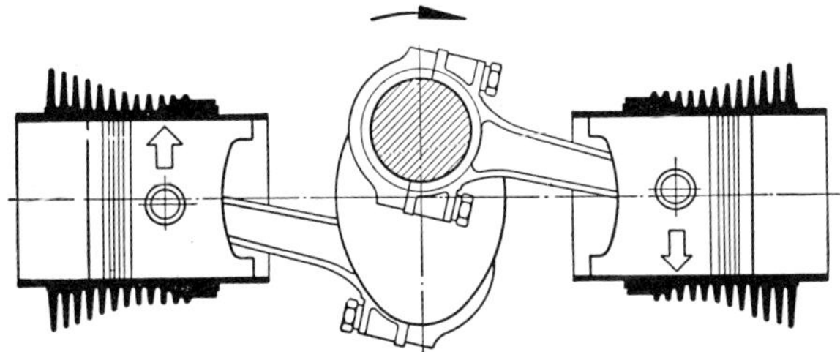

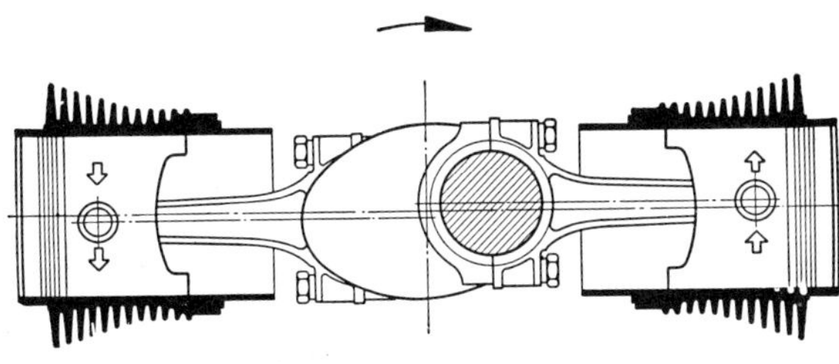

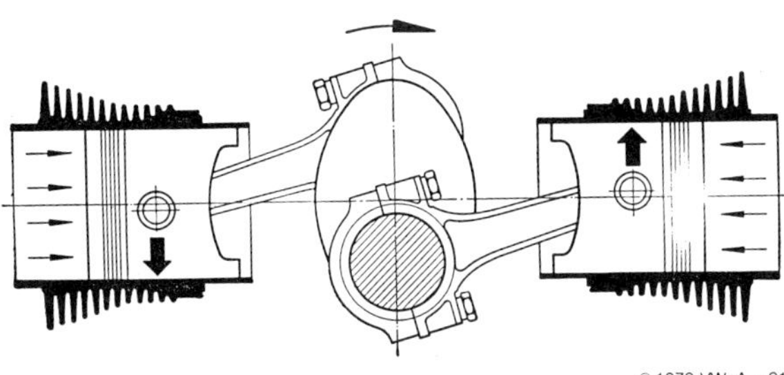

© 1972 VWoA—219

**Fig. 61.** Changing thrust of connecting rods in the four-cycle operation of the engine is indicated by the arrows. Offset of piston pin hole was designed to reduce piston slap as angle of thrust changes.

6. Check and install piston pin. Depending on tolerances between piston pin and bearing, the pin may be found to be a light push fit in the piston even when the piston is cold. This condition is quite normal. Even when the pin is loose enough to slide out of the piston under its own weight, there is no need to replace either pin or piston. To allow matching of sizes, the piston pin and the piston pin hole are color-marked.

   The clearance between piston pin and connecting rod bushing is 0.0004 to 0.0008 inch (0.01 to 0.02 mm). If the clearance is near the wear limit of 0.0016 inch (0.04 mm), install a new piston pin and bushing in the connecting rod.

   When the pin is not a push fit, you will have to heat the piston to obtain sufficient clearance. Use an oil bath at approximately 176 degrees F (80 degrees C). The resulting expansion will allow you to push the pin in with a drift.

   Place pin on a pilot and push on it until it makes contact with the circlip you have inserted at the opposite end of the bushing.

7. Insert second circlip. Make sure that both circlips fit properly in the grooves.

8. Check clearance between cylinder and piston.

2

### 11.3 Piston Clearance

The clearance between piston and cylinder wall is computed from measurements taken on the cylinder and on the piston. It is not measured directly with a feeler gauge.

The specifications for this fitting clearance between piston and cylinder are:

For 50 SAE bhp engine . . . . . . 0.0015 to 0.0019 inch (0.04 to 0.05 mm)

For 53 SAE bhp engine . . . . . . 0.0015 to 0.0023 inch (0.04 to 0.06 mm)

The permissible wear limit is 0.0078 inch (0.20 mm).

A dial gauge for inside diameters is used to measure the cylinder (Fig. 62). It should be set with a micrometer according to cylinder size. The measurement is taken from 0.04 to 0.06 inch (10 to 15 mm) below the upper edge of the cylinder.

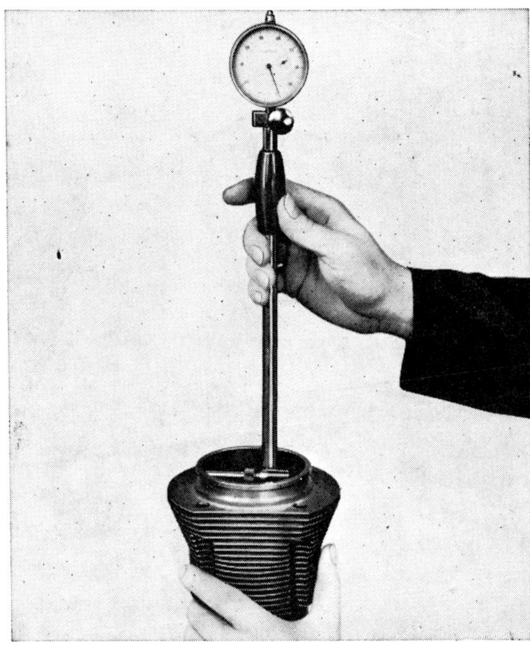

© 1972 VWoA—220

**Fig. 62.** Cylinder bore is measured with dial gauge for computation of clearance between cylinder and piston.

Although the nominal diameter of a piston is stamped on the crown (as shown in Fig. 54), you must make a close measurement to check the fitting clearance. You can use either a dial gauge (Fig. 63) or a micrometer caliper. Take the reading at the bottom of the piston skirt, at right angles to the axis of the piston pin.

**Fig. 63.** Piston diameter can be measured with dial gauge (as here) or with micrometer caliper for determination of fit between piston and cylinder.

If measurement of piston and cylinder shows that the running clearance is near 0.008 inch (0.2 mm), the piston and cylinder should be replaced with a set of the same size grading (standard or oversize). The difference in weight between pistons in an engine must not exceed 10 grams. Pistons must not be replaced individually if the cylinders to which they belong show signs of wear. If however, the cylinder of a damaged piston shows no sign of wear, the damaged piston usually can be replaced with one of matching size.

**NOTE** —

Only cylinders and pistons of the same size and weight gradings should be installed in an engine.

The oil consumption of the engine is an important factor in deciding whether or not a new cylinder and piston should be installed. If oil consumption is in excess of 1 quart per 600 miles (1 liter per 1000 km) the engine needs an overhaul.

## 12. FLYWHEEL/CRANKCASE ASSEMBLY

The fittings that secure the flywheel on the crankshaft and align it with respect to the crankcase can be seen in Fig. 64.

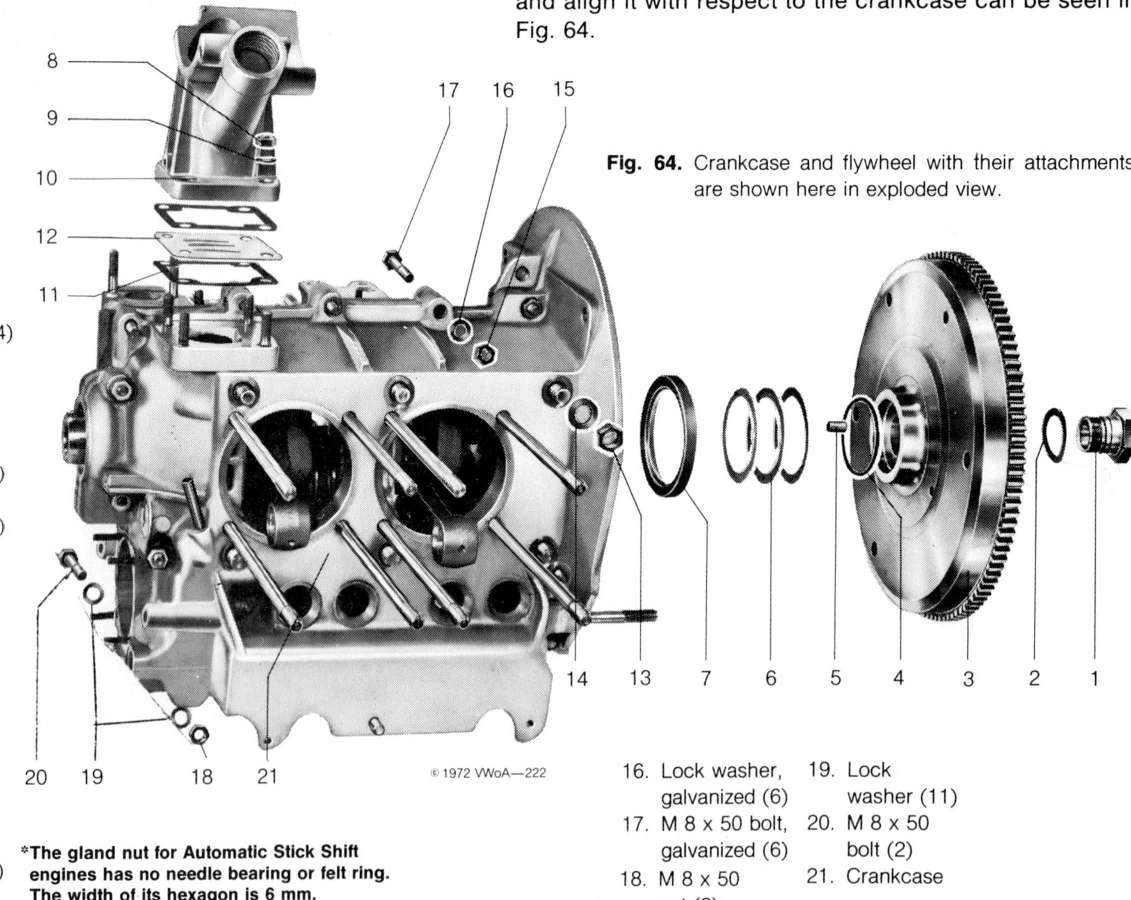




**Fig. 64.** Crankcase and flywheel with their attachments are shown here in exploded view.

1. Gland nut*
2. Lock washer
3. Flywheel
4. Rubber seal
5. Flywheel aligning pin (4)
6. Shim (3)
7. Crankshaft oil seal
8. M 8 nut, galvanized (4)
9. Lock washer, galvanized (4)
10. Generator support
11. Generator support gasket (2)
12. Oil deflector plate
13. M 12 x 1.5 nut (6)
14. Washer, 12.2 x 22
15. M 8 nut, galvanized (6)
16. Lock washer, galvanized (6)
17. M 8 x 50 bolt, galvanized (6)
18. M 8 x 50 nut (9)
19. Lock washer (11)
20. M 8 x 50 bolt (2)
21. Crankcase

***The gland nut for Automatic Stick Shift engines has no needle bearing or felt ring. The width of its hexagon is 6 mm.**

The gland nut (1) attaches the flywheel to the crankshaft, and four dowel pins (5) in the end of the shaft fix its position. Shims (6) control the axial play.

The gland nut has a needle bearing (which can be seen in Fig. 64) to support the main drive shaft. A metal gasket is fitted between flywheel and crankshaft. Oil seals are recessed at that fitting and in the crankcase at No. 1 main bearing. The oil seal lip fits over the flywheel flange, as shown in Fig. 65.

**Fig. 65.** Flywheel assembly is seen in cross section in this diagram.

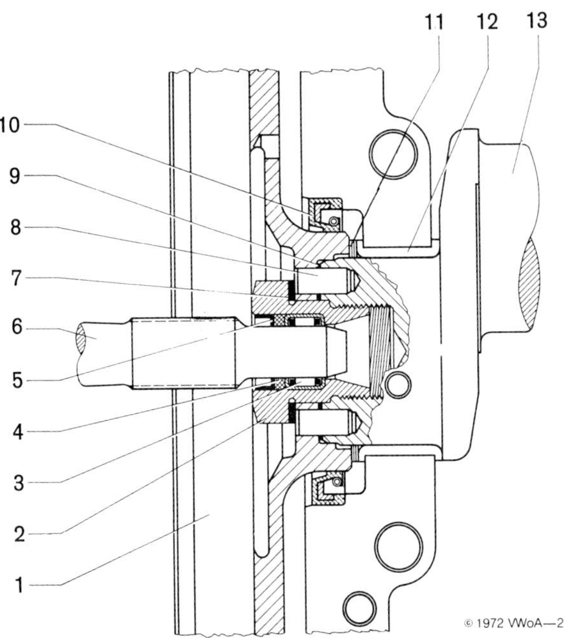


1. Flywheel
2. Gland nut
3. Needle bearing
4. Felt ring
5. Retaining ring
6. Main drive shaft
7. Lock washer
8. Dowel pin
9. Gasket
10. Oil seal
11. Crankcase
12. Crankshaft bearing
13. Crankshaft

## 12.1 Removing and Installing Flywheel

Since the engine was balanced when it was assembled at the factory, the position of the flywheel on the crankshaft is important and must be maintained. If you remove the flywheel, you must take precautions to make sure that you can re-install it in the original position.



**To remove:**

1. Before removal, mark positions of clutch, flywheel and crankshaft relative to each other to provide exact locations for correct re-installation.
2. Remove clutch and driven plate (see Fig. 66).

***WARNING —***
*The flywheel is very heavy. Be careful not to let it fall from the crankshaft as the gland nut is removed. A falling flywheel not only poses a danger to the mechanic, but may result in damage to the starter gear teeth machined into the rim of the flywheel itself. With wear, these teeth may also become very sharp at their outer edges. Care should be taken when handling the flywheel to avoid cutting your hands.*

2

**Fig. 66.** Special tool shown here is used in removal of flywheel after clutch, driven plate and gland nut have been taken off.

3. Remove gland nut.
4. Withdraw flywheel.

**To install:**

1. Check flywheel teeth for wear and damage. Gear rings that are slightly damaged can be re-machined. Up to 0.08 inch (2 mm) of metal at the clutch side of the gear ring can be removed. The teeth then must be chamfered to ensure proper engagement with the starter motor pinion.
2. Check dowel holes in flywheel and crankshaft.
3. Replace dowels if necessary.
4. Adjust crankshaft end play.
5. Check needle bearing in gland nut for wear (see

Fig. 67). The needle bearing should be lubricated with a very small amount (0.2 cc) of universal grease. Lubricate the felt ring with engine oil. Wipe off excess lubricant.

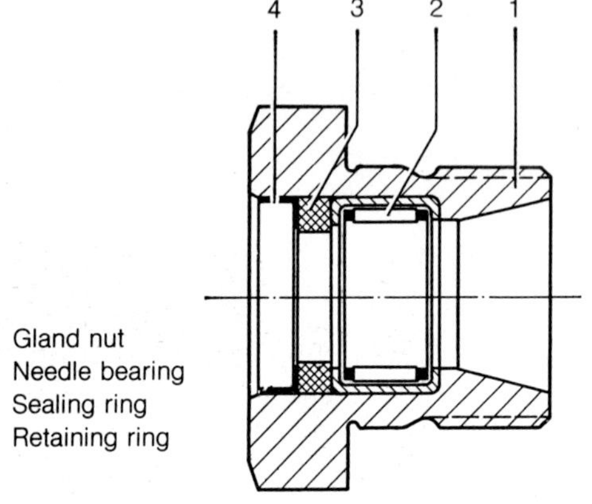


**Fig. 67.** Gland nut for flywheel is shown in cross section in this diagram.

6. Insert metal gasket for flywheel.

**NOTE —**
From chassis No. 116 796 901 (engine No. F0 741 385) the metal gasket between crankshaft and flywheel has been replaced with a rubber seal. See **12.4 Crankshaft End Play.**

7. Observe balance marks. Taking the mark on crankshaft for the reference point, install new flywheel or new clutch with its balance mark 180 degrees from the crankshaft mark.

| Part | Balance mark |
|---|---|
| Flywheel | Paint dot and 0.2-inch (5 mm) hole on face toward clutch |
| Clutch | Paint line on outer edge of clutch pressure plate. |

8. Tighten gland nut to 217 ft. lbs. (30 mkg).
9. Check flywheel for trueness. Maximum run-out allowed is 0.012 inch (0.3 mm).

**NOTE —**
From chassis No. 117 000 003 and engine No. H0 204 001 the 1500 engine has a new starter and a flywheel with a different number of teeth. The new flywheel has 130 teeth, instead of 109, and the outside diameter has been increased by 4 mm to 276 mm. The transmission housing also was changed to accommodate the increased flywheel diameter. The space for the clutch in the housing was enlarged by machining. In addition, the diameter of the hole for the starter pinion shaft was reduced from 0.491 inch to 0.432 inch (12.48 mm to 10.98 mm).

## 12.2 VW Automatic Stick Shift Drive Plate

In place of a flywheel, engines for the VW Automatic Stick Shift have a drive plate attached to the crankshaft with a gland nut (tightening torque 217 ft. lbs., or 30 mkg). The torque converter is attached to this drive plate with four socket-head M8 bolts, which must be removed when the engine is to be removed.

A special retaining ring (see Fig. 68) is used to keep the drive plate from turning while the gland nut is loosened or tightened.

**Fig. 68.** Retaining ring, tightened with wing nuts, keeps Automatic Stick Shift drive plate from turning when gland nut on crankshaft is loosened or tightened.

## 12.3 Removing and Installing Crankshaft Oil Seal
(engine assembled)

A good crankshaft oil seal leaks a small quantity of oil to lubricate the sealing lips and prevent them from burning. The presence of a thin smear of oil on the walls of housing (together with dust from the clutch linings) does not necessarily indicate that oil seal is defective.

**To remove:**

1. Take off flywheel. Inspect oil seal lip contact surface on flywheel flange.
2. Carefully pry out old oil seal.

**To install:**

1. Clean oil seal recess in crankcase and coat it with a thin film of sealing compound. If necessary,

chamfer the outer edge slightly (Fig. 69) with a scraper to avoid damage to outer edge of seal. Clean metal chips from recess.

© 1972 VWoA—227

**Fig. 69.** Scraper cuts slight chamfer on outer edge of oil seal recess to protect seal during installation.

2. Install new oil seal, using special tool. Screw tool into crankshaft and insert oil seal by tightening the guide piece. Oil seal must bed squarely on bottom of recess (see Fig. 70).

© 1972 VWoA—228

**Fig. 70.** Guide piece, the circular part below wrench, is used to seat oil seal squarely on bottom of recess in crankcase.

3. Remove tool.
4. Put flywheel back on crankshaft, observing location marks. Lubricate lip of oil seal.

### 12.4 Crankshaft End Play

The crankshaft end play (axial clearance) should be 0.003 to 0.005 inch (0.07 to 0.13 mm). The wear limit is 0.006 inch (0.15 mm). The end play is measured with engine assembled and flywheel fitted.

2

**To measure:**

1. Install flywheel with shims and metal gasket on engines up to No. F0 741 385 but without oil seal.
2. Attach dial gauge bracket to crankcase (Fig. 71).

© 1972 VWoA—234

**Fig. 71.** End play on crankshaft is measured on flywheel with dial gauge attached to crankcase. Thickness of shim to take up play is calculated from measurement.

3. Move crankshaft back and forth along its axis and measure movement on dial gauge.
4. Calculate thickness of third spacer washer to be used. The reading taken minus 0.10 mm (end play) gives thickness of third shim needed.
5. Remove flywheel.
6. Install oil seal and O-ring inside flywheel.
7. Install flywheel with three shims and new metal gasket, or O-ring.
8. Recheck end play.

## 13. CRANKCASE

In all work on the crankcase it is important to keep in mind that the two halves were machined together to very close tolerances. Never try to pry the halves apart with a sharp tool. Tapping on the right half with a rubber mallet should be enough to separate the halves. Because of the close tolerances involved, the halves are always replaced as a pair.

## 13.1 Disassembling and Assembling Crankcase

**CAUTION —**
*Do not use sharp instruments or corrosive chemicals on the crankcase. Exercise care during all procedures.*

**To disassemble:**

1. Unscrew oil pressure switch.
2. Remove oil filler.
3. Remove oil strainer.
4. Remove oil pump.
5. Remove crankcase nuts.
6. Hold cam followers of right half of crankcase in position with retaining springs.
7. Remove right half of crankcase by tapping with a rubber mallet. Do not force screwdrivers or other sharp tools between joining faces (Fig. 72).

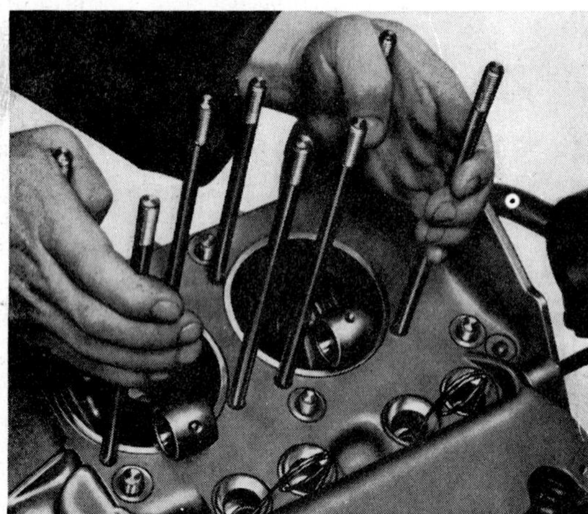



**Fig. 72.** Crankcase disassembly must be accomplished without forcing screwdrivers or other sharp instruments between joining faces of crankcase halves. Tapping with rubber mallet will be sufficient to separate halves.

8. Remove crankcase oil seal.
9. Remove camshaft end plug.
10. Lift out camshaft and crankshaft.
11. Remove cam followers.
12. Remove No. 2 crankshaft and camshaft bearing shells and take out camshaft.
13. Remove oil pressure relief valve.

**To assemble:**

1. Examine crankcase for exterior damage and cracks.
2. Use a non-corrosive solvent to remove all traces of old sealing compound from joining faces.
3. Make sure that joining faces are perfectly even and clean.

**CAUTION —**
*The halves of the crankcase are machined as a pair and must be replaced in pairs only.*

4. Join crankcase halves and tighten nuts to the prescribed torque. Measure crankcase bores for crankshaft bearings. A special dial gauge and micrometer are available for making these measurements. See **22. Engine Technical Data.**
5. Take crankcase apart again.
6. If necessary for smooth installation, slightly chamfer edges of the bearing bores.
7. Flush out oil passages and carefully blow them out with compressed air.
8. Check oil suction pipe for tightness and leaks; if necessary, secure the pipe with a peening tool (see Fig. 73).

**Fig. 73.** Oil suction pipe should be checked for loose fit and leaks at points indicated by black arrows. If necessary, use peening tool to secure pipe tightly in place.

9. Check studs for tightness. If tapped holes are worn, put in Heli-Coil inserts.

10. Check cam followers and the bores in the crankcase. Specifications for 1500 engine call for bore of 0.7480 to 0.7488 inch (19.00-19.02 mm) with wear limit of 0.75 inch (19.05 mm).
11. Insert cam followers.
12. Insert crankshaft bearing dowel pins (see Fig. 74).

© 1972 VWoA—231

**Fig. 74.** Dowel pins for crankshaft bearings are inserted at four points indicated by black arrows.

13. Insert bearing shells for No. 2 main bearing and camshaft and coat them lightly with oil.
14. Install crankshaft and camshaft, making sure that timing marks on timing gears are aligned properly. Check gear backlash and camshaft end play.

**NOTE —**
From chassis No. 117 198 502, engine No. H0 398 526, all M 12 x 1.5 crankcase studs in the 1500 engine are sealed with rubber seals, which fit between the crankcase halves. On early versions of the engine you allow for the seals by countersinking the stud holes in the crankcase half without studs. Prior to assembly of the crankcase halves, slide seals over studs until they bear against crankcase.

15. Hold cam followers of right half of crankcase in position with retaining springs.
16. Install camshaft end plug, using sealing compound (see Fig. 75).
17. For engines equipped with VW Automatic Stick Shift, the camshaft end plug must be installed in

© 1972 VWoA—232

**Fig. 75.** End plug of camshaft (white arrow) is installed in reverse position on engines equipped with Automatic Stick Shift.

the reverse position; that is, with the outside face toward the camshaft.

18. Spread even film of sealing compound on joining faces of the crankcase halves. On no account should the compound enter the oil passages of crankshaft and camshaft bearings.
19. Join crankcase halves and tighten nuts. Torque the M 12 nuts to 24 to 26 ft. lbs. (3.4 to 3.6 mkg). Torque the M 8 nuts to 14 ft. lbs. (2 mkg). First tighten the M 8 nut near the M 12 stud of the No. 1 crankshaft bearing. Then fully tighten the M 12 nuts (see Fig. 76). Observe this tightening sequence strictly. Go through torque procedure only once.

© 1972 VWoA—233

**Fig. 76.** M 8 nut (white arrow) must be tightened before M 12 nuts are tightened to join halves of crankcase.

2

**NOTE —**
Before introduction of the rubber seals on the 1500 engine (from chassis No. 117 070 165 and engine No. H0 230 323) the center M 12 x 1.5 crankcase studs near No. 2 bearing were sealed in production with sealing nuts. Washers are not installed. The sealing nut goes on stud with the plastic ring toward crankcase.

These sealing nuts should be torqued to 18 ft. lbs. (2.5 mkg) instead of the previously specified 25 ft. lbs. (3.5 mkg). When possible, use these new sealing nuts.

20. Turn crankshaft to check for ease of movement.
21. Install oil pressure relief valve.

## 14. CAMSHAFT

The camshaft, which turns at half engine speed, operates the oil pump and drives the valve gear. Fig. 77 shows the camshaft in relation to the rest of the crankcase assembly.

### 14.1 Removing and Installing Camshaft

**To remove:**

1. Open crankcase.
2. Remove camshaft.
3. Remove camshaft bearing shells.

**To install:**

1. Inspect riveted joint between camshaft timing gear and camshaft.

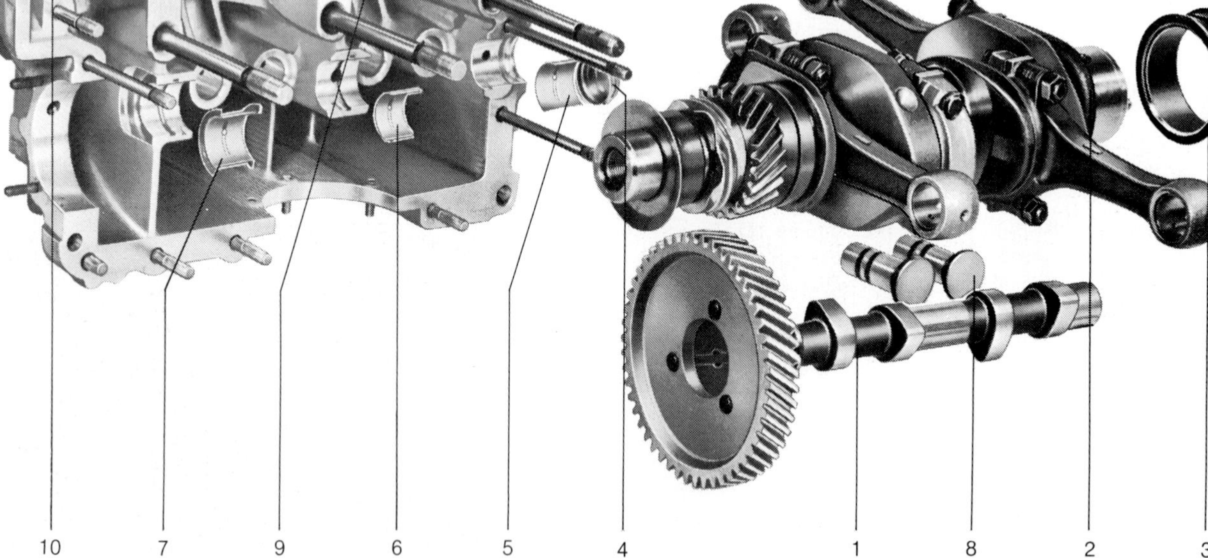


**Fig. 77.** Crankshaft and camshaft assemblies are shown here in an exploded view of 1500 engine case. Not shown but also part of the crankshaft and camshaft assemblies are: dowel pin for crankshaft bearing No. 2, shell for crankshaft bearing No. 2, shells for camshaft bearings No. 1, No. 2 and No. 3, and four cam followers.

1. Camshaft
2. Crankshaft and connecting rods
3. Main bearing No. 1
4. End cap for camshaft bore
5. Camshaft No. 1 bearing shell
6. Camshaft No. 2 bearing shell
7. Left shell for No. 3 camshaft bearing (with thrust shoulder)
8. Cam follower (4)
9. Shell for crankshaft No. 2 bearing
10. Dowel pin for crankshaft bearing (4)
11. Crankcase joint seal (6)
12. Left crankcase half

2. Check camshaft bearing points and cam lobes for wear. The lobes must be perfectly smooth and square, free of scoring.

**NOTE —**
Use oilstone to remove slight scoring. Smooth surface with 100 to 120-grit stone and polish with 280 to 320-grit stone (see Fig. 78).

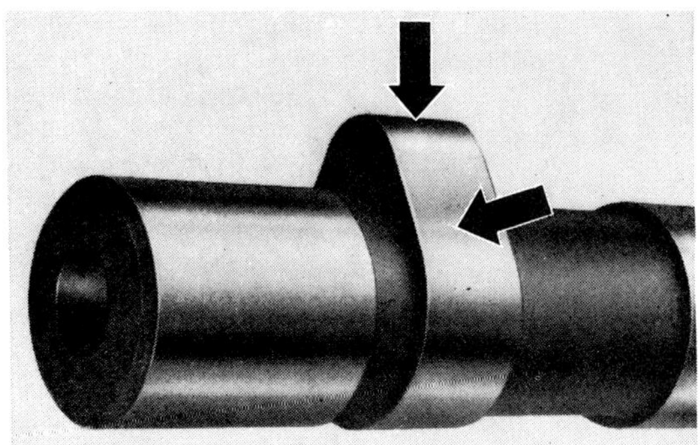

© 1972 VWoA—236

**Fig. 78.** Camshaft lobes must be smooth and square at the points indicated by the arrows.

3. Check camshaft for run-out. The maximum allowed at center journal is 0.04 mm (see Fig. 79).

© 1972 VWoA—237

**Fig. 79.** Camshaft run-out is measured with dial gauge on center bearing in set-up like this.

4. Examine camshaft timing gear for wear and tooth contact.

5. Break edges of bores for camshaft bearing shells at the joint and smooth them to prevent seizure due to pressure on bearings.

6. Check bearing shells for wear and damage. If necessary, replace with new shells.

7. When installing bearing shells, engage tabs in recesses in crankcase (see Fig. 80).

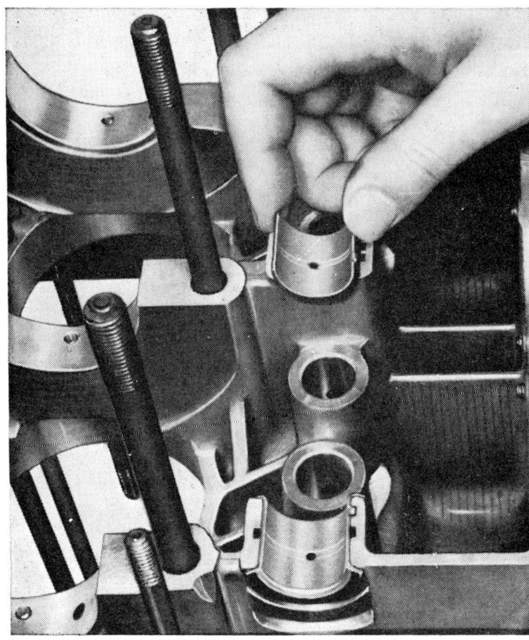

© 1972 VWoA—238

**Fig. 80.** Bearing shells for camshaft are installed to engage tabs in crankcase recesses.

**NOTE —**
No. 3 camshaft bearing takes axial thrust, and shell in left-hand side of crankcase has shoulder on each side to receive this thrust (see Fig. 81).

© 1972 VWoA—239

**Fig. 81.** No. 3 bearing, next to timing gear, takes axial thrust of crankshaft. Shoulders on No. 3 bearing shell can be seen in the picture. Shells for No. 1 and No. 2 bearings have no shoulder.

2

8. Coat bearing journals and cam lobes with engine oil.

9. When installing camshaft, locate timing gear tooth marked "O" between the two crankshaft timing gear teeth that exhibit center punch markings (see Fig. 82).

**Fig. 82.** Tooth marked "O" on camshaft timing gear (white arrow) goes between the two teeth with center punch marks on crankshaft timing gear.

10. Check end play. The end play at the thrust bearing is 0.0015 to 0.0051 inch (0.04 to 0.13 mm) and the wear limit is 0.006 inch (0.16 mm).

11. Check camshaft timing gear for backlash. If the camshaft and crankshaft gears are to run quietly, play between them must be kept at the minimum. To check, rock the gears back and forth while gradually turning the camshaft timing gear through a complete revolution. If excessive play does exist, this check will reveal it.

Camshafts with gears of various sizes are available as replacement parts to reduce backlash. The marking on a replacement gear (−1, +1, +2, etc.) tells in hundredths of a millimeter how much the pitch radius differs from the design size.

**NOTE** —
Each camshaft timing gear has an "O" on the outer face as a reference point for correct meshing with the crankshaft timing gear. The crankshaft timing gear is obtainable in one size only and has no special marking except the punch marks on two adjoining teeth (step 9 above). See Fig. 82.

## 15. CRANKSHAFT

The crankshaft, which was shown with the camshaft in Fig. 77 as part of the crankcase assembly, is seen disassembled in Fig. 83.

**Fig. 83.** Crankshaft assembly for the 1500 engine is shown in this exploded view. One disassembled connecting rod with piston pin is included in group.

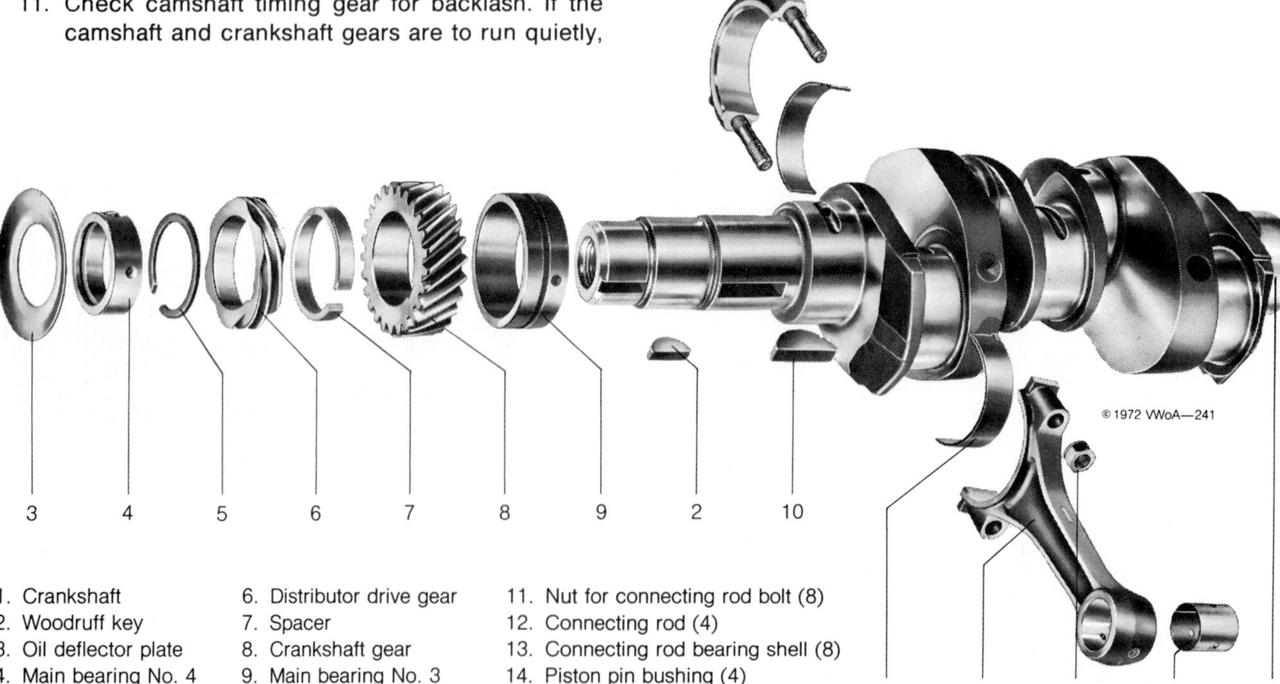




1. Crankshaft
2. Woodruff key
3. Oil deflector plate
4. Main bearing No. 4
5. Circlip
6. Distributor drive gear
7. Spacer
8. Crankshaft gear
9. Main bearing No. 3
10. Woodruff key
11. Nut for connecting rod bolt (8)
12. Connecting rod (4)
13. Connecting rod bearing shell (8)
14. Piston pin bushing (4)

## 15.1 Disassembling and Assembling Crankshaft

**To disassemble:**

1. With circlip pliers remove the distributor drive gear retaining ring (see Fig. 84).

© 1972 VWoA—242

**Fig. 84.** Drive gear for distributor is shown in place on crankshaft. Circlip pliers are used to remove gear retaining ring.

2. Using repair press (Fig. 85) press distributor drive gear, spacer and timing gear off crankshaft.

© 1972 VWoA—243

**Fig. 85.** Repair press and supporting plate are used in removal of gears from crankshaft.

3. Being careful not to alter the press fit, polish out light seizure marks on seating surfaces.

**NOTE** —
Apply rust-inhibiting oil or grease, before storing crankshaft.

**To check:**

1. Check crankshaft for run-out, cracks and wear. Use "ringing" test to detect cracks. When struck a sharp blow with a metal instrument, a crankshaft without cracks gives a characteristic ringing sound. If necessary, regrind or install a replacement. See the following:

| Run-out at bearings 2 and 4 (Bearings 1 and 3 on V blocks) | Journal out-of-round | Out-of-balance |
|---|---|---|
| max. 0.0008 inch 0.02 mm | max. 0.0011 inch 0.03 mm | max. 12 cmg |

2. Clean crankshaft and blow out oil passages with compressed air.
3. Check crankshaft timing gear and distributor drive gear for contact. Look for signs of seizure.

**To assemble:**

1. The timing gear is a shrink-fit on the crankshaft. Heat gear to about 176°F (80°C) in oil bath and press it on shaft. Be sure that chamfer on the gear is toward No. 3 bearing when you press the gear on crankshaft. Slide on spacer. See Fig. 86.

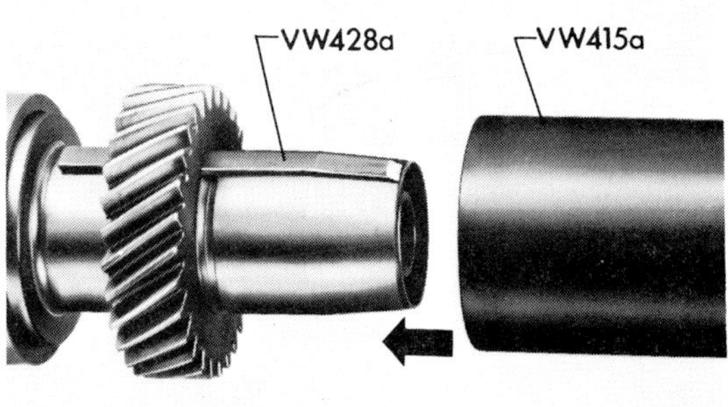


© 1972 VWoA—244

**Fig. 86.** Guide sleeve is used to press heated (176 degrees F) crankshaft gear on crankshaft. Arrow shows direction of movement. Gear is installed with chamfer toward No. 3 bearing.

2

2. Install distributor drive gear by the same method.
3. Slide on retaining ring (see Fig. 87). Tapered guide tube will prevent damage to crankshaft journal. After gears have cooled, test for tight seating.

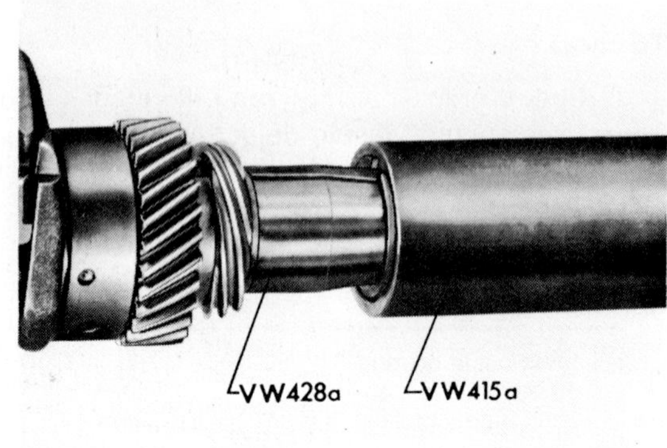




**Fig. 87.** Retaining ring for distributor drive gear is installed on crankshaft with guide tube.

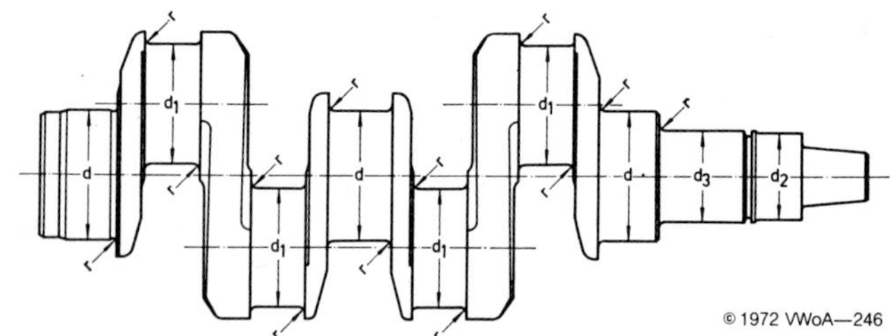




**Fig. 88.** Crankshaft dimensions are given in **Table b.** Gears that are a press fit on the main journals (marked **d** on diagram) must have diameters of 1.6533 to 1.6538 inches (41.995 to 42.006 mm). The radii (labeled **r**) should be 0.08 to 0.10 inch (2.0 to 2.5 mm). Crankshaft timing gear and distributor drive gear are a press fit at $\mathbf{d_3}$, 1.6533 to 1.6538 inches (41.995 to 42.006 mm).

## 15.2 Grinding Crankshaft

A crankshaft that needs regrinding should be taken to a specialty shop. This work requires skill and precision machinery that ordinarily is not available to the individual car owner or at the small general repair shop.

**Table b** gives specifications for the regrinding procedure. Read the dimensions with reference to Fig. 88.

Precision in grinding the radii measurement **r** in Fig. 88 is of great importance to the life of the crankshaft. The specifications are 0.08 to 0.10 inch (2.0 to 2.5 mm). Try for 2.5 mm. Polish after grinding.

The edges of the oil passage openings in the crankshaft will be sharp after grinding. Chamfer them slightly.

Crankshaft timing gear and distributor drive gear must be a press fit on crankshaft (see Fig. 86 and Fig. 87). Specifications call for diameters of 1.6533 to 1.6538 inches (41.995 to 42.006 mm). If gears are worn from repeated removal and re-installation, chromium plating or metal spraying will restore press fit.

On no account are the crankshaft bearing shells to be remachined.

### Table b. Specifications for Regrinding Crankshaft

| | **Main journals Nos. 1, 2, and 3 d** | | **Connecting rod journals ($d_1$)** | | **Main journal No. 4 ($d_2$)** | |
|---|---|---|---|---|---|---|
| | **Nominal diameter** | **Lapped diameter** | **Nominal diameter** | **Lapped diameter** | **Nominal diameter** | **Lapped diameter** |
| **Standard** | 2.1654 in.<br>55.00 mm | 2.1650 in.<br>54.990 mm<br>2.1642 in.<br>54.971 mm | 2.1654 in.<br>55.00 mm | 2.1654 in.<br>54.996 mm<br>2.1646 in.<br>54.983 mm | 1.5748 in.<br>40.00 mm | 1.5748 in.<br>40.00 mm<br>1.5742 in.<br>39.984 mm |
| **1st Undersize** | 2.1555 in.<br>54.75 mm | 2.1551 in.<br>54.740 mm<br>2.1543 in.<br>54.721 mm | 2.1555 in.<br>54.75 mm | 2.1554 in.<br>54.746 mm<br>2.1549 in.<br>54.733 mm | 1.5650 in.<br>39.75 mm | 1.5650 in.<br>39.750 mm<br>1.5643 in.<br>39.734 mm |
| **2nd Undersize** | 2.1457 in.<br>54.50 mm | 2.1453 in.<br>54.490 mm<br>2.1445 in.<br>54.471 mm | 2.1457 in.<br>54.50 mm | 2.1455 in.<br>54.496 mm<br>2.1450 in.<br>54.483 mm | 1.5551 in.<br>39.50 mm | 1.5551 in.<br>39.50 mm<br>1.5545 in.<br>39.484 mm |
| **3rd Undersize** | 2.1358 in.<br>54.25 mm | 2.1354 in.<br>54.240 mm<br>2.1347 in.<br>54.221 mm | 2.1358 in.<br>54.25 mm | 2.1359 in.<br>54.246 mm<br>2.1352 in.<br>54.233 mm | 1.5453 in.<br>39.25 mm | 1.5453 in.<br>39.250 mm<br>1.5447 in.<br>39.234 mm |

## 16. CONNECTING RODS

Since the balance of the moving parts in an engine is of the highest importance, weight of each connecting rod in comparison with weights of the other three rods must be checked carefully. The rod is stripped of bearing shells before weighing, but other fittings are left in place.

### 16.1 Checking and Installing Connecting Rods

**To check:**

1. Inspect connecting rods for external damage.

 **NOTE —**
 Connecting rod bolts must not be driven or pressed out. If bolts are damaged, the complete connecting rod must be replaced. The nuts are always replaced, never re-installed.

2. Weigh connecting rods (see Fig. 89). The difference in weight between any two connecting rods in the same engine must not exceed 10 grams. If one rod is replaced, all must be reweighed. Connecting rods in two weight ranges only are supplied as replacement parts. If matching weights cannot be obtained by replacement, remove metal from the heavier connecting rods at the points indicated in Fig. 89. A reduction of approximately 8 grams in weight can be obtained. The two weight ranges available in replacement parts are given here:

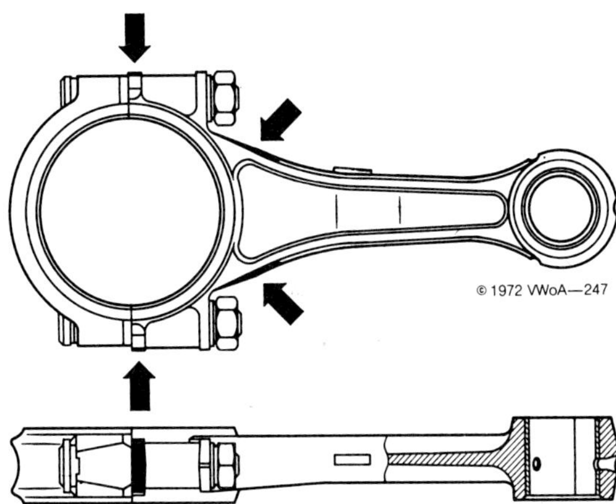


**Fig. 89.** Connecting rod for 1500 engine can be reduced in weight by grinding at points indicated by arrows.

| 1/1300, 1500 | Weight range (brown) in grams | Weight range (gray) in grams |
|---|---|---|
| | 580-588 | 592-600 |

3. Check piston pin bushing. At room temperature the piston pin should be a push fit into new bushing (see Fig. 90).

**Fig. 90.** Piston pin should be push fit (as here) in new bushing at room temperature.

4. Check connecting rod for correct alignment.

**To install:**

1. A connecting rod and cap will each have certain markings on one side, near the joint. When rod and cap are assembled, these markings must be on same side of the assembly.

2. On installation the forged mark on connecting rod must be up (see Fig. 91).

**Fig. 91.** Forged mark (black arrows) must be upward when connecting rods are installed.

2

3. Assemble rods with bearing shells on crankshaft and tighten bolts slightly. Check with feeler for good alignment between rod and crankshaft. Then tighten bolts to specified torque.
4. With rubber mallet tap connecting rod lightly on each side to relax slight strains set up between the bearing halves when connecting rod bolts are tightened (Fig. 92).

**Fig. 92.** Mallet tap on each side of connecting rod relaxes tension between bearing halves after connecting rod bolts are tightened.

5. Measure axial play of connecting rods with feeler gauge (see Fig. 93). Specifications are:
   New: 0.004 to 0.016 inch (0.1 to 0.4 mm)
   Wear limit: 0.0028 inch (0.7 mm)

**Fig. 93.** Feeler gauge is used as here to measure axial play of connecting rod. Play for new rod should be 0.004 to 0.016 inch (0.1 to 0.4 mm).

6. Lock nuts with peening tool (see Fig. 94).

**Fig. 94.** Peening tool applied at indicated point will lock nut on connecting rod bolt.

## 16.2 Repairing Connecting Rods

Slightly bent connecting rods can be straightened, and the bushings, if worn, can be replaced.

**To repair:**

1. Press bushing out on repair press.
2. Place connecting rod in special alignment device (Fig. 95).

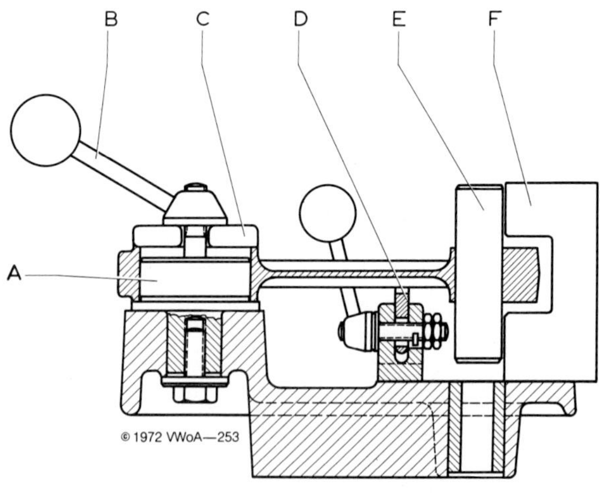


A. Mandrel
B. Locking lever
C. Washer
D. Support
E. Pin
F. Gauge

**Fig. 95.** Straightening device for connecting rods is seen here in cross section. Tool corrects alignment of rods.

3. Turn mandrel of device to bring machined face at right angle to center line of connecting rod. Fig. 96 shows position of rod.

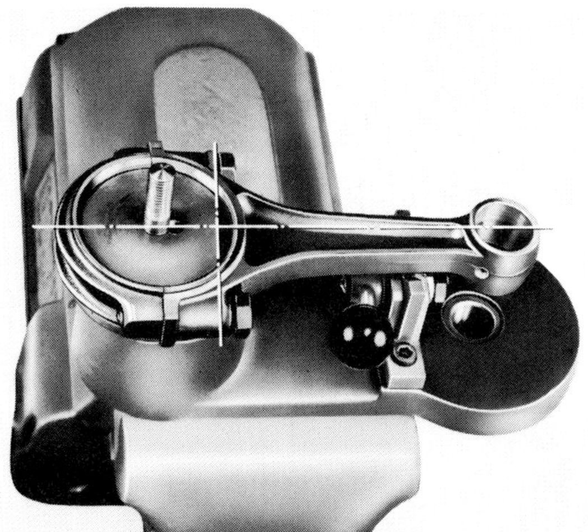

© 1972 VWoA—254

**Fig. 96.** Crankshaft end of connecting rod is over mandrel and eye end over hole in base plate when rod is in position for straightening.

4. Insert pin **E** (Fig. 95) into connecting rod and push it toward mandrel **A** with two fingers to prevent tilt between mandrel and large end of connecting rod eye and pin.
5. Use gauge to check connecting rod for twist and parallelism. Fig. 97 illustrates the operation. If deviations are found, tighten locking lever and straighten connecting rod with the bar.

© 1972 VWoA—255

**Fig. 97.** Perpendicular straightedge checks alignment of pin in eye of connecting rod for parallelism test on special device.

6. Press in bushings with repair press.
7. Using holes in rod as guides, drill oil holes 3.5 mm in diameter into bushings.
8. Insert reamer through connecting rod eye containing bushing and corresponding hole in device (Fig. 98). The conical bushing ensures correct centering of piston pin bushing. After tightening locking lever and support, ream bushing. The reamed bushing bore must be free of scoring and chatter marks. The piston pin must be a light push fit unoiled. Installation of an oversize piston pin in an attempt to eliminate excess clearance between piston pin and bushing will not work. A new bushing must, in all cases, be installed and reamed to size.

**2**

© 1972 VWoA—256

**Fig. 98.** Piston pin bushing is reamed while connecting rod is locked in straightening device.

9. Recheck connecting rod for parallelism and twist, as described previously, but this time with piston pin installed. Slight deviations can be corrected by inserting a bar into the piston pin bushing and straightening rod.

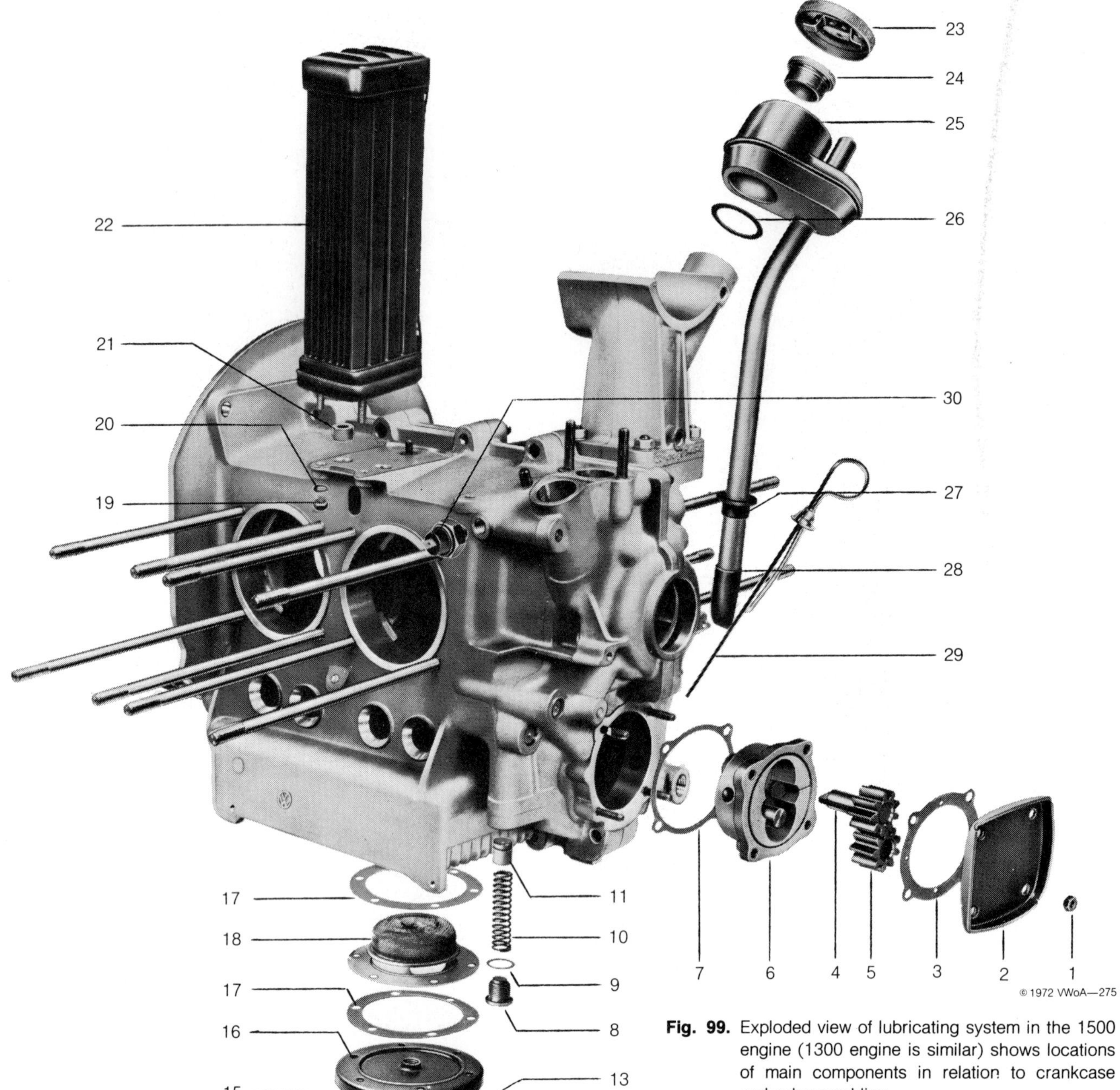


**Fig. 99.** Exploded view of lubricating system in the 1500 engine (1300 engine is similar) shows locations of main components in relation to crankcase and subassemblies.

1. M 8 sealing nut (4)
2. Oil pump cover
3. Oil pump cover gasket
4. Drive shaft
5. Oil pump gear
6. Oil pump housing
7. Oil pump housing gasket
8. M 18 x 1.5 plug
9. Seal
10. Spring
11. Piston for oil pressure relief valve
12. M 6 cap nut (6)
13. Seal (6)
14. Oil drain plug
15. Seal
16. Oil strainer cover
17. Gasket (2)
18. Oil strainer
19. M 6 nut (3)
20. Lock washer (3)
21. Oil cooler seal (2)
22. Oil cooler
23. Oil filler neck cap
24. Gland nut for breather
25. Oil filler and breather assembly
26. Seal
27. Grommet
28. Breather rubber valve
29. Dipstick
30. Oil pressure switch

## 17. ENGINE LUBRICATION SYSTEM

The oil pressure relief valve, which is installed between the oil pump and the oil cooler, regulates oil flow in the VW engine lubrication system (Fig. 99 and Fig. 100), and it is the first part to check when anything seems to be wrong in the system.

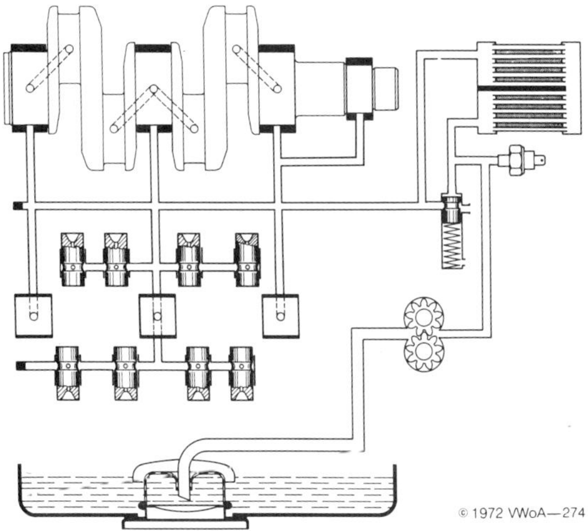

**Fig. 100.** Lubricating system of the engine is shown in this schematic. Geared pump is on line between sump (at bottom) and air cooler (top right). The spring-operated oil pressure relief valve is at right end of main gallery running length of case. Passages leading to bearings are shown. Oil drains from all points into sump, where pump picks it up again.

The location of the valve in relation to the rest of the lubrication system can be seen in the schematic, and its installation in the crankcase is shown in the exploded view of Fig. 99. The sequence that follows—Fig. 101, Fig. 102, and Fig. 103—illustrates how the valve functions through the successive stages of engine warm-up. A brief study of those illustrations will convince you that correct operation of this valve is essential to the functioning of the entire lubrication system.

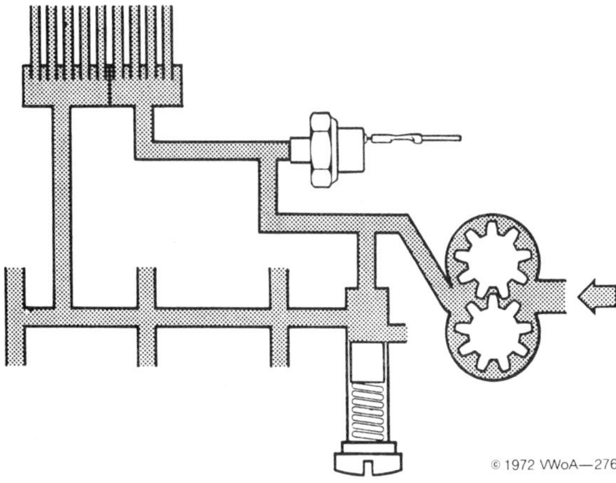

**Fig. 101.** In cold engine oil is thick and pressure very high. As heavy oil flows in from pump (right), it forces down plunger of pressure relief valve. Oil flows directly to lubrication points along main gallery (at lower left) and back into sump (to right of pressure relief valve).

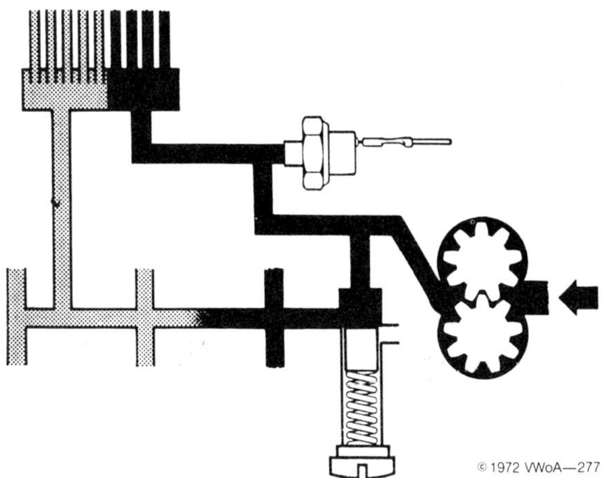

**Fig. 102.** In warming engine oil is thinner, exerts less pressure. Plunger of oil pressure relief valve now can rise to block off by-pass port back to sump. Oil flows to lubrication points along gallery both directly and by way of oil cooler (at top).

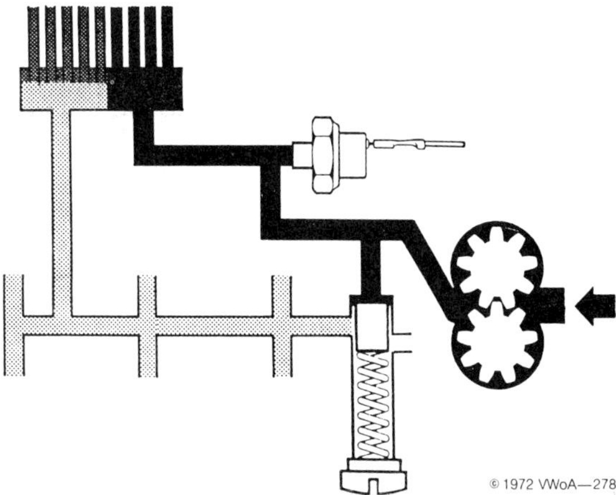

**Fig. 103.** In hot engine pressure is low. Plunger of pressure relief valve now can rise to highest position, blocking gallery to left and by-pass port at right. Now all oil must flow through oil cooler on way to lubrication points.

### 17.1 General Description

#### Cold Engine

When engine oil is cold and thick, the pressure is high. As in Fig. 101, the oil pressure bears the valve plunger down against the valve spring. The plunger is forced below the by-pass port, which leads back to the crankcase sump (in the picture the by-pass port is the opening that leads off to right). Now the plunger is in its lowest position. Some oil is seeping into lubrication points to left of plunger, and some is returning to sump.

#### Warming Engine

As oil warms, it thins, and the pressure drops. Now the valve spring can force the plunger upward, blocking the by-pass port. Oil flows directly to lubrication points by way of gallery to left of valve and also through oil cooler, at top of diagram. Valve blocks return to sump.

#### Hot Engine

At operating temperature oil is hot and thin, the pressure low. As in Fig. 103, plunger rises to highest position and now blocks oil gallery as well as by-pass port. All oil must pass through the oil cooler on way to lubrication points.

### 17.2 Crankcase Ventilation

Oil fumes from the crankcase are drawn from the filler neck through the air cleaner into the carburetor, to be burned in cylinders with fuel mixture. Components making up this ventilation system are shown in Fig. 104.

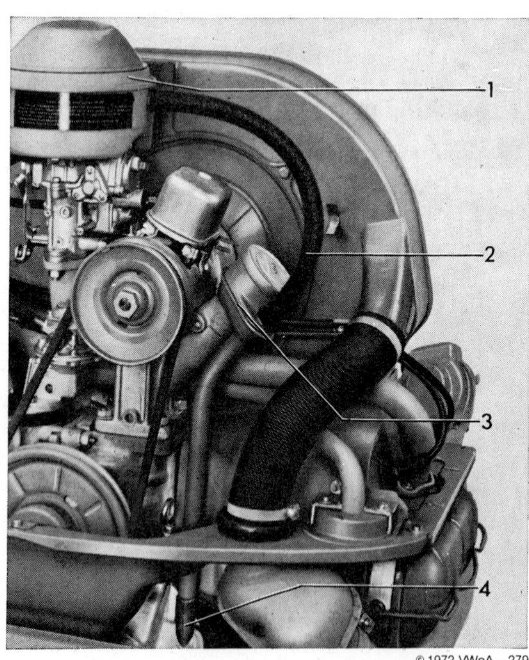




**Fig. 104.** Ventilation system for crankcase includes: air cleaner (1); hose (2); oil filler (3); and rubber drain valve (4). Fumes are drawn through the system into the carburetor and burned with fuel/air mixture in the engine.

On the 1500-cc engine, from chassis No. 118 000 003 and engine No. H0 874 200, an oil deflector plate (Fig. 105) is installed between the crankcase and the generator support to keep oil from being thrown out through the crankcase breather. With some modification this plate can be installed on earlier engines. Gaskets are fitted above and below the plate.

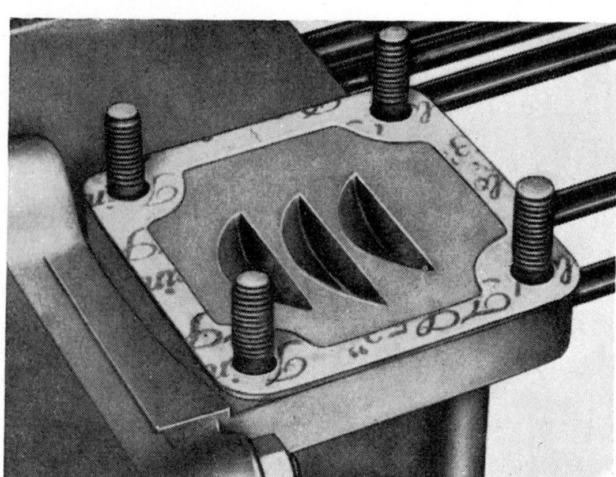



**Fig. 105.** Oil deflector plate between crankcase and generator keeps thrown oil away from crankcase breather. Upper side of plate is marked "Top". Plate is installed as shown.

### 17.3 Removing and Installing Oil Filler and Breather

**To remove:**

1. Pull breather hose off.
2. Remove threaded ring, as in Fig. 106.
3. Remove oil filler along with drain pipe.

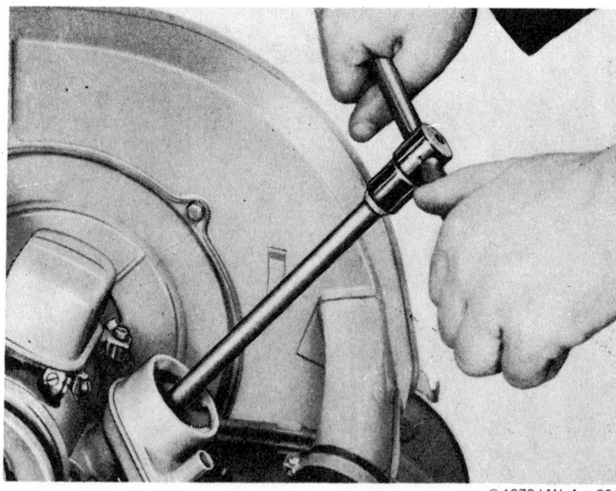



**Fig. 106.** T-wrench unscrews gland nut for removal of oil filler and breather assembly.

**To install:**

1. Put rubber grommet on water drain pipe.
2. Slide rubber valve onto drain pipe (Fig. 107) until button engages in hole in pipe.
3. Fit gasket between generator support and oil filler and install filler.

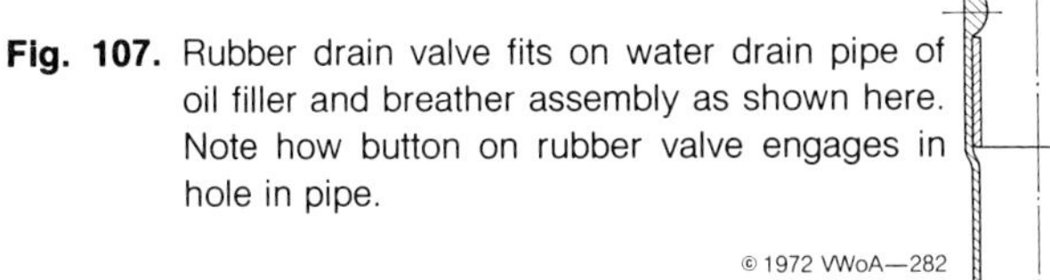

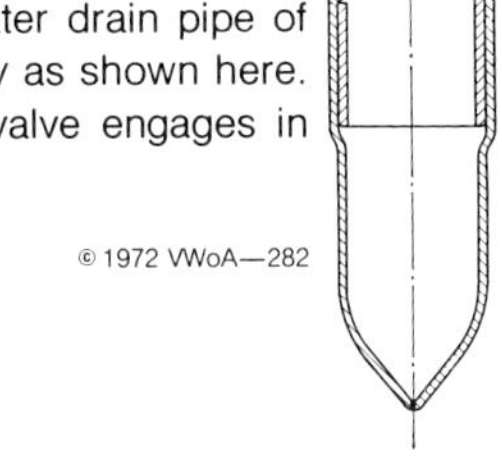

**Fig. 107.** Rubber drain valve fits on water drain pipe of oil filler and breather assembly as shown here. Note how button on rubber valve engages in hole in pipe.



## 17.4 Removing and Installing Oil Strainer (no oil in engine)

When reading the following instructions, look at the exploded view of the oil strainer assembly in Fig. 108, which shows the components of the assembly.

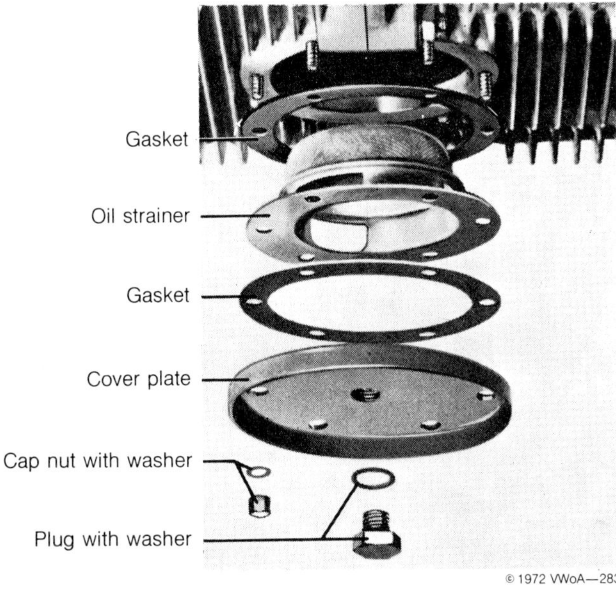




**Fig. 108.** Oil strainer assembly breaks down into parts shown in this exploded view.

**To remove strainer:**

**NOTE —**
For instructions on changing oil, see **LUBRICATION AND MAINTENANCE.**

1. Remove cap nuts on oil strainer plate.
2. Remove oil strainer plate.
3. Remove strainer and gaskets.

**NOTE —**
If plastic-coated gasket is hard to remove, loosen with 5 percent ammonia solution.

**To install:**

1. Clean strainer and remove traces of old gaskets.
2. Replace gaskets.
3. Re-install strainer. Check pick-up tube for correct seat in strainer. If necessary, bend strainer. Check measurements noted in Fig. 109.

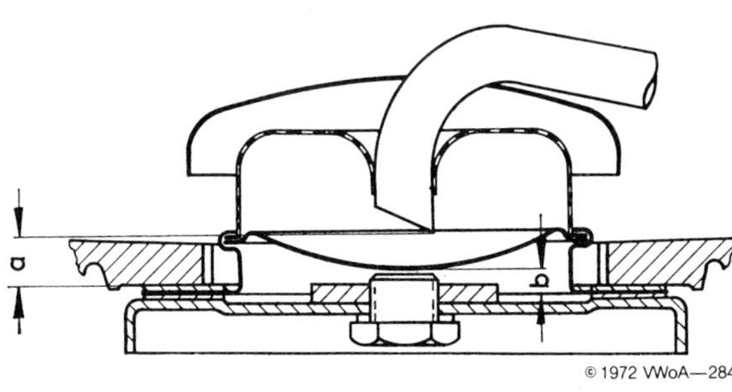




**Fig. 109.** Suction pipe seats in oil strainer as shown in this drawing. Specifications for measurements labeled on diagram are: "a", 0.35 to 0.43 inch (9 to 11 mm), and "b", 0.196 to 0.275 inch (5 to 7 mm).

4. Remove traces of old gasket from contact face of plate. Straighten bent or distorted plate. For good seal contact face must be undistorted.
5. Replace all copper washers.
6. To avoid bending plate, be careful not to over-tighten nuts.

A spring loaded valve (Fig. 110) in the oil strainer allows oil to flow to engine if the oil strainer becomes blocked. This part is installed in 1500 engines from chassis No. 118 045 837.

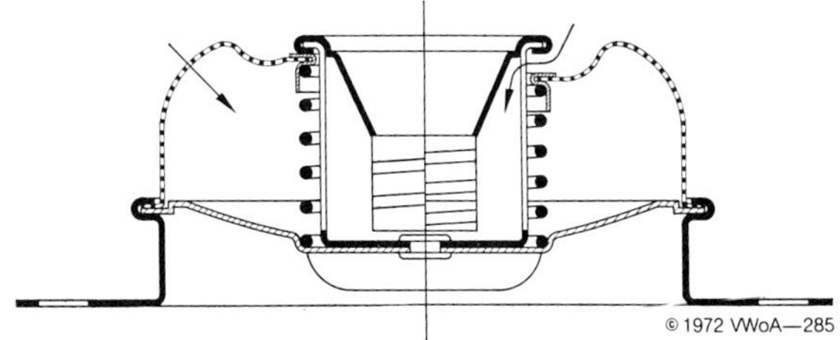



**Fig. 110.** Oil strainer by-pass opens under action of spring-loaded valve, allowing oil to flow to intake pipe if strainer mesh is blocked.

## 17.5 Removing and Installing Oil Pressure Relief Valve

Any trouble in the oil circulation system, particularly oil cooler leaks, is a signal to check the oil pressure relief valve (Fig. 111).

1. Plunger
2. Spring
3. Gasket
4. Plug

**Fig. 111.** Oil pressure relief valve, which forces oil to pass through cooler when engine warms up, is shown in exploded view.

If plunger sticks at top of bore when oil is cold and thick, there is danger of leaking from cooler.

If the plunger sticks at the bottom, oil will flow directly back to the sump, and the engine will not receive sufficient lubrication.

**To remove valve:**

1. Unscrew threaded plug.
2. Remove spring and plunger. A stuck plunger can be removed by screwing a tap M 10 (10 mm metric thread) into it.

**To install:**

1. Check plunger and bore in crankcase for signs of seizure. Carefully remove burrs or other distortions. Install new plunger if necessary.
2. Check spring. Correct specifications are:

| | Length | Load in lbs. (kg) |
|---|---|---|
| **Unloaded** | 2.44-2.52 inches (62-64 mm) | 0 |
| **Loaded** | 0.93 inch (23.6 mm) | 17.1 (7.75) |

In the 1500 engine, from chassis 117 054 916 and engine H0 225 117, piston (plunger) of oil pressure relief valve is modified. This version of piston has annular groove, which allows oil to pass directly to the sump, relieving pressure and lowering engine oil temperature.

## 17.6 Removing and Installing Oil Cooler

***CAUTION —***
*If the engine oil is found to be contaminated with metal particles or if the crankshaft bearings are found to be breaking down, it is advisable to replace the oil cooler.*

**To remove:**

1. If engine is in place on car, take off engine compartment lid and fan housing.
2. Use offset box wrench to remove oil cooler retaining nuts (Fig. 112).
3. Lift off cooler.

**Fig. 112.** Oil cooler is seated in bracket on top of crankcase, exposed to cooling air flow from fan. Retaining nuts are removed with offset wrench.

**To install:**

1. Check oil cooler for leaks. Make sure the mounting studs are secure (see Fig. 113).

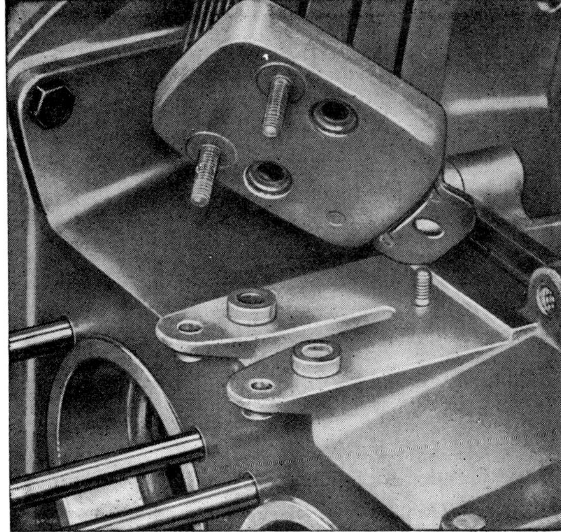

© 1972 VWoA—288

**Fig. 113.** Attaching studs for oil cooler are exposed when cooler is lifted off its bracket.

2. Test cooler at 85 psi (6 kg/cm$^2$) pressure.
3. If cooler leaks, check oil pressure relief valve.
4. Make sure that baffle plates are not loose.
5. Use new seals.
6. Install new seals and cooler. Tighten retaining nuts.

## 17.7 Removing and Installing Oil Pump
(single and double pump)

You can remove the pump while the engine is in the car if you first take off the rear engine cover plate, the crankshaft pulley and the cover plate under the pulley.

Housing, intermediate plate and cover of double oil pump are a matched set. Therefore, if one of these requires replacement, entire pump assembly must be removed. For exploded view of single pump see Fig. 114.

**To remove:**

1. Use a pencil or scribe to make accurate location marks that will fix the position of the pump housing relative to the crankcase. The location marks will enable you to return the pump to its original position when you re-install it.

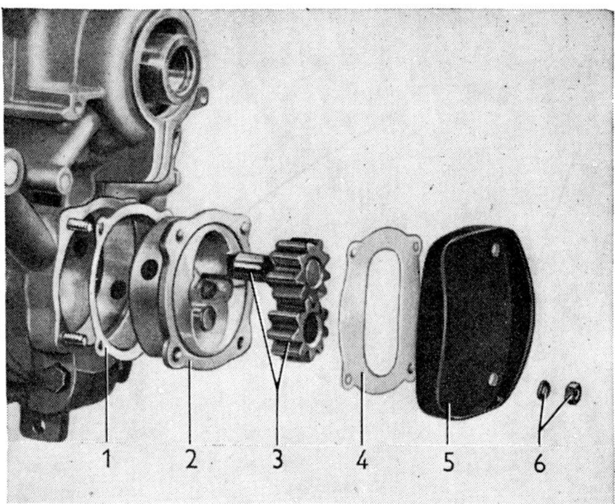


© 1972 VWoA—289

1. Gasket
2. Oil pump body
3. Gears
4. Gasket
5. Cover
6. Nut and washer

**Fig. 114.** Oil pump components are seen here in exploded view.

2. Remove retaining nuts on pump cover and take off cover and gasket.

**NOTE** —
If sealing nuts are removed, make sure on re-installation that you put the nuts back with the plastic rings toward the oil pump cover. Use a 5 percent ammonia solution to remove remaining plastic-coated gasket material.

3. Take out pump gears.
4. Remove oil pump body from crankcase with extractor (see Fig. 115).

© 1972 VWoA—290

**Fig. 115.** Oil pump, which works off camshaft, is removed from crankcase with extractor.

**To install:**

1. Before starting to assemble pump, check the body for wear, especially in the gear seating. Wear in pump body will result in loss of pressure.
2. Check idler gear shaft for tightness. If needed peen it securely in position. Measurement marked "a" in Fig. 116 should be between 0.02 and 0.04 inch (0.5 to 1 mm). If peening or other adjustment cannot meet specification, replace pump body.

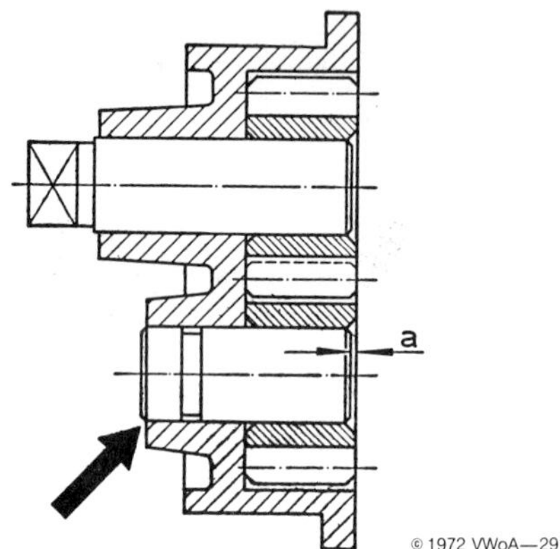


**Fig. 116.** Pump body, shown here in cross section, may wear and allow pressure drop. Idler gear must be tight at point indicated by arrow. Text gives specifications for measurement "a"

3. Check gears for wear. Backlash of 0 to 0.008 inch (0 to 0.02 mm) is permitted.
4. Using square and feeler gauge, as in Fig. 117, check end play. Without gasket, it should be 0.004 inch (0.1 mm).

**Fig. 117.** Axial play of gears in oil pump is checked with straight-edge and feeler gauge in method shown here. Maximum allowable end play without gasket is 0.004 inch (0.1 mm).

5. Check pump body mating surface on crankcase for dirt and damage.
6. Install pump body with gasket but without sealing compound.
7. Hold pump body in place against crankcase.
8. Insert pilot (Fig. 118) into pump body in place of the pump drive shaft and turn camshaft 360 degrees (one complete rotation of the camshaft or two of the crankshaft). This operation will align pump correctly for insertion of pump drive shaft into slot in camshaft.

**Fig. 118.** Pilot holds oil pump body in correct position on crankcase for insertion of pump gears.

9. Mark pump body and crankcase to give check of oil pump position after cover has been installed and tightened.
10. Remove oil pump pilot. Insert gears.
11. Check cover. Machine or replace worn covers.
12. Replace gaskets without sealing compound and install cover. When tightening nuts, do not disturb position of pump body.

## 17.8 Double Oil Pump
(Automatic Stick Shift engine)

Engines for the VW Automatic Stick Shift are equipped with a double oil pump (Fig. 119) which supplies oil to the engine and to the torque converter via separate circuits. The pumps are installed in tandem, separated by a plate with two gaskets, and both are driven from the camshaft. The pump cover holds two connections for the converter oil lines and a pressure relief valve. The valve prevents oil pressure in the converter circuit from rising above 38 to 52 psi (2.7 to 3.7 kg/cm$^2$).

2

**Fig. 119.** Double pump for Automatic Stick Shift engine is shown in exploded view.

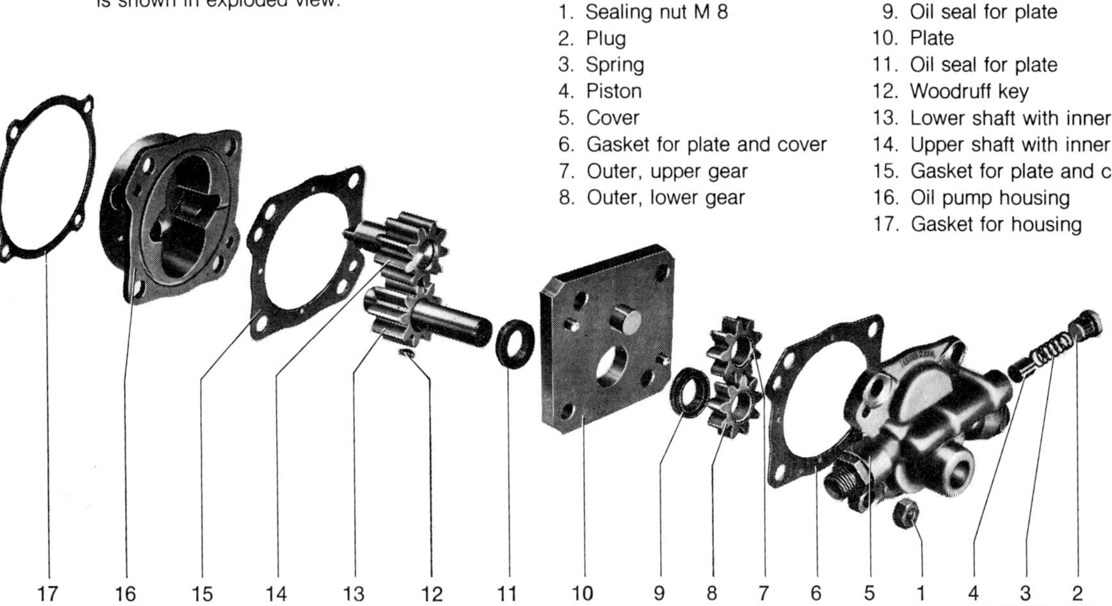

1. Sealing nut M 8
2. Plug
3. Spring
4. Piston
5. Cover
6. Gasket for plate and cover
7. Outer, upper gear
8. Outer, lower gear
9. Oil seal for plate
10. Plate
11. Oil seal for plate
12. Woodruff key
13. Lower shaft with inner gear
14. Upper shaft with inner gear
15. Gasket for plate and cover
16. Oil pump housing
17. Gasket for housing

## 18. IGNITION SYSTEM

The ignition system produces sparks in the four engine cylinders and times the sparking to cause combustion of the fuel and air mixture in each cylinder just as the piston reaches the top of the compression stroke. The system (see Fig. 120) consists of a primary circuit and a secondary circuit. The primary is the low voltage circuit receiving current from the battery (or from the generator by way of the battery). The secondary is a high voltage circuit receiving current from the coil. The secondary produces the sparks.

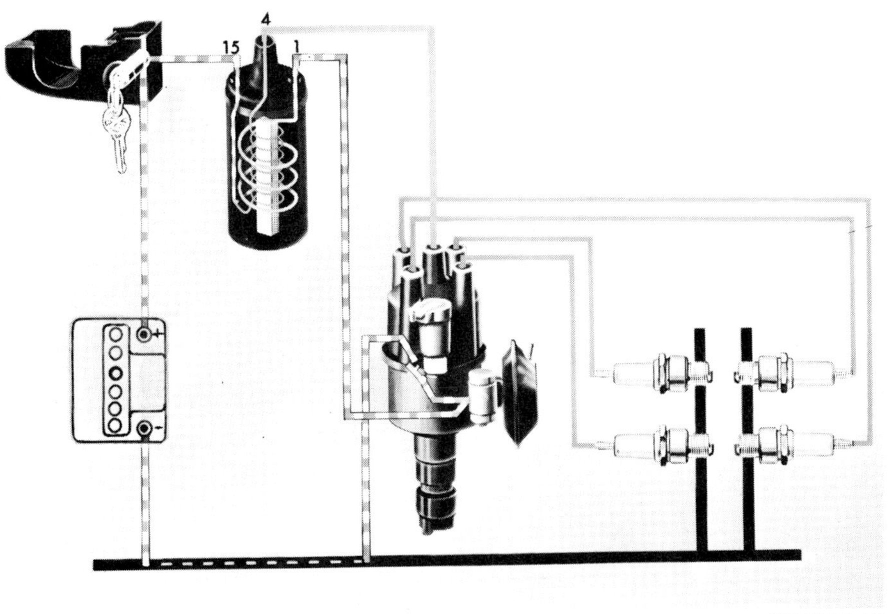


**Fig. 120.** Ignition system, shown in schematic, supplies spark that fires fuel/air mixture in cylinders. Dotted line connects components of primary (low voltage) circuit. Solid line connects components of secondary (high voltage) circuit. Lowest horizontal line is ground.

## 18.1 General Description

The units of the primary circuit are the battery, ignition switch, primary windings of the ignition coil, the contact breaker points in the distributor and the condenser. In Fig. 120 a dotted line connects these components. The secondary circuit units are the distributor rotor, distributor cap, high tension wires and spark plugs. A solid line connects them in the figure.

When the contact breaker points in the distributor are closed, current flows from the battery through the ignition switch, to the primary windings in the coil and through the breaker points to ground. The engine crankshaft turns the distributor shaft, and a cam on the distributor shaft opens the contact breaker points. When the points open, the flow of current in the primary circuit is interrupted.

It is a scientific fact that a magnetic field always appears around a wire carrying an electric current. It is also a fact that if you make a wire cut through a magnetic field (or make a magnetic field cross a wire) a voltage is generated in the wire. Both of these phenomena are put to work in the ignition system of your car.

A magnetic field accompanies the flow of current in the primary circuit. When the breaker points in the distributor interrupt this current flow, the magnetic field around the primary circuit collapses. The coil consists of a few turns of primary winding and a great many more of secondary winding. In the collapse of the primary magnetic field, magnetic lines of force cut across the many turns of wire in the secondary winding, generating voltage. Because there are many turns of wire in the coil, this voltage is very high. Each time the breaker points open, this high voltage is produced in the secondary circuit.

The high voltage current flows from the coil to the spark plug terminals in the distributor cap. A high tension current flows through the plugs in a certain sequence. Inside the cylinder the current jumps the spark plug gap, producing a spark. It is this spark that ignites the fuel/air mixture. The sequence is repeated in each cylinder, timed to produce the spark as the piston completes its compression stroke.

## 18.2 Ignition Coil

The coil functions as a transformer in the ignition system, stepping up voltage from 12 volts at the battery to approximately 20,000 at the plugs. The coil consists of a laminated iron cover wound with a few turns of heavy wire (the primary circuit) and many turns of fine wire (the secondary). The connections (Fig. 121) are:

Terminal 15 to ignition/starter switch
Terminal 1 to distributor (contact breaker)
Terminal 4 to distributor cap (the high tension lead).

**Fig. 121.** Ignition coil has connections shown here: terminal 15 to ignition/starter switch; terminal 1 to contact breaker in distributor and terminal 4 to distributor cap (high tension lead).

### Maintenance of Coil

The coil insulating cap must be kept clean to prevent short circuits and tracking across the cap.

At high coil temperatures a wax-like substance may appear at the bottom of the coil. It has no significance.

### Inspection of Coil

The ignition coil is tested by measuring the spark it produces. This test can be performed either on the engine or on the bench. The minimum voltage at the coil should be 9.6 (12 V system) or 4.8 (6 V). When you have determined that coil voltage is adequate and that the distributor is in working order, disconnect lead 4 at the distributor cap and hold it about half an inch from the crankcase. Have someone crank the engine. If no spark occurs, the coil is faulty and must be replaced, provided the condenser is known to be in order.

## 18.3 Distributor

The distributors used in the cars covered in this Manual are shown in **Table c.**

***WARNING —***
*Whenever repairs are made on engines with an exhaust Emission Control System, it is essential to have the engine, the ignition timing and the carburetor adjusted in accordance with the manufacturer's specifications in order to maintain a low emission level.*

## Table c. Distributor Specifications

| Model/Engine | from Engine no. | Distributor | Basic Ignition Setting |
|---|---|---|---|
| 1300/50 hp | F0 000 001 | Bosch 113 905 205 K<br>VW 113 905 205 L | 7.5° before TDC |
| 1500/53 hp | H0 204 001 | | |
| 1500/53 hp<br>with exhaust emission control | H5 000 001 | Bosch 113 905 205 M | 0° (TDC) |
| 1500/53 hp<br>Automatic Stick Shift<br>with exhaust emission control | H5 077 366 | Bosch 113 905 205 P | |



The distributor (seen in exploded view in Fig. 122) distributes the high voltage current from the coil to each of the four spark plugs in a precise firing order.

As engine speed increases, the travel time of each piston on each of its strokes shortens. For best results, the fuel/air mixture must then be fired earlier on each compression stroke. This advance in firing order is accomplished by a vacuum spark advance, a centrifugal spark advance or a combination of both. Ignition timing to suit all conditions of engine speed and load can be obtained with these devices, which are described below and in the text and illustration on the following page.

1. Breaker plate with ground
2. Condenser
3. Vacuum advance unit
4. Sealing ring
5. Distributor cap
6. Rotor
7. Distributor shaft
8. Fiber washer
9. Contact breaker arm with spring
10. Return spring
11. Contact breaker point
12. Distributor housing
13. Steel washer
14. Driving dog
15. Pin
16. Locking ring

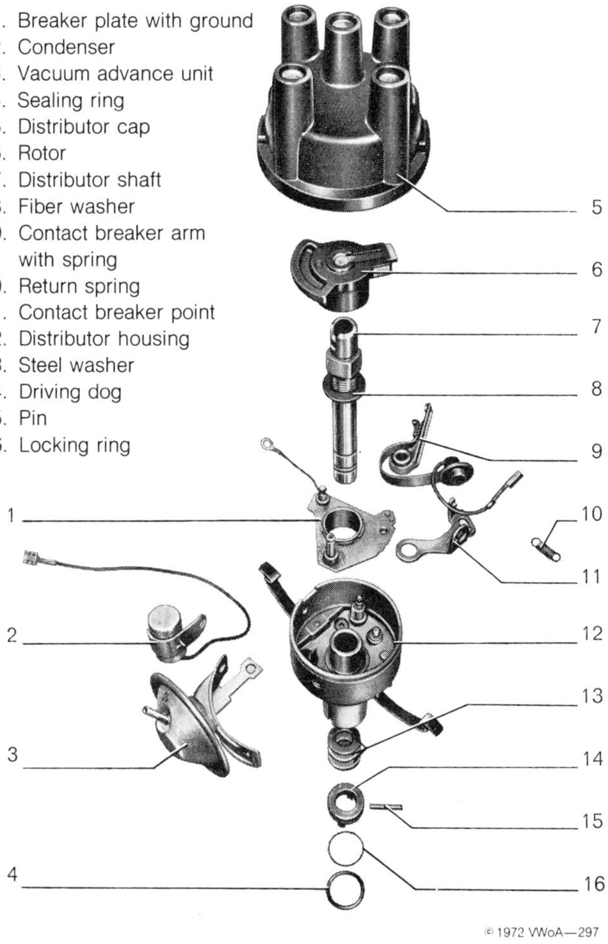

© 1972 VWoA—297

**Fig. 122.** Bosch distributor breaks down into parts shown in this exploded view.

### Vacuum Advance

A vacuum line from the carburetor leads to the vacuum unit on the distributor. The vacuum moves a diaphragm in the unit. A pull rod transmits the diaphragm movement to the contact breaker plate, turning it against the rotation of the distributor shaft. This change in the position of the breaker plate makes the contact points break the circuit earlier in respect to the rotation of the distributor shaft. Since the distributor shaft works off the crankshaft the points are now breaking earlier in respect to rotation of the crankshaft.

When the engine slows down and the carburetor vacuum drops, a return spring moves the contact breaker plate back to its original position.

### Centrifugal Advance

As the distributor shaft turns faster, two weights on the distributor carrier plate fly outward, exerting a pull on the contact breaker cam. The cam turns in the direction of the rotation and thereby advances the timing. With a decrease in speed, return springs pull the weights back into the original positions.

When the two advance mechanisms are operating together, the vacuum advance is pulling the plate against the shaft rotation while the centrifugal advance is pulling the cam ahead of the rotation. Both movements are directed toward causing ignition of the fuel/air mixture earlier in the travel of the piston toward TDC (Top Dead Center) on the compression stroke.

Distributors having only vacuum advance are used on the vast majority of cars covered in this manual. However, the engines used with the Automatic Stick Shift in 1969 are fitted with distributors having both vacuum and centrifugal advance mechanism.

### Spark Advance Malfunctions

Spark advance errors can cause a wide variety of operating problems. Lost performance and poor fuel economy are the inevitible result of faulty spark timing that originates in this way. However, in addition to reducing performance and economy, improper spark advance operation can eventually lead to very serious engine trouble. Both the car owner and service mechanic should constantly remain alert to operating symptoms that might indicate the presence of spark advance malfunctions that are beginning to develop. The following information will not only help in diagnosing spark advance trouble but offers several valuable suggestions for preventing their occurrence.

Any time the spark fails to advance, as it might if the vacuum line connecting the distributor with the carburetor were disconnected or had developed leaks, there will be a noticeable loss of power with rising vehicle speeds. In his attempt to maintain a satisfactory level of performance, the driver would have to depress the accelerator pedal much further than normal and fuel economy would begin to suffer. More important, the resulting increase in fuel consumed would lead to a pronounced rise in engine operating temperature, as would the extra burden of work placed or various engine components by the reduced level of efficiency.

Such overheating can be very harmful to an engine if it is allowed to continue for long periods. Therefore, a thorough check of the spark advance system should always be a part of every tune-up and should never be overlooked when attempting to discover the cause of lost power or reduced economy.

Occasionally dirt and hardened grease inside the distributor will cause the breaker plate to bind or become sluggish in its movements and the advance mechanism will not be able to move it. A serious possibility is that the plate will jam in its fully advanced position and remain there while the engine is being operated at low speeds under heavy loadings. The result of this condition could be preignition, or early firing of the fuel/air mixture in the cylinders of the engine. In extreme cases preignition has been known to burn holes in the tops of pistons.

The first warning of preignition is a "pinging" sound from the engine which persists during acceleration. It resembles the noise of a handfull of marbles being dropped on a steel plate. Many drivers believe that "pinging" is an indication that the engine is producing its maximum power. This is not true. In reality, preignition results in a loss of power. If this symptom becomes obvious in your engine, check the operation of the spark advance and make sure that the spark timing is set properly. Distributors can be checked with the help of a graph such as the one in Fig. 123.

Loose, stretched, rusted or broken springs in the distributor spark advance mechanism can also permit the ignition timing to become over-advanced. Another possible cause of improper spark timing is poor lubrication on the distributor shaft cam. If the wrong type of grease is used on the cam and breaker point rubbing block, or if the cam and rubbing block have received no lubrication at all, there will be excessive friction between the two parts. As a result, the rotation of the cam will tend to carry the contact points and breaker plate along with it fighting the action of the vacuum advance unit and causing the spark to become more and more retarded with increasing engine speeds.

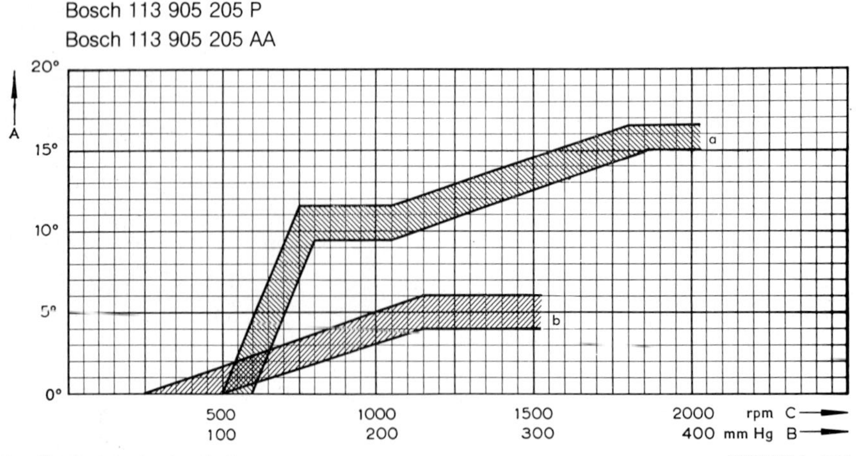


**Fig. 123.** Advance curve for distributors having both vacuum and centrifugal advance. Testing details for other types are on page 64.

## 18.4 Condenser

The condenser (also known as the capacitor) is attached to the distributor and connected in parallel with the contact breaker. A basic condenser consists of a roll of two layers of very thin metal foil separated by sheets of insulating material. The assembly is sealed in a can. The function of the condenser is to hasten collapse of the magnetic field by draining off a surge of self-induced current in the primary winding and to reduce arcing at the points.

## 18.5 Maintenance of Distributor

The normal color of the contact breaker points is a dull slate-gray. In the course of time, burning from the current or arcing may erode, pit or crater the points or cause a build-up of metal on them. While minor wear ordinarily does not interfere with operation of the system, severe burning or build-up can affect engine performance. If any trouble is experienced, the points should be replaced. This procedure is described in detail in **18.8 Replacing Breaker Points.**

Apart from replacing or adjusting the breaker points, maintenance of the distributor is a simple operation but one requiring some care.

**To service distributor:**

1. Working carefully, blow out the inside of distributor with compressed air.
2. Carefully clean fiber block and surface of distributor cam lobe.
3. Apply a small amount of the lithium-base, multipurpose grease to cam lobe surface, spreading evenly. Be careful. It is important to keep the points free of grease.

***CAUTION*—**
*In the heat and sparking of normal operation, grease on the points will carbonize. When lubricating the fiber block on the breaker arm, make sure that you keep the points absolutely clean.*

The sparking that occurs in normal operation of the car subjects the rotor and the four segments of the distributor cap to a certain amount of wear. If the cap cracks or rotor arm burns, trouble may occur. If high-tension leakage and arcing are to be avoided, the cap must be kept clean and dry, inside and out. When mounting the cap, check the spring-loaded button that makes contact with the rotor. Replace the button if necessary.



## 18.6 Adjusting Contact Breaker Points

This adjustment is one of the standard procedures of the engine tune-up. Formerly it was a regular practice to file metal build-up off the points, but today it is customary to replace worn points.

**To adjust:**

1. With ignition OFF, remove distributor cap and rotor.
2. Turn engine until fiber block on breaker arm rests on highest point of cam lobe.
3. Loosen lock screw of fixed breaker point.

***CAUTION*—**
*Do not allow oil or grease to come in contact with the points (for instance, by way of feeler gauge blades). Grease on points will cause misfiring or premature burning of points. When points have been adjusted, ignition timing must be re-set. An alteration of 0.004 inch (0.1 mm) in gap between points alters ignition timing by about 3 degrees.*

4. Insert screwdriver between the two small pins on the contact breaker plate (Fig. 124) and in the slot at the end of the fixed point. (The pins are shown as item 1 in Fig. 125.) Twist screwdriver until clear-

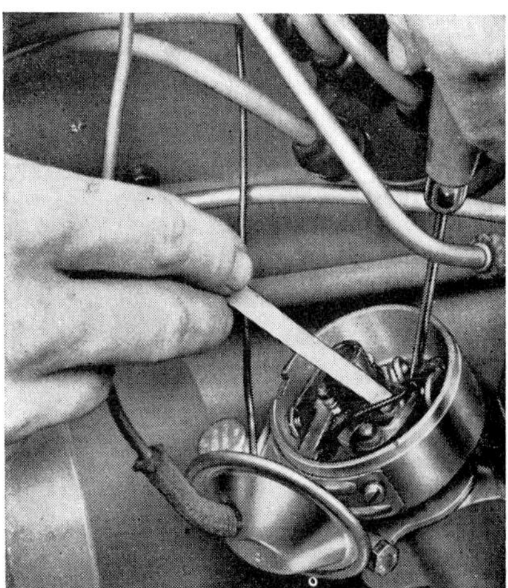



**Fig. 124.** Point gap is adjusted by inserting screwdriver blade between two pins on distributor contact breaker plate and into notch on moveable half of breaker point set and then turning screwdriver. Clearance should be 0.016 inch (0.4 mm) between points.

ance of 0.016 inch (0.4 mm) is obtained. While twisting screwdriver, use feeler gauge to measure the gap.

5. Holding correct gap with screwdriver, tighten lock screw.

The points will open and close at the proper times only if there is no excessive radial play in the distributor shaft bearings.

### 18.7 Dwell Angle

The dwell angle (also known as the cam angle) is the number of degrees the distributor cam turns while the distributor breaker points are closed. The width of the breaker point gap controls this measurement. Decreasing the gap increases dwell angle. Since the build-up of the magnetic field of the primary circuit depends on the length of time the points are closed, the dwell angle obviously is important. If the dwell angle is too small, the magnetic field will collapse too soon and voltage at the spark plugs will be insufficient.

Use of a feeler gauge to adjust the breaker points gap gives an indirect setting of dwell angle. A dwell angle meter, which measures voltage across the points, gives greater accuracy, and use of one is recommended for adjustment of the dwell angle.

The dwell angle for all Bosch distributors listed in **Table c** is 44 to 50 degrees for new points or 42 to 58 degrees for old points.

### 18.8 Replacing Breaker Points

When points are badly burned or too worn for further adjustment, they must be replaced. The points are always replaced as a set.

**To remove:**

1. Remove distributor cap and rotor.
2. Pull cable off.
3. Remove screw holding fixed contact point.
4. Remove circlip on breaker arm shaft (if applicable).
5. Lift contact breaker point out, complete.

**To Install:**

1. Go through steps of removal procedure in reverse.
2. Make sure that breaker arm washers are in correct positions.
3. Adjust contact breaker gap and firing point timing.

### 18.9 Static Ignition Timing
(engine not running)

Fig. 125 gives you a picture of the distributor parts you will be working on in the following procedures.

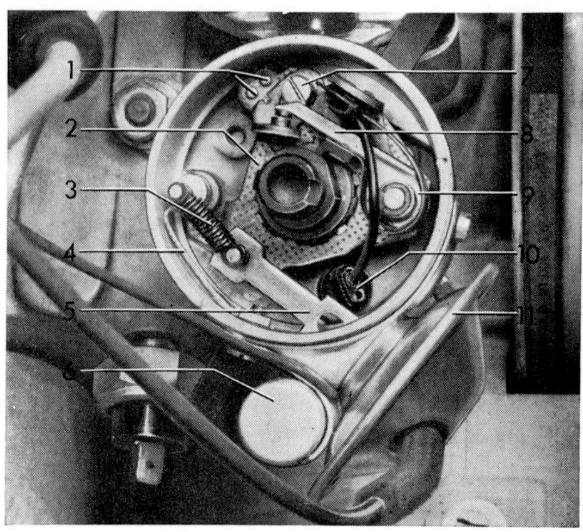




1. Pins and adjusting slot
2. Advance plate
3. Return spring
4. Ground connection
5. Pull rod
6. Condenser
7. Retaining screw
8. Breaker point
9. Breaker arm spring
10. Low tension cable
11. Vacuum unit

**Fig. 125.** Breaker points and other Bosch distributor parts involved in dwell and ignition timing are seen here in position in the distributor housing.

**NOTE —**
You will need a test light for this work.

Before you can set the ignition timing, you must check the breaker point gap, as in the procedure outlined earlier.

On the crankshaft pulley of your car you will find either two or three notches. The number depends on the model year of the car. These notches are reference points for setting the ignition timing. You read the markings with reference to the crankcase joint. When each mark is in line with the crankcase joint, it is showing you that the crankshaft has been turned a certain number of degrees away from the point where the piston of cylinder No. 1 was at Top Dead Center. That is, if you turned the crankshaft back (counter-clockwise) the same number of degrees, the piston of cylinder No. 1 would again be at the top of its compression stroke. You have a definite point from which to measure as you adjust the timing of the ignition. Always turn the crankshaft pulley clockwise to eliminate any play in gears and to minimize errors.

On engines manufactured before August 1967 there are two marks:

| | |
|---|---|
| Left | 7.5 degrees before TDC |
| Right | 10.0 degrees before TDC |

On engines manufactured from August 1967 there are three marks:

| | |
|---|---|
| Left | 0 degrees (at TDC) |
| Center | 7.5 degrees before TDC |
| Right | 10.0 degrees before TDC |

**To time:**

1. Crank the engine until the appropriate mark (see **22. Engine Technical Data**) on the crankshaft pulley lines up with crankcase joint. The distributor rotor arm must be approximately in line with the No. 1 cylinder mark on rim of the distributor base.

 **NOTE —**
 The ignition can be set only when the piston of No. 1 cylinder is at TDC. On some engines No. 3 cylinder fires 4 degrees of crankshaft rotation later than No. 1 cylinder.

2. Loosen clamp nut on distributor retainer.
3. Connect one lead of test light to terminal 1 of ignition coil and the other to ground.
4. Switch on ignition.
5. Rotate distributor body clockwise until contact points are closed. Then turn it slowly counterclockwise until the breaker points just begin to open and the test light lights up. See Fig. 126.

 **NOTE —**
 When turning distributor housing, avoid small rotations; try to make the turns sizable to compensate for play in linkage.

**Fig. 126.** Test light is used in the procedure for ignition timing. See text for explanation.

6. Tighten clamp nut.
7. Re-install rotor and distributor cap.

The ignition is correctly timed for all four cylinders if the test light lights up and the appropriate mark on the pulley is exactly in line with the crankcase joint.

2

## 18.10 Ignition Timing
(engine running)

***WARNING —***
*Keep clear of the fan belt. Never wear a necktie or loose clothing when you are going to work on a running engine. If your hair is long, restrain it in some way. Entanglement of your hair in the fan belt could lead to very serious injury.*

You will need a stroboscopic timing light to set the basic ignition timing on any engine with an Emission Control System. Use of a strobe is recommended also for other engines. The method of setting the basic firing point with a strobe while the engine is running is more accurate than the static method. Operation of the engine eliminates backlash in the ignition distributor drive shaft. When you hook up the test light, follow the procedure recommended by the manufacturer.

Regardless of method used, engine running or not running, the engine oil temperature must be between 68 and 160 degrees F (20 to 70 degrees C) when the basic ignition timing is set.

## 18.11 Testing Condenser

The condenser not only reduces arcing at the points but also affects ignition voltage. If poor spark is causing troubles with starting, it may be a defective condenser that is at fault. Whenever the ignition is timed, the condenser should be checked.

A condenser tester can be used to check the condenser for internal breakdown, insulation loss and capacitance.

**To check if condenser tester is not available:**

1. Remove distributor cap.
2. Turn crankshaft until breaker points are fully open.
3. Disconnect cable 1 at ignition coil.

4. Connect one lead of test light at terminal 1 on ignition coil and other lead to distributor cable (see Fig. 127).

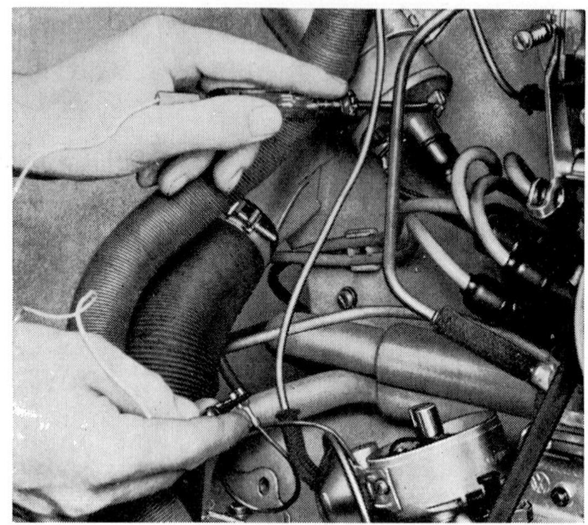


**Fig. 127.** Test light is connected at ignition coil (upper lead) and distributor cable (lower lead) for condenser test described in text.

5. Turn on ignition. If test light comes on, condenser is grounded and should be replaced.
6. Remove test light and reconnect cable 1 between distributor and ignition coil.
7. Remove main high tension cable (No. 4) from distributor cap and hold it about 0.25 inch (10 mm) from a suitable ground.
8. Switch on ignition. Open and close points quickly with small screwdriver. If spark does not jump the distance given, repeat check with a condenser known to be in order.

## 18.12 Removing and Installing Condenser

Only condensers of specified types should be used as replacements. Condensers with wrong capacitances for the system will cut the service life of the points.

**To remove:**

1. Turn off ignition.
2. Disconnect wire at terminal on distributor.
3. Remove screw fastening condenser to distributor and disconnect condenser.

Installation is the reverse of removal. Breaker point gap and ignition timing must be re-adjusted.

## 18.13 VW Distributor

The vacuum advance unit of the VW distributor (see Fig. 128) controls the spark advance over the entire speed range. A ball joint connects the vacuum unit pull rod to the contact breaker plate, which is mounted off center on a steel leaf spring.

Procedures for removal and installation of the VW distributor, adjustment of the ignition timing and condenser testing are the same as for the Bosch distributor.

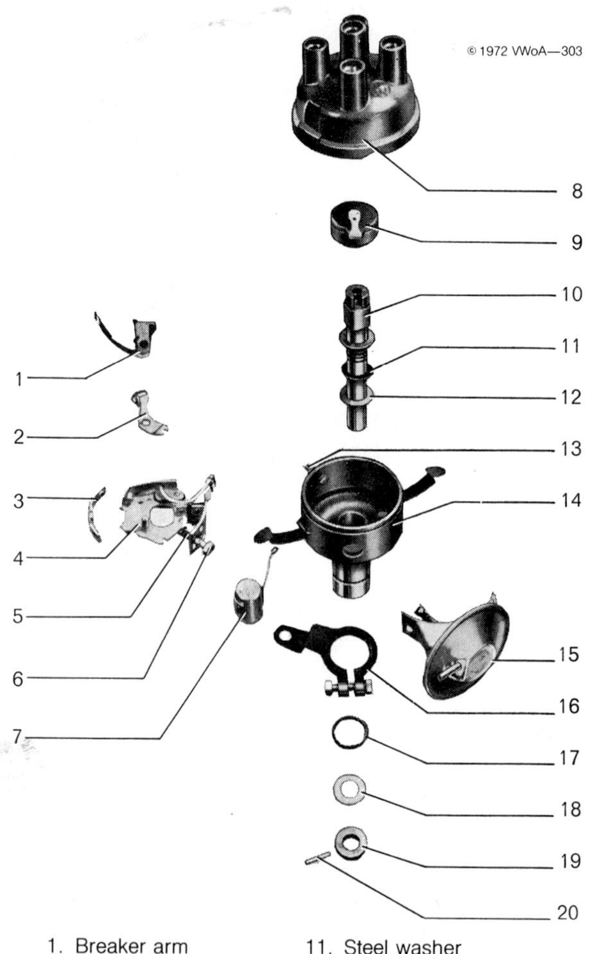


1. Breaker arm
2. Fixed breaker point
3. Stop bracket
4. Breaker plate
5. Spring
6. Threaded rod with nut and lock washer
7. Condenser
8. Distributor cap
9. Rotor
10. Distributor shaft
11. Steel washer
12. Fiber washer
13. Low tension cable
14. Distributor housing
15. Vacuum advance unit
16. Clamp bracket
17. Sealing ring
18. Fiber washer
19. Driving dog
20. Pin

**Fig. 128.** VW distributor, shown here in exploded view, differs in some details from Bosch distributor pictured in Fig. 122.

## 18.14 Maintenance of VW Distributor

Maintenance procedures for the VW distributor also are the same as for the Bosch. There are minor differences in the procedure for adjusting contact breaker points. Fig. 129 shows the parts involved.

1. Primary connection with cable
2. Securing screw
3. Leaf spring
4. Hexagon head screw
5. Stop bracket
6. Breaker arm
7. Breaker arm spring
8. Pull rod
9. Fixed point
10. Adjusting slot
11. Threaded rod
12. Spring
13. Leaf spring for breaker plate
14. Breaker plate

**Fig. 129.** VW breaker points are shown here in view comparable to Fig. 125, which shows Bosch breaker points.

**To adjust points:**

1. With ignition OFF, remove distributor cap and rotor.
2. By rotating crankshaft, turn distributor shaft until points are fully open.
3. Loosen securing screw (shown at 2 in Fig. 129) of breaker point.
4. Insert screwdriver between slot (10) in breaker plate and breaker fixed point. Turn screwdriver left or right until clearance of 0.016 inch (0.4 mm) is obtained.

> ***CAUTION —***
> *Do not allow oil or grease to come in contact with points. Grease or oil there will cause premature burning or misfiring. When points have been adjusted, ignition timing must be reset as a change of 0.04 inch (0.1 mm) in the point gap changes ignition timing about 3 degrees.*

5. Tighten securing screw.
6. Check clearance on all four cam lobes.

> ***CAUTION —***
> *When points are adjusted, contact breaker plate must not be moved from basic position. Otherwise, point gap will be altered.*



**To replace points:**

1. Remove distributor cap and rotor.
2. Remove fixed point securing screw (2).
3. Loosen bolt (4) securing breaker arm spring. (A specially ground 7 mm open-end wrench can be used here.)
4. Lift out breaker arm.
5. Remove fixed point with insulator. Installation is reverse of removal. Point gap and ignition timing must be adjusted.

**To replace condenser:**

1. Unscrew nut from terminal 1 on distributor and take off low tension cable and washers.
2. Remove condenser securing screw and take condenser out.

Installation of a condenser takes place in the reverse order. Only condensers of the recommended type should be used as replacements. Condensers with incorrect capacitance will shorten service life of the points.

## 18.15 Removing and Installing Distributor

For basic ignition settings see **Table c** in **18.3 Distributor.**

**To remove:**

1. Disconnect both cables between coil and distributor and pull hose off vacuum unit.
2. Take off distributor cap.
3. Rotate crankshaft pulley to TDC and distributor rotor to No. 1 position. If crankshaft pulley lacks the notch at 0°, you can obtain the approximate TDC position by aligning the rotor with the No. 1 cylinder mark on the distributor housing rim.
4. Remove large nut from distributor retaining bracket.
5. Remove distributor with bracket. Be careful not to drop or lose spring under distributor.

**To install:**

1. Check to be sure that crankshaft pulley is still at TDC (both valves closed.) Fig. 130 shows position.

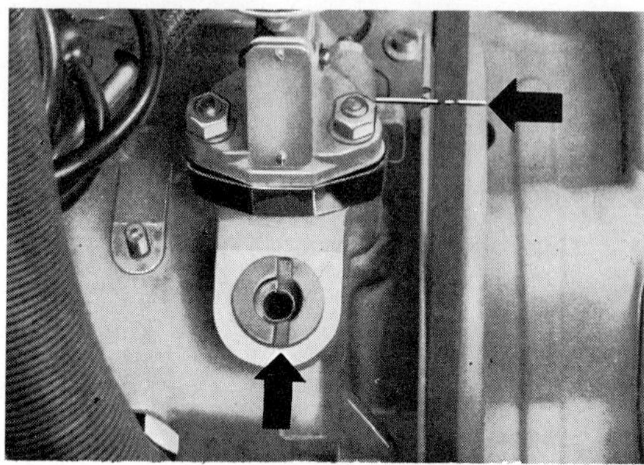

© 1972 VWoA—305

**Fig. 130.** Slot (lower arrow) in distributor drive pinion lines up in this position when piston of No. 1 cylinder is at TDC. Note also that timing notch (upper arrow) on crankshaft pulley is lined up with crankcase joint. This position is basic reference point for ignition timing.

**NOTE ——**
The slot in the distributor drive shaft should be almost parallel with pulley and offset toward pulley. Timing mark on pulley should align with crankcase joint.

2. Check that distributor rotor arm points to mark for No. 1 cylinder on distributor housing (Fig. 131).

© 1972 VWoA—306

**Fig. 131.** Line through rotor arm of distributor also passes through No. 1 cylinder mark on rim of distributor housing. Arm must be in this position for distributor shaft to engage properly in drive pinion slot. Note second line (lower center of picture) through timing notch on crankshaft pulley and crankcase joint.

3. Insert distributor with bracket. Turn rotor back and forth until distributor engages in drive shaft slot.
4. Adjust ignition timing.

## 18.16 Removing and Installing Distributor Drive Shaft

This procedure requires removal of fuel pump, which works off an eccentric cam on the distributor drive shaft.

**To remove:**

1. Take off distributor cap and turn engine until distributor rotor points to No. 1 cylinder mark on distributor housing rim (or position of appropriate crankshaft pulley notch shows TDC).
2. Remove large distributor bracket retaining nut. Pull out distributor along with bracket. Be careful not to lose spring below distributor.

**NOTE ——**
Taking distributor and bracket out together avoids damage to seal.

3. Remove fuel pump with intermediate flange with gasket (or gaskets) and push rod. Note number and placement of gaskets. Be careful not to let push rod drop into crankcase.
4. Take spacer spring out of distributor drive shaft.
5. Withdraw drive shaft with an expander-type removal tool by lifting and turning the shaft to the left (see Fig. 132).

***CAUTION ——***
*Do not drop the two washers under drive shaft into engine.*

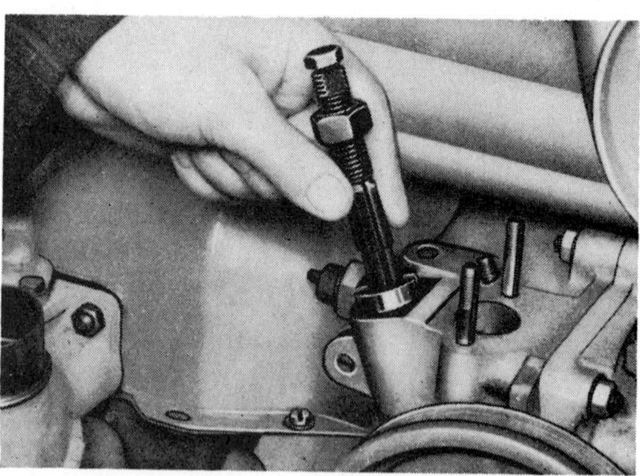

© 1972 VWoA—307

**Fig. 132.** Drive shaft of distributor is withdrawn with special tool after No. 1 cylinder has been set at TDC.

6. Using a magnet, remove the two washers under drive shaft. If engine has been removed and is on stand, and if oil has been drained, rotate engine to let washers fall out.

**To install:**

1. Check eccentric and spiral gear on drive shaft for wear. If spiral gear shows excessive wear, teeth of distributor drive gear on crankshaft must also be checked.
2. Check washers under drive shaft for wear. Replace them if necessary (see Fig. 133).

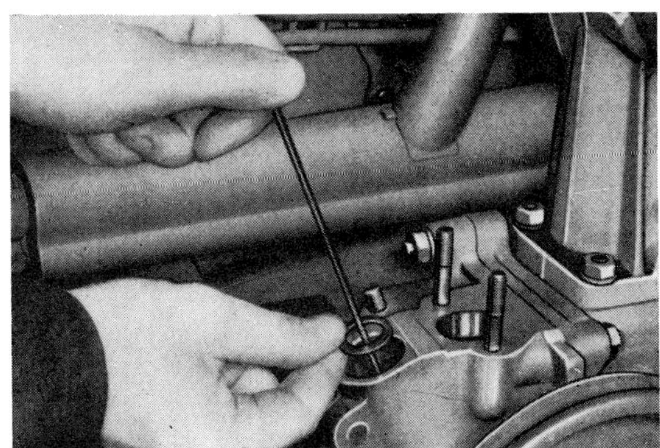

© 1972 VWoA—308

**Fig. 133.** Magnet picks up washers on which distributor drive shaft seats.

***CAUTION*** —
*Do not drop washers into engine.*

3. Install washers.
4. If crankshaft has been turned, reset No. 1 piston to TDC of compression stroke.
5. Install distributor drive shaft (see Fig. 134).

© 1972 VWoA—309

**Fig. 134.** Drive pinion must be turned to basic reference position (see Fig. 130) before distributor drive shaft is installed.

When installed in engines with emission control devices, distributor drive shaft should be turned counterclockwise 30 degrees (one tooth to left). Slot of drive shaft should then point to stud for attaching fuel pump, as shown in Fig. 130. With TDC correctly set, the vacuum unit is then at right angle to longitudinal axis of car.

## 18.17 Disassembling and Assembling Distributor

2

Study of the exploded views of the Bosch and VW distributors (Fig. 122 and Fig. 128) will be helpful preparation for this procedure.

**To disassemble:**

1. Remove contact breaker points.
2. Remove vacuum unit.
3. Mark location of centrifugal weights.
4. Mark position of driving dog in relation to shaft and distributor housing (see Fig. 135).

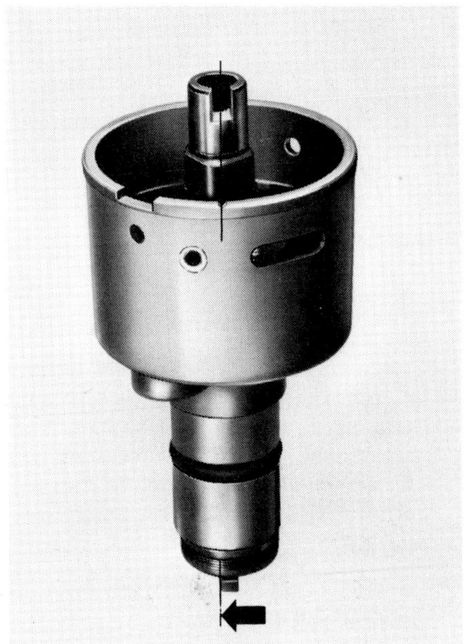

© 1972 VWoA—310

**Fig. 135.** Driving dog must line up with line (arrow) running through No. 1 cylinder mark on distributor housing rim and notch in cam on drive shaft. Mark dog position before disassembly.

5. Knock pin out of driving dog with punch.
6. Take driving dog off, note position and number of washers.

**To check:**

1. If radial play between shaft and housing is excessive, fit a new shaft and eliminate axial play with washers. If bushings in the distributor housing are badly worn, replace distributor.
2. If breaker plate has too much rock, fit a new plate. If the wear is in distributor housing, install a new distributor.

**To assemble:**

1. Oil distributor shaft.
2. Install steel and fiber washers in correct number and order.
3. Install the driving dog on shaft in the correct position (Fig. 135).
4. Install centrifugal weights as marked.

## 18.18 Checking Distributor on Test Stand

A distributor test stand is used to check cam offset, vacuum advance, centrifugal advance and dwell angle. There are various types of test stands on the market, but all have variable speed motors, tachometers, vacuum pumps and vacuum measuring gauges with a range of 0 to 100 mm (mercury).

**To test distributor:**

1. Clamp distributor in position and make sure that it turns smoothly.
2. Check dwell angle (see **18.7 Dwell Angle**). It may be necessary to adjust the contact gap and thus the dwell angle.
3. Set speed at 500 rpm. Note that at this speed the centrifugal advance mechanism has not started to operate.
4. Connect hose between vacuum pump and vacuum unit on distributor. Obtain full vacuum with pump.
5. Check vacuum unit for leakage. A vacuum of 100 mm of mercury should remain constant for about 1 minute with the vacuum line sealed.
6. With decreasing vacuum, measure vacuum advance. At as many points as possible measure the vacuum to the vacuum unit and read off actual advance figures obtained on test stand scale. The values must be inside the shaded area of the advance curves (see Fig. 136). If they are outside this area, repeat test with a new vacuum unit.
7. Run off speed sensitive advance curves on test stand. These values must also be within the shaded area in Fig. 136.

Bosch 111 905 205 T
Bosch 113 905 205 K
VW 113 905 205 L

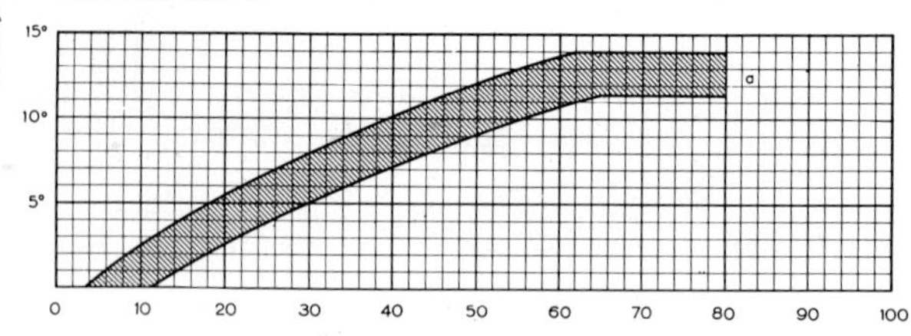


Bosch 113 905 205 M
Bosch 113 905 205 T

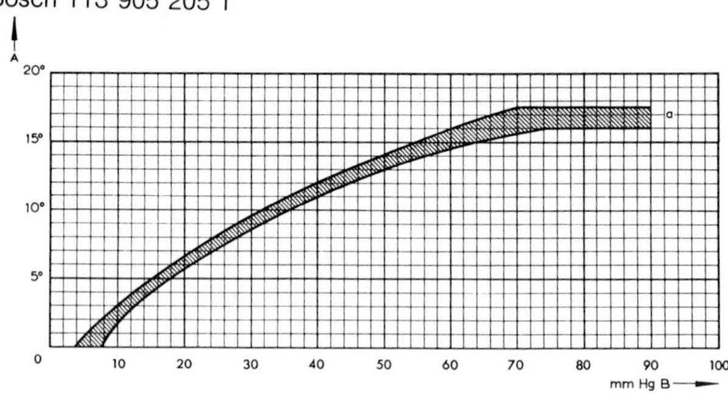




**Fig. 136.** Advance curves for distributors on test stand are given here for the distributors used on cars covered in this Manual. The advance in degrees of distributor shaft rotation is plotted against the vacuum in millimeters of mercury.

## 18.19 Spark Plugs

Spark plugs must resist very high electrical, mechanical, chemical and thermal stresses. Therefore, the quality of the plugs will have a considerable effect on engine performance. The intensity of the spark under varying conditions will influence starting, idle, acceleration and maximum engine output.

### Types

Spark plugs are classified according to their ability to dissipate heat. Plugs manufactured by Bosch, Beru and Champion may be used as well as others that comply with specification. See **22. Engine Technical Data.** The general specifications for the plugs are:

| | |
|---|---|
| Spark plug thread diameter | 14 mm |
| Spark plug gap | 0.024 to 0.028 inch (0.6 to 0.7 mm) |

The gap is shown as measurement "a" in Fig. 137.

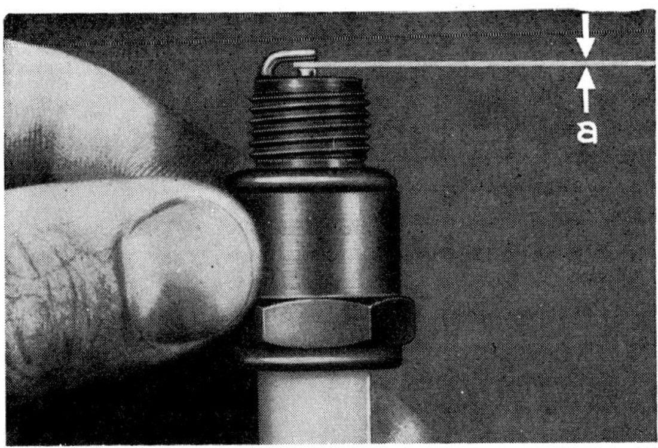


**Fig. 137.** Spark gap between electrodes of spark plug can be adjusted by bending upper electrode. The gap, shown as "a" in picture, should measure 0.024 to 0.028 inch (0.6 to 0.7 mm).

### Maintenance and Inspection

Spark plugs should be cleaned and the gaps checked at intervals of 6000 miles. It is advisable to install new plugs every 12,000 miles.

**NOTE** —
Do not forget washers when installing spark plugs.

To an experienced mechanic, the appearance of the spark plug gives immediate evidence of the adjustment and operating condition of the engine. The following diagnoses are generally applicable and should be of help to you.

| Color | Condition |
|---|---|
| gray | good carburetor setting<br>good plug performance |
| black | mixture too rich |
| light gray | mixture too lean |
| oiled up | plug failure or piston ring leakage |

In normal operation burning increases plug gap. If the increase is too great, the plug may fail to operate. The gap is measured with a gauge and adjusted to the correct value by bending the ground (outer) electrode (see Fig. 137).

In winter it is permissible to reduce the spark gap temporarily from 0.028 to 0.020 inch (0.7 to 0.5 mm) to make starting easier in the cold weather.

A number of testing devices for spark plugs are in use where the sparking occurs under pressure of 85 to 114 psi (6 to 8 kg/cm$^2$) and can be watched through an inspection hole.

Spark plugs should be cleaned in a sand blasting apparatus designed for the purpose and usually combined with appliances for testing. In an emergency you can clean spark plugs by scraping them with a piece of wood.

## 19. CLUTCH

The standard transmission cars covered in this Manual have a single-plate clutch of the dry disk type to transfer power from engine to transmission. Fig. 138 shows the clutch in cross section. The clutch cover, which carries the pressure plate, thrust springs, release levers and release ring, is bolted to the flywheel. The driven plate, to which the friction linings are riveted, is splined to the main drive shaft. When engaged, the spring-loaded pressure plate forces the driven plate

2

**Fig. 138.** The clutch is shown in this cutaway drawing as it would be seen by a person standing at the left side of the car. The engine would be at right.

1. Operating shaft
2. Release bearing
3. Main drive shaft
4. Release ring
5. Release lever
6. Bolt and special adjusting nut
7. Release lever spring
8. Thrust spring
9. Cover
10. Needle bearing for gland nut
11. Driven plate
12. Flywheel
13. Lining
14. Pressure plate

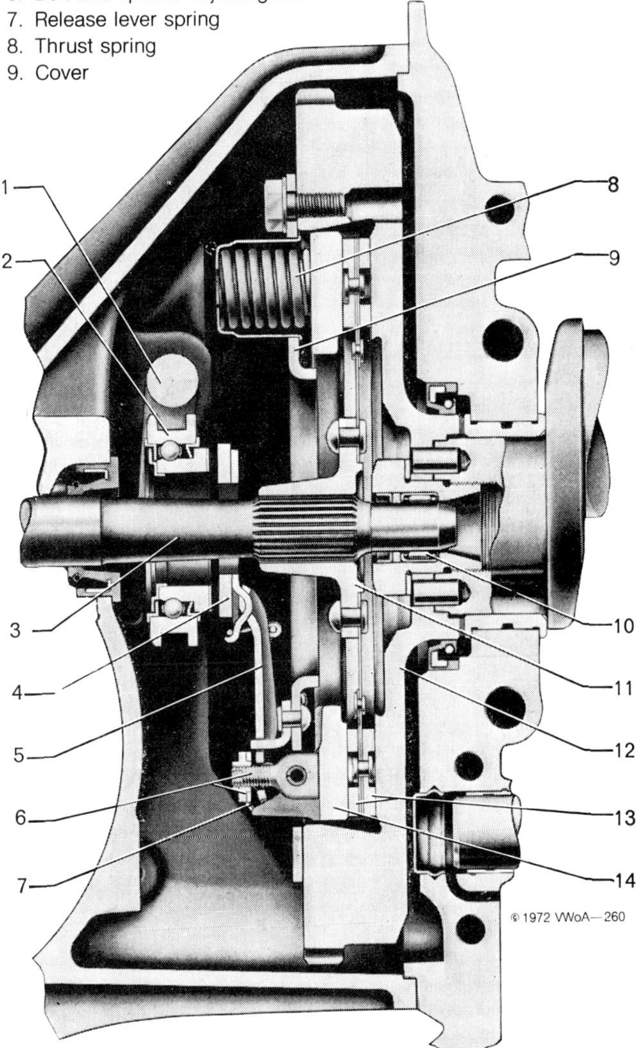

against the flywheel. The flywheel turns the driven plate, and the driven plate, by means of the spline, turns the main drive shaft. Thus engine output is transferred to the transmission.

## 19.1 Operation

(part number references are from Fig. 138)

To release the clutch, the driver depresses the clutch pedal. A cable transmits this pedal movement to the clutch operating lever, which is mounted on the outside of the transmission case. The lever turns the clutch operating shaft (1), which is inside the transmission case, and the two lugs on the shaft release fork push the release bearing (2) along the main drive shaft (3) toward the flywheel (12). With the bearing pushing on them, through the release ring (4), the three release levers (5) force the clutch pressure plate (14) away from the driven plate (11). Once the pressure plate has been moved away by the levers, the driven plate can disengage from the flywheel. In Fig. 138 the direction of the pressure plate and driven plate movement would be to the left.

The release bearing is a ball bearing with a plastic ring. It requires no maintenance. The cable linkage between the clutch pedal and the clutch is described in the **BODY AND FRAME** section of the Manual.

## 19.2 Adjustments

Servicing of the clutch is limited to adjusting the free play of the clutch pedal as the linings wear. VW specifications call for a free play of $^{13}/_{32}$ to $^{13}/_{16}$ inch (10 to 20 mm). No other adjustment is made unless the clutch is disassembled for replacement of parts. The procedure that is done in that case requires a special clutch adjustment gauge.

A diaphragm spring clutch (Fig. 139) is available as a replacement part on 1968 and 1969 cars. This clutch engages more rapidly than the clutch with coil springs does, and it requires less pedal pressure. In case of wear or damage the entire diaphragm spring clutch assembly must be removed and replaced. No replacement parts for it are available.

**Fig. 139.** Diaphragm spring clutch can be used as replacement for clutch with coil springs.

## 19.3 Removing and Installing Clutch

When any part of the clutch requires replacement, it is advisable also to replace the clutch pressure plate, clutch disk and possibly the release bearing if they appear worn.

**To remove clutch:**

1. Mark clutch and flywheel for accurate relocation.
2. Release clutch cover securing bolts evenly and diagonally (see Fig. 140). To prevent distortion from uneven tension of the thrust springs, give each bolt one or two turns at a time.
3. Take off clutch pressure plate and disk.

**Fig. 140.** Clutch pressure plate and cover come off flywheel after securing bolts have been removed.

**To install:**

1. Check clutch disk contact surface on flywheel. Surface cracks and grooves can be removed by regrinding or machining. Replace flywheel if necessary.
2. Check driven plate.
3. Check main drive shaft splines. Driven plate must slide freely on splines without sloppy radial movement.
4. Check bearing points of clutch operating shaft in transmission case. Replace worn bushings.

5. Check release bearing. The ball bearing requires no maintenance. Wipe it with clean cloth. Do not wash it in gasoline or other solvent. Replace a noisy or rough bearing.
6. Engage both clips fully in release bearing. Then, holding bearing against release fork on clutch operating shaft, grasp each clip with long-nosed pliers and snap it over lug on release fork.
7. If you are re-installing a release bearing that has been on the car, roughen the plastic ring with emery cloth and lubricate bearing contact surface with a molybdenum disulfide compound (Moly-Kote®). If it is a new replacement bearing, spraying the contact surface with Moly-Kote® will be sufficient.
8. Lubricate a new or old needle bearing for the gland nut with a very small quantity of universal grease. Lubricate the felt ring on bearing with engine oil. Wipe off excess lubricant.
9. Clean drive shaft splines of grease. Coat working surfaces lightly with molybdenum disulfide powder, applying with small brush or clean cloth.
10. Attach driven plate and pressure plate to flywheel. Observe the balance marks. Use pilot made from drive shaft to center driven plate correctly.
11. Tighten securing bolts evenly in criss-cross pattern to 18 ft. lbs. (2.5 mkg).

The adjustment of a clutch release ring (or plate) installed in the car should be checked with the clutch checking device or with straight edge and depth gauge. See Fig. 141.

© 1972 VWoA—263

**Fig. 141.** Clutch release ring adjustment is made with straight-edge and depth gauge as here or with special device as in Fig. 142.

The gap between clutch release plate and flywheel should be 1.05 to 1.07 inches (26.7 to 27.3 mm). The maximum run-out for the release plate should be 0.12 inch (0.3 mm). If these measurements cannot be obtained, remove clutch pressure plate and adjust according to tasks 8 through 11 of the clutch assembly procedure. The fit of clutch release ring and bearing can be checked also with procedure illustrated in Fig. 142.

2

© 1972 VWoA—264

**Fig. 142.** Magnetic bridge is device for measuring distance between flywheel and contact surface of release bearing and determining whether they are parallel.

The 200 mm diameter clutch on the 53 SAE bhp engine is equipped with nine thrust springs—six white and three red with gold-bronze stripes.

## 19.4 Clutch Release Bearing

Slight oscillation between the plastic ring on the release bearing and the clutch release ring may cause a whistling sound. The noise is harmless and does not affect the service life or functioning of the release bearing. Experience has shown that lubricating the plastic ring with molybdenum-disulfide paste (Moly-Kote® type) will stop the noise. There is no need to replace the bearing because of the whistle.

As lubrication of the release bearing ordinarily would involve engine removal, which requires time and special equipment, a method of lubricating the bearing from outside the transmission case has been developed.

**To lubricate bearing:**

**NOTE —**
If the instructions are followed closely and the spraying done as described, there will be little chance of spreading lubricant on the clutch linings.

1. Lift vehicle and drill a 10 mm hole in transmission case at point shown in Fig. 143.

**Fig. 143.** Drilled hole at point marked with black dot opens transmission case for lubrication of plastic ring on clutch release bearing. View here is from under car, below and to right of transmission case. Distance "a" from engine across engine mounting to drilling point is 2.6 inches (67 mm). Distance "b" from prominent rib on transmission case to drilling point is 0.4 inch (10 mm). Intersection of "a" and "b" locates the point. Hole is 0.4 inch in diameter. Procedure does not require engine removal.

2. Increase separation between release bearing and release ring by unscrewing nut on clutch cable about five turns.

3. Fit tube about 5½ inches long (140 mm) to molybdenum disulfide spray can. (Be sure that spray compound contains no oil or grease.) Spray can with long tip is shown in Fig. 144.

4. Through hole you have drilled in transmission case spray the plastic ring on the release bearing and the release ring but do not continue spraying longer than two seconds.

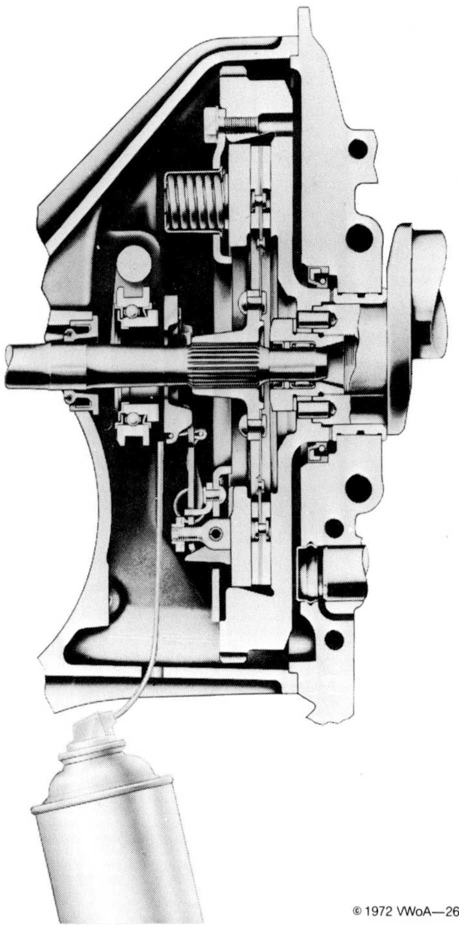



**Fig. 144.** Spray can tip is inserted through hole in transmission case to lubricate plastic ring on clutch release bearing. Five-inch tip on can will reach ring. See text for details.

5. Close hole in transmission case with a rubber insert.

6. Re-adjust clutch pedal free play.

## 19.5 Disassembling and Overhauling Clutch
(coil spring type)

The manufacturer balances the assembled clutch dynamically, and this balance must be maintained. It is important, therefore, when disassembling the clutch (Fig. 145) that you mark the positions of release levers and clutch to give you a guideline for re-assembly. Otherwise, you will risk having an unbalanced assembly.

The maximum allowable unbalance is 15 cmg, as measured by a special machine.

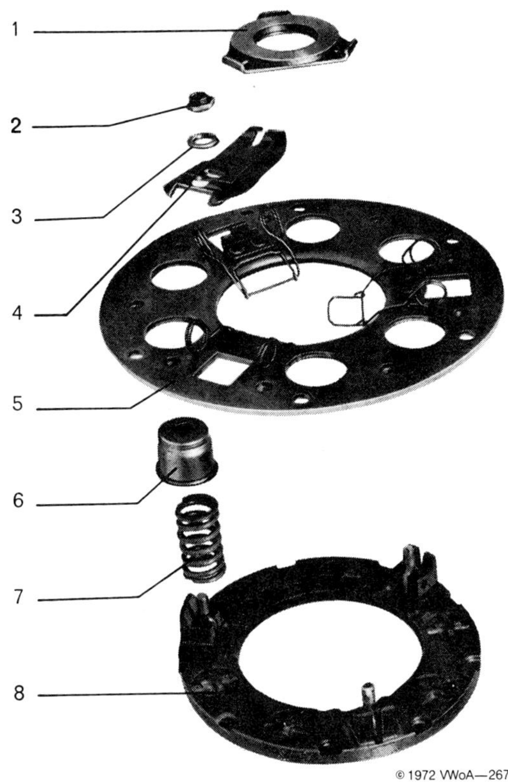




1. Release ring
2. Adjusting nut
3. Washer
4. Release lever (3)
5. Clutch cover
6. Spring cap
7. Spring (6)
8. Pressure plate

**Fig. 145.** Clutch assembly breaks down into the parts shown in this exploded view. This clutch has six coil springs.

**To disassemble:**

1. Place clutch with proper spacer ring (either 180 or 200 mm in diameter) in flywheel and mount assembly in vise. Depress release plate with clutch adjusting and repair tool (see Fig. 146).

**Fig. 146.** Adjusting nuts are removed with wrench after clutch has been inserted in flywheel and compressed with special clutch adjustment tool.

2. Take off special adjusting nuts.

***WARNING —***
*The clutch is under powerful spring tension. Be careful.*

3. Release holding device slowly and disassemble clutch.

**To check clutch:**

1. Disassemble clutch.
2. Inspect pressure plate for warping and scoring. Warped or grooved plates should be remachined, reground or, if necessary, replaced. Uneven contact pattern on plate will cause chattering.
3. Check tightness of pins in pressure plate.
4. Test clutch springs for uniformity. Variations in pressure should be as low as possible. Though clutch springs are heat-resistant, they do settle a little from clutch friction. New springs and settled springs must not be combined in same assembly because the differences in tension would be too great. Springs must be installed in complete sets.
5. Check clutch cover for warpage or cracks. Straighten a warped cover; replace a cracked one.
6. Check release levers and replace if warped, cracked or worn.
7. Replace lever springs if they are weak.
8. Inspect release ring. If it is worn where levers make contact, install new one.

2

## 19.6 Troubleshooting the Clutch

The most common complaints about clutches can be separated into the classes listed in **Table d.** The table breaks clutch troubles down into symptoms, probable causes and recommended remedies.

## 19.7 Assembling and Adjusting Clutch

This procedure requires special equipment.

**To assemble:**

1. Insert release lever pins in pressure plate. Slots in pins must be turned (see Fig. 147).

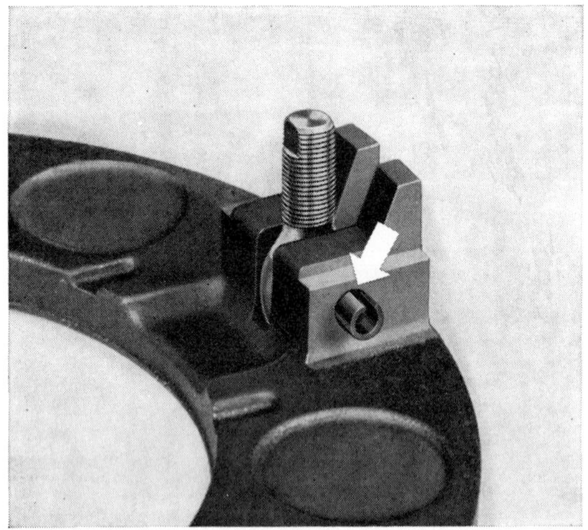



**Fig. 147.** Slot (arrow) in clutch release lever pin must be turned away from pressure plate (as here) when pin is inserted in pivoting point on plate.

2. Insert pressure plate with appropriate spacer ring (a special tool) in flywheel. Insert seats, thrust springs and caps and install clutch cover.

**NOTE —**
The marks you made on the release levers, clutch cover and pressure plate before disassembly must line up. Make sure that spring seats are positioned correctly in pressure plate (see Fig. 148).

3. Compress clutch carefully with special adjusting and repair tool. Make sure that square holes in clutch cover are free of damage and that locating lugs fit in flywheel recesses.

**Fig. 148.** Pivoting point (arrows) for release lever must enter square opening in clutch cover at assembly. Locating marks on levers, cover and plate will be helpful.

***WARNING —***
*The clutch is under powerful spring tension. To avoid accident and possible injury, take care to keep parts under control.*

4. Insert the six securing bolts with spring washers and tighten to 18 ft. lbs. (2.5 mkg).
5. Using lithium grease, lightly lubricate release levers at pivoting points and install them. Put on washers and special nuts and make trial adjustment of release levers. Use new adjusting nuts (Fig. 149) and pins, never old ones.

**Fig. 149.** Special adjusting nuts (black arrows) are used at clutch release lever pivoting points.

## Table d. Clutch Troubleshooting

| Symptom | Cause | Remedy |
|---|---|---|
| 1. Noise | a. Needle bearing in flywheel gland nut worn<br>b. Driven plate fouling pressure plate<br>c. Release lever springs weak or tension unequal<br>d. Release bearing defective | a. Replace gland nut and fill with universal grease*<br>b. Replace or straighten driven plate*<br>c. Replace springs<br>d. Fit new bearing* |
| 2. Chatter or grabbing | a. Transmission case not tightly mounted<br>b. Sag of cable guide tube insufficient or excessive<br>c. Contact of pressure plate uneven<br>d. Release plate not running true<br>e. Tension of thrust springs unequal<br>f. Cushion segments set unevenly | a. Tighten mounting bolts and nuts<br>b. Correct sag to 1 to $1\frac{13}{16}$ inches (25 to 45 mm)<br>c. Replace or regrind pressure plate*<br>d. Adjust or replace release plate*<br>e. Replace thrust springs*<br>f. Reset cushion segments or replace clutch driven plate |
| 3. Dragging or incomplete release | a. Excessive pedal free play<br>b. Sag of cable guide tube too great<br>c. Driven plate not running true<br>d. Cushion segments set unevenly<br>e. Plate linings broken<br>f. Main drive shaft not running true with gland nut (installation tolerances)<br>g. Needle bearing in gland nut defective or insufficiently greased.<br>h. Splines on main drive shaft or clutch driven plate dirty or burred<br>i. Felt ring in gland nut too tight on main drive shaft<br>j. Stiffness in pedal cluster clutch cable and the operating shaft | a. Adjust clutch clearance to $\frac{13}{32}$ to $\frac{13}{16}$ inch (10 to 20 mm) at clutch pedal<br>b. Correct sag to 1 to $1\frac{13}{16}$ inches (25 to 45 mm)<br>c. Straighten or replace driven plate<br>d. Reset cushion segments or replace clutch driven plate*<br>e. Install new linings or replace clutch driven plate*<br>f. It is sometimes sufficient to loosen the engine mounting bolts, move the engine slightly and re-tighten the bolts. If not check gland nut. If thread is damaged or there is excessive play between inner and outer thread the gland nut cannot be centered correctly*<br>g. Replace gland nut or grease needle bearing with universal grease after cleaning*<br>h. Clean splines. Remove burr*<br>i. Lubricate felt ring or replace gland nut with one which has a better fitting felt ring*<br>j. Grease parts thoroughly with universal grease |
| 4. Slipping | a. Lack of pedal free play due to lining wear<br>b. Grease or oil on clutch linings | a. Adjust clutch clearance: $\frac{13}{32}$ to $\frac{13}{16}$ inch (10 to 20 mm) at clutch pedal<br>b. Replace clutch linings. Replace engine or transmission oil seal if necessary* |

***It is recommended that you take your car to an Authorized VW Dealer shop or a recognized clutch specialty shop for this repair.**

6. With lithium grease lubricate the grooves for release levers on release plate. Install release plate and insert return springs.

7. Operate clutch a few times to settle parts in place. Then adjust gap between clutch release plate and flywheel. Use straight edge and depth gauge as in Fig. 150 and keep release levers pressed to the outside. The adjusted gap should be 1.050 to 1.075 inches (26.7 to 27.3 mm).

**Fig. 150.** Clearance between clutch release plate and flywheel is measured with straightedge and depth gauge.

8. Check release plate. Maximum run-out allowed is 0.012 inch (0.3 mm). See Fig. 151.

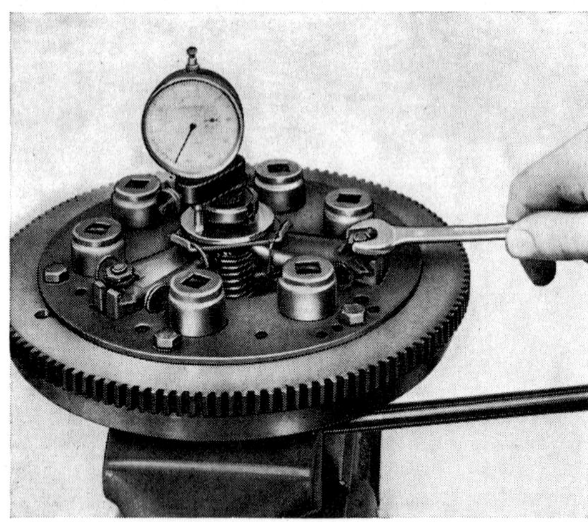

© 1972 VWoA—273

**Fig. 151.** Run-out of clutch release plate must be held to maximum of 0.012 inch. Dial gauge is used here in check.

9. Lock adjusting nuts.
10. Unscrew mounting bolts. To prevent distortion of clutch, keep release plate depressed with the adjusting and repair tool while you loosen the bolts.

## 20. Repairing Tapped Holes

A Heli-Coil or similar thread insert can be used when machined threads for a screw or bolt (in the crankcase or cylinder head, for example) have been broken or otherwise damaged. This simple repair sometimes will save replacement of a large or expensive part.

An assortment of threaded studs is available for the VW crankcase and cylinder heads. With them to choose from, you can count on obtaining an interference fit with the Heli-Coil inserts.

**Designation:**
Heli-Coil assortment for Volkswagen

**Thread sizes:**
M 6 x 1 (VW interference fit)
M 7 x 1 standard
M 8 x 1.25 (VW interference fit)
M 10 x 1.5 (VW interference fit)
M 10 x 1.5 standard
M 12 x 1.5 standard
M 14 x 1.25 standard
M 14 x 1.5 standard

**Sequence of operations:**

1. Read manufacturer's instructions regarding the insert you are using.
2. Enlarge the damaged tapped hole to nominal diameter.
3. Cut new thread with appropriate Heli-Coil tap and clean.
4. Place insert, tang first, into chamber of installing tool.

**NOTE —**
The tang of the insert must enter tool first to engage slot at bottom of chamber. With tang in slot, turn tool slowly until the tensioning sleeve turns insert. Then place installing tool over newly tapped hole and screw the thread insert in the required depth. Withdraw tool. The insert should be from a fourth of a thread to a thread and a half below surface.

5. Use pliers to break off tang of insert.

## 21. Bench Testing Engine

A test stand with water brake is most suitable for testing an engine. On this type of stand the load can be adjusted to fit test requirements on fuel consumption and engine performance. In these tests engines with new pistons, cylinders and bearings and reconditioned cylinder heads are to be regarded as reconditioned engines. Several preliminaries should precede the actual test.

1. Let engine warm up gradually at medium speed and under light load.
2. Check engine for leaks, noise, oil pressure, fan operation and performance.

### 21.1 Preparation for Testing

***WARNING —***
*When bench testing engine always have a fire extinguisher ready. Make sure that engine is securely mounted. Have adequate ventilation. Make provision for effective dispersal of exhaust gases.*

The bench test requires an engine tune-up if it is to give satisfactory results.

**To adjust engine:**

1. Adjust valve clearance.

2. Adjust contact points and set ignition.
3. Check belt tension.
4. Fill engine with 5.3 pints (2.5 liters or 4.4 imperial pints) of SAE 10 W or 20 W/20 engine oil.

## 21.2 Starting Engine

Crank engine several times by hand. If engine has not been in operation for some time, it is advisable to inject a few drops of oil into the carburetor air intake while starting.

> ***WARNING —***
> *Never wear a necktie or loose clothing when you are going to work on a running engine. If your hair is long, restrain it in some way. Entanglement of your hair in the fan belt could lead to very serious injury.*

As soon as engine has started and picked up speed, the oil pressure warning light should go out. If it stays on, the oil pump is not circulating oil and bearing and friction surfaces are not receiving lubrication.

The red generator warning light also should go out at fast idle speed.

## 21.3 Bench Procedure

Warming-up time on the test bench generally can be held to 30 minutes.

The engine when warm should be run on a water brake:

10 minutes at 1500 rpm
under load of 6.6 pounds (3 kg)
20 minutes at 2000 rpm
under load of 13.2 pounds (6 kg)

## 21.4 Checks on Bench

**1. Fuel system.** When engine is running, check fuel pump, fuel lines and carburetor for leaks and test fuel pump pressure. Adjust idle speed with engine warm.

**2. Generator, fan.** Check generator operation. The fan must not scrape against the housing.

**3. Fuel consumption, performance.** Check fuel consumption at end of half-hour run. With brand name fuels, engine should perform satisfactorily. Finally, engine output is measured and compared with values obtained from performance graphs. A variation of ± 5 percent is permissible to compensate for manufacturing tolerances and differences in test conditions.

**4. Compression check.** The compression is checked with throttle fully open and engine warm. Spark plugs are removed and engine turned over with starter.

## 21.5 Final Inspection

2

### Checking for Oil Leaks

After full-load and fuel consumption test on dynamometer, check engine for leaks. Special attention should be paid to valve push rod tubes, oil pump, oil cooler, and the crankcase joints.

### Re-check

Prior to re-installation of engine in car, check valve clearance and belt tension. The air cleaner should be cleaned and filled with specified amount of oil.

## 21.6 Partly Reconditioned Engines

If an engine has been partly reconditioned (that is, valves replaced and lapped in), the full-load test must not be carried out until the engine has attained operating temperature, 140 to 176 degrees Fahrenheit (60 to 80 degrees Centigrade).

## 21.7 Storage of Engines

Engines to be stored for a long time require special protection against corrosion. Any fuel or combustion gases remaining in the engine will become chemically active and attack cylinder walls, valve guides, etc. To prevent damage it is recommended either that anti-corrosion oil be injected through the carburetor air intake on the last engine rotation or that the spark plugs be removed for injection of anti-corrosion oil directly into each cylinder.

The exterior of the engine should be sprayed with the same anti-corrosion oil.

## 21.8 Testing Engines with Automatic Stick Shift

When Automatic Stick Shift engines are to be run on test stands, a certain amount of preparatory work is necessary. These engines have a drive plate instead of flywheel and vacuum connections on carburetor and intake manifold. In addition, the Automatic Stick Shift engine has a second oil pump for the converter oil feed, and it lacks the two engine mounting studs.

The following additional parts are required and should be available on every test stand:

| | Part No. |
|---|---|
| 1. Drive flange | |
| 2. Four M 8 bolts | 001 301 095 |
| 3. ATF tank | 113 142 199 |
| with dipstick | 113 142 235 |
| 4. ATF pressure hose | 113 142 245 |
| with suction hose | 113 142 249 |

Cut off banjo unions and join hoses with adapter and hose clamps.

**To mount engine for test:**

1. Attach drive flange to drive plate on engine with the four bolts.
2. Screw the two lower engine mounting studs into the crankcase.
3. Connect oil tank to double pump (Fig. 152).
4. Seal the vacuum connections on carburetor and intake manifold.

**Fig. 152.** Test set-up for the Automatic Stick Shift engine includes connection of ATF tank with the dual pump.

## 21.9 Fuel Consumption Tests on Dynamometer

The table gives time (in seconds) required to burn 6.1 cubic inches (100 cc) of fuel at a given speed (rpm) and brake loading lbs. (kg).

| Brake Loading lbs. (kg) | Engine Speed rpm | Time in seconds |
|---|---|---|
| 12.5 (5.7) | 2500 | 67-72 |
| min. 21 (9.6) | 4000 | 26-28 |

Fig. 153 and Fig. 154 show graphically the performance of (respectively) the 1300 and 1500 engines on cars covered in this Manual.

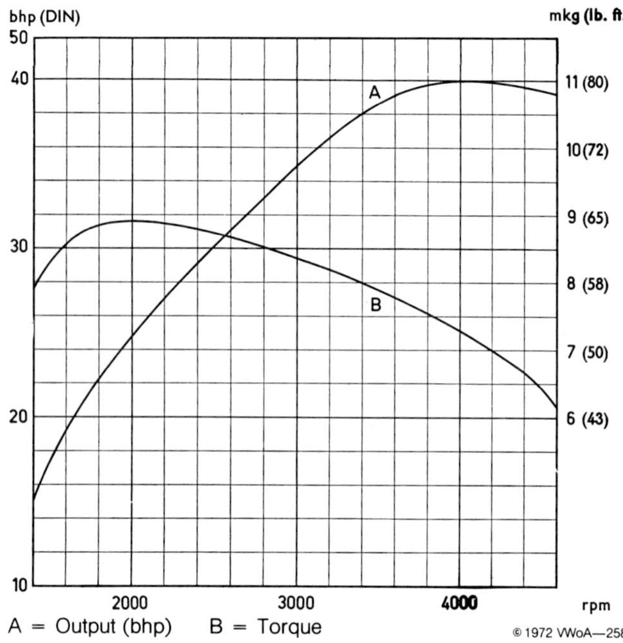




**Fig. 153.** 1300 engine output in brake horse power (European units) and in torque is graphed here for engine speeds from zero to 4,600 revolutions per minute. Curve A gives horsepower (axis at left), curve B torque (axis at right).

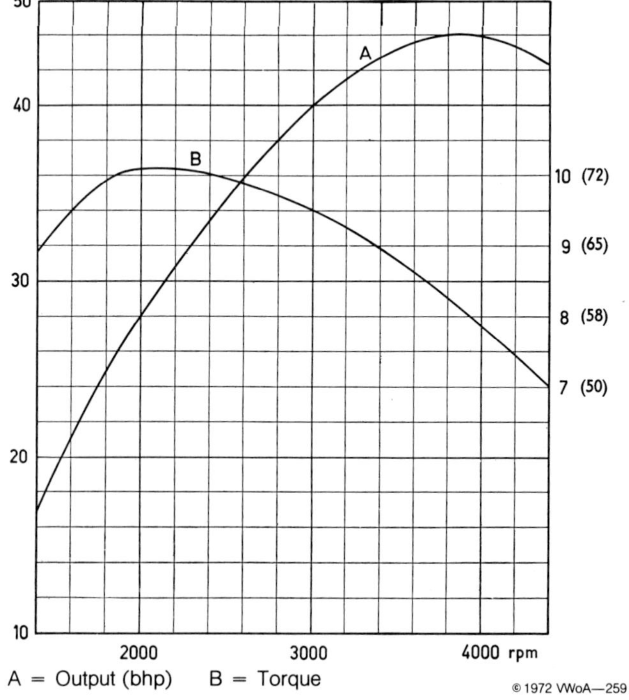




**Fig. 154.** 1500 engine output in brake horsepower (European units) and in torque is graphed here for engine speeds from zero to 4,400 revolutions per minute. Curve A gives horsepower (axis at left), Curve B torque (axis at right).

## 22. ENGINE TECHNICAL DATA

### I. General Description

2

| Type | | 1/1300 | 1/1500 |
|---|---|---|---|
| Engine code letter | | F | H |
| Design | | Air-cooled, four-stroke, four-cylinder engine, bolted to transmission and rear axle to form one unit, installed in rear of vehicle | |
| No. of cylinders | | 4 | |
| Cylinder layout | | Horizontally opposed pairs | |
| Bore | inches (mm) | 3.03 (77) | 3.27 (83) |
| Stroke | inches (mm) | 2.72 (69) | |
| Capacity | cubic inches (cc) | 78.4 (1285) | 91.1 (1493) |
| Compression ratio | | 7.3:1 | 7.5:1 |
| Output | DIN bhp/rpm | 40/4000 | 44/4000 |
| | SAE bhp/rpm | 50/4600 | 53/4200 |
| Torque* | DIN mkg/rpm | 8.9/2000 | 10.2/2000 |
| | SAE lb. ft./rpm | 69/2600 | 78/2600 |
| Mean piston speed | meters per sec./rpm | 9.2/4000 | |
| | feet per min./rpm | 1811/4000 | |
| Octane requirement | | 87 | 91 |
| Dry weight | lbs. (kg) | 244 (111) | 250 (114) |
| Ignition | | | |
| Coil | | 6-volt (1966)<br>12-volt (1967 on) | |
| Distributor | | See Table b in ENGINE section | |
| Firing point (ignition/combustion) | before TDC | 7.5° | 7.5°** |
| Firing order | | 1-4-3-2 | |
| Dwell angle | | 44-50° new or 0.016 to 0.020 inch (0.4 to 0.5 mm) breaker gap (old points 42-58°) | |
| Spark plugs | | Heat value 145 | |
| Bosch | | W 175 T 2 | |
| Beru | | 175/14/3 | |
| Champion | | L 88-A | |
| Spark plug thread | | M 14 x 1.25 x 12.7 | |
| Spark plug gap | inches (mm) | 0.024 to 0.028 (0.6 to 0.7) | |
| Cooling | | Air cooling by radial fan on generator shaft | |
| Air quantity | cubic feet (liters)/ sec. at rpm | 20 (550)/4000 | 21 (575)/4000 |
| Lubrication | | Pressure feed by gear type pump | |
| Oil cooling | | Oil cooler in fan air stream | |
| Oil strainer | | Located in center of oil sump | |
| Oil pressure indicator | | By warning light | |
| Oil capacity | | 5.3 U.S. pints (2.5 liters) | |
| Oil consumption | U.S. pints/ 1000 miles | 1 to 3.4 | 1.7 to 3.4 |
| | liter/1000 km | 0.3 to 1.0 | 0.5 to 1.0 |
| Cylinder heads | | One for each pair of cylinders, aluminum alloy with cooling ribs | |
| Valve seat inserts | | Shrunk-in, sintered steel | |
| Valve guides | | Shrunk-in, special brass | |
| Spark plug threads | | Cut in cylinder head | |
| Valve mechanism | | 1 camshaft below crankshaft, cam followers in crankcase, push rods and rocker arms | |
| Valve timing with 0.04 inch (1 mm) clearance: | | Valve timing check requires a gap above standard | |
| Intake opens before TDC*** | | 7°30′ | |
| Intake closes after BDC | | 37° | |

continued on next page

## I. General Description (continued)

| Type | 1/1300 | 1/1500 |
|---|---|---|
| Exhaust opens before BDC | 44°30′ | |
| Exhaust closes after TDC | 4° | |
| Valves | 1 intake, 1 exhaust per cylinder | |
| Exhaust valves | With heat-resistant coating on surfaces | |
| Arrangement | Overhead | |
| Clearance: intake | 0.006 inch (0.15 mm) with engine cold | |
| exhaust | 0.006 inch (0.15 mm) with engine cold | |
| Valve springs | 1 spring per valve | |
| Cylinders | Individual cylinders of special gray cast iron with cooling fins | |
| Distance between centers | 4.41 inches (112 mm) | |
| Pistons | Light alloy with steel insert | |
| Piston Pins | Floating, secured by circlips | |
| Piston rings | 2 compression, 1 oil | |
| Crankcase | Two-piece magnesium alloy, separated vertically through crankshaft and camshaft bearings | |
| Camshaft | Gray cast iron, three bearings | |
| Camshaft bearings | Thin-wall steel shells with white metal layer | |
| Camshaft drive | Helical gears | |
| Crankshaft | Forged high quality steel, four bearings | |
| Main bearings, 1, 3 and 4 | Aluminum bushings, lead coated | |
| Main bearing, 2 (center bearing) | Split shells, three-layer | |
| Main bearings, 1-3 | 2.165 inches (55 mm) diameter | |
| Main bearing 4 | 1.575 inches (40 mm) diameter | |
| Connecting rod journals | 2.165 inches (55 mm) diameter | |
| Flywheel | Forged, with integral starter ring | |
| Connecting rods | Forged with H-section shaft | |
| Connecting rod bearings | Three-layer, thin wall shells | |
| Piston pin bearings | Pressed-in steel bushings with lead-bronze layer | |
| Clutch | Coil spring clutch (replacement may be diaphragm type) | |
| Type | Single disk, dry | |
| Total lining area | 43 sq. inches (268 cm²) | 56 sq. inches (363 cm²) |
| Pressure | 761-816 lb. (345-370 kg) | 788-865 lb. (357.5-392.5 kg) |

*The unit of torque technically is the pound-foot but it is customary among automotive engineers and mechanics to speak of foot-pounds of torque.

**Automatic Stick Shift and/or Exhaust Emission Control will be 0° (TDC)

***Top Dead Center (TDC) is position of piston at end of stroke (spark plug end)

## II. Introduction Dates of Engine Modifications

(from August 1967)

| Type/ Model | Introduction date | Chassis No. | Engine No. | Modification |
|---|---|---|---|---|
| 1 | 29 May 68 | 118 889 936 | H 5359314 | Clutch plate with torsion springs |
| 1 | 2 Feb 68 | 118 524 391 | H 5207880 | Piston pins in one size class only |
| 1 | 1 Aug 68 | | H 5427383 | Distributor with one-piece breaker contacts |
| 1 Automatic Stick Shift and/or Emission Control | 14 Aug 68 | | H 5455668 | |
| 1 | 1 Feb 68 | 118 520 745 | | Coil with improved sealing |
| 1/1500 | 5 Nov 68 | 119 310 977 | H 5563170 | Cylinder head cover gaskets made of a mixture of asbestos cork and rubber |

## III. Tolerances and Wear Limits

In these pages the term "wear limit" refers to a specific measurement. If in the course of an overhaul a part is found to be approaching a wear limit (or to have arrived at the wear limit), the part should not be re-installed in the car. When the wear limit of pistons and cylinders is evaluated, engine oil consumption should also be considered.

2

| | 1/1300 | | 1/1500 | |
|---|---|---|---|---|
| | **Tolerances (new parts)** | **Wear limit** | **Tolerances (new parts)** | **Wear limit** |
| **Cooling** | | | | |
| Thermostat . . . . . . . . . opening temperature | 149-158°F (65-70°C) | — | 149-158°F (65-70°C) | — |
| Fan . . . . . . . . . . . . . . . . out-of-balance | max. 4 cmg | — | max. 5 cmg | — |
| Belt pulley radial run out | max. 0.030 in. (0.8 mm) | — | — | — |
| **Oil System** | | | | |
| 1. Oil pressure (SAE 30 oil only at 158°F (70°C) and 2500 rpm) | approx. 42 psi (3 kg/cm²) | 28 psi (2 kg/cm²) | approx. 42 psi (3 kg/cm²) | 28 psi (2 kg/cm²) |
| 2. Oil pressure relief valve spring | | | | |
| Length loaded | 0.929 in. (23.6 mm) | — | 0.929 in. (23.6 mm) | — |
| Load | 17 lbs. (7.75 kg) | — | 17 lbs. (7.75 kg) | — |
| 3. Oil pump (gears/housing without gasket) | | | | |
| Axial play | — | 0.004 in. (0.1 mm) | — | 0.004 in. (0.1 mm) |
| Backlash | 0.008 in. (0.0-0.2 mm) | — | 0.008 in. (0.0-0.2 mm) | — |
| 4. Oil pressure switch points open at . . . . . . . . . . . . . . . . . . . . pressure | 2.1-6.3 psi (0.15-0.45 kg/cm²) | — | 2.1-6.3 psi (0.15-0.45 kg/cm²) | — |
| 5. Dipstick | | | | |
| Upper mark . . . . . . . . . . . oil capacity | 5.3 U.S. pints (2.5 liters) | — | 5.3 U.S. pints (2.5 liters) | — |
| Lower mark . . . . . . . . . . . oil capacity | 2.6 U.S. pints (1.25 liters) | — | 2.6 U.S. pints (1.25 liters) | — |
| Quantity required to fill from lower mark | 2.7 U.S. pints or 1⅓ U.S. quarts | — | 2.7 U.S. pints or 1⅓ U.S. quarts | — |
| **Cylinder Head and Valves** | | | | |
| 1. Cylinder seating depth in cylinder head | 0.538-0.542 in. (13.7-13.8 mm) | — | 0.540-0.544 in. (13.75-13.85 mm) | — |
| 2. Combustion chamber capacity | 44-46 cc* | — | 48-50 cc | — |
| 3. Rocker arms . . . . . . . . inside diameter | 0.7086-0.7094 in. (18.00-18.02 mm) | 0.7102 in. (18.04 mm) | 0.7086-0.7094 in. (18.00-18.02 mm) | 0.7102 in. (18.04 mm) |
| 4. Rocker shaft . . . . . . . . . . . diameter | 0.7074-0.7078 in. (17.97-17.98 mm) | 0.7067 in. (17.95 mm) | 0.7074-0.7078 in. (17.97-17.98 mm) | 0.7067 in. (17.95 mm) |
| 5. Valve springs | | | | |
| Length loaded | 1.220 in. (31.0 mm) | — | 1.220 in. (31.0 mm) | — |
| Load | 117-135 lbs. (53.2-61.2 kg) | — | 117-135 lbs. (53.2-61.2 kg) | — |
| 6. Valve seats | | | | |
| a) Intake . . . . . . . . . . . . . . . . width | 0.05-0.06 in. (1.3-1.6 mm) | — | 0.05-0.06 in. (1.3-1.6 mm) | — |
| b) Exhaust . . . . . . . . . . . . . . width | 0.066-0.08 in. (1.7-2.0 mm) | — | 0.066-0.08 in. (1.7-2.0 mm) | — |
| c) Intake seat angle | 45° | — | 45° | — |
| d) Exhaust seat angle | 45° | — | 45° | — |
| e) Outer correction angle | 15° | — | 15° | — |
| f) Inner correction angle | 75° | — | 75° | — |

**continued on next page**

### III. Tolerances and Wear Limits (continued)

| | 1/1300 | | 1/1500 | |
|---|---|---|---|---|
| | **Tolerances (new parts)** | **Wear limit** | **Tolerances (new parts)** | **Wear limit** |
| 7. Valve guides: | | | | |
| Intake . . . . . . . . . . . inside diameter | 0.3149-0.3156 in. (8.00-8.02 mm) | 0.3172 in. (8.06 mm) | 0.3149-0.3156 in. (8.00-8.02 mm) | 0.3172 in. (8.06 mm) |
| Exhaust . . . . . . . . . . inside diameter | 0.3149-0.3156 in. (8.00-8.02 mm) | 0.3172 in. (8.06 mm) | 0.3149-0.3156 in. (8.00-8.02 mm) | 0.3172 in. (8.06 mm) |
| 8. Valve stems: | | | | |
| Intake . . . . . . . . . . . . . . . diameter | 0.3125-0.3129 in. (7.94-7.95 mm) | 3.109 in. (7.90 mm) | 0.3125-0.3129 in. (7.94-7.95 mm) | 3.109 in. (7.90 mm) |
| Exhaust . . . . . . . . . . . . . . diameter | 0.3114-0.3118 in. (7.91-7.92 mm) | 0.3098 in. (7.87 mm) | 0.3114-0.3118 in. (7.91-7.92 mm) | 0.3098 in. (7.87 mm) |
| out-of-round | 0.0004 in. (0.01 mm) | — | 0.004 in. (0.01 mm) | — |
| 9. Valve guide/valve stem: | | | | |
| Intake . . . . . . . . . . . . . . . . . rock | 0.008-0.009 in. (0.21-0.23 mm) | 0.031 in. (0.8 mm) | 0.008-0.009 in. (0.21-0.23 mm) | 0.031 in. (0.8 mm) |
| Exhaust . . . . . . . . . . . . . . . . rock | 0.011-0.012 in. (0.28-0.32 mm) | 0.031 in. (0.8 mm) | 0.011-0.012 in. (0.28-0.32 mm) | 0.031 in. (0.8 mm) |
| 10. Valve head: | | | | |
| Intake . . . . . . . . . . . . . . . diameter | 1.299 in. (33.0 mm) | — | 1.397 in. (35.5 mm) | — |
| Exhaust . . . . . . . . . . . . . . diameter | 1.181 in. (30.0 mm) | — | 1.259 in. (32.0 mm) | — |
| 11. Valve clearance (cold): Intake and exhaust setting | 0.006 in. (0.15 mm) | — | 0.006 in. (0.15 mm) | — |
| 12. Compression pressure (with engine warm, throttle open, all plugs out, gauge in plug seat and engine turned by starter) | | | | |
| a) Standard . . . . . . . . . . . . . . . psi / kg/cm² | 106-135 (7.5-9.5) | 92 (6.5) | 114-142 (8.0-10.0) | 100 (7.0) |
| b) Difference between cylinders . . . . psi / kg/cm² | — | max. 21 (1.5) | — | max. 21 (1.5) |
| Cylinders and Pistons | | | | |
| Two oversizes, each of 0.5 mm | | | | |
| 1. Cylinder . . . . . . . . . . . . out-of-round | 0.0004 in. max. (0.01 mm) | — | max. 0.0004 in. (0.01 mm) | — |
| 2. Cylinder/piston . . . . . . . . . . clearance | 0.0015-0.0019 in. (0.04-0.05 mm) | 0.008 in. (0.20 mm) | 0.0015-0.0019 in. (0.04-0.05 mm) | 0.008 in. (0.20 mm) |
| 3. a) Upper compression ring . side clearance | 0.0027-0.0035 in. (0.07-0.09 mm) | 0.0047 in. (0.12 mm) | 0.0027-0.0035 in. (0.07-0.09 mm) | 0.0047 in. (0.12 mm) |
| b) Lower compression ring . side clearance | 0.0019-0.0027 in. (0.05-0.07 mm) | 0.0039 in. (0.10 mm) | 0.0019-0.0027 in. (0.05-0.07 mm) | 0.0039 in. (0.10 mm) |
| 4. Oil ring . . . . . . . . . . . . . side clearance | 0.0012-0.0019 in. (0.03-0.05 mm) | 0.0039 in. (0.10 mm) | 0.0012-0.0019 in. (0.03-0.05 mm) | 0.0039 in. (0.10 mm) |
| 5. a) Upper compression ring . . . . . . . gap | 0.012-0.018 in. (0.30-0.45 mm) | 0.035 in. (0.90 mm) | 0.012-0.018 in. (0.30-0.45 mm) | 0.035 in. (0.90 mm) |
| b) Lower compression ring . . . . . . . gap | 0.012-0.018 in. (0.30-0.45 mm) | 0.035 in. (0.90 mm) | 0.012-0.018 in. (0.30-0.45 mm) | 0.035 in. (0.90 mm) |
| 6. Oil ring . . . . . . . . . . . . . . . . . . gap | 0.010-0.016 in. (0.25-0.40 mm) | 0.037 in. (0.95 mm) | 0.010-0.016 in. (0.25-0.40 mm) | 0.037 in. (0.95 mm) |
| 7. Weight difference between pistons in one engine | max. 5 grams | max. 10 grams** | max. 5 grams | max. 10 grams** |
| 8. Piston weight in grams | | | | |
| Standard | | | | |
| – Weight (brown) | 298-310 | | 370-380 | |
| + Weight (gray) | 306-318 | | 378-388 | |

### III. Tolerances and Wear Limits (continued)

| | 1/1300 | | 1/1500 | |
|---|---|---|---|---|
| | Tolerances (new parts) | Wear limit | Tolerances (new parts) | Wear limit |
| Crankcase | | | | |
| 1. Bores for crankshaft bearings | | | | |
| a) Bearing Nos. 1-3 . . . . . . . . diameter | 2.5590-2.5597 in. (65.00-65.02 mm) | 2.5601 in. (65.03 mm) | 2.5590-2.5597 in. (65.00-65.02 mm) | 2.5601 in. (65.03 mm) |
| b) Bearing No. 4 . . . . . . . . . diameter | 1.9685-1.9697 in. (50.00-50.03 mm) | 1.9700 in. (50.04 mm) | 1.9685-1.9697 in. (50.00-50.03 mm) | 1.9700 in. (50.04 mm) |
| 2. Bore for seal at flywheel end diameter | 3.5433-3.5452 in. (90.00-90.05 mm) | — | 3.5433-3.5452 in. (90.00-90.05 mm) | — |
| 3. Bore for camshaft bearings . . . . diameter | 1.0825-1.0852 in. (27.5-27.52 mm) | — | 1.0825-1.0852 in. (27.5-27.52 mm) | — |
| 4. Bore for oil pump housing . . . . . diameter | 2.7560-2.7580 in. (70.00-70.03 mm) | — | 2.7560-2.7580 in. (70.00-70.03 mm) | — |
| 5. Bore for cam followers . . . . . . diameter | 0.7480-0.7489 in. (19.00-19.02 mm) | 0.750 in. (19.05 mm) | 0.7480-0.7489 in. (19.00-19.02 mm) | 0.750 in. (19.05 mm) |
| Camshaft | | | | |
| 1. Bearings 1-3 . . . . . . . . . . . . diameter | 0.9837-0.9842 in. (24.99-25.00 mm) | — | 0.9837-0.9842 in. (24.99-25.00 mm) | — |
| 2. Run-out at center bearing (shaft between centers) | 0.0008 in. (0.02 mm) | 0.0016 in. (0.04 mm) | 0.0008 in. (0.02 mm) | 0.0016 in. (0.04 mm) |
| 3. Camshaft/bearings (taking housing preload into account) . . . . . . . . radial clearance | 0.0008-0.0019 in. (0.02-0.05 mm) | 0.0047 in. (0.12 mm) | 0.0008-0.0019 in. (0.02-0.05 mm) | 0.0047 in. (0.12 mm) |
| Thrust bearing . . . . . . . axial clearance | 0.0016-0.0051 in. (0.04-0.13 mm) | 0.0063 in. (0.16 mm) | 0.0016-0.0051 in. (0.04-0.13 mm) | 0.0063 in. (0.16 mm) |
| 4. Camshaft gear . . . . . . . . . . . backlash | 0.00-0.0019 in. (0.00-0.05 mm) | — | 0.00-0.0019 in. (0.00-0.05 mm) | — |
| 5. Cam follower . . . . . . . . . . . . diameter | 0.7463-0.7471 in. (18.96-18.98 mm) | 0.7452 in. (18.93 mm) | 0.7463-0.7471 in. (18.96-18.98 mm) | 0.7452 in. (18.93 mm) |
| 6. Bore/cam follower . . . . . radial clearance | 0.0008-0.0023 in. (0.02-0.06 mm) | 0.0047 in. (0.12 mm) | 0.0008-0.0023 in. (0.02-0.06 mm) | 0.0047 in. (0.12 mm) |
| 7. Push rod . . . . . . . . . . . . . . . run-out | 0.012 in. (0.3 mm) | — | 0.012 in. (0.3 mm) | — |
| Crankshaft and Connecting Rods | | | | |
| Three undersizes, each of 0.25 mm | | | | |
| 1. a) Bearings No. 1-3 . . . . . . . diameter | 2.1640-2.1648 in. (54.97-54.99 mm) | — | 2.1640-2.1648 in. (54.97-54.99 mm) | — |
| b) Bearing No. 4 . . . . . . . . . . diameter | 1.5739-1.5748 in. (39.98-40.00 mm) | — | 1.5739-1.5748 in. (39.98-40.00 mm) | — |
| c) Crank pins . . . . . . . . . . . diameter | 2.1644-2.1653 in. (54.98-55.00 mm) | — | 2.1644-2.1653 in. (54.98-55.00 mm) | — |
| 2. Crankshaft at No. 2 and 4 bearings (Nos. 1 and 3 on V blocks) . . . . . . . . run-out | — | 0.0008 in. (0.02 mm) | — | 0.0008 in. (0.02 mm) |
| 3. Crankshaft . . . . . . . . . . out-of-balance | max. 12 cmg | — | max. 12 cmg | — |
| 4. Main journals . . . . . . . . . . out-of-round | — | 0.0011 in. (0.03 mm) | — | 0.0011 in. (0.03 mm) |
| 5. Crank pins . . . . . . . . . . . out-of-round | — | 0.0011 in. (0.03 mm) | — | 0.0011 in. (0.03 mm) |
| 6. Crankshaft/main bearings (taking housing preload into account) | | | | |
| a) Bearings Nos. 1-3 . . . radial clearance | 0.0016-0.0047 in. (0.04-0.10 mm) | 0.007 in. (0.18 mm) | 0.0016-0.0047 in. (0.04-0.10 mm) | 0.007 in. (0.18 mm) |
| b) Steel bearing No. 2 . . radial clearance | 0.0011-0.0035 in. (0.03-0.09 mm) | 0.0066 in. (0.17 mm) | 0.0011-0.0035 in. (0.03-0.09 mm) | 0.0066 in. (0.17 mm) |
| c) Bearing No. 4 . . . . . radial clearance | 0.0019-0.004 in. (0.05-0.10 mm) | 0.0074 in. (0.19 mm) | 0.0019-0.004 in. (0.05-0.10 mm) | 0.0074 in. (0.19 mm) |
| 7. Crankshaft/No. 1 main bearing . . . axial clearance | 0.0027-0.0051 in. (0.07-0.13 mm) | 0.006 in. (0.15 mm) | 0.0027-0.0051 in. (0.07-0.13 mm) | 0.006 in. (0.15 mm) |

continued on next page

2

### III. Tolerances and Wear Limits (continued)

| | 1/1300 | | 1/1500 | |
|---|---|---|---|---|
| | Tolerances (new parts) | Wear limit | Tolerances (new parts) | Wear limit |
| 8. Crank pin/connecting rod . . . . . . . . . . . . . . . radial clearance | 0.0008-0.0027 in. (0.02-0.07 mm) | 0.006 in. (0.15 mm) | 0.0008-0.0027 in. (0.02-0.07 mm) | 0.006 in. (0.15 mm) |
| axial clearance | 0.004-0.016 in. (0.1-0.4 mm) | 0.028 in. (0.7 mm) | 0.004-0.016 in. (0.1-0.4 mm) | 0.028 in. (0.7 mm) |
| 9. Connecting rod weight | | | | |
| − Weight (brown or white) | 580-588 grams | — | 580-588 grams | — |
| + Weight (gray or black)*** | 592-600 grams**** | — | 592-600 grams**** | — |
| 10. Weight difference between connecting rod in one engine***** | max. 0.161 oz (5 grams) | max. 0.322 oz. (10 grams) | max. 0.161 oz (5 grams) | max. 0.322 oz (10 grams) |
| 11. Piston pins . . . . . . . . . . . . diameter | 0.8658-0.8661 in. (21.996-22.000 mm) | — | 0.8658-0.8661 in. (21.996-22.000 mm) | — |
| 12. Connecting rod bushing . . . . . diameter | 0.8664-0.8667 in. (22.008-22.017 mm) | — | 0.8664-0.8667 in. (22.008-22.017 mm) | — |
| 13. Piston pin/bushing . . . . radial clearance | 0.0004-0.0008 in. (0.01-0.02 mm) | 0.0016 in. (0.04 mm) | 0.0004-0.0008 in. (0.01-0.02 mm) | 0.0016 in. (0.04 mm) |
| 14. Flywheel (measured at center of friction surface) | | | | |
| . . . . . . . . . . . . . . . . . . . . runout | max. 0.012 in. (0.3 mm) | — | max. 0.012 in. (0.3 mm) | — |
| . . . . . . . . . . . . . . . . out-of-balance | max. 20 cmg | — | max. 20 cmg | — |
| Shoulder for oil seal outside diameter . . . | 2.7519-2.7598 in. (69.9-70.1 mm) | 2.7322 in. (69.4 mm) | 2.7519-2.7598 in. (69.9-70.1 mm) | 2.7322 in. (69.4 mm) |
| Machining tooth width | — | 0.08 in. (2.0 mm) | — | 0.08 in. (2.0 mm) |
| 15. Clutch plate . . . . . . . . out-of-balance | max. 5 cmg | — | max. 5 cmg | — |
| Clutch | | | | |
| 1. Complete clutch out-of-balance | max. 15 cmg | — | max. 15 cmg | — |
| 2. Pressure plate . . . . . . . . . . . . run-out | — | 0.004 in. (0.10 mm) | — | 0.004 in. (0.10 mm) |
| 3. Release ring . . . . . . . . . . . . . . run-out | max. 0.012 in. (0.3 mm) | — | max. 0.012 in. (0.3 mm) | — |
| 4. Flywheel/release ring distance | 1.0511-1.0747 in. (26.7-27.3 mm) | — | 1.0511-1.0747 in. (26.7-27.3 mm) | — |
| 5. Clutch springs | **lt. blue** / **dk. blue** | | **white** **** / **red** | |
| Length loaded | 1.1495 inches 29.2 mm) / 1.1495 inches (29.2 mm) | — | 1.1495 inches (29.2 mm) / 1.1495 inches (29.2 mm) | — |
| Load new | 132-141 lbs. (60-64 kg) / 136-145 lbs. (62-66 kg) | — | 98-109 lbs. (44.5-49.5 kg) / 75-81 lbs. (34-37 kg) | — |
| 6. Clutch plate . . . . . . . . . . . . . . run-out (measured at 175 or 195 mm) | 0.016 in. max. (0.4 mm) | — | max. 0.020 in. (0.5 mm) | — |
| 7. Free play at clutch pedal | 0.4-0.8 in. (10-20 mm) | — | 0.4-0.8 in. (10-20 mm) | — |

***1 cubic inch = 16.39 cc**
****At replacement**
*****Supplied as replacement part**
******Only for 1/1500**
*******During repair**

## IV. Performance Data, Type 1

| Model | 11/1300* | 11/1500* | 11/1500** | 14/1500 | 14/1500** | 15/1500 | 15/1500** |
|---|---|---|---|---|---|---|---|
| Maximum and cruising speed<br>mph<br>(kph)<br>at an engine speed of rpm | 75<br>(120)<br>4010 | 78<br>(125)<br>3950 | 75<br>(120)<br>4150 | 83<br>(132)<br>4150 | 74<br>(128)<br>4350 | 78<br>(125)<br>3950 | 75<br>(120)<br>4150 |
| Mean piston speed at maximum road speed feet per minute<br>(meters per second) | 1814<br>(9.22) | 1791<br>(9.10) | 1879<br>(9.55) | 1879<br>(9.55) | 1968<br>(10) | 1791<br>(9.10) | 1879<br>(9.55) |
| Road speed at an engine speed of rpm<br>1st gear . . . . . . . . . . mph (kph)<br>2nd gear . . . . . . . . . . mph (kph)<br>3rd gear . . . . . . . . . . mph (kph)<br>4th gear . . . . . . . . . . mph (kph) | 4000<br>17 (28)<br>33 (52)<br>52 (84)<br>74 (120) | 4000<br>19 (30)<br>34 (55)<br>56 (90)<br>79 (127) | 4000<br>31 (50)<br>50 (81)<br>72 (115)<br>— | 4000<br>19 (30)<br>34 (55)<br>56 (90)<br>79 (127) | 4000<br>31 (50)<br>51 (82)<br>73 (117)<br>— | 4000<br>19 (30)<br>34 (55)<br>56 (90)<br>79 (127) | 4000<br>31 (50)<br>51 (82)<br>73 (117)<br>— |
| Acceleration times (through the gears) seconds<br>from 0-31 mph (0- 50 kph)<br>from 0-50 mph (0- 80 kph)<br>from 0-62 mph (0-100 kph) | 6.0<br>14.0<br>26.0 | 6.0<br>13.0<br>23.0 | —<br>15.0<br>— | 6.0<br>13.0<br>22.0 | —<br>15.0<br>— | 6.0<br>13.0<br>23.0 | —<br>15.0<br>— |
| Fuel consumption according to DIN 70030***<br>miles/U.S. gallon<br>liters/1000 km | 27.7<br>8.5 | 26.7<br>8.8 | 25.3<br>9.3 | 27.7<br>8.5 | 26.1<br>9.0 | 26.7<br>8.8 | 25.3<br>9.3 |
| Oil consumption<br>U.S. pints/1000 miles<br>liter/1000 km | 1.0-3.4<br>0.3-1.0 | 1.7-3.4<br>0.5-1.0 | 1.7-3.4<br>0.5-1.0 | 1.7-3.4<br>0.5-1.0 | 1.7-3.4<br>0.5-1.0 | 1.7-3.4<br>0.5-1.0 | 1.7-3.4<br>0.5-1.0 |

***11 Beetle  14 Karmann Ghia  15 Convertible**
****Automatic Stick Shift**
*****Fuel consumption according to German Industrial Standard DIN 70030: Measured at 3/4 of the maximum speed (top limit = 68 mph) on a level, dry surface (max. gradient upwards or downwards = 1.5%); all tires with specified pressures, with a load corresponding to half of the difference between the maximum permissible weight and the curb weight; calm weather (max. wind speed = 6.7 mph); over a distance of approximately 6 miles, which should be driven first in one direction and then immediately back in the other direction. Atmospheric pressure 745 to 765 T, or (Standard day) and an outside temperature between 50-86°F.**
**Tolerance for testing fuel consumption = +5%.**

## V. Tightening Torques

| | 1/1300, 1/1500 lb. ft. (mkg) | | 1/1300, 1/1500 lb. ft. (mkg) |
|---|---|---|---|
| 1. Spark plugs | 25 (3.5) | 9. Cylinder head nuts* | 23 (3.2) |
| 2. Special nut for fan | 43 (6.0) | 10. Flywheel bolts | 217 (30.0) |
| 3. Nut for small pulley | 43 (6.0) | 11. Crankcase nuts** and M 8 bolts | 14 (2.0) |
| 4. Bolt for large pulley | 33 (4.5) | 12. Crankcase nuts** and M 12 or M 10 | 25 (3.5) |
| 5. Nut for oil pump | 14 (2.0) | 13. Connecting rod nuts*** or bolts | 24 (3.3) |
| 6. Oil drain plug | 33 (4.5) | 14. Bolts for clutch | 18 (2.5) |
| 7. Sealing nut for oil strainer cover | 5 (0.7) | 15. Engine mounting nuts | 22 (3.0) |
| 8. Rocker shaft nuts | 18 (2.5) | 16. Bolts for converter | 22 (3.0) |

***See Figs. 36 and 37 for tightening sequence**
****Sealing ring outwards**
*****Replace, lubricate contact surfaces**

# Section 3

# FUEL SYSTEM

3

## Contents


**1. Fuel Tank** . . . . . . . . . . 4
- 1.1 Removing and Installing Tank (vehicles prior to August 1967) . . . . . 4
- 1.2 Removing and Installing Tank (vehicles after August 1967) . . . . . 4
- 1.3 Treating Corroded Fuel Tank . . . . . 5

**2. Fuel Pump** . . . . . . . . . . 6
- 2.1 Removing and Installing Fuel Pump . . . . 7
- 2.2 Fuel Pump Troubleshooting . . . . . 8

**3. Oil Bath Air Cleaner** . . . . . . . . 8
- 3.1 Cleaning Filter . . . . . . . . 10
- 3.2 Adjusting Bowden Cable (1500 cc engines after August 1967) . . . . . . 11

**4. Carburetor** . . . . . . . . . . 11
- 4.1 Automatic Choke . . . . . . . 12
- 4.2 Idle System . . . . . . . . 15
- 4.3 Main Circuit . . . . . . . . 16
- 4.4 Accelerator Pump . . . . . . . 16
- 4.5 Power Fuel System . . . . . . . 17
- 4.6 Removing and Installing Carburetor . . . . 17
- 4.7 Disassembly of Carburetor . . . . . 18
- 4.8 Cleaning Carburetor . . . . . . 19
- 4.9 Carburetor Troubleshooting . . . . . 20
- 4.10 Checking and Assembling Upper Section . 20
- 4.11 Checking and Assembling Lower Section . 20
- 4.12 Checking Electromagnetic Pilot Jet . . . . . 20
- 4.13 Carburetor Adjustment . . . . . . 22
- 4.14 Main Jet with Altitude Corrector . . . . . . 22

**5. Checking The Fuel System** . . . . . . 23

**6. Engines With Exhaust Emission Control System** 23
- 6.1 Throttle Positioner . . . . . . . 23
- 6.2 Removing and Installing Throttle Positioner 26
- 6.3 Tuning of Engines with Exhaust Emission Control System . . . . . . . 27
- 6.4 Exhaust Emission Control Troubleshooting 28

**7. Driving Habits and Fuel Consumption** . . . . . . 28
- 7.1 Driving Habits . . . . . . . . 28
- 7.2 Power Loss . . . . . . . . 30
- 7.3 Natural Forces . . . . . . . 30
- 7.4 Weather . . . . . . . . . 31
- 7.5 Traffic Conditions . . . . . . . 31

**8. Fuel System Technical Data**
- I. Carburetor Jets and Settings . . . . . 32
- II. Fuel Pump . . . . . . . . . 32
- III. Other Data . . . . . . . . . 32

**TABLES**

- a. Fuel Pump Troubleshooting . . . . . . 9
- b. Carburetor Troubleshooting . . . . . . 21
- c. Exhaust Emission Control Troubleshooting . . . 28

# Fuel System

The fuel system includes all the components necessary to store gasoline, to mix the gasoline with air in the proper proportions for good combustion under varying engine conditions and to deliver this mixture to the engine intake manifold. In the Volkswagens of the years covered in this Manual the system consists of the fuel tank and fuel lines, a mechanical pump of the diaphragm type and a carburetor with automatic choke. Fig. 1 shows the location of the various components in a sedan.

The fuel tank, which holds 10.5 U.S. gallons (8.8 Imperial gallons or 40 liters), is under the front hood. The fuel line from the tank to the pump runs through a tunnel in the car frame. The pump, which is bolted to the top of the crankcase, works off an eccentric cam on the distributor drive shaft. The delivery of fuel to the carburetor is

© 1972 VWoA—1

**Fig. 1.** Beetle has fuel system in the arrangement shown here. Model shown is 1967. On 1968 and 1969 models fuel tank filler neck is above the right front fender, and the breather pipe leads back to the tank.

regulated by the amount of fuel in the carburetor float bowl. The oil bath air cleaner for the downdraft carburetor has a warm air control intake pipe for preheating the fuel/air mixture in cold engine starts (see Fig. 2).

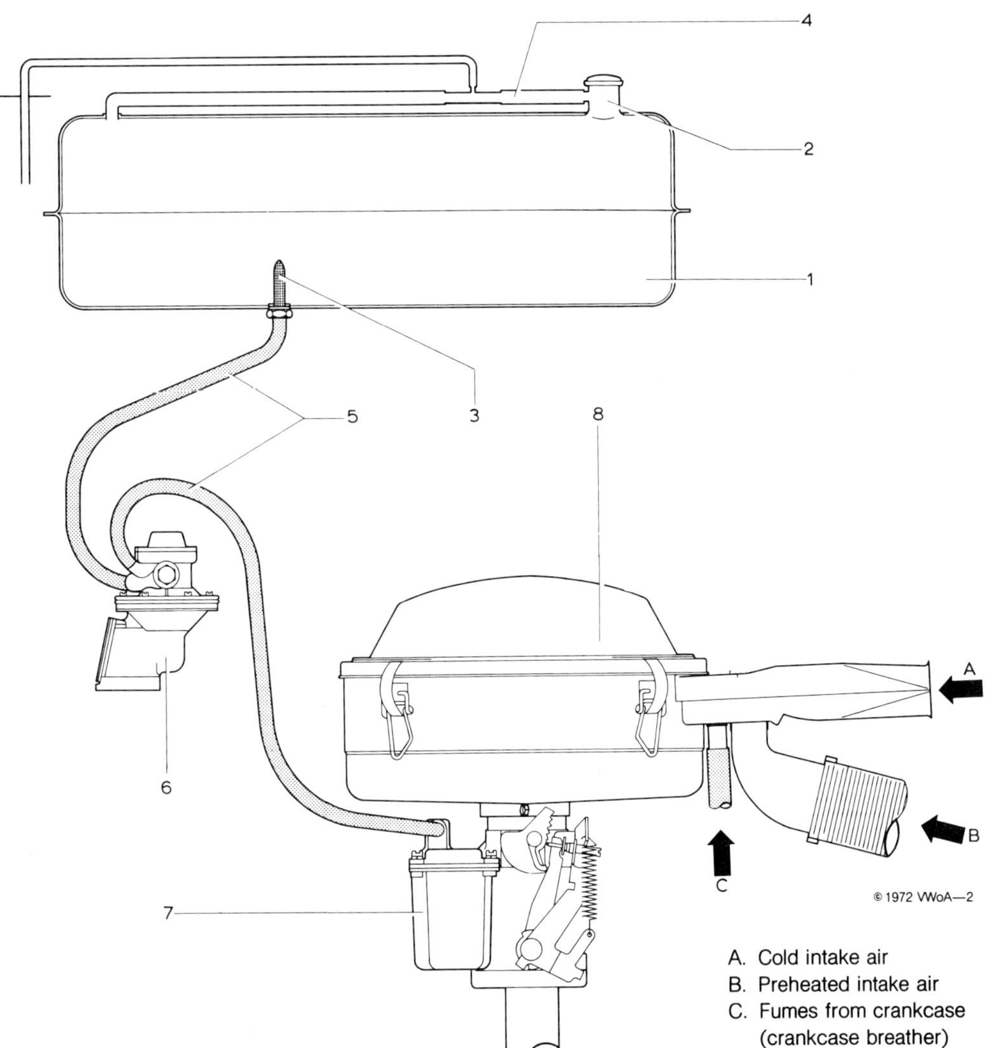

**Fig. 2.** Schematic of the fuel system shows connections between units. Tank (1) is filled at filler neck (2) and ventilated by breather pipe (4). Fuel passes through strainer (3) and line (5) to and away from fuel pump (6) which pumps to carburetor (7). At intake A cold air enters air cleaner (8) on the way to carburetor to mix with fuel. Preheated air enters at B. Fumes from crankcase enter at C.

## 1. FUEL TANK

The fuel tank capacity of 10.5 gallons includes a reserve of 1.3 U.S. gallons (1.1 Imperial gallons or 5 liters). A float-operated sending unit connected by cable to the fuel gauge on the driver's instrument panel indicates the level of fuel. On cars prior to 1968 this is a separate gauge, mechanically operated. From the 1968 model on the gauge is on the speedometer dial and is electrically operated. (For descriptions of the gauges see **ELECTRICAL SYSTEM.)**

At the tank outlet there is a fuel screen which can be removed for cleaning, but this operation rarely is needed. On cars manufactured prior to August 1967, the tank filler is under the hood, on the left side. Cars after that date have the tank filler neck outside, at the right front fender.

Repair of VW fuel tanks by owners is not recommended. Instructions for cleaning a corroded tank are given below, but in case of severe damage the tank should be replaced.

### 1.1 Removing and Installing Tank
(vehicles prior to August 1967)

***WARNING —***
*Fuel and fumes always present the danger of explosion and fire. Disconnect battery. Keep fire extinguisher handy. Do not attempt to weld tank or any other component of the fuel system.*

**To remove:**

1. Lift out spare wheel, jack and tools.
2. Remove luggage compartment lining.
3. Remove cover of sending unit (center of tank top) and disconnect fuel gauge cable. Depending on car model, operation of cable may be mechanical or electrical.
4. Pull fuel hose at bottom of tank from the line in car frame and plug it with pencil or 8 mm bolt. Leave hose and clip on tank pipe.
5. Remove fuel tank breather pipe. This is the small-diameter hose that on 1968-69 models carries gasoline fumes from filler neck back into tank. The breather pipe on earlier cars released the fumes to the air.
6. Remove four retaining screws and lift tank out.

***WARNING —***
*Do work on the fuel system in a well-ventilated place. Treat tank containing fumes as you would treat a potential bomb.*

**To install:**

1. Place anti-squeak seal for tank in position. If the seal is damaged, replace it.
2. Connect fuel hose to pipe in frame.
3. Install breather pipe (see Fig. 3).

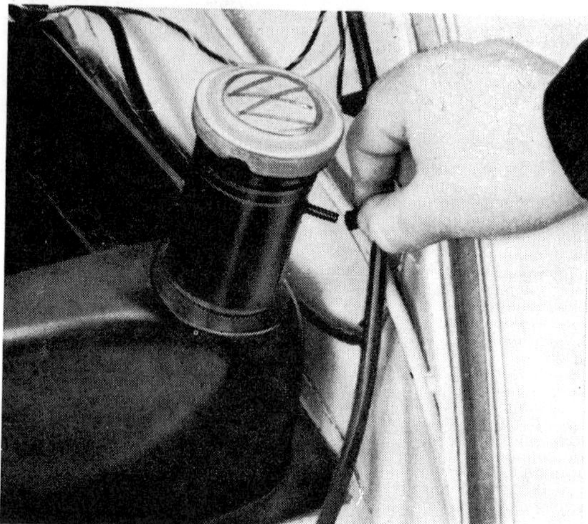



**Fig. 3.** Breather pipe on 1966 and 1967 models has simple connection at fuel tank filler neck.

4. Connect fuel gauge cable at sending unit cover.
5. Connect battery and adjust fuel gauge (see **ELECTRICAL SYSTEM).**

**To clean:**

1. Flush tank thoroughly with clean fuel. Carefully blow it out with compressed air.
2. Inspect interior for corrosion, especially at bottom of tank.

### 1.2 Removing and Installing Tank
(vehicles after August 1967)

***WARNING —***
*Disconnect battery against danger of sparking from a short circuit. Keep fire extinguisher handy. Do not attempt to weld tank or any other component of fuel system.*

**To remove:**

1. Lift out spare wheel, jack and tools.
2. Remove luggage compartment lining.
3. Pull off fuel gauge cable for sending unit.
4. Pull fuel hose from line in frame and plug with pencil or bolt. Leave hose and clip on fuel tank pipe. Filler neck and breather hose connections are now accessible, as shown in Fig. 4.

© 1972 VWoA—4

**Fig. 4.** Fuel tank attachments on 1968 and 1969 models are arranged as shown here. Note breather pipe connection.

5. Remove large clamp from boot on breather pipe and take off boot and pipe.

***CAUTION —***
*For this procedure fuel tank should be not more than half full. Drain off fuel over that amount.*

6. Loosen clamp for filler neck hose connection and pull connection from tank.
7. Remove retaining screws (four) and lift out tank.

**To install:**

1. Put anti-squeak seal in position. Replace if damaged.
2. Connect fuel hose to pipe in frame.
3. Attach breather pipe to tank (see Fig. 5).
   a. Moisten boot with glycerine and slip boot and clamp on breather pipe. The pipe is seated properly when its flared end extends about 0.04 inch (1 mm) from bottom of boot.
   b. Connect breather pipe with boot to fuel tank and secure clamp (see Fig. 5).

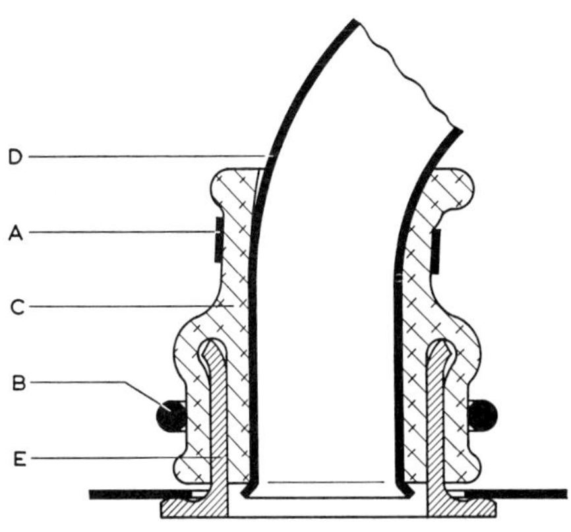


© 1972 VWoA—5

A. 22 mm diameter clamp
B. Hose clamp
C. Boot
D. Breather pipe
E. Connecting flange

**Fig. 5.** Boot for breather pipe is assembled as shown here.

## 1.3 Treating Corroded Fuel Tank

Being heavier than gasoline, water from the fuel may collect at the bottom of the tank and cause rusting, which can contaminate the rest of the fuel system and in time lead to engine failure. A rusted fuel tank should be replaced or cleaned.

There are two standard agents for cleaning rusted fuel tanks:

A. Derusting phosphate agent (commercially available) which should be mixed in a solution of one part agent to 10 parts of water (or according to manufacturer's instructions).

B. Aqueous solution of hydrochloric acid (industrial muriatic acid, specific gravity 1.19) in the proportion of 20 parts hydrochloric acid solution to 80 parts water and one part inhibitor.

Cleaning with agent A is the preferred treatment since the agent is milder and leaves a protective phosphate film. Both methods require immediate rinsing with a soluble oil mixture (one part machine coolant, a mineral oil type, to 20 parts of water). If the tank is not rinsed thoroughly, rust will form again.

**Procedure:**

1. Seal feed pipe and set tank horizontally on rack.
2. Fill tank with solution A or B. Make sure solution comes up to tank filler. Otherwise, acid fumes will attack the tank wall above the fluid.

3. Leave cleaning solution in tank for a long enough time to remove rust. Forty minutes may be sufficient for a very small accumulation of rust; a severe case may require eight hours. For best results leave cleaning solution in tank over night.
4. Immediately after treatment with cleaning agent, pour out solution and pour in from 1 to 1.3 U.S. gallons (4 to 5 liters) of rinsing solution. Rock tank vigorously to slosh rinse over the entire interior.
5. Drain tank and blow it out with compressed air to dry it. Rinse will leave the interior coated with a thin film of oil that should prevent further rusting.

Chemicals for cleaning the tank can be obtained from dealers in industrial chemicals or mineral oils. The drug store is another source for muriatic acid. The cleaners can be used ten or fifteen times. They should be kept in glass containers.

## 2. FUEL PUMP

The fuel pump delivers fuel from the tank to the float bowl (also known as the float chamber) of the carburetor, and the flow continues or stops according to how much fuel there is in the bowl. When the bowl fuel level is high enough to close the float needle valve, the flow ceases though the pumping action continues. As the fuel is used up and the float sinks enough to open the needle valve again, the flow resumes.

The pump, a cutaway view of which is shown in Fig. 6, is divided into the cover and the body section. The two sections are bolted together with the main pumping diaphragm between them. The upper part (the cover) contains a suction valve, a delivery valve and diaphragm cut-off valve that stops fuel flow when the engine is not running. The body of the pump houses the rocker mechanism which operates the pumping diaphragm. This diaphragm is made of several layers of a clothlike material riveted to a pull rod (see Fig. 6).

The pump is seated on a plastic intermediate flange with gaskets, and the whole assembly is bolted to the crankcase on studs. A push rod riding on the eccentric lobe of the distributor shaft travels up and down in this flange to operate the rocker arm. As the distributor shaft turns (once every two revolutions of the engine), the eccentric forces the rod up against one end of the rocker. The other end of the rocker then pulls the diaphragm down against the diaphragm spring. This movement leaves a vacuum above the diaphragm.

Under the influence of the vacuum, the suction valve lifts off its seat, allowing fuel from the tank to flow into the pump. At the same time, the push rod is riding downward on the turning eccentric, freeing the rocker arm. Now the loaded diaphragm spring can push the diaphragm back upward. This movement forces fuel out the delivery valve to the carburetor. The cycle repeats in every full turn of the distributor shaft.

The delivery pressure of the pump is related to the compression of the diaphragm spring in the suction stroke. The spring force has been calculated to allow regulation of the pumping action by the level of fuel in the carburetor. The spring is strong enough to pump when the carburetor needle valve is open but not strong enough to pump when the carburetor fuel level is high and the needle valve closed. Then pressure builds up in the line until it overpowers the diaphragm spring and

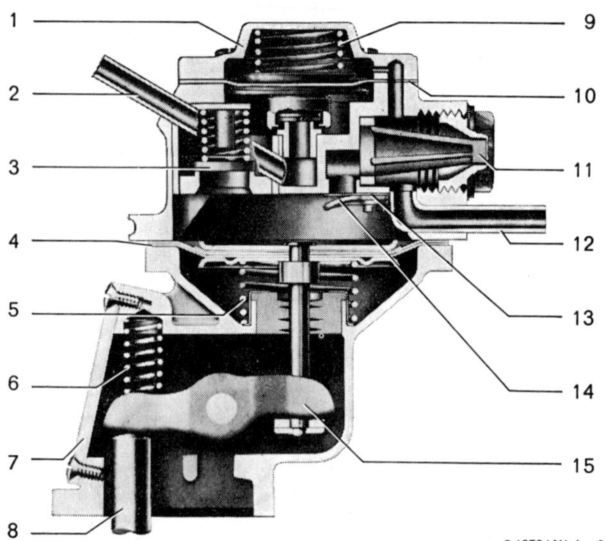


1. Fuel pump cover
2. Delivery pipe
3. Delivery valve
4. Diaphragm
5. Diaphragm spring
6. Spring
7. Inspection cover
8. Push rod
9. Cut-off diaphragm spring
10. Cut-off diaphragm
11. Fuel filter
12. Intake pipe
13. Suction valve
14. Suction valve retainer
15. Pump operating lever

**Fig. 6.** Fuel pump, seen here in cross-section, receives fuel at intake (12) and delivers it to carburetor delivery pipe (2). The pumping mechanism is a simple linkage of diaphragm (4) and the rocker arm operating lever (15) driven by push rod (8). Diaphragm moves fraction of an inch.

interrupts fuel flow. Under normal conditions the diaphragm moves only a fraction of an inch. At 3400 rpm it has a minimum delivery capacity of 400 cc of fuel per minute.

The diaphragm cut-off valve at the top of the pump is a single stage mechanism. When the engine is not running, spring pressure on the valve shuts off fuel flow. When the engine is started, the pressure of the outgoing fuel under the pumping action of the main diaphragm forces the cut-off valve open.

There is a hole in the main body of the pump to ventilate the chamber under the diaphragm. It serves also as a drain for any fuel that may enter the chamber.

The fuel pump causes almost no problems. The moving parts are splash-lubricated continuously from the crankcase, and the cleaning of the filter is the only regular maintenance required. **Table e** in **LUBRICATION AND MAINTENANCE** specifies the intervals for this cleaning.

## 2.1 Removing and Installing Fuel Pump

Fig. 7 gives an exploded view of the fuel pump.

***WARNING—***
*Before starting work on any unit of the fuel system, disconnect battery to prevent accidental short circuits. Keep fire extinguisher handy.*

**To remove:**

1. Pull hoses from pump.
2. Unscrew nuts at flange.
3. Lift off pump.
4. Remove push rod, intermediate flange and gaskets.

**To adjust pump stroke:**

1. Place two new gaskets on the crankcase studs for pump and install the intermediate flange on top of them.
2. Insert push rod in flange, tapered end down, to ride on eccentric cam of distributor drive shaft.

***WARNING—***
*Make sure that ignition is off.*

3. Turn engine by hand until push rod rises to its highest point of travel.

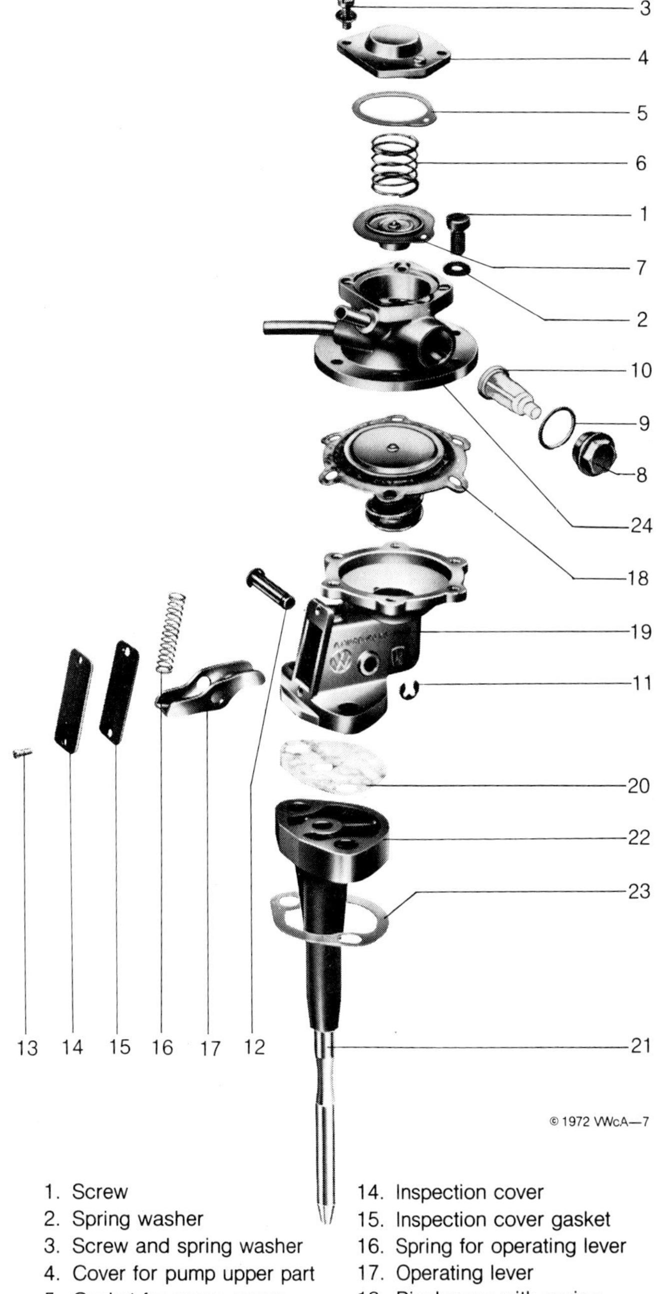

1. Screw
2. Spring washer
3. Screw and spring washer
4. Cover for pump upper part
5. Gasket for pump cover
6. Spring for cut-off valve
7. Diaphragm cut-off valve
8. Plug
9. Sealing ring 15.2 x 18.5 x 1
10. Fuel filter
11. Circlip
12. Operating lever pin
13. Screw
14. Inspection cover
15. Inspection cover gasket
16. Spring for operating lever
17. Operating lever
18. Diaphragm with spring and guide halves
19. Pump housing
20. Gasket under pump
21. Push rod
22. Intermediate flange
23. Gasket under intermediate flange
24. Pump upper part

**Fig. 7.** Pump parts are shown in exploded view. The gaskets (20 and 23) above and below intermediate flange (22) as replacement parts are both of the large-opening type (23). The older type shown at (20) has been discontinued.

4. Measure projection of rod above the flange; that is, from tip of rod to upper flange surface. Fig. 8 illustrates procedure. Measurement should be 0.51 inch (13 mm).

© 1972 VWoA—8

**Fig. 8.** Push rod stroke is measured from intermediate flange surface to highest and lowest points of rod travel. Difference of the two measurements gives stroke. See text.

5. Turn engine again to bring rod this time to lowest point of travel. Measure from tip of rod to surface of flange. Measurement should be 0.31 inch (8 mm). Total pump stroke should be about 0.16 inch (between 4 and 5 mm).
6. Set stroke to correct measurement by removing a flange gasket or by adding one (or more).

**To Install:**

1. Fill lower chamber of pump with universal grease.
2. Place one or more gaskets on crankcase studs to adjust push rod stroke (see above) and install intermediate flange on them.
3. Insert push rod in flange.

***CAUTION —***
*Always install intermediate flange on crankcase before inserting push rod. Otherwise, rod may slip through flange into crankcase.*

4. Fit gasket over intermediate flange. Install pump with inspection cover at left. Attach with nuts. After engine has been brought to working temperature, retighten nuts but do not over-tighten.

**NOTE —**
Gaskets of same type (large center opening) are now used above and below intermediate flange. This type formerly was used only between flange and crankcase.

5. Connect fuel hoses and secure with clips or clamps.
6. Check seating of fuel line rubber grommet in engine front cover plate.
7. Connect battery.

**To check pump pressure:**

1. Connect fuel pressure gauge between the pump delivery pipe and fuel line to carburetor.
2. Start engine and accelerate to 3400 rpm. Gauge should show pressure of about 2.8 psi.

### 2.2 Fuel Pump Troubleshooting

The most common symptoms of fuel pump troubles, together with the probable causes and recommended remedies, are charted in **Table a.** Except in emergency, it is not customary to attempt to repair upper part of pump. It is replaced instead.

## 3. OIL BATH AIR CLEANER

Four variations of the oil bath air cleaner are found on the VW cars (including the Karmann Ghias) covered in this Manual. On the Beetle models the cleaner is positioned above the carburetor and clamped to it. The Karmann Ghia cleaner is attached to a bracket at the right side of the engine compartment. (The lower profile of the Karmann Ghia engine lid requires this arrangement.) The oil bath and the filter for keeping dirt and dust out of the carburetor are the same on all four cleaners. The differences are found in the arrangements for preheating carburetor air for cold engine starts.

On the 1966 Beetle the air cleaner (see Fig. 9) has a single air intake duct. The 1967 air cleaner (Fig. 10) has two intakes, one on either side. The intake ducts have weighted flap valves which admit preheated air to carburetor for starting and then, as engine vacuum builds up, are switched to cold air for warm engine operation. Preheated air is drawn from around cylinders.

A third variation of air cleaner appears on 1500 cc engines after August 1967. On this model the engine thermostat indirectly operates intake duct flap of the air cleaner by means of a Bowden cable. (The cable is a steel wire enclosed in a spiral wire casing. It can transmit

## Table a. Fuel Pump Troubleshooting

| Symptom | Probable Cause | Remedy |
|---|---|---|
| 1. Fuel leaking at joining faces of pump | a. Slotted screws loose<br>b. Diaphragm cracked | a. Tighten screws.<br>b. Replace diaphragm. |
| 2. Fuel leaking at diaphragm rivets | Diaphragm damaged at assembly | Replace diaphragm. |
| 3. Fuel leaking through diaphragm itself | Diaphragm material damaged by solvent in fuel | Replace diaphragm. |
| 4. Diaphragm damaged, apparently from excessive pump stroke | Pump incorrectly installed, gasket too thin | a. Install pump correctly with additional gasket. Replace diaphragm.<br>b. Check push rod stroke. |
| 5. Pump pressure low | a. Pump incorrectly installed, gasket too thick<br>b. Spring pressure low | a. Install pump correctly, removing one gasket if necessary.<br>b. Stretch spring to lengthen or, if necessary, replace. |
| 6. Carburetor flooding | a. Pump pressure excessive, forcing needle valve down. Pump gasket too thin<br>b. Spring pressure excessive | a. Install pump correctly. Check push rod stroke. Add gasket if needed.<br>b. Replace spring or, if necessary, press spring together to shorten. |
| 7. Insufficient fuel delivery | Valves leaky or sticking | Replace top half of pump.* |

*It is not usual practice to repair the upper half of the pump. Except in emergency, a defective upper half will be replaced.

3

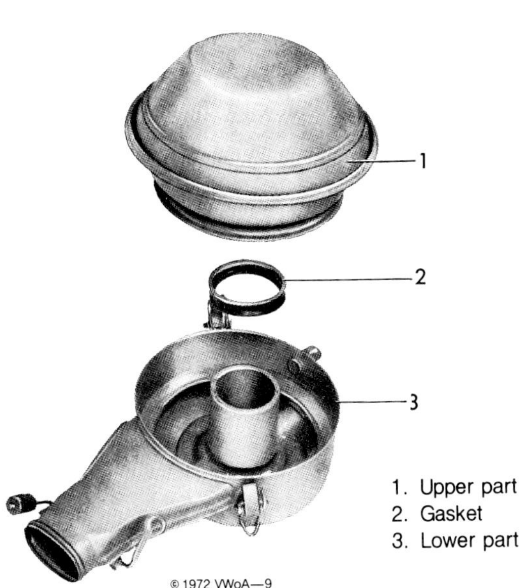


**Fig. 9.** Air cleaner with single intake appears on 1300 cc engine of 1966 cars. Mesh filter is in upper part (1) and oil bath in lower part (3). Gasket (2) completes fitting. Cleaning fluid is never used on mesh filter.

motion in a fixed direction.) An increase in engine temperature causes thermostat to expand. When thermostat expands, the engine air cooling flaps open and the Bowden cable shuts the intake duct flap of the cleaner against the flow of preheated air to the carburetor.

**Fig. 10.** Two intakes distinguish oil bath air cleaner for 1967 cars. Each has warm air control flap.

The fourth cleaner (the Karmann Ghia type) differs from the others only in its location at the side of the engine compartment and in the method of attachment.

All models of the air cleaner consist of two parts. The upper part holds the mesh filter. The lower part has the oil bath and the intake tube (or tubes). Two quick-release clips hold the parts together. Air on the way to the carburetor must cross the oil bath and pass through the oil-soaked mesh, where dirt particles are caught.

Cold air enters the cleaner directly at the intake duct (see Fig. 2). Warm air is drawn from around the engine to the intake duct through a hose (or hoses). At the duct the weighted balance arm on the flap valve can hold the valve open to warm air so long as the engine is cold and the vacuum low. When the engine speeds up and the vacuum increases, the flap valve yields to the pressure differential. The valve closes against the warm air, and cold air from the outside rushes in.

At idle and medium speeds the carburetor receives only preheated air, which helps to prevent the formation of ice in the carburetor jets. The intake duct flaps can be fixed to stay closed against the warm engine air, but this practice is recommended only for climates where the outside temperature remains very high.

The oil bath air cleaner also receives fumes from the crankcase. The lower part of the cleaner is fitted with an adapter which is connected by hose to the oil filler neck. When the engine is operating, the vacuum draws the fumes to the cleaner.

Air makes a hissing noise when it rushes into the cleaner intake. Besides filtering engine air, the oil bath cleaner muffles this noise.

### 3.1 Cleaning Filter

A dirty filter element in the cleaner not only reduces engine output but can cause premature engine wear. If the car is driven on very dusty roads, the cleaner requires frequent checking, even as often as every day under extreme conditions. The filter element in the upper part of the cleaner traps all the dust drawn in with the engine air, and the oil in the lower part washes out this dirt. In time a layer of sludge forms on the bottom of the cleaner. When this sludge comes within $\frac{3}{16}$ inch of the oil level, the bottom section of the cleaner must be emptied, cleaned and refilled with fresh oil.

The cleaner must be removed, of course, for cleaning. The bottom part should be cleaned thoroughly and filled to the mark (0.95 pint) with fresh engine oil. In temperate climates use SAE 30 oil the year around. In a very cold climate use SAE 10 W. The filter element normally does not require cleaning, and no fuel or solvent should ever be used on it. If it accumulates enough dirt to block the air inlets on the underside, scrape off the encrusted dirt with a piece of wood.

Removal and disassembly of the early Beetle cleaners are simple operations. A few more steps are required for the cleaners on the 1500 engines and the Karmann Ghia cleaners. The procedure for the Karmann Ghia cleaners (see Fig. 11) follows.

**To remove:**

1. Loosen clamp A (Fig. 11) on intake elbow and take elbow off cleaner.

**Fig. 11.** Bracket at right side of engine compartment holds oil bath air cleaner on the Karmann Ghia models. See text for explanation of disassembly procedure.

2. Pull off crankcase ventilation hose (B).
3. Loosen clamp C on the hot air intake hose and remove hose.
4. Hold screw D for the warm air control flap cable with pliers and loosen the hexagon nut.
5. Loosen screw E on the outer cable retainer and pull out cable.
6. Release clamp F securing the cleaner to the bracket and take off the cleaner.
7. Unfasten the three upper clamps and remove upper part of cleaner. When you set upper part down, do not upend it. Always keep this part upright just as it sits on the cleaner. Otherwise, you may jar loose dirt particles that will enter the carburetor.

**To install:**

1. After assembling cleaner, fasten it to the bracket in the engine compartment with the two clamps.
2. Work the warm air control flap to make sure that it moves freely. Connect cable.
3. Push casing of Bowden cable into its retainer and the cable itself into the clamp screw as far as they will go and secure both.
4. Carefully tighten clamp on the intake elbow.

### 3.2 Adjusting Bowden Cable
(1500 cc engines after August 1967)

The Bowden cable (see Fig. 12) works between the warm air control flap of the air cleaner and the right regulating flap on the fan housing. The latter flap admits cool air to the engine. The thermostat operates the regulating flap, which is linked by the cable to the warm air control flap of the air cleaner. Thus, the thermostat indirectly controls the flow of warm air to air cleaner and carburetor.

1. Basic adjustment with engine cold (for this procedure both warm air control flap and cooling air regulating flap are closed):
   a. Push cable housing onto the air cleaner intake as far as it will go. Push other end into retainer on the cooling fan housing. Secure.
   b. Push inner wire of cable into clamp on warm air flap lever and secure.
   c. Push inner wire into clamp on cooling air regulator. Spring coil on intake control lever should be slightly compressed and flap completely closed.
2. Adjustment when air cleaner has been removed (independent of engine temperature):
   a. Push cable housing into retainer and inner wire into clamp and secure.

© 1972 VWoA—12

**Fig. 12.** Bowden cable fitting on 1500 cc engines with warm air control flap is shown at (1) and (2). Flexible hose (A) brings warm air from engine to duct (B). Regulator flap (3) and warm air control flap (2) are connected by cable (1). Thermostat controls warm air flaps. When engine is hot, connection at (2) is pulled to left.

## 4. CARBURETOR

All carburetors work on the same physical principles. The function of the carburetor is to prepare a mixture of fuel and air in the right proportions for good engine performance under all conditions of temperature, speed and load. The various makes of carburetor differ in details and arrangements, but if you understand the principles, you will usually be able to figure out the working of any particular model, including the Solex carburetors used in Volkswagens. By tracing all the tubes, drillings and passageways, from each inlet to each outlet, you can get a clear idea of how the several circuits (or systems) of the carburetor are arranged and how they are supposed to operate.

3

**NOTE** —
To see how the carburetor is used by the Automatic Stick Shift servo see **AUTOMATIC STICK SHIFT.**

Carburetors work on pressure differences. Fluids (including air and vaporized gasoline) flow from regions of high pressure to regions of low pressure. In everyday language, we say that the fluids are "drawn" or "sucked" by a "vacuum". While this usage is not technically correct, it is descriptive and widely understood, and this Manual will follow it. The vacuum on which carburetor operation depends is created by: (1) the suction of the pistons in the engine cylinders and (2) the flow of air through the venturi (see Fig. 13) in the barrel of the carburetor. It is a scientific fact that a fluid flowing through a pipe speeds up when it enters a constriction (the venturi) and that the acceleration is accompanied by a drop in pressure. By means of valves, mainly the choke and throttle valves, the various passageways of the carburetor can be opened to, or closed off from, these vacuums, and fuel and air can thus be made to flow through the carburetor to the engine in different amounts and proportions to suit engine operation.

The Solex 30 PICT-1 carburetor for the 1300 cc and 1500 cc engines (Fig. 13) is similar in design to the reliable carburetors on previous models of VW cars. The Solex 30 differs from the earlier Solex 28 PICT-1 mainly in the diameter of the bore measured at the flange connection to the intake manifold and in the specifications for some of the fuel jets. A new feature of the Solex 30 is electro-magnetic control of the pilot jet.

The carburetor consists of cast upper and lower sections, with a gasket fitted between them. Five screws hold the two castings together. The upper casting contains the automatic choke, the connection pipe for the fuel line, the float needle valve and an angled drilling that ventilates the float chamber to the air intake. The connection pipe is pressed in; the needle valve is screwed in. On the Karmann Ghia 1300 carburetors the power fuel line also is pressed in.

**Fig. 13.** Solex 30 PICT-1 carburetor for VW 1300 cc engines from 1966 is shown in cross section.

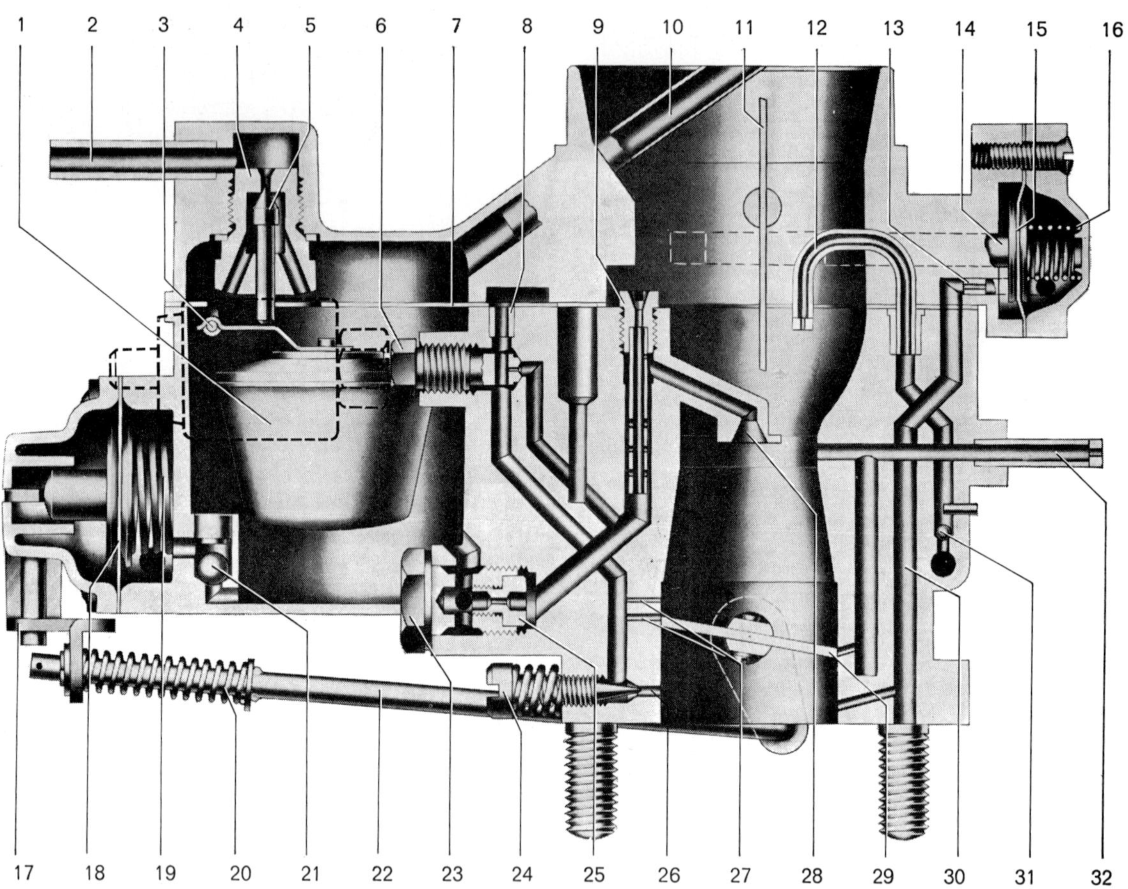


1. Float
2. Fuel line
3. Float lever
4. Float needle valve
5. Float needle
6. Electro-magnetic pilot jet
7. Gasket
8. Pilot air drilling
9. Air correction jet with emulsion tube
10. Float bowl vent tube
11. Choke valve
12. Accelerator pump discharge tube
13. Jet in vacuum drilling
14. Diaphragm rod
15. Vacuum diaphragm
16. Spring for vacuum diaphragm
17. Pump lever
18. Pump diaphragm
19. Pump spring
20. Spring
21. Ball check valve for accelerator pump
22. Pull rod for accelerator pump
23. Main jet carrier
24. Volume control screw
25. Main jet
26. Idle port
27. By-pass port
28. Discharge arm
29. Throttle valve
30. Vacuum drilling
31. Ball check valve in accelerator pump drilling
32. Vacuum connection



The lower casting of carburetor has float chamber and float, mixing chamber and all parts needed to prepare suitable mixtures of fuel and air for efficient combustion under various operating conditions. The throttle valve, working off throttle valve lever, is at the bottom of mixing chamber. The accelerator pump, connected by connecting link and pump lever to the throttle shaft, is in a housing cast integral with the float chamber. The outlets of the passageways of the idle circuit are below the throttle valve. The idle circuit is in effect an auxiliary carburetor that takes over the preparation of the fuel-air mixture when the throttle valve is almost closed.

## 4.1 Automatic Choke

The automatic choke provides a rich mixture for starting the cold engine. As the engine warms up, the choke valve gradually opens to admit more air and weaken the mixture. The choke system also increases the idle speed to keep the engine running smoothly while it warms up to operating temperature.

The automatic choke system has four main parts:

**1. The choke valve** (shown at 11 in Fig. 13) is a disk

mounted off-center on its shaft across the air intake of the carburetor. Because of the off-center mounting, the air pressure on the disk is greater on one side of the shaft than on the other. As the engine sucks air through the carburetor with increasing force, the choke valve tends to turn on its shaft and open.

**2. The fast idle cam,** which is shaped like a balance weight, pivots freely on the choke valve shaft until engaged by the operating lever, which is solidly attached to the shaft (see Fig. 14). When the choke valve closes, the operating lever turns the cam. The camming action is directed against the idle adjustment screw, which is linked to the throttle valve. When the choke is closed for a cold start, the cam bears on the idle screw to open the throttle slightly and thus increase idle speed. When the engine warms and the choke valve opens, the fast idle cam is free to pivot around. The idle adjusting screw then comes to rest on a lower step of the cam. The idle speed drops from the fast idle of the cold engine to the normal idle of the warm engine.

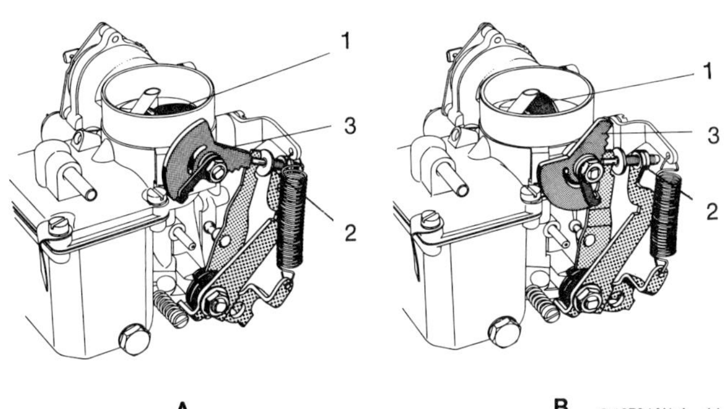


**Fig. 14.** Fast idle cam is illustrated here. At (A) choke valve (1) is closed. Idle adjustment screw (2) rests on highest step of cam (3). At (B) choke valve is open. Cam has swung around freeing the idle adjustment screw, which comes to rest on lowest step of cam. Movement of idle screw arm changes engine idle from fast to normal speed.

**3. The vacuum diaphragm** (see Fig. 15) is arranged to move under the influence of engine vacuum which causes it to pull on a two-arm lever that is riveted to the choke valve shaft. A drilling connects the diaphragm chamber to the region of high vacuum below throttle valve. When the engine starts up and creates a quickly rising vacuum, the diaphragm pulls choke valve slightly open.

**4. The automatic choke control** mechanism (Fig. 16) is a bimetal spring with a heater element, which warms up when the ignition is turned on (see Fig. 17). The

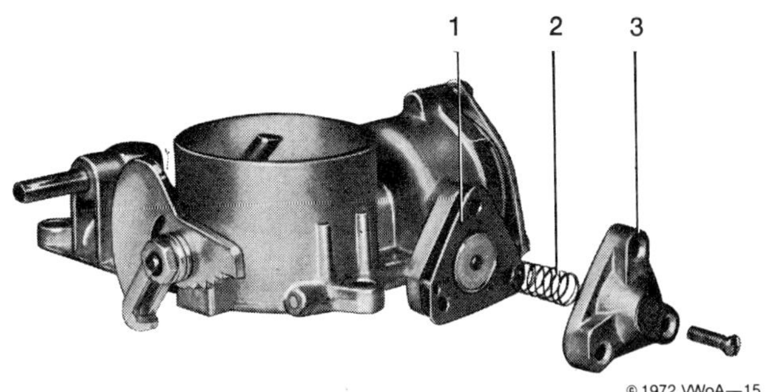


**Fig. 15.** Vacuum diaphragm unit, shown in exploded view, consists of diaphragm (1), diaphragm spring (2) and cover (3). Vacuum under throttle moves diaphragm, which is linked to choke valve. Choke opens to weaken the mixture.

3

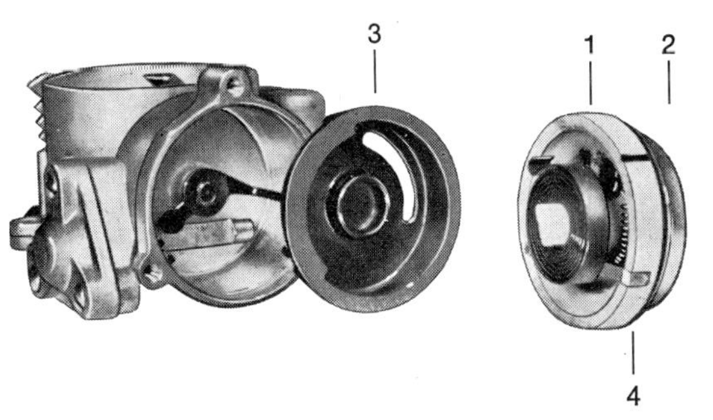


**Fig. 16.** Automatic choke control is shown here in exploded view. Bimetal spring and heater element are contained in ceramic cover (1). Metal cap (2) insulates unit. Plastic insert (3) in carburetor housing supports spring. Ceramic rod (4) separates spring and heater element. Lever on choke valve shaft can be seen at back of housing.

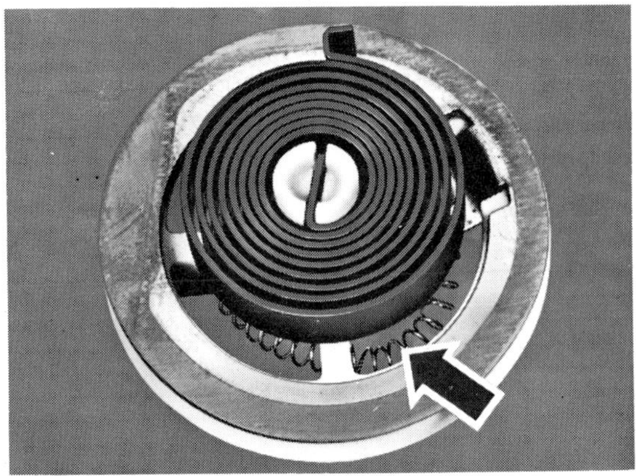


**Fig. 17.** Bimetal spring of automatic choke control, when heated, moves in a counter-clockwise direction to allow choke valve to open. Arrow points to electric heater element. When cold, hook on end of spring moves in clockwise direction, pulling choke valve closed.

spring when cold tends to hold choke valve closed. Warmed by the heater element, it relaxes, allowing choke to open.

A small housing in the upper casting of the carburetor holds the ceramic choke control unit, which has a metal cap. The heater element and bimetal spring are inside this ceramic part. The hook-shaped end of the spring engages the angled arm of the lever on the choke valve shaft. A plastic insert fits inside the control unit housing in the carburetor casting. The insert supports the bimetal spring laterally and provides heat insulation. A ceramic rod separates heater element and spring.

Under change of temperature, the bimetal spring expands or contracts. These movements affect the position of the angled arm lever of the choke valve shaft. As the spring uncurls at low temperature, the choke valve closes, shutting off the main air supply, and the engine receives the rich mixture required for a cold start. This turning movement of the choke valve shaft is transmitted to the fast idle cam through the operating lever. Thus it is the force exerted by the bimetal spring that determines on which step of the cam the idle adjustment screw comes to rest (see Fig. 18).

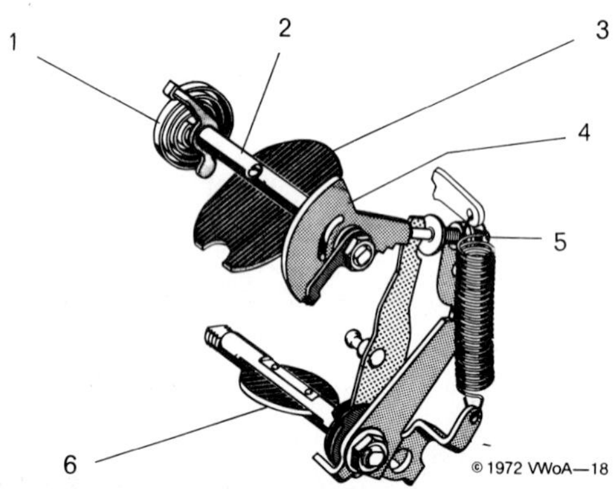


**Fig. 18.** Choke and throttle linkages adjust the airflow and fuel delivery to provide engine with right mixture for combustion under varying conditions. When bimetal spring (1) allows choke valve shaft (2) to turn and open (or close) choke valve (3), fast idle cam (4) acts on idle adjustment screw (5) and thus is acting on throttle (6).

From the foregoing description it will be seen that several forces work together to open the choke valve. First, the inrush of air striking the unbalanced choke valve gives the choke valve shaft a turning motion. At the same time, heat from the heater element in the automatic control unit is relaxing the bimetal spring and reducing its closing effort. (Current flows from terminal 15 on the coil to the tab connector on the automatic choke cover when the ignition is turned on. After ignition, it takes two to three minutes for the choke valve to open fully.) A third force on the choke valve comes from the movement of the vacuum diaphragm. A slight opening of the throttle valve opens the vacuum diaphragm drilling to vacuum below the throttle. The pull rod attached to the diaphragm engages the arm of the lever on the choke valve shaft. As the diaphragm moves under the influence of the vacuum, the rod pulls on the lever. The choke opens only a little under this force, but the resulting increase in air flow is enough to weaken the rich starting mixture.

The inrush of air to the carburetor and the closing effort of the cold bimetal spring are opposing forces. Exposed to both at the same time, the choke valve in the Solex 30 carburetor flutters for the first few seconds after the engine has started. But since the bimetal spring soon loses tension in the heat from the heater element, the choke valve begins to open. The vacuum under the throttle valve builds up to move the diaphragm and open the choke farther. The steadily increasing air flow into the venturi creates sufficient vacuum under the choke to draw fuel from the emulsion tube through the discharge tube. As soon as the bimetal spring warms up, the choke valve opens all the way, and the engine begins receiving the proper mixture of air and fuel for normal operation. Fig. 19 shows the situation.

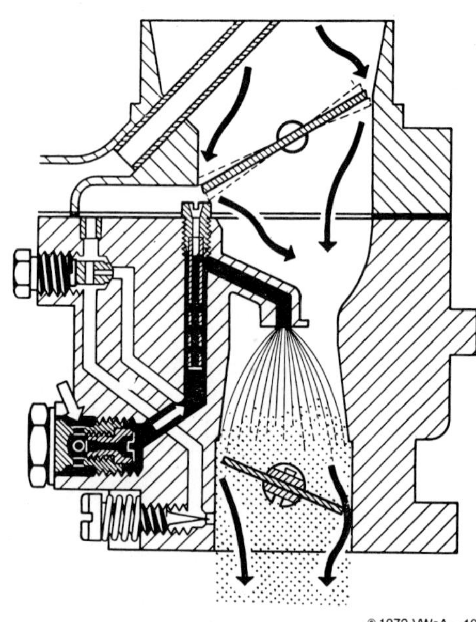


**Fig. 19.** In cold engine start vacuum under choke valve draws fuel (white arrows) to emulsion tube and discharge arm, where it is sprayed down into the mixing chamber below venturi. Black arrows show air flow around choke valve.

The VW driver is instructed to depress the accelerator pedal to the floor and release it before starting a cold engine. The explanation is to be found in the design tying the bimetal spring, choke valve and fast idle cam together. Depressing the pedal operates the throttle linkage and moves the idle adjustment screw enough to release the fast idle cam. Now the bimetal spring can close the choke and the carburetor will provide the rich mixture needed for a cold start. The driver must actuate the starter as soon as the ignition is switched on. Otherwise, current will flow to the heater element which will warm the bimetal spring, allowing the choke to open.

When the car first moves off after a cold start, contact between fast idle cam and idle adjustment screw prevents stalling of the engine. If accelerator pedal is released, the engine does not slow down automatically to pre-set idle speed. Instead, the adjustment screw comes to rest on one of the steps of the cam, and engine continues to run at fast idle. For the engine to slow to the pre-set idle speed on release of the accelerator pedal, the idle adjustment screw must be resting on the lowest step. That is, the choke must be open all the way.

## 4.2 Idle System

The idle system, shown schematically in Fig. 20, supplies fuel and air in proper mixtures and amounts for idle speeds. When the throttle is almost closed, as at idle, air speed in the venturi is reduced. Vacuum is too low to draw fuel from the main discharge arm. Below the throttle, however, the vacuum is very high. The idle system operates on this vacuum and through a drilling that discharges below the throttle valve.

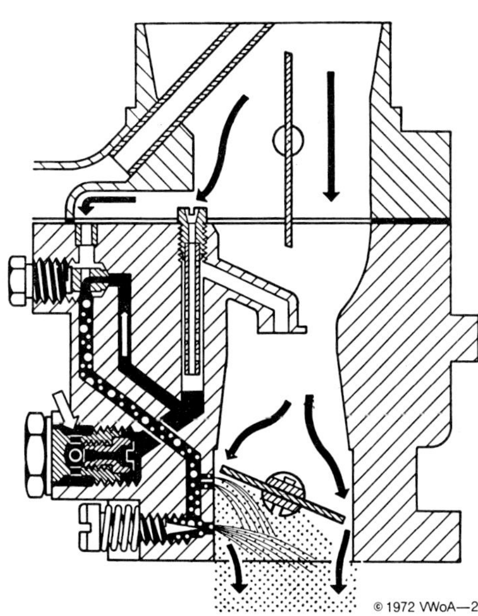



**Fig. 20.** At idle vacuum under choke is too low to draw fuel from discharge arm. Instead, high vacuum under throttle draws fuel from idle circuit discharge ports below throttle. Air (black arrows) has been mixed with fuel at pilot jet. Volume control screw setting determines flow.

Fuel for the idle system comes from the float chamber. It passes through the main jet into a drilling that leads up to the electro-magnetic pilot jet. Turning on the ignition activates the solenoid of the pilot jet, retracting its needle cutoff valve. Fuel for the idle system now can pass. Air is drawn from the air-bleed drilling above this jet to mix with the fuel. The fuel-air mixture then goes into the passage that leads past the volume control screw and discharges below the throttle. Turning the volume control screw, as shown in Fig. 21, controls the amount of mixture available to the engine at idle speed. Adjustment of this screw will affect the idle performance of the engine.

**Fig. 21.** Volume control screw is indicated by arrow. Adjusting position of this screw is part of engine tune-up procedure.

Adjustment of the idle speed screw determines idle rpm of the engine (see Fig. 22). Specifically, the setting of this screw fixes the opening of the throttle valve when the engine is running and driver's foot is off the accelerator pedal. The idle speed should not be too high or

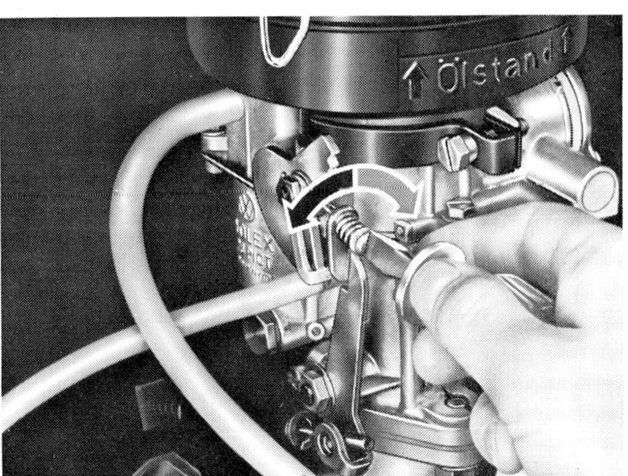




**Fig. 22.** Idle adjustment screw increases engine speed when turned to right, decreases speed when turned to left.

too low, and the adjustment will require correction from time to time. The setting will have a significant effect on fuel consumption.

Just above the volume control discharge hole, there are two other small discharge holes. These are the by-pass ports. The drillings to these ports tap the idle fuel system passage above the volume control screw. When the throttle valve is fully closed, the by-pass ports are above the valve, shielded from the vacuum below it. A slight opening of the throttle valve uncovers the ports and thus exposes them to the vacuum. The rush of air toward the intake manifold now draws additional fuel from the idling system and combines it with the mixture already coming from the volume control discharge port. This extra fuel helps to smooth the transition from idle speed to normal operation.

## 4.3 Main Circuit

The main circuit of the carburetor supplies fuel for normal operation of vehicle above idle speeds. This circuit, which includes vertical well, air correction jet and emulsion tube, goes into operation only when vacuum at the venturi tube in the carburetor intake passage is high enough to draw fuel from the discharge arm.

Factors affecting the vacuum are size of venturi, engine speed (pumping action) and throttle opening. The discharge arm outlet is at the narrowest diameter of venturi tube, where the effect of the vacuum is greatest. The arm sprays its mixture of fuel and air straight down toward the mixing chamber of the carburetor.

When fuel for this circuit leaves the float chamber, it passes through the main jet and up the drilling to the emulsion tube in the vertical well. The air correction jet admits air directly into the emulsion tube. The level of fuel in the well is the same as in the float chamber, but as the engine pumping action increases, increasing the vacuum, more and more fuel is drawn from the discharge arm. The level of fuel at the emulsion tube lowers, uncovering holes in the tube. Now air from the air correction jet can flow out these holes in the emulsion tube to mix with the fuel coming from the main jet. As engine speed increases, air from the air correction jet progressively weakens the mixture that is being sprayed from the discharge arm. The ratio of air in the air-fuel mixture increases with speed, and the velocity of the main air stream soon becomes high enough to atomize the discharge arm mixture for good combustion.

## 4.4 Accelerator Pump

The accelerator pump, shown schematically in Fig. 23, delivers a single spurt of fuel to enable the engine to pick up speed smoothly when the throttle is opened suddenly. Without this extra fuel delivered under pressure by the pump, there would be a lag in the adjustment of the fuel-air mixture needed for smooth acceleration. (By pushing the accelerator pedal down before you turn on the ignition you make the spurt of fuel from the accelerator pump available to the engine for the rich mixture needed in a cold start.)

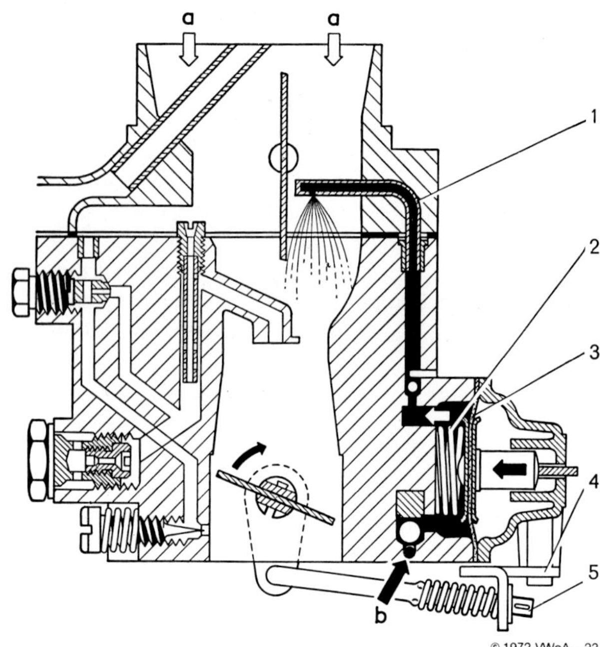


**Fig. 23.** Accelerator pump delivers spurt of fuel to enrich mixture for smooth acceleration at low and medium speeds. When driver releases accelerator pedal, spring (2) forces diaphragm (3) to rest position, opening chamber to fuel (b) from float chamber. Through linkage of pump lever (4) and connecting rod (5) next opening of throttle valve moves diaphragm in direction of black arrow. Diaphragm forces fuel into injection tube (1), which sprays it into venturi. Arrows at (a) show direction of airflow. Arrow at (b) indicates fuel passage between float chamber and pump.

A housing next to the float chamber, in the lower section of the carburetor, holds the pump. A connector rod and lever working off the throttle shaft operate it. Closing of throttle valve actuates the suction stroke. The linkage allows spring to move the pump diaphragm, drawing in fuel from the float chamber through a ball valve. The reverse action occurs when the accelerator pedal is depressed. The linkage then forces the diaphragm down against the spring. Fuel in the pump chamber is forced into a drilling that leads it past another ball valve to a discharge tube below the choke valve (see Fig. 24), where the fuel is sprayed into the mixing chamber. The discharge arm is designed to keep the spray of fuel close to the wall of the inlet so that in a cold start the fuel can pass the fluttering choke valve.

**Fig. 24.** Injector tube of accelerator pump circuit is indicated by arrow. View is venturi from above.

The suction stroke of accelerator pump begins when throttle opens and ends when throttle opening is approximately 30 degrees. The additional fuel from the pump is available only in the low through medium speed range. If the accelerator pedal is depressed to the floor, a spring on the connector rod holds the pump diaphragm in its forward position. Until the throttle is closed again, the pump chamber is shut off from the fuel supply.

### 4.5 Power Fuel System

The power fuel system (see Fig. 25) provides additional fuel flow for maximum output under full load and at high engine speeds. A drilling carries fuel from the float chamber to a calibrated injection tube pressed into the upper part of the carburetor. This tube which is shown in Fig. 25, extends into the air intake (Fig. 26) above the main circuit discharge arm. At low and medium rpm the vacuum in this region of the intake is too low to draw fuel from this tube, but under full load, when engine speed and intake vacuum are very high, fuel begins to flow to enrich the mixture coming from the main discharge arm.

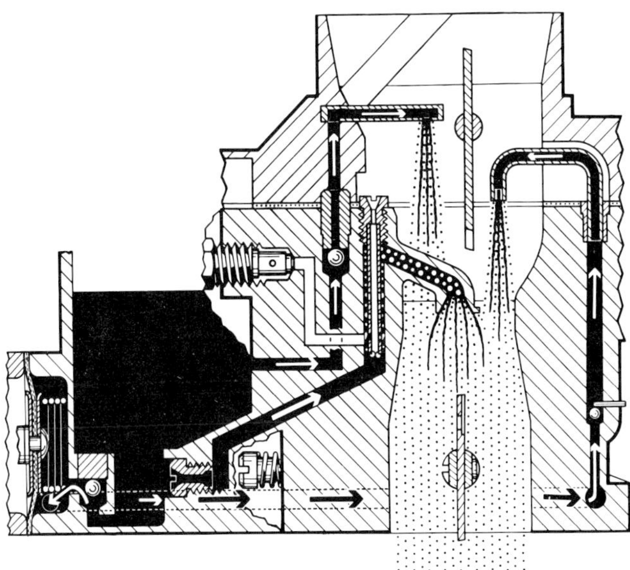



**Fig. 25.** Power fuel system draws fuel from float chamber to upper part of carburetor and discharges it through arm above choke valve. Arrows show fuel flow in Solex 30 PICT-2 carburetor under full load. Fuel is coming from the main discharge arm, accelerator pump arm and the power system arm for the richest possible mixture.

**Fig. 26.** Injector tube of power fuel circuit is seen in this view of carburetor intake from below. Right arrow points to discharge hole, left arrow to drilling for circuit.

At full throttle the fuel chamber of the accelerator pump is empty and the diaphragm at the limit of its delivery stroke, but further enrichment of the mixture can be obtained through this accelerator circuit. At this time the vacuum at the end of the power system injection tube in the intake passage is high enough to draw fuel from the float chamber through the accelerator system ball valves and to the spraying tube.

### 4.6 Removing and Installing Carburetor

The following instructions apply to carburetors on engines prior to August 1967. The carburetors and air cleaners on engines after August 1967 have additional attachments and emission control devices. Instructions for disassembling and adjusting them appear later.

***WARNING —***
*Disconnect battery before starting to work on any component of the fuel system. Keep fire extinguishers handy.*

**To remove:**

1. Detach preheater pipe from air cleaner intake tube.
2. Pull crankcase breather pipe off air cleaner.

3

***WARNING —***
*Unless engine has been stopped long enough to cool, be careful of burns from touching hot metal.*

3. Loosen clamp screw on air cleaner and remove cleaner (see **3. Oil Bath Air Cleaner).**
4. Take fuel hose and vacuum hose off carburetor (see Fig. 27).

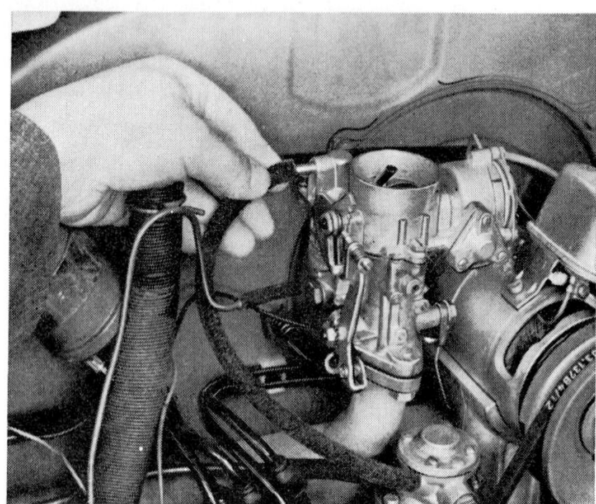

© 1972 VWoA—27

**Fig. 27.** Fuel hose from fuel pump is pulled from carburetor in removal procedure.

5. Pull off automatic choke and electromagnetic pilot jet cables.
6. Detach accelerator cable from throttle valve lever.
7. Unscrew nuts (two) and lift carburetor off intake manifold (see Fig. 28).

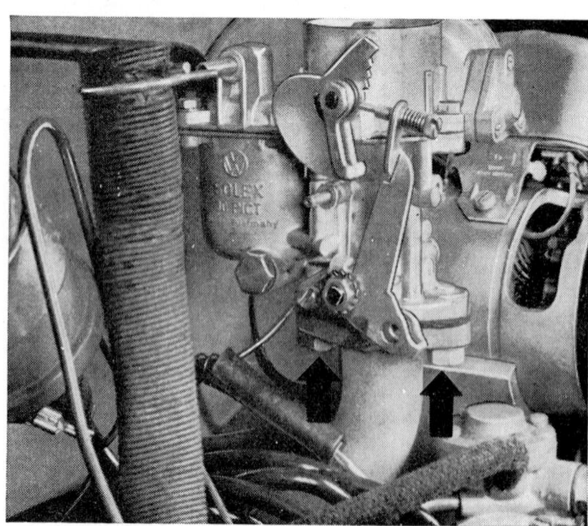


© 1972 VWoA—28

**Fig. 28.** Mounting nuts that hold carburetor on intake manifold are indicated by two black arrows.

**To install:**

1. Fit new gasket on intake manifold flange.
2. Position carburetor and tighten nuts evenly but do not overtighten.
3. Secure fuel hose with clamp.
4. Secure accelerator cable, allowing play of 0.04 inch (1 mm) between throttle valve lever and stop on carburetor body when accelerator pedal is fully depressed.
5. When the engine is warm, set idle at 800 to 900 rpm for standard engine, 900 for automatic stick shift. (See **4.13 Carburetor Adjustment.)**

## 4.7 Disassembly of Carburetor

1. Remove carburetor.
2. Remove the five screws that hold the two castings together (see Fig. 29). Lift off upper section.

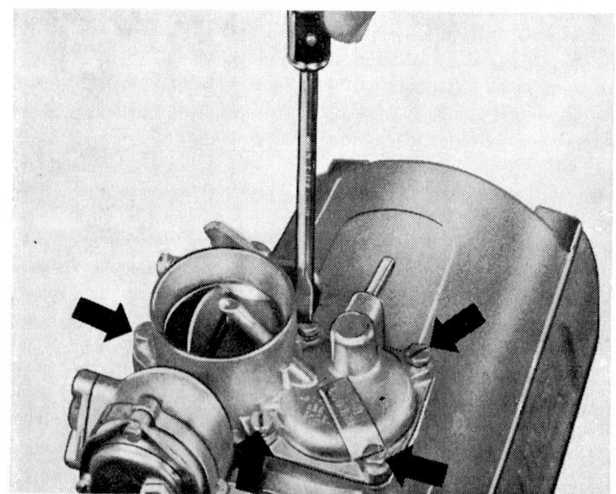

© 1972 VWoA—29

**Fig. 29.** Screws fastening upper and lower parts of carburetor together are indicated by black arrows.

3. Remove float from float chamber.
4. Screw float needle valve out of upper section.
5. Remove three automatic choke cover screws. Take off retaining ring and spacer.
6. Take off the ceramic plate, bimetal spring, heater element and plastic cap as a unit.
7. Remove electromagnetic pilot jet and air correction jet with emulsion tube (see Fig. 30).
8. Screw out main jet carrier with main jet (Fig. 31).
9. Screw out volume control screw.
10. Remove accelerator pump lever cotter pin from connector rod (see Fig. 32).
11. Remove four accelerator pump cover retaining screws and take off cover, diaphragm and spring.

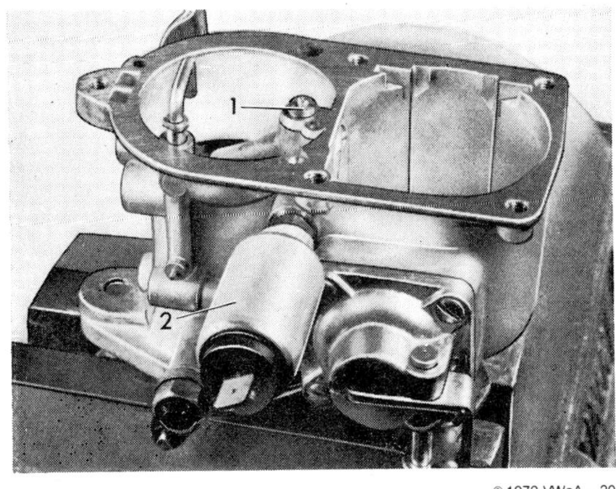


© 1972 VWoA—30

**Fig. 30.** Air correction jet (1) is unscrewed with emulsion tube after upper part of carburetor has been removed. Electromagnetic pilot jet is at (2).

© 1972 VWoA—31

**Fig. 31.** Main jet (1) is at left of volume control screw (2). Both are removed in disassembly of carburetor.

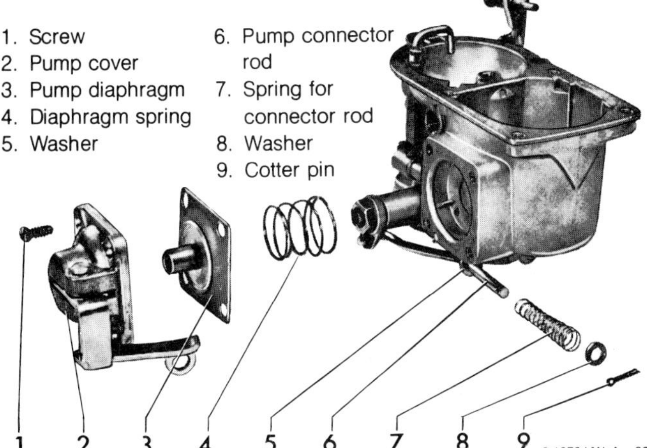


© 1972 VWoA—32

**Fig. 32.** Accelerator pump breaks down into parts shown in this exploded view. Note housing in carburetor body.

## 4.8 Cleaning Carburetor

***WARNING —***
*Fumes from the carburetor are highly explosive. Clean carburetor in well-ventilated room where smoking is prohibited. Keep fire extinguisher handy.*

1. Clean all metal parts, but not the ceramic automatic choke cover, in carburetor cleaning fluid.
2. Use two wrenches to unscrew pilot jet from cutoff valve (Fig. 33). Do not grip valve in a vise; excessive force might distort valve, causing needle to stick.

***CAUTION —***
*Never use pins or pieces of wire to clean jets. Probes may damage or enlarge calibrated drillings.*

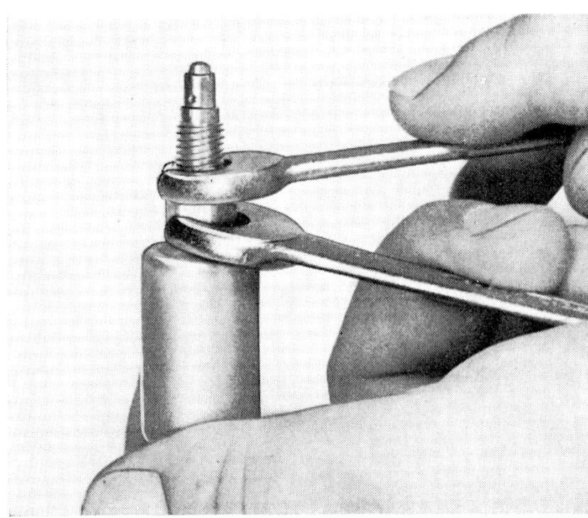

© 1972 VWoA—33

**Fig. 33.** Pilot jet is removed from cut-off valve with two wrenches as shown. Vise would damage the valve.

3. Blow out jets, valves and drillings with compressed air.

***CAUTION —***
*Do not attempt to clean a carburetor with compressed air with the top in place and the carburetor fully assembled. The pressure could damage the float, causing it to gradually become filled with gasoline and sink to the bottom of the bowl.*

3

### 4.9 Carburetor Troubleshooting

While all of the troubles listed in **Table b** are symptoms of carburetor malfunction, as stated, some may also be symptoms of trouble with the spark plugs or engine timing. These difficulties are discussed in **ENGINE.**

### 4.10 Checking and Assembling Upper Section

1. Check float needle valve for leakage. Needle pressed lightly against its seat should seal valve against compressed air.
2. Check condition and location of needle valve gasket.
3. Check gasket between upper and lower section. Replace if damaged or hardened.
4. Check choke valve shaft and fast idle cam for freedom of movement.
5. Check heater element and bimetal spring of automatic choke control unit. If either is damaged, replace entire unit.
6. When attaching ceramic cover, make sure ceramic rod is positioned correctly between heater element and bimetal spring.
7. Make sure that hooked end of bimetal spring engages angled arm of lever on choke valve shaft.
8. Loosely position outer cap and retaining ring with three screws and spacers.
9. Turn cap until paint mark on ceramic cover is in line with the center mark on choke housing. Tighten screws but do not overtighten.
10. Lightly oil fast idle cam on the choke valve shaft.

### 4.11 Checking and Assembling Lower Section

1. Check accelerator pump diaphragm (see Fig. 32) for leakage and replace if necessary.
2. While tightening pump cover screws, press pump lever away from float chamber to make sure diaphragm is in pressure stroke position.
3. Snap clip on pump rod leaving gap of 0.012 to 0.020 inch (0.3 to 0.5 mm) between clip and pump lever (Fig. 34).
4. Put float in hot water to check for leakage. If bubbles appear, float must be replaced.

**Fig. 34.** Axial play of 0.012–0.020 inch is left on accelerator pump rod as indicated at (a) when pump is assembled.

***WARNING —***
*Do not put damaged floats in an incinerator. An explosion might result.*

5. Compare float weight and sizes of all jets against Fuel System Technical Data **I. Carburetor Jets and Settings.**
6. Check throttle shaft clearance. Excessive clearance will allow air to leak past throttle valve. Leakage would affect starting and idle. Bushing for shaft may be needed.
7. Check volume control screw. The tapered area must not be grooved, bent, dented or show any other sign of pressure.
8. Check position of accelerator pump injector tube below the choke valve (see Fig. 26). When throttle is open, fuel must spray straight down from tube and pass throttle valve without touching venturi walls. Align tube if spray is not straight down.

### 4.12 Checking Electromagnetic Pilot Jet

1. Make sure ignition is off.
2. Pull cable off terminal.
3. Check that set screw is in all the way.
4. Switch ignition on and touch pilot jet terminal with cable end. The needle should move in and out with ticking noise as contact is made or broken.

   Cable end off terminal: needle moves toward carburetor to close jet.

   Cable end touching terminal: needle moves away from carburetor to open jet.

## Table b. Carburetor Troubleshooting

| Symptom | Probable Cause | Remedy |
|---|---|---|
| 1. Engine does not start (tank has fuel, and ignition is working) | a. Automatic choke not working properly<br>b. Choke valve sticking<br>c. Bimetal spring unhooked or broken<br>d. Ceramic plate broken<br>e. Float needle valve sticking and carburetor flooding | a. Check vacuum diaphragm for freedom of movement.<br>b. Apply penetrating fluid to free choke valve shaft.<br>c. Re-connect spring or, if broken, replace complete ceramic plate (when installing, match index marks).<br>d. Replace ceramic plate (when installing match index marks).<br>e. Clean or replace float needle valve.<br><br>If a large quantity of fuel has passed from flooded carburetor into engine, switch on ignition and before starting wait one minute for automatic choke to open. Then depress accelerator pedal to open throttle. |
| 2. Engine runs continuously at fast idle | a. Automatic choke not switching off<br>b. Heater element defective | a. Check heater element and both connections.<br>b. Replace complete ceramic plate. |
| 3. Engine idles unevenly or stalls | a. Idle adjustment incorrect<br>b. Pilot jet blocked<br>c. Loose or disconnected vacuum line on Automatic Stick Shift | a. Adjust idle to 900 rpm.<br>b. Clean jet.<br>c. Tighten connection or replace line. |
| 4. Engine "runs-on" when ignition is switched off | a. Idle mixture too rich<br>b. Idle speed too fast | a. Weaken idle mixture (by turning volume control screw to right).<br>b. Regulate idle speed.<br>c. Check electromagnetic cut-off valve if other remedies fail. |
| 5. Exhaust bangs when vehicle is overrunning the engine | Idle mixture slightly weak | Enrich mixture (by turning volume control screw to left). |
| 6. Transition from idle to normal running is poor | a. Accelerator pump dirty (pump passages blocked, ball sticking)<br>b. Torn diaphragm<br>c. Idle adjustment incorrect<br>d. Amount of fuel injected is incorrect | a. Clean accelerator pump and check action.<br>b. Replace diaphragm.<br>c. Adjust idle.<br>d. Adjust amount. |
| 7. Engine stalls when accelerator pedal is released suddenly | Idle mixture too rich | Adjust idle. |
| 8. Engine runs unevenly (surges) with black smoke at low idle and smokes badly as idle speed increases. Spark plugs soot-up quickly and misfire | a. Excessive pressure on float needle valve<br>b. Float leaking<br>c. Float needle valve not closing | a. Check fuel pump pressure and reduce if necessary.<br>b. Replace float.<br>c. Check needle valve and replace if necessary. |
| 9. Engine runs unevenly at full throttle, misfires and cuts out or lacks power* | Fuel starvation | a. Clean main jet.<br>b. Clean float needle valve.<br>c. Check fuel pump pressure and increase if necessary.<br>d. Clean fuel tank. |
| 10. Fuel consumption is excessive | a. Jet sizes not properly matched<br>b. Excessive pressure at float needle valve<br>c. Float leaking<br>d. Float needle valve not closing<br>e. Automatic choke not working properly | a. Install correct set of jets. Check spark plug condition.<br>b. Check fuel pump pressure and reduce if necessary.<br>c. Replace float.<br>d. Check needle valve and replace if necessary.<br>e. Check as at Symptom 2. |

*A poor transition and a tendency to stall at idle can also be caused by insufficient ignition advance, inadequate breaker point gap or dirty spark plugs. Always check ignition system when in doubt.

5. Replace pilot jet valve if faulty or if engine continues to run after ignition is turned off.

**NOTE —**
Turning set screw for adjustment of valve is possible only on early versions. On newer versions of jet, or when replacement part has been used, no adjustment can be made.

6. To adjust pilot jet, turn set screw next to terminal clockwise to close valve, counter-clockwise to open valve.

## 4.13 Carburetor Adjustment

Every carburetor is tested at the factory and adjusted on the engine for operation with standard fuels. Any alteration in settings, such as replacing jets with other than specified sizes, is detrimental to engine operation under normal conditions. Specifications for the carburetors installed on all cars covered in this Manual are given in **8. Fuel Section Technical Data.**

The idle adjustment requires resetting from time to time. For this tuning the engine must be warm to keep the adjustment screw from coming to rest on a step of the fast idle cam.

**To adjust:**

1. Attach tachometer according to manufacturer's instructions.
2. Turn idle adjustment screw (Fig. 35) to set idle at 800 to 900 rpm.

**Fig. 35.** Engine tune-up, required from time to time, includes resetting of idle adjustment. (Text gives procedure.)

3. Turn volume control screw (Fig. 36) in slowly until engine speed begins to drop, then turn screw out until engine runs at highest idle speed. Turn screw counter-clockwise no more than one half turn.

**Fig. 36.** Idle mixture is adjusted by turning volume control screw to highest idle speed, then back half turn.

4. Reset idle if necessary. The idle adjustment is correct if the warm engine continues to run after throttle has been opened and closed suddenly with the clutch pedal depressed.

## 4.14 Main Jet with Altitude Corrector

Atmospheric pressure decreases with increase in altitude, and in high mountains the change is sufficient to affect carburetors. Adjustments will be needed. For delivery of a satisfactory mixture at high altitudes the main jet carrier can be replaced with an altitude corrector having the correct main jet. This device, shown schematically in Fig. 37, may be obtained from authorized VW dealers in high mountain regions.

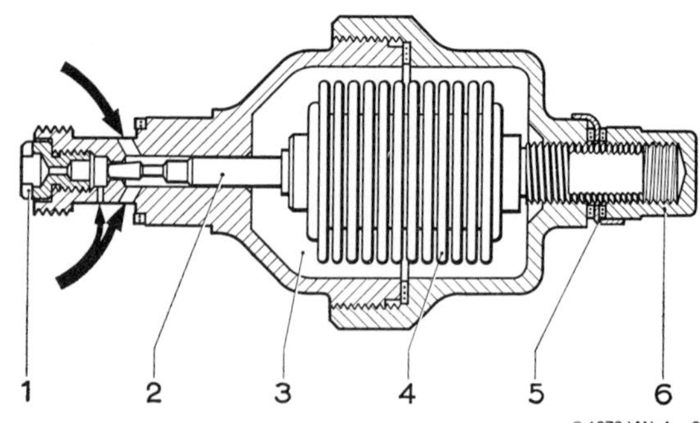




1. Main jet
2. Needle
3. Pressure chamber
4. Pressure unit
5. Lock
6. Regulating nut

**Fig. 37.** Altitude corrector replaces main jet carrier for better mixture at high altitudes.

Fuel from the float chamber comes to the main jet (1) through drillings indicated by the arrows in Fig. 37. It also flows into the pressure unit chamber (3). The pressure unit (4) expands or contracts with changes in atmospheric pressure, and this expansion or contraction moves needle (2) in the passage to the main jet. When the pressure unit expands at high altitude, the needle throttles fuel flow to the main jet to suit atmospheric conditions. At sea level the needle retracts to a position where it has no influence on fuel consumption.

> **NOTE** —
> When the altitude corrector unit is assembled the pressure unit is set with regulating nut (6) and locked with pressure plate (5). The setting must on no account be changed.

## 5. Checking the Fuel System

If the supply of fuel to the carburetor is interrupted, make the following sequence of checks:

1. Make certain there is fuel in the tank. If so, go to step 2.

> ***WARNING*** —
> *When working on fuel system, always use extreme caution and keep a fire extinguisher handy.*

2. Disconnect fuel line at the carburetor. Operate starter to activate fuel pump.
   a. If fuel is delivered: Check pump pressure. Inspect carburetor float needle valve and carburetor jets for dirt and other foreign matter. Catch some of the fuel from the pump in a clean glass or bottle and inspect it for dirt or other foreign matter.
   b. If no fuel is delivered: Go to step 3.
3. Disconnect fuel pump inlet line.
   a. If fuel flows out: Check fuel pump for leaks. Retighten screws and connections. If necessary, remove and disassemble pump for closer check.
   b. If no fuel flows: Go to steps 4 and 5.
4. Remove and clean fuel tank.
5. Blow out fuel line with compressed air.

## 6. Engines with Exhaust Emission Control System

The exhaust from gasoline engines contains poisonous carbon monoxide and unburned hydrocarbons. The amounts of carbon monoxide and hydrocarbons in the exhaust depend to a large extent on the ratio of fuel-to-air in the combustion mixture. The ignition timing and the temperature and condition of the engine are also of some importance. Since the mixture varies according to engine operating conditions, the composition of the exhaust gases also varies.

Production of engines with the exhaust emission control system began in August, 1967, with engine No. H 5 000 001. The system includes a special carburetor and other components. The Solex 30 PICT-2 carburetor shown in Fig. 38 incorporates devices for reducing the levels of carbon monoxide and hydrocarbons in the exhaust gases. Fig. 39 shows an exploded view of this carburetor. 3

The throttle positioner is another component in the VW system for control of emissions. (Engines for VW Automatic Stick Shift vehicles do not require the throttle positioner.) Whenever adjustments are made or maintenance is performed on engines with the exhaust emission control system, it is essential to observe all the manufacturer's specifications if the required low levels of emission are to be preserved.

### 6.1 Throttle Positioner

The throttle positioner comes into play in deceleration when the vehicle is over-running the engine. That is, the driver has taken his foot off the accelerator pedal, but the car continues to move and the engine to suck in fuel. Instead of the engine driving the car, the motion of the car is turning the engine. Since the throttle is closed, the air flow is inadequate. The mixture delivered to the cylinders is out of balance with engine rpm. Combustion is not complete.

The purpose of the throttle positioner is to keep the throttle open in deceleration long enough to prevent emission of unburned rich fuel mixture into the atmosphere. With the throttle partly open, the engine continues to take in an air-fuel mixture that is still combustible even in deceleration. Besides reducing the emission of hydrocarbons from the tailpipe, the throttle positioner also prevents backfiring in the muffler.

**Fig. 38.** Solex 30 PICT-2 carburetor, shown in cross-section, is emission control carburetor on 1500 cc engines.

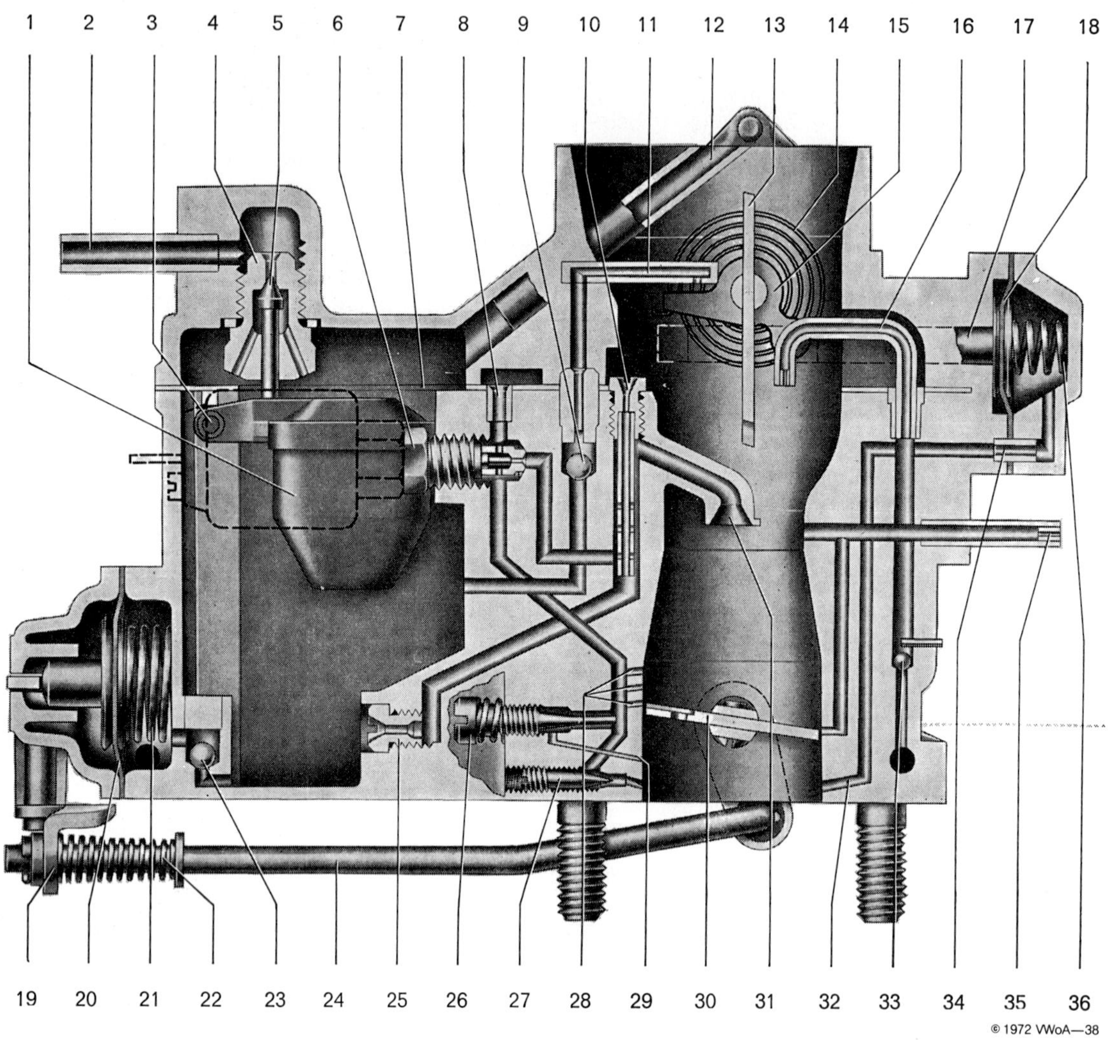


1. Float
2. Fuel line
3. Float lever
4. Float needle valve
5. Float needle
6. Pilot jet
7. Gasket
8. Pilot air drilling
9. Ball check valve in power fuel system
10. Air correction jet with emulsion tube
11. Power fuel tube
12. Float bowl vent tube
13. Choke valve
14. Bimetal spring
15. Operating lever
16. Accelerator pump discharge tube
17. Diaphragm rod
18. Vacuum diaphragm
19. Pump lever
20. Pump diaphragm
21. Spring
22. Push rod spring
23. Ball check valve for accelerator pump
24. Pump connector rod
25. Main jet
26. Volume control screw
27. Fuel metering screw*
28. By-pass port
29. Idle port
30. Throttle valve
31. Discharge arm
32. Vacuum drilling
33. Ball check valve in accelerator pump drilling
34. Jet in vacuum drilling
35. Vacuum connection
36. Diaphragm spring

***Caution: Do not change the adjustment of this screw.**

**Fig. 39.** Exploded view of Solex 30 PICT-2 carburetor shows relation among the different sub-assemblies.

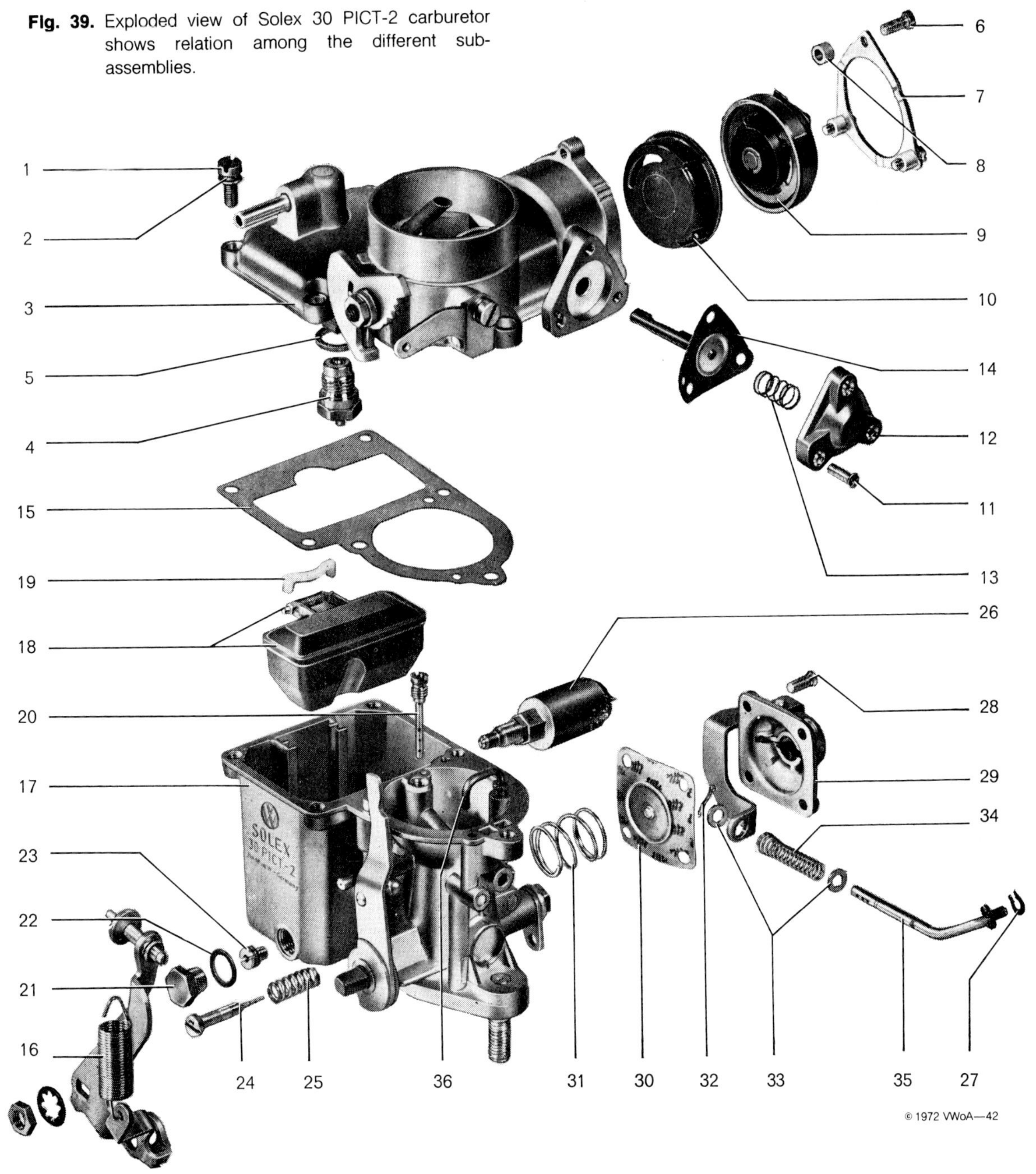

3

1. Screw for carburetor upper part
2. Spring washer
3. Carburetor upper part
4. Float needle valve 1.5 mm diameter
5. Washer for float needle valve
6. Screw for retaining ring
7. Retaining ring for cap
8. Spacer for retaining ring
9. Choke unit with spring and heater element
10. Plastic cap
11. Fillister head screw
12. Cover for vacuum diaphragm
13. Diaphragm spring
14. Vacuum diaphragm
15. Gasket
16. Return spring for accelerator cable
17. Carburetor lower part
18. Float and pin
19. Bracket for float pin
20. Air correction jet
21. Plug for main jet
22. Plug seal
23. Main jet
24. Volume control screw
25. Spring
26. Pilot jet cut-off valve "A"
27. Circlip
28. Fillister head screw
29. Cover for pump
30. Pump diaphragm
31. Spring for diaphragm
32. Cotter pin 1.5 x 15 mm
33. Washer 4.2 mm
34. Spring for connector rod
35. Connector rod
36. Injector tube for accelerator pump

As shown in Fig. 40, the vacuum (V) created below the throttle valve in deceleration becomes effective in chamber (A). Diaphragm (1) moves to the left against spring (2). The valve (3) attached to diaphragm (1) opens, and the vacuum in chamber (A) becomes effective in chamber (B). Now the vacuum can pull diaphragm (4) against spring (5). This motion is transmitted to pull rod (6), which actuates a lever to open the throttle valve. The stop washer (7) limits the pull rod stroke.

When the intake manifold vacuum decreases, spring (2) can press diaphragm (1) to the right, closing valve (3). A connection to the atmosphere is exposed by the movement of valve (3) to eliminate the vacuum in chamber (B), and the spring (5) now can move diaphragm (4) to the left, allowing the throttle valve to close.

The outside air that eliminates the vacuum in chamber (B) is admitted through hole (10) into the housing (C) of the altitude corrector. It passes through the plastic foam filter (9) and into chamber (B) by way of a drilling (8) in valve (3).

The altitude corrector (11), which presses on valve (3), is installed with a small preload. The arrangement automatically compensates for changes in vacuum and pressure, and the existing atmospheric pressure never affects the operation of the throttle positioner.

The throttle positioner is set with adjusting screw (12). Grub screw (13) locks adjusting screw (12).

## 6.2 Removing and Installing Throttle Positioner

Since repairs to the throttle positioner are not feasible, this part must be replaced. Instructions for removal and installation of new throttle positioner are given here.

**To remove:**

1. Disconnect pull rod from carburetor (see Fig. 41).
2. Remove three screws. Take off retaining ring and throttle positioner.
3. Pull off vacuum hose.

**Fig. 40.** Throttle positioner is an emission control device used with the Solex 30 PICT-2 carburetor. See text for descriptions of the operations labeled A, B, C, and V.

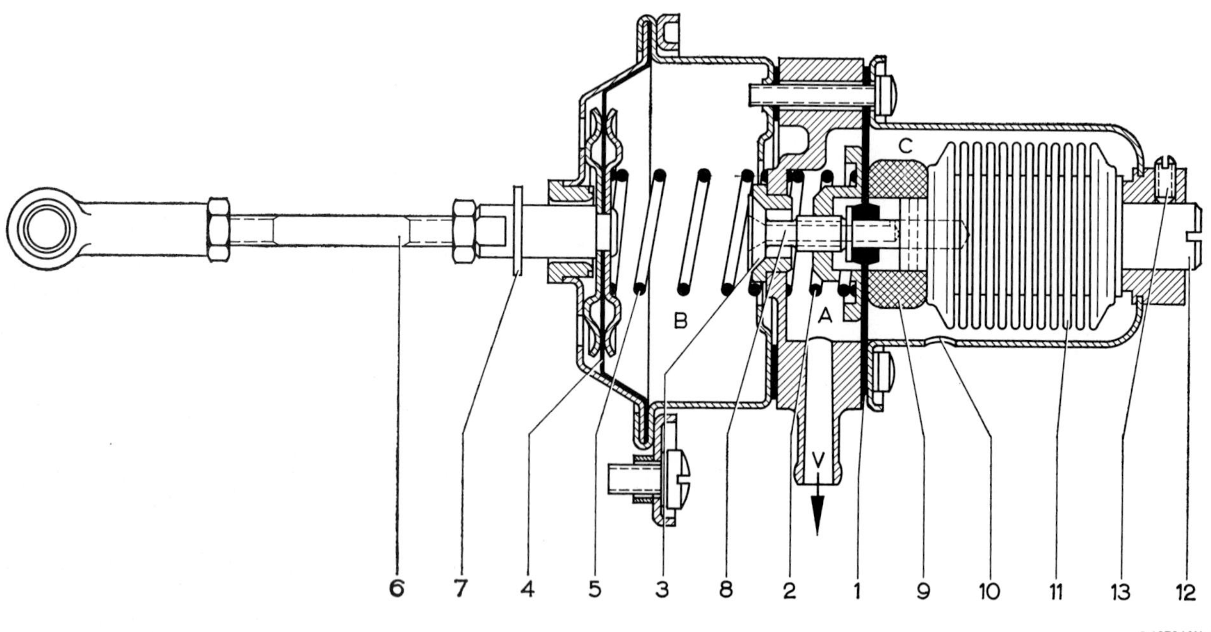


1. Diaphragm
2. Spring
3. Valve
4. Diaphragm
5. Spring
6. Pull rod
7. Washer
8. Drilling
9. Filter
10. Air hole
11. Altitude corrector
12. Adjusting screw
13. Lock screw

© 1972 VWoA—40

**Fig. 41.** Removal of throttle positioner requires removal of screws indicated by three black arrows at right after pull rod, indicated by fourth arrow, has been disconnected.

**To install:**

1. Reverse operations of removal.
2. Check adjustment. Correct if necessary.

## 6.3 Tuning of Engines with Exhaust Emission Control System

Before you attempt to adjust any part of the exhaust emission control system, check the engine, ignition and fuel systems. Functioning of exhaust emission control system depends on good condition of other systems. To check and adjust ignition system see **ENGINE.**

### Adjusting Idle

1. With engine warm use tachometer to set idle speed at 850 rpm with the idle adjusting screw (see Fig. 35).
2. Turn volume control screw (2) to the right until speed starts to drop. From this position turn the volume control screw to the left until engine runs fastest (see Fig. 36).

**NOTE —**
Variations in engine speed when volume control screw is turned are slight. Even when the volume control screw is turned in all the way, engine continues to run.

3. If necessary, regulate engine speed again with idle adjusting screw.

### Adjusting Throttle Positioner

**NOTE —**
This adjustment should be made only when engine is properly warmed up and after ignition timing has been checked. The choke valve of the automatic choke must be fully open.

**To adjust:**

1. Connect tachometer according to manufacturer's instructions and run engine.
2. Hold an open-end wrench behind the stop washer on the pull rod of the throttle valve positioner and pull on the wrench until the stop washer bears against the throttle positioner housing. Be careful not to pull down on the throttle positioner while you are pulling against the stop washer. 3
3. Note engine speed. It should be between 1700 and 1800 rpm.
4. Increase engine speed to 3000 rpm and release the throttle valve lever. Count the seconds between the instant you release the lever and the instant the throttle valve closes. The elapsed time should be between 3 and 4 seconds.
5. If it takes less than 3 seconds for throttle valve to close, turn the adjusting screw on the altitude corrector to the right. This screw is shown at (1) in Fig. 42. If it takes more than 4 seconds for the throttle valve to close, turn adjusting screw to the left.

© 1972 VWoA—41

**Fig. 42.** Adjusting screw of the throttle valve positioner is indicated at (1). Turning the screw to right or left speeds up or slows closing of the throttle.

6. Tighten lock screw on the adjusting screw and repeat check of the throttle valve closing time.

**NOTE —**
Movement of the adjusting screw changes only the response time. Push rod length determines final rpm.

### 6.4 Exhaust Emission Control Troubleshooting

The most common malfunctions of the exhaust emission control components are charted in **Table c,** with the causes and remedies. Remember, however, that the condition of the spark plugs and the ignition timing should be checked before you give your attention to emission control troubleshooting.

## 7. DRIVING HABITS AND FUEL CONSUMPTION

In theory, any vehicle leaving an assembly line should perform as well as any other vehicle produced on the same line. Nevertheless, practice has shown over and over again that considerable differences in fuel consumption will be found among vehicles of the same type.

When you fail to obtain the mileage you expect of your car, your first thought may be to blame the vehicle. It is necessary, however, to look also at the traffic conditions you regularly meet and at your own driving habits. Often, the explanation of high fuel consumption is to be found there.

Five factors influence the fuel consumption of a motor vehicle.

1. Driving habits
2. Power loss
3. Natural forces resisting motion
4. Weather
5. Traffic conditions

None of these five factors ever operates apart from the others, but it is easier to discuss them singly.

### 7.1 Driving Habits

Driving habits, which may reflect traffic conditions or the driver's approach to driving or a combination of both, have by far the greatest influence on fuel consumption.

The charts in Fig. 43 illustrate some relationships between acceleration and fuel consumption and between car speeds and engine rpm in the so-called "optimum" torque range. The data were taken from the performance of a run-in series production vehicle carrying two persons and traveling on a level surface, without headwind. The curves show the fuel consumption in liters per 62 miles (100 kilometers).

Look first at the upper chart, which shows fuel consumption plotted against speed, given in kilometers per hour for 2nd, 3rd and 4th gears. (A kilometer is approximately three-fifths of a mile. A liter is slightly more than a U.S. quart.) Fuel consumption is plotted vertically, speed horizontally. On each of the three curves the lower section, marked "A", shows fuel consumption at constant speed. The upper section, marked "B", shows fuel consumption under full throttle acceleration. The differences speak for themselves.

When accelerator pedal is depressed gradually for a reasonable acceleration to some selected constant speed, the surge of power is relatively small. The fuel consumption curve does rise, as shown in the graph for 4th gear, but it remains in lowest third of the field of the entire graph. For contrast, look at section "B" of the same 4th gear curve. Full throttle acceleration shoots fuel consumption to values more than twice those on

**Table c. Exhaust Emission Control**

| Symptom | Cause | Remedy |
|---|---|---|
| 1. Idle poor, resists adjustment | Dirt in idle system | Clean carburetor, adjust idle as prescribed. |
| 2. Idle too fast | a. Throttle valve sticking | a. Free throttle valve lever and pull rod, or replace. A bent pull rod must be replaced. |
| | b. Throttle valve positioner out of adjustment | b. Adjust throttle valve positioner as prescribed. |
| | c. Throttle valve positioner can not be adjusted | c. Replace throttle valve positioner. |
| 3. Backfiring when car is coasting | Throttle valve positioner out of adjustment | Adjust throttle valve positioner as specified or replace it. In extreme cases, set cut-in speed to max. 1900 rpm. |

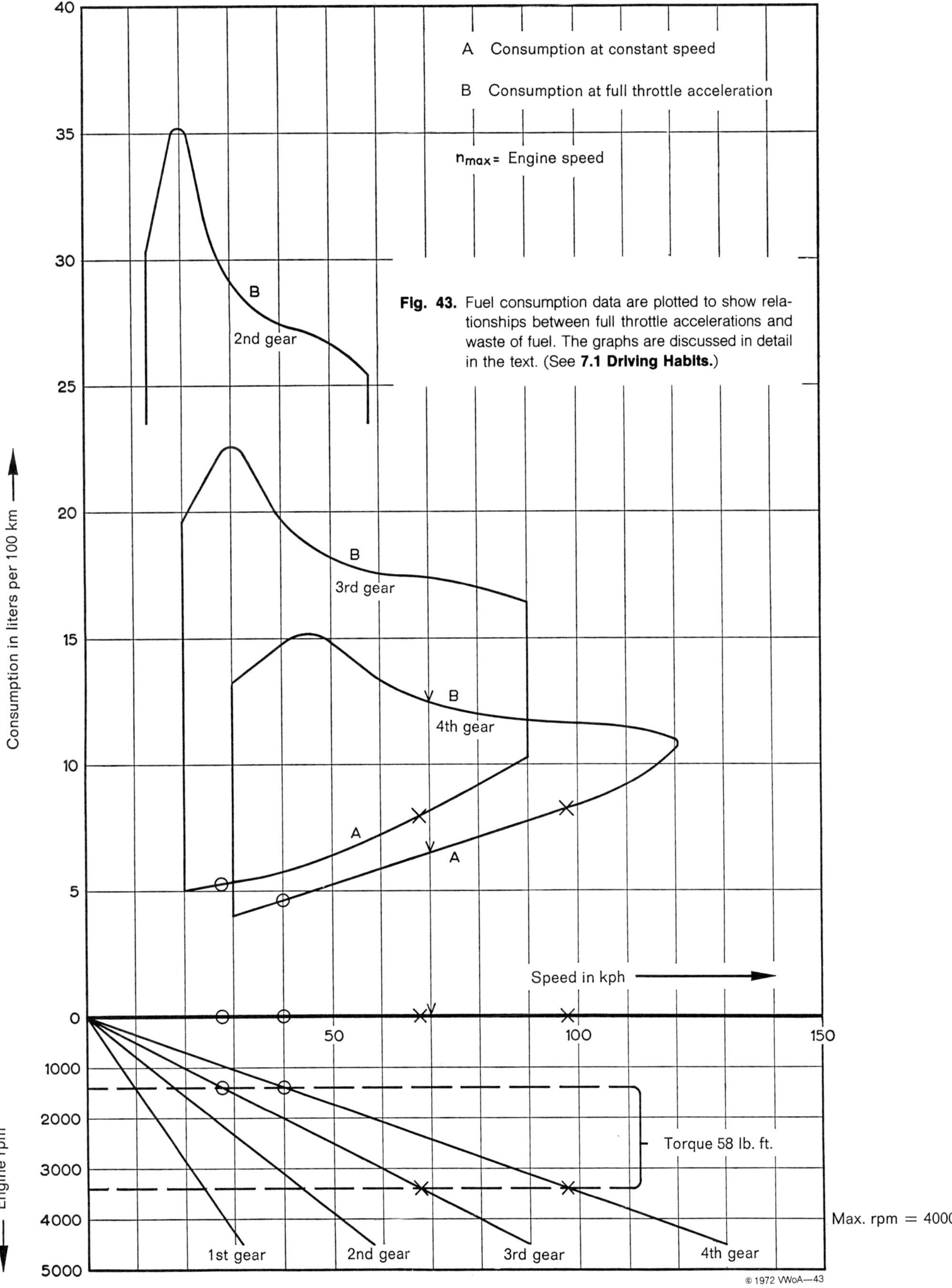


**Fig. 43.** Fuel consumption data are plotted to show relationships between full throttle accelerations and waste of fuel. The graphs are discussed in detail in the text. (See **7.1 Driving Habits.**)

3

curve "A." A specific example can be seen at speed marked "v." By tracing across to vertical axis on the left, you will see that speed "v" corresponds to fuel consumption of perhaps 7.5 liters on the "A" curve, but it rises to at least 12 liters on full-throttle acceleration "B" curve. A heavy foot on the pedal almost doubles fuel consumption. And, significantly, the particular speed chosen for the example is not at the maximum height of the "B" curve. Other points on the graph could have been picked where fuel consumption would have been even higher.

Now look at the consumption curves for 2nd and 3rd gears. The difference between minimum consumption and maximum consumption at full-throttle acceleration is much greater than in 4th gear. In 3rd gear, for example, to accelerate the vehicle from 20 to 50 kph (12 to 31 mph) requires only a small depression of the accelerator pedal, resulting in a very small rise in the fuel consumption curve. But under full throttle acceleration fuel consumption jumps immediately to three to four times the amount required for normal driving.

As the curves show, full throttle acceleration in 2nd gear sends the fuel consumption up to values several times greater than those for normal driving, and maximum consumption in 1st gear is higher still. For this reason, 1st gear should be reserved for moving off. High acceleration in 1st should be avoided.

At low speeds in heavy traffic full-throttle accelerations will not bring any noticeable gain in performance but will waste gas. The driver who trains himself to depress the accelerator pedal only a third or a half of its travel instead of all the way when he wants to pick up speed will save a considerable amount of fuel. Every time the brakes are applied the energy that was taken from the burning of fuel and translated into the car's motion is converted back to heat in the braking system and lost. As always, smooth, steady driving, with as few abrupt stops and strong accelerations as possible, will prove to be the most economical. It is rarely possible in today's traffic to keep fuel consumption on the lowest third of the graph, but fuel economy is one of the goals of a skilled driver.

The best compromise between engine performance, fuel economy and acceleration is achieved by driving in the "optimum" torque range, as charted in the lower part of Fig. 43. The diagram shows speeds in each of the four gears in relation to engine rpm. The "optimum" torque range lies between the two dashed horizontal lines; that is, between 1200 and 3200 rpm. The intersections of these lines with the solid lines representing gear speeds mark the lower and upper limits for best performance in the individual gear speed ranges. The lower limit intersections are marked "O" and the upper limit intersections "X". You will find similar "O" and "X" designations at the corresponding points on the fuel consumption curves in the diagram above.

For economical driving, especially in city traffic, we recommend the lower speed range. Car speeds and engine rpm near the intersections marked "O" on the diagram will give the most economical performance. The often heard opinion that low rpm are hard on the engine is no longer true. So long as the engine runs smoothly and without jerking, low rpm will not be damaging. Nevertheless, when traffic conditions and safety (others' as well as your own) permit or demand accelerating and passing, the next lower gear should be selected. If possible, engine speeds should not exceed the upper limits for the optimum torque range. As the diagrams make plain, the rate of fuel consumption goes up with speed. The rise in fuel consumption at speeds above "X" in 4th gear should serve as a reminder that driving in this range is uneconomical. Accelerating up to the limit in 1st, 2nd and 3rd gears not only is expensive but frequently leads to exceeding maximum engine speeds (rpm). Fast starts, flat-out acceleration in each gear and continuous high speed driving on the turnpikes all cost money. These considerations are of first importance when you are seeking the causes of poor performance or low mileage. Observe the red markings on face of speedometer dial for safe acceleration and minimum engine wear.

## 7.2 Power Loss

Power loss can have a marked effect on the performance of a vehicle and its fuel consumption. Because the frictional resistance of engine, gears and axles is greater before break-in, the car just off the assembly line will burn more fuel than one that has been well run-in. On the other hand, a car that is poorly maintained or in need of repair is likely to show a rise in fuel consumption and loss of output.

## 7.3 Natural Forces

Natural forces resisting motion of a vehicle will include the frictional, gravitational and inertial forces the car must overcome while rolling over the ground and moving through the air, climbing and accelerating.

(a) Rolling resistance comes from friction between the wheel and its bearing and friction in the flexing of the tire shape on the surface of the road. The internal structure of the tires, their size and the air pressure, as well as the design of the tread, have major effects on the distortion of the tire shape and, consequently, on the rolling resistance. The condition of the road also enters the picture. Obviously, an unpaved country track or a muddy or snow-covered one will offer greater resistance to the vehicle's wheels than a dry asphalt road or concrete highway will.

(b) Air resistance increases as the square of the speed. When you double the speed of your car from 30 to 60 miles, the air resistance is not doubled but multiplied by four. Every vehicle of a given shape has the same air resistance, but its resistance can be increased considerably if you add roof racks for luggage, ski racks, mud deflectors, pennants or other accessories that stick out from the car body and thus change its original shape.

(c) Climbing resistance depends not only on the slope of the incline but also on the weight of the vehicle and thus on gravity.

(d) Acceleration resistance depends on the magnitude of the change in speed or direction. Every body tends to remain in its present state of rest or motion. To set a resting body in motion or to change the motion of a moving body you have to overcome this tendency, which is called the body's inertia. In the case of a car overcoming inertial forces requires extra fuel.

## 7.4 Weather

The weather affects engine output and fuel consumption enough for the experienced driver to be able to note the differences. The effects of changes of temperature, atmospheric pressure, relative humidity and oxygen content of the air could be measured in the cylinders if we had sufficiently elaborate and sensitive apparatus. Short trips in cold weather with a cold engine always use more fuel than would be consumed in the same kind of driving in summer. Further, the force and direction of the wind, which also are characteristics of the weather, have a much greater effect on fuel consumption and engine output than many realize.

From the foregoing explanations of the various environmental factors affecting the performance of cars it will be apparent that in actual day-to-day operation series production vehicles of the same type will be subjected to greatly differing conditions. In consequence, it is impossible to give precise figures for the performance, maximum speed, acceleration and fuel consumption of any series type. A wide range of values must be allowed.

3

## 7.5 Traffic Conditions

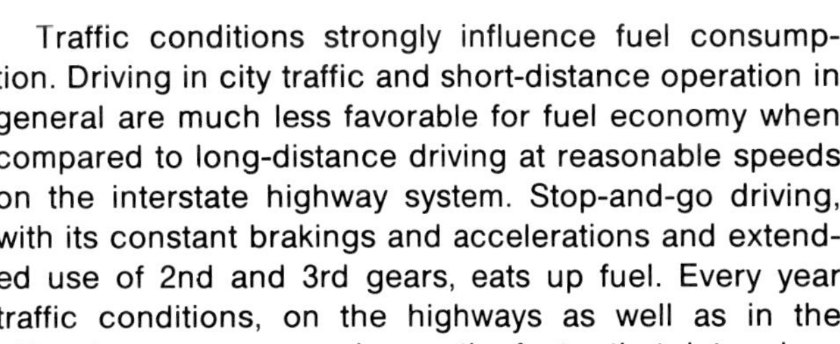

Traffic conditions strongly influence fuel consumption. Driving in city traffic and short-distance operation in general are much less favorable for fuel economy when compared to long-distance driving at reasonable speeds on the interstate highway system. Stop-and-go driving, with its constant brakings and accelerations and extended use of 2nd and 3rd gears, eats up fuel. Every year traffic conditions, on the highways as well as in the cities, become more and more the factor that determines what mileage the driver can expect from his car.

## 8. FUEL SYSTEM TECHNICAL DATA

### I. Carburetor Jets and Settings

| | | | | |
|---|---|---|---|---|
| Transmission | Manual | Manual | Manual | Automatic |
| Engine capacity and output | 1300/50 bhp SAE | 1500/53 bhp SAE | 1500/53 bhp SAE | 1500/53 bhp SAE |
| Engine No., from | F 0 000 001 | H 0 204 001 | H 5 000 001 | H 5 077 366 |
| Solex carburetor type | 30 PICT-1 | 30 PICT-1 | 30 PICT-2 | 30 PICT-2 |
| Part No. | 113 129 023 D<br>141 129 023 M | 113 129 025 B | 113 129 027 H | 113 129 027 J |
| Modification No. | VW 132-2 | VW 104-1 | VW 126-1/2 | VW 167-2 |
| Venturi | 24.0 mm dia. | 24.0 mm dia. | 24.0 mm dia. | 24.0 mm dia. |
| Main jet | 0.125 | 0.120 | X 116 | X 116 |
| Air correction jet | 125z* | 125z** | 125z** | 125z |
| Pilot jet | g55 | g55 | g55 | 55 |
| Idle air jet drilling | 150 | 150 | 135 | 140 |
| Auxiliary fuel jet | — | — | — | — |
| Auxiliary fuel jet drilling | — | — | — | — |
| Idle cut-off valve | electromagnetic with fuel jet | | electromagnetic with fuel jet | |
| Float needle valve | 1.5 mm dia. | 1.5 mm dia. | 1.5 mm dia. | 1.5 mm dia. |
| Fuel level | — | — | 19.5±1 | 19.5±1 |
| Float needle valve washer | — | — | 1.0 mm | 1.0 mm |
| Float weight | 5.7 grams | 5.7 grams | 8.5 grams | 8.5 grams |
| Injection quantity, cc/stroke | 1.3-1.6 | 1.05-1.35 | 1.05-1.35 | 1.05-1.35 |
| Cotter pin position/washer | — | — | — | — |
| Return drilling | — | — | — | — |
| Power fuel jet | *** | 50 | 60 | 60 |
| Distance from accelerator pump to housing joint | — | — | — | — |
| Throttle valve gap | — | — | — | — |
| Emulsion tube | Integral part of air correction jet | | Integral part of air correction jet | |
| Emulsion tube carrier | — | — | — | — |

***Type 1 K.G.: 170z **Type 1 K.G.: 135z **Type 1 K.G.: 75**

### II. Fuel Pump*

| Type | from Engine No. | Part No. | Identification mark | Minimum delivery capacity** cc/mm | rpm | Maximum delivery pressure in psi |
|---|---|---|---|---|---|---|
| 1 | F 0 000 001*** | 113 127 025 A | VW 7 | 400 | 3400 | 3-5 |

* Mechanical diaphragm type, with cut-off valve in upper part  ** Via 1.5 mm dia. float needle valve  *** and Type 1/1500 from Engine No. H 0 204 001

### III. Other Data

Fuel tank capacity . . 10.5 U.S. gallons (8.8 Im. gals.; 40 liters)
Air cleaner . . . . . . Oil-bath type with preheater tube

Fuel filter. Strainer in fuel tank, filter in fuel pump
Fuel gauge. Dash mounted unit (either mechanical or electrical)

Capacities
Oil bath cleaner (fill up to mark):
1300 . . . . . . . . . . . . . . . . 0.53 U.S. pints (0.25 liter)
1500 . . . . . . . . . . . . . . . . 0.8 U.S. pints (0.4 liter)
1500 (Karmann Ghia - 1967 model) . . . 0.63 U.S. pints (0.3 liter)
1500 (Karmann Ghia - 1968 model). . . 0.95 U.S. pints (0.45 liter)

# Section 4

# FRONT AXLE

## Contents

4


**1. General Description** . . . . . 5
- Axle Beam . . . . . 5
- Springing and Suspension . . . . . 5
- Wheels . . . . . 7
- Shock Absorbers . . . . . 7
- Lubrication . . . . . 7
- Maintenance . . . . . 7

**2. Removal and Disassembly of Axle** . . . . . 7
- 2.1 Removing and Installing Front Axle . . . 7
- 2.2 Disassembling Front Axle . . . . . 9
- 2.3 Removing and Installing Brake Drums . . 10

**3. Front Wheel Bearings** . . . . . 11
- 3.1 Removing and Installing Front Wheel Bearings . . . . . 11
- 3.2 Checking and Adjusting Front Wheel Bearings . . . . . 14

**4. Steering Knuckles** . . . . . 15
- 4.1 Removing and Installing Steering Knuckle . . . . . 16
- 4.2 Checking Steering Knuckle Spindle and Steering Arm . . . . . 18

**5. Stabilizer Bar** . . . . . 18
- 5.1 Removing and Installing Stabilizer Bar . . 18

**6. Torsion Arms and Ball Joints** . . . . . 19
- 6.1 Removing Torsion Arms . . . . . 19
- 6.2 Checking Ball Joints (torsion arm installed) . . . . . 20
- 6.3 Checking Ball Joints (torsion arm removed) . . . . . 21
- 6.4 Replacing Ball Joints . . . . . 22
- 6.5 Installing Torsion Arm . . . . . 23
- 6.6 Fitting Shock Absorber Pin . . . . . 23

**7. Torsion Bars** . . . . . 24
- 7.1 Removing and Installing Torsion Bars . . 24

**8. Front Axle Needle Bearings and Metal Bushings** . . . . . 25
- 8.1 Removing Upper and Lower Needle Bearings . . . . . 25
- 8.2 Removing Upper and Lower Metal Bushings . . . . . 25
- 8.3 Installing Needle Bearings and Metal Bushings . . . . . 26

**9. Shock Absorbers** . . . . . 27
- 9.1 Checking Shock Absorbers . . . . . 27
- 9.2 Replacing Shock Absorbers . . . . . 27
- 9.3 Removing and Installing Shock Absorbers . . . . . 27
- 9.4 Heavy Duty Shock Absorbers . . . . . 29

**10. Steering** . . . . . 29
- 10.1 Description and Operation . . . . . 29
- 10.2 Lubrication . . . . . 29
- 10.3 Maintenance . . . . . 29
- 10.4 Steering Troubleshooting . . . . . 31
- 10.5 Removing and Installing Steering Damper 31

10.6 Removing and Installing Tie Rods . . . . 32
10.7 Removing and Installing Steering Wheel 33
10.8 Removing and Installing Steering Column (1966 and 1967 cars) . . . . . . . . . . . 34
10.9 Removing and Installing Column Tube . 35
10.10 Energy-absorbing Steering Column . . . 36
10.11 Removing and Installing Energy-absorbing Column . . . . . . . . . 37
10.12 Steering Gearbox . . . . . . . . . . . . . . 38
10.13 Checking and Adjusting Roller Steering . 39
Axial Play of Steering Roller . . . . . . . . 40
10.14 Wheel Position . . . . . . . . . . . . . . . . 40
10.15 Front Wheel Alignment . . . . . . . . . . 41
10.16 Steering Geometry . . . . . . . . . . . . . 41
Camber and King Pin . . . . . . . . . . . . 41
Caster . . . . . . . . . . . . . . . . . . . . . 42
Toe-in and Toe-out (Toe) . . . . . . . . . . 42
Alignment Check . . . . . . . . . . . . . . . 43
Checking and Adjusting Camber . . . . . 43
Checking and Adjusting Toe Angle . . . 44
Adjusting Wheel Lock Angle . . . . . . . . 45
10.17 Troubleshooting the Steering System . . 45

**11. Front Axle Technical Data** . . . . . . . . . . . . 46
I. General Data . . . . . . . . . . . . . . . . . 46
II. Specifications for Vehicle Alignment . . . 46
III. Tolerances and Wear Limits . . . . . . . . . 47
IV. Torque Specifications . . . . . . . . . . . . 48

**TABLES**

a. Steering Troubleshooting . . . . . . . . . . . . . 31
b. Troubleshooting the Steering System . . . . . . 45

# Front Axle

On the cars covered in this Manual, the front axle, the front wheels, the steering mechanism and the suspension make up a linked system in which the functioning of each part or assembly affects the functioning of all the others. They are tied together in the steering geometry of the car. A change in any single element in the geometry necessarily leads to a change in the whole system.



Tire wear and the handling qualities of the car are evidence of how well or how badly the front axle system is working. Since both tire wear and car handling are factors in road safety, the importance of keeping the front axle components and assemblies in correct adjustment and good condition should be emphasized. Correct adjustment means not only adjustment of single working parts but also adjustment of linkages to other units and to the whole system.

In the VW system for the front end, the wheels are suspended independently. A simple linkage of transverse torsion bars with twin trailing arms achieves this result, which prevents the transfer of road shock from one wheel to the opposite wheel. The trailing arms are composed of torsion arms tied to the torsion bars and joined at ball joints to the steering knuckles.

Rubber buffers limit the up-and-down wheel movements on very rough roads, and these buffers are progressive in their action. Thus, the harder the blow on the buffer from a severe bump, the stronger the springing reaction to smooth out the ride.

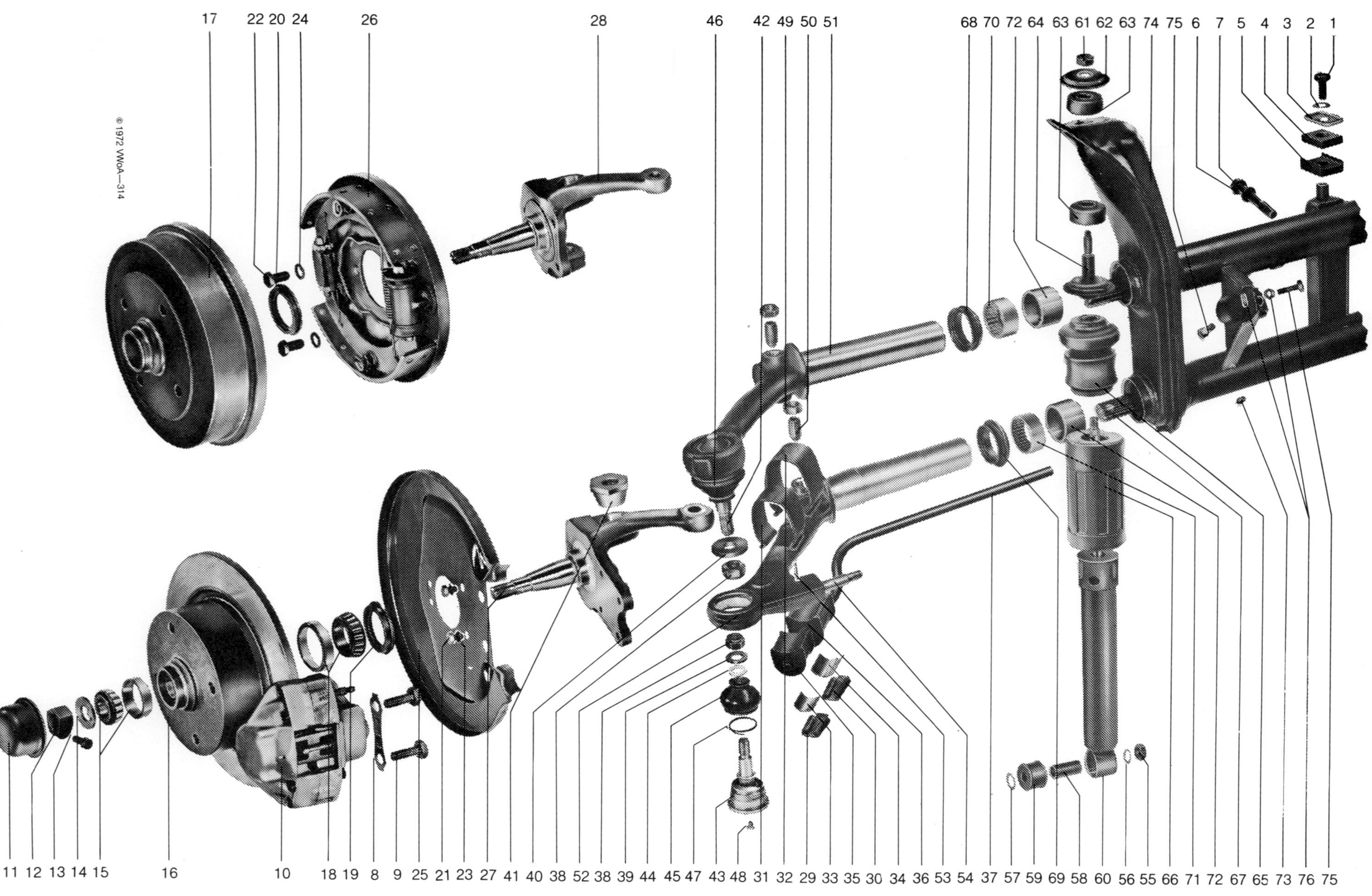
17 22 20 24 26 28 46 42 49 50 51 68 70 72 64 63 61 62 63 74 75 6 7 5 4 3 2 1
© 1972 VWoA—314
11 12 13 14 15 16 10 18 19 8 9 25 21 23 27 41 40 38 52 38 39 44 45 47 43 48 31 32 29 33 35 30 34 36 53 54 37 57 59 69 58 60 56 55 66 71 72 67 65 73 76 75

## 1. GENERAL DESCRIPTION

The linkages of the various components and assemblies of the front axle system can be visualized if you read the following brief descriptions with reference to the pictures and parts lists of Fig. 1 and Fig. 2.

### Axle Beam

The axle beam consists of two rigidly joined tubes bolted to the frame head at four places and to the car body at two places. The tubes hold torsion bars from which the front wheels are suspended. Side plates welded at ends of tubes strengthen beam and provide upper mounting points for telescopic shock absorbers.

> ***WARNING —***
> *Before any work on the front axle is undertaken, it is important to understand procedures and to have the right equipment. The steering system is absolutely essential to control of the car. Wrong adjustment of any component may endanger lives.*
> *For any procedure in which the front end is to be raised from the ground the equipment should include suitable stands to support the car safely. Cinder blocks and other makeshift supports are dangerous and should never be used.*

Since the axle beam has been welded into a rigid unit and since its original form must be preserved, it is never repaired. An axle beam that has been bent in a collision or damaged in some other way must be replaced.

### Springing and Suspension

The torsion bars from which the front wheels are independently suspended are packs of ten leaves anchored at the center to prevent twisting and side play. Seen in cross section, each bar is shaped like a cross.

The torsion arms fit over the ends of the torsion bars. They are fixed to the bars with set screws and mounted in metal bushings and needle bearings pressed into the tubes. A stabilizer bar connects the lower torsion arms. It is attached with rubber bushings and clips.

The steering knuckles carrying the spindles (stub axles) for the wheels are attached to the torsion arms at maintenance-free ball joints. The ball joints, which are pressed into eyes in the arms, have threaded pins (studs). The steering knuckles are fastened to the ball joint pins with nuts. Each upper ball joint fits in an eccentric bushing with which the camber (tilt) of the front wheel on that side of the car can be adjusted.

**Fig. 1.** Disassembled axle with ball joints is shown in these exploded views. Brake drum assembly is seen at upper left, disc brake assembly at lower left. Except as noted in the identification key, all parts for the axle come in pairs. Note the eccentric bushing (41) for the upper ball joint. Camber (tilt) of the wheel is adjusted by turning this eccentric bushing.

1. Bolt M 10 x 25
2. Lock washer
3. Plate
4. Rubber packing, upper
5. Rubber packing, lower
6. Bolt, M 12 x 1.5 x 90
7. Lock washer
8. Lock plate
9. Bolt M 10
10. Brake caliper
11. Dust cap
12. Clamp nut for wheel bearing
13. Screw for clamp nut M 7 x 18
14. Thrust washer
15. Outer tapered roller bearing
16. Disc
17. Drum
18. Inner tapered roller bearing
19. Seal for disc
20. Seal for drum
21. Bolt M 7 x 10 (6)
22. Bolt M 10 x 18 (3)
23. Lock washer (6)
24. Lock washer (3)
25. Cover
26. Front wheel brake and backing plate
27. Steering knuckle for disc brake
28. Steering knuckle for brake drum
29. Retainer, small
30. Retainer, large
31. Clamp, small
32. Clamp, large
33. Plate, small
34. Plate, large
35. Rubber mounting, small
36. Rubber mounting, large
37. Stabilizer (1)
38. Self-locking nut M 12 x 15 (4)
39. Washer, small
40. Washer, large
41. Eccentric bushing for camber adjustment
42. Upper ball joint
43. Lower ball joint
44. Ring 13.8 for rubber boot (4)
45. Boot for lower joint
46. Boot for upper joint
47. Ring for rubber boot (4)
48. Plug (4)
49. Hex. nut (6)
50. Set screw for torsion bar (6)
51. Torsion arm, upper
52. Torsion arm, lower
53. Pin
54. Pin for shock absorber
55. Hex. nut M 10
56. Lock washer 10.5
57. Lock washer 12.5
58. Sleeve for rubber bushing
59. Rubber bushing
60. Shock absorber
61. Nut
62. Plate for shock absorber bushing
63. Shock absorber bushing (4)
64. Pin for buffer
65. Buffer
66. Tube
67. Torsion bar—10 leaves
68. Seal for upper torsion arm
69. Seal for lower torsion arm
70. Needle bearing, upper
71. Needle bearing, lower
72. Metal bushing for torsion arms (4)
73. Grease fitting (4)
74. Axle beam (1)
75. Bolt M 8 x 25
76. Nut M 8

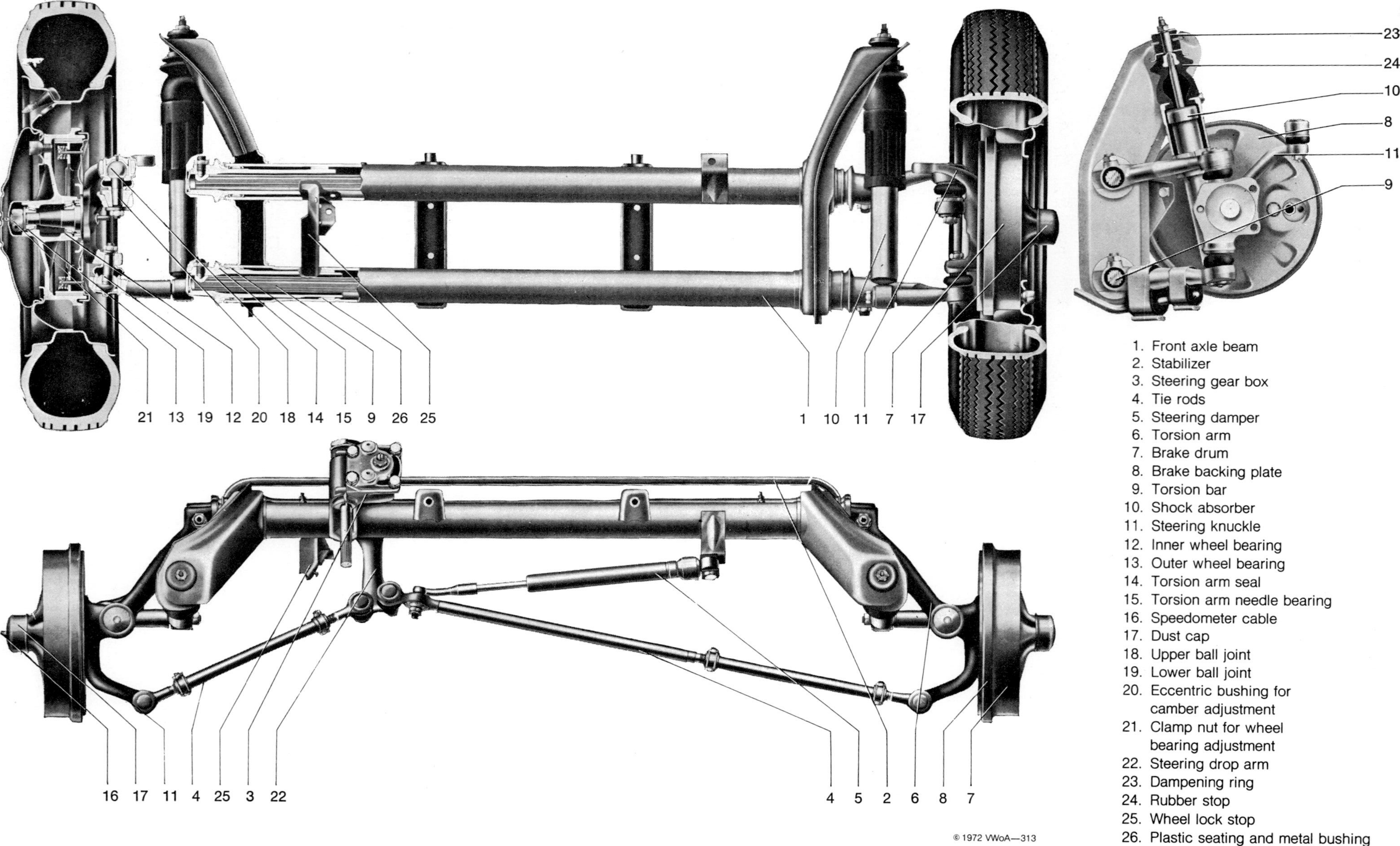


1. Front axle beam
2. Stabilizer
3. Steering gear box
4. Tie rods
5. Steering damper
6. Torsion arm
7. Brake drum
8. Brake backing plate
9. Torsion bar
10. Shock absorber
11. Steering knuckle
12. Inner wheel bearing
13. Outer wheel bearing
14. Torsion arm seal
15. Torsion arm needle bearing
16. Speedometer cable
17. Dust cap
18. Upper ball joint
19. Lower ball joint
20. Eccentric bushing for camber adjustment
21. Clamp nut for wheel bearing adjustment
22. Steering drop arm
23. Dampening ring
24. Rubber stop
25. Wheel lock stop
26. Plastic seating and metal bushing

**Fig. 2.** The front axle of a Beetle is shown here in three views. At the bottom, the axle is shown as seen from the driver's seat. Above, the axle has been tipped forward 90 degrees from the lower position. The view now is from directly behind the axle. At upper right, the view is from the center of the axle toward the inside of the right front wheel. Note the connection of the steering arm (22) and the tie rods (4). It is side-to-side movement of the arm that turns the wheels.

### Wheels

The brake drum and wheel hub are a single casting. The wheel turns on two tapered roller bearings on the spindle.

### Shock Absorbers

The hydraulic shock absorbers, which reduce bouncing and pitching of the car on rough roads, are designed specifically for the car's characteristics and should be replaced only with shock absorbers of the same type. The shock absorbers have rubber buffers to cushion road shock progressively.

### Lubrication

If the job is to be done properly, the front wheels must be off the ground when the front axle is lubricated. That is, the axle must be free of load. The axle requires lubrication every 6,000 miles or once a year, whichever comes first. In preparation for the job the four nipples on the axle should be cleaned thoroughly to keep dirt from entering the joints with the grease. It also is important to keep grease and oil off the tires and brake hoses. Every trace should be wiped off at once.

At every lubrication service, the dust boots on the maintenance-free tie rod ends must be checked for damage and security. A damaged boot can be replaced but only if it is known for certain that no dirt has entered the tie rod end ball socket. Usually a damaged boot is a signal to install a new tie rod end as well as a new boot.

Steering ball joints with damaged dust boots can be cleaned by pumping in grease to force out the dirt. Only worn steering ball joints need replacement.

A multi-purpose grease with a lithium base is recommended for use on the front axle. Only brands of good quality should be used.

### Maintenance

To maintain the riding qualities and the operational safety of the car, it is necessary to check the front axle and steering gear regularly and to stick to the maintenance schedule. (You will find schedule in **LUBRICATION AND MAINTENANCE**.)

The following operations are included in regular maintenance:

1. Check air pressure in tires and inspect them for wear and damage.
2. Check axial end play of lower steering ball joints (every 6,000 miles).
3. Inspect dust boots on steering ball joints and tie rod ends, and check security of tie rods.
4. Check and adjust toe and camber.
5. Check and adjust steering gear box.
6. Clean front wheel bearings, pack them with grease and adjust free play (every 30,000 miles).

## 2. Removal and Disassembly of Axle

Most work that will be done on the front axle can be done with the axle in place. It rarely is necessary to remove the axle unless the axle beam has been damaged and in that event the beam must be replaced.

If the car has been in an accident and there is reason to think that the axle beam has been bent, use a straightedge to check the tubes for distortion. But never try to straighten a damaged axle beam. Replace it.

### 2.1 Removing and Installing Front Axle

Since typical adjustments can be made with axle in place on the car, you usually will install or repair the axle only when replacing a damaged beam.

> ***CAUTION —***
> *On the Karmann Ghia models it is possible to damage the brake disc or the brake disc shield if the front axle assembly is not handled carefully in removal or installation. For this reason, always use a floor jack and a front axle cradle when removing or installing the front axle.*

**To remove axle:**

1. With car on ground, loosen wheel bolts. Raise car and take off front wheels.
2. Pull off fuel hose between tank and chassis and plug it.
3. Remove fuel tank. (See **FUEL SYSTEM**).
4. Loosen clip on steering column tube and pull horn cable connector off steering column. Now pull the column complete with steering wheel off the coupling flange.
5. Remove cotter pin from speedometer cable at dust cap of left front wheel and pull cable out of steering knuckle.
6. Disconnect brake hoses at brackets and plug them with bleeder valve dust caps.

7. Detach steering damper from bracket (see Fig. 3) on axle beam.

© 1972 VWoA—315

**Fig. 3.** Steering damper is attached to axle beam at bracket shown here. Damper absorbs road shock and stabilizes steering arm.

8. After bending up lock plates and removing nuts, press end of long tie rod off with a tool, as shown in Fig. 4. Take out tie rod and steering damper.

© 1972 VWoA—316

**Fig. 4.** Tie rod end is removed from steering knuckle with special tool.

9. Remove the two bolts that secure car body (see Fig. 5) to axle beam.

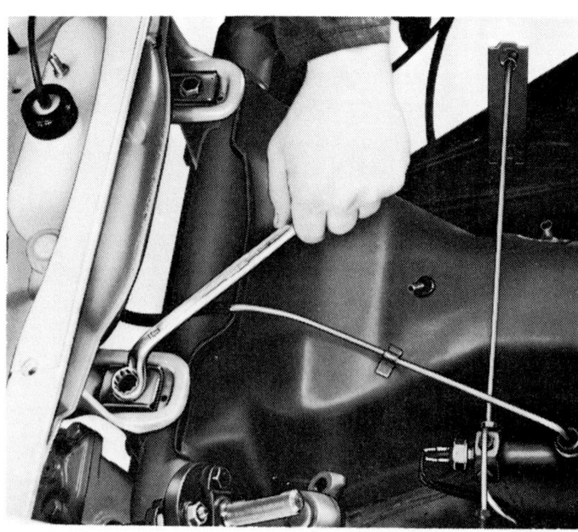
© 1972 VWoA—317

**Fig. 5.** Two bolts attach car body to front axle.

10. Loosen the four bolts securing axle to frame head, as in Fig. 6.

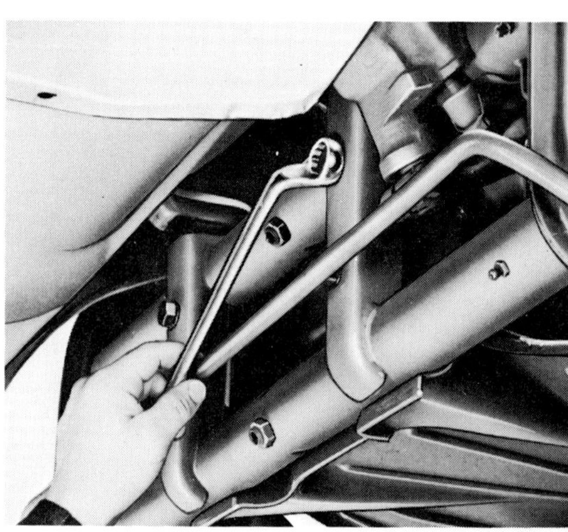
© 1972 VWoA—318

**Fig. 6.** Four bolts attach front axle to frame head.

11. Position floor jack and a suitable front axle adapter. Remove screws, take axle off, and place on a stand.

**To install axle:**

1. Place axle on adapter and using a chain, position it at proper angle for installation. (See Fig. 7.) Put a rubber spacer on each threaded bushing on the front axle.

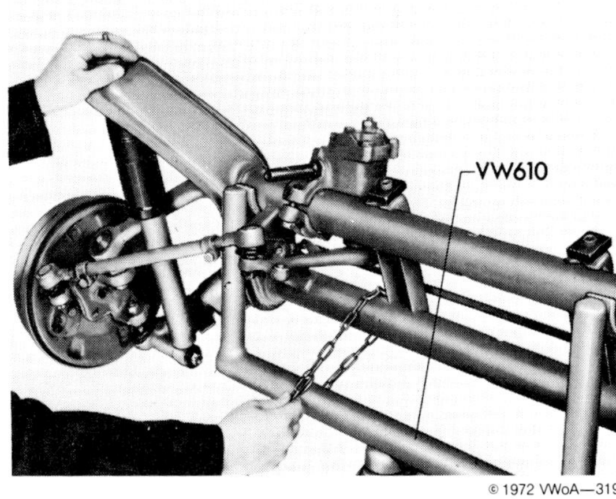


**Fig. 7.** Adapter cradle and chain hold front axle at correct angle for installation.

2. Use new spring washers for the securing bolts.
3. With torque wrench tighten the front axle securing bolts to 36 ft. lbs. (5.0 mkg).
4. Tighten the body bolts on front axle to 14 ft. lbs. (2.0 mkg). Do not forget rubber spacers, washers for spacers and spring washers. Fig. 8 illustrates the arrangement.

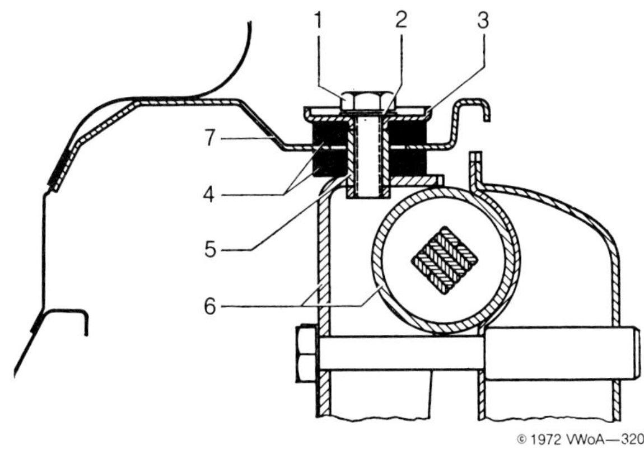


1. Body bolt
2. Lock washer
3. Washer for spacer
4. Rubber spacer
5. Threaded bushing
6. Axle
7. Car body

**Fig. 8.** Axle attachment to frame head and car body is seen here in cross section. Body bolt (1) is tightened to 14 ft. lbs.

5. Tighten tie rod end nuts and secure with cotter pins.
6. Install steering damper bolt in the front axle bracket, using a new lock plate. Tighten bolt to 29 to 32 ft. lbs. (4.0 to 4.5 mkg) and secure it. The new lock plate should be installed with the opening of the "U" to the front and the angled surface on the bracket.
7. Center the steering gear with the aid of the marking ring on the worm spindle. (See Fig. 9.) Place steering column on column coupling so that the steering wheel spoke is horizontal. Secure steering column clamp screw with a new lock plate.

**Fig. 9.** Vertical dashed line shows alignment of marking ring split with rib on steering gearbox. This is a factory adjustment. When worm and roller were meshed correctly, ring was driven on spindle to mark position. This view of gearbox is from above.

8. Check toe, camber and caster.

***WARNING*** 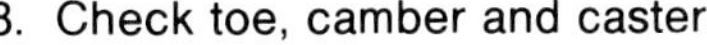
*Be careful not to twist brake hoses on installation.*

9. Install brake lines.
10. Bleed brake system and adjust brakes (see **BRAKES**).

## 2.2 Disassembling Front Axle

The following sequence is recommended for disassembling the front axle:

1. Remove tie rods and steering damper.
2. Remove steering gear box.
3. Remove brake drums.
4. Remove brake backing plates.
5. Remove shock absorbers.
6. Remove steering knuckles.
7. Remove stabilizer.
8. Remove torsion arms together with ball joints.

4

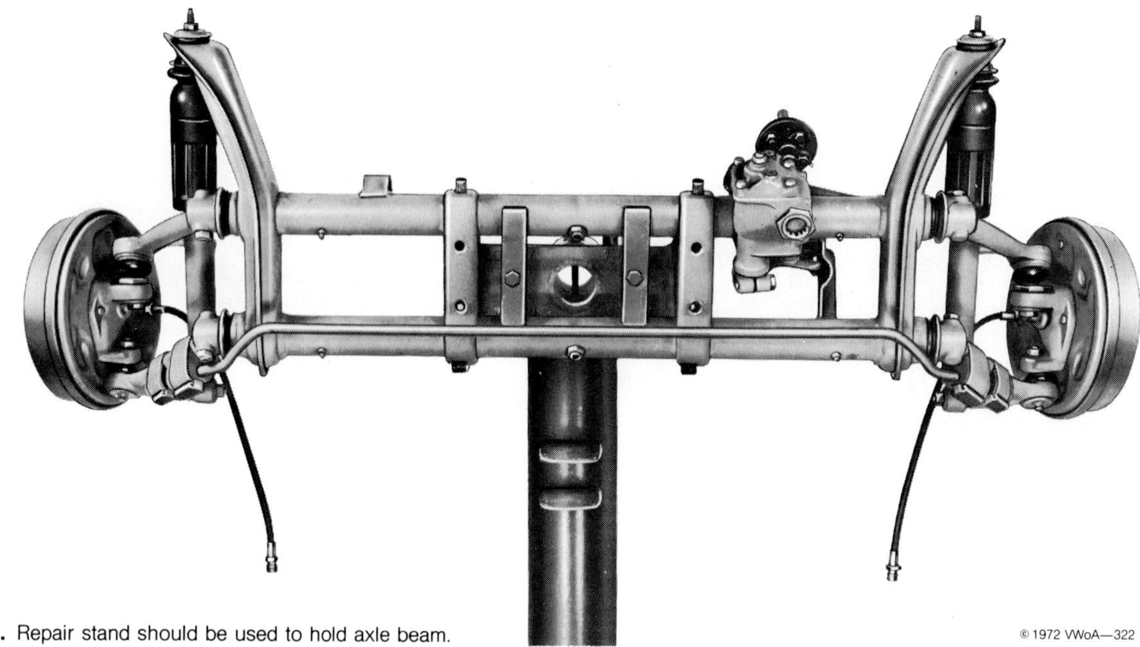

**Fig. 10.** Repair stand should be used to hold axle beam.



9. Remove torsion bars.

**NOTE —**
The final two steps (10 and 11) are taken only when the parts are to be replaced, not re-installed.

10. Drive out needle bearings for upper and lower torsion arms.
11. Drive out torsion arm metal bushings.

When work is to be done on the axle, it is advisable to keep the axle beam mounted on a repair stand (Fig. 10) with securing plate and clamps.

## 2.3 Removing and Installing Brake Drums

All the Beetles covered in this Manual are equipped with drum brakes. Karmann Ghias of the same years have disc brakes on the front wheels. For work on disc brakes see **BRAKES.**

**To remove brake drums:**

***WARNING —***
*Never attempt to loosen wheel bolts while car is on lift. You could topple the car off lift. Always have car on ground for this work.*

1. After loosening wheel bolts, raise car, take off front wheels, and back off brake shoes.
2. Remove cotter pin from speedometer cable in cap of left front wheel and pull speedometer cable out of steering knuckle.
3. Pull off dust cap, as shown in Fig. 11.

***CAUTION —***
*The left-hand steering knuckle has a left-hand thread.*

**Fig. 11.** Special tool is used to pull dust cap off stub axle.

4. Loosen bolt in clamp nut and take off nut (Fig. 12).

© 1972 VWoA—324

**Fig. 12.** Clamp nut bolt (under wrench) must be loosened for removal of nut, outer tapered roller bearing and brake drum.

5. Take thrust washer out. Carefully move brake drum out and away from brake shoes.
6. Take off drum, being careful not to drop bearings.

**To install:**

1. Clean brake drum, hub of drum, bearing, brake mechanism, backing plate and steering knuckle with suitable cleaning fluid. Dirt and dust from brake lining act as abrasives. Keep them out of bearings.
2. Check friction surface of brake drum. Inspect wheel bolt threads.
3. Check bearings for wear and damage. Install new bearings if necessary.
4. Check condition of grease seals.
5. Lubricate bearings with lithium grease of correct specification. Grease should be pressed into cages and between rollers. Grease bearing seat lightly. Fill hub of drum with grease but do not put grease in dust cap.

   **NOTE —**
   Use grease of good quality only. Do not mix different brands or types of grease. Some combinations can be harmful. The amount of grease required per wheel is about 2 ounces (50 grams).

6. Place drum on spindle of steering knuckle. Slide outer bearing on spindle.
7. Install thrust washer.
8. Adjust front wheel bearings. See **3.2 Checking and Adjusting Front Wheel Bearings.**



## 3. FRONT WHEEL BEARINGS

As shown in Fig. 1, each brake drum (or disc) on the front axle turns on an inner tapered roller bearing and an outer tapered roller bearing. The bearings are of different outside diameters, the inner one being the larger.

### 3.1 Removing and Installing Front Wheel Bearings

The removal and installation of the inner and outer wheel bearings are basically the same for drum and disc brakes, but the disc brake procedure takes a couple of extra steps.

**To remove:**

*WARNING —*
*Never attempt to loosen wheel bolts while the car is on a lift. You could topple the car off the lift. Always have car on the ground for this work.*

4

1. After loosening wheel bolts, raise car and remove front wheel. On car with drum brakes the brake shoe adjustment must be loosened first to allow removal of drum.
2. Remove cotter pin from speedometer cable in left front wheel and pull cable out of steering knuckle.
3. Remove dust cap with a tool (Fig. 11).

*CAUTION —*
*Do not attempt to remove disc brake caliper assembly until it has cooled to temperature of surroundings.*

4. On cars with disc brakes:
   a. Bend up lock plates on caliper securing screws and remove screws.
   b. Remove brake caliper and attach it to brake hose bracket with wire. Do not let caliper hang by the hose. (By leaving hose on caliper, you avoid having to bleed brakes.)

*CAUTION —*
*The left steering knuckle has a left-hand thread. Turn nut to right to loosen.*

5. Loosen bolt in clamp nut and take off nut (Fig. 12).
6. Remove bearing thrust washer.
7. Remove brake drum or brake disc.

**NOTE —**
Special adapter with lugs must be installed in the brake drum. The lugs of the adapter drop into the grooves in the hub and engage with the shoulder on the bearing wheels.

8. Press inner bearing and grease seal out of brake drum on a press (Fig. 13).

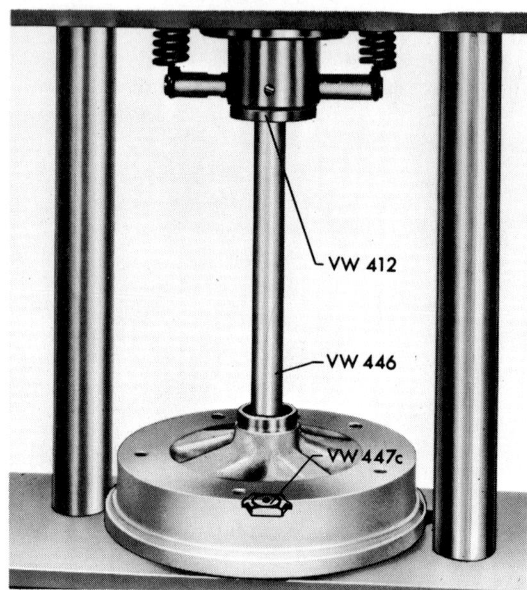




**Fig. 13.** Press is used to press out the inner and outer bearings and grease seal after removal of brake drum.

9. Press out the outer race of outer bearing.

**To install:**

1. After carefully cleaning all parts in suitable cleaning solvent, check for wear and damage.

**NOTE —**
Dirt and dust rubbed from brake linings are abrasive. Keep them out of bearing seats.

2. Check brake drum or brake disc for damage to wheel bolt threads. Check braking surface for damage.
3. Check dimensions of brake drum or disc.
4. Check bearings for wear and damage. Install new ones if necessary.
5. Check bearing seats on spindle of steering knuckle (stub axle) for size and for signs of seizure. Fig. 14 table gives specifications.

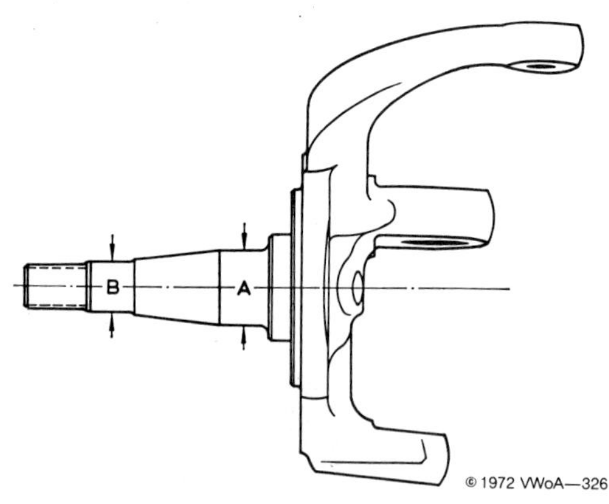




**Bearing Seat Tolerances**

| | Minimum | Maximum |
|---|---|---|
| A | up to chassis No. 118 857 239 | |
| | 1.0618 in. (26.97 mm) | 1.0622 in. (26.98 mm) |
| A | from chassis No. 118 857 240 | |
| | 1.1413 in. (28.99 mm) | 1.1417 in. (29.00 mm) |
| B | 0.6870 in. (17.45 mm) | 0.6874 in. (17.46 mm) |

**Bearing Tolerances**

| | | |
|---|---|---|
| inner | up to chassis No. 118 857 239 | |
| | 1.0626 in. (26.99 mm) | 1.0629 in. (27.00 mm) |
| inner | from chassis No. 118 857 240 | |
| | 1.1417 in. (29.00 mm) | 1.1420 in. (29.01 mm) |
| outer | 0.6874 in. (17.46 mm) | 0.6880 in. (17.48 mm) |

**Fig. 14.** A and B indicate bearing seats on stub axle.

6. To check the spindle and steering arm you may have to remove the backing plate (Fig. 15) and press out the outer tie rod end. The checking procedure requires a special measuring block with dial indicator.

**Fig. 15.** Backing plate (splash shield) of brake drum must be removed, for check of stub axle.

For drum brakes:

a. Place special measuring block over spindle and press firmly against the shoulder for the inner wheel bearing (see Fig. 16). Set dial gauge to zero and check spindle by making one complete turn with the device. The dial gauge should show a deflection not exceeding 0.006 inch (0.15 mm).

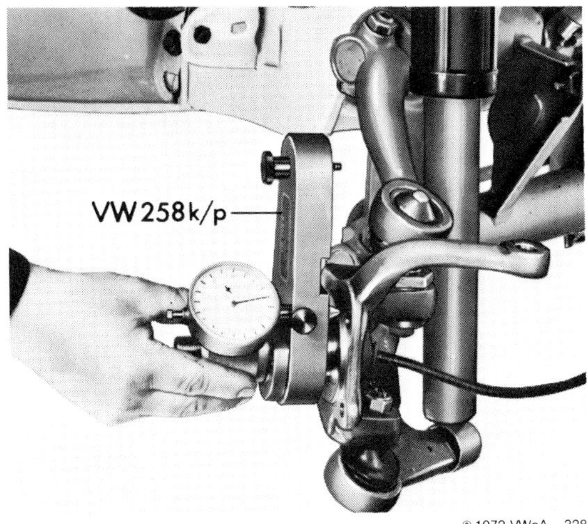


© 1972 VWoA—328

**Fig. 16.** Stub axle is checked for trueness with a special device, which is pressed against shoulder for inner bearing and rotated 360 degrees. Deflection must not exceed reading of 0.006 inch (0.15 mm) on dial.

b. Check steering arm with a special steering knuckle gauge, as shown in Fig. 17. The gauge must be flush with the steering knuckle flange and positioned with dowel pins bottoming in tapped holes in steering knuckle. Steering knuckle is in order if hole in gauge (A) and eye of arm are in line and side face of steering arm eye is parallel with matching surface on gauge (B).

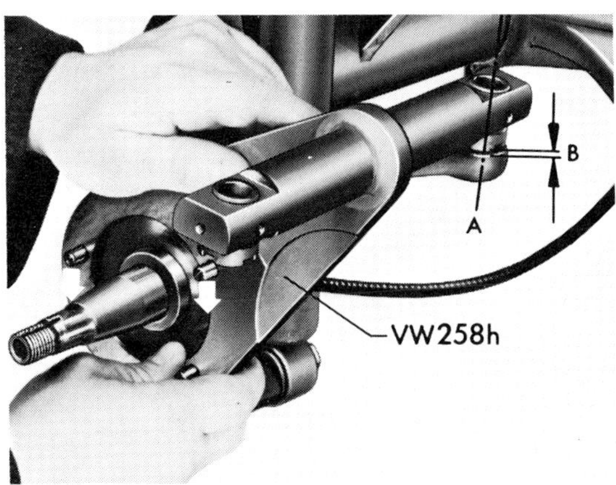


© 1972 VWoA—329

**Fig. 17.** Steering knuckle is checked with device that fits over stub axle, as shown here. Hole in the knuckle arm must line up with tolerance hole on gauge (A) and the side faces of the eye and hole must be parallel (B).

For disc brakes:

a. Bolt dial gauge holder to arm of the measuring device as shown in Fig. 18 and insert gauge.
b. With a master gauge set dial gauge to zero. (Preload on dial gauge should be as small as possible.)

© 1972 VWoA—330

**Fig. 18.** Mounting flange of disc brake caliper is checked with dial gauge in the measuring set-up shown.

4

c. Place measuring device on spindle (Fig. 19).

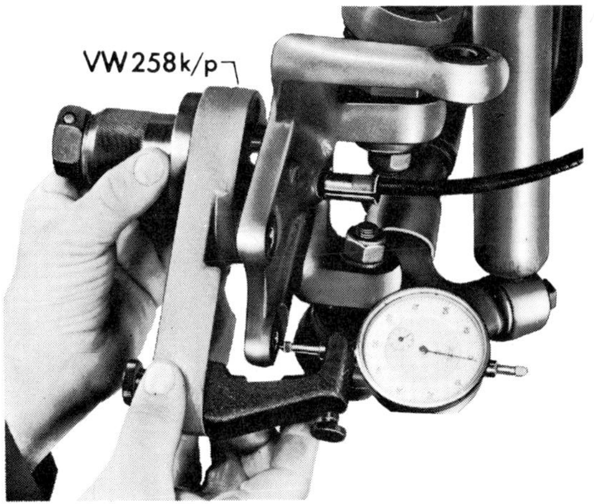


© 1972 VWoA—331

**Fig. 19.** Needle deflection when device is swung across caliper mounting surface must not exceed 0.002 inch (0.05 mm). This check is disc brake equivalent of drum brake test shown in Fig. 16.

Using a thrust washer and the wheel bearing adjustment clamp nut, press device against inner bearing shoulder. Holding device against shoulder will eliminate errors of movement. Tighten clamp nut by hand until the device can just be swung from side to side.

d. Swing device to bring dial gauge feeler onto the brake caliper mounting surface. The deflection shown on gauge must not be more than ± 0.002 inch (0.05 mm) at both caliper mounting points. Have surfaces spotless for the measurement.

**NOTE —**
The letters **R** and **L** ("right" and "left") on the measuring device indicate which set of dowel pins is to be inserted when checking the installed steering knuckles. Gauge must be swung in right direction if readings are to be valid when checking right-hand (R) or left-hand (L) steering knuckle.

***WARNING —***
*Do not attempt to straighten a bent steering knuckle. Install a new one.*

e. Check steering arm with steering knuckle gauge. In this procedure (Fig. 20) the gauge must be level on the steering knuckle flange near the spindle. The knuckle is in good condition if the steering arm bore lines up with the gauge tolerance bore (A), and if the face of the steering arm eye is parallel to the matching surface of the gauge (B). Procedure is similar to check of knuckle for brake drum (Fig. 17).

**Fig. 20.** Steering knuckle gauge is used in check on knuckle for disc brake also. As in Fig. 17 (drum brake), eye in knuckle arm and tolerance bore in gauge must line up (A) with faces parallel (B). Note dowel pins (black arrows) for use on knuckle on other side of car. Gauge is marked for right and left knuckles.

7. Press in outer race of inner bearing with a press. Install cage and inner race.
8. Check condition of seal. Using a rubber hammer, drive seal in by tapping it lightly, first on one side and then on the other. Make sure that the seal does not tilt.
9. On a press, press in outer race of outer bearing.
10. Lubricate bearings with lithium-based grease. Pack grease between the cages and rollers and lightly grease bearing seats. Fill hub of drum with grease but keep it out of hub cap.

**NOTE —**
Use only grease of specified ingredients and good quality. Do not mix different brands and types of grease as some combinations can be harmful. About 2 ounces (50 grams) will be required for each wheel.

11. Place brake drum or brake disc on steering knuckle. Insert bearing cage and push inner race of the outer bearing onto spindle.
12. On cars with disc brakes, install caliper. Use new lock plates. Tighten securing bolts on drum brakes to 43 ft. lbs. (6 mkg) or on disc brakes to 29 ft. lbs. (4 mkg). Lock securing bolts.
13. Adjust bearings as instructed in **3.2 Checking and Adjusting Front Wheel Bearings.**

## 3.2 Checking and Adjusting Front Wheel Bearings

Correct adjustment of the tapered roller bearings on which the front wheels turn is very important. In a very short time incorrect adjustment can damage or destroy the bearings. For this reason follow the instructions closely if you undertake the adjustments outlined here.

**To check:**

1. Lift front of vehicle.
2. Check that brake drum or brake disc turns freely. Brake linings must not rub.
3. Pull off dust cap.

4. Check bearing play as follows:
   a. Unscrew one wheel bolt and screw in threaded pin of dial gauge bracket.
   b. Set bracket to have dial gauge pin touching the clamp nut.
   c. Move wheel in and out (as in Fig. 21) and read gauge for axial play.

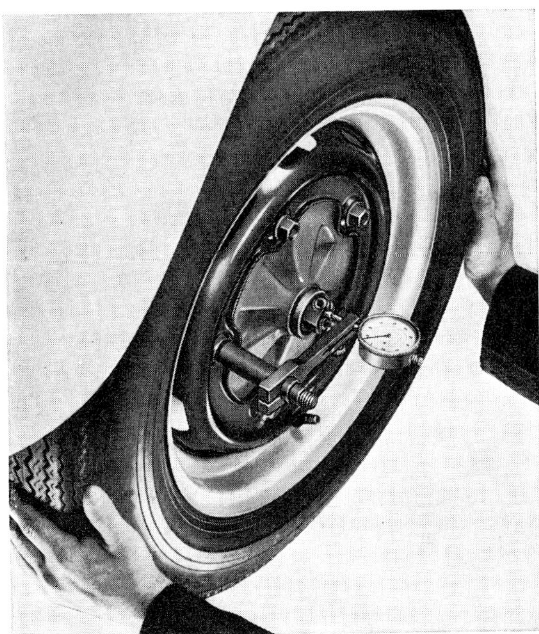

© 1972 VWoA—333

**Fig. 21.** Axial play of wheel is tested with dial gauge mounted in place of wheel bolt, as shown here. When wheel is moved in and out, gauge should read 0.001 to 0.005 inch.

The limits for axial play are 0.001 to 0.005 inch (0.03 to 0.12 mm). If the play is outside these limits, adjust bearings.

**NOTE** —
Near the upper limit, an axial movement of the wheel can be felt. This much play is permissible and requires no adjustment. If front axle noises are heard, then readjustment of the bearings will be needed. In such a case, keep as near the lower limit as possible, say from 0.001 to 0.003 inch (0.03 to 0.06 mm).

**To adjust:**

1. Loosen screw in clamp nut.
2. Tighten clamp nut to put bearing rollers in contact with shoulder of the inner race. Keep turning the wheel to prevent excessive tightening of the bearing. In Fig. 22, the right hand is turning wheel.

© 1972 VWoA—334

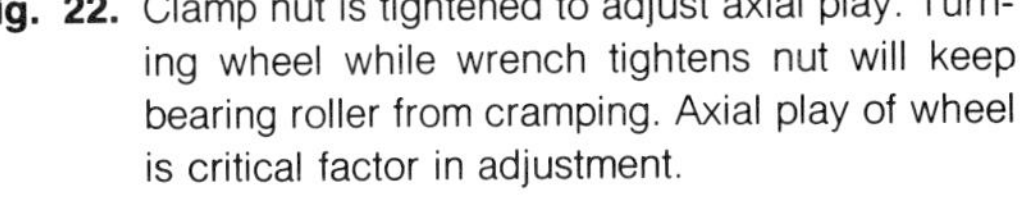

**Fig. 22.** Clamp nut is tightened to adjust axial play. Turning wheel while wrench tightens nut will keep bearing roller from cramping. Axial play of wheel is critical factor in adjustment.

3. Slack off the clamp nut until axial play is between 0.001 and 0.005 inch (0.03 to 0.12 mm) when wheel is moved in and out.

***WARNING*** —
*To give sufficient clamping force regardless of screw torque, the slot in the clamp nut must be 0.098 to 0.118 inch (2.5 to 3.0 mm) wide.*

4. Tighten clamp nut screw to 7 to 9 ft. lbs. (1 to 1.3 mkg). For tight fit hold strictly to these values. It is the reverse of procedure shown in Fig. 12.
5. Recheck adjustment.
6. Put on bearing dust cap after making sure that it is grease-free.

## 4. STEERING KNUCKLES

Maintenance-free ball joints connect the steering knuckle to the torsion arms (Fig. 1). The ball joints are pressed into the torsion arms. A tapered stud with nut connects the ball joint and knuckle.

A steering knuckle can be on or off the car when it is checked for distortion or other wear or damage. The critical measurements require special tools.

## 4.1 Removing and Installing Steering Knuckle

***WARNING —***
*Do not attempt to loosen or tighten wheel nuts when the car is on a lift. You could topple the car over. Always have car on the ground when you loosen or tighten wheel nuts.*

**To remove:**

1. Lift car and take off the front wheel.
2. For drum brakes:
   Detach brake hose at hose bracket and plug brake line with bleeder valve dust cap.

   For disc brakes:
   Unscrew brake caliper (see Fig. 23) and attach it to hose bracket with a piece of wire.

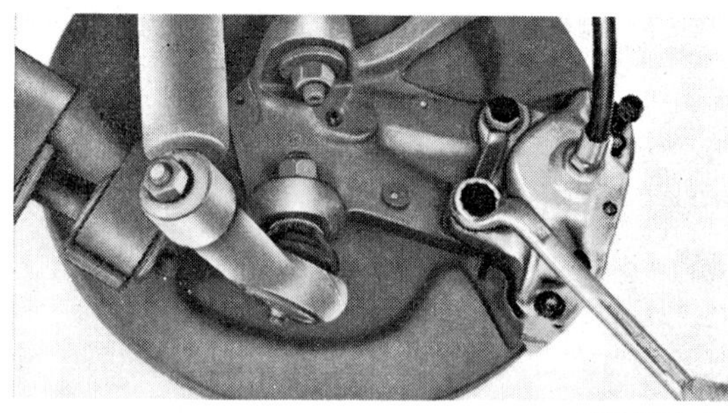



**Fig. 23.** Two bolts fasten brake caliper to backing plate (cover). Allow caliper to cool before removing it.

***CAUTION —***
*Make sure that caliper has cooled before removing it.*

3. Press out outer tie rod end.

**NOTE —**
It is possible to remove the steering knuckle without disconnecting the brake hose and later having to bleed the brakes. Turn the steering wheel to give the brake hose maximum slack and then take off the backing plate. Hang the plate, with hose attached, by a wire, being careful not to kink the hose.

4. Remove brake drum and backing plate or brake disc and splash shield.
5. Unscrew hexagon nut on lower ball joint and, using removal tool, press ball joint out of steering knuckle. A very tight lower ball joint can be loosened. With the extractor tool in place and exerting pressure, tap the knuckle with a steel hammer at the exact point indicated by arrow in Fig. 24. Ball joint will then pop out.

**NOTE —**
Before pressing out the ball joint, screw a cap nut M 10 x 1 or M 12 x 1.5 (depending on pin thread) on the ball joint to protect the thread. Screw it on as far as it will go so that the thrust will be taken at the base of the nut and not by the threads alone. Do not, however, screw the nut on too tightly or the pin then will turn with the nut and make the nut difficult to remove after the joint has been pressed out.

**Fig. 24.** Lower ball joint can be loosened by tapping steering knuckle eye at point indicated by arrow. Extractor tool has been applied to the joint.

6. Unscrew nut on upper ball joint and loosen eccentric bushing for camber adjustment, as shown in Fig. 25. When doing repair work on the lower ball joint, always remove upper joint. The removal procedure is the same as for the lower joint.

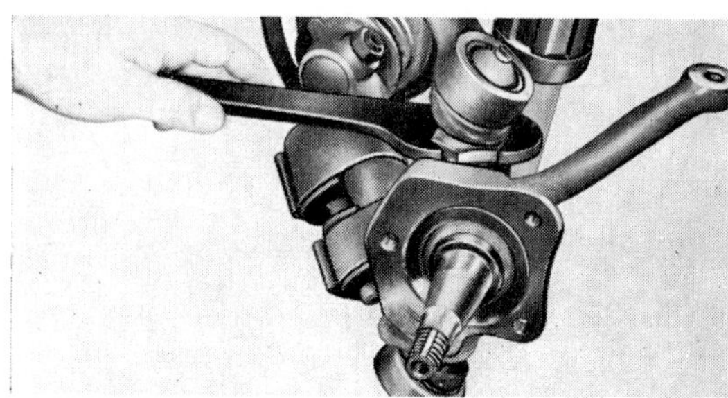



**Fig. 25.** Eccentric bushing on upper ball joint can be loosened with wrench after nut below ball joint is taken off. Bushing controls wheel camber.

7. Lift the upper torsion arm (Fig. 26) with tool and remove steering knuckle.

© 1972 VWoA—338

**Fig. 26.** Special tool lifts upper torsion arm for removal of steering knuckle.

**To install:**

1. Check bearing seats for wear and size. See Fig. 14 and accompanying table.
2. Visually check spindle and knuckle for distortion.

> ***CAUTION —***
> *Do not attempt to straighten a bent steering knuckle. Always replace bent knuckles.*

3. Install steering knuckle. Make sure that notch (Fig. 27) in the eccentric bushing for camber adjustment is toward front of car.

© 1972 VWoA—339

**Fig. 27.** Notch (black arrow) in the eccentric bushing for camber adjustment must be toward front of car when steering knuckle is installed.

> ***WARNING —***
> *Use only self-locking hexagon nuts and never re-use old nuts.*

4. Torque ball joint nut (see Fig. 28) to the following specification:

| | |
|---|---|
| M 10 x 1 | 29 to 36 ft. lbs. (4 to 5 mkg) |
| M 12 x 1.5 | 36 to 51 ft. lbs. (5 to 7 mkg) |

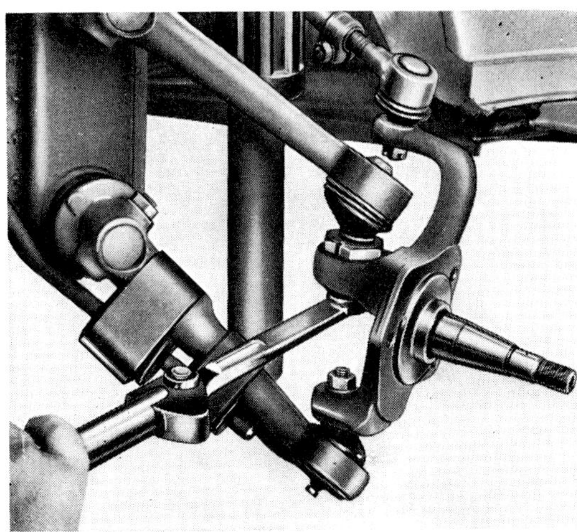

© 1972 VWoA—340

**Fig. 28.** Ball joint nut is being tightened here to a specified torque, depending on size of the nut. See text.

4

5. Tighten shock absorbers as far as they will go. Do not omit damper ring and plate for damper ring.
6. Tighten tie rod end nuts and secure with cotter pin.

> ***CAUTION —***
> *On disc brake tighten caliper securing bolts to torque of 29 ft. lbs. (4 mkg). Always use new lock plates.*

7. Install backing plate and brake drum or splash shield and brake disc.
8. Adjust wheel bearings in accordance with instructions given in **3.2 Checking and Adjusting Front Wheel Bearings.**
9. Install brake hoses free of twist. Bleed brake system.
10. Adjust toe-in and camber.

### 4.2 Checking Steering Knuckle Spindle and Steering Arm

Differences in the steering knuckles require some differences in these procedures for cars with drum brakes on the front wheels (Beetles) and cars with disc brakes (Karmann Ghias). Special measuring devices used when installing and checking wheel bearings are also used here.

**To check drum brakes:**

1. Place special measuring bracket with dial indicator (Fig. 16) on spindle (stub axle) and press it firmly against shoulder of inner wheel bearing. Set dial gauge to zero and check spindle for distortion by turning axle one revolution. The deflection of the dial gauge needle must not exceed 0.006 inch (0.15 mm).
2. Check steering arm with special gauge shown in Fig. 17. The gauge must be flush against the steering knuckle flange with dowel pins bottoming in the tapped holes in the steering knuckle.

   The steering knuckle is serviceable (see Fig. 17) if the hole in the steering arm is in line with the hole on the gauge (A) and if the side face of the steering arm eye is parallel with the matching face on the gauge (B).

**To check disc brakes:**

1. Bolt dial gauge holder to arm of measuring device (Fig. 18) and insert gauge.
2. Set dial gauge to zero with master gauge. Preload on the dial gauge should be as small as possible.
3. Position steering knuckle in measuring device as in Fig. 19 and swing the caliper mounting surface under the dial gauge feeler. Contact surfaces on knuckle and gauge must be spotless if check is to give valid result. The dial gauge needle deflection must not be more than ± 0.002 inch (0.05 mm) at either caliper mounting point.
4. Check steering arm with a steering knuckle gauge, as in Fig. 20. The steering knuckle flange must be level on the gauge, near the stub axle. The steering knuckle is in good condition if the steering arm bore is in line with hole in gauge (A) and if side face of the steering arm eye is parallel with corresponding face on gauge (B).

***CAUTION —***
*Do not attempt to straighten a bent steering knuckle. Always replace bent knuckles.*

## 5. STABILIZER BAR

The stabilizer bar, also called the anti-sway bar, prevents excessive roll or sway on turns. Running across the front of the car, the bar ties the two lower torsion arms together.

### 5.1 Removing and Installing Stabilizer Bar

Clamps with rubber bushings fasten the bar to the lower torsion arms.

**To remove:**

1. After loosening wheel bolts, raise vehicle and take off front wheels.
2. Bend up lugs on the clips, as in Fig. 29, and take clips off the clamps on both sides.

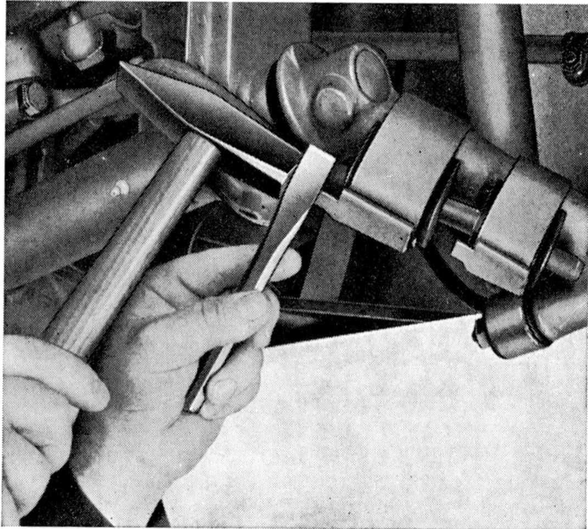


**Fig. 29.** Clip lugs are bent up for removal of clips and clamps holding stabilizer.

3. Open clamps and take out metal plates.
4. Lift clamps off and remove stabilizer.

**To install:**

1. Check stabilizer bar, rubber bushings, clips, plates and clamps for damage. Install new parts where necessary.
2. Install clamps with slot tapering toward steering knuckle (see Fig. 30).

© 1972 VWoA—342

**Fig. 30.** Slot in clamp tapers toward steering knuckle when correctly located for installation of stabilizer bar.

3. Compress clamps with slip joint pliers or some similar tool and slide on clips. The lugs on the clips must be toward the axle beam, as in Fig. 31.

© 1972 VWoA—343

**Fig. 31.** Lugs on stabilizer bar clips are toward axle beam when positioned correctly.

4. Bend down lugs to secure clips.

## 6. Torsion Arms and Ball Joints

The inner ends of the torsion arms fit over the torsion bars in the upper and lower axle tubes. Set screws fasten the arms and bars together. At the outer ends ball joints connect the arms and the steering knuckles.

### 6.1 Removing Torsion Arms

Bent torsion arms or torsion arms with worn bearing surfaces must be replaced, complete with new ball joints.

**To remove torsion arm:**

1. Take off steering knuckle complete with brake drum, as in Fig. 32.

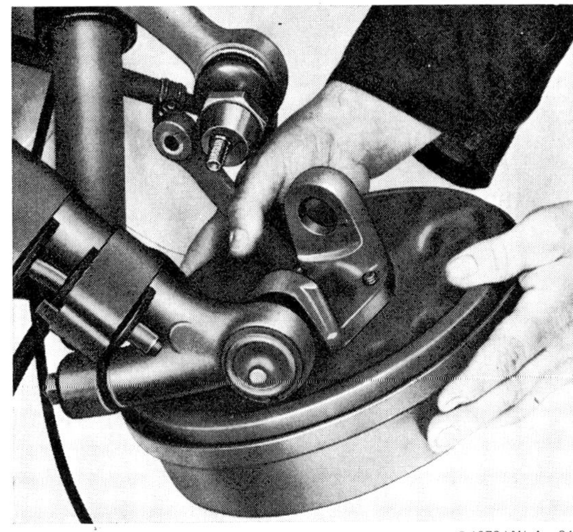

© 1972 VWoA—344

**Fig. 32.** Steering knuckle with brake drum attached is taken off for removal of torsion arm.

4

2. If lower torsion arm is to be removed also, take off stabilizer.
3. Loosen lock nuts on torsion arm set screws and screw out. See Fig. 33.

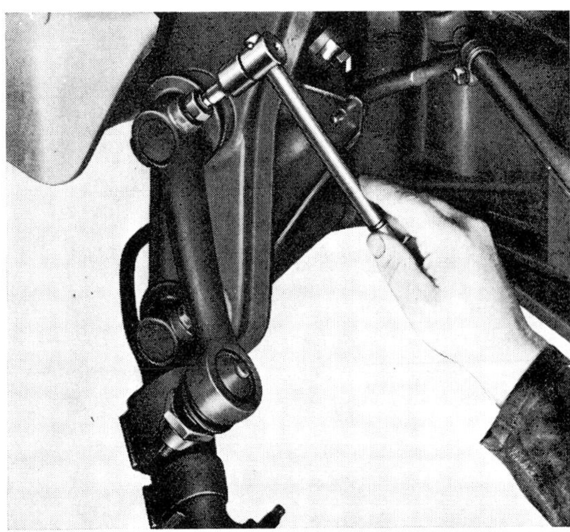

© 1972 VWoA—345

**Fig. 33.** Lock nuts on securing pins for torsion arm are loosened and pins removed.

4. Pull torsion arms out of axle tubes.
5. If necessary, take sealing rings out of axle tubes.

**To check torsion arms:**

1. Clean torsion arms and ball joints thoroughly.
2. Check bearing seats on torsion arms for wear.
3. Take plug out of tapped hole for the grease nipple in ball joint and screw in plug of the special test plate used in these procedures. Fig. 34 shows the plug.

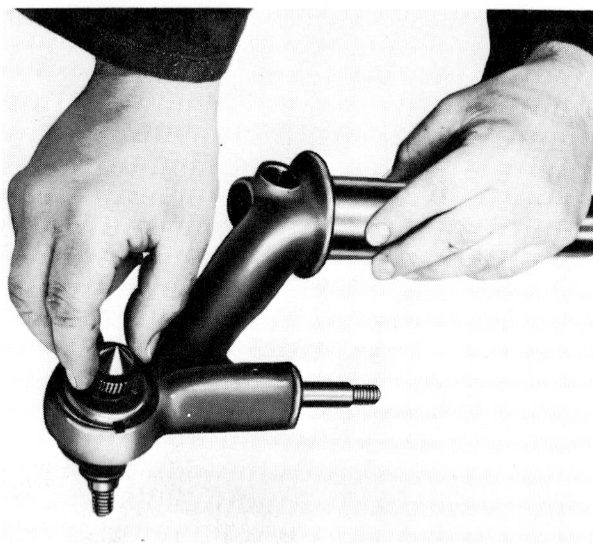



**Fig. 34.** Test plate plug is screwed into tapped hole for grease nipple on torsion arm ball joint.

4. Locate torsion arm bushings in test plate.
5. Place torsion arm in test plate. See Fig. 35. The top must touch the small boss on the plate. If it does not make contact, the torsion arm is bent.

**Fig. 35.** Torsion arm is on test plate for check of straightness. Bent arm is replaced.

***CAUTION —***
*Bent torsion arms or arms with worn bearing surfaces should be replaced complete with steering ball joints.*

6. Seal ball joints with new plastic plugs.

**NOTE —**
Always screw plugs in. Never drive them in.

## 6.2 Checking Ball Joints
(torsion arm installed)

The axial play of an installed ball joint can be measured. The procedure requires a special lever tool and vernier caliper.

**To check:**

1. Lift vehicle and turn wheels to one side.
2. Place lever between upper and lower torsion arms as shown in Fig. 36.

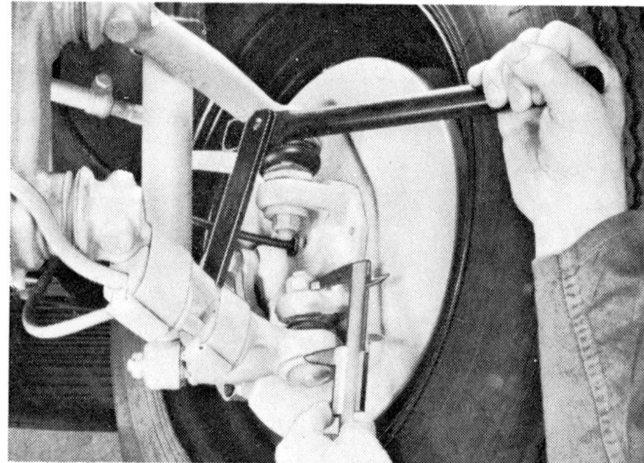



**Fig. 36.** Ball joint play is checked with special lever and vernier caliper. Lever works between upper and lower torsion arms to expand ball joint. Before-and-after caliper readings give play.

3. Place vernier caliper on the joint with one jaw on the lower torsion arm and the other jaw on bottom section of steering knuckle and read the measurement. Without removing caliper, press lever down to expand the arms. Take second reading from vernier caliper. Subtract first reading from second to get play of ball joint.

Maximum play (upper and lower) when new: 0.02 inch (0.5 mm)
Wear limit:
Upper ball joint: 0.08 inch (2.0 mm)
Lower ball joint: 0.04 inch (1.0 mm)

### 6.3 Checking Ball Joints
(torsion arm removed)

**To check:**

1. Carefully clean torsion arms and ball joints.

   **NOTE —**
   Only grease with lithium base is to be used in ball joints.

2. Check ball joint play by moving pin in and out axially and measuring with vernier caliper. With one jaw of caliper on the ball joint cover and the other on end of threaded pin, take readings with pin at limits of travel. Fig. 37 shows the measurement.

   Maximum play, new: 0.02 inch (0.05 mm)
   Wear limit:
   Upper ball joint: 0.08 inch (2.0 mm)
   Lower ball joint: 0.04 inch (1.0 mm)

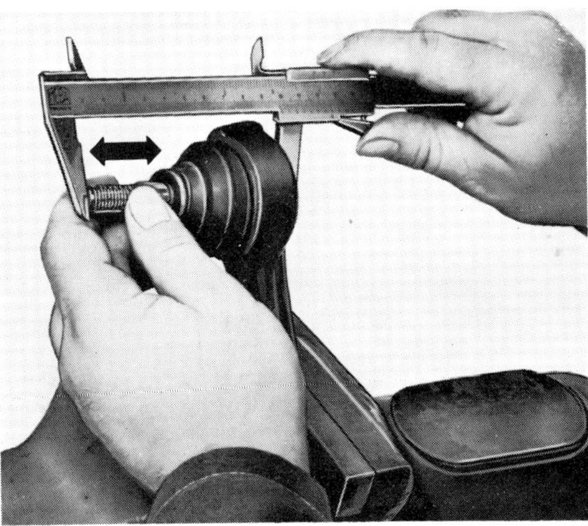

© 1972 VWoA—349

**Fig. 37.** Vernier caliper measures play as threaded pin is moved in and out of ball joint. Arrows show pin movement.

***WARNING —***
*Used ball joints must not be reinstalled.*

3. Check ball joint boots (rubber seals) and replace if damaged.

   **NOTE —**
   If there is a possibility that dirt may have entered a damaged ball joint, thoroughly clean the joint in a suitable cleaning solvent. Then remove plug from the tapped hole for grease nipple. Screw in nipple and force lithium grease through the joint until every trace of dirt has been removed.

4. Use 0.04 inch (1.0 mm) wire or steel retaining ring, depending on type of ball joint, to secure new boot to joint housing. Do not expand these boots or rings more than necessary.

The ball joint stud pivots along the major axis (that is, the longer diameter) of an oval cutout in the joint under the boot. This axis must line up in the driving direction of the joint.

The location of the steel retaining ring that holds the rubber boot is critical because improper installation can lead to puncturing of the boot. The opening in the ring must be 90 degrees from the operating angle of the ball joint pin. This location will prevent the ring ends from cutting into the boot.

When pressing the ball joint into a torsion arm, make sure that the notch in boot lines up with the notch at the eye of the torsion arm, as in Fig. 38. This alignment allows the stud to pivot in the correct driving direction. 4

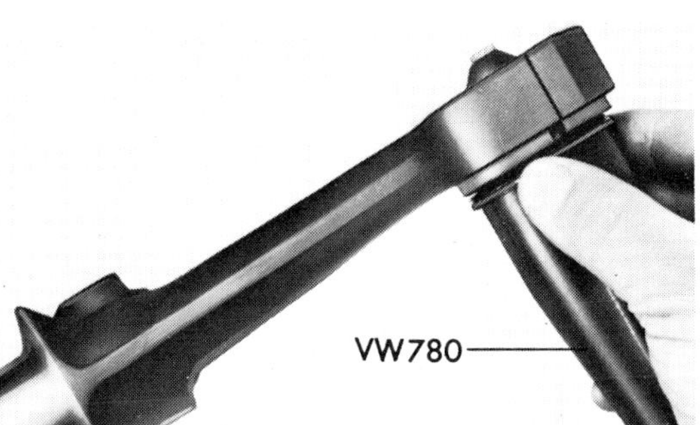


© 1972 VWoA—350

**Fig. 38.** Steel retaining ring for ball joint boot must be installed with gap in ring (just above thumbnail) at angle of 90 degrees from operating axis of threaded pin.

A press and adapter are used to press out upper ball joints.

**NOTE —**
Ball joints that originally were secured with wire can be fitted with metal rings. Wire, however, cannot be used on joints originally fitted with the metal rings.

5. Grease ball joints again with lithium grease. While pumping grease in, lift edge of boot all around pin. To avoid damage, lift with a round rod only. After greasing, move pin back and forth through its operating angle at least twice to permit excess grease to escape.

6. Install new plastic retaining ring (if available) for the boot on the ball joint pin. Use installing sleeve

similar to one used in step 3 (see Fig. 39). Make sure that retaining rings are not twisted.

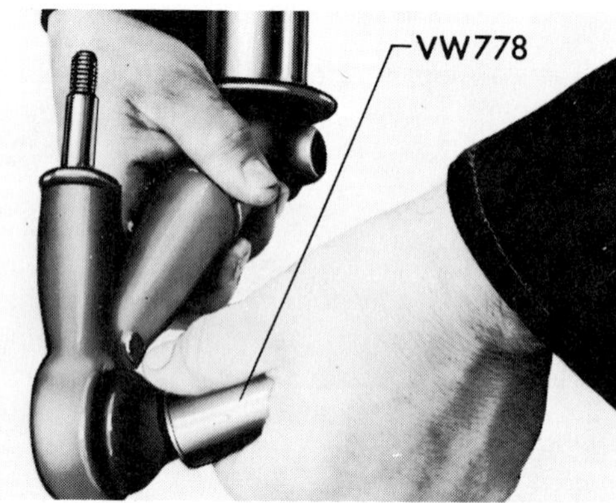




**Fig. 39.** Special sleeve prevents twisting of plastic retaining ring when ring is installed on boot for ball joint pin.

7. Unscrew grease nipples and seal tapped holes with new plugs. With holes plugged, it is unlikely that someone unfamiliar with VW procedures will be able to fill the joints with wrong kind of grease.

**NOTE —**
Always screw in the plugs. Never drive them.

## 6.4 Replacing Ball Joints

For reasons having to do with manufacture, the ball joints on your car may be slightly different from the standard part. The other than standard joints are 0.016 inch (0.4 mm) oversize in the diameter across the knurled ring. Upper and lower ball joints in either case are quite similar but can be distinguished. The upper joint has a longer threaded stud to hold the eccentric nut for adjusting camber. The distinguishing marks on the two kinds of ball joints are illustrated in Fig. 40. It is important to be able to recognize the differences because the sizes are not marked on the joints.

**NOTE —**
1. When installing a ball joint always make sure that the notch is turned to the driving direction of the joint because the stud under the boot operates along a cutout in that direction.
2. The notch on the boot must align with the notch on the ball joint collar.
3. The ends of wire or clamp holding boot must be 90 degrees from stud notch in ball joint to prevent puncturing boot.
4. Notch in ball joint collar must align with notch in torsion arm. This alignment insures that travel of stud will be in driving direction.

**Fig. 40.** Distinguishing marks are clues to ball joint sizes. Standard M 12 x 1.5 joint at left has two square notches, 180 degrees apart, in shoulder. Oversize M 10 x 1 and M 12 x 1.5 joint has additional vee notch (black arrow) at 45 degrees from square notch. Square notches on collar fix fitting position for ball joint when it is installed. See text for details.

**To replace upper ball joints:**

1. Use press and special tools to press out ball joints. To prevent the ball joint from jumping out, screw a nut on the threaded bolt of the joint.

***WARNING —***
*Used ball joints must not be reinstalled.*

2. If necessary, use special tool to press eccentric bushing off ball joint.

3. Press in new ball joint.

**NOTE —**
When pressing a new ball joint in, be sure that notch in boot is in line with notch in torsion arm eye, as in Fig. 41. Make sure plastic cap is protecting rubber boot.

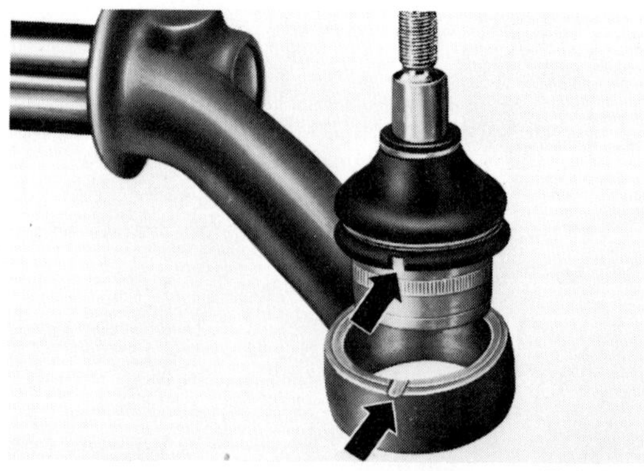



**Fig. 41.** Notches in ball joint and torsion arm eye must line up.

**To replace lower ball joints:**

1. Remove rubber boot and press out lower ball joint on repair press.

> ***WARNING —***
> *Under no conditions is a used ball joint to be re-installed in a torsion arm.*

2. Press new joint in. Make sure that notch in joint collar lines up with notch in torsion arm eye. See Fig. 42.

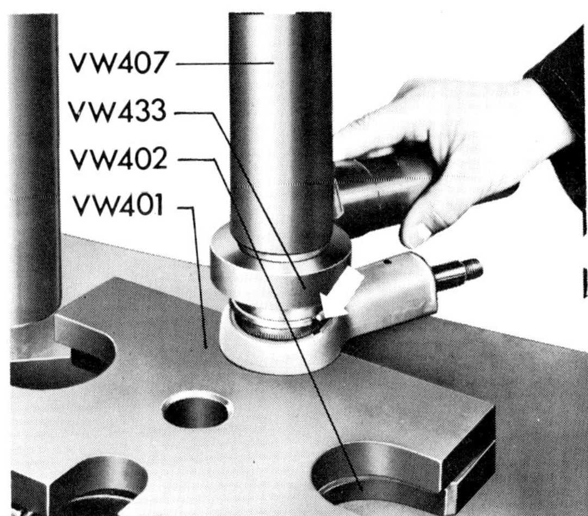




**Fig. 42.** Notches (arrow) in ball joint and torsion arm eye are aligned when joint is pressed into arm in this press set-up.

## 6.5 Installing Torsion Arm

Before undertaking this procedure, check condition of the torsion arm sealing rings. Install new parts where necessary.

**To install:**

1. Attach torsion arm on torsion bar. Put in set screws and secure them with lock nuts.
2. Install all other parts. Grease the front axle thoroughly with lithium-based grease.
3. Adjust camber and toe-in.

## 6.6 Fitting Shock Absorber Pin

When it is necessary to fit a new shock absorber mounting pin in the torsion arm, an oversize pin (Fig. 43) may be obtained as a replacement part. The hole in the torsion arm must be bored out and reamed for this pin.

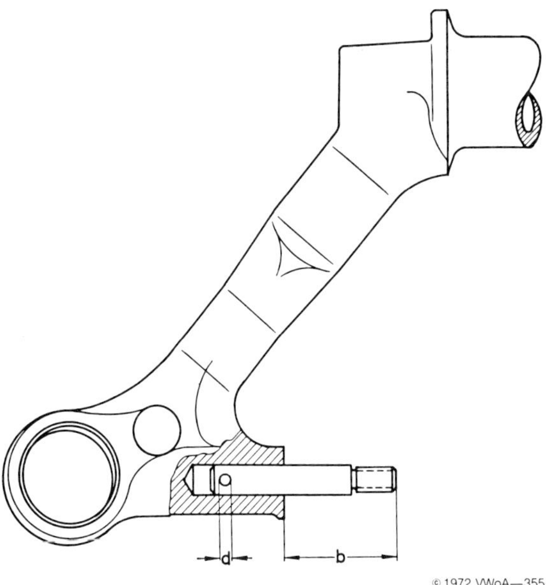




4

**Fig. 43.** Shock absorber pin in torsion arm can be replaced with oversize pin. Dimensions of interest are those labeled "d" and "b". See text.

**To remove pin:**

1. Remove torsion arm.
2. Drive lock pin out.
3. Pull old mounting pin out.

**To remove broken pin:**

1. Centerpunch remaining fragment and drill a 0.12 inch (3 mm) pilot hole in it.
2. Drill out remainder of broken part with 0.42 inch (10.75 mm) drill. Usually fragment will come out with last few turns of drill.

**To install pin:**

1. Drill out hole in torsion arm with 0.48 inch (12.3 mm) drill and ream it with 12.5 P8 (12.455 to 12.482 mm) diameter reamer. If reamer of this size is not available, oversize pin can be ground down to fit the drilled-out hole. A light interference fit of 0.0004 to 0.0020 inch (0.01 to 0.05 mm) must be obtained. Pin then can be driven in with a mallet.
2. Press the oversize pin in until it projects 1.77 to 1.79 inches (45.0 to 45.5 mm) (dimension "b" in Fig. 43).
3. Drill a 0.157 to 0.160 inch (4.00 to 4.08 mm) hole (dimension "d" in Fig. 43) in the pressed-in oversize pin.
4. Secure with lock pin.

## 7. TORSION BARS

The front axle torsion bars, which allow up-and-down movement of the front wheels, consist of 10 spring steel leaves each. The two outer leaves of each bar are split lengthwise. Viewed in cross-section, the bars are cross-shaped. The bars must be greased liberally to prevent corrosion.

### 7.1 Removing and Installing Torsion Bars

The torsion bars are anchored at their centers in bushings inside the axle tubes and secured with Allen-head screws. If cracked or broken, the bars must be replaced. In all work with torsion bars you will find them much easier to handle if you tape them into a secure bundle. Any strong tape will do.

**To remove:**

1. Remove steering knuckles.
2. Remove torsion arm on one side.
3. Loosen lock nut of torsion bar set screw in axle tube.
4. Remove Allen-type screw with 8 mm hexagon wrench, as in Fig. 44.

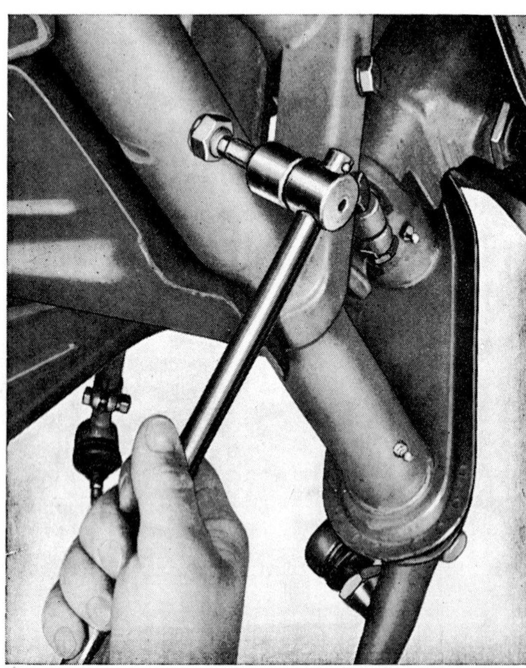



**Fig. 44.** Set screw of front axle torsion bar is removed with 8 mm hexagon wrench.

5. Pull torsion arm out with torsion bar. (See Fig. 45.)

**NOTE —**
A torsion bar is heavy and packed with grease. It is not necessary in removal to mark the bars because the position of the bars for re-installation is obvious.

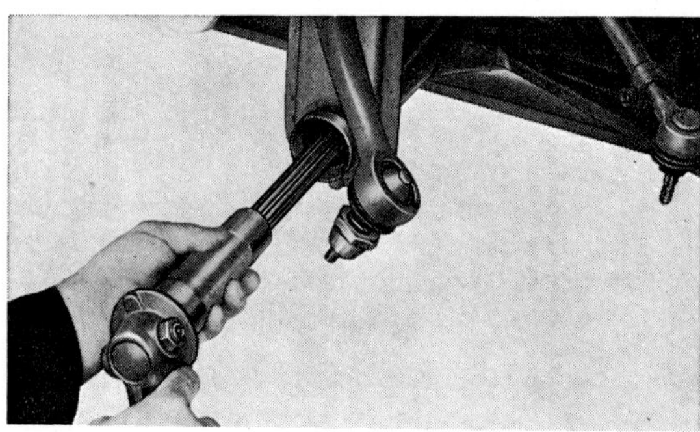



**Fig. 45.** Torsion bar is a heavy bundle of steel leaves, requiring a firm hold when it is pulled from axle tube.

**To install:**

1. Clean torsion bars and examine them for cracks and breakage. Replace bars if necessary.
2. Check torsion arms, needle bearings and bushings. Install new parts where necessary.
3. Before installing, coat bars liberally with multi-purpose grease to prevent corrosion.

   **NOTE —**
   Grease fittings on torsion tube housings lubricate moving parts of torsion arms. A lithium based grease is used.

4. When inserting the torsion bars, check the number of leaves and align countersunk recesses with torsion arm set screws. (See Fig. 46.)

**Fig. 46.** Leaves of torsion bar should be counted and position of countersunk recesses noted before installation.

5. Align the recess in the center of the bar with the hole for the set screw. Tighten center screw and secure with lock nut.
6. Install all other parts and lubricate axle with multi-purpose grease.

## 8. FRONT AXLE NEEDLE BEARINGS AND METAL BUSHINGS

The metal bushings of the front axle assembly are subject to little wear and rarely need replacement. But if wear is noted on the torsion arm bearing surface, the metal bushing should be replaced as well as the torsion arm. It may be impractical to replace bushings because the work is time-consuming and requires measuring devices not readily available. Replacement of the complete axle beam may be more expedient.

**To check axle bushings:**

1. Remove both steering knuckles complete with drums. Take out torsion arms and torsion bars.
2. With an internal gauge, measure wear on metal bushing, as in Fig. 47. The wear limit for upper and lower bushings is 1.47 inches (37.38 mm).

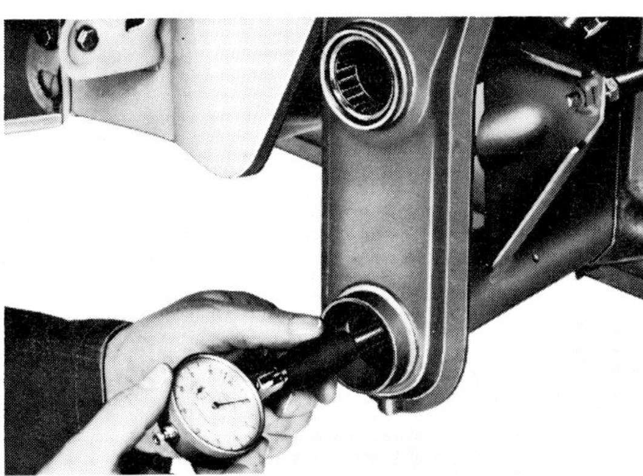



**Fig. 47.** Metal bushing for torsion bar is gauged for wear in this procedure. Bar must be removed for measurement.

### 8.1 Removing Upper and Lower Needle Bearings

This procedure requires an extractor with special washers.

**To remove:**

1. Attach special washers for lower needle bearing to extractor as shown in Fig. 48. Insert tool into axle tube and press washer against shoulder of needle bearing.

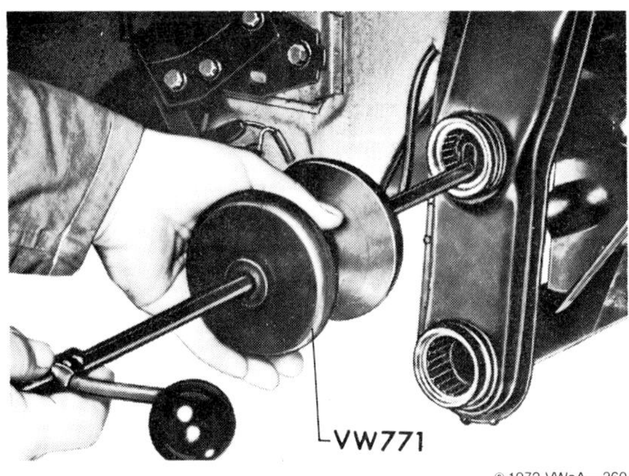




**Fig. 48.** Needle bearing is removed from axle tube beam with special extractor.



2. Pull bearing out.

### 8.2 Removing Upper and Lower Metal Bushings

Fig. 49 shows this assembly in cross-section. Study the diagram before starting this work.

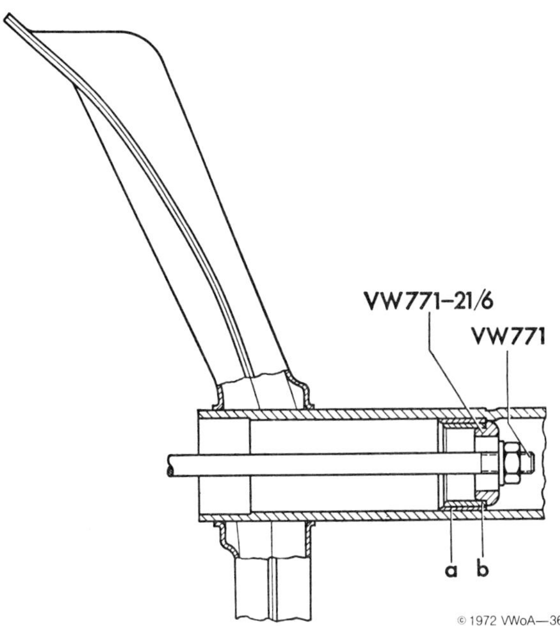




**Fig. 49.** Metal bushing is pulled from axle tube with extractor as in removal of needle bearing (Fig. 48). Cutaway diagram shows fit of plastic sleeve (a) and metal bushing (b) inside axle tube.

**To remove:**

1. Insert extractor into axle tube with washer attached and place washer against bushing.

*CAUTION* —
*The plastic sleeves for the bushings do not wear. Since sleeves remain in the axle tube, extreme care when driving out bushings is necessary to avoid damaging sleeves.*

2. Pull metal bushing out as with needle bearings.

## 8.3 Installing Needle Bearings and Metal Bushings

This procedure calls for care and may require replacement of the axle beam.

**To install:**

1. Clean axle tubes, particularly at needle bearing and bushing seats.
2. Check condition and dimensions of needle bearing seats in axle tube, using dial gauge as in Fig. 50.

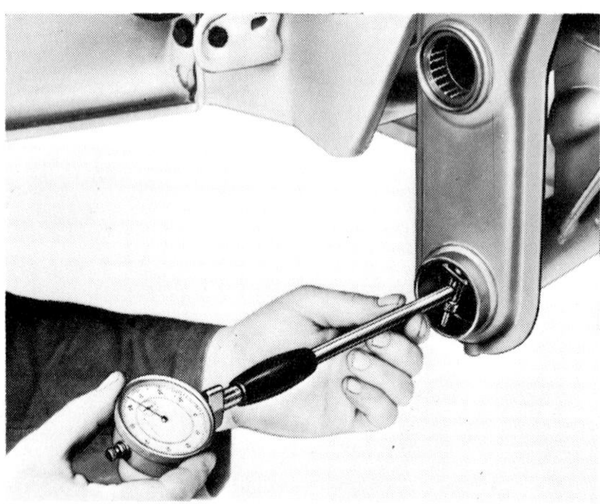

© 1972 VWoA—362

**Fig. 50.** Needle bearing seat in axle tube is measured before oversize bearing is fitted.

**NOTE** —
You may find that oversize needle bearings were installed in the axle of your car. When fitting new needle bearings, you must measure tubes. Inside diameters of bores are:

**Standard inside diameters of bores**
Upper: 1.810 to 1.809 inches (45.99 to 45.97 mm)
Lower: 1.968 to 1.967 inches (49.99 to 49.97 mm)

**Oversize inside diameters of bores**
Upper: 1.818 to 1.817 inches (46.19 to 46.17 mm)
Lower: 1.976 to 1.975 inches (50.19 to 50.17 mm)

Bearings to match these dimensions are:

| | Standard | Oversize |
|---|---|---|
| Upper needle bearing: | 1.811 inches (46.0 mm) | 1.819 inches (46.2 mm) |
| Lower needle bearing: | 1.969 inches (50.0 mm) | 1.976 inches (50.2 mm) |

If the seats in the axle tubes are no longer within the tolerances given, a new axle beam must be installed. It is not possible to machine the seats to fit.

*CAUTION* —
*When installing metal bushings be careful not to damage the plastic sleeves. Damaged plastic sleeves cannot be replaced. Clean needle bearings carefully. Check diameters of bearings and bushings.*

3. Lubricate needle bearing seats lightly with universal grease.
4. Drive in new upper metal bushing and upper needle bearing with special tool (see Fig. 51). The needle bearing should be installed with marking on shoulder toward end of axle. Bushing should go in far enough for shoulder on drift to make contact with axle tube.
5. Drive new lower metal bushing and lower needle bearing in with a drift until shoulder on drift makes contact with the axle tube.
6. Re-install all parts. Lubricate axle thoroughly with multi-purpose grease.

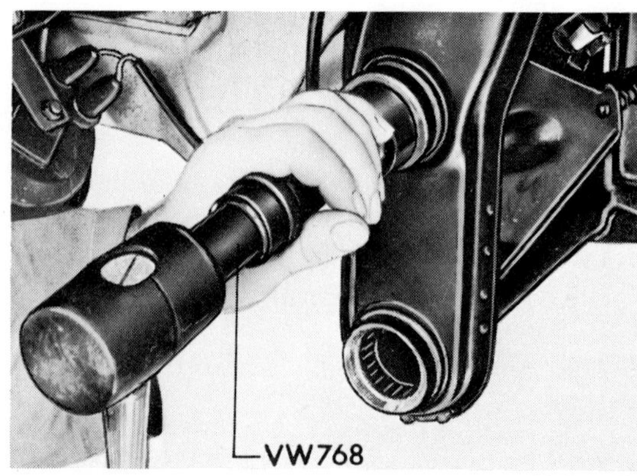


© 1972 VWoA—363

**Fig. 51.** New bushings and bearings are driven to specified depths in the axle tubes with special drifts.

**NOTE —**
If special drifts for this work are not available, drive metal bushings and needle bearings into axle beam to the dimensions given below and illustrated in Fig. 52.

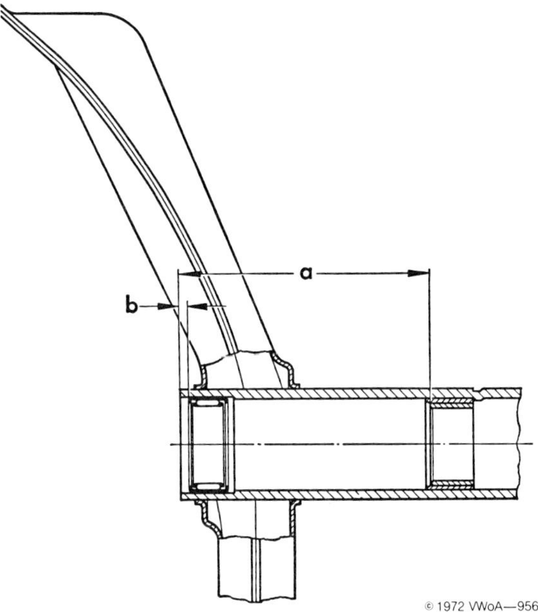


**Fig. 52.** Seating dimensions for metal bushings and needle bearings in axle tube are illustrated here. See text and accompanying table for measurements at "a" and "b".

**Metal bushings (dimension "a"):**
Upper: 4.80 to 4.88 inches (122 to 124 mm)
Lower: 5.20 to 5.28 inches (132 to 134 mm)

**Needle bearings (dimension "b"):**
Upper: 0.138 to 0.146 inch (3.5 to 3.7 mm)
Lower: 0.197 to 0.205 inch (5.0 to 5.2 mm)

## 9. SHOCK ABSORBERS

The front axle of the Volkswagen is equipped with double-acting telescopic hydraulic shock absorbers. The resistance of the shock absorber is progressive. That is, the faster the wheel bounces on a rough road the greater damping effect the shock absorber exerts.

The shock absorbers are matched precisely to the suspension characteristics of the vehicle. Heavy duty shock absorbers may be obtained at your Authorized VW Dealer for cars that are going to be driven continually over bad roads.



### 9.1 Checking Shock Absorbers

You can check the action of a shock absorber by slowly stretching and compressing it by hand. Try to hold it in the position it has on the car. The shock absorber should operate at an even pressure and smoothly over the entire stroke. If in doubt, compare your shock absorber with a new one of the same manufacture. The damping action in both directions must be clearly felt to the end of the stroke. Shock absorbers that have been stored for a long time may have to be "pumped" several times to restore the full action.

Knocking noises coming from around the front wheels when the car is in operation may be symptoms of shock absorber defects.

VW shock absorbers require no maintenance, but if found to be defective they must be replaced. The shock absorber has a large enough supply of fluid to sustain a small leak. As long as the shock absorber continues to function satisfactorily, a trace of leakage should not be regarded as the signal for replacement of the part. It is not possible, however, to top up the fluid.

4

### 9.2 Replacing Shock Absorbers

It is not always necessary to replace both shock absorbers on the axle if one is found defective, but usually shocks are replaced in pairs.

When replacing shock absorbers, make sure that the new ones you are installing are for the front axle. The wrong shock absorbers will impair the driving characteristics of the car.

### 9.3 Removing and Installing Shock Absorbers

Shock absorbers (Fig. 53) from different manufacturers but with the same damping characteristics can be

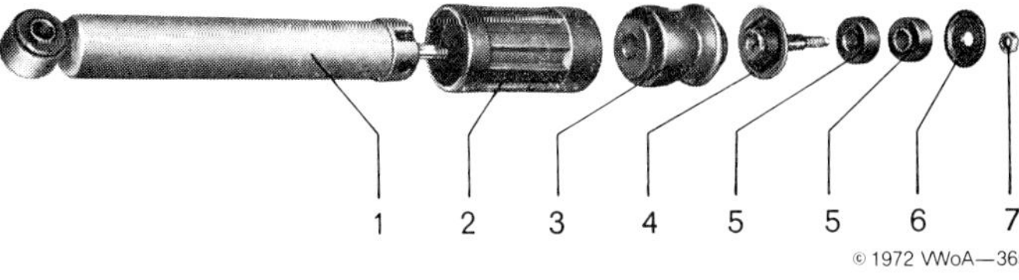


1. Shock absorber
2. Outer tube
3. Buffer
4. Buffer pin or stud
5. Bushings or damping rings for pin
6. Plate for bushings
7. Hexagon nut

**Fig. 53.** Shock absorber breaks down into the parts shown in this exploded view.

interchanged on the front axle. Before such parts are installed, however, an Authorized VW Dealer should be consulted regarding the interchangeability of the components.

**To remove shock absorbers:**

1. Lift car and take off front wheel.
2. Lift brake drum assembly high enough to relax torsion arm tension.
3. Remove nut that attaches shock absorber to front axle side plate.

**NOTE —**
It may be necessary to hold shock absorber at the buffer pin or stud nut with a 42 mm open-end wrench. See Fig. 54.

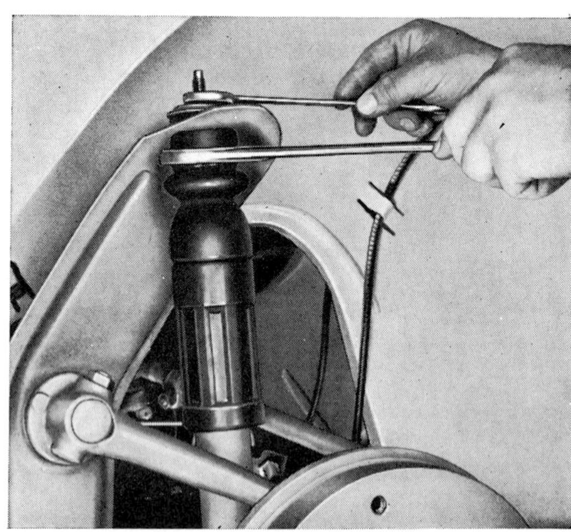
© 1972 VWoA—366

**Fig. 54.** 42-mm wrench on buffer stud gives good hold for removal of shock absorber.

4. Disconnect lower attachment. Pull shock absorber down, pivot out of way and remove.

**To remove seized attaching nut:**

1. If you cannot loosen the nut attaching shock absorber to side plate, remove rubber stop and protective tube from the rubber stop bolt.
2. Hold lower end of bolt with pliers. With open-end wrench screw piston rod of shock absorber out of buffer stud. The wrench should be applied at the flat spot on the piston rod, as in Fig. 55.
3. Remove nut from pin in torsion arm.

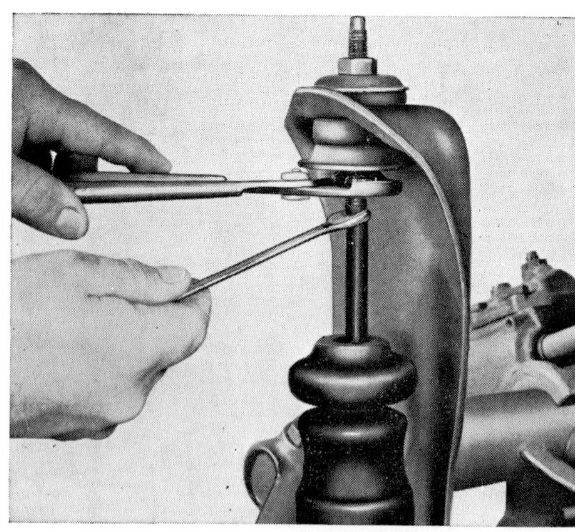
© 1972 VWoA—367

**Fig. 55.** Seized nut complicates procedure for unfastening shock absorber from side plate. See text.

4. Carefully lower wheel from support.
5. Take shock absorber off.

**To install shock absorber:**

1. Check shock absorber for wear and damage. Replace if necessary.
2. Pull buffer off stud and unscrew stud from piston rod, as in Fig. 56. Check damping rings, buffer stud and buffer, and replace parts where necessary.

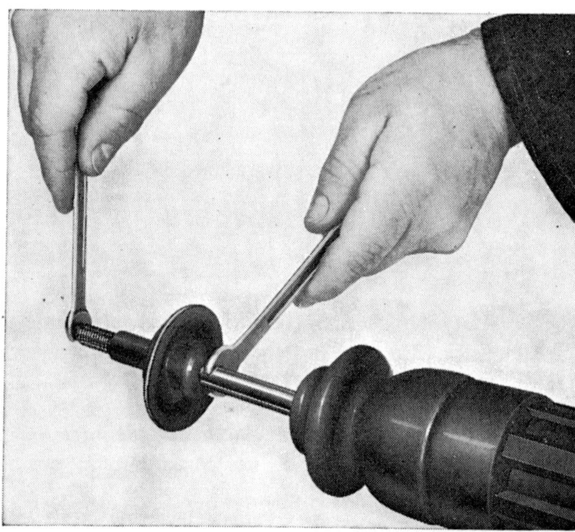
© 1972 VWoA—368

**Fig. 56.** Buffer stud is unscrewed from shock absorber piston rod.

3. Check shock absorber bushings for wear and replace parts if necessary.

4. Check pin in torsion arm for wear and replace pin if necessary.
5. Lightly grease pin in torsion arm.
6. Place shock absorber on torsion arm and tighten securing nut by hand.
7. Place damping ring (bushing) on buffer stud with shoulder facing up. Fig. 57 shows correct position of ring.

**Fig. 57.** Damping ring goes on shock absorber buffer stud with shoulder of ring up, as shown here.

8. Pass piston rod through hole in axle side plate. Install second damping ring plate.
9. Lift torsion arm or wheel and fully tighten nut on stud for rubber buffer to:
   M 10 14 ft. lbs. (2 mkg)
   M 12 x 1.5 22 to 25 ft. lbs. (3.0 to 3.5 mkg)
10. Tighten nut for shock absorber mounting pin on torsion arm to 22 to 25 ft. lbs. (3.0 to 3.5 mkg).

## 9.4 Heavy Duty Shock Absorbers

Heavy duty shock absorbers which will give good service in tropical heat and under continuous heavy load, and which are not easily damaged by stones, are available. They are particularly suited to very bad road conditions. It should be noted, however, that heavy duty shock absorbers will affect the riding quality of the car.

> ***CAUTION*** —
> *Heavy duty shock absorbers should be installed on front and rear axles at the same time.*

# 10. STEERING

The VW sedans and Karmann Ghias of the years covered in this Manual are equipped with a worm-and-roller steering gear. The steering column is mounted inside a tube attached to the car body and is connected to the steering worm at a disk coupling of rubberized fabric. Two types of column are found in these model years. The energy-absorbing steering column on 1968–69 cars differs in construction from the column on earlier cars.

## 10.1 Description and Operation

The steering gear box is clamped to the upper tube of the axle beam. Inside the box the steering worm meshes with the rollers. Turning the steering wheel turns the worm, which gives the transversely mounted roller shaft a rotary movement. The drop arm (also called steering gear arm or Pitman arm) is attached to roller shaft. Rotation of shaft causes drop arm to move tie rods from side to side, pushing one while it pulls the other.

4

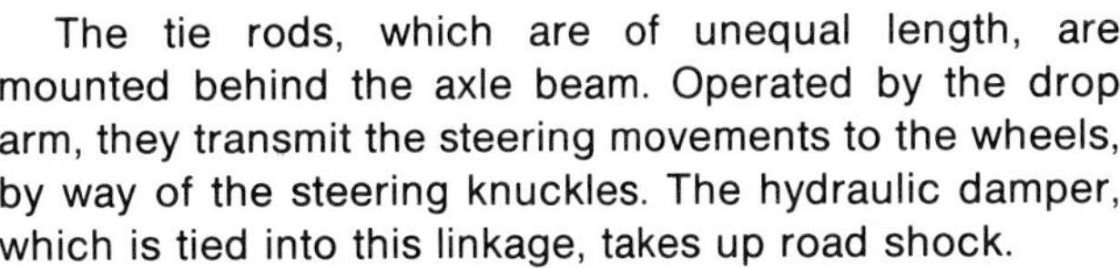

The tie rods, which are of unequal length, are mounted behind the axle beam. Operated by the drop arm, they transmit the steering movements to the wheels, by way of the steering knuckles. The hydraulic damper, which is tied into this linkage, takes up road shock.

In the gearbox a needle bearing supports the roller. The worm runs in two ball thrust bearings. The roller shaft turns in bronze bushings. The steering worm is adjusted by a shim under the upper ball bearing. The meshing depth of the roller in the worm is adjusted by means of a screw in the steering box cover. These parts are shown in cutaway and cross section views in Fig. 58. The steering linkage (drop arm, tie rods and damper) is shown in Fig. 59. You will find these two figures on the next page.

## 10.2 Lubrication

The steering gearbox requires no lubrication, provided it was filled on installation. If trouble occurs, replace the gearbox. The capacity of the gearbox is about a third of a pint (160 cc), and transmission grease is the lubricant used.

## 10.3 Maintenance

The adjustment of the steering gearbox should be checked at the intervals specified in the maintenance chart. Prompt and correct adjustment of the steering has a considerable influence not only on the handling characteristics of the car but also on the service life of the steering assemblies.

**Fig. 58.** Steering mechanism of VW Beetle is shown in cross section. Upper view of steering column and gearbox is from the left side. Lower view of gearbox and drop arm (or steering arm) is from above, shows worm-roller mesh.

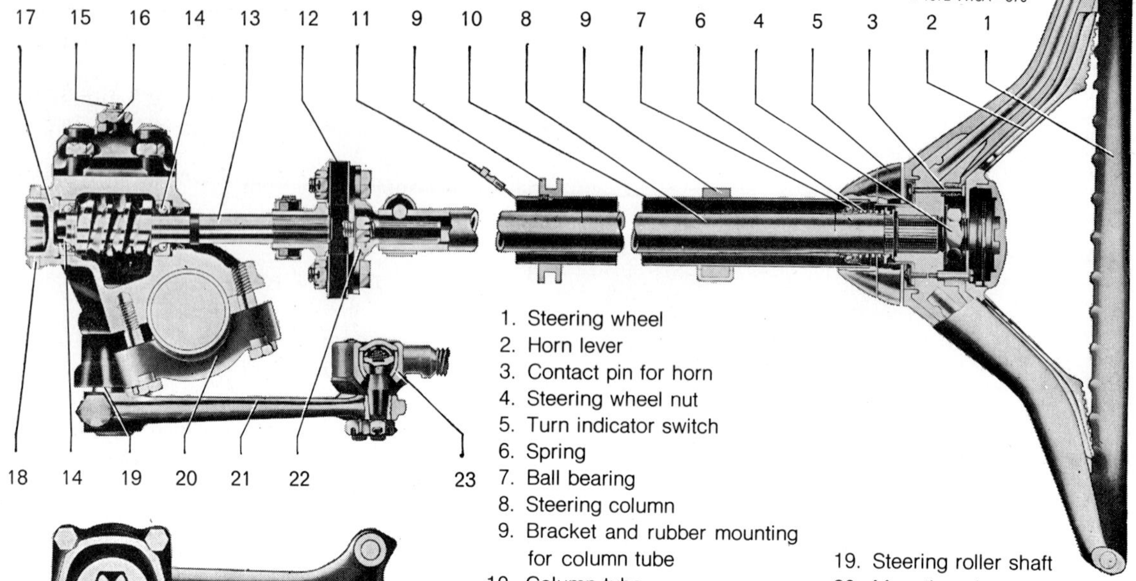

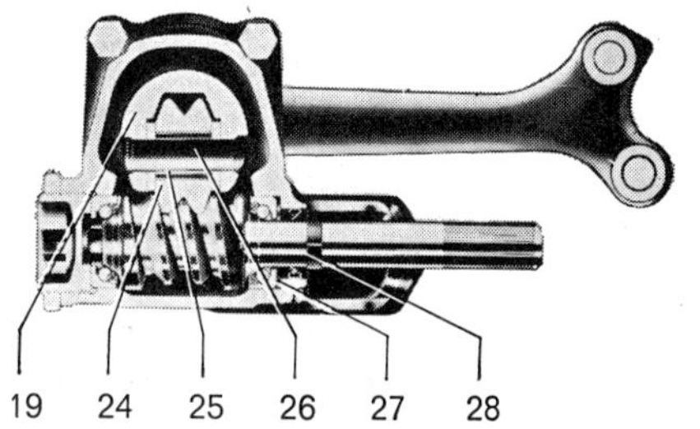

1. Steering wheel
2. Horn lever
3. Contact pin for horn
4. Steering wheel nut
5. Turn indicator switch
6. Spring
7. Ball bearing
8. Steering column
9. Bracket and rubber mounting for column tube
10. Column tube
11. Connection for horn cable
12. Steering column coupling
13. Worm spindle
14. Thrust bearing
15. Roller shaft adjusting screw
16. Lock nut
17. Worm spindle adjusting screw
18. Lock nut
19. Steering roller shaft
20. Mounting clamp
21. Drop arm
22. Tab for ground connection
23. Tie rod end
24. Steering roller
25. Roller needle bearing
26. Pin for roller
27. Shim
28. Marking ring for enter position

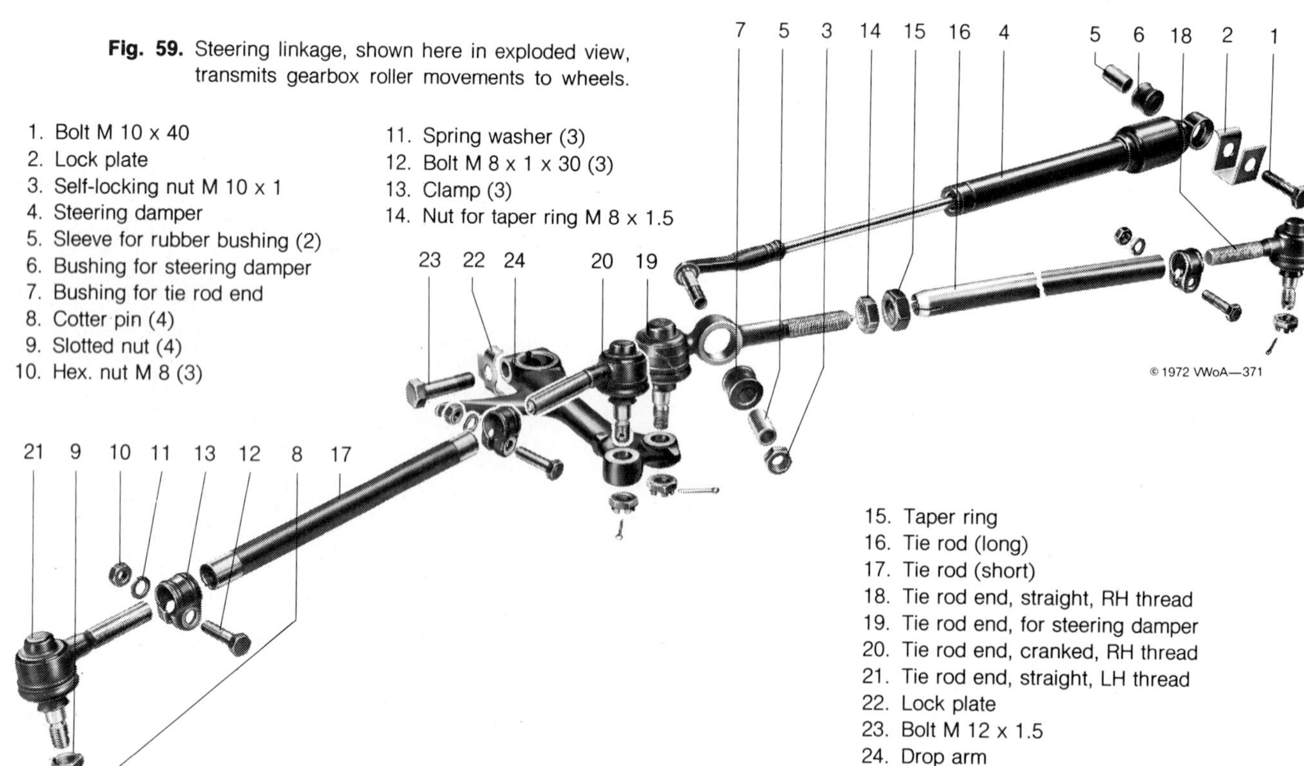


**Fig. 59.** Steering linkage, shown here in exploded view, transmits gearbox roller movements to wheels.

1. Bolt M 10 x 40
2. Lock plate
3. Self-locking nut M 10 x 1
4. Steering damper
5. Sleeve for rubber bushing (2)
6. Bushing for steering damper
7. Bushing for tie rod end
8. Cotter pin (4)
9. Slotted nut (4)
10. Hex. nut M 8 (3)
11. Spring washer (3)
12. Bolt M 8 x 1 x 30 (3)
13. Clamp (3)
14. Nut for taper ring M 8 x 1.5
15. Taper ring
16. Tie rod (long)
17. Tie rod (short)
18. Tie rod end, straight, RH thread
19. Tie rod end, for steering damper
20. Tie rod end, cranked, RH thread
21. Tie rod end, straight, LH thread
22. Lock plate
23. Bolt M 12 x 1.5
24. Drop arm

## Table a. Steering Troubleshooting

| Symptom | Cause | Remedy |
|---|---|---|
| 1. Steering is stiff from lock to lock, jams or fails to return automatically to straight-ahead position | a. Front axle inadequately lubricated<br>b. Steering gear out of adjustment | a. Jack up front end of car and lubricate front axle.<br>b. Check steering gear adjustment. |
| 2. Front wheels do not self-center, although there is no tightness in steering system | Front wheels improperly adjusted | Check and adjust front wheel alignment (caster, camber and toe-in). |
| 3. Steering gear has excessive play | a. Steering gear improperly adjusted<br>b. Steering gear set worn | a. Check steering gear adjustments.<br>b. Replace steering gear set. |
| 4. Tie rod ends have excessive play | Tie rod ends worn | Replace tie rod ends. |
| 5. Front wheel suspension shows excessive play | Worn bearing points (torsion arms, stub axle, and front wheel bearing) | Check adjustments of torsion arms and front wheel bearings. Adjust parts with excessive play or replace if necessary. |
| 6. Car pulls to one side | a. Tire pressures uneven. (Car pulls to side on which pressure is low)<br>b. Tires unevenly worn. (Car pulls to side on which wear is worse)<br>c. Toe not adjusted properly<br>d. Steering damper defective<br>e. Difference between camber of front wheels excessive. (Car pulls to one side if camber differs more than 20 minutes of angle between sides) | a. Correct tire pressures.<br>b. Switch tires around the car or get new tires.<br>c. Adjust toe angle.<br>d. Replace damper.<br>e. Check camber and correct. |

### 10.4 Steering Troubleshooting

**Table a,** which appears above, lists various steering problems, the probable causes and suggested remedies.

### 10.5 Removing and Installing Steering Damper

Any erratic action of the damper is cause for replacement.

**To remove:**

1. Lift vehicle and take off front wheels.

2. Unlock and remove bolt in bracket on axle beam, as in Fig. 60.

**Fig. 60.** Bolt (arrow) fastens steering damper to bracket on front axle beam.

3. Remove nut at tie rod eye (see Fig. 61) and take damper off.

© 1972 VWoA—373

**Fig. 61.** Nut at tie rod eye must be removed before the steering damper can be detached from steering linkage.

**To install:**

1. Check steering damper. Work plunger by hand. Plunger should move slowly and uniformly. If there is a flat spot anywhere in the range of movement, damper must be replaced.
2. Check rubber bushing and sleeve in damper for wear and damage. Also check bushing and sleeve on tie rod end. Replace with new parts as required.

**NOTE ——**
The damper fluid cylinder cannot be disassembled.

a. Press sleeve out of bushing on press using a tapered pilot.

**NOTE ——**
Usually bushing can be pressed out of eye without tools.

b. Press in new bushing.
c. Insert sleeve in bushing and press it in. Use press with cylindrical pilot as in Fig. 62. Grease pilot lightly.

3. Check bushing and sleeve where damper attaches to tie rod.
4. Tighten inner nut at tie rod eye to 18 ft. lbs. (2.5 mkg) and secure with new lock nut.
5. Install bolt in bracket on axle with a new lock plate. Install lock plate with open end of "U" pointing forward and short angled part on the bracket.
6. Tighten bolt to 18 ft. lbs. (2.5 mkg) and lock.

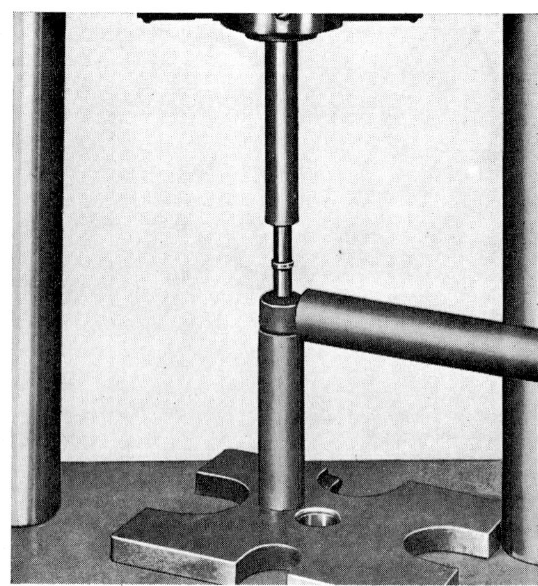

© 1972 VWoA—374

**Fig. 62.** Sleeve for rubber bushing in eye of steering damper must be pressed out, but rubber bushing usually can be pushed out without tools.

## 10.6 Removing and Installing Tie Rods

Since the tie rod ends are ball joints, you should reread **6. Torsion Arms and Ball Joints** before undertaking these procedures.

If your work requires you to remove the tie rods, you will have to adjust front wheel toe angle after you have re-installed the rods.

**To remove tie rods:**

1. Lift car and take off front wheels.
2. Remove cotter pins and nuts from tie rod ends.
3. Detach steering damper at tie rod.

***CAUTION ——***
*When removing tie rod ends be careful to avoid damaging the rubber boots. Take pains not to squeeze grease out of seals here or at any other part of the steering system. Steering service life will be satisfactory only if joints are properly packed with grease. Damaged boots must be replaced.*

4. Press tie rod ends out with special tool.

***WARNING ——***
*Bent tie rods must be replaced, not straightened.*

**To install:**

1. Check tie rods for damage.
2. Check tie rod ends for wear and tightness. If there is any play or if the pin cannot be moved by hand, replace the tie rod end. The thread on the pin must be undamaged.
3. Check rubber boots for damage.

**NOTE —**
If a tie rod end boot has been punctured, replace the tie rod. Dirt probably has entered the joint.

4. Check bushing on steering damper for wear and replace if necessary.
5. Install both tie rods with the left-hand threads on the left, as the driver would see it.
6. Tighten tie rod end nuts and insert cotter pins.
7. Loosen clamp nuts.
8. Twist both ends of each rod in the same direction (front or rear) to align them correctly.
9. With ends aligned, tighten nut for the tapered ring or clamp nut.
10. Secure steering damper to tie rod.
11. Adjust toe angle.

## 10.7 Removing and Installing Steering Wheel

**To remove:**

1. Disconnect battery ground strap.
2. Carefully remove horn lever cover with a screw-driver.
3. Disconnect horn ground cable at horn lever.
4. Remove steering wheel nut (Fig. 63) and take off the spring washer.

© 1972 VWoA—376

**Fig. 63.** Steering wheel nut is removed with wrench.

5. Remove steering wheel with horn lever.

**To install:**

1. Make sure that brass washer is positioned properly. When wheels are in straight-ahead position, cut-away section of washer points to right (Fig. 64).

© 1972 VWoA—377

**Fig. 64.** Brass washer under steering wheel nut is located correctly on steering column (as here) if cutaway sector of washer is toward driver's right when front wheels are in straight-ahead position.

4

2. Place steering gearbox in center position and install steering wheel with the spoke horizontal. Tongue of cancelling ring must engage recess in brass washer. Fig. 65 shows correct position of spoke.

**NOTE —**
Steering gearbox is centered when split in ring (circlip) lines up with raised boss on gearbox.

© 1972 VWoA—378

**Fig. 65.** Steering wheel spoke should be horizontal (as here) when steering is in straight-ahead position.

3. Install spring washer and nut and tighten to 36 ft. lbs. (5.0 mkg). The distance between turn indicator switch and steering wheel hub must be 0.04 to 0.08 inch (1.0 to 2.0 mm). Measurement is shown as distance "a" in Fig. 66. The distance can be varied as required by moving column on the upper coupling flange. If only a small adjustment is needed, distance "a" may be obtained on early model cars by moving the signal switch. If you fail to obtain specified clearance, disassemble and start over. Check each step carefully.

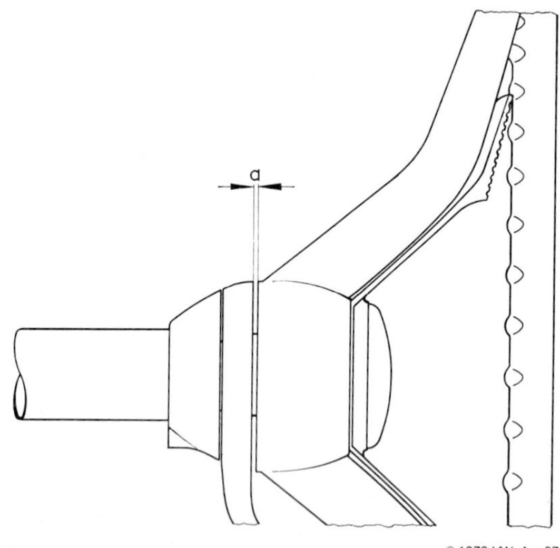


© 1972 VWoA—379

**Fig. 66.** Steering wheel hub should be separated from turn indicator switch (distance "a") by 0.04 to 0.08 inch.

4. Connect horn cable to horn lever.

## 10.8 Removing and Installing Steering Column (1966 and 1967 cars)

The procedure differs somewhat for cars with steering ignition lock.

**To remove column:**

1. Unlock and remove bolt in clamp on steering column and take off clamp. Fig. 67 shows the operation.

2. Pull horn cable off connection on steering column coupling.

3. Remove column.
   a. On cars without steering/ignition lock:
      (1) Loosen steering wheel nut slightly and pull column out of tube complete with steering wheel.

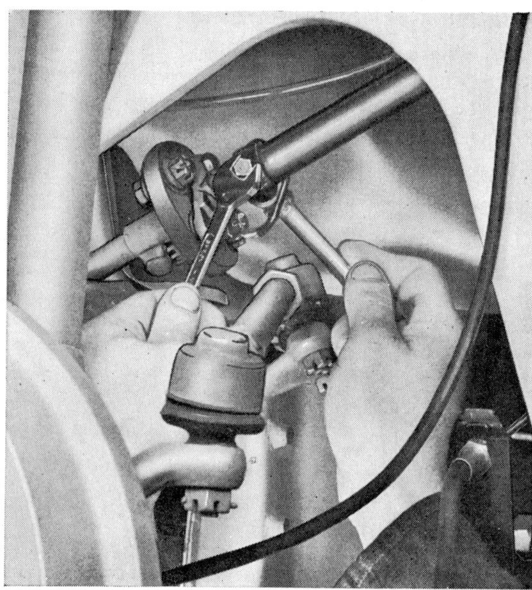

© 1972 VWoA—380

**Fig. 67.** Steering column clamp at coupling to worm spindle comes off after bolt has been unlocked and removed.

   b. On cars with steering/ignition lock:
      (1) Take steering wheel off.
      (2) Loosen turn signal indicator switch screw and take switch off. It is necessary to disconnect cables in the switch harness and pull the cable a little way out of the instrument panel.
      (3) Pull column out of tube complete with bearing. Drive bearing out through lock shells on the column, but take care not to damage it. The shells, which are spot-welded on the column, have recess for the ignition lock pin.

4. Press circlip out of column and take off brass washer, thrust spring and support ring. Fig. 68 shows the parts.

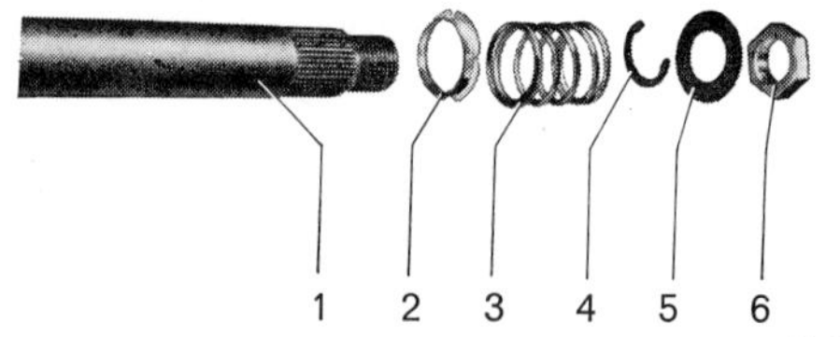


© 1972 VWoA—381

1. Steering column
2. Support ring
3. Thrust spring
4. Circlip
5. Spring washer
6. Steering wheel nut

**Fig. 68.** Upper end of steering column breaks down into parts shown in this exploded view.

**To install:**

1. Check condition of ball bearing for steering column and install a new bearing if necessary. Fig. 69 shows the parts.

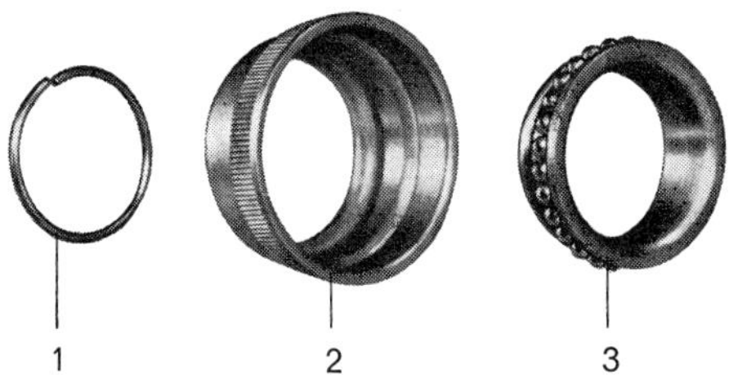


1. Circlip
2. Outer race
3. Inner race with the ball bearings

**Fig. 69.** Ball bearing on column below steering wheel is seen here in exploded view.

**NOTE** —
The ball bearing on the steering column is packed with special grease and requires no maintenance.

2. Install steering column.
3. Place ring on column with shoulder upward. Install thrust spring and brass washer and secure with circlip.
4. Turn brass washer to have cut-out segment at right when wheels are in straight-ahead position.
5. Set steering gear in the centered position and install steering wheel with spoke horizontal. Tongue of canceling ring must engage in cut-out in the brass washer.
6. Install spring washer and tighten wheel securing nut to 36 ft. lbs. (5.0 mkg).
7. Set space between steering wheel hub and indicator switch 0.04 to 0.08 inch (1.0 to 2.0 mm) by moving steering column on coupling. (See step 3 of "To install" in **10.7 Removing and Installing Steering Wheel**.)
8. Install screw for column clamp with new lock plate. Tighten screw and lock it.

## 10.9 Removing and Installing Column Tube

**To remove:**

1. Disconnect horn cable from connection on column coupling.
2. Remove steering wheel.
3. Loosen clamp screw for turn signal switch and pull switch off column tube. It will be necessary to disconnect the turn signal cables and pull the cable harness a little way out of the instrument panel.
4. Take circlip off column and remove brass washer, thrust spring and ring.
5. On cars without steering/ignition lock:
   a. Disconnect column tube.
   b. Remove screws and take off column tube bracket.

   On cars with steering/ignition lock:
   a. Drill out the special shear screws and take off steering lock. The operation is shown in Fig. 70.

**Fig. 70.** Special shear screws must be drilled out for removal of steering/ignition lock. See text.

6. Twist column tube back and forth and pull it out of the rubber mounting in the front partition.

**To install:**

1. Check column bearing and install new one if needed.

   **NOTE** —
   The ball bearing on the steering column is packed with special grease and requires no maintenance.

2. Check upper and lower rubber mountings. Replace if damaged.
3. Install column tube.

**CAUTION —**
*On vehicles with the steering/ignition lock, the special screw heads must not be twisted off until steering wheel has been installed and hub-to-switch clearance set correctly.*

4. Before tightening clamp screw, push switch onto stop on tube.
5. Place ring, spring and brass washer on the column in proper order and secure with circlip.
6. Install steering wheel and adjust hub to switch clearance by moving the column tube. Fig. 66 gives the important dimension. Make sure that steering gear is centered before you install wheel.
7. Connect cables to flasher relay and to connector on column coupling.
8. Check steering wheel operation.

## 10.10 Energy-absorbing Steering Column

From 1968 models on, the cars covered in this Manual are equipped with an energy-absorbing steering column. The key to the design is the expanded metal tubular section indicated at A in Fig. 71. Under impact this section would collapse to absorb the energy. Forces working on the steering column axially, as would be typical of a head-on collision, would push the expanded metal section together. A lateral impact would deform it sideways. Again, the column would absorb energy.

The column tube is attached to the underside of the dash panel with a special mounting that consists of guide pieces fastened with plastic rivets. The rivets are designed to shear off when impact forces are exerted against the steering wheel. The guide pieces slide out of the mounting. Column and tube then would be pushed through the hole in the partition to deform the energy-absorbing system.

**WARNING —**
*Since the energy-absorbing section in the steering column is designed to collapse when stressed beyond a certain point, it must be checked carefully for cracks or distortion whenever the car has been in an accident. Even slight visible damage in the energy-absorbing section calls for replacement of the complete steering column.*

**Fig. 71.** Energy-absorbing steering column appears on all Volkswagens from the 1968 model on. Collapsible metal section at (A) yields under impact to absorb collision energy. Dashboard mounting at (B) has plastic rivets that shear off under impact, allow wheel and tube to go forward and deform section at (A). Energy is absorbed.

## 10.11 Removing and Installing Energy-absorbing Column

The disassembled energy-absorbing steering column is shown in Fig. 72.

1. Lock plate
2. Hexagon nut
3. Bolt
4. Clamp for steering column
5. Support for column
6. Circlip for column
7. Contact ring
8. Allen head M 8 x 22 bolt (secures column switch to column tube)
9. Allen head M 8 x 35 bolt (secures column switch to mounting plate for column tube)
10. Spring washer
11. Column tube
12. Bushing tor column tube
13. Steering column
14. Allen head M 8 x 12 bolt (for mounting plate)
15. Column mounting plate

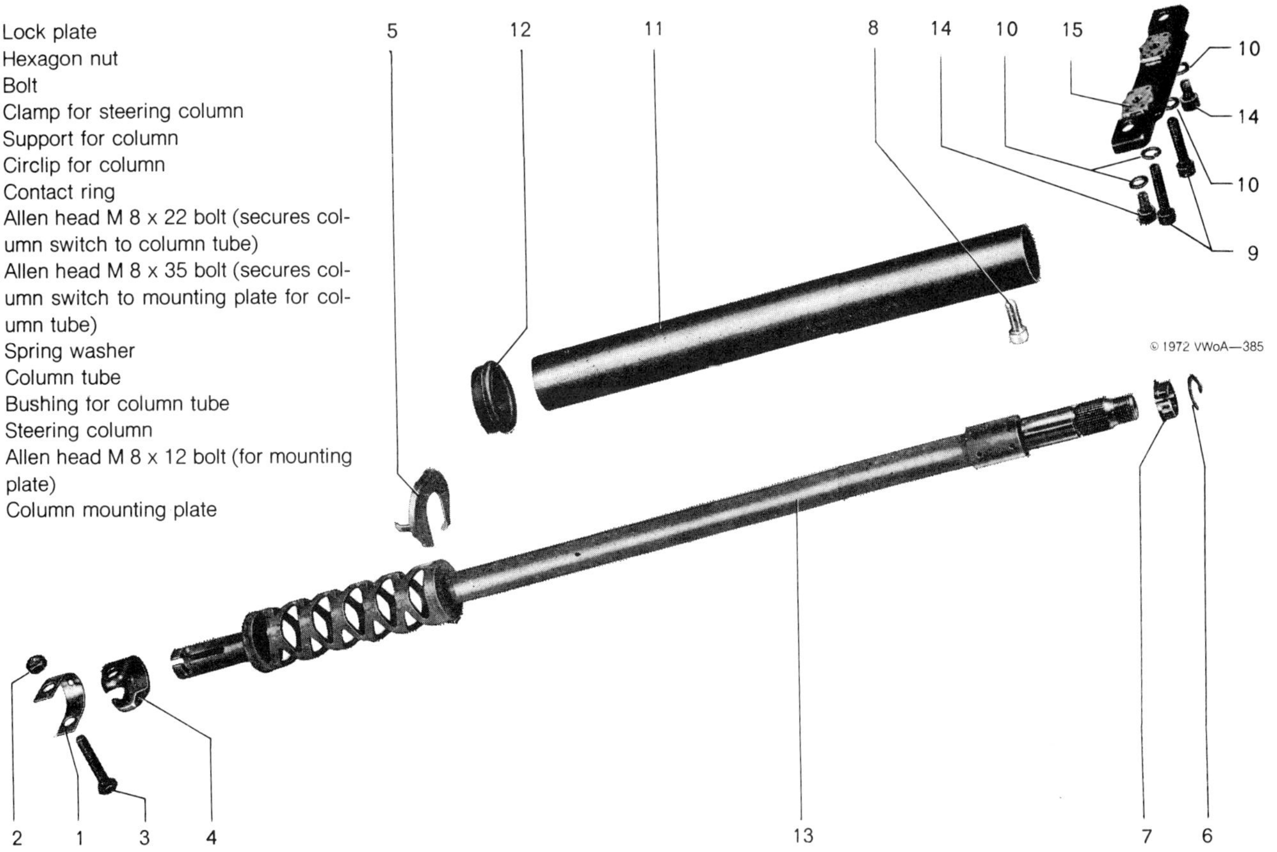

**Fig. 72.** Exploded view shows breakdown of parts of the energy-absorbing safety steering column on all VW cars from 1968. Attaching plate (15) has plastic rivets.

**To remove:**

1. Disconnect battery ground strap.
2. Remove fuel tank.
3. Disconnect ground cable from terminal on steering coupling (arrow A in Fig. 73). Unlock nut for clamp on steering column and remove nut (arrow B). Bend up tongues of support ring for steering column and remove support (arrow C).
4. Remove steering wheel, then take out circlip for steering column. Turn ignition key to "Fahrt" or unlock steering wheel.

**Fig. 73.** Ground cable is disconnected from terminal on steering coupling (A). Arrow (B) points to nut on steering column clamp. Arrow (C) indicates support ring. See text.

5. Remove securing screws from steering column tube and three Allen head clamp bolts from steering column switch (indicated by arrows in Fig. 74).

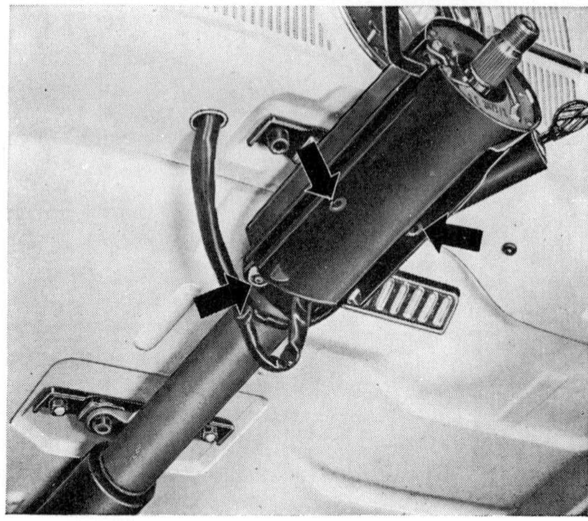



**Fig. 74.** Three clamp bolts (black arrows) hold steering column switch.

6. Take steering column switch off column and suspend it to remove tension from wiring harness.
7. Pull column tube with steering column up and out.

**To install:**

1. Make sure that clamp for column tube is firmly and correctly installed. Closed side must face driving direction, as indicated by arrows in Fig. 75. Tighten securing screws to 4 to 7 ft. lbs. (1.5 to 1 mkg).

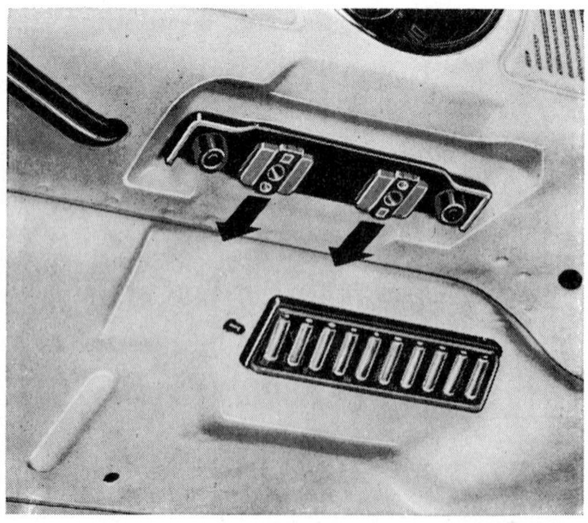



**Fig. 75.** Clamp for steering column tube is positioned correctly when closed side is toward front of car. Black arrows indicate the direction.

2. Insert column tube into rubber support on forward cross panel.
3. Push steering column into column tube and attach to steering coupling. Do not forget steering column clamp.
4. Insert contact ring into bearing from below.
5. Install steering column switch.
6. Lightly tighten clamp bolt for steering column switch.
7. Insert circlip for steering column tube.
8. Set steering to center position (marking ring on steering worm must align with seam on cast housing).
9. Install clamp bolt and new lock plate for clamp on steering column. Tighten and lock clamp bolt.
10. Connect horn ground cable.
11. Install steering column support ring. Lock it by bending over the tongues.
12. Install steering wheel. Make sure that turn signal lever is in center position. Otherwise, canceling cams will be damaged by tongue of canceling ring. Torque attaching nut for steering wheel to 36 ft. lbs. (5 mkg).
13. Move steering column switch in elongated holes so that distance between steering wheel hub and steering wheel switch is 0.04 to 0.08 inch (1.0 to 2.0 mm). This measurement is distance "a" on Fig. 66.

***CAUTION —***
*Observe torque specifications.*

14. Make sure that steering column and tube are properly aligned. Torque all bolts to 4 to 7 ft. lbs. (0.5 to 1.0 mkg) and in the following sequence:
    a. Column switch to attaching plate bolts.
    b. Column switch to column tube bolts.

## 10.12 Steering Gearbox

If the steering gearbox is damaged or requires repair it is advisable to replace it on an exchange basis with your local Authorized VW Dealer.

**To remove box:**

1. Lift car and take off left front wheel.
2. Detach tie rods from steering drop arm.
3. Unscrew clamp nut on steering column clamp.

4. Disconnect cable on steering coupling contact.
5. Pull steering column off steering column flange.
6. Mark steering gearbox clamp. Unlock and remove nuts and take off clamp, as in Fig. 76.
7. Remove steering gearbox.

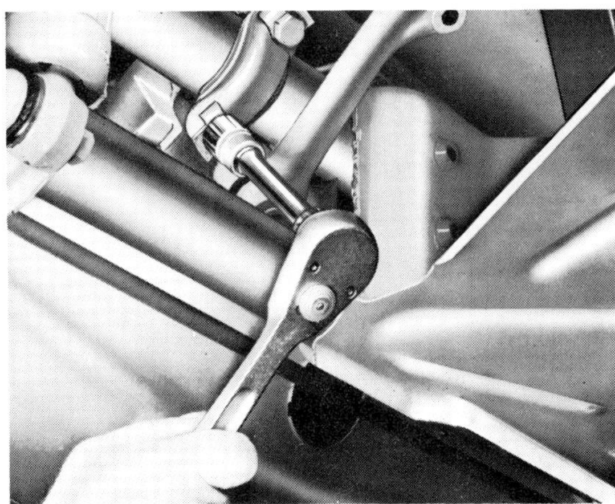

© 1972 VWoA—389

**Fig. 76.** Gearbox clamp comes off after removal of nuts.

**To install:**

1. Check and adjust steering gear. Disassemble if necessary and replace damaged or worn parts with new ones.

**NOTE —**
When a new steering gear is installed, the steering center position must be established. A special device is used for this procedure after the appropriate steering drop arm has been installed on the roller shaft. Mark center position with dab of paint after marking ring has been positioned on the worm spindle.

2. Install steering gearbox on upper beam of axle tube between the two welded-on stops. Use new lock plates and do not tighten bolts fully at first.
3. Set steering to center position and push steering column onto flange, with steering wheel spokes horizontal.
4. Align steering gear to bring steering column as close as possible to center.

**NOTE —**
Stop welded to axle tube and appropriate cutouts in bracket (Fig. 77) fix steering gear angle. The numeral 13 on bracket marks cutout for sedan, 14 for Karmann Ghia.

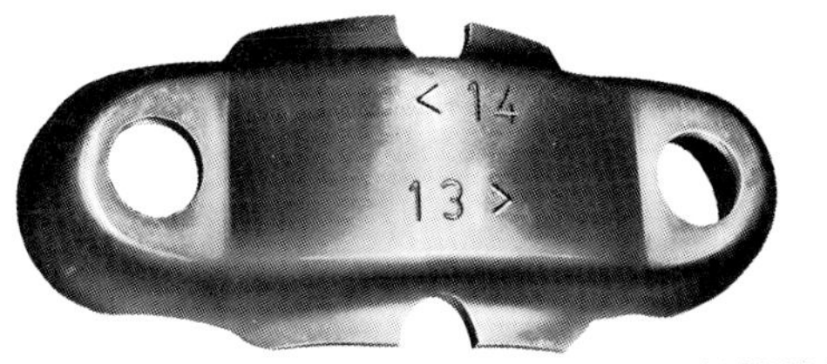


© 1972 VWoA—390

**Fig. 77.** Gearbox bracket has a cutout for the Beetle and another one for the Karmann Ghia. When bracket is on axle tube with arrow at 13 pointing forward, installation is for Beetle. When arrow at 14 points forward, the installation is for Karmann Ghia. Cutouts limit steering gear angle.

5. Tighten steering gearbox bracket bolts to a torque of 18 to 22 ft. lbs. (2.5 to 3.0 mkg) and lock them with locking plates.
6. Use new lock plate for steering column clamp.
7. Tighten tie rod nuts and secure them with cotter pins.

4

***CAUTION* —**
*Wheel toe angle must be checked after each removal and installation of the steering gear and each alteration of the installation position.*

8. Check toe.

## 10.13 Checking and Adjusting Roller Steering

The roller steering should be checked at regular maintenance inspection and, if necessary, adjusted.

**To check:**

1. With car on ground, turn front wheels to straight-ahead position.
2. With your finger at end of the spoke, move the steering wheel lightly back and forth until you feel resistance in both directions. The steering adjustment, as well as the tie rods and steering coupling, will determine the range of this movement when the steering system is at center position. Measured on the circumference of the wheel, movement up to 1.0 inch (25 mm) is allowable.

Excessive play at the center position can arise at three points. Checks and adjustments are made in a certain sequence. The places to look are indicated in Fig. 78.

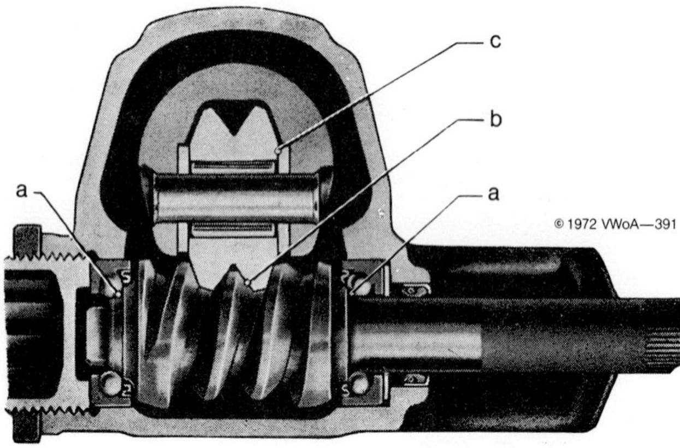


**Fig. 78.** Three points indicated here should be checked when play at center steering position is excessive: axial play of worm (a); play between roller and worm (b); roller axial play (c).

Axial play of the worm (point "a" in Fig. 78) is determined by turning the worm back and forth at the steering coupling. The car must be raised for this check.

**To adjust axial play:**

1. Turn steering wheel to left or right.
2. Loosen the lock nut of the steering worm adjusting screw. (Large nut at end of shaft.)
3. Turn the steering worm back and forth at the steering coupling and at the same time tighten the adjusting screw until no play is noticeable.
4. Hold adjusting screw and tighten lock nut to 36 to 43 ft. lbs. (5 to 6 mkg).
5. Turn steering worm from lock to lock. During rotation no unusually tight position should be noticeable. If there is one (or more), the adjusting screw is too tight. The adjustment must then be corrected.

If play in the steering cannot be eliminated by adjusting the worm, the roller-to-worm setting (point "b" in Fig. 78) must be adjusted. When steering is in center position there should be no play between roller and worm. The roller-to-worm adjustment can be made with the car raised. To check the adjustment, however, the car must be on the ground.

**To adjust play between roller and worm:**

1. Turn steering wheel 90 degrees to left or right.
2. Loosen lock nut of roller shaft adjusting screw.
3. Loosen the adjusting screw approximately one turn.
4. Tighten the adjusting screw until you feel the roller make contact with the steering worm.
5. Hold the adjusting screw and tighten the lock nut to 16 to 18 ft. lbs. (2.2 to 2.5 mkg). The upper limits are maximums.
6. With car on the ground, check the adjustment when steering wheel is turned 90 degrees to each side. The play must not exceed 1 inch (25 mm), measured on circumference of steering wheel. If there is more play on one side, the adjustment of the roller to toe worm at the 90 degree position should be repeated on this side.
7. Check wheel toe angle and correct if necessary.
8. Road test the car. If the steering does not return to within 45 degrees of the centered position after taking a corner at 10 to 12 mph, the roller is too tight. The adjustment procedure should then be repeated. Otherwise, the worm and roller will be damaged.

**Axial Play of Steering Roller**

If the specified range at center position cannot be obtained by adjusting the steering worm and roller shaft, the steering roller axial play (point "c" in Fig. 78) must be checked. For this operation the steering gear must be removed and disassembled. As previously mentioned, it is recommended that you have this adjustment done in the shop of your Authorized VW Dealer.

## 10.14 Wheel Position

Whether your car handles easily and rides smoothly depends on the functioning of all the parts of the front axle assembly and the steering mechanism and upon the alignment and tilt of the wheels. The importance of the following points cannot be emphasized too strongly:

1. All parts of the front axle and the steering mechanism must have the amount of play that the design calls for. This freedom of movement results from regular lubrication.
2. The steering gear must be set correctly.
3. The front wheels must run true. That is, the wheel bearings must be adjusted properly. Each wheel must be in balance within the specified limits. Wheel runout must not exceed the allowed limit.
4. The alignment of the front axle and front wheels must be correct.
5. Tire pressure must be as specified, and the wear on the tires must be even.
6. The shock absorbers must be in good working order. (The functioning of the shock absorbers can be tested by bouncing the car.)

When aligning the front end, you should observe the following three fundamental points:

1. Have the car on a level surface.
2. Have the spare wheel in the car and the fuel tank full, but otherwise have the car unloaded.
3. Follow the instructions of the manufacturer of the equipment you are using.

The relation of these points to correct steering geometry and wheel position will be discussed in the following pages but not necessarily in the order in which the points are listed above.

## 10.15 Front Wheel Alignment

The instructions set forth in the following procedures are of a general nature. Manufacturers of alignment equipment should furnish you with specific instructions for the use of their products. And always follow the manufacturer's instructions for the specific equipment you are using. In outlining the alignment procedure we will follow this sequence:

1. Front wheels
   a. Camber
   b. Caster
   c. Toe-in
   d. Turning angle
   e. Toe-out
2. Rear wheels
   a. Camber
   b. Toe
3. Track (involves both front and rear wheels)

## 10.16 Steering Geometry

The steering geometry of the car consists of four specific angles involving components of the axle, steering and wheel assemblies. Together with the springing of the car, these four angles are the main factors that affect steering. We list the angles here and then discuss them in detail on subsequent pages:

1. Camber of front wheels
2. Steering axis inclination (on older cars with king pins instead of ball joints this angle is called king pin inclination)
3. Caster
4. Toe-angle of front wheels when in straight-ahead position.

If only one of these four angles is changed by wear or by damage in a collision, the springing and steering geometry of the car will be disturbed. All the other angles can be correct, but distortion of one will upset the alignment of the whole front end. The results of such misalignment can include:

1. Excessive tire wear
2. Hard steering
3. Pulling off to one side
4. Poor road holding, especially on wet or icy roads and poor cornering
5. Front wheel shimmy

These dangerous possibilities underline the importance of having the camber, king pin or steering axis inclination, caster and toe angle of a car checked at regular inspections. Adjustment of the components for correct steering geometry requires a certain mechanical skill and also requires some understanding of the theory. The principal points will be covered in the following discussions.

4

### Camber and King Pin Inclination

Camber, as illustrated in Fig. 79, is defined as the inclination of the wheel away from the vertical. The wheel leans outward in positive camber, inward in nega-

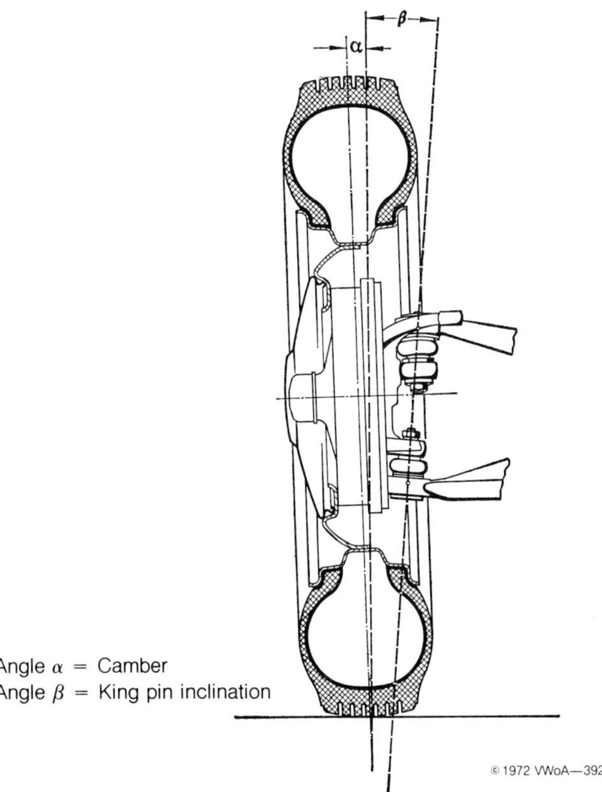


**Fig. 79.** Camber of wheel is shown here as angle $\alpha$ (alpha). Since wheel tilts outward here, camber is positive. Angle $\beta$ (beta) is the king pin or steering axis inclination from the vertical. Note that the line determining angle $\beta$ runs through the ball joints. See text.

tive camber. This discussion will focus on positive camber. Camber exists because the wheel spindle (or stub axle) is not at a right angle to the line that passes through the king pin on earlier cars or through the two ball joints on later cars. Camber can be adjusted by turning the eccentric bushing in the upper torsion arm, as described later in this section.

King pin inclination is the angle between the steering axis (the line through the upper and lower ball joints or through the king pin) and a vertical line from the road through the steering knuckle pivot point, as seen from the front of the car. This angle also is shown in Fig. 80.

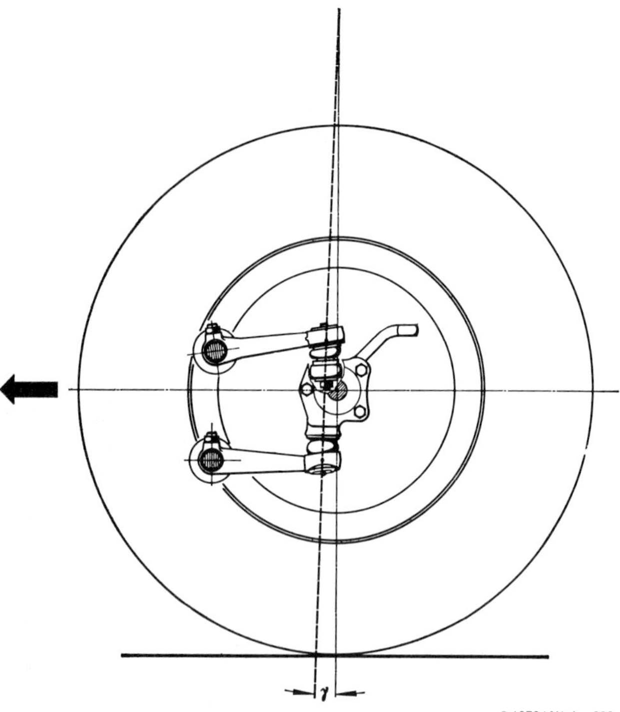


**Fig. 80.** Caster of wheel is shown as angle $\gamma$ (gamma). Note that caster is the fore-and-aft inclination of the steering axis, whereas king pin inclination measures the side-to-side tilt of axis. Arrow shows direction of travel. Dotted line is steering axis. Solid line is vertical.

Camber and king pin inclination are adjusted to establish the optimum relationship between the point where the steering axis meets the road and the point where the center line of the wheel meets the road. If the first point falls outside the second point, the wheel toes in. If it falls inside (that is, toward the middle of the car) the wheel toes out. The optimum distance between the two points has been determined over years of experience. When the two points are close together, the car wheels tend to follow the straight-ahead direction of travel. The heavy steering knuckle assembly helps to reduce road shock instead of passing it on to the steering linkage—and eventually to the driver. The tendency of the tires to scuff on turns is held to a minimum.

### Caster

Caster is defined as the angle between the steering axis and a vertical line through the wheel hub as seen from the side of the car. Fig. 80 shows the angle. In positive caster the angle is to the front of the car, from the vertical line through the hub. In negative caster the angle is toward the rear.

Caster is important in steering because it tends to bring the wheel back into a straight-ahead direction of travel. Caster also helps to pull the car out of a turn. The steering axis tends to lead the wheel. A crude illustration of the effect is given when you push a chair that is on casters. Regardless of the direction of push, the caster on each leg quickly swings around to follow the leg, which in this example is a counterpart of the steering axis.

Insufficient caster makes the vehicle tend to wander under the influence of various forces it encounters from potholes, uneven road surface, and side wind. The car does not come out of curves properly. Too much caster makes steering difficult. Increased force must be applied to turn the steering wheel to counteract the tendency of the wheels to remain in the straight-ahead position.

### Toe-in and Toe-out (Toe)

The combination of positive camber and road resistance tends to make the wheel turn outward, as viewed from the front of the car. The amount of play in the front wheel bearings, the wheel suspension and the joints of the tie rods will all affect this tendency. Toe-in, pictured in Fig. 81, compensates for it. In toe-in the wheels point

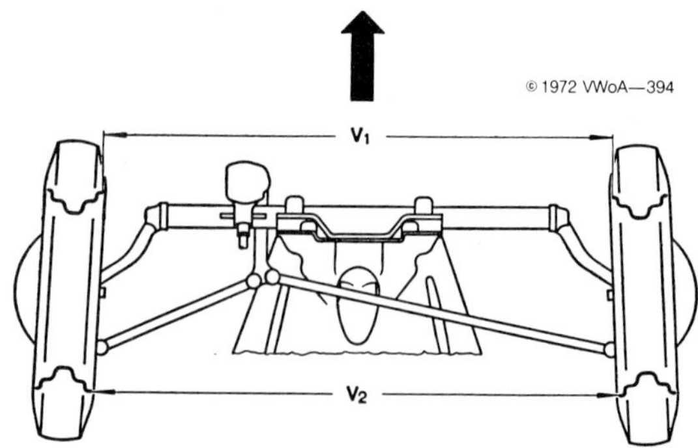


**Fig. 81.** Toe-in is illustrated in this view of the front axle, looking down. The heavy arrow indicates the direction of travel. The wheels "toe in" when the distance $V_1$ is less than the distance $V_2$. Toe-in keeps the tracks of the wheels parallel when the car is moving straight ahead.

inward. This adjustment keeps the wheels rolling on parallel tracks when the car is moving forward.

When cornering, inner wheel travels on a smaller circle than outer wheel does, and therefore must turn at a sharper angle. The forces set up by this difference in turning angle change the toe-in position of the wheels on the straightaway to toe-out on curves (Fig. 82).

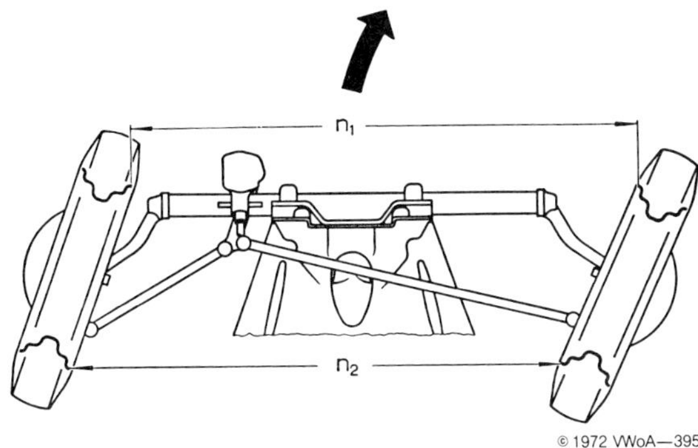


**Fig. 82.** Toe-out is illustrated in this view of the front axle, looking down. The heavy arrow indicates the direction of travel. The wheels toe out when the distance $n_1$ is greater than the distance $n_2$. Since the inside wheel turns more sharply on a curve, some toe-out is necessary.

If steering is incorrectly adjusted or if a steering arm is bent, scuffing will occur on turns. That is, to make a turn the tire will have to slide along surface of road instead of rolling on it. Scuffing causes excessive tire wear.

### Alignment Check

Correct wheel alignment is of vital importance to the road-holding quality of a car. Variations from specified values for toe angle and camber can affect handling qualities noticeably and will cause abnormal tire wear.

If the road-holding of a car is poor, if the tires show abnormal wear or if it is suspected that a collision has disturbed the wheel alignment, a careful check of the axle alignment and rear wheel setting is in order. Necessary adjustments should be made and parts replaced where needed. A complete check can be carried out only with the use of an optical device which can measure misalignment to the required number of decimal places to satisfy technical specifications. However, if an optical axle alignment gauge is not available, the camber and toe can be measured with less complicated instruments. The test preparations should accomplish the following:

1. Tire pressure must be correct.
2. Car must be on a level surface.
3. Car should be unloaded except for spare wheel and full tank of fuel.
4. The steering gear has been adjusted properly.
5. Linkage has been checked for excessive play.
6. Front wheel bearings have been adjusted properly.
7. Vehicle has been bounced up and down to work shock absorbers.

### Checking and Adjusting Camber

This procedure requires use of a special device called a protractor. The device has a leveling bubble and measures inclination of a surface from the vertical.

**To check:**

1. Have the front wheels of the car as nearly as possible in the straight-ahead position on a level surface. Center the steering according to the second step of the procedure for installing the steering wheel.
2. Place the protractor (Fig. 83) on the wheel rim, marking contact point with chalk.

**Fig. 83.** Protractor is device with leveling bubble used to measure inclination of wheel from vertical.

3. Set the device to bring the level marked "axle beam/angle" to the center position.
4. Read camber angle.
5. Roll vehicle forward half a turn of the wheels.

6. Place protractor on the rim at the chalk mark and take another reading. The camber angle of the wheel is the average of the two readings.
7. Repeat the procedure on the other front wheel.

An eccentric bushing on each upper ball joint controls the camber of the wheel on that side of the car.

**To adjust:**

1. Set protractor to prescribed value (see **Front Axle Technical Data**) and place it on chalk marks.
2. Loosen hexagon nut on upper ball joint and turn eccentric bushing until the bubble in the bubble level centers. (See step 6 in **4.1. Removing and Installing Steering Knuckle**.) In its base position the notch in the eccentric bushing points in the driving direction. The bushing can be turned to move the notch a maximum of 90 degrees to the left and 90 degrees to the right of the base position.
3. After adjusting camber, tighten the cam securing nut to:
   M 10 x 1    29 to 36 ft. lbs. (4 to 5 mkg)
   or
   M 12 x 1.5    36 to 51 ft. lbs. (5 to 7 mkg)

If it has not been necessary to back off the self-locking nuts on ball joints more than one thread when adjusting camber, do not replace them with new ones.

### Checking and Adjusting Toe Angle

A track gauge, shown in Fig. 84 is required for these procedures.

**To check:**

1. Place front wheels in straight-ahead position. (Center steering wheel.)
2. Position track gauge in front of wheels (Fig. 84).

**Fig. 84.** Track gauge is the set-up shown here for adjusting toe angle and checking alignment of wheels.

3. Locate the gauge pins on the wheel rims level with the wheel centers.
4. Set gauge to zero and make a chalk mark on rim at point of pin contact on wheel.
5. Roll vehicle forward half a turn of the wheels.
6. Position track gauge behind wheels and locate pins on rims at chalk mark made previously.
7. Take the reading and check against **Front Axle Technical Data** at end of section.

Toe is adjusted by lengthening or shortening the tie rods. When tie rods are located behind front axle (as on the VW), lengthening them increases toe-in. During this adjustment procedure, the steering must remain in the center position, as set by the marking ring on the worm spindle. If center position is disturbed in adjustment of toe-in, it must be re-set. To keep steering centered while toe adjustment is made, you must be careful to lengthen or shorten both tie rods by same amount.

The left ends of both the long and short tie rods have left-hand threads. Therefore, lengthen rods by turning adjusting sleeves (or tubes) toward front of car. Shorten rods by turning sleeves toward rear of car.

**To adjust:**

1. Loosen clamp nuts on short tie rod.
2. Loosen long tie rod.
   a. On 1966–67 cars by loosening clamp nuts.
   b. On 1968–69 cars by loosening the nut for the tapered ring or clamp nut.
3. Correct toe.
   a. Turn tie rod sleeves toward front of car to increase toe-in.
   b. Turn tie rod sleeves toward rear of car to decrease toe-in.
4. Retighten clamp nuts.
5. Recheck center position of steering.
6. Check toe-in adjustment.
7. Road test car.

**NOTE —**
If steering wheel spoke is at an angle when driving straight ahead, steering center position needs correction. One tie rod must be lengthened, the other shortened by the same amount. If tie rods are shortened or lengthened, then toe-in is not changed. Which rod is to be lengthened and which shortened will depend on angle of the steering wheel spoke (Fig. 85). Under no condition is position of spoke to be changed by repositioning steering wheel on column.

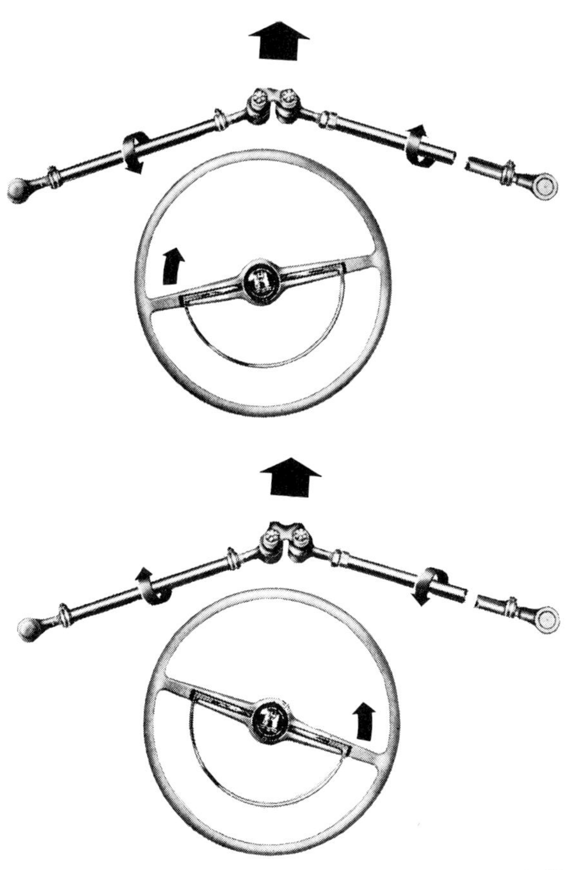


**Fig. 85.** Tie-rod adjustment is required when steering wheel spoke is at an angle in straight-ahead driving. Correction above requires shortening of right rod, lengthening of left rod by same amount. Arrows around rods show directions of turn for adjusting sleeves to make correction. Situation below is just the opposite, and it requires the opposite adjustments of the tie rods, as shown.

**Adjusting Wheel Lock Angle**

The steering geometry is arranged to make the inside wheel turn more sharply on a curve than the outside wheel does. In other words, the angle of turn of the inside wheel is greater than the angle of turn of the outside wheel. The difference is only a few degrees but is significant in improving the handling quality of the car and in reducing tire wear.

The amount of turn possible on either side to the wheel lock is limited. Contact of the back of the steering knuckle with the torsion arm link of the outside wheel on the curve stops the movement. The angles of maximum lock are:

| Model | Inside Wheel | Outside Wheel |
|---|---|---|
| All types | 34 ± 2 degrees | 27 to 28 degrees |

This adjustment gives the car a turning circle of about 36 feet (11 meters). Various factors, mainly faults in the steering geometry, can cause deviations from these values.

## 10.17 Troubleshooting the Steering System

**Table b** lists some steering system troubles that may be encountered. Probable causes and recommended remedies are given.

***WARNING —***
*Road safety depends on correct functioning of the steering system. Rather than risk a malfunction, take your car to an Authorized VW Dealer's workshop for all work on the steering system.*

**Table b. Troubleshooting the Steering System**

| Symptom | Cause | Remedy |
|---|---|---|
| 1. Lock angle of one wheel too big or too small | Steering geometry not correct | Check the difference in outside wheel turn when the inside wheel is turned 20 degrees.<br>Check drop arm, tie rods and steering arms for distortion. |
| 2. Turning circle too large at full lock on either side. | Lock angle too small on both sides | Grind down the front boss for backplate securing screw on both steering knuckles until the lock angle is correct. |
| 3. Turning circle too small at full lock on either side (wheels rubbing fenders) | Lock angle too great on both sides | Use a longer backplate screw M 10 x 1.5 and tighten to 29 to 33 ft. lbs. (4.0 to 4.5 mkg). Grind off the projecting end of the bolt till the lock angle is correct. |
| 4. Turning circle too large or too small at full lock on one side only | Lock angle of both wheels too large or too small on one side | Apply the remedy given at 2 or 3 to one wheel only. If the defect is apparent on the left-hand lock, carry out the repair to the right-hand wheel and vice-versa. |

Adjustment of the wheel lock angles is obtained through the two adjustable stop screws on the front axle beam, shown in Fig. 86.

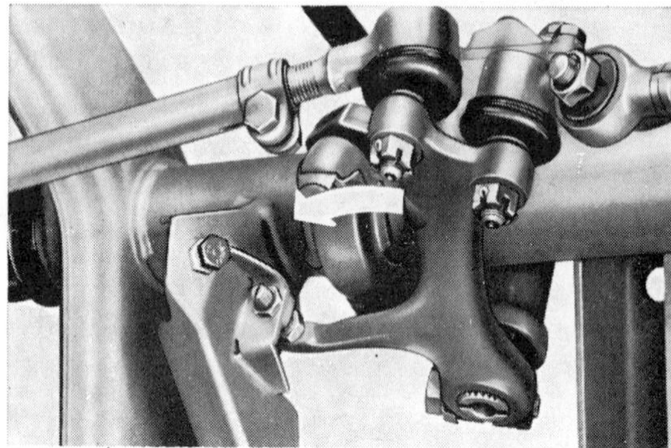

© 1972 VWoA—399

**Fig. 86.** Wheel lock angle is adjusted with screws in the steering stop on the axle beam, just ahead of the white arrow. Drop arm is in contact with other end of one screw now. When arm turns in direction of arrow, another part will make contact with visible end of the other screw. Screws can be turned in or out.

When correcting the wheel lock, the screws in the steering stops on the axle beam must be set so that there is always a gap of 0.4 ± 0.04 inch (10 mm ± 1 mm) between upper torsion arm and tire. See Fig. 87.

© 1972 VWoA—400

**Fig. 87.** Clearance between upper torsion arm and tire must be maintained through steering stop screw adjustments (Fig. 86). Here feeler gauge is used to check gap, which should be kept at 0.4 ± 0.04 inch.

This measurement, which is taken with the vehicle lifted and the wheels turned to full lock, gives adequate clearance between wheel housing and wheels under all load conditions.

## 11. FRONT AXLE TECHNICAL DATA

### I. General Data

| | | |
|---|---|---|
| Wheelbase | | 94.5 in. (2400 mm) |
| Track, front (at permissible total weight) | drum brakes | 51.6 in. (1310 mm) |
| | disc brakes | 51.8 in. (1316 mm) |
| Turning circle between curbs | | 34.2 ft. (10.5 m) |
| Turning circle between walls | | 36 ft. (11.0 m) |
| Torsion arm/Tire gap—in wheel lock condition | | 0.4 ± .04 in. (10 mm ± 1 mm) |
| Front axle load at permissible total weight | | 1080 lbs. (490 kg) |
| Stabilizer bar diameter | | 0.47 in. (12 mm) |
| Torsion bars | length | 37.6 in. (954 mm) |
| | number of leaves | 10 |
| Steering gear ratio | | 19.4 |
| Overall steering ratio | Sedan<br>Karmann Ghia | 14.35<br>14.14 |
| Steering wheel turns from lock | | 2½ |
| Steering wheel hub/switch gap | | 0.04-0.08 in. (1-2 mm) |

### II. Specifications for Vehicle Alignment

| | |
|---|---|
| Test conditions: Instrument and wheel mirrors properly set<br>Vehicle unladen<br>Correct tire pressures (for permissible total weight)<br>Suspension free of tension<br>Vehicle aligned correctly | |
| Note<br>All track values preceded by the sign + refer to toe-in, − refer to toe-out. | |
| 1. 10 angular minutes equal a toe angle of (with 15″ wheels) | 0.05″ (1.2 mm) |
| 2. Total toe-in without pressure on wheels (front) | +30′ ± 15′ |
| 3. Total toe-in with pressure on wheels (front) | +5′ ± 15′ |
| 4. Pressure applied to wheels (front) | 22 ± 4 lbs. (10 ± 2 kg) |
| 5. Maximum permissible difference between tow-in values (wheels pressed—not pressed) | maximum 25′ |

## II. Specifications for Vehicle Alignment (continued)

| | |
|---|---|
| 6. Front wheel camber in straight-ahead position | 0° 30′ ± 20′ |
| Maximum permissible difference between left and right sides | 30′ |
| 7. Difference in wheel angle at 20° lock to left and right (not pressed) | |
| to the left | −1° 20′ ± 30′ |
| to the right | −2° 10′ ± 30′ |
| Maximum permissible difference between sides | 1° |
| 8. Offset between stub axles in direction of motion | maximum 0.314 in. (8 mm) |
| 9. Caster angle of a wheel (front), | 3° 20′ ± 1° |
| corresponds to the camber difference of a wheel on a steering lock from 20° left to 20° right | 2° 15′ ± 40′ |

**Rear Axle Specifications***

| Vehicles with Swing Axles | |
|---|---|
| Test conditions: Spring plates (torsion bars) correctly set (after at least 300 miles in use) | |
| 1. Camber: | |
| Model 11 Beetle from chassis No. 117 000 001 | +1° ± 1° |
| Model 14 K.G. from chassis No. 147 000 003 | +15′ ± 1° |
| Model 15 Beetle Convertible up to chassis No. 157 000 002 | +15′ ± 1° |
| All models (includes K.G.) up to chassis No. 116 1021 298 | +2° 30′ ± 1° |
| 2. Permissible minimum camber: | |
| Model 11 Beetle from chassis No. 117 000 001 | −1° |
| Model 14 K.G. from chassis No. 147 000 003 | −1° 30′ |
| Model 15 Beetle Convertible up to chassis No. 157 000 002 | −1° 30′ |
| All models (includes K.G.) up to chassis No. 116 1021 298 | 0° |
| 3. Maximum permissible camber difference between sides | 20′ |
| 4. Total toe with camber correctly set | −5′ ± 10′ |
| 5. Maximum permissible toe deviation in wheel alignment | 10′ |

| Vehicles with Double Joint Rear Axles | |
|---|---|
| 1. Camber, all models | −1° 20′ ± 40′ |
| 2. Maximum permissible camber difference between sides | 45′ |
| 3. Total rear wheel toe with camber correctly set | 0° ± 15′ |
| 4. Maximum permissible toe deviation in wheel alignment | 10′ |

***The rear axle must conform to these specifications before any alignment work is attempted on the front axle.**

4

## III. Tolerances and Wear Limits

| Designation | | On Installation | Wear Limit |
|---|---|---|---|
| **Axle beam** | | | |
| 1. Torsion arm bearings in axle beam | | | |
| a. Seat for upper needle bearing | diameter | 1.809-1.810 in. (45.97-45.99 mm) | — |
| Needle bearing | diameter | 1.811 in. (46.0 mm) | — |
| Thrust rings | diameter | — | — |
| Oversize | diameter | 1.817-1.818 in. (46.17-46.19 mm) | — |
| Needle bearing | diameter | 1.819 in. (46.2 mm) | — |
| Thrust rings | diameter | — | |
| b. Seat for lower needle bearing | diameter | 1.967-1.968 in. (49.97-49.99 mm) | — |
| Needle bearing | diameter | 1.968 in. (50.0 mm) | — |
| Oversize | diameter | 1.975-1.976 in. (50.17-50.19 mm) | — |
| Needle bearing | diameter | 1.976 in. (50.2 mm) | — |
| 2. Bearing bushing for: | | | |
| a. Torsion arm, upper | ream out to | 1.463-1.465 in. (37.20-37.25 mm) | 1.47 in. (37.38 mm)**** |
| b. Torsion arm, lower | ream out to | 1.463-1.465 in. (37.20-37.25 mm)* | 1.47 in. (37.38 mm)**** |
| 3. Torsion arm | twist | max. 0.02 in. (0.5 mm)* | — |

continued on next page

### III. Tolerances and Wear Limits (continued)

| Designation | | On Installation | Wear Limit |
|---|---|---|---|
| **Steering knuckle, link pins, ball joints** | | | |
| 1. Steering knuckle/stub axle | distortion | .006 in. (0.15 mm)* | — |
| Steering knuckle/disc caliper | contact surface distortion | ± 0.002 in. (0.05 mm)** | |
| 2. Torsion arm link pin | diameter | 0.706-0.705 in. (17.94-17.91 mm) | 0.700 in. (17.80 mm) |
| 3. Ball joints, upper | play | max. 0.02 in. (0.5 mm) | 0.08 in. (2.0 mm) |
| Ball joints, lower | play | max. 0.02 in. (0.5 mm) | 0.04 in. (1.0 mm) |
| 4. Wheel bearings (taper roller) | play | 0.001-0.005 in. (0.03-0.12 mm)*** | — |

***From Chassis No. 116 000 001  **Karmann Ghia  ***If axle is noisy, adjust to lower limit  ****Valid only for metal bushings**

### IV. Torque Specifications

The quality grading of bolts and nuts according to DIN standards as used previously is being replaced by a tensile strength classification according to ISO (European) regulations. During a transitional period, bolts and nuts will be used which can be marked either according to the old system (quality grade) or according to the new standards (tensile strength). Bolts with equivalent qualities can be interchanged.

| Location | Description | Thread | Quality Grade | Tensile Class | mkg | ft. lb. |
|---|---|---|---|---|---|---|
| Front axle to frame | bolt | M 12 x 1.5 | 8 G | 8.8 | 5.0 | 36 |
| Body bolt to front axle | bolt | — | — | — | 2 | 14 |
| Shock absorber to axle beam side plate | nut | M 10<br>M 12 x 1.5 | 6 G<br>10 K | 6<br>10.9 | 2.0<br>3.0-3.5 | 14<br>22-25 |
| Shock absorber to lower torsion arm | nut | M 10 | 6 G | 8 | 3.0-3.5 | 22-25 |
| Steering damper to axle | bolt | M 10 | 8 G | 8.8 | 4.0-4.5 | 29-32 |
| Steering damper to tie-rod | nut | M 10 x 1 | 6 G | 8 | 2.5 | 18 |
| Tie-rod to steering knuckle and drop arm | slotted nut | M 12 x 1.5<br>M 10 x 1 | 8 G<br>— | 10<br>8 | 3.0*<br>2.5* | 22*<br>18* |
| Lock nut for taper ring on tie-rod | nut | M 14 x 1.5 | 6 G | — | 2.5 | 18 |
| Bolt in clamp for tie-rod | bolt | M 8 x 1 | 8 G | 8.8 | 1.5 | 11 |
| Set screw for torsion bar | socket hd. screw | M 14 x 1.5 | CK 15 Kv | — | 4.0-5.0 | 29-36 |
| Lock nut for set screw | nut | M 14 x 1.5 | 6 G | — | 4.0-5.0 | 29-36 |
| Screw for wheel bearing clamp nut | socket hd. screw | M 7 | 10 K | 10.9 | 1.0-1.3 | 7-10 |
| Brake backing plate to steering knuckle | bolt | M 10 | 9 S 20 K | — | 5 | 36 |
| Caliper to steering knuckle | bolt | M 10 | 10 K | 10.9 | 4.0 | 29 |
| Steering ball joint to steering knuckle | self-locking nut | M 12 x 1.5<br>M 10 x 1 | 6 S<br>— | 8<br>— | 5.0-7.0<br>4.0-5.0 | 36-51<br>29-36 |
| Steering gearbox to front axle | bolt | M 10 | 8 G | 8.8 | 2.5-3.0 | 18-22 |
| Worm shaft to steering coupling | bolt | M 8 | 10 K | 10.9 | 2.0-2.5 | 14-18 |
| Drop arm to roller shaft | bolt | M 12 x 1.5 | 8 G | 8.8 | 7.0 | 51 |
| Lock nut for drop arm shaft adjusting screw | nut | M 10 x 1 | 5 S | — | 2.5 | 18 |
| Lock nut for worm spindle adjusting screw | nut | M 35 x 1.5 | 9 S K 20 | — | 5.0-6.0 | 36-42 |
| Cover for steering gear housing | bolt | M 8 x 1.25 | 8 G | — | 2.0-2.5 | 14-18 |
| Cancelling ring to steering wheel | fillister hd. screw | AM 3.5 | 8 G | 8.8 | 0.5 | 3.5 |
| Steering wheel to column | nut | M 18 x 1.5 | 6 G | — | 5.0 | 36 |
| Steering column tube attaching plate to instrument panel | bolt | — | — | — | 0.5-1 | 4-7 |
| Steering column switch to attaching plate | bolt | — | — | — | 0.5-1 | 4-7 |
| Column switch clamp to housing | bolt | — | — | — | 0.5-1 | 4-7 |
| Steering coupling flange to disc | nut | M 8 | 6 G | 8 | 1.5 | 11 |
| Column to coupling flange | bolt | M 8 | 10 K | 10.9 | 1.5 | 11 |

***Turn further to cotter pin hole if necessary**

# TRANSMISSION AND REAR AXLE

## Contents


**1. General Description (manual transmission)** . . 4
- Transmission Case . . . . . . . . . . . . . 4
- Transmission . . . . . . . . . . . . . . . . 4
- Final Drive . . . . . . . . . . . . . . . . . 6
- Rear Suspension . . . . . . . . . . . . . . 6
- Lubrication . . . . . . . . . . . . . . . . . 6

**2. Removing and Installing Rear Axle (complete with transmission)** . . . . . . . . . . 6
- 2.1 Removing and Installing Clutch Release Bearing . . . . . . . . . . . . . . . . . 8
- 2.2 Removing and Installing Clutch Operating Shaft . . . . . . . . . . . . . . . . . 9
- 2.3 Replacing Oil Seal for Main Drive Shaft . . 10
- 2.4 Replacing Oil Seal or Rear Wheel Bearing 11
- 2.5 Removing and Installing Rear Axle Tube and Shaft (swing axle) . . . . . . . . . . . 13
- 2.6 Replacing Rear Axle Boots (rear axle installed) . . . . . . . . . . . . . 16

**3. Transmission and Final Drive** . . . . . . . . . . 17
- 3.1 Removing and Installing Differential and Transmission (swing axle) . . . . . . . . . 19
- 3.2 Disassembling and Assembling Gear Carrier . . . . . . . . . . . . . . . . . . 23
- 3.3 Adjusting Shift Forks . . . . . . . . . . . . 26
- 3.4 Disassembling and Assembling Drive Pinion . . . . . . . . . . . . . . . . . . . 28
- 3.5 Adjustment of Concave Washer . . . . . . 32
- 3.6 Calculating Shim Thickness . . . . . . . . 33
- 3.7 Disassembling and Assembling Main Drive Shaft . . . . . . . . . . . . . . . . . . . 34

**4. The Differential** . . . . . . . . . . . . . . . . . . 35
- 4.1 Disassembling and Assembling Differential (swing axle) . . . . . . . . . . . . . . . . . 36
- 4.2 Removing and Installing Differential (standard transmission, double-joint axle) 37
- 4.3 Disassembling and Assembling Differential (double-joint axle) . . . . . . . . . . . . . 40
- 4.4 Axial Play (double-joint axle) . . . . . . . . 43

**5. Adjustment of Pinion and Ring Gear** . . . . . . 44
- 5.1 Gear Fit . . . . . . . . . . . . . . . . . . . 44
- 5.2 What Needs Adjusting and When . . . . . 45
- 5.3 Adjusting Pinion (swing and double-joint axles, standard transmission) . . . . . . . 47
- 5.4 Finding Measurement **e** (swing axle differential) . . . . . . . . . . . 47
- 5.5 Finding Measurement **e** (double-joint axle) 48
- 5.6 Finding $S_3$ Shim Thickness . . . . . . . . . 49
- 5.7 Adjusting Ring Gear (swing axle) . . . . . 50
- 5.8 Adjusting Ring Gear (double-joint axle, standard transmission) . . . . . . . . . . . 55

**6. Gearshift Lever** . . . . . . . . . . . . . . . . . 59
- 6.1 Removing and Installing Gearshift Lever (all cars) . . . . . . . . . . . . . . . . . . . 59
- 6.2 Removing and Installing Shift Rod . . . . . 60


5

**7. Torsion Bars (swing axle)** . . . . . . . . . . . . 61
7.1 Removing and Installing Torsion Bars . . . 61

**8. Spring Plates** . . . . . . . . . . . . . . . . . . . 63
8.1 Setting Spring Plates . . . . . . . . . . . . 63

**9. Rear Wheel Alignment** . . . . . . . . . . . . . . 65
9.1 Checking Rear Wheel Alignment Graphically . . . . . . . . . . . . . . . . . . 67
9.2 Checking Toe-in/Toe-out Angles and Axle Alignment by Calculation . . . . . . . . . . 67
9.3 Correcting Toe-in/Toe-out and Alignment 67
9.4 Rear Wheel Camber . . . . . . . . . . . . 68
Measuring Camber . . . . . . . . . . . . . 68
Adjusting Camber . . . . . . . . . . . . . . 68
9.5 Wheel Alignment Check . . . . . . . . . . 68

**10. Shock Absorbers** . . . . . . . . . . . . . . . . . 69
10.1 Removing and Installing Shock Absorbers (rear axle) . . . . . . . . . . . . . . . . . . 69
10.2 Shock Absorber Specifications . . . . . . 69

**11. Equalizer Springs** . . . . . . . . . . . . . . . . . 70
11.1 Removing and Installing Equalizer Springs 70

**12. Double-joint Axle** . . . . . . . . . . . . . . . . . 71
12.1 General Description . . . . . . . . . . . . . 71
Drive Shafts . . . . . . . . . . . . . . . . . 72
12.2 Removing and Installing Constant Velocity Joints . . . . . . . . . . . . . . . . . . . . . 73
12.3 Disassembling and Assembling Constant Velocity Joints . . . . . . . . . . . . . . . . 75
12.4 Removing and Installing Double-joint Axle 77
12.5 Adjusting Torsion Bars . . . . . . . . . . . 81
12.6 Adjusting Axle . . . . . . . . . . . . . . . . 83
12.7 Aligning Rear Wheels . . . . . . . . . . . . 83
12.8 Disassembling and Assembling Diagonal Arm . . . . . . . . . . . . . . . . . . . . . . 84

**13. Transmission and Rear Axle Technical Data**

Technical Data on the **TRANSMISSION AND REAR AXLE** will be found under **23. Transmission Technical Data** in **AUTOMATIC STICK SHIFT.**

**TABLES**

a. Circlip Thicknesses . . . . . . . . . . . . . . . . . 32
b. Sleeve Lengths . . . . . . . . . . . . . . . . . . . 44
c. Required Adjustments for Repaired Parts . . . . 46
d. Symbols Used in Ring Gear/Pinion Adjustment . 46
e. Shim Measurements . . . . . . . . . . . . . . . . 49
f. Shims Supplied as $S_3$ Replacement Parts . . . . 49
g. Shims Supplied as $S_1$ and $S_2$ Replacement Parts 54
h. Shim Combinations ($S_1$ and $S_2$) . . . . . . . . . . 54
i. Shim Thicknesses ($S_1$) . . . . . . . . . . . . . . . 57
j. Shims Supplied as $S_2$ Replacements Parts . . . . 58
k. Shim Combinations (double-joint axle) . . . . . . 58
l. Rear Wheel Camber Angles and Track Values . . 64
m. Fault Diagnosis Chart . . . . . . . . . . . . . . . 68
n. Rear Shock Absorber Specifications . . . . . . . 69
o. Spring Plate Setting Angles . . . . . . . . . . . . 82
p. Setting Data for the Double-Joint Rear Axle (empty) . . . . . . . . . . . . . . . . . . . . . . . 84

# Transmission and Rear Axle

In the VW cars covered in this Manual the engine, transmission and rear axle are bolted together to form a single assembly mounted at the rear of the vehicle. Two types of transmission are found in these cars, the standard manual transmission and the Automatic Stick Shift. There are also two types of rear axle, the swing half-axle and the double-joint axle. The 1966, 1967 and 1968 cars with manually-operated transmission have the swing axle. The 1969 cars with manual shift have the double-joint axle, and so do all the cars equipped with Automatic Stick Shift.

5

**NOTE —**
This section **(TRANSMISSION AND REAR AXLE)** covers in full the swing and double-joint axles. It also covers the Automatic Stick Shift components that are identical with Standard Transmission parts. For descriptions and discussions of parts unique to the Automatic Stick Shift cars see Section 6 **(AUTOMATIC STICK SHIFT).**

## 1. GENERAL DESCRIPTION
(manual transmission)

The manual transmission offers four forward speeds and reverse. The gear shift lever with which the different speeds are selected is installed in a housing on the car frame tunnel, between the two front seats. As shown in Fig. 1, the lever works in the familiar H-shift pattern. In the shift to reverse, the lever is first depressed, then moved all the way to the left and to the rear.

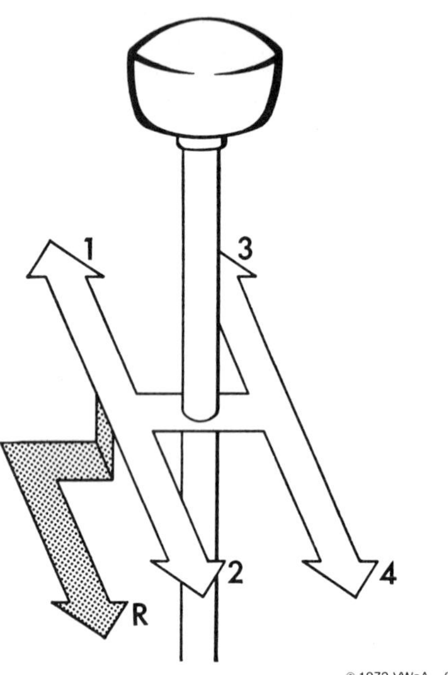


**Fig. 1.** Gearshift pattern is the familiar H one, shown here. When shifting, press clutch pedal all the way down and follow the H-pattern. Attempting to move lever diagonally can jam the linkage.

The Automatic Stick Shift, which will be described in detail in a later separate section, offers three forward driving ranges and reverse. The Automatic Stick Shift operates in an H-pattern roughly similar to the pattern for the manual transmission but requires less shifting of gears in normal operation of the car.

### Transmission Case

The transmission case, which contains the transmission, final drive and differential (see Fig. 2), is die-cast in one piece of light alloy metal. It is attached to the car frame at three points with rubber mounts. At the rear of the case there is an integral housing for the clutch with a flange to which the engine is attached. The gear carrier closes the forward end of the case and holds the selector shafts and the front bearings for the gear shafts. Midway inside the case there is a deeply-ribbed partition separating the transmission from the differential. The bearings for the main drive shaft from the engine and for the pinion drive to the ring gear are fitted in this partition. At each side of the transmission case, somewhat toward the rear, a rear axle tube is attached to the hemispherical surface of a cover for the final drive.

### Transmission

The manual transmission is fully synchronized in the forward speeds, with the gears in constant mesh for quiet operation. The synchronizing units are of the balk or block type, consisting of the hub or clutch gear with shifting plates, the stop rings and operating sleeve. (You will hear other names for comparable parts in similar systems—for instance, "shifter" plate, "blocking" or "balk" ring and "synchronizer" sleeve.) The synchronizer unit for 1st and 2nd gears is on the drive pinion shaft, the unit for 3rd and 4th gears on the main drive shaft.

The purpose of the synchromesh transmission, of course, is to prevent clashing of gears when they are engaged while the car is moving. The synchromesh brings the mating gears to the same speed before the engagement is made. This equalization of speed is accomplished through the braking effect of friction between matching coned surfaces on the stop ring and the gear to be engaged.

The shift fork moves the sleeve and hub against the stop ring and toward the gear to be engaged. As the matching coned surfaces on ring and gear come together, the frictional braking effect quickly equalizes the speeds. Under the rotational forces involved, the stop ring turns just enough to allow the ends of the three shifting plates of the synchronizer unit to enter three slots on the circumference of the stop ring. Now the ring is held to the same rotational speed as the synchronizer unit. Under continuing pressure from the shift fork, the sleeve slides across chamfered teeth on the stop ring to mesh with chamfered teeth on the driven gear. The engagement is complete, and since the hub of the unit is splined (or keyed) to the shaft, the driven gear and shaft must turn together.

For correct operation of the synchros it is of the utmost importance to release the clutch completely. The clutch pedal travel (see **19. Clutch** in **ENGINE** section) should be checked regularly. Insufficient declutching or dragging of the clutch plate (by distortion of the plate or damage to the plate lining) wears the synchronizer stop rings rapidly. A broken plate lining can lock the clutch plate and prevent synchronization, making it impossible to shift.

Use only approved clutch linings. Whenever the engine has been removed make sure on re-installation that the clutch releases fully. With engine running, declutch and shift into reverse several times to check the work.

**Fig. 2.** Transmission case with gears is shown in cutaway view from the side (upper) and from above (lower). The right side of the pictures is toward the rear of the car.

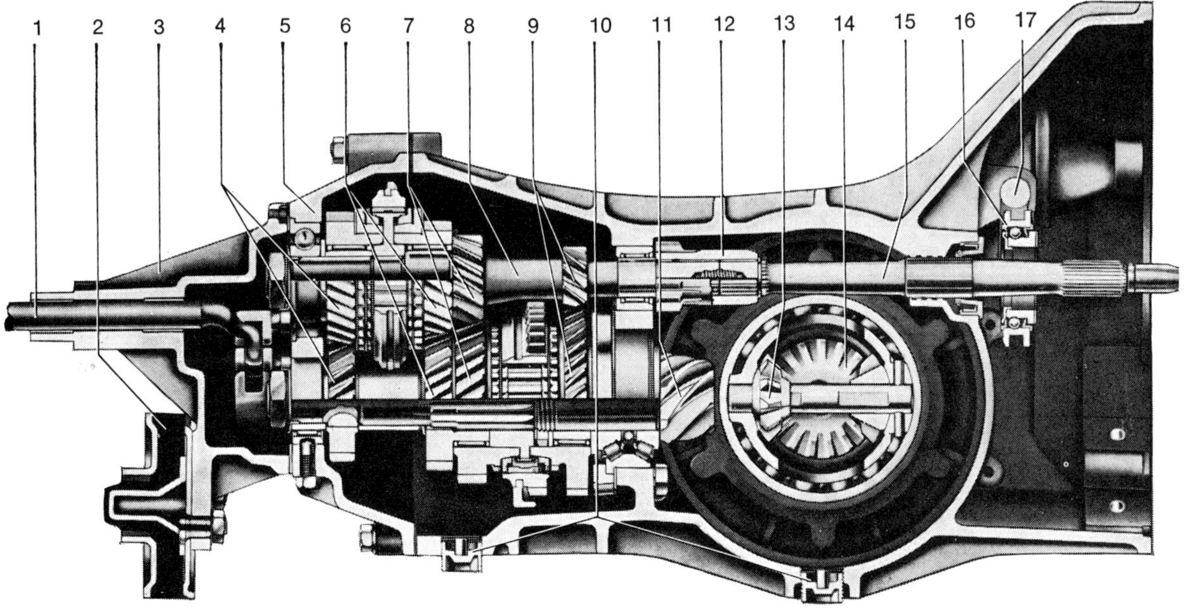

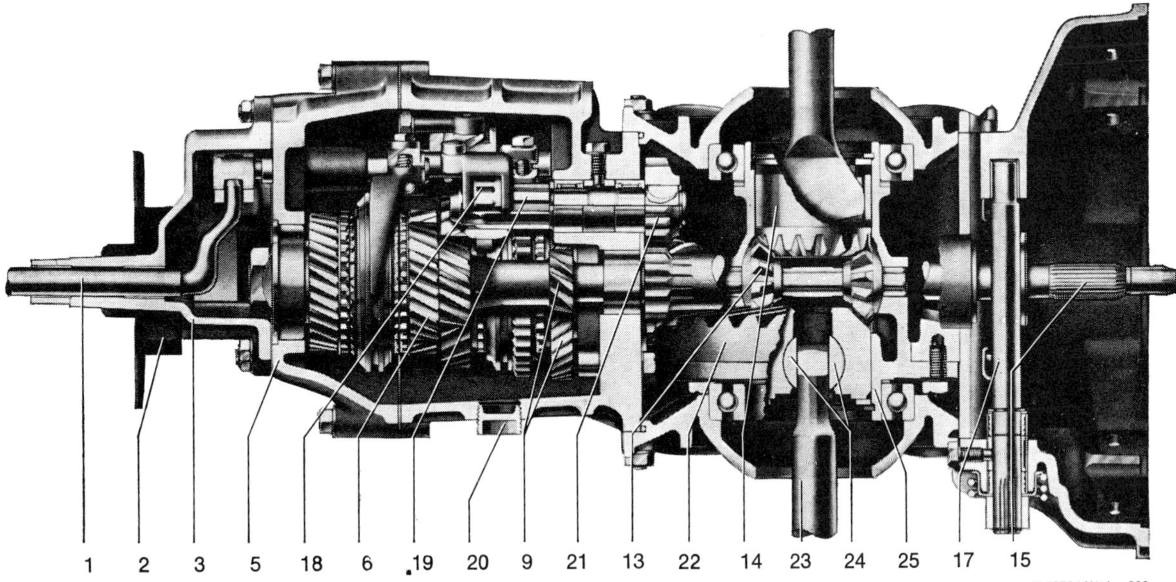




1. Inner shift lever
2. Bonded rubber mounting
3. Gearshift housing
4. 4th gear
5. Gear carrier
6. 3rd gear
7. 2nd gear
8. Main drive shaft, front
9. 1st gear
10. Oil drain plugs
11. Drive pinion
12. Reverse gear
13. Differential pinion
14. Differential side gear
15. Main drive shaft, rear
16. Clutch release bearing
17. Clutch operating shaft
18. Reverse sliding gear
19. Reverse shaft
20. Oil filler plug
21. Reverse drive gear
22. Ring gear
23. Rear axle shaft
24. Fulcrum plate
25. Differential housing

### Final Drive

The helically-cut drive pinion turning the ring gear (also known as crown wheel) transmits the engine power to the rear axles and wheels by way of the two bevel differential side gears. Silent operation and service life of the final drive mechanism depend on precise adjustment of the drive pinion and ring gear. The differential side gears allow the rear wheels to turn at different speeds (or one wheel to turn while the other is stopped). This arrangement is necessary because in the same length of time the outside wheel must travel farther than the inside wheel on a turn.

### Rear Suspension

The rear wheels are sprung independently on all models of the car. The trailing spring plate at either end of the rear axle transmits road shock from the wheel to the torsion bar on that side. A spline arrangement anchors the torsion bars at the center of the cross tube. A progressive rubber bumper attached to spring plate and housing for the axle shaft bearing helps to smooth out road bumps in the upper range of the deflection. Hydraulic double-acting shock absorbers dampen road shock by snubbing excessive rebound.

The splines in the torsion bars and spring plates were designed to allow accurate adjustment of the rear wheel suspension.

### Lubrication

The hypoid oil specified for the transmission case lubricates the transmission gears and the differential. Used oil should be drained by removing both magnetic oil drain plugs while the oil is still warm. The plugs should be cleaned carefully before re-installation and the transmission then refilled. See section on **LUBRICATION AND MAINTENANCE.**

## 2. REMOVING AND INSTALLING REAR AXLE (complete with transmission)

The procedure for removing the rear axle with transmission is different for cars prior to 1969 and the 1969 models. Several more steps are required for the earlier models. The following steps are necessary for 1966, 1967 and 1968 cars. Dotted instructions, on the other hand, comprise the complete procedure for 1969 cars.

***WARNING—***
*If you intend to disassemble the rear axle after it has been removed from the vehicle, loosen the axle shaft nuts before lifting the vehicle. If you try to loosen the nuts on the raised car, you will topple the car off the lift.*

**To remove:**

•1. Move shift lever into reverse, 2nd or 4th gear.

•2. Lift up rear seat and disconnect battery.

•3. Remove inspection cover for frame-end near battery.

•4. Remove the bolt of the shifting rod coupling and push transmission shift rod to rear. (See Fig. 3.)

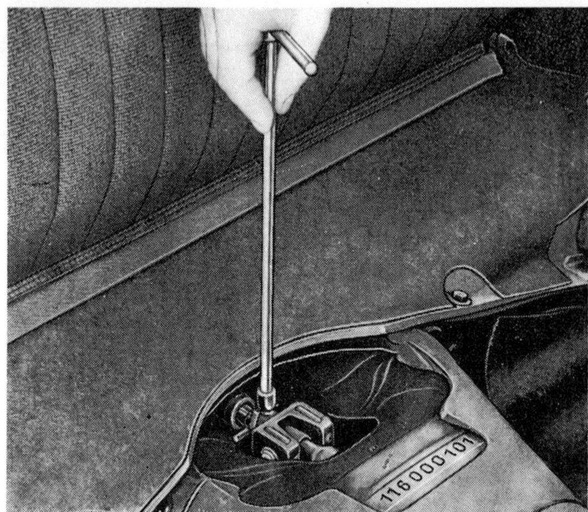




**Fig. 3.** Shifting rod coupling is exposed when inspection cover under rear seat is taken up. Bolt is removed here for withdrawal of coupling from transmission shift rod. (Note location of chassis number.)

5. Take off rear wheels.

•6. Remove engine.

7. Disconnect and cap rear brake hoses.

8. Detach brake cables at parking brake. Remove brake and withdraw cables from guide tubes.

•9. Loosen clamps on axle rubber boots. (On 1969 version disconnect inboard CV joints, hang and cap them.)

10. Remove lower shock absorber mounting bolts.

11. With chisel, carefully cut matching marks on the spring plate and housing of the axle shaft bearing for the correct location in reinstallation. (See Fig. 4.)

***CAUTION—***
*Provide a suitable support for the suspension.*

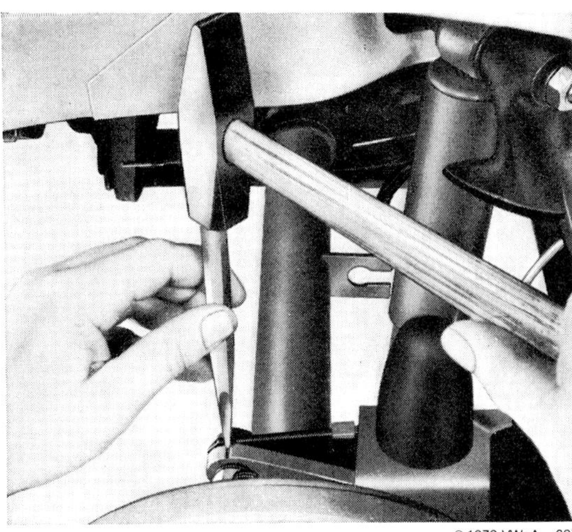
© 1972 VWoA—627

**Fig. 4.** Matching mark is cut on spring plate in line with groove on housing for rear axle bearing to facilitate re-installation.

12. Remove bolts at housing of rear axle shaft bearing. (See Fig. 5.)

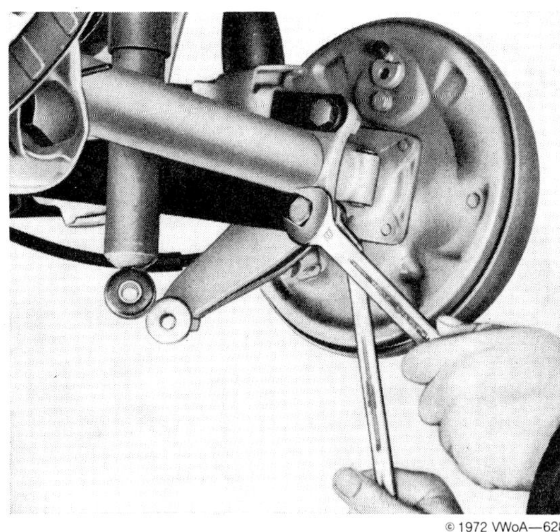
© 1972 VWoA—628

**Fig. 5.** Bearing housing on rear axle is held with bolts, which are taken off here for removal of axle.

•13. Disconnect clutch cable from clutch operating shaft lever, which is on the left cover of final drive. Slide off the rubber boot and withdraw cable and sleeve from the bracket.

•14. Disconnect cable terminals 30 and 50 at starter.

•15. Remove attaching nuts at front mounting of the transmission case (Fig. 6).

© 1972 VWoA—630

**Fig. 6.** Front transmission mounting is seen here. Nuts are taken off prior to removal of the rear axle.

•16. Push floor jack under car and clamp rear axle cradle to rear axle. (For 1969 version use same jack but with adapter for transmission alone.)

•17. With 27 mm box wrench, remove the two bolts at transmission carrier (see Fig. 7).

5

© 1972 VWoA—631

**Fig. 7.** Two bolts shown here fasten transmission carrier to car frame. Carrier and transmission case are bolted together through rubber mountings. Note position of transmission jack here.

•18. Withdraw axle toward the rear on the floor jack and carefully lower jack.

When you are taking the axle off the floor jack, be careful to protect the main drive shaft which protrudes from the case.

**NOTE —**
Now that you are ready to disassemble the transmission or final drive, keep the following points in mind:

•1. **Cleanliness** when you are working on the transmission and final drive is most important. Keep the components clean, but don't scrape dirt off with sharp tools. Use the appropriate solvents instead.
•2. The components you will be handling are **heavy**. When you are lifting or carrying them, be careful.
•3. Some springs are **compressed** and will jump out when tension is relaxed. Be careful.
•4. Follow instructions **closely** and measure **carefully**.

**To install:**

•1. Use floor jack to lift rear axle into position on car. On 1969 car only, use cradle adapter on jack to lift the transmission.

•2. Grease the two transmission carrier mounting bolts and tighten them.

•3. Tighten nuts of mounting plate at front of transmission case.

**NOTE —**
When installing a new rear axle, you should follow the specified sequence in tightening the mounts. First, tighten the nuts of the bonded rubber mounting at the front of the transmission case. Then tighten the nuts of the rear bonded rubber mounting. This procedure will prevent distortion and premature wear of bushings. Follow same sequence if transmission case has been replaced.

•4. Move shift lever into neutral and connect shift rod coupling. Make sure that the point of the coupling screw drops into the recess in correct alignment. Secure screw with a piece of wire. Incorrect installation may make it difficult or even impossible to shift down to 2nd gear and 1st gear, and under certain conditions a shift to 2nd might end up in reverse with the possibility of serious damage to the transmission.

5. Adjust rear wheels. The holes in the spring plates for the bearing flange screws are slotted to allow correct positioning of axle shafts. Make sure the wheels are reset to the previously marked original position.

6. Torque spring plate mounting bolts to 80 ft. lbs. (11 mkg).

7. Securely tighten lower shock absorber mounting bolts.

•8. After engine has been re-installed, adjust clutch pedal free-play to 13/32 to 13/16 inch (10 to 20 mm).

***WARNING —***
*To attempt to loosen or tighten axle shaft nuts while the car is on the lift is very dangerous. You will topple the car over. Always tighten or loosen axle nuts with the car on the ground (Fig. 8).*

© 1972 VWoA—632

**Fig. 8.** Rear axle shaft nuts are torqued (or loosened) only when the car is on the ground, never on a lift.

9. Tighten rear axle shaft nuts with a torque wrench to 217 ft. lbs. (30 mkg), as in Fig. 8. If the cotter pin cannot be inserted at this torque, turn on to the next slot.

10. Bleed and adjust brake system (see **BRAKES**).

**NOTE —**
When installing a new rear axle or replacing the frame, a spring plate or a front-mounting for the transmission case, you must re-adjust the rear wheels. A special optical instrument should be used to align the rear wheels and set up the track, but if one is not available, line up the matching marks in the sides of the spring plates and on the axle flanges. When the optical instrument is used, the marks are matched and then measurements are taken to allow correction of wheel alignment when necessary. Moving the axle flange 1 mm changes toe-in toe-out by 8 minutes.

## 2.1 Removing and Installing Clutch Release Bearing

**To remove:**

1. Remove engine.

***WARNING —***
*The release bearing retaining springs are under tension. Before removing a spring, cover it with a rag.*

2. Take off release bearing retaining springs, as in Fig. 9.

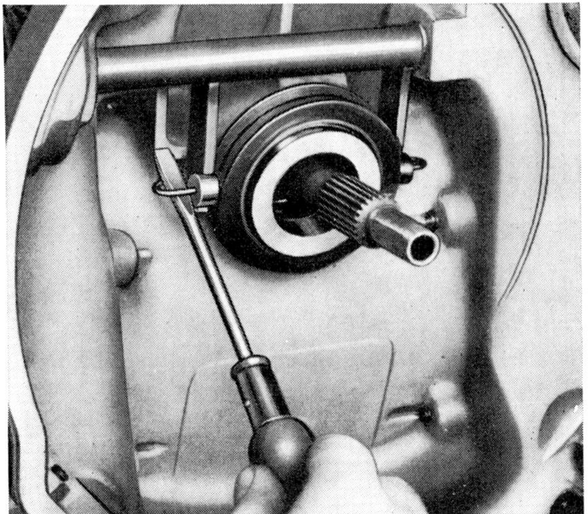

© 1972 VWoA—633

**Fig. 9.** Clutch release bearing is attached to the operating shaft fork with spring retaining clips. Use screwdriver to pry springs loose, but be careful. Springs are under tension.

3. Withdraw release bearing.

**To install:**

1. Check release bearing. The ball thrust bearing requires no maintenance. Wipe it with a clean cloth but do not wash it in gasoline or other solvent. If it is dirty inside or noisy, replace it.
2. With medium sandpaper or emery cloth, lightly smooth the plastic coating of the release bearing and coat the polished surface with molybdenum disulfide (Moly-Kote®) paste. Spraying with Moly-Kote® is sufficient lubrication for a new bearing.
3. Lubricate contact points between fork and bearing lightly with lithium grease. Slide bearing on.
4. Install retaining clips, as in Fig. 10 (see **ENGINE**).

© 1972 VWoA—634

**Fig. 10.** Retaining clip for clutch release bearing must hook snugly around arm of operating shaft fork.

5. Make sure retaining clips fit properly. Bent end must engage behind arm of fork, "a" in Fig. 11.

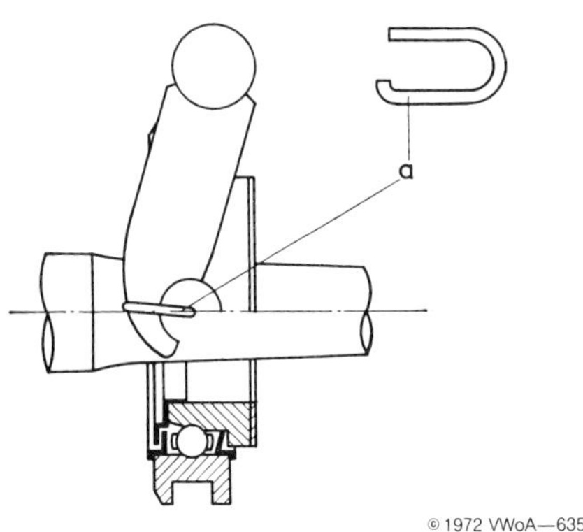


© 1972 VWoA—635

**Fig. 11.** Bent end of clutch release bearing retaining clip is indicated at "a" in this diagram of assembly.

6. Check clutch pedal play after installing engine and adjust if necessary.

## 2.2 Removing and Installing Clutch Operating Shaft

5

**To remove:**

1. Remove clutch release bearing.
2. Remove clutch operating lever circlip (see Fig. 12).

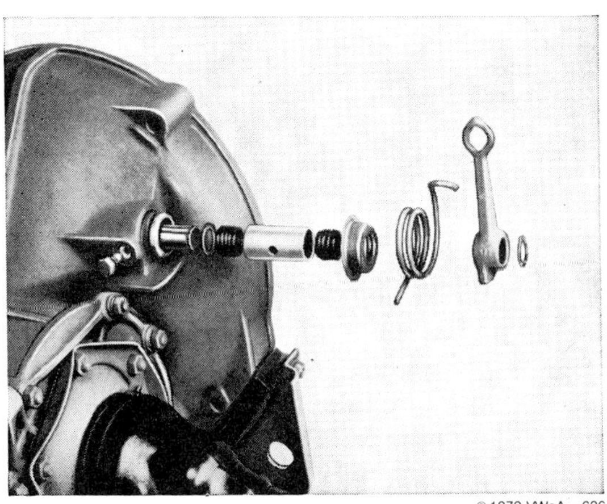

© 1972 VWoA—636

**Fig. 12.** Clutch operating shaft is shown disassembled. From right, parts are: lock ring, operating lever, return spring, return spring seat, rubber bushing, shaft bushing, rubber bushing washer.

3. Take off lever, return spring and seat.

4. Remove operating shaft bushing lock bolt (Fig. 13).

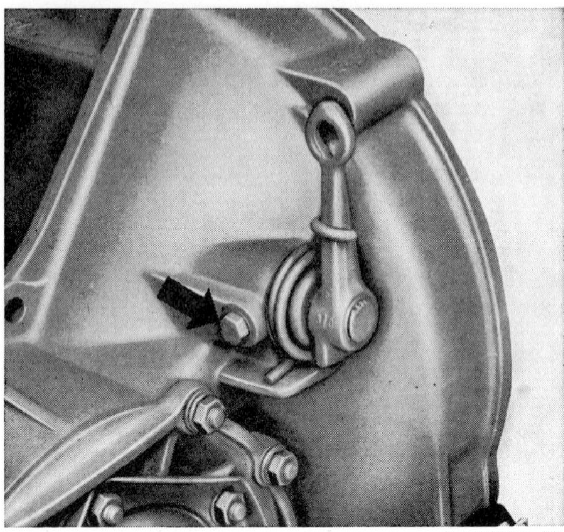



**Fig. 13.** Lock bolt for clutch operating shaft bushing is indicated by the black arrow. Operating lever is in place here.

5. Slide operating shaft to the left, remove bushing, washer, and spacer sleeve.
6. Remove operating shaft to the right, as in Fig. 14.

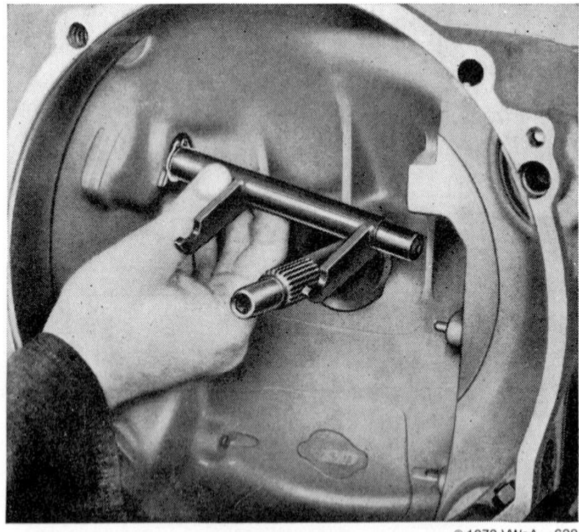



**Fig. 14.** Clutch operating shaft is removed from transmission case after disassembly.

**To install:**

1. Check right hand bushing in the transmission case and replace it if worn.
2. Lubricate operating shaft with lithium grease and install it.
3. Check left bushing and washer for wear. Replace them if necessary.
4. Screw in lock bolt but make sure that cylindrical part of bolt fits in hole in bushing.
5. Check return spring and replace if weak.
6. Push lever on and install circlip.
7. Check position of clutch pedal (see **BODY AND FRAME**).

## 2.3 Replacing Oil Seal for Main Drive Shaft

The following procedures can be carried out with rear axle in place or removed.

**To remove seal:**

1. Remove engine.
2. Remove clutch release bearing.
3. Carefully pry out the damaged seal as in Fig. 15.

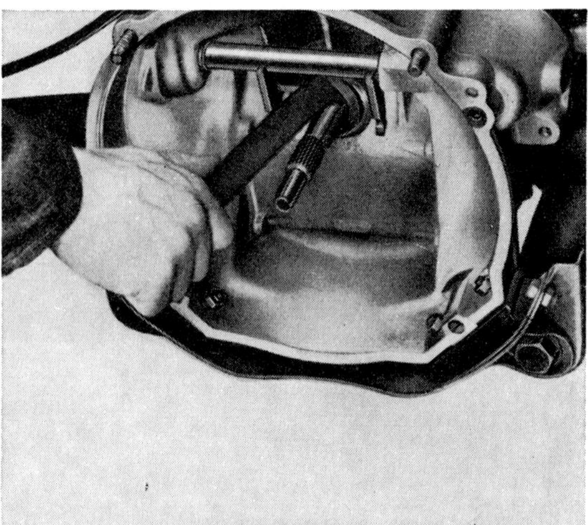



**Fig. 15.** Oil seal around the main drive shaft behind the clutch release bearing is pried out of the transmission case.

**To install:**

1. Lightly coat the exterior of the oil seal with sealing compound. Lubricate main drive shaft and seal lip.

***CAUTION*** —
*Be careful to keep the spring around the seal lip in place.*

2. Slide oil seal onto main drive shaft and drive it into position, as in Fig. 16.

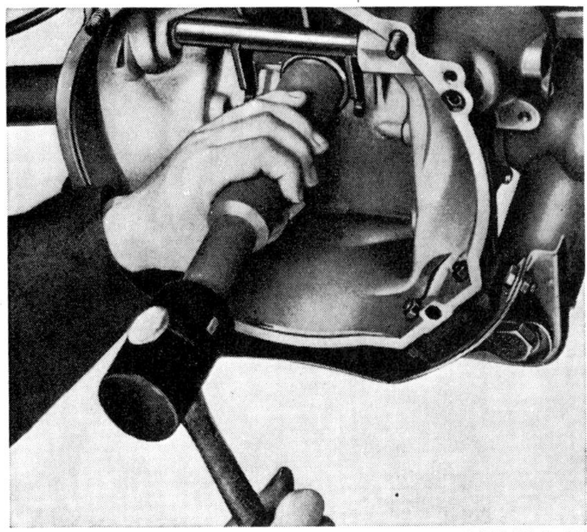

© 1972 VWoA—640

**Fig. 16.** Mallet and sleeve are used here to drive oil seal into place on main drive shaft at rear of case.

**NOTE ——**
On cars from chassis No. 117 812 292, the machined surface at rear end of main drive shaft has been extended and fitted with a new oil seal. The new seal has two lips, one for sealing and the other to keep out dust. The new shaft and seal can be installed in earlier transmissions.

## 2.4 Replacing Oil Seal or Rear Wheel Bearing

Since both the oil seal and wheel bearing are in the same assembly on the rear axle shaft, the removal and installation procedures are the same. The bearings can be removed with the axle on or off the car, but removal of the bearing flange requires a hydraulic press.

**NOTE ——**
A certain amount of oil seepage at the rear wheels is permitted, but leakage calls for replacement of the seal. Experience has shown that a new O-ring and paper gasket will stop leakage.

If only the bearings are to be replaced (axle on car), disconnect the backing plates and suspend them from the car. This way you avoid having to disconnect the brake hoses and parking brake cables.

***WARNING ——***
*To attempt to loosen or tighten axle shaft nuts while the car is on the lift is dangerous. You can topple the car off the lift. Always have the car on the ground when you loosen or tighten axle nuts.*

**To remove:**

1. Take off axle shaft nut and remove brake drum.
2. Remove cover retaining bolts and take off cover and oil seal.
3. Remove brake backing plate and paper gasket.
4. Take off outer spacer, gasket between spacer and ball bearing, washer, and cover gasket.
5. Remove rear wheel bearing and take off inner spacer (see Fig. 17).

© 1972 VWoA—641

**Fig. 17.** Inner spacer ring is pulled off rear axle shaft with puller tool shown in operation here.

5

**To install:**

1. Inspect ball bearing closely and replace it if worn or damaged.
2. Replace both sealing rings.
3. Inspect oil seal. If any sign of damage or poor fit is visible on the lip, replace the seal.
4. Inspect the outer spacer. It must not be scored or cracked or show rust. To prevent damage to the oil seal lip by friction, lightly coat the spacer with oil. Make sure that all components to be installed are absolutely clean. Fig. 18 on the following page shows exploded view of parts.

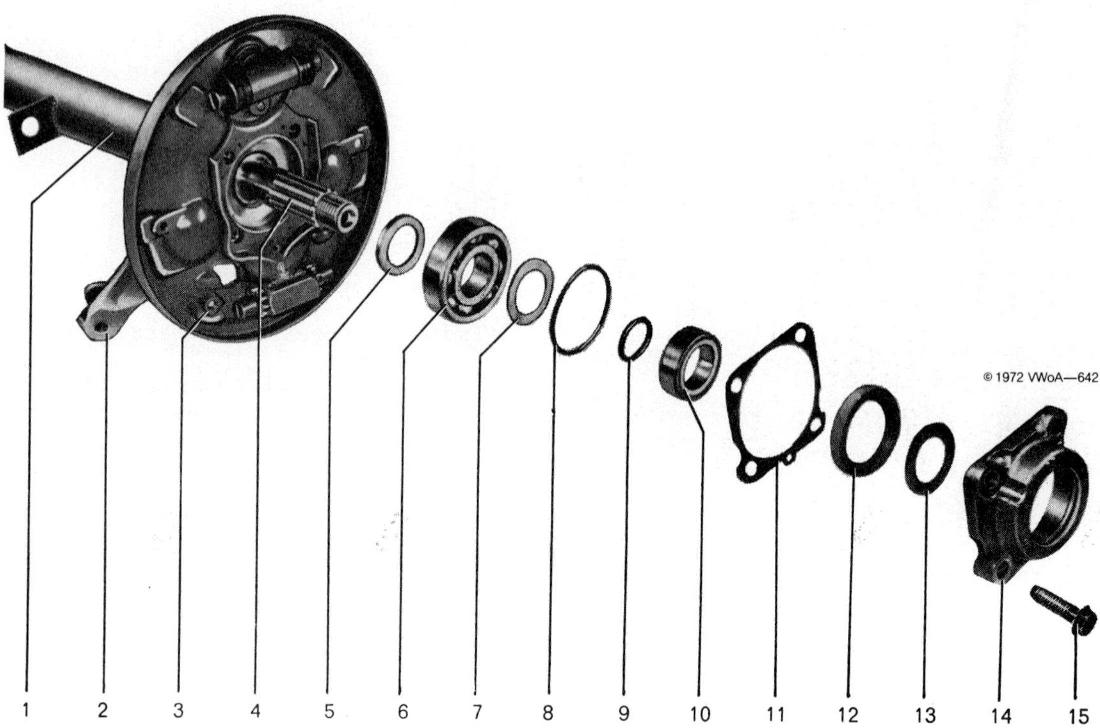


**Fig. 18.** Rear wheel bearing assembly is shown in exploded view.

1. Rear axle tube
2. Bearing housing
3. Brake backing plate
4. Axle shaft
5. Inner spacer
6. Ball bearing
7. Washer
8. Sealing ring
9. Sealing ring
10. Outer spacer
11. Paper gasket
12. Oil seal
13. Oil deflector
14. Cover
15. Bolt

5. Use drift to install bearing.
6. Clean oil drain hole in bearing cover.
7. Install bearing cover, as in Fig. 19.

**Fig. 19.** Cover for rear wheel bearing is installed on axle shaft with oil drain hole down.

8. Check splines in break drum hub. Replace break drum if splines are worn.

***WARNING —***
*There is danger of serious accident from trying to loosen or tighten axle shaft nuts with the vehicle on a lift. Always have car on the ground for these operations.*

9. Torque rear axle shaft nut to 217 ft. lbs. (30 mkg) and secure it with a new cotter pin.
10. Check transmission oil level and refill if necessary. Oil should be up to edge of filler hole.
11. Adjust brakes (see **BRAKES**) and bleed if hydraulic lines were disconnected.

## 2.5 Removing and Installing Rear Axle Tube and Shaft
(swing axle)

**NOTE —**
You will find it easier to remove and install the rear axle tube and shaft if you first take the axle off the car. With the axle removed, you will be able to make the necessary adjustments in any direction. When the axle is on the car, you do not have the same freedom of movement.

**To remove:**

1. Withdraw brake drum. Remove bearing cover and brake backing plate and pull off rear wheel ball bearing. The relative positions of these parts can be seen schematically in Fig. 20 and in exploded view in Fig. 21.

**Fig. 20.** Cross section of assembly at wheel end of swing axle shows location of bearing and flange.

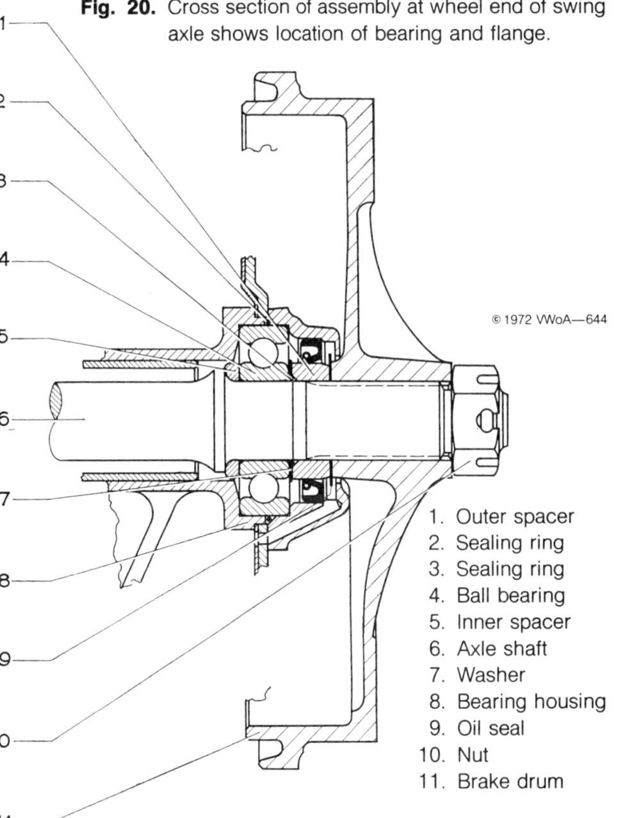

**Fig. 21.** Swing rear axle is shown here pulled out of the transmission case and partly disassembled. The exploded view is arranged to show how the inboard parts are assembled on the axle shaft and also how the shaft fits into the differential gear.

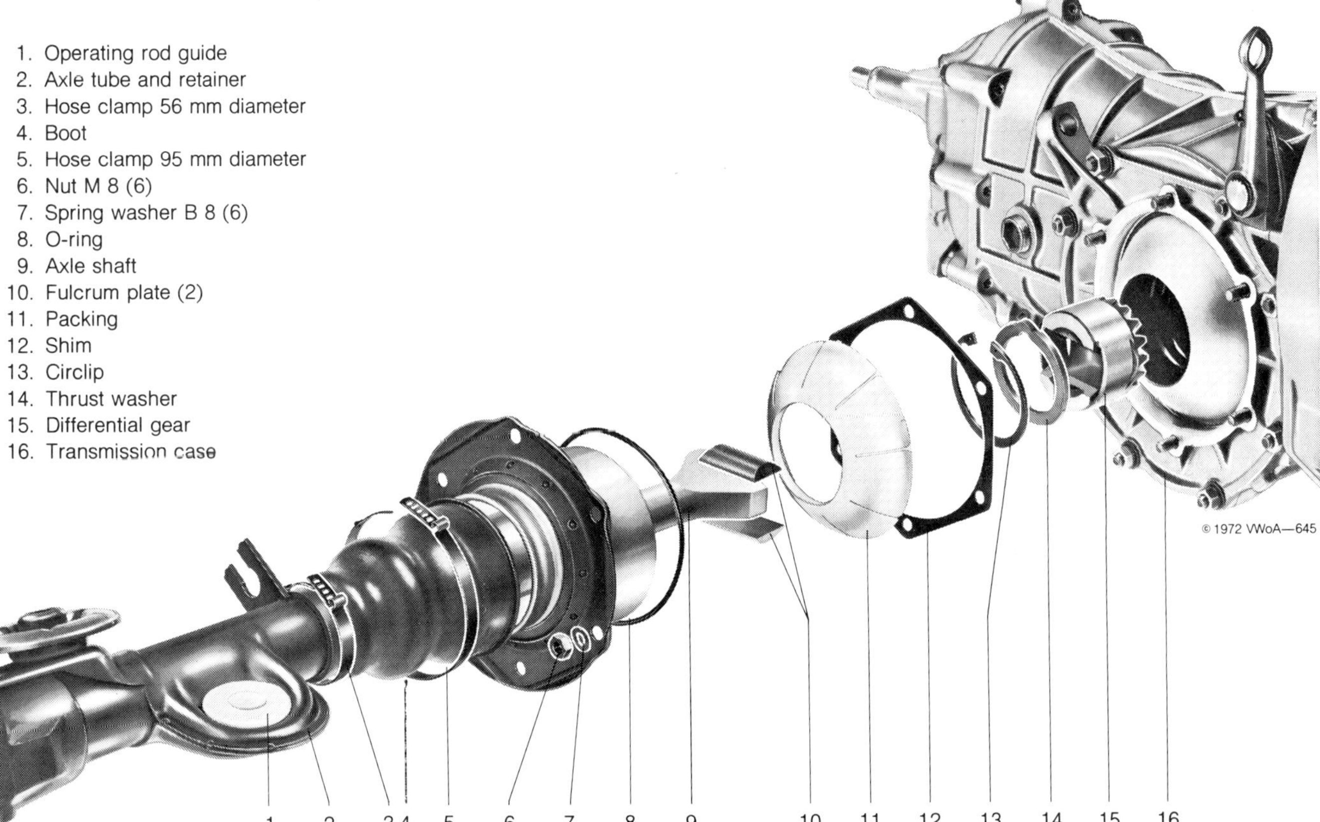

2. Remove nuts for axle tube retainer, as in Fig. 22.

**Fig. 22.** Axle tube retainer is attached to transmission case with nuts being removed here.

3. Withdraw rear axle tube along with retainer and take off gasket and plastic packing.
4. Remove differential side gear lock ring (Fig. 23).

**Fig. 23.** Lock ring (circlip) that secures differential side gear must be removed before axle shaft can be withdrawn.

5. Remove differential side gear thrust washer and withdraw axle shaft, as in Fig. 24.

6. Remove differential side gear and fulcrum plates from differential housing.

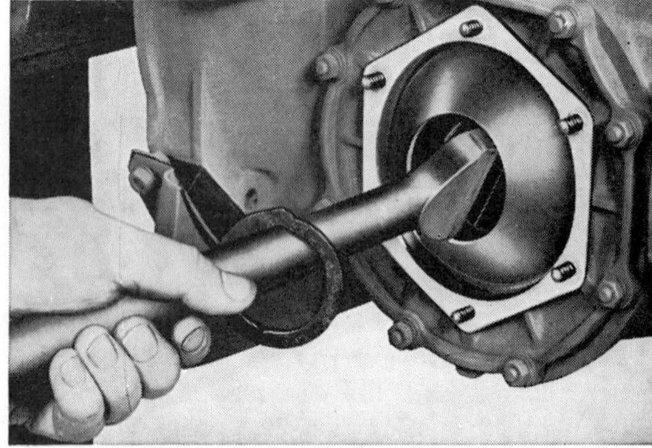



**Fig. 24.** Axle shaft is withdrawn from differential side gear after removal of lock ring (circlip) and thrust washer. Washer can be seen on shaft, just ahead of thumb.

7. Drive lock pin out of housing for axle shaft bearing at other end of shaft.
8. Loosen axle boot clamps.
9. Press axle tube out of bearing housing (Fig. 25).

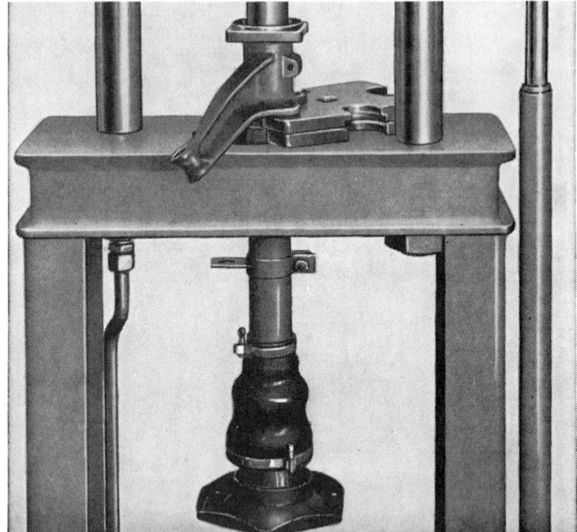



**Fig. 25.** Axle tube is pressed out of bearing housing with this set-up. Housing is part resting on thrust plates on press platform.

**NOTE —**
When performing step 9, be careful not to damage the housing. A damaged housing must not be put back in the car.

**To install:**

1. Clean axle tube retainer and axle tube retainer seat on final drive cover.

2. Check axle boot for damage and replace if necessary.

> ***CAUTION*** —
> *Operate press carefully to avoid damage to bearing housing. A damaged housing must be replaced.*

3. Before pressing the bearing housing into place, thoroughly clean and oil all seating surfaces.
4. Lower end of assembly must be supported when housing is pressed into place. Bring press cross member up against axle tube retainer to provide support and put spacers or blocks under cross member. Raise cross member 3½ inches.
5. Press housing into place.
6. Check axle shaft, differential side gear, and thrust washer. Replace damaged or worn parts, but note following instructions. The fitting clearance between the flat end of the rear axle shaft (measured across the ball-shaped sides) and the inner diameter of the differential side gear must fall in the range 0.001 to 0.004 inch (0.03 to 0.1 mm). Fig. 26 shows the measurement. Adequate clearance is necessary to prevent axle noise or seizure. Rear axle shafts and differential side gears fall into three tolerance groups and should be matched accordingly. A paint spot in a recess identifies the gear group. Axle shaft has a painted ring 6 inches from flat end.

| Paint mark | Side Gear inner diameter | Axle Shaft outer diameter |
|---|---|---|
| yellow | 2.3595 to 2.3610 inches (59.93 to 59.97 mm) | 2.3570 to 2.3582 inches (59.87 to 59.90 mm) |
| blue | 2.3614 to 2.3622 inches (59.98 to 60.00 mm) | 2.3586 to 2.3598 inches (59.91 to 59.94 mm) |
| pink | 2.3626 to 2.3638 inches (60.01 to 60.04 mm) | 2.3602 to 2.3610 inches (59.95 to 59.97 mm) |

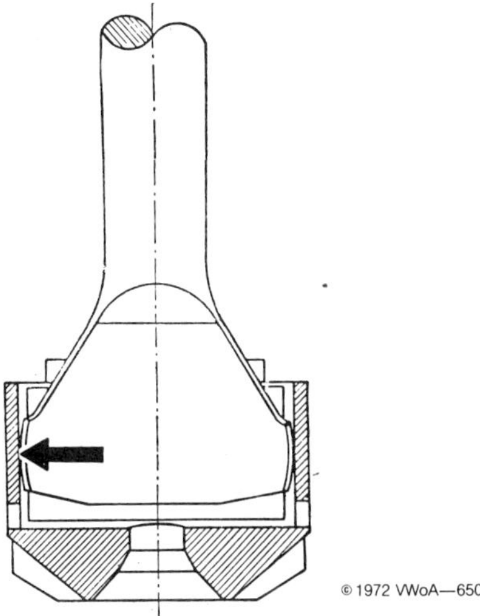


**Fig. 26.** Fitting clearance between axle shaft and inner diameter of differential gear is measured at point indicated by the black arrow. See text.

7. Check rear axle drive shaft for run-out at ball bearing seat (splined end). The permissible run-out is 0.002 inch (0.05 mm). If run-out is no more than slightly above the acceptable tolerance, it is permissible to cold-straighten the shaft.

> **NOTE** —
> On cars from chassis No. 117 580 250 the rear axle tube retainer has been modified and paper gaskets used as shims have been discontinued. Later axle tube is adjusted with hard paper shims. In either case axle tube must not bind but be free to move without looseness. Sealing is done with an O-ring. When installing later retainer, make sure that shims (3 in Fig. 27) are placed on the rear axle tube retainer (2) before you install the O-ring (4). If this sequence is not followed, shims will bend and cause leakage.

5

**Fig. 27.** Retainer assembly for rear axle tube is shown in exploded view.

1. Final drive cover
2. Retainer
3. Gaskets
4. O-ring

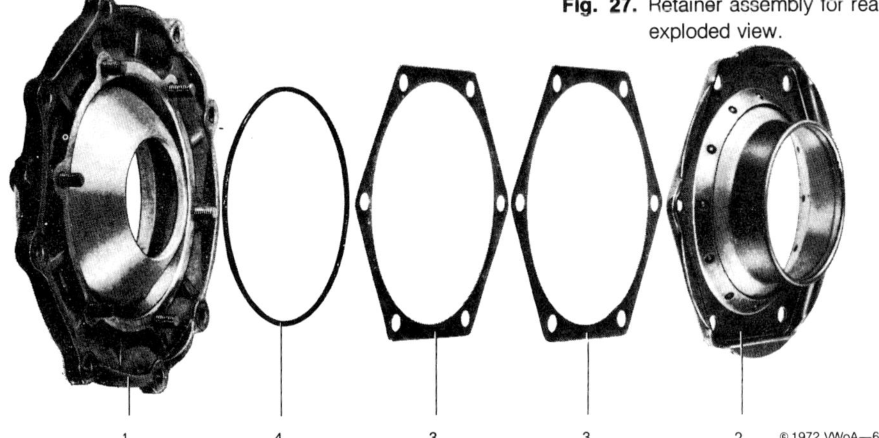

***CAUTION —***
*Improper clearance between axle shaft and fulcrum plates may cause noise or seizure.*

8. Clearance between axle shaft and fulcrum plate should be 0.001 to 0.010 inch (0.035 to 0.244 mm). If you find excessive clearance, install oversize fulcrum plates (faces of these are grooved) or replace worn parts. Note previous instructions regarding fit. Fig. 28 shows measurement of clearance.

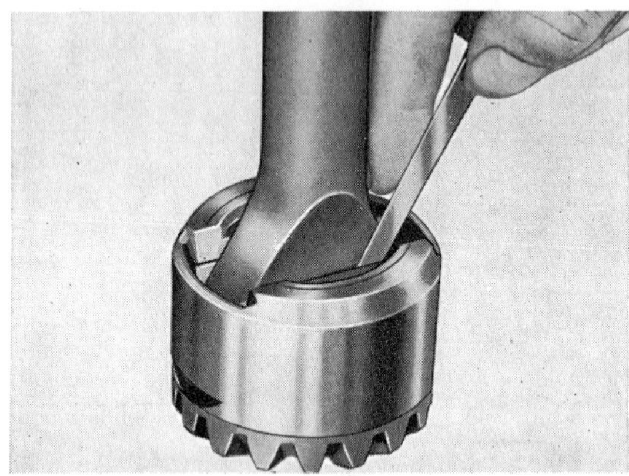



**Fig. 28.** Feeler gauge is used, as here, to check the clearance of the rear axle shaft/fulcrum plates/differential side gear. See text.

9. Insert differential side gear, axle shaft (Fig. 29) and thrust washer into differential housing and secure with lock ring.

**Fig. 29.** Differential housing receives assembly of rear axle shaft and differential side gear.

10. Rear axle tube should be installed without end play. Select an axle tube retainer gasket of appropriate thickness. Maximum end play of 0.008 inch (0.2 mm) must not be exceeded. Torque nuts of axle tube retainer to 14 ft. lbs. (2 mkg).
11. Put hose clamp in place at axle tube end but do not tighten clamp until the axle is installed. Otherwise, twisting may damage the boot.

## 2.6 Replacing Rear Axle Boots
(rear axle installed)

A split axle boot is available. If you use it, you can avoid having to disassemble the axle.

**To remove boot:**

1. Remove retaining clamps.
2. Cut damaged axle boot and take it off.
3. Clean axle tube and axle tube retainer.

**To install:**

1. Lightly coat joining faces of the split axle boot with sealing compound.
2. Make sure that diameter of boot at the transmission end is correct: 3.5 inches (89 mm).
3. Tighten axle boot screws. Install and tighten retaining clamps.

**NOTE —**
Do not overtighten axle boot screws and retaining clamps. The tightening should be done with the rear axle level. Make sure the boot is not distorted or strained. See Fig. 30.

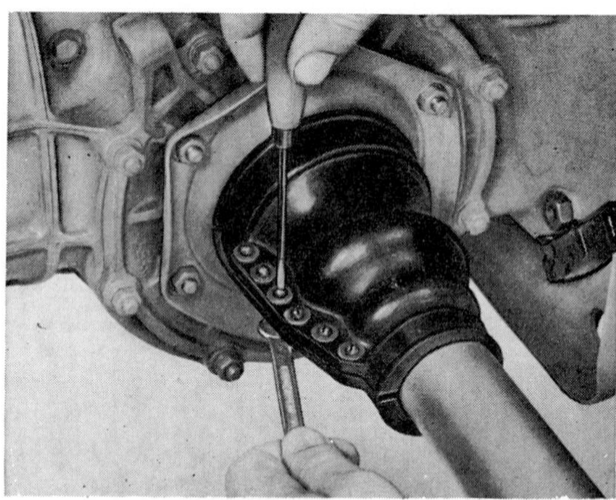



**Fig. 30.** Axle boot is held on rear axle tube with screws and retaining clamps. Excessive tightening of screws or clamp can distort and damage boot.

## 3. TRANSMISSION AND FINAL DRIVE

As shown in Fig. 31 and Fig. 32, the final drive and differential assemblies of the standard transmission 1969 cars, which have the double-joint rear axle, are somewhat different from those of the standard transmission 1966, 1967 and 1968 cars, which have the swing rear axle. These differences require somewhat different procedures in removal and installation, disassembly and reassembly. In the following discussions these differences will be noted where appropriate.

1. Differential
2. Final drive cover, left
3. Final drive cover, right
4. Ball bearing (2)
5. O-ring
6. Shim $S_1$
7. Shim $S_2$
8. Nut M 8 (16)
9. Lock washer (16)
10. Flat washer (16)
11. Transmission



**Fig. 31.** Final drive for 1966, 1967 and 1968 cars with manual transmission and swing half-axle is shown here in exploded view.

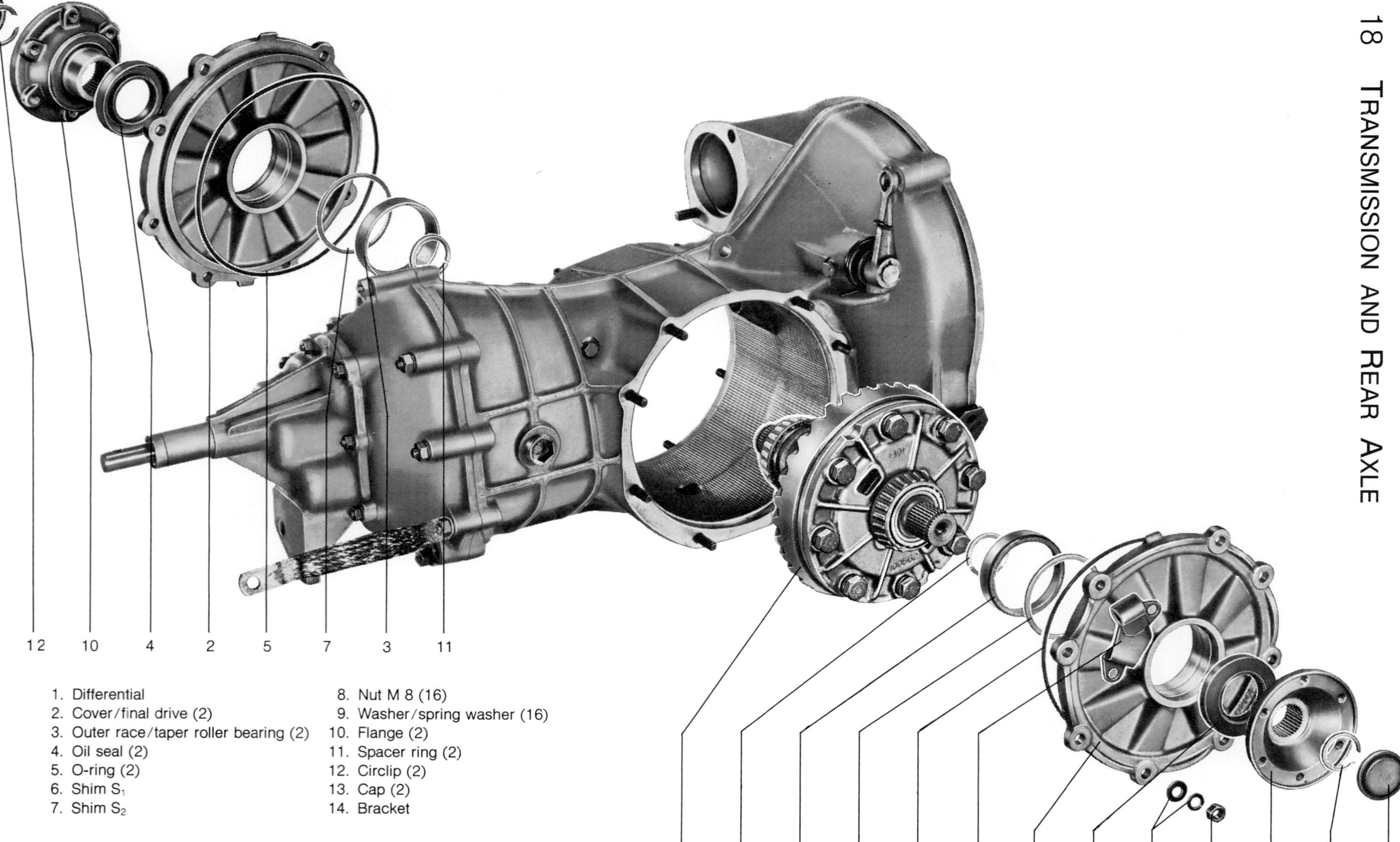


1. Differential
2. Cover/final drive (2)
3. Outer race/taper roller bearing (2)
4. Oil seal (2)
5. O-ring (2)
6. Shim $S_1$
7. Shim $S_2$
8. Nut M 8 (16)
9. Washer/spring washer (16)
10. Flange (2)
11. Spacer ring (2)
12. Circlip (2)
13. Cap (2)
14. Bracket

© 1972 VWoA—656

**Fig. 32.** Final drive for 1969 cars with manual transmission and double-joint axle is shown here in exploded view.

### 3.1 Removing and Installing Differential and Transmission
(swing axle)

When repairing the transmission, it is advisable to remove and install the differential complete with axle shafts. For this operation remove the right wheel bearing housing on the axle shaft and press the differential out to the left, complete with the final drive cover.

> **NOTE** —
> When you are working on the transmission, cleanliness is absolutely essential. Dirt not only wears or damages parts but also can give you false readings in the adjustment procedures.
>
> Keep your workbench, your tools and the transmission components clean, but do not use sharp instruments to scrape off dirt. Use appropriate solvents instead.

**To remove:**

1. Remove nuts holding gearshift housing, gasket and inner shift lever.
2. Pry off all lock plates for drive pinion and main drive shaft nuts.
3. Engage reverse and 3rd/4th gear to lock transmission.
4. Remove drive pinion and main drive shaft nuts and take off lock plates. (Do not re-install the used nuts.) Fig. 33 shows the operation.

© 1972 VWoA—657

**Fig. 33.** Nuts on front ends of drive pinion and main drive shaft can be removed after two gears have been engaged to keep shafts from turning. View is of gear carrier (front) end of transmission case.

5. Remove gear carrier stud nuts and take off battery ground strap.
6. Turn transmission case to bring left-hand final drive cover upward.
7. Remove the nuts holding the left final drive cover (Fig. 34).

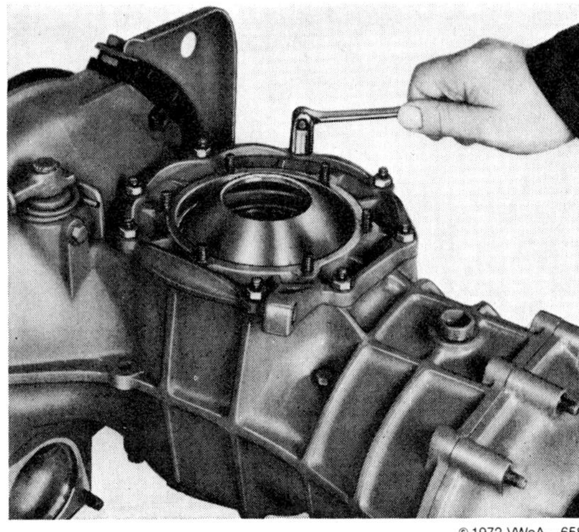

© 1972 VWoA—658

**Fig. 34.** Transmission case on stand is turned 90 degrees for removal of left final drive cover.

8. With special tool, remove final drive cover. Position the tool thrust plate on the differential housing flange as in Fig. 35 and attach the spindle to two of the axle tube retainer studs.

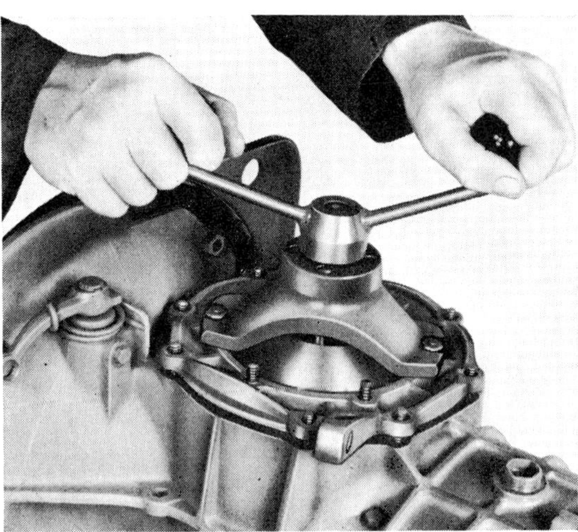

© 1972 VWoA—659

**Fig. 35.** Left final drive cover is lifted from the transmission case with special spindle tool shown here.

> **NOTE** —
> To facilitate re-assembly, take note of the arrangement and thickness of the differential shims as you are removing the differential.

5

9. Using same procedure, position spindle and thrust plate on the right final drive cover and press out differential. (Procedure for disassembly of differential is given in **4.1. Disassembling and Assembling Differential**.)

10. Loosen reverse gear retaining ring on main drive shaft. Slide gear to rear. Unscrew shaft to separate it into two sections. See Fig. 36.

© 1972 VWoA—660

**Fig. 36.** Reverse gear is removed from main drive shaft here before shaft is screwed apart for removal from case.

11. Take off reverse gear and retaining ring, and withdraw the rear section of main drive shaft to the rear. Be careful not to damage oil seal.
12. Take off right-hand final drive cover.
13. Pry down lock plates of bolts attaching bearing retainer for drive pinion and remove bolts (Fig. 37). Take care not to damage the pinion teeth.

© 1972 VWoA—661

**Fig. 37.** Retainer for drive pinion bearing is unbolted for removal of the gear train.

14. Using special tool (Fig. 38), carefully push gear train out of case.

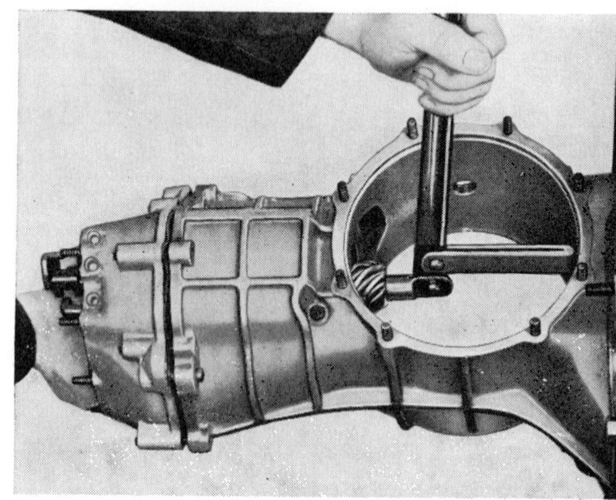

© 1972 VWoA—662

**Fig. 38.** Gear train is pushed to the front out of transmission case with the special lever shown here.

**NOTE —**
To facilitate re-assembly, take note of thickness of the pinion shims, hereafter referred to as $S_3$.

15. Remove circlip with circlip pliers (Fig. 39) and take reverse drive gear off reverse gear shaft.

© 1972 VWoA—663

**Fig. 39.** Circlip (lock ring) securing reverse drive gear on reverse gear shaft is removed with circlip pliers shown here.

16. Remove Woodruff key and withdraw reverse gear shaft and thrust washer from transmission case.
17. Remove bolt that secures spacer sleeve for the reverse gear shaft needle bearings.

18. Using a drift (Fig. 40), drive out needle bearings for reverse gear shaft and spacer sleeve.

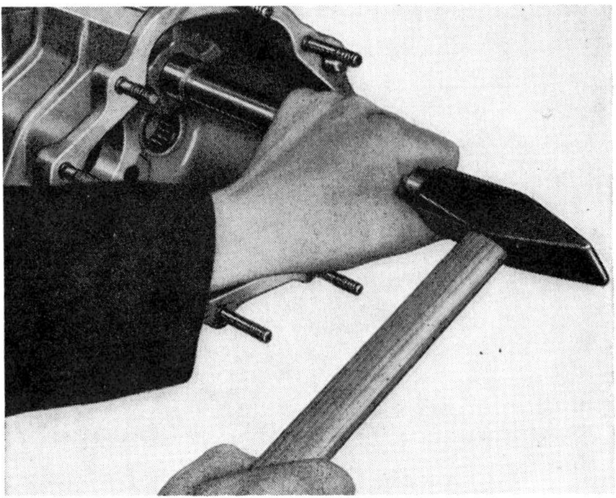

© 1972 VWoA—664

**Fig. 40.** Needle bearings for reverse gear shaft and spacer sleeve are driven out of transmission case.

19. Remove bolt that secures needle bearing on the main drive shaft.
20. With drift, drive out main drive shaft needle bearing.
21. Remove ball bearings from left and right final drive covers, using press as in Fig. 41.
22. Remove clutch release bearing and operating shaft.

© 1972 VWoA—665

**Fig. 41.** Ball bearing is pressed out of final drive cover with the set-up shown here.

For installation of a new transmission case the pinion and ring gear must be adjusted. When a final drive cover is replaced, setting backlash of the ring gear is the only special adjustment required.

**To install:**

1. Clean and inspect transmission case and final drive covers for damage. Replace damaged parts.
2. Inspect starter bushing for wear. Replace if necessary.
3. Check the clutch operating shaft for free play. Lubricate shaft if needed.
4. Check all bearings before re-installation and replace if necessary.

**NOTE —**
When new differential bearings are installed, the ring gear must be adjusted.

5. Insert needle bearings for reverse gear shaft and spacer sleeve and secure.
6. Install main drive shaft needle bearing with a drift and secure.
7. Insert Woodruff key into reverse gear shaft and install gear shaft thrust washer and drive gear. Check circlip for proper tension.
8. Place drive pinion shims on bearing and screw two studs (approximately 4 inches long) into bearing retainer. Studs (Fig. 42) prevent the retaining ring from turning when transmission is installed.

5

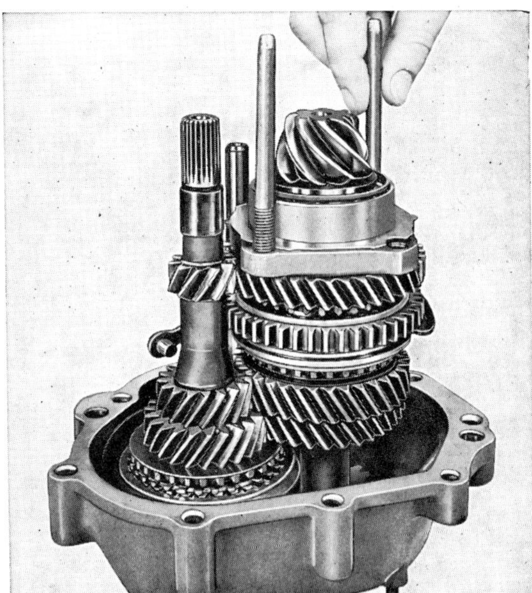

© 1972 VWoA—666

**Fig. 42.** Two studs 4 inches long are screwed into bearing retainer to keep retaining ring from turning when the transmission is installed in the case.

9. Push the reverse selector fork and slide gear on reverse lever. Engage reverse gear.

10. Insert transmission into transmission case. Use a new gear carrier gasket. Position pinion with rubber mallet.

> **NOTE —**
> Use only grade 10 K bolts on the bearing retainer.

11. Tighten bearing retainer bolts to 36 ft. lbs. (5 mkg). Use new lock plates.

> **NOTE —**
> Make sure that a flat on head of each bolt near the extended selector rod faces the bearing, but be careful not to exceed specified torque (Fig. 43). When bolts have been locked, engage 1st gear to check that the rod is free.

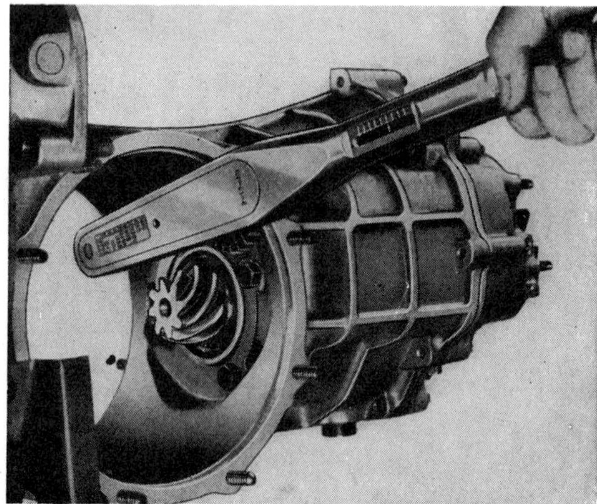



**Fig. 43.** Bearing retainer bolts are torqued to 36 ft. lbs. in installation of the transmission.

12. Apply oil to the tip of the oil seal before installing the rear half of the main drive shaft. Screw halves of drive shaft together, backing off until splines for the reverse gear are in line. Do not screw shaft sections tightly together. Make sure that reverse gear circlip has correct pre-tension.

13. Press ball bearings into left and right final drive covers.

14. Check differential and repair it if necessary. (See later discussion.)

15. Install right final drive cover with a new gasket. Tighten nuts to 22 ft. lbs. (3 mkg). The final drive covers tend to settle slightly after car has been running. Check nuts at 300 miles after a repair and tighten if necessary.

16. Install differential in transmission case (Fig. 44), making sure that shims are inserted correctly. Install left cover with flat and lock washers.

**Fig. 44.** Differential goes into left side of the transmission case as shown here.

17. Torque gear carrier stud nuts to 14 ft. lbs. (2 mkg).

18. Block transmission by engaging both reverse gear and either 3rd or 4th gear.

19. Torque main drive shaft and pinion nut to 87 ft. lbs. (12 mkg), then back off and retighten to 43 ft. lbs. (6 mkg). Secure with lock plate. See Fig. 45.

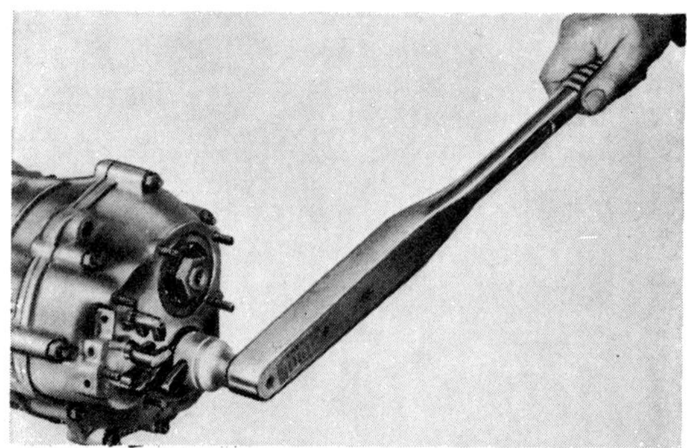



**Fig. 45.** Retaining nuts on drive pinion and main drive shaft are torqued and secured with lock plates. See text.

20. After making sure the three selector shafts are in neutral, attach gear shift housing.

> **NOTE —**
> When the transmission case, differential housing, final drive cover or other part directly affecting adjustment of ring gear has been replaced, the ring gear must be readjusted. (See later description of gear adjustment.)

21. Install axle shafts, tubes and wheel bearing housings.

## 3.2 Disassembling and Assembling Gear Carrier

An exploded view of the gear train removed from the standard transmission case is given in Fig. 46. Study of the position of the parts in relation to each other will help you to visualize the following repair procedures.

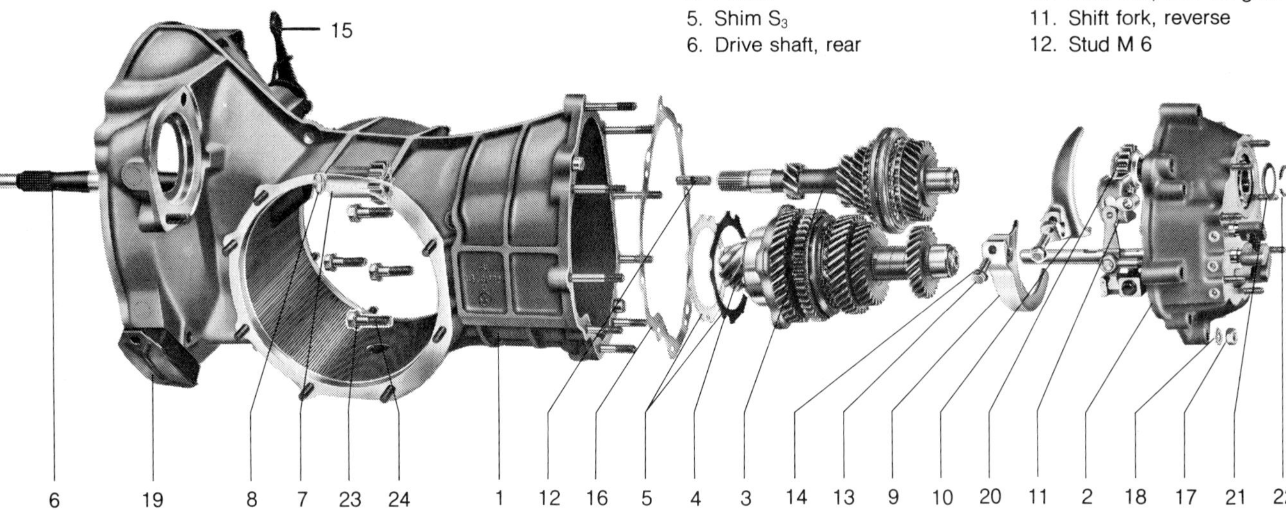


1. Transmission case
2. Gear carrier
3. Drive shaft, front
4. Pinion
5. Shim $S_3$
6. Drive shaft, rear
7. Drive gear, reverse
8. Circlip
9. Shift fork, 1st/2nd gear
10. Shift fork, 3rd/4th gear
11. Shift fork, reverse
12. Stud M 6
13. Bolts (2)
14. Spring washer B 6 (2)
15. Clutch lever
16. Gasket/gear carrier
17. Hexagon nut (9)
18. Spring washer B 8 (9)
19. Bonded rubber mounting
20. Sliding gear/reverse
21. Dished washer
22. Circlip
23. Washer B 10 (4)
24. Bolts (4)

**Fig. 46.** Gear train for manual transmission is seen here removed from the transmission case.

5

**NOTE —**
When you are working on the transmission, cleanliness is absolutely essential. Dirt not only wears or damages parts but also can give you false readings in your adjustment procedures.

Keep your workbench, your tools and the transmission components clean, but do not use sharp instruments to scrape off dirt. Use appropriate solvents instead.

**To disassemble:**

1. Remove reverse shift fork and reverse sliding gear from reverse lever.
2. Remove shims from drive pinion bearing. Take note of shim thicknesses.
3. Place gear carrier in vise equipped with aluminum jaw covers. Loosen locking screws (Fig. 47) of the 1st-and-2nd and 3rd-and-4th shift forks, and remove shift fork for 1st and 2nd gears.
4. Withdraw selector shaft for 3rd and 4th gears from shift fork and remove transmission from gear carrier.

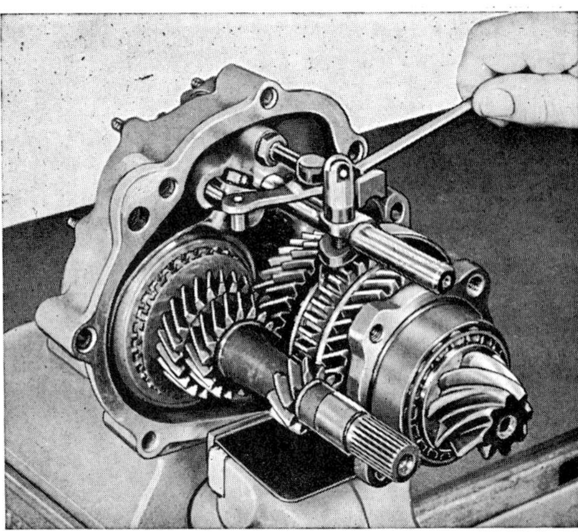


**Fig. 47.** Gear carrier with gear train is shown here in vise in preparation for disassembly. Shift fork locking bolt is being removed.

***WARNING***—
*The dished washer below the circlip is under tension and will pop out.*

5. Remove circlip or nut from main drive shaft and take off dished washer. Use special pliers on circlip.

***WARNING***—
*When pressing transmission out of gear carrier, be careful to avoid injury. Be sure to keep a firm hold on heavy components. If you let them fall, they will be damaged.*

6. Press transmission out of gear carrier. Fig. 48 shows the set-up on press. The drive pinion should be guided carefully to prevent tilting, which might damage gear or needle bearing in gear carrier.

**NOTE**—
When pressing the gears out, you will find it a good idea to hold pinion and drive shaft together with a strong rubber band, as shown in Fig. 48.

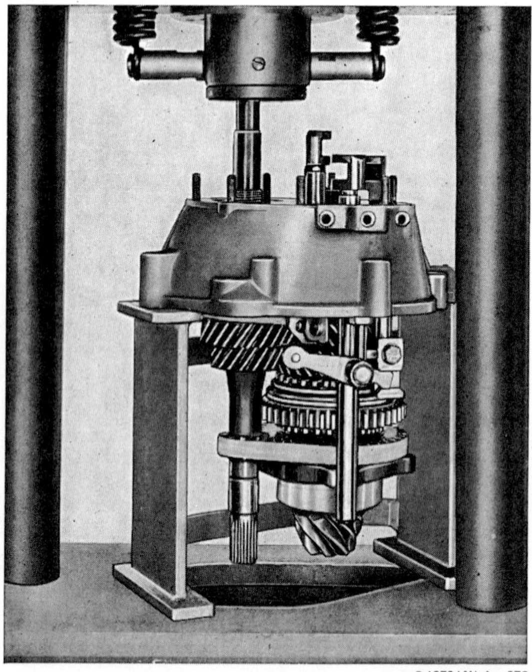



**Fig. 48.** Rubber band holds pinion and drive shaft together as transmission is pressed out of gear carrier. Keep a firm hold on the heavy parts to prevent them from falling.

7. Remove bolt securing drive pinion needle bearing and press out needle bearing. See Fig. 49.

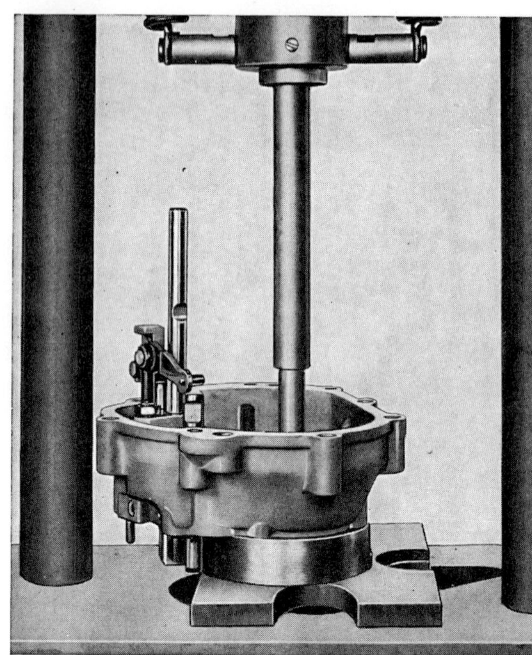



**Fig. 49.** Main drive shaft bearing is pressed out of gear carrier with press set-up shown here. Similar procedure is followed in pressing out needle bearing.

8. Press main drive shaft bearing out of gear carrier, as in Fig. 49.

9. Re-install gear carrier in vise (use aluminum jaws) and remove bolt from reverse lever guide, as in Fig. 50.

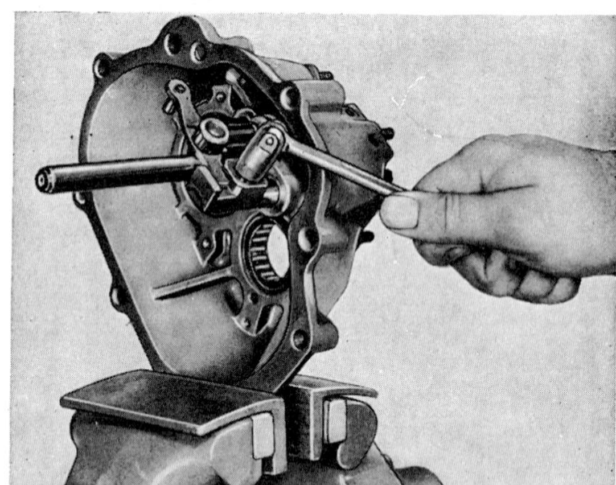



**Fig. 50.** Reverse lever guide bolt is removed with gear carrier in vise. Note aluminum jaw covers on the vise.

10. Withdraw reverse gear selector shaft and remove reverse lever guide.
11. Withdraw selector shaft for 1st and 2nd gears and remove reverse lever from the support.
12. Remove selector shaft for 3rd and 4th gears.
13. Take out interlock plungers and balls.
14. Remove plugs from shaft locking bores. Loosened plug is being removed in Fig. 51.
15. Remove springs with a small screwdriver.

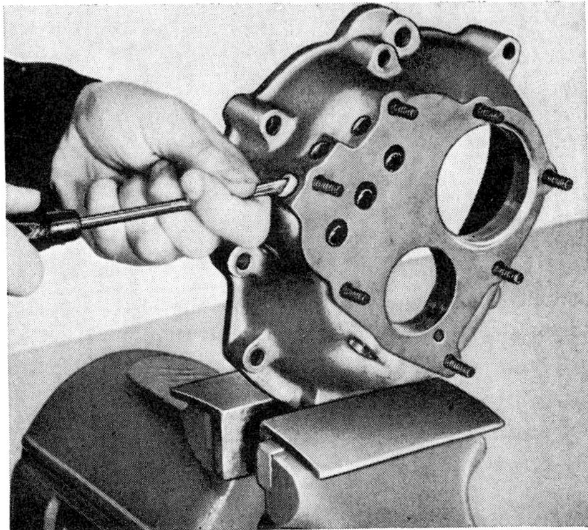



**Fig. 51.** Plug in gear carrier bore for selector shaft interlock plunger is removed here. Usual procedure is to thread plug for M 6 bolt.

**To assemble:**

1. Check selector shaft locking springs and replace if necessary. Free length of detent springs should be 1.0 inch (25 mm), wear limit 0.9 inch (23 mm). The force applied to overcome detent ball grooves on the shafts should be approximately 33 to 44 lbs. (15-20 kg). If difficult gear shifting is experienced, the resistance should be tested with drive pinion and main driveshaft removed.
2. Insert springs into holes (Fig. 52) and seal holes with new plugs.
3. Install reverse selector shaft with reverse lever and reverse lever guide.
4. Install selector shafts for 1st-and-2nd and for 3rd-and-4th gears, making sure not to omit the two interlock plungers. Engage a gear to check for proper interlocking. The selector shaft next to the one just used must be locked. When 1st or 2nd gear is engaged, the two other selector shafts should be locked.
5. Check drive pinion needle bearing and main drive

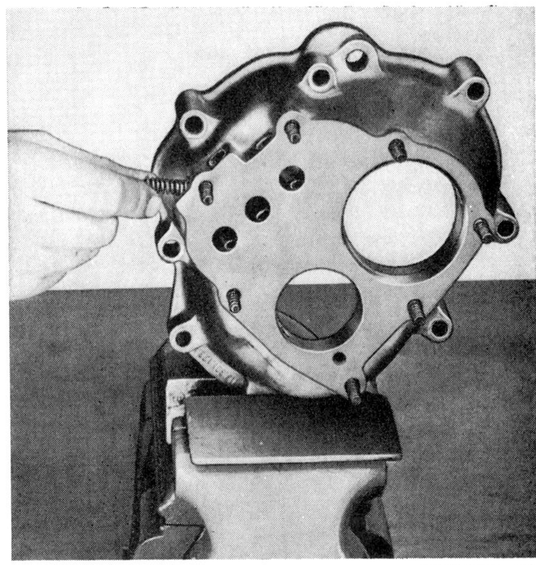



**Fig. 52.** Detent spring for selector shaft interlock mechanism is inserted in gear carrier and holes plugged.

shaft ball bearing. Replace as necessary. Install pinion needle bearing in the gear carrier and secure.

5

6. Place gear carrier on support and press main drive-shaft ball bearing into position. (Fig. 53.)

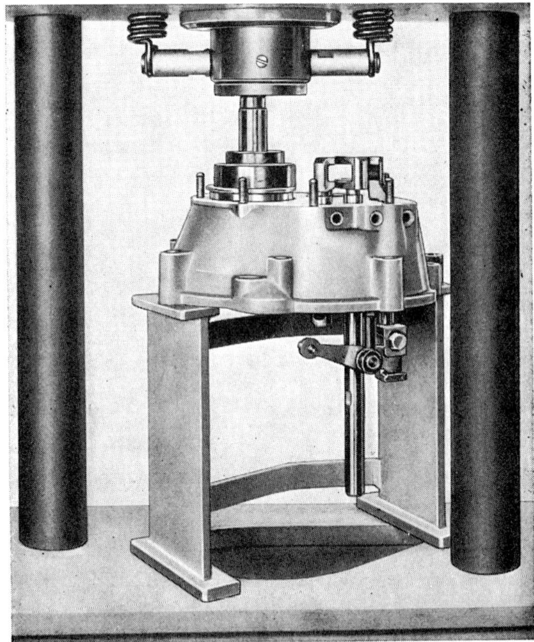



**Fig. 53.** Ball bearing for main drive shaft is pressed into gear carrier supported as in this set-up.

7. Check shift forks for wear. The clearance between forks and operating sleeves should be 0.004 to 0.012 inch (0.1 to 0.3 mm). Replace worn parts.

8. Check main drive shaft and drive pinion for wear or damage.

9. Make sure the shift fork for 3rd and 4th gears is positioned in the operating sleeve. When transmission is pressed into gear carrier, the drive pinion should lift slightly. Insert selector shaft all the way into the fork and check that the shift fork for 3rd and 4th gears does not jam.

**NOTE** —
When pressing the transmission into position, you will find it a good idea to hold drive pinion and main drive shaft together with a rubber band. Stretch band around the operating sleeve for the 1st and 2nd gears and the main drive shaft. See Fig. 54.

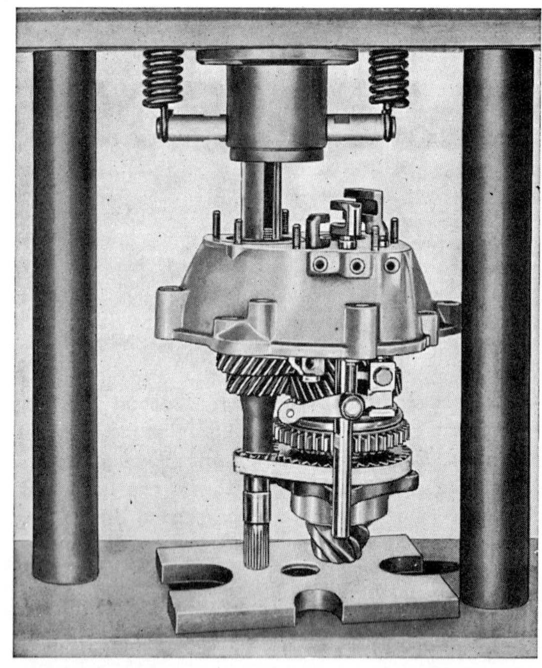



**Fig. 54.** Transmission is pressed into gear carrier. Note that 3rd/4th gear selector fork is installed. As in removal procedure (Fig. 48), heavy rubber band holds pinion and main drive shaft together.

10. Place dished washer on the shaft, install a new circlip and press down with tube until circlip snaps into groove. Then squeeze circlip all around with a suitable pair of pliers (water-pump pliers, for example).

11. Install 1st and 2nd shift fork.

12. Attach reverse gear shift fork with reverse sliding gear on reverse lever.

13. Adjust shift forks. (See description following.)

On cars from chassis No. 117 812 292 method of securing drive shaft in gear carrier has been changed. A dished washer and lock ring replace nut and lock plate. Install circlip with special pliers. Be careful because dished washer is under heavy tension. Press washer on with tube as in Fig. 55, until it snaps into place.

**NOTE** —
When circlip is in place, squeeze it all around with pliers until it bottoms in the groove.

**Fig. 55.** New circlip is pressed on main drive shaft in gear carrier with tube shown here. Circlip will snap into place.

### 3.3 Adjusting Shift Forks

For correct adjustment of the shift forks a special appliance is almost a necessity. The pinion and drive shaft are installed in the appliance in the same positions relative to each other that they will occupy in the transmission case. To make sure of the fit the $S_3$ shim of proper thickness for axial location of the pinion is used in the appliance. The thickness of the paper gasket between gearshift housing and appliance spacer sleeves also is taken into account.

If the appliance is a pre-1961 model, some reworking may be necessary before it will accept the fully synchronized transmission.

**To adjust forks:**

1. Install complete gear carrier in appliance including gasket, pinion with shim, drive shaft and reverse gear. Attach with the four nuts. Fig. 56 shows the set-up.

© 1972 VWoA—680

**Fig. 56.** Special appliance holds gear carrier with drive pinion and main drive shaft for adjustment of shift forks. Arrows point to securing nuts.

2. Insert two diagonally-opposed bearing retainer bolts and tighten them. See Fig. 57.

© 1972 VWoA—681

**Fig. 57.** Diagonally opposite bolts (two arrows numbered 1) fasten special appliance and retainer for drive pinion bearing together. Single arrow at left points to shim $S_3$ which locates axial position of pinion.

***CAUTION —***
*The shift fork for 1st/2nd gears (wider fork) is installed with profile toward gear carrier. The profile of the 3rd/4th gear fork is away from carrier.*

3. Push selector shaft for 3rd/4th gears into shift fork and tighten clamp bolt.

4. Install shift fork for reverse and 1st gear and tighten clamp bolt.

**NOTE —**
On transmissions with pinion and main shaft nuts, place setting appliance crank on the drive shaft splines and brace handle against vise (Fig. 58) to prevent shaft from turning. Engage 1st gear.

© 1972 VWoA—682

**Fig. 58.** Crank of test appliance is splined on main drive shaft and braced against appliance plate to keep shaft from turning while 1st or 2nd gear is engaged. See text.

5

5. First tighten nuts on pinion and drive shaft to 88 ft. lbs. (12 mkg) and then back them off. Retighten to 44 ft. lbs. (6 mkg) and lock them.

6. Insert lower selector shaft (for 1st/2nd gear) in the notch for 2nd gear. Slide operating sleeve with fork over the coupling teeth until sleeve is against the 2nd gear. Center shift fork in operating sleeve groove and tighten clamp bolt. See Fig. 59.

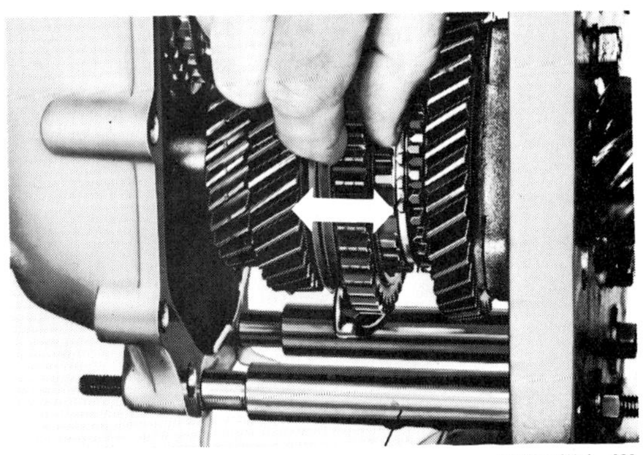

© 1972 VWoA—683

**Fig. 59.** Shift fork is centered in groove of synchro operating sleeve to provide clearance between fork and groove.

***CAUTION —***
*The shift forks must not rub against or exert pressure on the sides of the groove in the operating sleeve when transmission is in neutral or after a gear is engaged. There must always be clearance.*

7. While turning transmission, use forks to select both gears and neutral several times. Check clearance between shift fork and operating sleeve in each position. If necessary, change the shift fork position until both end positions give the same clearance between fork and sleeve groove. Tighten clamp bolt to 18 ft. lbs. (2.5 mkg).

***CAUTION —***
*For correct adjustment of 3rd and 4th gears the ball bearing in the gear carrier must be pressed in fully.*

8. Insert upper selector shaft (for 3rd/4th gears) in the notch for 3rd gear. Adjust fork for 3rd/4th gears in the same way you did for 1st/2nd gear in previous procedure. Tighten clamp bolt to 18 ft. lbs. (2.5 mkg).

***CAUTION —***
*When adjusting the reverse sliding gear, make sure that there is no axial play at the shift fork. If necessary, loosen support for reverse lever and press reverse lever in direction of sliding gear (arrow in Fig. 60) until only the running clearance remains.*

**Fig. 60.** Black arrow indicates direction in which relay lever is to be pushed for adjustment of reverse sliding gear (see text). Lever support must first be loosened by backing off bolt at lower right.

9. Adjust the reverse gear shift fork to center sliding gear between operating sleeve and the 2nd gear on the drive shaft. Reverse gear must engage fully with the reverse gear on the pinion after shift is made. Tighten bolt in the relay lever guide to 14 ft. lbs. (2 mkg).

**NOTE —**
If necessary, the relay lever support (eye rod) can be adjusted further to bring the distance from center of eye to carrier flange to 1.50 to 1.54 inches (38.2 to 39.0 mm).

10. Engage reverse gear and check alignment of teeth on sliding gear and operating sleeve (Fig. 61). Correct as necessary.

**Fig. 61.** Reverse gear alignment is seen between two thin vertical white lines in picture. Here the reverse gear and operating sleeve gears are in perfect mesh.

11. Check selector shaft interlock. When a gear is engaged, it must not be possible to engage another gear. The selector shafts must be interlocked one against the other.

**NOTE —**
For disassembly of the shift housing see **AUTOMATIC STICK SHIFT**. A similar procedure is explained there.

## 3.4 Disassembling and Assembling Drive Pinion

The following procedures are the same for all types of transmission on the cars covered in this Manual.

**To disassemble pinion:**

1. Remove securing nut or circlip (depending on installation). Press out inner race of needle bearing and 4th gear, and remove Woodruff key for 4th gear.
2. Take off spacer sleeve, concave washer shims and concave washer or spring spacer and circlip. Exploded view in Fig. 62 shows the parts.

1. Shim(s) $S_3$
2. Drive pinion
3. Woodruff key for 4th gear
4. Tapered roller bearing
5. Thrust washer for 1st gear
6. Needle bearing inner race (1st gear)
7. Needle cage (1st gear)
8. Thrust washer for needle bearing (1st gear)
9. Round nut
10. Shims, end play 1st gear

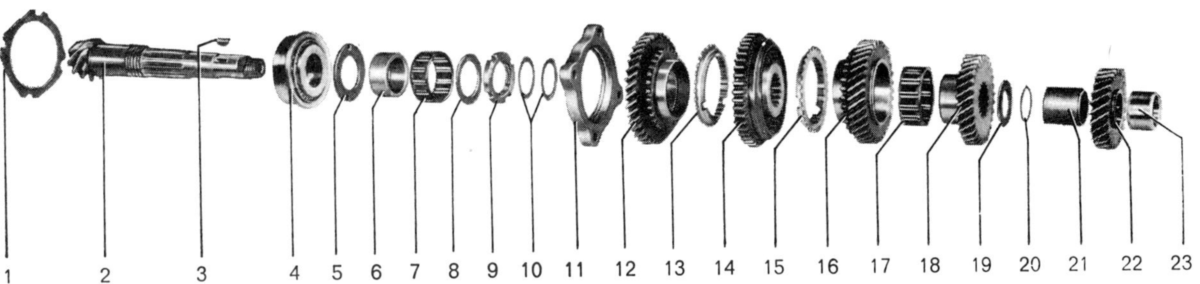




**Fig. 62.** Drive pinion assembly is shown in exploded view. Front of car is to the right.

11. Tapered roller bearing retainer
12. 1st gear
13. Synchronizer stop ring (1st gear)
14. Clutch gear 1st and 2nd gears and reverse gear
15. Synchronizer stop ring (2nd gear)
16. 2nd gear
17. Needle cage (2nd gear)
18. 3rd gear
19. Concave washer
20. Shims for concave washer or circlip
21. Spacer sleeve or spring
22. 4th gear
23. Inner race, needle bearing in gear carrier and circlip (not shown)

5

3. Remove 3rd and 2nd gears, needle cage and synchronizer stop ring for 2nd gear.
4. Remove clutch gear for 2nd and 1st gears including springs, shifting plates and operating sleeve. Disassemble, but note positions.
5. Remove synchronizer stop ring, 1st gear and roller bearing retainer.
6. Remove the shims for 1st gear.
7. Using 32 mm box wrench in conjunction with the assembly appliance, take off round nut. Fig. 63 shows set-up.

**Fig. 63.** Round nut is removed from drive pinion with box wrenches while pinion is held in special appliance in vise.

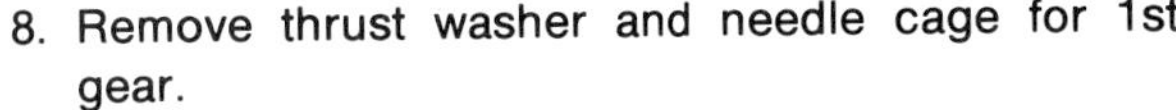

8. Remove thrust washer and needle cage for 1st gear.
9. Press out inner race of needle bearing, thrust washer, 1st gear and roller bearing.

**To inspect pinion assembly:**

1. Examine drive pinion for wear and damage. If necessary, replace drive pinion and ring gear as a pair. Note matching numbers on pinion and ring gear. (See **5. Adjustment of Pinion and Ring Gear**.)
2. Check condition of roller bearing and needle bearings. Replace if necessary.

**NOTE** —
If the gear set or roller bearing is replaced, the drive pinion and ring gear will require readjustment.

3. Check gears for wear and damage. Replace worn or damaged parts.

**NOTE —**
Damaged 3rd and 4th gears must always be replaced in pairs. The 1st and 2nd gears are replaced in pairs only if the teeth have been damaged.

4. Check all parts of the synchronizer clutch gear for wear.
   a. With wire brush, clean the internal cone surface of the stop rings.
   b. Check clearance between the stop ring face and clutch teeth of the corresponding gear. Specified clearance (see Fig. 64) is 0.43 inch (1.1 mm). If the clearance is near the wear limit 0.024 inch (0.6 mm), replace stop ring. Poor condition or incorrect operation of clutch will cause premature wear of stop rings.

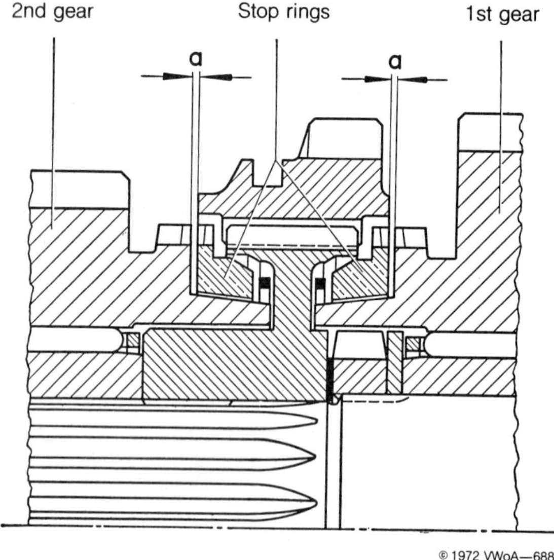


**Fig. 64.** Clearance between face of synchronizer stop ring and clutch teeth of corresponding gear is illustrated here. Clearance "a" should be 0.043 inch (1.1 mm).

   c. If a gear will not engage when the clutch is fully released, the teeth of the stop ring may be too far out of line with splines of operating sleeve. Worn slots in synchronizer stop ring can cause this condition.
   d. Replace worn parts.

5. Check condition of thrust washers and shims. Re-

**To assemble:**

1. Heat inner races of the tapered roller bearing and 1st gear needle bearing to about 212 degrees F (100 degrees C) install on drive pinion.

**NOTE —**
Two types of double-tapered roller bearings are found on cars covered here. One has a spacer race between the two inner races. The other has slightly wider inner races which are in contact with each other.

2. At this time install on pinion only the double-tapered roller bearing, thrust washer for 1st gear and inner needle bearing race.

3. When bearings on drive pinion have cooled (in kerosene) to nearly room temperature, use a press to seat them completely. Apply pressure of about 3 tons, read from gauge. See Fig. 65.

**Fig. 65.** Cooled bearings are pressed home on drive pinion in the assembly set-up shown here.

4. Now install 1st gear needle bearing cage and thrust washer and tighten round nut to 108 to 144 ft. lbs. (15 to 20 mkg). See Fig. 66.

**NOTE —**
Do **not** lock round nut. The drive pinion must be readjusted if the double-tapered roller bearing or the transmission case or the drive pinion is replaced.

**Fig. 66.** Round nut torque is specified at 108 to 144 ft. lbs. (15 to 20 mkg). Nut is tightened while the drive pinion is held in the special appliance in vise.

5. Install pinion as now assembled in transmission housing and tighten retainer bolts to 36 ft. lbs. (5 mkg). To help align pinion, attach gear carrier (with bearing in place) to housing.

6. Attach torque gauge and check torque. (If you will look ahead to Fig. 107, you will see a picture of the set-up.) Turn pinion 15 to 20 revolutions in each direction and while continuing to turn, read the torque. Then remove pinion from transmission case. On pinion shafts having a round nut with locking shoulder, peen the shoulder down into pinion splines at three equally-spaced points. See Fig. 67. Be sure not to damage splines. Remove pinion shaft from housing.

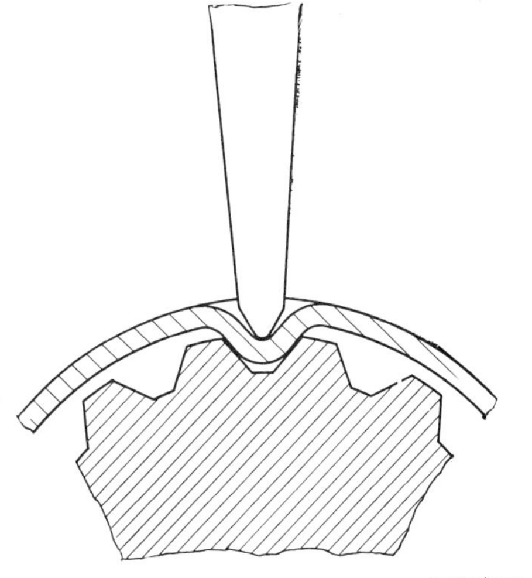

© 1972 VWoA—691

**Fig. 67.** Locking shoulder of round nut is peened into pinion splines at three points, 120 degrees apart. If peening cracks or splits nut, replace it.

**NOTE —**
It is essential to check the turning torque and to use the right torque wrench for the check. When new bearings are installed, the torque should be 5 to 18 in. lbs. (6 to 21 cmkg). If the bearings are run in (300 miles or more on the road), the torque should be 1.7 to 6.1 in. lbs. (2 to 7 cmkg). The bearing must **not** have zero (0) torque or any end play. If the torque is not in the specified range, the bearing, housing, or pinion must be replaced.

***CAUTION —***
*Replace damaged gears in matched sets only.*

7. Slide on roller bearing retainer, 1st gear, shims, and 1st gear synchronizer stop ring.

**NOTE —**
The synchronizer stop rings for the 1st and 2nd gears have approximately the same inside diameter. Be careful not to mix them up. The stop ring for 1st gear can be recognized (Fig. 68) by the small recesses for the shifting plates, and by the larger number of internal oil scraper grooves.

© 1972 VWoA—692

**Fig. 68.** Synchronizer rings for 1st (shown at left) and 2nd (shown at right) gears exhibit differences. Locking recesses (upper arrow) for shifting plates are smaller on 1st gear ring, which has more internal oil scraper grooves (lower arrow).

8. Assemble synchronizer unit for 1st and 2nd gears. Slide operating sleeve on clutch gear with its shifting plate slots in line with clutch gear slots. Put the shifting plates into position, and install the two snap rings, offset to one another. Make sure that the ends of each snap ring engage behind the shifting plates.

**5**

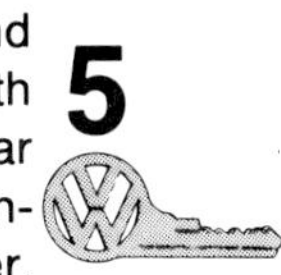

9. Slide 1st gear synchronizer stop ring and assembled 1st gear synchronizer unit on the drive pinion. The longer hub should be toward the drive pinion splines. Turn 1st gear synchronizer stop ring until the shifting plates engage in the slots.

10. With feeler gauge, check end play between thrust washer and 1st gear. Correct as necessary. The lower play limit is preferred. See Fig. 69 for measurements. Fig. 70 on the following page shows how feeler gauge is used.

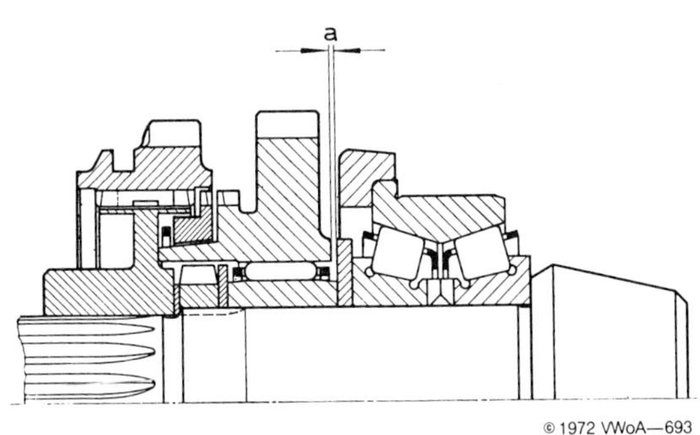


© 1972 VWoA—693

**Fig. 69.** End play between thrust washer and 1st gear, shown here as measurement "a", should be 0.004 to 0.010 inch.

**Fig. 70.** Feeler gauge is used as shown here to check axial play between installed thrust washer and 1st gear.

11. Slide on the gear synchronizer ring, 2nd gear with needle bearing and 3rd gear. Secure with circlip using circlip pliers.
12. Measure the axial play of 3rd gear with a feeler gauge and adjust by installing circlip of appropriate size. **(Table a.)** The play should be 0.004 to 0.010 inch (0.10 to 0.25 mm), kept as near as possible to the lower limit. Fig. 71 shows measurement.

**Fig. 71.** Suitable circlip adjusts 3rd gear axial play. Measurement of play is made with feeler gauge as shown here.

13. Install concave washer, after having determined the proper thickness. See **3.5 Adjustment of Concave Washer.**
14. Heat 4th gear and needle bearing inner race in an oil bath to 212 degrees F (100 degrees C) before pressing into position.

**Table a. Circlip Thicknesses**

| Thickness S | Part No. | Color |
|---|---|---|
| 1.45 | 113 311 381 | plain |
| 1.60 | 113 311 382 | black |
| 1.75 | 113 311 383 | blue |
| 1.90 | 113 311 384 | brown |
| 2.05 | 113 311 385 | grey |
| 2.20 | 113 311 386 | copper |

15. Slide shim(s) for concave washer and split spacer (or spacer spring) on the pinion shaft.
16. Insert Woodruff key for 4th gear in drive pinion.
17. Slide 4th gear on drive pinion with wide shoulder toward spacer sleeve.
18. Press in 4th gear, split spacer or spacer spring and needle bearing inner race until fully seated. Secure with nut (or circlip). See Fig. 72.

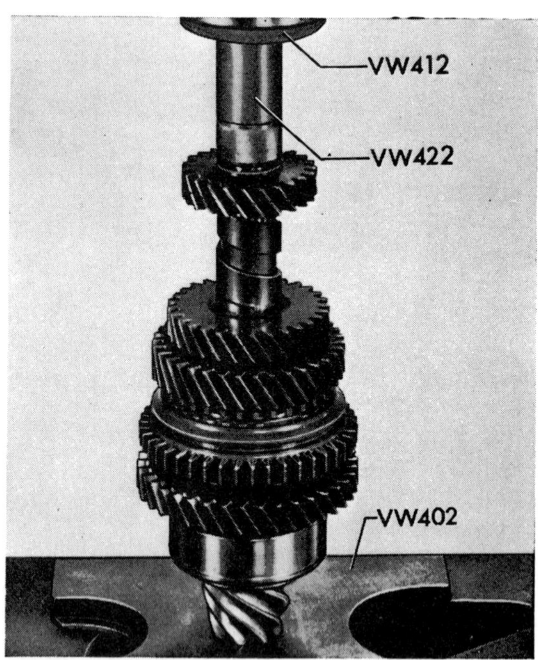



**Fig. 72.** Inner race for needle bearing is pressed on drive pinion with 4th gear after the race and gear have been heated in oil to approximately 212 degrees F (100 degrees C).

### 3.5 Adjustment of Concave Washer

The concave washer on the drive pinion must be adjusted to give a spring deflection of 0.0066 to 0.0074 inch (0.16 to 0.18 mm). When installed, the washer exerts a pressure of approximately 220 lbs. (100 kg) on the 3rd gear and the clutch gear for 1st and 2nd gear. When installed on the drive pinion, these parts must have a minimum backlash of 0.002 inch (0.05 mm). Pressure from the washer keeps gears snug on shaft.

The quiet running of the rear axle will be adversely affected if the clutch gear and 3rd gear are tightly seated without any backlash. This is the case when the concave washer is adjusted too tightly. If the maximum spring deflection is exceeded, the 2nd gear will tend to jump out of engagement.

**To measure adjustment:**

1. Assemble the drive pinion up to and including the 3rd gear.

 **NOTE —**
 The clutch gear for 1st and 2nd gear and the 3rd gear should not be seated tightly on the drive pinion. Check by hand for end play.

2. Use the repair press to position clutch gear for 1st and 2nd gears and the 3rd gear. The end play of the 1st gear should be 0.004 to 0.010 inch (0.10 to 0.25 mm). Fig. 73 shows measurement on press set-up.

© 1972 VWoA—697

**Fig. 73.** Repair press is used for measurement of 1st gear end play. Feeler gauge is used as shown here. See text.

3. Replace the tracer pin on dial indicator with an extension 1.1 inches (28 mm) long. Slide measuring sleeve of adjusting device onto the drive pinion as far as the shoulder for the 4th gear. Set the dial indicator to zero. Fig. 74 shows set-up.

© 1972 VWoA—698

**Fig. 74.** Measuring sleeve of adjusting device is set on drive pinion with dial indicator in procedure to determine shim thickness. See text for details.

4. Slide drive pinion spacer sleeve onto the measuring pin of the adjusting device.
5. Lift measuring sleeve off drive pinion. Slide it onto measuring pin of the adjusting device and position it firmly on the spacer sleeve. The dial indicator reading (Fig. 75) now shows the difference between length of spacer sleeve and distance from 4th gear shoulder to 3rd gear.

5

© 1972 VWoA—699

**Fig. 75.** Dial reading with measuring sleeve moved to pinion spacer sleeve gives difference between spacer sleeve length and distance from 4th gear shoulder to 3rd gear. See text.

### 3.6 Calculating Shim Thickness

The concave washer and the spacer sleeve separate 3rd and 4th gear on the drive pinion. The washer is 0.041 inch (1.09 mm). We also know the length of the spacer sleeve. If we take into consideration this information plus the measurement obtained in the previous procedure, we can calculate the thickness of the shim needed to give proper fit of the parts on the drive pinion. It will be the measurement obtained on adjusting device (1) minus the sum of the concave washer thickness and the spring travel (2).

(1) − (2) = shim thickness

Example **only:**

| | |
|---|---|
| 1. Adjusting device measurement | 0.07 inch (1.84 mm) |
| a. Washer thickness | 0.04 inch (1.04 mm) |
| b. Washer spring travel | + 0.01 inch (0.17 mm) |
| 2. (a.) + (b.) = | 0.05 inch (1.21 mm) |
| (1.) − (2.) = | 0.07 inch (1.84 mm) |
| | − 0.05 inch (1.21 mm) |
| (1.) − (2.) = | 0.02 inch (0.63 mm) |

Therefore, required shim thickness is 0.02 inch (0.63 mm).

The following thicknesses of shim (given in mm) are available: 0.15, 0.20, 0.25, 0.30, 0.40, 0.60, 0.80, 1.00 and 1.20. The shims should be measured carefully with a micrometer before installation.

Finally, shim thickness is checked by placing the shims under the spacer sleeve on the measuring pin of the adjusting device. Press the measuring sleeve down firmly. The dial indicator reading must not exceed .048 ± 0.0004 inch (1.21 ± 0.01 mm) (thickness of concave washer + **spring travel**).

## 3.7 Disassembling and Assembling Main Drive Shaft

An exploded view of the components of the main driveshaft is given in Fig. 76. Study of this picture will help in visualizing the following procedures:

**To disassemble drive shaft:**

1. Remove thrust washer, 4th gear, needle cage and stop ring.
2. Remove 4th gear needle bearing inner race, clutch gear for 3rd and 4th gear.
3. Remove needle cage for 3rd gear.
4. Disassemble synchro unit for 3rd and 4th gears.

**To inspect front section of shaft:**

1. Check the splines of reverse gear for wear.
2. Check needle bearing contact surfaces for wear.
3. Check 1st and 2nd gears for damage and wear.
4. Place front main drive shaft between two centers and check at contact surface of 3rd gear and needle bearing for run-out. Maximum permissible run-out: 0.0006 inch (0.015 mm).

**NOTE ——**
If wear or run-out is excessive, the front main drive shaft should be replaced, but the 1st and 2nd gears on the pinion need not be replaced.

5. Check needle bearings and 3rd and 4th gears for damage and wear. Replace gear trains if necessary, but only in pairs.
6. Check all synchronizer components for wear:
   a. Clean internal cone surfaces of synchronizer stop rings with wire brush.
   b. Check clearance between stop ring face and clutch teeth of gears with feeler gauge. The specified clearance, shown as "a" in Fig. 77 is 0.039 inch (1.00 mm). If clearance is near the wear limit of 0.024 inch (0.6 mm) stop rings

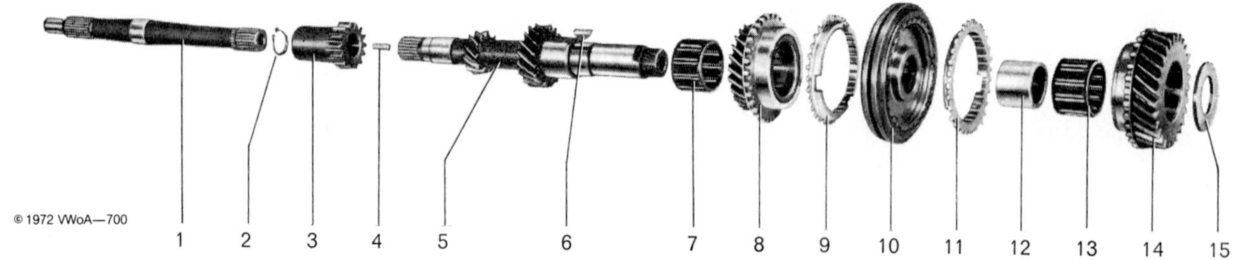


1. Main drive shaft, rear half
2. Circlip for reverse gear
3. Reverse gear on drive shaft
4. Stud
5. Main drive shaft, front half
6. Woodruff key for clutch gear
7. Needle cage (3rd gear)
8. 3rd gear
9. Synchronizer stop ring (3rd gear)
10. Clutch gear (3rd and 4th speeds)
11. Synchronizer stop ring (4th gear)
12. Needle bearing inner race (4th gear)
13. Needle cage (4th gear)
14. 4th gear
15. Thrust washer (4th gear)

**Fig. 76.** Main drive shaft is shown here in exploded view. Front of car would be at the right.

should be replaced. Premature wear of stop rings indicates poor clutch condition or incorrect operation of clutch.

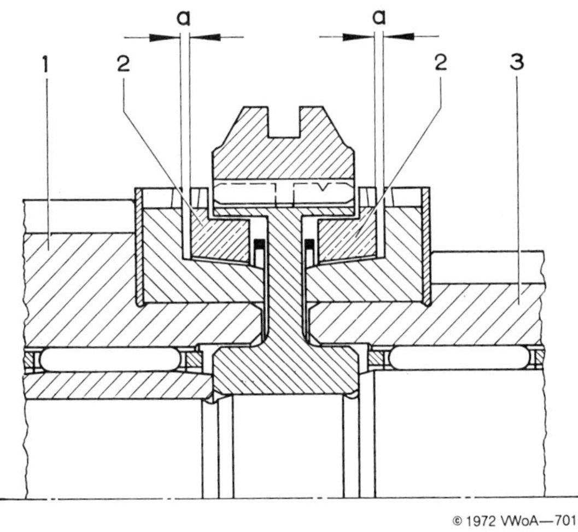


1. 4th gear
2. Synchro stop rings
3. 3rd gear

**Fig. 77.** Clearance between stop ring faces and clutch teeth of 3rd and 4th gears is shown here. Clearance is "a". See text.

c. If a gear will not engage when clutch is fully released, the stop ring teeth may be too far out of line with the splines of the operating sleeve. Worn slots in the stop ring cause this condition.

7. Check 4th gear thrust washer for wear and replace if necessary.

**To inspect rear section of shaft:**

1. Check main drive shaft pilot for wear.
2. Check splines for wear and damage.
3. Check oil seal (mating) surface for scoring and signs of wear.
4. Check reverse gear on main drive shaft for wear and damage. Replace gear if necessary.

**To assemble main drive shaft:**

1. Assemble synchro unit for 3rd and 4th gears, observing following points:
   a. Replace clutch gears and operating sleeves in pairs only.
   b. Install operating sleeve with the groove 0.039 inch (1 mm) deep toward 4th gear. The clutch gear has chamfer on 3rd gear side to facilitate assembly.
   c. Assemble clutch gear/operating sleeve with etched matching marks in line. These marks are shown at "C" in Fig. 78. For correct assembly the marks must line up.

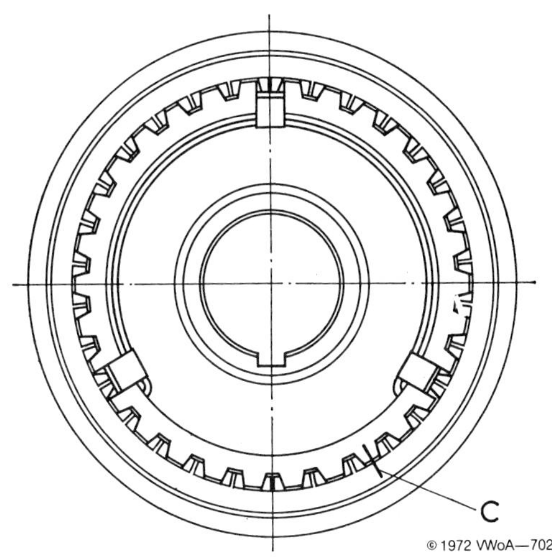


**Fig. 78.** Etched line shown here at "C" marks assembly position for clutch gear/operating sleeve of synchro unit.

5

   d. Install shifting plates and snap rings. Make sure that the two rings are offset from each other and that the ends of the rings engage behind the shifting plates.
2. Place synchronizer stop ring on coned surface of 3rd gear. Slide needle bearing cage with 3rd gear onto main drive shaft.
3. Insert Woodruff key in drive shaft. Position clutch gear on shaft to have the $\frac{1}{32}$ inch (1 mm) groove toward 3rd gear until the synchronizer stop ring engages with the shifting plates. (This groove is on same side as etched marking line.) Press clutch gear into position.
4. Using repair press, press 4th gear needle bearing inner race into position.
5. Slide needle cage, 4th gear and thrust washer on shaft.

## 4. THE DIFFERENTIAL

The 1966, 1967 and 1968 cars with manual transmission all have the swing rear half-axle and use the same differential. The 1969 cars equipped with manual transmission have the double-joint rear axle and the type of differential found with the Automatic Stick Shift.

## 4.1 Disassembling and Assembling Differential
(swing axle)

**NOTE —**
Instructions for removing the differential were given in step 9 of **3.1 Removing and Installing Differential and Transmission.**

**CAUTION —**
*Do not let ring gear drop on vise jaws. The teeth could be damaged.*

3. Knock ring gear off housing with a drift.
4. Remove pin, drive out differential pinion shaft with a drift and take out differential pinions. Fig. 80 shows the disassembled differential for swing axle.

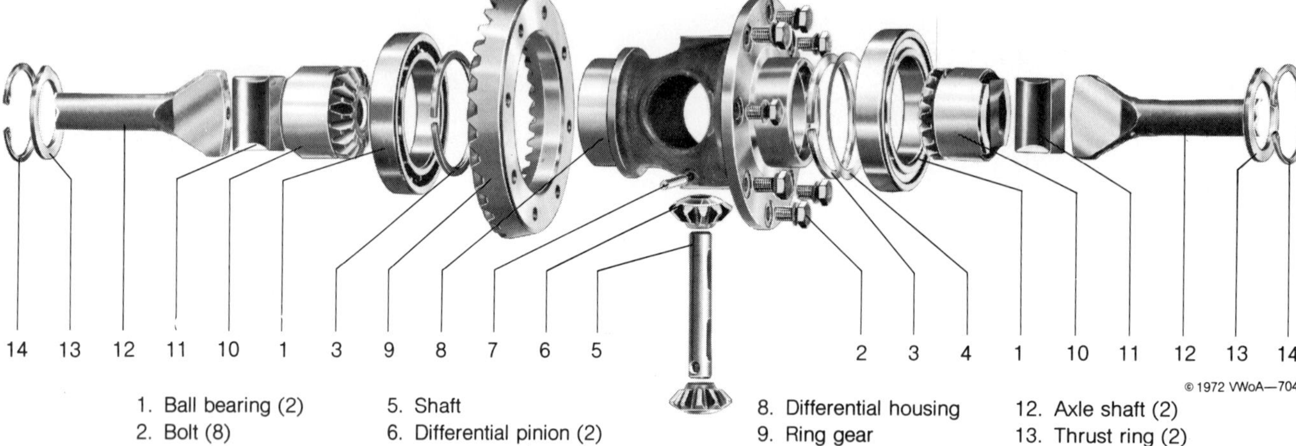


1. Ball bearing (2)
2. Bolt (8)
3. Spacer ring (2)
4. Shim
5. Shaft
6. Differential pinion (2)
7. Pin for shaft
8. Differential housing
9. Ring gear
10. Differential gear (2)
11. Fulcrum plate (4)
12. Axle shaft (2)
13. Thrust ring (2)
14. Circlip 65 mm dia. x 2.5

**Fig. 80.** Differential for cars with manual transmission and swing half-axle is shown here in exploded view. The two differential pinions (6) on the shaft (5) engage with the differential side gears (10) when assembled.

**To disassemble:**

1. Place differential in holding fixture.
2. Take off lock wire and the attaching bolts for the ring gear (also known as crown wheel). Fig. 79 shows the gear in fixture.

**Fig. 79.** Holding fixture for differential is used, as here, when the ring gear attaching bolts are removed.

**To assemble:**

1. Check differential housing for wear and damage, particularly on differential pinion thrust surfaces. Replace parts as necessary.

   **NOTE —**
   When the differential housing has been replaced, the ring gear must be re-adjusted.

2. Peen new differential shaft pin to lock it, as shown in Fig. 81.

**CAUTION —**
*The contact surfaces of housing and ring gear must be clean. Use oilstone to remove any burrs and pressure marks.*

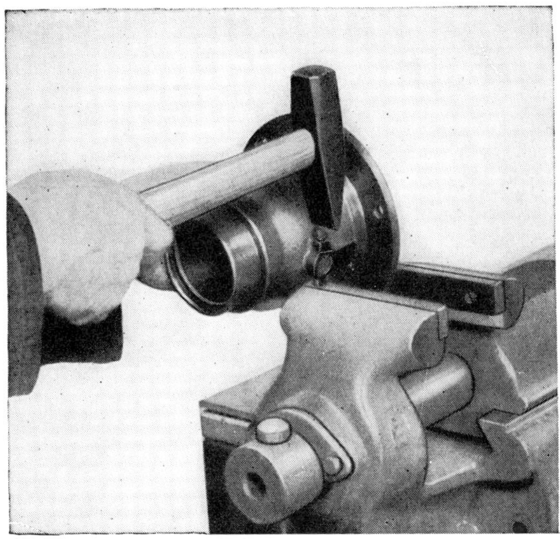

© 1972 VWoA—705

**Fig. 81.** Lock pin for differential pinion shaft is peened after assembly in differential housing.

3. Heat ring gear to about 212 degrees F (100 degrees C). With two locating pins install gear on housing. See Fig. 82.

© 1972 VWoA—706

**Fig. 82.** Heated ring gear is installed on differential housing after burrs and pressure marks have been removed from contact surfaces with oilstone.

***CAUTION —***
*Use only the specified self-locking bolt with spring washers to secure ring gear.*

4. Tighten ring gear bolts to correct torque and secure with lockwire.

5. Turn the differential gears and check axial play. The gears should turn smoothly without jamming.

**NOTE —**
Check backlash between differential gears and pinions. Select thrust rings of thickness that will allow easy installation of circlip. The play between shoulder of gears and thrust rings should be 0.002 to 0.008 inch and should be the same on both sides. Use feeler gauge to measure.

## 4.2 Removing and Installing Differential
(standard transmission, double-joint axle)

On 1969 cars with standard transmission the differential complete with ring gear, tapered roller bearings and drive shaft flanges are of the type designed for the Automatic Stick Shift. The final drive covers house shims for the ring gear, outer races for the tapered roller bearings and oil seals for the drive shaft flanges.



**To remove:**

1. Remove starter. Mount transmission on a transmission stand.
2. Pierce cap in flange with a screwdriver and pry it out. Remove circlip and pry flange off. Do not remove final drive cover at this stage. See Fig. 83.

© 1972 VWoA—756

**Fig. 83.** Flange is pried off final drive cover after cap has been pierced and cap and circlip removed.

3. Rotate transmission 180 degrees and take out the flat, washer-like spacer ring.
4. Remove left cap, circlip, flange, and spacer ring.

Remove nuts and pull off cover with a bridge. See Fig. 84.

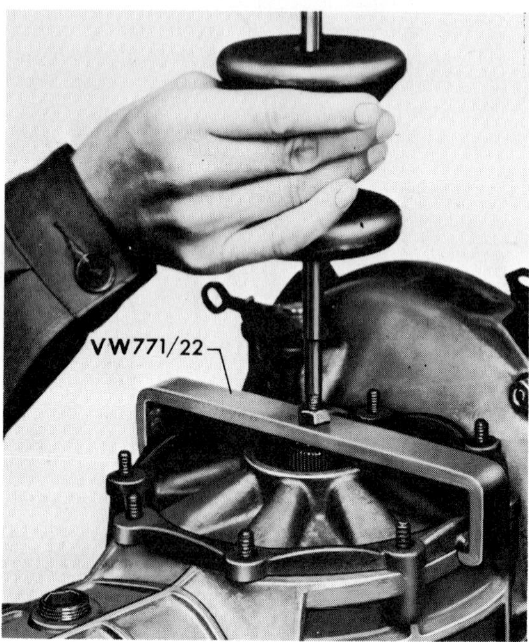


© 1972 VWoA—757

**Fig. 84.** Bridge is used to pull off final drive cover.

5. Press oil seal out of final drive cover (Fig. 85).

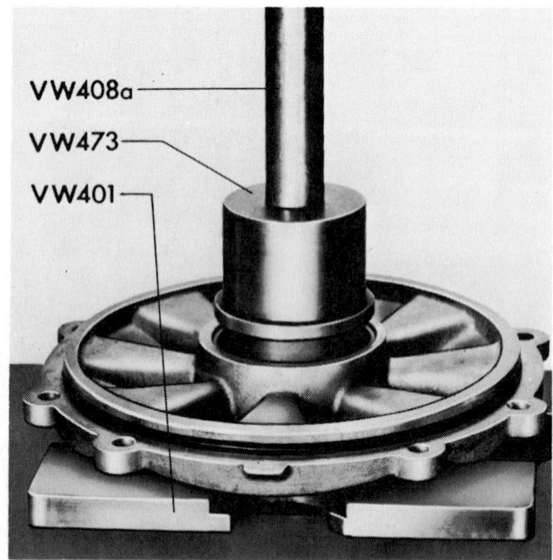


© 1972 VWoA—758

**Fig. 85.** Oil seal is pressed out of final drive cover with the set-up on press shown here.

6. Press out outer race of bearing (Fig. 86).

© 1972 VWoA—943

**Fig. 86.** Outer race of tapered roller bearing is pressed out of final drive cover with this set-up.

***CAUTION*** —
*Covers, bearing outer races and shims must not be mixed up if they are to be used again. As you remove these parts, mark them for relocation.*

7. Take shims off bearing outer race or from cover.
8. Take O-ring off cover.
9. Lift out differential.
10. Take off right final drive cover.

**To install:**

1. Check bearings and oil seals. Replace parts where necessary.
2. Place correct shims in the final drive covers and press in the outer races of bearings, as in Fig. 87.

© 1972 VWoA—944

**Fig. 87.** Bearing outer race is pressed into final drive cover with this set-up.

**NOTE —**
If you are going to adjust the preload or backlash of a tapered roller bearing, you will have to make some precise measurements. For these procedures install the covers first without shims or oil seals. See **5. Adjusting Pinion and Ring Gear.**

3. Coat oil seals lightly with oil and press them all the way into covers. Install O-rings and oil them lightly. Fig. 88 shows installation set-up.

© 1972 VWoA—945

**Fig. 88.** Oil seal is pressed into final drive cover with tools shown here.

4. Install the right cover and tighten nuts to specified torque.
5. Rotate housing 180 degrees in fixture and slide new circlip and reverse gear on the rear section of main shaft. Screw both sections of main shaft together. Then back off one spline, slide on reverse gear and secure with circlip.
6. Install differential (complete with bearings) in its housing and oil the bearings with hypoid oil.
7. Place cover on ring gear side and tighten nuts to specified torque. Drive in oil seal with tool as shown in Fig. 89.

© 1972 VWoA—946

**Fig. 89.** Final drive cover on ring gear side of differential is installed and nuts torqued to specifications. It may be necessary (as here) to drive in oil seal with a tube before installing flange.

8. Insert spacer rings, slide on flanges and secure with new circlips. To help assembly, lift the differential side gear and at the same time press the flange down with a puller and an M 10 stud. You will be squeezing the spacer washer together until the circlip can snap into the groove. See Fig. 90.

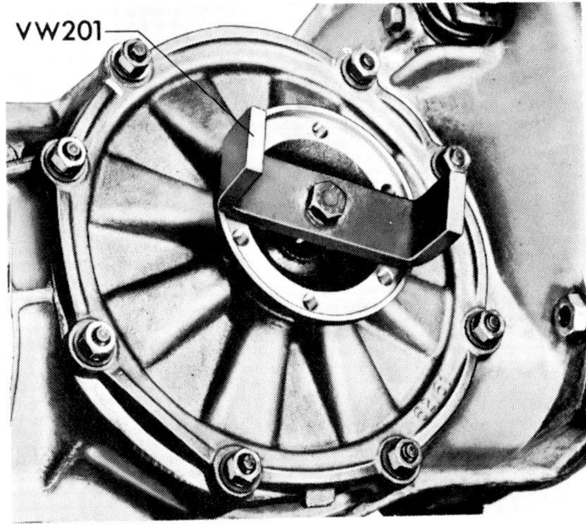


© 1972 VWoA—759

**Fig. 90.** Puller is used to pull flange down into cover, squeezing spacer washer until circlip seats in groove.

5

9. Drive new caps into flanges with tool in Fig. 91.

© 1972 VWoA—760

**Fig. 91.** New cap is driven into flange with a driving sleeve in set-up shown here.

## 4.3 Disassembling and Assembling Differential
(double-joint axle)

The following procedures are the same for 1969 cars with manual transmission and cars with the Automatic Stick Shift. The call-out numbers in Fig. 92 are given in the instructions to help you to visualize the procedures.

1. Differential housing
2. Cover for differential housing
3. Differential gear (long shaft)
4. Differential gear (short shaft)
5. Thrust washer (2)
6. Differential pinion (2)
7. Shaft/differential pinion
8. Pin for shaft
9. Spacer sleeve
10. Ring gear
11. Bolts with spring washers (8)
12. Tapered roller bearing/inner race (2)

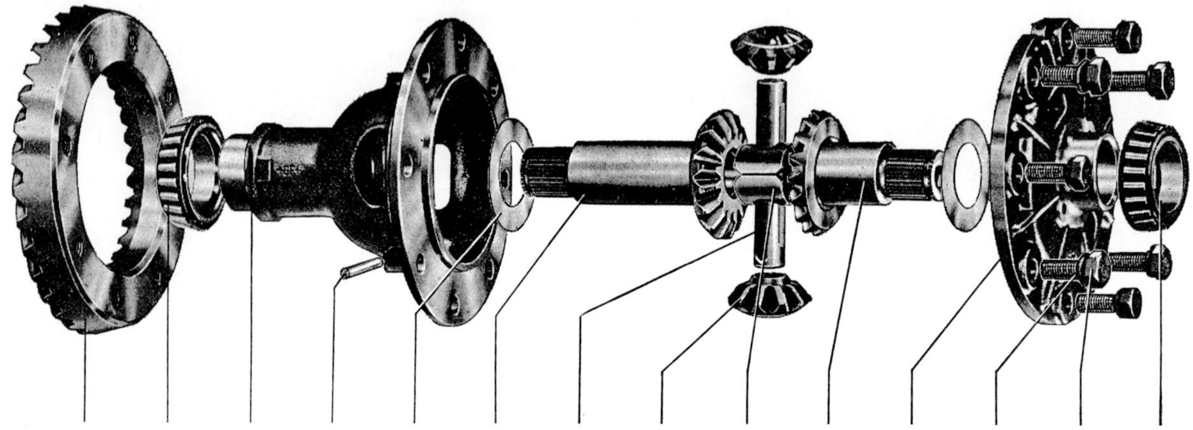

**Fig. 92.** Differential is shown here in exploded view.

**To disassemble:**

1. Put soft covers on the vise jaws to protect differential. Then secure differential in vise, as in Fig. 93.

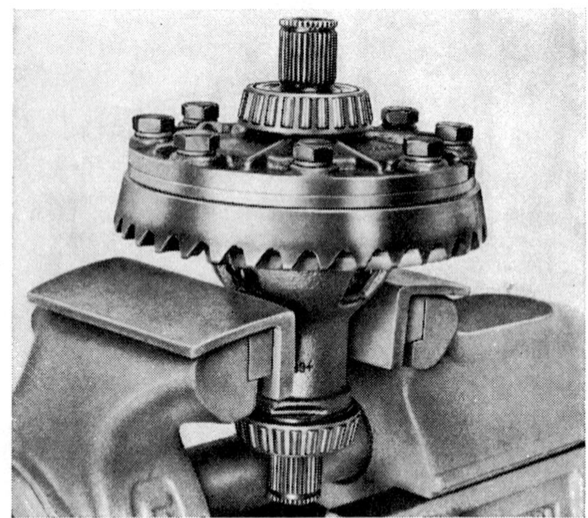



**Fig. 93.** Soft jaw covers protect differential while it is in vise.

2. Remove ring gear bolts (11). With drift (Fig. 94) carefully punch ring gear (10) off shaft. Make sure that ring gear teeth do not hit vise jaws. Use rags to protect them.

**Fig. 94.** Drift is used to press ring gear off housing after ring gear bolts have been removed. Rag under ring gear protects teeth.

3. Pull cover (2) off differential housing (1). (Fig. 95.)

© 1972 VWoA—947

**Fig. 95.** Cover of differential housing is pulled off with this set-up.

4. Take out differential gear (4) and thrust washer (5).
5. With drift drive out retaining pin (8) and shaft (7). See Fig. 96. Take out spacer sleeve (9), pinions (6), side gear (3) and thrust washer (5).

© 1972 VWoA—948

**Fig. 96.** Differential pinion shaft is driven out of differential housing in direction indicated by arrow after retaining pin has been removed.

6. Press bearing inner race off differential cover first, as in Fig. 97.

© 1972 VWoA—936

**Fig. 97.** Bearing inner race is pressed out of differential cover with set-up shown here.

5

7. Now press other bearing inner race (12) off differential housing with set-up shown in Fig. 98.

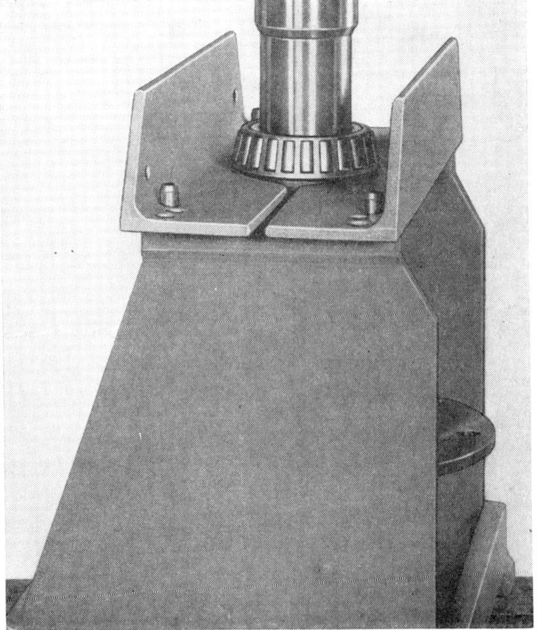

© 1972 VWoA—937

**Fig. 98.** Special support assembly shown here is used to press bearing inner race off differential housing.

**To assemble:**

1. Check bevel gears, thrust washers, thrust surfaces in housing, cover, ring gear, bolts and spacer sleeve. Replace worn or damaged parts.
2. Heat inner race of tapered roller bearing to 212 degrees F (100 degrees C) and install it on housing. For correct seating (Fig. 99), apply pressure of 3 tons.

© 1972 VWoA—938

**Fig. 99.** Tapered roller bearing is pressed onto differential housing after being heated to 212 degrees F.

3. Insert side gear with long shaft and thrust washer into differential housing.

**NOTE ——**
If insufficient backlash has damaged gear teeth in a differential not fitted with a spacer sleeve, the sleeve should be service-installed. (See **4.4 Axial Play**.)

4. Install differential pinions, spacer sleeve and shaft. Secure shaft with new pin. Using center punch and a block for support, peen pin at both ends, as in Fig. 100.

**NOTE ——**
If housing, cover, a side gear or a thrust washer has been replaced, axial play between the side gears will require re-adjustment. Service installation of spacer sleeve is necessary when grinding of end faces of differential gears is required. (See **4.4 Axial Play**.)

© 1972 VWoA—949

**Fig. 100.** Retaining pin for differential pinion shaft is peened at both ends after installation.

5. Heat ring gear to 212 degrees F (100 degrees C) and install on housing with two guide pins, as in Fig. 101.

**NOTE ——**
Contact surfaces of housing and ring gear must be clean. Use oilstone to remove burrs and pressure marks.

© 1972 VWoA—939

**Fig. 101.** Ring gear, heated to 212 degrees F, is installed in differential cover with this set-up.

6. Heat bearing inner race to 212 degrees F (100 degrees C) and install on cover. Apply pressure of 3 tons to seat race fully.

7. Place cover with thrust washer and side gear on housing and insert bolts. Tighten bolts diagonally to specified torque.

**NOTE** —
Use only specified, new bolts and spring washers.

The differential bevel gears must turn smoothly and without jamming.

## 4.4 Axial Play
(double-joint axle)

The spacer sleeve between the bevel gears in the differential keeps the backlash correct even when there is axial pressure on the side gears. Obviously, the fitting of this assembly calls for precision. If the housing, the differential cover, a side gear or the spacer sleeve itself must be replaced, the length of the spacer will require adjustment.

**To adjust axial play:**

1. Place side gear (short shaft) and both thrust washers into differential cover. Slide bevel gear on shaft and press tightly against cover. Hold short shaft with suitable clamping device. Fig. 102 shows the operation.

2. Place side gear (long shaft) into differential housing.

© 1972 VWoA—753

**Fig. 102.** Side gear (short shaft) with two thrust washers is installed in differential cover with this set-up.

3. Assemble differential. Place shortest spacer sleeve (part No. 004 517 241) on top of short shaft bevel gear. (Fig. 103 illustrates procedure to find shortest sleeve.) Attach housing, including long shaft, to cover with four M 8 x 20 bolts and washers on ring gear side.

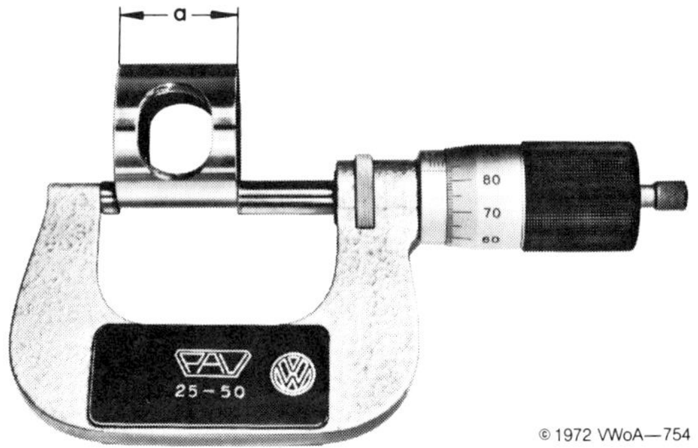


© 1972 VWoA—754

**Fig. 103.** Shortest spacer sleeve, found by actual measurement with micrometer, is used as standard for adjustment of axial play in differential. Dimension to be measured is shown here as "a".

5

4. Attach measuring bar and dial indicator with extension to end face of side gear, as in Fig. 104. Make sure that the indicator extension is in contact with edge of housing neck.

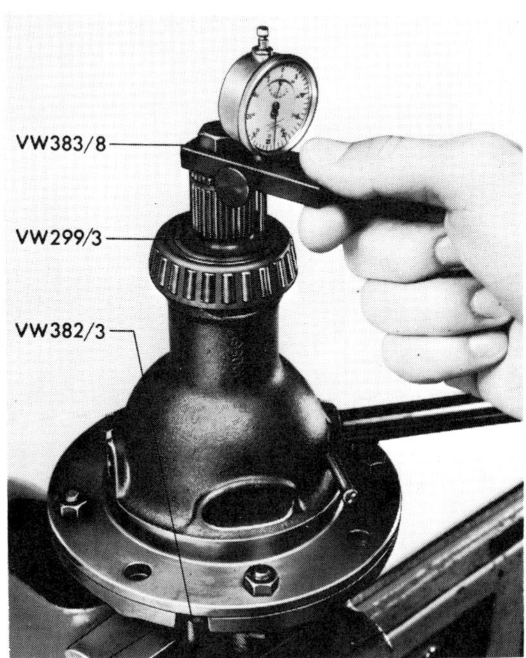


© 1972 VWoA—755

**Fig. 104.** Axial play between differential bevel gears is measured with this set-up of measuring bar and dial indicator. Dial indicator extension is in contact with edge of differential housing neck.

5. Move side gear up and down and note amount of play shown on dial.
6. Add play measurement to sleeve length. Look up result in **Table b**, in column under "x" (range). Entries on same line in other columns give sleeve length "l" and part number.

### Table b. Sleeve Lengths*

| "x" (Range) | "l" (Sleeve length) | Part number |
|---|---|---|
| 28.82 to 28.90 | 28.77 | 004 517 241 |
| 28.91 to 28.99 | 28.86 | 004 517 242 |
| 29.00 to 29.08 | 28.95 | 004 517 243 |
| 29.09 to 29.18 | 29.04 | 004 517 244 |

***Lengths in millimeters**

7. Disassemble differential. Remove measuring sleeve and replace with sleeve of length determined in step 6. Reassemble differential, exactly as before. Recheck play, which now should be from 0 to 0.005 inch (0 to 0.14 mm). Completely re-assemble differential.

## 5. ADJUSTMENT OF PINION AND RING GEAR

In both cars with the swing rear axle and cars with the double-joint rear axle, the quiet running and service life of the final drive depend on precise adjustment between the drive pinion and the ring gear. Every gear set has one particular setting at which it runs smoothly, and even a few hundreths of a millimeter are important in determining that setting. Adjusting the pinion and ring gear is not a task for most do-it-yourselfers, and certainly not for every car owner, but if you are interested in learning how your car works, you will find the following discussion profitable. This particular adjustment is the same on all cars covered in this Manual.

### 5.1 Gear Fit

At the factory the drive pinion and ring gear in your car were machined as a pair and fitted with a master gauge to the dimension shown as $\mathbf{R_o}$ in Fig. 105. This measurement is the distance from the center line of the ring gear to the face of the pinion and is 2.3110 inches (58.70 mm). At this setting there is no backlash between the gears; that is, the ring gear cannot be turned in either direction.

At this standard setting your drive pinion and ring gear were then put on a testing device to determine the adjustment at which they would run most silently together. The pinion was moved back and forth along its axis (horizontal arrows in Fig. 105) and at the same time the ring gear was lifted out of full mesh (vertical arrows) until the best setting was found. This deviation from the standard setting $\mathbf{R_o}$ is given as **r**, and the final distance from centerline of ring gear to face of drive pinion in the adjusted setting is $\mathbf{R_o}$ plus **r**; which, as shown in Fig. 105, gives **R**. At the same time the backlash introduced into the setting must not exceed 0.15 to 0.25 mm. That is, the ring gear can be turned by hand against the drive pinion not less than 0.15 mm but not more than 0.25 mm. The value of **r** and other pertinent information is stamped on the faces of the pinion and ring gear in each set of gears. The stampings are shown in the figure.

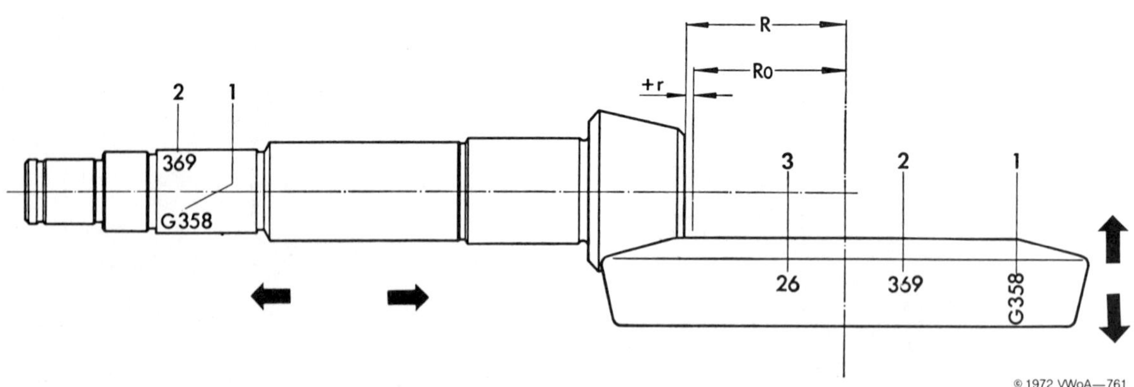


**Fig. 105.** Gear fit in final drive is illustrated in this diagram of drive pinion and ring gear setting. Measurement $\mathbf{R_o}$ is set with factory master gauge at 2.3110 inches (58.70 mm). Measurement **r** is further adjustment required to make particular gear set silent-running. Factory sets this deviation from $\mathbf{R_o}$ to obtain **R**. Value of **r** in hundredths of a millimeter is shown at 3. Code number at 1 gives type and number of gear teeth. Identification at 2 gives matching number of the gear set. Large arrows show directions in which pinion and ring gear can be moved for adjustment.

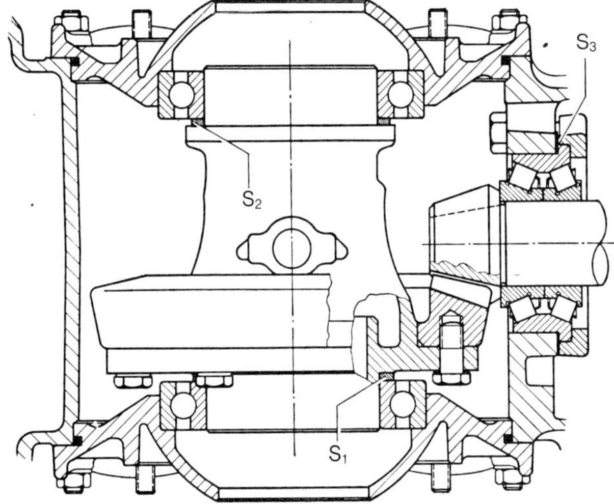


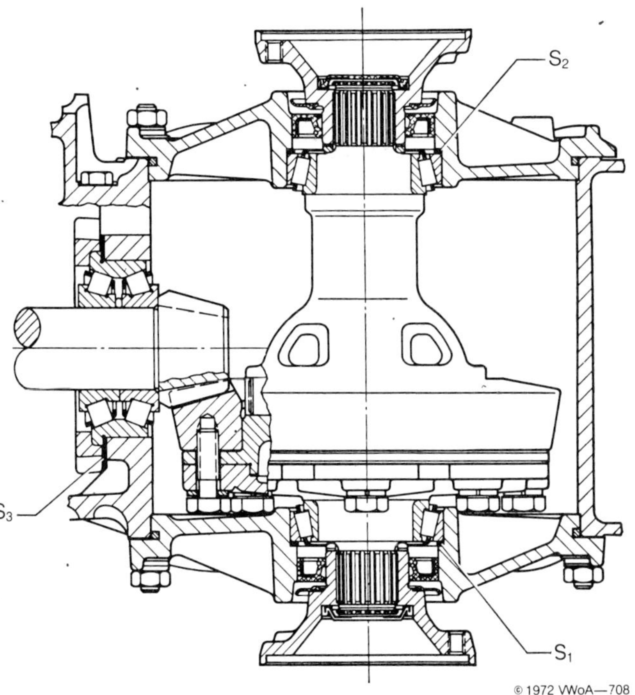


$S_1$ Shim at ring gear end of differential
$S_2$ Shim at end opposite ring gear
$S_3$ Shim for pinion

**Fig. 106.** Shims required to adjust drive pinion and ring gear are shown in these diagrams. Upper diagram shows assembly for swing axle, lower diagram for double-joint axle. Shim $S_3$ between roller bearing and differential housing determines distance from center of ring gear to drive pinion face. Shim $S_1$ at ring gear end of differential and shim $S_2$ at opposite end together make up total shim thickness **S** which controls ring gear backlash. Arrows in Fig. 105 show movements controlled by shims.

The marking G on a gear set means a Gleason gear set, K a Klingelnberg gear set. The number given with either initial is the gear ratio. For example, G 358 means a Gleason gear set with 35 teeth on ring gear, and 8 on pinion gear.

The value **r** is always given in hundreds of a millimeter. For example, the number 26 at the **r** position means that **r** for that set of gears equals 0.26 mm (0.010 inch).

The gear set usually needs re-adjusting only when parts directly affecting the adjustment have been replaced. When the differential housing, a final drive cover or a differential tapered roller bearing has been replaced, it is sufficient to reset the ring gear only. Both pinion and ring gear, however, will need re-adjustment if the transmission case or the complete gear set has been replaced. If the double-tapered roller bearing for the pinion is replaced, only the pinion needs re-adjustment. The object of the adjustment, of course, is to set the gears to give the same quiet running they provided when your car left the factory.

The first step in this adjustment is to locate the pinion by placing shims between the double-tapered roller bearing and the transmission housing. The resulting measurement from ring gear centerline to pinion end face should correspond exactly with the dimension $\mathbf{R_o}$ plus **r** obtained at the factory.

5

The ring gear is then installed and adjusted to give the specified backlash and a certain preload between it and the tapered roller bearing. The amount of preload is measured by the friction obtained in the tapered roller bearings when the ring gear is rotated. Fig. 106 shows where adjustments are measured. For these measurements you will need a special torque gauge.

***CAUTION—***
*Care and cleanliness during all assembly work and measuring operations are an absolute necessity if correct results are to be obtained.*

## 5.2 What Needs Adjusting and When

As in the other major assemblies and systems of the car, replacement or adjustment of one part often requires re-adjustment of other parts. **Table c** on the following page lists the adjustments that will be required when individual transmission or differential components are replaced. Use of this Table will save you unnecessary work.

**NOTE—**
For conversion purposes 1 mm = 0.03937 inch. (See conversion table at end of **GETTING STARTED**.)

### Table c. Required Adjustments for Repaired Parts

| Part replaced | Parts to be adjusted | | |
|---|---|---|---|
| | Pinion | Shift forks | Ring gear* |
| Transmission case | X | X | X |
| Final drive covers | | | X |
| Differential ball bearings | | | X |
| Differential tapered roller bearings | | | X |
| Pinion double tapered roller bearing | X | X | X |
| Ring gear and pinion | X | X | X |
| Differential housing | | | X |
| Differential housing cover | | | X |

***Includes adjustment of differential bearings**

### Table d. Symbols Used in Ring Gear/Pinion Adjustment

| Symbol | Designation | Dimension |
|---|---|---|
| S | Total shim thickness ($S_1$ + $S_2$) is found by computing differential housing length from housing internal dimension or from tapered roller bearing preload | mm (can be from 0.95-2.10 mm) |
| $S_1$ | Shim at ring gear end of differential | See table for thickness |
| $S_2$ | Shim at opposite end | See table for thickness |
| $S_3$ | Shim between double tapered roller and housing | See table for thickness |
| r | Deviation from $R_o$ marked on ring gear | 1/100 mm (can be from 0.05 to 0.65 mm) |
| $R_o$ | Length of master gauge on special test machine | 58.70 mm |
| R | Position of pinion in relation to ring gear centerline at quietest running point (nominal dimension) | $R = R_o + r$ |
| $Sv_o$ | Backlash | Given in 1/100 mm |
| $Sv_o$ A | Average backlash; average of $Sv_o$ readings | Given in 1/100 mm |
| e | Difference between zero setting on mandrel and actual pinion position without shims | 0.10 to 0.50 mm |
| $\Delta S_1$ | Axial movement of ring gear to the specified mean backlash (correction value) | Given in 1/100 mm |
| w | Correction factor for gear set concerned | |
| h | Ring gear lift from no-play mesh position to mean backlash position | Given in 1/100 mm (see Shim table) |
| G 358 | Gear set G = Gleason 358 | Ring gear/pinion ratio 35/8 |
| K | Gear set K = Klingelnberg | |
| J | Length of final drive housing between ball bearings | |
| L | Length of differential housing | |
| P | Preload on ball bearings | |

*CAUTION* —
*Care and cleanliness in all assembly and measuring operations are essential if the results are to be satisfactory.*

The following steps give the basic sequence for adjustment of the ring gear set after the necessary measurements have been made. The dimensional references are to Fig. 106.

1. Determine and adjust pinion $S_3$ and check.
2. Determine total shim thickness **S**.
3. Adjust ring gear backlash and establish $S_1$.
4. Determine $S_2$, add preload of 0.07 mm per side and assemble differential.
5. Check backlash.

**Table d** lists symbols used in the instructions on adjustment of ring gear and pinion. Shims are available in millimeter sizes only, and dimensions are given in mm to conform.

## 5.3 Adjusting Pinion
(swing and double-joint axles, standard transmission)

This procedure does not apply to the Automatic Stick Shift.

*CAUTION* —
*The pinion must be adjusted if the transmission case, the double-tapered roller bearing or the gear set itself has been replaced. For accurate measurement you must have all surfaces spotlessly clean.*

**To adjust:**

1. Assemble pinion up to needle bearing for 1st gear. Tighten round nut to correct torque but do not lock it.
2. Install pre-assembled pinion in the transmission case without shim $S_3$. Tighten bearing retainer screws or retaining ring to correct torque.

**NOTE** —
To help align the pinion in the housing, it is a good idea to install the gear carrier.

*CAUTION* —
*Before installing the pinion, lubricate bearing with hypoid oil. If bearing is dry or lubricated with any other oil, the test results will be inaccurate.*



3. Measure preload (turning torque) by checking double tapered roller bearing preload. Use a torque gauge, adapter and a 32 mm socket. Fig. 107 shows set-up.

**Fig. 107.** Torque gauge is used to check the double-tapered roller bearing preload that was obtained with the shim $S_3$ fitting.

Test results should be:

5

| | new bearing | used bearing (after 30 miles running) |
|---|---|---|
| Turning torque | 5 to 18 in. lbs. (6 to 21 cmkg) | 2.6 to 6 in. lbs. (3 to 7 cmkg) |

## 5.4 Finding Measurement "e"
(swing axle differential)

This measurement can be obtained only with special mandrel and setting block shown in Fig. 108.

**Fig. 108.** Special mandrel used to obtain measurement **e** is shown here with dial indicator.

**To find measurement:**

1. Using press and special adapters, check that ball bearings are tight in the final drive covers.

> ***CAUTION —***
> *When installing the cover, do not use a mallet. Pounding could loosen bearings and upset subsequent measurement from bearing to bearing. Pull cover down by uniformly tightening the eight nuts.*

2. Install right final drive cover and tighten nuts to correct torque.
3. Place mandrel on setting block, install dial indicator with 5 mm extension in the mandrel and zero the dial indicator with 1 mm preload. See that the setting block and mandrel contact surfaces are spotlessly clean. Fig. 108 shows mandrel on block.
4. Place mandrel in transmission case, install left final drive cover and tighten nuts.
5. While watching dial indicator through the hole in the mandrel, bring extension pin into contact with pinion end face. Then turn slowly until indicator shows the maximum reading, as in Fig. 109.

**Fig. 109.** Installed mandrel measures distance from mandrel zero to drive pinion face. Dial is read through open end of mandrel and opening for axle in left final drive cover. Pinion face is to left of dial.

> **NOTE —**
> If the ring gear also requires adjustment, the housing dimension J should be measured when pinion is adjusted. (See **5. Adjustment of Pinion and Ring Gear.**)

## 5.5 Finding Measurement "e"
(double-joint axle)

1. Take oil seals and shims out of both final drive covers, install bearing outer races again and press on with proper tool.
2. Install right final drive cover on transmission case. Place setting appliance on cover and tighten nuts to correct torque, as in Fig. 110.

**Fig. 110.** Setting appliance shown here is used to install right final drive cover for measurement of value **e** of differential for double-joint axle.

3. Insert dial indicator (3 mm range) with 18 mm extension in measuring mandrel. Zero dial indicator on setting block with 1 mm preload.
4. Rotate transmission housing 180 degrees and place mandrel in housing. Install left final drive cover and tighten nuts.
5. Press right bearing outer race against mandrel by turning spindle of the setting appliance until mandrel can just be turned by hand.
6. Watch dial indicator through the hole in the mandrel while bringing extension pin into contact with pinion end face. Turn slowly until dial shows the maximum reading (starts to reverse direction). Note this reading as **e** but take the preload (1 mm) into consideration.
7. Read off the deviation **r** already on the ring gear and find thickness of shim $S_3$.
8. Install pinion with shims $S_3$ and tighten bearing retainer bolts or pinion retaining nut to correct torque.

### 5.6 Finding $S_3$ Shim Thickness

Example **only**:

> **NOTE —**
> In this case $\mathbf{R_o}$ and **R** of tool used are equal.

For this example we will take $\mathbf{R_o}$ to be 58.70 mm and the measured reading **e** from the mandrel/setting block to be 0.48. Subtracting **e** from $\mathbf{R_o}$ will give the actual measurement to the pinion face without shims.

$$\mathbf{R_o} = 58.70 \text{ mm}$$
$$\mathbf{e} = \underline{0.48 \text{ mm}}$$
$$\mathbf{R_o} - \mathbf{e} = 58.22 \text{ mm} \quad \text{(actual measurement)}$$

The adjustment **r** is added to $\mathbf{R_o}$ to obtain the quietest running. The value of **r** for each gear set is marked on the ring gear. For this example we take **r** to be 0.18 mm. Then

$$\mathbf{R_o} = 58.70 \text{ mm}$$
$$\mathbf{r} = \underline{0.18 \text{ mm}}$$
$$\mathbf{R_o} + \mathbf{r} = 58.88 \text{ mm} \quad \text{(nominal pinion measurement)}$$

To find the $S_3$ shim thickness required we subtract the actual measurement $(\mathbf{R_o} - \mathbf{e})$ from the nominal pinion measurement $(\mathbf{R_o} + \mathbf{r})$

$$\mathbf{R_o} + \mathbf{r} = 58.88 \text{ mm}$$
$$\mathbf{R_o} - \mathbf{e} = \underline{58.22 \text{ mm}}$$
$$S_3 = 0.66 \text{ mm} \quad \text{(shim thickness required)}$$

Combining these two calculations gives us the following simple formula:

$$S_3 \text{ nominal} = \mathbf{e} + \mathbf{r}$$

In our example this would be:

$$\mathbf{e} = 0.48 \text{ mm}$$
$$\underline{+\mathbf{r} = 0.18 \text{ mm}}$$
$$S_3 \text{ nominal} = 0.66 \text{ mm}$$

(Remember that **r** is given for each gearset.)

This example shows how the thickness of the shim $S_3$ is obtained. According to the simple formula, it is necessary only to find the dimension **e** between pinion end face and mandrel (0.48 mm in example). The sum of **e** and **r** then gives us the shim thickness for $S_3$ (0.66 mm in example), and from this we are able to find an actual shim thickness of 0.65 mm as shown in **Table e.** The shim combination from the table to fit this example would be No. 5 + No. 1.

The shims listed in **Table e** should be measured carefully before you use them. Take readings with a micrometer at several points on the shim. Check for burrs or damage and use only shims in perfect condition.



### Table e. Shim Measurements

| Calculated shim thickness required | Shim No. | Shim thickness | $S_3$ actual |
|---|---|---|---|
| 0.33-0.37 | 2 + 1 | 0.20 + 0.15 | 0.35 |
| 0.38-0.42 | 4 | 0.40 | 0.40 |
| 0.43-0.47 | 3 + 1 | 0.30 + 0.15 | 0.45 |
| 0.48-0.52 | 5 | 0.50 | 0.50 |
| 0.54-0.57 | 4 + 1 | 0.40 + 0.15 | 0.55 |
| 0.58-0.62 | 6 | 0.60 | 0.60 |
| 0.63-0.67 | 5 + 1 | 0.50 + 0.15 | 0.65 |
| 0.68-0.72 | 7 | 0.70 | 0.70 |
| 0.73-0.77 | 6 + 1 | 0.60 + 0.15 | 0.75 |
| 0.78-0.82 | 8 | 0.80 | 0.80 |
| 0.83-0.87 | 7 + 1 | 0.70 + 0.15 | 0.85 |
| 0.88-0.92 | 9 | 0.90 | 0.90 |
| 0.93-0.97 | 8 + 1 | 0.80 + 0.15 | 0.95 |
| 0.98-1.02 | 10 | 1.00 | 1.00 |
| 1.03-1.07 | 9 + 1 | 0.90 + 0.15 | 1.05 |
| 1.08-1.12 | 9 + 2 | 0.90 + 0.20 | 1.10 |
| 1.13-1.17 | 10 + 1 | 1.00 + 0.15 | 1.15 |
| 1.18-1.22 | 10 + 2 | 1.20 | 1.20 |
| 1.23-1.27 | 6 + 5 + 1 | 0.60 + 0.60 + 0.15 | 1.25 |
| 1.28-1.32 | 10 + 3 | 1.00 + 0.30 | 1.30 |

Note:—
Measure the shims at several points with a micrometer. Check shims for burrs and damage. Use only shims which are in perfect condition.

5

**Table f** lists shims supplied as replacement parts.

### Table f. Shims Supplied as $S_3$ Replacement Parts

| Shim No. | Part No. | Thickness (mm) |
|---|---|---|
| 1 | 113 311 391 | 0.15 |
| 2 | 113 311 392 | 0.20 |
| 3 | 113 311 393 | 0.30 |
| 4 | 113 311 394 | 0.40 |
| 5 | 113 311 395 | 0.50 |
| 6 | 113 311 396 | 0.60 |
| 7 | 113 311 397 | 0.70 |
| 8 | 113 311 398 | 0.80 |
| 9 | 113 311 399 | 0.90 |
| 10 | 113 311 400 | 1.00 |
| 11 | 113 311 401 | 1.20 |

> **NOTE —**
> It is a good idea to set the preload of the differential tapered roller bearings before installing the pinion. Pinion is then installed as a complete unit with transmission. This method usually avoids having to readjust the differential tapered roller bearing after measurements have been rechecked.

**To check shim measurements** (swing axle):

1. Using the setting block, zero dial indicators with 1 mm preload. Fig. 111 on next page shows set-up.

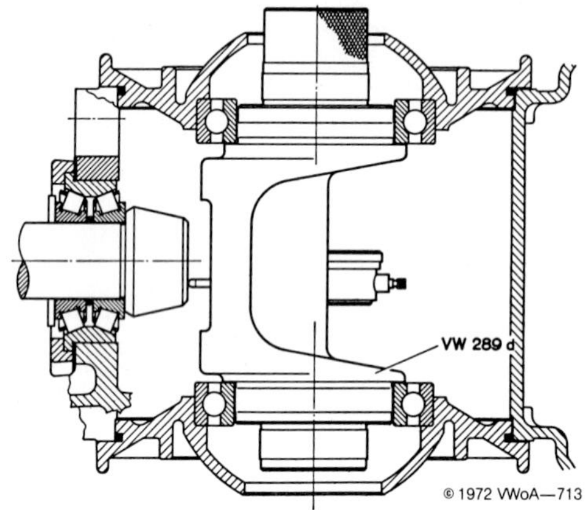


**Fig. 111.** Swing axle measurement is shown here. Dial indicator pin is on face of drive pinion. Dial should show **r** ± 0.04 mm. See text.

2. Check all measurements.

**NOTE ——**
If shim $S_3$ has been selected correctly, the dial indicator read counterclockwise (red figures) should now show the deviation **r** within a tolerance of ± 0.04 mm.

**To check shim measurements** (double-joint axle):

1. Using setting block, zero dial indicator with 1 mm preload. Fig. 112 shows set-up.

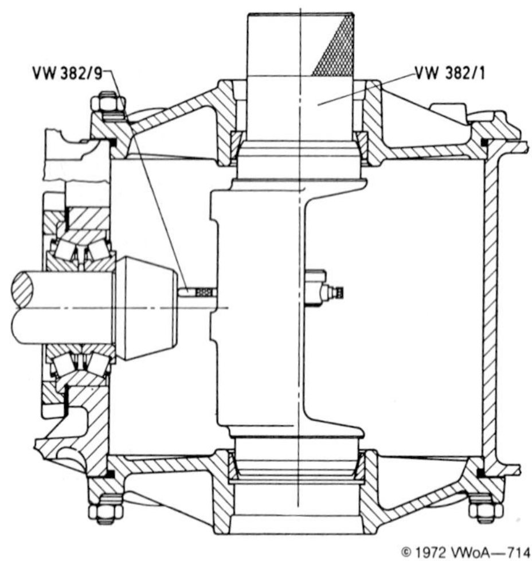


**Fig. 112.** Double-joint axle measurement is shown here. If $S_3$ shim thickness is correct, dial will show **r** ± 0.04 mm. Dial indicator pin is on drive pinion face.

**NOTE ——**
If the shim $S_3$ has been selected correctly, the dial indicator read counterclockwise (red figures) should now show deviation **r** within a tolerance of ± 0.04 mm.

2. Check all measurements.
3. Take out measuring mandrel.

## 5.7 Adjusting Ring Gear (swing axle)

The ring gear needs adjusting only when the parts that directly affect the ring gear setting have been replaced. These parts are: gear set, transmission case, differential housing, final drive covers, ball bearings.

This procedure will require measurement of the depth **(J)** of the transmission case; measurement of the length **(L)** of the differential housing, and adjustment of axial play **(C)** of the ring gear. In this case axial play is the backlash.

**To measure "J":**

1. Attach dial indicator bracket to one of the studs for the axle tube retainer. Place indicator in bracket and set to zero, as in Fig. 113.

**Fig. 113. J** measurement to find depth of transmission case is made with this set-up. Dial indicator pin is resting on lip of mandrel. Dial is zeroed.

2. Rotate transmission case 180 degrees to let mandrel drop on inner race of ball bearing in the left

final drive cover. The reading now shown on the dial indicator is added to the length of the mandrel. This addition gives the internal dimension of the case **J**, which is required for ring gear adjustment. Fig. 114 shows dial gauge after rotation of case.

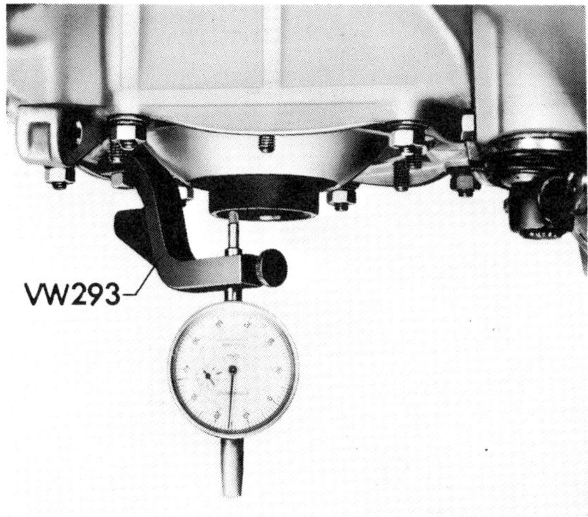




**Fig. 114.** Mandrel, which had been resting on opposite drive cover, falls against dial indicator pin when transmission case is rotated 180 degrees. Reading on dial plus mandrel length then gives **J**.

| Example: | |
|---|---|
| Length of mandrel | 107.88 mm |
| indicator reading | + 1.82 mm |
| Case dimension **J** | 109.70 mm |

3. Take off indicator bracket and screw nut back on left cover.
4. Rotate transmission case back to upright position. Install spindle on right cover and bolt in place.
5. Press left final drive cover off with the spindle and pull mandrel out of transmission case.

**To measure "L":**

1. Equip dial indicator with a 28 mm extension from the setting appliance and insert into the device. Place adjusting plate on the polished surface for the differential and set the dial indicator to zero. See Fig. 115.
2. Raise the dial indicator extension and insert the differential into the device. Measure the housing at several points and take the average of the readings. See Fig. 116.

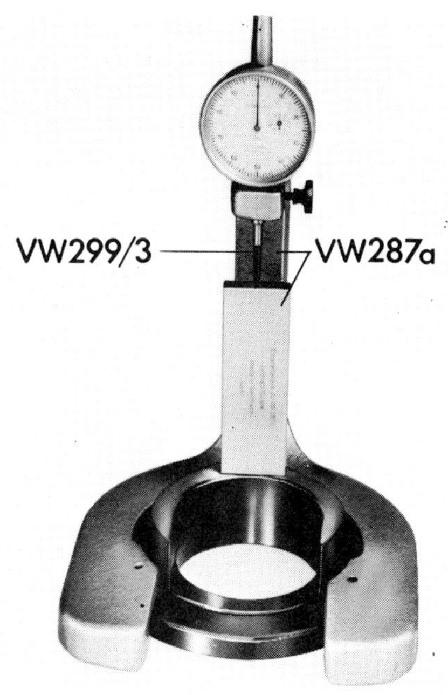




**Fig. 115. L** measurement on differential housing requires special bracket shown here. Dial indicator is set to zero when pin rests on adjusting block 102.51 mm long.

5

**Fig. 116.** Differential housing, with ring gear in place, is set on bracket and readings taken at several points around rim. Length is then easily computed. See text.

3. The dial indicator reading is added to the nominal dimension of the adjusting block to obtain the length of the differential housing **L**.

Example:

| | |
|---|---|
| Nominal dimension of adjusting block | 102.51 mm |
| Dial indicator reading | + 0.39 mm |
| Length of differential housing **L** | 102.90 mm |

**NOTE** —
If the proper measuring device is not available the length of the differential housing can be obtained with a caliper square.

**To adjust "C"** (transmission installed):

1. Place the differential between the two thrust plates of measuring device. Insert retaining bolts from the ring gear side and tighten the nuts. Fig. 117 shows set-up.

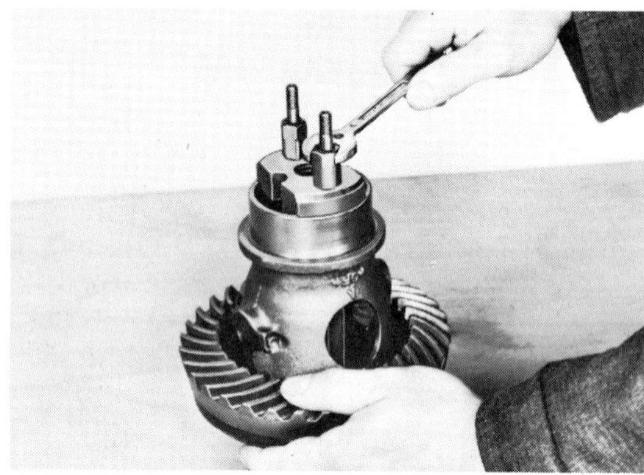



**Fig. 117.** Thrust plates are bolted on differential in first step of procedure to measure ring gear axial play.

2. Attach bracket (Fig. 118) to gear carrier to secure pinion shaft.

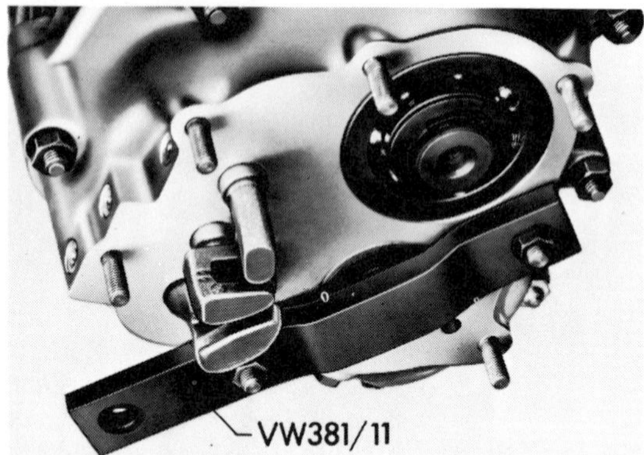




**Fig. 118.** Bracket on gear carrier holds drive pinion in place for measurement of ring gear axial play. Measurement is made with differential installed.

3. Install right final drive cover and differential in the transmission case.
4. Insert 2.8 mm gauge ring on the ring gear side and install left final drive cover. Nuts for both final drive covers must be tightened diagonally to correct torque.
5. Position tool spindle on the left final drive cover. Fully tighten the spindle attaching nuts.
6. Rotate transmission 180 degrees. Attach bracket of indicator for measuring ring gear backlash to the clamping bolts. Attach bracket to the two thrust plates with two of the axle tube retainer nuts, as in Fig. 119.

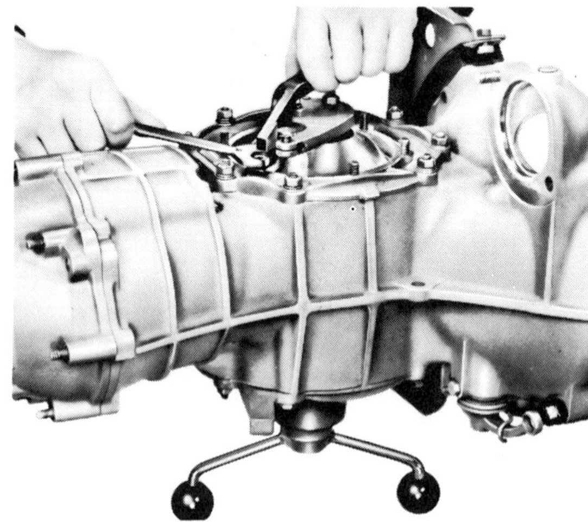



**Fig. 119.** Backlash indicator bracket is attached to the two clamping bolts that are holding the differential between thrust plates. Differential is in the transmission case.

7. Attach bracket of indicator for axial adjustment of the differential. Install dial indicator with extension.

***CAUTION*** —
*To prevent errors of measurement as a result of axial play in the differential bearings, be careful to bottom ring gear in the housing. Also, when setting dial indicator make sure that the ball bearing in the left cover is seated correctly. Retighten spindle, back it off and check the dial indicator setting.*

8. With spindle, pull differential all the way into the bearing in the left cover. Release spindle pressure and set indicator for axial adjustment to 2.8

mm (thickness of setting ring) or to the actual dimension of the measured spacer ring. Fig. 120 shows set-up schematically.

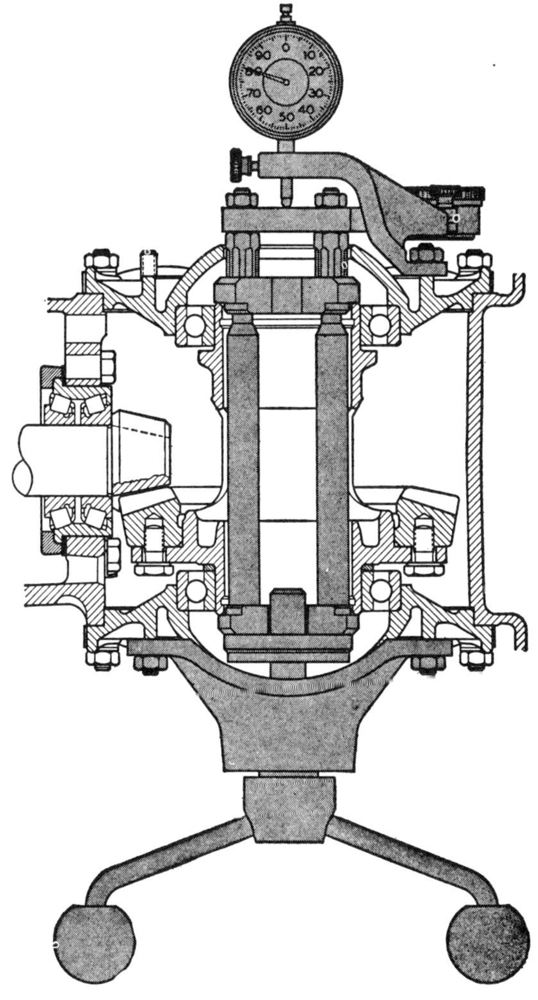



**Fig. 120.** Assembled apparatus for measuring ring gear axial play is shown here in cross section. Spindle is used to draw differential into transmission case. Drive pinion is at center left in the picture. Note two gauges in set-up. Vertical gauge measures axial play. Horizontal gauge (barely visible at upper right behind vertical gauge bracket) measures backlash. See text.

9. Using lever already attached to differential, which will touch the dial gauge, turn differential in both directions and find midway position (backlash). See Fig. 121.

10. Note ring gear backlash. Push the differential slowly toward the pinion with the spindle until a backlash of 0.20 to 0.22 mm is obtained. Fig. 121 shows operation.

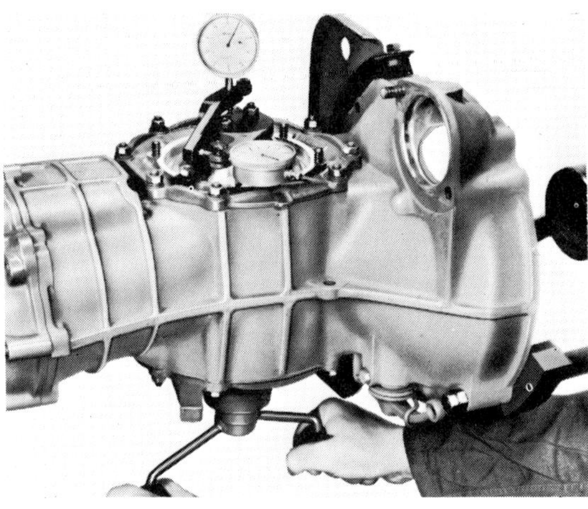



**Fig. 121.** Backlash in ring gear is adjusted in measuring procedure by moving differential toward drive pinion. Spindle is turned to move differential. See text.

**NOTE —**
When measuring ring gear backlash, you must back off the spindle each time. The axial movement of the differential should automatically correspond with the reading shown on the dial indicator. The thickness of shim $S_1$ at the ring gear end can be read directly from the dial indicator for the differential axial movement.

5

Example **only**:

| | |
|---|---|
| Initial dial indicator setting (thickness of setting ring inserted) | 2.80 mm |
| Axial movement needed to get correct amount of backlash | + 0.35 mm |
| Final indicator reading ($S_1$) | 3.15 mm |

The shim $S_2$ is calculated from the dimension **J** in the housing between the two ball bearings, the length of the differential housing **L** and $S_1$.

Example:

| | |
|---|---|
| **J** | 109.70 mm |
| −**L** | −102.90 mm |
| $-S_1$ | − 3.15 mm |
| $S_2$ | 3.65 mm |

Finally, the installation preload on the final drive covers must be even on the two sides. The preload for both covers is 0.14 mm. Therefore addition of 0.07 mm shim thickness on each side is required. The final shim thickness in this example is:

$$S_1 = 3.15 + 0.07 = 3.22 \text{ mm}$$

$$S_2 = 3.65 + 0.07 = 3.72 \text{ mm}$$

Shims supplied as replacement parts are listed in **Tables g** and **h**.

## Table g. Shims Supplied as $S_1$ and $S_2$ Replacement Parts

| Shim No. | Part No. | Thickness (mm) |
|---|---|---|
| 1 | 113 517 199 | 2.80 |
| 2 | 113 517 201 | 2.90 |
| 3 | 113 517 203 | 3.00 |
| 4 | 113 517 205 | 3.10 |
| 5 | 113 517 207 | 3.20 |
| 6 | 113 517 209 | 3.30 |
| 7 | 113 517 211 | 3.40 |
| 8 | 113 517 213 | 3.50 |
| 9 | 113 517 215 | 3.60 |
| 10 | 113 517 217 | 3.70 |
| 11 | 113 517 219 | 3.80 |
| 12 | 113 517 221 | 3.90 |
| 13 | 113 517 245 | 0.25 |

## Table h. Shim Combinations ($S_1$ and $S_2$)

| Nominal shim thickness found for $S_1$ or $S_2$ | Shim thickness* (mm) | Shim No. |
|---|---|---|
| 2.98-3.02 | 3.00 | 3 |
| 3.03-3.07 | 3.05 | 1 + 13 |
| 3.08-3.12 | 3.10 | 4 |
| 3.13-3.17 | 3.15 | 2 + 13 |
| 3.18-3.22 | 3.20 | 5 |
| 3.23-3.27 | 3.25 | 3 + 13 |
| 3.28-3.32 | 3.30 | 6 |
| 3.33-3.37 | 3.35 | 4 + 13 |
| 3.38-3.42 | 3.40 | 7 |
| 3.43-3.47 | 3.45 | 5 + 13 |
| 3.48-3.52 | 3.50 | 8 |
| 3.53-3.57 | 3.55 | 6 + 13 |
| 3.58-3.62 | 3.60 | 9 |
| 3.63-3.67 | 3.65 | 7 + 13 |
| 3.68-3.72 | 3.70 | 10 |
| 3.73-3.77 | 3.75 | 8 + 13 |
| 3.78-3.82 | 3.80 | 11 |
| 3.83-3.87 | 3.85 | 9 + 13 |
| 3.88-3.92 | 3.90 | 12 |
| 3.93-3.97 | 3.95 | 10 + 13 |

***Measure shims at several points with a micrometer. Check for burns and damage. Only use shims which are in good condition.**

11. After having checked all readings, take off the indicator bracket. Press off left final drive cover, place spindle on right cover and press differential out of transmission case.
12. Screw front and rear parts of main drive shaft together, back off one spline, slide reverse gear on and install circlip, making sure to use new one.
13. Install shims $S_1$ and $S_2$ with the chamfer towards the differential (center of housing). Thin shims (if needed) go between thick shim and ball bearing.
14. Tighten nuts attaching the final drive covers to the correct torque.
15. Recheck ring gear backlash at several positions. The tolerance for the backlash is 0.15 to 0.25 mm, and individual measurements must not vary more than 0.05 mm from one another. Fig. 122 shows operation.

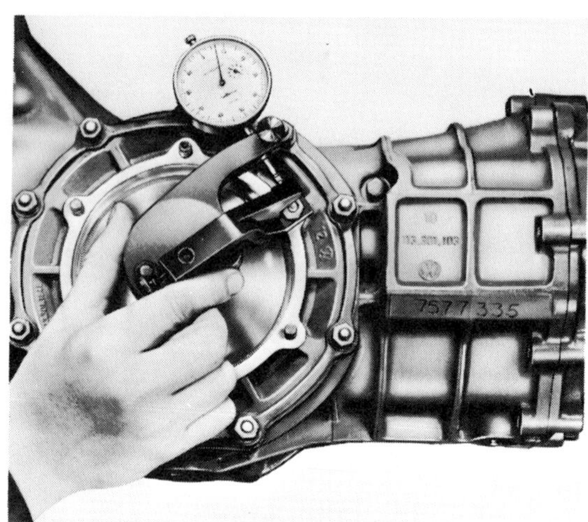



**Fig. 122.** Backlash measurement is made with set-up shown here. Device is anchored to ring gear. When it is turned it bears against dial indicator pin.

16. Take off dial indicator.
17. Remove clamping bolts and take thrust plates out through the holes for the axle shafts, as shown in Fig. 123.

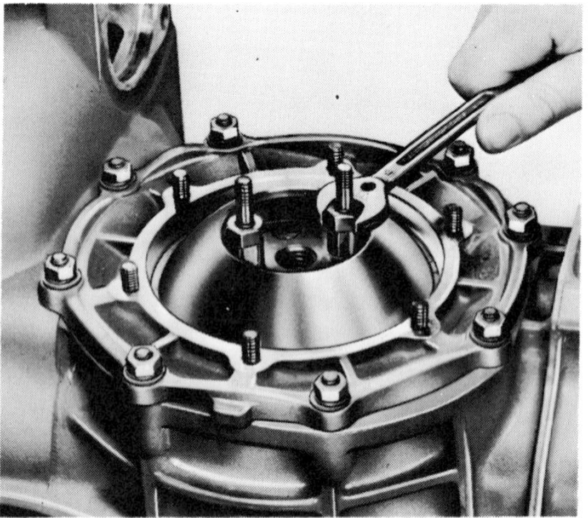



**Fig. 123.** Clamping bolts and thrust plates are removed from differential through openings for axle shafts after ring gear measurements have been made.

## 5.8 Adjusting Ring Gear
(double-joint axle, standard transmission)

The ring gear will need adjusting only when parts that directly affect the ring gear or tapered roller bearing setting have been replaced. These parts are: gear set, transmission case, differential housing, differential housing cover, final drive covers, tapered roller bearings. Tapered roller bearings which have been run with play must always be replaced. In any work on the ring gear, care and cleanliness are essential if satisfactory results are to be obtained. Fig. 124 shows schematically the set-up for ring gear adjustment.

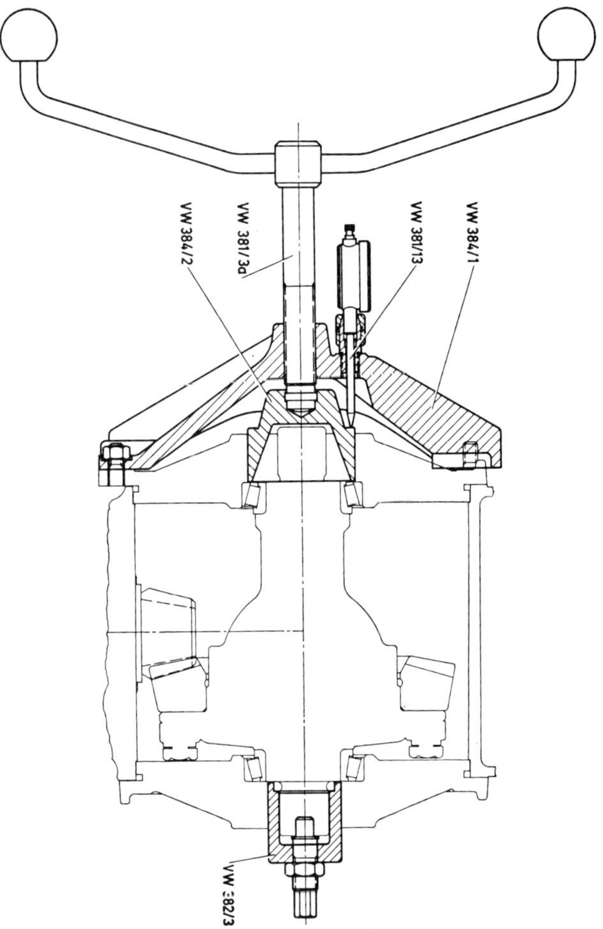


**Fig. 124.** Special tools used in adjustment of ring gear in the differential for the double-joint axle are shown shaded in this schematic of the set-up. Although sketch shows pinion in place, it must be removed during procedure.

**To adjust tapered roller bearings** (pinion removed):

1. Press oil seals and bearing outer races out of final drive covers. Take out shims and press bearing races back in again. Make sure that all races are seated properly.
2. Install right cover (Fig. 125) on transmission case. Place setting appliance on cover and tighten nuts diagonally to correct torque.

**NOTE** —
It is advisable to remove the O-rings when making this adjustment.

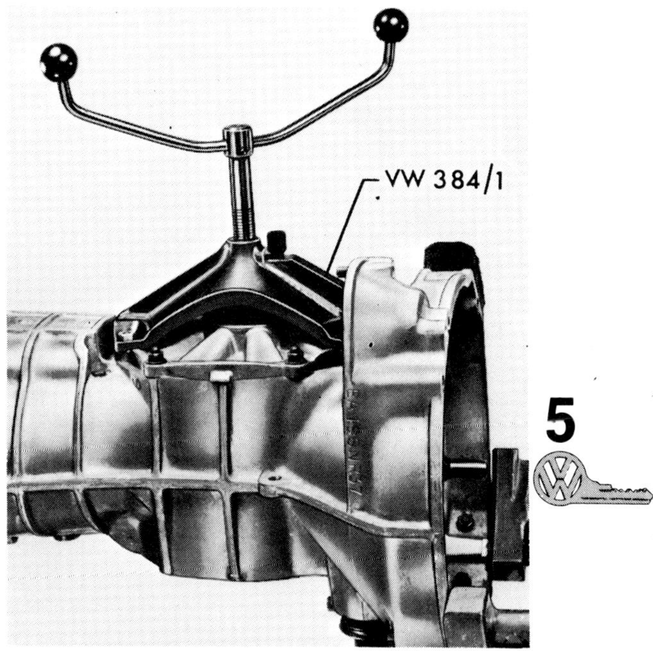


**Fig. 125.** Setting appliance is shown on right final drive cover of transmission case. Cover nuts are tightened diagonally to specified torque.

***CAUTION*** —
*Before you install differential, oil the bearings with hypoid transmission oil. If bearings are dry or have been lubricated with other oils you will get incorrect results.*

3. Rotate housing 180 degrees and place differential in housing. Ring gear should be on the left side.
4. Install left cover and tighten nuts. Attach clamping sleeve on ring gear without lever.
5. Rotate transmission to bring ring gear up. Turn spindle of the setting appliance carefully until the thrust piece is just touching the bearing outer race without play. Take care that the bearing race is not moved at this time.

5

6. Install dial indicator with extension (52 mm) in the appliance and zero indicator with 3 mm preload. Fig. 126 shows set-up.

© 1972 VWoA—728

**Fig. 126.** Dial indicator set at zero for a 3 mm preload is installed as shown for ring gear adjustment.

7. Press in bearing outer race by turning spindle until no play in differential bearings can be detected.
8. Rotate transmission 90 degrees. Place torque gauge with 10 mm socket on the clamping sleeve (Fig. 127) and turn differential in both directions several times.

© 1972 VWoA—729

**Fig. 127.** Torque gauge on spindle of special tool is used to turn differential in both directions after transmission case has been rotated to standard position.

9. Screw spindle in farther and increase pressure on bearings until the required preload (turning torque) is obtained.

***CAUTION —***
*Increase the torque very slowly while taking repeated readings. If the specified torque is exceeded, the side cover must be removed, the bearing race pressed back to the original position and the adjustment repeated.*

The turning torque should be as follows:

| new bearings | used bearings* |
|---|---|
| 16 to 19 in. lbs.<br>(18 to 22 cmkg) | 2.6 to 6.1 in. lbs.<br>(3 to 7 cmkg) |

***After running at least 30 miles**

10. Take dial indicator reading (red figures). This value should be used as the dimension for the total shim thickness **S**. Example: **S** = 1.65 mm.
11. Remove right cover and differential. Press bearing race in again until fully seated in right cover.
12. Install transmission with the $S_3$ shim as previously determined. Check the measurement (see **5.3 Adjusting Pinion**).

**To adjust backlash** (transmission installed):

***CAUTION —***
*Make sure that the bearing outer races are properly seated in the covers.*

1. Install right final drive cover and special setting appliance.
2. Install rear part of main drive shaft. Place differential in housing with clamping sleeve already attached. Install final drive cover on ring gear side, attach dial indicator holder and tighten bolts diagonally to correct torque.
3. Using the crank handle attached to the main drive shaft, turn differential (thus turning drive shaft, 4th gear and pinion) and at the same time push in the bearing outer race. Do this with the setting appliance until the dial indicator shows the total **S** reading previously arrived at. The preload on the tapered roller bearings, which was determined previously by the torque test, can now be obtained.

**NOTE —**
Engage the 4th gear to make this check easier.

4. Attach pinion retaining bracket on the gear carrier and tighten nuts by hand.

5. Screw lever into clamping sleeve. Install dial indicator (3 mm range) with extension (6 mm) in the dial indicator holder. Have edge of clamping cylinder on the indicator flush with edge of holder.

6. Turn ring gear with crank handle as before (thus turning driveshaft, 1st gear and pinion) until lever is touching dial indicator pin. Then turn carefully until indicator has a preload of 1.5 mm. Be careful not to damage the indicator. See Fig. 128.

**Fig. 128.** Backlash adjustment of ring gear requires dial indicator set-up shown here.

7. Secure pinion with retaining bracket in position shown in Fig. 129.

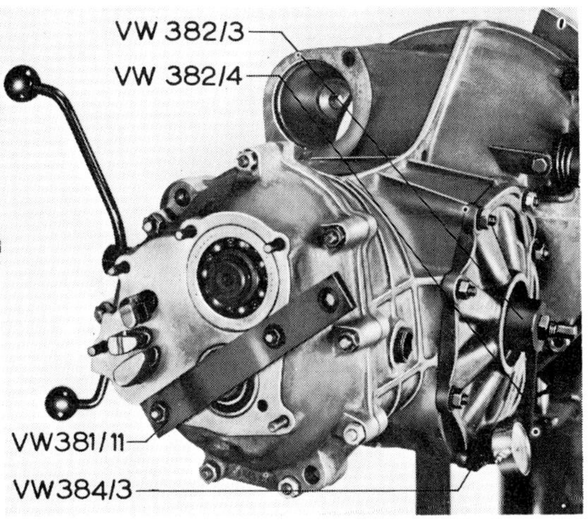




**Fig. 129.** Retaining bracket on gear carrier holds drive pinion in place for ring gear adjustment.

8. Turn ring gear as far as it will go and set dial indicator to zero. Turn ring gear in other direction and read off backlash $Sv_o$. Write this figure down.

9. Loosen lock nut in clamping sleeve on differential and the nuts securing pinion retaining bracket. Turn ring gear and take three further readings at intervals of 90 degrees. Add the readings together (including that in step 8) and divide by four to find average.

***CAUTION*** —
*If the readings obtained in this check vary by more than 0.06 mm from one another, there is something wrong with the installation of the ring gear or with the gear set itself. Check assembly operations and replace gear set if necessary.*

To find $Sv_o$ average (example):

| | |
|---|---|
| 1st reading | 1.10 |
| + 2nd reading | 1.12 |
| + 3rd reading | 1.13 |
| + 4th reading | 1.11 |
| Total | 4.46 |
| Divide by 4 | 1.115 = 1.12 |

5

The maximum difference between readings shown is 0.03 mm (1.13-1.10).

10. Determine the thickness of $S_1$ shim (ring gear side). The thickness for $S_1$ shim can be worked out from the backlash $S_{vo}$ average as follows:
    a. From **Table i**:
    For $S_{vo}$ average of 1.12 mm the Table shows $S_1$ shim thickness of 0.92 mm.

## Table i. Shim thicknesses ($S_1$)

| **Backlash Svo mean Svo** | **Shim thickness G 833 K 833** | **Backlash Svo mean** | **Shim thickness G 833 K 833** |
|---|---|---|---|
| 0.20 | 0.00 | 0.36 | 0.16 |
| 0.21 | 0.01 | 0.37 | 0.17 |
| 0.22 | 0.02 | 0.38 | 0.18 |
| 0.23 | 0.03 | 0.39 | 0.19 |
| 0.24 | 0.04 | 0.40 | 0.20 |
| 0.25 | 0.05 | 0.41 | 0.21 |
| 0.26 | 0.06 | 0.42 | 0.22 |
| 0.27 | 0.07 | 0.43 | 0.23 |
| 0.28 | 0.08 | 0.44 | 0.24 |
| 0.29 | 0.09 | 0.45 | 0.25 |
| 0.30 | 0.10 | 0.46 | 0.26 |
| 0.31 | 0.11 | 0.47 | 0.27 |
| 0.32 | 0.12 | 0.48 | 0.28 |
| 0.33 | 0.13 | 0.49 | 0.29 |
| 0.34 | 0.14 | 0.50 | 0.30 |
| 0.35 | 0.15 | 0.51 | 0.31 |

**continued on next page**

## Table i. Shim thicknesses ($S_1$) (continued)

| Backlash | Shim thickness | Backlash | Shim thickness |
|---|---|---|---|
| 0.52 | 0.32 | 0.86 | 0.66 |
| 0.53 | 0.33 | 0.87 | 0.67 |
| 0.54 | 0.34 | 0.88 | 0.68 |
| 0.55 | 0.35 | 0.89 | 0.69 |
| 0.56 | 0.36 | 0.90 | 0.70 |
| 0.57 | 0.37 | 0.91 | 0.71 |
| 0.58 | 0.38 | 0.92 | 0.72 |
| 0.59 | 0.39 | 0.93 | 0.73 |
| 0.60 | 0.40 | 0.94 | 0.74 |
| 0.61 | 0.41 | 0.95 | 0.75 |
| 0.62 | 0.42 | 0.96 | 0.76 |
| 0.63 | 0.43 | 0.97 | 0.77 |
| 0.64 | 0.44 | 0.98 | 0.78 |
| 0.65 | 0.45 | 0.99 | 0.79 |
| 0.66 | 0.46 | 1.00 | 0.80 |
| 0.67 | 0.47 | 1.01 | 0.81 |
| 0.68 | 0.48 | 1.02 | 0.82 |
| 0.69 | 0.49 | 1.03 | 0.83 |
| 0.70 | 0.50 | 1.04 | 0.84 |
| 0.71 | 0.51 | 1.05 | 0.85 |
| 0.72 | 0.52 | 1.06 | 0.86 |
| 0.73 | 0.53 | 1.07 | 0.87 |
| 0.74 | 0.54 | 1.08 | 0.88 |
| 0.75 | 0.55 | 1.09 | 0.89 |
| 0.76 | 0.56 | 1.10 | 0.90 |
| 0.77 | 0.57 | 1.11 | 0.91 |
| 0.78 | 0.58 | 1.12 | 0.92 |
| 0.79 | 0.59 | 1.13 | 0.93 |
| 0.80 | 0.60 | 1.14 | 0.94 |
| 0.81 | 0.61 | 1.15 | 0.95 |
| 0.82 | 0.62 | 1.16 | 0.96 |
| 0.83 | 0.63 | 1.17 | 0.97 |
| 0.84 | 0.64 | 1.18 | 0.98 |
| 0.85 | 0.65 | 1.19 | 0.99 |
| | | 1.20 | 1.00 |

b. By calculation:

Multiply $S_{vo}$ average by correction factor **w** and subtract axial ring gear lift **h** to get $S_1$.

$S_1 = (S_{vo} \text{ average} \times \mathbf{w}) - \mathbf{h}$.

In this Formula:

$S_1$ = Thickness of shim on ring gear side

$S_{vo}$ average = Average measured backlash without shims

**w** = Correction factor

**h** = Axial ring gear lift (with ring gear in horizontal position) from the no-play mesh position to average backlash position. In this case it will be a constant value 0.02 mm.

**NOTE —**

Because the correction factor in this case is **1**, ring gear lift and backlash are identical.

| Gear Set | Correction factor w | Lift h |
|---|---|---|
| G 338/358 | 1.00 | 0.20 |
| K 835 | 1.10 | 0.22* |

*Automatic Stick Shift

In our example:

$S_1 = (1.12 \text{ mm} \times 1) - 0.20 \text{ mm}$
$S_1 = 0.92 \text{ mm}$

11. Determine thickness of $S_2$ shim (end opposite to ring gear). In the procedure for adjusting tapered roller bearings, a value of 1.65 mm was obtained for the required total shim thickness **S**. $S_2$ is easily obtained by subtracting $S_1$ from **S**:

$S_2 = \mathbf{S} - S_1$
$S_2 = 1.65 \text{ mm} - 0.92 \text{ mm}$
$S_2 = 0.73 \text{ mm}$

**Table j.** lists available shims; **Table k.** lists shim thicknesses.

## Table j. Shims Supplied as $S_2$ Replacement Parts

| Shim No. | Part No. | Thickness (mm) |
|---|---|---|
| 1 | 113 517 201 A | 0.15 |
| 2 | 113 517 202 A | 0.20 |
| 3 | 113 517 203 A | 0.30 |
| 4 | 113 517 204 A | 0.40 |
| 5 | 113 517 205 A | 0.50 |
| 6 | 113 517 206 A | 0.60 |
| 7 | 113 517 207 A | 0.70 |
| 8 | 113 517 208 A | 0.80 |
| 9 | 113 517 209 A | 0.90 |
| 10 | 113 517 210 A | 1.00 |
| 11 | 113 517 211 A | 1.20 |

## Table k. Shim Combinations (double-joint axle)

| Nominal shim thickness found for $S_1$ or $S_2$ | Shim thickness* (mm) | Shim No. |
|---|---|---|
| 0.28-0.32 | 0.30 | 3 |
| 0.33-0.37 | 0.35 | 1 + 2 |
| 0.38-0.42 | 0.40 | 4 |
| 0.43-0.47 | 0.45 | 1 + 3 |
| 0.48-0.52 | 0.50 | 5 |
| 0.53-0.57 | 0.55 | 1 + 4 |
| 0.58-0.62 | 0.60 | 6 |
| 0.63-0.67 | 0.65 | 1 + 5 |
| 0.68-0.72 | 0.70 | 7 |
| 0.73-0.77 | 0.75 | 1 + 6 |
| 0.78-0.82 | 0.80 | 8 |
| 0.83-0.87 | 0.85 | 1 + 7 |
| 0.88-0.92 | 0.90 | 9 |
| 0.93-0.97 | 0.95 | 1 + 8 |
| 0.98-1.02 | 1.00 | 10 |
| 1.03-1.07 | 1.05 | 1 + 9 |
| 1.08-1.12 | 1.10 | 2 + 9 |
| 1.13-1.17 | 1.15 | 1 + 10 |
| 1.18-1.22 | 1.20 | 11 |
| 1.23-1.27 | 1.25 | 1 + 5 + 6 |
| 1.28-1.32 | 1.30 | 3 + 10 |

***Reminder: The shims should be measured carefully at several points with a micrometer. Check shims for burrs or damage. Use only shims which are in perfect condition.**

**NOTE —**
Shims should be measured carefully at several points with a micrometer. Check for burrs or damage and use only shims in perfect condition.

12. Install $S_1$ shim on ring gear side and $S_2$ on other side.
13. Install right final drive cover complete with bearing outer race, oil seal and O-ring and tighten nuts to correct torque.
14. Install differential with clamping sleeve already attached. Install left cover without oil seal.
15. Check backlash. It must be measured at four points 90 degrees apart and should be:
$$S_{vo} = 0.15 \text{ to } 0.25 \text{ mm}$$

**NOTE —**
Individual readings must not differ from one another by more than 0.05 mm.

16. Take off left cover and sleeve again. Press oil seal into cover with tube and completely assemble transmission. See **4.2 Removing and Installing Differential**.

## 6. GEARSHIFT LEVER

A change in the gearshift lever was made in the period covered by this Manual. On cars produced after August 1967 the lever is straight. On the later version the ball has no guide pin and the head of the shift rod has no slot. The shift rod of the later version is shortened to fit the relocated mounting in the frame tunnel.

### 6.1 Removing and Installing Gearshift Lever
(all cars)

Incorrect adjustment of the stop plate in the gear shift lever assembly can be a cause of shifting difficulties. When removing the lever, be careful to mark the position of the stop plate as a guide for re-installation.

**To remove:**

1. Put shift lever in neutral position and take up front floor mat.
2. Mark plate as a guide for re-installation. Remove bolts attaching gearshift lever ball housing to the frame tunnel.
3. Take off gearshift lever, ball housing, rubber boot, and spring as a unit. Turn spring to clear the pin, as in Fig. 130.
4. Take off stop plate.
5. Clean all parts.

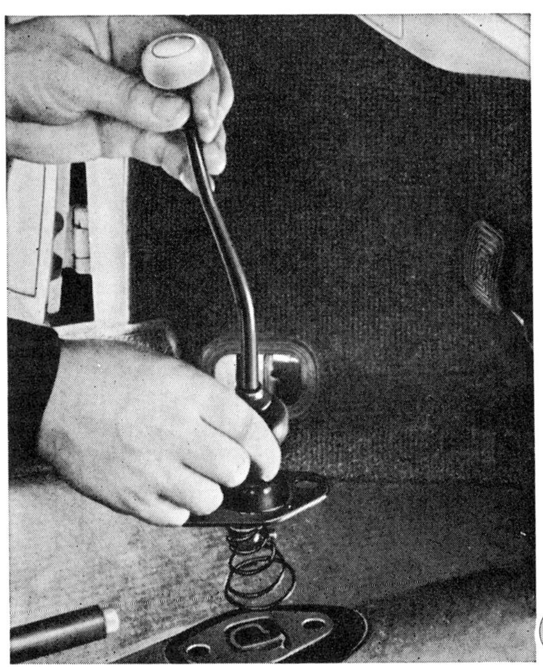

5

© 1972 VWoA—732

**Fig. 130.** Gearshift lever with attachments comes off as unit when housing is unscrewed from frame tunnel.

**To install:**

1. Check gearshift lever collar, stop plate, and gearshift lever ball socket in shifting rod for wear. Replace worn parts.
2. Make sure the gearshift lever locating pin is secure (Fig. 131). Check spring in steel ball for tension. Replace if necessary.

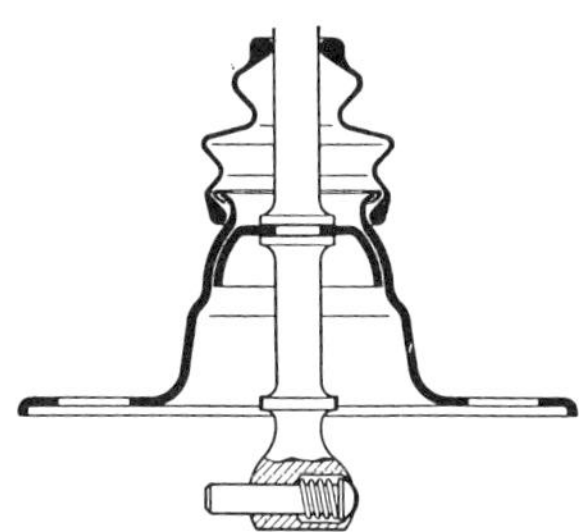

© 1972 VWoA—733

**Fig. 131.** Locating pin for gearshift lever assembly is held in place by spring tension, as shown in this schematic.

3. When installing stop plate, have the upward projecting lip of opening at the right, as in Fig. 132.

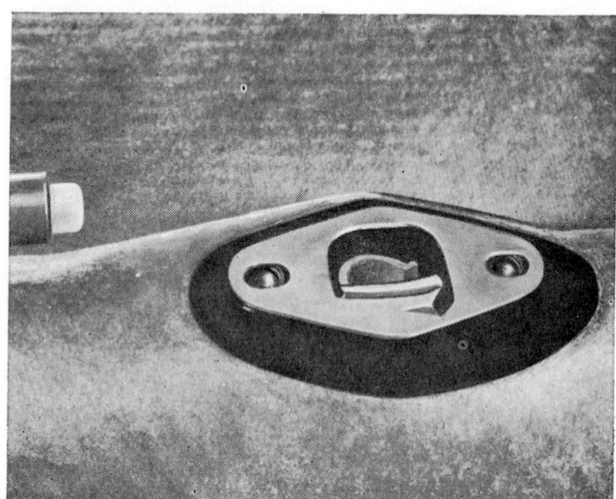

© 1972 VWoA—734

**Fig. 132.** Stop plate of gearshift lever assembly is installed with turned-up edge to the right. In this picture turned-up edge faces you.

4. Grease all moving parts with universal grease.
5. Attach lever ball housing. The straight (lower) section of gearshift lever should stand vertical in neutral position. The gearshift lever locating pin engages in slot in ball socket.

**NOTE —**
The stop plate must seat in the hollow flange of the ball housing, as shown in Fig. 133.

© 1972 VWoA—735

**Fig. 133.** Hollow flange of ball housing is underneath the stop plate for the gearshift lever.

6. Check condition of gearshift lever rubber boot. Replace if damaged.
7. Recheck position of gearshift lever by engaging the gears. Correct if necessary.

On an occasional new or overhauled transmission it may be found that one gear is difficult to engage, apparently from failure to synchronize properly. An accumulation of improper tolerances at the conical surfaces of gear and synchronizer stop ring can cause this difficulty. The trouble usually appears in the first 100 miles and ceases as the mating parts run in.

Do not regard this shifting difficulty as a symptom calling for disassembly of the transmission. Frequent shifting of the gears in the wear-in period ordinarily will do the trick. If you find you cannot engage a gear, return to neutral, declutch and try again. Do not apply force to engage the gears, however. Forcing might cause the synchronizer stop rings to seize on the gears or give rise to other damage.

## 6.2 Removing and Installing Shift Rod

**To remove:**

1. Take up front floor mat and remove gearshift lever.
2. Take out rear seat.
3. Remove inspection cover on frame tunnel.
4. Disconnect gearshift rod coupling.
5. Take off front bumper.
6. Remove frame head cover.
7. Withdraw shift rod from the coupling, using a pair of combination pliers, and push it toward the frame head. See Fig. 134.
8. Completely withdraw shift rod through the openings in the body.

**NOTE —**
Ordinarily there is no need to replace the plastic bushing in the frame tunnel behind the opening for the gearshift lever. If a replacement is necessary, however, proceed as follows:

a. Remove bushing from the shift rod guide with a pair of pliers.
b. Attach wire ring to the bushing. Insert the new bushing through the shift lever opening. Then, starting from the slot, press bushing fully into the shift rod guide.

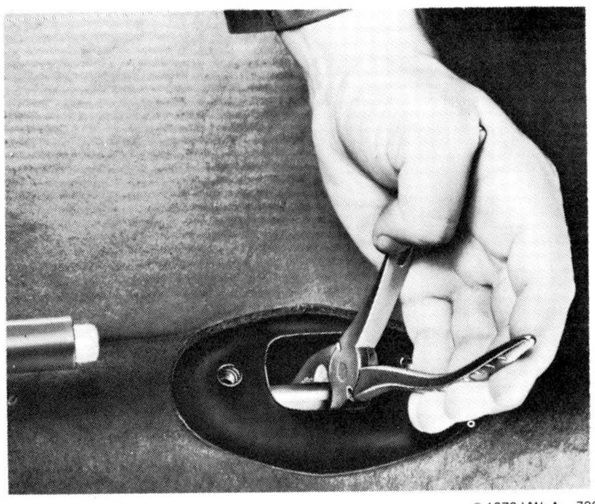

© 1972 VWoA—736

**Fig. 134.** Shift rod is withdrawn from coupling with pliers, as shown here, and pushed toward frame head.

**To install shift rod:**

1. Check rod for distortion. Replace if necessary.
2. Coat the entire rod lightly with universal grease.
3. Insert shift rod through openings in body into the shift rod guide in the tunnel. See Fig. 135.

© 1972 VWoA—737

**Fig. 135.** Insertion of shift rod from front end of car is shown here. Rod goes in opening under latch for front hood. Car shown is 1966 model.

**NOTE —**
Since December 1965, on cars from chassis No. 116 412 701, the gearshift rod pin has been replaced with a slotted, expanding sleeve with screw and securing cap. When screw is turned, sleeve seats itself firmly in the gearshift rod coupling pin.

**NOTE (continued)**
The expanding sleeve can be installed as a replacement. In this installation make sure that the expanding sleeve is pushed through before you tighten the screw. This procedure prevents play at the washer causing noises. When removing and installing the gearshift rod coupling, remove the gearshift lever to allow rotation of the gearshift rod.

4. Install shift rod coupling.
5. Adjust shift lever.

## 7. TORSION BARS (swing axle)

The rear wheels are sprung independently. A splined tube welded to the frame rear cross member anchors the torsion bars at the inner ends. The splined outer ends of the torsion bars carry the hubbed spring plates which have slotted holes to permit adjustment. The spline connections also allow adjustment of the suspension. A rubber bumper is attached to the spring plate and axle shaft housing to prevent metal-to-metal contact when the suspension bottoms. Double-acting telescopic shock absorbers snub excessive rebound.

### 7.1 Removing and Installing Torsion Bars

**NOTE —**
Any removal or replacement of parts in the rear axle may require readjustment or re-alignment unless the same parts are re-installed. Put matching marks on adjoining parts to assist in reassembly.

**To remove:**

1. Loosen rear wheel mounting bolts.
2. Support car in a horizontal position on jack stands and take off rear wheel.
3. Disconnect parking brake cables at parking brake lever and pull them a little to the rear.
4. Mark the position of the spring plate in relation to the housing of the rear axle shaft bearing. Chisel a matching mark on the spring plate in perfect alignment with the groove in the housing, as was done in removal of rear axle.
5. Take out lower shock absorber mounting bolts.
6. Take out bolts at axle shaft bearing housing.
7. Pull rear axle toward the rear until it clears spring plate.
8. Remove bolts that attach spring plate hub cover. Take off cover.

9. Pull spring plate off torsion bar, as in Fig. 136.

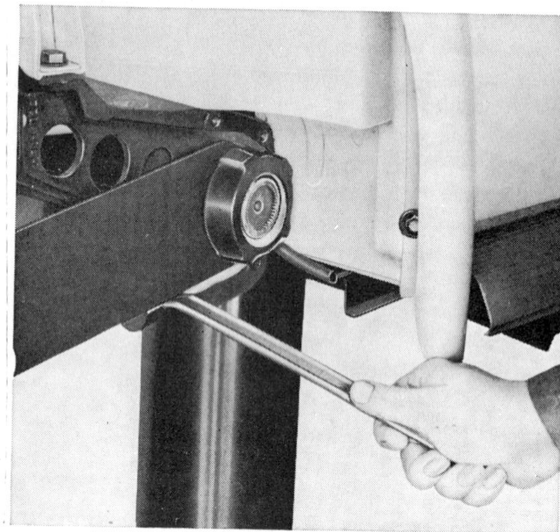



**Fig. 136.** Spring plate is pulled off right torsion bar.

10. Remove about five of the bolts that fasten the forward section of the fender. Pulling fender away from car, withdraw the torsion bar. See Fig. 137.

**NOTE —**
Be careful to protect the paint on the torsion bar. Even slight damage can expose the metal to corrosion and eventual fracture.

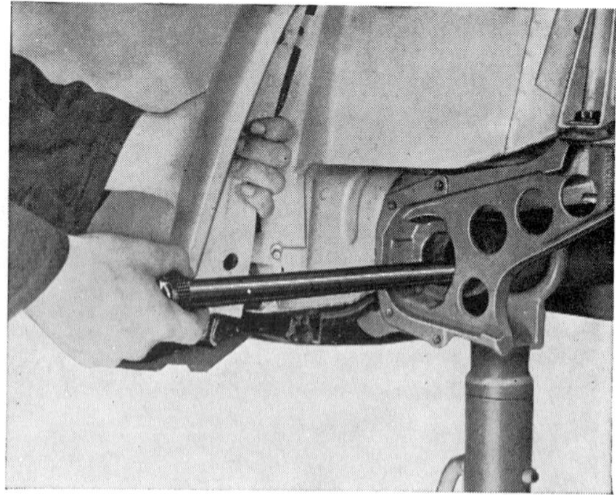



**Fig. 137.** Torsion bar is withdrawn from frame cross tube.

**To install torsion bars:**

1. Inspect splined ends of torsion bars and painted surfaces for damage. Make sure there is no sign of rust. Replace bars if any damage is found.
2. Grease splines of torsion bar.
3. Install torsion bar and spring plate and adjust.

**NOTE —**
The torsion bars are prestressed in manufacture. Be careful not to mix up the left and right bars. "R" for right and "L" for left are on the faces of the outer ends.

4. Coat the rubber bushing (Fig. 138) with talcum powder. Make sure that the thicker part of the bushing (marked **Oben**) is always at the top.

**Fig. 138.** Rubber bushing is installed on torsion bar end with German word **Oben** at top, as shown here.

5. Attach cover and tighten bolts uniformly. If necessary, use two longer bolts to pull cover down until bolts of specified length can be installed without difficulty.
6. Lift spring plate with a tensioner (Fig. 139) until lower edge of plate is higher than the lower stop in the cross tube flange.

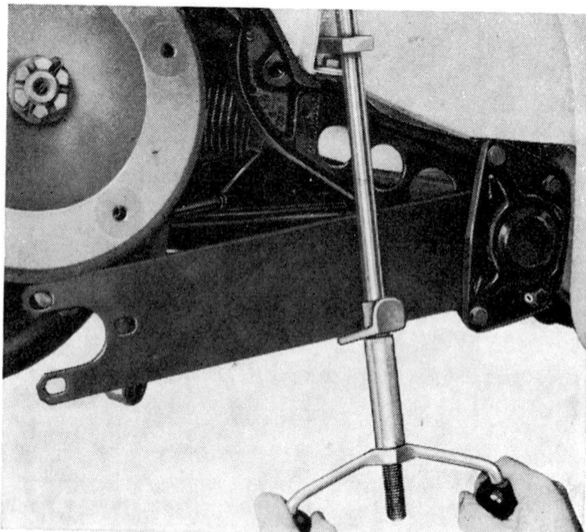



**Fig. 139.** Tensioner is used as shown here to raise spring plate for installation of plate hub cover.

7. Install and tighten the spring plate hub cover.
8. Clean mating faces between spring plate and housing of axle bearing.
9. When bolting housing and spring plate together, use the mark you made on the spring plate when you removed the torsion bar. Have this mark in perfect alignment with the groove in the axle bearing housing.

**NOTE** —
If a new rear axle, frame, spring plate or front transmission mounting has been installed, the rear wheels must be re-aligned. An optical gauge is needed to set the track and wheel alignment accurately, but if one is not available, set the wheels to bring the marks in the sides of the spring plates in line with the marks in the housings of the axle shaft bearings. When an optical gauge is used, the parts are installed with marks aligned and the alignment then checked with the instrument and corrected where necessary. A 1-mm movement of the housing changes the toe of the wheels 8 minutes.

10. Tighten mounting bolts of the housing of axle bearing to a torque of 80 ft. lbs. (11 mkg).
11. Reconnect cable to parking brake and adjust the brake.

## 8. SPRING PLATES

Correct wheel alignment and adequate spring travel under all loads for which the car was designed are essential to good roadholding. These conditions can be obtained only if both spring plates are set at exactly the same angle. When one side has been set, the angle of the other plate should be checked and corrected as necessary.

### 8.1 Setting Spring Plates

The specified spring plate setting angle with the torsion bars free of tension is 17 degrees 30 minutes to 18 degrees 20 minutes. The number of splines on the inner and outer ends of the torsion bars is different to allow accurate setting of the spring plate angle:

Inner end: 40 splines
Outer end: 44 splines



Turning the torsion bar by one inner end spline changes the angle 9 degrees. Turning the spring plate one spline gives an angle change of 8 degrees 10 minutes. This combination allows a minimum correction of 50 minutes in the spring plate angle. (Nine degrees minus 8 degrees 10 minutes equals 50 minutes.) A special protractor with a bubble level is used to measure the spring plate angle in the installation procedure.

**To set spring plate:**

1. Insert torsion bar in cross tube inner splines.

**NOTE** —
The torsion bars are prestressed in manufacture. Do not mix up the right and left hand bars. The bars are marked on the outer ends with the letters "R" (right) and "L" (left).

2. Attach spring plate.
3. Set protractor in door opening to zero its scale to the horizontal position of the axis of the car. Adjust protractor (Fig. 140) to bring the bubble on the "axle beam/angle" scale to the center position.

5

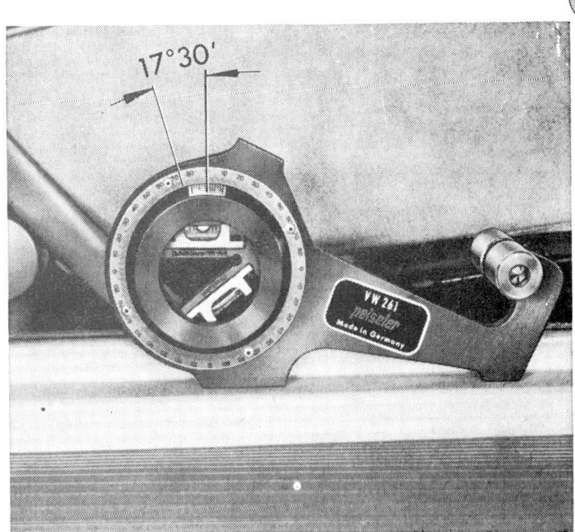


© 1972 VWoA—742

**Fig. 140.** Protractor for setting spring plates is shown here. With protractor in door opening, bubble is centered and then level carrier is turned 17 degrees 30 minutes.

4. Now turn the bubble level carrier 17 degrees 30 minutes from center position.
5. Place protractor on the untensioned spring plate on the same side of the car. Eliminate play in the plate mounting by lifting plate in the working direc-

tion. Note the angle, reading from the back side of the instrument as in Fig. 141.

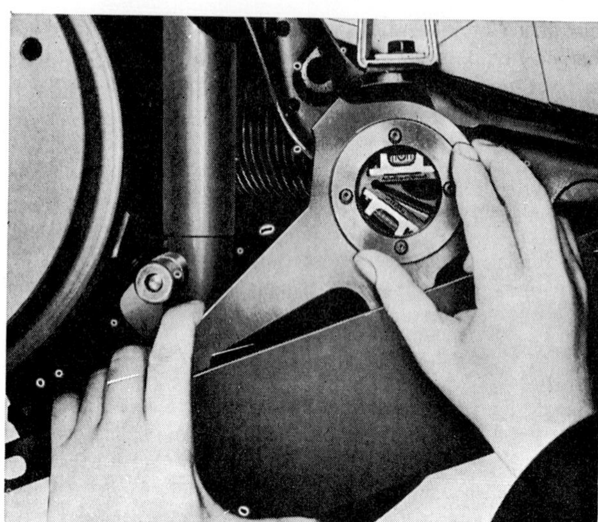

© 1972 VWoA—743

**Fig. 141.** Spring plate angle can be calculated from bubble position when protractor is placed on plate.

6. Correct spring plate setting as necessary.
   a. A bubble deviation of one graduation from center position indicates an error of 50 minutes in the setting of the spring plate. To correct the error, bar and spring plate must each be turned one spline (but in opposite directions). In the required adjustment turn the spring plate in the same direction you would have to turn the level carrier in order to bring the bubble to center position.
   b. Deviations too large to be read from the protractor scale can be found easily. The deviation is equal to the angle through which the level must be turned to bring the bubble back to center position.
   c. The angle of deviation established in step b is translated by a simple calculation into the number of splines the torsion bar and spring plate must be turned (in opposite directions, in this case) for the correction. You divide the angle of deviation (step b) by 50 minutes, which is, as we saw earlier, the smallest correction possible. In the calculation round off the remainder upward to 50 minutes if the angle is too flat (as in the first of the following two examples). If the angle is too open (second example) ignore the remainder. Either way, the specified tolerance of 50 minutes is preserved.

In **Table I**, the rear wheel camber angle and track values (toe) have been revised to include the settling that occurs with new torsion bars. The Table therefore is valid only for cars that have run at least 300 miles. Different readings will be obtained if the angles are checked any earlier. If a correction is to be made on a car showing some mileage, both torsion bars must be reset. Otherwise, there is a risk of upsetting the driving characteristics with two different camber angles.

**NOTE** ——
When any alignment work is undertaken, the instructions of the equipment manufacturer should be followed.

The camber angle given in the Table as the permissible minimum is for guidance only. The camber should not be smaller than this angle even after considerable mileage.

## Table I. Rear Wheel Camber Angle and Track Values

| Model | Introduction | Chassis numbers | Spring plate setting angle* | Camber angle after 300 miles | Permissible minimum camber angle | Total track | Permissible deviation in wheel alignment |
|---|---|---|---|---|---|---|---|
| **A - Without equalizer spring** | | | | | | | |
| VW 1200 and 1300, Convertible and Karmann Ghia | from Aug. 59 to July 66 | from 2 528 668 to 116 1 021 298 | 17°30′ + 50′ | 2°30′ ± 1° | 0° | −5′ ± 10′ | max. 10′ |
| **B - With equalizer spring** | | | | | | | |
| VW 1500 | from Aug. 66 | from 117 000 001 | 20° + 50′ | 1° ± 1° | −1° | −5′ ± 10′ | max. 10′ |
| VW Convertible and Karmann Ghia | from Aug. 66 | from 147 000 003 from 157 000 002 | | 15′ ± 1° | −1°30′ | | |

***Spring plate angle can be calculated from bubble position when protractor is placed on plate.**

Examples:

| | |
|---|---|
| 1. Protractor reading on door sill | 40′ |
| Desired angle for spring plate setting | +17°30′ |
| Actual measured angle | 16°50′ |
| Total actual angle of spring plate (Includes 40′) | 18°10′ |
| Difference between 18°10′ and 16°50′ | 1°20′ |

1°20′ = 80′

80′ divided by 50′ = 1 plus 30′ remainder.

As the angle of the spring plate was too low, the remainder of 30 minutes is rounded off up to 50 minutes. The torsion bar and spring plate are turned 2 splines in opposite directions.

| | |
|---|---|
| 2. Protractor reading on door sill | 30′ |
| Desired angle for spring plate setting | +17°30′ |
| Actual measured angle of spring plate | 20°20′ |
| Total actual angle of spring plate (Includes 30′) | 18° |
| Difference between 18° and 20°20′ | 2°20′ |

2°20′ = 140′

140′ divided by 50′ = 2 plus 40′ remainder

As the angle of the spring plate was too high, the remainder of 40 minutes is discarded.

## 9. REAR WHEEL ALIGNMENT

Toe-in and toe-out of rear wheels are defined as they were for front wheels (see **FRONT AXLE**). The angle of the wheels in relation to the longitudinal axis of the car determines toe-in or toe-out. If the wheels are closer together at the front than at the rear they are said to toe-in (+). If they are farther apart at the front than at the rear, they are said to toe-out (−). If both wheels are parallel with the longitudinal axis of the vehicle, the angle is zero. In this last case (angle = 0) the wheel alignment and longitudinal axis are said to be in line with one another. Axle alignment is obtained from the wheel angle. See Fig. 142.

It is important to know that even when wheel angles fall within the specified limits for toe-in/toe-out, the wheel alignment can still deviate too far from the longitudinal axis of the car. This condition arises when the axle is not at a right angle to the axis. Wheel angles must satisfy not only the specifications for toe-in/toe-out but also the tolerance set for the position of the axle in relation to the longitudinal axis of the car.

Both toe-in/toe-out readings and deviation in axle alignment can be checked by calculation and by graphical methods. An evaluation diagram for checking the correctness of rear axle alignment is shown as Fig. 143, on the following page.

5

**Fig. 142.** Wheel position on this car will show deviation from specified alignment because the rear axle is not at a right angle to the axis of the vehicle.

© 1972 VWoA—744

**Fig. 143.** Evaluation diagram provides graphical analysis of rear axle alignment, on the basis of toe-in/toe-out. The two small scales below the large square illustrate the example given in text. The small scale at lower left shows angle of left rear wheel. Small scale at right gives right rear wheel angle. See text for explanation.

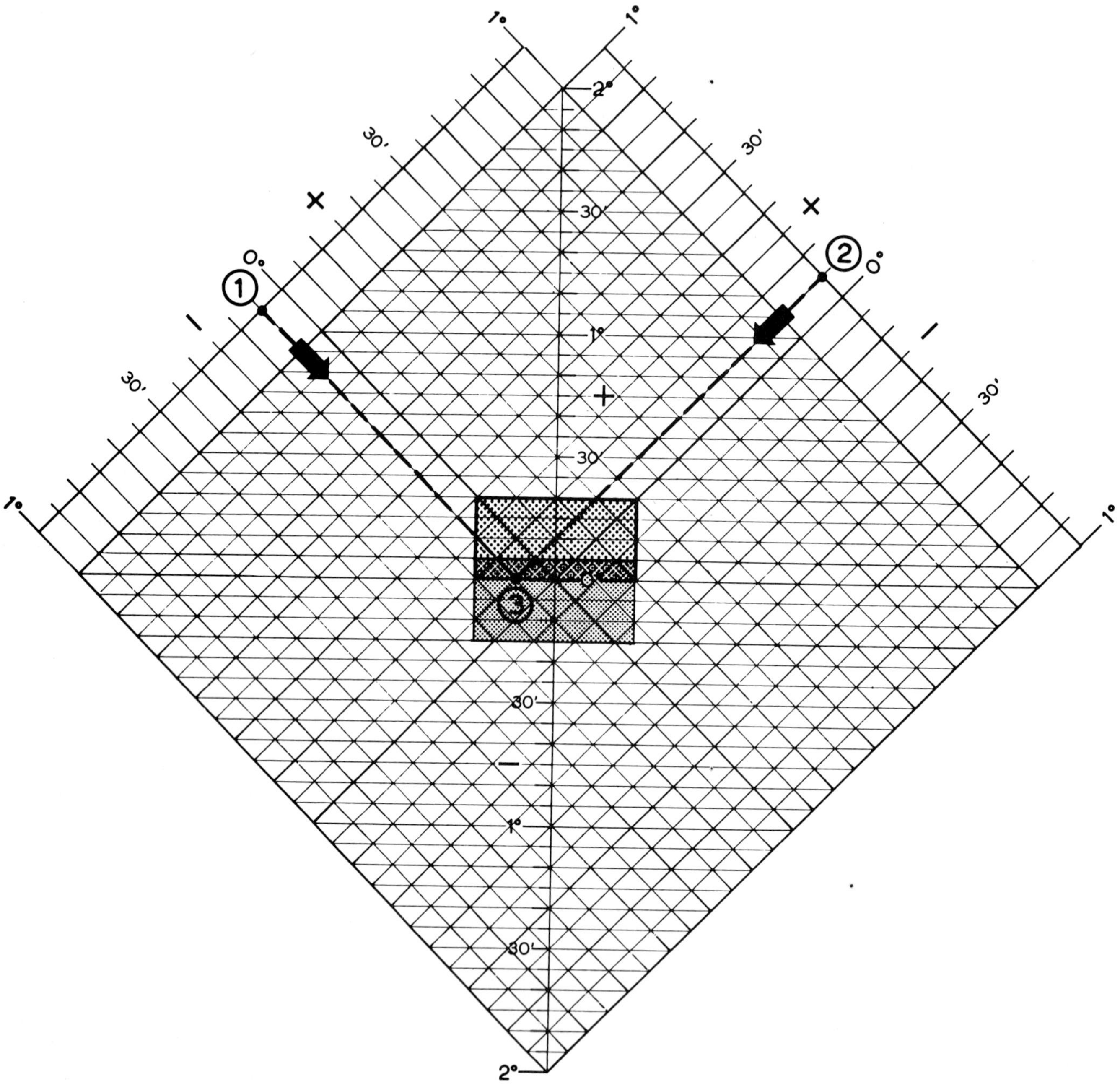

## 9.1 Checking Rear Wheel Alignment Graphically

The diagram of Fig. 143 is turned 45 degrees out of the position in which you would expect to find a conventional graph, but otherwise it will not present any complications.

The toe-in or toe-out of the rear wheels is plotted on the upper sides of the big square, left wheel alignment at left, right wheel alignment at right. The point marked 0 at either side represents a wheel exactly parallel to the car axis. All toe-in values (either left or right) go above the points marked 0, all toe-out values below. Thus, at the point shown as 1, a toe-out of 5 minutes of angle is plotted for the left wheel. At the point shown as circled 2 (right side) a toe-in of 5 minutes of angle is plotted for the right wheel. Dotted lines are drawn from these points (arrows) perpendicular to the sides of the big square and extended inward until they intersect. The location of this intersection of the perpendicular lines is what interests us here.

At the center of the big square you will see a small rectangle divided into two parts (upper and lower) by the shading. If the position of the rear wheels on a swing axle is correct, the dotted lines will intersect in the lower rectangle with the fine shading. For a double-joint axle the intersection should fall in the upper (coarsely shaded) section of the center rectangle. In both cases the rear wheel angles and the axle alignment will be within the specified tolerance range for the type of axle.

There is an overlap of 5 minutes of the upper and lower sections of the center rectangle. The height and width of those smaller rectangles represent the specified tolerances for, respectively, the wheel angle and axle alignment.

## 9.2 Checking Toe-in/Toe-out Angles and Axle Alignment by Calculation

If an evaluation diagram is not available, the toe-in/toe-out angle and axle alignment can be checked by calculation.

In these calculations the values for the toe-in/toe-out of the two rear wheels are added algebraically (that is, with reference to the plus and minus signs) to obtain a total toe-in/toe-out for the rear wheel position. If the values for both wheels have the same sign (either plus or minus) you add the values and give the result the same sign. If the values have different signs (one plus and one minus) you subtract the numerically smaller value from the larger one and give the result the sign of the larger value.



For example, two possible rear wheel situations are illustrated in Fig. 144, one at (A) and the other at (B). In each case the two smaller scales at the top show the toe-in or toe-out of, respectively, the left rear wheel and the right rear wheel. The larger scale below combines the readings for the individual wheels into a total **rear wheel position.** (The scales are divided from 0 to 1 degree or 0 to −1 degree in increments of 5 minutes and 10 minutes.)

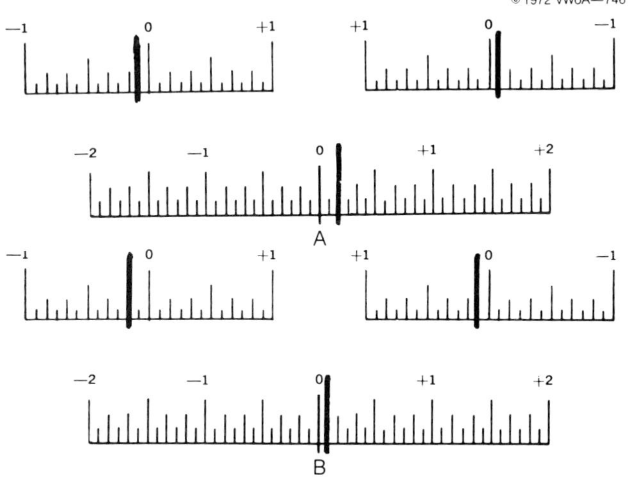


**Fig. 144.** Calculation of total rear wheel position is illustrated in diagrams (A) and (B). Two small upper scales in each set give toe-in or toe-out for each rear wheel (left/right). Larger scale below combines readings into total rear wheel position for the axle. Smallest division on scale represents 5 minutes. Next division represents 10 minutes. The numbered divisions (−1, 0, 1, etc.) represent degrees.

Accordingly, the diagram at (A) gives 5 minutes of toe-out for each wheel. Therefore, the total wheel position (lower scale) is minus 5 plus minus 5 equals minus 10.

$$[(-5) + (-5) = -10]$$

In the diagram at (B) the left wheel has 10 minutes of toe-out and therefore a value of minus 10, while the right wheel has 5 minutes of toe-in and is plus 5. The total is minus 10 minus plus 5 equals minus 5.

$$[(-10) - (+5) = (-5)]$$

In each case the computation gives the actual deviation of wheel alignment from the longitudinal axis of the car.

## 9.3 Correcting Toe-in/Toe-out and Alignment

The actual deviation of the rear wheels from the longitudinal axis (as computed from the previous procedure or otherwise determined) may require a change in the position of one wheel or both wheels. On the cars covered in this Manual the slots in the spring plates allow for such changes in wheel position. A chart **(Table m)** of faulty wheel positions and recommended remedies follows.

**Table m. Fault Diagnosis Chart**

| Defect | Cause | Remedy |
|---|---|---|
| 1. Too much toe-out (−) on both wheels | Axle tubes incorrectly set | Move both axle tubes forward in spring plates. |
| 2. Too much toe-in (+) on both wheels | Axle tubes incorrectly set | Move both axle tubes to rear in spring plates. |
| 3. Toe-in/toe-out angles differ | Axle tubes incorrectly set | Move appropriate axle tube in spring plate. |
| 4. Toe-in/toe-out angles differ considerably (on old vehicles) | Spring plate rubber bushings damaged | Fit new rubber bushings and correct angles. |
| 5. Deviation in alignment is excessive | Axle tubes incorrectly set | Change position of wheels by moving axle tubes. |
| 6. Camber angle too large, but the same on both wheels | Spring plates incorrectly set | Set spring plates properly. |
| 7. Camber angle too small, but the same on both wheels | Torsion bars settled | Set spring plates properly. |
| 8. Camber angles different | a. Spring plates set unevenly<br>b. Friction in spring plate rubber bushings uneven or excessive<br>c. Spring plate rubber bushings damaged | a. Set plates correctly.<br>b. Coat bushings with talcum on installation.<br>c. Fit new bushings. |

## 9.4 Rear Wheel Camber

The camber of the rear wheels is the sideways inclination or tilt of the wheels from a vertical line drawn through the point where the tire makes contact with the road, as seen from the rear of the vehicle. (See **10.16 Steering Geometry** in **FRONT AXLE**.) If the wheel is exactly vertical to the road surface, the camber angle is zero. If the top of the wheel is inclined outward, the camber angle is positive (+). If the inclination is inward, the camber angle is negative (−). The rear wheel camber angles are specified for an unloaded car with spring plates set correctly. The angles should be as nearly as possible the same on both sides. Basically, the setting of the torsion bars controls this condition.

### Measuring Camber

Because torsion bars tend to settle slightly, the camber angle should not be measured until the vehicle has been driven at least 300 miles. The permissible minimum camber angle is only an approximate figure, but the angle should not fall below this figure even after the vehicle has covered a considerable mileage.

### Adjusting Camber

The rear wheel camber angle can be changed by adjusting the torsion bars. The specifications should be observed.

When carrying out repairs on the rear axles of high mileage vehicles, always adjust both torsion bars to avoid upsetting the ride characteristics as a result of different camber angles.

## 9.5 Wheel Alignment Check

Before you begin a wheel alignment check, always inspect the running gear carefully for visible signs of damage. If you find none, check the car for the following:

1. Tire pressures must be correct.
2. Car must be unloaded except for full tank of fuel.
3. Steering must be adjusted properly.
4. Steering linkage must be free of excess play.
5. Front wheel bearings must be properly adjusted.

6. Spring plates must be correctly set.
7. Car must be aligned and bounced to settle suspension.

After making the checks and correcting any damage found, you are ready to proceed with the alignment check. Systematically cover the following:

a. On front axle:
   Camber of front wheels
   Toe-in/toe-out of front wheels
   Caster angle of front wheels
   Difference in wheel angle on lock
   Stub axle offset (as an additional check if suitable measuring equipment is available)
b. On rear axle:
   Camber of rear wheels
   Toe-in/toe-out of rear wheels
   Alignment of rear axle

## 10. SHOCK ABSORBERS

In design the shock absorbers for the rear axle are basically the same as those for the front axle. The instructions given in **FRONT AXLE** for checking the action of shock absorbers apply also to rear axle shocks.

### 10.1 Removing and Installing Shock Absorbers (rear axle)

**To remove:**

1. Lift vehicle and take off rear wheel.
2. Remove shock absorber securing nuts (Fig. 145) and take shock absorber off.

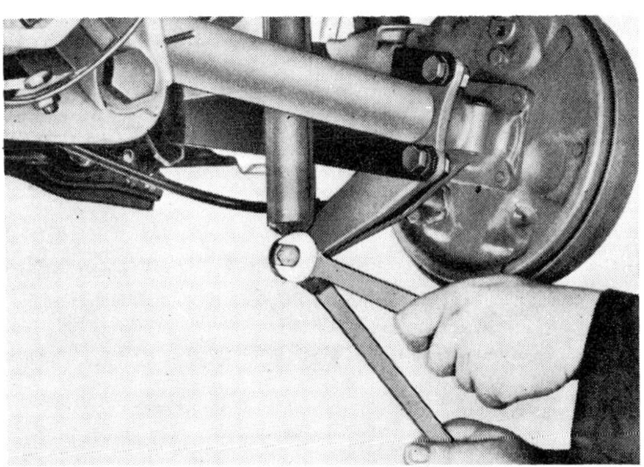

© 1972 VWoA—747

**Fig. 145.** Securing nuts are taken off for removal of rear axle shock absorber.

**To install:**

1. Check shock absorber and replace if necessary.

**NOTE —**
See **FRONT AXLE** for instructions.

2. Check rubber bushings for wear and replace them if necessary.
3. Install new spring washers.
4. Torque securing nuts to 43 ft. lbs. (6 mkg). Heavy duty shock absorbers are available for heavy duty use.

**NOTE —**
Instructions on the installation and adjustment of the heavy duty shock absorbers are given in the **FRONT AXLE.**

**To remove rubber bushing:**

1. Press out bushing sleeve with a guide.
2. Press out bushing.

**To install rubber bushings:**

1. Coat bushing with talcum powder and press it into eye of shock absorber.
2. Use tapered pilot to press sleeve into bushing. Coat bushing and pilot lightly with glycerine or brake cylinder paste.

5

### 10.2 Shock Absorber Specifications

**Table n** gives specifications for rear shock absorbers on cars covered in this Manual.

**Table n. Rear Shock Absorber**

| Make | Part no. (stamped on) | Remarks |
|---|---|---|
| Boge | 113513031 N | Can be paired with 113513031 P Color: red-brown |
| Fichtel & Sachs | 113513031 P | Can be paired with 113513031 N Color: red-brown |

Damping force:

At a test speed of 100 cycles per minute (CPM) and a stroke of 2.95 inches (75 mm).

Draw stage = 344.9 − 31.96 lbs. (156.6 − 14.5 kg)
Pressure stage = 132.24 − 15.43 lbs. (60 − 7 kg)

## 11. Equalizer Springs

The equalizer spring is a side-to-side torsion bar connected to the axle tubes. You will find it mounted under the luggage compartment floor, behind the rear set. The spring mechanism includes two levers slanted in opposite directions and two operating rods (Fig. 146). The purpose of the equalizer is to provide an additional progressive spring action to assist the torsion bars when under load. Because the operating levers slant in opposite directions, the action of the equalizer spring does not affect body roll, and the front axle assembly is thereby enabled to absorb more roll to give better cornering of the vehicle.

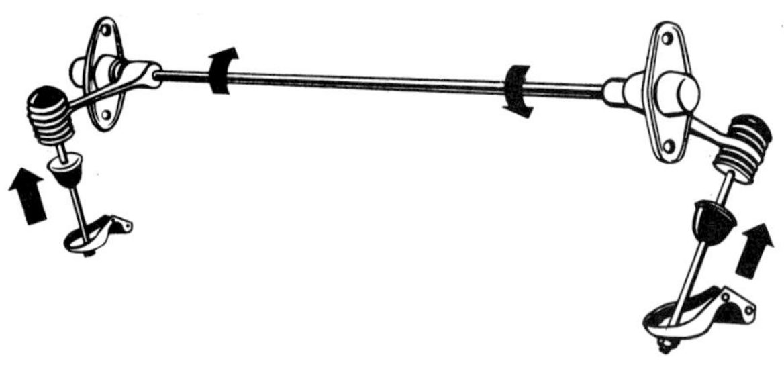



**Fig. 146.** Equalizer spring assists rear torsion bars with the springing action illustrated by the black arrows. Note the opposing action of the two operating levers.

### 11.1 Removing and Installing Equalizer Springs

**To remove:**

1. Disconnect battery ground strap.
2. Loosen wheel mounting bolts.

> ***WARNING —***
> *Do not attempt to loosen or tighten wheel bolts when car is on a lift. You can topple the car off the lift. Always have car on the ground when you loosen or tighten wheel bolts.*

3. Raise vehicle and take off wheels.
4. Remove operating rod nuts on mounting, as in Fig. 147.

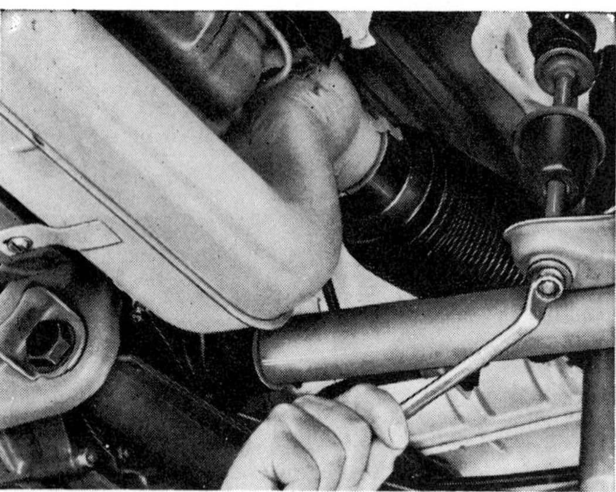



**Fig. 147.** Operating rod for equalizer spring is unbolted here from the operating rod guide.

5. Remove rubber caps and unscrew operating rod nuts on the levers (Fig. 148).

**Fig. 148.** Operating lever for equalizer spring is unbolted here from the operating rod guide.

6. Remove operating rods and rubber buffers.
7. Unscrew nuts for supports and remove supports and rubber bushings.
8. Loosen the lock nut and socket head bolt securing the left lever on the equalizer spring a few turns until the lever can be removed.
9. Withdraw equalizer spring and right lever to the right.
10. Check operating rod guide rings and replace if necessary. You can take the rings off with a screwdriver.
11. Unscrew two nuts on each side (Fig. 149) and take left and right guides off axle tube flange.

**Fig. 149.** Two nuts (black arrows) fasten guide for operating lever of equalizer spring assembly to the axle tube flange.

12. Check equalizer spring, rubber bushings, damping rings, guide tubes and rubber stops. Replace them if necessary.

**To install:**

1. Push lever on equalizer spring. Note that left lever is marked "L". The left lever must point downward toward the rear, and the clamping screw toward the front. Install the right lever as shown in Fig. 150.

**Fig. 150.** Support for equalizer spring assembly is shown here in exploded view.

2. Tighten clamping screw and lock it.
3. Install equalizer spring, together with lever, from the right.
4. Install supports and rubber bushings. Place a hard rubber washer between lever and support.
5. Install operating rods. The long operating rod is installed on the right side. Place a damping ring above and below the levers. Install protective caps.

**NOTE —**
For best seating of the damping rings, the operating rods should be attached to the levers first. The levers must not rest in the guides.

6. Insert operating rods into guides. Install washers and tighten nuts.
7. Install all other parts.

## 12. DOUBLE-JOINT AXLE

The 1969 cars with the manual transmission (and all cars with Automatic Stick Shift) have the double-joint rear axle instead of the swing rear axle.

As the name suggests, each drive shaft of the rear axle has two joints. The inner joint is at the transmission case. The outer joint is at the wheel. Both are ball joints of the constant velocity type. The design was developed to eliminate the variations in driven shaft rpm that are characteristic of ordinary universal joints.

### 12.1 General Description

At the inner CV joint on the double-joint rear axle the transfer of power is from the flange on the differential to the outer housing of the joint. From the outer housing, power is transferred through the balls to the joint hub and then by splines to the drive shaft. At the outer joint the sequence is reversed. That is, power flows from drive shaft to splines to outer housing and finally, to rear wheel shaft.

5

The constant velocity joints compensate for movement of the wheel shaft relative to the flange on the differential. The balls move in grooves inside the joints on paths that allow variation in total shaft length without introducing variation in shaft rpm. The drive shaft as a result maintains a correct position. Fig. 151 shows CV joint construction in cross section.

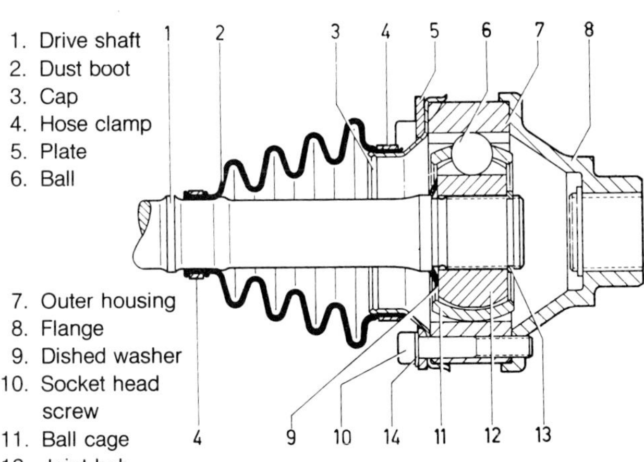


**Fig. 151.** Constant velocity joint is shown here in cross section.

**Fig. 152.** Double-joint axle with Automatic Stick Shift is seen here from below and slightly behind wheels.

The design of the double-joint axle has each independently suspended rear wheel mounted in an arrangement of trailing diagonal control arm and trailing link. The trailing link, which usually is called the spring plate, is bolted to the housing of the wheel bearing and splined on the transverse torsion bar. The diagonal arm is attached to a bracket welded on the cross tube in which the torsion bar is installed. Fig. 152 and Fig. 168 show the complete assembly. The diagonal arm pivots at the bracket. The torsion bar allows up and down movement of the spring plate. In other axles side thrust acts directly on the gearbox, but this design transmits the thrust to the car frame.

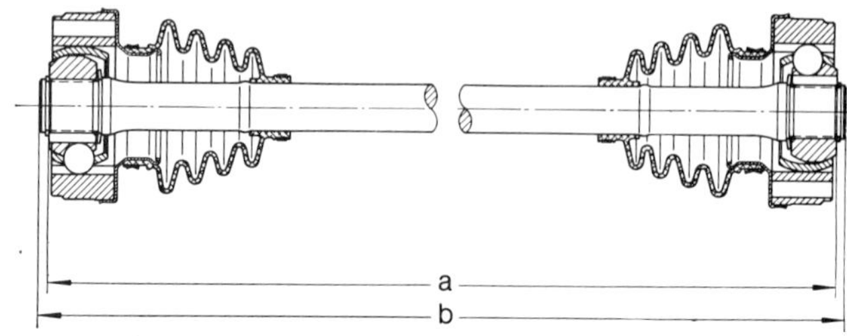




**Fig. 153.** Coded lengths of drive shaft are shown here: "a" is distance between CV joints; "b" is overall length. See V. Double Joint Shafts in Automatic Stick Shift Technical Data.

## Drive Shafts

The different types of VW cars require rear axle drive shafts of different lengths, depending on the transmissions installed, but the cars we are discussing here, those with Automatic Stick Shift as well as those with manual transmission, take the same shaft.

The drive shafts carry stamped code numbers, which refer to measurements illustrated in Fig. 153. A number stamped in the end of the shaft is coded to measurement "b", the total shaft length. Another stamped number is coded to "a", which is shaft length measured between the ball joints. Shafts with the same "b" measurement can differ in the "a" measurement, depending on the location of two dished washers.

The shaft for the cars under discussion here is part No. 113 501 211 (without joints) and carries code number 1 stamped on the end and elsewhere on the shaft for the two measurements. The lengths, dimensions "a" and "b", are given in millimeters. They are:

| | |
|---|---|
| Length "a" between joints | 405.3 mm (15.9 inches) |
| Total length "b" | 415.5 mm (16.3 inches) |

Fig. 154 shows a double-joint rear axle drive shaft with the joint at one end disassembled. The dished washer at (7) is one of the two that determine measurement "a" in shaft length.

**Fig. 154.** Drive shaft for double-joint axle is seen here with one CV joint removed from shaft. Washer (7) is critical in measurements. Quantities shown in parenthesis are for one shaft. See text.

1. Drive shaft
2. Constant velocity joint (2)
3. Dust boot (2)

© 1972 VWoA—895

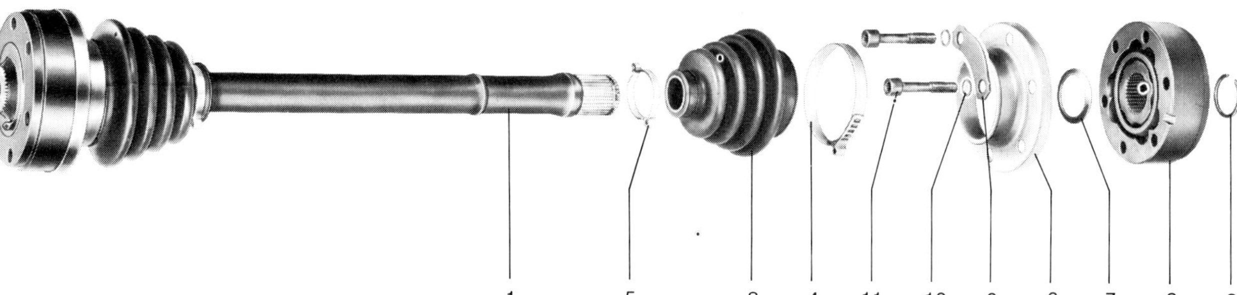

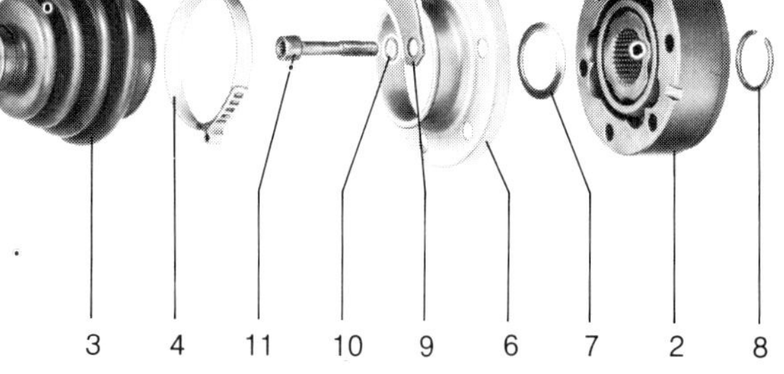


4. Hose clamp, large (2)
5. Hose clamp (2)
6. Cap (2)
7. Dished washer (2)
8. Circlip (2)
9. Plate (6)
10. Lock washer (12)
11. Socket head screw M 8 (12)

## 12.2 Removing and Installing Constant Velocity Joints

When the car is on a lift, the drive shafts hang down from the inner ball joint. With a shaft in this position, you will have to turn the wheel to get at all the socket head screws which fasten the ball joint cap to the flange on the differential. The easiest procedure is to set the parking brake and then remove the two uppermost screws. Release brake and turn wheel to bring two more screws into position for removal. Set brake and repeat procedure until all the screws are out.

**To remove joint:**

1. Take out six socket-head screws holding shaft to differential flange (see above). Tilt shaft downward and remove.
2. Loosen clamp and slide back dust boot, as shown in Fig. 155.

© 1972 VWoA—896

**Fig. 155.** Clamps holding dust boot on CV joint have been loosened here.

3. Remove circlip from ball hub.
4. Drive cap off joint with a drift, as in Fig. 156.

5

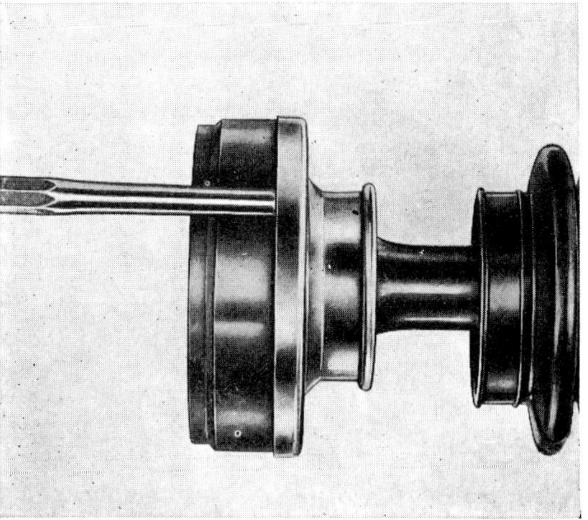

© 1972 VWoA—897

**Fig. 156.** Cap is driven off CV joint with drift as shown here.

**NOTE —**
After removing the protective cap, be careful about tilting the ball hub. If it tilts more than 20 degrees in the outer part of the joint, the balls can fall out.

5. Slide outer part with balls onto ball hub.

6. While supporting hub, press drive shaft out of ball hub and take off dished washer. Fig. 157 shows the set-up.

© 1972 VWoA—898

**Fig. 157.** Hub of CV joint is supported on plate while drive shaft is pressed out.

**To install:**

1. Check drive shaft, dust boot, constant velocity joint, protective cap and dished washer for wear and damage and replace if necessary.

> ***CAUTION —***
> *If any part of a CV joint is damaged, worn or out of order, the joint must be replaced. New joints come packed in grease of the cosmoline type. You remove this cosmoline with clean solvent. After the cleaning, pack the joint with molybdenum disulfide grease (Moly-Kote®). See the procedure for disassembly of CV joints.*

2. Install new clamps (see Fig. 154).
3. Slide guide sleeve over the drive shaft splines and slide boot into position, as in Fig. 158.

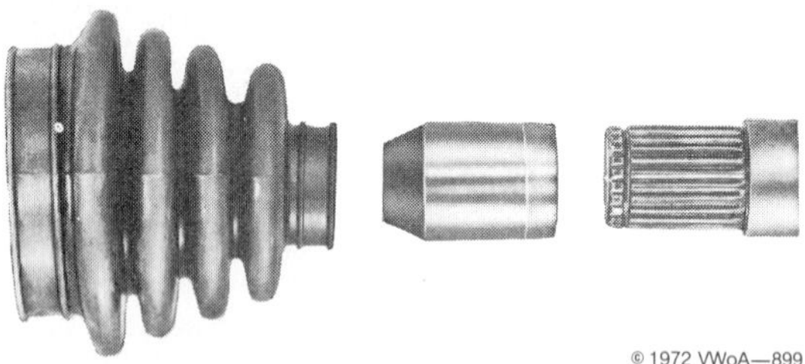

© 1972 VWoA—899

**Fig. 158.** Sleeve (center) fits over splines on drive shaft (right) for installation of dust boot (left).

> **NOTE —**
> The large diameter of outer part of joint (see arrow in Fig. 159) should be toward boot.

© 1972 VWoA—900

**Fig. 159.** Larger diameter (arrow) on CV joint is toward dust boot when joint is installed. Smaller diameter is toward differential flange at transmission end of drive shaft and toward axle shaft flange at the wheel end.

4. Put dished washer and constant velocity joint on drive shaft and press them into place together. For this operation, support the shaft on beam under press table, as in Fig. 160.

© 1972 VWoA—901

**Fig. 160.** Beam under press supports drive shaft while dished washer and CV joint are pressed on shaft.

5. Install new circlip, pressing it down until it snaps into groove.
6. Squeeze circlip all around until clip seats fully in groove. (Water pump pliers, as in Fig. 161, are useful here.)

**Fig. 161.** Circlip (retaining ring) on end of drive shaft is squeezed with pliers until it snaps into groove.

7. Repack constant velocity joint. Use Moly-Kote® grease. Amount of grease per joint: 3.2 ounces (90 grams).

**NOTE —**
Pack about two-thirds of the grease between outer part of joint, protective cap and dust boot. Pack remainder into open joint from the front. All contact surfaces between joint, cap and seal, cap and shaft must be free of grease.

8. Attach both clamps and tighten.

**NOTE —**
Install clamps in positions that do not interfere with removal or replacement of socket head screws. Use clamps as nearly like original equipment as possible. These clamps have lugs which are pinched together. This arrangement prevents damage to the seal.

9. Squeeze boot by hand to force grease into joint from behind.
10. Install drive shaft and tighten socket head screws to specified torque.



## 12.3 Disassembling and Assembling Constant Velocity Joints

We include these procedures only in case CV joints are to be cleaned. You do not repair CV joints or replace individual parts of a joint. The CV joint is replaced only as an assembly.

**NOTE —**
Study the pictures closely and proceed slowly, exercising care in the assembly. Tight tolerances make new CV joints difficult to disassemble. Before you take a CV joint apart, be sure to make some matching marks with chalk or crayon across adjacent parts to guide you in re-assembly. A line across a radius would do.

**To disassemble:**

1. Press constant velocity joint off drive shaft. (See procedure for removal in **12.2 Removing and Installing Constant Velocity Joints**.)
2. Swivel ball hub and cage into position shown in Fig. 162. Do this by pressing hub and cage on the side nearest to you towards the left as in Fig. 162. Then press ball cage all the way out of the outer ring.

5

3. Press balls out of cage.

**Fig. 162.** Ball cage is at right angle to outer ring when in position to be pressed out of CV joint. Arrow shows direction to press in.

4. Turn hub into position shown in Fig. 163. Channel in hub will be in line with outside edge of cage. Tip out hub, which now has room to clear inside of cage. These channels are machined in outer and inner races of joint. The balls ride in them.

**Fig. 163.** Ball hub of CV joint is turned to bring long channel (arrows) in hub in line with edge of cage. Channel allows enough play to let you tip hub out of cage.

5. Carefully clean and dry all parts of the CV joint. Pack with Moly-Kote® grease as you would a bearing. Remove excess grease.

**NOTE —**
The ball hub and outer ring of a CV joint are a matched set and must not be mixed up. The six balls of each joint were selected for grouping to a specified tolerance. If you are disassembling more than one joint at a time, make sure that you put back all parts exactly as they were.

**To assemble:**

1. Check outer ring (outer race), ball hub (inner race), ball cage and balls for wear. Excessive radial play in the joints will cause noise under load changes. Replace noisy joints.

**NOTE —**
If you find any parts of a CV joint faulty, replace the entire joint.

2. Insert hub into cage. This operation is the reverse of step 4 of the disassembly procedure. With the edge of the cage in the hub channel (Fig. 163) for clearance, press and swivel the hub into the cage.

3. Press balls into cage, as in Fig. 164. If necessary, pack in Moly-Kote® grease to hold the balls in the cage.

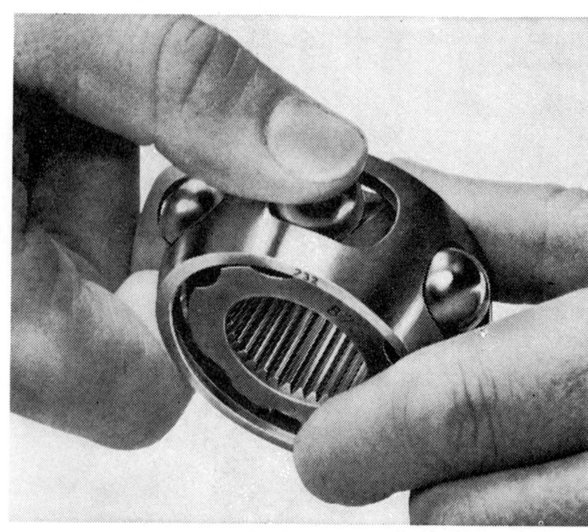



**Fig. 164.** Balls for CV joint are pressed into cage as shown here.

**NOTE —**
Before proceeding further, it is a good idea to stop for a moment here and study how the inner and outer races of the CV joint fit together and how the assembled joint goes on the axle shaft. Note that the splines in the hub are chamfered at one end. This is the end that receives the axle shaft splines and therefore must point toward the shaft (not toward the transmission case at one end or at the wheel at the other end) when the joint is installed on the shaft. Note also that the larger diameter of the outer race (also called the housing) is also toward the shaft (not toward case or wheel) when installed. Therefore, when you think of bringing the hub and outer race together for assembly, you would picture the chamfered end of the hub approaching the **smaller** diameter of the outer race.

If you put the hub and outer race on a bench in this position relative to each other, you will note that on each part there is a difference in the spacing between the channels in which the balls ride. A wide spacing alternates with a narrow spacing, as shown in Fig. 165. When the joint is assembled, a narrow spacing on the hub (shown as "b" in Fig. 165) must be lined up with a wide spacing in the outer race ("a" in Fig. 165). You can force the hub and outer race together in a different alignment, but if you do, the joint will lock up solidly and be useless. Now you should be ready to continue with the assembly.

4. Hold the outer race vertical and insert the hub with cage and balls into it as in Fig. 165. The hub and outer race are now assembled into a unit.

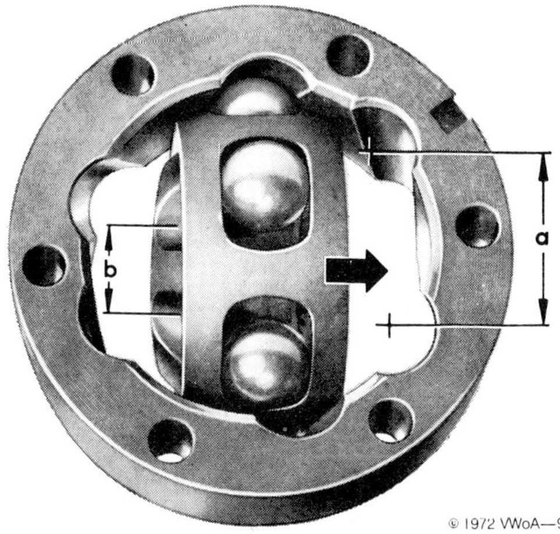


**Fig. 165.** Hub of CV joint is pivoted into place in outer race. Letter "b" indicates narrow, raised sector of hub that must be in line with wide cut-out "a" on outer race. The outer race on this joint has a notch on the rim showing that it is an early version. The beveled surface seen in Fig. 166 is the later version of this notch. The basic move in the procedure illustrated here is to bring the narrow sector on the hub into the wide cut-out on the outer race. See VI. Constant Velocity Joints in Automatic Stick Shift Technical Data.

5. While holding the cage firmly, pivot the hub in the direction indicated by the single arrow in Fig. 166. As the hub pivots, the two balls will move to the highest position on the hub (double arrows), approaching the channels in the outer race.

**Fig. 166.** Balls must align (arrows) with channels before hub can be pressed into CV joint.

6. Check alignment of hub and outer race before final assembly of joint.
   a. Remember that the chamfered ends of the internal splines of the hub point toward the contact shoulder on the drive shaft.
   b. Remember that the chamfered ends of the splines also are at the larger diameter of the outer race when assembled.
   c. Remember that the smaller diameter of the outer race faces the differential flange surface on the transmission case or the axle shaft flange on the wheel end.
7. At point indicated by arrow in Fig. 167, press cage firmly until hub swings into place.

**Fig. 167.** Finger pressure applied at point indicated by arrow will force correctly positioned hub into outer ring of CV joint.

8. Check joint for action. If you can move the ball hub back and forth by hand over the full range, you have assembled the joint correctly.

5

### 12.4 Removing and Installing Double-joint Axle

The suspension assembly for rear wheel on a double-joint axle is shown in Fig. 168, on the following page. The partly exploded view gives a clear picture of the relationship of spring plate and diagonal arm.

> ***WARNING***—
> *When car is on lift it is dangerous to loosen or tighten wheel shaft nuts. Loosen or tighten the nuts only when car is on the ground.*

**Fig. 168.** Suspension system for rear wheel on double-joint axle is shown disassembled here. Fitted bolt (10) fastens trailing diagonal arm (2) to cross tube carrying torsion bar. Spring plate (3), suspended on torsion bar, attaches to diagonal arm with bolt (15) and bolt (12).

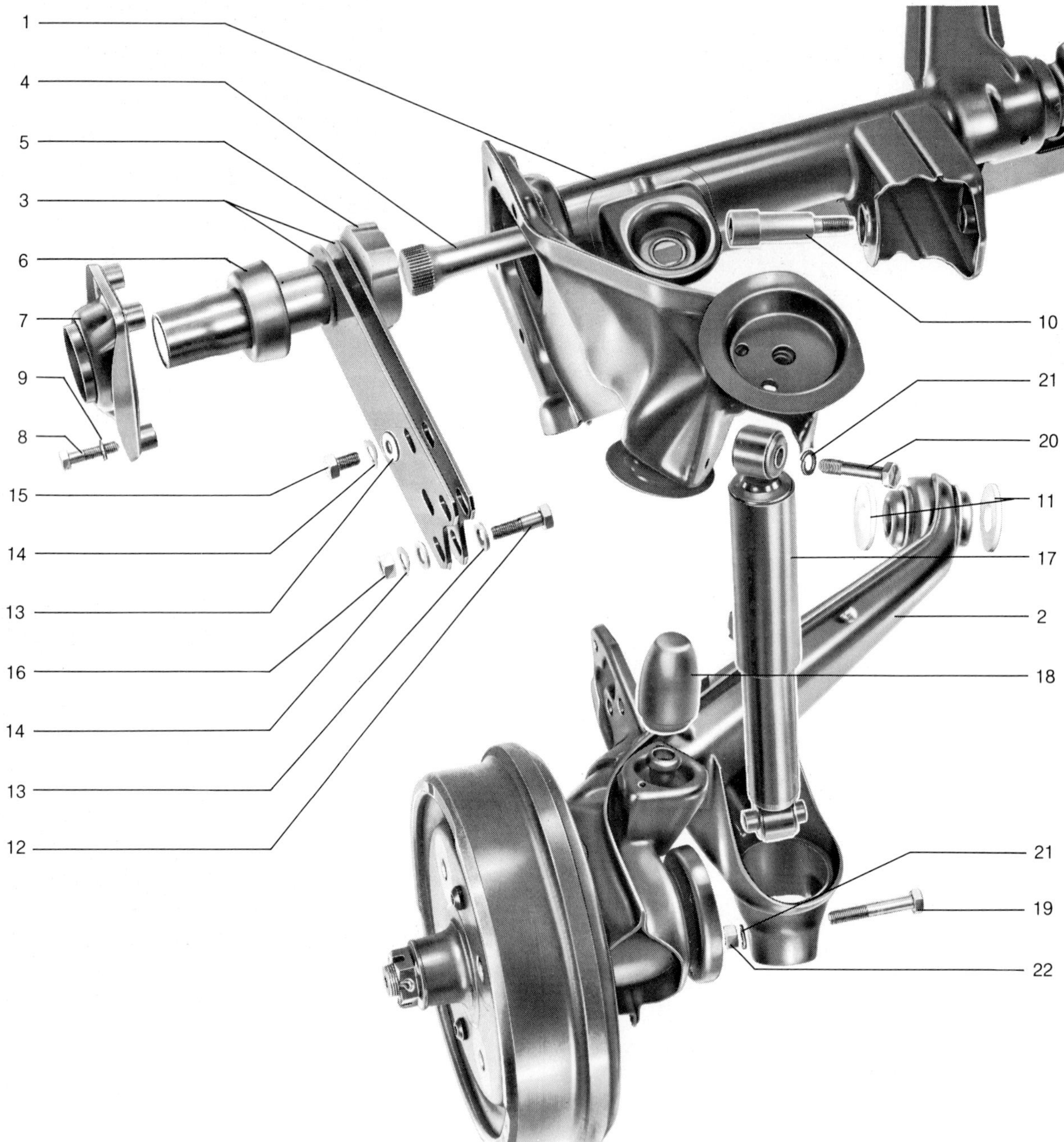


1. Frame or sub-frame
2. Diagonal arm (complete)
3. Double spring plate
4. Torsion bar
5. Rubber bushing, inner left
6. Rubber bushing, outer
7. Cover for spring plate hub
8. Bolt M 10 x 35 (4)
9. Lock washer B 10 (4)
10. Fitted bolt
11. Spacer (2)
12. Bolt M 12 x 40 (3)
13. Washer A 13 (7)
14. Lock washer (4)
15. Bolt M 12 x 20
16. Nut M 12 (3)
17. Shock absorber
18. Rubber stop
19. Bolt M 12 x 70
20. Bolt M 12 x 50
21. Lock washer B 12 (2)
22. Nut M 12

**To remove axle:**

1. Loosen wheel shaft nuts, which hold brake drums.
2. Detach drive shaft at wheel ends and cover CV joints with plastic cap, as in Fig. 169.

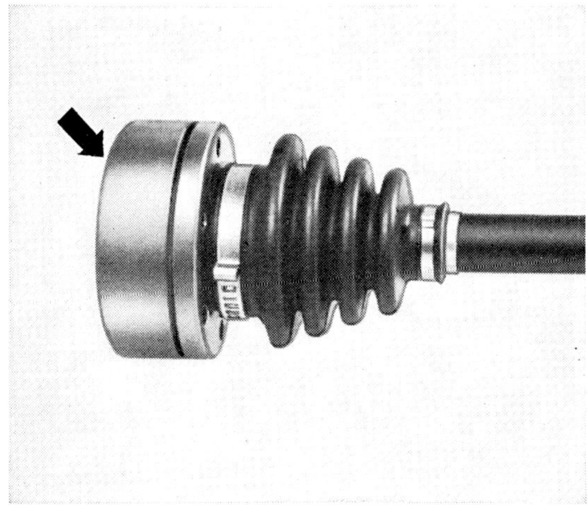



**Fig. 169.** Plastic cap (arrow) protects CV joint when drive shaft has been detached.

3. Remove wheel shaft nuts and pull brake drums off. Disconnect brake lines and parking brake cable. Remove backplate.
4. Remove lower shock absorber bolts.

**NOTE —**
If you are disassembling only the wheel bearings, take off brake drums and backing plates but do not disconnect either brake lines or parking brake cables. Hang backing plates on car with pieces of wire. By leaving brake lines connected, you avoid having to bleed brakes.

5. Mark location of spring plate and diagonal arm with a chisel mark at top and bottom, as shown by arrows in Fig. 170.

***CAUTION —***
*Support spring plate with jack.*

6. Remove nuts and bolts holding spring plate and arm together but note position of bolts.

**NOTE —**
If you find it necessary to replace a spring plate or diagonal arm, you will have to correct the rear wheel alignment when you reassemble the rear axle.

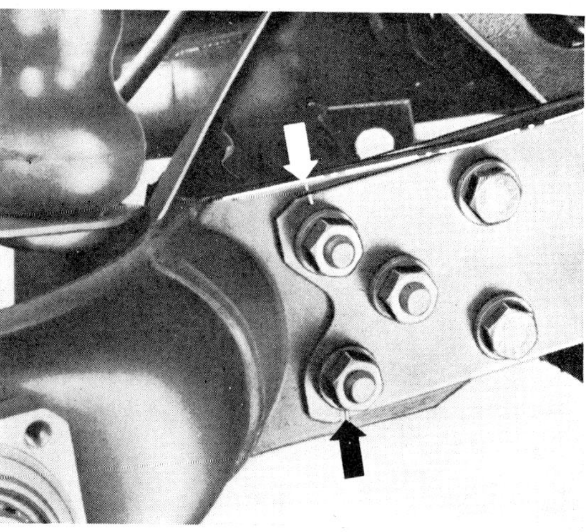



**Fig. 170.** Chisel cuts (arrows) locate the match for reassembly of spring plate and diagonal arm. Note differences in bolt installation.

7. Remove socket-head screw which attaches diagonal arm to bracket and take arm off. Fig. 171 shows the screw.

5

**Fig. 171.** Socket head screw, shown with wrench in it, attaches diagonal arm to bracket.

**NOTE —**
Be careful to note positions of special washers. They must go back in same locations.

8. Remove bolts that hold cover on spring plate hub. Take off cover.

**NOTE —**
It is possible also to remove spring plate with the diagonal arm installed.

9. Using tire iron, lift spring plate off lower stop as in Fig. 172.

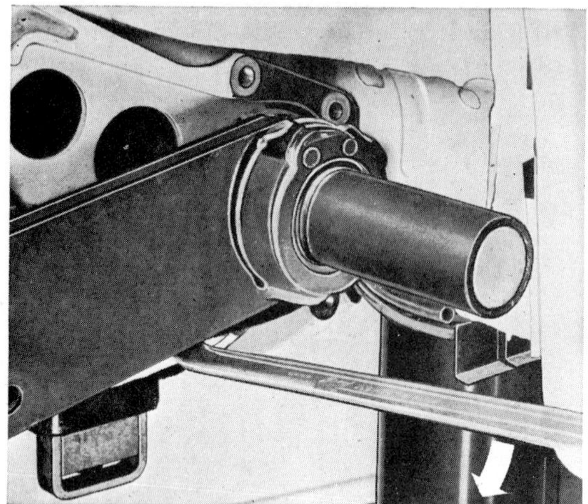



**Fig. 172.** Tire iron holds spring plate off lower stop while bolts are taken out for removal of plate.

10. Remove five bolts at front of fender to free torsion bar.

11. Take off spring plate and pull out torsion bar.

**NOTE —**
You can fish out pieces of broken torsion bar with a smaller tube flared at the end. You can also remove the opposite torsion bar and knock out broken pieces with a long bar.

**To install:**

1. Check torsion bar, rubber bushings and spring plates for wear and damage and replace parts as necessary.

**NOTE —**
The protective paint on torsion bars prevents corrosion, which can lead to fatigue failure. It is most important that this protective coating should remain intact. Repaint any bare spots on bars.

2. Grease torsion bar splines.

**NOTE —**
Torsion bars are prestressed in their working directions and therefore should not be installed in the wrong position. Each axle has a left bar and a right bar. You will find "L" stamped on the end face of the left bar, "R" on end face of right bar.

3. Before you install spring plate, coat the inner and outer rubber bushings with talcum powder, not graphite. The bushings were designed to remain in a fixed position in relation to the spring plate, allowing only elastic movement. Graphite would permit the spring plate to slip and turn in the bushings. The rubbing would cause premature wear. See Fig. 173.

**Fig. 173.** Talcum powder on rubber bushings keeps spring plate from turning in the bushings.

**NOTE —**
When installing the inner and outer bushings for torsion bars, position them with the German word **Oben** at the top. Take note that the inner and outer bushings are different.

4. Install spring plate and outer bushing and adjust torsion bar.

**NOTE —**
When attaching the double spring plate and diagonal arm, separate the spring plate leaves with a large nut or similar object. You will then be able to insert the flange on the diagonal arm for bolting.

5. Secure spring plate hub cover (Fig. 174) with two bolts, using longer than standard bolts if necessary. Insert diagonal arm flange between spring plate leaves.

6. Using special tool (tensioner), lift spring plate onto lower stop and hold. Tighten bolts in hub cover.

***CAUTION —***
*Use only the tensioner intended for this job when you install spring plates.*

**Fig. 174.** Two long bolts hold spring plate hub cover until diagonal arm can be attached.

7. Install remaining bolts in hub cover. If you used long bolts in step 5, replace them now with specified bolts. Tighten all bolts to specified torque. Re-install all the special washers in their original positions.
8. Secure extended diagonal arm to bracket with bolt. Tighten bolt to correct torque and lock it by peening the metal shoulder on the bracket, as shown in Fig. 175.

**Fig. 175.** Peening metal shoulder at point indicated by arrow locks fitted bolt holding diagonal arm.

**NOTE ——**
To prevent tension in bonded rubber bushings, have the diagonal arm in the extended position when you tighten this bolt. Watch the location of the washers. When installing a new arm, check spacing for the drive shafts and correct as necessary. (See **12.6 Adjusting Axle**.)

9. Attach arm to spring plate. Watch alignment marks. Tighten nuts and bolt to correct torque.

**NOTE ——**
When a new spring plate or diagonal arm is installed, rear wheel alignment must be checked on an alignment rig and corrected as necessary.

10. Attach backing plate and bearing cover for rear wheel shaft to diagonal arm and tighten bolts to correct torque.
11. Grease constant velocity joint lightly with Moly-Kote® and install shaft. (Use new lock washers, installing them with convex side towards screw head.) Tighten socket head screws to specified torque.

**NOTE ——**
Contact surfaces of shaft flange and joint must be free of grease.

***WARNING ——***
*It is dangerous to loosen or tighten the wheel shaft nuts when car is on a lift. Loosen or tighten these nuts only when car is on the ground.*

**5**

12. Install brake drum, tighten slotted nut to 217 ft. lbs. (30 mkg) and secure with cotter pin.
13. Bleed and adjust brakes.

## 12.5 Adjusting Torsion Bars

The setting angle for the torsion bar is given in degrees of deviation from the horizontal along the longitudinal axis of the car. The longitudinal axis is the line running the length of the car through the center of gravity of the car. A protractor with bubble level is used for the measurement of the deviation, and the measurement is taken with the torsion bars free of load. The first step of the procedure is to find the deviation of the car axis from the true horizontal. This deviation is taken into account in determining the setting angle.

The number of splines at the two ends of a torsion bar are not the same. Instead, they are:

| | |
|---|---|
| Inner end: | 40 splines |
| Outer end: | 44 splines |

The difference in the number of splines makes possible a relatively fine adjustment between torsion bar and spring plate. Turning the inner end of a torsion bar one spline changes the angle by 9 degrees, whereas turning the spring plate back one spline at the other end of the bar changes the angle by 8 degrees 10 minutes in the opposite direction. Combining the two turns gives an adjustment of 9 degrees minus 8 degrees 10 minutes, which equals 50 minutes. This is the smallest adjustment that can be made.

> **NOTE —**
> On cars with considerable mileage, always adjust both torsion bars since the bars tend to settle in use.

**To adjust:**

1. Determine deviation of car axis from the horizontal. For this measurement set the protractor on the tunnel cover by the driver's seat, as in Fig. 176, and press down on it firmly. Read the gauge and make a note of the reading.

© 1972 VWoA—917

**Fig. 176.** Protractor resting on frame tunnel measures angle of car axis from the horizontal.

2. Place spring plate on torsion bar and position protractor on plate as in Fig. 177. Measure angle. While measuring the angle, lift the plate in order to eliminate any play in the splines.

© 1972 VWoA—918

**Fig. 177.** Spring plate angle is measured with protractor in this position.

3. If the angle you read from the gauge differs from the specified setting of the plate by more than 50 minutes, you will have to make an adjustment.

4. Depending on the deviation (whether plus or minus from specified setting), turn torsion bar one spline forward or back and spring plate one spline in the opposite direction. (This procedure applies to either side of axle.)

5. Install spring plate bearing cover and assemble rear wheel suspension.

**Table o** gives the spring plate setting angles for the cars covered in this Manual. Note that measurements for

### Table o. Spring Plate Setting Angles

| | Model | Transmission Type* | Chassis number from | to | Torsion bar length mm | Diameter mm | Spring plate setting |
|---|---|---|---|---|---|---|---|
| Swing Axle (Without Equalizer Spring) | all | 1 | 2532 668 | 116 1021 297 | 552 | 22 | 17°30′±50′ |
| Swing Axle (With Equalizer Spring) | all | 1 | 117 000 001 | 118 1016 098 | 552 | 21 | 20° + 50′ |
| Double-joint Axle | all | 2<br>1, 2 | 118 000 001<br>119 000 001 | | 676 | 22 | 20°30′+50′ |

***1 Standard 2 Automatic Stick Shift**

both swing and double-joint axles and both manual and Automatic Stick Shift are included. In the column headed "Transmission Types", the manual shift is designated "1" and the Automatic Stick Shift "2". Linear measurements are specified in millimeters.

## 12.6 Adjusting Axle

In order to understand why certain procedures are followed to adjust the double-joint axle, you need to visualize the mounting of the power/drive unit, the mounting of the diagonal arms and spring plates and the linkages through which power is transmitted from final drive to wheel shafts.

The power/drive unit consists of engine, transmission and final drive. At the front of the transmission a bonded rubber mounting attaches this unit to the frame cross-tube. At the rear the carrier, which is bolted to the engine, supports the unit, and rubber bushings secure it to the frame at the sides. The rear cross-tube, with its torsion bars and brackets for the diagonal control arms, ties this assembly together with the rear wheel suspension. You will find a picture of this assembly in the **FRAME** section.

The short drive shafts, with two constant velocity joints on each shaft, transmit torque from final drive to wheel shafts. Swivel motion in the constant velocity joints compensates for relative movement between final drive flanges and wheel shaft flanges. If manufacturing tolerances are not to restrict this swivel motion, the distance between wheel shaft flanges must be set when the suspension is at the lowest point of its up-and-down travel. Also, the engine/transmission unit must be centered between the wheel shaft flanges.

On the cars covered in this Manual the adjustments required are for wheel toe (track angle) and camber. All washers on attaching arms are installed on the outside of the arms. When a diagonal arm has been replaced or repaired, the following checks and adjustments are made:

1. Check distance between wheel shaft flanges and the centering of engine/transmission unit with suspension at bottom of travel.
2. Make sure that washers are installed as shown for correct version in Fig. 178.
3. The spring plate, which is made up of two plates, is bolted to the diagonal arm with four bolts. Note that bolt holes are elongated to allow you to adjust wheel toe by adjusting the diagonal arm position. Because wheel toe angle and distance between flanges are dependent on each other, both toe angle and diagonal arm setting must always be checked when the rear axle is adjusted.

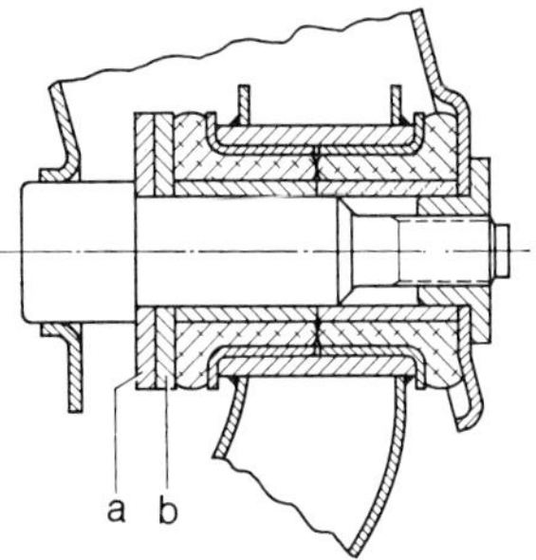

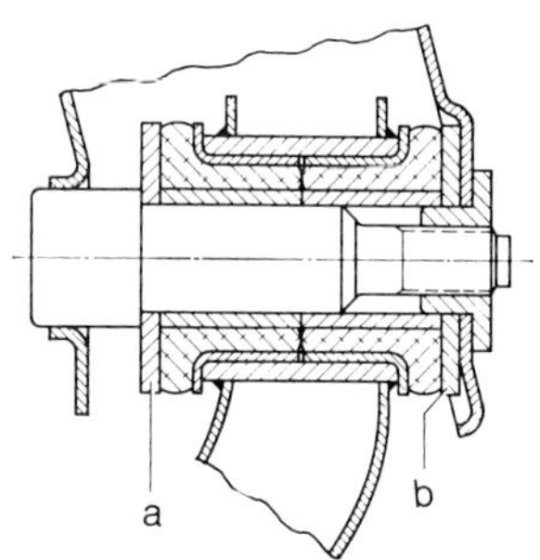




**Fig. 178.** Spacer washers (a and b) at diagonal arm mounting on bracket are shown correctly installed at left for cars covered in this Manual. On these cars installation at right is wrong.

4. To center engine (small corrections), loosen all transmission mounting bolts and rotate engine clockwise or counterclockwise.
5. To check distance between wheel flanges, use special measuring bar. With car on lift and wheels hanging freely, place bar between wheel shaft flanges. Make sure that ends of bar are not in contact with lock plates on flanges. When axle is in proper adjustment, pointer on bar will line up with center rib on transmission case, and measuring sleeve on bar will come between two tolerance marks on bar.



## 12.7 Aligning Rear Wheels

For this procedure the car must be unloaded, the tires correctly inflated, and the suspension settled. Since there is a variety of alignment equipment on the market, no single set of instructions can be applied. Follow the instructions of the manufacturer of the equipment you are using.

**To set wheels:**

1. Check tire pressure and correct if necessary.
2. Put car on wheel alignment stand and lock parking brake. Mount testing equipment.
3. Take the following readings: camber, toe angle and track. If track is not within the tolerance of 10 minutes, correct by moving wheels in or out.
4. If total toe-in angle exceeds 15 minutes and camber exceeds −2 degrees, loosen the four mounting bolts on spring plate and diagonal arm to obtain largest possible positive camber angle.
5. Adjust toe angle. After obtaining desired toe adjustment, recheck camber and re-adjust if necessary. If camber varies by more than 45 minutes, it will also be necessary to adjust the torsion bars.

### Table p. Setting data for the double-joint rear axle (empty)

| Model | Torsion bar diameter | Spring plate angle | Camber after 300 miles | Total toe angle | Permissible deviation in wheel alignment |
|---|---|---|---|---|---|
| all | 22 mm | 20°30′ + 50′ | − 1°20′ ± 40′ | 0′ ± 15′ | max. 10′ |

**NOTE —**
Adjustment of torsion bars does not influence the camber setting of the double-joint rear axle as much as it does the swing axle. If torsion bars are readjusted, try to attain the specified value of 25 degrees.

**Table p** gives specifications for an unloaded double-joint rear axle.

## 12.8 Disassembling and Assembling Diagonal Arm

To assist you in visualizing the relationships of the parts, the following instructions refer to components by the call-out numbers given in Fig. 179.

**To disassemble:**

1. Clamp diagonal arm flange in a vise.
2. Remove slotted nut (17) and brake drum (15) if attached.
3. Remove bolts (14) holding bearing cover (11). Take off cover with O-ring (10), outer spacer (12) and backing plate (9).
4. Knock shaft (2) out with a soft drift or press it out with a puller with 10-inch (250 mm) jaws, as in Fig. 180. Take out inner spacer (3).

**Fig. 180.** Puller is used to remove wheel shaft from diagonal arm.



**Fig. 179.** Diagonal arm assembly, with wheel shaft, wheel backing plate and brake drum, is shown in exploded view.

1. Diagonal arm
2. Rear wheel shaft
3. Spacer, inner
4. Oil seal (2)
5. Circlip 62 x 2 DIN 472
6. Ball bearing
7. Spacer sleeve
8. Roller bearing
9. Backing plate (complete)
10. O-ring
11. Bearing cover
12. Spacer, outer
13. Spring washer A10 (4)
14. Bolt (4)
15. Brake drum
16. Bonded rubber-bushing (
17. Slotted nut
18. Cotter pin 5 x 45 DIN 94

5. Pry inner oil seal (4) out, as in Fig. 181.

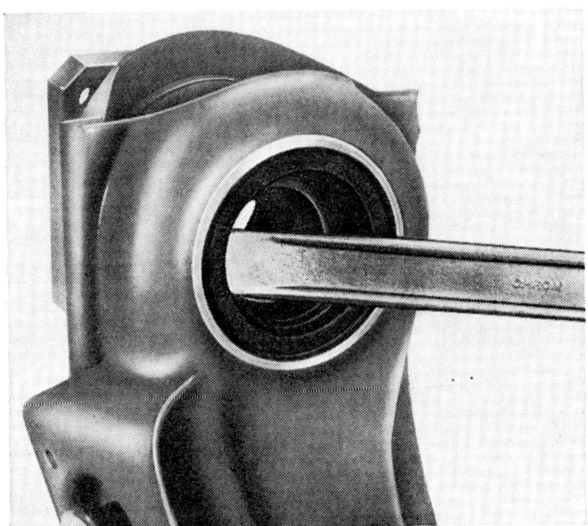

© 1972 VWoA—922

**Fig. 181.** Tire iron is used to pry out inner oil seal.

6. Take circlip (5) off and knock ball bearing (6) out with a drift, as in Fig. 182.

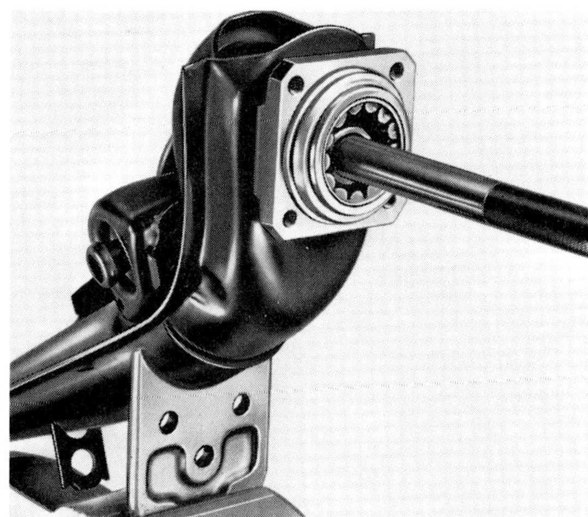

© 1972 VWoA—923

**Fig. 182.** Drift is used to knock out ball bearing.

7. Take out spacer sleeve (7) and inner race of roller bearing (8) as in Fig. 183. Knock outer race out with a drift.

***CAUTION***
*Be ready to catch bearing race when it comes loose. If it falls on concrete or into dirt, it may be damaged.*

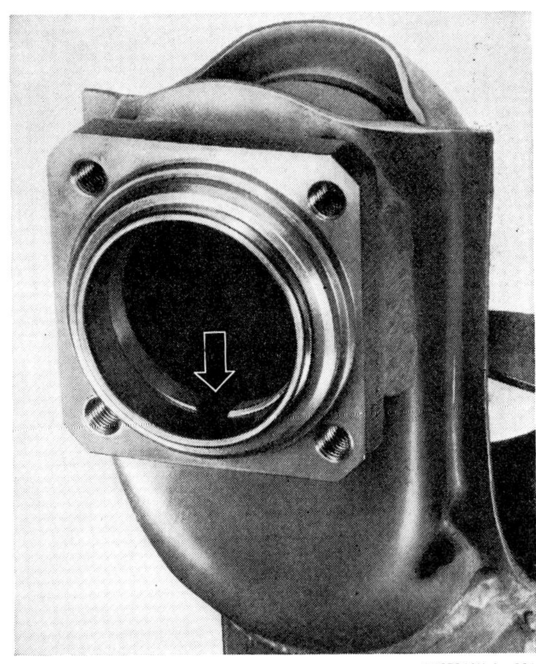

© 1972 VWoA—924

**Fig. 183.** Spacer sleeve for diagonal arm roller bearing is indicated by arrow.

8. Press inner sleeve of bonded bushing out with drift, as in Fig. 184. If drift sticks, press it out from opposite direction using another drift of same size.

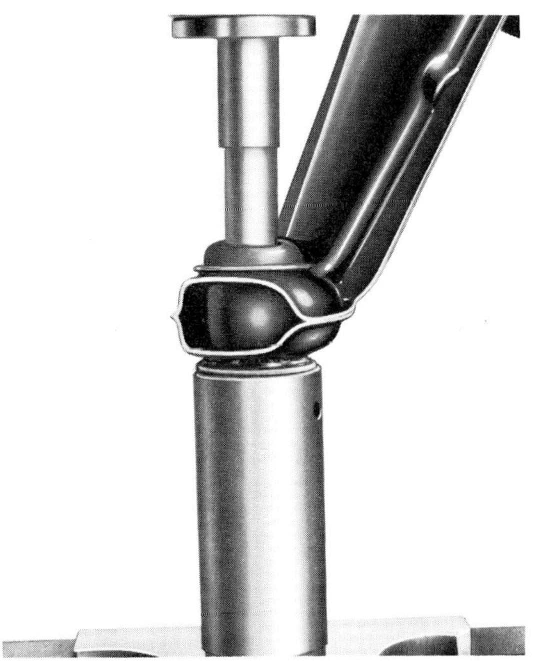

© 1972 VWoA—925

**Fig. 184.** Inner sleeve of bonded bushing is pressed out with drift.

**NOTE —**
The lower rubber bushing will come out at this time.

9. Remove upper rubber cushion either by pushing up with a suitable drift or by carefully prying out.
10. Slide extractor up from the bottom into flanged sleeve. Open extractor hooks to engage in recess between upper and lower flanged bushing inserts.

***WARNING —***
*Make sure your feet and hands are not underneath the plate while you are pressing out the bushing. Position a plate or restrainer to keep flanged bushing and extractor from falling.*

11. Press down on extractor with drift until lower flanged bushing drops down into plate cut-out, as in Fig. 185.

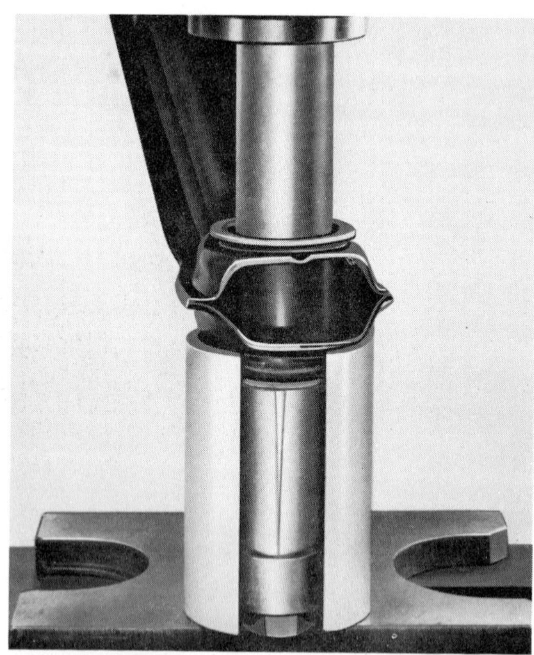



**Fig. 185.** Flanged bushing is pressed out with set-up shown here.

12. Turn arm upside down and repeat previous procedure.

**NOTE —**
If proper tools are not available, it is possible to remove flanged bushings by carefully punching them out.

**To assemble:**

1. Check bonded rubber bushing, oil seals, wheel shafts and spacer rings for wear and damage or scoring. Replace damaged parts.
2. Press one bonded rubber bushing in as far as it will go, as in Fig. 186.

**Fig. 186.** Bonded rubber bushing is pressed into diagonal arm as shown here.

3. Press second bonded rubber bushing in as far as it will go, as in Fig. 187.

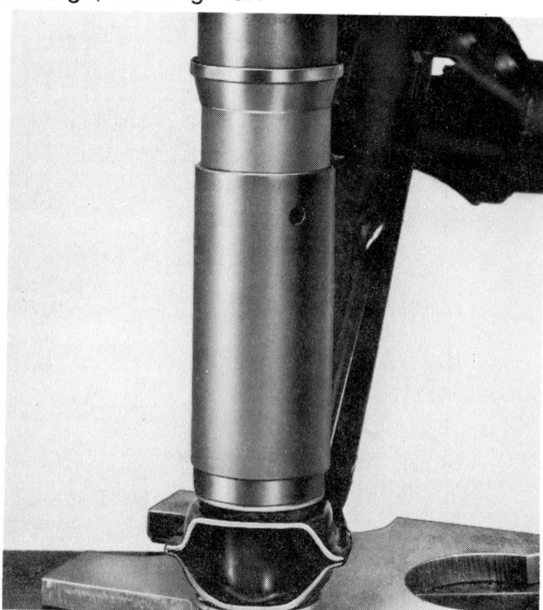



**Fig. 187.** Second bushing is installed in arm from opposite direction.

4. Drive or press in ball bearing, as in Fig. 188.

© 1972 VWoA—929

**Fig. 188.** Ball bearing can be driven or, as here, pressed into diagonal arm.

5. Install circlip and drive in oil seal.
6. Pack 2 ounces (60 grams) of multi-purpose grease into hub of diagonal arm and grease ball bearing and oil seal lip. Drive shaft in or press it in lightly against bearing inner race.
7. Install spacer sleeve. Grease and drive in outer race of roller bearing. Use bearings with rollers on outer race only, as in Fig. 189.

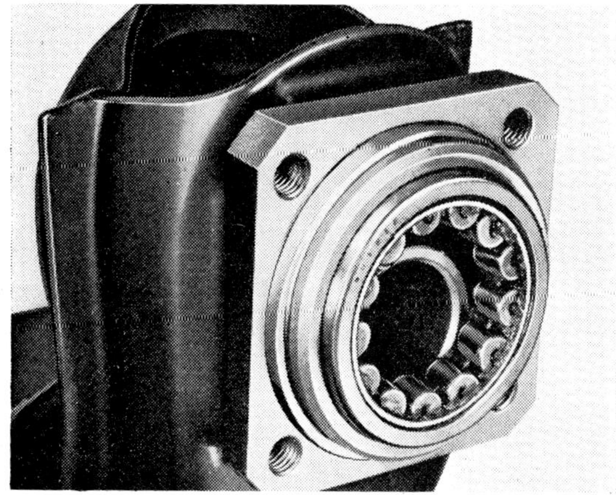

© 1972 VWoA—930

**Fig. 189.** Outer race of roller bearing is driven into diagonal arm after installation of spacer sleeve.

8. Press bearing inner race on with outer spacer, thrust piece and slotted nut, as in Fig. 190.

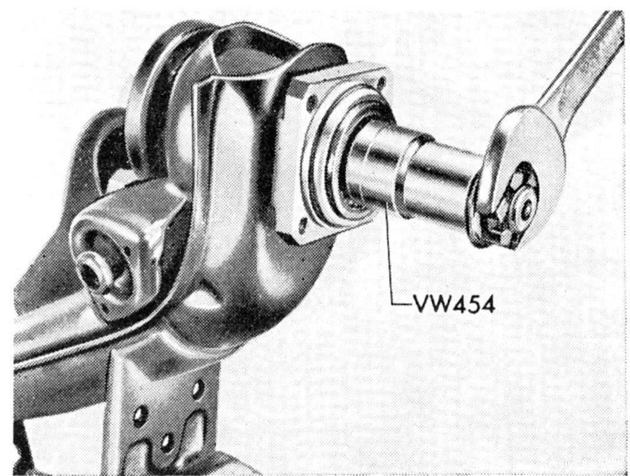


© 1972 VWoA—931

**Fig. 190.** Slotted nut goes on end of drive shaft after outer spacer and thrust piece.

9. Press oil seal into bearing cover (Fig. 191) and fill double lip with grease.

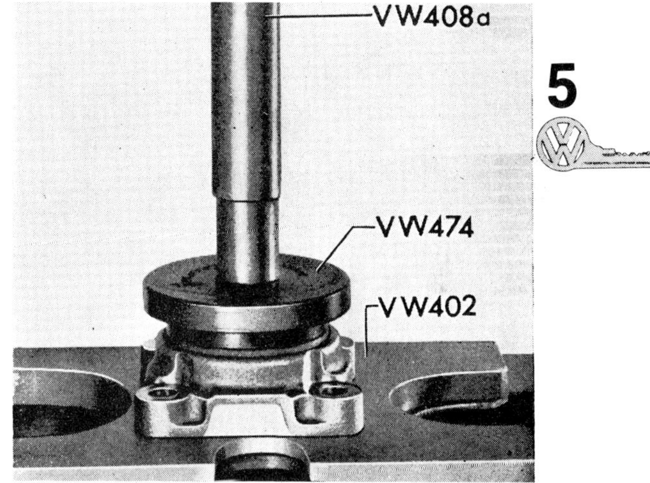


© 1972 VWoA—932

**Fig. 191.** Oil seal is pressed into bearing cover with this set-up.

5

10. Install backing plate and bearing cover, spacer and new O-ring. Tighten bolts to correct torque.
11. Install brake drum and slotted nut.

***WARNING*** —
*Car must be on ground when slotted nut on axle is loosened or tightened to avoid danger of toppling vehicle off lift.*

12. Tighten slotted nut to specified torque. See Technical Data in **AUTOMATIC STICK SHIFT.**

# AUTOMATIC STICK SHIFT

## Contents


**1. Operation of Automatic Stick Shift** . . . . . . . . 4
- Changing the Drive Range . . . . . . . . . 4
- Stopping . . . . . . . . . . . . . . . . . . . . 4
- Maneuvering . . . . . . . . . . . . . . . . . 4
- Parking . . . . . . . . . . . . . . . . . . . . . 4
- Towing . . . . . . . . . . . . . . . . . . . . . 4

**2. Design and Working Principles** . . . . . . . . . . 5
- 2.1 Controls and Warning Devices . . . . . . . 7
- Temperature Warning Device . . . . . . . 7
- 2.2 Torque Converter . . . . . . . . . . . . . . . 8
- 2.3 ATF Circulation . . . . . . . . . . . . . . . . 9
- 2.4 Clutch . . . . . . . . . . . . . . . . . . . . . 9
- Clutch Control . . . . . . . . . . . . . . . . . 9
- 2.5 Selector Lever . . . . . . . . . . . . . . . . 12
- 2.6 Gearbox . . . . . . . . . . . . . . . . . . . 12

**3. Automatic Stick Shift Maintenance** . . . . . . . . 12
- 3.1 Troubleshooting the Automatic Stick Shift Clutch . . . . . . . . . . . . . . . . . . . . . 12

**4. Removing and Installing Transmission** . . . . . 12
- Road Test . . . . . . . . . . . . . . . . . . . 18
- Pressure Test . . . . . . . . . . . . . . . . . 18
- Stall Speed Test . . . . . . . . . . . . . . . 18

**5. Removing and Installing Converter Housing and Shift Clutch** . . . . . . . . . . . . . . . . . . . . 18

**6. Adjusting Clutch** . . . . . . . . . . . . . . . . . . 21
- 6.1 Checking Clutch Play . . . . . . . . . . . . 22
- 6.2 Adjusting Speed of Engagement . . . . . . 23

**7. Removing and Installing Clutch Carrier Plate (clutch removed)** . . . . . . . . . . . . . . . . . . 23

**8. Replacing Converter Seal and Bushing** . . . . . 25

**9. Cleaning Torque Converter** . . . . . . . . . . . . 27

**10. Removing and Installing Control Valve** . . . . . 28

**11. Selector Lever** . . . . . . . . . . . . . . . . . . 31
- 11.1 Selector Lever Contact . . . . . . . . . . . 31
- 11.2 Disassembling and Assembling Selector Lever Mechanism . . . . . . . . . . . . . . . 31

**12. Removing and Installing Tanks** . . . . . . . . . 33
- 12.1 Vacuum Tank . . . . . . . . . . . . . . . . 33
- 12.2 ATF Tank . . . . . . . . . . . . . . . . . . 33

**13. Removing and Installing Differential** . . . . . . 34

**14. Removing and Installing Transmission Gears** 38

**15. Disassembling and Assembling Main Drive Shaft** . . . . . . . . . . . . . . . . . . . . . . . 41

# 2 Automatic Stick Shift


**16. Disassembling and Assembling Drive Pinion** . . 43

**17. Disassembling and Assembling Gear Carrier** . 46

**18. Adjusting Selector Forks** . . . . . . . . . . . . . 48

**19. Disassembling and Assembling Gearshift Housing** . . . . . . . . . . . . . . . . . . . . . . 49

**20. Disassembling and Assembling Transmission Case** . . . . . . . . . . . . . . . . . . . . . . . . 50

**21. Final Drive** . . . . . . . . . . . . . . . . . . . . . 52

**22. Adjusting Pinion and Ring Gear** . . . . . . . . . 52

22.1 Adjusting Pinion . . . . . . . . . . . . . . . 54

22.2 Adjusting Ring Gear . . . . . . . . . . . . 57

22.3 Adjusting Ring Gear Backlash . . . . . . . 58

22.4 Removing Side Cover Oil Seals . . . . . . 60

**23. Transmission Technical Data** . . . . . . . . . . 61

I. Transmission Data . . . . . . . . . . . . 61

II. Tolerances, Wear Limits and Settings . . 61

III. Ratios . . . . . . . . . . . . . . . . . . . 62

IV. Torsion Bar Adjustment (spring plates unloaded) . . . . . . . . . 63

V. Double Joint Shafts—Drive Shafts . . . 63

VI. Constant Velocity Joints . . . . . . . . . 63

VII. Tightening Torques . . . . . . . . . . . . 64

VIII. Table of Correction Factors . . . . . . . 65


**TABLES**


a. Troubleshooting Chart . . . . . . . . . . . . . . . 13

b. Differential Replacements . . . . . . . . . . . . . 53

c. Explanation of Symbols and Measurements . . . 55

d. Shims for Final Drive Adjustment . . . . . . . . . 56

# Automatic Stick Shift

The VW Automatic Stick Shift, which was offered as optional equipment for the 1500 engine on cars covered in this Manual, sharply reduces the amount of gear-changing required in ordinary driving, and it does away with the clutch pedal altogether.

> **NOTE —**
> Some transmission and rear axle components are the same on both cars with manual transmission and cars with Automatic Stick Shift. These parts are described in **TRANSMISSION AND REAR AXLE.** This section is devoted to components found only on the Automatic Stick Shift.

6

In place of the four forward speeds of the standard manual transmission with clutch pedal, the Automatic Stick Shift allows you to select a **drive range** for operation of the car. You can start or stop without having to work a clutch pedal with your foot, and in each drive range you have available a wider range of speed than a single gear in the manual transmission would have provided. Since only occasional changes from one range to another are required, driving is easier. With Automatic Stick Shift you operate the hand lever only about a tenth as often as you would have to shift gears in a car with a manual transmission.

In the Automatic Stick Shift system a **selector lever** on the frame tunnel at the driver's right hand takes the place of the conventional gearshift lever of the manual transmission. The appropriate movement of the selector lever gives a choice of four driving ranges (including reverse) and a neutral position.

## 1. Operation of Automatic Stick Shift

The operations in the different drive ranges (Fig. 1) are as follows:

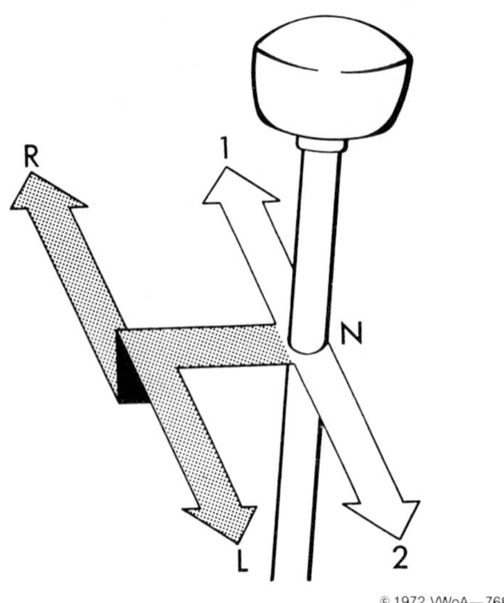


**Fig. 1.** Shift pattern for Automatic Stick Shift selection of drive ranges is shown here.

**N (Neutral)** For starting the engine you must have the selector lever in this position. The engine should be at idle when you move the lever from **N** to a drive range. When the engine is cold, the car may start to move in **N** unless you apply the foot brake.

**L (Low)** You select this range when a heavy load is to be put on the engine. For example, you would move the selector lever to **L** for moving off on a steep hill with the car loaded or for driving at low speed over very rough terrain. The drive range **L** will give speeds from 0 to about 34 miles an hour.

**1 (Moving Off and Accelerating)** For moving off in normal traffic and for rapid acceleration **1** is the drive range you select. Speeds in this range are from 0 to approximately 55 mph.

**2 (Drive)** This is the range for highway driving and accelerating at medium and high speeds.

**R (Reverse)** To engage reverse, you must depress the selector lever slightly to overcome a safety catch. Then move the lever to **R.**

### Changing the Drive Range

When you put your hand on the selector lever and move it, even slightly, you close the circuit to the solenoid in the servo mechanism that operates the Automatic Stick Shift clutch.

**To select a drive range:**

1. Release accelerator pedal.
2. Push selector lever to position for desired drive range.
3. Take hand off selector lever.

> ***CAUTION*** —
> *Do not touch the selector lever unless a change of drive range is intended. The selector switches are so sensitive that the slightest movement of the lever will put the clutch servo in operation.*

When the engine is pulling hard, the temperature of the automatic transmission fluid (ATF) in the torque converter can rise above normal. This overheating calls for a change in driving range. For this reason there is a warning light (red) in the speedometer. If the light comes on, you should select the next lower drive range to allow the torque converter ATF to cool down.

### Stopping

When you make a short stop at a traffic light or in a traffic jam, you stay in the range in which you have been driving, but apply the foot brake. Unless braked, the car tends to move forward when a drive range is engaged.

### Maneuvering

For close maneuvering and parking, **L** is the driving range to use alternately with reverse. In the changes from **L** to **R** (and vice versa) the foot brake easily holds the car against the slight tendency to creep forward in neutral.

### Parking

To park the car you move the selector lever to **N** and apply the parking brake firmly. In the Automatic Stick Shift system there is no equivalent for engaging a gear to hold a parked car.

### Towing

When necessary, the Automatic Stick Shift car can be towed to start the engine. Select drive range **L** and with ignition ON have the car pulled at a minimum speed of 15 mph (25 kph). At a lower speed the torque converter does not provide a fluid coupling to turn the engine.

## 2. DESIGN AND WORKING PRINCIPLES

The basic differences from the standard transmission are found in two main components of the Automatic Stick Shift. First, the hydrodynamic torque converter (as well as the shift clutch) transfers engine power to the transmission gear train of the Automatic Stick Shift. Second, an electrically activated servo mechanism, instead of the driver's foot, operates the Automatic Stick Shift clutch. The servo works on pressure differences between the atmosphere and vacuum in the carburetor venturi and intake manifold. A connected vacuum tank stabilizes the system.

The torque converter is a hydraulic clutch or fluid coupling between engine and clutch plate, and it is also a turbine capable of multiplying engine torque. This multiplication is greatest at relatively low engine rpm (just above 2,000 to 2,250) when turbine torque output is 2.1 times engine torque output. With increasing engine rpm, multiplication of torque tapers off. At highway speeds the ratio has fallen to approximately one to one.

The transmission case, which is a three-piece light alloy metal casting, holds the torque converter, clutch, transmission and final drive. You can see the arrangement in Fig. 2 and in Fig. 3 on the following page. Comparison with cutaway views of the standard transmission will reveal similarities as well as differences. The servo for the shift clutch is attached at the rear of the left side of the transmission case.

**Fig. 2.** Transmission case for Automatic Stick Shift is seen here in cross section.

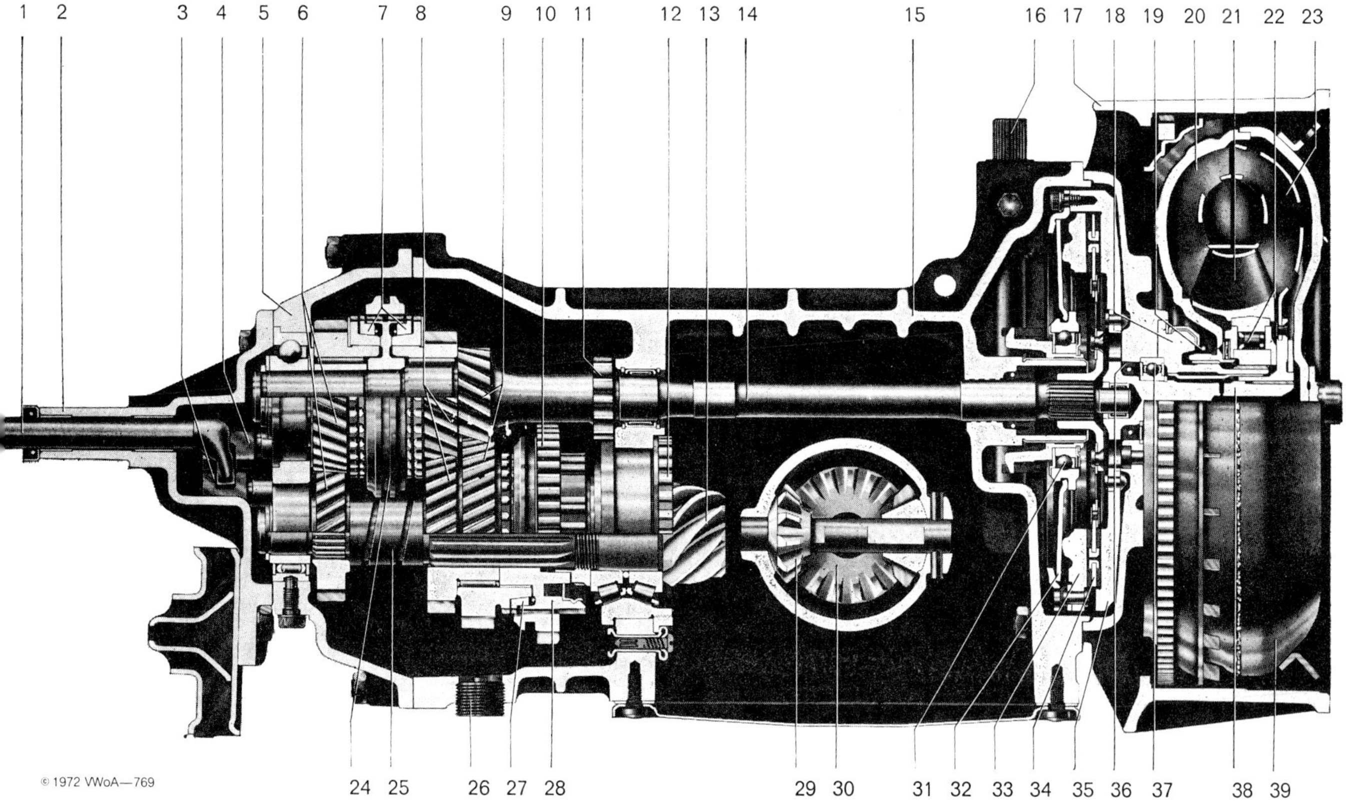

6

1. Inner shift lever
2. Gearshift housing
3. Low/reverse shift rod
4. **1/2** shift rod
5. Gear carrier
6. **2** speed gears
7. **1/2** gear synchronizer rings
8. **1** speed gears
9. Low speed gears
10. Operating sleeve for low/reverse gear
11. Reverse gear drive
12. Retaining ring for pinion
13. Pinion
14. Drive shaft
15. Transmission case
16. Shift clutch release shaft
17. Converter housing
18. Support tube for one-way clutch
19. Seal for converter
20. Impeller
21. Stator
22. One-way clutch
23. Turbine
24. **1/2** gear operating sleeve
25. **1/2** gear spacer spring
26. Magnetic oil drain plug
27. Low gear synchronizer ring
28. Synchronizer hub low/reverse gear
29. Differential pinion
30. Differential side gear
31. Clutch release bearing
32. Diaphragm spring
33. Pressure plate
34. Clutch plate
35. Carrier plate
36. Oil seal for converter housing
37. Bearing for turbine shaft
38. Turbine shaft
39. Torque converter

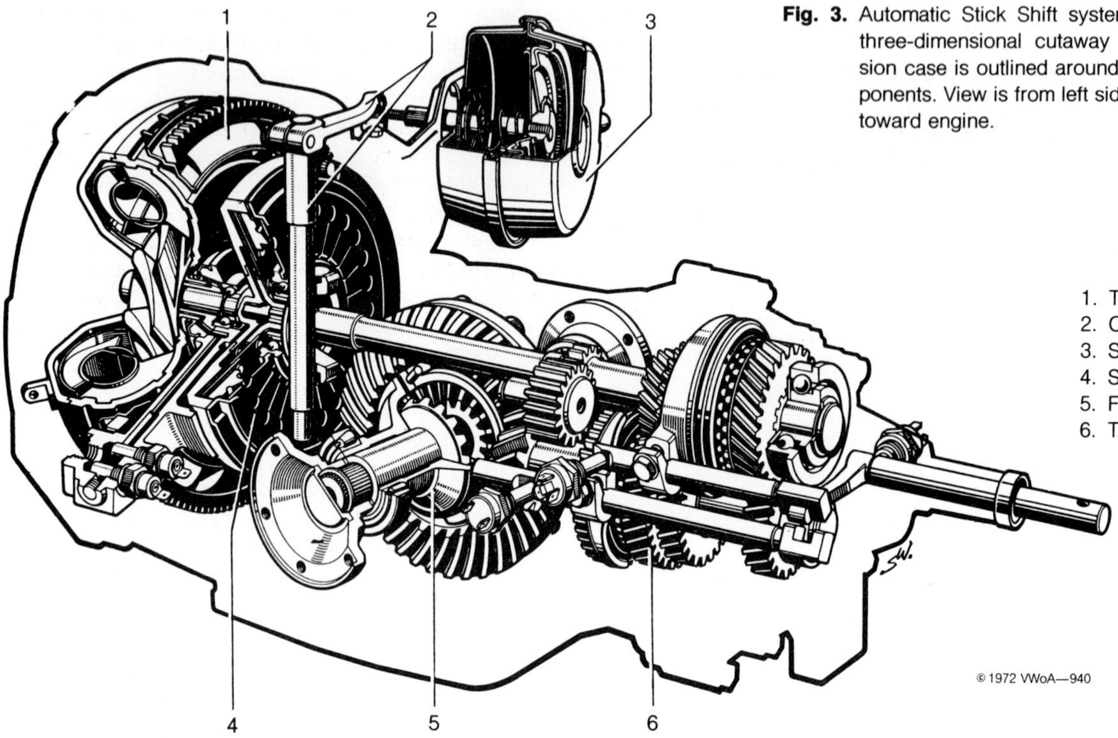

**Fig. 3.** Automatic Stick Shift system is seen here in a three-dimensional cutaway view. The transmission case is outlined around the assembled components. View is from left side of car looking back toward engine.

1. Torque converter
2. Clutch shaft
3. Servo
4. Shift clutch
5. Final drive
6. Transmission

Fig. 4 shows schematically the arrangement of the Automatic Stick Shift hydraulic and vacuum systems. On the car the control valve is at the left of the engine compartment. The vacuum tank is under the left fender. Hoses connect the intake manifold, control valve and vacuum tank, as shown in Fig. 4.

Cars with Automatic Stick Shift have a dual oil pump in place of the single engine oil pump of the standard transmission cars. Driven from the camshaft, the double oil pump has one circuit for engine oil and another for ATF for the torque converter. The ATF reservoir for this second circuit is under the right rear fender. The hoses carry fluid from reservoir to pump to torque converter and back to filler neck of the reservoir.

1. Torque converter
2. Clutch
3. Clutch lever
4. Servo
5. Control valve
6. Vacuum tank
7. Oil tank
8. Oil pump
9. Carburetor

A. Pressure line
B. Return line
C. Vacuum line-intake manifold/control valve
D. Vacuum line-vacuum tank/control valve
E. Vacuum line-servo/control valve
F. Vacuum line-reduction valve/venturi

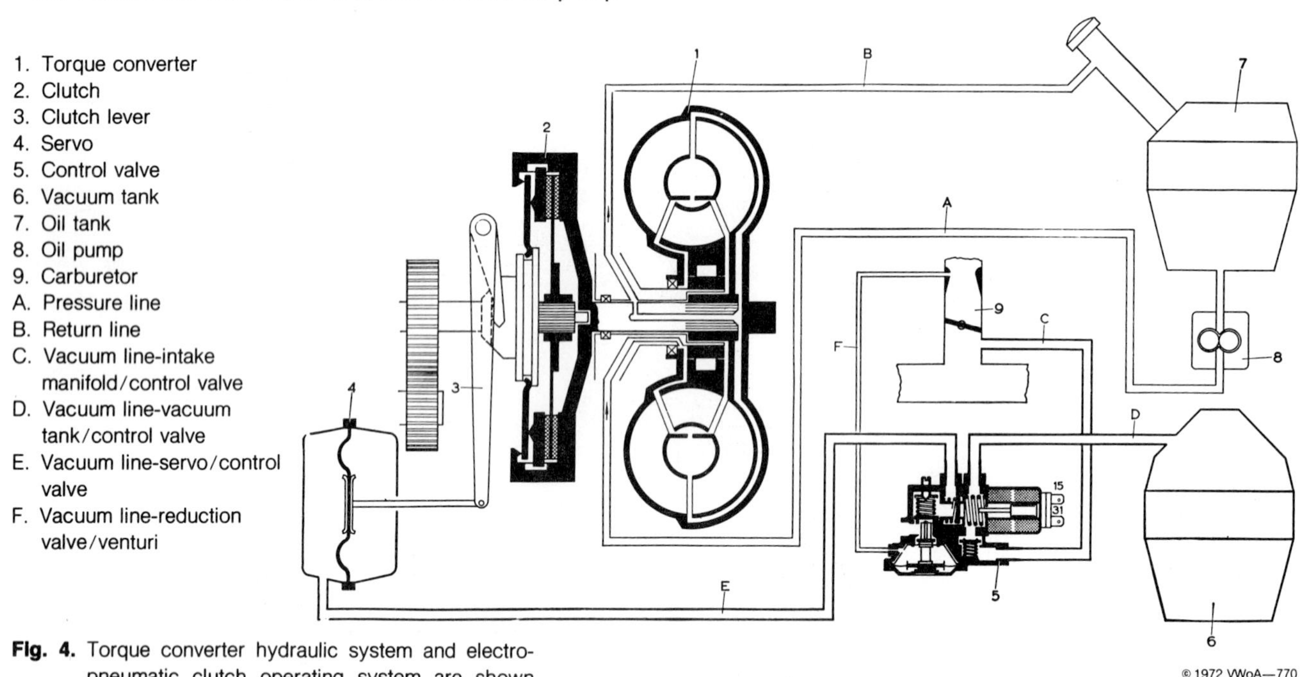

**Fig. 4.** Torque converter hydraulic system and electro-pneumatic clutch operating system are shown schematically.

## 2.1 Controls and Warning Devices

The contact for activating the solenoid of the servo control valve is just below the selector lever. The neutral safety switch is screwed into the shift housing. The selector switch, which is in the transmission case, connects a red warning light in the speedometer to one of two temperature switches in the torque converter ATF flow. Selector lever position determines which switch is connected.

The warning light receives its power from terminal 15 on the speedometer. The solenoid is connected to terminal 15 on the ignition coil. An in-line 8-amp fuse protects the circuit. Fig. 5 shows the arrangement of the electrical circuit schematically.

### Temperature Warning Device

Within each drive range the torque converter supplies the amount of torque the load on the engine calls for. But on a long steep hill or when the car is towing a trailer in drive range **2,** the ATF in the torque converter can overheat. The red warning light in the speedometer then comes on to tell you that the torque converter ATF is too hot. In such a case it is necessary to select the next lower drive range.

Of the two warning light switches in the ATF return flow, switch 1 closes at a temperature of 257 degrees F (125 degrees C) and is connected to the warning light in drive range **2.** Temperature switch 2 closes at a temperature of 284 degrees F (140 degrees C) and is connected to the warning light in drive range **1.** A third switch operated by the selector lever connects either switch 1 or switch 2.

When the ATF temperature in drive range **2** reaches 257 degrees F (125 degrees C) and the driver in response to the warning light selects drive range **1,** the light should go out. But if the temperature of the ATF then continues to rise, the warning light comes on again at 284 degrees F (140 degrees C). The driver must then select drive range **L.** In this range the ATF is adequately cooled under all load conditions. No warning signal in the **L** range is necessary.

**NOTE —**
The following modifications have been made in replacement parts for the warning circuit: The switch for the temperature range 257 to 275 degrees F (125 to 135 degrees C) and the control switch have been eliminated. In the modified system the switch for the temperature range 284 to 302 degrees F (140 to 150 degrees C) operates the red light in the speedometer, and the light stays on until the ATF fluid has cooled. Previously, the light went off as soon as the driver downshifted. Replacement of the converter housing, shift rods or transmission case now calls for conversion of the temperature warning device to the modified system. A longer cable is required to connect the warning light with the 284 to 302 degrees F temperature switch directly. The existing holes for the temperature and control switches of the earlier system must be sealed with plugs and washers.



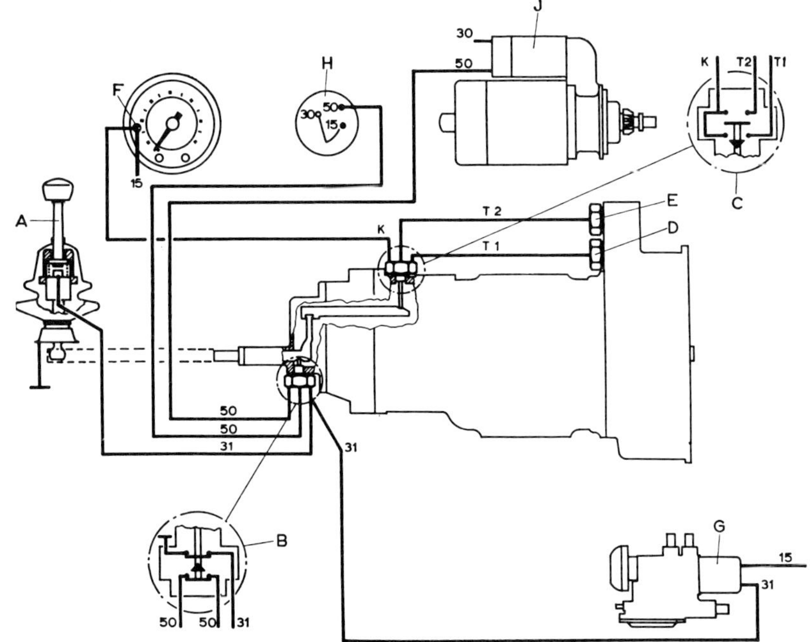


A. Selector lever and contact
B. Neutral safety switch and idle contact
C. Selector switch
D. Temperature switch for drive range **2**
E. Temperature switch for drive range **1**
F. Warning light
G. Solenoid for control valve
H. Ignition switch
J. Starter

**Fig. 5.** Electrical circuit for the Automatic Stick Shift is shown schematically here.

## 2.2 Torque Converter

The torque converter, which is supported on a tube pressed into the cover of final drive, has four main parts: housing, impeller, turbine and stator. Since you will have no occasion to disassemble the converter, the description of these four parts will be kept brief. In case of damage or failure, the converter is replaced, not repaired. Fig. 6 gives a cutaway view of the converter.

1. The housing is made up of two round, saucer-shaped sheet metal casings welded together around the rims to form a hollow container. On the outside the housing carries the starter ring gear and cooling fins. The engine crankshaft turns this assembly by way of the drive plate, which is fastened to the rear of the housing with four M 8 bolts.
2. The impeller, which is often called the pump, is the driving member of the converter. It is a vaned wheel rigidly attached inside the front half of the converter housing. When the engine crankshaft spins the housing, the impeller turns with it.
3. The turbine is the driven member of the converter. This part is an independent, vaned wheel in the rear half of the housing. It is attached to the turbine shaft, which extends forward through the hubs of the stator and impeller to the transmission gears. Rotation of the turbine turns the turbine shaft and thus the transmission gears.
4. The stator is a smaller vaned wheel in the narrow gap between impeller and turbine. The stator turns on a one-way roller clutch on the support tube. It rotates only in the direction of crankshaft rotation.

When the crankshaft spins the converter housing, and with it the impeller, the curved vanes of the impeller pick up ATF and by centrifugal force throw the fluid against the curved vanes of the turbine. The force of the thrown ATF starts the turbine turning and also the turbine shaft. The curved vanes of the impeller and turbine are so designed that the force of the thrown fluid causes the turbine to turn in the same direction as the impeller, and thus in the same direction as the engine crankshaft.

Fluid leaving the turbine strikes the stator vanes, which turn it back at the most favorable angle against the vanes of the impeller. Thus energy remaining in the fluid from the turbine is added to energy the impeller is receiving from the crankshaft. And since the stator can turn only in the engine direction, there is also a reaction

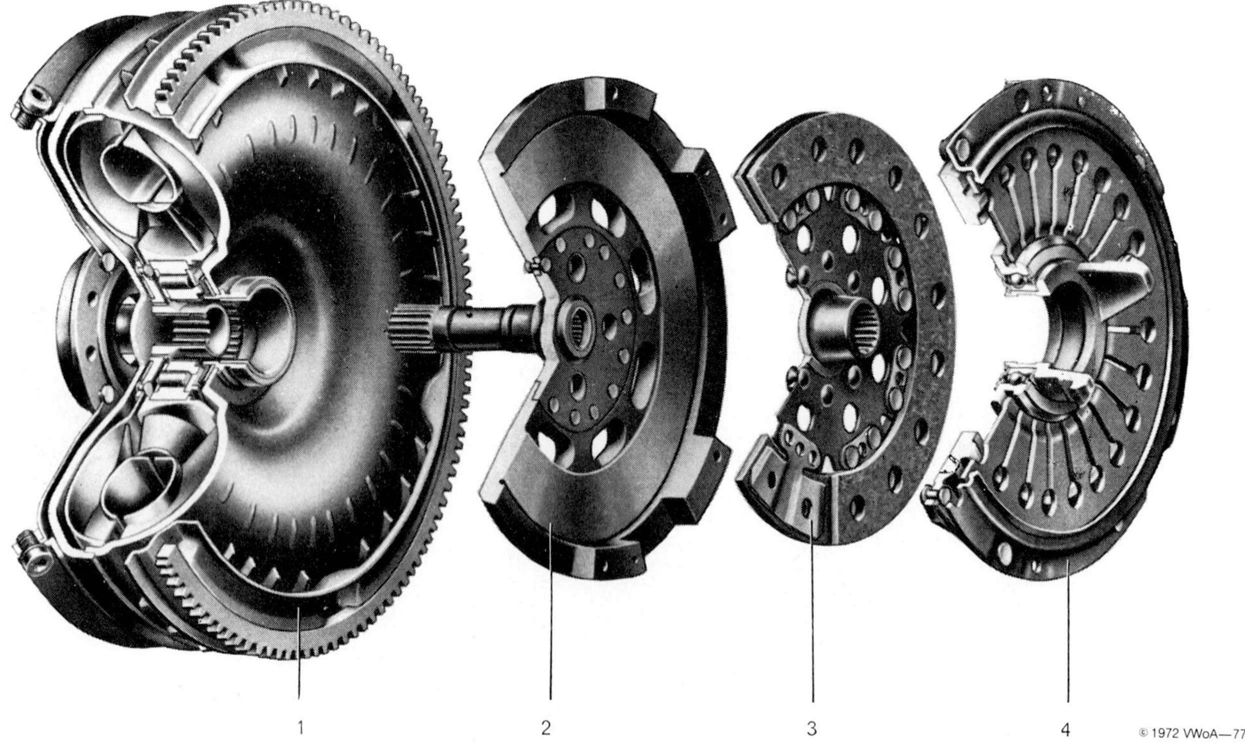


1. Torque converter 2. Carrier plate 3. Clutch plate 4. Pressure plate and diaphragm spring

**Fig. 6.** Torque converter assembly is shown here in exploded view.

force to be added to the system. From this combination of added forces, the turbine becomes a torque multiplier. Roughly, the torque is increased by the number of revolutions the impeller makes for one revolution of the turbine. As the turbine picks up rpm, the torque multiplication diminishes.

The sequence just described enables the torque converter to handle the stopping and moving off of the car without the clutch work and gear shifting required for a standard transmission. At engine idle the impeller is not throwing oil against the turbine vanes hard enough to transfer sufficient power to set the car in motion. But as soon as the throttle is opened to increase engine speed, the turbine begins to exert the greatest torque multiplication of which it is capable. From a stop the car can readily overcome its inertia and move off. The engine speed at which the turbine ceases to transfer usable power to the gear train is called the stall speed. It is from 2000 to 2250 rpm.

## 2.3 ATF Circulation

A jet in the return ATF line maintains the fluid pressure in the converter. The ATF pump has a pressure relief valve to hold pressure below the specified maximum limit. Circulation of the fluid makes it possible to keep the temperature of the converter ATF within specified limits.

## 2.4 Clutch

The design of the transmission requires some means of interrupting power transfer when a change in drive range is to be made. Since it is not possible to interrupt the operation of the converter at high engine rpm, the VW Automatic Stick Shift has a semi-automatic clutch between converter and gearbox. Fig. 6 shows the components of the clutch assembly. The clutch is of the dry, single-plate type with a diaphragm spring. As stated earlier, a vacuum-actuated servo with a line to the intake manifold operates this clutch by way of a release lever and shaft.

### Clutch Control

The control valve (Fig. 7) opens and closes the vacuum connection between intake manifold and servo. When movement of the selector lever actuates the solenoid, this valve controls the engagement or release of the clutch. The valve also controls the speed of the engagement action once a range has been selected. This latter control is automatic, depending on throttle valve position (engine load).



1. Reducing valve
2. Spring for reducing valve
3. O-ring
4. Washer
5. End cap
6. Adjusting screw
7. Cap
8. Main valve spring
9. Connection to servo
10. Main valve seat
11. Connection to vacuum tank
12. Main valve
13. Housing with connections
14. Spacer spring
15. Solenoid
16. Terminal
17. Air filter
18. Hose connection
19. Washer
20. Rubber washer
21. Compensating port
22. Adjusting screw
23. Pressure spring
24. Spacer
25. Cover
26. Double diaphragm
27. Housing cover
28. Support washer
29. Spring for check valve
30. Check valve
31. Connection to manifold

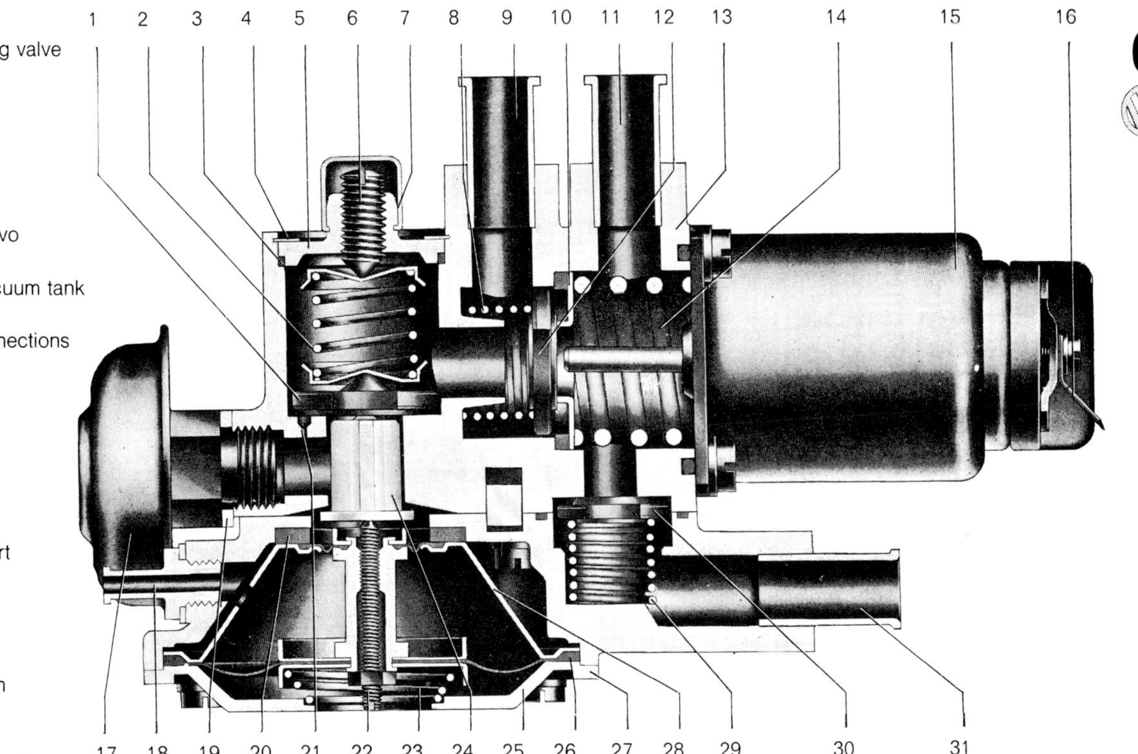


**Fig. 7.** Control valve for clutch servo in the Automatic Stick Shift system is shown here in cross section.

In the sequence of Figs. 8, 9 and 10 you can see how the servo works. The different colors in the pictures represent the different pressure conditions in the system. The following description of the servo will refer to the colors in those figures and to the letters used to identify the various components of the system. Fig. 7 also is pertinent to the discussion since it shows a cross section of the control valve.

Starting with Fig. 8, you can follow the operation of the clutch servo by comparing the changes in the blocks of color in the sequence of pictures. When selector lever (A) is moved to engage a drive range (other than **N**) the contact (red) is closed and solenoid (B) of the control valve energized. The conditions illustrated in Fig. 8 have now been established.

The energized solenoid actuates main valve (C), thus connecting the vacuum side of the servo to the engine intake manifold (H). At the same time, the main valve is closing the connection to the outside atmosphere (yellow). Pressure in the vacuum chamber (dark blue) of the servo falls abruptly. Because pressure on the other side of the servo diaphragm (J) is now much greater (yellow), the diaphragm must move in the direction of the black arrow. The operating rod on the diaphragm pulls on the clutch lever to disengage the clutch through the clutch lever shaft and release bearing. Power transfer to the transmission is interrupted. Selection of another drive range can proceed.

The automatic disengagement of the clutch takes about a tenth of a second. You could not do it as fast with a clutch pedal.

When you take your hand off the selector lever after changing the drive range, you are allowing the circuit to the solenoid to open again. The solenoid, returning to its original position, closes the main valve. The pressure difference between the vacuum side of the servo and the atmosphere is compensated (eliminated) by air flow through the reducing valve (D) and the compensating port (K). The operating rod on the servo diaphragm now moves in the direction of the black arrow in Fig. 9. The clutch engages.

Depending on engine load (throttle position), this operation of engaging the shift clutch can proceed at two different speeds:

1. Immediate engagement after selection of a drive range, as in Fig. 9, or
2. Delayed engagement, as in Fig. 10 when the engine is braking the car.

Suppose you depress the accelerator pedal after selecting a drive range. For illustration we go back to Fig. 9. The open throttle valve creates a high vacuum (dark blue) in the thin hose between the carburetor venturi (G) and the diaphragm chamber (E) above the control valve vent diaphragm (F). The pressure difference between the atmosphere and the vacuum forces vent diaphragm (F) upward to open reducing valve (D). Opening of the reducing valve admits atmospheric pressure (yellow) to the servo chamber under the diaphragm (J), and this pressure forces the diaphragm with its clutch operating rod to move in the direction of the black arrow. The clutch engages at once and transmits full converter torque.

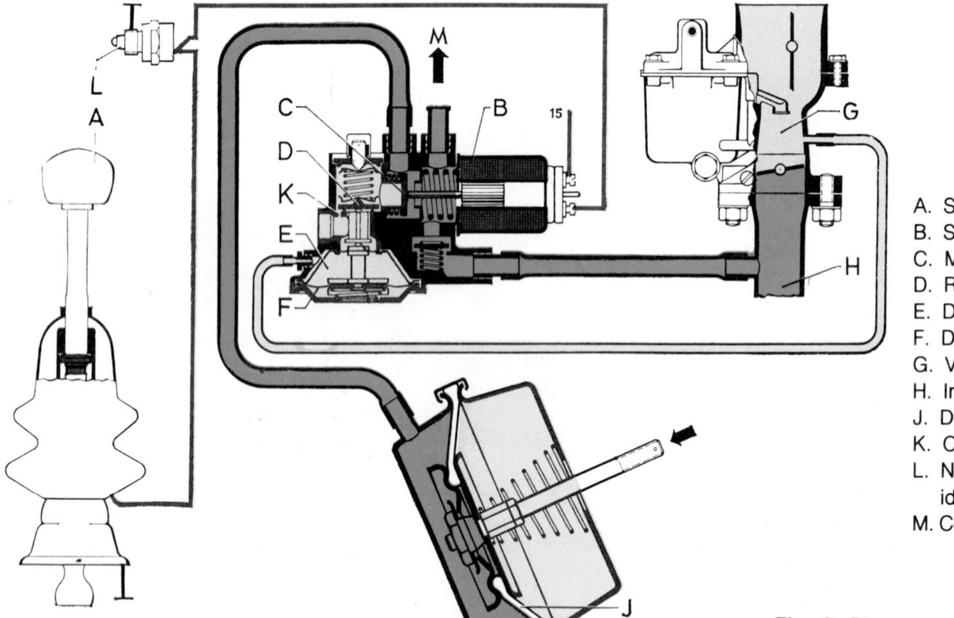


A. Selector lever
B. Solenoid
C. Main valve
D. Reducing valve
E. Diaphragm chamber (venting)
F. Diaphragm in control valve
G. Venturi
H. Intake manifold
J. Diaphragm in servo
K. Compensating port
L. Neutral safety switch and ground for idle
M. Connection for line to vacuum tank

**Fig. 8.** Disengagement of Automatic Stick Shift clutch is illustrated here. See text.

The situation is different when you select a driving range but keep your foot off the accelerator pedal. Since throttle opening controls vacuum in the venturi (see **FUEL SYSTEM**) and since the clutch servo mechanism operates on venturi vacuum, you might expect the combination of drive range selection with acceleration to produce different results from those you get from the combination of drive range selection without acceleration. Fig. 10 illustrates the distribution pressure in the system in the latter situation, and you will be able to see how it leads to delayed engagement of the clutch.

In this situation you do not want the clutch to grab but to engage gradually and smoothly. Since the throttle valve is closed, the vacuum in the venturi (G) is low (light blue). The vacuum in the thin hose from the venturi does allow the vent diaphragm (F) to move and open the reducing valve briefly, but it is not high enough to hold the reducing valve open and thus to eliminate the pressure differential altogether. Instead of vacuum, as in Fig. 8, or full atmospheric pressure, as in Fig. 9 under the servo diaphragm (J), there is now an intermediate pressure (green). This intermediate pressure is rising. When it

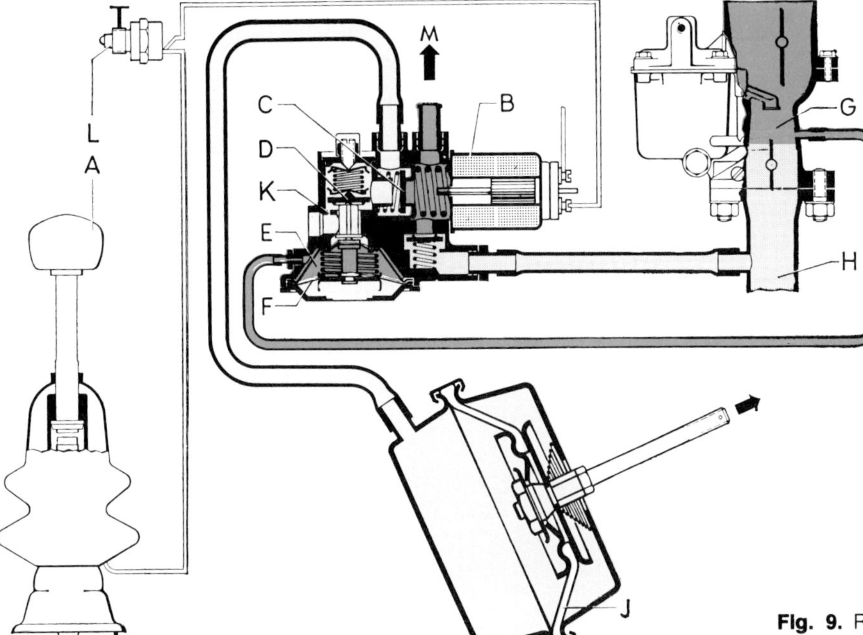


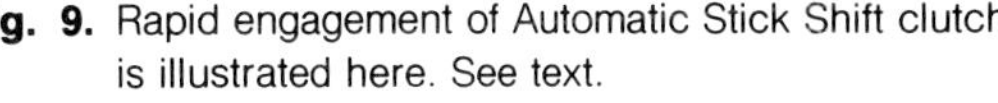
**Fig. 9.** Rapid engagement of Automatic Stick Shift clutch is illustrated here. See text.

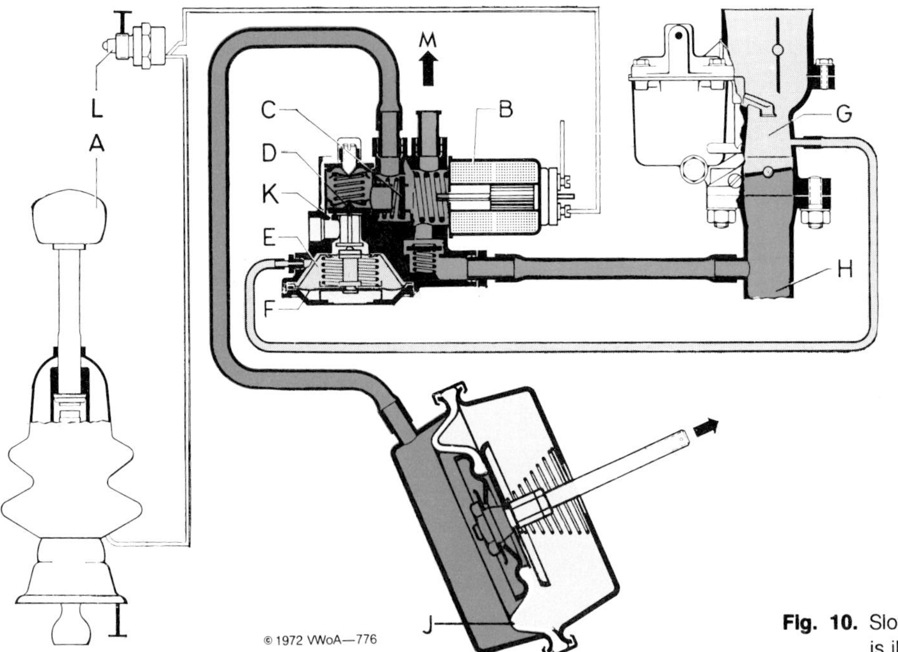


**Fig. 10.** Slow engagement of Automatic Stick Shift clutch is illustrated here. See text.

reaches a certain value, which is determined by pretension on the reducing valve spring, the reducing valve can close. The compensating port (K) then allows gradual equalization of pressure in the servo, and the operating rod moves in the direction of the black arrow. The clutch engages smoothly.

Thus, in the Automatic Stick Shift system clutch engagement adapts to actual driving conditions. The weight of your foot on the accelerator pedal determines whether clutch engagement will be slow or fast.

### 2.5 Selector Lever

The sensitive contact in the selector lever makes and breaks the ground connection in the circuit to the control valve solenoid. The contact is designed to close only on forward and rearward movements of the lever in the directions of drive range selection, not on side-to-side movements. This restriction prevents disengagement of the clutch, which would cause the engine to race, if you accidentally jiggle the lever. Obviously, the contact does not close when you intentionally move lever sideways in changing to or from reverse or low drive range.

A second contact in the neutral safety switch is always connected to ground when the selector lever is in neutral. The neutral safety switch is in the gearshift housing and is operated by the inner shift lever. This contact keeps the shift clutch circuit closed while the selector lever moves through neutral in the change to another drive range.

### 2.6 Gearbox

The mechanical gears in the VW Automatic Stick Shift system are basically the same as in the four-speed fully synchronized manual transmission, except that the former has only three forward ranges and reverse. Automatic Stick Shift gear sets and ratios are the same as the 2nd, 3rd, 4th and reverse gears of the fully synchronized manual transmission. The words gear, speed and range really are synonymous when used in reference to the transmission. The Automatic Stick Shift gearbox, like the gearbox for manual transmission, is balk-synchronized with blocking stop rings, and gears are in constant mesh for silent operation. Main difference is in elimination of standard 1st gear. The great increase in torque at low converter turbine rpm makes a 1st gear unnecessary.

## 3. AUTOMATIC STICK SHIFT MAINTENANCE

Proper care of your car calls for a regular schedule of maintenance of the Automatic Stick Shift System. There are standard maintenance procedures and schedules for the torque converter, final drive and rear axle. You will find them listed in charts under **LUBRICATION AND MAINTENANCE.**

> **NOTE —**
> On newer versions of the transmission case or replacement cases the drain plug may have been eliminated. For cases with no plug use only hypoid oil conforming with MIL-L-2105-B. This oil may be used in all transmissions. If you have the new type of transmission case (without drain plug) remove pan, drain oil and replace pan and oil. Do this only at the first 600-miles interval or 600 miles after installation of new transmission or differential gears. MIL oil requires changing only when a gearset is replaced.

> **NOTE —**
> In working on the Automatic Stick Shift you may come on differences in model years or changes in spare parts. Every effort has been made to call attention to these differences and changes in these notes. Read all the procedures carefully with the possibility of model differences in mind.

### 3.1 Troubleshooting the Automatic Stick Shift Clutch

**Table a** (opposite) lists possible malfunctions of the Automatic Stick Shift clutch. You will find a column of clutch symptoms given with the possible (or probable) causes and recommended remedies.

## 4. REMOVING AND INSTALLING TRANSMISSION

The procedure given here includes removal of the engine. Removal of the A.S.S. engine differs in various details from removal of standard transmission engine.

**To remove:**

1. Move shift lever into **2** range if possible.
2. Disconnect battery ground strap.
3. Remove inspection cover for frame-end near battery. Detach gearshift rod coupling with T-handle wrench and disengage coupling. Push rod to rear.
4. Disconnect control valve cables and vacuum hoses. Remove rear cover plate to prevent seal damage.
5. Disconnect accelerator cable from carburetor. Disconnect cables from generator, carburetor, ignition coil and oil pressure switch.
6. Detach ATF pressure line to converter at transmission and raise line to keep ATF from running out.

## Table a. Troubleshooting Chart

| Symptom | Possible cause | Remedy |
|---|---|---|
| 1. Shift clutch slips at full throttle, not just after shifting | ATF on clutch linings, clutch defective, linkage incorrectly adjusted | Install new plate. Eliminate ATF leakage. Install new clutch and adjust linkage. Check for play in clutch linkage. |
| 2. Clutch slips excessively after range has been selected | a. Reducing valve adjusting screw in too far<br>b. Hose between carburetor and valve venting diaphragm leaking or off<br>c. Venting diaphragm defective<br>d. Filter blocked | a. Adjust correctly (see Control Valve Adjustment).<br>b. Install new hose.<br>c. Install new diaphragm.<br>d. Clean filter. |
| 3. Clutch is not disengaging properly | a. Linkage not adjusted properly<br>b. Leakage in hose or vacuum tank<br>c. Servo diaphragm defective<br>d. Needle bearing in clutch defective | a. Adjust.<br>b. Eliminate leakage.<br>c. Install new servo.<br>d. Install new needle bearing and seal in clutch carrier plate. |
| 4. Clutch is not disengaging at all | a. Circuit to solenoid interrupted, switch contacts burned or dirty<br>b. Poor ground to frame<br>c. Hoses kinked or collapsed (no air passage), servo diaphragm faulty, excessive voltage drop in wire to solenoid | a. Eliminate fault. Install new fuse. Clean contacts or install new switch.<br>b. Check ground connection.<br>c. Install new solenoid, hose or servo. May be necessary to install a relay to eliminate voltage drop. |
| 5. Engine stalls during range selection | Hose from control valve to servo leaking, servo diaphragm leaking | Install new hose or new servo. |
| 6. Engine stalls and cannot be restarted | Hose from manifold to control valve loose or defective, hose from control valve to vacuum tank loose or defective, tank leaking | Secure hose or install new one or replace vacuum unit. |
| 7. Clutch does not engage after range selection | a. Shift lever contacts sticking<br>b. Short in wire from contacts to solenoid<br>c. Control valve solenoid sticking | a. Clean and free contacts. Install new contacts if necessary.<br>b. Eliminate short or install new wire.<br>c. Install new solenoid. |
| 8. Clutch grabs after range is selected | ATF or grease on clutch linings, friction surface of carrier plate distorted | Install new carrier plate or machine old one. |
| 9. Vehicle jerks at idle speed when lever is released after range selection | a. Idle speed too high<br>b. Control valve adjustment incorrect | a. Adjust idle.<br>b. Adjust control valve. |
| 10. Converter is noisy (high-pitched hissing) | Insufficient ATF in converter circuit, pressure low, converter losing ATF at pump hub or at welded seam between impeller and turbine | Add ATF. Disassemble and check pump. Replace seal on pump hub, or replace converter. |
| 11. Acceleration is poor though engine output is normal and Automatic Stick Shift is working properly | Converter faulty. Check stall speed with aid of electronic tachometer. Stall speed should be between 2000 and 2250 rpm* | If actual stall speed is considerably below the normal, converter must be replaced. |
| 12. Warning lights do not work. (The lights can be checked by removing the wire at the temperature switch and holding against ground) | Light or wire faulty, selector or temperature switch defective | Replace light. Repair wire or replace defective switch. |

***This test should last only long enough for a reading of tachometer.**

7. Lift vehicle.

**NOTE —**
If transmission (gearbox) is to be disassembled drain oil at this time. Oil should be hot. It is not necessary, however, to drain ATF. Merely close off the hose after disconnecting it as described in text.

8. Detach ATF suction line and seal it with a soldered-up union M 16 x 1.5, as in Fig. 11.

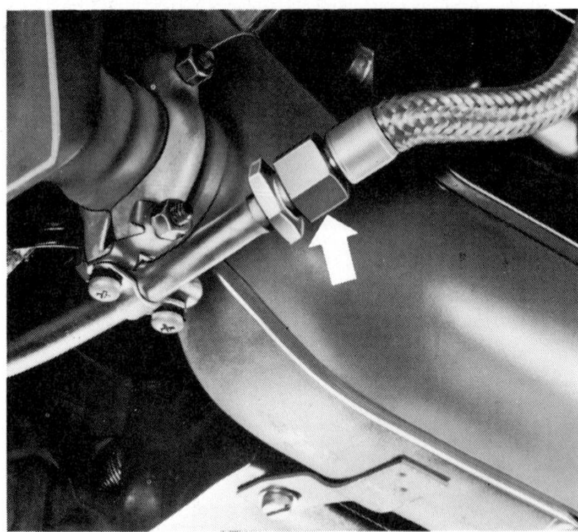



**Fig. 11.** Soldered-up union (M 16 x 1.5) is indicated by black arrow.

9. Remove four M 8 bolts from drive plate through access hole in transmission case. Turn engine with V-belt pulley to bring bolts, one at a time, into view.

**NOTE —**
If engine cannot be turned it is not possible to remove the converter/drive plate bolts. In such a case remove engine with converter to get at bolts (Fig. 12). When this procedure is followed, be sure to replace converter oil seal.

10. Pinch fuel hose closed and pull it off carburetor.

11. Disconnect heater flap cables and detach heater hoses from engine.

12. Pull accelerator cable out of guide tube.

***WARNING —***
*Before loosening upper engine mounting bolts, support engine with jack and engine adapter plate.*

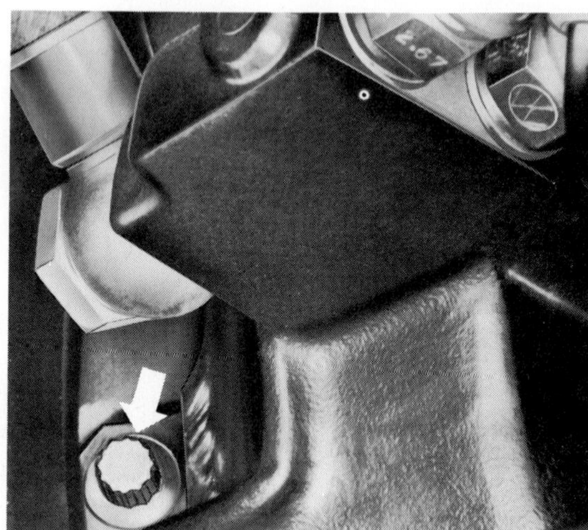



**Fig. 12.** Bolt (arrow) fastens drive plate to torque converter. This is one of four bolts accessible through hole in transmission case.

13. Remove two lower engine mounting bolts, as in Fig. 13.

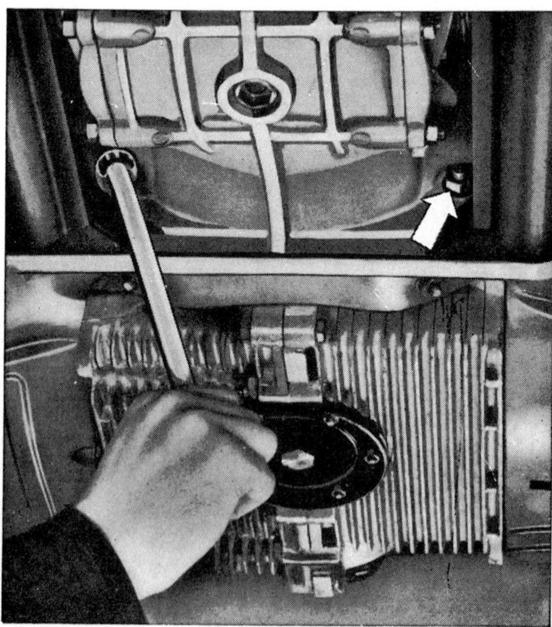



**Fig. 13.** Lower engine mounting bolts are shown here. Wrench is on one. Arrow points to other. Mounting is the same as for standard transmission.

14. Remove the two upper engine mounting nuts, as in Fig. 14.

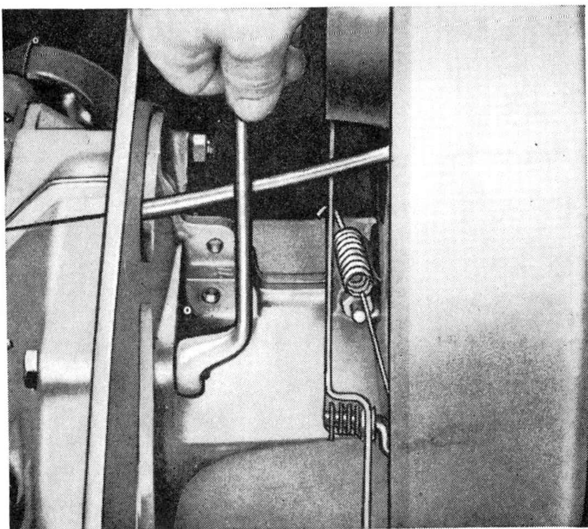
© 1972 VWoA—163

**Fig. 14.** Upper engine mounting bolts are shown here. Wrench is on one. Other can be seen in background.

15. Lower jack and tilt engine down slightly at the rear until it can be pulled out.
16. Hold torque converter with suitable retainer, as in Fig. 15.

© 1972 VWoA—781

**Fig. 15.** Retainer is metal strap attached to hold torque converter in place while transmission is removed. Strap is secured to stud in transmission case (at upper right of picture). It is possible to remove the converter also at this time, but if you do, be careful not to damage the seal.

17. Apply parking brake and remove drive shaft screws alternately at inner joints (Fig. 16). You can hang the inner ends of the drive shafts on wire hooks. However, if the car must be moved the drive shafts should be taken out completely.

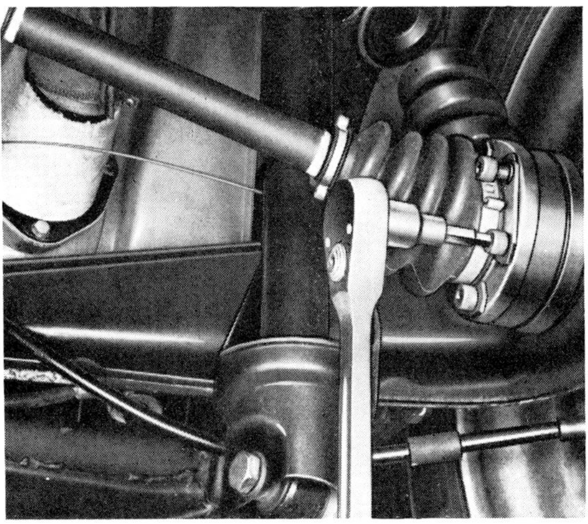
© 1972 VWoA—782

**Fig. 16.** Six socket head screws fasten wheel drive shaft to flange at each wheel.

**NOTE —**
Cover joints with plastic caps to keep dirt out.

***CAUTION —***
*To avoid breaking seals, be careful when you remove unions.*

18. Remove ATF hose banjo unions (upper arrow in Fig. 17) at transmission and seal off connections. Pull off connections at temperature switches (lower arrow).

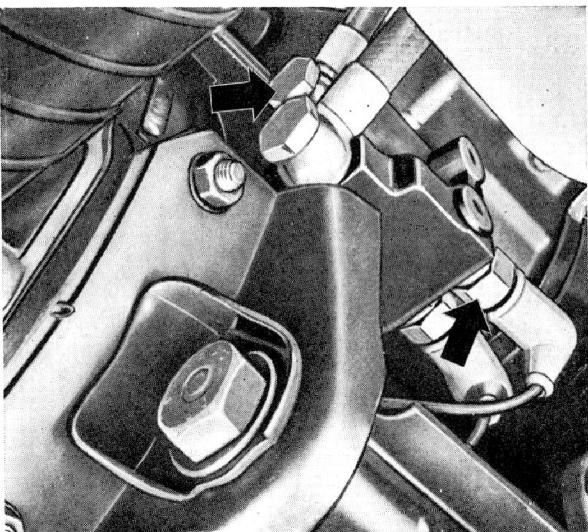
© 1972 VWoA—783

**Fig. 17.** Banjo union for ATF hose is indicated by black arrow at left. Arrow at right indicates connections at temperature switches.

19. Loosen clamp for vacuum hose on servo and pull hose off.
20. Disconnect cables from starter connections 30 and 50, as in Fig. 18.

**Fig. 18.** Starter connections 30 and 50 are indicated by black arrows.

21. Slide back rubber cap and pull off three-pin plug for oil temperature switch (arrow in Fig. 19). Pull off connection for back-up light.

**Fig. 19.** Three-pin connector (arrow) from temperature switches is attached to plug in selector switch.

22. Push back rubber cap and pull three-pin plug off neutral safety switch on side of gearshift housing. Also remove nuts at front transmission mounting (see Fig. 20).

**Fig. 20.** Nuts, two lower black arrows, fasten transmission at the front mounting. Arrow at upper left points to three-pin plug on neutral safety switch.

***WARNING —***
*Before starting the procedure for removal of transmission case, support the transmission as shown in Fig. 21.*

23. Loosen bolts at rear transmission mounting and finish removal of bolts. Carefully withdraw transmission from vehicle.

**Fig. 21.** Plate to hold heavy transmission on floor jack is shown here in place.

**NOTE —**
Now that you are ready to disassemble the transmission or final drive, keep these points in mind:

1. Cleanliness in these procedures is absolutely essential. Keep your workbench,

**NOTE (continued)**
your tools and the transmission components clean, but do not use sharp instruments to scrape off dirt. Use appropriate solvents instead.
2. Transmission components are heavy. While you have them in a press or while you are handling them, be careful.
3. Some springs are compressed and will pop out when restraints are removed. Be careful.
4. Follow instructions closely and make your measurements carefully.

**To install:**

1. With floor jack and plate raise transmission into engine compartment and snug down nuts for front transmission mounting. Loosely insert bolts for rear transmission mounting.
2. Push on hose for clutch servo and tighten clamp.
3. Insert new washers and connect ATF hoses. Tighten banjo unions.
4. Connect three-pin plug to neutral safety switch.

**NOTE —**
Make sure that slot in plug and lug on the switch are aligned properly.

5. Push on three-pin plug of oil temperature control switch.
6. Connect cables to terminals 30 and 50 on starter.

***CAUTION —***
*Clean rear wheel shaft flanges. Contact surfaces of the joint flanges must be free of grease. See that clearance between inner joints of drive shafts and car frame fork is adequate.*

7. Remove plastic protective caps (if they have been used) from universal joints. Slide new lock washer on screw as in Fig. 22 and attach joint to flange. Tighten screws. Install washers with convex sides toward screw heads. Fig. 22 shows the installation.

***CAUTION —***
*When tightening the transmission support bolts, lift transmission and align it to keep joints from rubbing on frame fork.*

8. Tighten transmission bolts and nuts to proper torque.



9. Remove retaining plate and transmission jack before installing engine.
10. Slowly and carefully lift engine and center it in vehicle.

**NOTE —**
Align engine with studs in transmission (through bolts). Tighten upper nuts and then lower ones to required torque. Be careful not to damage Heli-coil inserts.

11. While slowly turning the crankshaft pulley, insert the four M 8 securing screws through access hole in the converter housing. Tighten them first by hand and then to specified torque.

**NOTE —**
If you let the M 8 securing screws drop into the transmission case, you may have to remove the engine to retrieve them. But try a magnet first, of course.

12. Install heater hoses. Connect heater flap cables and adjust them. Connect fuel hose and attach ATF suction line union.
13. Connect vacuum hoses at carburetor and intake manifold and all the electrical wiring you previously disconnected.
14. Attach ATF pressure line union. Fill transmission and ATF tank as described in **LUBRICATION AND MAINTENANCE.**
15. Insert gearshift rod coupling. Tighten the screw and secure it with wire.
16. Connect battery ground strap.

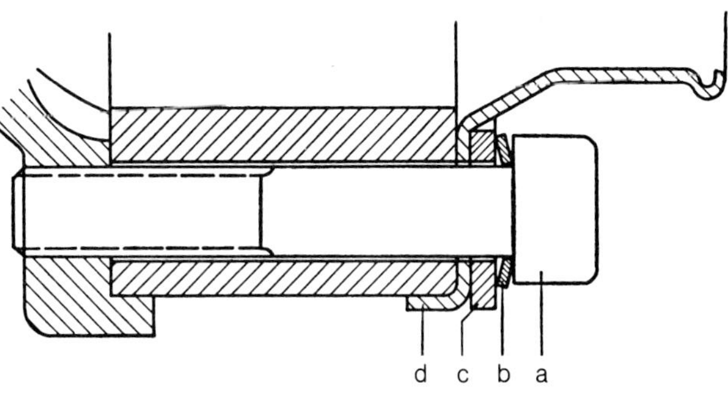


a. Socket head screw
b. Lock washer
c. Packing or spacer
d. Protective cap

**Fig. 22.** Lock washers under socket-head screws fastening constant velocity joints to flanges at transmission case are installed as shown in this diagram. Note that convex side of washer is toward screw head.

17. Start engine. Check flow, pressure and leakage while engine runs.

> ***WARNING —***
> *Before undertaking a pressure check, road test or stall speed check of a re-installed Automatic Stick Shift, read carefully the subsection on bench testing engines in* ***ENGINE.*** *Pay particular attention to all the WARNING notes. With this background you can begin the testing. Start the engine and let it run at idle until ATF is flowing back to the tank continuously. If return flow has not started after 2 or 3 minutes, you will have to bleed the lines. It may be necessary to check the suction and pressure hoses for blockage.*

18. Check transmission by shifting through the ranges with the engine running.

### Road Test

Take the car on the road and drive it in all ranges and under various road conditions. Note particularly the speed of clutch engagement when shifting down and when accelerating.

After road test, check transmission for leaks.

### Pressure Test

If the converter ATF seals leak, measure the ATF pressure in the converter circuit (see Fig. 23).

**Fig. 23.** Pressure gauge connection for testing ATF pressure in torque converter circuit is indicated by arrow.

If pressure is too high, check pump ATF pressure relief valve. Also check inside diameter of the pressure hoses. Hoses with restrictions (badly fitted connections) must be replaced.

### Stall Speed Test

This test provides a rapid check of converter functioning, but you should perform it only if the car cannot reach specified maximum speed or if the acceleration is poor.

1. Connect electronic tachometer according to manufacturer's instructions. Start engine and hold car with foot brakes and parking brake.

> ***CAUTION —***
> *In this test converter ATF heats up very quickly. Do not continue test longer than the time required to read instruments.*

2. Put selector lever in position **2** and depress accelerator pedal briefly to full throttle. After first accelerating, engine will run at a reduced speed, which is known as the stall speed. Stall speed should be 2000-2250 rpm.

If an engine in correct adjustment does not reach the specified stall speed, the converter is faulty. If the engine speed is higher than specified, the shift clutch requires adjustment.

## 5. REMOVING AND INSTALLING CONVERTER HOUSING AND SHIFT CLUTCH

> **NOTE —**
> Experience has shown that the torque converter rarely leaks. If there is a leak near the one-way clutch support (see Fig. 24), replace the support seals. Even if the converter itself is covered with ATF, it should not on this evidence alone be replaced. If the converter hub on a car with high mileage shows deep scoring or if the bushing or starter ring gear shows damage, the converter should be replaced.

**To remove shift clutch:**

1. Pull torque converter off one-way clutch support tube and remove from car. Close off hub opening.
2. Secure transmission on repair stand. Disconnect clamp screw in clutch operating lever and pull off lever. Remove nuts between clutch housing and transmission case. You will find two screws accessible from the differential housing after the trans-

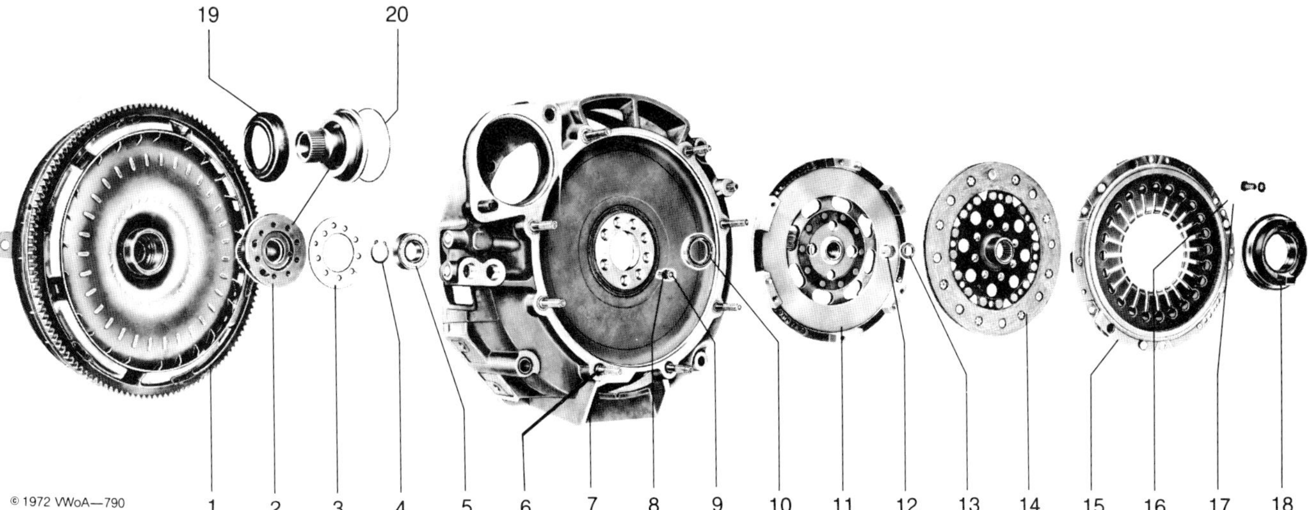


1. Torque converter
2. One-way clutch support
3. Gasket
4. Circlip for carrier plate
5. Ball bearing
6. O-ring for stud (2)
7. Converter housing
8. Spring washer (8)
9. Socket head screw (8)
10. Seal*
11. Clutch carrier plate
12. Needle bearing
13. Seal/carrier plate
14. Clutch plate
15. Diaphragm clutch pressure plate
16. Spring washer (6)
17. Socket head screw
18. Release bearing
19. Seal/converter
20. O-ring/one-way clutch

***To improve the sealing effect of this part, modifications have been made in the one-way clutch support and the torque converter. While the older parts are still available, use of the modified replacements should be considered. The latter must be replaced as a set.**

**Fig. 24.** Torque converter and clutch assembly is seen here in exploded view.

mission cover has been removed (arrows in Fig. 25). If cap nuts have been used instead of ordinary nuts, put them back when assembling.

© 1972 VWoA—791

**Fig. 25.** Nuts (black arrows) that fasten the clutch housing to the transmission case are accessible from the differential housing after the transmission cover has been removed.

**NOTE —**
When the shift clutch is repaired, there is no need to drain the transmission oil if you hold the clutch upright when you remove it. Block the breather hole in the gearshift housing.

3. Pull clutch housing off transmission case studs. Turn clutch lever shaft to disengage fork from release bearing. Remove both lower engine mounting bolts.

**6**

***CAUTION —***
*Do not wash release bearing. Merely wipe it dry.*

4. Remove bolts with 8 mm socket wrench (12-point). Remove diaphragm clutch and clutch plate. Loosen bolts evenly to prevent distortion of diaphragm clutch. Remove release bearing from clutch.

**To install:**

1. Check clutch plate, pressure plate and release bearing for wear and damage. If necessary replace parts. Check clutch carrier plate needle bearing and seal in clutch carrier plate for wear. Replace worn parts.
2. If the clutch is oiled up with ATF, replace the clutch carrier plate seal (converter sealing). If transmission oil is leaking, replace seal in transmission case (main drive shaft sealing).

3. Pull seal out with hooks as in Fig. 26, and seat new seal with tube.

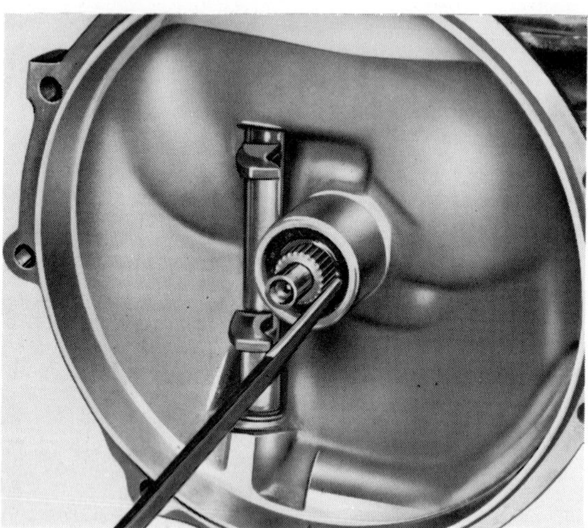

© 1972 VWoA—792

**Fig. 26.** Hooks are used to pull out seal for shift clutch.

4. Some converters have a slight chamfer on the hub to accommodate the oil seal. You may find burrs on this chamfer. Carefully remove them. Then polish and round chamfer to protect oil seal from damage when converter is inserted.

5. Lightly coat release bearing guide on transmission case neck and both lugs (arrows in Fig. 27) with lithium grease containing $MoS_2$ additive. Insert bearing clutch.

© 1972 VWoA—793

**Fig. 27.** Release bearing lugs (black arrows) require lubrication (see text) before bearing is installed.

6. Apply lithium grease to needle bearing of carrier plate. Install clutch plate and clutch, centering plate with clutch pilot made from a shortened main drive shaft (Fig. 28). (A similar procedure was used to center the clutch plate on the fly wheel of the standard transmission. See **TRANSMISSION AND REAR AXLE**.) Tighten clutch screws evenly by hand and then with wrench to specified torque.

© 1972 VWoA—794

**Fig. 28.** Clutch pilot made from a section of main drive shaft is shown in position centering clutch carrier plate while one of six socket-head screws is tightened.

7. Insert two lower engine mounting bolts from the front. Check sealing rings on all eight studs (arrows in Fig. 29). Replace any that are worn or damaged.

**NOTE —**
On some transmissions aluminum sealing rings and cap nuts will be found on these studs.

© 1972 VWoA—795

**Fig. 29.** Sealing rings on bolts for lower engine mounting are indicated by black arrows. Bolts are inserted from front.

8. Install transmission case on the converter housing studs. Insert clutch lever shaft behind the release bearing lugs and put bearing on its guide at the end of the transmission case. (This guide is also called the transmission case neck.)
9. Tighten nuts evenly by hand. Then torque them to specifications with a wrench.
10. Install clutch operating lever and adjust clutch setting.

## 6. ADJUSTING CLUTCH

The following instructions give you a basic setting for the installation of a new clutch plate:

1. Attach clutch servo to bracket on transmission.
2. Slide clutch operating lever on clutch lever shaft. The clutch operating lever (arrow in Fig. 30) should make contact with the clutch housing. Tighten the clamping screw a little.

© 1972 VWoA—810

**Fig. 30.** Operating lever for shift clutch is indicated by black arrow. Lever should be in contact with clutch housing.

3. With reference to the measurements indicated in Fig. 31, adjust clearance "a" to 0.335 inch (8.5 mm) and distance "b" to 3.03 inches (77 mm).

4. Push servo rod all the way into servo unit. Turn clutch lever on clutch shaft in direction of clutch servo until measurement between eye of lever and eye of threaded sleeve on servo rod is 1.574 inches (40 mm). This measurement is shown as "c" in Fig. 32. Torque clutch operating lever clamp screw to 18 ft. lbs. (2.5 mkg).

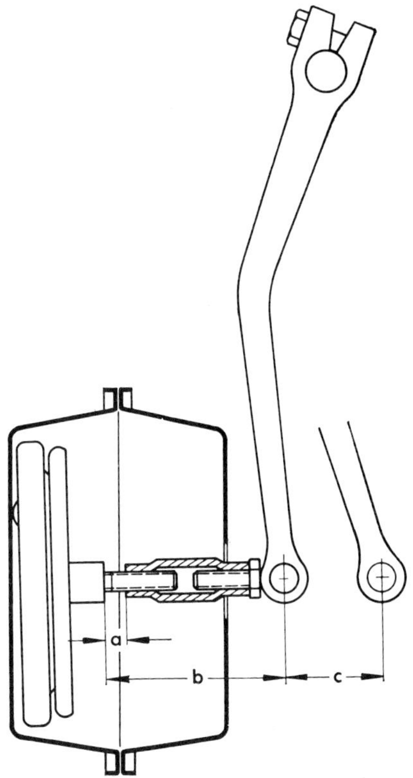


© 1972 VWoA—811

**Fig. 31.** Threaded sleeve on servo rod is adjusted to give measurement of 0.335 inch (8.5 mm) for "a" (distance from end of sleeve to hub of servo diaphragm) and measurement of 3.03 inches (77 mm) for "b" (distance from hub to eye of sleeve). Measurement "c" is illustrated in Fig. 32.

6

© 1972 VWoA—812

**Fig. 32.** Measuring jig is used to set eye of clutch lever 1.574 inches (40 mm) from eye of servo rod. This is distance "c" shown in Fig. 31.

5. Connect clutch operating lever with servo rod of clutch servo (Fig. 33). Insert plastic sleeves. Insert bolt from above, install washer below and secure with cotter pin.

© 1972 VWoA—813

**Fig. 33.** Servo rod (black arrow) and shift clutch lever are attached in assembly shown here. Bolt is inserted from above and secured below with cotter pin.

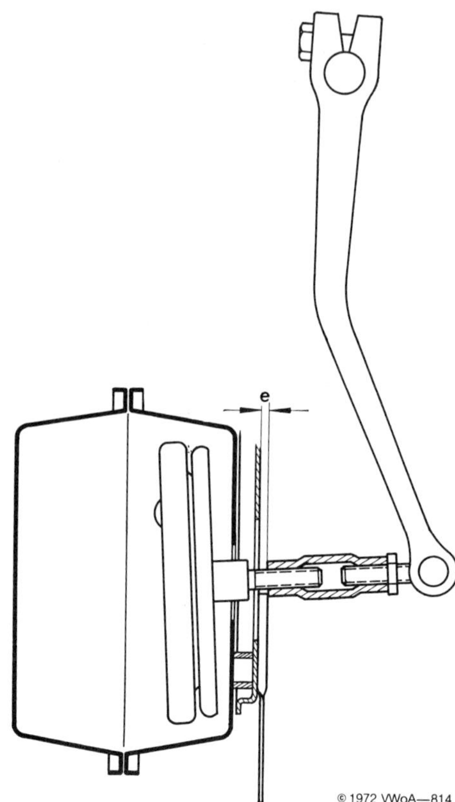


© 1972 VWoA—814

**Fig. 34.** Clearance "e" between upper edge of clutch servo mounting bracket and lower edge of adjusting sleeve on servo rod must be less than 0.157 inch (4 mm).

## 6.1 Checking Clutch Play

Normal wear on the clutch lining will in time reduce clutch clearance, but if the clutch is to engage fully, a certain minimum clearance must be maintained. Otherwise, the clutch will slip, and slipping causes excessive heating and increased wear. Clutch play must be checked and, if necessary, adjusted every 6000 miles.

For this inspection of the clutch you will need a gauge made of sheet metal 0.040 inch (1 mm) thick. Cut the piece to measure 0.157 (4 mm) at one end and 0.275 inch (6.5 mm) at the other.

**To check clutch:**

1. Pull off vacuum hose at clutch servo. Use narrow end (0.157 inch) of metal gauge to measure clearance from upper edge of bracket to lower edge of adjusting nut. If the servo rod of the clutch servo (with linkage connected) can be pulled out a distance of 0.157 inch (4 mm) or more, the clutch requires adjustment. In Fig. 34 this measurement is shown at "e".

**To adjust:**

1. Pull vacuum hose off clutch servo. Barely loosen lock nut and leave in loose position.
2. Turn adjusting nut five or five and a half turns away from sleeve. The separation between adjusting nut and lock nut (shown as "d" in Fig. 35) should then be 0.275 inch (6.5 mm). Gauge this distance with the wider end of your sheet metal gauge.

© 1972 VWoA—815

**Fig. 35.** Separation "d" between adjusting sleeve and lock nut is 0.275 inch (6.5 mm) in clutch adjusting procedure.

3. Screw lock nut up against adjusting nut in its new position and tighten. Push on vacuum hose and tighten clamps.

**NOTE —**
If the clutch already has been adjusted and the clutch operating lever is in contact with the clutch housing, further adjustment is not possible. The clutch plate is worn and must be replaced.

4. Road test vehicle to check adjustment. If you can accelerate without slipping of the clutch and if you can engage the reverse gear, the adjustment is correct.

## 6.2 Adjusting Speed of Engagement

The control valve of the VW Automatic Stick Shift is adjusted to give smooth clutch engagement after selection of a drive range. In use, however, improvement of the clutch plate contact pattern may cause the clutch to grab. An adjustment of the reducing valve in the control valve can compensate for the grabbing. To a great extent, in fact, it is possible to fit clutch engagement time to the car owner's driving habits.

***CAUTION —***
*When the clutch engages too softly (slowly), increased heat (and consequently increased wear of the clutch linings) results. There is a simple test to tell whether the engagement time of your clutch is correct. Select the lower drive range but do not accelerate. About 1 second after you take your hand off the gearshift lever the clutch should engage fully. A servo control valve, though not defective, may not be in best adjustment to suit the car owner's driving habits. If you are not satisfied with the engagement of your clutch, study the troubleshooting charts and make appropriate adjustments, working slowly and carefully.*

1. Clutch engages too quickly
   Remove protective cap. Turn adjusting screw (indicated by arrow in Fig. 36) between a quarter and a half turn clockwise and replace cap.

**NOTE —**
When reducing valve is set to basic position, the adjusting screw should be out of the cover about two threads.

2. Clutch engages too slowly
   Turn adjusting screw (arrow in Fig. 36) between a quarter and half turn counterclockwise and replace cap.



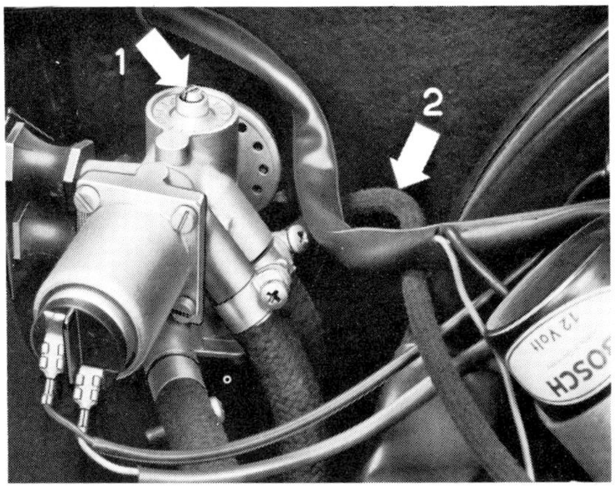



**Fig. 36.** Adjusting screw (arrow #1) on control valve is turned clockwise to slow clutch engagement, counter-clockwise to speed it up. Arrow #2 points to vacuum line.

## 7. Removing and Installing Clutch Carrier Plate
(clutch removed)

These instructions will be easier to follow if at each step you refer back to Fig. 24. Call-out numbers of the parts in the illustration are given here to assist you.

6

**To remove plate:**

1. Remove converter (1) from one-way clutch support (2) and cover opening for the turbine shaft. Take converter housing (7) off assembly support.
2. Remove socket head screw (6 mm) through openings in clutch carrier plate (11), as in Fig. 37.

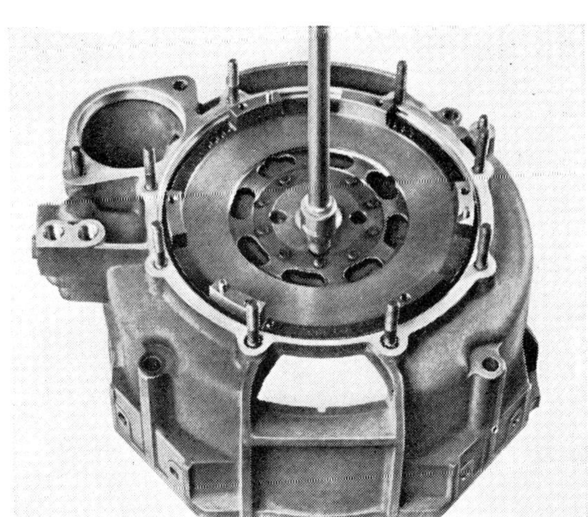


**Fig. 37.** Openings in clutch carrier plate allow removal of eight 6 mm socket head screws.

3. Remove one-way clutch support tube (2) from converter housing (7). Use drift (Fig. 38). Take off gasket (3).

© 1972 VWoA—797

**Fig. 38.** Drift is applied as here to remove one-way clutch support tube from converter housing.

4. Remove circlip (4) from turbine shaft of clutch carrier plate and with mallet knock out carrier plate, as in Fig. 39.

© 1972 VWoA—798

**Fig. 39.** Rubber mallet is used to knock clutch carrier plate out of converter housing after circlip on turbine drive shaft has been removed.

5. Pull seal (10) and needle bearing out of carrier plate with a puller, as in Fig. 40.

***CAUTION*** —

*Replace damaged or noisy bearings. Bearings with or without sealed cages can be used.*

© 1972 VWoA—799

**Fig. 40.** Puller is applied as shown here to pull seal and needle bearing out of clutch carrier plate.

6. Knock ball bearing (5) out with drift (Fig. 41) and adapter.

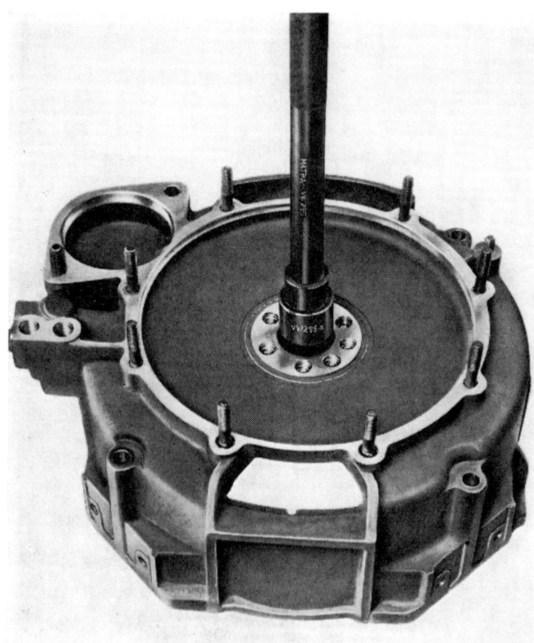

© 1972 VWoA—800

**Fig. 41.** Ball bearing is forced out of converter housing with drift as shown here.

7. Using drift, knock out seal (10).

**To install:**

1. Using a sleeve as in Fig. 42 insert ball bearing in converter housing. Support the plate and force the bearing all the way to the stop.

© 1972 VWoA—801

**Fig. 42.** Drift is used to drive ball bearing into converter.

2. Drive in seal with the sealing lip up (toward the converter).
3. Drive turbine shaft of carrier plate into ball bearing and insert circlip.
4. Push one-way clutch support tube into converter housing. Insert gasket between support and housing. Insert bolts through openings in carrier plate and tighten. Coat bolts with gasket cement D3.

**NOTE —**
When inserting gasket and one-way clutch support tube, make sure that ATF feed and return drillings are open. These large drillings are opposite each other. Before installing the one-way clutch support with O-ring, remove all traces of burr from housing and moisten O-ring with ATF to prevent damage when support is inserted.

5. Install needle bearing and seal for main drive shaft. Use the kind of punch shown in Fig. 43. Coat bearing with lithium grease when installing.

© 1972 VWoA—802

**Fig. 43.** Special punch is used to install needle bearing and seal on main drive shaft.

## 8. REPLACING CONVERTER SEAL AND BUSHING

Since the converter is welded together, it can be replaced only as an assembly. In most cases the converter itself rarely leaks, and leakage in the assembly usually can be stopped by replacing the seal.

**To replace the seal:**

1. Remove engine, pull converter off one-way clutch support and cover hole in hub.
2. Insert hook behind edge of seal and by prying upward at opposite points pull off seal. Fig. 44 shows use of hook.

© 1972 VWoA—803

**Fig. 44.** Hook inserted under edge of converter seal is used to pry seal off one-way clutch support.

3. Moisten inside of new seal with ATF and slide seal on one-way clutch support.
4. Using block and rubber mallet as in Fig. 45, drive seal into place. Make sure seal goes in without tilting.

**Fig. 45.** Block and rubber mallet are used to drive converter seal into place.

5. Install clamping bar across the installation block, as in Fig. 46, and tighten nuts alternately and evenly until bar makes contact with converter housing.

**NOTE —**
This procedure seats seal properly. There is a new type of clutch support that has a saw tooth on the circumference to secure the seal. On a support without the saw tooth groove, the metal collar of the seal must be peened into the annular groove of the support at three places (120 degrees apart). Use the point of puller hook, as in Fig. 46, for the peening.

6. Remove bar and block. Install converter and engine.

***CAUTION —***
*Be very careful when pushing the converter onto the one-way clutch support. If you let the converter tilt, you will stretch the seal and damage the converter hub bushing.*

7. Perform pressure test.

**Fig. 46.** Point of puller hook is used to peen metal collar of converter seal into groove of one-way clutch support of earlier type.

**To replace converter bushing:**

1. Check hub for scoring by oil seal.
2. Check starter ring and air deflector plate for security. Insert turbine shaft and make sure that turbine turns easily. De-burr starter ring.
3. Check bushing for wear. Replace if scored.
4. Using extractor with adapter as in Fig. 47, pull out bushing.

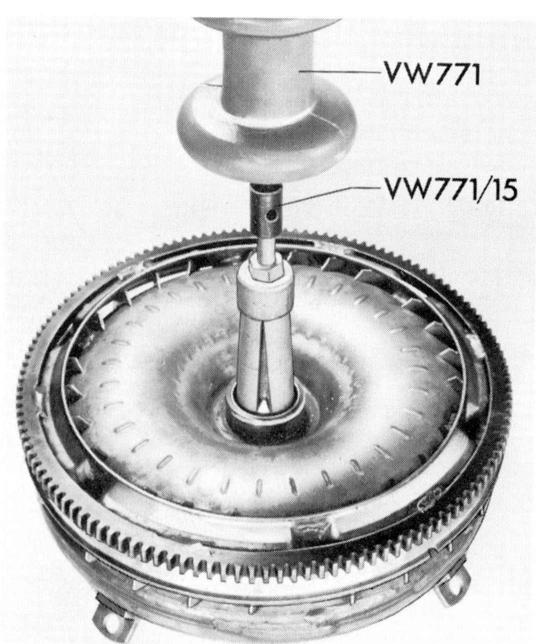




**Fig. 47.** Extractor, in set-up like this, is used to pull out torque converter bushing.

5. Install new bushing with press and tube (Fig. 48).

**Fig. 48.** Special press tool and tube are used when installing torque converter bushing.

**NOTE —**
The inside diameter of the installed bushing must fall within the tolerance 35.98 to 36.03 mm. If the diameter is smaller than the lower limit, the bushing will seize. The specified wear limit for this bushing is 36.05 mm. Use this value as a general guide.

## 9. CLEANING TORQUE CONVERTER

Contaminants from a damaged oil pump or converter bushing could enter the torque converter. With a siphoning device like the one pictured in Fig. 49, it is possible to remove almost all the ATF from a converter, enabling you to restore a contaminated one to service.

**To drain converter:**

1. Place converter on a horizontal surface and insert plug of siphon as shown in Fig. 50.
2. Push suction pipe into converter hub until pipe bottoms.
3. Place an empty oil container (about 2 quarts) below converter to catch fluid. To start siphoning action blow on tube numbered (2) in Fig. 50.

**NOTE —**
Use a suction pipe of very small diameter in the siphon. Fluid in the converter runs from the vanes to hub very slowly, and a large hose would drain accumulation too quickly. You would have to re-start the siphon repeatedly. You may have to experiment before you find the right combination.

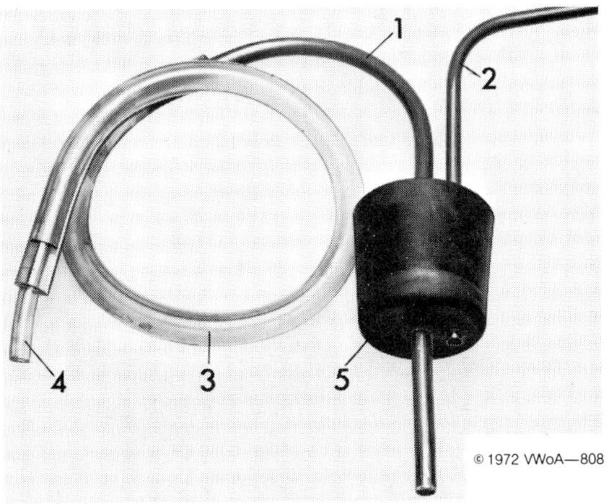


| Designation | Qty. | Material |
|---|---|---|
| 1. Tube 3/16 in. x 8 in. (4 x 200 mm)* | 1 | Steel or copper |
| 2. Tube 1/8 in. x 6 in. (3 x 150 mm)* | 1 | Steel or copper |
| 3. Hose 1/4 in. x 14 in. (6 x 350 mm)* | 1 | PVC |
| 4. Hose 1/8 in. x 1 1/4 in. (3 x 30 mm)* | 1 | PVC |
| 5. Plug 1 1/2 in. dia. (35 mm) | 1 | Rubber, conical |

*** Use nearest standard size**

**Fig. 49.** Siphon for draining torque converter can be made with materials shown here.

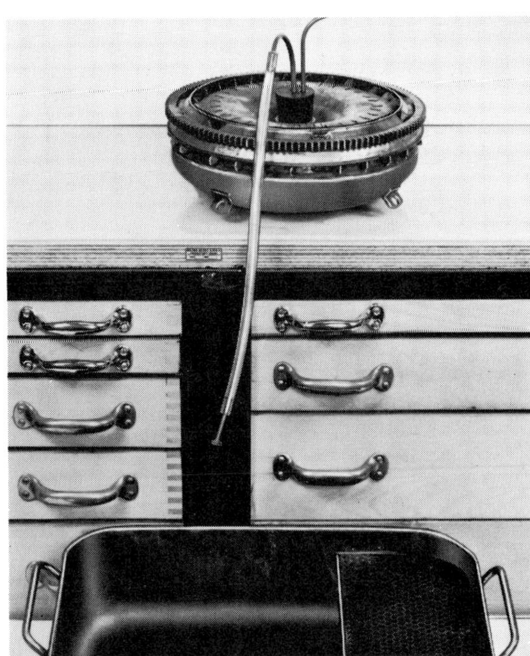


**Fig. 50.** Set-up for siphoning ATF from torque converter is shown here. Blowing into short tube starts operation.

4. Let converter drain overnight. Up to 4.2 pints (2 liters) of ATF can be siphoned off.

6

## 10. REMOVING AND INSTALLING CONTROL VALVE

In the following instructions call-out numbers from Fig. 51 are used to describe the various parts and help you to locate their positions in the assembly.

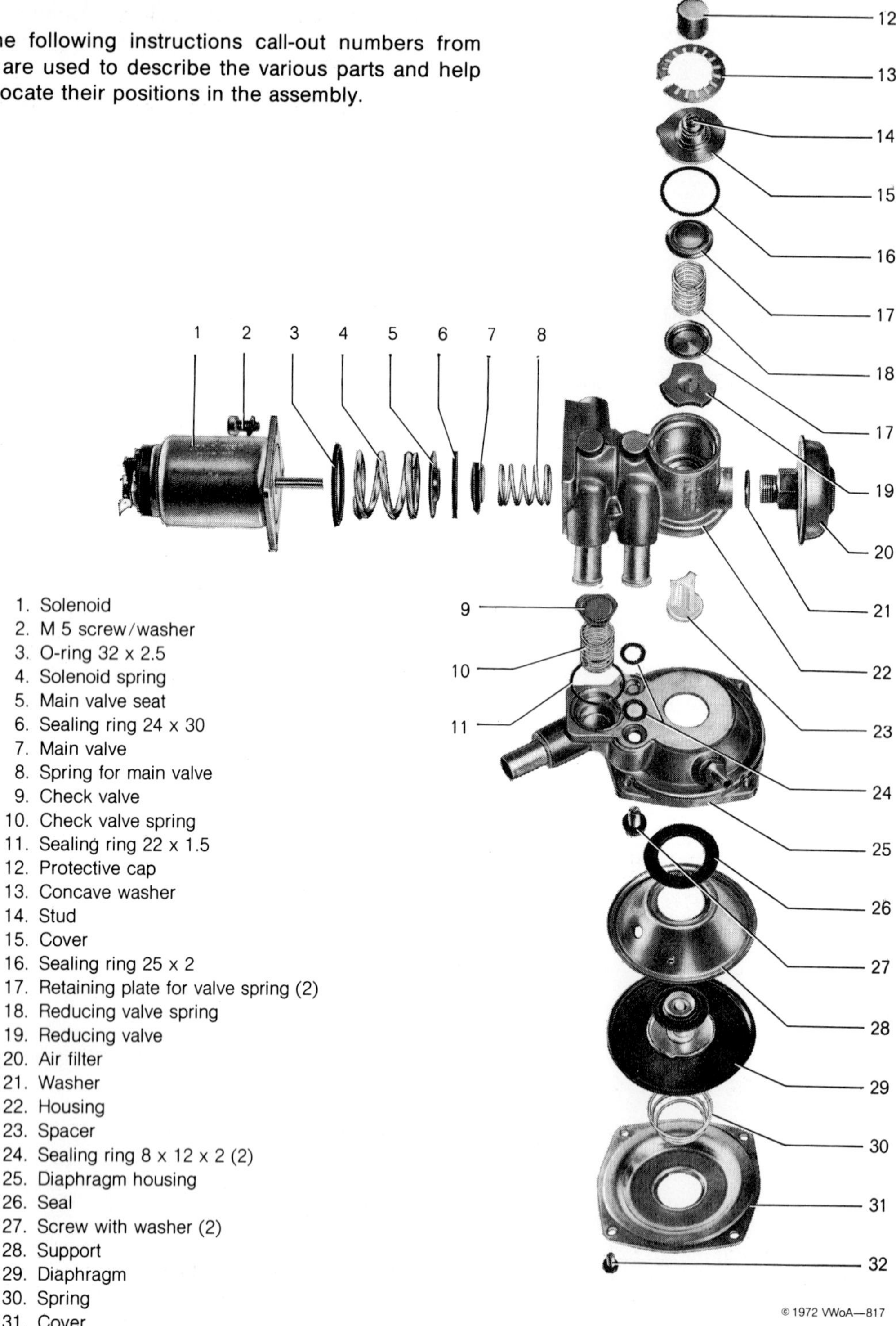


**Fig. 51.** Control valve for Automatic Stick Shift clutch is shown here in exploded view.

**To remove valve:**

1. Pull off wire (black) at connection 15 and ground wire (brown) at solenoid.
2. Loosen vacuum hose clamps and pull hoses off control valve.
3. Take out three screws at bracket and remove control valve.

For another view of control valve see Fig. 10.

**To disassemble:**

1. Remove bracket. With screwdriver remove special (concave) washer (13) for cover (15).
2. Take off cover (15) with seal (16). Remove spring for reducing valve (18) and reducing valve (19).
3. Remove screws (32) at cover (31) and take out spring (30), diaphragm (29), support washer (28), and rubber washer (26) with spacer (23).
4. Remove two screws (27) in housing cover and take off housing with hose connections (22).
5. Lift out check valve (9) with spring (10) and sealing ring (11).
6. Screw out solenoid (1) and remove sealing ring (3), spacer spring (4), valve seat (5), seal (6), main valve (7) and spring (8).
7. Unscrew air filter (20) and remove.

**To assemble:**

1. Check solenoid, valve seats, valve springs, diaphragms, seals and sealing rings. Replace if necessary.
2. Install check valve and attach housing to housing cover.
3. Insert spacer and assemble diaphragm. If a new diaphragm is installed, the clearance of the reducing valve must be checked and, if necessary, reset.
4. Screw stud housed in diaphragm in or out until you obtain the position illustrated in Fig. 52. When you press the diaphragm down, the dome of the spacer should protrude a certain distance above the valve seat in the housing. This distance is obtained by subtracting measurement "b" in the illustration from measurement "a". The result should be between 0.012 to 0.016 inch (0.3 to 0.4 mm).
5. Secure stud.
6. Be sure that compensating port and valve seat of reducing valve are clean. Install reducing valve (19), replace cover with sealing ring and install spring washer.
7. Install main valve (7) and screw on solenoid (1).

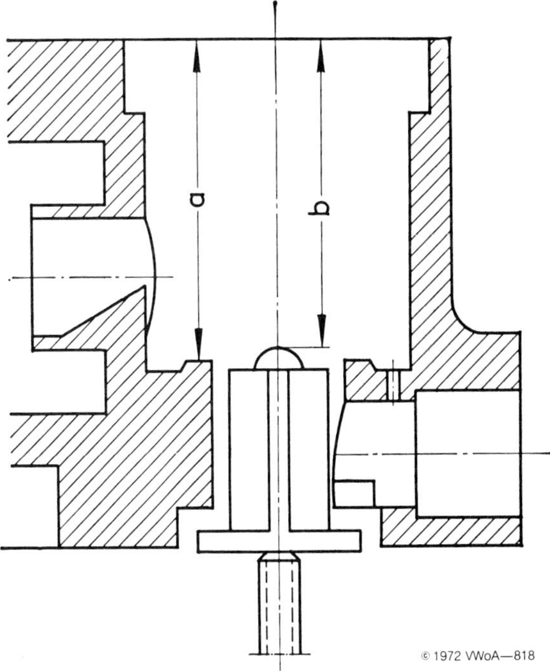


**Fig. 52.** Dome on spacer should protrude 0.012 to 0.016 inch (0.3 to 0.4 mm) above valve seat in diaphragm housing. This distance is measurement "a" minus measurement "b".

6

**To install:**

1. Attach bracket and install control valve in engine compartment.
2. Push on vacuum hoses and tighten clamps.

> **NOTE —**
> Use reinforced vacuum hoses only.

3. Connect wire 15 (black) to left plug and ground wire (brown) to right plug.
4. Road test vehicle to check adjustment of reducing valve. The speed of clutch engagement, whether slow or fast, depends on this adjustment.

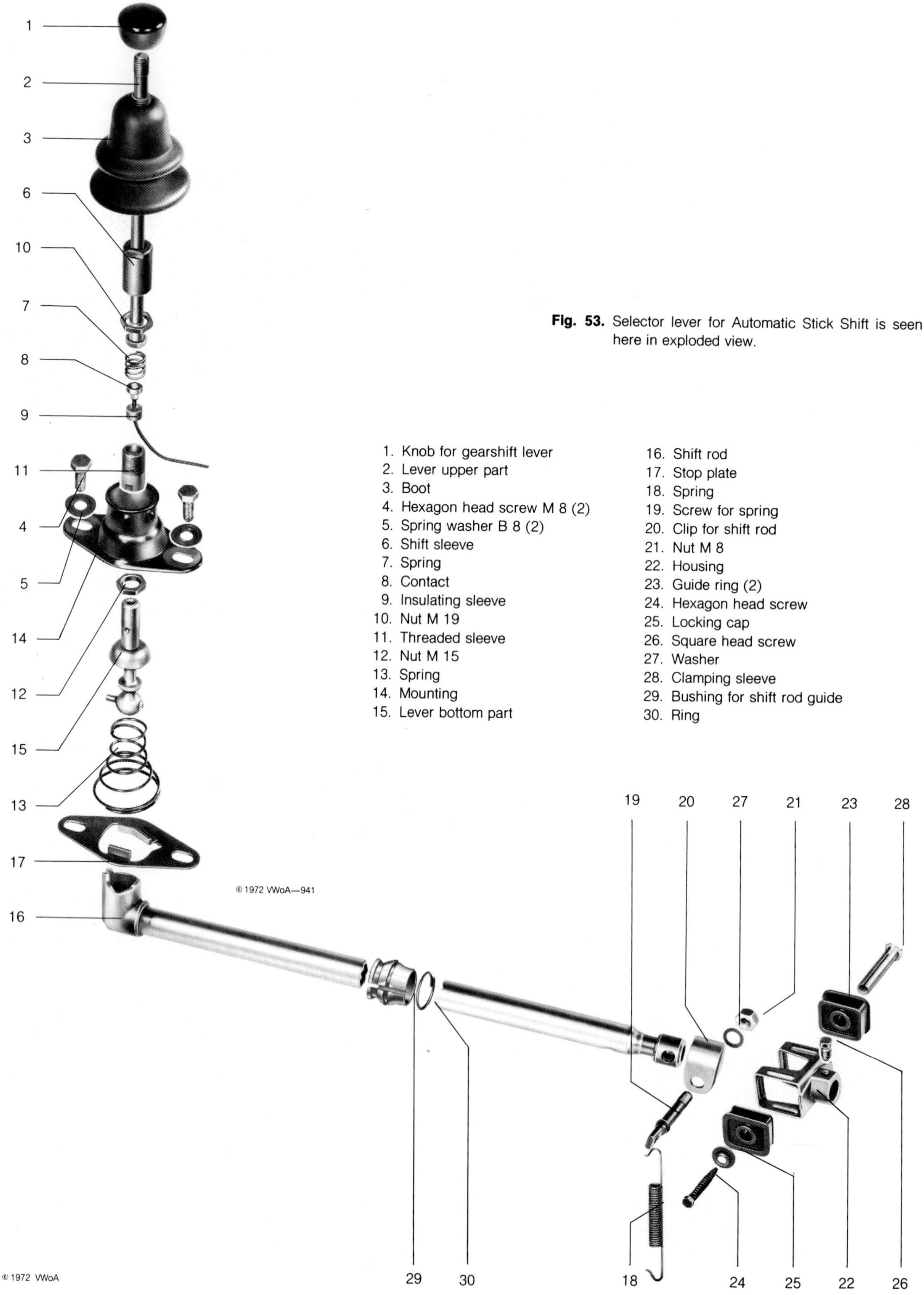

**Fig. 53.** Selector lever for Automatic Stick Shift is seen here in exploded view.

1. Knob for gearshift lever
2. Lever upper part
3. Boot
4. Hexagon head screw M 8 (2)
5. Spring washer B 8 (2)
6. Shift sleeve
7. Spring
8. Contact
9. Insulating sleeve
10. Nut M 19
11. Threaded sleeve
12. Nut M 15
13. Spring
14. Mounting
15. Lever bottom part
16. Shift rod
17. Stop plate
18. Spring
19. Screw for spring
20. Clip for shift rod
21. Nut M 8
22. Housing
23. Guide ring (2)
24. Hexagon head screw
25. Locking cap
26. Square head screw
27. Washer
28. Clamping sleeve
29. Bushing for shift rod guide
30. Ring

## 11. SELECTOR LEVER

The selector lever of the Automatic Stick Shift looks something like the gearshift lever for the manual transmission, but the two are quite different in component parts, connections and installation. Fig. 53 (opposite page) gives an exploded view of the Automatic Stick Shift selector lever.

### 11.1 Selector Lever Contact

The selector lever contact, which closes the electric circuit to the valve solenoid for selection of a drive range, requires inspection every 6,000 miles. Check it for dirt or corrosion and for play. Remember that the circuit should not close when the lever is moved from side to side. Clean the contact. If necessary, replace the assembly.

**NOTE ——**
To clean or replace the selector lever contact, loosen the lock nut on the shift sleeve and screw off the sleeve.

### 11.2 Disassembling and Assembling Selector Lever Mechanism

**To disassemble:**

1. Under the rear seat you will find the connector for the selector lever contact ground wire. (Fig. 54.) Disconnect the wire.

2. Remove the bolts that hold the selector lever mounting. Take the lever assembly out as a complete unit.

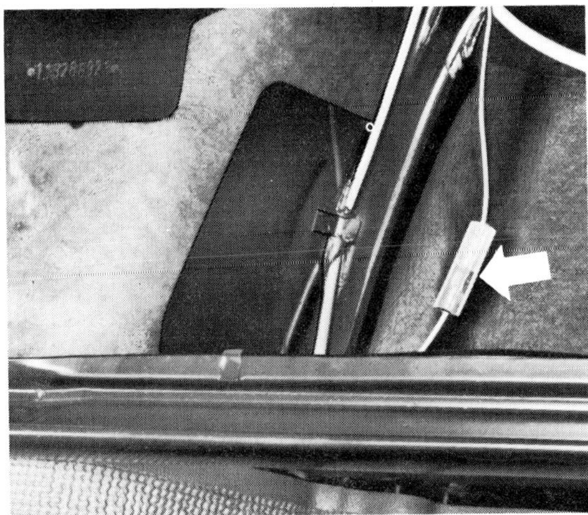

© 1972 VWoA—942

**Fig. 54.** Connector (arrow) under rear seat connects ground lead from selector lever contact with ground wire to frame.

3. Remove frame fork inspection cover. Take out shift rod coupling pin. Remove clamp and disconnect spring. See Fig. 55.

© 1972 VWoA—952

**Fig. 55.** Shift rod coupling is shown here. Arrow 1 points to hex head screw shown as part 24 in Fig. 53. Arrow 2 points to screw for spring, part 19 in Fig. 53. Arrow 3 indicates M 8 nut, part 21 in Fig. 53. The U-shaped part is the housing, part 22. The square head screw above the housing is part 26.

4. Remove both cover plates in the front panels and the cover plate on the frame head. (See **BODY**.) Pull shift rod out through front of car with pliers.

Study of Fig. 53 will help you in the following assembly procedure.

**To assemble:**

1. If the bushing in the shift rod mounting (Fig. 56) is to be replaced, fit the wire ring around the bushing first. Then press on bushing, starting from slot.

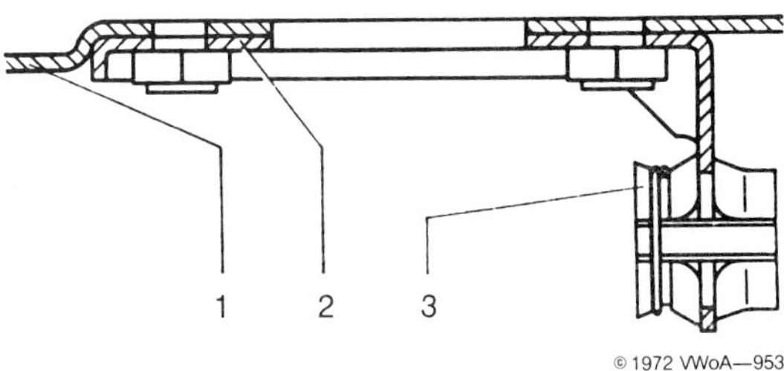


© 1972 VWoA—953

**Fig. 56.** Bushing for shift rod mounting is shown at 3. It is part 29 in Fig. 53. Also shown here are frame tunnel (1) and shift rod guide (2).

2. Lightly grease shift rod along entire length. Insert rod in tunnel at front of car and pass it through the bushing.
3. Install clamp, insert pin in shift rod coupling, tighten screw and connect spring.
4. Adjusting selector lever contact
   a. Clean contacts or replace with new ones before attempting adjustment.
   b. Screw shift sleeve together until contacts touch. Then unscrew contact a half turn. Contact gap then should be 0.25 to 0.40 mm. See Fig. 57.

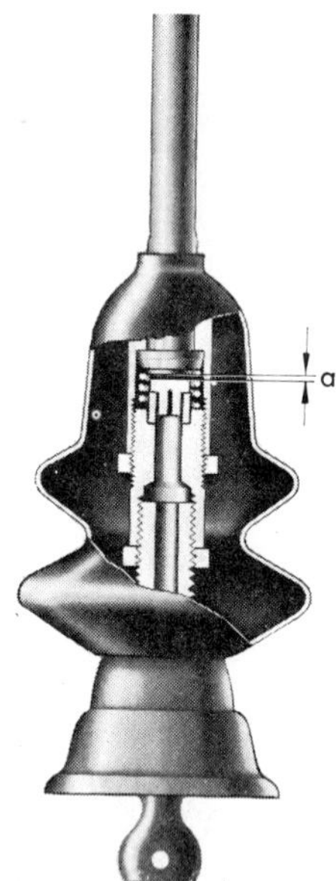


**Fig. 57.** Contact gap in selector lever assembly, shown here as clearance "a", is adjusted with threaded steel sleeve. Gap should be 0.010 to 0.016 inch (0.25 to 0.40 mm).

**NOTE —**
After adjustment of the contacts the shift sleeve may be out of alignment with the centerline of the car. In that case loosen the lower M 15 lock nut and move the lever into line.

5. Install the selector lever, with mounting and the spring and stop plate as a unit. Secure with bolts.
6. Adjust selector lever.
   a. Move lever into drive range **L**.
   b. Carefully align lever in the **L** position. The lever should not tilt to either side but should incline backward about 10 degrees from the vertical.
   c. Loosen the bolts a little. Then, holding the lever to keep it from moving, press the stop plate under the mounting to the left until it makes contact with the shoulder on the lever. Fig. 58 illustrates this adjustment.

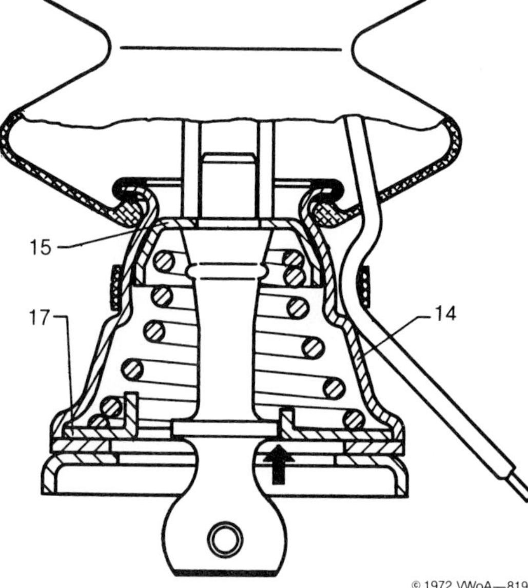


**Fig. 58.** Stop plate adjustment under lever mounting is shown here. Black arrow points to contact of plate with shoulder on lever. Call-out numbers in picture refer to Fig. 53: mounting (14); bottom part of lever (15); stop plate (17).

   d. With lever in the position obtained in the three previous steps, retighten the mounting bolts. Then shift through all the drive ranges. You should be able to engage any range easily and without sticking.

7. Secure ground lead for selector lever contact at the lever mounting (Fig. 59). Route lead under rear seat and connect to ground wire. Re-install boot.

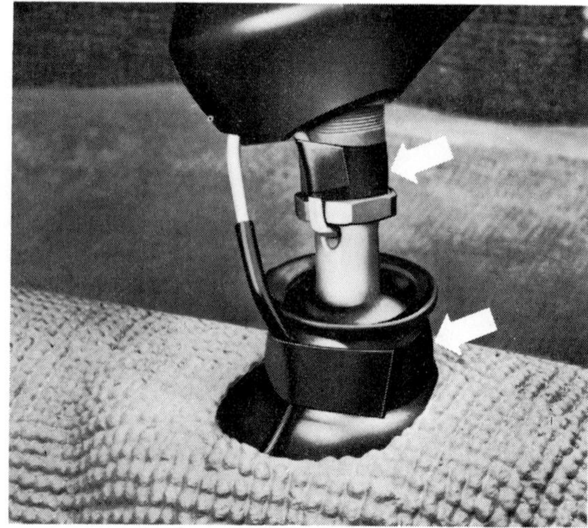


**Fig. 59.** Ground lead connection for selector lever contact is indicated by upper arrow. Lower arrow points to mounting.

## 12. REMOVING AND INSTALLING TANKS

Cars with Automatic Stick Shift have two tanks, the vacuum tank and ATF tank, not found on cars with standard transmission.

### 12.1 Vacuum Tank

On sedans the vacuum tank is under the left fender, but on Karmann Ghias it is in the housing for the right rear wheel, behind the engine compartment trim.

**To remove tank:**

1. Disconnect hose clamp and pull off vacuum hoses.
2. Remove retaining strap bolts (Fig. 60) and take off tank.

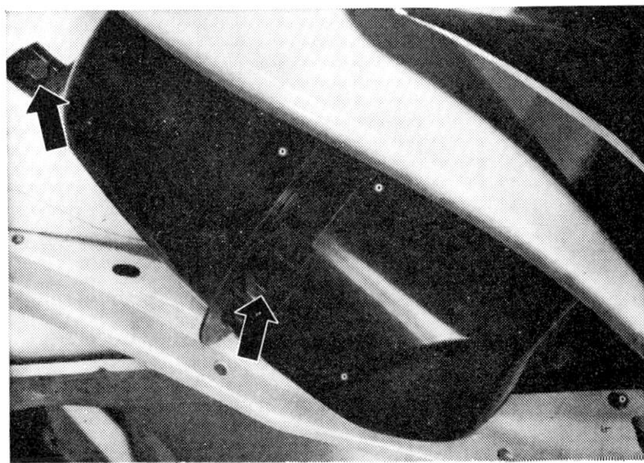

© 1972 VWoA—821

**Fig. 60.** Bolt (center arrow) in retaining strap and bolt (arrow at left) through bracket hold vacuum tank.

3. Remove bolts at bumper bracket and remove bracket.

To install tank, go through above procedure in reverse order.

### 12.2 ATF Tank

On sedans the ATF reservoir is under the right rear fender. On Karmann Ghias the tank is in the engine compartment, at the right.

**To remove ATF tank:**

1. Disconnect return line at ATF filler (upper arrow in Fig. 61). Catch fluid and dispose of it.
2. Remove trim plate and rubber seal at quarter panel.
3. Disconnect pump suction line at ATF tank and drain off ATF (lower arrow in Fig. 61). Dispose of fluid.

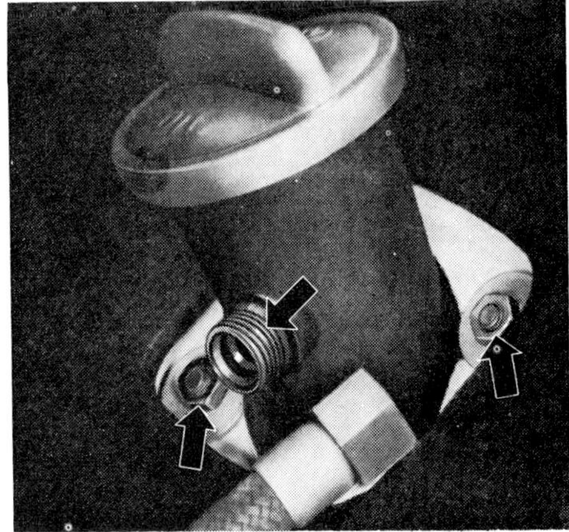

© 1972 VWoA—822

**Fig. 61.** ATF tank has connection for return line in filler neck (upper arrow at center). Lower arrows point to fasteners.

4. Remove retaining strap bolt (Fig. 62) and take off ATF tank.

© 1972 VWoA—823

**Fig. 62.** Suction line from ATF tank to dual pump is indicated by lower black arrow. Upper arrow points to bolt on retaining strap.

5. Remove bolts in bumper bracket and take off bracket. Recheck fluid level.

Installation takes place in reverse order.

6

## 13. Removing and Installing Differential

The differentials for 1969 cars with manual transmission and for cars with Automatic Stick Shift are identical, but the removal procedures are different.

Before the differential can be removed, it is necessary to take out the transmission and the starter. To help you to visualize the procedures, the following instructions give call-out numbers from Fig. 63 when referring to the various parts in the assembly. Study this and the other illustrations carefully before you begin your work, and make sure that you have at hand all the seals and gaskets you will need in re-assembly. If you have to leave parts exposed while you are working, either cover them or spray them with a preservative.

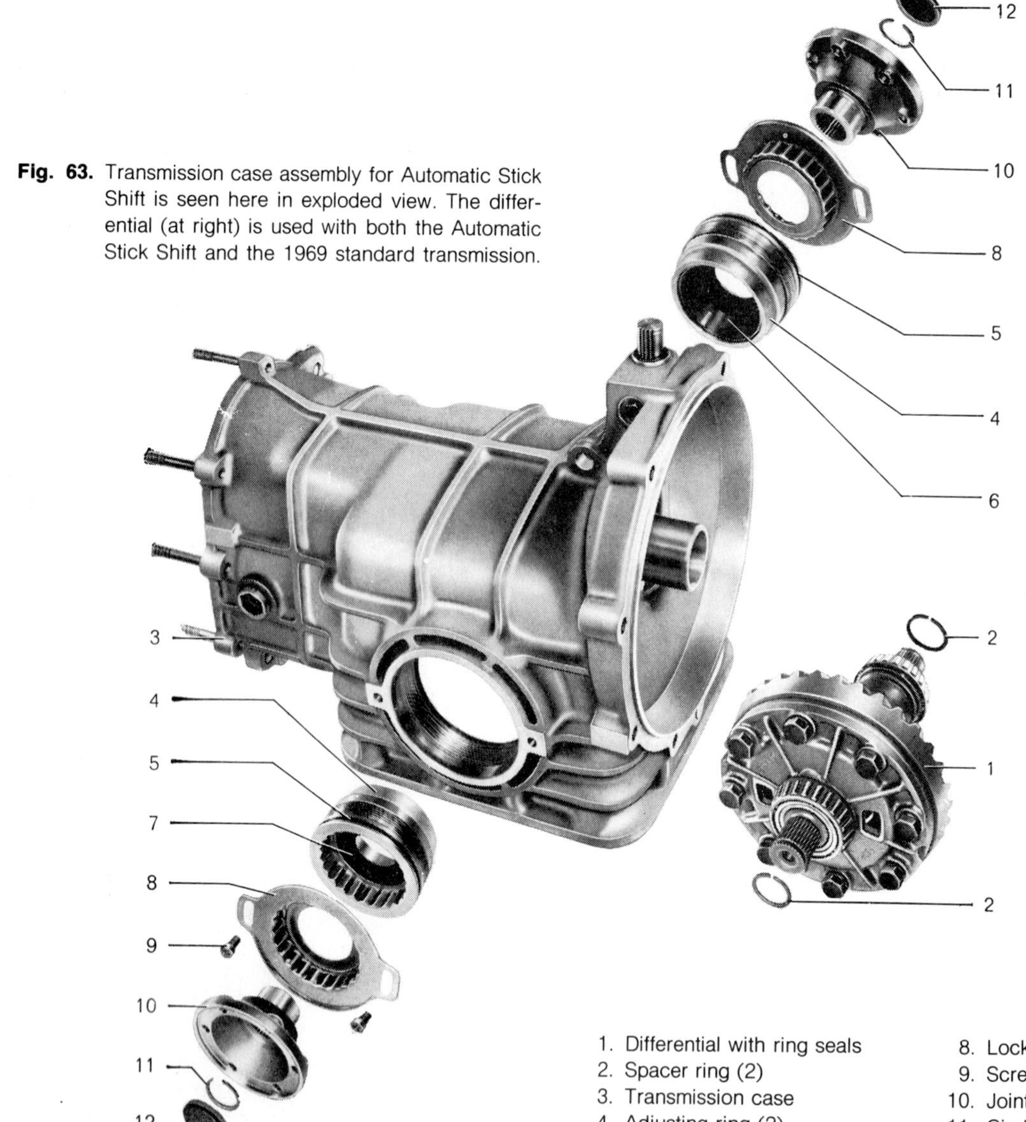


**Fig. 63.** Transmission case assembly for Automatic Stick Shift is seen here in exploded view. The differential (at right) is used with both the Automatic Stick Shift and the 1969 standard transmission.

1. Differential with ring seals
2. Spacer ring (2)
3. Transmission case
4. Adjusting ring (2)
5. O-ring (2)
6. Roller bearing/outer race (2)
7. Seal (2)
8. Lock plate (2)
9. Screw (Phillips head) (4)
10. Joint flange (2)
11. Circlip (Lock ring)
12. Cap (2)
    Sealing cap* (2)

***To prevent corrosion between case or adjusting rings and lock plates, install sealing cap as a modification. Always coat the measuring surface with rust preventive, even if sealing caps are not used. The flat surface against which the lock plate rides on adjusting ring is for making measurements of the depth of the adjusting ring when the ring is screwed into the transmission case.**

**To remove differential:**

1. With screwdriver, as in Fig. 64, pierce caps (12) at the flanges for the constant velocity joints and remove caps.

© 1972 VWoA—825

**Fig. 64.** Cap in flange for constant velocity joint is pierced with screwdriver and pried out. Note position of lock plate (part 8 in Fig. 63).

2. Remove lock ring (11) with angled circlip pliers and pry off joint flanges (10) with two levers, as shown in Fig. 65.

© 1972 VWoA—826

**Fig. 65.** Two levers are used to pry off the differential side gear shaft.

3. Remove screws (9) on lock plates (8) for adjusting rings (4) and take off lock plates.

**NOTE ——**
If you are not re-adjusting the differential, you will need reference points for re-installing the bearing rings. Either mark the rings for location on the transmission case or, using the flat measuring surface, carefully measure the depth of installation in the case and note the values for later use.

4. Screw out and remove bearing rings (4), Fig. 66.

© 1972 VWoA—827

**Fig. 66.** Star-shaped socket is used to screw out bearing ring.

6

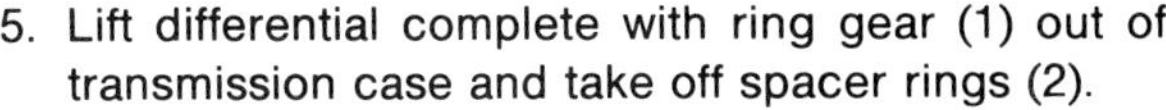

5. Lift differential complete with ring gear (1) out of transmission case and take off spacer rings (2).

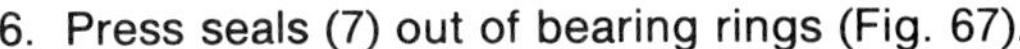

6. Press seals (7) out of bearing rings (Fig. 67).

© 1972 VWoA—828

**Fig. 67.** Seals are pressed out of bearing rings with set-up shown here.

7. Press the roller bearing outer races (6) out of the bearing rings (4) and take off O-rings (5), as in Fig. 68.

**Fig. 68.** Outer race of roller bearing is pressed out of bearing ring with this set-up.

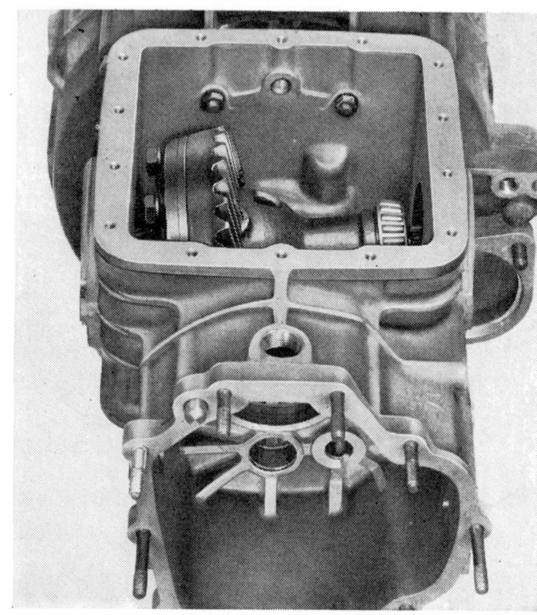



**Fig. 69.** Differential with ring gear goes into transmission case as shown here. View is from front of transmission case.

**To install:**

1. Check tapered roller bearing, spacer rings, seals, O-rings and differential. Replace worn or damaged parts.
2. Insert differential with ring gear into transmission, as in Fig. 69.

**NOTE ——**
On differential repairs that require re-adjustment of the roller bearings, you must screw in the left bearing ring without a seal. (See **22.2. Adjusting Ring Gear**.)

3. Install transmission and tighten retaining ring to specifications.
4. Press the outer rings of tapered roller bearings (6) all the way into bearing ring.
5. Press in seal (7), as in Fig. 70. Install new O-rings.
6. Screw bearing rings into transmission case as marked in step 3 of removal procedure. Be sure to set them according to scribed mark or measured depth of insertion.

**Fig. 70.** Seal is pressed in place with set-up shown here.

**NOTE —**
Coat thread of bearing rings with lithium grease containing $MoS_2$ (Molybdenum disulfide) additive.

7. Coat surfaces of bearing rings and housing with preservative to prevent corrosion on measuring surfaces. Fig. 71 shows the parts.

**Fig. 71.** Bearing ring and housing are coated with preservative to prevent corrosion.

8. Insert both lock plates and attach with two screws (9) each. Fig. 72 shows plate and screws in place.

**Fig. 72.** Lock plate is attached with two Phillips head screws.

9. Insert spacer rings (2), slide on joint flanges (10) and install new circlips.

**NOTE —**
If necessary, you could use the device shown in Fig. 73 with a stud to lift the side gear while simultaneously pressing down the joint flange. This set-up compresses the spacer ring until the circlip snaps into place.

**Fig. 73.** Bracket is applied as shown here to press down flange and spacer ring to allow correct installation of lock ring (circlip).

10. Drive in new end caps (12), as in Fig. 74.

**Fig. 74.** Special installing sleeve is used to drive new end caps into flanges.

**NOTE —**
For disassembly and assembly of the transmission case and adjustment of axial play, see the sections on the double-joint axle in **TRANSMISSION AND REAR AXLE**.

## 14. REMOVING AND INSTALLING TRANSMISSION GEARS

The gear trains and operating parts for the drive ranges **L**, **1** and **2** of the Automatic Stick Shift correspond in function to 1st, 2nd and 3rd gears in the standard transmission.

In the following instructions the parts call-out numbers refer to the designations in Fig. 75.

> **NOTE —**
> Installation of an anti-rotation shoulder bearing of the new type requires the following procedure for torquing the retaining nut: Torque the pinion retaining nut to 159 ft. lbs. (22 mkg). Because the special C-wrench increases leverage, set the torque wrench to 130 ft. lbs. (18 mkg). The bearing shoulder has notches which bear on notches in the transmission case. The notches prevent rotation of the bearing when the bearing is pressed against the case.

The differential can be left in the transmission case when the transmission gears are removed.

**To remove transmission:**

1. Remove gearshift housing nuts and take off gearshift housing with inner transmission lever (not shown).
2. Remove nuts (14) at gear carrier (12).
3. Take off bolts at transmission cover and remove cover and gasket. Drain fluid (if it has not already been drained).

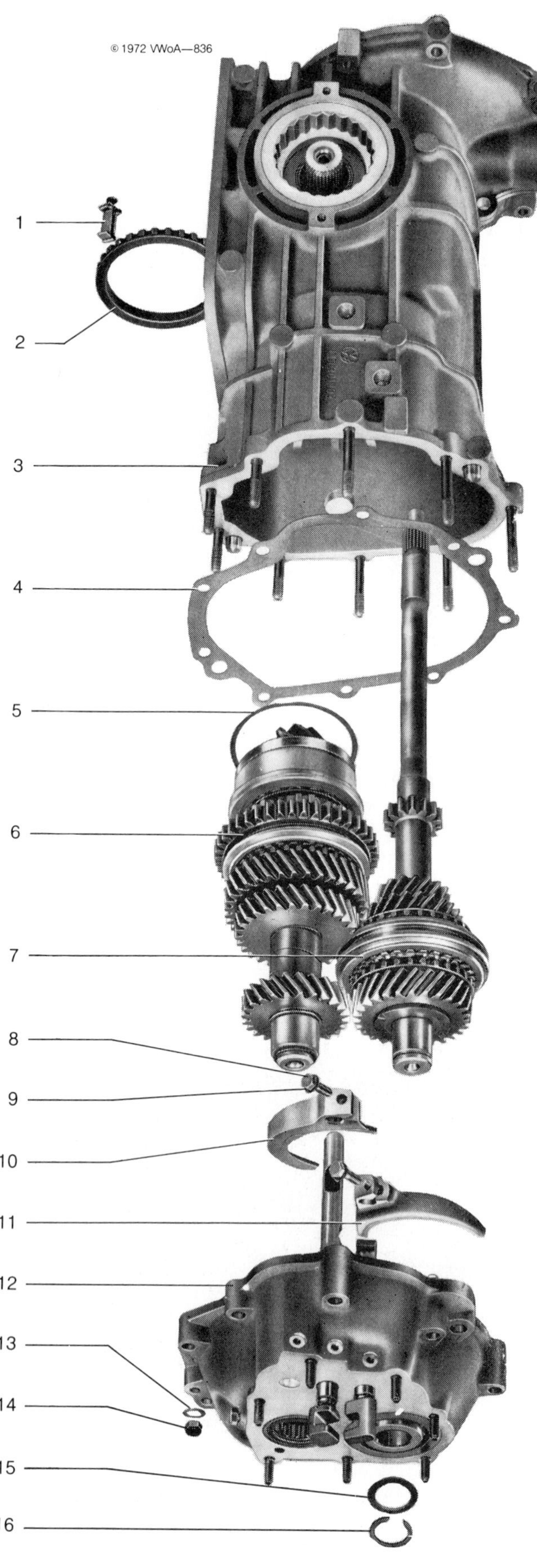


1. Lock
2. Pinion retaining nut
3. Transmission case
4. Gasket/Gear carrier
5. Shim $S_3$
6. Drive pinion
7. Main drive shaft
8. Clamping bolt (2)
9. Spring washer (2)
10. Selector fork, reverse and **1** gear
11. Selector fork, **2** and **3** gear
12. Gear carrier
13. Spring washer (9)
14. Nut (9)
15. Dished washer
16. Lock ring

**Fig. 75.** Transmission gears for Automatic Stick Shift are shown here with transmission case, shift forks and gear carrier. **L**, **1** and **2** range gears are identical to 2nd, 3rd and 4th gears of standard transmission. Lock on your car may be different version of lock shown here (1).

4. Take out lock (1). Using special wrench and breaker bar, loosen retaining nut (2) of double-tapered roller bearing.

**NOTE —**
Lock (1) comes in two versions.

5. With special C-wrench, screw retaining nut (2) away from bearing until nut just touches ring gear. Fig. 76 shows operation.

© 1972 VWoA—837

**Fig. 76.** Retaining nut is screwed off bearing with special C-wrench shown here.

6. With removal tool, press transmission out until retaining nut again is in contact with case. See Fig. 77.

© 1972 VWoA—838

**Fig. 77.** Hinged lever is used to press transmission out of case. Alternately, retaining nut is loosened and lever worked until nut is completely off bearing.

7. Alternately loosen retaining nut and press out transmission until nut clears bearing completely. Press out bearing, along with transmission carrier, and separate from case. Note the thickness and number of shims $S_3$ for drive pinion adjustment. Old shims must be used again if parts affecting drive pinion adjustment are re-installed.

8. Clamp gear carrier (12) in vise or install it in special appliance for adjusting selector fork. Remove clamping bolts (8) and take out selector fork (10) for 1st and reverse gear.

9. Pull selector shaft for **2** and **3** gear out of selector fork (11).

***WARNING —***
*The dished washer (15) is under tension. Be careful when removing it.*

10. Use circlip pliers to remove lock ring or circlip (16) from main drive shaft (7) as shown in Fig. 78. Take off dished washer (15).

***CAUTION —***
*Guide both shafts carefully to prevent damaging the splines. Be sure that selector forks do not jam.*

6

© 1972 VWoA—839

**Fig. 78.** Circlip (lock ring) is removed from main drive shaft with special pliers while gear carrier is held in fixture.

11. Take gear carrier out of vise and place in a suitable holding device.

12. With carrier and holding device in press set-up as shown in Fig. 79 (below) press out the main drive shaft.

© 1972 VWoA—840

**Fig. 79.** Gear carrier rests on special support while main drive shaft is pressed out.

**To install:**

1. Check dished washer, selector shaft, pinion and main drive shaft (complete) and gear carrier. Overhaul or replace worn or damaged parts.
2. Engage selector fork for **2** and **3** gears in the operating sleeves.
3. Position pinion (6) and main drive shaft on plate under press as in Fig. 80.

***CAUTION*** —
*Guide main drive shaft and pinion carefully in order to avoid damaging the splines. Make sure that selector fork for **2** and **3** gears is in correct position.*

4. Carefully place gear carrier over standing shaft and press on main drive shaft.
5. Slide spring washer (15) on main drive shaft. Put new lock ring (16) on shaft and press it down until it snaps into groove. Fig. 81 shows set-up.

© 1972 VWoA—841

**Fig. 80.** Main drive shaft (at right) rests on special tube in engagement with pinion (at left) for installation in gear carrier.

© 1972 VWoA—842

**Fig. 81.** Press set-up for installation of pinion and main drive shaft in gear carrier is shown here.

6. With joint or water pump pliers squeeze lock ring all around until it bottoms in groove. Fig. 82 shows this step.

**Fig. 82.** Circlip (lock ring) is squeezed all around with special pliers until it snaps into groove at end of main drive shaft.

7. Install and adjust selector forks (see **18. Adjusting Selector Forks**).
8. Attach assembled gear carrier with spacer and gasket to transmission case. Use a rubber mallet to drive in the pinion and main drive shaft. If transmission has a locating screw for the double-tapered roller bearing, align the opening in the bearing outer race with hole in housing.

**NOTE**
Since the differential is in place, you must install the retaining nut of the double-tapered roller bearing while you are driving in the carrier case.

9. Tighten retaining nut to 101 to 115 ft. lbs. (14 to 16 mkg). If the special C-wrench is used with the torque wrench, tighten only to 87 ft. lbs. (12 mkg).
10. Tighten gear carrier nuts diagonally. Insert retaining nut lock plate and tighten screws.

**NOTE**
On transmissions with locating screw, insert locking clip and align for correct installation of screw (Fig. 83). When driving transmission in, see that opening in bearing outer race coincides with hole in transmission case.

**Fig. 83.** Lock plate for retaining nut can be seen under screw head at top of nut.

11. Attach gearshift housing with transmission shift lever and tighten nuts.
12. Install transmission cover with gasket and tighten bolts diagonally.

6

## 15. DISASSEMBLING AND ASSEMBLING MAIN DRIVE SHAFT

Fig. 84 gives an exploded view of the main drive shaft assembly. Call-out numbers from the figure are used in the following instructions to identify the various parts. Study of the figure will quickly reveal the similarities between the transmissions for the Automatic Stick Shift and standard models.

1. Main drive shaft
2. Lock ring
3. Dished washer
4. Gear—**3***
5. Gear—**2**
6. Synchronizing ring **2** and **3** gear
7. Woodruff key
8. Clutch gear (complete)
9. Thrust washer **3** gear
10. Needle cage **2** and **3** gear (2)
11. Inner race/needle bearing **3** gear

**Fig. 84.** Main drive shaft for Automatic Stick Shift is shown in exploded view.

7 1 5 10 6 8 6 4 10 9 11 3 2



***Replacement parts for 1 and 2 drive range (3rd and 4th gear) may differ from original parts.**

**To disassemble:**

1. Remove lock ring (2), dished washer (3), thrust washer (9), **3** gear (4), needle bearing (10) and synchronizer stop-ring (6).
2. Press off inner race of needle bearing (11), clutch gear with operating sleeve (8) and **2** gear (5). Fig. 85 shows set-up.

© 1972 VWoA—846

**Fig. 85.** Special pilot and plate are used when thrust washer, **3** gear, needle bearing and stop ring are pressed off main drive shaft.

3. Take out Woodruff key (7).
4. Disassemble synchronizer hub.

**To assemble:**

1. Check gears (with particular attention to clutch gear teeth), operating sleeve thrust washer, main drive shaft, clutch gear, needle bearings, bearing races and Woodruff key. Replace any worn or damaged parts.
2. Press synchronizing rings into gears and measure clearance with a feeler gauge. See Fig. 86.

© 1972 VWoA—847

**Fig. 86.** Clearance "a" between synchronizer stop ring (above) and gear (below) is measured with feeler gauge. When assembly is installed, "a" should be 0.043 inch (1.1 mm). The wear limit is 0.024 inch (0.6 mm).

3. Install **2** gear with needle bearing and synchronizer stop ring.
4. Install Woodruff key.
5. Assemble clutch gear for **2** and **3** gears. Note matching mark (indicated by arrow in Fig. 87).

© 1972 VWoA—848

**Fig. 87.** Matching mark for assembly of clutch gear for **2** and **3** gears is indicated by black arrow.

**NOTE —**
Operating sleeve and clutch gear are matched. Replace them in pairs only.

6. Assemble springs offset from each other by 120 degrees, as shown in Fig. 88. The angled ends of springs must engage over the clutch keys.

© 1972 VWoA—849

**Fig. 88.** Angled ends of clutch gear springs must engage over clutch keys (shift plates). Springs are installed offset from each other by 120 degrees.

7. Press assembled clutch gear into position on shaft. Groove on operating sleeve must point toward **3** gear. This groove is indicated by arrow in Fig. 89.

**Fig. 89.** Groove 1 mm deep (indicated by black arrow) on operating sleeve must be toward **3** gear and chamfer on side of clutch gear hub toward **2** gear when clutch gear is assembled for installation on main drive shaft.

8. Heat inner race of needle bearing for **3** gear to approximately 212 degrees F (100 degrees C). Slide heated race on shaft and apply force of 3 tons to press it home.
9. Install needle bearing, synchronizer stop ring and thrust washer for **3** gear.

## 16. DISASSEMBLING AND ASSEMBLING DRIVE PINION

Fig. 90 gives an exploded view of the drive pinion assembly. The call-out numbers also appear in the following instructions to help you to visualize the repair procedures. The similarities in drive pinion for Automatic Stick Shift and standard models will be apparent when you study the figure.

**To disassemble pinion:**

1. While firmly holding down **3** gear, remove circlip (16) with pliers.
2. Using press set-up shown in Fig. 91, press off **3** gear (13) and needle bearing inner race (15).

**Fig. 91.** **3** gear and inner race of needle bearing are pressed off pinion together if inner race is tight.

3. Take off spacer spring (14). With pliers, remove circlip (12) which limits **2** gear axial play.
4. Take off **2** gear, **1** gear (10) with synchronizer ring

6

1. Pinion*
2. Double-tapered roller bearing**
3. Round nut
4. Shim
5. Clutch gear (assembly)
6. Clutch key (not shown)
7. Key spring (not shown)
8. Operating sleeve (not shown)
9. Synchronizing ring (**1** gear)
10. **1** gear
11. **2** gear
12. Circlip
13. **3** gear
14. Spacer spring
15. Needle bearing inner race
16. Circlip
17. Shim $S_3$ (pinion adjustment)
18. Needle bearing (**1** and **2** gear)

**Fig. 90.** Drive pinion for Automatic Stick Shift is shown here in exploded view.

***Replacement parts for gear, pinion gear shaft and ring gear set may differ from the originals.**
****Replacement part for this bearing may be of the new anti-rotation shoulder type, which also requires new shims and transmission case.**

(9), needle bearing (18) for **1** gear, clutch gear (5) with operating sleeve and shim (4).

5. In special appliance remove round nut (3).
6. Press double-tapered roller bearing (2) off pinion (1). Fig. 92 shows press set-up.

**Fig. 92.** Double-tapered roller bearing is pressed off pinion with set-up shown here.

7. Remove operating sleeve, clutch keys (shift plates) and springs from synchronizer hub.

**To assemble:**

1. Check double-tapered roller bearing, needle bearing and races, gears, clutch keys and clutch gear. Replace worn or damaged parts.
2. Check synchronizer teeth on gear, synchronizer ring and operating sleeve.
3. Press synchronizer ring over cones on gear and measure clearance with feeler gauge, Fig. 93.

**Fig. 93.** Synchronizer stop ring (above) is pressed on cone of **1** gear (below) to leave clearance ("a") of 0.043 inch (1.1 mm). Wear limit for "a" is 0.024 inch (0.6 mm).

***CAUTION*** —
*When replacing gears, note that **2** and **3** gears may be replaced only in pairs.*

4. Heat inner races of double-tapered roller bearing to about 212 degrees F (100 degrees C) and install bearing on pinion. The lettering on the inner races should line up when the races are in place on the pinion. When the races have cooled to room temperature, apply a force of 3 tons on the press to seat them fully. Fig. 94 shows the press set-up.

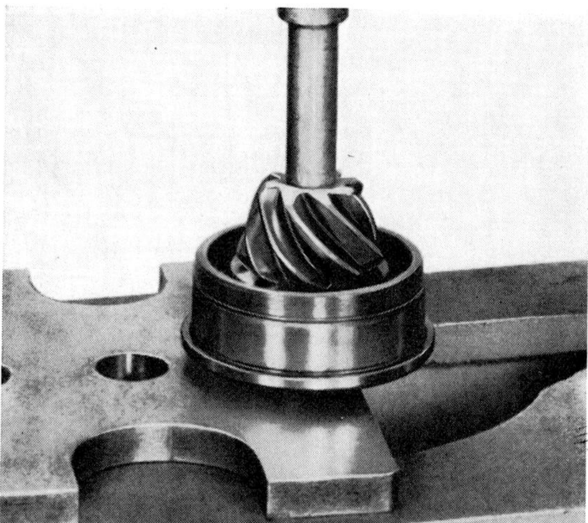



**Fig. 94.** Inner race of double-tapered roller bearing is heated to 212 degrees F (100 C) before bearing is pressed on pinion in set-up shown here.

5. Set up pinion in special holding device with knurled knob. This appliance holds the pinion while you turn a new round nut on. Use a long socket and turn the nut toward the pinion gear. Fig. 95 illustrates the set-up.

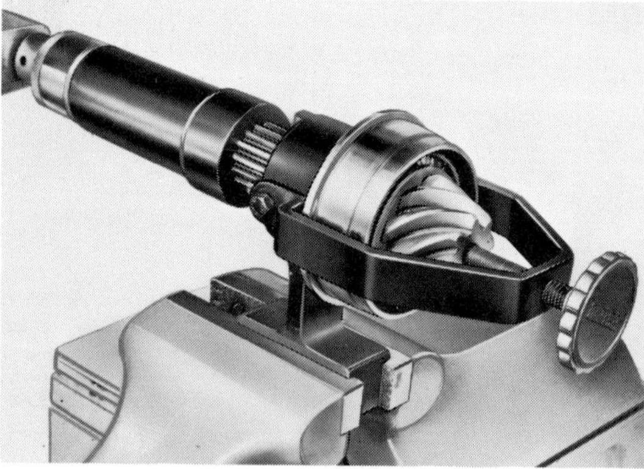



**Fig. 95.** New round nut is screwed on drive pinion from left while pinion is held in special appliance shown here.

6. Check turning torque of double-tapered roller bearing with special torque wrench.
   Specified values are:

| | |
|---|---|
| New bearing | 5.16 to 18.06 in.lb. (6 to 21 cmkg) |
| Used bearing (after at least 30 miles on road) | 2.58 to 6.02 in.lb. (3 to 7 cmkg) |

**NOTE —**
Do not proceed to step 7 until you have performed step 6.

7. Using blunt chisel, peen locking shoulder of round nut into pinion splines at three places (120 degrees apart). Be careful not to crack or burr shoulder while peening. See Fig. 96.

**Fig. 96.** Locking shoulder of round nut is peened into pinion splines at three places with blunt chisel. Indentation of one lock is visible here.

8. The axial setting of the drive pinion assembly requires that the thickness of the round nut shim be determined by measurement and a simple calculation. (The round nut is shown at (3) and the shim at (4) in Fig. 90.) The axial setting (gear tooth alignment) of the clutch gear and **1** gear must be from 1.74 to 1.75 inches (44.40 to 44.50 mm). As illustrated in Fig. 97, this measurement (shim thickness "x") is taken from the bearing contact shoulder on the pinion to the upper edge of shim.

   a. Place pinion on plate and use depth gauge to measure from end of pinion gear to plate to find "a", as at left, top of Fig. 97.
   b. Measure from end of pinion to bearing inner race to find "b", as at center of Fig. 97.
   c. Subtract "b" from "a" to find "x", as at right (bottom) of Fig. 97. (a − b = x)

9. With shim in position measure distance "x". Make sure tolerances have been kept.

6

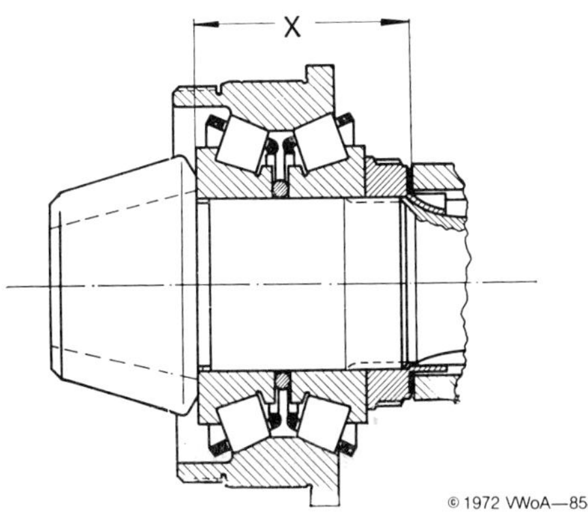




**Fig. 97.** Shim required for round nut is calculated from measurements shown here. Distance from face of pinion to plate (top) is "a". Distance from face of pinion to bearing inner race (center) is "b". With shim installed, distance "x" (bottom) must be 1.74 to 1.75 inches (44.40 to 44.50 mm). "a" minus "b" plus shim equals "x".

**NOTE —**
Shims are available in steps of 0.05 from 0.55 to 0.85 mm.

10. Assemble pinion up to **2** gear and adjust axial play of the gear. Play should be 0.004 to 0.010 inch (0.10 to 0.25 mm) with circlip installed. Measure by inserting feeler gauge between gear and circlip, Fig. 98. Keep to lower limit if possible.

**Fig. 98.** Feeler blade between **2** gear and circlip (lock ring) measures axial play for gear. Play should be 0.004 to 0.010 inch (0.10 to 0.25 mm).

11. Install spacer spring and **3** gear.

12. Heat needle bearing inner race to 212 degrees F (100 degrees C). Press race together with **3** gear on pinion as far as it will go. Fig. 99 shows set-up.

13. Install circlip with pliers.

**Fig. 99.** Inner race of needle bearing, heated to 212 degrees F (100 degrees C) is pressed on pinion with **3** gear in this set-up.

**NOTE —**
If inner race is not tight, first press **3** gear on as far as it will go. Then heat inner race, install and secure with circlip.

## 17. Disassembling and Assembling Gear Carrier

The numbers designating parts in the disassembly procedures are call-outs from Fig. 100.

**Fig. 100.** Gear carrier is shown with selector shafts in exploded view.

1. Plug (2)
2. Plug (3)
3. Ball/gear lock (2)
4. Spring/gear lock (2)
5. Plug
6. Screw/needle bearing
7. Washer (screw/needle bearing)
8. Gear carrier
9. Outer race/needle bearing
10. Ball bearing
11. Selector shaft **1** and **R** gears
12. Interlock plunger for selector shafts
13. Selector shaft **2** and **3** gears

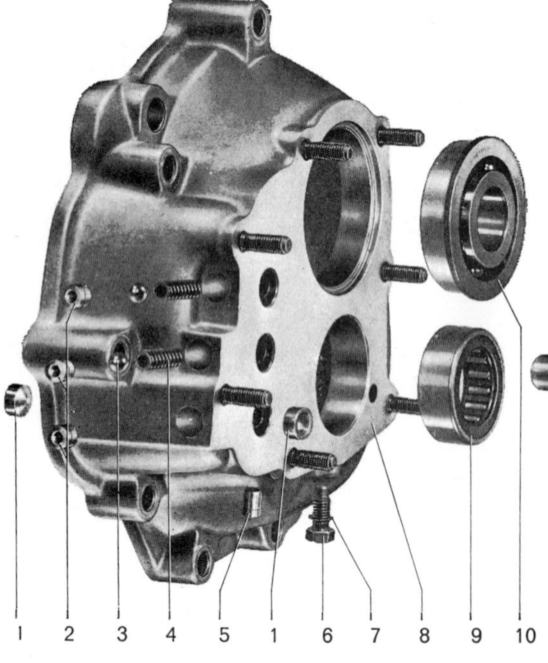

**To disassemble carrier:**

1. Put gear carrier (8) in vise with soft jaw covers, as in Fig. 101.

© 1972 VWoA—862

**Fig. 101.** Carrier is held in vise for removal of selector shafts, detent balls and interlock plunger.

2. Remove selector shafts (11) and (13). Take out detent balls (3) and interlock plunger (12).
3. Pull out plugs (2) for detent springs (4). It will be necessary to cut an M 6 thread in the plugs and remove by bolt as in Fig. 102.

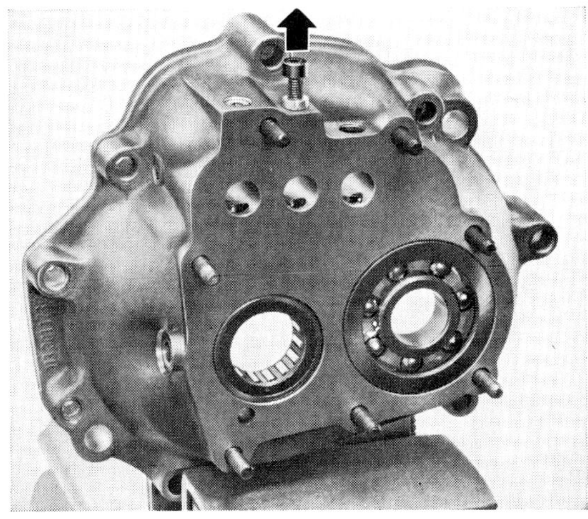

© 1972 VWoA—863

**Fig. 102.** Plug for detent spring is threaded for bolt and removed in direction indicated by black arrow.

4. Remove springs with small screwdriver.
5. Remove screw (6) for needle bearing.



6. Press out needle bearing (9). Fig. 103 shows set-up.

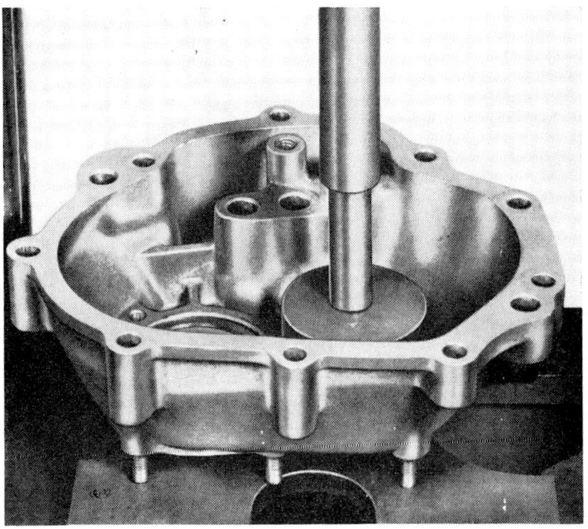

© 1972 VWoA—864

**Fig. 103.** Needle bearing for main drive shaft is pressed out of carrier with this set-up.

7. Press out ball bearing (10), as in Fig. 104.

© 1972 VWoA—865

**Fig. 104.** Ball bearing for drive pinion is pressed out of carrier with this set-up.

**To assemble:**

1. Check bearings, selector shafts, interlock plunger springs and gear carrier. Replace worn or damaged parts.
2. Check shaft detent springs (especially if gear shifting has been difficult). Free length of springs should be 0.9 to 1.0 inch (23 to 25 mm). The force

applied on the selector shaft to overcome the grooves must be no greater than 33 to 44 lbs. (15 to 20 kg).

3. Press in needle bearing as in Fig. 105 and secure with screw.

© 1972 VWoA—866

**Fig. 105.** Carrier rests on support for installation of needle bearing.

4. Press in ball bearing in same way as above.
5. Install springs and drive in plugs.
6. Install selector shafts. After installing **1** shaft, interlock the plunger between shafts before installing **2** shaft.

## 18. ADJUSTING SELECTOR FORKS

Adjustment of the selector forks is aimed at smooth and positive selection of drive ranges. The forks engage with the synchronizer hub grooves and slide them along the shaft. The amount of play allowed is limited.

Adjustment of the selector forks requires special equipment, which includes a support for the gear carrier. There is also a special shift fork setting device. This is a metal plate carrying five studs and with a number of precisely located holes drilled through it. When held in this appliance, the pinion and drive shaft are engaged as they would be in the transmission.

To locate the axial position of the pinion in the appliance, it is necessary to install a shim of the correct thickness $S_3$ for the specific assembly. $S_3$ is on the drive pinion shim that separates the tapered roller bearing from the final drive housing and thus determines the axial location of the pinion in its engagement with the ring gear.

Later on you will see how this shim is used in adjustment of the pinion.

**NOTE —**
A certain length was set for the studs on the shift fork setting appliance in order to eliminate the need for a gasket in the procedure to adjust the selector forks. The set-up compensates for gasket thickness and allows final adjustment of the forks. Some relocation of the studs is possible to allow mounting of the gear carrier.

**To adjust shift forks:**

1. Install gear carrier, pinion with shim and drive shaft on the appliance and secure with four nuts.
2. Screw retaining nut on double-tapered roller bearing and hand tighten with C-wrench.
3. Push selector shaft in **2** and **3** gear fork and loosely install clamp bolt.
4. Install selector fork for **1** and **R** gears and loosely insert clamp bolt. Fig. 106 shows assembly.

© 1972 VWoA—867

**Fig. 106.** Shift fork setting device holds gear carrier for installation of selector fork for **1** and **R** gears.

5. Pull lower selector shaft out all the way (**1** gear and **R**) into the detent groove for **1**. Slide operating sleeve and fork over the synchro teeth until it is against **1** gear. Center fork in operating sleeve groove and tighten the clamp bolt.

***CAUTION —***
*The selector forks must not rub or put pressure on the sides of the groove in the sleeve when in neutral, or after a gear is fully engaged. (There must always be clearance.)*

6. While turning the transmission, select **1, R** and **neutral** several times. Keep checking clearance between fork and sleeve groove in each position. In reverse gear the operating sleeve makes contact with a stop pressed into the hub. If necessary, change selector fork setting until clearance is equal between selector sleeve and gear sleeve and also at the stop in both end positions. Tighten clamp bolt (Fig. 107) to specified torque.

© 1972 VWoA—868

**Fig. 107.** Selector fork for **1** and **R** gears is shown in place on shaft with clamp bolt installed.

7. Move upper selector shaft (for **2** and **3** gears) into detent groove for **3** gear. Then adjust fork as for **1** and **R** gears. Tighten clamp bolt to specified torque.
8. Check interlock mechanism. Gently pull or push both selector rods at the same time. When one gear is engaged, it must not be possible to engage any other gear. The shafts should be interlocked, one against the other.

## 19. DISASSEMBLING AND ASSEMBLING GEARSHIFT HOUSING

When reading the following instructions, look at the exploded view of the gearshift housing in Fig. 108. The numerical designations for parts in the instructions refer to the call-out numbers in the picture.

**Fig. 108.** Gearshift housing is seen here in exploded view.

© 1972 VWoA—869

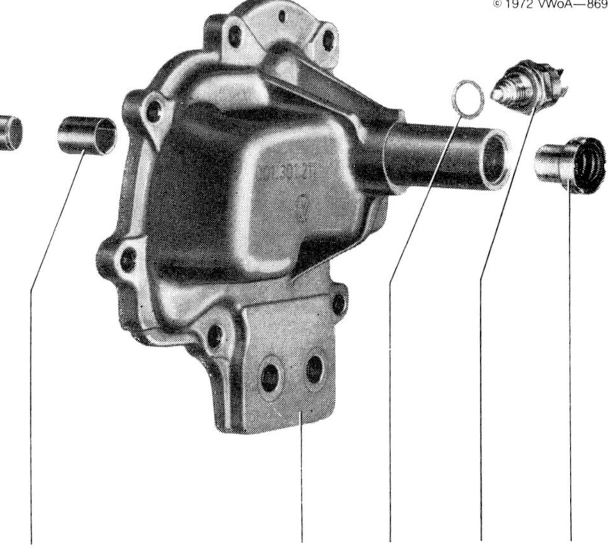


1. Inner selector lever
2. Guide bushing
3. Gearshift housing
4. Seal
5. Neutral safety switch
6. Bushing with seal

**To disassemble case:**

1. Remove bushing and seal (6) with a pair of slip joint pliers, shown in Fig. 109.

6

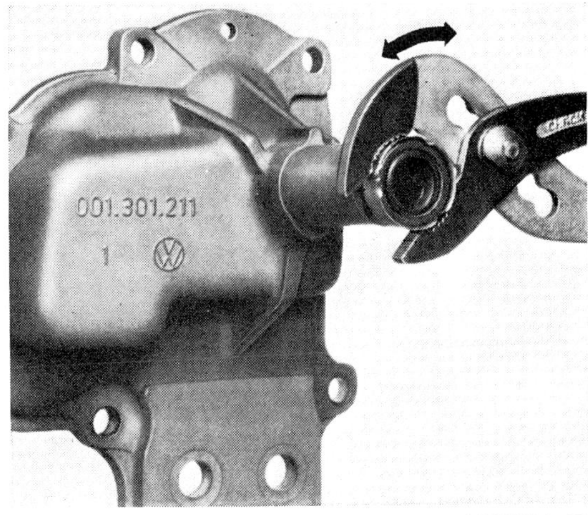


© 1972 VWoA—870

**Fig. 109.** Bushing with seal is removed from gearshift housing with water pump pliers.

2. Pull out inner selector lever (1) and with screwdriver press inner slotted guide bushing (2) together at the slot and pull it out.
3. Screw out neutral safety switch (5) with seal (4).

**To assemble:**

1. Press in new guide bushing, as shown in Fig. 110.

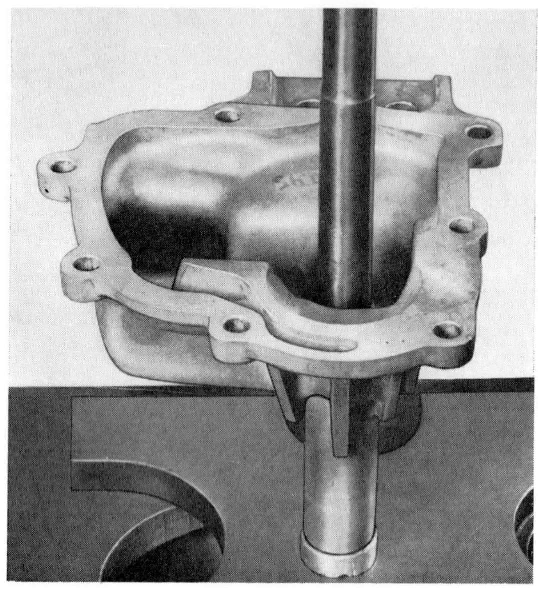

© 1972 VWoA—871

**Fig. 110.** New guide bushing is pressed into gearshift housing with this set-up.

2. Press in bushing with seal. Fig. 111 shows set-up.

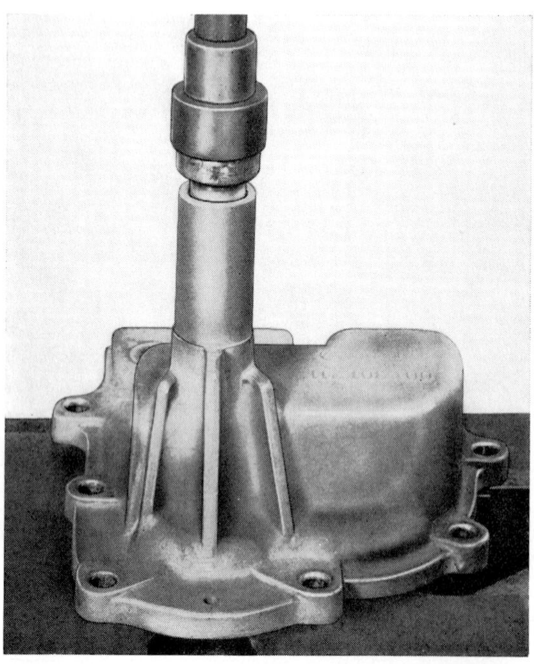

© 1972 VWoA—872

**Fig. 111.** Special punches are used to press bushing with seal into place in gearshift housing.

**NOTE —**
If range selection is difficult, the bushings of the transmission shift lever should be reamed out to 0.591 to 0.592 inch (15.03 to 15.05 mm). Make sure that the seal is not damaged.

3. Install neutral safety switch with seal.

## 20. DISASSEMBLING AND ASSEMBLING TRANSMISSION CASE

An exploded view of the transmission case is given in Fig. 112 (opposite page), and the call-out numbers from the figure are used in the following instructions to help you to visualize the procedures.

**To disassemble case:**

***WARNING —***
*Washer below lock ring (circlip) is under tension. Be careful when removing lock ring.*

1. Remove lock ring (22) for reverse idler gear (26). For this operation compress spring washer (23) with a slotted piece of pipe and a clamp.
2. Drive out reverse gearshift (27) with idler gear (26).
3. Remove lock ring (20) for main drive shaft needle bearing (21) with small screwdriver and drive out bearing, as in Fig. 113.

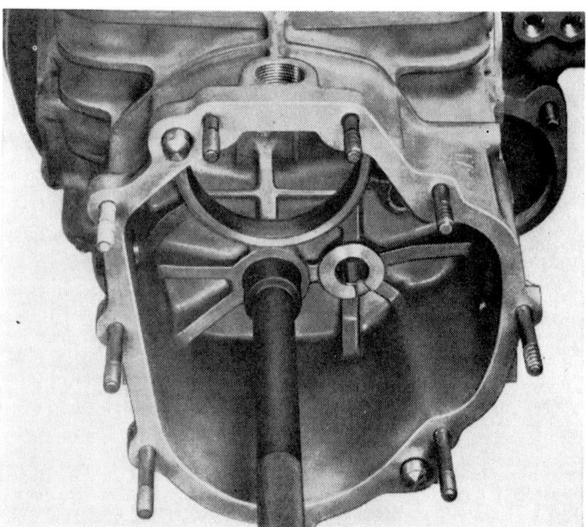

© 1972 VWoA—874

**Fig. 113.** Needle bearing for main drive shaft is driven out of transmission case with drift, as shown here.

**Fig. 112.** Transmission case assembly is shown here in exploded view. Main drive shaft, pinion, differential have been removed.

1. Thrust washer
2. Bearing sleeve
3. Rubber seal (2)
4. Spacer bushing
5. Lock ring
6. Clutch operating shaft
7. Guide sleeve
8. Spring washer
9. Bolt (bearing sleeve)
10. Seal/main drive shaft
11. Transmission case
12. Gasket
13. Cover/oil sump
14. Spring washer (14)
15. Bolt M 7 (14)
16. Seal
17. Oil drain plug
18. Plug
19. Plug/oil filler
20. Lock ring (2)
21. Needle bearing
22. Lock ring
23. Dished washer
24. Thrust washer
25. Needle bearing (2)
26. Idler gear
27. Reverse shaft



***CAUTION—***
*To avoid damaging the case, apply only moderate pressure and do not position tool at lip of transmission case neck.*

4. Pry out main drive shaft seal (10). Work with tool as near top of seal as possible. Once loosened, seal comes out easily.
5. Take lock ring (5) for clutch operating shaft (6) out of groove and screw out bearing sleeve lock screw.
6. Push shaft upward, take off bearing sleeve (2) and then pull shaft down and out.
7. Withdraw lower slotted bushing (7) of operating shaft by pressing slot together with screwdriver.

**To assemble:**

1. Check all components. Replace worn or damaged parts.

***CAUTION—***
*The needle bearing can be damaged when you drive it in unless you rest the drift against the side of the bearing which has lettering on it. The metal is thicker on that side.*

2. Insert one lock ring for needle bearing (Fig. 114) and press in bearing.

6

**Fig. 114.** Lettering on needle bearing marks side with heavier metal. Drift should be held against this side when bearing is driven into place.

3. Insert second lock ring.
4. Drive in thrust washer (24). Then slide needle bearings and idler gear on reverse shaft. Drive assembled reverse shaft into transmission case. Make sure that lug of thrust washer engages with special cut-out in the case.

**NOTE** —
If needle bearings are replaced, make sure that the replacements carry the same color markings.

5. Insert concave washer and new lock ring. With piece of pipe (see step 1 of disassembly procedure) and clamp compress assembly until ring snaps into groove. Then squeeze ring all around with a pair of slip joint pliers.
6. Drive in main drive shaft seal, as in Fig. 115. Drive shaft can be in place for this operation.

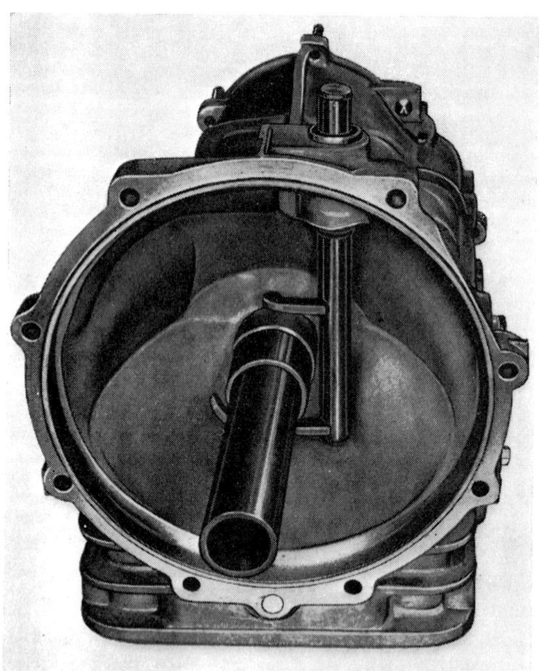



**Fig. 115.** Seal for main drive shaft is driven into transmission case.

7. Drive in lower slotted bushing with drift. Use new bushing.
8. Slide thrust washer and new lock ring as far as possible on reverse shaft and insert shaft from below.
9. Insert lock ring into groove and install bearing sleeve with seals and spacer bushing.
10. Screw in lock bolt for bearing sleeve and install clutch lever.

## 21. Final Drive

The basic requirements for satisfactory operation of the final drive are the same for cars with Automatic Stick Shift and cars with standard transmission. Careful adjustment of ring gear and pinion is essential if the rear axle is to give long service and run silently. For this reason, ring gear and pinion are matched at the factory and run together on special testing machines to check the contact pattern of gear engagement and the quietness of operation.

In the factory mating of pinion and ring gear different degrees of mesh are tried until the position of most quiet running is found. Basically, the adjustment seeks an accommodation between the ideal gear engagement, where the centers of pinion and ring gear would meet, and the practical requirements of manufacturing tolerances. Both pinion and ring gear are restricted to in-and-out movement, as suggested by the black arrows in Fig. 116 (opposite page), and the right combination of the movements must be found for satisfactory adjustment.

## 22. Adjusting Pinion and Ring Gear

In this adjustment the engagement of pinion and ring gear is set first on a special test machine with a master gauge, which establishes a distance $\mathbf{R_o}$ from the center of the ring gear to the face of the drive pinion. This distance is shown in Fig. 116 (opposite page). It measures 2.31 inches (58.70 mm). With the pinion and ring gear in the position shown in the figure, the pinion is moved back and forth along its axis while at the same time the ring gear is lifted until backlash between the two is within the specified tolerance, which is 0.006 to 0.010 inch (0.15 to 0.25 mm). At the adjustment where the quietest running is observed, the distance between center of ring gear and face of pinion will deviate from the standard gauge distance $\mathbf{R_o}$. This deviation, called $\mathbf{r}$, can be from 0.002 to 0.026 inch (0.05 to 0.65 mm). For each set it is stamped, in hundredths of a millimeter, on the ring gear. The adjusted distance for quietest running is called **R**, nominal measurement for the set.

$$\mathbf{R} = \mathbf{R_o} + \mathbf{r}$$

Each gear set carries certain stampings, divided between pinion and ring gear, which give information concerning the fitting of the set. An example of the stampings is given in Fig. 116.

1. The marking "G 358" means a Gleason gear set with ratio of 35/8 teeth.
2. Matching number of gear set.
3. Deviation **r** from the $\mathbf{R_o}$ master gauge used in factory production machines. The deviation is always given in 0.01 mm. For example, "26" means **r** = +0.26 mm (0.010 inch).

$\mathbf{R_o}$ = Length of master gauge $\mathbf{R_o}$ = 2.311 inches (58.70 mm)

**R** = Actual dimension between ring gear centerline and end face of pinion at the quietest running position for this particular gear set.

Usually a gear set needs readjusting only when parts directly affecting the adjustment have been replaced. When the differential housing, a final drive cover or a differential tapered roller bearing has been replaced, it is sufficient ordinarily to reset the ring gear. But both pinion and ring gear must be adjusted if the transmission case or the complete gear set has been replaced. If the double-tapered roller bearing for the pinion is replaced, only the pinion will need re-adjustment. **Table b** summarizes the re-adjustments required by various replacements.

The object of every adjustment is to return the gear set to the quiet running position established at the factory. The basic sequence of operations in adjusting a gear set is:

1. Adjust pinion and check.
2. Adjust the differential tapered roller bearings ring gear.
3. Adjust ring gear backlash and check.

First the pinion must be located by placing shims between the double-tapered roller bearing and the transmission housing. This measurement from ring gear centerline to pinion end face should equal the measurement **R** obtained at the factory.

Next, the ring gear is installed and adjusted to establish a certain preload between the tapered roller bearings, and to have the specified backlash in the engagement with the pinion teeth. The amount of preload is measured by the friction obtained in the tapered roller bearings when the ring gear is rotated. Finally, the ring gear is measured for backlash and checked.

## Table b: Differential Replacements

| Part replaced | Parts to be adjusted | | |
|---|---|---|---|
| | **Pinion** | **Shift forks** | **Ring gear*** |
| Transmission case | X | X | X |
| Adjusting ring | | | X |
| Differential tapered roller bearings | | | X |
| Pinion double tapered roller bearings | X | X | |
| Ring gear and pinion | X | X | X |
| Differential housing | | | X |
| Differential housing cover | | | X |

***Includes adjustment of both differential bearings**

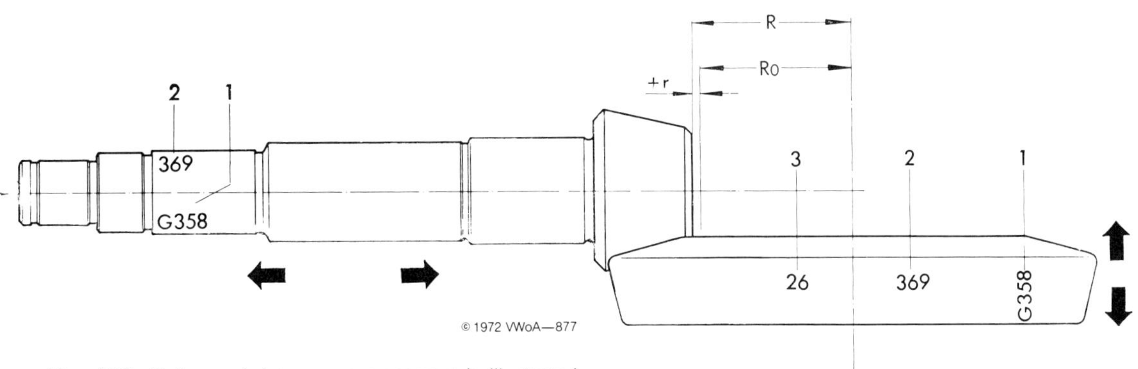


**Fig. 116.** Pinion and ring gear engagement is illustrated here. Horizontal arrows indicate directions of pinion movement. Vertical arrows show directions of ring gear movement. Measurement $\mathbf{R_o}$, from center of ring gear to face of pinion, is set at factory. Measurement **r**, which can be plus or minus, is adjustment to obtain most quiet engagement of gearset. Meanings of other symbols are explained in text.

Standard shims, in steps of 0.10 mm, are available to obtain the adjustments required for the gear set. The location of these shims is shown in Fig. 117, and they are described in **Table c** (opposite page), which summarizes all the measurements and coding pertinent to final drive adjustments.

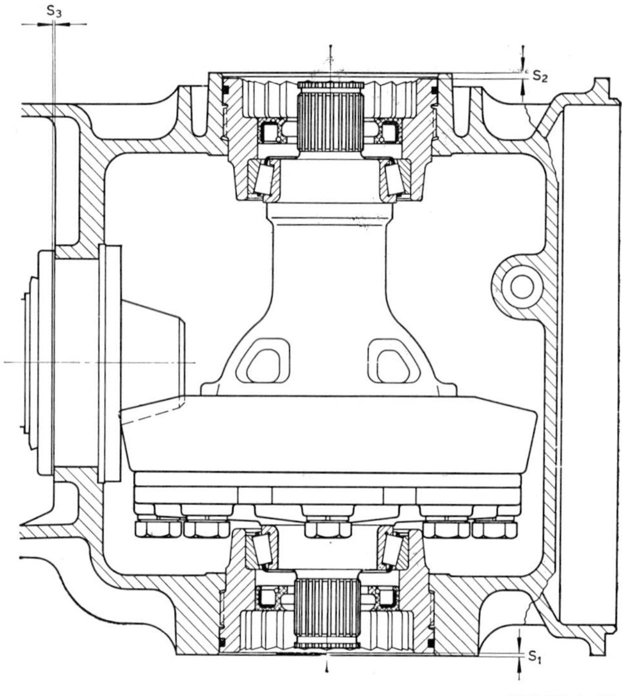




**Fig. 117.** Shims to adjust engagement of pinion and ring gear and the backlash of ring gear are installed at locations indicated here. See text for explanation.

*CAUTION—*
*If you are to obtain satisfactory results from adjustment of ring gear and pinion, you must maintain conditions of maximum cleanliness and exercise maximum care in your work.*

## 22.1 Adjusting Pinion
(see **Table c**)

*CAUTION—*
*The pinion must be adjusted if the transmission case, the double-tapered roller bearing or the gear set itself has been replaced.*

1. Assemble pinion up to the double-tapered roller bearing. Tighten round nut to specified torque but do not lock it.

2. Install pre-assembled pinion in the housing without shim $S_3$. Install retaining ring and tighten to 101 to 115 ft. lb. (14 to 16 mkg). If special C-wrench is used with the torque wrench, tighten only to 87 ft. lbs. (12 mkg). Fig. 118 shows special wrench.

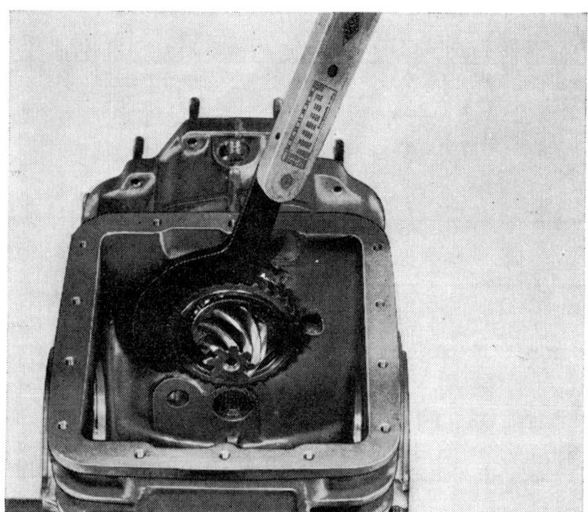



**Fig. 118.** Retaining nut on pinion is tightened with special wrench shown here.

3. Lightly lubricate bearings with hypoid oil. Attach a quarter-inch drive socket to the torque gauge to hold it in place. Turn pinion rapidly in each direction fifteen or twenty turns and take torque reading while continuing to turn. Fig. 119 shows arrangement.

**Fig. 119.** Torque gauge is used in this set-up to turn pinion for check of the turning torque of tapered roller bearing.

## Table c. Explanation of Symbols and Measurements

| Symbol | Reference | Measurement |
|---|---|---|
| $S_1$ | Screw-in depth of ring (ring gear end) | 0.01 mm |
| $S_2$ | Screw-in depth of ring (opposite end) | 0.01 mm |
| $S_3$ | Shims between double-tapered roller bearing and housing | See table of thickness |
| **r** | Deviation from $R_o$ marked on ring gear | 0.002-0.026 inch (0.05-0.65 mm) |
| **$R_o$** | Length of master gauge on special test machine | $R_o$=2.31 inches (58.70 mm) |
| **R** | Position of pinion in relation to ring gear at quietest running point (nominal measurement) | $R = R_o + r$ |
| $Sv_o$ | Backlash | 0.01 mm |
| $Sv_o$ average | Average backlash (average of $Sv_o$) | 0.01 mm |
| e | Difference between zero setting on mandrel and actual dimension of pinion without shims | from 0.004 to 0.020 inch (0.10 to 0.50 mm) |
| $S_1$ | Axial movement (change necessary) of ring gear to the specified average backlash (correction value) | 0.01 mm |
| w | Correction factor for individual gear set | |
| h | Ring gear lift from no-play position with pinion of individual gear set | 0.01 mm |
| Effective screw in depths $S/S_1$ and $S_2$ | Measurement from transmission case to bearing ring | 0.01 mm |
| G 358 | Gear set G+Gleason 358, ratio of 35:8 | |
| K 835 | Gear set K=Klingelnberg 835, ratio of 35:8 | - |

6

**NOTE —**
You need to check the turning torque only on new bearings, but make sure that used bearings have no axial play.

Use hypoid oil only to lubricate bearings when assembling. If bearings are dry or lubricated with some other lubricant, the test results will be inaccurate.

4. Insert dial indicator of 0.118 inch (3 mm) range with 0.708 inch (18 mm) extension in special measuring mandrel and zero indicator on setting block with preload of 0.040 inch (1 mm). Fig. 120 shows indicator in mandrel.

5. Screw in left adjusting ring (ring gear side) with special tool to bring ring 0.040 inch (1 mm) below surface of housing.

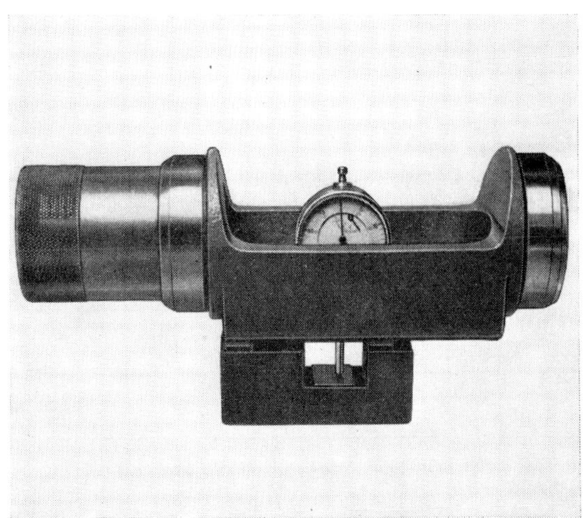



**Fig. 120.** Measuring mandrel, with dial gauge installed and zeroed on setting block, is used in pinion adjustment. See text.

6. Insert mandrel through hole for right-hand adjusting ring, as in Fig. 121. Screw in adjusting ring with special tool until the mandrel can just be turned by hand.

**Fig. 121.** Position of mandrel in differential housing for adjustment of pinion is shown here. Note that end of mandrel protrudes from opening for adjusting ring on right side (lower side in picture) of differential housing.

7. Swing dial gauge pin onto end of pinion and find highest point. Read off measurement and record as **e,** taking into account the 0.040 inch (1 mm) preload on gauge.

**NOTE —**
For accurate results, all surfaces must be spotlessly clean.

8. Read off deviation **r** on ring gear and work out thickness of shim $S_3$.
9. Swing mandrel slightly on its two pivots. Remove retaining ring with special wrench and press pinion out of housing.
10. Push selected and measured shims $S_3$ over double-tapered roller bearing. Drive in pinion again and tighten retaining ring to correct torque.
11. Check that dial gauge in mandrel is zeroed with setting block for a preload of 0.040 inch (1 mm) and correct setting if necessary.
12. Swing mandrel to bring gauge pin onto pinion end-face and find highest point. Read gauge but take preload 0.040 inch (1 mm) into account.
13. Remove pinion and recheck reading.

**NOTE —**
If shims $S_3$ have been selected correctly, the reading should be within ± 0.0016 inch (0.04 mm) of the deviation **r** marked on pinion.

From the foregoing procedures and measurements we derive a simple formula:

$$S_3 = \mathbf{e} + \mathbf{r}$$

## Table d: Shims for Final Drive Adjustment

| Shims Number | Part Number | Thickness (mm) |
|---|---|---|
| 1 | 002 311 391 | 0.15 |
| 2 | 002 311 392 | 0.20 |
| 3 | 002 311 393 | 0.30 |
| 4 | 002 311 394 | 0.40 |
| 5 | 002 311 395 | 0.50 |
| 6 | 002 311 396 | 0.60 |
| 7 | 002 311 397 | 0.70 |
| 8 | 002 311 398 | 0.80 |
| 9 | 002 311 399 | 0.90 |
| **$S_3$ nominal dimension ranges with appropriate shims** | | |
| **$S_3$ nominal range** | **$S_3$ actual** | **Shim numbers** |
| 0.275-0.325 | 0.30 | 3 |
| 0.325-0.375 | 0.35 | 1 + 2 |
| 0.375-0.425 | 0.40 | 4 |
| 0.425-0.475 | 0.45 | 1 + 3 |
| 0.475-0.525 | 0.50 | 5 |
| 0.525-0.575 | 0.55 | 1 + 4 |
| 0.575-0.625 | 0.60 | 6 |
| 0.625-0.675 | 0.65 | 1 + 5 |
| 0.675-0.725 | 0.70 | 7 |
| 0.725-0.775 | 0.75 | 1 + 6 |
| 0.775-0.825 | 0.80 | 8 |
| 0.825-0.875 | 0.85 | 1 + 7 |
| 0.875-0.925 | 0.90 | 9 |
| 0.925-0.975 | 0.95 | 1 + 8 |

Example (see required values given on **Table d**)

1. Actual dimension/setting block/mandrel — 58.70 mm
   −measured reading — −0.48 mm
   Actual dimension/pinion (without shims) — 58.22 mm

***CAUTION —***
*In the following example, as in all other examples in this Manual, the values given are for illustration only. Never use any value taken from an example as a setting for any part in your car. These hypothetical values are intended only to make the examples instructive and realistic, not to supply specifications for adjustments or repairs.*

| | |
|---|---|
| 2. Design dimension $R_o$ | 58.70 mm |
| +deviation **r** | |
| (marked on ring gear) | +0.18 mm |
| Nominal pinion dimension **R** | |
| (for quietest running) $R_o + r$ | 58.88 mm |

| | |
|---|---|
| 3. Nominal pinion dimension **R** | 58.88 mm |
| −actual pinion dimension | |
| (in housing without shims) | −58.22 mm |
| Required thickness of shims $S_3$ | 0.66 mm |

If the $S_3$ measurement exceeds the actual shim dimension, use the next thicker shim. Measure shims carefully at several points with a micrometer and check them for burrs or damage. Use only shims in perfect condition.

**Table d** lists shims available as replacement parts.

## 22.2 Adjusting Ring Gear
(see **Table c**)

Once the pinion has been properly located, the ring gear must be adjusted relative to it. (See Fig. 122.) Ring gear axial play is determined by the two adjusting rings which move the differential (ring gear) as a unit from side to side. We have to find axial play and turning torque.

The ring gear needs adjusting only if parts directly affecting ring gear and tapered roller bearing settings are replaced. These parts are: transmission case, differential housing, differential housing cover, tapered roller bearings, adjusting rings and gear set.

When repairing the differential, always re-adjust bearings that have been in use. If, however, the bearings show any signs of axial or radial play, replace them.

**To adjust:**

1. Install differential in transmission case complete with attached ring gear.
2. Press oil seal out of bearing ring on opposite side of ring gear. Press outer races of tapered roller bearings into adjusting rings, forcing them into firm contact with shoulder. Attach dial gauge to measuring bar with an 0.118 inch (3 mm) preload. Zero the gauge.
3. Screw in ring on ring gear side to bring outer edge 0.006 inch (0.15 mm) below measuring surface on the case.
4. Screw in other ring until differential is supported firmly but without preload.
5. Attach sleeve from torque gauge on ring gear side. Tighten nut and install torque gauge with a 10 mm

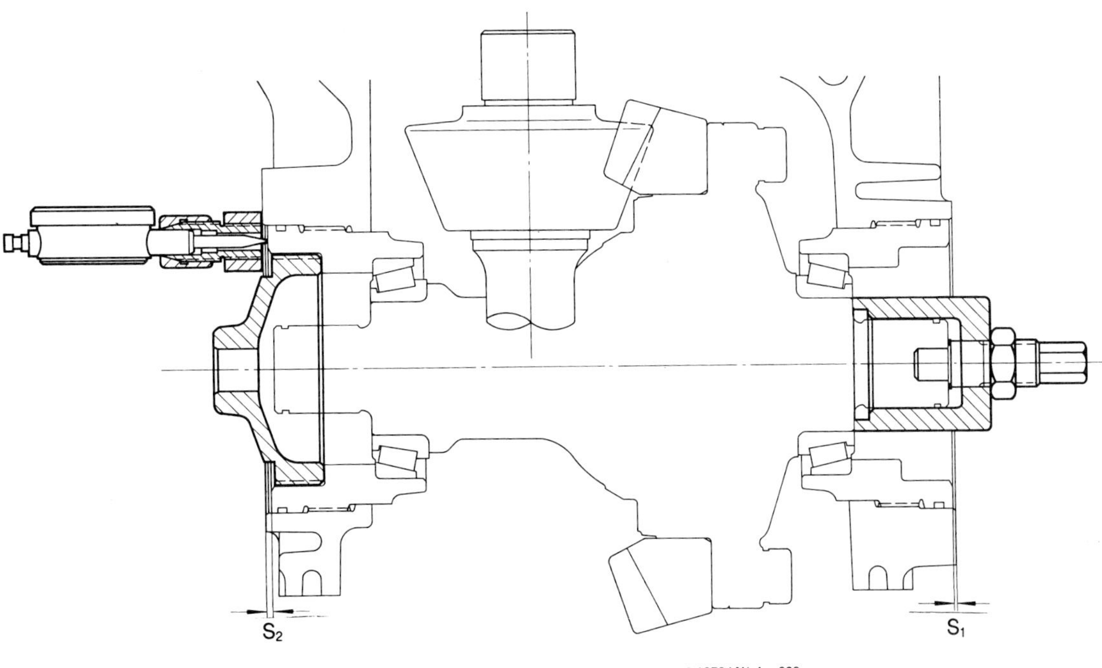


**Fig. 122.** Adjusting ring screw-in depths that determine ring gear position. (Final drive shown is not for a car covered by this Manual, but the adjustments are the same as those for the Automatic Stick Shift final drive.) $S_1$ is the screw-in depth of the adjusting ring on the ring gear side of the differential; $S_2$ is the screw-in depth of the adjusting ring at the opposite side. A dial indicator is shown in position to measure the $S_2$ screw-in depth.

6

socket. Turn differential in both directions while oiling the tapered roller bearings with hypoid oil. Fig. 123 shows set-up.

© 1972 VWoA—884

**Fig. 123.** Torque gauge is used as shown to turn ring gear while tapered roller bearing is lubricated with hypoid oil.

**NOTE** —
Use hypoid transmission oil only to lubricate tapered roller bearings. If bearings are dry or have been lubricated with other oil, the measurements you make will be incorrect.

6. Slowly increase bearing preload by screwing in the ring (opposite end of ring gear) while turning differential rapidly. Continue until the specified value is reached.
7. Measure depth $S_1$ and $S_2$ of the bearing rings with a bridge as shown in Fig. 124. Note readings.

© 1972 VWoA—885

**Fig. 124.** Bridge with dial gauge is installed as shown to measure depths $S_1$ and $S_2$ of bearing rings. Text gives specifications.

Tapered roller bearing preload should be:

| | |
|---|---|
| New bearing | 15.48 to 18.92 in. lb. (18 to 22 cmkg) |
| Used bearing (after at least 30 miles on road) | 2.58 to 6.02 in. lb. (3 to 7 cmkg) |

8. Install transmission gears and tighten retaining ring to specified torque.

## 22.3 Adjusting Ring Gear Backlash
(see **Table c**)

This adjustment is not undertaken until the drive pinion has been adjusted.

**Procedure:**

1. Attach measuring lever to sleeve, as in Fig. 125.

© 1972 VWoA—886

**Fig. 125.** Special sleeve with lever is installed on differential at ring gear end for adjustment of ring gear backlash.

2. Install dial gauge of 0.118 inch (3 mm) range with 0.236 inch (6 mm) extension pin in gauge holder. Edge of dial gauge clamping bushing must be flush with edge of holder, as in Fig. 126.

© 1972 VWoA—887

**Fig. 126.** Dial gauge with extension pin (0.236 inch) is installed in holder with gauge clamp bushing (black arrow) flush with holder edge.

3. Secure holder to transmission with two bolts as in Fig. 127.

© 1972 VWoA—888

**Fig. 127.** Gauge holder is secured to transmission case with two bolts as shown.

4. Turn ring gear to bring measuring lever just in contact (Fig. 128) with dial gauge pin. Keep turning ring gear carefully until gauge has preload of 0.060 inch (1.5 mm). Do not damage dial gauge.

**NOTE** —
By setting the preload of 0.06 inch (1.5 mm) you are ensuring that the measuring surface of the lever will be on the vertical centerline of the ring, as shown in Fig. 129.

5. Secure pinion with clamping bar in position shown in Fig. 130.

© 1972 VWoA—889

**Fig. 128.** Measuring lever is in contact here with dial gauge pin. Preload of 0.06 inch then is cranked in.

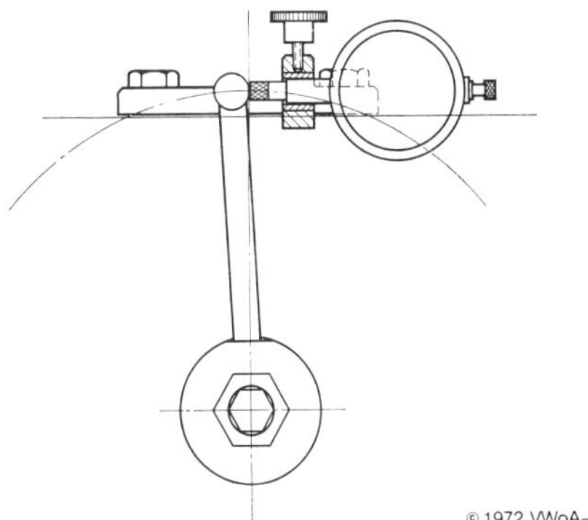

© 1972 VWoA—890

**Fig. 129.** Dial gauge pin makes contact with measuring lever in set-up for backlash adjustment.

6

© 1972 VWoA—891

**Fig. 130.** Clamping bar bolted across front of gear carrier secures pinion position for adjustment.

6. Turn ring gear as far as it will go and set dial gauge to zero. Now turn in opposite direction and read off backlash $Sv_o$. Make note of reading.
7. Loosen lock nut in sleeve, turn ring gear and take three more readings and divide by four to obtain the average.

Finding $Sv_o$ average (example):

***CAUTION —***
*Never use values given in examples as values for setting actual parts in car. They are for illustration only.*

1st reading $Sv_o$ = 0.0208 inch (0.53 mm)
2nd reading $Sv_o$ = 0.0220 inch (0.56 mm)
3rd reading $Sv_o$ = 0.0212 inch (0.54 mm)
4th reading $Sv_o$ = 0.0204 inch (0.52 mm)
Total = 0.084 inch (2.15 mm)

$Sv_o$ average = Total/4
= 0.0844 inch (2.15 mm)/4
= 0.0211 inch (0.537 mm)
= 0.021 inch (0.54 mm)

***CAUTION —***
*If the $Sv_o$ readings you obtain vary by more than 0.002 inch (0.06 mm), from one another, there is something wrong with the ring gear installation or the gear set itself. Recheck assembly operations and replace gear set if necessary. The maximum difference between the backlash readings in the example we have given is 0.04 mm (0.56 to 0.52 mm), and real values must be in this neighborhood.*

8. Find the correction value $S_1$ (axial movement within specified average backlash).

| Gear set | Correction factor W | Lift h |
|---|---|---|
| G 358 | 1.00 | 0.20 |
| K 835 | 1.10 | 0.22 |

Finding $S_1$
$S_1$ = ($Sv_o$ average × W) − h
$S_1$ = (0.54 × 1.00) − 0.20
$S_1$ = 0.34

9. Working with adjusting ring on end opposite ring gear, screw the ring out the distance $S_1$ from the effective screw-in depth $S_2$. Screw in the adjusting ring on the ring gear side by the same amount. The preload requires that the adjusting ring opposite ring gear must be rechecked and relocated after the other ring has been screwed in. Make sure to stay within a tolerance of ± 0.01 mm.
10. Recheck backlash. It should be measured at four points 90 degrees apart and should give:
    $Sv_o$ = 0.006 to 0.010 inch (0.15 to 0.25 mm)

    Individual readings must not differ from one another by more than 0.002 inch (0.05 mm).
11. Apply preservative compound to adjusting rings and measuring surfaces on transmission case. Install locking plates and completely assemble transmission.

## 22.4 Removing Side Cover Oil Seals

The following instructions assume that the transmission has been removed, but the work can be done with the transmission installed. In the latter case, be scrupulous about removing dirt and cleaning surfaces.

**To remove:**

1. Remove six screws holding constant velocity joint at transmission end.
2. Detach constant velocity joint. Move axle out of way.
3. Pry out rubber sealing cap with pliers.
4. Remove circlip.
5. Remove drive flange.
6. Remove two Phillips head screws.
7. Remove lock plate with sealing cap.
8. Remove rubber cushion.
9. Remove drive flange spacer.
10. Pry out old oil seal.

**To install:**

**NOTE —**
Make sure that seal recess is clean. Moisten seal lip with hypoid oil before installing it.

1. Press new seal in place.

**NOTE —**
Make sure that the seal is centered and fully seated.

2. Follow steps of removal procedure but in reverse order. Tighten constant velocity joint screws to specified torque.

## 23. TRANSMISSION TECHNICAL DATA

### I. Transmission Data

| Type/Model* | Transmission type** | Code letter | Final drive ratio | Engine capacity | Remarks | Manufactured from | Manufactured to |
|---|---|---|---|---|---|---|---|
| 113, 114, 115 | 1 | AB | 8:35 | 1300 | Swing axle | Aug. 65 | July 66 |
| 113, 114, 115 | 1 | AC | 8:33 | 1500 | Swing axle | Aug. 66 | July 68 |
| 113, 114, 115 | 1 | AH | 8:33 | 1500 | Double-joint axle | Aug. 68 | July 69 |
| 113, 114, 115 | 2 | BA | 8:35 | 1500 | Automatic Stick Shift | Aug. 68 | July 69 |

***113 Sedan 114 Karmann Ghia 115 Convertible**
****Type of transmission: 1 = Four speed manual transmission**
**2 = Automatic Stick Shift**

### II. Tolerances, Wear Limits and Settings

| Part | Fully synchronized transmission New installation inch (mm) | Fully synchronized transmission Wear limit inch (mm) | Automatic Stick Shift New installation inch (mm) | Automatic Stick Shift Wear limit inch (mm) |
|---|---|---|---|---|
| **A. Manual transmission** | | | | |
| 1. 1st gear . . . . . . . . . . . . . end play | .004-.010* (0.10-0.25)* | — | — | — |
| 2. 3rd gear . . . . . . . . . . . . . end play | .004-.010* (0.10-0.25)* | — | .004-.010* (0.10-0.25)* | — |
| 3. 4th gear . . . . . . . . . . . . . end play | .004-.010 (0.10-0.25) | — | .004-.010 (0.10-0.25) | — |
| 4. Synchromesh units clearance "a" between coupling teeth and synchronizer ring | | | | |
| 1/2 gears . . . . . . . . . . . clearance | .043-.070 (1.1-1.8) | .024 (0.60) | .043-.070 (1.1-1.8) | .024 (0.60) |
| 3/4 gears . . . . . . . . . . . clearance | .039-.070 (1.0-1.8) | .024 (0.60) | .043-.070 (1.1-1.8) | .024 (0.60) |
| 5. Shift fork/operating sleeves for 1/2 and 3/4 gears . . . . . . . . . . . clearance | .004-.012 (0.10-0.30) | — | .004-.012 (0.10-0.30) | — |
| 6. Preload of pinion tapered roller bearing Turning torque . . . . . . . . . . . . new | 5.2-18.3 in.lbs. (6-21 cmkg)** | — | 5.2-18.2 in.lbs. (6-21 cmkg) | — |
| used (more than 30 miles) | 2.6-6.1 in.lbs. (3-7 cmkg)** | — | 2.6-6.1 in.lbs. (3-7 cmkg) | — |
| **B. Drive shaft** | | | | |
| Drive shaft, front (surface for 3rd gear needle bearing) . . . . . . . . . . . . run-out | max. 0.0007 (0.02) | — | — | — |
| **C. Gearbox and gearshift housing** | | | | |
| 1. Preload of transmission case halves or final drive covers on the differential ball bearings . . . . . . . . . . . . . . . . . . | .005 (0.14) | — | — | — |
| 2. Preload of final drive covers on taper roller bearings Turning torque . . . . . . . . . . . . new | 15.7-19.1 in.lbs. (18-22 cmkg) | — | 15.7-19.1 in.lbs. (18-22 cmkg) | — |
| used (more than 30 miles) | 2.6-6.1 in.lbs. (3-7 cmkg) | — | 2.6-6.1 in.lbs. (3-7 cmkg) | — |
| 3. Plastic packing/transmission case/axle tube/tube retainer. . . . . . . clearance | .000-.008 (0.00-0.20) | — | — | — |
| 4. Shift rod shifting pressure | 30-44 lbs. (15-20 kg) | — | 14 lbs. (6.5 kg) | — |
| 5. Gearshift housing bushings . . . . inside diameter | .592-.591 (15.05-15.03) | .600 (15.25) | .592-.591 (15.05-15.03) | .600 (15.25) |
| 6. Inner shift lever. . . . . . . . . . diameter | .590-.588 (15.00-14.96) | .580 (14.75) | .590-.588 (15.00-14.96) | .580 (14.75) |
| 7. Preload of gearshift housing | .0008-.0043 (0.02-0.11) | — | — | — |
| 8. Starter bushing . . . . . inside diameter | .493-.494 (12.55-12.57) | .497 (12.65) | .493-.494 (12.55-12.57) | .497 (12.65) |
| 9. Starter shaft/bushing. . radial clearance | .003-.005 (0.09-0.14) | .010 (0.25) | .003-.005 (0.09-0.14) | .010 (0.25) |

**continued on next page**

6

## II. Tolerances, Wear Limits and Settings (continued)

| Part | Fully synchronized transmission New installation inch (mm) | Fully synchronized transmission Wear limit inch (mm) | Automatic Stick Shift New installation inch (mm) | Automatic Stick Shift Wear limit inch (mm) |
|---|---|---|---|---|
| **D. Final drive** | | | | |
| 1. Play at differential gears with differential housing bolted together . . . . . . axial | .010-.017 (0.25-0.45)*** **** | — | .010-.017 (0.25-0.45)*** | — |
| 2. Play between differential housing and cover/gear shaft radial. . . . . . . . old | .001-.003 (0.03-0.08) | .005 (0.12) | — | — |
| new | .001-.002 (0.025-0.06) | .005 (0.12) | — | — |
| 3. Double tapered roller pinion bearing Preload (turning torque) . new bearings | 5.2-18.2 in.lbs. (6-21 cmkg) | — | 5.2-18.2 in.lbs. (6-21 cmkg) | — |
| used bearings (used more than 30 miles) | 2.6-6.1 in.lbs. (3-7 cmkg) | — | 2.6-6.1 in.lbs. (3-7 cmkg) | — |
| 4. Tapered roller bearings for differential Preload . . . . . . . . . . new bearings | 15.8-19.3 in.lbs. (18-22 cmkg) | — | 15.8-19.3 in.lbs. (18-22 cmkg) | — |
| used bearings (used more than 30 miles) | 2.6-6.1 in.lbs. (3-7 cmkg) | — | 2.6-6.1 in.lbs. (3-7 cmkg) | — |
| 5. Backlash (measured at pitch circle diameter) | .006-.010 (0.15-0.25) | — | .006-.010 (0.15-0.25) | — |
| 6. Rear axle shafts: | | | | |
| a. Flange/fulcrum plates/differential gears (4 parts). . . . . . . clearance | .0015-.009 (0.04-0.24) | .010 (0.25) | — | — |
| b. Flange/differential gears (measured across the convex faces) . clearance | .001-.004 (0.03-0.10) | .008 (0.20) | — | — |
| c. Measured at bearing seat shaft between centers . . . . . run-out | Max. .0019 (0.05) | — | — | — |

***Try to keep to lower limit (0.04 inch/0.10 mm)**
****Valid for all transmissions with double-joint axle**

*****Differentials with spacer sleeve: 0-.005 inch (0-0.14) wear limit: .008 inch (0.20)**
******For all transmissions used together with double-joint rear axle**

## III. Ratios

| Gears | Fully synchronized transmission | Automatic Stick Shift | |
|---|---|---|---|
| | **No. of teeth Ratio** | **No. of teeth Ratio** | |
| 1st gear | 38/10 | 35/17 | |
| 2nd gear | 35/17 | 29/23 | |
| 3rd gear | 30/23 | 24/27 | |
| 4th gear | 24/27 | — | |
| Reverse | 21/14 x 44/17 | 43/14 | |
| Reverse from August 1967 | 20/14 x 43/17 | — | |
| **Ratio** | | | |
| 1st gear | 3.80 | 2.06 | |
| 2nd gear | 2.06 | 1.26 | |
| 3rd gear | 1.26* | 0.89 | |
| 4th gear | 0.89 | — | |
| Reverse | 3.88 | 3.07 | |
| Reverse from August 1967 | 3.62 | — | |
| Torque increase max. | — | 2.1 | |
| **Final drive** | **1300** | **1500** | **Automatic Stick Shift** |
| Klingelnberg | — | 4.125 | 4.375 |
| Gleason | 4.375 | 4.125 | 4.375 |

***Up to Chassis No.: 116 1 021 298 (1.32)**

## IV. Torsion Bar Adjustment (spring plates unloaded)

| Type | Model | Transmission Type* | Installed from Chassis No. | Installed to Chassis No. | Torsion Bar Length in. (mm) | Torsion Bar Diameter in. (mm) | Setting |
|---|---|---|---|---|---|---|---|
| **Without equalizer spring** | | | | | | | |
| 1 | all | 1 | 252 8 668 | 116 1021 297 | 22.4401 (552) | .866 (22) | 17° 30′ ± 50′ |
| **With equalizer spring** | | | | | | | |
| 1 | all | 1 | 117 000 001 | 118 1016 098 | 21.732 (552) | .826 (21) | 20° + 50′ |
| **With double-joint axle** | | | | | | | |
| 1 | 113-117<br>141-143<br>151 | 1 + 2 | 118 000 001** | — | 26.614 (676) | .866 (22) | 20° 30′ + 50′ |

*Transmission types: 1 = Four speed manual, 2 = Automatic Stick Shift
**Vehicles with manual transmission from Chassis No. 119 000 001

## V. Double Joint Shafts—Drive Shafts

| Type | Transmission Type* | Code Number On end of shaft | Code Number Shaft assembly | Length, inch (mm) Shaft dimension "b" | Length, inch (mm) Complete shaft dimension "a" | Part No. Shaft (without joints) |
|---|---|---|---|---|---|---|
| 1 | 1 | 1 | 1 | 16.375 (415.5) | 15.955 (405.3) | 113 501 211 |
| | 2 | 1 | 1 | 16.357 (415.5) | 15.955 (405.3) | 113 501 211 |

*Transmission: 1 = Four speed manual, 2 = Automatic Stick Shift

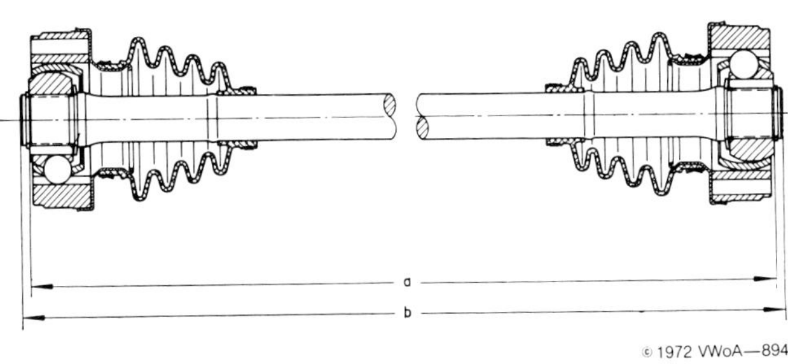


Double Joint Drive Shaft

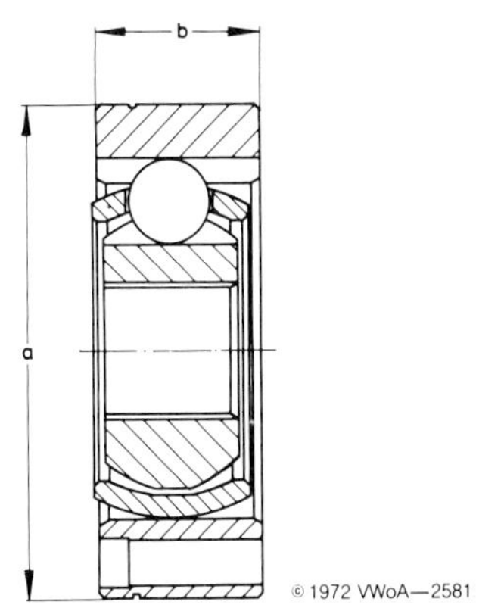


Constant Velocity Joint

## VI. Constant Velocity Joints

| Type | Part No. | Diameter "a" inch (mm) | Width "b" inch (mm) | Ball diameter inch (mm) | Grease per joint | Designation | New installation | Wear limit |
|---|---|---|---|---|---|---|---|---|
| 1 | 113 501 331 | 3.582-.003 (91-0.1) | 1.259-.011 (32-0.3) | .624 (15.88) | 60 grams multi-purpose grease with $MoS_2$ additive | Shaft, run-out | .019 in. (0.5 mm) | — |
| | | | | | | Turning torque in tapered roller bearings (rear wheel bearings) | max. 17.4 in. lb. (20 cmkg) | — |

## VII. Tightening Torques

| Part | Thread | ft/lbs | mkg |
|---|---|---|---|
| **Transmission and Rear Axle (fully synchronized) all Types** | | | |
| Drive pinion round nut | | | |
| 1. For double ball bearing | M 35 x 1.5 | 87 | 12.0 |
| 2. For double tapered roller bearing | M 35 x 1.5 | 144 | 20.0 |
| Pinion bearing retainer bolt | M 10 x 1.5 | 36 | 5.0 |
| Pinion nut | M 22 x 1.5 | 43* | 6.0* |
| Drive shaft nut | M 22 x 1.5 | 43* | 6.0* |
| Reverse lever guide bolt | M 7 x 1 | 14 | 2.0 |
| Selector fork bolt | M 8 x 1.25 | 18 | 2.5 |
| Nuts for gearshift housing | M 7 x 1 | 11 | 1.5 |
| Ring gear bolt | M 10 x 1.5 | 43 | 6.0 |
| Final drive cover nuts | M 8 x 1.25 | 22 | 3.0 |
| Axle tube retainer nuts | M 8 x 1.25 | 14 | 2.0 |
| Rear wheel bearing retainer bolt | M 10 x 1.5 | 43 | 6.0 |
| Oil drain plug | M 24 x 1.5 | 14 | 2.0 |
| Oil filler plug | M 24 x 1.5 | 14 | 2.0 |
| Rear axle shaft nut | M 24 x 1.5 | 217 | 30.0 |
| Transmission carrier on frame | M 18 x 1.5 | 166 | 23.0 |
| **Additional torques for transmission and rear axle (Automatic Stick Shift)** | | | |
| Temperature switch/Selector switch/Starter safety switch | M 14 x 1.5 | 18 | 2.5 |
| Converter to drive plate screws | M 8 x 1.25 | 18 | 2.5 |
| Retaining nut for tapered roller bearing | M 80 x 1 | 115 | 15 |
| Nut for converter housing | M 8 x 1.25 | 14 | 2.0 |
| Bolt for one-way clutch support | M 6 x 1 | 11** | 1.5** |
| Bolt for clutch carrier plate | M 6 x 1 | 11 | 1.5 |
| Bearing lock bolt | M 8 x 1.25 | 7 | 1.0 |
| Clamp bolt for clutch lever | M 8 x 1.25 | 18 | 2.5 |
| Screw for transmission oil pan and lock plate | M 7 x 1.25 | 7 | 1.0 |
| Union for oil pressure line | M 12 x 1.5 | 25 | 3.5 |
| Union for oil return line | M 14 x 1.5 | 25 | 3.5 |
| Screw for drive shaft | M 8 x 1.25 | 25 | 3.5 |
| Bolt in diagonal arm | M 14 x 1.5 | 87 | 12.0 |

***Tighten first to 12 mkg (87 ft. lbs) then back off and finally tighten to 6 mkg (43 ft. lbs)**

****Use new bolts**

**CAUTION: These listings do not include fasteners of Quality Grade or Tensile Class. Always check the Parts List to make sure that a fastener is specified for the use you have in mind.**

## VIII. Table of Correction Factors

| Correction factor $\Delta S_1$ in conjunction with backlash $Sv_o$ | | | | | |
|---|---|---|---|---|---|
| **Backlash** | **Correction factor (G 358)** | **Correction factor (K 835)** | **Backlash** | **Correction factor (G 358)** | **Correction factor (K 835)** |
| 0.20 | 0.00 | 0.00 | 0.70 | 0.50 | 0.55 |
| 0.21 | 0.01 | 0.01 | 0.71 | 0.51 | 0.56 |
| 0.22 | 0.02 | 0.02 | 0.72 | 0.52 | 0.57 |
| 0.23 | 0.03 | 0.03 | 0.73 | 0.53 | 0.58 |
| 0.24 | 0.04 | 0.04 | 0.74 | 0.54 | 0.59 |
| 0.25 | 0.05 | 0.05 | 0.75 | 0.55 | 0.60 |
| 0.26 | 0.06 | 0.07 | 0.76 | 0.56 | 0.62 |
| 0.27 | 0.07 | 0.08 | 0.77 | 0.57 | 0.63 |
| 0.28 | 0.08 | 0.09 | 0.78 | 0.58 | 0.64 |
| 0.29 | 0.09 | 0.10 | 0.79 | 0.59 | 0.65 |
| 0.30 | 0.10 | 0.11 | 0.80 | 0.60 | 0.66 |
| 0.31 | 0.11 | 0.12 | 0.81 | 0.61 | 0.67 |
| 0.32 | 0.12 | 0.13 | 0.82 | 0.62 | 0.68 |
| 0.33 | 0.13 | 0.14 | 0.83 | 0.63 | 0.69 |
| 0.34 | 0.14 | 0.15 | 0.84 | 0.64 | 0.70 |
| 0.35 | 0.15 | 0.16 | 0.85 | 0.65 | 0.71 |
| 0.36 | 0.16 | 0.18 | 0.86 | 0.66 | 0.73 |
| 0.37 | 0.17 | 0.19 | 0.87 | 0.67 | 0.74 |
| 0.38 | 0.18 | 0.20 | 0.88 | 0.68 | 0.75 |
| 0.39 | 0.19 | 0.21 | 0.89 | 0.69 | 0.76 |
| 0.40 | 0.20 | 0.22 | 0.90 | 0.70 | 0.77 |
| 0.41 | 0.21 | 0.23 | 0.91 | 0.71 | 0.78 |
| 0.42 | 0.22 | 0.24 | 0.92 | 0.72 | 0.79 |
| 0.43 | 0.23 | 0.25 | 0.93 | 0.73 | 0.80 |
| 0.44 | 0.24 | 0.26 | 0.94 | 0.74 | 0.81 |
| 0.45 | 0.25 | 0.27 | 0.95 | 0.75 | 0.82 |
| 0.46 | 0.26 | 0.29 | 0.96 | 0.76 | 0.84 |
| 0.47 | 0.27 | 0.30 | 0.97 | 0.77 | 0.85 |
| 0.48 | 0.28 | 0.31 | 0.98 | 0.78 | 0.86 |
| 0.49 | 0.29 | 0.32 | 0.99 | 0.79 | 0.87 |
| 0.50 | 0.30 | 0.33 | 1.00 | 0.80 | 0.88 |
| 0.51 | 0.31 | 0.34 | 1.01 | 0.81 | 0.89 |
| 0.52 | 0.32 | 0.35 | 1.02 | 0.82 | 0.90 |
| 0.53 | 0.33 | 0.36 | 1.03 | 0.83 | 0.91 |
| 0.54 | 0.34 | 0.37 | 1.04 | 0.84 | 0.92 |
| 0.55 | 0.35 | 0.38 | 1.05 | 0.85 | 0.93 |
| 0.56 | 0.36 | 0.40 | 1.06 | 0.86 | 0.95 |
| 0.57 | 0.37 | 0.41 | 1.07 | 0.87 | 0.96 |
| 0.58 | 0.38 | 0.42 | 1.08 | 0.88 | 0.97 |
| 0.59 | 0.39 | 0.43 | 1.09 | 0.89 | 0.98 |
| 0.60 | 0.40 | 0.44 | 1.10 | 0.90 | 0.99 |
| 0.61 | 0.41 | 0.45 | 1.11 | 0.91 | 1.00 |
| 0.62 | 0.42 | 0.46 | 1.12 | 0.92 | 1.01 |
| 0.63 | 0.43 | 0.47 | 1.13 | 0.93 | 1.02 |
| 0.64 | 0.44 | 0.48 | 1.14 | 0.94 | 1.03 |
| 0.65 | 0.45 | 0.49 | 1.15 | 0.95 | 1.04 |
| 0.66 | 0.46 | 0.51 | 1.16 | 0.96 | 1.06 |
| 0.67 | 0.47 | 0.52 | 1.17 | 0.97 | 1.07 |
| 0.68 | 0.48 | 0.53 | 1.18 | 0.98 | 1.08 |
| 0.69 | 0.49 | 0.54 | 1.19 | 0.99 | 1.09 |
| 0.70 | 0.50 | 0.55 | 1.20 | 1.00 | 1.10 |

# BRAKES

## Contents


**1. General Description** . . . . . 4
Foot Brakes . . . . . 6
Parking Brake . . . . . 6

**2. Brake Fluid Reservoir** . . . . . 6
2.1 Reservoir Mountings . . . . . 7
2.2 Reservoir Connections . . . . . 7
2.3 Brake Fluid Reservoir Maintenance . . . 8

**3. Compensating Port (master cylinder)** . . . . . 8

**4. Master Cylinder** . . . . . 8
4.1 Push Rod . . . . . 8
4.2 Check Valve . . . . . 9
4.3 Primary Cup . . . . . 10
4.4 Removing and Installing Master Cylinder 10
4.5 Repairing Master Cylinder . . . . . 11

**5. Brake Lines and Hoses** . . . . . 12
5.1 Brake Lines . . . . . 12
Tube Connections . . . . . 12
5.2 Brake Hoses . . . . . 13
5.3 Replacing Brake Hoses . . . . . 13

**6. Drum Brakes** . . . . . 14
6.1 Description . . . . . 14
6.2 Removing and Installing Brake Drums (front wheels) . . . . . 15
6.3 Reconditioning Brake Drums (front wheels) . . . . . 16
6.4 Replacing Front Brake Shoes . . . . . 16
6.5 Removing and Installing Brake Drums (rear wheels) . . . . . 18
6.6 Removing and Installing Rear Brake Shoes . . . . . 19
6.7 Reconditioning Brake Drums (rear wheels) . . . . . 20

**7. Wheel Cylinders** . . . . . 20
7.1 Removing and Installing Front Wheel Cylinders . . . . . 21
7.2 Repairing Front Wheel Cylinders . . . . . 22
7.3 Removing and Installing Rear Wheel Cylinders . . . . . 22

**8. Parking Brake Lever** . . . . . 23
8.1 Removing and Installing Parking Brake Lever . . . . . 23
8.2 Removing and Installing Parking Brake Cables . . . . . 24

**9. Bleeding the Brakes** . . . . . 24
9.1 Brake Fluid . . . . . 24
9.2 Brake Cylinder Paste . . . . . 24
9.3 Flushing Brake System . . . . . 24
9.4 Procedure for Bleeding . . . . . 25
9.5 Changing Brake Fluid . . . . . 25

**10. Adjusting Drum Brakes** . . . . . 26
10.1 Adjusting Parking Brake . . . . . 26
10.2 Relining Brake Shoes . . . . . 27
10.3 Machining Specifications . . . . . 27

# 2 BRAKES


**11. Dual Circuit Drum Brakes** . . . 28
11.1 General Description . . . 28
11.2 Brake Fluid Reservoir . . . 29
11.3 Tandem Master Cylinder . . . 29
11.4 Brake System with Warning Device . . . 30
11.5 Brake Light Switch . . . 30
11.6 Residual Pressure Valve . . . 30
11.7 Repairing Tandem Master Cylinder . . . 32
11.8 Bleeding the Brakes . . . 32
11.9 Testing Brake Light Switch . . . 33
11.10 Testing Brake Warning Device Switch . . . 33
11.11 Removing and Installing Brake Light Switch/Warning Device Switch . . . 33

**12. Disc Brakes (Karmann Ghia)** . . . 33
12.1 General Description . . . 34
12.2 Disc Brake Operation . . . 34
12.3 Tandem Master Cylinder . . . 36
12.4 Brake Pads . . . 36
12.5 Checking Brake Pads . . . 36
12.6 Removing and Installing Brake Pads . . . 37
12.7 Removing and Installing Brake Caliper . . . 40
12.8 Repairing Brake Caliper . . . 40
12.9 Checking Brake Discs . . . 42
12.10 Reconditioning Brake Discs . . . 42
12.11 Removing and Installing Brake Disc . . . 42
12.12 Removing and Installing Brake Disc Shield . . . 44
12.13 Bleeding the Brakes . . . 44
12.14 Adjusting Brakes . . . 44
Front Brakes . . . 44
Rear Brakes . . . 44
12.15 Brake Troubleshooting . . . 45

**13. Wheels and Tires** . . . 47
13.1 Wheels . . . 47
13.2 Tires . . . 47
Tire Dimensions . . . 48
Inflation Pressures . . . 48
13.3 Tubeless Tires . . . 48
13.4 Changing Tires . . . 48
13.5 Checking Tires . . . 50
Roadworthiness . . . 51
Inflation Pressure . . . 51
Abnormal Wear . . . 52
13.6 Driving Habits . . . 53
Road Surface . . . 53
Incorrect Wheel Alignment . . . 53
Impact Fractures . . . 54
13.7 Summary of Abnormal Tire Wear . . . 55
13.8 Wheel Rotation . . . 56
13.9 Replacing Tires . . . 56
13.10 Wheel Balancing . . . 56
13.11 The Weather and Tire Life . . . 57
13.12 Anti-skid Qualities of Tires . . . 57
13.13 Winter Tires and Snow Chains . . . 58
13.14 Radial-Ply Tires . . . 58
Tubeless Radials . . . 59

**14. Brake Technical Data** . . . 59
I. Brakes and Wheels: Tolerances, Wear Limits and Settings . . . 59
II. Tire Data . . . 60
III. Tightening Torques . . . 60


**TABLES**


a. Pedal Strokes . . . 26
b. Brake Drum Specifications . . . 27
c. Brake Troubleshooting . . . 45
d. Summary of Tire Wear . . . 55
e. Tire Characteristics . . . 57

# Brakes

Three different hydraulic brake systems are found among the cars covered in this Manual. The 1966 sedans and convertibles have single-circuit drum brakes. Sedans and convertibles of later years have dual-circuit drum brakes (Fig. 1). The Karmann Ghias also have the dual-circuit system but have disc brakes instead of drum brakes on the front wheels. The three systems will be described in detail after a brief discussion of some of the principles on which hydraulic brakes operate.

In work on brakes many procedures are the same for single-circuit and dual-circuit systems. Where this is the case, we will give full details of the procedure for the single-circuit system. When we come to the equivalent procedure in the dual-circuit system, we will put the emphasis on differences between components of the two systems. By emphasizing significant details and differences, we will try to keep repetition at a minimum.

1. Brake fluid reservoir
2. Brake master cylinder
3. Drum brakes
4. Parking brake
5. Front brake circuit
6. Rear brake circuit

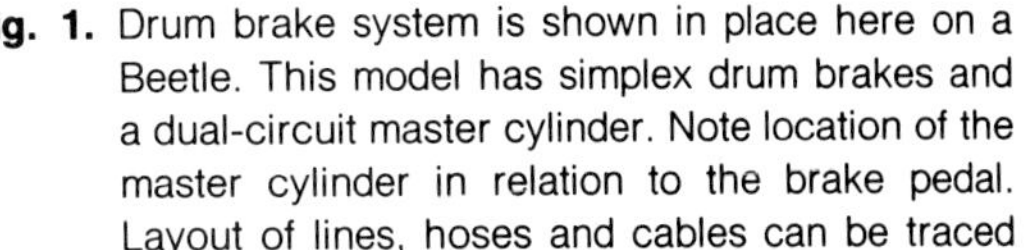

**Fig. 1.** Drum brake system is shown in place here on a Beetle. This model has simplex drum brakes and a dual-circuit master cylinder. Note location of the master cylinder in relation to the brake pedal. Layout of lines, hoses and cables can be traced through car.

## 1. GENERAL DESCRIPTION

In the hydraulic (fluid) brake system a comparatively low pressure on the brake pedal gives a high and equal braking pressure at the four wheels. The system is designed both to multiply the force of the driver's foot on the brake pedal and to deliver the same braking pressure at each wheel to keep the car from swerving when the brakes are applied.

The mechanical leverage of the brake pedal causes the first increase in applied force. Then the pedal moves a piston (or pistons) in the master cylinder to convert the pedal force into hydraulic pressure throughout the entire system. At the wheels other pistons apply the multiplied hydraulic pressure against the brake drums (or brake discs) to slow or stop the car. The scientific law underlying the operation of hydraulic brakes is well known: Pressure applied to an incompressible fluid in a closed vessel or a closed system is transmitted uniformly in all directions and equally to every square inch of the vessel or system.

The number of pistons in the master cylinder depends on whether the system is single- or dual-circuit. The piston action in the cylinder forces the brake fluid into the lines and through the lines and hoses to the wheels, where the pressure moves other pistons. In drum brakes the wheel cylinder pistons force the brake shoes outward against the brake drums. In disc brakes the caliper pistons force pads inward against the discs. Either way, the brake system works on friction. It is the function of brakes to absorb the kinetic energy (energy of movement) of the car. Through friction the brakes convert that energy into heat, which then is given up to the atmosphere.

You can think of the brakes on your car as a power-absorbing machine. While it takes from 15 to 20 seconds to accelerate your car to a speed of 60 miles an hour, you may have to call on the brakes to absorb all the energy—that is, to stop the car—in a fraction of the time. This picture gives some idea of the power your brake system must be able to exert for safe driving and of the amount of energy the brakes must drain off in the form of heat. Remember, braking and heat go together. Never touch any part of a brake until you have given it time to cool.

Fig. 2 gives a schematic view of a hydraulic brake system. While the components sketched in the figure are for a single-circuit system with drum brakes, there are enough basic similarities to make the illustration a useful reference for a discussion of the dual-circuit system and

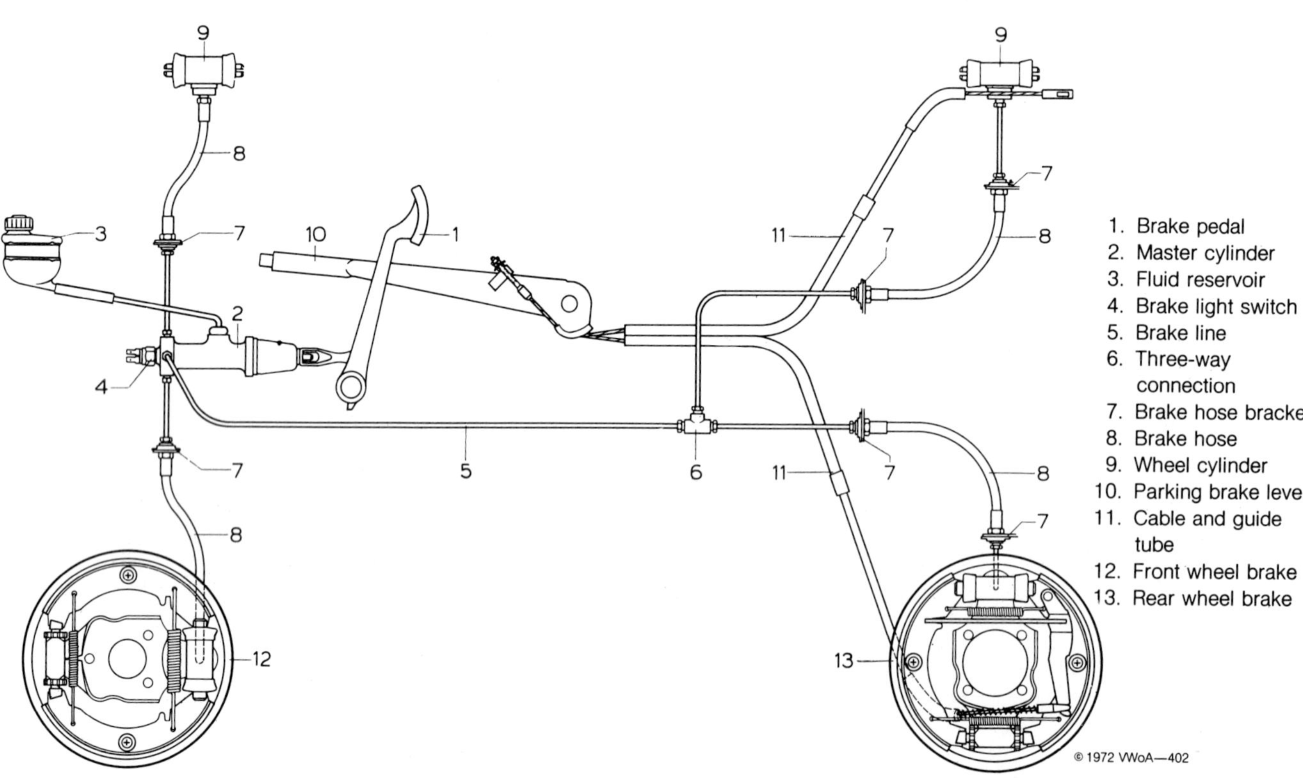


**Fig. 2.** Schematic of the Beetle hydraulic brake system is given here. The system shown is single-circuit with drum brakes. Karmann Ghias of the years covered in this Manual are equipped with disc brakes on front wheels.

disc brakes as well. The figure shows 13 components altogether, but for a quick picture of the operation of a hydraulic brake system, it is better to concentrate on four main assemblies.

1. The brake fluid reservoir keeps the volume of working fluid constant and provides space for expansion of heated fluid. The reservoir stabilizes the system.
2. The master cylinder converts the driver's push on the brake pedal into hydraulic pressure in the system. The single-circuit master cylinder on 1966 cars has one piston. The dual-circuit cylinder on later cars has two.
3. The hydraulic lines and hoses connect the master cylinder to the brakes at the four wheels, transmitting hydraulic pressure to the wheel cylinders on drum brakes or to the brake calipers on disc brakes.
4. The hydraulic pressure works on pistons to force a braking part against a moving part of the wheel assembly to slow or stop the car by friction. In drum brakes the wheel cylinder piston forces the brake shoes outward against the rotating brake drum. In disc brakes the opposing caliper pistons force brake pads inward to squeeze the turning disc.

The fluid reservoir and the master cylinder together compose the heart of the hydraulic brake system. Fig. 3 shows these parts in cross section. There is a back-and-forth flow of brake fluid between the reservoir and cylinder through the cylinder intake port, which is shown at (13) in Fig. 3, and the compensating port (10). This flow is necessary to keep the volume constant in the rest of the system where the fluid actually works the brakes.

The difference between a single-circuit hydraulic brake system and a dual-circuit system is simply stated.

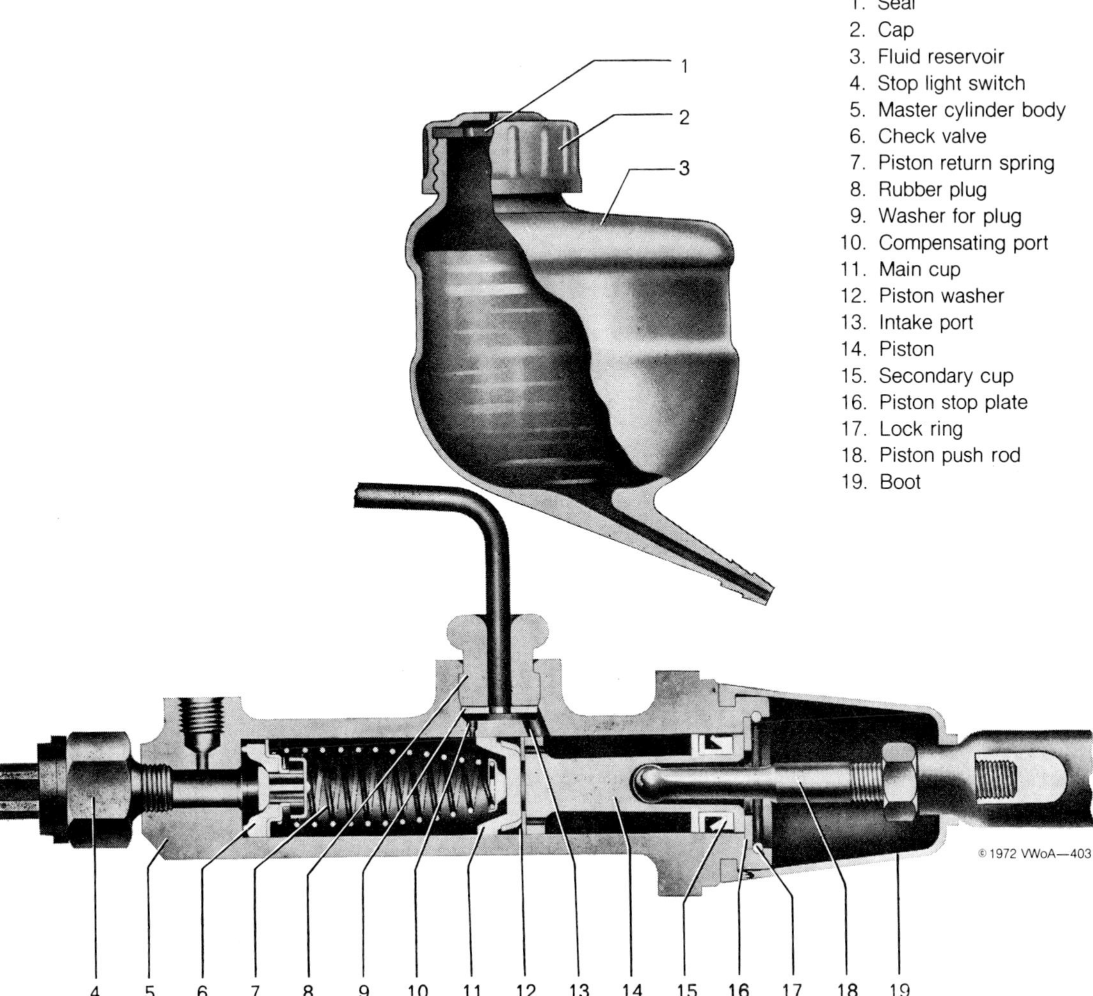


**Fig. 3.** Cutaway view of the fluid reservoir (above) and master cylinder (below) shows working parts of the heart of single-circuit hydraulic brake system. Inside diameter of cylinder is 0.687 inch (17.46 mm). Piston stroke is 1.299 inches (33 mm). Brake pedal works directly on push rod.

In a single-circuit system the hydraulic pressure for the brakes on all four wheels is generated by one piston working in a single pressure chamber in the master cylinder. A dual-circuit system has two pressure chambers in the cylinder, each with its own piston. One chamber generates pressure for the brakes on the front wheels. The other generates pressure for the rear wheel brakes. There is no connection between the two systems. This is a safety measure. If one circuit fails, the other continues to operate. With one circuit out, the car can still be brought to a stop, though the stopping distance will be greater than when both circuits are working.

### Foot Brakes

When you push the brake pedal down, the two brake shoes at each wheel in a drum brake system put uniformly increasing pressure on the brake drum. When you take your foot off the pedal, return springs force the shoes and the wheel cylinder pistons back to rest positions. Brake fluid returns to the master cylinder through a check valve. Rubber cups on all the pistons in the system hold the hydraulic pressure and prevent leaks. Though the details differ, the main hydraulic action is roughly similar for disc brakes.

### Parking Brake

The parking brake, which you operate by pulling up on the hand lever, works on the rear wheel brakes only and exerts its force mechanically, not hydraulically. Cables running through guide tubes in the car frame transmit the movement of the hand lever to levers that apply force on the rear wheel brake shoes.

## 2. BRAKE FLUID RESERVOIR

Differences in the mountings and connections for the reservoir and in the reservoir itself appear in the model years covered by this Manual. Some of these differences can be seen in Fig. 4, Fig. 5 and Fig. 6.

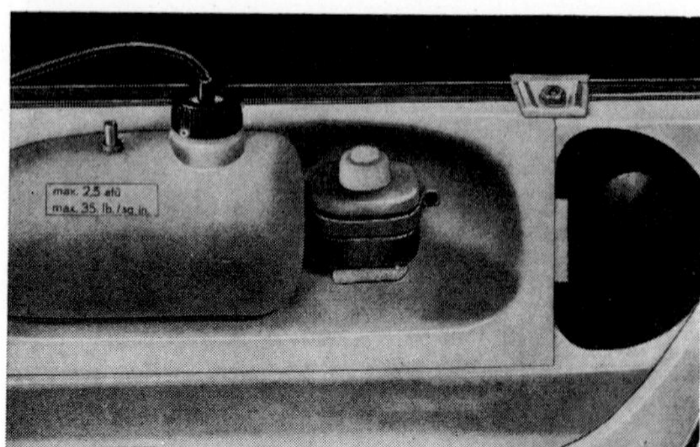




**Fig. 4.** Brake fluid reservoir in 1966 and 1967 Beetles is mounted on plate on left side panel in front of luggage compartment.

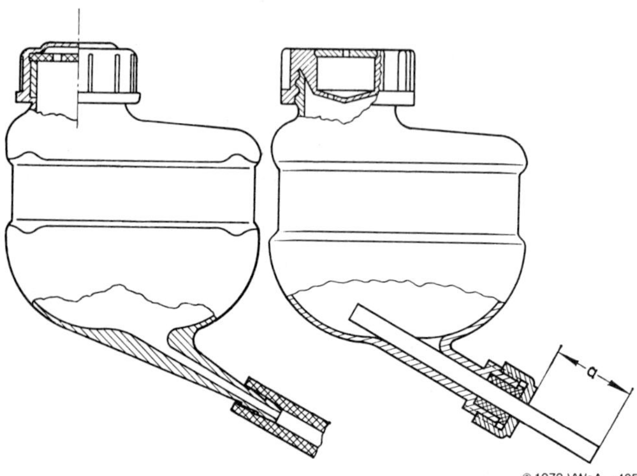




**Fig. 5.** Connections on brake fluid reservoirs are either of the push-on type (left) or the threaded type (right). Push-on connection is the earlier version. On threaded connection distance labeled "a" in picture measures 0.9 inch (23 mm).

**NOTE** ——
Only brake fluid reservoirs and brake lines of designs dated after April 1967 are now available as spare parts. If you have to replace any of these components, be sure to obtain the new parts. Replacement of any section of a brake line requires replacement of the entire line.

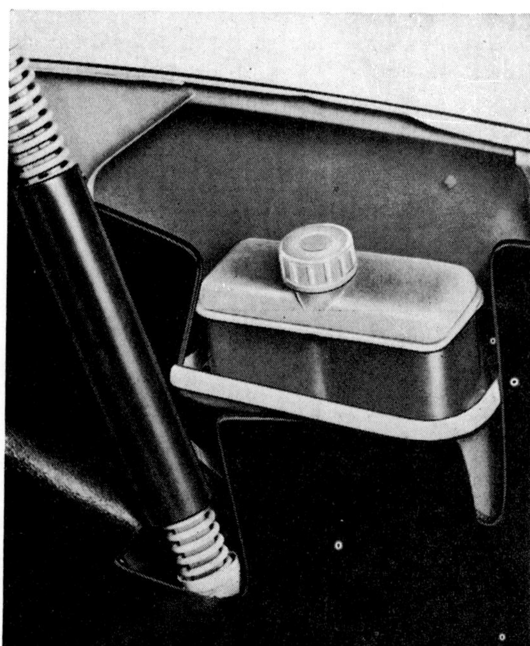



**Fig. 6.** Brake fluid reservoir in 1968 and 1969 Beetles is different from earlier version (Fig. 4). It is mounted on plate on left side panel of front luggage compartment.

## 2.1 Reservoir Mountings

In the 1966 sedans the reservoir is mounted (Fig. 4) behind the spare wheel, in the front luggage compartment. A line with rubber sleeves connects it to the master cylinder.

From May 12, 1966, chassis No. 116 872 032, all cars have been equipped with a brake fluid reservoir that has a threaded connection. The line and connecting hose between the reservoir and the master cylinder has been modified accordingly. Fig. 5 shows the change in connections.

All sedans and convertibles from August 1, 1967, have the reservoir on a plate attached to the left front side panel, as shown in Fig. 6.

On Karmann Ghia models the reservoir is on a plate behind the instrument panel cover in the front luggage compartment. The shape of the reservoir has been changed and the method of securing it. One of the two tabs on the bottom of the reservoir goes into a slot in the mounting plate. A screw through the other tab holds the reservoir in place. Fig. 7 shows this model.

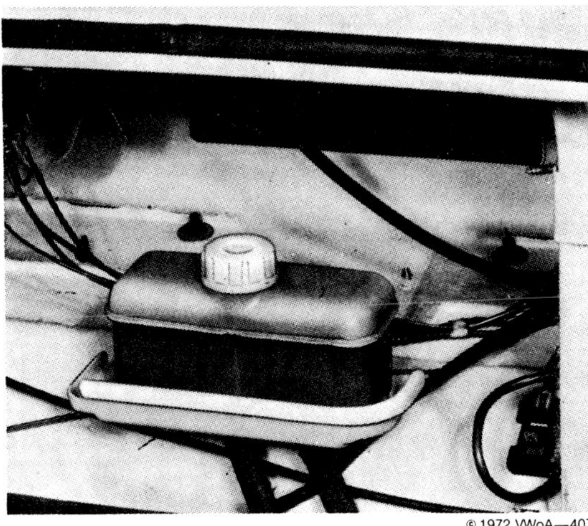

© 1972 VWoA—407

**Fig. 7.** Karmann Ghia model of the brake fluid reservoir differs from others and is mounted behind the instrument panel cover in the front luggage compartment.

## 2.2 Reservoir Connections

In April 1967 a change was made in the size of the connecting line from the brake fluid reservoir to the master cylinder (except for a short length of the line in the reservoir). Models affected and dates were:

Sedan with dual-circuit brakes, from chassis No. 117 626 506, April 1, 1967
Karmann Ghia, from chassis No. 147 657 893, April 17, 1967
Convertible, from chassis No. 157 658 059, April 17, 1967

The earlier line was 6 mm in diameter with wall thickness of 0.7 mm. The new line has the same wall thickness but is 8 mm in outside diameter. Only 8 mm lines are available as replacement parts. If you need parts for a car with 6 mm lines, convert to the 8 mm size.

There is a change also in the fitting of the line at the master cylinder. Instead of fitting directly into the cylinder, as the earlier model did, the line now is connected by means of an 8 mm hose and an elbow on the cylinder. An adapter hose connects the 6 and 8 mm lines.

When installing the rubber plug that seals the elbow at the master cylinder (Fig. 8), be sure to turn the elbow in the right direction. Do not re-use the metal washer for the plug. Install a new one.

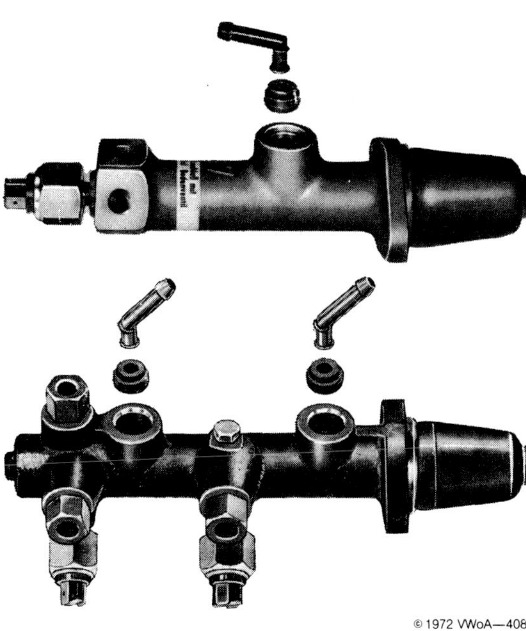

© 1972 VWoA—408

**Fig. 8.** Master cylinders in VW cars are either single-circuit (above) or dual-circuit (below). In the dual-circuit cylinder the front piston applied pressure on the front wheel brakes and the rear piston on the rear wheel brakes. If one set of brakes should fail, the other would remain in operation, but a greater distance would be required to stop the car.

7

***WARNING*** —

*Use only genuine VW brake fluid or a brake fluid that meets SAE recommendation J 1703. Since the fluid is both poisonous and damaging to finishes, be careful not to spill it on yourself or any painted surface.*

### 2.3 Brake Fluid Reservoir Maintenance

Care of the brake fluid reservoir is simple but important.

**To service reservoir:**

1. Make sure that the vent in the reservoir cap is open. Without this opening, operation of the master cylinder piston might create a vacuum in the reservoir or build up pressure to disrupt the entire brake system. (If you are doing any painting around the reservoir, be careful not to plug the vent with paint.)
2. Before you fill the reservoir or take off the cap, always clean the cap and the top of the reservoir thoroughly. It is most important to keep dirt out of the brake system. Before you open the reservoir, take a second look to make sure that the cap and the area around it are absolutely clean.
3. Keep fluid level in reservoir about three-quarters of an inch (15 to 20 mm) below the cap.

## 3. COMPENSATING PORT
(master cylinder)

As you can see in Fig. 3, the compensating port (10) actually is in the master cylinder, but this vent, which also is called the by-pass port, is so important to the system that it deserves separate discussion. By allowing flow between the reservoir and master cylinder, the compensating port serves as a balance for the entire system.

Since brake fluid expands when hot and contracts when cooling, a rise or fall in temperature increases or diminishes the total volume of fluid. To stay in balance, the brake system must be capable of accommodating these changes in volume. Otherwise, a rise in temperature from braking in hilly country, for example, could expand the fluid enough to keep continuing pressure on the wheel cylinder pistons and cause the brakes to drag. At the other end of the scale, a severe drop in temperature might reduce the working volume enough to impair braking. In this situation more fluid must be fed into the system.

The compensating port provides automatic regulation of brake fluid volume to meet these conditions. At high temperatures the excess fluid can flow from the pressure chamber in the master cylinder into the reservoir. In a fluid shortage the flow is from reservoir into cylinder pressure chamber by way of the compensating port. When your foot is off the brake pedal and the system is at rest, the main cup (11) on the cylinder piston is just behind the port. When you apply the brakes, the piston moves forward and the primary cup then covers the port, sealing the pressure chamber. Further movement of the piston forces brake fluid out of the chamber and into the lines to build up hydraulic pressure on the wheel cylinder pistons and thus against the brake shoes or the brake discs.

***CAUTION —***
*Use brake fluid only to wash brake parts. The use of gasoline or other petroleum products can leave traces behind that will eventually lead to deterioration of the rubber parts in the brake system.*

## 4. MASTER CYLINDER

The components of a single-circuit master cylinder are seen in cross section in Fig. 3. When you push the brake pedal down, you are indirectly applying force to the push rod (18). In turn, the push rod pushes the piston (14) forward. This movement of the piston in the sealed pressure chamber forces brake fluid under pressure into the lines. When you take your foot off the pedal, the direction of flow reverses. Pressure in the system then causes the fluid to flow back through the check valve (6) into the cylinder and through the compensating port (10) into the reservoir.

### 4.1 Push Rod

The factory has set the push rod to leave clearance of 0.04 inch (1 mm) between the tip of the rod and the bottom of the recess in the rear of the piston. This clearance is sufficient to keep the compensating port open. Unless the brake pedal is depressed, the piston will not move forward enough to close the port. This push rod clearance **must not** be changed. In Fig. 9, the clearance is shown as **S.**

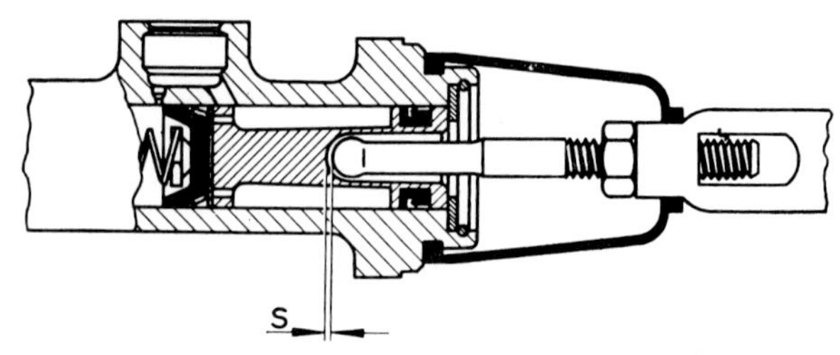


**Fig. 9.** Push rod working off brake pedal transmits driver's braking action to master cylinder piston. Seen in cross section here, rod enters cylinder at right and extends into recess in piston. Clearance of 0.04 inch (dimension **S** here) must be left between rounded end of push rod and bottom of piston recess.

***WARNING —***
*The compensating port must always be open when the brake system is at rest. Otherwise, expanding hot brake fluid will cause the brakes to drag.*

The play between push rod and piston is not set on the rod but at the stop bracket for the brake pedal. The adjustment is explained in the procedure for installing the master cylinder. In Fig. 10 the measurement **x** shows the equivalent pedal play. The clearance of 0.04 inch in the cylinder equals play of 3/16 to 9/32 inch (5 to 7 mm) at **x.**

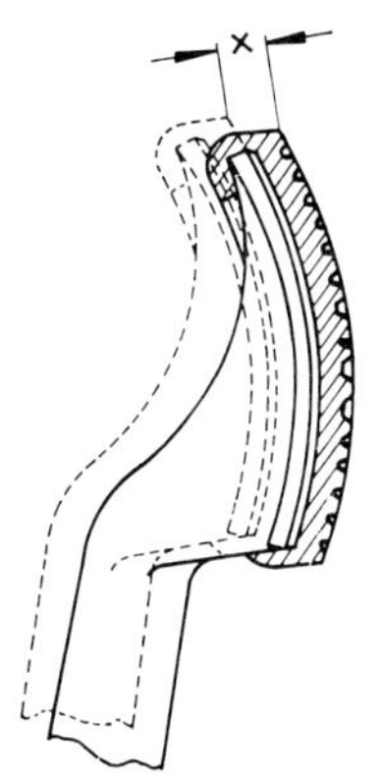


**Fig. 10.** Brake pedal play, shown here as measurement **x,** is directly related to push rod clearance in the master cylinder piston (Fig. 9). Pedal play **x** is adjusted to 3/16 to 9/32 inch (5 to 7 mm).

***WARNING —***
*The factory has set the length of the push rod (Fig. 11) in your car, and this setting must not be changed.*

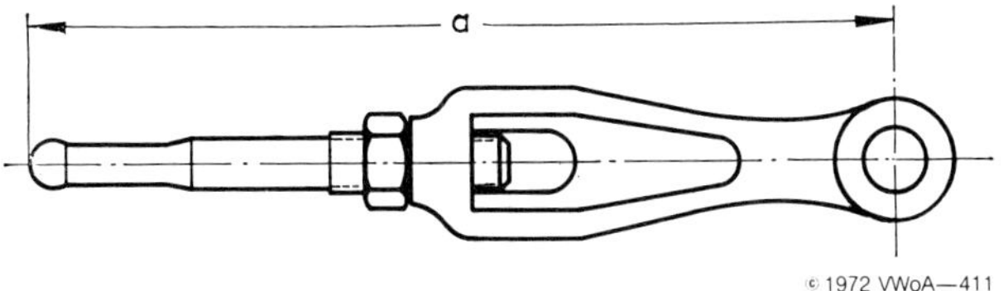


**Fig. 11.** Push rod length (measurement **a**) is a factory setting and **must not** be altered.

## 4.2 Check Valve

The double-acting check valve at the front end of the master cylinder controls brake fluid flow between the pressure chamber and brake lines. The valve reacts to pressure change anywhere in the system. In braking, the piston forces fluid under pressure past the valve and into the lines. When the brake pedal is released, the flow reverses. The tension of the return springs for the wheel cylinder pistons and the brake shoes builds up enough pressure in the lines to lift the check valve off its seat. The fluid in the lines then can flow back into the cylinder and reservoir. The valve action is illustrated in Fig. 12.

As the fluid flows back into the cylinder, pressure in the lines falls but never drops all the way to zero. The valve spring you can see in Fig. 12 is preloaded to shut off the return flow when pressure in the lines has fallen



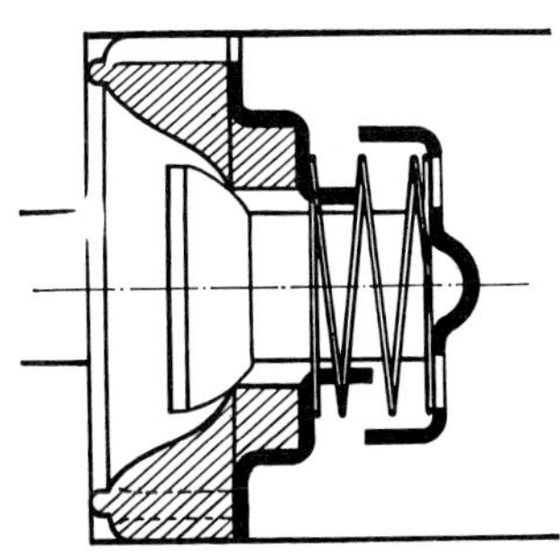

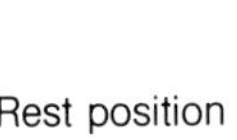


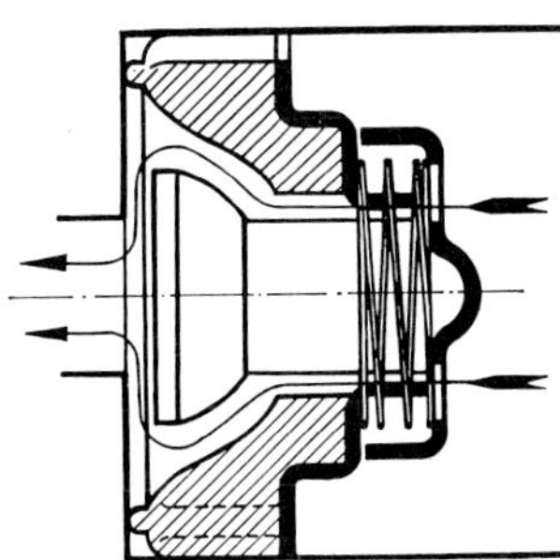

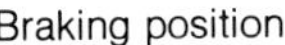


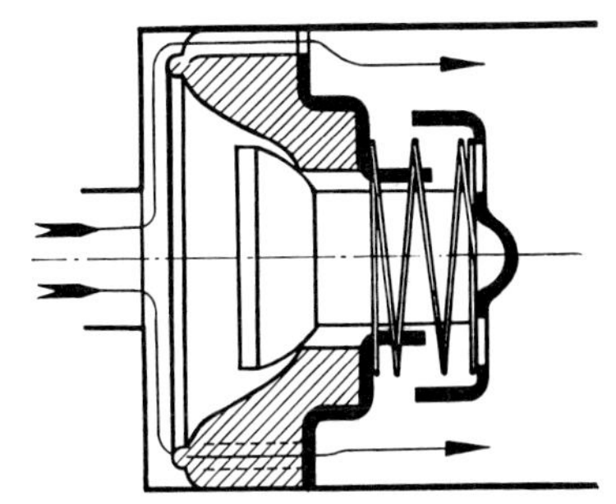


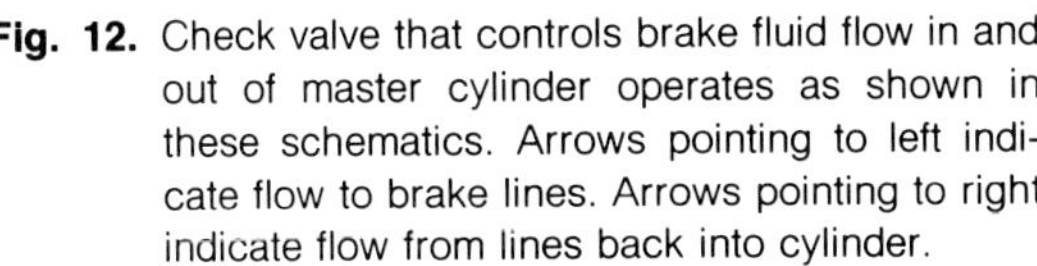

**Fig. 12.** Check valve that controls brake fluid flow in and out of master cylinder operates as shown in these schematics. Arrows pointing to left indicate flow to brake lines. Arrows pointing to right indicate flow from lines back into cylinder.

to a certain small value. Thus the check valve automatically maintains at all times a small residual pressure in the lines and the wheel cylinders. This pressure keeps the lines full right up to the wheel cylinders. With the wheel cylinder pistons already under this residual pressure, sudden increase in pressure from the brake pedal causes almost instantaneous movement of the wheel cylinder pistons and thus almost instant braking action.

The residual pressure also has a sealing effect. It forces the cups on the wheel cylinder pistons into close sealing contact with the cylinder walls to keep brake fluid from leaking out and air from leaking in.

### 4.3 Primary Cup

The piston of the master cylinder is thicker at the ends than in the middle. This shape leaves room for brake fluid between the central section of the piston and the cylinder wall. It also provides relief in the bearing of piston and bore. Otherwise, the entire length of the piston would be a tight fit. At each release of the brake pedal, withdrawal of the piston under pressure of the return spring would then leave a vacuum in the front end of the cylinder. Air could be drawn into the system to fill that vacuum.

Instead, the annular (doughnut-shaped) space between the piston and cyiinder wall behind the primary cup fills with brake fluid from the reservoir. There are drillings through the front end of the piston and cup washer and grooves through the primary cup. Brake fluid in the annular space can flow through these openings. When the brake pedal is released and the return spring drives the piston back to the rear of the cylinder, this flow occurs. Brake fluid from the annular space goes forward and fills the vacuum in the brake line end of the cylinder. The secondary cup seals the annular chamber behind the piston. This arrangement blocks off any inflow of air that would reduce or destroy the efficiency of the brake system.

### 4.4 Removing and Installing Master Cylinder

Before you undertake to remove the master cylinder (or reservoir) for inspection and cleaning, you should take note of several points regarding preparations for reinstallation of the parts:

1. Clean all parts in alcohol and dry them. Prior to re-assembly, lubricate the parts with VW brake cylinder paste.
2. When inspecting parts, reject any that show signs of corrosion.
3. Replace all rubber parts.

   **NOTE —**
   Once they are removed, rubber parts change shape, and experience has shown that it is not good practice to use them again. We strongly recommend using only new replacements.

4. Store brake fluid in airtight containers. Never reuse fluid that has been bled from the brake system or fluid that has been kept in open cans.

**To remove master cylinder:**

**NOTE —**
Prior to removal, make sure that parts and work area are clean.

1. Remove master cylinder plug with line.
2. Disconnect brake light wire from switch.
3. Carefully remove brake lines (Fig. 13) and plug them. Drain and catch brake fluid.

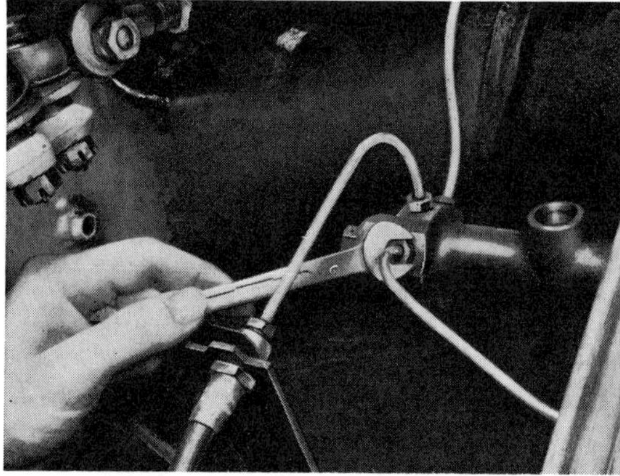



**Fig. 13.** Brake line to rear wheels is being disconnected here from a single-circuit master cylinder.

4. Bend up lock plate at push rod hinge pin and remove pin.
5. Loosen brake pedal stop bracket and take out push rod. The length of the push rod must not be changed.
6. Remove master cylinder securing bolts. Be careful not to drop spacers. Take cylinder out toward the front (Fig. 14).

**Fig. 14.** Securing bolts are taken out and master cylinder removed toward the front of the car.

**To install:**

1. Insert spacer for master cylinder in front cross member (Fig. 15).

© 1972 VWoA—415

**Fig. 15.** Spacer for master cylinder is inserted in front cross member before installation of cylinder and push rod.

2. Install master cylinder complete with push rod. Make sure that boot is properly located.

**NOTE ——**
Always use a new lock plate on push rod pin. Examine stop plate for wear or distortion. Replace plate if bent or damaged. Do not forget lock washer on bolt for stop plate.

3. Adjust brake pedal by moving stop plate (Fig. 16)

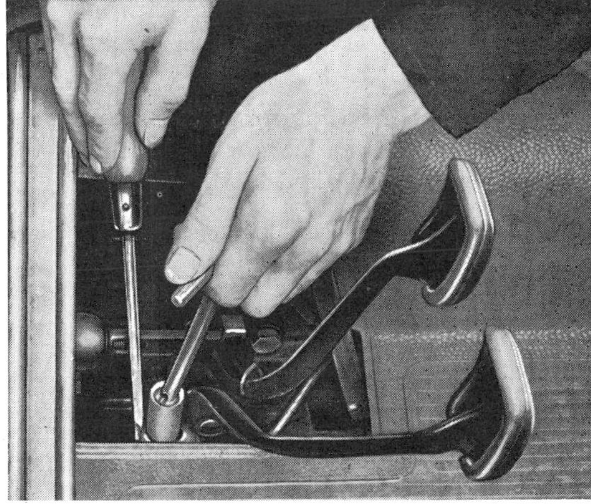

© 1972 VWoA—416

**Fig. 16.** Pedal cluster stop plate is moved to give required clearance of push rod in master cylinder piston.

until the clearance shown in Fig. 10 is obtained. Be careful not to let clutch pedal go beyond its stop. Further movement would disconnect it from the cable in the tunnel.

4. Check clutch pedal free play. (See **FRAME**.)
5. Moisten plastic elbows and sealing plugs with brake fluid to facilitate installation. Install plugs, elbows and brake lines. Connect brake light wire.
6. Be careful when installing the push rod boot. Any dirt here could damage the master cylinder seal.
7. Fill reservoir with fresh brake fluid (SAE specification J 1703).
8. Bleed brake system. After replacing reservoir cap, make sure that cap vent hole is open.
9. Recheck brake pedal plate free play. Apply brakes several times and check for leakage.
10. Take car on road to check brakes. Make sure that brake lights are working.

## 4.5 Repairing Master Cylinder

***CAUTION ——***
*Two different manufacturers supply master cylinders for the cars covered in this Manual. While the cylinders complete with component parts are interchangeable regardless of make, individual parts are not interchangeable between the two makes.*

If you need replacement parts for repair of the master cylinder in your car, look for the manufacturer's name on the cylinder and then ask by name for the specific repair kit for that make of cylinder.

Do not buy spare parts indiscriminately without reference to the specific make of the master cylinder in your car.

7

Kits for master cylinder repair are put together as a total package. That is, when you use a kit to make a repair on your cylinder, you must install the entire contents of the kit, even though only one part in the cylinder may be worn or damaged.

**To disassemble cylinder:**

***WARNING ——***
*Do not change push rod adjustment (factory only).*

1. Remove rubber boot.
2. Remove lock ring.

3. Remove stop washer and piston.
4. Take out piston washer, primary cup, return spring and check valve. Fig. 17 shows relation of these parts to each other.
5. Screw out the brake light switch.

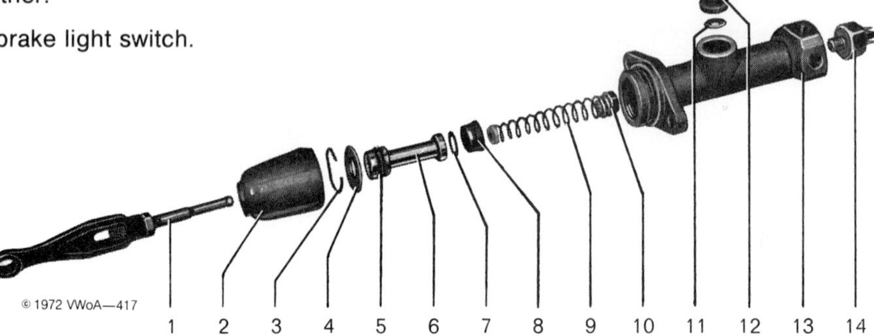


**Fig. 17.** Master cylinder, single circuit, breaks down into the parts shown in this exploded view. Brake fluid from reservoir enters cylinder by elbow through sealing plug (12).

1. Push rod
2. Boot
3. Lock ring
4. Stop washer
5. Secondary cup
6. Piston
7. Piston washer
8. Primary cup
9. Return spring
10. Check valve
11. Washer for plug
12. Sealing plug
13. Cylinder housing
14. Brake light switch

**To assemble:**

1. Clean all parts. Use alcohol or brake fluid only.
2. Check parts for wear. The compensating port must be open and free of burrs. The piston when clean and dry must be a suction fit in the cylinder.
3. Coat piston with VW brake cylinder paste.
4. Check seating of lock ring.
5. Be sure that rubber sealing plug for elbow is properly installed, and that elbow when installed is turned in the proper direction.

## 5. BRAKE LINES AND HOSES

The brake lines run along the frame of the car carrying brake fluid from the master cylinder to the wheels. Brake hoses connect the lines to the wheel cylinders. There is one wheel cylinder at each wheel.

### 5.1 Brake Lines

The brake lines consist of 4.75 x 0.72 mm steel tubing. Since this tubing is adequate for all pressures likely to occur in the system, no trouble should arise as long as the tubing remains tightly secured to the chassis to prevent vibration and rubbing.

#### Tube Connections

The tube ends are double flared, as shown in Fig. 18, for extra protection against splitting and leakage. When the union nuts at connections are tightened, the tube ends are forced to a close fit against beveled faces in the unions. Fig. 18 illustrates this tight joint.

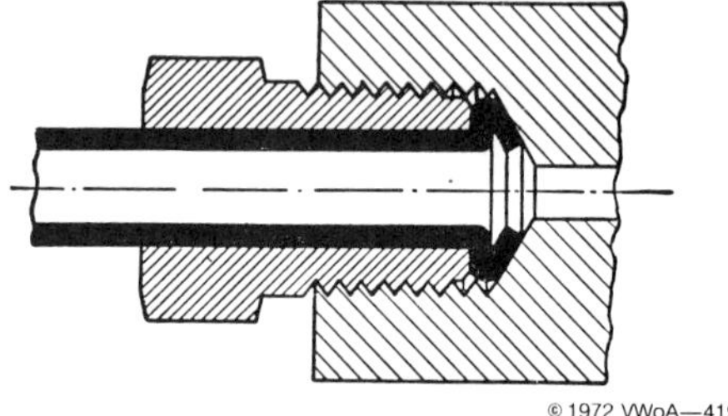


**Fig. 18.** Double flare at end of brake line tube is seen here against cavity inside the union connection. Flare strengthens tube against splits from tightening strains.

Before you tighten union nuts in the brake lines, moisten the flared ends of the tubing with a few drops of brake fluid.

***WARNING —***
*When checking the brake system for leaks, carefully inspect all brake lines for signs of corrosion or other damage. Look for dents or cracks from rocks or distortion from twisting. In your inspection also look over the lines where they are exposed along the frame tunnel. Never try to repair a brake line. Use only new lines when making repairs. You can get flared and shaped replacement tubes from your authorized VW dealer. Use of substitutes is not recommended.*

## 5.2 Brake Hoses

Brake hoses are supposed to hang freely, without twists. Fig. 19 shows a correctly suspended hose. When you install a brake hose, be careful not to leave a sharp bend at the connection. Turn the wheel and make sure that the hose remains free throughout the movement. The hose must not chafe against the chassis or any other part of the body when the car is in motion.

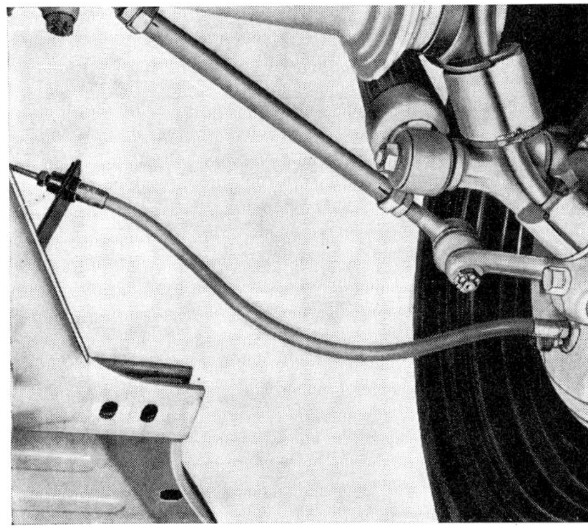

© 1972 VWoA—418

**Fig. 19.** Brake hose should hang down free of twists, as shown here. When installing the hoses, exercise care.

The axle should be unloaded when front wheel brake hoses are installed. Raise the front end of the car for this procedure.

***WARNING*** —
*Paint, grease, oil, gasoline and kerosene are damaging to brake hoses. Do not paint the hoses on your car or leave them in contact with petroleum products for any length of time. When you are greasing the car, keep watching for grease on the brake hoses. Wipe off every trace of grease at once.*

Every time you disconnect a brake hose or brake line you must bleed the brake system. (See **9. Filling and Bleeding the Brakes**.) Top up the reservoir as necessary with fresh, unused brake fluid of recommended make and specifications. Check tightness of brake hose connections at the wheel cylinders and brake line connections at cylinder unions. The specified torque is 10 to 14 ft. lbs. (1.5 to 2.0 mkg).

**NOTE** —
From August 1, 1966, chassis No. 117 000 002, a different length of front wheel brake hose has been used to fit a change in the location of the brake hose bracket on the lower part of the frame head. If you need a front brake hose replacement, be sure to ask for the correct length for your car. Cars with double-joint rear axles require brake hoses longer than the hoses found on swing-axle cars.

***WARNING*** —
*Never try to repair brake hoses. Replace worn or damaged hoses.*

## 5.3 Replacing Brake Hoses

**To remove:**

1. Take wheel off.
2. Loosen union nut and remove hose clamp from bracket.
3. Pull out hose.
4. Remove hose from wheel cylinder.

**To install:**

**NOTE** —
Before starting the installation, read (or re-read) instructions at the beginning of this subsection on brake hoses.

1. Install hose, taking care not to cross-thread fittings.
2. Check location and position of hose at all wheel positions.
3. Bleed brakes and plug bleeder valves with dust caps.

7

## 6. DRUM BRAKES

The drum brakes on front wheels (Fig. 20) differ somewhat from the rear wheel brakes, but both work on the same principle. The wheel cylinder pistons force the brake shoes against the brake drums to slow the car by friction. On the front wheels the shoes work vertically, up and down. On the rear wheels the shoes apply the force horizontally. The parking brake works only on the rear wheels.

### 6.1 Description

The ends of the brake shoes ride in slots in the wheel cylinder pistons and adjusting screws, as shown in Fig. 20. This free mounting makes the shoes self-centering.

In each brake the wheel cylinder and anchor block are bolted directly to the steering knuckle. This attachment provides a positive location for the brake and rigid support. The backing plate, besides giving the shoes lateral support, serves as a cover to keep out dirt and water.

A guide spring with cup and pin is attached to the backing plate to keep each brake shoe in constant contact with the backing plate. Two return springs pull the shoes back to rest positions when the brakes are released. The thickness of the brake linings can be checked through inspection holes in the brake drums. When the linings are worn down to a thickness of $^{13}/_{64}$ inch (2.5 mm), they must be replaced.

1. Adjusting nut
2. Anchor block
3. Front return spring
4. Adjusting screw
5. Guide spring with cup and pin
6. Cylinder
7. Rear return spring
8. Backing plate
9. Brake shoe with lining

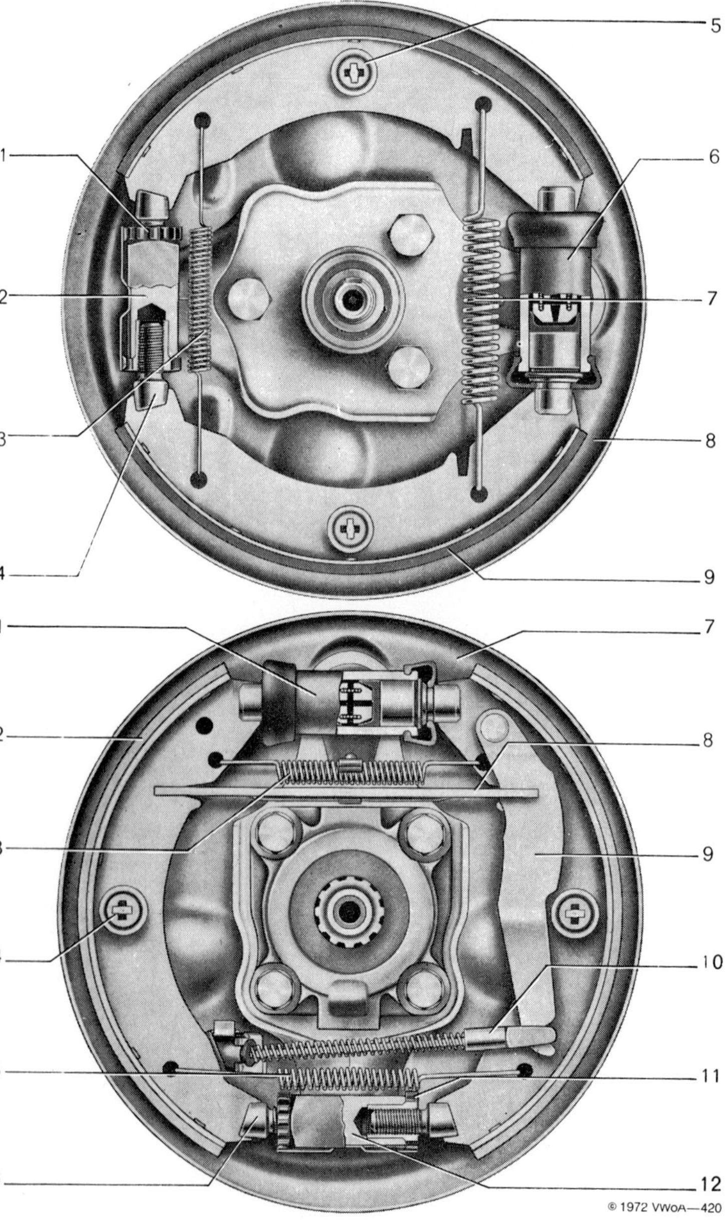


**Fig. 20.** Drum brake assemblies for front (top picture) and rear (bottom picture) wheels are seen here with the brake drums removed. Note thrust of brake shoes is vertical on front wheels, horizontal on rear wheels. Parking brake operates lever (9) on rear wheel by means of cable (10) to force upper end of lever against the rear brake shoes (at right).

1. Cylinder
2. Brake shoe with lining
3. Upper return spring
4. Spring with cup and pin
5. Lower return spring
6. Adjusting screw
7. Backing plate
8. Connecting link
9. Lever
10. Brake cable
11. Adjusting nut
12. Anchor block

## 6.2 Removing and Installing Brake Drums
(front wheels)

An exploded view of the front wheel drum brake is given in Fig. 21 to show the locations of the various parts of the assembly.

**Fig. 21.** Front wheel drum brake is shown with steering knuckle in exploded view of the parts.

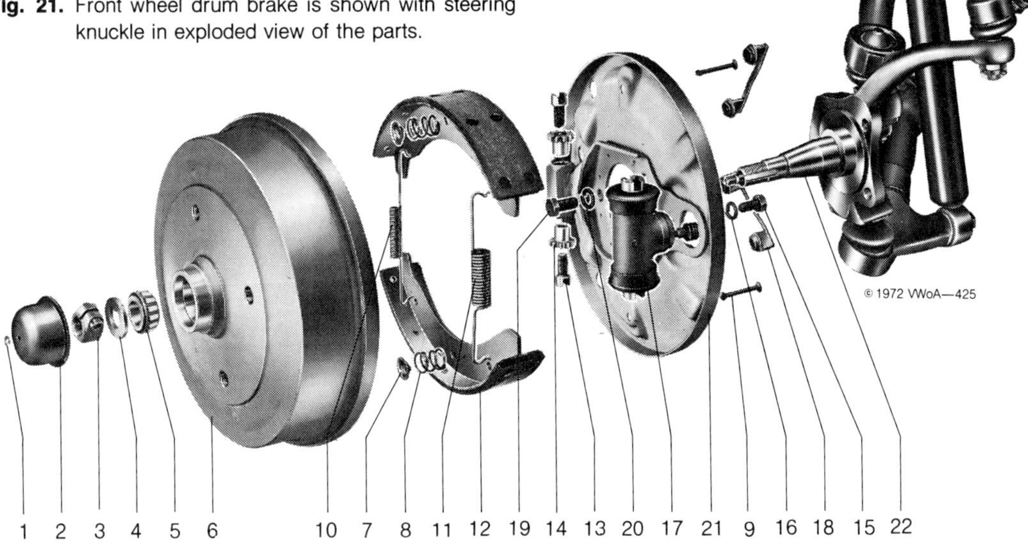


1. C-washer
2. Dust cap
3. Clamp nut
4. Thrust washer
5. Wheel bearing
6. Brake drum
7. Spring plate (2)
8. Spring (2)
9. Retaining pin (2)
10. Return spring
11. Return spring
12. Brake shoe (2)
13. Adjusting screw (2)
14. Adjusting nut (2)
15. Bolt
16. Lock washer
17. Wheel brake cylinder
18. Sealing plugs (2)
19. Bolt (3)
20. Lock washer (3)
21. Backing plate
22. Steering knuckle

© 1972 VWoA—421

**Fig. 22.** Dust cap is pried off with special tool. C-washer for speedometer cable drive must be removed before left front wheel can be taken off.

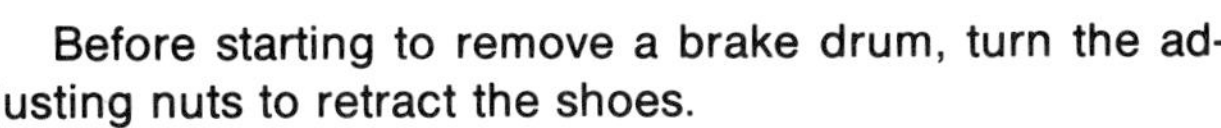
Before starting to remove a brake drum, turn the adjusting nuts to retract the shoes.

**To remove drum:**

1. Pull off dust cap (Fig. 22) and, if you are working on the left front wheel, remove the speedometer cable C-washer.
2. Remove clamp nut and take off drum.

**To install:**

Before installing a brake drum make sure that the wheel bearing is correctly positioned. (See **FRONT AXLE**.)

1. Be sure braking surface of drum is clean. Install brake drum, bearing and clamp nut. Install wheel. When tightening clamp nut, rotate wheel.

2. Position dial indicator as in Fig. 23 and adjust bearing play. Specified play: 0.001 to 0.005 inch (0.03 to 0.12 mm).

© 1972 VWoA—422

**Fig. 23.** Bearing play should be measured at several points after brake drums have been installed or re-installed on car. Allowed play is 0.001 to 0.005 inch.

**NOTE ——**
The play should be measured (Fig. 23) at several points on the circumference of the wheel.

3. Tighten socket head bolt to prescribed torque, as in Fig. 24.

© 1972 VWoA—423

**Fig. 24.** Bolt on the brake drum clamp nut is torqued before dust cap is installed on hub.

## 6.3 Reconditioning Brake Drums (front wheels)

Worn, scored or out-of-round brake drums often can be made serviceable by machining (turning), as illustrated in Fig. 25. The turning dimensions (as well as all other tolerances) are given in **Table b.**

© 1972 VWoA—424

**Fig. 25.** Worn brake drums can be reworked by turning on machine tools like this one. Brake drums that have been turned require shoes with oversize linings.

***CAUTION ——***
*Oversize linings must be used on brake shoes for reconditioned drums, and these linings must be matched with the radius of the turned drums.*

## 6.4 Replacing Front Brake Shoes

**NOTE ——**
Before removing brake shoes, you should check the operation of the wheel cylinders. This is a two-man job. One carefully works the brake pedal while the other watches the cylinder and shoes.

**To remove:**

1. Take front wheel off.
2. Remove bearing dust cap (on the left wheel, the C-washer for the speedometer cable drive must be removed first).
3. Loosen brake shoes by turning adjusting screws and pull drum off.

4. Secure wheel brake cylinder with wire to prevent piston from expanding when brake shoes are removed. Remove shoe retainer spring cups, springs and pins. (See Fig. 26.)

© 1972 VWoA—426

**Fig. 26.** Shoe retainer spring cups, springs and pins hold brake shoe against backing plate.

5. Detach front return spring (Fig. 27).

© 1972 VWoA—427

**Fig. 27.** Return springs are detached for removal of front wheel drum brake shoes.

6. Press one shoe out of the slot in the adjusting screw and take shoes off.

**To install:**

***CAUTION —***
*Be careful to keep parts as clean as possible. Use lubricants sparingly. Keep grease and oil from coming in contact with brake shoes. Clean brake shoes with medium grit sand paper.*

1. Check brake linings to make sure that you are installing the same type on both wheels of the same axle. Specified widths for linings are:
   1.181 inches (30 mm) (1966 and 1967 models)
   1.574 inches (40 mm) (1968 and 1969 models)
2. Install brake shoes. Make sure that the stronger return spring and the cut-out for the push rod in the brake shoe web are near the wheel cylinder.

***CAUTION —***
*Be sure to free up the adjusting screws before you reinstall shoes. Align the angled slots in the adjusting screws to receive the shoe ends. Hook return springs in from the front to keep them from contact with other parts of the brake.*

3. Install brake shoe pins, retainer springs and spring cups.

**NOTE —**
The brake shoe pins are 1.574 inches (40 mm) long. It is essential that the pins on the same axle be of the same length.

4. Center brake shoes.
5. Check condition of grease seal before reinstalling brake drum.
6. Adjust front wheel bearings (see **FRONT AXLE**).
7. Adjust and bleed brake system. Do not forget bleeder valve dust caps.
8. Test brakes before moving off and then on the road.

***CAUTION —***
*After new brake shoes have been installed, you will find the braking effect different. The brakes may not be as efficient as you expected. Test the brakes cautiously, and be sure to readjust them after approximately 300 miles.*

## 6.5 Removing and Installing Brake Drums
(rear wheels)

An exploded view of the rear wheel with drum brake is given in Fig. 28. Note differences from front wheel assembly.

1. Cotter pin
2. Slotted nut
3. Brake drum
4. Spring plate (2)
5. Spring (2)
6. Retaining pin (2)
7. Return spring (2)
8. Brake shoe (2, one with lever)
9. Connecting link
10. Return spring
11. Clip
12. Adjusting nut (2)
13. Adjusting screw (2)

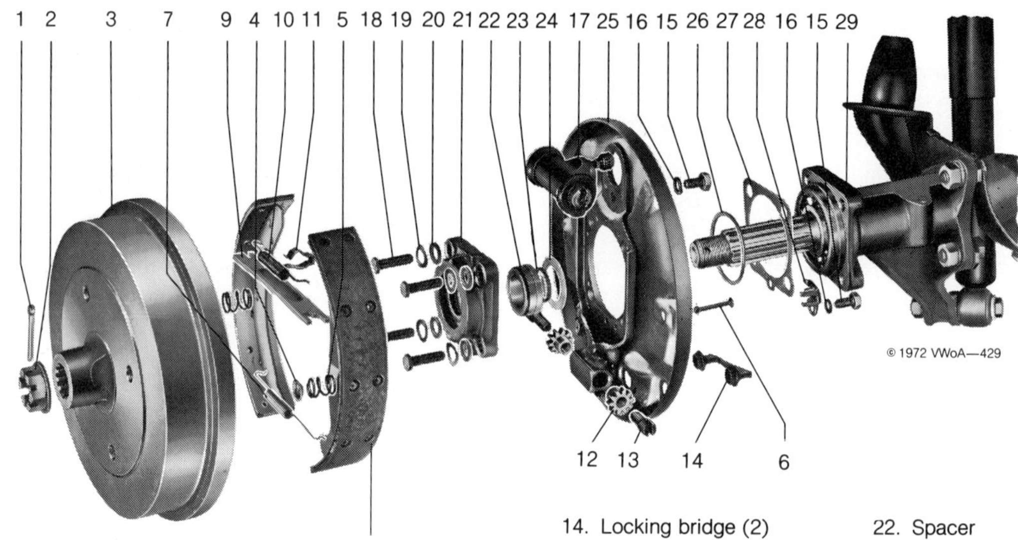


14. Locking bridge (2)
15. Bolt (2)
16. Lock washer (4)
17. Wheel brake cylinder
18. Bolt (4)
19. Spring washer (4)
20. Washer
21. Rear wheel bearing cover
22. Spacer
23. Seal
24. Washer
25. Brake backing plate
26. Seal
27. Gasket
28. Brake cable bracket
29. Wheel bearing housing

**Fig. 28.** Rear wheel brake drum is shown with wheel bearing housing in this exploded view.

***WARNING —***
*You are risking a serious accident if you try to loosen or tighten wheel nuts when the car is up on a lift. You can topple the car over. Always lower the car to the ground before applying force to the wheel nuts.*

Before starting to remove the rear brake drums, back off the brake shoes by turning the adjusting screws. Make sure that the parking brake is off.

**To remove drum:**

1. Remove cotter pin and nut.
2. Lift car.
3. Remove wheel and install puller as shown in Fig. 29.

**NOTE —**
On an older car you may find the brake drum corroded to the splines of the axle shaft. Use a puller to remove the drum, as in Fig. 29.

**Fig. 29.** Puller device will remove brake drum that is corroded to stub axle splines. Be sure to use spacer between puller spindle and axle stub to protect thread. Apply penetrating oil while turning. Do not hit puller with hammer. A blow would damage differential gears.

**To install drum:**

1. Before installing drum, lubricate splines lightly but do not get oil on any other parts.

> ***WARNING—***
> *It is dangerous to torque axle shaft slotted nuts when car is on a lift.*

2. Tighten slotted nut while turning drum until fully home. Install wheel and lower car to ground. Tighten slotted nut to correct torque. If necessary, turn farther to align cotter pin with hole.
3. Insert cotter pin.

## 6.6 Removing and Installing Rear Brake Shoes

**To remove:**

1. Take off rear wheel and brake drum. Check rear wheel cylinders.
2. Secure wheel cylinder piston with wire and remove shoe retainer spring cups, springs and pins.
3. Unhook lower shoe return spring.
4. Disconnect parking brake cable (Fig. 30).

© 1972 VWoA—430

**Fig. 30.** Parking brake cable is disconnected from lever that operates rear wheel brake shoe.

5. Secure wheel brake cylinder. Remove brake shoes with lever (Fig. 31), connecting link, upper return spring and clip.

© 1972 VWoA—431

**Fig. 31.** Brake shoes come off rear wheel with lever, connecting link and upper return spring clip.

6. Remove circlip and take parking brake lever off brake shoe (Fig. 32).

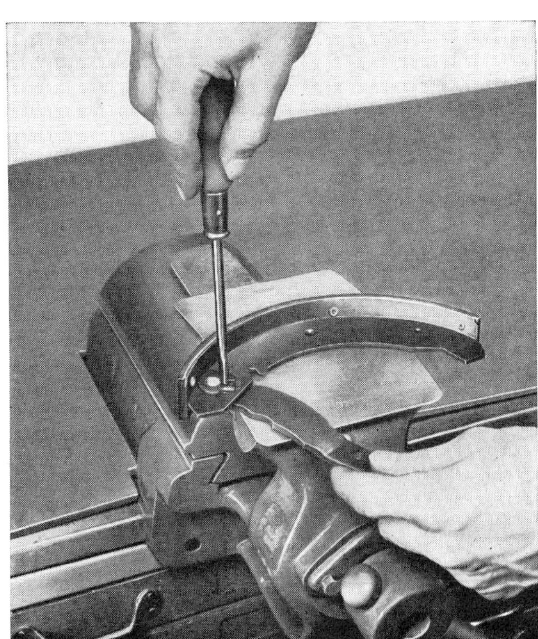

© 1972 VWoA—432

**Fig. 32.** Lever for parking brake is attached to rear brake shoe with circlip.

**To install:**

> ***CAUTION—***
> *Be careful to keep all brake parts clean. Replace worn parts.*

7

1. When replacing brake shoes, be sure linings of the same type are used for both wheels on the same axle. Specified lining widths are:

| | |
|---|---|
| 1966 model | 1.181 inches (30 mm) |
| 1967-1969 models | 1.574 inches (40 mm) |

2. Free up adjustment screws and install brake shoes with lever, connecting link, upper return spring and clip. Connect brake cable.

> ***CAUTION —***
> *Align angled slots in the adjusting screws correctly to receive brake shoe ends, as illustrated in Fig. 33.*

**Fig. 33.** Angled slots in adjusting screws must be positioned correctly (dashed lines) to receive shoe ends.

3. Hook lower return spring to shoes.
4. Install spring cups, retainer springs and pins. The pins should be 1.259 inches (32 mm) long. It is essential that all pins on the same axle be of the same length.
5. Reinstall drum.
6. Tighten axle shaft nut while turning drum to seat drum. Install wheel. Lower car to ground.

> ***WARNING —***
> *Do not torque axle nut with car up on lift.*

7. Torque axle shaft nuts to 217 ft. lbs. (30 mkg) and fit cotter pins.

> **NOTE —**
> If the cotter pin hole is not open when the nut has been tightened to correct torque, turn nut farther until cotter pin can be inserted.

8. Adjust brakes and bleed system. Do not forget the bleeder valve dust caps. Adjust parking brake.

> ***WARNING —***
> *Before you take your car on the road, be aware that repaired or re-installed brakes may not yet be up to full braking efficiency. Test brakes first on an off-street driveway or parking lot.*

9. Test brakes on the road. Be sure to readjust relined brakes after 300 miles.

### 6.7 Reconditioning Brake Drums
(rear wheels)

The comments on reconditioning front wheel drums apply here as well. See **Table b.**

## 7. WHEEL CYLINDERS

The function of the four wheel cylinders is to apply hydraulic pressure to the brake shoes on their respective wheels. Each brake drum has one cylinder. Each cylinder has two pistons, which transmit the pressure uniformly but in opposite directions. An exploded view of a wheel cylinder is given in Fig. 34, top of next page.

Each of the two pistons in a wheel cylinder has a cup behind it to act as a seal. Two cup expanders connected by a spring separate the two cups. Spring tension keeps the rims of the cups in contact with the cylinder wall to maintain the seal behind the pistons.

When the brakes are applied, fluid under pressure from the master cylinder pushes the cups and pistons of the wheel cylinders outward against the brake shoes to force the shoes into contact with the brake drums.

A bleeder valve is screwed into a hole in the cylinder between the two pistons. The valve allows air to be bled from the brake system. In this procedure fresh fluid is forced through the system while the valve is open. The pressurized fluid forces any air in the system to bubble out of the valve.

Rubber boots at the ends of the cylinder keep out dirt and moisture.

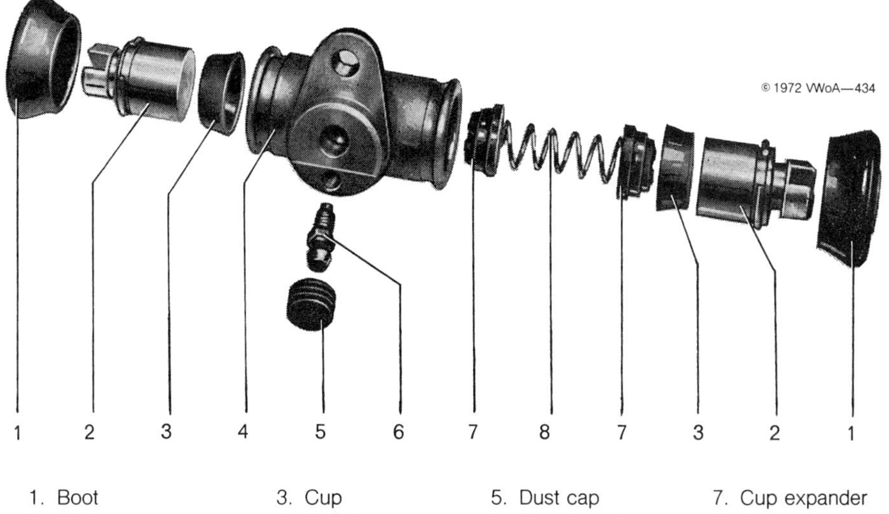


**Fig. 34.** Wheel cylinder is shown here in exploded view.

The cylinders for the front and rear wheels differ in size but are otherwise identical. The diameters are:

Front 0.874 inch (22.20 mm)
Rear 0.750 inch (19.05 mm)

## 7.1 Removing and Installing Front Wheel Cylinders

**To remove:**

1. Take wheel off, loosen brake shoes and remove drum.
2. Disconnect hose and plug brake line with bleeder valve dust cap.
3. Remove shoe retaining spring cups, spring and pins.
4. Remove front return spring. Secure wheel cylinder with wire to keep inner spring from forcing piston out.
5. Pull either shoe out of the adjusting screw slot and take off shoes.
6. Remove adjusting screws and take off wheel cylinder (see Fig. 35).

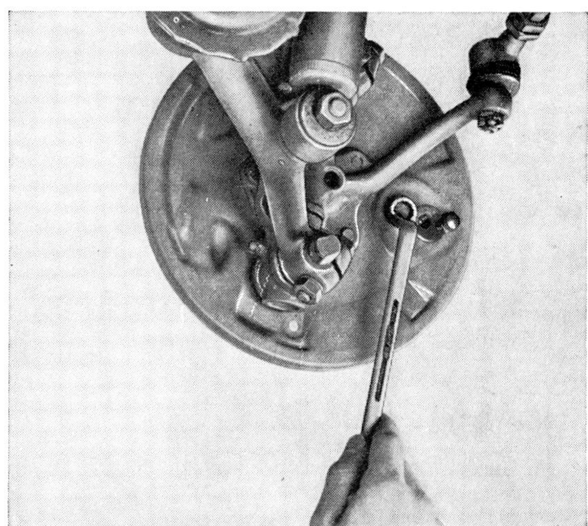


**Fig. 35.** Single bolt attaches front wheel brake cylinder. As here, it is removed from behind backing plate.

**To install:**

1. Install wheel cylinder. If fitting a new cylinder check that the inside diameter is 0.874 inch (22.2 mm).
2. Install hoses, as described in **5.3 Replacing Brake Hoses.**

3. Install brake shoes, as described in **6.4 Replacing Front Brake Shoes.**
4. Install the brake shoe pins, retainer springs and spring cups.
5. Center brake shoes.
6. Check condition of grease seal before fitting brake drum.
7. Adjust front wheel bearings.
8. Adjust and bleed brakes. Do not forget bleeder valve dust caps.
9. Test brakes on the road.

### 7.2 Repairing Front Wheel Cylinders

**To disassemble:**

1. Remove wheel cylinder, as in previous procedure.
2. Remove both boots.
3. Take out piston, cups, cup expanders and spring.
4. Screw out bleeder valve.

**To assemble:**

1. Clean all parts in alcohol or brake fluid.
2. Examine all parts for wear. Do not hone or machine the sliding surfaces to remove visible wear marks, but rather replace part.
3. Fit new cups of the correct size.
4. Coat pistons with VW Brake Cylinder Paste and install them.

### 7.3 Removing and Installing Rear Wheel Cylinders

**To remove:**

1. Take off wheel, loosen brake adjustment, and remove drum. (See **6.2** and **6.5 Removing and Installing Brake Drums**.)
2. Remove spring cups, brake shoe retainer springs and pins.
3. Unhook lower shoe return spring.
4. Disconnect parking brake cable.
5. Remove brake shoes with lever, connecting link, upper return spring and clip.
6. Disconnect brake line and seal with bleeder valve dust cap.
7. Remove bolts and take off cylinder. (See Fig. 36.)

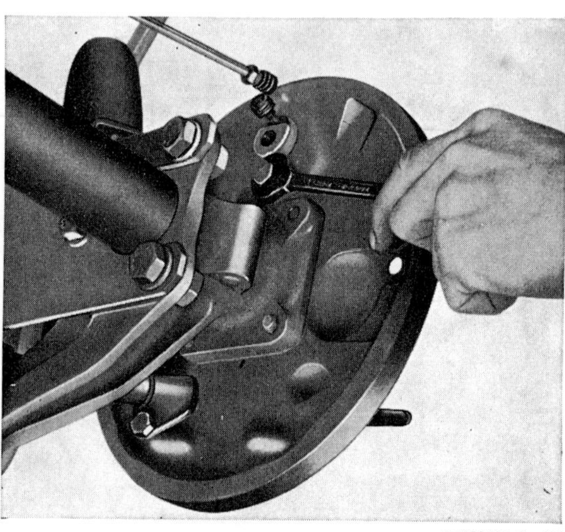



**Fig. 36.** Two bolts attach rear wheel brake cylinder. They are removed from behind backing plate.

**To install:**

1. Install wheel cylinder. The inside diameter of a new cylinder should be 0.750 inch (19.05 mm).
2. Connect brake line.
3. Install brake shoes with lever, connecting link, upper return spring and clip. Connect parking brake cable.
4. Hook lower return spring to brake shoe.
5. Install spring cups, retainer springs and pins.

***WARNING —***
*You are risking a serious accident if you try to loosen or tighten wheel nuts when the car is up on a lift. You could topple the car over. Lower car to the ground for this work.*

6. Tighten axle shaft nuts to 217 ft. lbs. (30 mkg) and secure with new cotter pin. Turn to next cotter pin hole if necessary.
7. Adjust brakes and bleed system. Do not forget bleeder valve dust caps. Adjust parking brakes.
8. Test brakes on the road.

***WARNING —***
*Before you take your car on the road, be aware that repaired or re-installed brakes may not yet be up to full braking efficiency. Test brakes first on off-street driveway or parking lot.*

## 8. PARKING BRAKE LEVER

The components of the parking brake lever assembly are shown in Fig. 37.

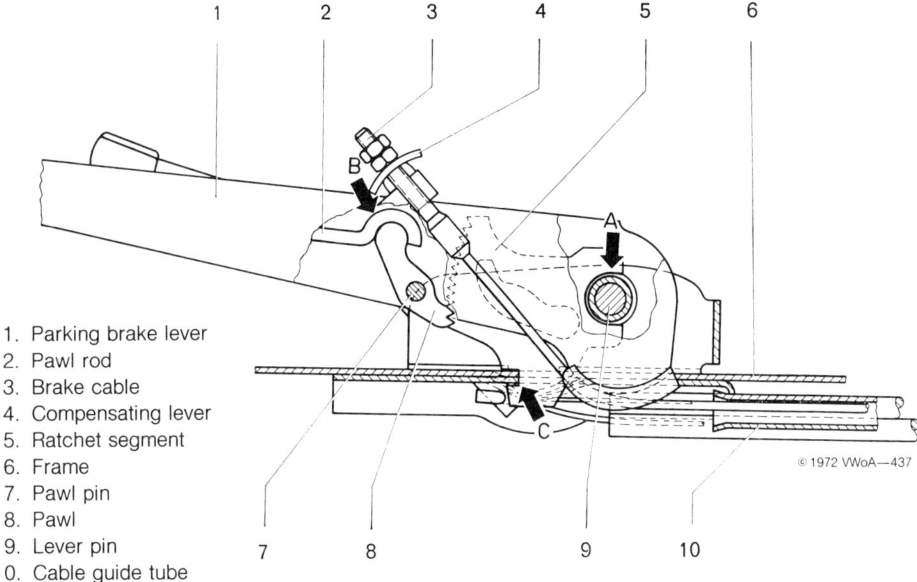


**Fig. 37.** Parking brake lever is shown with attachments in this cutaway diagram. See text for explanation of the points indicated by the black arrows at A, B and C.

### 8.1 Removing and Installing Parking Brake Lever

**To remove:**

1. On 1966 and 1967 models take front seats out and remove rear floor covering. (Not necessary on 1968 and 1969 models.)
2. Pull off cover of parking brake lever (see Fig. 37).
3. Remove lock and adjusting nuts from cables. Take off compensating lever.
4. Remove circlip from lever pin and take pin out.
5. Without pressing release button, push lever to the rear until it can be lifted out with the ratchet segment.
6. Press release button and take out ratchet segment.

**To install:**

1. Disassemble lever. Clean pawl rod, press button, pawl spring and ratchet segment. Grease all parts and assemble.
2. With reference to Fig. 37, insert ratchet segment so that the recess fits over the tube in lever (A) and the teeth engage in pawl. Make sure that rounded end of pawl is positioned correctly (B).
3. Insert lever from above, guiding threaded ends of cables to the sides.

**NOTE —**
Slot in the ratchet segment (Fig. 38) must engage frame edge when lever is inserted, as seen at (C) in Fig. 37.

7

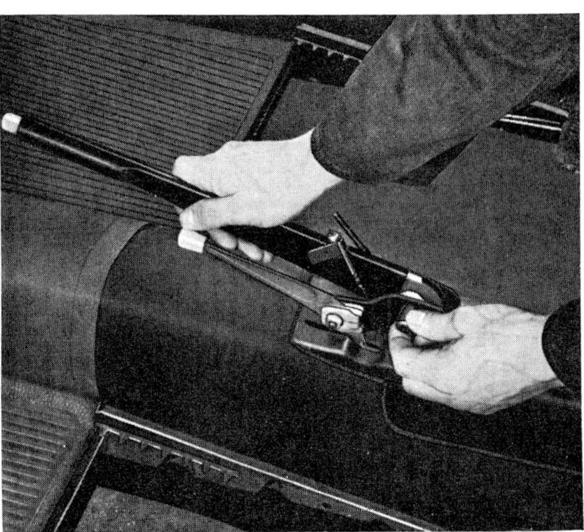


**Fig. 38.** Ratchet segment fits over lever pin (9) at point indicated by arrow and labeled (A) in Fig. 37.

4. Grease lever pin, install and secure with circlip.
5. Fit compensating lever.
6. Attach cables and adjust parking brake.
7. Fit lock nuts.
8. Install lever cover.
9. Replace rear floor covering and re-install front seats.
10. Road test car and check parking brake.

### 8.2 Removing and Installing Parking Brake Cables

**To remove:**

1. Release parking brake and detach cable from lever.
2. Remove rear wheel and brake drum.
3. Remove brake shoes.
4. Detach cable clip from backing plate.
5. Pull cable with guide hose out of backing plate and cable guide tube and replace with one of identical length.

**NOTE ——**
From August 1, 1966, chassis No. 117 000 002, the rear wheel track was increased. All models have been equipped with longer parking brake cables and modified rear brake lines.

**To install:**

1. Clean cables and guide tube.
2. When installing new cables, recheck length.
3. Lubricate cables well with universal water-repellent grease.
4. Adjust parking brake.
5. Check parking brake on the road.

## 9. BLEEDING THE BRAKES

***WARNING ——***
*Brake fluid is poisonous. Never try to siphon brake fluid by sucking on a drainage tube. The fluid also is damaging to paint.*

Every time you disconnect a brake hose or line you must bleed the brake system and then top it up. If the brake pedal action feels spongy or pedal travel is excessive, it is time to bleed the brakes.

The hydraulic brake system must be free of air bubbles if it is to work properly. Otherwise, movement of the master cylinder piston will not cause an immediate, uniformly proportional movement of all the pistons at the wheels. To give this immediate response the fluid in the system must be incompressible. But air is compressible. Since it is compressible, air in the brake system will squash under pressure instead of transmitting the pressure uniformly as brake fluid does.

Brake fluid is hygroscopic—that is, it absorbs moisture from the air. Water is incompressible like brake fluid, but its boiling point is lower. Under severe braking conditions, water in the system will vaporize to produce the same situation as having air in the lines. Freezing of trapped water in winter gives the system a sluggish response to braking. Further, water in the system corrodes the master cylinder and wheel cylinders. The system must be bled from time to time to get rid of water as well as air. Change brake fluid every two (2) years.

### 9.1 Brake Fluid

Only VW brake fluid or another fluid complying with SAE specification J 1703 should be used in the brake system of your car. These fluids will perform reliably regardless of weather. The recommended fluids will not damage the structure or surface of any of the seals or other components of the brake system.

Never re-use brake fluid that has been taken from the brake system of your car. Besides falling below specifications, old fluid can introduce both dirt and water into the system. Always top up with fresh fluid from a previously unopened container.

### 9.2 Brake Cylinder Paste

Never use mineral oil or grease to lubricate the sealing parts of the hydraulic brake system. VW brake cylinder paste, which is neutral in respect to the sealing materials in the system and which improves the sliding qualities of pistons and cups.

Before installing a brake system cylinder (master or wheel), disassemble it, wash it thoroughly in alcohol and dry it. Then coat the piston (or pistons) and the inside walls of the cylinder with brake cylinder paste before assembling. Any time there is occasion to take a cylinder apart, use this paste.

### 9.3 Flushing Brake System

Never use anything but brake fluid to flush the brake system. Use alcohol for cleaning pistons and other components, but not for flushing the system.

## 9.4 Procedure for Bleeding

Bleeding the brakes is a job for two persons. While one works the brake pedal, the other does the bleeding.

> **NOTE —**
> Submerge the drain hose in brake fluid in a glass jar, so you can watch for air bubbles as the bleeding progresses. Once air bubbles cease to appear, shut off bleed valve.

**To bleed:**

1. Place the fluid container on the reservoir (as shown in Fig. 39) to keep the reservoir full during the bleeding process.

© 1972 VWoA—439

**Fig. 39.** Container of fluid is placed on reservoir to keep system full while brakes are bled.

2. Take dust caps off bleeder valves on wheel cylinders. Start bleeding at the wheel cylinder which is farthest from the master cylinder (see sequence in Fig. 40).

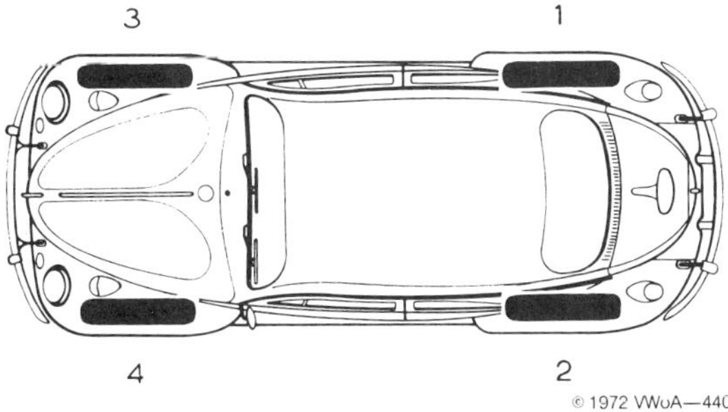


© 1972 VWoA—440

**Fig. 40.** Bleeding sequence for brake system is given by numbers at the wheels. Procedure starts at right rear wheel (1).

> ***WARNING —***
> *Brake fluid is poisonous. It also is damaging to paint.*

3. Place bleeder hose on wheel cylinder bleeder valve.
4. Loosen bleeder valve about one turn.
5. Depress the brake pedal quickly and allow it to return slowly. Continue to depress and release pedal until bubbles no longer appear in the sight tube in the bleeder hose or in the glass jar. (See Fig. 41.)

© 1972 VWoA—441

**Fig. 41.** Bleeding apparatus shown here is more elaborate than necessary. Clean glass jar partly filled with brake fluid is sufficient. See text.

6. Depress pedal once more and hold at lowest position until bleeder valve has been closed.
7. Take off bleeder hose and secure dust cap.
8. Repeat process on each wheel in turn.

## 9.5 Changing Brake Fluid

At least once every two years the brake fluid in your car should be changed. The procedure is basically the same as bleeding the brakes.

**Table a. Pedal Strokes**

| | |
|---|---|
| **a. Cars with single circuit brakes:** | |
| Rear, right bleeder valve open | 12 pedal strokes = approx. 80 cc of fluid |
| Rear, left bleeder valve open | 8 pedal strokes = approx. 70 cc of fluid |
| Front, right bleeder valve open | 8 pedal strokes = approx. 70 cc of fluid |
| Front, left bleeder valve open | 8 pedal strokes = approx. 70 cc of fluid |
| **b. Cars with dual circuit brakes:** | |
| Front, right bleeder valve open | 30 pedal strokes = approx. 100 cc of fluid |
| Front, left bleeder valve open | 15 pedal strokes = approx. 50 cc of fluid |
| Rear, right bleeder valve open | 25 pedal strokes = approx. 80 cc of fluid |
| Rear, left bleeder valve open | 10 pedal strokes = approx. 30 cc of fluid |

**To drain and replace fluid:**

1. Using a plastic squeeze bottle or a siphoning apparatus (never your mouth), remove as much fluid as possible from the reservoir. Then add fresh brake fluid. (Keep the plastic bottle or siphon for use with brake fluid only.)
2. Change the fluid in the cylinders and lines. This procedure is bleeding the brakes on a grand scale. The brake pedal will have to be depressed many times and the bleeder valves opened and closed for each action of the pedal.

**NOTE —**
Be alert to keep the refill container from running dry in the course of this operation.

3. During Step 2 catch the used brake fluid in a measuring glass. To make sure that the entire system is filled with new fluid, the number of pedal strokes must be compared with the amount of fluid to be taken from each bleeder valve. **Table a** gives the specifications.

## 10. ADJUSTING DRUM BRAKES

In the course of use, normal wear on the brake linings reduces the clearance between the brake shoes and brake drums. The wear shows up in extra travel of the brake pedal. When the extra travel becomes excessive, the brake shoes must be adjusted. The adjusting is done at each wheel.

**To adjust brake shoe:**

**NOTE —**
Before making any adjustment of the brakes, check play of front wheel bearing.

1. Raise car and release parking brake.
2. Depress brake pedal as far as possible several times to center brake shoes in the drums.
3. Turn the wheel to be adjusted until hole in brake drum is in line with one of the adjusting nuts.
4. Insert screwdriver through the hole (Fig. 42) and turn adjuster, using screwdriver as a lever, until a light drag is noted when the wheel is turned by hand. Then back off adjuster three or four teeth to allow the wheel to turn freely.

**NOTE —**
If the brakes are far out of adjustment it may be necessary to again center the shoes once or twice during the course of adjustments.

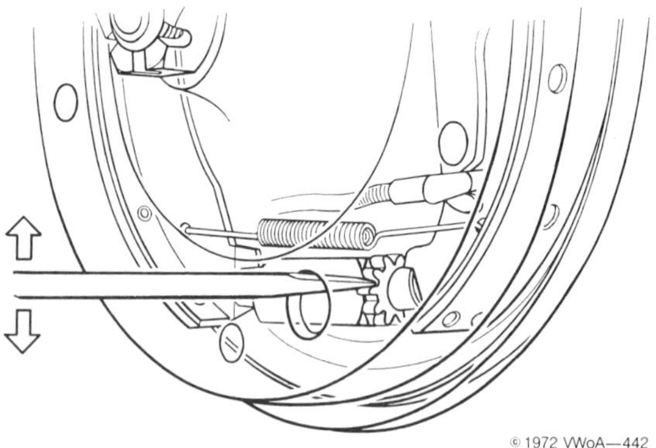


**Fig. 42.** Screwdriver inserted through hole in brake drum turns adjuster to change clearance between brake shoe and brake drum.

5. Repeat the procedure on the other adjusting nut. Note that the two nuts turn in opposite directions.
6. Repeat the procedure on the other wheels.
7. Road test the brakes.

### 10.1 Adjusting Parking Brake

Make sure that foot brakes are properly adjusted before you adjust the parking brake. The parking brake cables are adjusted at the parking brake lever. The adjusting screws are accessible through slots in the sides of the parking brake lever boot (shown in Fig. 43).

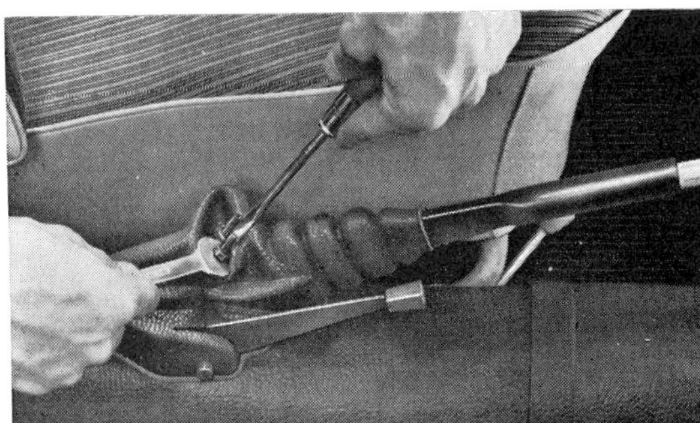

© 1972 VWoA—443

**Fig. 43.** Adjusting screws for parking brake are accessible through slots in side of brake lever boot.

**To adjust:**

1. Lift the car.
2. Fold back slots in boot to get at adjusting screws and loosen locknuts.
3. Tighten adjusting nuts but leave the rear wheels still turning freely when the parking brake is off.
4. Apply parking brake two notches. Check whether braking effort on both wheels is the same. At about four to five notches you no longer should be able to turn the wheels by hand.

   **NOTE** —
   The compensating lever must be horizontal when parking brake is applied.

5. Tighten locknuts.
6. Fit boot again. The cover flaps for the slots must be pushed inward.
7. Road test the brake.

## 10.2 Relining Brake Shoes

When it is necessary to replace brake shoe linings, always replace both linings on both wheels on the axle. That is, replace the linings on both front wheels or both rear wheels, never on one wheel alone. This procedure will ensure uniform braking. By the same token, use linings of the same quality on both wheels.

Replace oil-soaked brake linings. Washing old brake linings in fuel or some other solvent is useless. As soon as the brakes warm up, the oil deep in the porous material will ooze to the surface.

**To reline shoe:**

1. Remove brake shoes.
2. Take off old linings carefully to avoid distorting or otherwise damaging the shoes.
3. Clean shoes and remove burrs from rivet holes.
4. Rivet new linings, beginning with center rivet and working outward (Fig. 44).

© 1972 VWoA—444

**Fig. 44.** Brake lining is riveted on shoe. Riveting should be done from center of lining outward to ends. Lining must make uniform contact.

Be sure to fit the new linings so that they do not overhang the sides of the shoes. A lining should make contact with the entire surface of the shoe. Otherwise, the brakes will be noisy and inefficient. To reduce tension in the linings, be careful to press the rivets straight in.

The linings for front and rear wheel shoes are of different widths:

| | | |
|---|---|---|
| Front | 1.6 inches (40 mm) | |
| Rear | 1.2 inches (30 mm) | |
| | 1.6 inches (40 mm) | August 1967 |

## 10.3 Machining Specifications

The specifications for reworking scored, worn or out-of-round brake drums are given in **Table b.**

7

### Table b. Brake Drum Specifications

| Size | Brake drum diameter | |
|---|---|---|
| | front | rear |
| Original | 0.050 + .008 in. (230.1 + 0.2 mm) | 0.055 + .008 in. (230.0 + 0.2 mm) |
| a | 9.098 + .008 in. (231.1 + 0.2 mm) | 9.094 + .008 in. (231.0 + 0.2 mm) |
| b | .157 in. (4 mm) | .157 in. (4 mm) |
| c | 9.103 in. (231.5 mm) | 9.103 in. (231.5 mm) |

The general procedure for reworking brake drums follows:

1. Turn the internal diameter of the drum to the appropriate measurement in line "a" of table. The wall thickness remaining after this work must be not less than the appropriate measurement shown on line "b". The braking surface of the drum must not taper more than 0.004 inch (0.1 mm). The maximum axial run-out allowed is 0.010 inch (0.25 mm). Measurement "c" gives the wear limit.
2. Be sure to fit oversize linings to match the new dimensions of reconditioned brake drums.

## 11. Dual Circuit Drum Brakes

Cars of the model years 1967 through 1969 (except Karmann Ghias) are equipped with dual circuit drum brakes. Most of the components of this system are the same as in the single-circuit system, and the same maintenance procedures apply to them. The differences will be emphasized in the following discussions.

### 11.1 General Description

The dual-circuit brake system has a tandem master cylinder and a two-chamber fluid reservoir in place of the single circuit cylinder and reservoir previously described. In basic design, the tandem cylinder is like two single cylinders fitted one behind the other. The forward pressure chamber of the cylinder is connected to the front wheel brakes. The rear pressure chamber is connected to the rear wheel brakes. Fig. 45 gives cutaway views of the tandem cylinder and the two-chamber fluid reservoir.

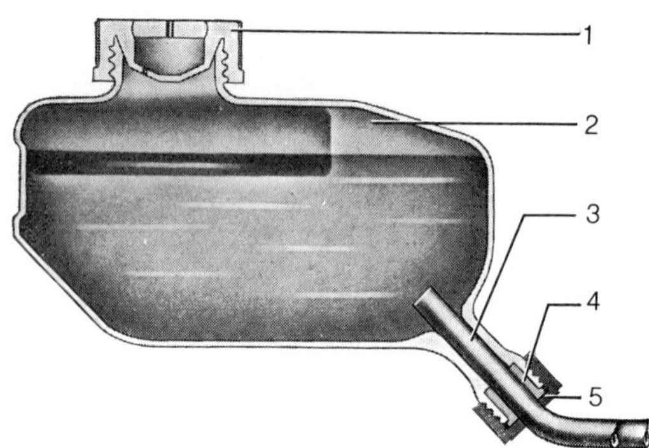


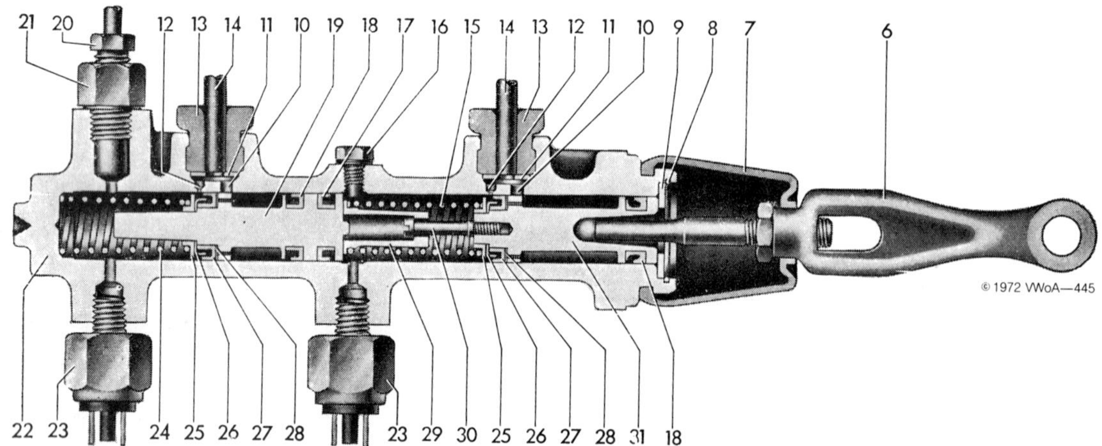


**Fig. 45.** Master cylinder for dual-circuit brake system is shown in the cross section with the later model brake fluid reservoir. Note relationship of the two pistons.

1. Screw cap
2. Brake fluid reservoir
3. Feed line
4. Feed line seal
5. Line securing nut
6. Push rod
7. Boot
8. Spring ring
9. Stop ring
10. Feed port
11. Sealing plug washer
12. Compensating port
13. Sealing plug
14. Feed line
15. Rear brake circuit piston spring
16. Stop screw and seal
17. Seal
18. Secondary cup
19. Front brake circuit piston
20. Brake line union nut
21. Residual pressure valve
22. Master cylinder housing
23. Brake light switch
24. Front brake circuit piston spring
25. Spring plate
26. Support ring
27. Primary cup
28. Cup washer
29. Stop sleeve
30. Stroke limiting screw
31. Rear brake circuit piston

The connections of the two-chamber reservoir and the tandem cylinder divide the hydraulic brake system into two completely independent systems capable of operating individually. If for any reason the pressure fails in one system, the intact second system is capable of bringing the car to a stop, but in a greater distance.

Suppose a leak occurs in the front circuit. The action of the brake pedal pushes both master cylinder pistons (and the fluid between them) forward until the front piston comes to a stop against the end of the cylinder housing. The rear piston then builds up pressure in the fluid between the two pistons, and this pressure is transmitted

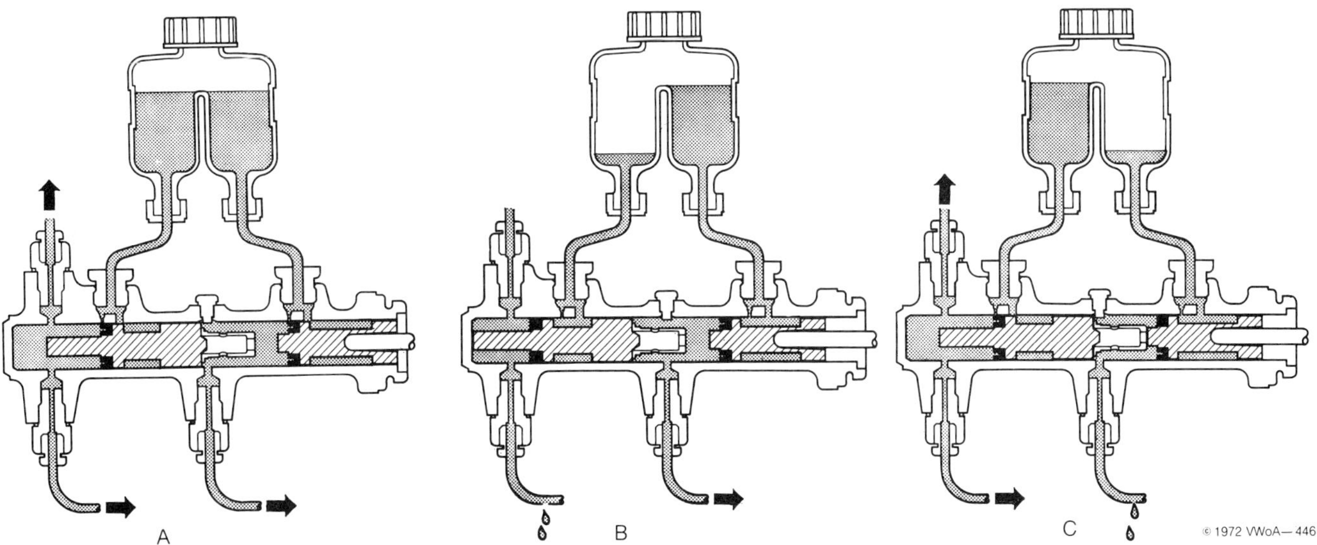


**Fig. 46.** Dual-circuit system keeps one set of brakes in operation if other fails. Three possible conditions are shown here: both circuits intact (A); front circuit out, rear circuit operating (B); rear circuit out, front circuit operating (C). See text for explanation.

throughout the rear circuit. Fig. 46 illustrates what happens in both a front-circuit leak and rear-circuit leak.

In a rear-circuit leak the rear piston goes forward to bear against the stop sleeve and exert mechanical force on the front piston, which then builds up pressure in the front circuit. The failure of either circuit increases the travel of the brake pedal considerably, and a greater distance is required to stop the car.

## 11.2 Brake Fluid Reservoir

The brake fluid reservoir for the dual-circuit brake system has separate lines leading from the chambers to the brake circuits. This division of the fluid supply is necessary to ensure that one brake circuit will continue to function if the other loses brake fluid.

Always fill the brake fluid reservoir to the upper edge of the securing strap. The fluid level must be above the dividing wall between the two chambers.

## 11.3 Tandem Master Cylinder

Fig. 47 illustrates the operating sequence of the tandem master cylinder.

When the brake pedal is depressed, the push rod (1) forces the rear piston (2) forward. The primary cup (3) covers the compensating port (4) to close the rear pressure chamber (I). Pressure then builds up in chamber (I) and forces front piston (5) forward. The front primary cup (7) covers the front compensating port (6) to close the front pressure chamber (II). The pressure in the two chambers forces the fluid into the lines for the two circuits and to the wheel cylinders.

The internal dimensions of the tandem cylinder are:

| | | |
|---|---|---|
| Diameter | 0.75 inch | (19.05 mm) |
| Total stroke | 1.10 inches | (28.00 mm) |
| Front circuit stroke | 0.61 inch | (15.50 mm) |
| Rear circuit stroke | 0.49 inch | (12.50 mm) |

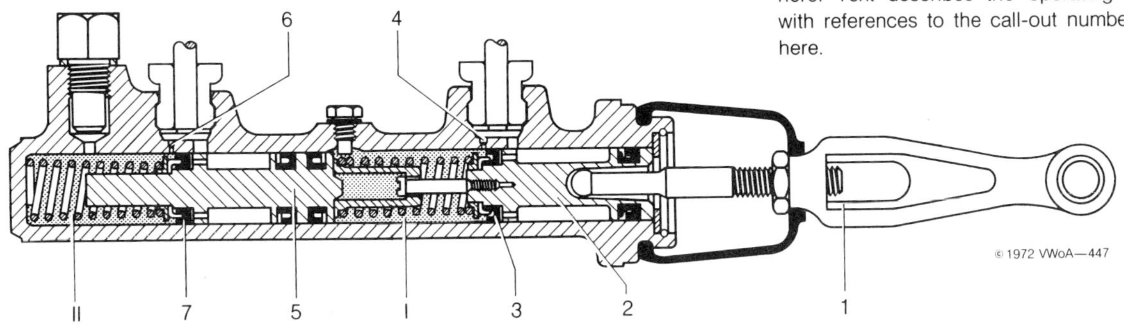


**Fig. 47.** Master cylinder without warning switch is shown here. Text describes the operating sequence with references to the call-out numbers shown here.

## 11.4 Brake System with Warning Device

Cars from August 1, 1967, chassis No. 118 000 001, are fitted with a warning device to indicate when one of the brake circuits is defective. The device consists of an auxiliary chamber on the master cylinder with two small pistons to operate a switch controlling a warning light on the instrument panel.

Two drillings, one to each pressure chamber in the master cylinder, connect the warning device to the brake system. Springs force the two small pistons together with the contact pin of the switch between them. The drillings from the pressure chambers of the master cylinder are at either end of the warning device assembly, as shown in Fig. 48. If the pressure collapses in either brake circuit, the pressure differential between the intact and collapsed circuit then forces the small pistons toward the drilling for that circuit. The movement operates the warning light switch.

## 11.5 Brake Light Switch

The tandem master cylinder has a brake light switch for each circuit (Fig. 49).

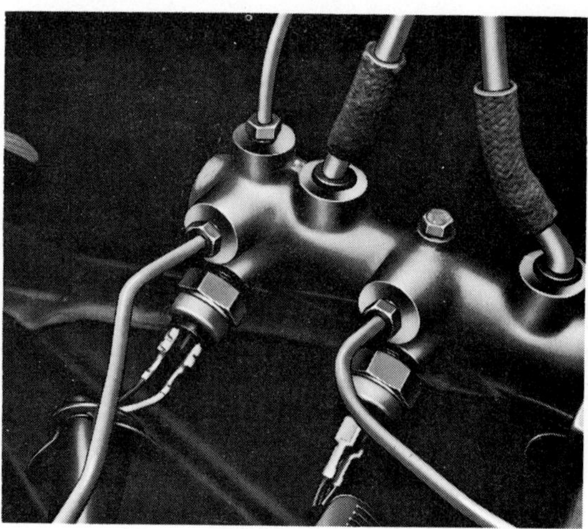


**Fig. 49.** Brake light switches are provided for both circuits on tandem master cylinder. Switches are just below brake line connections on cylinders.

**Fig. 48.** Warning light switch is in housing connected by drillings to the master cylinder pressure chambers. This diagram shows relative position of switch.

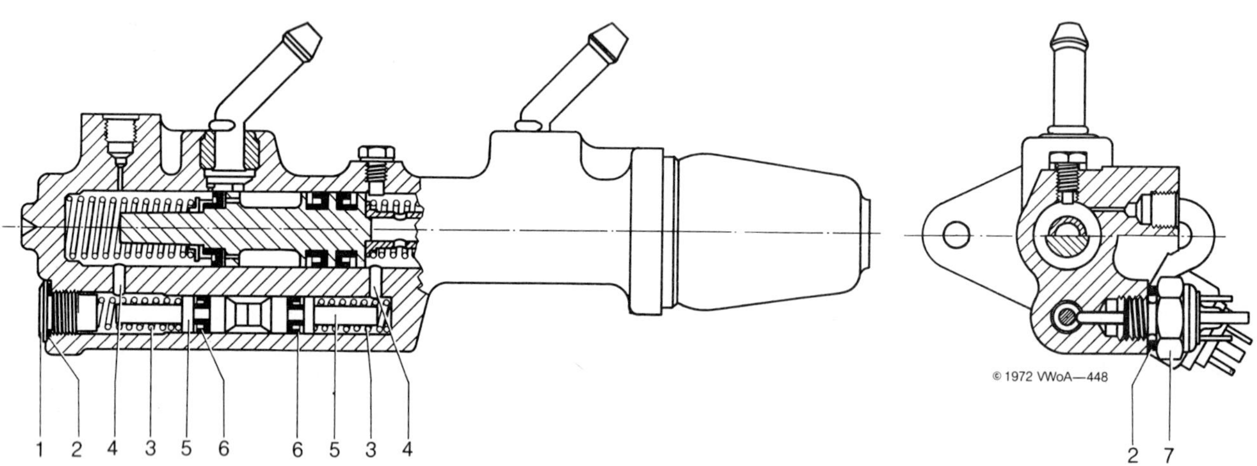


1. Plug
2. Washer
3. Spring
4. Connecting drilling
5. Piston for warning device
6. Piston cup
7. Switch

## 11.6 Residual Pressure Valve

In the tandem master cylinder residual pressure valves take the place of the check valve in the single-circuit system. A residual pressure valve is screwed into each connection on the tandem master cylinder. A master cylinder thus has three such valves, two for the front brake circuit and one for the rear brake circuit.

The three diagrams in Fig. 50 illustrate the operations of the residual pressure valves when the brakes are in the "off" position (A); when the brakes are applied (B), and when the brakes have just been released (C).

In the "off" position the residual pressure spring (1) working on the sleeve (2) forces the seal (3) against the shoulder of the support (7) to seal off the cylinder. The spring (6) working on the sleeve (5) presses the ball (4) against the seal to shut off the brake lines.

When the brakes are applied, rising hydraulic pressure overcomes spring pressure to lift the ball off its seat. Brake fluid flows around the ball, through the slotted sleeve into the brake lines. When the brakes are released, the higher pressure in the lines overcomes spring pressure (1). The seal lifts from its seat, and brake fluid flows past the ball back into the cylinder.

The spring (1) is designed to hold a low residual pressure in the brake system so that force applied at the brake pedal is transferred directly to the brake system without lag from lost movement. Fig. 51 shows a disassembled tandem master cylinder.

**Fig. 50.** Residual pressure valve operates in the three positions shown here: brakes off (A); brakes on (B) and brakes just released (C). See text.

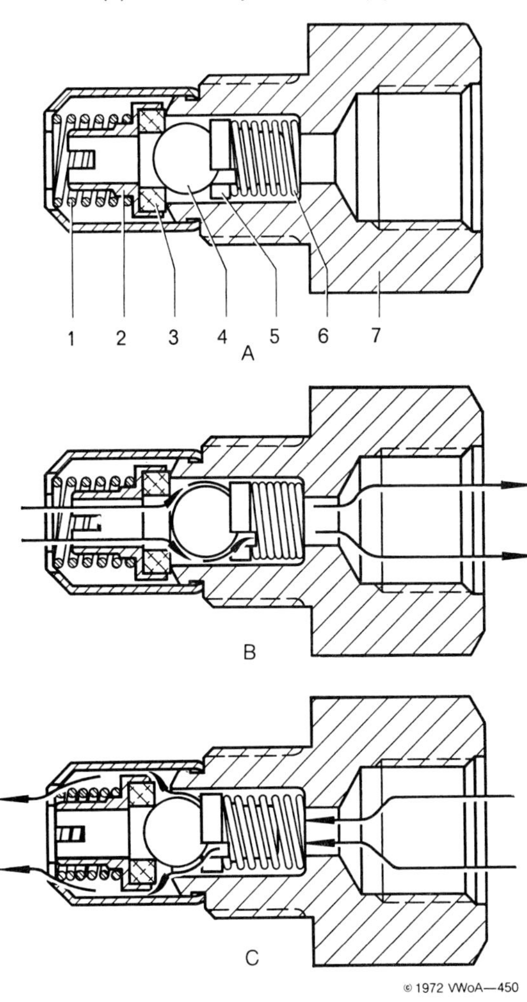

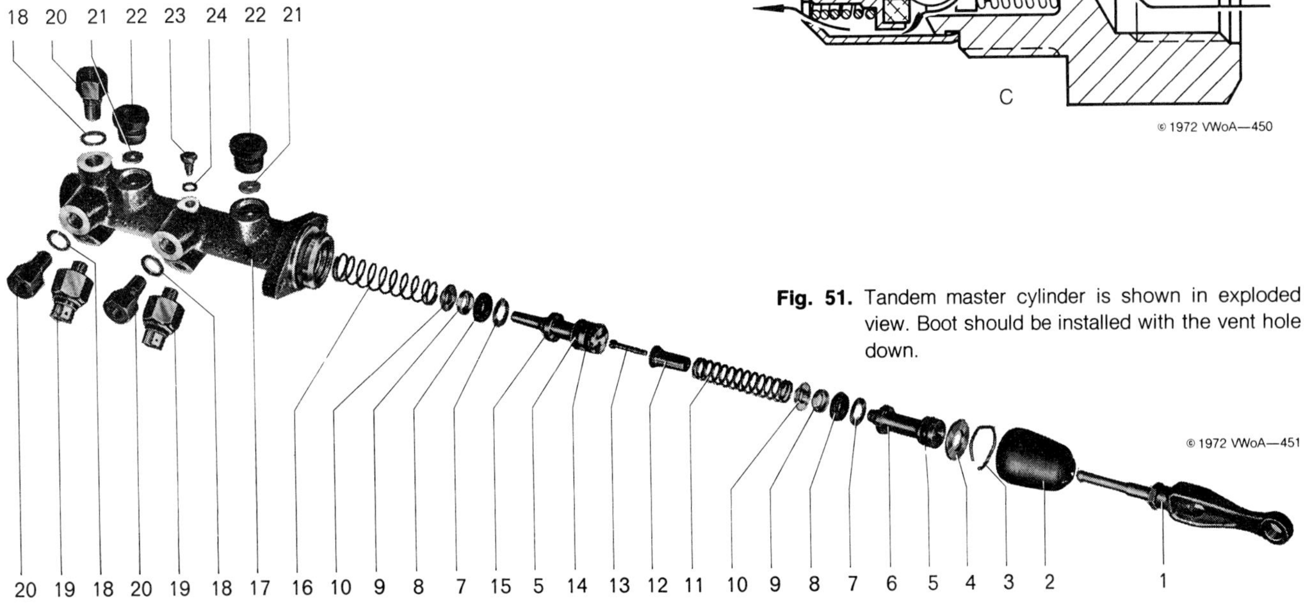

**Fig. 51.** Tandem master cylinder is shown in exploded view. Boot should be installed with the vent hole down.

© 1972 VWoA—451

1. Push rod
2. Boot
3. Spring ring
4. Stop ring
5. Secondary cup
6. Rear brake circuit piston
7. Cup washer
8. Primary cup
9. Support washer
10. Spring plate
11. Rear brake circuit piston spring
12. Stop sleeve
13. Stroke limiting screw
14. Seal
15. Front brake circuit piston
16. Front brake circuit piston spring
17. Master cylinder housing
18. Residual pressure valve seal
19. Brake light switch
20. Residual pressure valve
21. Sealing plug washer
22. Sealing plug
23. Stop screw
24. Stop screw seal

## 11.7 Repairing Tandem Master Cylinder

**CAUTION —**
*Two manufacturers supply the tandem master cylinders and repair kits that are available from VW dealers. To prevent malfunction of the brake system, be sure you have the correct repair kit for the master cylinder in your car. The repair parts put in the kit made by one manufacturer must not be installed in the housing of a tandem brake master cylinder made by another manufacturer. When carrying out repairs on the master cylinder, you must install all the parts of the repair kit together, even if only one internal part of the master cylinder has been damaged.*

*To avoid confusion, note the following part numbers:*

*ATE Repair Kits 111 698 181 B*
*Schaefer Repair Kits 111 698 183 A*

**To disassemble master cylinder:**

**WARNING —**
*Do not change push rod adjustment. The factory setting must be kept.*

1. Remove boot.
2. Unscrew stop screw.
3. Remove spring ring for stop ring.
4. Remove internal parts of cylinder.
5. Unscrew residual pressure valves and brake light switch.

**To assemble:**

1. Clean all parts, using alcohol or brake fluid only.

**CAUTION —**
*Be sure that the compensating ports are not blocked or burred.*

2. Check parts for wear.

**NOTE —**
With exception of the secondary cup for the rear brake circuit piston, all cups are of the same shape and the same size and therefore interchangeable.

3. Install cups on pistons with installing sleeve, as seen in Fig. 52.

**Fig. 52.** Piston cup has been placed over conical cup sleeve (right) for installation on piston (left).

4. Hold master cylinder housing with the opening downward. Then place cup washer, primary cup, support washer, spring plate and conical spring on the front brake circuit piston and insert piston vertically into the housing. This sequence is necessary. If you try to put the piston in horizontally, the parts will fall off.
5. Assemble rear brake circuit piston, cup washer, primary cup, support washer, spring plate, stop sleeve cylindrical spring and stroke limiting screw, and insert into master cylinder.
6. Install stop washer and spring ring.
7. Install stop screw and seal after checking that hole for screw is not covered by front brake circuit piston. If hole is covered, push the parts farther inside the cylinder with the push rod while you screw in the stop screw.
8. Screw residual pressure valve and brake light switch into master cylinder housing and tighten to a torque of 11 to 14 ft. lbs. (1.5 to 2.0 mkg).
9. Install protective cap boot with breather hole downward.
10. Install sealing plugs with large diameter ridge toward receptacle on master cylinder.
11. Before installing cylinder in car, insert elbows into plugs, turning them to point in the correct direction.

**NOTE —**
You will need a cup sleeve for installation of the front secondary cup on the front piston. The sleeve will make installation of the cups easier.

## 11.8 Bleeding the Brakes

When bleeding both circuits of the dual-circuit brake system, always start with the front one. When bleeding the brakes after some repair in one of the circuits, it is sufficient to bleed only the circuit in which the repair was made.

## 11.9 Testing Brake Light Switch

**NOTE —**
This procedure can be used on the single circuit master cylinder also.

**To test switch:**

1. Disconnect wires from brake light switch (Fig. 53) for front or single brake circuit. Switch on ignition and operate foot brake. Brake lights should work.
2. Connect wires and repeat test on brake light switch for rear brake circuit (if applicable).
3. If either test fails to switch on the brake lights, replace the defective switch.

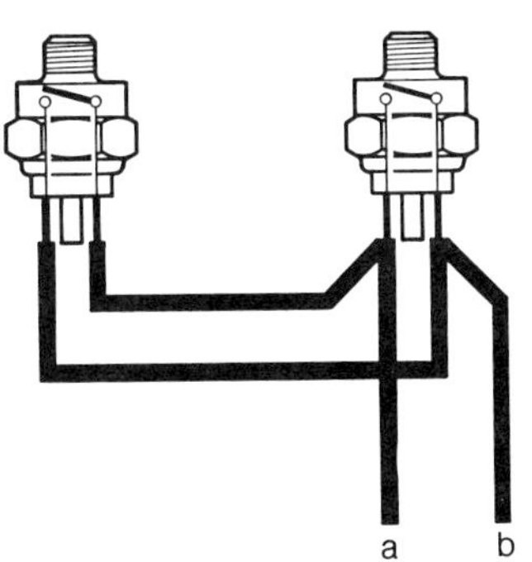


**Fig. 53.** Wiring schematic shows hook-up of brake light switches. Wire "a" goes to terminal 15. Wire "b" leads to the brake lights. Switch at the left is for front wheel brakes, right for rear wheels.

## 11.10 Testing Brake Warning Device Switch

Before you test or replace switch, make sure that the bulb is not dead.

**To test:**

1. Turn on ignition and test warning light by pressing the pushbutton. Warning light should come on. If it does not, replace bulb.
2. Remove warning device switch from master cylinder, but be careful not to remove brake light switches.
3. Depress plunger on warning device switch and observe warning light. If light does not come on, replace switch.

## 11.11 Removing and Installing Brake Light Switch/Warning Device Switch

Look at Fig. 53 and Fig. 54 to see the connections and hook-up of the switches.

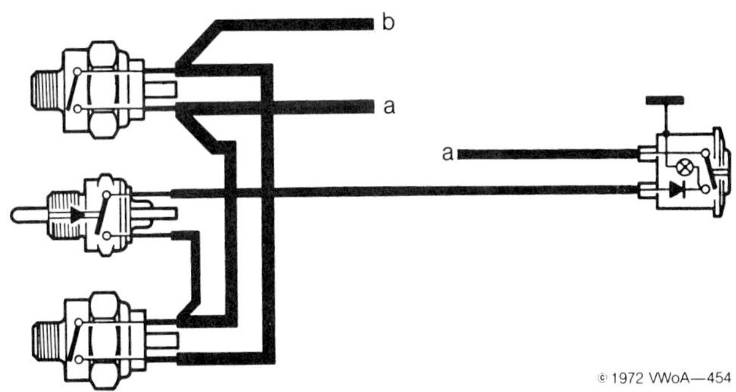


**Fig. 54.** Connections for brake light switch and warning device switch are shown in this wiring diagram. Wire "a" goes to terminal 15, wire "b" to brake lights.

1. Disconnect wires from brake light switch or warning device switch and unscrew switch. Have a cloth to catch any fluid.
2. Install new brake light switch/warning device switch and connect wires according to wiring diagram.
3. After installing brake light switch, bleed appropriate brake circuit. Bleeding is not necessary for the warning device switch.

7

## 12. DISC BRAKES
(Karmann Ghia)

The Karmann Ghia models of the years covered in this Manual have drum brakes on the rear wheels but are equipped with disc brakes on the front wheels. The brake system is dual circuit and, apart from the discs, is substantially the same as the system on the other cars of 1967 through 1969. Car disc brakes were developed from brakes designed originally for the high landing speeds of jet aircraft.

## 12.1 General Description

The main parts of a disc brake (see Fig. 55) are the disc, which turns with the wheel, and the caliper, which contains the hydraulically-operated braking mechanism. A splash shield bolted to the steering knuckle protects the inner surface of the disc from dirt and stones. The road wheel gives protection for the outer surface.

**Fig. 55.** Disc brake assembly consists of the splash shield (1); brake disc (2) and caliper (3). The caliper, which is bolted to the steering knuckle, contains the two pistons and the two brake pads. The disc turns on the steering knuckle spindle. The assembly shown here is for the right front wheel of a Karmann Ghia.

The brake caliper is at the back of the wheel, behind the axle. It consists of an inner and an outer housing, one at each side of the brake disc. Four bolts hold the two housings together, and two bolts secure the entire caliper to the steering knuckle.

A cylindrical bore for a piston is machined into each caliper housing. Under hydraulic pressure from the tandem master cylinder, the two pistons move toward the brake disc, which intersects their opposing directions of travel. In other words, the disc spins in a plane between the faces of the two pistons and perpendicular to the lines of travel of the pistons. A rubber seal at the rear of each piston and a rubber boot in a groove at the front prevent leakage of brake fluid and keep out dirt and moisture.

A recess roughly triangular in shape is machined in the lower third of the face of the piston to hold a piston retaining plate. The plate slides along a flat surface in the caliper housing toward the disc. Its function is to keep the piston from turning under the forces of braking. The piston is correctly positioned in the housing when a line drawn along the upper edge of this recess in the face makes an angle of 20 degrees with the surface on which the retaining plate slides. There is a special gauge to fix the piston in this position. The parts mentioned here are shown in Fig. 56.

The actual braking force is applied to the disc by brake pads sliding ahead of the pistons in grooves in the caliper housings. Spreader springs press the pads against the pistons to eliminate vibration and thus reduce noise.

The inner housing of the caliper has a threaded fitting for connection to the hydraulic system and a bleeder valve. Internal passages for the brake fluid connect the piston bores in the two housings.

## 12.2 Disc Brake Operation

When the brake pedal is depressed, hydraulic pressure from the master cylinder forces the pistons and brake pads against the friction surfaces of the disc with equal pressure on both sides. The movement of the pistons pulls on the elastic rubber seals on the piston skirts, distorting them slightly, as shown in Fig. 57.

When the brake pedal is released and the brake system is relieved of pressure, the rubber seals, acting like springs, pull the caliper pistons away from the disc and back into rest position.

The spreader springs force the brake pads back and allow the disc to rotate freely again. The clearance between brake pads and brake disc when the brakes are off depends upon the elasticity of the rubber seal. It is approximately 0.006 inch (0.15 mm). This clearance does not increase as the brake pads wear. When the pistons have to cover a distance greater than the deflection of the rubber seals, they slip through the seals. The brake pads adjust themselves automatically according to the amount of wear.

**Fig. 56.** Exploded and cutaway views show the parts of the disc brake assembly (above) and the parts in place in the caliper (below).

1. Bleeder valve dust cap
2. Bleeder valve
3. Brake caliper inner housing
4. Groove for rubber seal
5. Rubber seal
6. Brake caliper piston
7. Rubber boot
8. Spring ring
9. Piston retaining plate
10. Brake pad
11. Brake caliper outer housing
12. Caliper housing securing bolt
13. Brake disc
14. Brake pad retaining pin
15. Nut
16. Spreader spring
17. Fluid passage O-ring

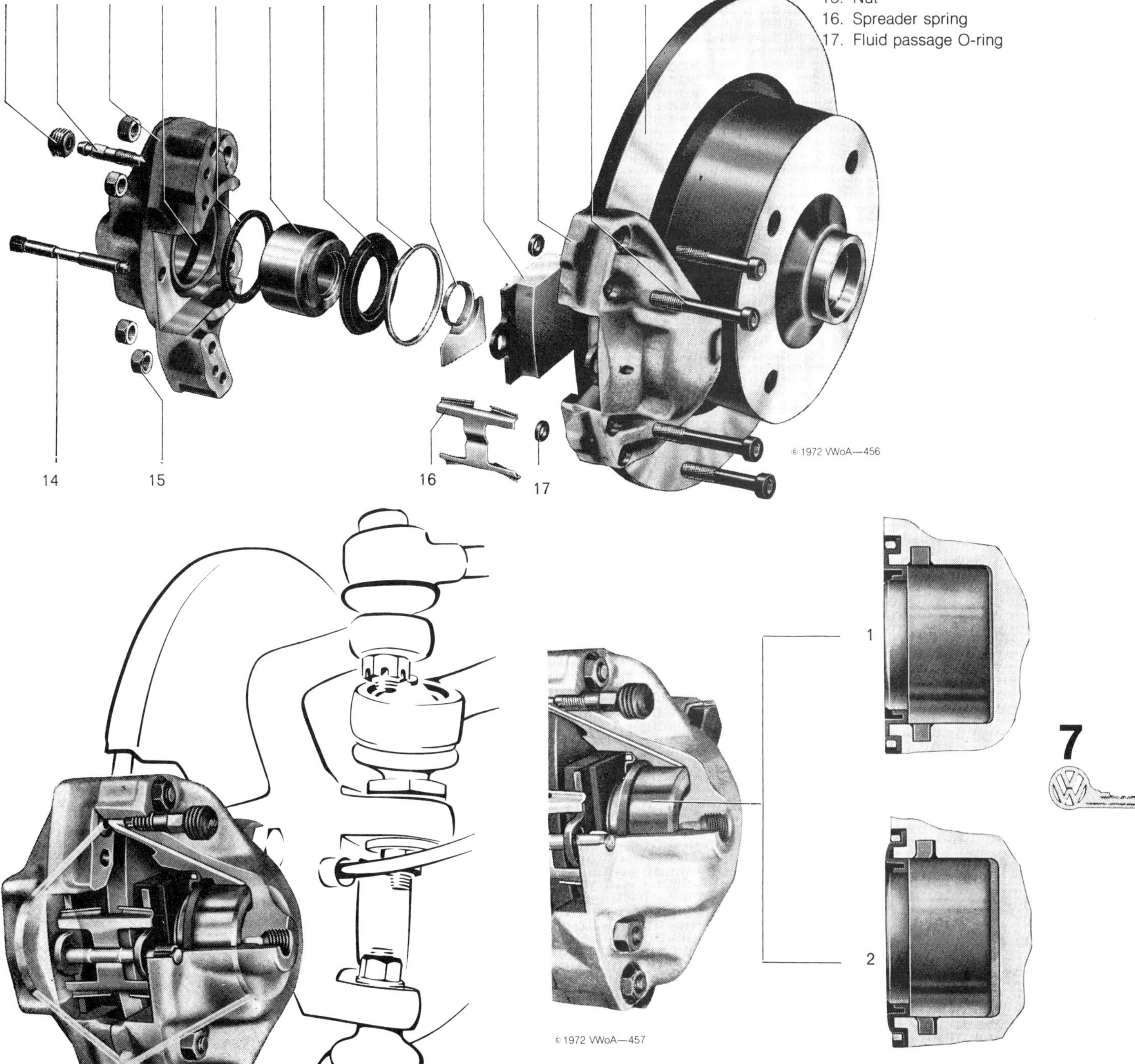


**Fig. 57.** Rubber seal on shoulder of caliper piston acts as spring to force brake pads off disc when brakes are released. Connecting line shows location of pad in caliper. At (1) pad is at rest and at (2) under braking pressure. Note deflection of seal (in braking position).

## 12.3 Tandem Master Cylinder

There is one major design difference in the tandem cylinder for disc brakes. In place of residual pressure valves, this cylinder has drillings of very small diameter leading to the exit ports where brake fluid leaves the pressure chambers. Disc brakes do not need valves. When the brakes are "off", the entire system is supposed to be without pressure. The exit port drillings, shown in Fig. 58, reduce the flow of brake fluid and thus make it possible to build up pressure quickly by pumping the brake pedal.

***CAUTION —***
*The tandem master cylinder for disc brakes is not interchangeable with tandem cylinders for drum brakes.*

**Fig. 58.** Exit ports in tandem master cylinder for disc brakes have small drillings (arrows) which reduce brake fluid flow and enable driver to "pump" brakes to build up pressure in the system. See text for details.

The internal dimensions of the tandem master cylinder for disc brakes are:

| | | |
|---|---|---|
| Diameter | 0.75 inch | (19.05 mm) |
| Total stroke | 1.10 inches | (28.00 mm) |
| Front circuit stroke | 0.55 inch | (14.00 mm) |
| Rear circuit stroke | 0.55 inch | (14.00 mm) |

**NOTE —**
The thread of the brake line connection on the disc brake tandem master cylinder is M 10 x 1 and the thread of the residual pressure valve connection on the drum brake tandem master cylinder is M 12 x 1. For this reason the two cylinders cannot be confused.

## 12.4 Brake Pads

The brake pads consist of a pad of friction material bonded to a metal plate. A layer of sound-deadening plastic is cemented to the back of the metal plate. The friction material has a groove 0.08 inch (2 mm) wide and 0.3 inch (8 mm) deep running in a radial direction. A water or oil film forming on the brake disc breaks on encountering this groove. By this means, good braking is maintained in bad weather. (See Fig. 59.)

**Fig. 59.** Brake pads, also known as friction pads, consist of friction material bonded to metal plate, which is slotted for attachment. Thin plastic layer behind metal plate dampens noise.

## 12.5 Checking Brake Pads

The brake pads must be checked for wear at the regular maintenance inspections, every 6,000 miles. Brake pads which have worn down to a thickness of 0.08 inch (2 mm) must be replaced. Fig. 60 shows this measurement at "a".

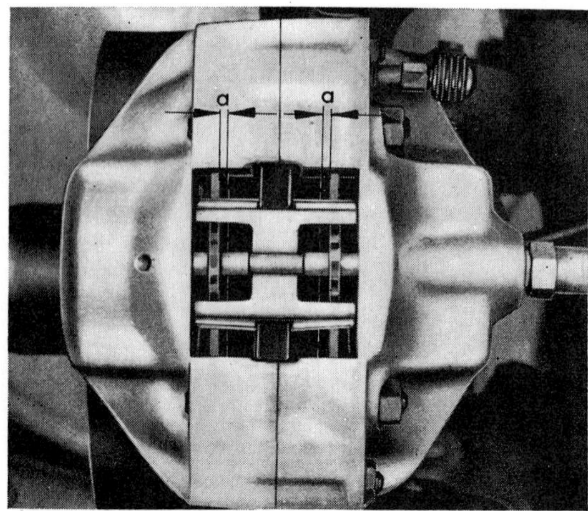




**Fig. 60.** Brake pad thickness, the measurement shown here at "a", must be checked regularly for wear.

**NOTE —**
Cars from September 18, 1967, chassis No. 118 142 061, have a different spreader spring in the brake caliper. One side of the spring surface that is in contact with the brake pad plate has been widened to give more support on the caliper housing cutout. The new spring reduces the rattling noises caused by play between brake pads and caliper housing. The new spring must be installed with the wider part downward. (See Fig. 61.)

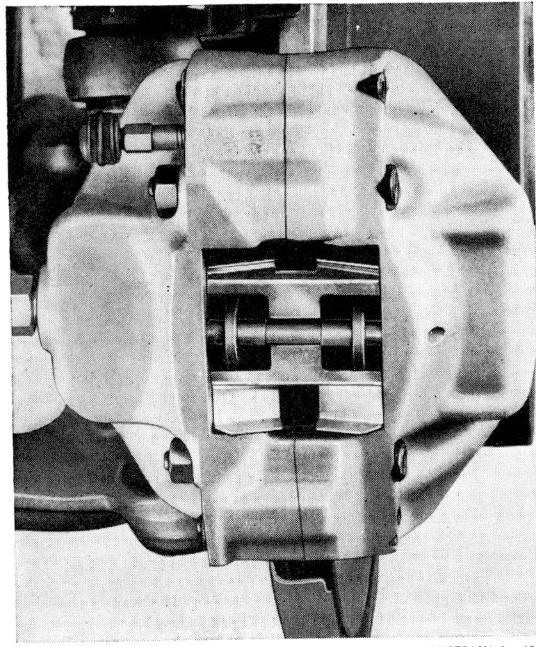

© 1972 VWoA—460

**Fig. 61.** Spreader spring presses brake pads against pistons. Later model spring shown here has wider contact with caliper housing to reduce noise.

## 12.6 Removing and Installing Brake Pads

***WARNING —***
*Always replace all four brake pads together. Never replace a single pad or the pads of only one wheel. The spreader springs of both calipers must be replaced with the brake pads.*

**To remove brake pads:**

1. Take off front wheel.
2. Using a punch, drive out brake pad retaining pin (Fig. 62).
3. Remove brake pad spreader spring.

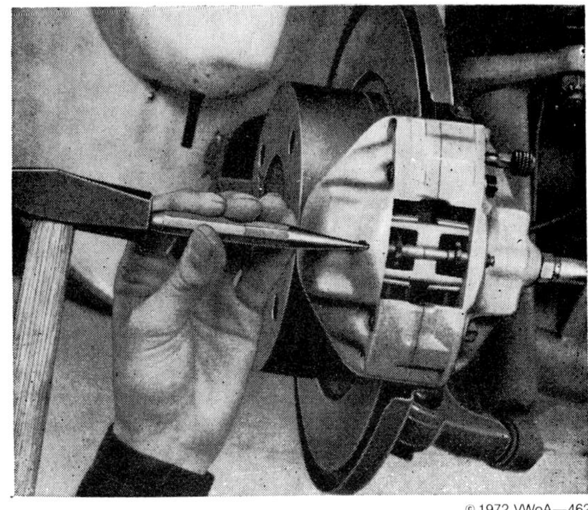

© 1972 VWoA—462

**Fig. 62.** Retaining pin is driven out with punch as first step in removal of disc brake pads.

***WARNING —***
*If you intend to put back a used brake pad, be sure to mark it and its housing for later matching. Pads must not be switched from inner to outer housing (or vice versa) or between wheels.*

4. Pull brake pads out of brake caliper, using extractor hooks. Fig. 63 shows the operation.

© 1972 VWoA—463

**Fig. 63.** Extractor hooks pull brake pads out of disc brake caliper.

**To install:**

1. Inspect pads carefully. Replace all cracked or oily pads and pads detached from the metal backing plate. Remember that all pads on the front wheels must be replaced together.

7

2. Using piston-retaining pliers, push both pistons back into end positions in the caliper housings. Fig. 64 shows operation.

© 1972 VWoA—464

**Fig. 64.** Special pliers push pistons to end positions in caliper for installation of brake pads.

**NOTE —**
Pushing the pistons back into the housings will force brake fluid back into the reservoir, which may overflow. Before starting the procedure remove some fluid from the reservoir, and use **new** fluid only to replace it.

3. Clean seating and sliding surfaces of brake pads in brake caliper. It will be necessary to remove the piston-retaining plates. After cleaning, blow out brake caliper with compressed air.

***CAUTION —***
*Use only alcohol for cleaning. Never use mineral oil or solvents. Sharp-edged tools must not be used.*

4. Check rubber boot (arrow in Fig. 65) for damage. Hardened, brittle or cracked boots must be replaced. To replace the rubber boot, the brake caliper must be removed.

© 1972 VWoA—465

**Fig. 65.** Rubber boot (arrow) on piston must be replaced if hardened or cracked.

5. Insert piston retaining plate. The circular part of the plate (arrow "a" in Fig. 66) must be firmly pressed into piston crown. Plate must lie below relieved part of piston (arrow "b"). When piston retaining plate is correctly installed, position of piston is correct. Corroded or damaged piston retaining plates must be replaced.

© 1972 VWoA—466

**Fig. 66.** Piston retaining plate must be inserted in piston crown with circular part (a) firmly in the crown and main part of plate below relieved section (b) of piston.

6. Align piston with the piston rotating pliers if necessary. Fig. 67 shows the operation.

© 1972 VWoA—467

**Fig. 67.** Special pliers hold pistons for rotation into correct position shown in Fig. 66.

7. Check position of piston again with a piston-setting gauge. Gauge is held against the lower guide surface in the brake caliper; that is, counter-

clockwise to the rotation of the brake disc (arrow in Fig. 68) when the vehicle is moving forward.

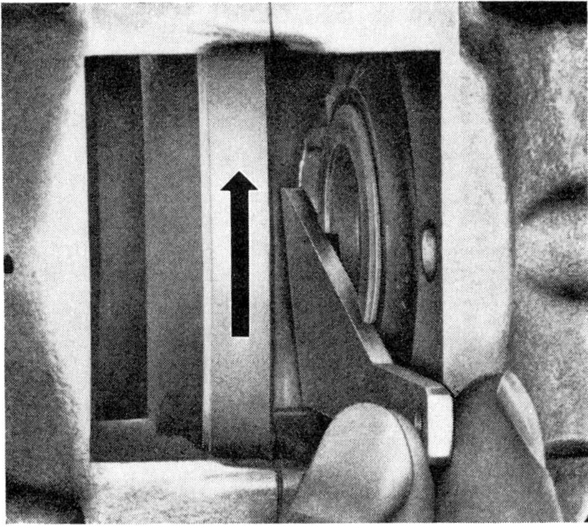


**Fig. 68.** Gauge applied to piston crown as shown checks position of piston with respect to brake disc. Arrow shows the direction of rotation of the disc.

8. Check brake disc for wear.

***WARNING —***
*If old brake pads are to be used again, they must go back in the exact locations they were in before removal. Before removing pads, mark them and calipers for later matching. Check those matching marks carefully before re-installing pads.*

9. Insert brake pads into brake caliper. The brake pads must be free enough (Fig. 69) to move back and forth in the brake caliper.

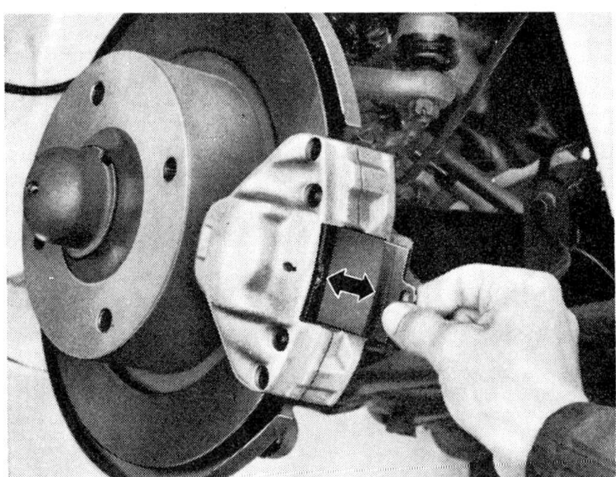


**Fig. 69.** Brake pad play should be free enough for pads to move back and forth in caliper.

10. Install new brake pad spreader spring.

***CAUTION —***
*Do not drive in brake pad retaining pin (Fig. 70) with punch smaller in diameter than the pin. The split clamping bushing can easily shear off shoulder (arrow in Fig. 71) if smaller punch is used. Use a hammer only to drive the pins in.*

**Fig. 70.** Retaining pin for brake pad, started here by hand, should be driven into caliper with hammer, not with a small punch.

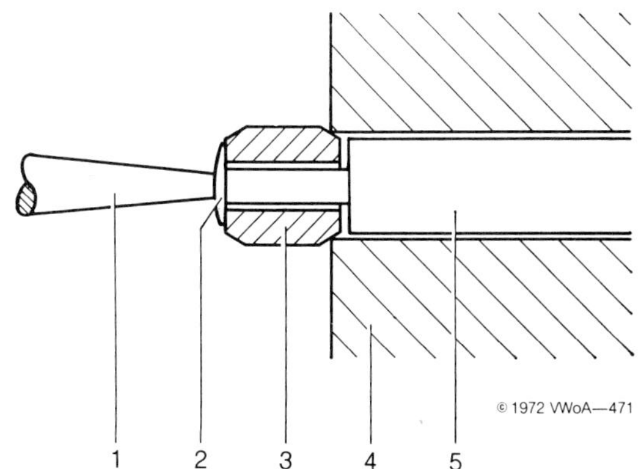


1. Punch
2. Endangered retaining pin shoulder
3. Split clamping bushing
4. Housing
5. Retaining pin

**Fig. 71.** Shoulder (2) of brake pad retaining pin (5) may shear if small punch (1) is used to drive pin into caliper.

7

11. Insert new retaining pin in caliper. Always replace old retaining pins. New ones are part of repair kit.
12. With car stationary, depress brake pedal several times to free pistons and brake pads, allowing them to take correct positions in respect to brake disc.
13. Check brakes on road test.

## 12.7 Removing and Installing Brake Caliper

***CAUTION —***
*Brakes get very hot. To prevent warping, remove brake caliper only after it has cooled down.*

**To remove:**

1. Take off front wheel.
2. Remove brake hose and close brake line with bleeder valve dust cap.
3. Bend down brake caliper lock plate on both bolts.
4. Unscrew brake caliper attaching bolts (Fig. 72), and discard lock plate.
5. Take off brake caliper.

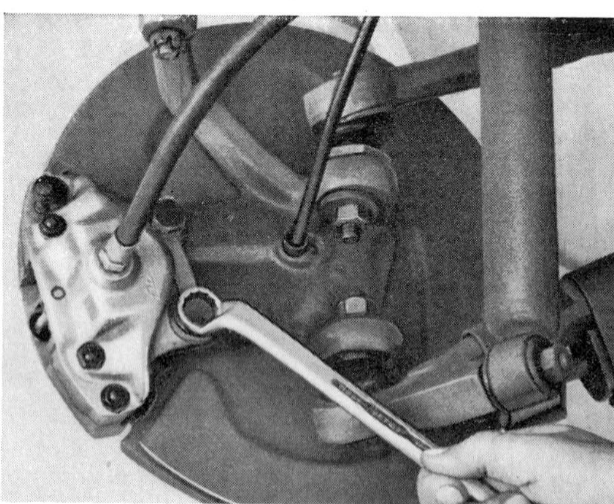



**Fig. 72.** Two bolts are taken off for removal of caliper.

**To install:**

***CAUTION —***
*When installing be careful to position brake caliper with the inner housing bleeder valve at the top. The attaching bolts and the lock plate must be replaced.*

1. Clean mating surfaces of brake caliper and steering knuckle.
2. Tighten brake caliper attaching bolts with a torque wrench.
   Bolt grade: 10 k
   Torque: 29 ft. lbs. (4 mkg)
3. Lock the bolts with lock plates.
4. Bleed brake system. Do not forget dust caps on the bleeder valves.
5. Depress brake pedal several times and check for leakage.

***WARNING —***
*Before you take your car on the road, be aware that repaired or re-installed brakes may not yet be up to full braking efficiency. Test brakes first on off-street driveway or parking lot.*

6. Road test brakes.

## 12.8 Repairing Brake Caliper

**To disassemble:**

1. Clean dirt off removed caliper.
2. Hold caliper by flange in vise with padded jaws.
3. Remove piston retaining plates.
4. Using screwdriver, carefully pry out rubber boot spring ring (Fig. 73). Be careful to avoid damaging rubber boot.

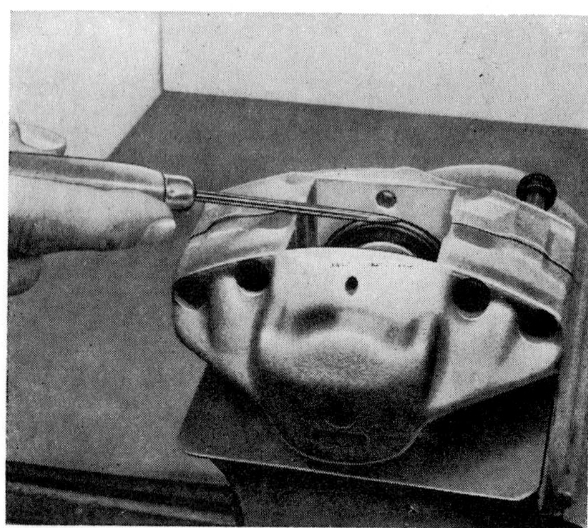



**Fig. 73.** Spring ring for rubber boot is pried out with screwdriver. Be careful to avoid damaging boot.

***CAUTION —***
*Do not use sharp-edged tool on the rubber boot.*

5. Remove rubber boot with plastic or rubber rod, as in Fig. 74.

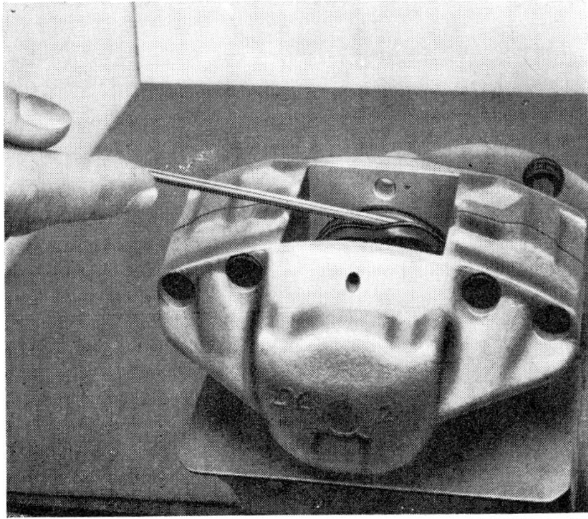

© 1972 VWoA—474

**Fig. 74.** Rubber boot is pried out with plastic or rubber rod. Do not use tool with sharp edge.

6. Insert hardwood or rubber block about a quarter of an inch thick in housing grooves to protect the piston. (See Fig. 75.)

© 1972 VWoA—475

**Fig. 75.** Hardwood block in housing grooves of caliper prevents damage when piston is blown out with compressed air. Tool holds other piston. See text.

7. Remove one piston from the brake caliper with compressed air. While doing this, you will have to hold the second piston with piston retaining pliers.

**NOTE —**
The cylinders can be repaired only one at a time. With one piston removed, no pressure can be built up in brake caliper to force out other piston. If a piston does not come out of caliper at first blast of air, it must be pushed back into original position with piston retaining pliers for a second try.

8. Remove rubber seal. Use only a plastic or rubber rod to pry with. (See Fig. 76.)

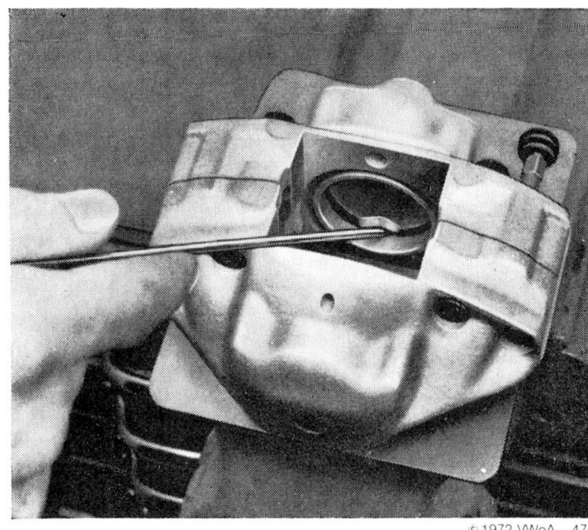

© 1972 VWoA—476

**Fig. 76.** Rubber seal is removed with plastic rod.

**To assemble:**

7

1. Clean all parts, using alcohol or brake fluid only.
2. Check parts for wear. If a cylinder is damaged, the complete brake caliper must be replaced.

***CAUTION —***
*The rubber seal, rubber boot, spring ring and piston-retaining plate must be replaced with new parts each time brake caliper is repaired.*

3. Put thin coat of VW brake cylinder paste on piston and new rubber seal and install the parts. When pressing the piston into the cylinder with the piston-retaining pliers, always use clamp that will keep piston from tilting.
4. Install new rubber boot and new spring ring.

5. Check position of piston with gauge as in Fig. 77 and correct with piston rotating pliers if necessary.

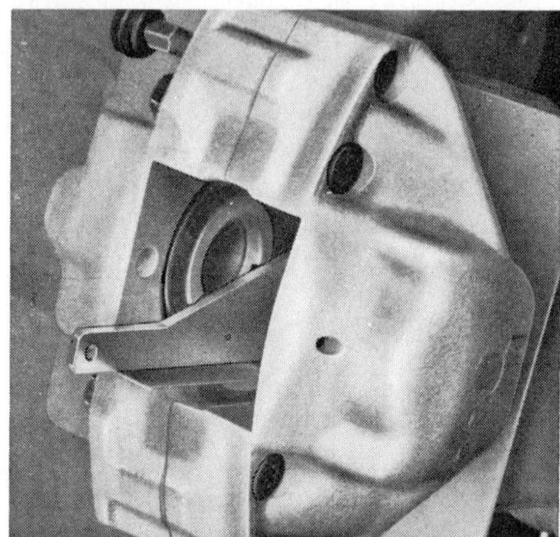



**Fig. 77.** Checking gauge established position of piston crown with respect to place of brake disc.

6. Install piston retaining plate. Fig. 78 shows correct position.

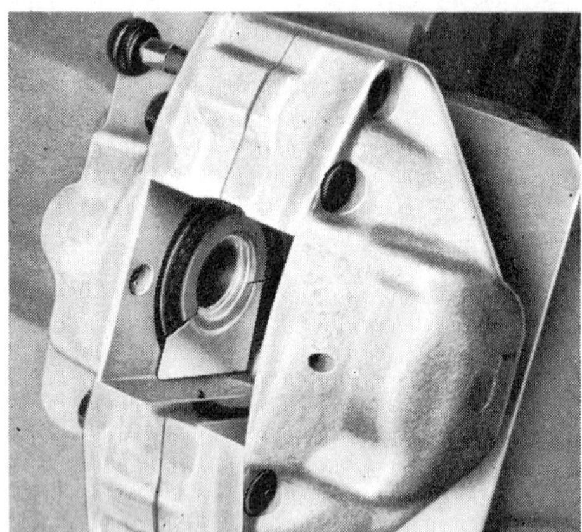



**Fig. 78.** Piston retaining plate fits in piston crown correctly after piston has been lined up with gauge as in Fig. 77.

7. Remove the second piston and go through same procedure.

## 12.9 Checking Brake Discs

Each time a repair is carried out, the brake discs should be checked for wear. Worn, scored or cracked brake discs must be replaced. Brake discs with a thickness of only 0.315 inch (8 mm), must be replaced.

## 12.10 Reconditioning Brake Discs

The brake discs can be reworked down to a thickness of 0.335 inch (8.5 mm). There are several restrictions, however. The disc must be reworked equally on both sides. The maximum permissible thickness variation is 0.0008 inch (0.02 mm). Measurements taken at several locations on the disc must not vary more than this amount.

The specified thickness for a new brake disc is 0.370 to 0.374 inch (9.4 to 9.5 mm). The minimum thickness allowed after reworking is 0.335 inch (8.5 mm). Wear limit of brake disc thickness is 0.315 inch (8 mm). The maximum thickness variation allowed is 0.0008 inch (0.02 mm). The maximum allowed runout of installed brake disc is 0.008 inch (0.2 mm).

## 12.11 Removing and Installing Brake Disc

**To remove:**

1. Take off front wheel.

> ***CAUTION*** —
> *The brake disc and caliper can become hot enough to inflict severe burns. Be careful. Let the brakes cool before you touch them. To prevent warping, do not remove disc until it has cooled to the temperature of its surroundings.*

2. Detach brake caliper from steering knuckle and hang it on tie rod with wire hook, as in Fig. 79, but not on brake line.

**Fig. 79.** Removed caliper should be hung from tie rod while brake disc is removed and installed.

3. Remove C-washer on left wheel and pull off dust cap.
4. Remove wheel bearing clamp nut and take off brake disc.

**To install:**

1. Install brake disc, bearing and clamp nut. While tightening clamp nut, rotate wheel.
2. Position dial indicator to measure bearing play (Fig. 80). Acceptable play: 0.001 to 0.005 inch (0.03 to 0.12 mm).

**NOTE —**
Measure play at several locations on the circumference.

© 1972 VWoA—480

**Fig. 80.** Axial play of brake disc should be measured at several points with dial indicator.

3. Tighten socket head screw to prescribed torque (Fig. 81).

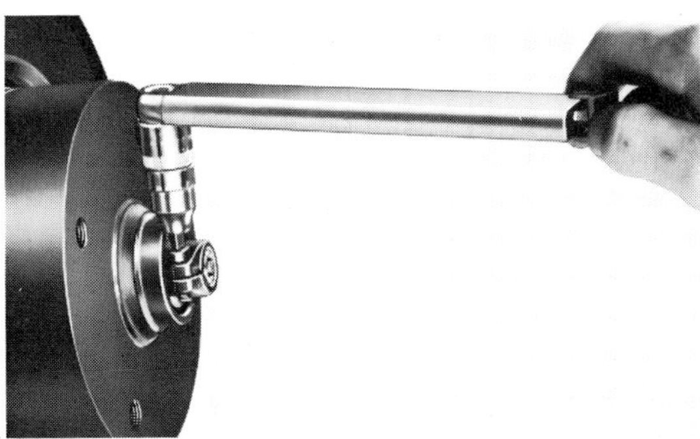

© 1972 VWoA—481

**Fig. 81.** Disc clamp nut must be tightened to specified torque.

***CAUTION —***
*Use new bolts and lock plate.*

4. Tighten caliper bolts to specified torque.
5. Install wheel. Tighten wheel bolts to specified torque.

**To check brake disc runout:**

1. Remove front wheel.
2. Remove brake pads.
3. Adjust front wheel bearing play as described in preceding procedure.
4. Insert measuring appliance in brake caliper grooves (Fig. 82) and tighten with wing nut.

© 1972 VWoA—482

**Fig. 82.** Special gauge for measuring brake disc runout is inserted in caliper grooves.

5. Attach dial gauge as in Fig. 82.
6. Turn brake disc slowly by hand and read gauge.

**NOTE —**
Tilting the brake disc in this procedure or moving it on its axis will give a false reading. The maximum permissible runout is 0.008 inch (0.2 mm). Brake disc with greater runout must be replaced.

7. Remove dial gauge.
8. Loosen the wing nut and remove the measuring appliance.
9. Install brake pads.
10. Check brakes on road.

***WARNING —***
*Before you take your car on the road, be aware that repaired or re-installed brakes may not yet be up to full braking efficiency. Test brakes first on off-street driveway or parking lot.*

## 12.12 Removing and Installing Brake Disc Shield

**To remove:**

1. Remove front wheel.
2. Detach brake caliper from steering knuckle and hang it on tie rod with a wire hook (Fig. 79).
3. Remove brake disc.
4. Unscrew splash shield attaching bolts and remove splash shield (Fig. 83).

© 1972 VWoA—483

**Fig. 83.** Splash shield is removed from steering knuckle after attaching bolts have been unscrewed.

**To install:**

1. Clean mating surfaces of splash shield and steering knuckle. If shield is damaged, replace it.
2. Install splash shield.
3. Check brake disc for wear.
4. Adjust front wheel bearing play as described in instructions for installing brake disc.
5. Install brake caliper. New attaching bolts and lock plate must be used.
6. Tighten attaching bolts to torque of 43 ft. lbs. (6 mkg).

> ***WARNING —***
> *Before you take your car on the road, be aware that repaired or re-installed brakes may not yet be up to full braking efficiency. Test brakes first on off-street driveway or parking lot.*

7. Check brakes on road.

## 12.13 Bleeding the Brakes

Two persons are required for the bleeding operation. While one works the brake pedal, the other drains off fluid at the bleeder valves.

**To bleed brakes:**

1. Place the fluid container on reservoir as in Fig. 39 to keep reservoir full during the bleeding operation.

> ***WARNING —***
> *Brake fluid is poisonous. Never suck on the end of a tube to start siphoning action. Use a mechanical pump or siphon apparatus.*

2. Start bleeding at wheel cylinder farthest from master cylinder. Take dust cap off bleeder valve on cylinder.
3. Place bleeder hose on wheel cylinder bleeder valve.
4. Depress and release brake pedal quickly and repeatedly until a resistance shows that pressure has built up in system.
5. Hold brake pedal in its lowest position.
6. Back off bleeder valve about one turn.
7. Close bleeder valve as soon as pressure has been released from system; that is, when no more fluid flows from bleeder hose. Do not release brake pedal until the bleeder valve has been closed.
8. Repeat operation on same wheel until no more air bubbles are visible in the transparent tube in the bleeder hose, or in the jar.
9. Remove bleeder hose and install dust cap.
10. Repeat operation on each wheel in turn.

## 12.14 Adjusting Brakes

### Front Brakes

The front wheel disc brakes do not require adjusting, but should be checked for wear.

### Rear Brakes

Brake lining wear increases clearance between brake shoes and drums as car is driven and will require adjustment. When distance pedal moves before brakes are applied becomes excessive, the brake shoes must be adjusted.

## 12.15 Brake Troubleshooting

**Table c** gives a comprehensive picture of brake troubles that conceivably might be encountered. The chart lists symptoms, probable causes and suggested remedies, but in the interests of safety we recommend that all brake adjustments and repairs be made at authorized VW repair shops.

### Table c. Brake Troubleshooting

| Symptom | Cause | Remedy |
|---|---|---|
| 1. Pedal travels all the way to floor in braking | Linings worn | a. Adjust brake shoes.<br>b. Do not adjust at pedal cluster. |
| 2. Pedal travel has spongy feel | a. Air in system<br>b. Insufficient fluid in reservoir | a. Bleed system.<br>b. Top up fluid and bleed system. |
| 3. Pedal travels a long way without braking action although shoes have been adjusted and system bled | a. Check valve in master cylinder defective | a. Replace parts in master cylinder.<br>b. Clean valve seat. Fit new valve if necessary. |
| 4. Braking action occurs only after pedal is pumped although new check valve has been fitted | a. Air in system<br>b. Spring weak | a. Bleed system.<br>b. Replace parts in master cylinder. |
| 5. Braking action decreases after shoes have been adjusted | a. Brake lines leaking<br>b. Damaged or defective cup in master or wheel cylinders | a. Tighten connections or fit new lines and hoses.<br>b. Fit new cup. If defective cup is in master cylinder, fit all new internal parts. |
| 6. Brakes overheat | a. Compensating port in master cylinder blocked<br>b. Insufficient clearance between brake pedal rod and master cylinder piston<br>c. Return springs weak<br>d. Rubber parts swollen by contact with unsuitable brake fluid | a. Clean master cylinder.<br>b. Adjust pedal clearance.<br>c. Fit new return springs.<br>d. Drain fluid, remove all rubber parts and flush system well with VW or similar brake fluid. Replace all parts in master cylinder. |
| 7. Brakes have unsatisfactory action despite high pedal pressure | a. Linings oiled-up<br>b. Unsuitable brake linings | a. Clean drums and fit new linings and seals if necessary.<br>b. Fit new linings. |
| 8. Brakes bind while car is in motion | a. Compensating port blocked, possibly by swollen cup<br>b. Brake fluid unsuitable<br>c. Incorrect brake pedal stop setting | a. Disassemble master cylinder and clear port.<br>b. Flush system well and fill with VW or similar fluid.<br>c. Check brake pedal stop and adjust to leave compensating port open when brakes are in rest position. |
| 9. Brakes chatter and tend to grab | a. Linings worn, rivets protruding<br>b. Drums out of round | a. Fit new linings or new rivets.<br>b. Turn drums out or fit new drums. |
| 10. Brakes squeak* | a. Unsuitable linings<br>b. Loose rivets, badly fitting linings<br>c. Brakes dirty<br>d. Backing plates distorted<br>e. Return springs weak<br>f. Poor lining contact pattern due to shoe distortion | a. Fit new linings. Use only approved parts.<br>b. Fit new rivets or possibly reline.<br>c. Clean brakes.<br>d. Check backing plates for distortion and fit new parts if necessary.<br>e. Fit new return springs.<br>f. Align shoes to make them vertical to back plate, with 0.0078 inch (0.2 mm) clearance at lining ends and contact across full width. |

continued on next page

7

## Table c. Brake Troubleshooting (continued)

| Symptom | Cause | Remedy |
|---|---|---|
| 11. Brakes give uneven braking action | a. Oil or grease on linings | a. Clean drums, fit new linings and seals or wheel cylinders if necessary. |
| | b. Poor contact between lining and drum due to brake shoe distortion | b. Shape shoes to leave 0.0078 inch (0.2 mm) clearance at lining ends. |
| | c. Brake shoes too tight in the adjusting screw slots or in wheel cylinder pistons | c. Free up shoes. |
| | d. Different types of linings on the axle | d. Fit new linings. |
| | e. Incorrect tire pressures or unevenly worn tires | e. Correct pressures or replace worn tires. |
| | f. Drums out of round or scored | f. Turn drums out or fit new drums. |
| | g. Drums distorted by unevenly tightened wheel bolts | g. Tighten wheel bolts to: 72 ft. lbs. (10 mkg) for five-bolt pattern or 87 to 94 ft. lbs. (12 to 13 mkg) for four-bolt pattern. If distortion is excessive replace brake drum. |
| | h. Contact area on wheel disk out of true and causing distortion in drum | h. Measure drum with wheel disk bolted on and try to reduce effect of distortion by mounting wheel in different positions. Interchanging wheels sometimes will correct condition. If not, fit a new wheel disk. |
| | i. Brake shoes not in contact with backing plate | i. Remove shoes and straighten or replace them. Fit new backing plates. |
| | j. Pistons tight in wheel cylinders | j. Free up pistons. |
| | k. Dirt in brake lines or hoses | k. Clean lines. Replace defective hoses. |
| 12. Brakes pulsate** | a. Front axle attaching bolts unevenly tightened or too loose | a. Back off attaching bolts and retighten to prescribed torque of 35 ft. lbs. (5 mkg). |
| | b. Brake drum distorted from unevenly tightened wheel bolts | b. Tighten wheel bolts to 72 ft. lbs. (10 mkg) for five-bolt pattern or 87 to 94 ft. lbs. (12 to 13 mkg) for four-bolt pattern. |
| | c. Seating surface of wheel disk of brake drum not flat; drum distorted | c. With drum bolted to wheel disk, check brake drum with special appliance for measuring out-of-round distortion. If the ovality is more than 0.004 inch (0.1 mm) try different drum-to-disk positions for less distortion. In some circumstances this can be achieved by interchanging the wheel disks. If ovality cannot be kept below the maximum permissible limit of 0.004 inch (0.1 mm), replace wheel disk. If suitable lathe is available, use it with dial gauge to check the brake drum for ovality while drum is bolted to wheel disk. If necessary, turn out brake drum while still bolted to wheel disk. |
| | d. Brake shoe webs too tight in adjusters or wheel cylinder pistons | d. Smooth shoe web ends and contact surfaces of adjusters and wheel brake cylinder pistons with crocus cloth and lubricate with high melting point graphite grease. |
| | e. Poor lining contact pattern from brake shoe distortion | e. Reshape brake shoes to leave 0.008 inch (0.2 mm) clearance at the lining ends, as shown in the illustration. © 1972 VWoA—765 |

***Vibration between brake shoes and linings and the brake drums causes this noise. The trouble can be of a mechanical nature, but atmospheric influences often are the cause. Moisture in the air can change the coefficient of friction of the brake linings. High humidity can cause a thin film of rust to form in the brake drums. When the linings are pressed against the rusted drums, squeaking noises occur. The noise stops as soon as friction dries the linings and polishes the drums again. This type of brake squeaking is usually heard when the vehicle has been standing for some time in damp air, overnight for example.**

****Do not try to remedy pulsating by installing the recessed cups that are made for the wheel cylinders of Type 3 vehicles only.**

## 13. WHEELS AND TIRES

Proper maintenance of the wheels and tires is essential to your safety on the road and to economy in the operation of your car. Good maintenance will include:

1. Tightening the wheel mounting bolts to specifications.
2. Inflating tires to specified pressures.
3. Inspecting tires regularly for damage and signs of wear.
4. Inspecting rims for damage, especially at flanges and shoulders.
5. Balancing wheels.

### 13.1 Wheels

Volkswagen cars are equipped with drop-center, rimmed wheels.

Rim size: 4 J x 15
Tire size: 5.60—15 tubeless

Fig. 84 shows the significant measurements on VW tires and rims.

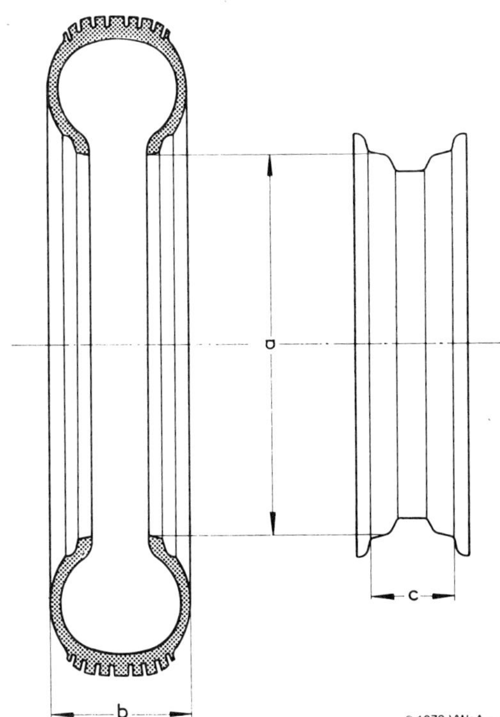


**Fig. 84.** Tires and wheels on VW cars must fit specifications shown here. Measurements are: "a", 15 inches; "b", 5.60 inches, and "c", 4 inches.

**_WARNING_ —**
*Distorted wheels should be replaced, not straightened. The maximum axial and radial run-out allowed is 0.06 inch (1.5 mm).*

The cars covered in this Manual may have road wheels of either the four-bolt or five-bolt pattern. The specified tightening torques for the two patterns are:

Four-bolt pattern 87 to 94 ft. lbs. (12 to 13 mkg)
Five-bolt pattern 72 ft. lbs. (10 mkg)

**NOTE —**
From production date October 10, 1967, chassis No. 118 227 175, all cars are equipped with four-bolt wheels and with rims of the hump type. Fig. 85 shows this rim.

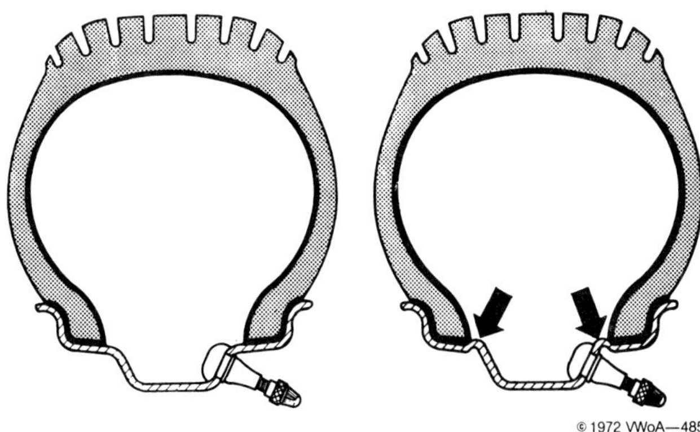


**Fig. 85.** Humps (black arrows) on shoulder of wheel rims are shown at right. This design, which appears on cars after 1968, holds tire beads in place against side forces. Earlier rim is shown at left.

The hump on the rim shoulder provides increased protection against side impact or blowout. With hump rims it takes a very severe force to dislodge the tire bead from the shoulder into the rim well.

### 13.2 Tires

The condition of the tires greatly influences the driving characteristics of a car and road safety. A reasonable amount of care will contribute to the reduction of wear and the increase of service life. Careful balancing of wheels and tires helps to reduce wear on both tires and wheel bearings and improves driving characteristics of the car.

Along with driving habits and the condition of road surfaces, incorrect tire pressures, faulty wheel alignment and excessive unbalance are all factors in rapid tire wear.

For better tire wear try to avoid overloading your car. On very hot days park the car in the shade if you can to keep the tires out of the intense sunshine. As far as possible try to protect the tires from contact with gasoline and oil.

### Tire Dimensions

Significant measurements on the 5.60—15 tires on your Volkswagen are:

| | |
|---|---|
| Outside diameter | 25.63 ± 0.24 inches (651 ± 6 mm) |
| Maximum operating width | 6.06 inches |
| Effective static radius | 11.97 ± 0.12 inches (304 ± 3 mm) |
| Effective dynamic radius | 12.17 ± 0.12 inches (309 ± 3 mm) |

**NOTE —**
From production date October 3, 1966, chassis No. 147 245 980, the VW 1500 Karmann Ghia models are fitted with 5.60 S 15 4 PR tires. When replacements are required, only tires so designated are to be provided for the 1500 Karmann Ghia. The inflation pressures are the same for these tires as for the 5.60—15 4 PR.

***WARNING —***
*Driving with tire pressures too low affects car handling and safety.*

### Inflation Pressures

For a car carrying one or two persons the following tire pressures are recommended:

Front 16 psi (1.1 kg/cm²)
Rear 24 psi (1.7 kg/cm²)

For fully loaded car:

Front 17 psi (1.2 kg/cm²)
Rear 26 psi (1.8 kg/cm²)

For high speed turnpike driving the pressures should be increased by 3 psi (0.2 kg/cm²).

To keep tire wear to a minimum and get the best possible ride, have your tires checked regularly and kept at the specified pressures.

## 13.3 Tubeless Tires

Special tools are available for changing tubeless tires. You will need two long tire irons with rounded edges, a tool for inserting the valve and a bead-breaker to force the tire bead from its seat in the rim.

When you are working on a tubeless tire, take great care not to damage the air-retaining lining. The sealing surface is shown at (5) in Fig. 86.

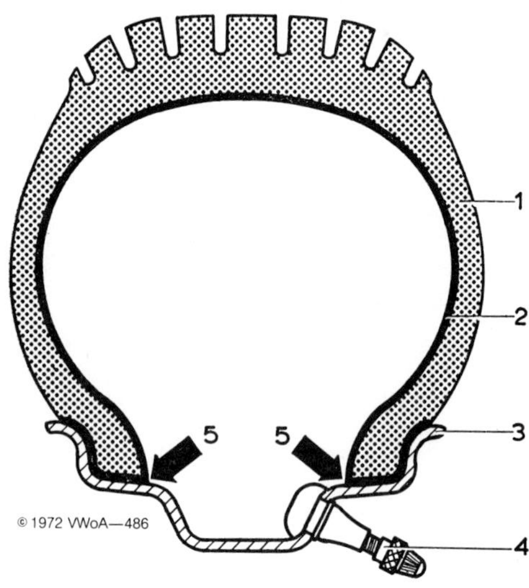


1. Tire
2. Air-retaining lining
3. Rim flange
4. Valve
5. Rim sealing surface

**Fig. 86.** Tubeless tire is shown here in cross section with its rim.

A rubber valve (Fig. 87) is used as standard equipment for tubeless tires.

© 1972 VWoA—487

**Fig. 87.** Rubber valve shown here is for tubeless tires on cars covered in this Manual.

## 13.4 Changing Tires

To mount or dismount tires on safety-type hump rims you will need a tool or appliance that can exert enough pressure or leverage to force the tire bead over the hump.

While it is possible to change tires with hand tools (tire irons, etc.), the use of power-assisted devices is recommended. Except in the unusual emergency, such equipment is generally available nowadays and should be used to prevent damage to tires and wheels, as well as unnecessary hard work.

When changing tires, make every effort to avoid damaging the rubber lining on the innner wall of the tire and the tire beads.

**To dismount tire:**

> ***WARNING —***
> *The air valve core is under pressure and can shoot out like a projectile. Be careful when removing it.*

1. Take off valve cap, unscrew valve core and relieve tire of all air.

> ***CAUTION —***
> *To avoid damaging the sealing lining on the bead, use only tools with smooth rounded edges.*

2. Detach tire bead from rim with a pneumatic appliance, as in Fig. 88.

© 1972 VWoA—488

**Fig. 88.** Pneumatic appliance is used here to break tire bead from wheel rim.

3. Pry tire walls one after the other over the rim edge. A special tool is shown in Fig. 89.

© 1972 VWoA—489

**Fig. 89.** Tire walls are pried over rim edge.

4. Check airtight lining inside the tire for damage and bruises between lining and wall. Inspect exterior of tire for embedded stones, cuts, grease and signs of uneven wear. (See tire wear patterns in this section.)
5. Pull valve out of rim with valve installing tool, and scrap. Never put back a used valve.

The tubeless radial ply tires were designed for use with the hump rim and should be mounted only on such rims. Inner tubes can be used in radial tires if the vehicle is to be driven continually on very bad roads or off roads altogether.

> ***WARNING —***
> *If radial tires are to be mounted on standard rims produced prior to production date October 10, 1967, chassis No. 118 227 175, inner tubes must be used.*

**To mount tire:**

1. Check rim for damage. Never mount tubeless tires on rims with damaged or distorted shoulders or flanges.

> ***WARNING —***
> *Do not attempt to straighten distorted rims. The maximum run-out of 0.06 inch must not be exceeded.*

2. Remove dirt from rim shoulders and flanges, using a wire brush if necessary. Before mounting tire, smooth all sharp edges.

**NOTE** —
To provide a better seal between tire and rim, the diameter of the tire beads is smaller than the rim shoulders. Moreover, the rim shoulders are not horizontal but inclined upward. As a result, tire beads are under some tension when positioned on the rim shoulders.

3. Insert valve, using valve installing tool as shown in Fig. 90.

**Fig. 90.** Valve is inserted in rim as first step of mounting tubeless tire.

**NOTE** —
In August 1968, rubber valve 43 GS/16 with a 0.77 inch (19.5 mm) diameter was replaced with the Type 2 wheel disc valve 43 GS/11.5, which has a diameter of 0.6 inch (15.2 mm). The hole for the valve in the wheel rim was modified accordingly. Both valves are still available at Authorized VW Dealers. When replacing a wheel, make sure that you use the valve of correct diameter.

4. Mount tire on rim. If there is a red dot on the tire wall (or two red dots), position the tire with the dot (or dots) near the valve. To facilitate mounting the tire, coat the rim shoulder with soft soap or with a special rubber lubricant sold for this purpose. The mounting procedure with a machine is shown in Fig. 91.

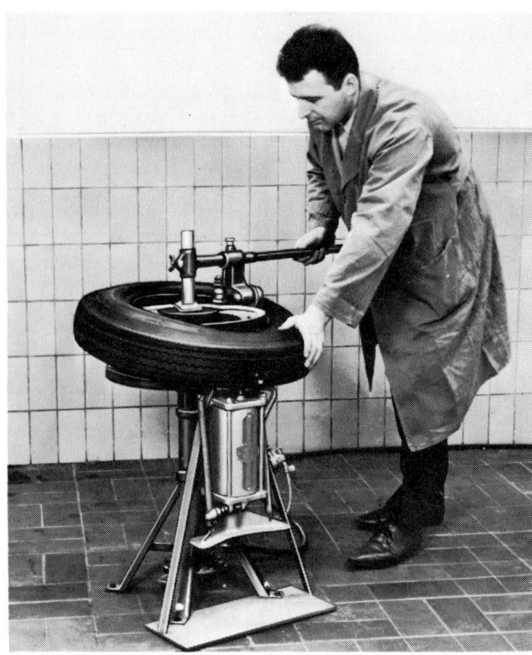



**Fig. 91.** Soap or special lubricant on rim makes mounting tire easier.

5. Remove valve core.
6. Inflate tire with an air blast of at least 51 psi (7 kg/cm$^2$). You should be able to hear the bead of the tire jump over the hump.
7. Insert valve core and inflate tire to correct pressure. Tubeless tires should always be stored in an upright position. If the tire walls have been pressed together from stacking or other improper storage, it is advisable to use a tensioning band around the tire tread when reinflating. The band spreads the tire walls, allowing them to seat properly on the rim shoulders.
8. Immerse wheel in water and check for leaks.
9. Balance wheel.
10. Install wheel and tighten bolts to prescribed torque.

## 13.5 Checking Tires

The tires should be checked regularly for damage, wear and correct pressure.

***WARNING*** —
*For maximum safety, always buy replacement tires that meet or exceed the specifications of the original tires with regard to size, load carrying capacity, tread patterns, etc.*

## Roadworthiness

Various laws and regulations make the driver responsible for keeping his car in a condition fit for the road. The state of the tires usually figures in the requirements.

Tires with tread at least 0.04 inch (1 mm) over the entire running surface are serviceable but at the limit for skid-free, safe operation. Tires worn past that point, even on a part of the tread, are not considered safe. Tires worn beyond the safety limit are shown in Fig. 92 and Fig. 93.

**Fig. 92.** Tread wear on this tire is at the safety limit. Only 0.04 inch (1 mm) of tread remains.

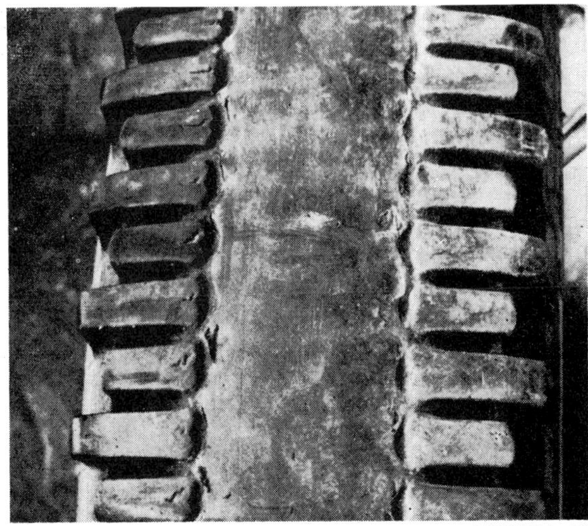



**Fig. 93.** Over-inflation causes abnormal wear at center of tread. The effects are evident here.

## Inflation Pressure

The life of your tires and the driving characteristics of your Volkswagen will depend a great deal on the tire inflation pressures. It is therefore essential to check the pressures at regular intervals—at least once a week because every tire loses a certain amount of pressure by diffusion of oxygen through the rubber.

Tubeless tires hold pressures much longer than is generally the case with tubes, but the notion that tubeless tires do not need the same attention you would give to tubes is false and dangerous. A noticeable loss of pressure from a tubeless tire is always an indication of something wrong in wheel, tire or valve. If your tire continues to lose pressure and you cannot detect leakage in the tire itself or at the sealing beads, investigate the following possibilities:

1. Leak at rim (fit new wheel).
2. Leak at valve (fit new valve or valve core).
3. Foreign matter or rough surface between rim shoulders and tire (clean or smooth off shoulders and tire beads).
4. Excessive looseness of tire on rim due to combination of unfavorable tolerances (replace wheel and tire).

If a tire continues to lose pressure, it is asking for trouble to pump it up and drive away. An under-inflated tubeless tire, like an under-inflated tube tire, will heat up from flexing of the sidewalls. The excessive heat will damage the tire. Since only the shoulders of the tire will be in contact with the road surface, the handling qualities of the car will suffer.

Always check the tires when they are cold. After fast driving the pressure is up. Never let air out of tires when warm from the road. The pressure will be too low when the tires cool down.

**NOTE —**
The simple type of pressure gauge tends to lose accuracy after long use. Remember that an error of only one or two pounds per square inch can cause abnormal tire wear. Compare your gauge with one that is known to be accurate.

You can detect valve core leakage by wetting a finger and holding it on the valve opening. A leaking valve core should be replaced.

Fig. 94 illustrates the three possible conditions of tire inflation.

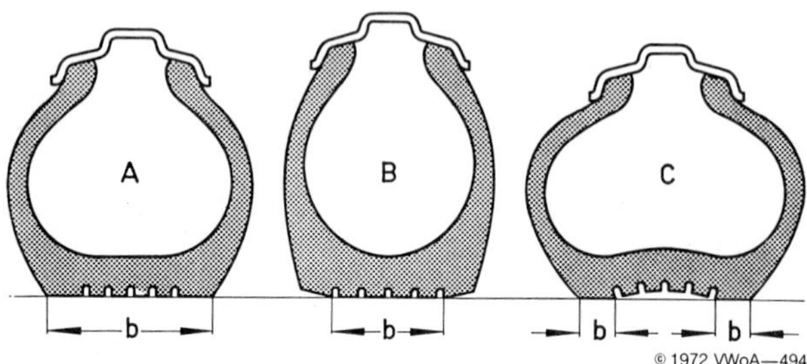


**Fig. 94.** Air pressure controls the cross sectional shape of tires, as shown here, and therefore influences wear. The shapes shown are: normal pressure (A), too high pressure (B), too low pressure (C). The distance "b" gives road contact for each shape.

A. At normal pressure the full width of the tire is in contact with the road surface, shoulder to shoulder. The tread wears evenly.

B. When the pressure is too high, the tread is curved, and the shoulders do not touch the road surface. The tire rides hard and tends to lose contact with the road. This increased slipping causes premature wear in the center of the tread. A very hard tire is more subject to impact fracture.

C. When the pressure is too low, the side walls of the tire curve excessively. Flexing increases tire temperature, and heat damages the carcass of the tire.

### Abnormal Wear

Causes of abnormal tire wear can be summarized as:

Under and over-inflation
Driving habits
Overloading of car
Road surface conditions
Improper wheel alignment

Fig. 95, 96, and Fig. 97 show graphically what under-inflation or over-inflation can do to tires. Fig. 98 and 99 demonstrate the results of driving habits on tire wear.

**Fig. 95.** Wear at sides of tread on this tire is result of under-inflation. Load bears too heavily on tire shoulders.

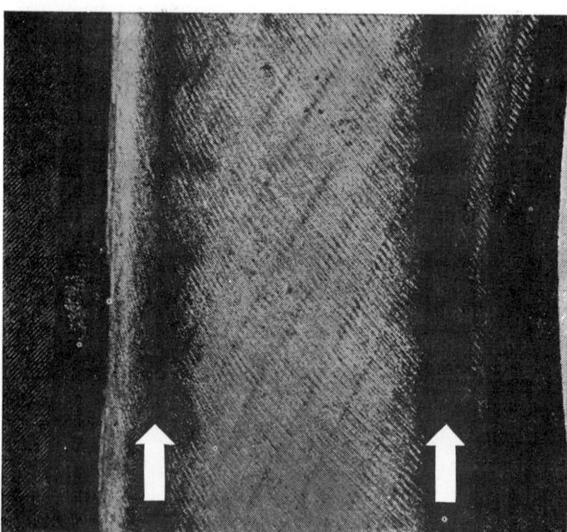


**Fig. 96.** Black stripes (arrows) are symptoms of structural change from over-heating of under-inflated tire. Under-inflation causes excessive flexing of tire.

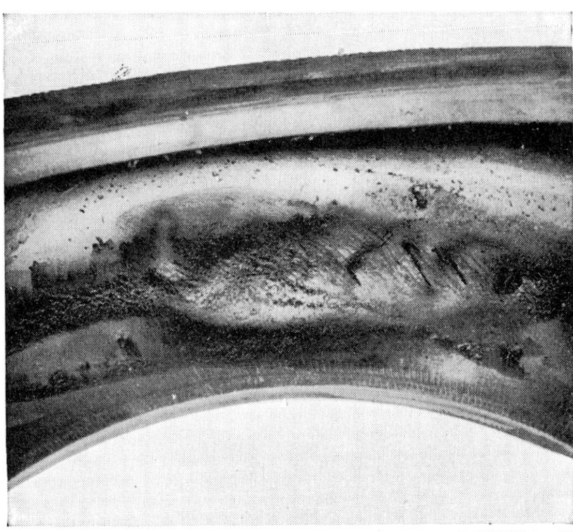

© 1972 VWoA—497

Fig. 97. Plies of this tubeless tire have separated from heat damage. Tire ran considerable distance with insufficient air pressure.

## 13.6 Driving Habits

The development of the interstate highway system and other highway improvements of recent years have increased the average speed of cars and trucks considerably. Tire wear does not necessarily increase in proportion to car speed. The wear on tires at 56 miles an hour (90 kmh) is roughly twice the wear at 37 mph (60 kmh). In the graph of Fig. 98 the normal life expectancy of a tire (100 per cent) is shown on the curve at its value for a speed of 37 mph.

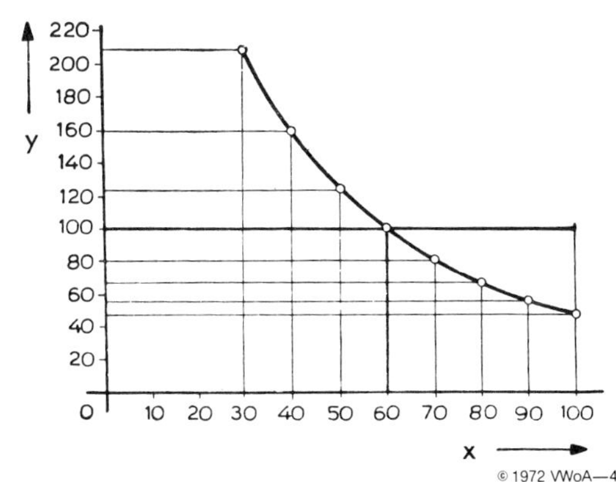


© 1972 VWoA—498

Fig. 98. Tire life is graphed here against an average speed of 37 miles an hour (60 kilometers per hour) as the normal. The x-values are speeds (in kmh) and the y-values represent comparative tire life. The normal life expectancy is given as 100, at 60 kmh. The expectancy goes down as the speed goes up, with heat as the main cause of shortened tire life.

The effect of violent braking at high speed on tires is suggested in Fig. 99, where the patch of tread was worn off as the tire slid along the highway. Locked brakes cause this kind of damage. Uneven braking force can cause extra wear on individual tires, and out-of-round brake drums also can be hard on tires.

© 1972 VWoA—499

Fig. 99. Isolated patch of worn tread is evidence of braking wear. Locked wheels caused this damage.

### Road Surface

Although a rough, anti-skid surface on a road can wear tire tread, this direct contact is by no means the only influence road conditions have on the service life of a tire.

7

On steeply cambered roads the tires are subjected to side thrust, which the driver tries to counteract by steering toward the center of the road. For this situation any variation from the specified toe-in setting of the front wheels has a particularly unfavorable result. If the toe-in is excessive, the wheel at the edge of the road is subjected to heavier stress. If the wheels toe-out, wear will be worse on the tire at the center of the road. Wear at one side of a tire and feathers at the edge of the tread are symptoms. Even when the toe settings are correct, there will be more wear on a steeply cambered road, but it will not be confined to one particular wheel.

### Incorrect Wheel Alignment

If the settings of the front or rear wheels are incorrect there will be a certain amount of irregular tire wear. As soon as signs of excessive tire wear are noticed, the following points should be checked:

Front wheel track
Wheel angle on steering lock
Position and track of rear wheels
Position of axles in relation to each other
Wheel base on both sides
Wheel camber
Setting of rear spring plates
Efficiency of shock absorbers

Improperly aligned wheels cause scrubbing. The front wheels run on one side. On the wheels on both axles scrubbing can cause spotty wear across the tread or only on one side of the tread. The right-hand side of the tread shows sharp-edged depressions with rubber feathers. On the other side the shoulder is rounded and the tread worn off. Fig. 100 gives an example.

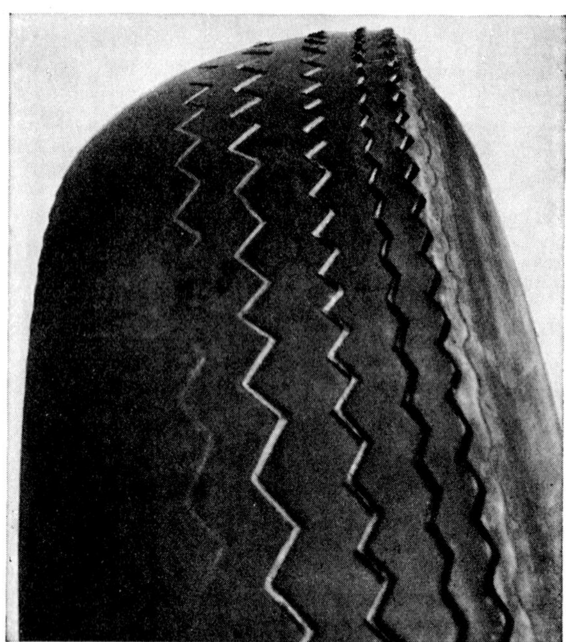



**Fig. 100.** Uneven wear on tread as seen on this tire results from improper wheel alignment. "Feathering" of tread at right is symptom. A chassis out of line from a collision can cause tire wear of this kind.

If it is suspected that the chassis of a vehicle is distorted and the wheels out of alignment from accident damage, the chassis should be checked.

### Impact Fractures

Driving rapidly over any sharp obstacle (the edge of a deep pothole, a projecting rail, a large sharp stone (Fig. 101) and so on, can lead to a local fracture of the casing cords.

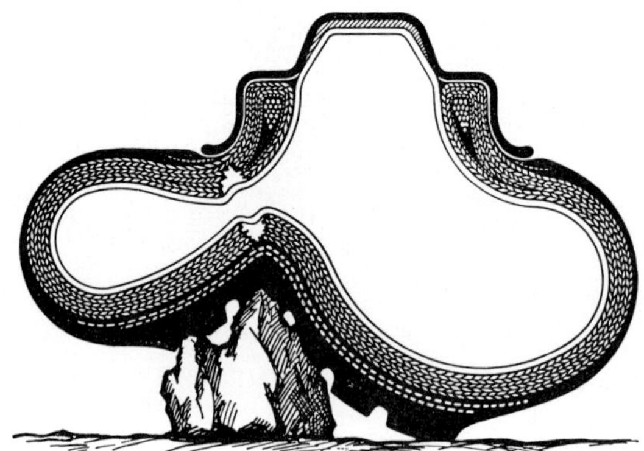



**Fig. 101.** Impact fracture is internal tear in casing cords from running over sharp objects or hitting obstacles. Fracture is shown at tire constriction above rock.

This serious type of damage is easily visible from inside the tire but usually impossible to detect from outside. It is therefore important to examine the interior of the tire if such damage is suspected. Only a few layers may be damaged at first, and the tire may not become unserviceable until later when the damage has spread. Failures of this nature can be avoided if the damage is recognized promptly. Fig. 101 shows how these fractures occur. Fig. 102a and 102b illustrate different forms the impact fractures may take.

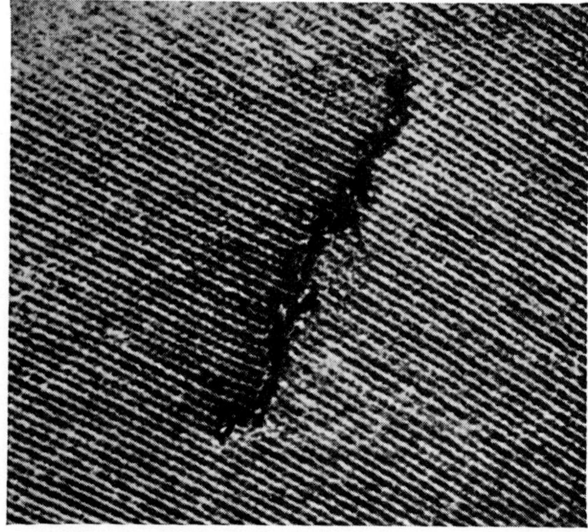



**Fig. 102a.** Single diagonal tear is the form of fracture seen here from inside the tire.

**Fig. 102b.** T-shaped fractures occurred in two places on this tire, at bottom and at top of picture. View is from inside of tire.

## 13.7 Summary of Abnormal Tire Wear

Irregular tire wear is usually caused by a combination of various defects as can be seen in the wear pattern of the example shown in Fig. 103. **Table d** gives a summary of types of abnormal wear and the causes.

1. Pressure too high = Center of tread worn.
2. Incorrect wheel settings = Scrubbing ridges on tread.
3. Cornering at high speed = Feathering, round shoulders
4. Violent braking = Small worn spots.
5. Rough road surface, winding roads = Scale-like roughness.
6. In addition to the external wear there is also the heat build-up which damages the carcass as well as the tread.

**Fig. 103.** Irregular wear from a combination of defects is seen on this tire.

### Table d. Summary of Tire Wear

| Type of wear | Cause |
|---|---|
| 1. Wear at both sides of tread | Under-inflation |
| 2. Wear at center of tread around tire | Over-inflation |
| 3. Spotty or irregular wear on one side of tread (gouges or waves) | Wheel is out of balance statically and dynamically. Lateral run-out is excessive. Play in wheel bearings is excessive |
| 4. Slightly worn spots in center of tread (cups) | Wheel is out of balance statically. Radial run-out is excessive |
| 5. Isolated badly worn spots in center of tread | Brakes are binding. Brake drum is out of round. Check brakes |
| 6. Stepped tread wear (heel and toe or saw tooth). In severe cases, fractures in fabric which also become visible externally in the course of time | Typical sign of overloading. Inspect inside of tire for fractures |
| 7. Feather edges on sides of tread | Typical sign of scrubbing wheel. Wheel alignment is incorrect. On rear wheels, check spring plate settings and efficiency of shock absorbers |
| 8. Ridge formation on one side of a front tire | Wheel is out of line and has been scrubbing. Wheel alignment is incorrect. Continuous driving on steeply cambered roads, fast cornering can be contributing factors |
| 9. Impact fracture in fabric, only visible inside tire at first | Driving over sharp stones, rails, etc., at high speeds causes this damage |

7

### 13.8 Wheel Rotation

If it is noted that the tires are wearing unevenly after a certain amount of use, the five wheels can be rotated as shown in Fig. 104.

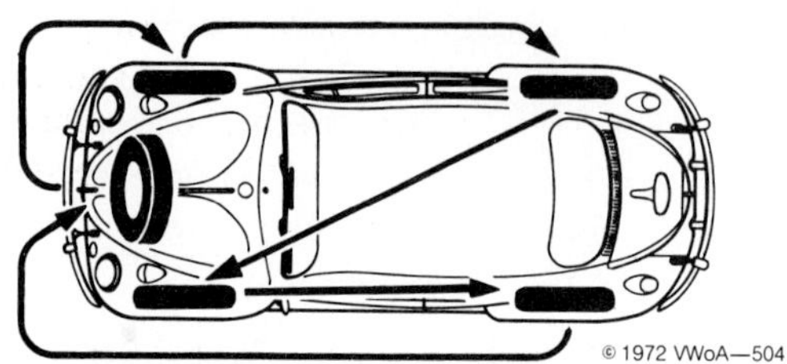


**Fig. 104.** Recommended sequence for rotation of tires to spread wear evenly is illustrated here.

**NOTE —**
Experience has shown that the cost of rotating tires is not offset by the benefits of evening the wear. In fact, rotating of the tires may upset the wear pattern. For the best information on the subject, consult a representative of the tire manufacturer.

### 13.9 Replacing Tires

The best time to put on a new tire is in the autumn because tire wear, on the average, is much higher in summer than in winter. At the same time there is also the advantage that the treads of a new tire grip better and reduce danger of skidding in the cold, wet season. Fig. 105 shows influence of the seasons on tire wear.

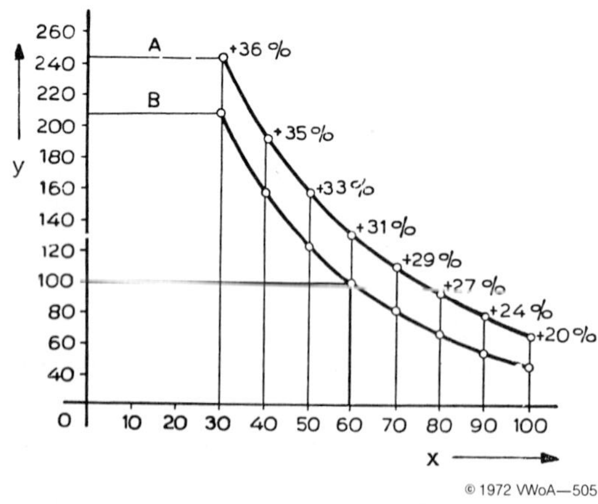



**Fig. 105.** Seasonal influence on tire wear is graphed here. The x-values show average speeds in kilometers per hour. The y-values show comparative tire life with 100 as the normal expectancy. Curve A is for winter and B for summer. The difference is obviously in favor of winter, by 20 to 36 per cent.

Always replace a tire when the tread is down to 0.04 inch (1 mm) thick. The tire is no longer safe.

### 13.10 Wheel Balancing

The riding qualities of the Volkswagen can be fully realized only if the wheels are properly balanced. Out-of-balance wheels can tramp and wobble enough to make the steering unsteady. The faster the vehicle is to be driven the more carefully the wheels must be balanced. Fig. 106 shows the effect of wheel balance on tires.

**Fig. 106.** Wheel balance made the difference in the wear on these two tires. Both tires traveled about the same distance, but balanced tire at left shows much less wear than tire on right which was on unbalanced wheel.

Wheels with repaired or retreaded tires must always be checked for balance. If apparatus for wheel balancing is not available, put such wheels on the rear axle only and cut your speed. Otherwise, severe damage may occur to the vehicle.

The word "unbalanced" refers here to uneven distribution of weight and material in a rotating body. A wheel is balanced when the weight is uniformly distributed a) statically and b) dynamically. In static balance the weight of the wheel disk with cap, tire and tube is evenly distributed around the axis of the wheel. A wheel not balanced statically (Fig. 107) will tend to tramp, shake or bounce when the vehicle is in motion.

Dynamic balance refers to uniform distribution of the weight in relation to the vertical centerline of the wheel.

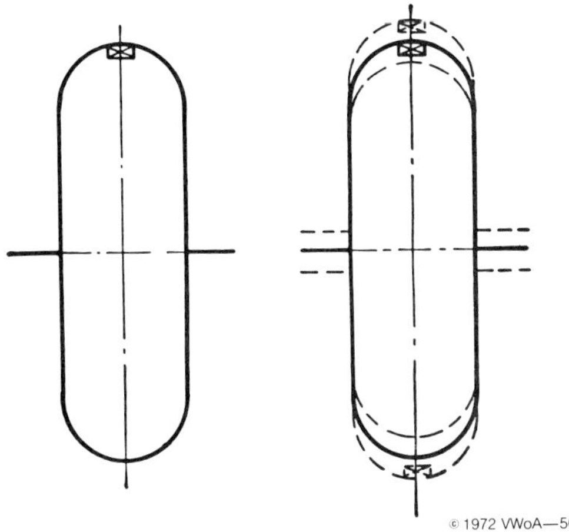
© 1972 VWoA—507

**Fig. 107.** Static imbalance (at right) is condition in which weight of wheel, tire and fittings is not distributed uniformly with respect to axle.

Lack of dynamic balance (Fig. 108) is noticed only when the car is moving and the wheels flutter or vibrate.

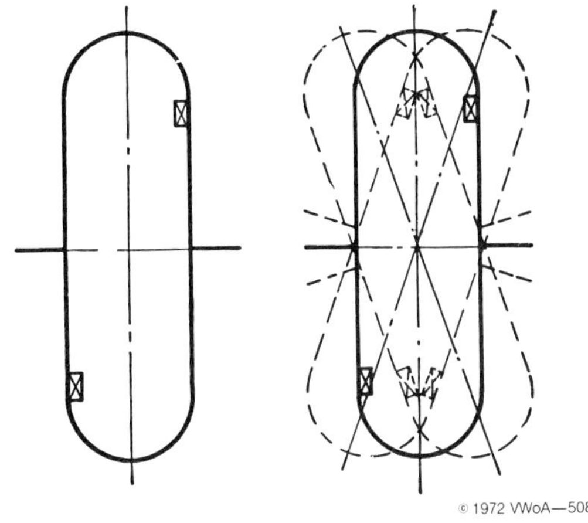
© 1972 VWoA—508

**Fig. 108.** Dynamic imbalance (at right) condition in which the weight of tire and wheel and fittings is not distributed uniformly with respect to the vertical centerline of the wheel.

Conditions of imbalance become more pronounced as the speed increases. At a certain wheel speed, forces which can do serious damage to the wheel bearings are set up.

Before they are balanced, wheels must be checked for lateral and radial run-out. The maximum lateral and radial run-out permitted is 0.059 inch (1.5 mm). Static balance can be checked on a simple appliance, but a special machine is required to check dynamic balance. The maker's instructions should be followed if you use one of these devices.

## 13.11 The Weather and Tire Life

Heat is the worst enemy of the tire. Under the influence of high temperatures, heavy loading and low tire pressure, the tire may heat up enough—especially in a long period of fast driving—for the structure of the tire to alter. Such an alteration if continued causes abnormal wear.

It is advisable to pay attention to the temperature of the tires on long fast trips.

Tire wear lessens when the road surface is wet. The water acts as a lubricant, reducing the frictional contact.

## 13.12 Anti-skid Qualities of Tires

The tendency of a car to skid is influenced by the condition of the tire tread, and the design of the tread is therefore of great importance to the steering stability of the car under bad road and weather conditions.

**Table e** shows performance characteristics of various types of snow tires.

7

***WARNING —***
*If radial tires are used, they must be mounted on all four wheels. The different handling characteristics of these tires require this uniformity.*

### Table e. Tire Characteristics

| Operating conditions | Snow w/studs radial-ply | Snow w/studs bias-ply | Snow radial-ply | Snow bias-ply | Standard radial-ply | Standard bias-ply |
|---|---|---|---|---|---|---|
| Dry | 0 | 0 | X | X | X | X |
| Wet | — | — | X | X | X | X |
| Snow | X | X | X | X | 0 | 0 |
| Ice | X | X | 0 | 0 | 0 | — |

**X** = Effective **0** = Restricted effectiveness **—** = Non-effective

## 13.13 Winter Tires and Snow Chains

The modern winter tire can cope with deep snow, slush, and ice much better than the tires of several years ago. The trouble is that winter weather is mixed with spells when the roads are quite open. In such conditions even the best winter tire cannot replace the ordinary tire.

With full recognition of the progress made by tire manufacturers towards the production of a universal winter tire, we still have to say that the ideal tire for all phases of winter driving has not yet been achieved.

The studded tire helps to reduce the risk of driving on ice. These tires are quite satisfactory when used on the Volkswagen. On ice and hard-packed snow, studded tires perform better than standard tires in moving off, accelerating, braking and cornering. On dry and wet roads they are not as good as standard tires.

As winter tires have a detrimental influence on the roadholding and cornering properties of every automobile, it is advisable to drive with normal tires until conditions really call for winter tires. In order to get the best roadholding and cornering when using winter tires, keep the tire pressures up and uniform. The advantages of snow and ice tires are even more noticeable if the tires are inflated to 3 psi above the pressure given for the standard tires. Do not under any conditions reduce pressures. The following instructions and recommendations also apply when using special tires and snow chains.

1. Tires 5.60—15
   a. You can use snow tires on all wheels without any special precautions.
   b. You should use snow tires on all wheels when snow conditions prevail for long periods.
2. Ice tires 5.60—15 (studs)
   You should use studded tires on all four wheels to get the full benefit when driving on ice and hard snow.
3. Snow chains 5.60—15
   a. You can use chains on rear wheels only with either standard or winter tires.
   b. Use only thin chains which do not stand more than 0.511 inch (13 mm) above tread and inner wall, including tensioner. Be careful to tension the chains correctly.

We advise all Volkswagen drivers **not** to drive vehicles equipped with winter tires at full speed on snow-free roads. Snow and ice reduce the adhesion and directional stability of tires. On snow and icebound roads, the old rules still apply: Drive slower. Accelerate and brake gently. If you stick to the rules, your tires will keep their directional stability.

***CAUTION*** —
*Refer to local motor vehicle laws to legality and seasonal use of studded tires.*

When using snow tires note the following points:

1. Studded snow tires
   Studded snow tires should be driven at moderate speeds for the first 200 miles to allow the studs to "bed in".
2. Tread depth
   Snow tires (with or without studs) must have a minimum tread depth of an eighth of an inch (4 mm).
3. Air pressures of snow tires
   The driving characteristics of bias-ply snow tires will be improved if they are inflated to 3 psi above the pressures for standard bias-ply tires. For radial-ply snow tires, the inflation pressure should always be held to the figure given on the tire sidewall.

***WARNING*** —
*Never exceed pressures marked on side wall.*

4. Snow tire usage
   Inquire about state or municipal regulations concerning the use of snow tires, especially **studded** snow tires.
5. Storage of winter tires
   You should mark the direction of rotation clearly on your snow tires before removing them from wheels. It does not matter if they remain on their own wheels. This is to make sure you can remount them to run in the same direction as before.

## 13.14 Radial Ply Tires

There is no general objection to the use of radial-ply tires on VW cars, but you should bear in mind that while they offer numerous advantages, these tires also have certain disadvantages. Long service life and improved directional stability in fast driving are the specific properties of radial-ply tires which make them appear superior to ordinary tires. The movement of rubber particles in the tire contact surface is restricted as the wheel rolls, and this restriction assures particularly good adhesion even on wet surfaces. The radial-ply tire is also distinguished by its limited flexing, which means low rolling resistance and a lower running temperature. All these features result in a long tire life.

These positive characteristics, however, are obtained at the expense of a certain loss of comfort. On some roads radial tires create far more noise in the vehicle than standard tires do. They also react more directly to steering changes. Radial-ply tires are ideal for fast driving but the best qualities are really apparent only on good roads. If you rarely take long trips or if you live where the roads are generally poor, you may not gain much from putting radials on your Volkswagen. Before you buy radials it is a good idea to have a test run in a Volkswagen fitted with this type of tire to see if they meet your individual requirements.

Generally speaking, the standard tires fitted at the factory give Volkswagen cars excellent driving characteristics and riding comfort. These tires represent the most favorable compromise with regard to service life, running characteristics and price. Particularly in respect to riding comfort, the standard tire is far superior to any radial-ply tire. The use of other types is therefore a matter for each individual.

### Tubeless Radials

Constant improvements in tires and introduction of the hump rims have made tubeless radial-ply tires possible. Use tubeless radials only with the hump type rims. You can install tubes in these tires if the car is to be driven on very bad roads.

If you want to put radials on rims without humps, be sure to use inner tubes with them.

## 14. BRAKE TECHNICAL DATA

### I. Brakes and Wheels: Tolerances, wear limits and settings

| Part | From Chassis No. | Up to Chassis No. | New installation inch (mm) | Wear limit inch (mm) |
|---|---|---|---|---|
| a. Master cylinder | | | | |
| Stroke | 115 000 001 | — | 1.299 (33.0) | — |
| Diameter | 115 000 001 | — | .687 (17.46) | — |
| b. Tandem master cylinder | | | | |
| Front wheel circuit stroke | 117 000 001 | — | .609 (15.5)* | — |
| Rear wheel circuit stroke | — | — | .491 (12.5) | — |
| Front wheel circuit stroke | 147 000 001 | — | .551 (14.0)** | — |
| Rear wheel circuit stroke | — | — | .551 (14.0) | — |
| Diameter | 117 000 001 | — | .749 (19.05) | — |
| c. Wheel cylinders | | | | |
| Front . . . . . . . . diameter | 167 3 351 | — | .873 (22.20) | — |
| Rear . . . . . . . . diameter | 167 3 351 | — | .749 (19.05) | — |
| d. Caliper | | | | |
| Cylinder . . . . . . . . diameter | 147 000 001 | — | 1.574 (40.0) | — |
| e. Brake drums*** | | | | |
| Front . . . . . . . . inside diameter | — | — | 9.058 + .008 (230.1 + 0.2) | 9.113 (231.5) |
| Rear . . . . . . . . inside diameter | — | — | 9.005 + .003 (230.0 + 0.2) | 9.113 (231.5) |
| Front and rear . . . . . . wall thickness | — | — | — — | .16 (4.0) |
| out of round | — | — | max. 0.004 (0.1) | — |
| taper | — | — | max. 0.004 (0.1) | — |
| lateral run-out | — | — | max. 0.016 (0.25) | — |
| Measured at friction surface . . . . . radial run-out | — | — | max. 0.006 (0.15) | — |
| f. Brake disc | | | | |
| thickness | — | — | .373-.372 (9.50-9.45) | .315 (8.0) |
| Disc after turning . . . . . . . thickness | — | — | min. 0.333 (8.5) | .315 (8.0) |
| Machining dimension. . . . . . . per side | — | — | max. 0.019 (0.5) | — |
| thickness tolerances | — | — | max. 0.0007 (0.02) | — |
| run-out | — | — | max. 0.007 (0.2) | — |
| g. Brake linings | | | | |
| Linings for brake shoes | | | | |
| Front . . . . . . . . width | — | — | 1.574 (40.0) | — |
| Rear . . . . . . . . width | — | — | 1.181 (30.0) | — |
| width | 118 000 001 | — | 1.574 (40.0) | — |
| front and rear thickness | — | — | .157-.149 (4.0-3.8) | .098 (2.5) |
| Friction pad for disc brake . . . . . thickness | — | — | .393 (10.1)**** | .078 (2.0) |

*Valid for drum brakes only
**Valid for disc brakes only
***The drum turning dimension for 0.002 inch (0.5 mm) oversize linings is 0.040 inch (1.0 mm) above the given dimension for all drums
****Without pad carrier plate



7

## II. Tire Data

| Model | VW 1300 and Karmann Ghia | | VW 1500 | |
|---|---|---|---|---|
| Tire (tubeless) | 5.60—15 4 PR* | | 5.60—15 4 PR | |
| Rim x wheel size<br>Radial run-out<br>Lateral run-out | 4 J x 15*<br>Max. 0.060 inch (1.5 mm) | | | |
| | **Inflation pressures in kg/cm² and (psi)** | | | |
| | **front** | **rear** | **front** | **rear** |
| a. up to 2 occupants<br>b. fully loaded | 1.1 (16)<br>1.2 (17) | 1.7 (24)<br>1.8 (26) | 1.1 (16)<br>1.3 (18) | 1.9 (27)<br>1.9 (27) |

***Model 14 (Karmann Ghia) from Chassis No. 147 000 001: 5.605-15 4 PR**

****Model 14 (Karmann Ghia) from Chassis No. 148 000 038: 4 1/2 J x 15**

**For prolonged high speed travel tire pressures on vehicles with bias-ply tires should be increased by 0.2 kg/cm² (3 psi).**

**Under no circumstance is the cold tire pressure to exceed the maximum inflated pressure marked on the tire.**

## III. Tightening torques

| Location | Part | Thread | ft/lb | mkg |
|---|---|---|---|---|
| **Master cylinder** | | | | |
| Stop screw in housing | bolt | M 6 | 3.5-7.0 | 0.5-1.0 |
| Residual pressure valve to housing | — | M 12 x 1 | 14 | 2.0 |
| Brake light switch to housing | — | M 10 x 1 | 14 | 2.0 |
| Master cylinder to frame | bolt | M 8 | 18 | 2.5 |
| Brake line to master cylinder* | union nut | M 10 x 1 | 11-14 | 1.5-2.0 |
| **Front wheel brakes** | | | | |
| Backing plate to steering knuckle | bolt | M 10 | 36 | 5.0 |
| Splash shield to steering knuckle | bolt | M 7 | 7.0 | 1.0 |
| Cylinder to backing plate | bolt | M 8 | 18 | 2.5 |
| Caliper housing | socket head screw | M 7 | 14-18 | 2.0-2.5 |
| Caliper to steering knuckle | bolt | M 10 | 29 | 4.0 |
| Bleeder valve in cylinder/caliper | — | M 6/77 | max. 3.5 | max. 0.5 |
| Hose to cylinder/caliper | — | M 10 | 11-14 | 1.5-2.0 |
| Screw for clamp nut | socket head screw | M 7 | 7 max. 9 | 1.0 max. 1.3 |
| **Rear wheel brakes** | | | | |
| Cylinder to backing plate | bolt | M 8 | 14-22 | 2.0-3.0 |
| Cover to bearing housing | bolt | M 10 | 43 | 6.0 |
| Brake drum to shaft | slotted nut | M 24/M 30 | 253 | 35.0 |
| **Wheels** | | | | |
| Wheel to drum/disc | bolt | M 14 x 1.5 | 87-94 | 12.0-13.0 |
| Wheel to drum/disc | bolt | M 12 x 1.5 | 72 | 10.0 |
| **Pedals** | | | | |
| Pedal bracket to frame | bolt | M 10 | 28-32 | 4.0-4.5 |
| Pedal stop plate to frame | bolt | M 8 | 14-18 | 2.0-2.5 |

***Valid for all brake line connections**
**CAUTION: Quality Grade or Tensile Class of listed threaded fasteners are not included. Always check with Parts List to make sure they are for the intended purpose.**

# Section 8

# LUBRICATION AND MAINTENANCE

## Contents


**1. Lubricants** . . . . . 3
- 1.1 Engine Oils . . . . . 3
- 1.2 Transmission Oils . . . . . 3
  - Automatic Transmission Fluid (ATF) . . . . 3
- 1.3 Grease . . . . . 3
- 1.4 Lubricant Additives . . . . . 4

**2. Maintenance** . . . . . 4
- Changing Engine Oil . . . . . 4
- Changing Transmission Oil . . . . . 6
- Automatic Stick Shift—Fluid Refilling . . . . 7
- 2.1 Steering Gear Box . . . . . 8
- 2.2 Front Axle . . . . . 8
- 2.3 Front Wheel Bearings . . . . . 8
- 2.4 Locks and Hinges . . . . . 9
- 2.5 Air Cleaner . . . . . 9
- 2.6 Lubricating Distributor . . . . . 9
- 2.7 Front Seat Runners . . . . . 9
- 2.8 Gearshift Lever . . . . . 9
- 2.9 Convertible Top Linkage . . . . . 9

**TABLES**
- a. Lubrication and Maintenance Chart . . . . . 11
- b. Maintenance Operations (emission control system) . . . . . 11
- c. Maintenance Operations (Automatic Stick Shift) . 11
- d. Lubrication Chart (Automatic Stick Shift) . . . . . 11
- e. Maintenance Chart . . . . . 12
- f. Lubricants . . . . . 12

# Lubrication and Maintenance

For reliability and economy of operation, your Volkswagen must have the benefits of thorough lubrication and regular maintenance. A good starting point is to give some thought to the oils and greases you will be buying for your car. Because the lubricating properties of car oils and greases must hold up over a wide range of operating conditions, you will be best served if you stick to known brands of high quality. The next step is to read the instructions and the maintenance schedules given in the next few pages of this Manual. If you will follow these recommended programs faithfully, you will greatly help to preserve the reliability and the good handling qualities of your car and to maintain its value.

The public's continuing demands for better performance on the road and for a more comfortable ride have influenced developments in lubricants. The oil companies now produce a large variety of oils and greases for cars, and in your own interest it would be good to know at least a little about the different grades of lubricants and the different purposes for which they were developed. The lubrication charts in these pages will give you the basic information you need.

Volkswagen does not endorse products by brand names, but it does recommend types of products in respect to technical specifications. The VW engineers have done much research on lubricants best adapted to use in VW cars, and the lubrication charts you will find elsewhere in these pages embody the results of this research. We recommend that you make use of the charts. Over the long run you will find yourself well repaid for the time spent on this reading.

## 1. LUBRICANTS

The oil in an engine operating at high rpm or under full load over a period of time becomes very hot, but so does oil at low rpm and under light load if the car is in the noonday sunshine or a hot climate. To measure differences in the properties of the oil in these two situations might not be easy, but the example illustrates how seemingly different conditions can impose similar requirements on lubricants. You need good oil and good greases.

### 1.1 Engine Oils

Every engine oil must meet one basic requirement: it must retain its lubricating properties over the whole range of operating temperatures, from the lowest to the highest. The oil must protect the metal from corrosion and it should resist chemical reactions, including oxidation. Oxidation thickens oil and can form a varnish-like film on pistons and valve stems.

When you go to buy oil, the property of most interest to you will be the viscosity. Viscosity is a measure of the resistance of the oil (or other fluid) to flow. That is, an oil of high viscosity is thicker than an oil of lower viscosity and slower to run.

Every change of temperature tends to change the viscosity of an oil. Heat thins the oil, reducing the protective film between moving parts. Cold thickens oil and increases its resistance to movement in the mechanism. This resistance contributes to slow starting in winter. A cold engine needs oil that is thin enough to flow at once to all the lubrication points. While the viscosity has no effect on lubricating properties as such, it does influence the flow to the parts to be lubricated.

The Society of Automotive Engineers (SAE) has established the SAE system of grading the viscosity of oils with numbers. According to the viscosities, oils are sold as SAE 30, SAE 20, SAE 10. High numbers signify thick oils, low numbers thin.

A well-known brand of HD (high detergent) oil should be used in VW engines, either new or rebuilt. The viscosity should be selected to suit the climate and the season as follows:

| | |
|---|---|
| SAE 40 | In hot, tropic climates |
| SAE 30 | In the warm seasons and all year round in hot climates. |
| SAE 20 W/20 | In winter |
| or | |
| SAE 10 W | Where the average temperature is below 5 degrees F (−15 degrees C). |
| SAE 5 W | In arctic climates with average temperatures below −13 degrees F (−25 degrees C). |



High detergent oils contain additives that improve resistance to oxidation and protect bearings from corrosion. The detergent property holds contaminants in suspension which otherwise would be deposited on engine parts. At oil changes the contaminants are drained off with the old oil. The HD oils suitable for the VW engine formerly were labeled "For Service MS" under the API classification of the American Petroleum Institute. (The "MS" stands for "motor severe.") Under a new classification system a variety of new designations has been introduced. The equivalent of MS is now SD. During the changeover oil cans may carry such designations as MS-SD. The system of grading engine oils by viscosity will continue.

### 1.2 Transmission Oils

For lubrication of the VW transmission and rear axle a hypoid SAE 90 gear oil should be used the year round. If the outside temperature is expected to remain below 14 degrees F (−10 degrees C), the thinner SAE 80 oil should be used.

Note the following:

1. If you are taking your car out of service for several months in winter, drain off the hypoid oil and refill the transmission with anti-corrosion oil. A rear axle should not be stored with hypoid oil in it.
2. Check the oil seals for leakage.

**Automatic Transmission Fluid**
(ATF)

Certain automatic transmission fluids (ATF) are specified for use in the torque converter of the VW Automatic Stick Shift. Use only an ATF which has the following on the label:

1. Brand name
2. DEXRON®
3. A five-digit number preceded by the letter "B". ATF without such descriptions on the label is not recommended for VW products.

### 1.3 Grease

All moving or bearing parts of the car are subject to a certain amount of wear. To keep repair costs at the minimum, have your car lubricated at regular intervals as outlined in **Tables a, c** and **d.** Regular lubrication is of great importance. Use the different greases specified for the different applications:

**High pressure grease** must be cold-resistant and water-repellent. The melting point must be above 230 degrees F (110 degrees C).

**Transmission grease** contains a large percentage of oil and has a low consistency. The melting point should be above 284 degrees F (140 degrees C).

**Multi-purpose grease** with a lithium base has a high melting point (at least 338 degrees F; 170 degrees C) and should be water-repellent and cold-resistant. For a very cold climate the grease should retain its lubricating properties down to −31 degrees F (−35 degrees C).

Moly greases are composed of a lithium-base grease and molybdenum disulfide. The melting point should be at least 356 degrees F (180 degrees C). Moly-Kote® is typical of those specifications.

### 1.4 Lubricant Additives

The VW engine has demonstrated that it does not require special lubricating agents or additives to give expected performance and service life while holding to normal consumption of fuel and oil. Though particular situations of severe pressure and temperature may at times occur, actual experience has shown that under all operating conditions the well-known standard brands of lubricants are adequate for the VW engine.

Tests carried out with various additives have shown that neither the performance nor the fuel oil consumption of a properly maintained VW engine has been improved enough to justify the cost of using additives regularly. As far as the VW engine is concerned, any type of additive, whether mixed with the fuel or the engine oil, is superfluous.

For this reason the VW Owner's Manual states that no additive of any kind should be mixed with HD oils.

## 2. MAINTENANCE

Under the heading of maintenance we include the procedures for changing engine oil and transmission fluid and refilling the Automatic Stick Shift tank as well as specific maintenance procedures for various separate components of the car.

### Changing Engine Oil

On a new or rebuilt VW engine the oil should be changed first at 300 miles, next at 3,000 miles and thereafter regularly at intervals of 3,000 miles.

The engine should be warm when the oil is drained (see ENGINE). The drain plug is removed and then the cover of the oil strainer. At every oil change, the strainer should be taken out and thoroughly cleaned and dried. Do not put back the old gaskets or the old copper washers on the cap nuts. Replace them with new ones.

The amount of oil specified for your VW engine is 5.3 U.S. pints (2.5 liters). You may find, however, that this amount will bring the oil level slightly above the top mark on the dipstick. The small discrepancy is due to manufacturing tolerances and is of no significance. Having the oil level slightly above the top mark, or between the two marks after some travel, does not adversely affect the oil circulation.

When changing oil, stick to the same type, and if possible, to the same brand. Attach a tag to the door post stating the brand, type and viscosity of the oil used. Do not put tags in the engine compartment as the engine cooling fan might suck them in.

The use of different types of oils is not recommended. If you can avoid it, do not mix brands of oil, even of the same type. Always follow the product manufacturer's recommendations.

If your driving is restricted to short distances and in city traffic only, it is a good practice, especially in winter, to have an additional oil change every 1500 miles. There are some other exceptions to the general recommendation of an oil change every 3,000 miles:

1. If your car is covering only a few hundred miles a month in city traffic, it is advisable to change the engine oil every six to eight weeks.
2. If you drive your car less than 6,000 miles a year, the oil should be changed at least twice in that time.
3. If you drive in an arctic climate (below −13 degrees F or −25 degrees C) you should change the oil every 750 miles. This short interval is recommended also for less severe winters when the car covers only a few hundred miles a month.

Before you change engine oil, there are several points to consider:

1. You will have to get rid of the old oil. Before you drain the engine, check with some authority about disposal. Do not pour the oil in a sewer, on the ground or in an open stream. The zoning regulations or environmental rules of your community will tell you how you can dispose of it. If getting rid of the old oil presents a real problem, we suggest that you have your oil changed at your Authorized VW Dealer or a service station.
2. If the engine oil is to carry away the accumulated foreign particles in the crankcase, it must be warm when you drain it.

3. You will need a suitable container to hold the old oil. Be sure that it is large enough for all the oil. A screen placed over the receptacle will reduce splashing.
4. When checking the oil shortly after an oil change, you will find that the oil has changed color. Do not be alarmed. In only a short time on the road even the best oil will darken.

**To drain engine oil:**

1. Run engine until oil is warm.
2. Shut off engine.
3. Place oil drain pan under engine.

> ***WARNING—***
> *When removing the drain plug with your fingers, hold your elbow as high as possible. This position will keep hot oil from running down your wrist and arm. Protect your eyes by wearing safety glasses.*

4. Use 21 mm wrench to loosen and remove plug, as in Fig. 1.

**To remove oil strainer:**

1. With an offset box wrench take off the six cap nuts holding oil strainer cover plate. Discard the six copper washers under the nuts. (See Fig. 2.)
2. Remove cover plate and oil strainer.
3. Remove and discard paper gaskets. Make sure that no piece of gasket is left on the strainer.
4. Wash the strainer plate, the plug and nuts in a suitable solvent.

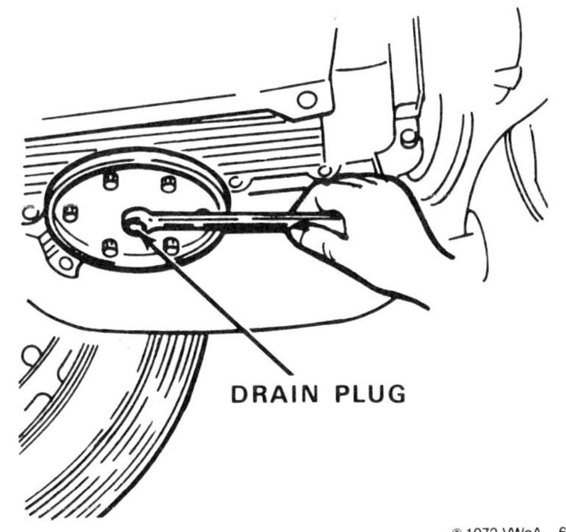


**Fig. 1.** Drain plug for crankcase is unscrewed with wrench.

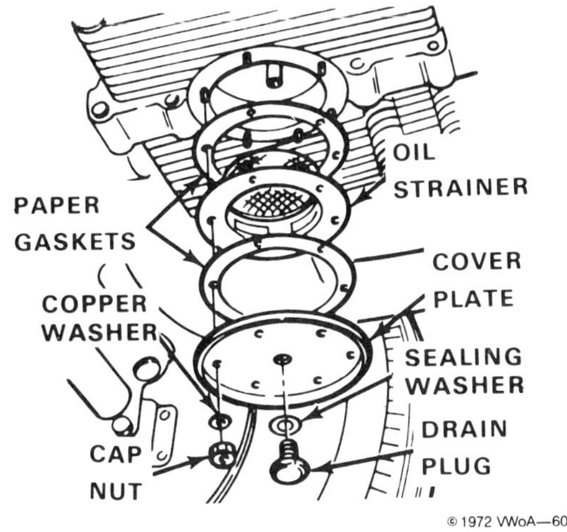


**Fig. 2.** Oil strainer breaks down into parts shown here.

**To install strainer:**

1. Put copper washer on plug and screw plug finger-tight on plate. Place a new gasket on each side of strainer.
2. Place strainer and gaskets on cover plate. Push strainer into housing. Rotate cover plate until holes are in line with mounting bolts. Push up on cover to seat it.
3. Screw on cap nuts. Use a new copper washer under each nut. Tighten all nuts finger-tight.
4. With torque wrench tighten each cap nut to 5 ft. lbs. in cross-pattern (see Fig. 3).
5. Torque plug to 25 ft. lbs.

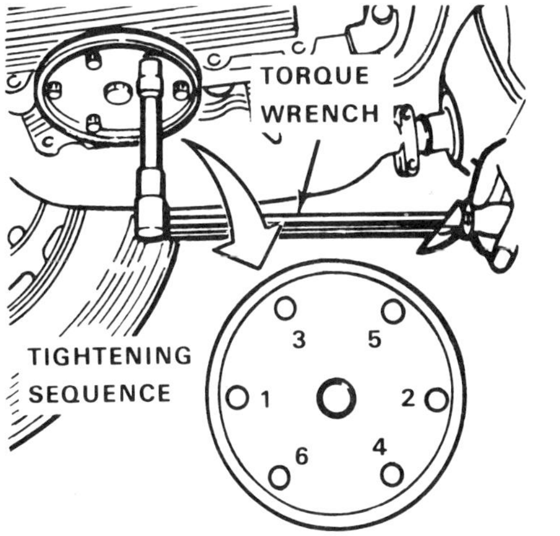


**Fig. 3.** Cap nuts on oil strainer should be tightened in sequence given by numbers shown here on strainer cover.

**To refill engine oil:**

1. Raise engine lid.
2. Unscrew and remove oil filler cap (see Fig. 4).
3. Pour in 5.3 U.S. pints (4.4 imperial pints) of oil labeled "for service MS" (or under new designation "SD"). Use the oil can opener/spout.

**NOTE —**
When topping-up, add engine oil until level reaches top mark on dipstick.

4. Pull dipstick out (Fig. 5) and wipe it off.
5. Insert dipstick, pushing it all the way down.
6. Pull dipstick out again and check oil level (Fig. 6). It should be on or near the top mark.
7. Put dipstick back. Install oil filler cap and tighten.

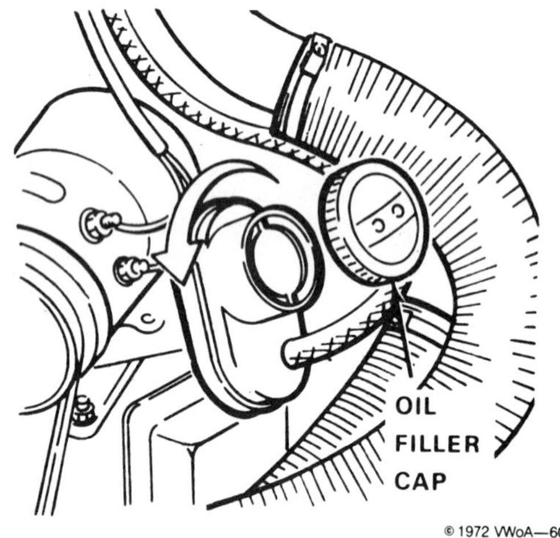


**Fig. 4.** Oil filler neck is in engine compartment, to right of the generator.

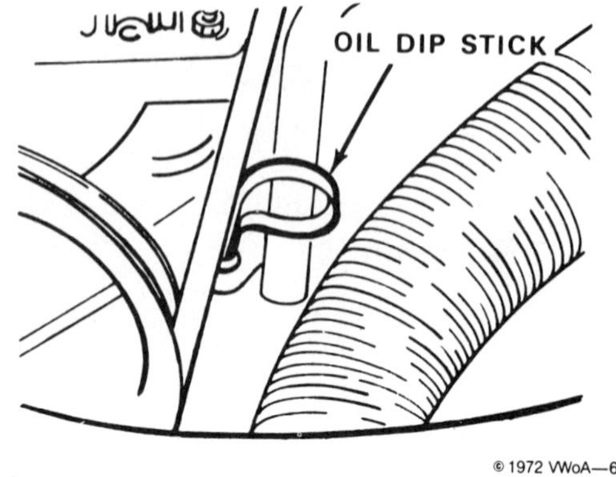


**Fig. 5.** Oil dipstick is at right of and just behind crankshaft pulley in the engine compartment.

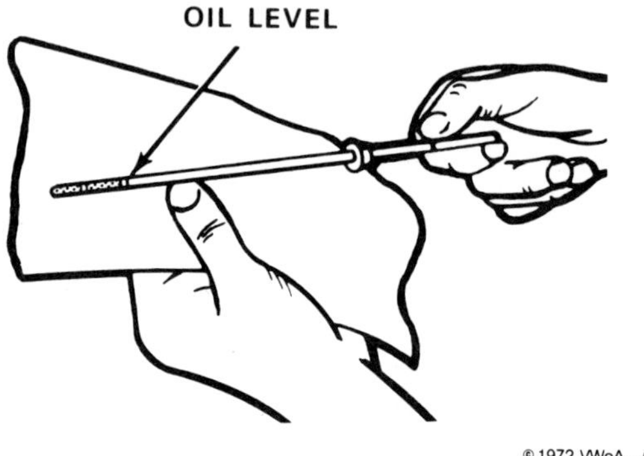


**Fig. 6.** Mark on dipstick indicates correct oil level.

The oil strainer and plate must be cleaned at each oil change. As the HD oils have a cleansing action, it is not necessary to flush the engine when changing the oil.

## Changing Transmission Oil

The oil in a new or rebuilt VW transmission is changed the first time after 300 miles on the road and thereafter at intervals of 30,000 miles. If fluid meeting military specifications MIL-L-2105B is used, changing will not be required.

***CAUTION —***
*Unless you are equipped to refill the transmission case with approved fluid and in recommended way, don't drain transmission case. If you are prepared for this task, be sure to read instructions before you begin.*

Before each change the car should be warmed up on the road. The drained transmission oil should still be warm. Both magnetic drain plugs should be removed for this operation, and they should be cleaned thoroughly before they are put back in the transmission.

For all cars covered in the Manual the initial filling of the fully synchronized transmission requires 6.3 U.S. pints of oil (5.3 imperial pints or 3.0 liters). On refill the transmission takes 5.3 U.S. pints (4.4 imperial pints or 2.5 liters). The oil level should come up just to the filler hole.

**NOTE —**
The fluid level in the transmission should be checked at specified intervals (see **Tables c, d** and **f**). You should leave replacement of transmission fluid and even topping-up to your VW dealer. The procedure requires a special filling apparatus. Further, vehicle must be level when it is raised to give access to filler plug. Transmission fluid is not generally available because it is not marketed in small enough quantities to fit your need.

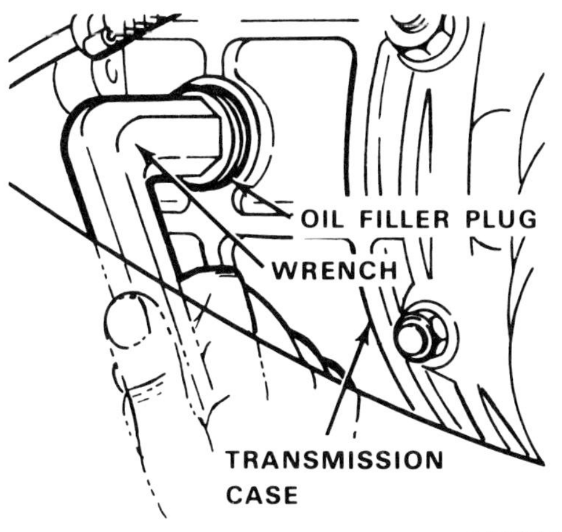


**Fig. 7.** Oil filler plug at left side of transmission case is removed with hex head wrench, as shown here.

**To change oil:**

1. Using hex-head wrench, remove the oil filler plug on the left side of the transmission case, as seen in Fig. 7.
2. With your finger check fluid level. Fluid should come just to edge of the opening (Fig. 8). If not, have your dealer or a service station attendant add more fluid.
3. Screw plug back into transmission case and tighten.

The amount of oil that will remain in the half axles of the swing axle at an oil change depends on whether there is a load on the rear axle. After refill with the correct amount (5.3 U.S. pints), the oil level in the transmission case will vary slightly, but the variation will not affect lubrication of the transmission and rear axle.

Sometimes the transmission fills very slowly. If the oil is poured in too fast, there may be an overflow as if the case were already full. In reality, not more than two or three pints have been poured. Since sufficient oil in the transmission case is essential to silent operation of the rear axle and a long service life for it, care is indicated here. It is good practice to pour about three U.S. pints, wait a few minutes and then pour the rest.

**NOTE —**
The refill capacity of the transmission of the VW Automatic Stick Shift is 6.3 U.S. pints of hypoid transmission oil.

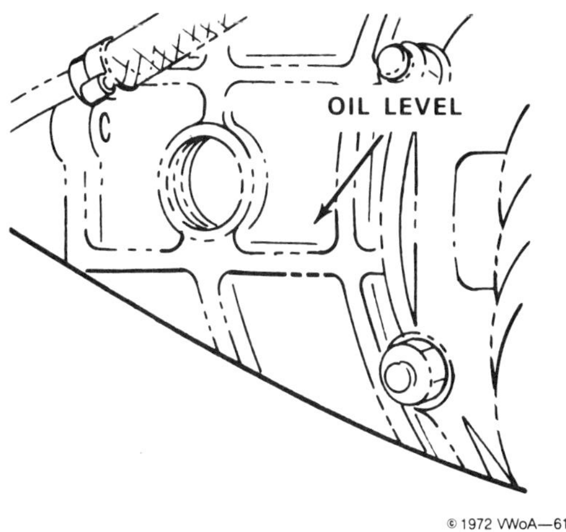


**Fig. 8.** Oil level for transmission case is indicated by arrow here. Check is made with finger.

### Automatic Stick Shift—Fluid Refilling

The automatic transmission fluid tank is on the right side of the engine compartment (Fig. 9).

***CAUTION —***
*Before you remove the filler cap, shut off engine.*

**To check fluid level:**

1. Remove filler cap, which has a dipstick attached. Using a clean lint-free cloth, wipe the dipstick.
2. Insert dipstick, pushing it all the way down.

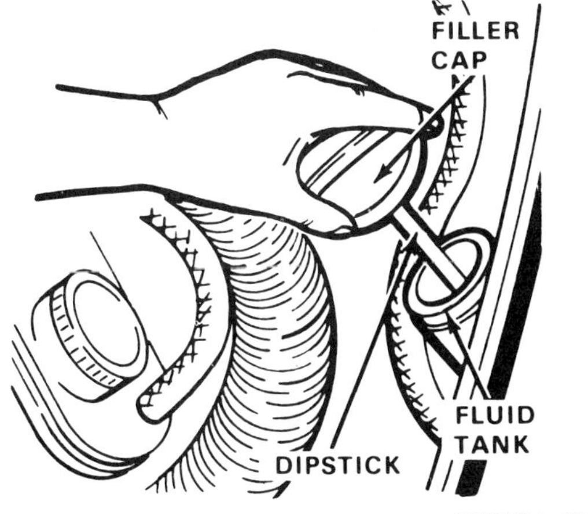


**Fig. 9.** Filler cap with dipstick for Automatic Stick Shift fluid tank will be found at the right side of the engine compartment.

8

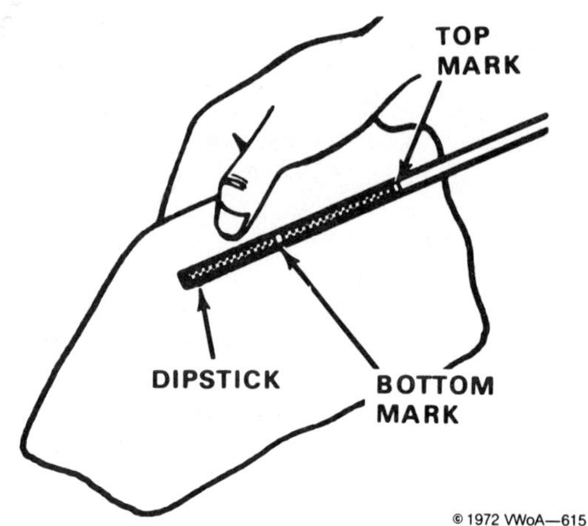


**Fig. 10.** Two marks (arrows) on dipstick indicate permissible range of fluid level.

3. Withdraw the cap and dipstick again. Check fluid level. It should be between the two marks (Fig. 10).

***CAUTION —***
*Do not fill the transmission above the top mark.*

4. If fluid is at or below bottom mark, add more to bring level near top mark. Screw filler cap back on.
5. Check line from transmission to fluid reservoir for leaks. Check transmission case for leakage at joints and openings (see Fig. 11).
6. If a line is leaking at a fitting, tighten fitting. Leakage from the transmission case requires maintenance (see **AUTOMATIC STICK SHIFT**).

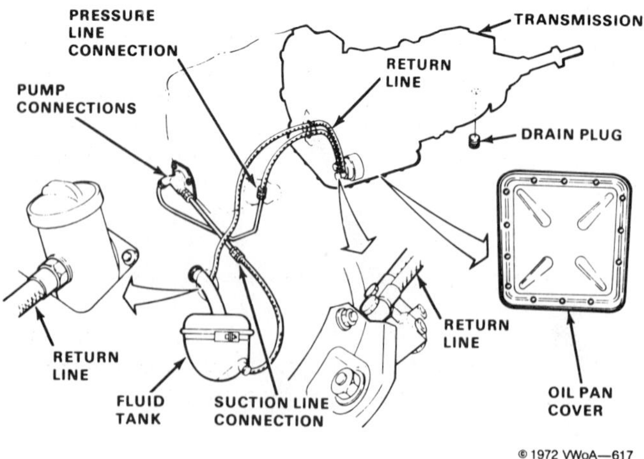


**Fig. 11.** Hydraulic system for cars with Automatic Stick Shift is shown schematically here.

## 2.1 Steering Gearbox

With occasional exceptions, the steering gearbox (roller type) is filled with a liquid transmission grease. Checking and topping-up of the steering gear is unnecessary. The grease is changed only when the steering mechanism is disassembled. A grease meeting the specifications in the table of lubricants should be used, but you may find it available only at an Authorized VW Dealer or an oil company distributor.

The exceptions are roller type steering boxes that will be found filled with gear oil. The same lubricant should be used to top up these boxes. Do not change to grease.

## 2.2 Front Axle

Adequate lubrication of the moving parts and joints in the front end of your car is required for good steering and springing. You will find four lubrication points on the front axle tubes.

Under normal operating conditions it is sufficient to grease the front axle every 6,000 miles. If, however, the car is driven mainly on bad roads, or if the total distance covered each year is less than 7500 miles (approximately 600 miles per month), it is advisable to grease the axle tubes every 3,000 miles.

**NOTE —**
The front end of the car should be raised for greasing. If sufficient grease is to reach the lubrication points, the load on the axle should be removed.

***CAUTION —***
*Do not let grease or oil come in contact with any part of the brake assemblies, particularly the brake shoes, drums and hoses. If you see any grease or oil on these parts, wipe it off at once.*

The grease nipples should be cleaned before lubrication. Damaged, blocked or missing nipples should be replaced. Continue with the greasing until fresh grease begins to emerge at the edges of the lubrication points.

## 2.3 Front Wheel Bearings

In assembly at the factory the front wheel bearings are packed with grease. They should be cleaned and packed with lithium grease at 30,000 miles and each time they are removed.

**To lubricate bearings:**

> ***CAUTION —***
> *Do not let grease or oil come in contact with any part of the brake assemblies, particularly the brake shoes, drums and hoses. If you see any grease or oil on these parts, wipe it off at once.*

1. Remove all old grease from wheel spindles and chamber between the bearing seats.
2. Remove old grease from races, cages and the rollers. Rinse out bearings.
3. Use the specified type of lithium grease to lubricate the bearings. Pack grease into cage and between the rollers. Grease bearing seats and rings lightly. Use only well-known brands of grease.
4. Pack the space between bearings with grease. Each wheel requires only about 2 ounces of grease.
5. Make sure that the dust caps are free of grease.
6. Adjust bearing as specified.

Never mix greases of different brands and types. Some chemical action may affect the lubricating properties and cause damage. Too much grease is harmful. Each wheel requires about 2 ounces (50 grams) of grease.

## 2.4 Locks and Hinges

Door hinges on all Karmann Ghia models are made of a material that requires no lubrication or maintenance. Hinges of sedans and convertibles and door and hood locks of all vehicles covered in this Manual do need lubrication according to the following procedures:

1. Clean and oil the sedan door hinges and the hood hinges.
2. Rub lock striker plates on the door frames with a lubricating paste based on molybdenum disulfide. Wipe off excess paste to save clothing.
3. Blow powdered graphite into keyholes of the locks. Dip key in graphite and work each lock several times.
4. Give door lock rods and exposed parts of locks a thin coat of grease.
5. If the door trim panels are removed for repair, lubricate the moving parts of lock mechanisms with universal grease.



## 2.5 Air Cleaner

The oil bath cleaner should be checked every 6,000 miles as specified in **Table a.** Clean lower part if necessary. In very dusty places, the cleaner must be checked more frequently, even as often as every day.

When there is only 5/32 to 3/16 inch (4 to 5 mm) of oil above sludge layer at bottom of the cleaner, the lower part should be cleaned carefully and filled to the mark with fresh SAE 30 engine oil. If oil level is more than 5/32 inch (4 mm) below the mark but with very little dirt showing, fresh oil can be added to bring level up to the mark.

The top part of the cleaner should not be cleaned with gasoline or other solvents. If the filter insert has become dirty enough to obstruct the air inlet holes on the underside, scrape off dirt with a stick.

When you put the upper section of the air cleaner down, always have the opening down, toward the surface. Do not turn it upside down.

## 2.6 Lubricating Distributor

The amount of grease on the breaker arm fiber block is checked during inspections and multi-purpose grease applied if necessary. See **ENGINE** for procedure.

## 2.7 Front Seat Runners

Grease runners for front seat lightly. Clean runners and apply grease to sliding surfaces.

## 2.8 Gearshift Lever

The gearshift lever is not greased in the course of the lubrication services, but if it has been removed it should be greased, if it seems dry. All moving parts—gearshift lever ball socket in shifting rod, spring and stop plate—should be cleaned and well greased with universal grease. At the same time, grease the shifting rod guide.

## 2.9 Convertible Top Linkage

In addition to the lubrication procedures already outlined, the sedan and Karmann Ghia convertible models need lubrication at the joints of the top mechanisms. The method is:

1. Open top.
2. Clean joints of the linkage.
3. Lubricate the joints, being very careful not to get oil on the top itself.

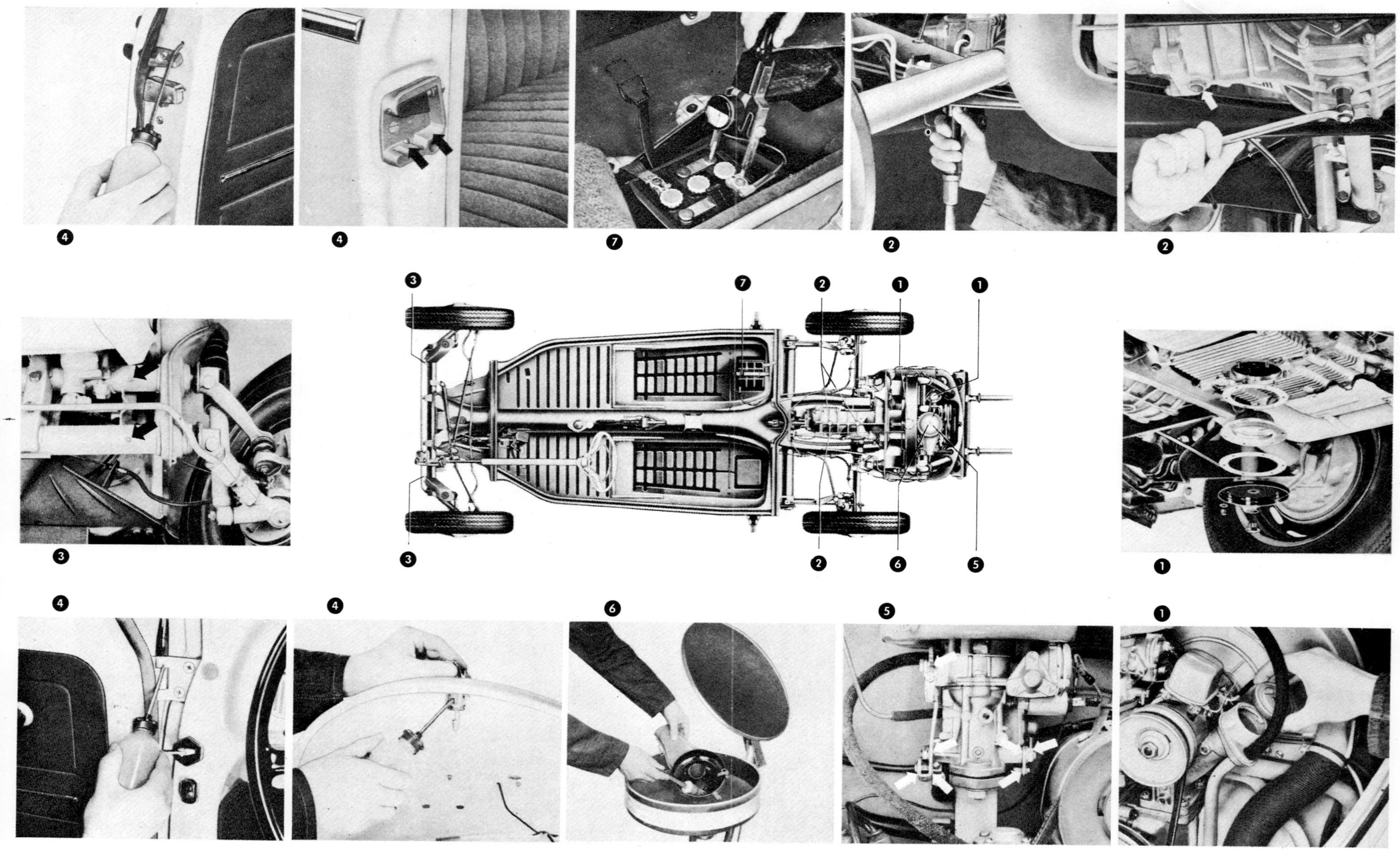

**Fig. 12.** Lubrication points and other parts involved in maintenance procedures are shown here. Key to numbers is given in first column of Table a, Lubrication and Maintenance Chart.

## Table a. Lubrication and Maintenance Chart

These lubrication and maintenance operations must be carried out at the intervals given. The numbers in the first column correspond to the numbering of the pictures in Fig. 12.

| Fig. No. | Operation | 300 miles after major overhaul | At 3,000, 9,000, 15,000 miles and so on | At 6,000 12,000, 18,000 miles and so on |
|---|---|---|---|---|
| 1 | Change engine oil and clean strainer. Check for leaks | X | X | X |
| 2 | Change rear axle oil. Clean magnetic oil drain plugs. Check for leaks | X | Only at 30,000, 60,000 miles and so on | |
| 2 | Check rear axle oil level. Check for leaks | | | X |
| 3 | Lubricate front axle | | | X* |
| 4 | Lubricate door and hood locks and door hinges | | X | X** |
| 5 | If grease or other lubricant has built up on carburetor linkage at points indicated in picture 5 of Fig. 12, clean thoroughly | | | X |
| 6 | Check air cleaner and clean lower part if necessary | | | X |
| 7 | Check battery, adding distilled water if necessary. Clean and grease terminals after connections have been clamped in place | | X | X |
| | Windshield washer; check fluid | X | X | X |

***Or at least once a year**
****Or at least every three months**

## Table b. Maintenance Operations
(emission control system)

Cars with the exhaust emission control device (throttle positioner) require the following additional service:

| Operation | 300 miles after major overhaul | At 6,000, 12,000, etc. miles |
|---|---|---|
| After road test, adjust ignition with strobe light. Check operation of throttle positioner | X | X |

## Table c. Maintenance Operations
(Automatic Stick Shift)

Cars with Automatic Stick Shift require the following maintenance work in addition to procedures specified for cars with standard transmissions.

| Operation | 300 miles after major overhaul | at 6,000, 12,000 miles etc. |
|---|---|---|
| Check rear axle constant velocity joint screws; tighten if necessary | X | X |
| Check constant velocity joint dust boots for leaks/damage | X | X |
| Check play at clutch servo piston rod; adjust if necessary | | X |
| Clean control valve air filter. Install dry. Wash in suitable fluid; blow out with compressed air | | X |
| Check and clean contacts of selector lever. Replace burned or damaged contacts. Adjust contact clearance | | X |
| Clean rear wheel bearings and pack with grease. Remove brake drums and rear wheel shafts for this procedure | | Only at 30,000, 60,000 miles, etc. |
| Clean transmission case magnetic drain plug. If transmission pan is leaking, retorque screws or remove, clean and re-install pan | X | X |
| Replace pan gasket. Recheck for leaks. If new rear axle or gearbox has been installed, check | At first 500 to 750 miles, thereafter at 30,000 mile intervals | |

## Table d. Lubrication Chart
(Automatic Stick Shift)

8

Cars with Automatic Stick Shift require the following additional lubrication checks and service:

| Operation | At 3,000 miles and at intervals of 3,000 miles thereafter |
|---|---|
| Check ATF level and top up* if required. Make visual check of converter for leaks | X |

***Use only well known name brand of ATF. DEXRON® and 5-digit number preceded by letter "B" must appear on label.**

Fill final drive and gear box with hypoid oil as before. Carry out lubrication procedures as for standard transmission.

## Table e. Maintenance Chart

| Operation | 300 miles after major overhaul | At 6,000, 12,000, 18,000 miles, etc. |
|---|---|---|
| Check rear axle shaft nuts and tighten if necessary | X | |
| Check fan belt and tighten or replace if necessary | X | X |
| Clean fuel pump filter | X | X |
| Check breaker points and replace if necessary. Grease distributor. Check breaker gap and ignition timing | X | X |
| Adjust valve clearance; fit new cylinder head cover gaskets | X | ·X |
| Clean spark plugs. Adjust plug gap. Check compression | | X |
| Check control flap for carburetor preheating | | X |
| Check rubber valve for crankcase ventilation, replace if worn or damaged. Check exhaust system for damage | | X |
| Adjust clutch pedal free-play | X | X |
| Check dust seals and fit of plug on ball joints. Check dust seals on tie-rod ends. Check tie-rod ends. Tightening if necessary | X | X |
| Check and adjust camber and toe-in of front wheels | | X |
| Check axial play of lower ball joints | | X |
| Clean, grease and adjust front wheel bearings (procedure to include removing and re-installing both brake drums) | | only at 30,000, 60,000 miles, and so on |
| Check and adjust play between steering gear roller and worm | | X |
| Check tire pressure and security of wheel bolts | X | |
| Check tire wear and damage and inflation pressures | | X |
| Check hydraulic brake system for leaks and damage. Check level of brake fluid. Adjust foot brakes and parking brake | X | X |
| Road test car, checking operation of foot brakes and parking brake. Check and adjust engine idle. Check heating and ventilating systems | X | X |
| Check thickness of brake linings | | X |
| Check operation of complete electrical system and adjust headlights | X | X |
| Check wiper blades and replace if necessary | | X |

## Table f. Lubricants

| Lubricant | Lubrication Points | Specifications | |
|---|---|---|---|
| Powdered graphite | Door key mechanisms | (local purchase item) | |
| Engine oil | Engine, oil bath air cleaner<br>Carburetor linkage<br>Door hinges | SAE 40<br>SAE 30<br>SAE 20 W/20* | In hot, tropic climates<br>In the warm seasons and all the year in countries with hot climates<br>In the winter |
| Hypoid oil | Transmission | SAE 90** | all the year |
| ATF | Torque converter | Automatic transmission fluid (DEXRON®) | |
| Universal grease | Door and hood locks | Cold-resistant, water repellent high pressure grease | |
| Lithium grease | Front axle, front wheel bearings, breaker arm fiber block | Multi-purpose grease | |
| Molybdenum-disulfide | Constant velocity joints and door lock striker plates | Moly-Kote® or similar | |

*** SAE 10 W where average temperature is below 5°F; SAE 5 W if below −13°F** **** SAE 80 all the year in countries with arctic climates**

# Section 9

# BODY AND FRAME

## Contents

### BODY

**1. General Description** . . . . . 4
Doors . . . . . 4
Hoods (lids) . . . . . 4
Windows . . . . . 4
Front Seats . . . . . 4
Rear Seats . . . . . 4
Interior Trim . . . . . 4
Insulation . . . . . 5
Heating . . . . . 5
Fresh Air Ventilation . . . . . 5
Luggage Compartment Capacity . . . . . 5
Exterior Trim . . . . . 6

**2. Fenders and Running Boards** . . . . . 6
2.1 Removing and Installing Front Fenders . . 6
2.2 Removing and Installing Rear Fenders . . 6
2.3 Removing and Installing Running Board . 7

**3. Hoods (Lids) and Hood Locks** . . . . . 8
3.1 Removing and Installing Front Hood Lock (prior to chassis No. 118 000 001) . . . . . 8
3.2 Removing and Installing Front Hood Lock (from chassis No. 118 000 001) . . . . . 9
3.3 Removing and Installing Rear Hood Lock 10

**4. Bumpers** . . . . . 11
4.1 Removing and Installing Bumper Bows (cars prior to 1968) . . . . . 11
4.2 Removing and Installing Front Bumper (prior to chassis No. 118 000 001) . . . . . 12
4.3 Removing and Installing Rear Bumper (prior to chassis No. 118 000 001) . . . . . 12
4.4 Removing and Installing Front and Rear Bumpers (from chassis No. 118 000 001) . 12

**5. Doors and Door Locks** . . . . . 13
5.1 Adjusting Striker Plate (cars prior to August 1966) . . . . . 13
Basic Adjustment . . . . . 14
5.2 Adjusting Striker Plate (cars after August 1966, from chassis No. 117 000 001) . . . 16
5.3 Removing and Installing Door . . . . . 19
5.4 Removing and Installing Door Window . . 20

**6. Heating and Ventilation Systems** . . . . . 23
6.1 Removing and Installing Front Footwell Heater Slides . . . . . 24
6.2 Removing Front Heater Hoses . . . . . 24
6.3 Adjusting Cables for Fresh Air Flaps (from chassis No. 118 000 001) . . . . . 25

**7. Steel Sliding Roof (sun roof)** . . . . . 25
7.1 Removing and Installing Sliding Roof Panel . . . . . 25
7.2 Removing and Installing Trim Lining . . . 27
7.3 Removing and Installing Guide Rails and Cables . . . . . 27

9

7.4 Adjusting the Cable . . . . . . . . . . . . . . 28
7.5 Vertical Adjustment of Sliding Roof Panel 29
7.6 Troubleshooting Sliding Roof . . . . . . . . 30
7.7 Sealing Roof Panel . . . . . . . . . . . . . . 30
7.8 Water Drain Channels . . . . . . . . . . . . 31

**8. Convertible Top** . . . . . . . . . . . . . . . . . . . 31
8.1 Adjusting Convertible Top (from chassis No. 157 250 033) . . . . . . 31
8.2 Replacing Rear Trim Molding (from chassis No. 157 250 033) . . . . . . 32
8.3 Adjusting Top Header . . . . . . . . . . . . 34

## FRAME

**9. General Description** . . . . . . . . . . . . . . . . 36

**10. Control Cables** . . . . . . . . . . . . . . . . . . . 37
10.1 Removing and Installing Clutch Cable . . 37
10.2 Clutch Operating Lever Spring . . . . . . 38
10.3 Adjustment of Clutch Pedal Free-play . . 38
10.4 Removing and Installing Accelerator Cable . . . . . . . . . . . . . . . . . . . . . 39
10.5 Removing and Installing Heater Flap Cable . . . . . . . . . . . . . . . . . . . . . 40
10.6 Cables for Rear Footwell Heating . . . . 41
10.7 Rear Footwell Heater Flaps . . . . . . . . 42

## TABLES

a. Troubleshooting Sliding Roof . . . . . . . . . . . 30

# Body and Frame

In line with VW practice, this Manual treats the body and frame under a single heading in this section but divides the discussion into two parts. The first part deals with the body and the second with the frame and the lines and control cables that run through the frame.

It was the unique shape of the body that first attracted the world's attention to the VW Beetle, but when the designers first drew that now familiar profile, they were more interested in engineering than in looks. Strength, aerodynamic properties and easy replacement of the parts most likely to be damaged were the main objectives. Among the results achieved have been a long service life and air-tight sealing.

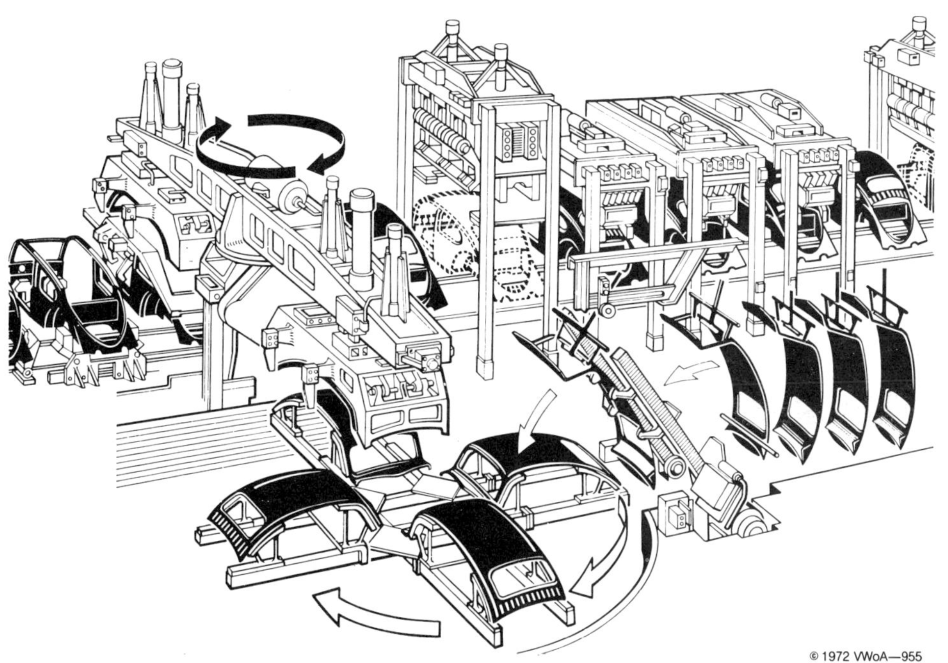


**Fig. 1.** Beetle bodies are put together in the factory in Wolfsburg, Germany, with fully automated presses and conveyor mechanisms like the ones in this drawing. Arrows indicate directions in which equipment turns when moving bodies from station to station of the assembly line.

# Body

## 1. General Description

The all-steel body of the VW Beetle consists of the parts shown in Fig. 2 welded together into a single unit. This solid unit is then bolted to the frame, which is essentially a platform of welded sheet metal stampings. Rubber sealing strips of U-section seal the joint between body and frame. The fenders and running board (sill panels) are bolted on. This method of fastening makes these parts readily detachable and easy to replace.

Partitions divide the two-door body into the luggage compartment in front, passenger compartment and engine compartment. The distinctive curved front hood, the curved sloping windshield, the convex roof panel and the sloping rear end are the conspicuous features of the celebrated body design, and in combination they make for exceptionally low air resistance. A series of slots below the rear window admits a flow of air to the engine compartment.

### Doors

The doors, which are 37.4 inches (950 mm) wide, are attached to pillars in the door frames on adjustable external hinges. Pushbuttons on the outside and handles on the inside of the doors operate the latch mechanisms on early cars covered in this Manual. On cars from chassis No. 118 000 001 on, triggers in the outer door handles replace the pushbuttons. On earlier cars the pushbutton in the door handle on the driver's side has a cylinder lock. An inside handle locks the other door. After chassis No. 118 000 001, both doors can be locked from the outside. The doors open to a maximum of about 80 degrees; a check strap with rubber buffer stops further movement. An adjustable striker plate on the door frame permits correct alignment of door with body panels.

### Hoods
(lids)

The hood for the front compartment, which contains the fuel tank, spare wheel and tools and includes the luggage compartment, has a lock. A cable operated by pull knob or lever (depending on model year) unlatches the hood lock. On sedans the knob is below the instrument panel at the left of the steering column. On the four-seater convertible (from chassis No. 158 000 005) and Karmann Ghia models (from chassis No. 148 000 004) the cable mechanism is in the glove compartment, on which a lock is optional. Two spring-loaded stays hold the front hood in the open position. The lock on the rear lid over the engine compartment is operated by pressing a button. A spring holds the lid in the open position.

### Windows

All windows are 0.17 to 0.20 inch (4.3 to 5.2 mm) thick. The one-piece windshield is 41.4 inches (1050 mm) wide and 14.2 inches (360 mm) high and is installed at an angle of 32 degrees. It is made of laminated safety glass. A one-piece weatherstrip (rubber seal) holds the windshield in place. Each door is equipped with a roll-down window and a vent window. Four-and-a-half turns are required to open or close the roll-down window. The rectangular rear window, which is 35.4 inches (900 mm) wide and 15.6 inches (359 mm) high, is installed at an angle of 53 degrees.

### Front Seats

The adjustable individual front seats travel in runners which rise slightly toward the front. For easier adjustment, the seats have springs to assist forward movement. The backrests are adjustable to three different positions, and on 1968 and 1969 cars there is a locking mechanism on the side. The seat frame is of tubular steel. The core consists of interlinked coil springs with a padding of rubberized hair. The springs in the backrests are of zig-zag design.

### Rear Seats

The backrest of the rear seat folds down. It can be held in the folded-down position with the hold-down strap hooked to the seat support. This arrangement provides a large addition to the space for luggage. The core of the back seat and backrest consists of zig-zag springs with a layer of rubberized hair padding.

### Interior Trim

The floor is covered with rubber mats. The lower part of the front partition and the frame tunnel are lined with rubber. The upper part of the front partition, the front quarter panels, the side members and the rear luggage compartment are lined with haircord carpeting. The roof, roof side members and the trim panels around the rear window are covered with leatherette. The door pillars are lined with leatherette trim. The door and quarter panels are covered with plastic material and trimmed with chrome molding. The right hand quarter panel has an ash tray. There is a pocket on the driver's door and an armrest on the passenger's side with decorative molding. Cars from chassis No. 117 000 001 on are equipped with armrests on both doors.

The rear view mirror is mounted by ball joint at the center of the upper windshield frame. There are two sun

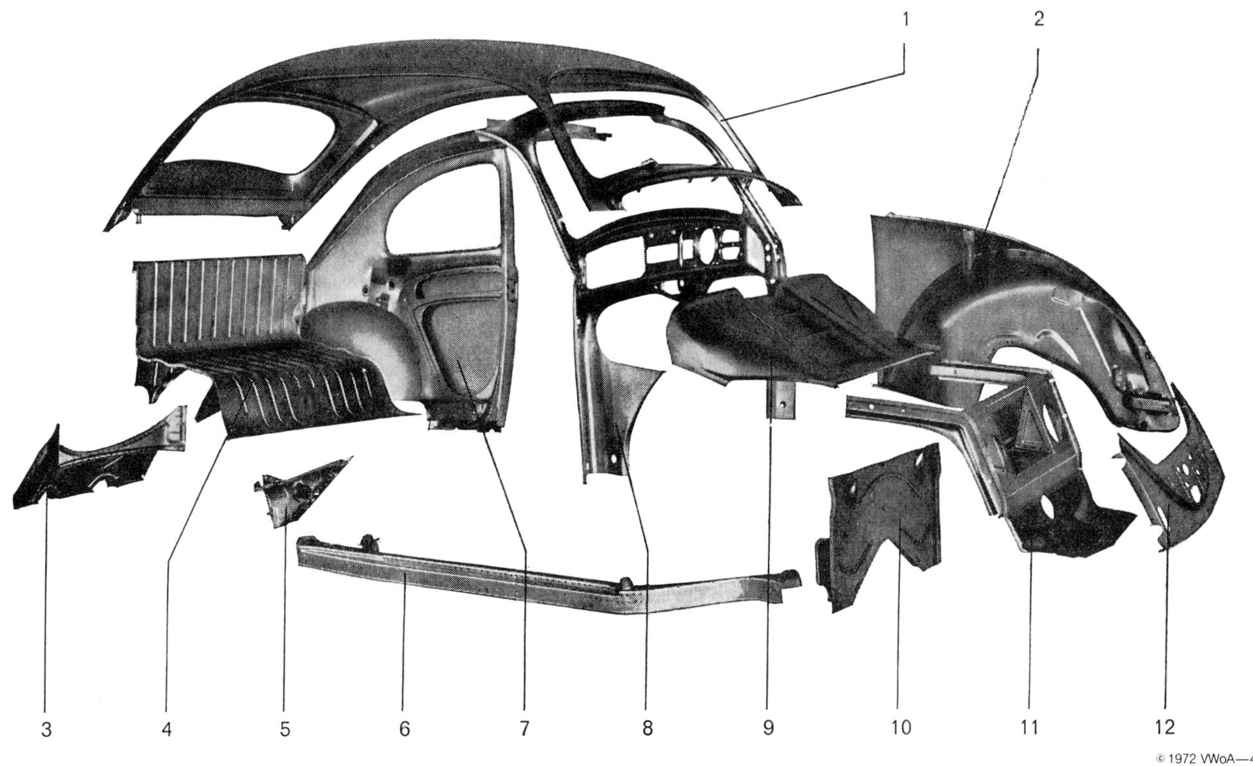


1. Roof
2. Side panel
3. Rear apron
4. Luggage compartment floor plate
5. Rear cross member
6. Side member
7. Quarter panel
8. Instrument panel
9. Front luggage compartment
10. Front cross panel
11. Reinforcement plate
12. Front apron

**Fig. 2.** Beetle body is made of these individual parts welded together into a unit.

visors. The instrument panel has a grab handle. Clothes hooks and assist straps are fitted to the door pillars. Safety-belt mounting points and safety belts are provided for driver and passengers.

### Insulation

A variety of materials are used in the Beetle for insulation from engine and road noise and heat and cold. Padding seals the openings on left and right between the rear luggage compartment and the rear quarter trim panels. Foam rubber fills the rear opening in the roof side members. There are panels of sound-absorbing material between the engine compartment and the rear of the luggage compartment and the wheel housings. The floor of the rear luggage compartment has a layer of cork felt. Bituminized felt covers the frame tunnel up to the front partition. Front luggage compartment is lined with cork felt. A layer of insulation material is cemented to inside of roof, doors, outer panels and rear quarter panels.

### Heating

Fresh air drawn in by the fan on the engine is heated in the heat exchangers. Double flaps on shafts in the front parts of the exchangers direct the flow of heated air to either the interior of the car or the outside. When the right-hand lever between the front seats is operated, a cable closes the outlet to the outside and opens the outlet to the interior. Sound-damping hoses and tubes in the frame side members then carry the warm air to outlets in the front footwell and to defrosters at the windshield. The outlets in the front footwell have slides to admit the warm air or shut it out. The left lever on the frame tunnel operates cables which open or close the rear heating outlets.

### Fresh Air Ventilation

On cars from chassis No. 118 000 001 fresh air enters through louvers in the front hood near the cowl. The fresh air flows through the control box to two separately regulated vents in the instrument panel below the windshield. Two rotary knobs at left and right above the ashtray, control the air flow.

### Luggage Compartment Capacity

The capacity of the rear luggage compartment with backrest up is 4.3 cubic feet (120 liters). When the backrest is down, the luggage space is increased by 10 cubic feet (280 liters). The compartment under the front hood holds about 5 cubic feet (140 liters).

### Exterior Trim

The running boards (sill panels) are rubber-covered. The bumpers, hub caps, turn signal, light housings, rims of headlights and taillights and the vent window frames are chrome-plated. The Volkswagen insignia is pressed into the hub caps.

The outside rear view mirror and the molding on the running boards are stainless steel.

Highly-polished anodized aluminum is used for all body, door and window moldings, as well as emblems and lettering.

## 2. FENDERS AND RUNNING BOARDS

On the VW the fenders and running boards (sill panels) are bolted together in an assembly that is also bolted to the car body. Ease of replacing these parts in case of damage was the main aim of the design.

### 2.1 Removing and Installing Front Fenders

**To remove:**

1. Raise car off the ground.
2. On cars after chassis No. 118 000 001 disconnect wires from horn. (See **ELECTRICAL SYSTEM**.)
3. Remove headlight and turn signal light assembly. (See **ELECTRICAL SYSTEM**.) Pull wires and protective sleeves from fender.
4. Remove bolt between fender and running boards (see Fig. 3).

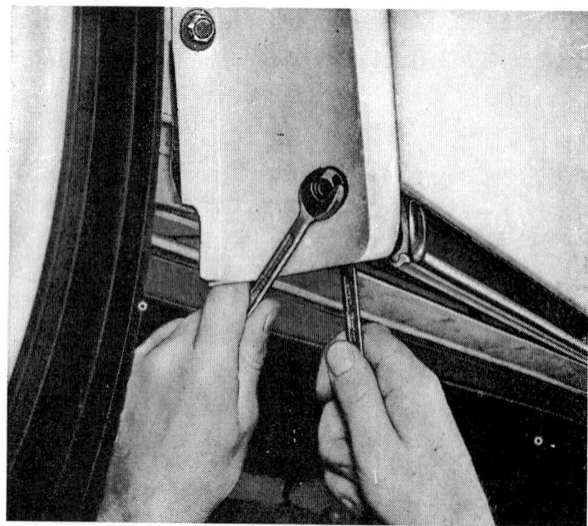



**Fig. 3.** Single bolt fastens front fender and running board together. Left fender is shown here.

5. Remove nine bolts securing fender (see Fig. 4).

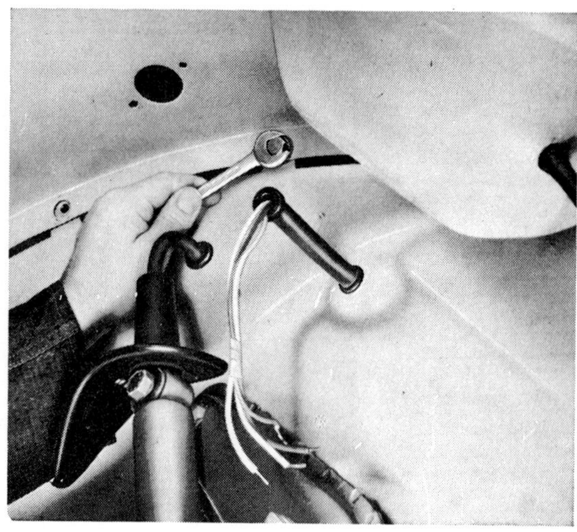



**Fig. 4.** Nine bolts secure front fender to body of car. Wires for headlights and turn signals must be pulled out before fender is removed.

6. Take off fender and beading.

**To install:**

1. Check beading, replace if damaged. Be careful about fitting the beading when you install fender.
2. Check all bolt threads and replace bolts with damaged threads. Lubricate bolts.
3. Fit new rubber washer between fender and running board.
4. Check headlight settings and correct as necessary. (See **ELECTRICAL SYSTEM**.)
5. Install bumper bracket, making sure that it is centered in fender opening. Also be sure that the rubber grommets are evenly fitted.

### 2.2 Removing and Installing Rear Fenders

**To remove:**

1. Raise car off ground.
2. Remove taillight assembly with gasket (see **ELECTRICAL SYSTEM**) and pull wires out of fender.
3. Remove bumper and brackets and take out bracket seals.
4. Remove bolt and nut between fender and running board.

5. Remove the nine bolts and one nut (ten bolts as of chassis No. 117 000 001) that secure the fender (see Fig. 5).

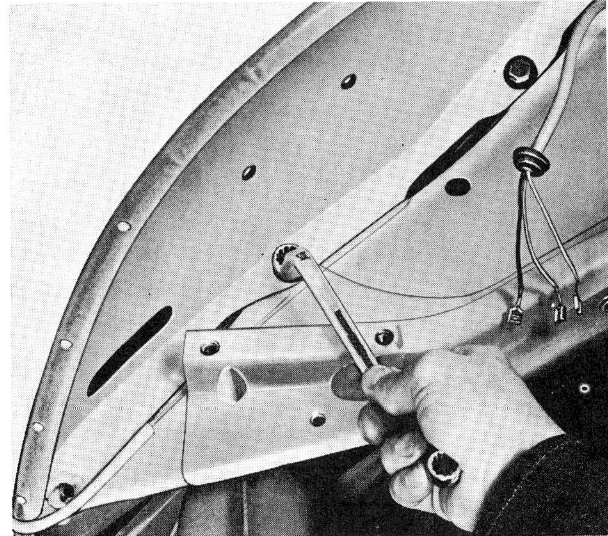

© 1972 VWoA—47

**Fig. 5.** Nine bolts and one stud or ten bolts, depending on model, attach rear fender to car body.

6. Take off fender and beading.

**To install:**

1. Check beading and replace if damaged. When you install fender, be careful about fit of beading.
2. Check threads in bolts and clean up with tap if necessary. Lubricate bolts.
3. Fit new rubber washer between the fender and running board if the old one is damaged or worn (see Fig. 6).

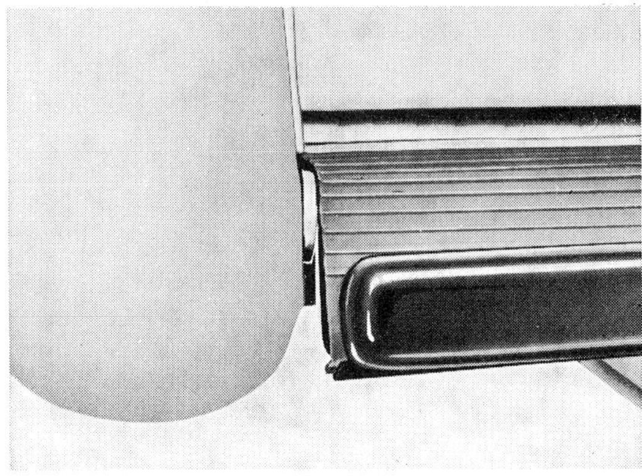

© 1972 VWoA—48

**Fig. 6.** New rubber washer must be fitted between fender (at left) and running board when fender is put back on car.

4. Install seals for bumper bracket in opening in fender. When bolting on the front bumper, be careful to fit the rubber seal properly.
5. Install taillight and connect wires. (See **ELECTRICAL SYSTEM.**) Before attaching lens, check the gasket and replace if necessary.
6. Check functioning of rear lights.

## 2.3 Removing and Installing Running Board

**To remove:**

1. Take out bolts and nuts that attach running board to front and rear fenders.
2. Take off nuts that attach running board to the body (see Fig. 7).

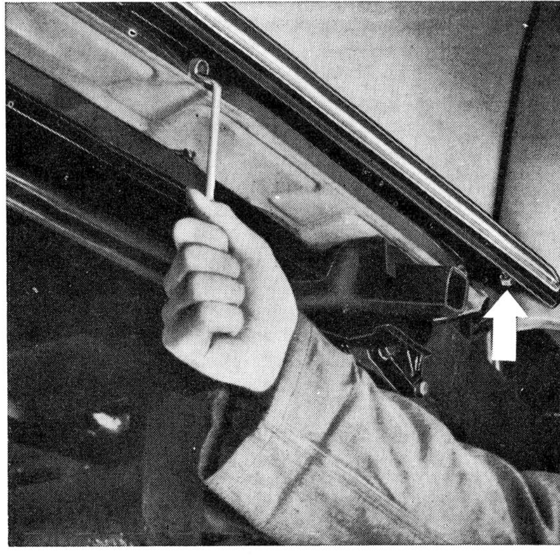

© 1972 VWoA—49

**Fig. 7.** Running board is bolted to car body as well as to fender. Arrow points to rear fender bolt.

3. Lift running board upward and off car.

**To install:**

1. Put running board in position between fenders. Slip flat washers on mounting bolts and start bolts through running board and body.
2. Place rubber washer between running board and fender and start nuts on bolts.
3. Tighten bolts on side member first. Then tighten the nuts and bolts at the ends.

9

## 3. HOODS (LIDS) AND HOOD LOCKS

The front hood lock is designed to unlatch if the cable breaks. Ordinarily the latch holds the pin on the hood bracket when the hood is closed, but in the event of a cable break the latch springs back automatically. The pin is freed, and the hood can be opened. This arrangement calls for the exercise of some care in fitting the cable.

### 3.1 Removing and Installing Front Hood Lock

(prior to chassis No. 118 000 001)

**To remove:**

1. Open the front hood.
2. Remove the two bolts (Fig. 8) holding the hood lock upper part and take off handle and lock bolt assembly.

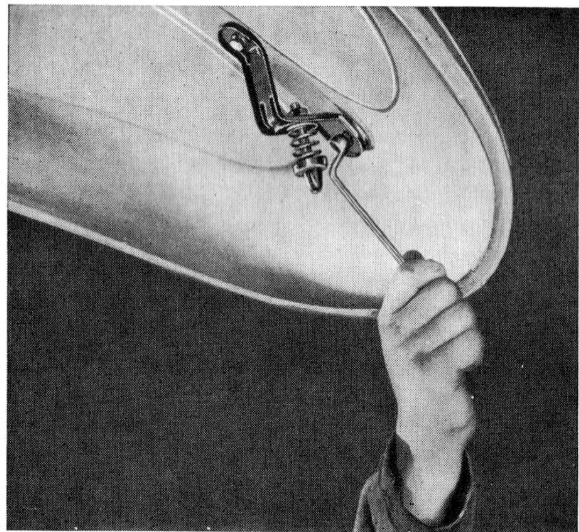



**Fig. 8.** Hood lock pin is part of assembly on inside of front hood. Two bolts secure this assembly to handle on outside of hood. Lock shown is for 1966 and 1967 cars.

3. Remove the three bolts securing the lock lower part (see Fig. 9).
4. Pull down on the cover plate of the lock assembly to remove it. Loosen the cable clamping screw (see Fig. 10). Remove lower part of lock.
5. Pull cable out of the guide tube.

**To install:**

1. Grease hood lock cable and insert it in guide tube.
2. The cable clamping screw is fixed to the crank under the latch plate. Turn the crank against the spring until the latch projects into the bolt opening. Then insert cable in lock and secure it with the clamping screw. Bend back excess cable.
3. Install lower part of lock and cover plate.
4. Attach hood handle and upper lock assembly.
5. Open and close hood several times to test length of lock pin and position of latch assembly. If necessary, correct the length of the lock pin at the adjusting nuts and adjust latch plate assembly by moving it in its slots (see Fig. 11).
6. Check adjustment of hood lock cable. If necessary, re-adjust cable after removing cover plate. Bend back excess cable.

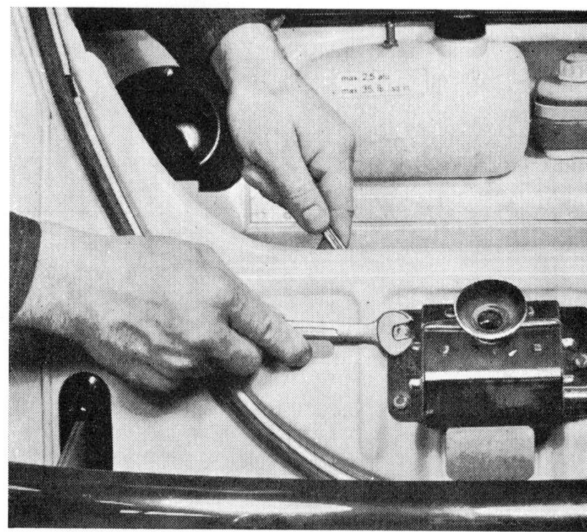



**Fig. 9.** Hood lock latch is in assembly attached to the front apron of car. Model shown is on 1966 and 1967 cars. Three bolts attach this part to apron.

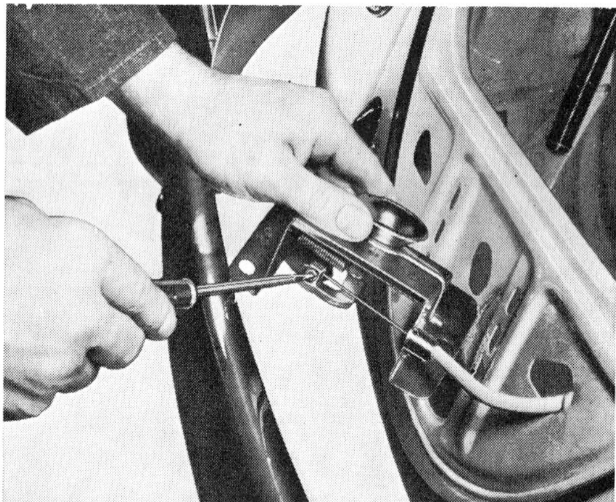



**Fig. 10.** Clamping screw attaches lock cable to latching mechanism. Pull on cable releases latch.

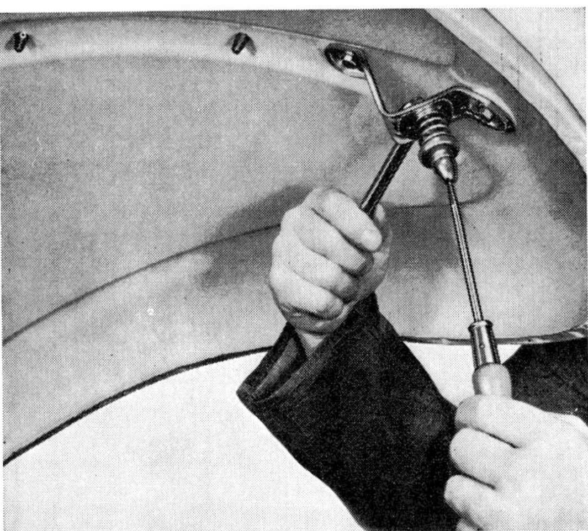



**Fig. 11.** Lock pin can be adjusted for length by screwing pin shaft in or out after lock nut above bracket has been loosened.

7. Grease lock pin.

## 3.2 Removing and Installing Front Hood Lock
(from chassis No. 118 000 001)

This hood lock is similar in basic latching mechanism to the earlier version but has a pushbutton in the handle which you depress to open the hood. The lower part of the lock is attached to a carrier on the front apron instead of to the apron itself. Pop rivets are the fasteners. A lever in the glove compartment controls the cable which releases the latch on the lock pin.

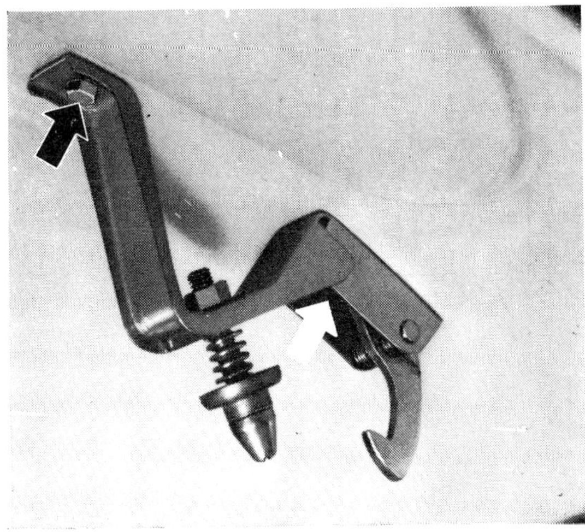



**Fig. 12.** Two bolts (arrows) fasten hood lock on 1968 and 1969 cars. Nut for adjusting pin length can be seen on pin shaft above bracket.

**Fig. 13.** Clamping screw for cable on later model (1968 and 1969 cars) of hood lock latch can be seen through hole (black arrow) in car apron.

**To remove hood lock completely as unit:**

1. Remove the two bolts (see Fig. 12).
2. Remove handle, plastic gasket and hood lock upper part.
3. Loosen cable clamping screw, working through the opening in the lock (see Fig. 13).
4. With flat chisel, cut off heads of pop rivets (as shown in Fig. 14).
5. Take out lower part of hood lock from below.

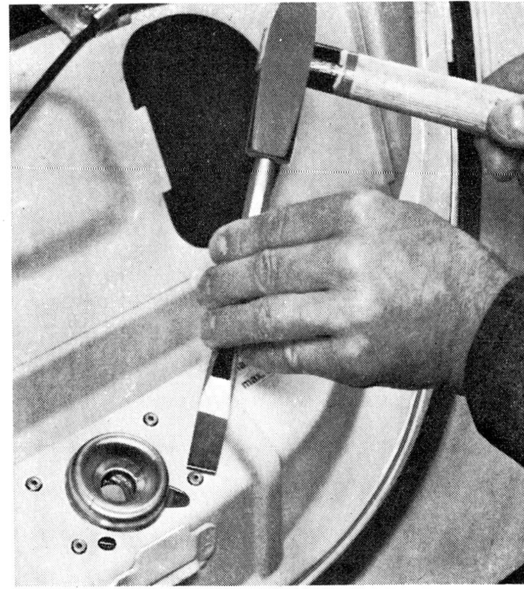



**Fig. 14.** Pop rivets fasten the lower part of the hood lock mechanism to the front apron on 1968 and 1969 cars. For removal of lock, rivets must be cut off with chisel, as shown here.

Before you start the installation procedure, inspect hood lock upper and lower parts for wear or damage and replace if necessary. Lubricate parts lightly. If a new hood lock cable is used, lubricate it lightly before you insert it in the guide tube.

**To install:**

1. Use clamping screw to push lock cable into guide of lock lower part and temporarily attach cable to the hook (see Fig. 15).

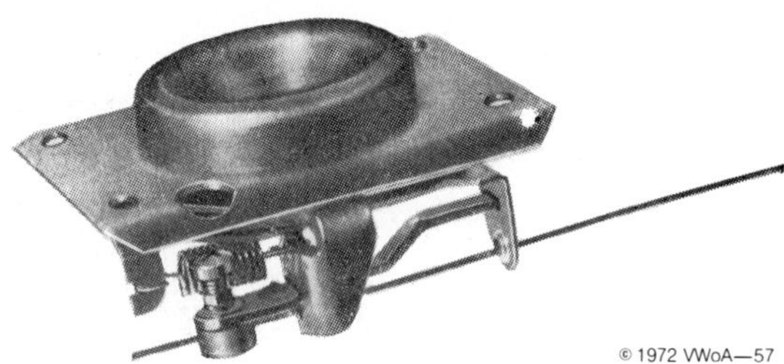

© 1972 VWoA—57

**Fig. 15.** Latch assembly of later model front hood lock is shown here removed from car. Cable that works latch is held by clamping screw, which goes into hook at lower left of assembly.

2. Attach lock lower part to the carrier on the apron with either rivets or screws (see Fig. 16).
3. Loosen clamping screw, pull lock cable taut and retighten clamping screw. Then secure the cable by bending it over behind clamping screw.
4. Position handle and plastic gasket on hood.
5. Push button into hood handle.
6. Insert both bolts and washers and tighten.

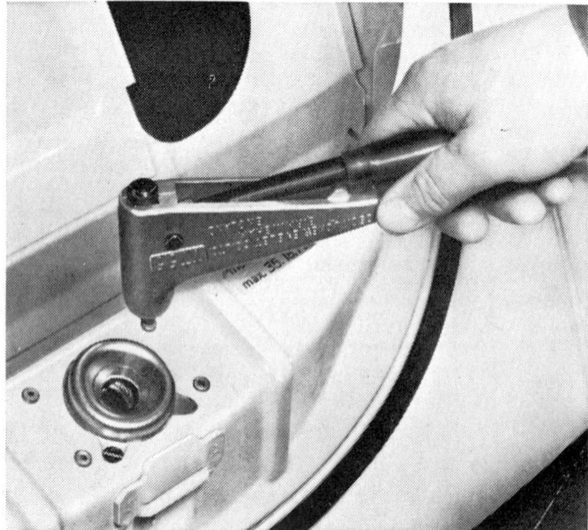

© 1972 VWoA—58

**Fig. 16.** Riveting tool is required if pop rivets are used to attach lower assembly of hood lock mechanism on later cars. Screws can be substituted for the pop rivets.

7. Open and close hood several times to check operation. If needed, change length of pin by backing off locknut and screwing pin in or out (Fig. 17).

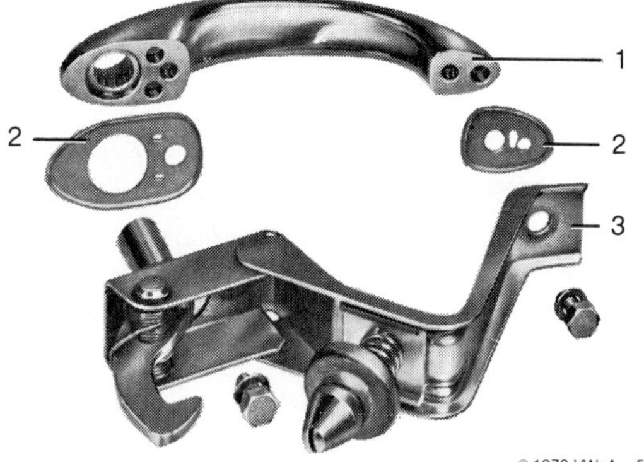


© 1972 VWoA—59

1. Hood handle  2. Packing  3. Hood lock upper part

**Fig. 17.** Front hood handle and upper assembly of later model hood lock are shown here disassembled.

### 3.3 Removing and Installing Rear Hood Lock

Two versions of the rear hood lock are found on cars covered in this Manual. In the early version, handle and lock are separate. From chassis No. 117 000 001 they are a single part.

**To remove:**

1. Open rear hood.
2. Take out the three Phillips screws on inside of hood (see Fig. 18).

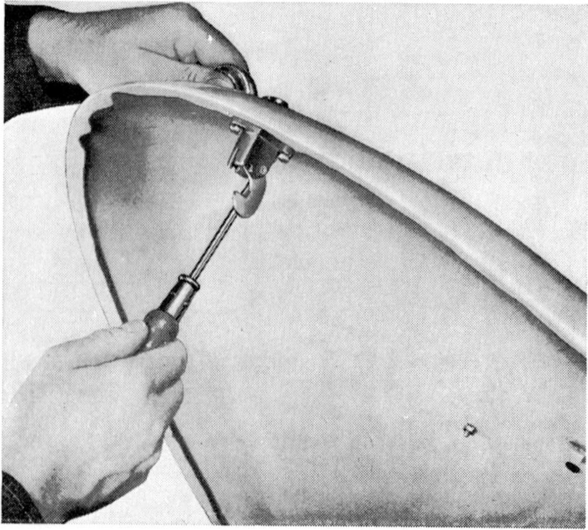

© 1972 VWoA—60

**Fig. 18.** Rear hood lock is fastened to hood with three Phillips screws on the underside.

3. Holding lock, pull off handle with packing.

**To install:**

1. Check lock, handle and packing. Replace worn or damaged items.
2. Hold lock in position on the inside of hood and install handle from above.
3. Fasten lock and handle together with Phillips screws (see Fig. 18).
4. Open and close hood several times to check installation. If necessary, correct position of lock by moving the striker plate (Fig. 19) in the slots provided for this adjustment.

   From chassis No. 118 000 001 on, the striker plate for the rear hood lock is welded to body. Adjustable rubber bumper keeps hood from rattling.

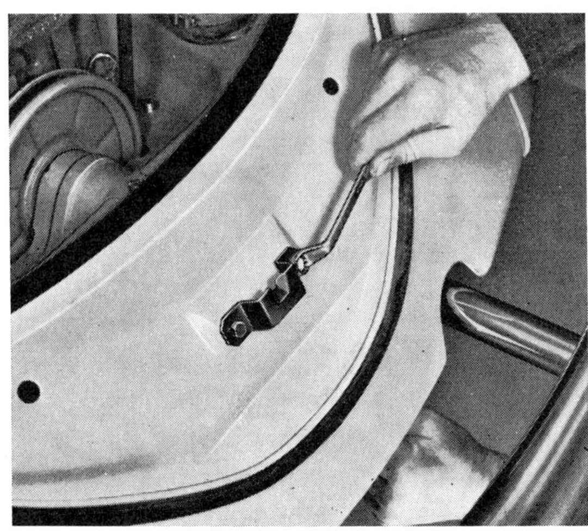



**Fig. 19.** Striker plate for rear hood lock on 1966 and 1967 cars is bolted (as here) to rear apron. On later cars it is welded.

## 4. BUMPERS

Depending on model years, two distinct designs of bumpers will be found on the cars covered in this Manual. The early version has bows and overriders to strengthen the assembly and give protection above the main bumper. In the later version bows and overriders have been eliminated and bumper height raised to compensate. The change came in 1968 cars, beginning at chassis No. 118 000 001. Obviously, procedures for removal and disassembly of the two versions differ in detail. We treat them separately in the following instructions.

### 4.1 Removing and Installing Bumper Bows
(cars prior to 1968)

**To remove:**

1. Take out the two bolts that secure overrider supports on each side.
2. Take out the attaching bolts and remove single bow from front bumper and two bows from rear bumper (see Fig. 20).

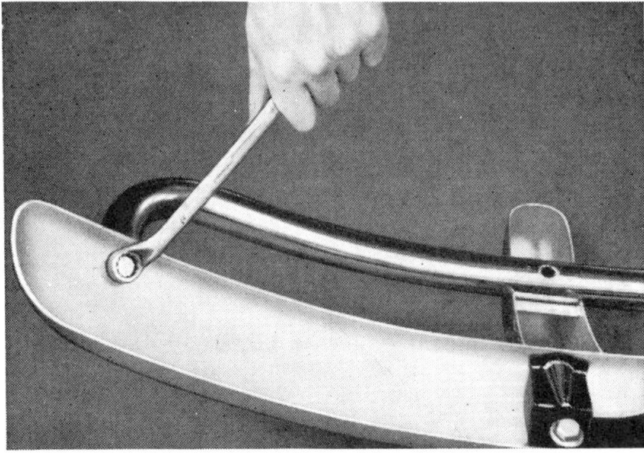



**Fig. 20.** Front bumper with single bow supporting overriders is seen here from the inside of assembly.

**To install:**

1. Check support seals and install them.
2. After fitting bows, insert supports and bolt them to car body with the bumper brackets (see Fig. 21).

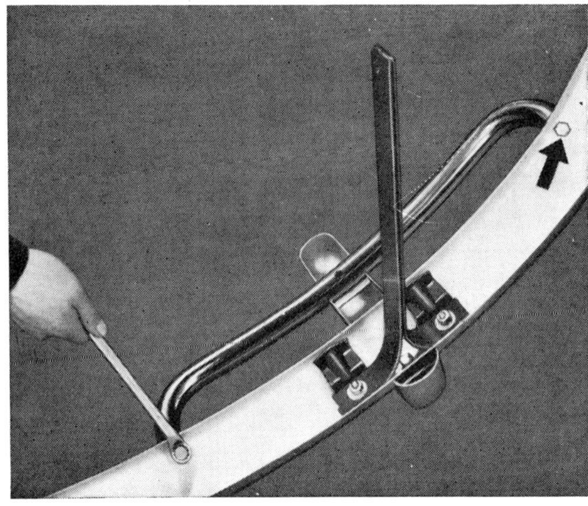



**Fig. 21.** Rear bumper is shown here with bracket, overrider and one of twin bows bolted in place.

9

### 4.2 Removing and Installing Front Bumper
(prior to chassis No. 118 000 001)

**To remove:**

1. Lift front hood and take out spare wheel.
2. Remove the two bolts at each side and take off bumper, the four reinforcement plates and overriders.
3. Remove bracket bolts (see Fig. 22) and pull brackets out of front apron.

**Fig. 22.** Bolt (white arrow) securing right front bumper bracket also fastens overrider support. Wrench is on other overrider bolt. Other bracket bolt is at left of arrow.

**To install:**

1. Check bracket seals and replace if worn or damaged. Fit seals in front apron opening.
2. Oil bolts and nuts lightly and bolt brackets to bumper.
3. Make sure that clearance between fender and bumper is uniform.

### 4.3 Removing and Installing Rear Bumper
(prior to chassis No. 118 000 001)

**To remove:**

1. Remove bumper bolts and nuts and take off bumper and four reinforcement plates.
2. Remove left and right overriders (see Fig. 23).

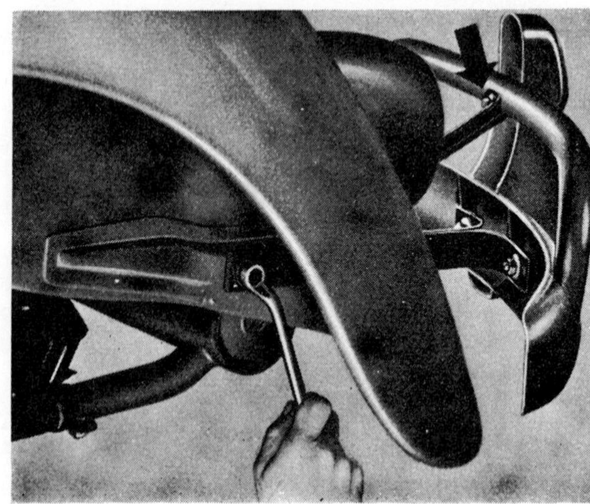



**Fig. 23.** Bolt under left rear fender secures overrider. Black arrow points to other overrider bolt.

3. Remove each bumper bracket and withdraw it through fender opening.
4. Take out bumper bracket seals.

**To install:**

1. Check bumper bracket seals for damage, replacing them, if necessary. Insert seals in the fender openings.
2. Install bumper and brackets.
3. Check clearance between bumper and fenders for uniformity.

### 4.4 Removing and Installing Front and Rear Bumpers
(from chassis No. 118 000 001)

Three bolts attach each bumper bracket at a quarter or side panel of the body, depending on whether it is a rear or front bumper. All attaching bolts are accessible from the outside. Rubber grommets seal the openings where the brackets pass through the fenders.

Before removing the front bumper, take the horn off the left side panel (see Fig. 24).

In installation be sure to center the bumper brackets in their fender openings before you tighten the bolts. Do not forget washers.

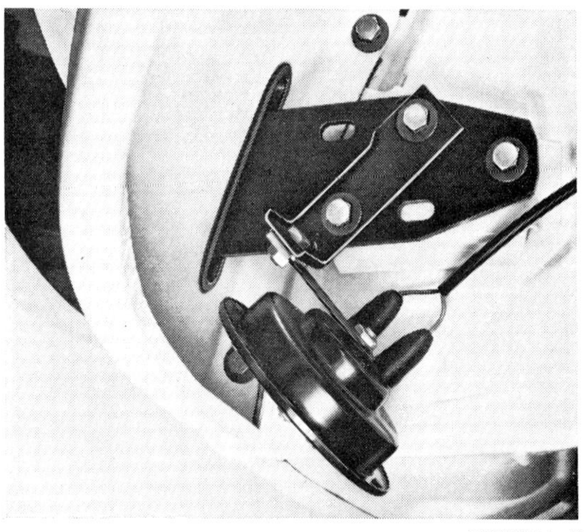



**Fig. 24.** Bumper bracket and horn are bolted together at left front body panel. Horn must be taken off before bracket can be withdrawn through fender opening.

**NOTE ——**
Put the rubber grommets in the fender openings before you insert the brackets. Prior to installation, lightly oil the bolt threads.

## 5. DOORS AND DOOR LOCKS

Since the body of a car in motion on any road undergoes vibration and some torsion from travel over uneven surfaces, the door latches are under fairly continuous stress. While the mechanism is designed to compensate for these forces, it is not unusual for door latches to require minor adjustment. Most of the time this adjustment can be made at the striker plate on the door frame. In case of damage it may be necessary to re-align the door. The procedures for adjusting the striker plates follow, first for an early version of the latch and then for a later latch of quite different design.

### 5.1 Adjusting Striker Plate
(cars prior to August 1966)

The latch housing on the door itself carries the latch bolt on the underside and the safety catch at the end. Fig. 25 shows the workings of these parts in relation to the striker.

When the door is closed, the latch bolt jumps the outer (safety) notch in the striker plate to engage in the inner notch. At the same time the inner surface of the striker plate drives the safety catch back into the latch housing to lock the latch bolt in the striker plate notch.

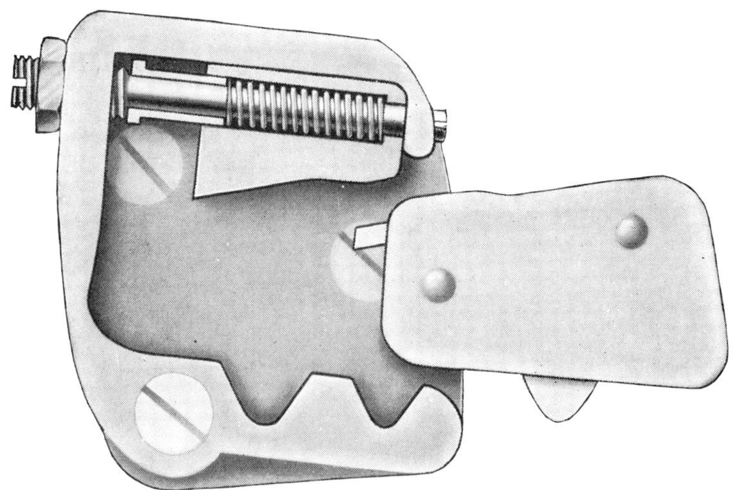

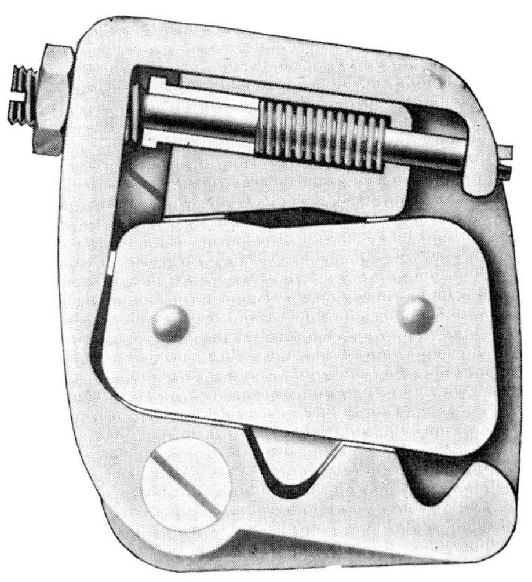



**Fig. 25.** Door latch mechanism on 1966 and 1967 cars is seen here in two cutaway views. In view at left door is almost closed, but the latching mechanism is not yet engaged. At right door is closed and securely latched. The striker plate, which is screwed to the door pillar in the car body, is the square part in background of the pictures. The latch housing, which is installed in the door itself, is the oblong object entering the striker plate from right. The protruding piece at underside of the housing is the latch bolt. The protruding piece at left face of the housing is the safety catch or safety slide. As the latch housing enters the striker plate, the bolt jumps over the first (safety) notch in plate to engage in the inner notch. At the same time, the safety catch, coming against the inner side surface of the plate, is forced back into the latch housing to lock the bolt. At the upper part of the striker plate the adjusting screw holds the plastic wedge. Turning the screw moves the wedge to left or right to bring less or more pressure on the latch housing to reduce or prevent rattling.

The adjustable plastic wedge at the top of the striker plate brings pressure on the latch housing and latch bolt to prevent rattling. All these parts must be adjusted in relation to each other. Replacement parts for this design of latch may be different from the originals. Consult your local authorized VW dealer.

### Basic Adjustment

1. Remove the striker plate.
2. Check the fit of the door in the opening. It is correctly aligned when:
   a. the gap between top of door and edge of roof is about equal to the gap between edge of door and side panel of body,
   b. the door is flush with the body side panel,
   c. the waistline moldings of door and body are in line,
   d. the door does not rub at top or bottom,
   e. the weatherstrip bears evenly around door and is uniformly compressed.
3. If necessary, adjust the door. You may have to loosen hinges and reposition the door.
4. Check functioning of the lock:
   a. The top surface of the latch housing must be smooth and the bottom smooth and perfectly flat. The openings for the latch bolt and the safety catch must not be worn at the edge.
   b. When the door handle is pulled, the latch bolt should retract completely into the housing, as shown in Fig. 26. If the latch does not retract, the door may be difficult to close or open.

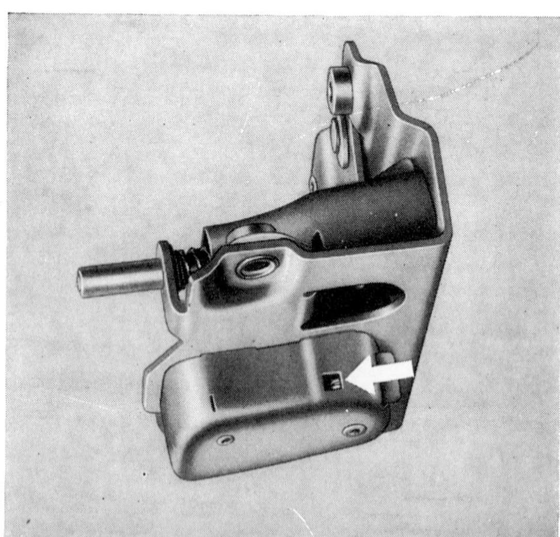



**Fig. 26.** Latch housing on the door mechanism removed from car is indicated by arrow. Top surface of the housing must be smooth and flat for easy operation.

5. Inspect striker plate (Fig. 27). If bearing surfaces for latch housing (A) and notch (B) are badly worn, the striker plate should be replaced.

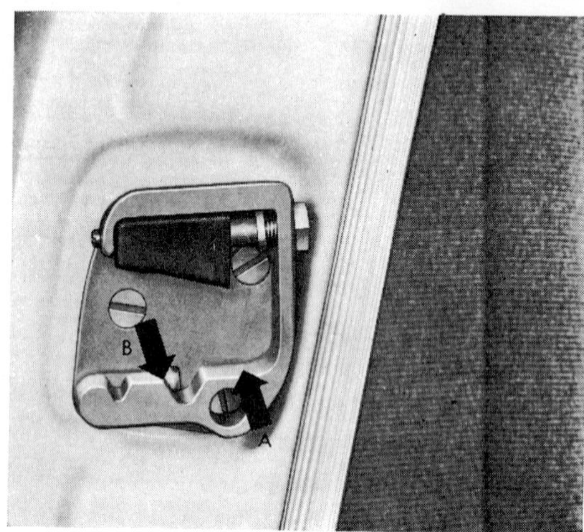




**Fig. 27.** Striker plate should be inspected for wear at (A), where latch housing bears, and at (B), where locking bolt engages. Heavy wear at these points calls for replacement of plate.

**NOTE —**
If the plastic wedge is scored or worn, replace it.

6. Install striker plate but do not tighten screws fully (see Fig. 28).
7. Loosen locknut on wedge adjusting screw and turn screw to right until the stop bushing is in contact with striker plate housing. This adjustment gives wedge maximum free movement.

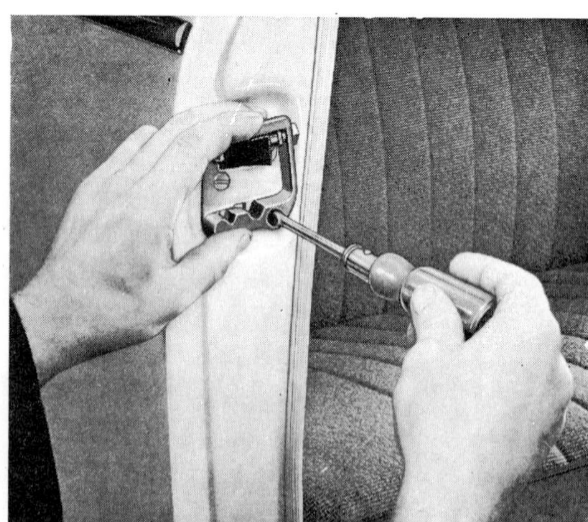



**Fig. 28.** Striker plate screws are left loose until plate position is adjusted.

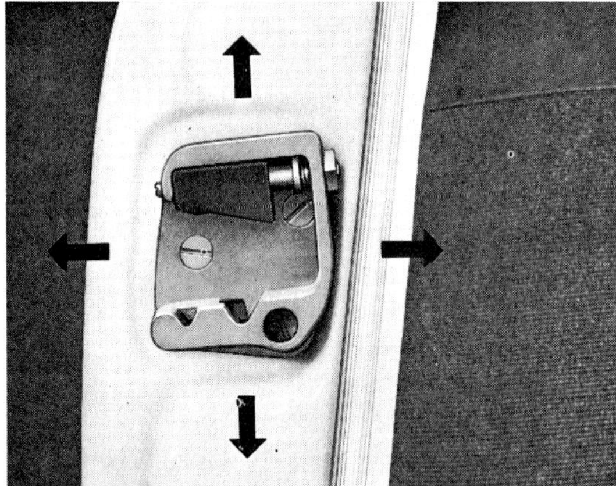


**Fig. 29.** Striker plate adjustments to correct door alignment are indicated by black arrows.

8. Adjust striker plate.
   a. Horizontal adjustment: Move striker plate to one side or other until door and rear quarter panel are flush with one another.
   b. Vertical adjustment: Position plate as shown in Fig. 29. The measurement (X) between the latch housing and the plastic wedge is greater than the measurement (Y) between the latch housing and the bearing surface above the lock notches (see Fig. 30).

**NOTE —**
When door is closed, the latch should strike bearing edge of the striker plate and be lifted by about 0.08 inch (2 mm), shown as (a) in Fig. 30.

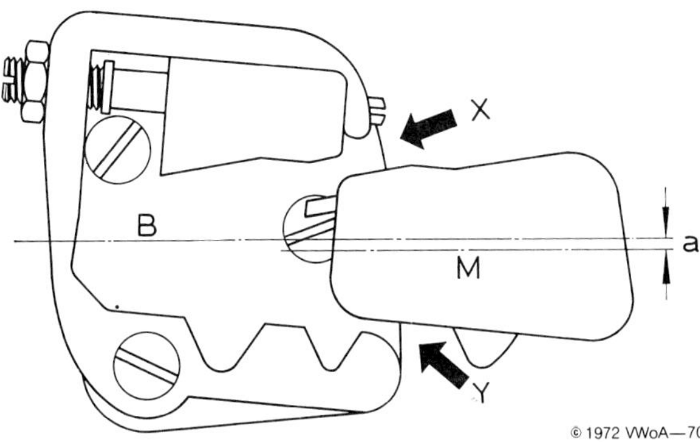


**Fig. 30.** Engagement of striker plate and latch housing should be adjusted to make measurement X between housing and wedge smaller than measurement Y between housing and plate bearing edge. Contact of housing with plate should lift housing approximately 0.08 inch (2 mm), shown here as measurement "a".

9. While holding the door almost shut, push weatherstrip aside to see how the latch housing will fit in the striker plate (Fig. 31).

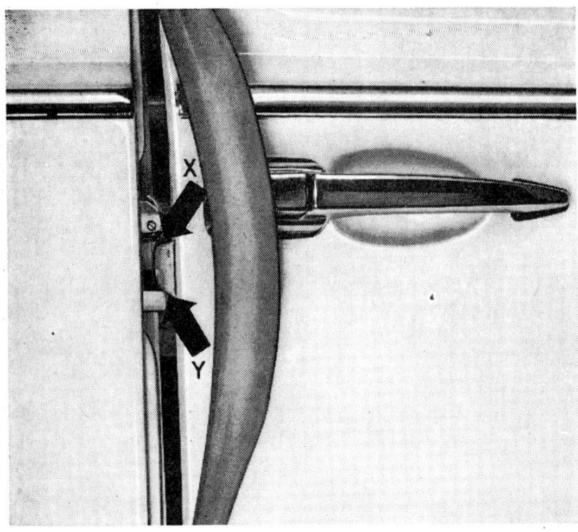


**Fig. 31.** Fit of latch housing with striker plate can be checked if weatherstrip is pushed aside when door is nearly closed. The X and Y arrows point to the measurements illustrated in Fig. 30.

10. With striker plate adjusted, open and close door several times to check bearing of latch on plate. If the latch housing does not bear evenly on striker plate, tilt plate slightly as in Fig. 32.
11. Tighten securing screws of striker plate.
12. Adjust plastic wedge.

An adjustable stop holds this wedge in place in

**Fig. 32.** Bearing surfaces (black arrows) on striker plate must make even contact with latch housing bearing surfaces. If not, striker plate must be tilted.

9

the striker plate under torsion and road shock and keeps it from moving when the door is closed (Fig. 33).

a. Loosen lock nut (1) of adjusting screw (3) while holding screw with screwdriver (Fig. 34).

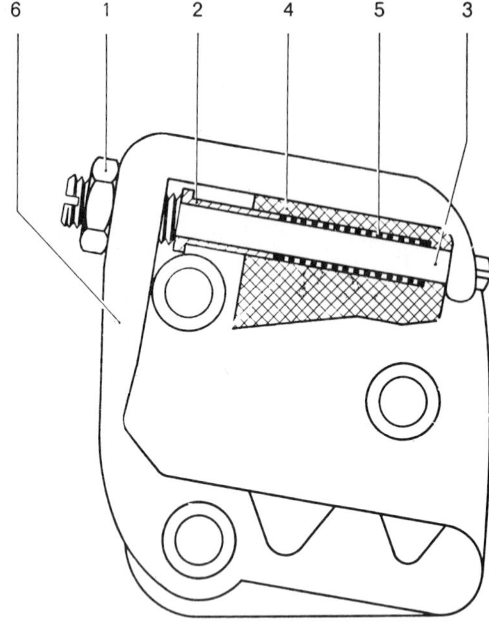


1. Lock nut
2. Stop
3. Adjusting screw
4. Plastic wedge
5. Spring
6. Body of striker plate

**Fig. 33.** Plastic wedge on striker plate is shown schematically here. Text gives adjustment procedure with reference to these parts numbers.

**Fig. 34.** Adjusting screw for plastic wedge in striker plate is turned with screwdriver at outer end while wrench holds lock nut at inner end.

b. Turn adjusting screw counter-clockwise to move stop (2) toward wedge. The position of wedge (4) will be correct when you feel increased resistance on opening door. If the resistance seems excessive or if the door springs back when you try to close it, you have moved the stop too far. Turn adjusting screw clockwise to reduce wedge pressure.

c. Holding the adjusting screw with screwdriver, tighten lock nut.

d. New striker plates may settle at first, requiring readjustment of the wedge. To re-adjust, repeat procedure given under a, b, c.

e. Spread a thin film of petroleum jelly or molybdenum disulfide paste on contact surfaces of door latch and wedge. Wipe off excess.

## 5.2 Adjusting Striker Plate

(cars after August 1966, from chassis No. 117 000 001)

The latching mechanism of this lock is exposed and its operation is self-evident. The bonded rubber wedge on the striker plate, unlike the wedge on the earlier latch, is not adjustable, but if necessary, it can be fitted with a shim to increase pressure on the latch and eliminate rattling. The shim, which is 0.02 to 0.04 inch (0.05 to 1.5 mm) thick, goes between wedge and the short angled arm of the striker plate. Revised replacement latches are available at your Authorized VW Dealer. It will be necessary to make sure that the new latch engages snugly with the wedge in the striker plate.

**To adjust:**

1. Take out four Phillips screws to remove striker plate (Fig. 35).

**Fig. 35.** Striker plate on 1968 and 1969 cars is fastened to moveable threaded plate in door frame by four Phillips head screws (black arrows).

2. Holding removed striker plate in your hand, apply it to the latch on the door, as shown in Fig. 36. Insert the striker plate stud into the lock latch and press upward on the plate to force the latch bolt into locking position.

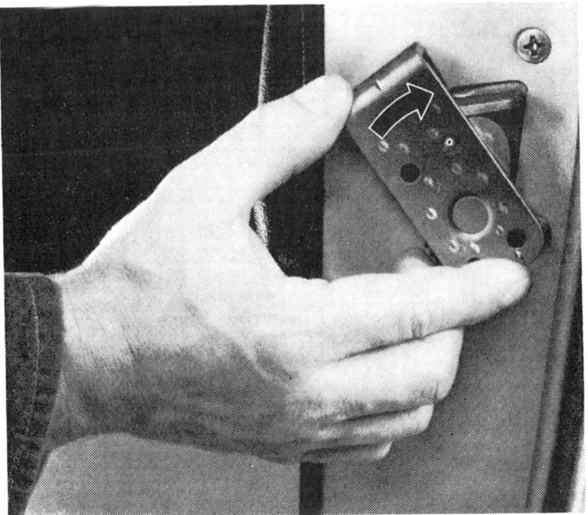

© 1972 VWoA—76

**Fig. 36.** Removed striker plate is applied to lock latch in door to test fit of striker plate wedge. When lock latch has been pressed into locking position on striker plate pin, plate is twisted as indicated by black arrow.

3. Twist striker plate upward, as in Fig. 36.
4. If you can feel play when moving striker plate up and down in the position of Fig. 37, you will have to either replace the wedge or shim it.

© 1972 VWoA—77

**Fig. 37.** Striker plate fit is tested by moving plate up and down (black arrows) on pin. If play is felt, rubber wedge needs shimming.

5. To install shim, unscrew two Phillips screws in angled part of striker plate, as in Fig. 38.

© 1972 VWoA—78

**Fig. 38.** Phillips screws (black arrows) on angled arm of striker plate must be removed for installation of shim.

6. Insert shim and screw it with wedge to striker plate. Fig. 39 shows wedge with shim installed.
7. After removing striker plate, correct the position of door in door opening by the following procedure:

© 1972 VWoA—79

**Fig. 39.** Shim between angled arm of striker plate and rubber wedge is indicated by black arrows. Shim is 0.02 to 0.06 inch (0.5 to 1.5 mm) in thickness.

a. If hinge screws are loose, tighten them.
b. If door and front panel are out of alignment, loosen hinges and move door in, out, up or down to obtain correct alignment.
c. If waistline of door and front panel are out of alignment, follow step (b).

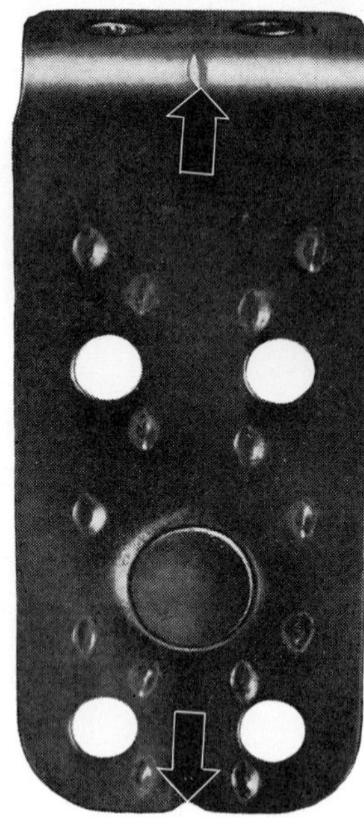



**Fig. 40.** Notches at top and bottom of striker plate (black arrows) provide reference points for adjustment of the plate in door frame recess.

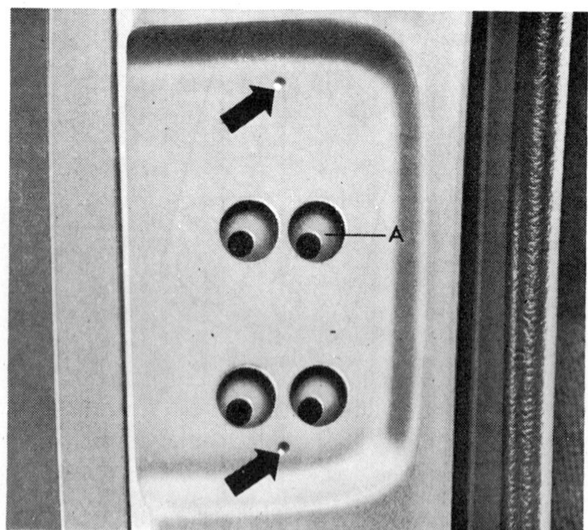




**Fig. 41.** Threaded plate for adjustable attachment of striker plate can be seen at A through holes in door frame recess. Dimples indicated by arrows give adjustment reference points to match with striker plate notches shown in Fig. 40.

d. If door and rear panel are out of alignment, install striker plate in approximate position and then adjust to obtain correct alignment.
e. If waistline of door and rear panel are out of alignment, follow step (d).

Fig. 40 and Fig. 41 show reference points on back of striker plate and in door frame for adjustments required in Steps (d) and (e) of above procedure. The striker plate adjustment will be correct when:

1. Door is flush with lock pillar.
2. Waistline of door and rear panel are flush.
3. No play can be felt between lock and striker plate when door is opened or closed by handle.
4. Door can be opened from inside without excessive effort.

Fig. 42 and Fig. 43 illustrate the procedure for adjusting the striker plate by rotating it about the pivot point under the stud.

1. If the door is hard to close and the pushbutton hard to operate, the striker plate is inclined too far inward at the top.
   Remedy: Rotate striker plate as at "a", Fig. 42.

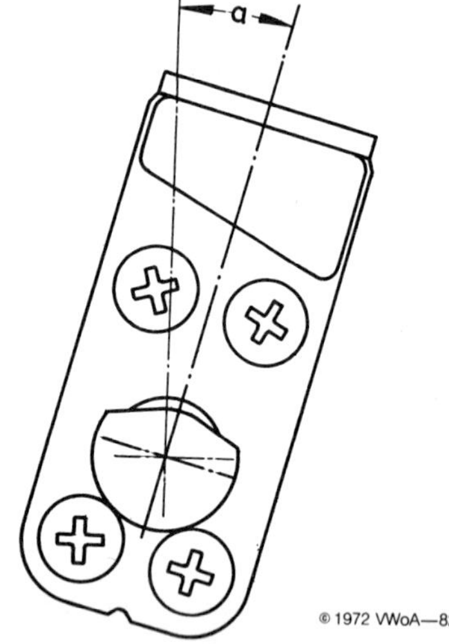




**Fig. 42.** Inward tilt of striker plate, as shown here for right-hand door, may make door hard to close, pushbutton hard to push. Remedy is to rotate plate counterclockwise. Approximate rotation required is shown at "a".

2. If the door springs back to safety position instead of staying closed when you slam it, the striker plate is inclined too far outward at top. The pushbutton opens door easily.
   Remedy: Rotate striker plate as at "a" in Fig. 43.

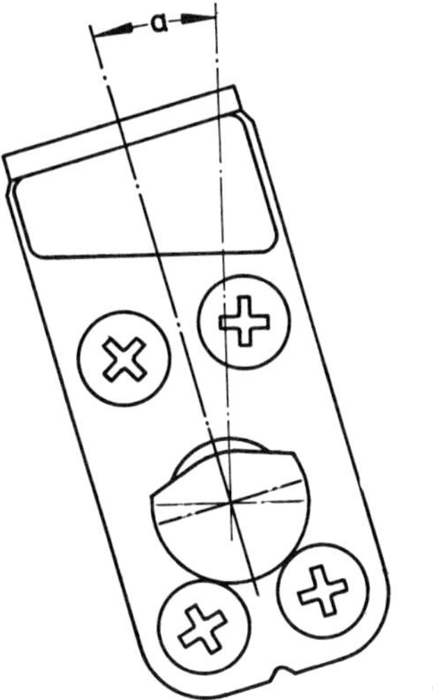


© 1972 VWoA—83

**Fig. 43.** Outward tilt of striker plate, as shown here for right-hand door, may cause door to spring back to safety position when closed. Remedy is to rotate plate clockwise. Approximate rotation required is shown at "a".

3. When the striker plate is set too high, it will be hard to open the door with the pushbutton. On opening the door will drop noticeably instead of holding its horizontal position.
   Remedy: Lower striker plate.
4. If the door when slammed springs out of the closed position and engages in the safety notch, the striker plate is set too low.
   Remedy: Move striker plate upward.

## 5.3 Removing and Installing Door

The door hinges are screwed into moveable plates. This method of attachment allows you to align the door with the outer panels.

**To remove:**

1. Take off door check strap pin.
2. Remove hinge screw cover plugs.
3. Loosen hinge screws with punch screwdriver (see Fig. 44) and then remove them with Phillips screwdriver.
4. Take door, complete with hinges, out of pillar.

**To install:**

1. Check door weatherstrip and fit new seal if necessary. Glue on new seal with universal adhesive D 12.

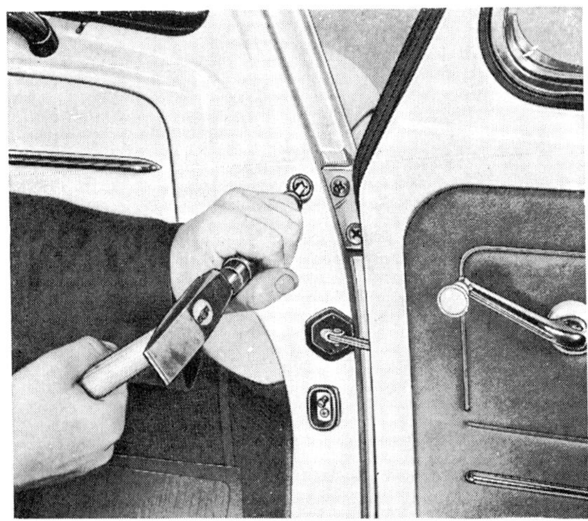

© 1972 VWoA—84

**Fig. 44.** Door hinge screws are loosened with punch screwdriver. They can then be removed with Phillips screwdriver.

2. Attach door. Make sure that seal has even contact all around opening and that you can open and close door without slamming it. The striker plate must be removed for this test (see Fig. 45).
3. Re-install striker plate, adjusting it for correct alignment of door with rear panel and for easy closing of door. (Detailed instructions are given under **5.1** and **5.2 Adjusting Striker Plates.**) The arrows in Fig. 45 point to four locations where the door-body panel alignment is critical.
4. Lubricate hinges. Clean oil slots and replace dust caps.

© 1972 VWoA—85

**Fig. 45.** Critical points of door-body fit are indicated by black arrows. At points indicated, adjoining surfaces should be flush, edges either aligned or evenly separated.

9

> **NOTE —**
> From chassis No. 117 496 043 shorter hinge pins were installed. The shorter pin leaves a small chamber in the top part of the hinge, which no longer has a lubricating groove. This chamber is filled with oil to lubricate the hinge. A small plastic plug keeps out dirt.

5. Give contact surfaces of the latch housing on the striker plate and on the wedge a light coating of petroleum jelly or molybdenum disulfide paste.

> **NOTE —**
> Use graphite powder only to lubricate door handle lock cylinders. Never use oil or grease on them. Dip key in graphite powder and turn the lock with it a few times.

## 5.4 Removing and Installing Door Window

**To remove:**

1. Press window crank and inner handle escutcheons against trim panel to expose retaining pins and knock out pins with a punch. Take off crank, handle and escutcheons.
2. On cars from chassis No. 118 000 001 use a screwdriver as shown in Fig. 46 to pry plastic cover loose from window crank handle. As in the illustration, use a scrap of wood under screwdriver blade to give leverage and protect trim panel. Take out Phillips head screw (Fig. 47) and remove handle and plastic ring.
3. On cars from chassis No. 117 000 001, use screw-

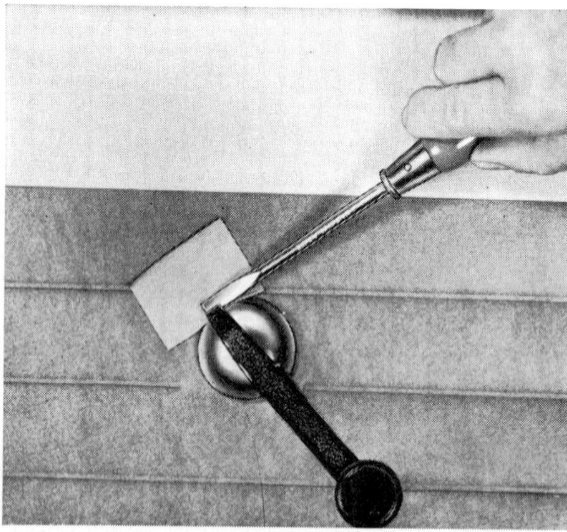



**Fig. 46.** Plastic cover of window crank handle is pried loose with screwdriver. For leverage and protection of door trim put scrap of wood under screwdriver blade.

**Fig. 47.** Phillips screw that attaches window crank is exposed when plastic cover of handle is freed.

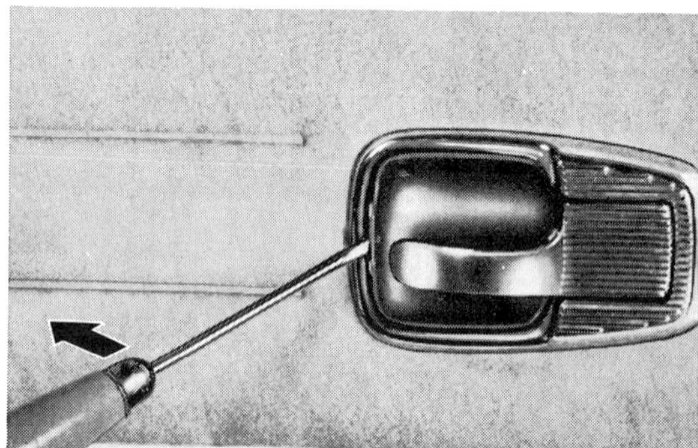



**Fig. 48.** Trim plate of inside door handle is pried off with screwdriver twisted in direction indicated by the black arrow.

**Fig. 49.** Escutcheon of inside door handle is fastened with Phillips screw (arrow) which is exposed when trim has been removed as in Fig. 48.

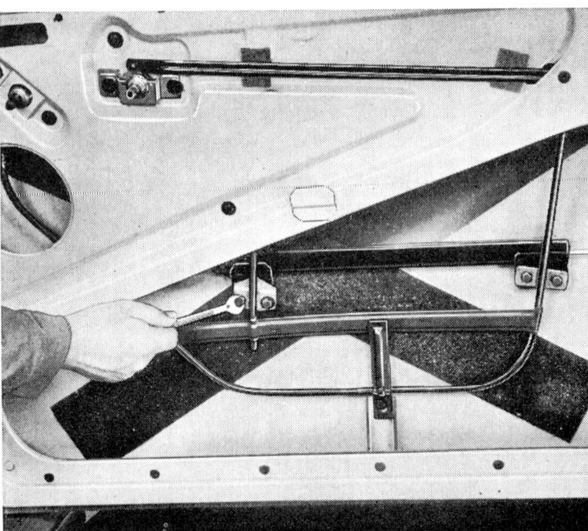

© 1972 VWoA—90

**Fig. 50.** Lift channel in which door window rests is fastened to lifting assembly with four bolts. Wrench here is on bolt at left end of channel.

driver as shown in Fig. 48 to pry out trim plate for inside door handle.

4. Remove exposed Phillips head screw (Fig. 49) and escutcheon.
5. Take off trim panel. Be careful not to damage panel or paintwork.

**NOTE —**
On passenger's side (and from chassis No. 117 000 001 on driver's side also) there is an arm rest retaining plate to hook trim on the arm rest support to the door inner panel. Pull trim panel away slightly, then lift it to clear.

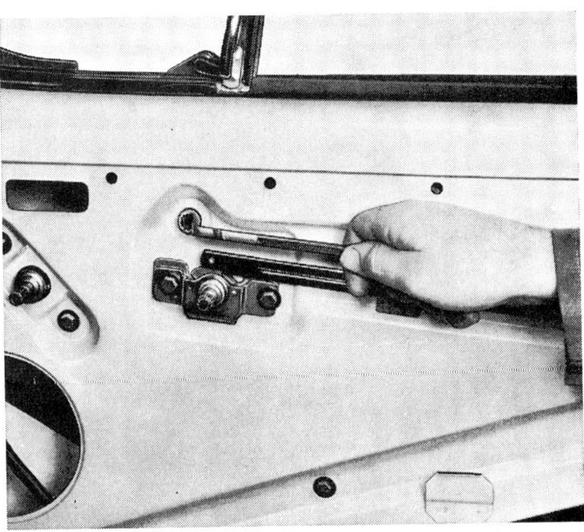

© 1972 VWoA—91

**Fig. 51.** Five bolts hold door window lifter and sixth one fastens vent wing.

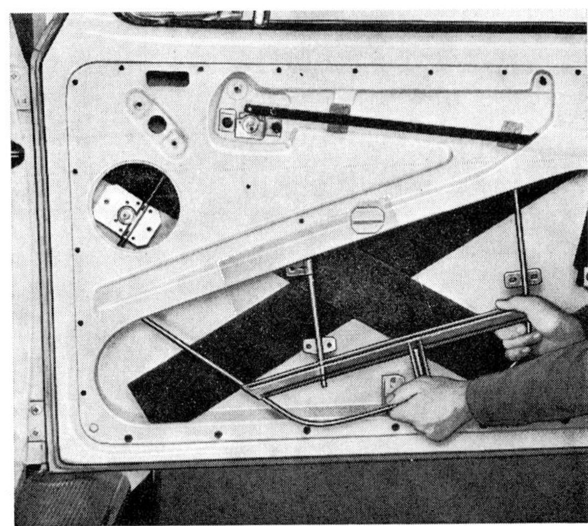

© 1972 VWoA—92

**Fig. 52.** Lifter assembly is removed through door panel opening after window on lifter channel has been pushed up as far as it will go.

6. Press retaining ring off check strap pin and take pin out.
7. Remove four bolts from window lifter channel, as in Fig. 50.
8. Push window upward. Remove five bolts in window lifter and one bolt for vent wing (see Fig. 51).
9. Press window lifter toward outer panel and take it out downward. Fig. 52 shows removal.
10. Pull window glass down, tilting it slightly as in Fig. 53, and take it out of door.
11. If necessary, remove window trim molding with

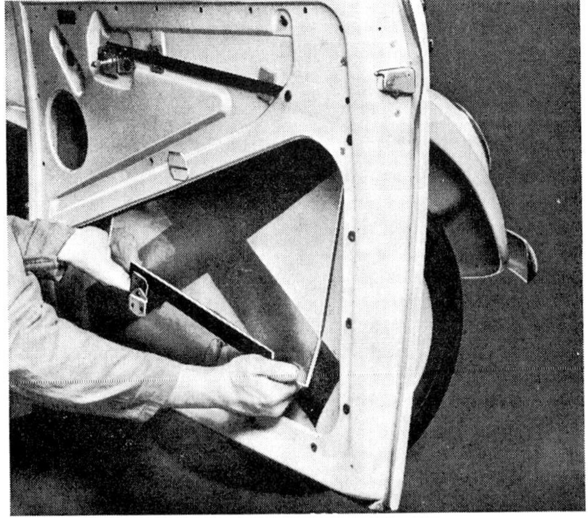

© 1972 VWoA—93

**Fig. 53.** Window on lifter channel comes out at opening in inside door panel. Window should be tilted slightly outward for this operation.

9

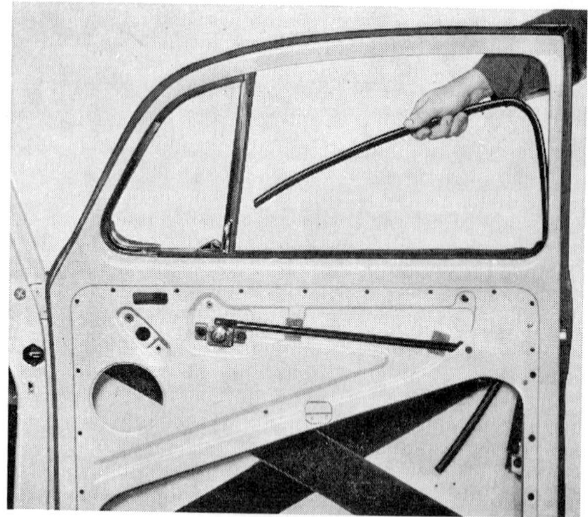

© 1972 VWoA—94

**Fig. 54.** Run channel for window is pulled out of window slot.

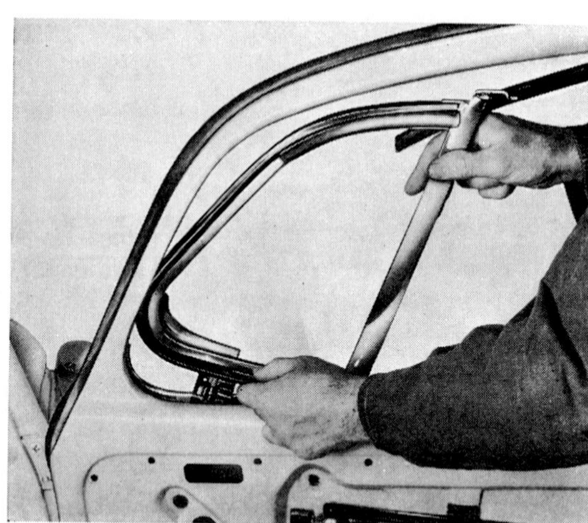

© 1972 VWoA—96

**Fig. 56.** Vent wing frame comes off after Phillips head screw in upper window frame and bolt on inner panel have been removed.

weatherstrip. It is advisable to press trim molding clips out from the rear.

12. Remove slot seal on door inner panel.
13. If necessary, pull rear run channel up out of window slot (Fig. 54).
    The window guide channel can be taken out downward after one bolt has been removed from mounting, as in Fig. 55.
14. Remove Phillips screw in upper window frame and bolt near remote control lock on inner panel. Then take out front window guide channel with vent wing frame (see Fig. 56).

**To install:**

1. Check guide channel, glass run channel and retaining clips for wear or damage and replace as necessary. The rear glass run channeling is supplied in straight pieces, cut to size. Before fitting, bend channel to shape and then press it into clips in door frame and rear guide channel (see Fig. 57).

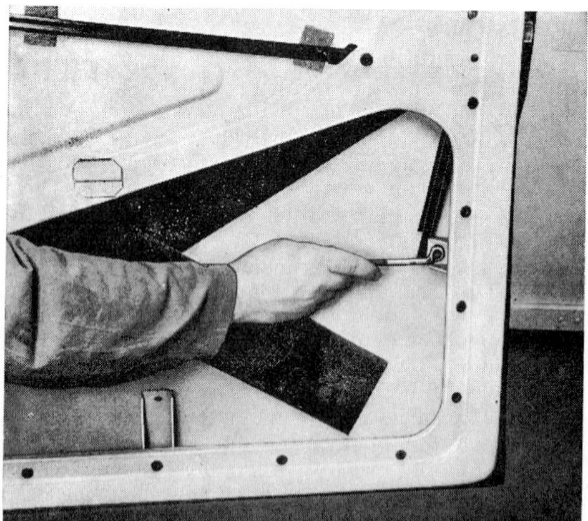

© 1972 VWoA—95

**Fig. 55.** Guide channel can be taken out through opening in inside door panel after one bolt has been removed, as shown here.

© 1972 VWoA—97

**Fig. 57.** Channeling for door window must be bent to shape before it is pressed into clips in door frame.

**NOTE —**
If lifter channel was taken off glass, it must be installed again. The distance shown as "a" in Fig. 58 should be about 3.15 inches (80 mm) measured along the straight bottom edge of glass.

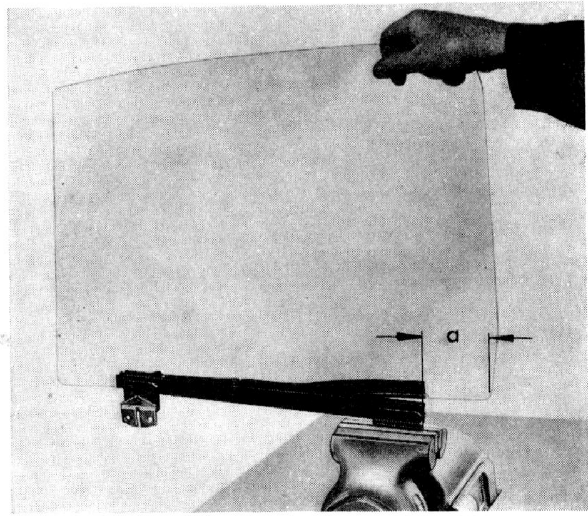


© 1972 VWoA—98

**Fig. 58.** Distance "a" along straight bottom edge of door window glass fixes setting of glass on lifter channel. Measurement "a" should be 3.15 inches (80 mm).

2. Coat lifter cable lightly with universal grease.
3. Check that damping strips on door are secure and that drain holes at bottom of door are clear.
4. Install glass run channel with vent wing frame and secure it.
5. Insert window into glass run channel from below and slide it upward.
6. Fit lifter and attach it to inner panel. Fig. 59 shows lifter with attachments.

**NOTE —**
If lifter cannot be pushed through the front window guide channel near the remote control lock, the vent wing must be lifted slightly.

7. Slide window down and attach lifter channel loosely to window lifter on each side. Open and close window a few times. Then tighten screws in window lifter channel.
8. Glue new sheet of plastic (Fig. 60) to door panel with universal adhesive D 12.
9. Fit rubber buffers, springs and trim panel. The large end of the conical springs must be toward trim panel.

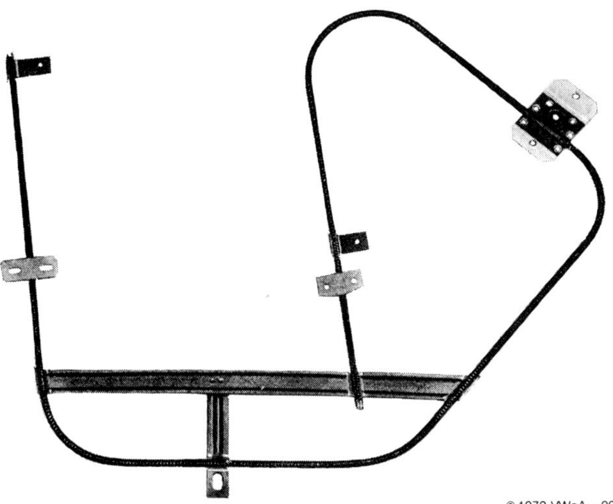

© 1972 VWoA—99

**Fig. 59.** Lifter assembly is shown without window and lifter channel. Installed lifter channel would be bolted to the two light-colored plates on vertical sections of the cable run.

10. Install window crank and inner handle at correct angles.
11. Operate window several times in order to check installation.

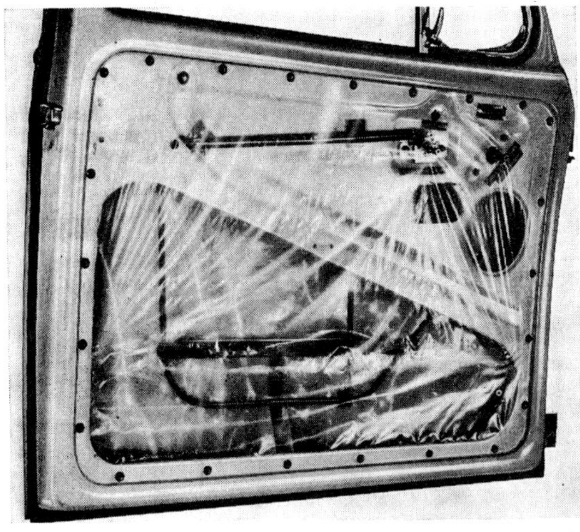

© 1972 VWoA—100

**Fig. 60.** Plastic sheet seals inside of door beneath the door trim.

9

## 6. HEATING AND VENTILATION SYSTEMS

Some changes in the fresh air system were made in 1968 cars beginning at chassis No. 118 000 001. These changes will be noted at the appropriate places in the following instructions.

## 6.1 Removing and Installing Front Footwell Heater Slides

**To remove:**

1. Carefully detach front lining near the warm air outlets and fold it back as in Fig. 61.

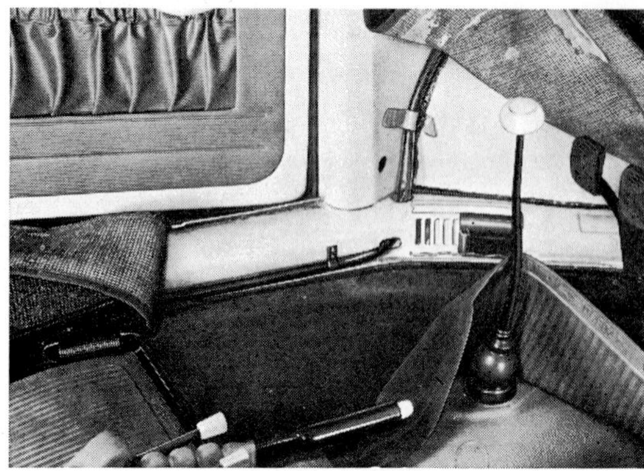

© 1972 VWoA—101

**Fig. 61.** Lining in front passenger compartment must be folded out of way for work on footwell heater slide. This is slide on driver's side.

2. Pull tensioning wire out of side member.
3. Pull slide forward out of upper groove (Fig. 62).

© 1972 VWoA—102

**Fig. 62.** Heater slide is removed to the front from guide after tensioning wire has been pulled out.

**To install:**

1. Check slide and retaining wire for wear or damage and replace if necessary.
2. Check upper groove on side member for damage and straighten if needed.
3. Insert slide and fit retaining wire.
4. Move the slide back and forth several times to check ease of movement. Straighten upper groove if necessary.
5. Coat front panel lining lightly with adhesive and stick it down again. Be careful about fit of lining material around outlet.

## 6.2 Removing Front Heater Hoses

The front heater hoses are a push fit on the adapter pipes. To remove hoses, bend up metal tabs (Fig. 63) and pull them off.

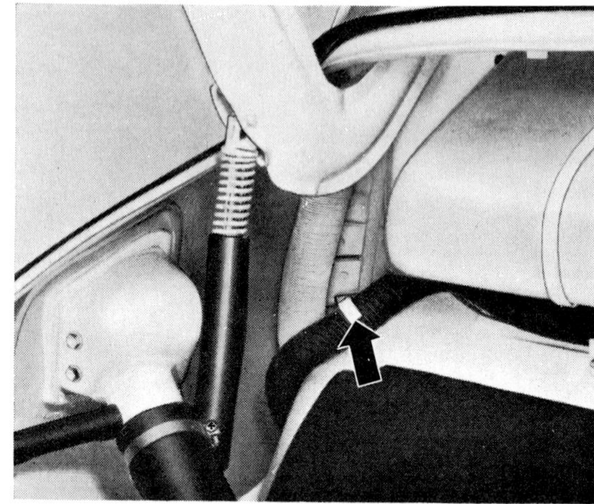

© 1972 VWoA—103

**Fig. 63.** Metal retaining tab (black arrow) secures front heater hose.

**NOTE —**
From chassis No. 118 000 001, it is necessary to remove the fresh air control box before removing front heater hoses (Fig. 64).

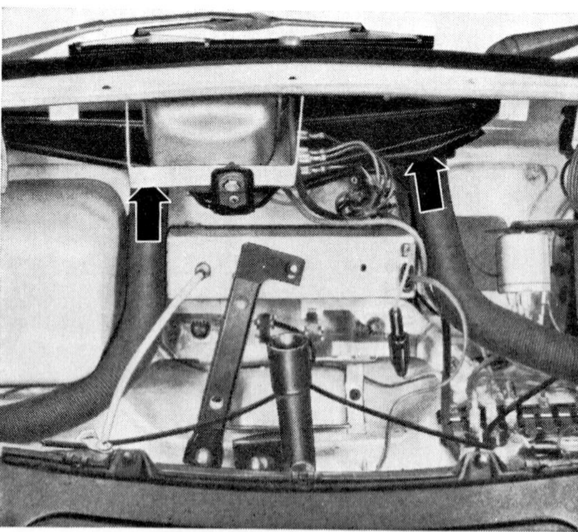

© 1972 VWoA—104

**Fig. 64.** Heater hoses on 1968 and 1969 cars are connected (black arrows) at sides of the air control box. On these models box must be removed before hoses can be taken off.

When re-installing heater hoses make sure that the securing metal tabs have a firm grip on the hoses to prevent rattling.

Do not attempt to remove heater hoses from bottom side member adapter pipes. Special tools are required to re-install the hoses on the pipes.

### 6.3 Adjusting Cables for Fresh Air Flaps
(from chassis No. 118 000 001)

This procedure will require removal of the elbow and water drain hose along with the fresh air control box.

**To adjust:**

1. Remove fresh air control box:
   a. Pull both hoses off fresh air control box.
   b. Remove one nut from elbow for water drain hose (single black arrow in Fig. 65).
   c. Remove three Phillips head screws (three black arrows in Fig. 65).

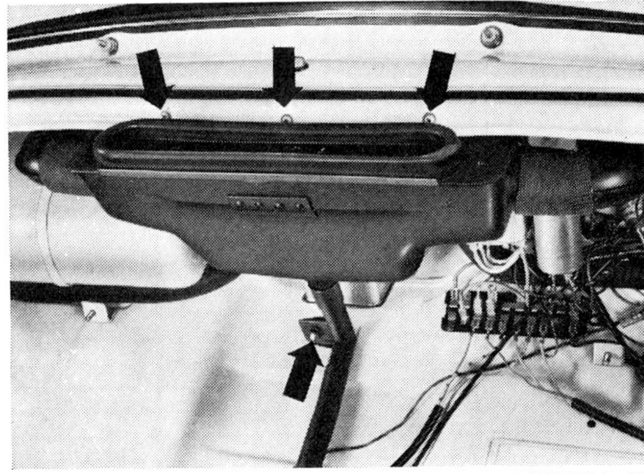



**Fig. 65.** Phillips head screws (three arrows at top) fasten fresh air control box to car body. Lower arrow points to bracket for nut on water drain hose elbow.

2. Remove fresh air control box with elbow and water drain hose in a downward direction.
3. Pull off elbow with water drain hose.
4. Adjust cables:
   a. Turn adjusting knob to stop (closed position).
   b. Loosen Phillips head screw for cable clamp (arrow in Fig. 66).
   c. Hold fresh air flap closed with control box lever and tighten Phillips head screw on cable clamp.

**Fig. 66.** Cable clamp on fresh air control box has Phillips head screw (black arrow).

5. Check operation of Bowden cables and controls.

To install fresh air control box, follow same procedure but in reverse order.

## 7. STEEL SLIDING ROOF
(sun roof)

The steel sliding roof is operated with a crank handle and can be cranked to any position between shut and all the way open. The roof measures 14.5 by 26 inches (375 by 665 mm).

A gear attached to the crank engages two cables which pull (or push) on the sliding roof at opposite sides. The hook-up is such that both cables move in the same direction at the same time. To open the roof, you turn the crank counter-clockwise. To close it, you crank in the clockwise direction. When not in use, the crank folds into a recess between the two sun visors.

### 7.1 Removing and Installing Sliding Roof Panel

**To remove:**

1. Open roof half way.
2. Remove trim panel at front. Carefully insert screwdriver between panel and roof and lever out the five clips.

3. Push trim panel to the rear as far as it will go, as shown in Fig. 67.

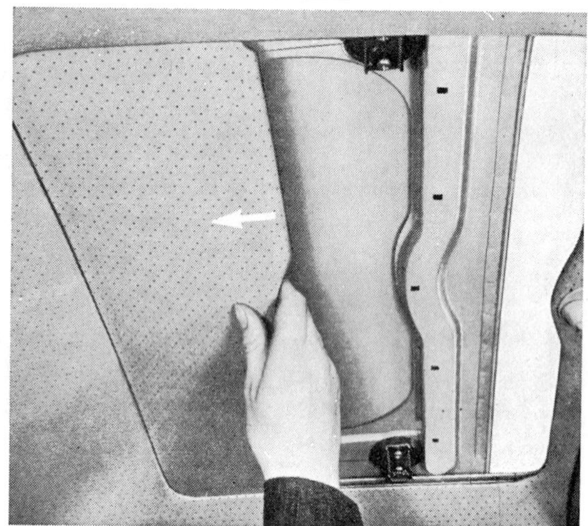

© 1972 VWoA—107

**Fig. 67.** Trim panel of roof lining is pushed to rear (white arrow) for removal of steel sliding roof.

4. Close the roof until an opening of about 2 inches remains.
5. Unscrew both front guides, as in Fig. 68.

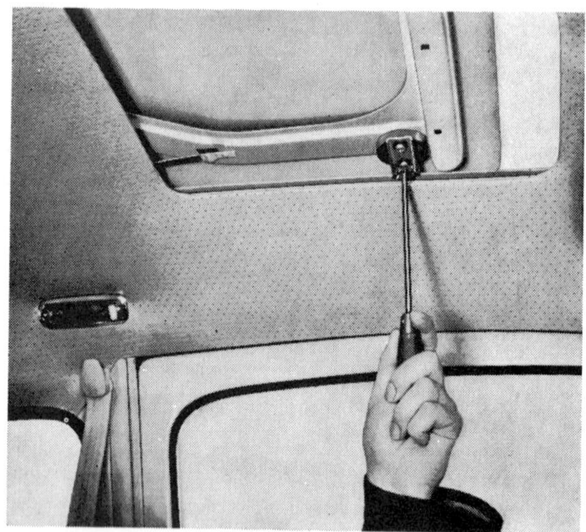

© 1972 VWoA—108

**Fig. 68.** Front guide in sliding roof control assembly is unscrewed while the roof is partly open.

6. Completely close roof. Unhook the leaf springs on left and right rear guides and turn springs to front. (Arrow in Fig. 69 shows turning direction.)
7. Pull rear guide brackets out of supports at left and right, as in Fig. 70.
8. Lift sliding roof panel out of opening, taking care to lift it evenly and to avoid damaging the seal.

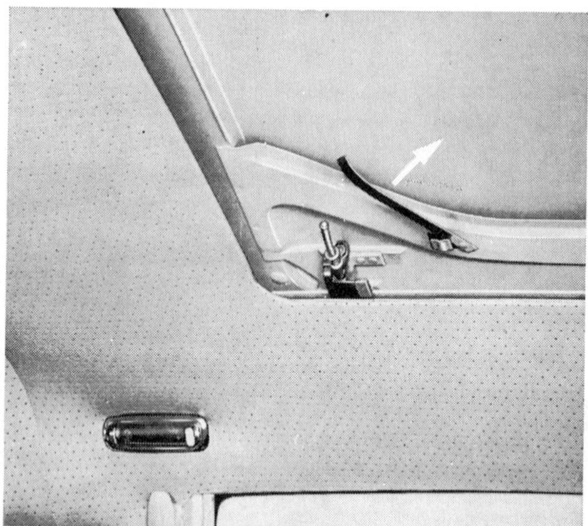

© 1972 VWoA—109

**Fig. 69.** Leaf spring on rear guide is unhooked and turned to front (white arrow) after roof has been closed.

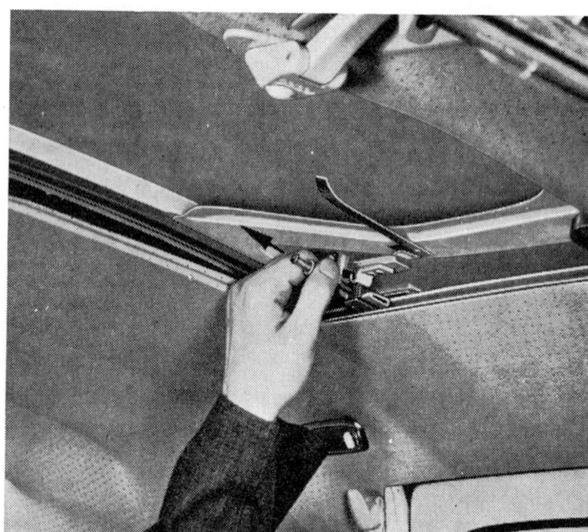

© 1972 VWoA—110

**Fig. 70.** Rear guide is pulled out (black arrow) of bracket on sliding roof. With both guides removed, sliding panel can be lifted out of opening.

**To install:**

1. Press trim lining down and insert roof panel at angle into the rear of the opening.
2. Slide panel to rear and lower front end slowly. Take care not to damage the seal.
3. Pull roof panel all the way to front.
4. Insert rear guide brackets into supports at left and right.
5. Install front guides at left and right.

6. Adjust sliding roof (see later sections on cable adjustment and vertical adjustment).
7. Open roof halfway and pull trim lining to front.
8. Attach trim lining by pressing clips into position, and check operation of roof.

## 7.2 Removing and Installing Trim Lining

Removal of the trim lining for the sliding roof panel requires removal of one side runner. In the installation procedure the trim lining and side runner must be inserted together.

## 7.3 Removing and Installing Guide Rails and Cables

**To remove:**

1. Remove sliding roof panel. Take out five Phillips head screws (Fig. 71) that fasten cover on cable guide housing.

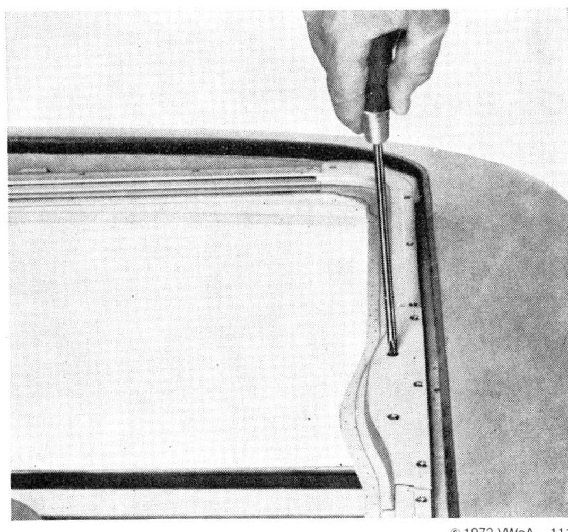

© 1972 VWoA—111

**Fig. 71.** Five Phillips head screws hold cover on central cable guide housing for sliding roof.

2. Remove cable guide housing cover to expose reinforcement plate (Fig. 72).
3. Take out reinforcement plate.
4. Remove four Phillips screws on each side and take off left and right upper guide channels.
5. Remove four Phillips screws from guide channels on each side.
6. Take side channels with cables, left and right front lower guide channels and trim panel out of roof opening (see Fig. 73).

© 1972 VWoA—112

**Fig. 72.** Reinforcement plate in the center guide housing is exposed when housing cover has been removed.

© 1972 VWoA—113

**Fig. 73.** Roof opening is shown here with the side and lower guide channels and the cables and trim panel removed.

**To install:**

1. Before pushing cables into the two rust-proof steel lower rails, check them carefully for wear, distortion and damage. Replace damaged parts. If one cable needs replacement it is advisable to replace both to ensure free movement of the roof without binding at either side. The new cables must not be shorter than the old ones.
2. When inserting the side rails into the roof opening, push the front plastic retainers all the way

into the mounting brackets. Otherwise, the rails will have side movement when the roof panel is opened or closed, and the panel will not slide properly. Fig. 74 shows the insertion.

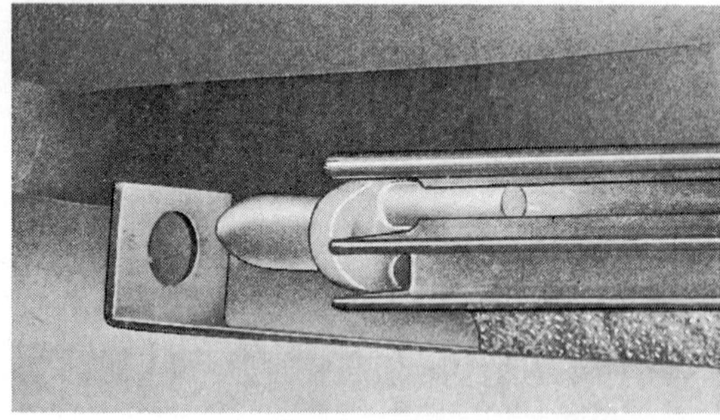


**Fig. 74.** Front plastic retainer on end of side runner for sliding roof must be pushed all the way into hole in mounting bracket or roof may bind.

3. Before you secure the side rails, insert trim panel into the lower groove and push it to rear as far as it will go.
4. Lubricate cables with a molybdenum disulfide grease.
5. Secure center cable channel by pressing retaining lugs into front of roof frame.
6. Cross cables and press them over drive gear.
7. Place reinforcement plate over center runner.
8. Press cover onto center channel and secure it with screws. Three Phillips tapping screws are used at the front, and three Phillips countersunk head screws at the rear.
9. Press upper parts of channel into roof frame on each side and secure.
10. Install sliding roof panel and adjust cables.

### 7.4 Adjusting the Cable

This procedure requires removal of the crank.

**To adjust:**

1. With roof partly open, detach trim panel and push it to rear.
2. Remove crank after taking off the small cap (as seen in Fig. 75).
3. Remove escutcheon.
4. Unscrew the two cable drive gear securing screws about six turns.
5. Pull drive gear down until gear no longer engages in cables (see Fig. 76).

1. Cap
2. Screw
3. Washer
4. Crank
5. Escutcheon
6. Drive gear screws
7. Drive gear

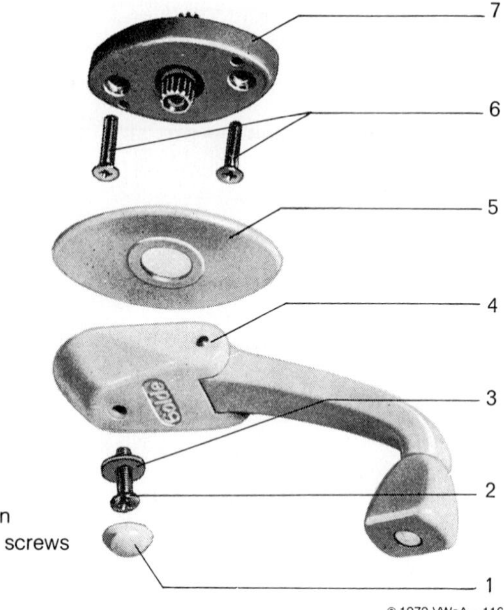



**Fig. 75.** Hand crank for sliding roof mechanism is shown in exploded view.

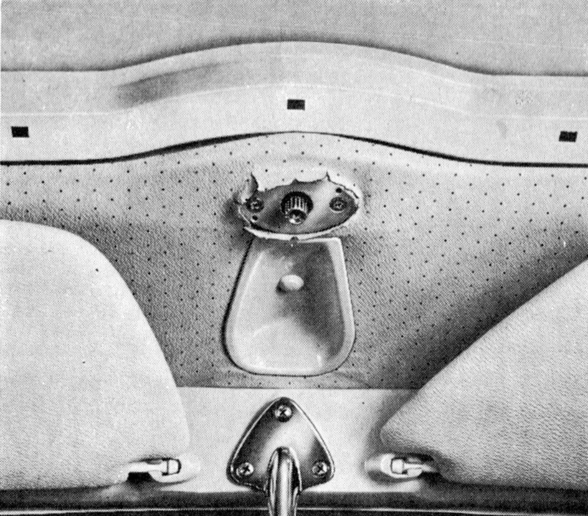


**Fig. 76.** Crank gear for steel sliding roof is exposed when the crank handle has been removed.

6. Pull the two rear guides with cables along guide rails to brackets on sliding roof (Fig. 77).
7. Turn pivoting part of each guide to the vertical position and insert its pin into bracket on sliding roof (see Fig. 78).
8. Turn drive gear shaft to right as far as it will go (maximum 12 turns).
9. Press cable drive gear up and secure. Gear must engage both cables.

© 1972 VWoA—117

**Fig. 77.** Rear guides with cables attached are pulled toward brackets on sliding roof after crank has been removed for cable adjustment. This is view of rear guide on left side of car.

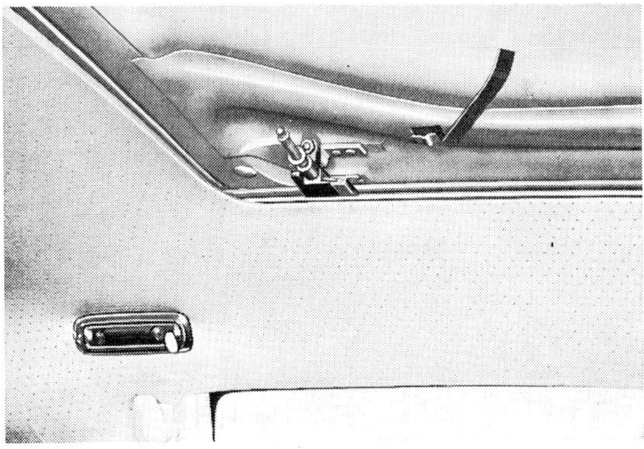

© 1972 VWoA—118

**Fig. 78.** Left rear guide is shown here after it has been turned to vertical position and attached to bracket on sliding roof. Same operation is performed on right rear guide.

10. Install escutcheon and crank.
11. Open and close roof to test cable adjustment.
12. Pull trim panel forward and attach it to roof panel.

## 7.5 Vertical Adjustment of Sliding Roof Panel

**To adjust front:**

1. Open roof slightly, detach trim lining and push to rear.
2. Close roof.
3. Loosen screws in front guides.
4. Adjust sliding roof panel to correct height by turning knurled nuts at left and right as in Fig. 79.

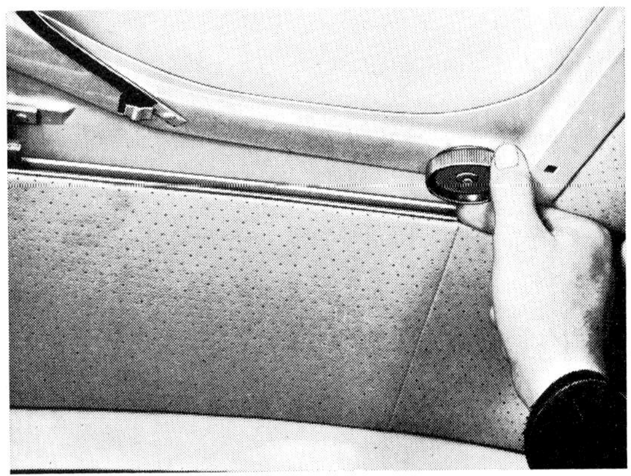

© 1972 VWoA—119

**Fig. 79.** Knurled nut at either side of roof opening controls vertical position of sliding roof on 1966 and 1967 cars.

**NOTE —**
From chassis No. 117 575 355 the two knurled nuts used for vertical adjustment were replaced with Phillips head countersunk screws.

5. Tighten front guide screws.
6. Pull trim lining forward and attach to panel.

**To adjust rear:**

1. Open roof halfway, detach trim lining and push to rear.
2. Close roof until rear guides are just about to lift on ramp.
3. Loosen nuts on upper pins, as in Fig. 80.

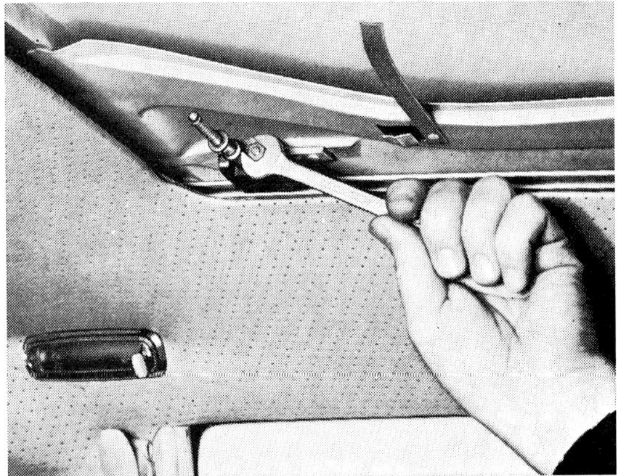

© 1972 VWoA—120

**Fig. 80.** Upper pin on rear guide, which holds sliding roof at roof bracket, must be moved to adjust vertical position of roof. Wrench here is loosening lock nut on pin.

9

4. Adjust position of guide upper pin to correct height with adjusting screw, as in Fig. 81.

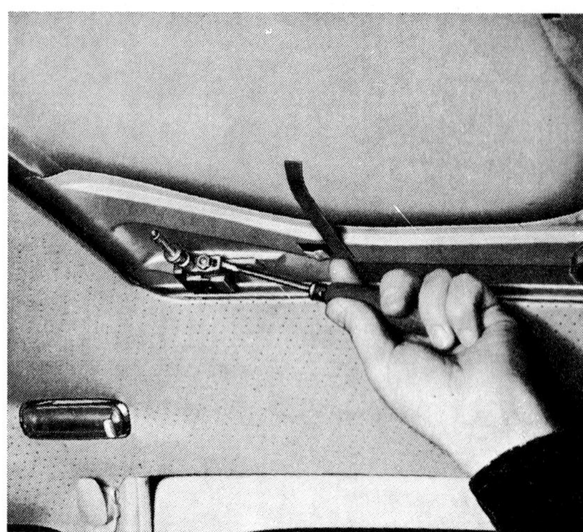



**Fig. 81.** Adjusting screw for pin in rear guide is being turned here to move pin to alter vertical position of roof.

5. Tighten nuts.
6. Check that roof slides without binding. If necessary, adjust cables.
7. Pull trim lining forward and attach to panel.

## 7.6 Troubleshooting Sliding Roof

Troubleshooting procedures applicable to the sliding roof on VW vehicles covered by this Manual are given in **Table a.**

## 7.7 Sealing Roof Panel

The long seal (velvet beading shown in Fig. 82) is cemented to the front and sides of the roof opening. The short seal is cemented to the rear edge of the roof panel. Make sure that the cementing of the short seal is continued around to the ends of the curved section of the rear panel. Fit the long seal to leave no space between seals when the roof is closed.

**Fig. 82.** Ramp for sliding roof is installed in water channel. This view is looking down on roof, rear of car at right. Note velvet beading around edge of sun roof.

An additional rubber seal is fitted at the rear of the roof panel. The panel must be removed for replacement of this seal.

### Table a. Troubleshooting Sliding Roof

| Symptom | Cause | Remedy |
|---|---|---|
| 1. Sliding roof panel lifts at one side | a. Lifter not running on ramp | a. Align ramps in sliding roof water channels correctly with lifter (cam-like angled metal lug of rear roof panel support). Set ramp to have contact point of lifter resting on center of ramp. At the moment front panel edge touches front seal, brackets must be at angle of 45 degrees. Locate ramps accordingly. Lifter contact point can be changed by tapping ramps forward or backward to change lifter contact point (see Fig. 81). |
| | b. Cable or drive gear damaged | b. Replace cables or drive gear. |
| | c. Guide brackets set too low | c. Adjust guide brackets properly. |
| 2. Sliding roof panel binds | a. Adjustment of cables incorrect | a. Adjust roof panel (cables and height). |
| | b. Cables or drive gear damaged | b. Replace cables or drive gear. |

### 7.8 Water Drain Channels

When water enters the roof opening, it runs along the water channels in the sliding roof frame and drains off through hoses in the front and rear roof members and side panels.

If the hoses are blocked, you can clean the front ones from above after opening the roof and the rear ones from below after removing the running boards. Either blow the hoses out with compressed air or probe them with a flexible steel wire (see Fig. 83).

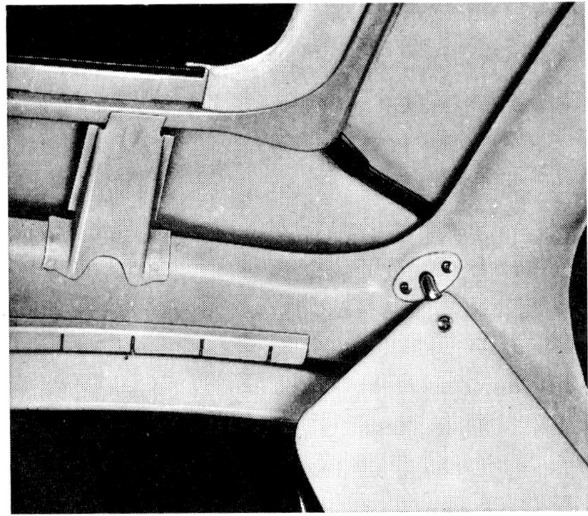



**Fig. 83.** Water drain channel is the black strip at elbow in ceiling trim just above sun visor pivot.

When fitting new hoses, keep them free of kinks. Seal the hoses to the pipes with universal adhesive.

## 8. CONVERTIBLE TOP

The framework for the convertible top consists of metal side members held together with a wooden bow for a cross piece at the front, a curved metal bow at the rear and three tubular bows hinged to the side members. Two main hinges support the assembly. The hinges are mounted in brackets bolted to the body pillars.

The top outer cover is made of polyvinyl chloride (PVC) material. A rubberized hair pad, which is sewed into a linen sheet and secured at the top linkage, gives the top shape and serves as insulation. Additional wadding fills out the top contours. A headlining of perforated leatherette covers the inside of the top.

Two spring catches hold the top in the folded position. A bent catch, by failing to hold securely, may allow the framework to rub. Straighten or replace a bent catch promptly because rubbing will leave friction marks on the top. Always cover the folded top with the protective boot to keep the material from flapping in the wind. Friction marks or tears will spoil the appearance of the top and the headlining.

Keep the hinge points of top linkages lubricated. When they look dry, apply a few drops of oil. Before oiling, wipe dirt off the joints.

### 8.1 Adjusting Convertible Top
(from chassis No. 157 250 033)

A tensioning cable in a metal channel attached to the rear body bow secures the convertible top cover to the rear and quarter panels. The arrangement allows some tightening of the convertible top cover when necessary. To prepare for the adjustment procedures, you must loosen both top latch mechanisms and raise top 15¾ inches (400 mm). Loosen the headliner at the rear on both sides. You are then ready to proceed.

**To adjust:**

1. Remove stud fasteners for boot cover and securing hook for rear seat backrest.
2. Detach carpeting from luggage compartment and sides of wheel housings.
3. Remove the two nails behind the rear seat backrest stops (arrow in Fig. 84).

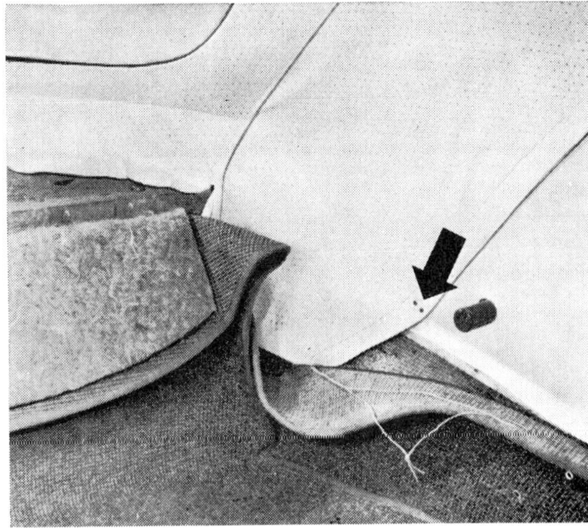



**Fig. 84.** Two nails (black arrow) behind stops for rear seat backrest must be taken out for adjustment of convertible top. Nails are exposed when luggage compartment carpeting is pulled away.

9

4. Position headliner near main bow.
5. Fig. 85 shows attachment of tensioning cable. Hold cable with wrench to prevent twisting and tighten adjusting nut with a second wrench, as in Fig. 86.

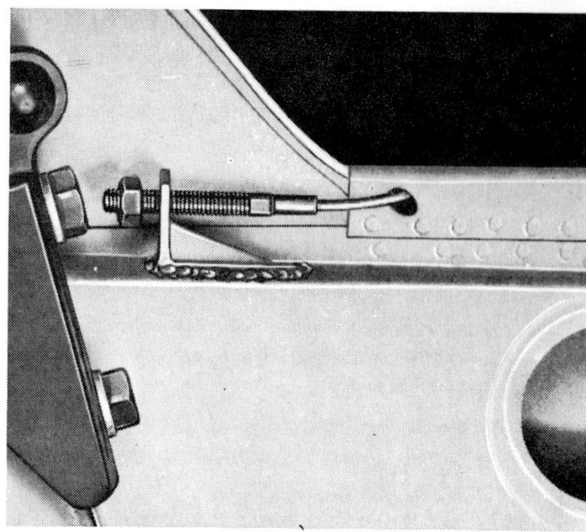



**Fig. 85.** Tensioning cable runs around rear bow of top and is adjusted by tightening or loosening nuts.

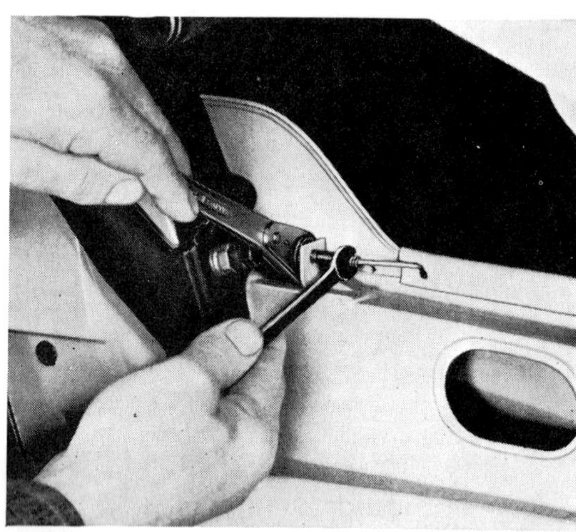



**Fig. 86.** Second wrench keeps tensioning cable from twisting when convertible top adjusting nut is turned.

**NOTE —**
Be sure to tighten adjusting nuts on both sides of top an equal amount.

6. Nail headliner and rubber straps to wooden strip on left and right sides and reglue carpeting.

## 8.2 Replacing Rear Trim Molding
(from chassis No. 157 250 033)

**To remove:**

1. Raise convertible top a little.
2. Remove Phillips head screws at ends of trim molding and carefully lift molding out of slot.

**To install:**

1. Mark centers of top cover and trim molding, as in Fig. 87.

**Fig. 87.** Location marks (vertical white lines) at centers of convertible top cover and trim molding above rear hood facilitate re-installation.

2. Press trim molding into slot, starting from center. If necessary, use wooden block to open slot for easier installation. Fig. 88 shows the operation.

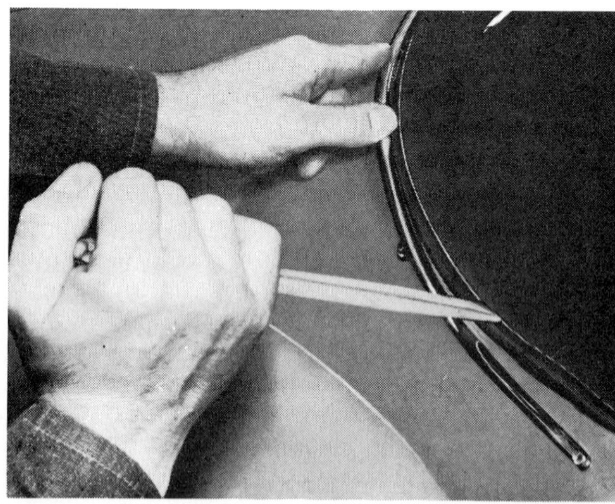



**Fig. 88.** Trim molding is pressed into slot on back of car and it may be necessary to pry slot open slightly. A wooden tool should be used.

3. For correct seating, twist trim molding upward at seams before pressing it into slot, as in Fig. 89.

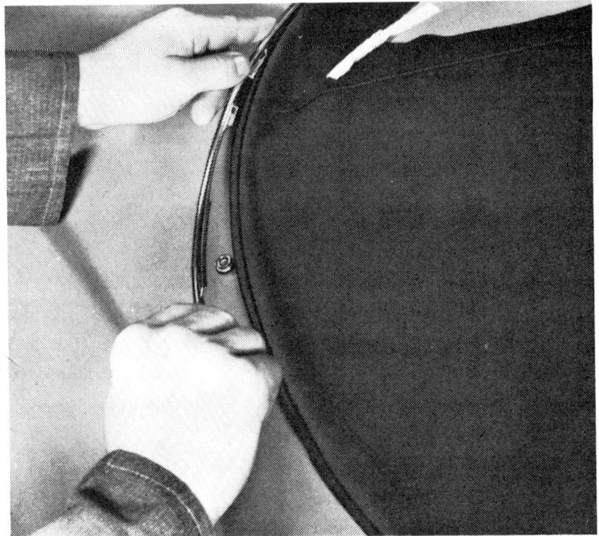

© 1972 VWoA—129

**Fig. 89.** Upward twist at seams will facilitate seating of trim molding.

4. If molding projects too far to one side, use wooden block as in Fig. 90 to move it back into position.

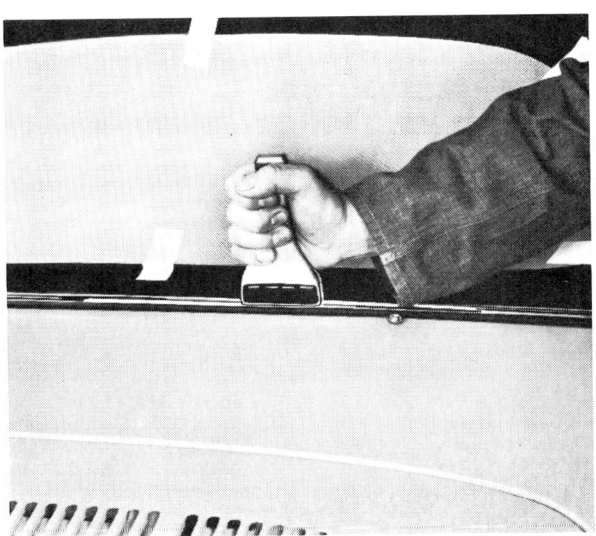

© 1972 VWoA—130

**Fig. 90.** Wooden tool is used to force trim molding into position in slot.

**NOTE —**
Fig. 91 gives pattern for construction of special block.

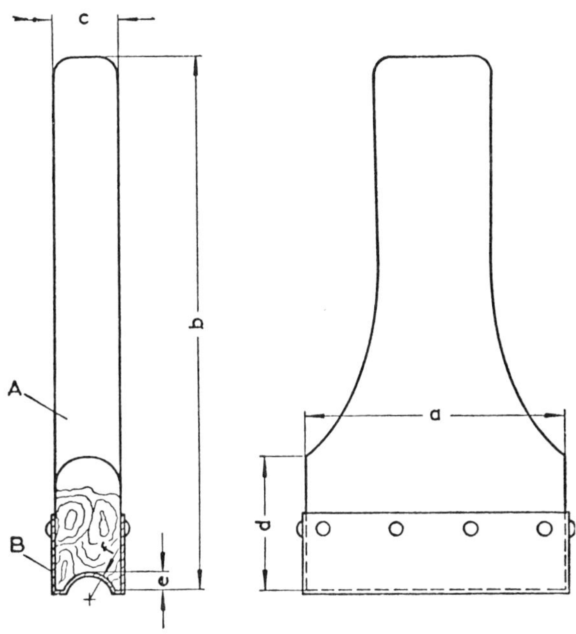


© 1972 VWoA—131

A. Special block
B. Leather cover (approximately 1/32 in. [1 mm] thick)

a = 2 3/4 inches (70 mm)
b = 5 1/2 inches (140 mm)
c = 21/32 inch (17 mm)
d = 1 3/8 inches (35 mm)
e = 3/16 inch (5 mm)
f = 9/32 inch (7 mm)

**Fig. 91.** Pattern for wooden tool used on trim molding is given here. Section labeled A is uncovered wood. Leather covering at B should be from quarter to half inch in height.

5. Tighten Phillips head screw on each end of trim molding, as in Fig. 92.

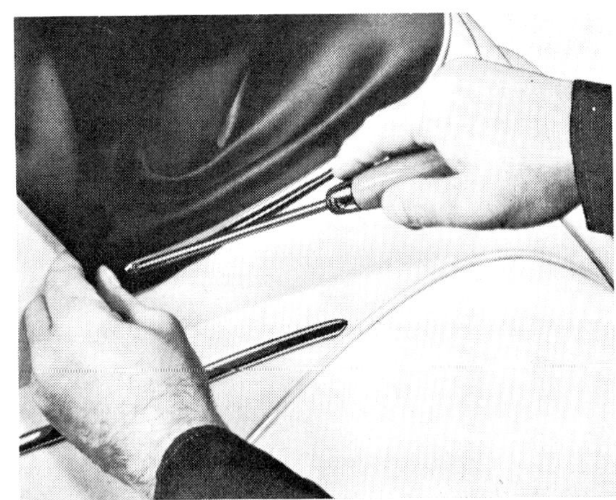

© 1972 VWoA—132

**Fig. 92.** Phillips head screws hold ends of convertible top trim molding.

9

From chassis No. 147 610 910, Karmann Ghia convertibles also are equipped with the modified top cover and tensioning cable. The instructions for adjusting the sedan top also apply to adjustment of the convertible top as well as to the replacement of the rear trim molding on these models.

### 8.3 Adjusting Top Header

If the convertible top is difficult to open or close, or if drafts, water leaks, or fluttering noises come from around the front header, the front part of the top cover needs adjustment.

**To adjust** (four-seater convertible from chassis No. 158 000 005):

1. Loosen lock nuts on hooks (arrow in Fig. 93).

**Fig. 93.** Lock nut (black arrow) allows adjustment of hook holding convertible top at front.

2. Move hooks in or out to adjust fit of header.
3. Retighten hook lock nuts.

**To adjust** (Karmann Ghia convertible):

1. Open top.
2. Remove cap nut (Fig. 94) and take off top lock handle.
3. Remove escutcheon for handle (Fig. 95).
4. Remove 12 Phillips head screws and cover plate from top header (Fig. 96).

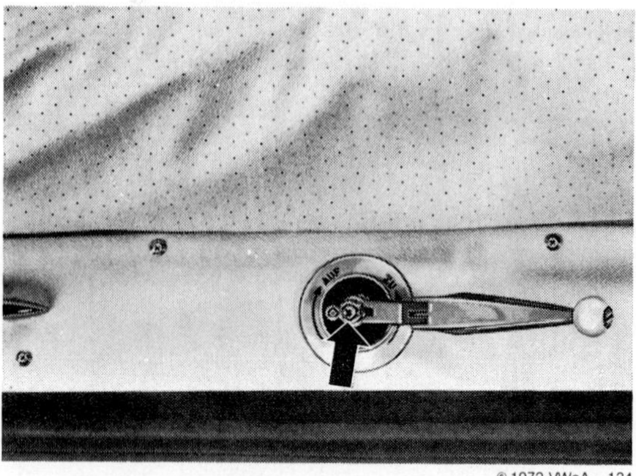



**Fig. 94.** Cap nut (black arrow) secures handle on lock assembly on Karmann Ghia convertible top.

**Fig. 95.** Escutcheon of top lock handle on Karmann Ghia convertible has two Phillips screws (arrows) for fasteners.

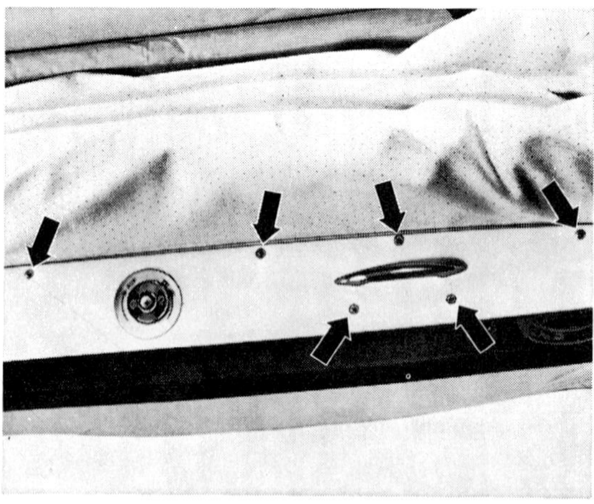



**Fig. 96.** Top header of Karmann Ghia convertible has 12 Phillips head screws. Black arrows point to six of the screws.

5. Remove 4 Phillips head screws from each locking cover (see Fig. 97). Remove both covers from the recesses.

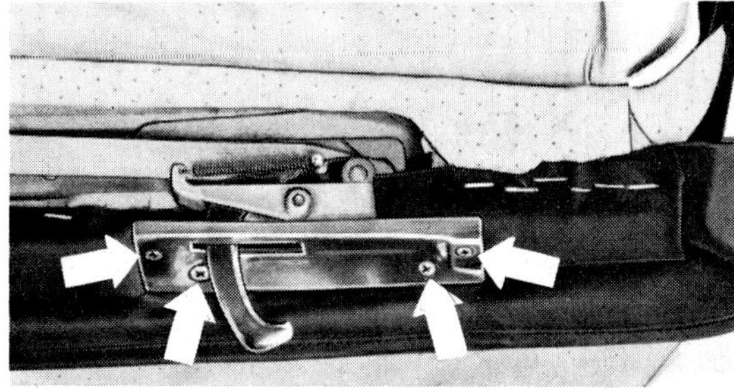
© 1972 VWoA—137

**Fig. 97.** Locking cover for Karmann Ghia convertible top is fastened with 4 Phillips head screws. There are two covers.

6. Tighten 10 screws on header for latching mechanism (Fig. 98).

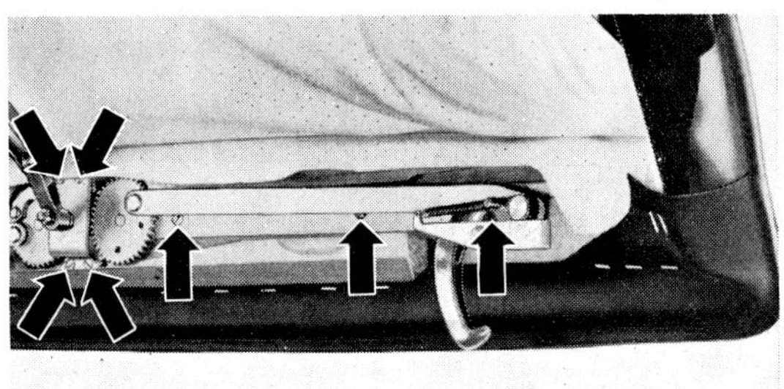
© 1972 VWoA—138

**Fig. 98.** Latching mechanism for Karmann Ghia convertible top is shown here with covers removed. Arrows point to the screws of various sizes used for fasteners.

7. Temporarily attach lock handle and check whether locking hooks engage properly with windshield frame. If not, bend hooks with pliers. Wrap plier jaws with cloth to prevent damage to hooks.

8. Attach cover plate, escutcheon, header cover, and handle for latching mechanism.

**NOTE —**
Make sure that when top is closed knob of folded handle points to right (see Fig. 99).

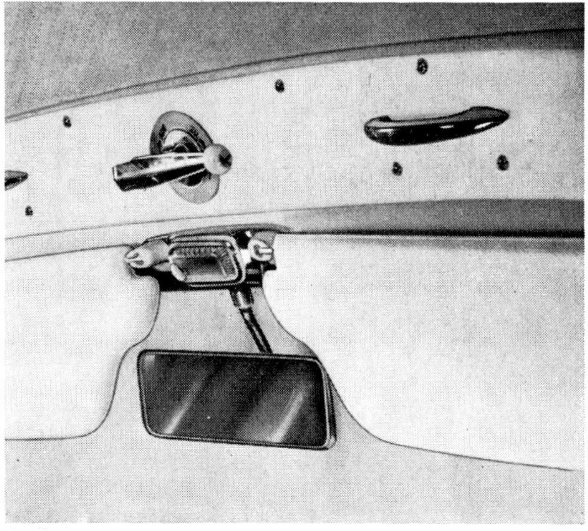
© 1972 VWoA—139

**Fig. 99.** Latching mechanism header on Karmann Ghia convertible has 10 Phillips head screws.

9

# Frame

## 9. GENERAL DESCRIPTION

The frame consists of a number of sheet metal stampings of various shapes welded together around the frame tunnel. As you can see in Fig. 100, the tunnel is a raised tube-like structure running the length of the frame. It is the backbone of the frame, the main supporting member.

The frame platform extends along the tunnel on either side from the front cross member to the frame end plate at the rear. It is made up of two sections of ribbed sheet metal (the floor plates) welded to the tunnel. The frame head is welded to the structure just ahead of the front cross member. The front axle assembly is attached to the frame head. At the rear the frame fork supports the transmission and engine. The cross tube is welded to the frame fork where the fork is joined to the tunnel. The tube carries the rear torsion bars and the spring plate supports of the rear axle assembly.

The flat bottom plate of the tunnel is reinforced with ribs. Guide tubes for the control cables of the clutch, accelerator, parking brake and heater control flaps run inside the tunnel, and the gearshift lever mechanism is also in it. These linkages are illustrated schematically in Fig. 101, which is a color plate appearing at the end of the Frame section. The upper surface of the tunnel has machined locations for the pedal cluster, gearshift lever, parking brake and heater controls. Welded reinforcements behind the mounting bracket for the parking brake lever serve as attaching points for the safety belts.

The runners for the front seats are on the floor plates. On each side a socket for the car jack is spot-welded at the front of the left floor plate. The front cross member, the channel-shaped edges of the floor plates and the frame end plate provide contact surfaces for attachment of the car body.

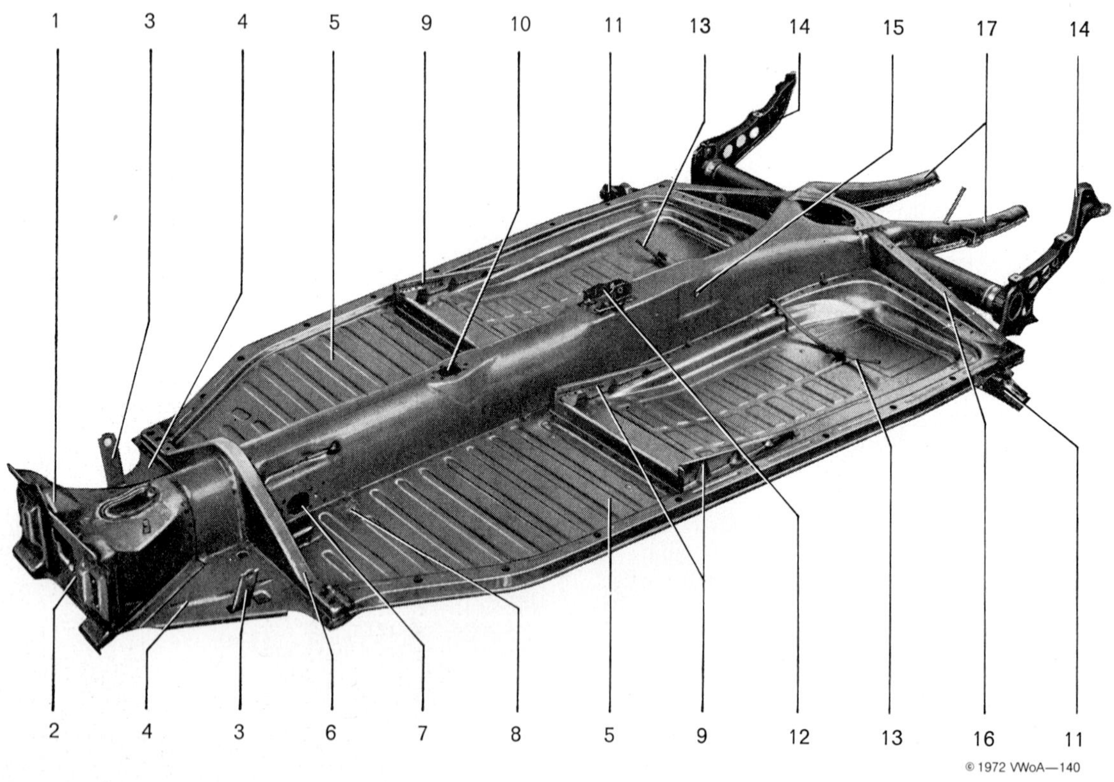


1. Frame head (upper part)
2. Frame head (front plate)
3. Brake hose retainer
4. Frame head (lower part)
5. Floor plate
6. Front cross member
7. Hole for pedal cluster
8. Accelerator pedal attachment
9. Seat runners
10. Hole for gearshift lever
11. Jack sockets
12. Parking brake lever and heater control mounting bracket
13. Guide tube for rear footwell heating control cable
14. Spring plate supports
15. Safety belt attachments
16. Frame end plate
17. Frame fork

**Fig. 100.** Beetle frame consists of sheet metal stampings welded around the frame tunnel.

On cars from August 1, 1966, chassis No. 117 000 001, there is a drainage depression in the bottom of the frame tunnel with a central drain hole in front of the frame fork. A rubber valve seals the hole. Water in the tunnel can drain out through a slot in the valve, but no water can get in.

If leaks occur on an older car, the rubber valve can be service-installed. The procedure is to drill a 9/16 inch (14 mm) diameter hole in the lower part of tunnel in front of the frame fork. Deburr and paint the edge of the hole. With a red-hot welding rod burn a notch in the shoulder of the rubber valve at right angles to the slot to allow water to run into the valve. The rubber valve must be installed with notch facing in the driving direction.

**NOTE —**
Cars from May 3, 1966, chassis No. 116 851 650, have a fabricated pedal cluster which was introduced in conjunction with a frame modification. The floor plate recess near the clutch and brake pedal stop is deeper than on earlier cars. The cast pedal cluster can still be used when frame or floor plates on older cars are replaced, but a special stop plate must be installed. The floor plate recess is too deep for the stop on the brake pedal to make contact with the old stop.

## 10. CONTROL CABLES

The locations of the control cables for the clutch, throttle and heating system are shown in the color plate of the frame (Fig. 101) at the end of this section. These cables run through the frame tunnel.

### 10.1 Removing and Installing Clutch Cable

**To remove:**

1. Raise rear end of car and take off left rear wheel.
2. Disconnect clutch cable from clutch operating lever on transmission case, as in Fig. 102.
3. Withdraw rubber boot from guide tube and pull clutch cable out of boot.
4. Remove the piston push rod in the brake master cylinder.

***WARNING —***
*Do not change setting of piston push rod. Safe functioning of hydraulic brakes depends on this setting. See* ***BRAKES****.*



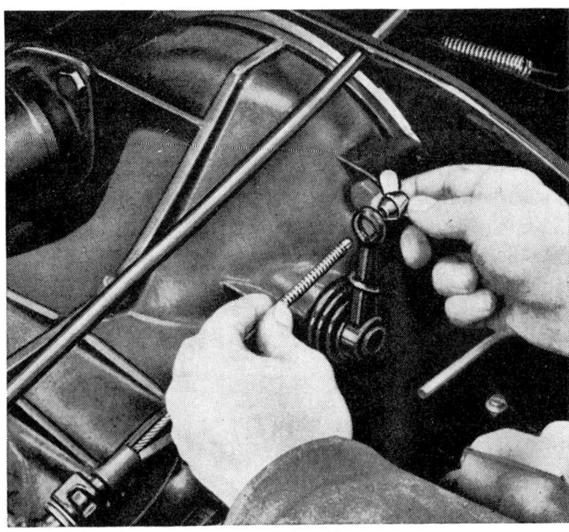



**Fig. 102.** Clutch cable attaches to clutch operating lever with wing nut shown here. Lever pivots on shaft in transmission case.

5. Disconnect accelerator cable.
6. Remove pedal cluster.
7. Pull clutch cable out through hole for pedal cluster in frame tunnel.

**To install:**

1. Grease clutch cable with universal grease.
2. Insert clutch cable. The best method is to thread the cable between the middle and index fingers of your left hand as in Fig. 103 to steady your aim and then push the cable through the pedal cluster into

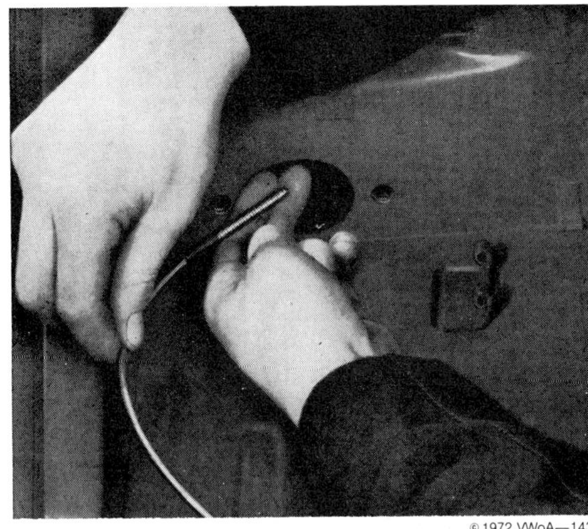



**Fig. 103.** Two fingers of left hand steady clutch cable for threading into guide tube under pedal cluster. See text.

9

the guide tube. Hold the fingers against the opening in the tunnel and keep pushing the cable with your other hand until the cable is well started in the guide tube. Then push the cable all the way through the tunnel, being careful not to twist or kink it.

3. Note position of rubber boot at end of guide tube.
4. Grease clutch cable eye and clutch pedal shaft with universal grease.
5. After you have attached the cable eye to the hook, hold clutch pedal in the position shown in Fig. 104 to keep the cable from falling off the hook. Have a helper keep cable under tension at other end.

**Fig. 104.** Pedal cluster is held in this position to keep clutch cable from falling off hook.

6. Check position of pedal stops. Push rod for brake master cylinder must have clearance of 0.04 inch (1 mm) in the piston (see **BRAKES**).
7. Grease clutch cable adjusting nut with universal grease.
8. Adjust clutch pedal free-play.
9. The clutch cable guide at the end of frame tunnel should sag 1 to 1¹³⁄₁₆ inch (25 to 45 mm). This measurement is shown as B in Fig. 105. Obtain this preload by inserting washers between the bracket on transmission and end piece of guide A.

On vehicles with fully synchronized transmissions too much sag in the cable guide tube can result in stiffness in clutch operation, noise or breakage of the cable. Shortening the guide tube at the rear end will correct this condition. The tube and cable must, of course, be removed for this work.

If the bend is insufficient, you can increase it by inserting washers between guide tube and the case boss on the final drive cover.

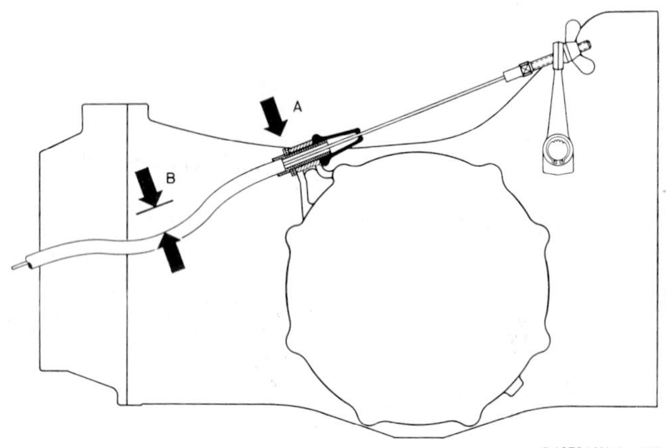




**Fig. 105.** Clutch cable guide should have sag (B) where cable guide leaves frame tunnel. Sag can be obtained by inserting washers at (A) between end of guide and bracket on transmission. See text for correct measurements.

## 10.2 Clutch Operating Lever Spring

This spring is on the transmission case. If it breaks, pry off the broken pieces with screwdriver and pliers. When installing a new spring, apply lubricant to prevent rusting.

## 10.3 Adjustment of Clutch Pedal Free Play

When the clutch is engaged, there should be clearance of 0.04 to 0.08 inch (1 to 2 mm) between the thrust ring of the release bearing and the clutch release plate. Because the transmission is in the way, you cannot make this measurement directly, but you can obtain it indirectly by measuring the clutch pedal free-play. Measured at the clutch pedal, this clearance is 0.4 to 0.8 inch (10 to 20 mm). You can obtain this clearance at the adjusting nut on the cable end.

As the wear on the clutch lining increases, clearance between the release bearing and the release plate diminishes until these two parts come in contact. See **19. Clutch** in **ENGINE**. This contact causes excessive wear and reduces clutch pressure. Slippage and burning of the lining can result.

**To adjust:**

1. Turn adjusting nut on cable end either in or out (Fig. 106) until the clutch pedal free-play is $^{13}/_{32}$ to $^{13}/_{16}$ inch (10 to 20 mm). Make sure that the wing nut lugs engage in grooves in the clutch operating lever.

   **NOTE —**
   Since wing nut rides under tension in a slotted recess, it may be hard to turn. Spray it with penetrating oil.

2. When adjustment is correct, grease thread and wing nut thoroughly.

© 1972 VWoA—146

**Fig. 106.** Wing nut on clutch cable can be turned in or out at the clutch operating lever to adjust free-play in clutch pedal.

## 10.4 Removing and Installing Accelerator Cable

The accelerator cable passes through the frame tunnel and fan housing of the engine in guide tubes. At one end it is attached to the accelerator pedal rod, at the other end to a swivel pin in the throttle valve lever. A plastic hose carries it between tunnel and front engine cover plate.

A spring on the carburetor returns the accelerator cable and closes the throttle when you take your foot off the accelerator pedal.

**To remove cable:**

**NOTE —**
Old cable will be packed with grease. Wipe it with rags in order to avoid getting grease on the upholstery.

1. Disconnect accelerator cable from throttle valve lever at carburetor.
2. Detach accelerator cable from connecting lever.
3. Pull accelerator cable forward through tube.

To help you visualize installation of cable see Fig. 107.

© 1972 VWoA—148

**Fig. 107.** Tubing for accelerator cable has rubber boot where tube leaves frame and passes over transmission case. Numbered parts shown here are rubber boot (1); accelerator tubing (2); and clutch cable (3).

**To install:**

1. Grease accelerator cable liberally with water-repellent universal grease.
2. Make sure that cable lies straight between guide tubes.
3. Make sure that rubber boot and plastic hose are correctly seated to keep water out of guide tubes.

   **NOTE —**
   You may have to put plastic tube back on the fan housing guide tube to allow cable to enter fan housing without binding.

4. Take extra care when attaching accelerator cable to throttle valve lever. Too much tension at full throttle might break the cable. Open throttle valve to allow clearance of about 0.04 inch (1 mm) between throttle lever and stop at carburetor body. Fully depress accelerator pedal and connect cable to throttle valve.

## 10.5 Removing and Installing Heater Flap Cable

This cable is in the shape of a Y with the arms joined at the control lever and the longer arm going to the right side. The cable must be replaced as a unit.

**To remove:**

1. Loosen terminal (Fig. 108).

© 1972 VWoA—151

**Fig. 108.** Heater flap cable is fastened below operating lever with clamping device indicated by arrow.

**NOTE** —
Be careful not to bend or break the heater flap cables while loosening the clamp.

2. Pull cable ends out of terminal.
3. Clean cable of corrosion to prevent damage to sealing plugs. Pull sealing plugs out of guide tube and slide them over the cables.
4. Remove parking brake cover and unscrew nut from right-hand heating operating lever, as in Fig. 109. Remove cable.

**NOTE** —
Old cable will be packed with grease. Handle with rags in order to avoid getting grease on the upholstery.

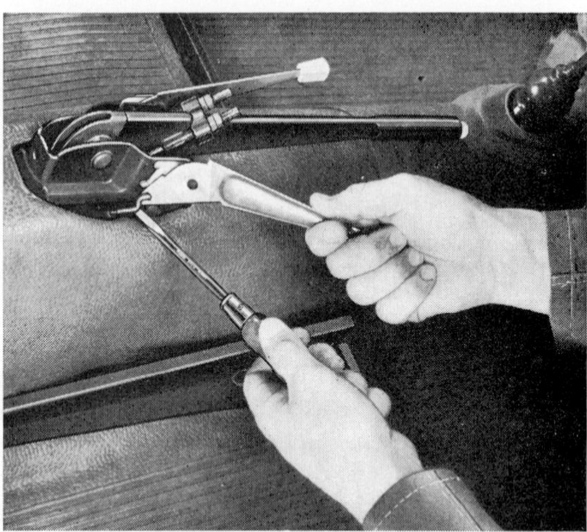

© 1972 VWoA—152

**Fig. 109.** Operating lever for heating system comes off mounting on parking brake assembly after nut has been removed. Use screwdriver to disengage cable end from lever.

**To install:**

1. Check all parts and replace if worn or damaged. Coat cables liberally with water repellent grease.
2. Push cables into tubes.
3. Hook lever into hook-shaped end of cable and attach lever to mounting with friction disks.
4. Seal the guide tubes carefully with plugs, as shown in Fig. 110.

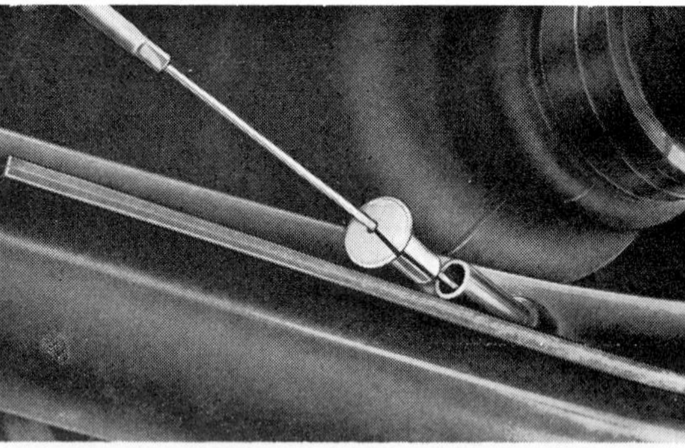

© 1972 VWoA—153

**Fig. 110.** Plug on cable seals heating system cable guide tube.

5. Clamp cables to heater flaps, making sure that flaps open and close fully. Work them a few times to test installation.

**NOTE** —
Loosening or tightening nut on lever mounting decreases or increases effort required to move lever.

## 10.6 Cables for Rear Footwell Heating

This cable is Y-shaped with the arms joined at the control lever. The cable must be replaced as a unit.

**To remove cable:**

1. Remove kick plates.
2. Loosen each clamp as in Fig. 111.

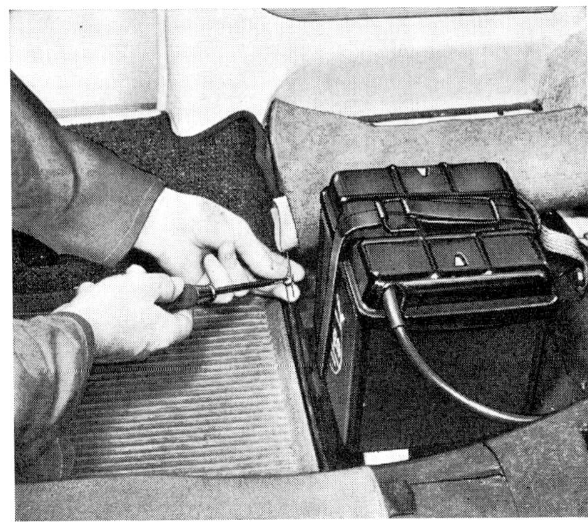

© 1972 VWoA—154

**Fig. 111.** Clamps hold cables for rear footwell heating.

3. Pull cable ends out of clamp.
4. Take off parking brake lever cover and remove nut from left heater lever.
5. Take lever and friction disks off mounting, disconnect cables and pull them out upward as in Fig. 112.

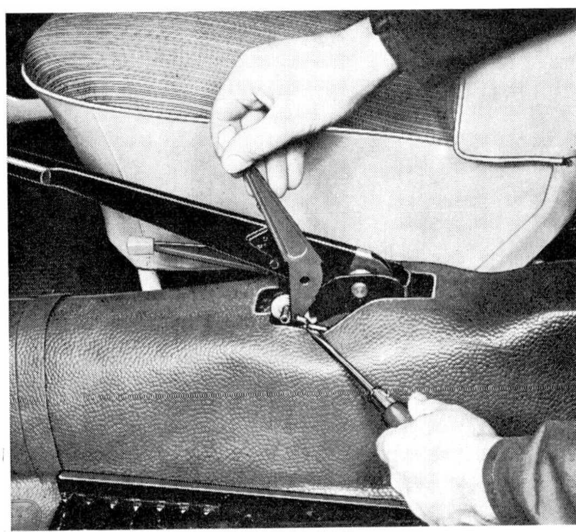

© 1972 VWoA—155

**Fig. 112.** Left heater lever on parking brake mounting controls flaps for rear footwell heating outlets.

**To install:**

1. Check all parts and replace if worn. Coat cable lightly with universal grease.
2. Push cable into guide tubes.

**NOTE —**
Longer arm of cable goes in lower guide tube.

3. Hook lever into hook-shaped end of cables and attach lever to mounting with friction washers.
4. Clamp cable to flaps, making sure that flaps open and close fully. Work flaps several times to test operation.

**NOTE —**
Loosening or tightening the nut decreases or increases the effort required to move the levers.

5. Install kick boards. See that rubber rings make correct contact with warm air outlets. See Fig. 113.

© 1972 VWoA—156

**Fig. 113.** Rubber rings on the kick boards in the rear footwell should make good contact with the warm air outlets.

9

## 10.7 Rear Footwell Heater Flaps

**To remove flaps:**

1. Remove kick boards.
2. Loosen clamps at cable ends and pull flaps off pivots in the warm air outlet pipe. Fig. 114 shows the attachment.

© 1972 VWoA—157

**Fig. 114.** Flaps to control flow from warm air outlets are installed in duct on pivots.

**To install:**

1. Check that spring clips are tight in flaps and replace if necessary.
2. Press flap on pivot. Move back and forth to make sure that spring clip is gripping pivot and that short cable can move freely.
3. Connect cable to flap (Fig. 115). Move lever back and forth a few times to check functioning. If necessary, correct cable length after loosening clamp.
4. Install kick boards. Make sure that rubber rings are in good contact with warm air outlets.

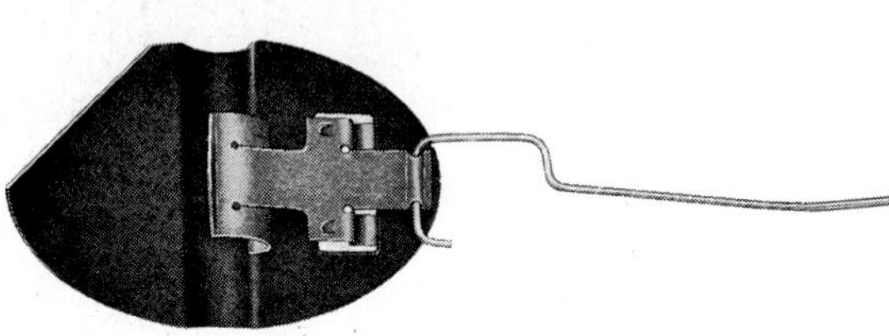

© 1972 VWoA—158

**Fig. 115.** Cable connection for pivoted flap in warm air outlet for back seat passengers is shown here.

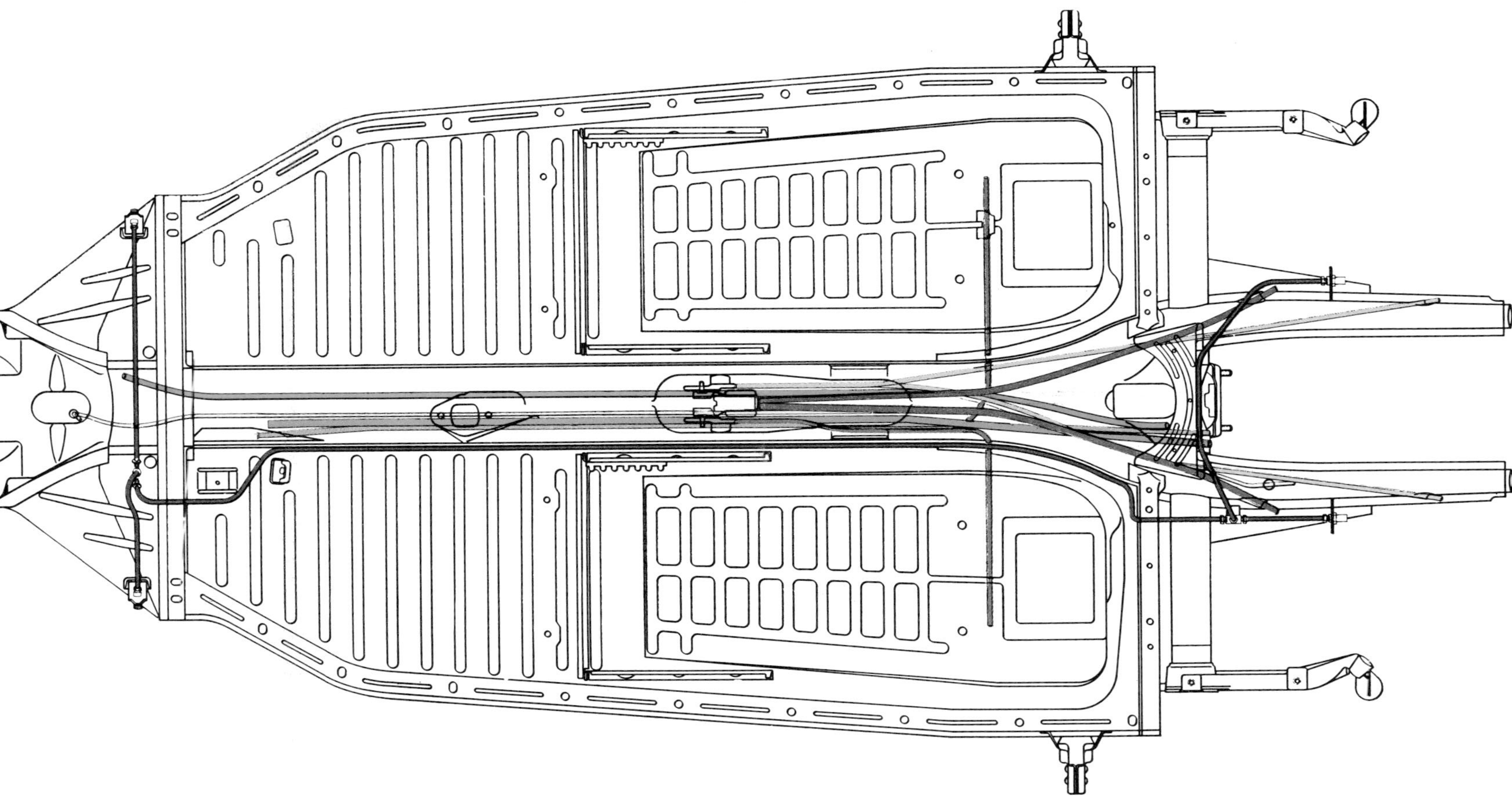


**Fig. 101. (Body and Frame)** Lines and cables run through the Beetle frame at the locations charted on this diagram.

# ELECTRICAL SYSTEM

## Contents


1. **Wiring Diagrams** . . . . . . . . . . 5

2. **General Description** . . . . . . . . . . 6
   - 2.1 The System . . . . . . . . . . 6
   - 2.2 Battery . . . . . . . . . . 6
   - 2.3 Starter Motor . . . . . . . . . . 6
   - 2.4 Generator . . . . . . . . . . 7
   - 2.5 Ignition System . . . . . . . . . . 7
   - 2.6 Lights . . . . . . . . . . 7
   - 2.7 Cables and Connections . . . . . . . . . . 8
   - 2.8 Windshield Wipers and Washers . . . . . . 8
   - 2.9 Instruments . . . . . . . . . . 8

3. **Battery** . . . . . . . . . . 8
   - Cell Voltage . . . . . . . . . . 8
   - Discharging . . . . . . . . . . 8
   - Charging . . . . . . . . . . 8
   - 3.1 Care of the Battery . . . . . . . . . . 9
     - Specific Gravity Testing . . . . . . . . . . 9
     - Electrolyte Level . . . . . . . . . . 9
     - Voltage Testing . . . . . . . . . . 9
     - Service Life . . . . . . . . . . 10
   - 3.2 Removing and Installing Batteries . . . . . 10
   - 3.3 Quick-charging . . . . . . . . . . 10
   - 3.4 Normal Current Charging . . . . . . . . . . 11
   - 3.5 Cold Weather Operation . . . . . . . . . . 11
   - 3.6 Storing the Battery . . . . . . . . . . 11

4. **Starter Motor** . . . . . . . . . . 12
   - 4.1 Types of Starter Motors . . . . . . . . . . 12
   - 4.2 Maintenance . . . . . . . . . . 14
   - 4.3 Starter Motor Troubleshooting . . . . . . . 14
   - 4.4 Removing and Installing Starter Motor . . 15
   - 4.5 Removing and Installing Solenoid . . . . . 15
   - 4.6 Checking Brushes and Commutator (Bosch starter) . . . . . . . . . . 16
   - 4.7 Testing Starter (installed) . . . . . . . . . . 17
   - 4.8 Bench-testing Starter . . . . . . . . . . 17

5. **Generator** . . . . . . . . . . 19
   - Connections . . . . . . . . . . 20
   - Warning Light . . . . . . . . . . 20
   - Maintenance . . . . . . . . . . 20
   - 5.1 Specifications . . . . . . . . . . 20
   - 5.2 Testing Generator and Regulator . . . . . 22
     - Testing No-load Voltage . . . . . . . . . . 22
     - Testing Charging Current . . . . . . . . . . 22
     - Testing Current Regulator . . . . . . . . . . 22
     - Testing Generator Without Regulator . . . 23
   - 5.3 Removing and Installing Regulator . . . . 23
   - 5.4 Checking Brushes and Commutator . . . . 24
   - 5.5 Removing and Installing Brushes . . . . . 24
   - 5.6 Removing and Installing Generator (engine in place) . . . . . . . . . . 24
   - 5.7 Generator Warning Light . . . . . . . . . . 25
   - 5.8 Generator Troubleshooting . . . . . . . . . . 25

6. **Lighting System (sedan and convertible)** . . . . 26
   - 6.1 Replacing Sealed Beam Unit and Parking Light Bulb (1966) . . . . . . . . . . 26
   - 6.2 Adjusting Sealed Beam Headlights . . . . 28

6.3 Aiming the Headlights . . . 28
6.4 Removing and Installing Front Turn Signal 29
6.5 Replacing License Plate Light . . . 29
6.6 Rear Lights . . . 30
6.7 Interior Light . . . 31
6.8 Replacing Bulbs for Warning and Instrument Lights . . . 32
6.9 Turn Signal System . . . 32
6.10 Emergency Flasher System . . . 33
6.11 Replacing Turn Signal Flasher Relay . . . 34
6.12 Brake Light Switch . . . 34
6.13 Oil Pressure Switch . . . 35
Testing Oil Pressure Switch . . . 36

**7. Lighting System (Karmann Ghia models)** . . . 36
7.1 Sealed Beam Headlights . . . 36
7.2 Rear Lights . . . 37
7.3 License Plate Lights . . . 37
7.4 Interior Light . . . 38

**8. Windshield Wipers** . . . 39
8.1 Wiper Motor . . . 39
8.2 Precautions . . . 40
8.3 Makes of Motor . . . 41
8.4 Troubleshooting and Maintenance . . . 41
8.5 Removing and Installing Wiper Motor and Linkage Assembly . . . 41
8.6 Removing and Installing Motor . . . 42
8.7 Replacing Wiper Shafts . . . 42
8.8 Replacing the Carbon Brushes . . . 43
8.9 Removing and Installing Wiper Switch . . 43
8.10 Wiper Blades . . . 43
8.11 Removing and Installing Wiper Blades . . 44
8.12 Troubleshooting Windshield Wiping System . . . 44
8.13 Replacing Blade Fillers . . . 46
8.14 Windshield Washing System . . . 47

**9. Horn** . . . 48
Maintenance . . . 48

**10. Replacing Fuses** . . . 49

**11. Rear Window Defogger** . . . 49

**12. Ignition/Starter Switch** . . . 50

**13. Karmann Ghia Accessories** . . . 51
13.1 Horns . . . 51
Maintenance . . . 51
Removal and Installation . . . 51
13.2 Turn Signal System . . . 52

**14. Instruments (sedan and convertible)** . . . 53
14.1 Speedometer . . . 53
Removing and Installing Speedometer . . 53
Speedometer with Fuel Gauge . . . 54
Operation of Electric Fuel Gauge . . . 54
Testing Electric Fuel Gauge . . . 54
Removing and Installing Speedometer Cable . . . 55
14.2 Mechanical Fuel Gauge (VW 1300 only) . 55
Removing and Installing Sending Unit . . 56
Removing, Installing and Adjusting Mechanical Fuel Gauge . . . 56
14.3 Karmann Ghia Instruments . . . 57
Clock . . . 57
Speedometer . . . 57

**15. Electrical System Technical Data** . . . 58

**TABLES**

a. Electrical Terminal Locations . . . 5
b. Starter Types . . . 12
c. Starter Motor Troubleshooting . . . 14
d. Starter Test Data . . . 18
e. Solenoid Switch Test Data . . . 18
f. Generator Performance Specifications . . . 20
g. Generator Troubleshooting . . . 26
h. Windshield Wiper Motor Troubleshooting . . . 41
i. Windshield Wiping System Troubleshooting Chart . . . 45

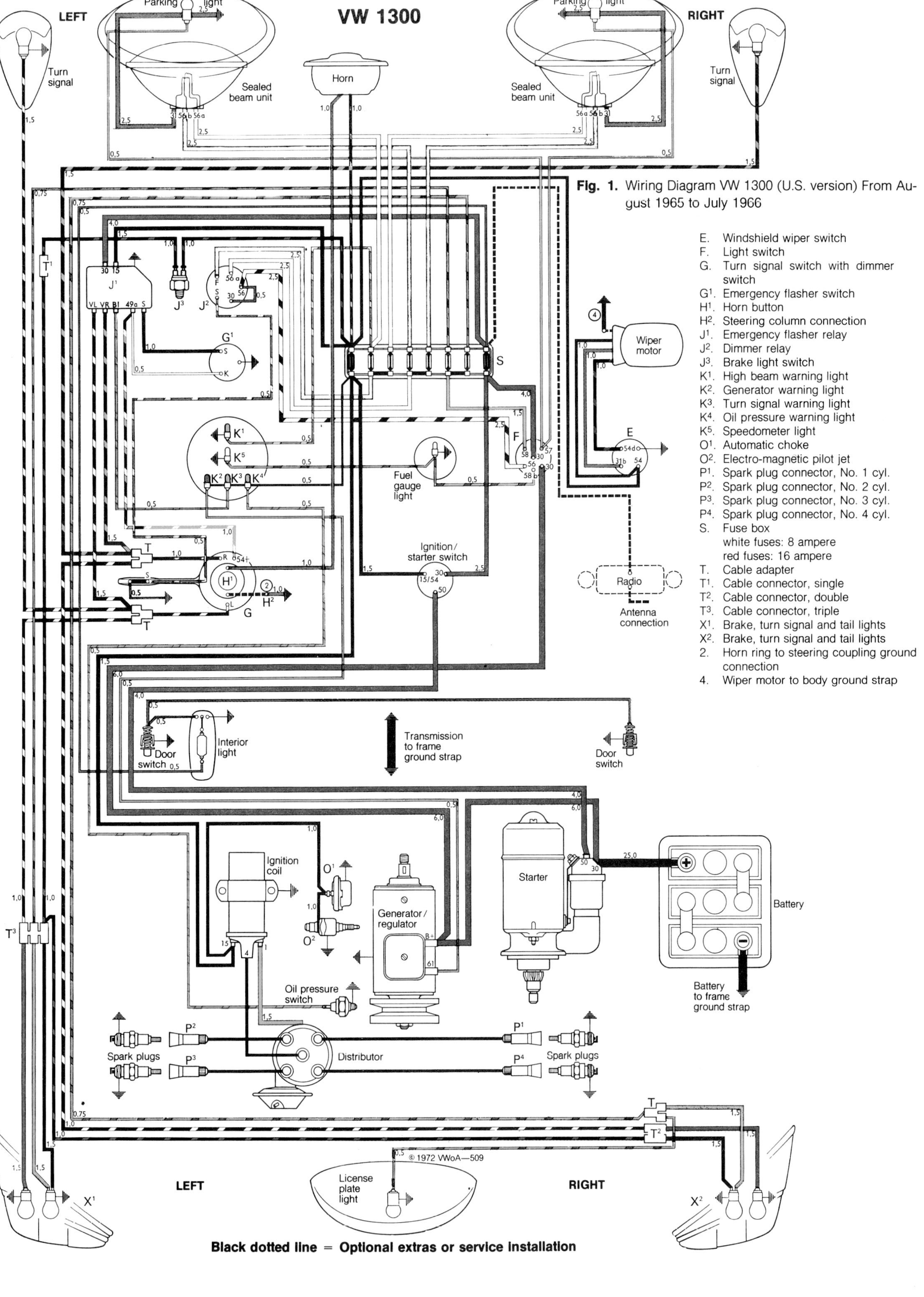


**Fig. 1.** Wiring Diagram VW 1300 (U.S. version) From August 1965 to July 1966

E. Windshield wiper switch
F. Light switch
G. Turn signal switch with dimmer switch
G1. Emergency flasher switch
H1. Horn button
H2. Steering column connection
J1. Emergency flasher relay
J2. Dimmer relay
J3. Brake light switch
K1. High beam warning light
K2. Generator warning light
K3. Turn signal warning light
K4. Oil pressure warning light
K5. Speedometer light
O1. Automatic choke
O2. Electro-magnetic pilot jet
P1. Spark plug connector, No. 1 cyl.
P2. Spark plug connector, No. 2 cyl.
P3. Spark plug connector, No. 3 cyl.
P4. Spark plug connector, No. 4 cyl.
S. Fuse box
white fuses: 8 ampere
red fuses: 16 ampere
T. Cable adapter
T1. Cable connector, single
T2. Cable connector, double
T3. Cable connector, triple
X1. Brake, turn signal and tail lights
X2. Brake, turn signal and tail lights
2. Horn ring to steering coupling ground connection
4. Wiper motor to body ground strap

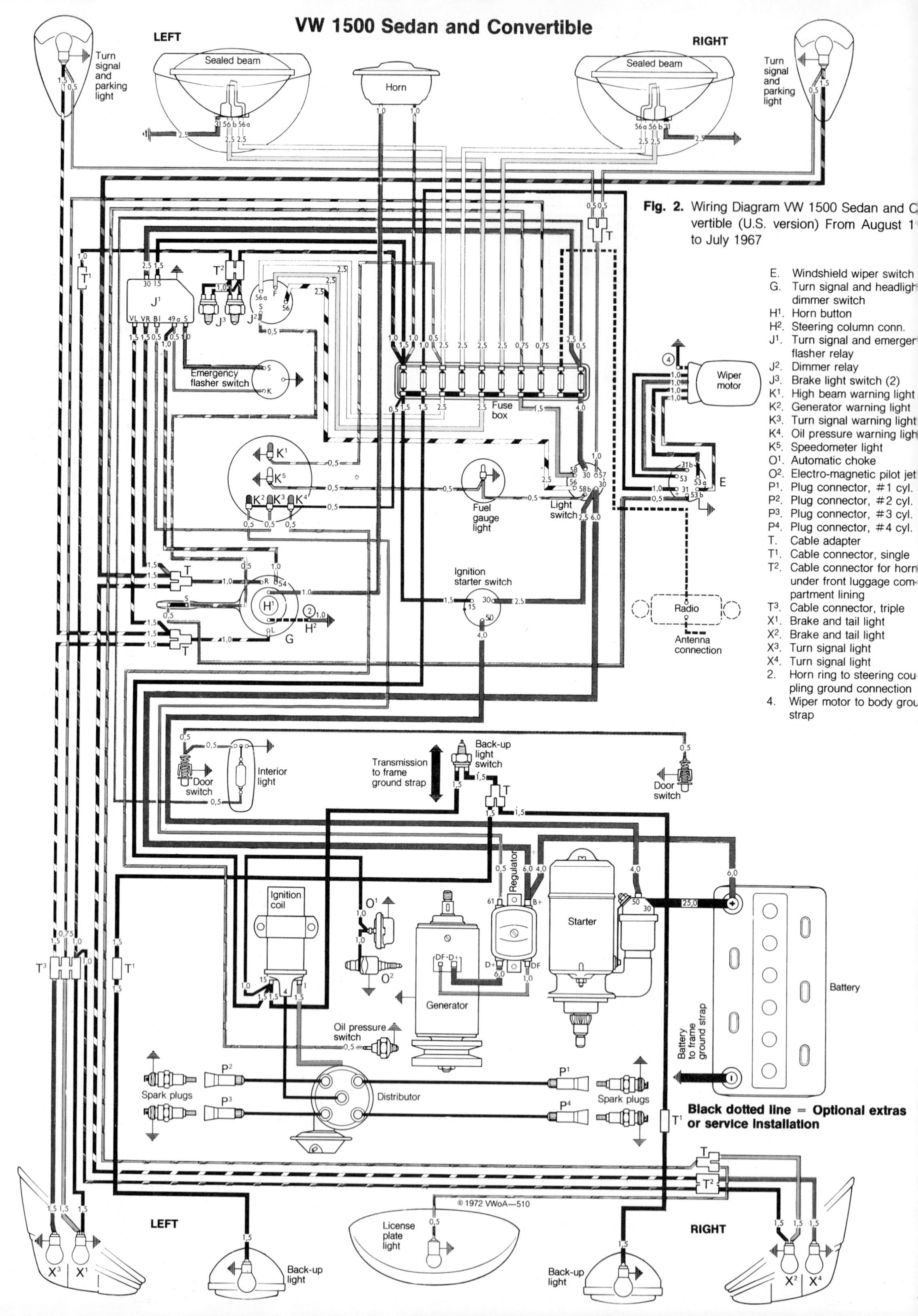


**Fig. 2.** Wiring Diagram VW 1500 Sedan and C vertible (U.S. version) From August 1 to July 1967

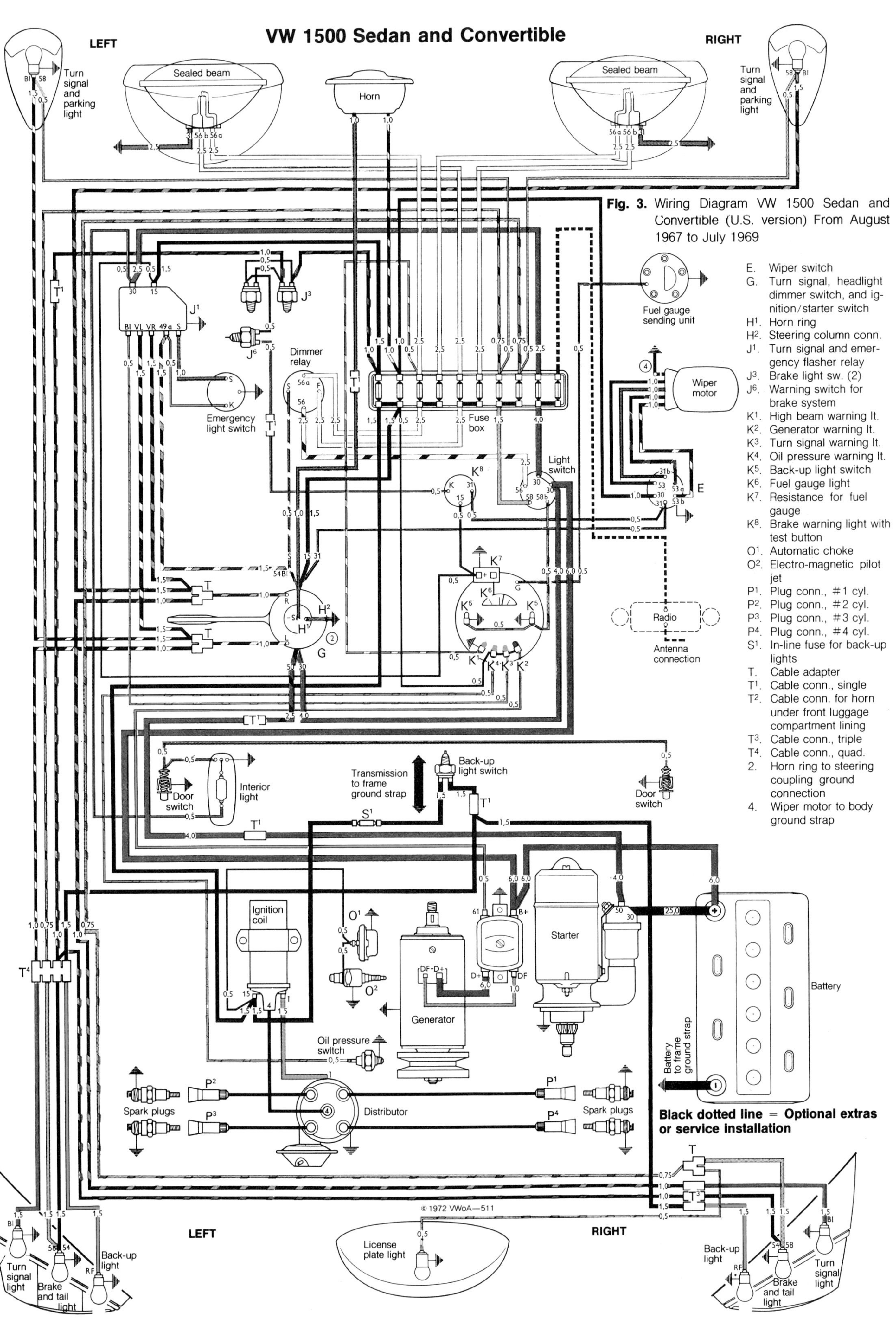


**Fig. 3.** Wiring Diagram VW 1500 Sedan and Convertible (U.S. version) From August 1967 to July 1969

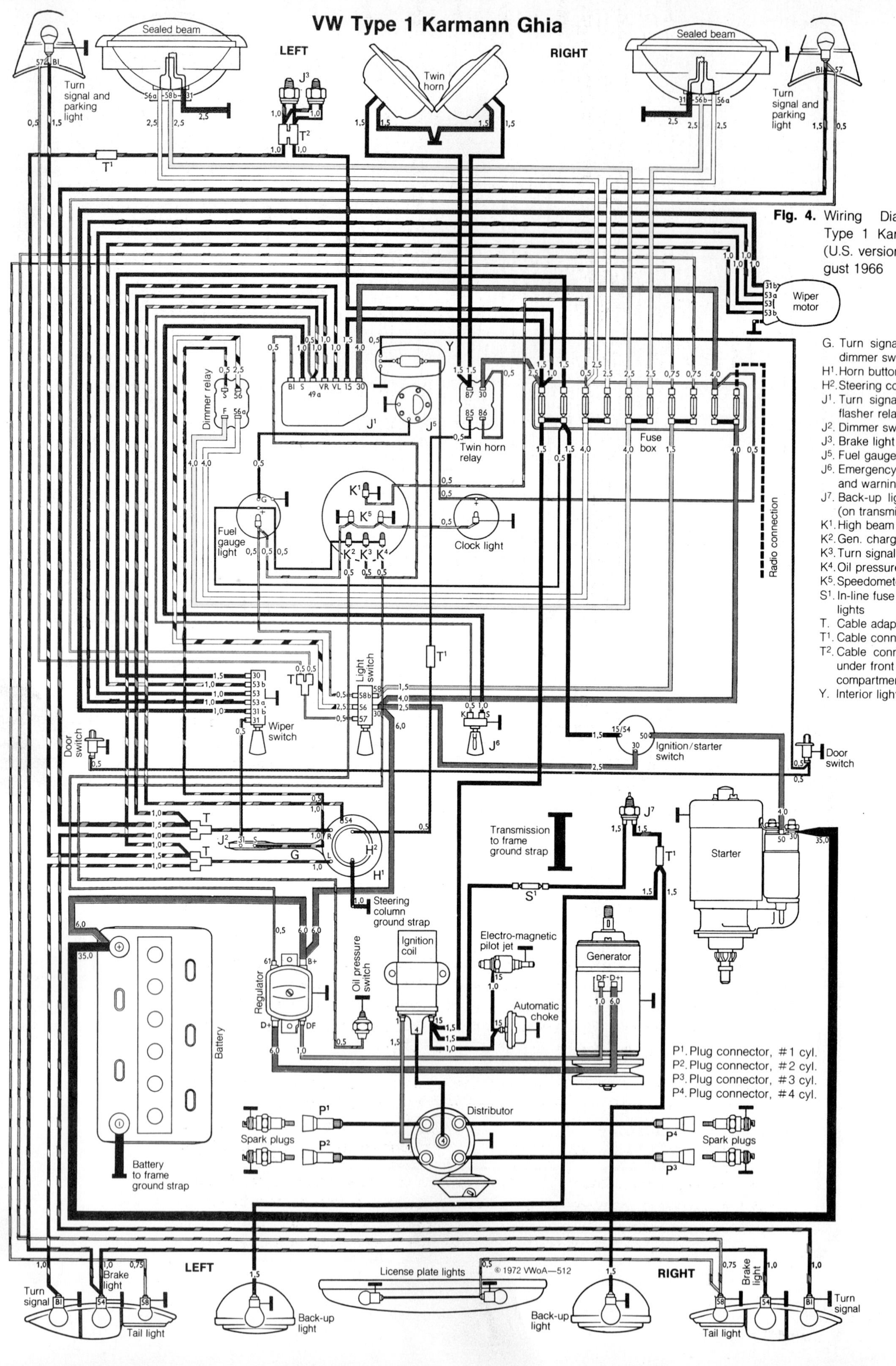


**Fig. 4.** Wiring Diagram Type 1 Karmann (U.S. version) Fro gust 1966

# Electrical System

The electrical system of the cars covered in this Manual includes many circuits with some fairly complex components. In the next few pages we explain simple but important facts about electric current and circuits. You may already be familiar with this material. If not, we hope that you will find this introduction useful when you are troubleshooting the electrical system in your car. Sometimes a little knowledge of the basic law relating to the voltage, current and resistance in a circuit can help to isolate a problem quickly.

The flow of electric current is similar in many respects to the flow of water in pipes, and it is useful to keep these similarities in mind when trying to find a short circuit. Both electric current and water need insulated pathways: the wire is the pathway for electric current and the pipe for water. Just as water flows from a point of higher pressure to a point of lower pressure, electric current has points of higher voltage and lower voltage. The size of the pipe affects water flow, and the size of a cable (as well as its material) affects electric current. A small electric cable offers more resistance than a large one. For both water and electric current the amount of flow (current) depends on pressure (voltage) and frictional drag (resistance).

A leak in a pipe drains off water from the main line, and a large break can divert the flow altogether. In the same way, a short circuit drains or diverts current away from the circuit components the circuit is supposed to operate.

Science describes current as a directed flow of negatively charged particles called electrons. The unit of measurement is the ampere (or amp), measured with an instrument called the ammeter. An ammeter is always connected into a circuit in series. That is, the instrument is connected into the circuit between the source of current and the load. The symbol for current is the capital letter I.

Voltage can be thought of as the electrical pressure that causes an electric current to flow when an insulated pathway is open to the circuit. The volt, measured with a voltmeter, is the unit of voltage. The voltmeter is always connected in parallel. That is, the voltmeter is connected across load. Symbol for voltage is capital letter E.

The resistance of an electric circuit depends on the kinds and amounts of materials in the circuit and their temperatures. The resistance is directly proportional to the length of a conductor and inversely proportional to its diameter. That is, a long cable offers more resistance than a short cable does, but a thick cable offers less than a thin one. The unit of resistance is the ohm. The instrument for measuring resistance is the ohmmeter, which has its own source of voltage. The resistor to be measured is removed from the circuit and the ohmmeter then is applied directly across it. The symbol for ohm is the Greek letter omega (Ω), but the capital letter R stands for the resistance of a circuit or component in ohms.

A simple mathematical formula ties the three fundamental properties of electric circuits together:

$$E = IR$$

The equation says that voltage (given in volts) equals the amount of current (given in amps) multiplied by the resistance (given in ohms).

We can manipulate the three terms of this equation, which is known as Ohm's law, to get two other equations:

$$I = \frac{E}{R} \qquad R = \frac{E}{I}$$

The first says that current equals the voltage divided by the resistance. The second says that the resistance equals the voltage divided by the current. With these three relationships, it is possible to analyze any direct current circuit to the extent that will be required for repair of the electrical system of a car.

For example, if the design of a circuit calls for the use of an 8-amp fuse to guard against overload in a 12-volt system, we can plug numbers into third equation to get:

$$R = \frac{12}{8} = 1.5$$

This result says that in this particular circuit we need resistance totaling 1.5 ohms. If the voltage remains constant and a short circuit somewhere cuts the resistance below 1.5 ohms, the rise in current will blow the fuse. The circuit was designed to carry only 8 amps of current, and the fuse was installed to protect the circuit components against any surge of current above 8 amps.

Electron flow from the storage battery of a car is, as we have said, in one direction only, from the negative pole of the battery. (The car body is the general conductor in the circuit.) Battery current is called direct current, as opposed to alternating current, which continually reverses its direction of flow.

In a series circuit the current is the same at every point in the circuit. A parallel circuit opens alternative paths to current flow, and the flow will be greatest in the branch with the lowest resistance. The total voltage of batteries connected in series is the sum of all the separate voltages, but the total voltage of batteries in parallel is only the lowest of the individual voltages.

Magnetic fields are associated with current flow, and it is such magnetic fields that cause the generator and the ignition system of your Volkswagen to work.

***CAUTION*** ―

*Before starting work on the electrical system of your car, always disconnect the battery at the negative (ground) terminal and keep it disconnected until you need power to test the repair. Otherwise, you are inviting short circuits that could ruin expensive equipment. When the engine is running, make sure that the generator and the voltage regulator are connected to the electrical system.*

## 1. WIRING DIAGRAMS

Appearing after the contents pages of this section are wiring diagrams (Figs. 1-4) that give schematic views of the main components and circuits of the VW electrical systems covered in this Manual. In the wiring diagrams, components are shown in outline and in approximately the positions they occupy relative to each other in the cars. The colors of the cables in the diagrams are the same as the colors of the corresponding cables in the cars. By comparing the component outlines and the cable colors of the diagrams with the actual parts and cables in the car you should be able to trace out any circuit. Note, however, that some differences exist in the electrical systems of the different model years and engines, and make sure you are following the right diagram for your car.

In line with European practice, the diagrams show terminal or connector numbers. These numbers correspond with numbers you will find on the actual parts. On such components as switches and relays you will find the identifying numbers at the connectors or close to them. The diagrams also have index numbers in smaller type along the wiring runs. These numbers indicate the gauge of the particular cables in millimeters squared.

**Table a** is a list of some of the numbers and the locations of the terminals that you will deal with frequently when working on the VW electrical systems.

### Table a. Important Terminal Locations

| Terminal No. | Location |
|---|---|
| B+ | on regulator, input from ignition switch |
| B 1 | on turn signal bulbs (4 locations) and front parking lights |
| D+ | on relay and generator |
| DF | on relay and generator |
| 1 | on coil, output to primary distributor lead |
| 4 | on coil, high tension output and on distributor high tension lead |
| 15 | hot lead, ignition switch controlled |
| 30 | hot lead, directly from battery |
| 31 | ground (general designation) |
| 31 b | ground, through switch, windshield wiper switch and motor |
| 50 | on both terminals of starter solenoid—ignition starter switch |
| 54 | on brake light bulbs, steering ignition switch and windshield wiper switch |
| 53 | windshield wiper switch and motor |
| 56 | light switch and dimmer relay |
| 56 a | dimmer relay, headlight low beam |
| 56 b | headlight high beam |
| 58 | on tail light bulbs, light switch and front parking lights |
| 58 b | light switch |
| 85,86,87 | twin horn relay |

Two versions of the fuse box are found in the cars covered in this Manual. Fig. 5 shows the locations of the various fuses in both versions. Note that over the years 1966-69 both 8-amp and 16-amp fuses were used.

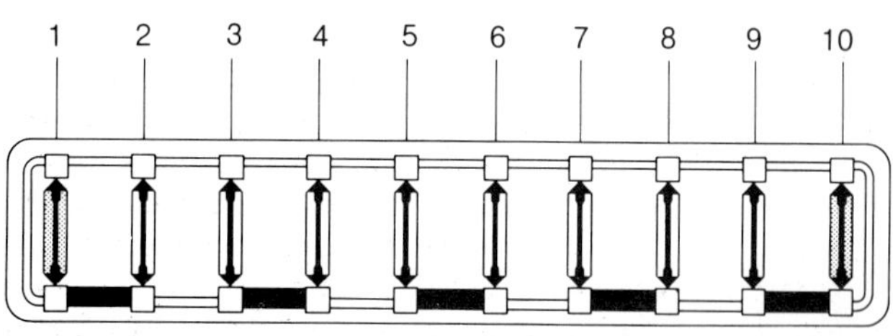


1. Horn; turn signals; brake light
2. Windshield wipers
3. High beam warning light; high beam, left
4. High beam, right
5. Low beam, left
6. Low beam, right
7. Parking light, left; tail light, right; license plate light
8. Parking light, right; tail light, left
9. Radio
10. Interior light; emergency flasher lights

**Fig. 5a.** Fuse locations are shown for 1966 and 1967 cars. The fuse at each end is 16 amps. All others are 8 amps.

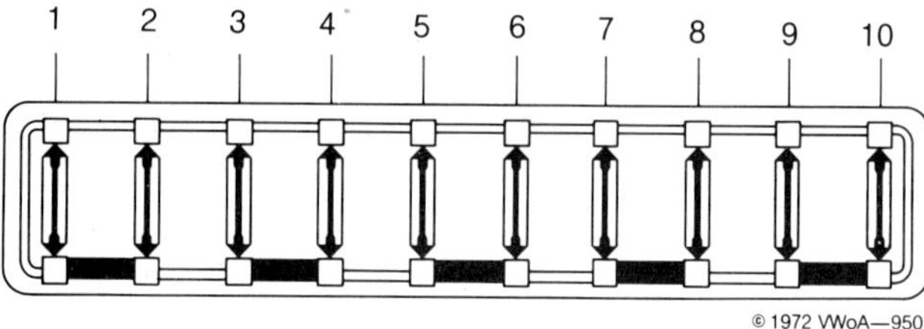


1. Turn signals; brake light; warning lights for brake operation and Automatic Stick Shift
2. Horn; windshield wipers
3. High beam warning light; high beam, left
4. High beam, right
5. Low beam, left
6. Low beam, right
7. Parking light, left; tail light, left
8. License plate light; parking light, right; tail light, right
9. Interior light; emergency flasher lights
10. Open for subsequent installation of electrical accessories

**Fig. 5b.** Fuse locations are shown for 1968 and later cars. All fuses are 8 amps.

## 2. GENERAL DESCRIPTION

The components of the VW electrical system are discussed in detail in later pages of this section of the Manual, but a brief general description of the main units (Fig. 6) is in order here to clarify the wiring diagrams and introduce the troubleshooting charts on later pages. For explanations of how the various components work and for repair and replacement procedures, see the detailed discussions under specific headings.

### 2.1 The System

The basic rating of the VW electrical system is either 6 or 12 volts, depending on the car model and year of manufacture. From the 1967 model on all cars operate on the 12-volt system. A label glued to the door hinge post on the driver's side identifies the car with the 12-volt system.

### 2.2 Battery

VW batteries are of the lead-acid type. The 6-volt battery consists of three cells and has a capacity of 66 ampere hours (Ah). This rating means that at a temperature of 68 degrees F (20 degrees C) the battery can produce a current flow of 3.3 amps for 20 hours before it is discharged. The 12-volt battery is composed of six cells and is rated at 36 Ah. On the cars covered in this Manual, except for the Karmann Ghia, the battery is installed under the rear seat, on the right-hand side of the frame. The Karmann Ghias have the battery in the engine compartment, on the left side.

The function of the battery is, first, to operate the starter motor and, second, when the engine is running to receive electrical energy that converts back to electrical energy. The battery balances the electrical system.

The negative pole of the battery is grounded.

### 2.3 Starter Motor

The VW starter motor is series-wound and has an overrunning clutch. Depending on the make of starter motor and year of car, the starter produces either 0.5 or 0.7 horsepower. (See **Table b.**) The starter/ignition switch controls the starter motor. When you turn the ignition key, you are actuating a solenoid switch, which engages the pinion with the ring gear on the flywheel and connects the starter motor to the battery.

## 2.4 Generator

The generator is the main source of electrical energy for the car. When the engine is running, the generator supplies direct current to the battery and through the battery to all the equipment of the electrical system. A cut-out relay and voltage regulator control generator out-put. The relay connects the generator to the electrical system only when a certain engine speed (cut-in speed) has been reached and generator voltage has risen above battery voltage. When generator voltage drops below battery voltage, the relay contacts open to prevent the battery from discharging through the generator. The voltage regulator keeps generator output constant and thereby prevents overloading of the electrical system. A red light on the speedometer face warns that generator voltage is less than battery voltage. The light should go out when engine is up to cut-in speed.

## 2.5 Ignition System

Apart from the starter motor circuit, VW treats the ignition system as a subassembly of the engine. You will find a detailed discussion of the ignition system, with repair procedures, under **ENGINE.**

## 2.6 Lights

The VW headlights are sealed beams with dual filaments and are flush-mounted in the fenders. The headlight units are adjustable horizontally and vertically in conformance with highway safety regulations. Parking lights are incorporated in the front turn indicators. The rear lighting includes two tail lights on the fenders and the license plate light on the rear hood. The two brake lights are with the turn signals and tail lights in housings in the rear fenders.

The main light switch is of the pull-push type. Turning this switch increases or decreases the brightness of the instrument panel lights. The turn signal lever on the steering column operates the switch for the turn signal lights, up for right turn and down for left turn. On the 1966 and 1967 cars a pushbutton on the lever works the switch for high and low beams of the headlights. On later cars, pulling the lever itself up toward the steering wheel operates the switch. A blue light on the speedometer dial shows when the high beams are on. The light to illuminate the interior of the car is operated by a contact door switch but can be turned on or off manually.

**Fig. 6.** Main cables and connections of the Beetle electrical system are shown here approximately as they are found in cars with 12-volt battery. The voltage regulator is under rear seat (just ahead of the left rear wheel). On 1966 Beetles the regulator was integral with the generator.

10

On cars covered in this Manual, the driver's warning lights (including the red generator warning light and the red or green oil pressure light) are on the speedometer face.

### 2.7 Cables and Connections

All components of the electrical system (except the heavy battery cables) have tab connectors. The cable terminals are of the push-on type, securely crimped to the cable ends for good contact.

> ***CAUTION —***
> *To avoid short circuits, always disconnect the battery ground strap before undertaking any work that requires the removal of cables.*

Electrical system repairs on VW cars are limited usually to the removal and replacement of worn or defective components and replacement or reconditioning of wiring. When replacing cables, it is important to use wire of the same gauge and length as the original. Otherwise, excessive voltage drop or undesirable cable tension may occur.

### 2.8 Windshield Wipers and Washers

The windshield wiper motor on cars after August 1966 is two-speed. When the motor is turned off, the blades return automatically to the parked position. A press button in the wiper switch on the instrument panel actuates the pneumatic windshield washer, which sprays the windshield from two jets in the center of the cowl panel. A translucent container with a capacity of one or two quarts (depending on car model) is behind the spare wheel, under the front hood.

### 2.9 Instruments

A flexible cable from the left front wheel drives the speedometer and odometer.

On cars prior to the 1968 model the fuel gauge is mechanically operated, connected by cable to the sending unit in the fuel tank. Cars after 1968 have an electrically operated gauge on the face of the speedometer. The operation of both types is described later in this section.

The fuse box under the instrument panel at the right of the steering column contains the fuses for the high and low headlight beams, parking lights, tail lights, brake lights, turn signals, the interior light, the windshield wipers and the horn.

## 3. BATTERY

Each cell of the VW battery (whether 6-volt or 12-volt) contains a set of positive lead peroxide ($PbO_2$) plates and negative spongy lead (Pb) plates with separators. The positive plates are chocolate-brown in color, the negative plates gray. An electrolyte covers the plates. In VW batteries the electrolyte is sulfuric acid ($H_2SO_4$) diluted with water to a specific gravity of 1.285. This specific gravity means that a given volume of the battery electrolyte weighs 1.285 times as much as an equal volume of water.

The cells are connected in series with heavy lead bars. A casing of acid-proof material contains the cells and electrolyte. On the 6-volt battery the cell connectors are exposed, but in the 12-volt version a plastic case completely encloses plates and connectors. The terminal posts of the battery are marked (+) and (−). The positive post is made thicker than the negative one.

#### Cell Voltage

The nominal voltage of each cell is 2 volts. Under charging, the voltage rises to a terminal voltage of 2.5 to 2.7 volts. When the charging current is shut off, the voltage drops. From the peak it falls in a very short time to 2.0 to 2.1 volts. Thus the voltage of fully-charged 6- and 12-volt batteries ranges from 6.0 to 6.3 volts and from 12.0 to 12.6 volts, respectively.

When the terminal voltage of a cell has dropped to 1.75 to 1.8 volts in the unloaded condition, the battery is fully discharged.

#### Discharging

In the electrolytic process that produces electric current from a battery, the acid attacks the metal plates, turning them into lead sulphate ($PbSO_4$). Electrons from the positive plates gather at the negative pole of the battery. At the opening of a suitable pathway (circuit) electric current flows.

When electric current is flowing from the battery and the chemical reaction is turning the plates into lead sulphate, the battery is discharging. Its potential for producing more electric current is being reduced. As the sulphate of the acid joins chemically with the lead, the proportion of water in the solution increases, and the specific gravity of the electrolyte drops.

#### Charging

The discharging of a lead-acid battery can be reversed. Sending a direct electric current back through the battery causes the lead sulphate to give back its sulphate to the electrolyte. The positive plates again become lead peroxide while the negative plates return to spongy lead. The electrolyte regains the original specific gravity. These are the chemical changes that occur when a battery is charged.

Only direct current (dc) can be used to charge lead batteries. The voltage should be 2.7 volts for each cell of the battery. The source of direct current and the battery are connected in parallel; that is, the negative pole of the source to the negative of the battery. The charging will build to a peak, called the terminal voltage. If charging is continued beyond terminal voltage, the water in the electrolyte will begin to decompose into hydrogen and oxygen. This condition is called "gassing."

When the electrical system is in good order, charging of the battery is an almost continuous process while the car is in motion.

## 3.1 Care of the Battery

The condition of the battery determines to a great extent whether engine starting will be reliable and rapid. The service life of a battery depends on regular checking and careful maintenance. The procedures are simple and quickly done. For a battery in constant use good maintenance requires only regular inspection of the external condition of the case and terminals and regular testing of the specific gravity and level of the electrolyte.

### Specific Gravity Testing

The specific gravity of the battery acid is accurate evidence of the state of charge. Specific gravity is tested with a hydrometer, which is a syringe-like instrument consisting of a glass cylinder with a freely-moving float inside. A calibrated scale is etched on the cylinder for measuring the position of the float when the hydrometer is full of electrolyte. There is a rubber bulb for sucking up the acid. The denser the acid is—that is, the higher the specific gravity—the higher the float will rise in the barrel of the hydrometer. The scale reading of the float position then gives the specific gravity. A correction for temperature is required. The values for different states of charge of the battery are:

| State of Charge | Specific Gravity |
|---|---|
| Fully discharged | 1.120 |
| Half discharged | 1.200 |
| Fully charged | 1.285 |

### Electrolyte Level

The level of the electrolyte in a battery in constant use will fall because of evaporation and electrolysis of the water (gassing). Evaporation will be greater in summer and in hot climates. In very hot weather it may be necessary to check the level as often as every week. The fluid should come up to the manufacturer's level mark inside the case (if a mark can be seen) or to a height of 3/16 inch (5 mm) above the plates and separators.

Only distilled water should be added to the battery. Tap water and rain (especially rain in smoggy industrial regions) contain chemicals detrimental to the service life of the battery. Care should be taken not to add too much water. If the level of electrolyte is too high, the battery may boil over on a long daylight run when the charging from the generator is continuous and the load on the electrical system is light.

In the unlikely event that you should find it necessary to add acid, a variety of products is available at local automotive supply stores. Follow the manufacturer's instructions carefully, and be sure to test the specific gravity afterward.

***WARNING —***
*Battery acid is highly corrosive and can cause severe burns. When working with the electrolyte always wear goggles, rubber gloves and apron. If electrolyte is spilled on the skin, flush at once with large quantities of water. If it gets into the eyes, call a doctor immediately.*

### Voltage Testing

The voltage of a battery or of an individual cell is always measured under a given electrical load. The instrument used is a discharge meter, which is a voltmeter connected in parallel with a known resistance for the test load. When the discharge meter is applied across the battery or the individual cell, the resistance draws a current of 80 to 100 amps.

On batteries with open tops allowing a test of the individual cells the meter is applied across each cell (see

Fig. 7). The plus point of the meter is pressed into the plus cell connector and the minus point into the minus connector. The voltage of all the cells should be approximately the same—normally 2.0 volts. If any cell differs from the others by more than 0.2 volt, it is sulphated or otherwise defective. If any cell shows a voltage under 1.6 volts in a heavy discharge test (lasting from 10 to 15 seconds), the battery is discharged.

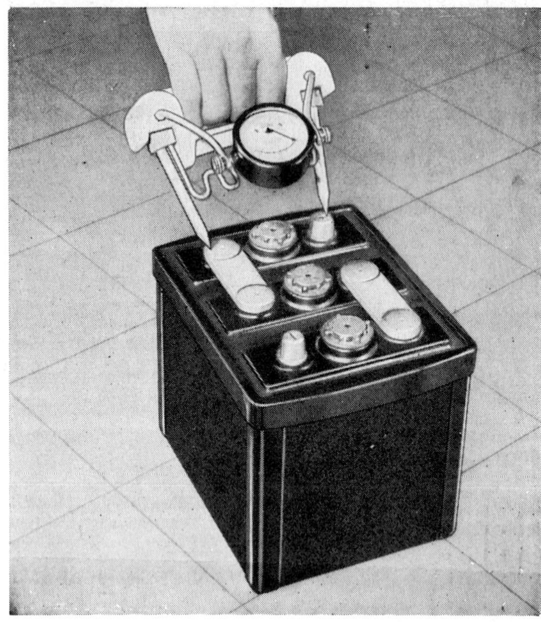

© 1972 VWoA—515

**Fig. 7.** Voltmeter is being used to test the voltage of one cell of a 6-volt battery.

Testing of individual cells of the newer type of batteries with enclosed plastic cases is not possible. A reading of the total voltage of the battery is taken instead. The discharge meter is applied, as before, in parallel. The resistance test load should be adjusted to at least 100 amps. The following values for the different states of charge will be found:

| Battery rating | Fully charged | Fully discharged |
|---|---|---|
| 6 volts | 6.3 volts | 4.8 volts |
| 12 volts | 12.6 volts | 9.6 volts |

A discharged battery should be recharged at once.

### Service Life

The properly maintained lead-acid battery should give good service over a period of two to three years, but neglect or abuse will shorten its life. The vibration of a moving car can crack the case of a battery that is not attached securely to the car frame. Prolonged efforts to start a reluctant engine ("grinding the battery") draw current of as much as 250 amps and constitute a severe drain on the battery.

The battery case should be inspected from time to time for cracks or holes or bulging and should be kept clean. If the electrolyte boils over or is spilled into dirt and grease on the case, it can establish a circuit between the battery terminals and gradually discharge the battery. The battery terminals should be wiped clean. After the cables have been connected, the terminals should be coated with a thin application of petroleum jelly or acid-resistant grease. A special cleaning agent and special brushes are available for removing heavy corrosion from the posts, and there is a tool for pulling off corroded cable connectors.

## 3.2 Removing and Installing Batteries

**To remove:**

1. Lift out rear seat of car.
2. Disconnect battery clamp.
3. Remove top cover of early model battery or flip up cover of later battery with plastic case.
4. Disconnect negative terminal (ground strap) first and then positive terminal.
5. Lift battery out of mounting.

**To install:**

1. Wipe battery terminals and cable connections clean. If necessary, brighten battery posts by rubbing with steel wool or sandpaper.
2. Coat terminals and connections with a thin application of petroleum jelly.
3. Follow in reverse order the steps of the procedure for removing the battery.

> ***WARNING —***
> *Charging causes a battery to gas. That is, pure hydrogen and oxygen are produced in the decomposition of excess water in the electrolyte. This is a highly explosive combination. Smoking and open flames should not be permitted in a room where batteries are charged. Also, precision tools should not be stored in the room. Exposure to the gases can damage them.*

## 3.3 Quick-charging

Under normal conditions the charging of a battery is a rather slow procedure in which the applied current (in amperes) is held to not more than 10 percent of rated capacity. That is, a charging current of 6.6 amperes would be used on a battery with a 66 Ah capacity. Experience has shown, however, that a higher current can be used to charge a good battery in considerably less time. For this emergency quick-charging, currents as high as 72 amps are used, depending on the battery and its state of charge. The time required for this quick-charging ranges from an hour for a battery with a specific gravity of 1.150 or less to 15 minutes for a battery with specific gravity of 1.200 to 1.225. Quick-charging is not suitable for batteries with specific gravity above 1.225.

Only sound batteries that are in regular use are quick-charged. Even for them the procedure should be restricted to emergencies, since repeated quick-charging will tend to reduce service life. Factory-new batteries are not suitable for quick-charging, nor are sulphated batteries. In fact, quick-charging can be used as a test of the condition of a battery. If the terminal voltage rises above 7.75 volts for a 6-volt battery (15.5 volts for a 12-volt battery) after three minutes of fast charge, the plates are sulphated or worn out. The battery should be replaced.

New batteries that are being put in service and old batteries that have been out of service for some time should be charged at the slow normal rate.

### 3.4 Normal Current Charging

A current as low as 5 percent of the rated capacity (Ah) of a battery can be used in normal charging, and should be used in the initial charging of new batteries.

In normal charging the battery is considered to be charged when it is gassing freely and when the voltage of the individual cells has risen to 2.5 to 2.7 volts. An hour or so after the charging current has been switched off, the voltmeter should be applied again, this time to find the "rest" voltage of the battery. It should be 2.1 or 2.2 for each cell.

### 3.5 Cold Weather Operation

Winter makes heavy demands on the car battery. Cold weather thickens oil and grease and makes the engine harder to turn over in starting. More important, low temperatures drastically reduce the capacity of a battery. For example, the capacity of a battery at 5 degrees F is only about half its capacity at 68 degrees F. Cold weather operation of a car calls for more careful maintenance of the battery. When the car is driven mainly in city traffic in the winter, it is advisable to have the battery removed every six weeks for thorough charging. The electrolyte level and specific gravity should, of course, be checked frequently.

In winter there is also the risk of freezing the battery. When the battery is discharging, its specific gravity is decreasing, and consequently the proportion of water in the electrolyte is rising. The higher the proportion of water the more susceptible the battery becomes to freezing. A frozen battery produces no current, but if it can be thawed slowly in a warm room, it usually can be restored to service.

The following table gives the freezing points of battery electrolyte at different specific gravity:

| Specific gravity | Freezing point |
|---|---|
| 1.285 | −92° F (−68° C) |
| 1.200 | −17° F (−27° C) |
| 1.120 | 12° F (−11° C) |

### 3.6 Storing the Battery

A battery that is out of use over a period of time discharges gradually. The rate of discharge depends on the temperature of the surroundings. At normal room temperature the discharge is about one percent of the battery capacity per day. Rising temperature increases the rate of discharge.

The plates of a battery stored in a warm room tend to sulphate. This formation of lead sulphate can be recognized as a gray coating on the plates. Beyond a certain point, this coating is difficult to reconvert. Since a badly sulphated battery cannot supply the heavy current required for starting the engine, a battery in this condition is no longer usable.

The following procedure to prevent self-discharging and sulphating is recommended for a battery that is to be taken out of service and stored for a long time:

1. Charge battery, test acid level and specific gravity and make necessary corrections.
2. Store battery in a cool, dry place.
3. Every six to eight weeks, discharge battery and recharge it.
4. Before returning battery to service, charge it with a very low current "trickle charge" (not over 3 amps).

Large differences in the individual cell voltages of a battery that has been out of service suggest that the plates are sulphated. A sulphated battery put on regular charge will start to gas almost immediately. A low current (maximum 3 amps) therefore should be used if the lead sulphate is to have time to reconvert gradually.

***WARNING*** —
*"Boosting" a sulphated battery at a high charging rate can cause an explosion.*

## 4. STARTER MOTOR

The series-wound starter motor (see Fig. 8) on VW engines draws heavy current from the battery in order to deliver very high torque (twisting force) for cranking the engine. The motor has a sliding drive gear (pinion) to engage the ring gear on the engine flywheel, and it turns the pinion by means of an overrunning clutch. Once the engine starts, the clutch slips its hold on the pinion, allowing the pinion to free-wheel at high speed while the armature shaft of the starter motor continues to rotate at its own much lower speed. If the high rpm of the pinion were forced on the armature shaft, the starter motor would quickly burn out.

A solenoid switch connected by cable to the ignition/-starter switch is attached to the housing of the starter motor, and the assembly is bolted to the transmission housing. A composition bushing in the transmission housing supports the armature shaft of the Bosch motor at the drive end. The VW starter motor does not require this bushing.

The solenoid switch has a dual function. First, the solenoid moves the shift fork or yoke, which thrusts the pinion along the armature shaft to the flywheel ring gear. Second, it closes the circuit between battery and starter motor armature. When pinion and ring gear engage, the pinion turns the flywheel and begins to crank the engine. Once the engine has started, the return spring forces the pinion out of engagement with the ring gear.

The ignition switch has a non-repeat latch, which prevents operation of the starter while the engine is running. Before the starting operation can be repeated, the ignition must be switched off.

**Fig. 8.** Wiring diagram shows starter motor hook-up.

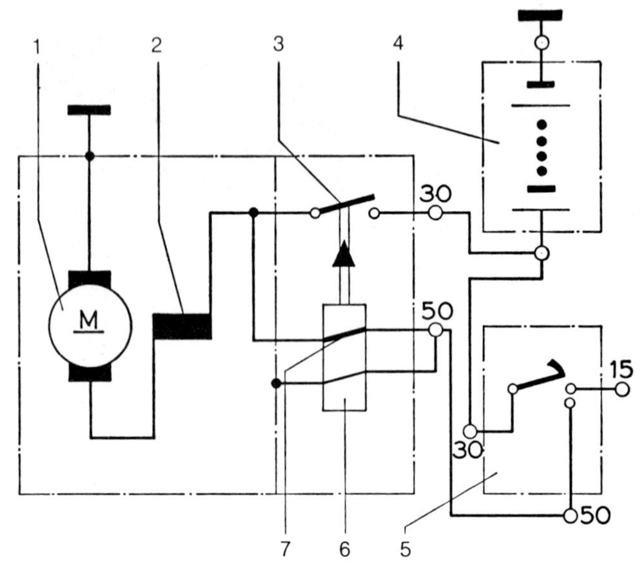


1. Armature
2. Field winding
3. Solenoid switch
4. Battery
5. Ignition/starter switch
6. Holding winding
7. Pull-in winding

### 4.1 Types of Starter Motors

**Table b** lists the types of starter motors that are installed in VW cars covered in this Manual. Figures 9, 10 and 11 show exploded views of these starter motors.

**Table b. Starter Types**

**(see Figs. 9, 10 and 11)**

| Model | From Chassis No. | Starter | Voltage | HP Rating |
|---|---|---|---|---|
| VW 1300 | 116 000 001-116 1021 300 | VW 113 911 021 A<br>Bosch 113 911 021 B | 6V | 0.5 hp |
| VW 1300 Ghia | 146 350 066-146 1021 300 | Bosch 141 911 021* | 6V | 0.5 hp |
| VW 1500 and VW 1500 Ghia | 117 000 001-117 999 000 | Bosch 211 911 023* | 12V | 0.7 hp |
| VW 1500 Automatic Stick Shift<br>VW 1500 and VW 1500 Ghia | 118 000 001<br>118 000 001-119 1200 000 | Bosch 003 911 023 A<br>VW 111 911 023 A | 12V<br>12V | 0.8 hp<br>0.7 hp |
| VW 1500 and VW 1500 Ghia | 118 000 001-119 1200 000 | Bosch 311 911 023 B | 12V | 0.7 hp |

***Starter has modified pinion and cannot be installed on older cars.**

**Fig. 9.** Bosch starter (113 911 021 B) breaks down into parts shown here.

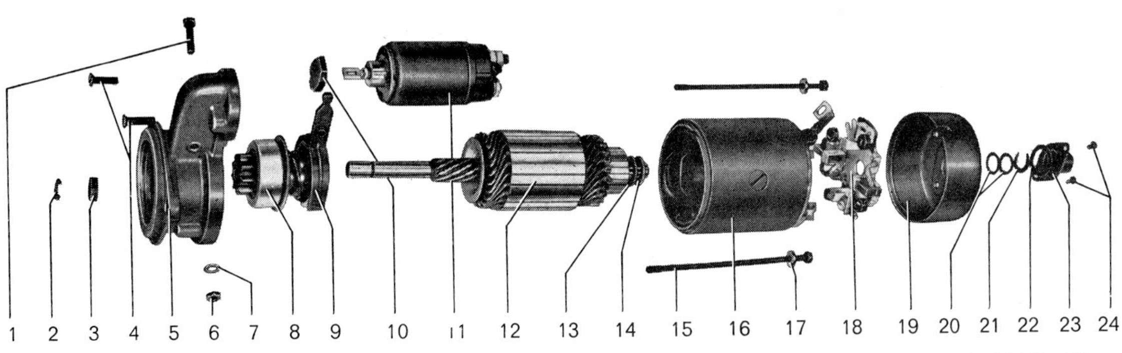


1. Lever bearing pin
2. Circlip
3. Stop ring
4. Securing screw
5. Mounting bracket
6. Nut
7. Spring washer
8. Pinion
9. Operating lever
10. Rubber seal
11. Solenoid
12. Armature
13. Steel washer
14. Synthetic washer
15. Through bolts
16. Housing
17. Washer
18. Brush holder
19. End plate
20. Shims
21. Lock washer
22. Sealing ring
23. End cap
24. Screws

**Fig. 10.** VW starter (113 911 021 A) breaks down into parts shown here.

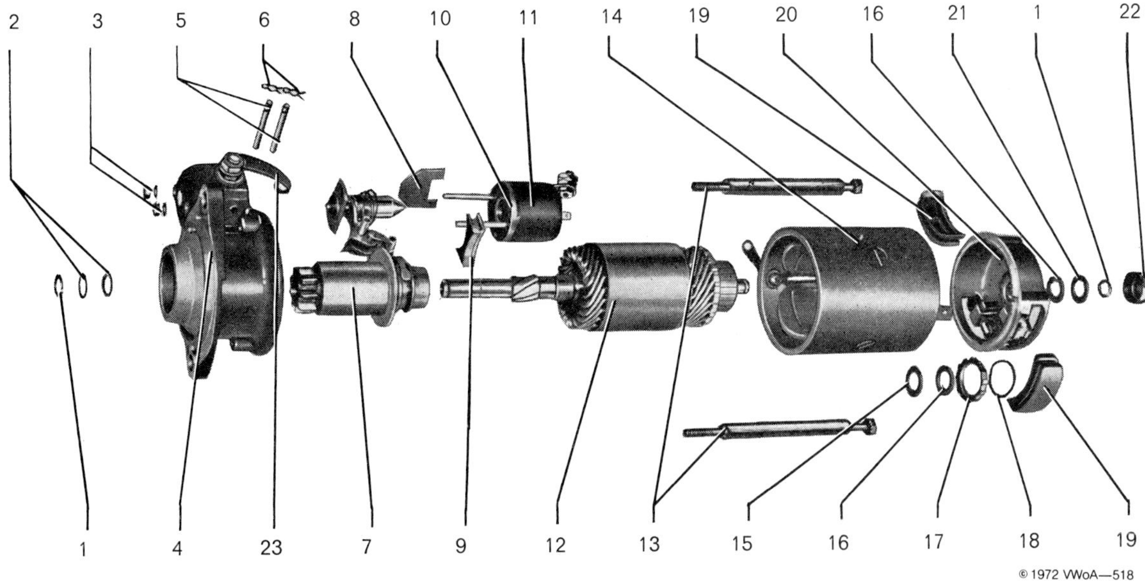


1. Circlip
2. Cup washer
3. Nuts and lockwashers
4. Intermediate bracket
5. Pivot pins
6. Spring clips
7. Drive pinion with linkage and solenoid core
8. Insulating plate
9. Molded rubber seal
10. Insulating disc
11. Solenoid housing
12. Armature
13. Through bolts
14. Housing and field assembly
15. Steel washer
16. Bronze washer
17. Friction washer
18. Thrust ring
19. Brush inspection cover
20. Commutator end plate
21. Steel washer
22. Cap
23. Connecting strip

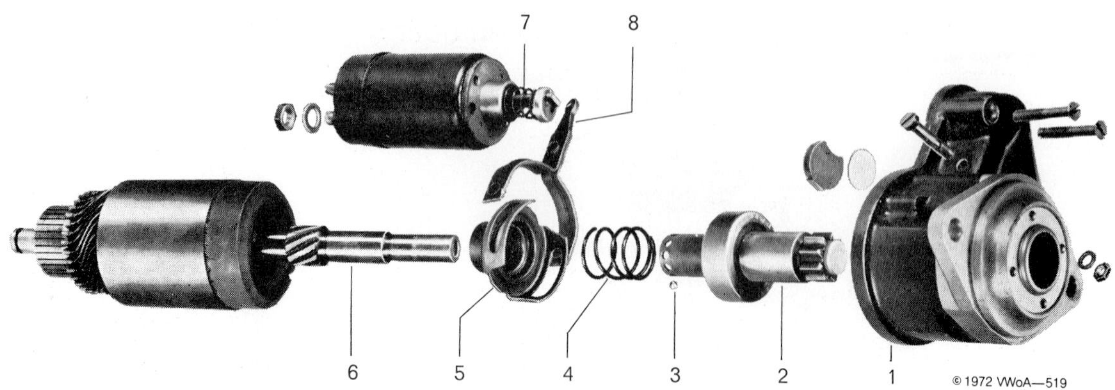


**Fig. 11.** Automatic Stick Shift starter (Bosch 003 911 023 A) differs from other models in some details.

1. Intermediate bearing
2. Starter drive
3. Steel balls (10)
4. Drive spring
5. Shift bush
6. Armature
7. Solenoid spring
8. Engaging fork

## 4.2 Maintenance

The armature bushings on the VW starter motor should be replaced when the motor is overhauled. When the engine is removed, the bushing for the starter motor armature should be inspected for wear and if badly worn should be replaced. Lightly coat starter shaft with molybdenum disulfide grease before installing the starter.

The brushes of the starter motor should move freely in their guides. When motor is undergoing repair, or if trouble with motor is experienced, remove the end cap for inspection of the brushes. Replace worn brushes and weak brush springs. If the commutator is rough and pitted or shows burned spots, the starter motor needs an overhaul. Scub a dirty or oily commutator with a clean cloth wrapped around a piece of wood and dampened with cleaning solvent.

## 4.3 Starter Motor Troubleshooting

Troubleshooting procedures applicable to all types of starters installed in VW vehicles covered by this Manual are given in **Table c.**

### Table c. Starter Motor Troubleshooting

| Symptom | Test and Diagnosis | Remedy |
|---|---|---|
| 1. Starter does not operate when ignition key is turned to start position | Turn on lights for test | |
| | a. Lights are out. Loose cables or poor ground connection. Battery run down | a. Check battery cables and connection. Test voltage of battery. Charge if necessary. |
| | b. Lights go out when key is moved to starting position. Insufficient current due to loose connections or corroded terminals | b. Clean battery terminals and cable clamps. Clean and tighten connections between battery starter motor and ground. |
| | c. Lights go dim when key is moved to starting position. Battery run down | c. Charge battery. |
| | d. Lights stay bright when key is moved to starting position. Make a jumper contact between terminals 30 and 50 at starter motor. If the motor operates, there is an open circuit in cable 50 to ignition-starting switch, or in cable 30 to lighting switch, or the ignition starting switch is defective | d. Eliminate open circuits. Replace defective parts. |
| | e. Lights stay bright and solenoid switch operates. Disconnect battery cable from terminal 30 at starter motor and connect it to terminal stud of connector strip. If the starter motor operates, the contacts of the solenoid switch are worn or dirty. | e. Replace solenoid switch. |

**continued on next page**

## Table c. Starter Motor Troubleshooting (continued)

| Symptom | Test and Diagnosis | Remedy |
|---|---|---|
| 2. Starter motor does not operate when battery cable is directly connected with terminal stud of connector strip | a. Brushes sticking<br>b. Brushes worn<br>c. Weak spring tension. Brushes do not make contact<br>d. Commutator dirty<br>e. Commutator rough, pitted or burned<br>f. Armature or field coils defective | a. Clean brushes and guides of brush holders.<br>b. Replace brushes.<br>c. Replace springs.<br>d. Clean commutator.*<br>e. Overhaul starter motor.*<br>f. Overhaul starter motor.* |
| 3. Starter turns too slowly or fails to turn engine over | a. Battery run down<br>b. Insufficient current flow due to loose or corroded connections<br>c. Brushes sticking<br>d. Brushes worn<br>e. Commutator dirty<br>f. Commutator rough, pitted or burned<br>g. Armature or field coils defective | a. Charge battery.<br>b. Clean battery terminals and cable clamps, tighten connections.<br>c. Clean brushes and guides of brush holders.<br>d. Replace brushes.<br>e. Clean commutator.*<br>f. Overhaul starter motor.*<br>g. Overhaul starter motor.* |
| 4. Starter motor makes usual sounds but cranks engine erratically or fails to crank | a. Drive pinion defective<br>b. Flywheel gear ring defective | a. Replace drive pinion.<br>b. Replace flywheel or remachine ring gear. |
| 5. Drive pinion does not move out of mesh | a. Drive pinion or armature shaft dirty or damaged<br>b. Solenoid switch defective | a. Overhaul starter motor.*<br>b. Replace solenoid switch. |

***Repair should be made at authorized VW repair shop or specialty shop.**

### 4.4 Removing and Installing Starter Motor

*CAUTION* —
*Disconnect battery ground strap before removing motor.*

**To remove:**

1. Disconnect terminal 30 at solenoid.
2. Disconnect cable from ignition/starter switch at terminal 50 of solenoid.
3. Remove nut in engine compartment while holding upper bolt (2 men or special wrench); then remove lower nut from stud which attaches starter motor to transmission case.
4. Withdraw starter motor.

**To install:**

1. Lubricate starter shaft bushing with multi-purpose grease.
2. Apply a good sealing compound between intermediate bracket and transmission case.
3. Slide starter on stud and secure transmission case with nut.
4. Insert long bolt and secure with nut.
5. Make sure terminals are clean and tight.

### 4.5 Removing and Installing Solenoid

**To remove:**

1. Remove nut and connector strip (see Fig. 12).

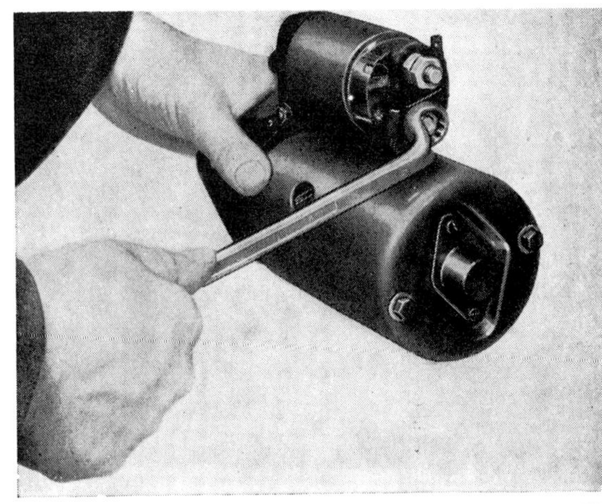

© 1972 VWoA—520

**Fig. 12.** Solenoid switch is shown in position on Bosch starter.

2. Remove two screws that fasten solenoid to intermediate bracket (see Fig. 13).

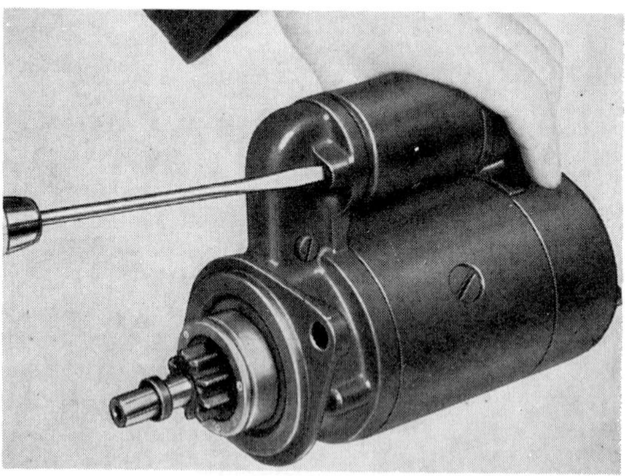

© 1972 VWoA—521

**Fig. 13.** Two screws fasten solenoid to intermediate bracket on starter motor.

3. Lift pull rod upward out of operating lever and withdraw solenoid.

**NOTE —**
Defective solenoid switches should be replaced. The setting should not be changed. When a new solenoid is installed, it is important to measure carefully the distance from switch flange to pull rod eye and adjust to specification shown in Fig. 14.

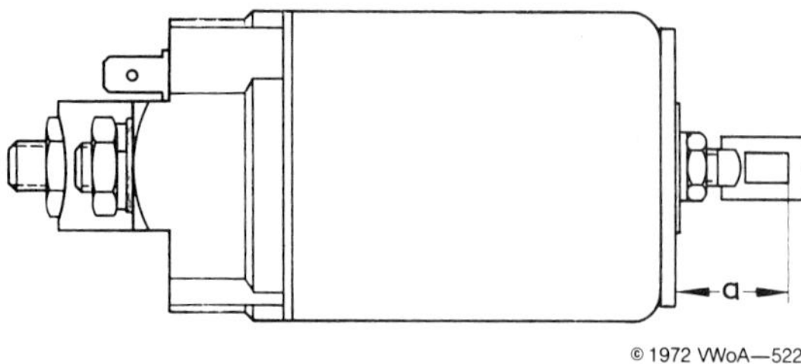


© 1972 VWoA—522

**Fig. 14.** Pull rod must be adjusted accurately when new solenoid is installed. With pull rod drawn in, distance "a" from switch flange to pull rod eye must be 0.780 to 0.788 inch (18.9 to 19.1 mm).

**To Install** (see Fig. 15):

1. Check seating of rubber gasket on starter mounting bracket.
2. Place small strip of plastic sealing compound on outer edge of solenoid end face.
3. Pull drive pinion out to bring forked end of shift lever out as far as possible toward solenoid switch clevis.
4. Insert solenoid and screw to intermediate bracket.

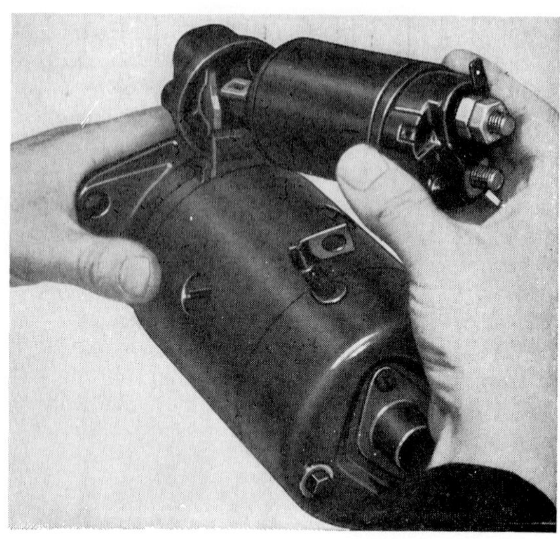

© 1972 VWoA—523

**Fig. 15.** Shift lever of starter motor is at opening of intermediate bracket as solenoid switch is installed.

5. Replace connector strip and nut.

## 4.6 Checking Brushes and Commutator (Bosch starter)

1. Remove end cap and sealing ring (see Fig. 16).

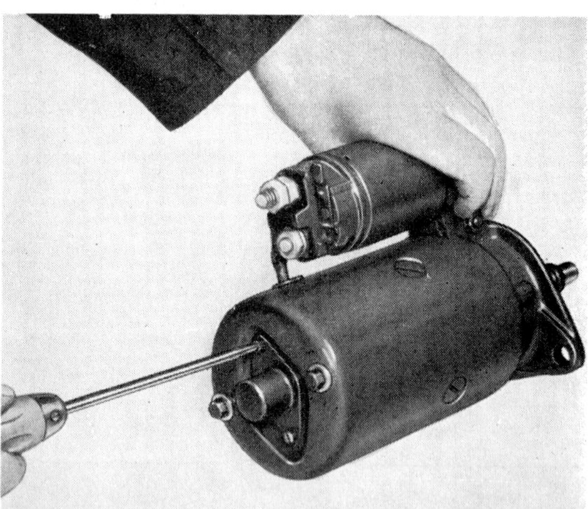

© 1972 VWoA—524

**Fig. 16.** End cap of starter (Bosch) is unscrewed in procedure to check brushes.

2. Remove lock washer and steel shims from drive shaft (see Fig. 17).
3. Remove through bolts and take off end plate.
4. Lift the four brushes from guides.

© 1972 VWoA—525

**Fig. 17.** Lock washer and shims on starter drive shaft are indicated by arrow.

5. Pull brush holder off armature shaft (see Fig. 18).

© 1972 VWoA—526

**Fig. 18.** Commutator and brushes of starter are exposed when brush holder (at right) is removed.

6. Unsolder two brushes on field coil connections and two brushes on brush holder.
7. Solder on four new brushes.
8. With clean rag soaked in solvent and wrapped on a piece of wood, clean oil and dirt from commutator.
9. Inspect surface of commutator for grooves or burn spots. Overhaul commutator if damaged.

When machining or heavy polishing of commutator is necessary, diameter must not be reduced below 1.35 inches (34.5 mm). After machining, insulation between bars should be undercut. When assembling, make sure rubber seal for the solenoid cable is properly seated.

## 4.7 Testing Starter
(installed)

When starter fails to crank, the first step in trouble-shooting is to check voltage at terminal 50 on solenoid switch. In a 12-volt system voltage available at this terminal should be at least 7 volts. If voltage is less than 7, the next step is to inspect the electrical system in general and to check wiring of starter circuit in particular.

The procedure for checking the starter circuit follows:

1. Make sure a charged battery is properly connected to the electrical system.
2. Raise car.
3. Connect terminals 30 and 50 with 11-gauge wire.

If starter engages when terminals 30 and 50 are connected, either the ignition switch or the wiring from switch to starter is faulty.

If starter does not engage when terminals are connected, further investigation is necessary. Remove starter motor for bench test.

## 4.8 Bench-testing Starter

A battery (or series of batteries) with rated capacity of 135 Ah is used when testing the operation and output of a starter motor on the test stand. (See Fig. 19). No weak-

© 1972 VWoA—527

**Fig. 19.** Test stand for starter motors has instruments, ring gear and brake.

## Table d. Starter Test Data

| | | | No-load test* | | | Load test | | | Stall torque test*** | | |
|---|---|---|---|---|---|---|---|---|---|---|---|
| Starter Type VW Part No. | Vehicle Type | Installed from — to | Current A | Voltage V | Speed** rpm | Current A | Voltage V | Speed** rpm | Current A | Voltage V | Solenoid Switch pull-in voltage V* |
| 111 911 023 | 1 | Aug 66—Dec 66 | | | | | | | | | |
| 211 911 023 | 1 | Aug 66—July 67 | 30-50 | 11.5 | 7400-9100 | 170-215 | 9 | 900-1300 | 220-275 | 6 | 7 |
| 111 911 023 A | 1 | Aug 68—July 69 | | | | | | | | | |
| 311 911 023 B | Automatic Stick Shift Models | Sept 67—July 69 | 35-55 | 11.5 | 6400-7900 | 160-215 | 9 | 1100-1400 | 250-300 | 6 | 7 |
| 003 911 023 A | | Sept 67— | | | | | | | | | |
| AL EEF 0.5/6L1<br>113 911 021 B<br>113 911 021 A | 1 | Aug 65—July 66 | 50-70 | 5.5 | 5400-6800 | 250-290 | 4.5 | 900-1200 | 430-515 | 3.5 | 3.3 |
| 141 911 021 | 14 | Jan 66—July 66 | 50-70 | 5.5 | 5400-6800 | 250-290 | 4.5 | 900-1200 | 430-515 | 3.5 | 3.3 |

*Checking temperatures 68°F (20°C) **Starter shaft speeds ***Starter braked to standstill

## Table e. Solenoid Switch Test Data

| | Current draw (amps.) 6-volt solenoid switch | | Current draw (amps.) 12-volt solenoid switch | |
|---|---|---|---|---|
| | Bosch | VW | Bosch | VW |
| Pull-in winding, max. | 89 | 43 | 35 | 30 |
| Holding winding, max. | 18 | 23 | 11 | 12 |

**These values are for a 6-volt—135 Ah power source or two 77 Ah batteries in parallel, a 12-volt—135 Ah power source or three 45 Ah batteries in parallel.**

er battery should be used. The following sequence of tests can be made:

1. No-load test.
2. Load test.
3. Stall torque test.
4. Pull-in of pinion under load.

If false readings from heating of starter or discharging of battery are to be avoided, it is important to perform the tests in the sequence given. Test data for starters installed in the cars covered in this Manual is given in **Tables d and e.**

**No-load test:**

1. Set up starter motor on test stand.
2. Adjust travel of pinion on shaft to allow pinion teeth to engage ring gear to full depth of ring gear.
3. Connect terminal 30 at starter to battery positive terminal; connect test stand cable to terminal 50 of solenoid switch.
4. Without braking flywheel, operate starter motor to let pinion run while fully engaged with ring gear on flywheel. Take readings for rpm, current consumption and battery voltage.

In no-load operation the starter speed should be high and current consumption low. Test stand readings along this line indicate that the armature is rotating freely in the bushings and that there is no short circuit in the windings or to ground.

**Load test:**

***CAUTION —***
*Load test should not take longer than 10 seconds.*

1. Apply test stand brake to reduce starter speed for the no-load reading to approximately 1000 rpm.
2. Measure current draw and battery voltage.

In this test if the battery voltage is too low or the starter is too hot, a lower reading for rpm will be given.

**Stall torque test:**

***CAUTION —***
*Test must not last longer than 5 seconds.*

1. Operate starter motor to crank flywheel.
2. Apply load by braking until flywheel stops briefly.
3. Release load immediately and turn off starter.

**Test of pinion pull-in:**

1. While braking slightly, switch starter on and off.
2. Observe whether the pinion is engaging fully with ring gear each time and whether it is disengaging smoothly.

## 5. GENERATOR

The generator converts mechanical energy from the engine into electric current for the battery, the sparkplugs (except at starting) and all the other components of the electrical system.

The generator works on electromagnetic induction. When a wire or coil of wire is moved in a magnetic field, voltage is induced on the wire or coil. In the VW generator the moving element is the armature, which is a winding of many coils of wire on a shaft. The fan belt, running from the pulley on the engine crankshaft, turns this shaft to spin the armature between the poles of an electromagnet. With voltage induced on the armature, electric current flows.

Although the VW generator is called a direct current (dc) generator, the current it produces is actually alternating current (ac). The direction of flow of an induced current is determined by the direction in which the wire or coil cuts the magnetic field. Since each rotation of the armature causes the coils of wire to cut the magnetic field in opposite directions, the resulting current alternates. But the battery can accept only direct current, so the VW generator has a mechanical switch that allows the generated current to pass in only one direction. The flow at the generator output terminal is therefore direct current. This mechanical switch is made up of the brushes and commutator.

A strap secures the VW generator to its support bracket above the engine. The armature spins in ball bearings. The commutator is on the pulley end of the armature. The other end of the shaft projects into the fan housing and carries the fan. On the 1966 sedan the voltage regulator is attached to the generator, but all later sedans have it under the rear seat. The Karmann Ghia regulator is mounted at the left side of the engine compartment. Besides keeping the generator output constant, the voltage regulator connects the generator to the electrical system at cut-in speed (see **2.4 Generator**) and opens the circuit when generator voltage falls below battery voltage.

### Connections

Electrical connections for generator are from terminal B+ (51) to terminal 30 at starter motor (battery lead); from terminal 61 to generator warning light (Fig. 20).

**Fig. 20.** Terminals at the voltage regulator are shown.

### Warning Light

The red warning light on the speedometer face is connected with terminal 61 and B+ of the regulator by way of terminals 15/54 in the ignition/starter switch. When the ignition is turned on, the red light comes on. As soon as generator voltage rises to approximately battery voltage, the light goes out.

Since generator armature carries the engine cooling fan on the front end of the shaft, the red warning light may also signal trouble in the belt drive. If fan belt should break, the armature would cease to turn, the voltage would drop and the light would come on and stay on.

### Maintenance

The ball bearings supporting the generator armature are packed with Bosch high-temperature grease, or another product of equivalent quality, but this lubrication is done only when the generator is overhauled. Ordinary grease should not be used. When the generator is undergoing repair, the brushes should be checked for wear and worn brushes replaced.

## 5.1 Specifications

**Table f** gives parts numbers and performance specifications for the generators and regulators used on Volkswagens with 1300 and 1500 engines; Figs. 21 and 22 show the generators.

### Table f. Generator Performance Specifications

**Generators**

| Model | Engine numbers | Generator | Regulator | Voltage |
|---|---|---|---|---|
| 1300 Sedan | F 0 000 001—F 0 940 716 | *111 903 021 H/111 903 021 J | integrally mounted | 6 Volt |
| 1300 Ghia | F 0 000 001—F 0 940 716 | 131 903 021 | 131 903 801 | 6 Volt |
| 1500 Sedan and Ghia | H 0 204 001—H 0 874 199 | 211 903 031 | 211 903 803 | 12 Volt |
| | H 0 874 200—H 0 976 397 | 211 903 031 A | 113 903 803 E | 12 Volt |
| | H 0 976 398—H 1 124 668 | 113 903 031 G | 113 903 803 E | 12 Volt |

**Test Data**

| Generator | Cut-in speed** | Cut-in voltage A | Return current A | No-load regulating voltage V | Regulated voltage underload V | Load current A | Nominal output |
|---|---|---|---|---|---|---|---|
| VW 111 903 021 J | 1350-1600 | 6.4- 6.7 | 2-9.0 | 7.4- 8.1 | 6.4- 7.3 | 34 | 180 Watts at 6 Volts and 2400 rpm. |
| Bosch 111 903 021 H | 1660-1950 | 6.2- 6.8 | 3-7.0 | 7.4- 8.1 | 6.4- 7.3 | 34 | 180 Watts at 6 Volts and 2500 rpm. |
| Bosch 131 903 021 | 1000-1050 | 6.2- 6.8 | 2-5.5 | 7.3- 8.0 | 6.3- 7.2 | 34 | 180 Watts at 6 Volts and 1500 rpm. |
| Bosch 211 903 031 | 1450 | 12.4-13.1 | 2.0-7.5 | 13.5-14.5 | 12.8-13.8 | 45 | 360 Watts at 12 Volts and 2000 rpm. |
| Bosch 113 903 021 G | 1450 | 12.4-13.1 | 2.0-7.5 | 13.5-14.5 | 12.8-13.8 | 45 | 360 Watts at 12 Volts and 2000 rpm. |

*see Figs. 8-21 and 8-22 **generator rpm, approximately twice engine rpm

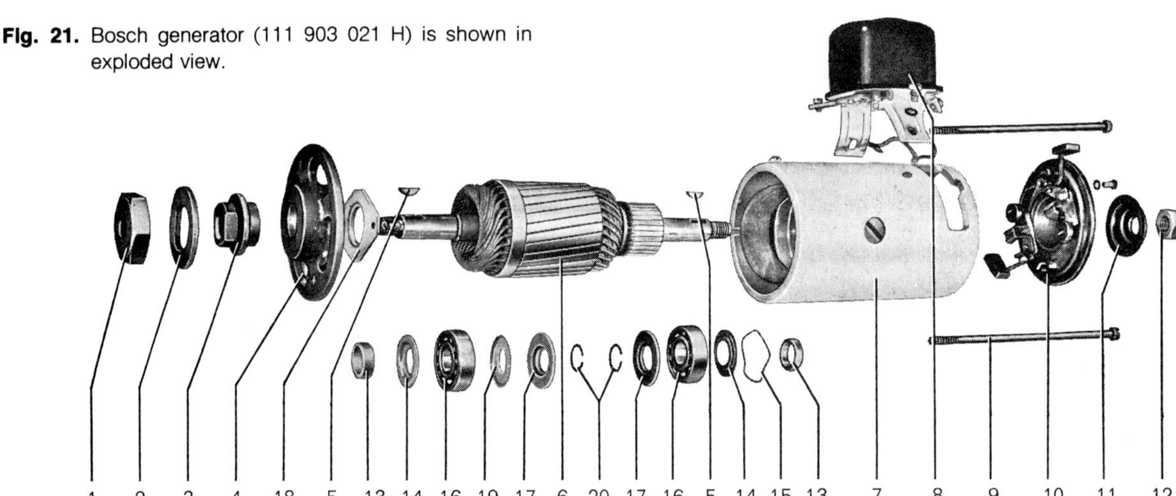


**Fig. 21.** Bosch generator (111 903 021 H) is shown in exploded view.

1. Fan nut
2. Carrier plate
3. Fan hub
4. End plate
5. Woodruff key
6. Armature
7. Housing and field assembly
8. Regulator
9. Through bolts
10. Brush holder end plate
11. Spacer washer
12. Pulley nut
13. Spacer ring
14. Oil slinger
15. Spring ring
16. Ball bearing
17. Oil slinger
18. Flange
19. Cover washer
20. Circlip

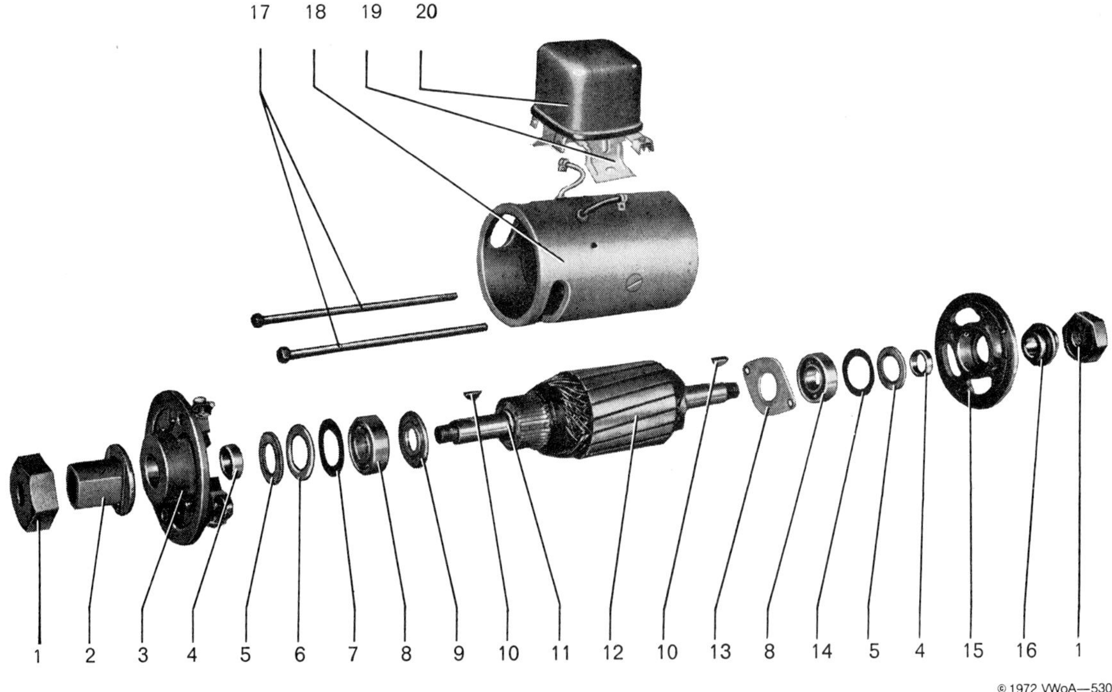


**Fig. 22.** VW generator (111 903 021 J) differs from Bosch in details, as seen in this exploded view.

1. Nut
2. Pulley hub
3. Brush holder end plate
4. Spacer ring
5. Felt washer
6. Retainer
7. Thrust ring
8. Ball bearing
9. Washer
10. Key
11. Spacer
12. Armature
13. Bearing retainer
14. Thrust ring
15. End plate
16. Fan hub
17. Through bolts
18. Housing and field assembly
19. Slotted screw
20. Regulator

10

## 5.2 Testing Generator and Regulator

The generator or the voltage regulator may need testing even when the red warning light is not indicating trouble. The light may be working properly, but the setting of the regulator may be off or the battery may be receiving insufficient current for adequate charge.

There is a series of tests for the generator and regulator, some of which are performed with the components in place and others with components on the bench. Good instruments for measuring current and voltage are required for these tests. The procedures follow.

### Testing No-load Voltage

1. Disconnect cable from terminal B+ (51) at the regulator. Connect positive lead of voltmeter to terminal B+ (51) at the regulator and ground negative lead.
2. Start engine and increase speed to 2000 rpm. Voltmeter should read 7.4 to 8.1 volts for 6-volt battery or 13.5 to 14.5 for 12-volt system.

**NOTE ——**
Cut-in speed (rpm) of so-called "early cut-in generators" is so low that in some cases engine rpm may have to be adjusted to the lowest idle speed.

3. When engine is turned off, the voltmeter needle should swing abruptly back to zero just before the engine stops completely. The needle movement indicates that regulator points are not sticking.

### Testing Charging Current

The battery may be receiving insufficient charge even when the regulator adjustment is correct.

**To test:**

1. Disconnect battery ground cable.
2. Disconnect cable from regulator terminal B+ and connect a suitable ammeter (50-0-50 A range) between cable and terminal.
3. Reconnect battery ground strap.
4. Run engine at high speed and turn on some electrical equipment.
5. Read ammeter. If no current output from the generator is shown, the regulator is defective and must be replaced.
6. Decrease engine speed. The ammeter needle should swing past zero mark into the negative range to indicate that current is flowing back from battery to generator. As the slowing engine reaches idle speed, the regular cut-out switch should operate. The ammeter will then swing back to zero.

### Testing Current Regulator

Since the charging current is dependent on the state of charge of the battery, the previous test could not check the regulator adjustment in isolation from the state of charge of the battery. The following further procedure is required. A voltmeter, ammeter and a sensitive variable resistance capable of carrying up to 50 amps will be needed. The test can be performed with generator in place or on the bench (see Fig. 23).

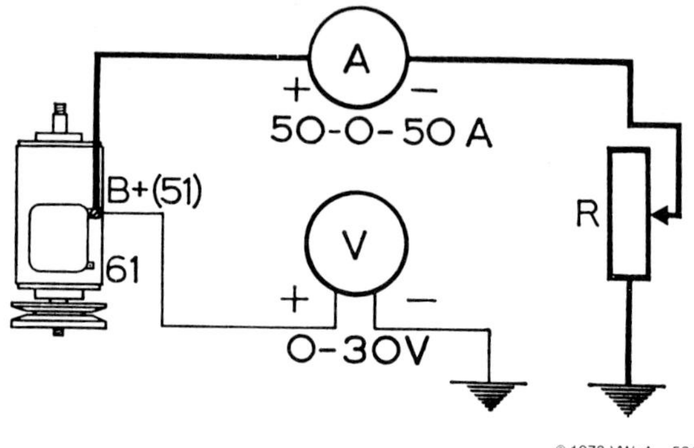


**Fig. 23.** Test hook-up shows functioning of regulator independent of battery. Required are ammeter (A), voltmeter (V) and sliding resistance (R). See text.

**To test:**

1. Disconnect the cable from terminal B+ (51) at the regulator.
2. Connect sliding resistance (R) in series with ammeter between terminal B+ (51) and ground.
3. Connect positive terminal of voltmeter to terminal B+ (51) on regulator and negative voltmeter terminal to generator ground.

**NOTE ——**
Use short cable of cross-section not less than 8-gauge. Check for good ground and terminal connections. Bad connections will give high resistance and false readings.

4. Start engine and check cut-in voltage. Accelerate to generator speed of approximately 4000 rpm (2000 engine rpm). Adjust resistance to "load current" specified in Table f. Voltage reading should match value given in table column headed "Regulated voltage under load."

If readings from this test are not within the specified limits, replace the regulator. It cannot be repaired. Attempts to clean the regulator or to change or file any settings can cause damage in the electrical system.

> **CAUTION ―**
> *The engine must be shut off and cable B+ (51) disconnected before the cable connections on the generator and regulator are connected or disconnected. A short circuit will ruin the regulator. Interchanging cables on the + (D+) (DF) terminals also will damage regulator.*

### Testing Generator Without Regulator

(see Fig. 24)

1. Disconnect both cables from regulator.
2. Connect cable F (DF) on generator to ground (D−).

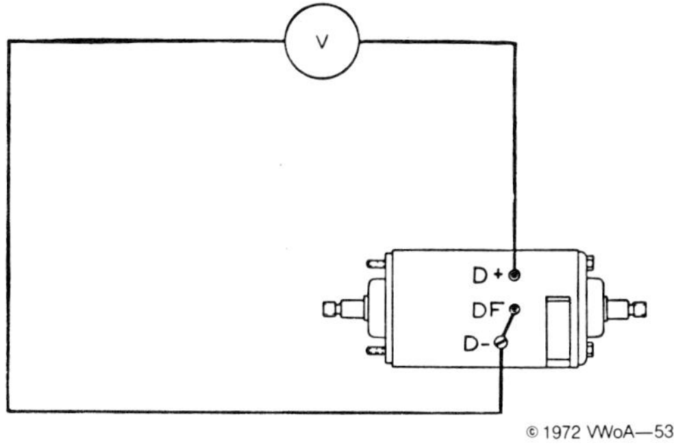


**Fig. 24.** Test hook-up for functioning of generator independent of regulator requires only voltmeter. See text.

3. Connect voltmeter positive terminal to + (D+) cable on generator and negative terminal to ground (D−).

> **CAUTION ―**
> *This test must be completed within a few seconds. Otherwise, generator field windings will burn out.*

4. Run generator at the following speeds momentarily and check voltages produced.

| Rpm* | Voltage |
|---|---|
| 1500 | About 6 V |
| 3000 | About 18 V |

*** Generator rpm is about twice engine rpm.**

5. If generator produces too low a voltage in this test or no voltage at all, it should be removed and overhauled.



## 5.3 Removing and Installing Regulator

The regulator is mounted on the generator only in 1966 sedans and convertibles (Fig. 25). The 1967, 1968 and 1969 models have the regulator under the rear seat, on the left side.

**Fig. 25.** Attached regulator on generator appears only on 1966 cars. See text for removal procedure.

On the Karmann Ghia (after August 1967) the regulator is mounted at the left side of the engine compartment (see Fig. 26). The wiring diagram for the Karmann Ghia shows cable connections for this mounting.

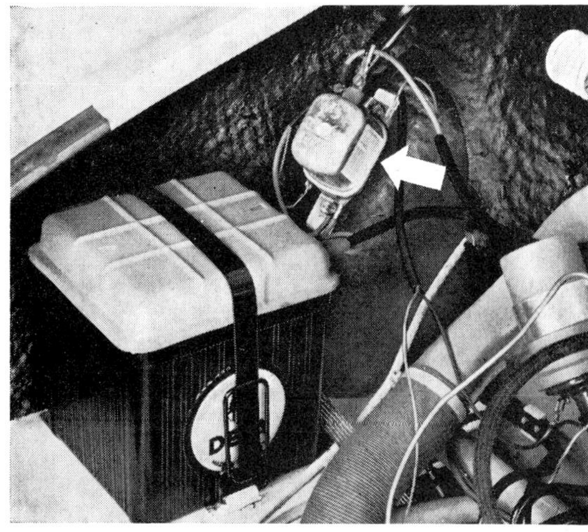


**Fig. 26.** Separate regulator in Karmann Ghia models is mounted at left of engine compartment, as indicated by the arrow.

***CAUTION —***
*Disconnect battery ground strap before starting to remove regulator.*

**To remove regulator:**

1. Disconnect cables from terminals B+ (51) and 61 at the regulator (see Fig. 25).
2. On 1966 sedans remove slotted screws that attach regulator to generator. Take off regulator.
3. Disconnect the two cables from terminals marked + (D+) and F (DF) at bottom of regulator.

**To install:** Procedure is reverse of removal procedure, but the following points should be noted:

1. The thick cable from the positive brush must be connected to terminal + (D+) at the bottom of the regulator.
2. The thin cable from the field windings must be connected to F (DF) terminal at the bottom of the regulator. If replacing the regulator does not correct trouble in the generator system, the generator itself is defective.

## 5.4 Checking Brushes and Commutator

Since brushes undergo constant friction while the engine is running and the generator armature is spinning, they wear down. The commutator may become rough or pitted and may show burn spots. A commutator in such condition will need remachining.

## 5.5 Removing and Installing Brushes

**To remove:**

1. Take off the generator brush cover (if your car has one).

   **NOTE —**
   The generator brushes are more accessible when the generator/fan pulley has been removed. In work on the installed generator it is a good idea to use a screwdriver that can hold a screw while you get it started. Otherwise, you may drop a screw into the generator housing and cause yourself a good bit of trouble getting it out.

2. Examine brushes. If too worn to protrude from the holders, they should be replaced with new brushes of the same type.
3. Disconnect battery ground strap.
4. On 1966 version disconnect the D+ and DF cables and remove both wires from generator terminals.
5. Remove the two screws holding the brush pigtails. Lift brush springs and take out brushes. Be careful not to drop screws or washers into the generator.

**To install:**

1. Use clean cloth dampened in solvent to wipe off dirty or oily commutator.
2. Replace brushes and pigtail screws.
3. Replace generator brush cover.
4. Reconnect the wires D+ and DF to the generator terminals.

If any springs need to be replaced or if the commutator needs remachining, it will be necessary to remove the generator.

## 5.6 Removing and Installing Generator
(engine in place)

***CAUTION —***
*Disconnect battery ground cable before removing generator.*

**To remove:**

1. Disconnect regulator cables.
2. Take off air cleaner and carburetor.
3. Take fan belt off.
4. Loosen generator retaining strap.
5. Remove engine cooling air thermostat.
   a. With chalk, mark location of thermostat bracket for correct replacement later.
   b. Insert socket through hole in air deflector plate (see **ENGINE**) to remove bolts, or remove deflector plate.
6. Detach warm air hoses from fan housing.
7. Remove the two fan housing screws and lift up housing. If it sticks, careful rocking will loosen it.
8. Remove the four bolts in the fan housing cover and take off generator and fan.

**To install:**

*CAUTION —*
*Before it is installed in the car, especially after the armature or field coils have been replaced, a re-assembled generator must be polarized to give the pole shoes residual magnetism of the correct polarity. This residual magnetism provides the magnetic field in which the armature turns when you start the engine. In the polarizing procedure you run the generator briefly as a motor. The hookup is as follows: from the negative pole of a battery to D− and DF terminals on the generator. From positive pole of battery to D+ terminal on generator.*

1. Follow steps of removal procedure in reverse order, paying careful attention to assembly of generator and fan cover, as outlined in Note.

   **NOTE —**
   Generators with outside diameter of 4.13 inches (105 mm) are cooled by air under pressure, and a modified fan cover is used with them. This combination of generator and modified cover must be assembled as shown in Fig. 27 and installed together. When the assembly is installed in fan housing, the air slots must face downward. Otherwise, cooling will be insufficient and damage will result.

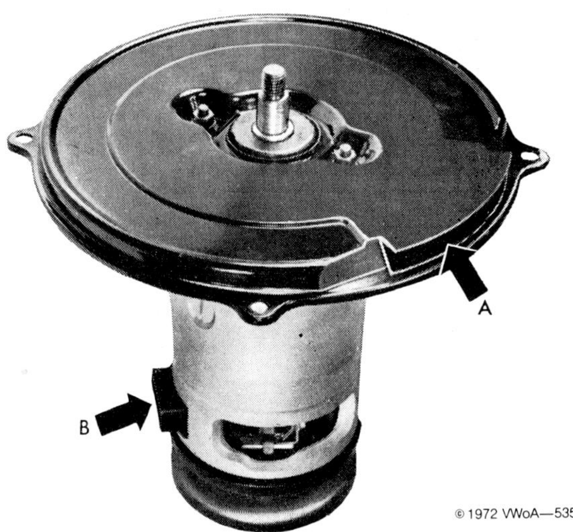


A. Cooling air slots B. Connections

**Fig. 27.** Fan cover and generator with pressure air cooling are mounted together. Assembly is positioned to have cover air slots (A) opening downward.



## 5.7 Generator Warning Light

If the generator and voltage regulator are known to be in order but the generator red warning light comes on while the car is in motion, there can be only one cause: an excessively high voltage drop is occurring in the connections between regulator terminal B+ and the warning light. This voltage drop can appear at any of the following points:

Regulator, terminal B+
Light switch, terminal 30
Fuse box, terminal 30 (fuse 1, lower)
Ignition/starter switch, terminal 30
Ignition/starter switch, terminal 15/54
Fuse box, terminal 15/54 (fuse 8, lower)

**To check:**

1. Start engine and run it at fast idle.
2. Turn on headlights, windshield wipers and turn signals.
3. Strip insulation at both ends of a 13-foot length of 12-gauge wire and connect one end to terminal B+ on voltage regulator.
4. With free end of cable touch in sequence all the listed connections while helper watches warning light.
5. If light goes out when a connection is touched, the fault has been found. The excessive voltage drop is between this connection and the connection just before it.

Loose connections, poor contacts in switches or damaged wires can cause excessive voltage drops. Clean corroded connections, tighten loose ones and replace damaged parts.

## 5.8 Generator Troubleshooting

Malfunctioning of the generator red warning light on the speedometer face can be a symptom of various troubles in the generator or voltage regulator. The red light should glow when the ignition is turned on, and it should go off as soon as the engine is up to the speed at which generator voltage equals battery voltage. Possible causes of and remedies for, malfunctions are given in **Table g.**

### Table g. Generator Troubleshooting

| Symptom | Cause | Remedy |
|---|---|---|
| 1. Ignition is on, but warning light does not glow | a. Discharged battery | a. Charge battery |
| | b. Broken battery case or plates | b. Replace battery |
| | c. Bulb burned out | c. Replace bulb |
| | d. Corroded and/or loose battery terminals | d. Clean and/or tighten terminals |
| | e. Loose connections and/or broken terminal wiring | e. Tighten and/or repair cables |
| | f. Ignition/starter switch defective | f. Replace ignition/starter switch |
| | g. Generator brushes do not make contact with commutator | g. Free the brushes or replace them. If necessary, replace the brush springs. |
| | h. Regulator faulty | h. Check regulator, replace if necessary |
| 2. Light stays on or flickers when engine is running | a. Fan belt broken or slips badly | a. Replace or adjust fan belt. |
| | b. Regulator faulty | b. Replace regulator |
| | c. Loose connections or broken wire | c. Check wires and connections |
| | d. Generator faulty | d. Check generator |
| | e. Commutator bars short-circuited | e. Clean commutator with fine polishing cloth |
| 3. Light goes out only at high speed | a. Generator faulty | a. Check generator |
| | b. Regulator faulty | b. Replace regulator |
| 4. Light remains on with the ignition switched off | a. Regular contact points sticking (burned) | a. Replace regulator |

## 6. LIGHTING SYSTEM
(sedan and convertible)

**NOTE —**
From the 1967 models on, all VWs are equipped with modified headlights, as shown in Fig. 28. The front fenders also have been modified. The headlight housing now is vertical to allow installation of the complete Type 3 sealed beam insert. The previously standard lens was discontinued. In the new model headlight removal of a screw in the six o'clock position permits removal of the chrome ring (bezel) around the unit. The adjusting screws are then exposed. The locations of these screws are the same as on the 1966 model. In the post-1967 arrangement the parking lights are combined with the front turn signals, and a twin-filament bulb provides the illumination.

The lighting systems of the sedan and convertible are sufficiently different from those of the Karmann Ghia models to warrant discussing them separately.

**Fig. 28.** Modified headlight on cars from 1967 model on has vertical housing. Front fender also was modified.

### 6.1 Replacing Sealed Beam Unit and Parking Light Bulb
(1966 cars only)

***CAUTION —***
*Before beginning procedure, make sure lights are off.*

**To remove:**

1. Loosen front rim retaining screw and pull out complete headlight unit (see Fig. 29).

© 1972 VWoA—537

**Fig. 29.** Sealed beam headlight and parking light come out of fender as unit after retaining screw is removed.

2. Pull headlight connector off sealed beam unit (see Fig. 30).
3. Disconnect the two cables from the parking light bulb socket.
4. Screw out parking light bulb.

***WARNING —***
*Lens retaining springs are under heavy tension. To prevent an accident, be careful when removing them.*

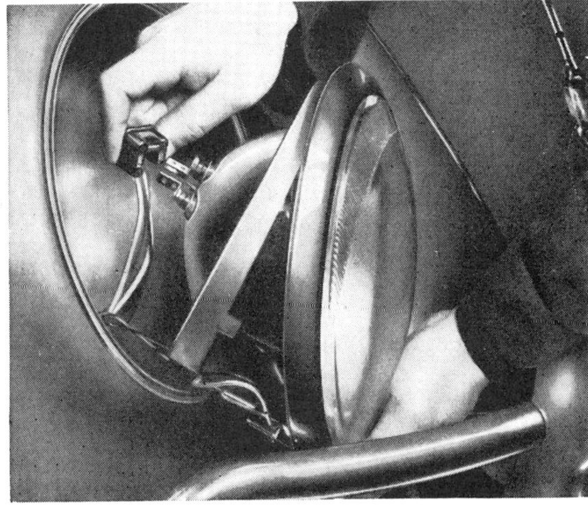

© 1972 VWoA—538

**Fig. 30.** Headlight connector is removed from sealed beam unit.

5. Remove lens retaining springs as shown in Fig. 31 Hold the lamp unit with one thumb controlling spring while other thumb hooks springs out of their seatings. Fig. 31 shows the operation.
6. Withdraw retaining ring and sealed beam unit.

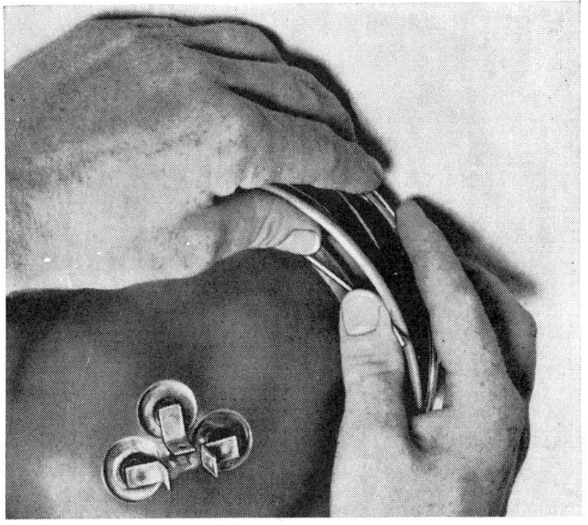

© 1972 VWoA—539

**Fig. 31.** Retaining springs of headlight unit are under heavy tension. Be careful when removing them. Hold spring with one thumb while prying with other thumb.

**To install:**

1. Use tabs and slots of the retaining ring as guides for correct location of sealed beam unit.
2. Connect cables.
3. Inspect rubber seal between front rim and car fender for proper seating.
4. Choose replacement parts from following table:

| | Standard Replacement | VW Part Number |
|---|---|---|
| **Headlights (sealed beam)** | | |
| 6-volt | 6006 | 111 941 161 A |
| 12-volt | 6012 | 111 941 261 A |
| **Parking Bulb** | | |
| 6-volt | 81 | N 17 719 1 |
| 12-volt | 1034 | N 17 738 2 |

5. Recheck headlight adjustment.

**To replace headlight glass:**

1. Remove headlight unit.
2. Detach connector and parking light cable.

***WARNING —***
*Exercise care when removing lens retaining springs. They are under heavy tension.*

10

3. Take out lens retaining springs.
4. Unscrew headlight adjusting screws as far as possible and detach spring clip. (See Fig. 32.)

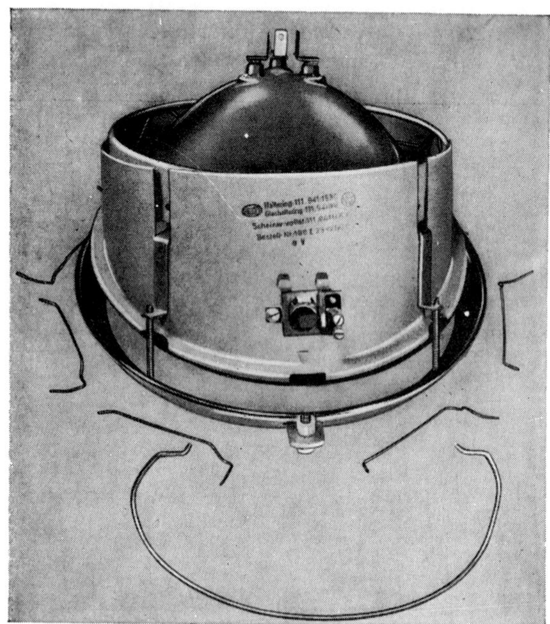



**Fig. 32.** Stripped headlight, with cables, lens, gasket and retaining springs removed, is shown here.

5. Lift retaining ring and sealed beam unit until headlight glass and gasket can be removed.
6. Place gasket on new glass and insert glass in rim so that the VW sign will be upright when installed and the arrow pointing down.
7. Position retaining ring and sealed beam unit and check the seating of gasket between rim and retaining ring.
8. Insert retaining springs.
9. Adjust headlights.

## 6.2 Adjusting Sealed Beam Headlights

Each headlight has two screws by which the lateral and vertical aim of the lights can be adjusted to conform to highway safety regulations. As shown in Fig. 33, screw A controls vertical aim. Screw B controls lateral aim.

**Adjustments**

| Screw | Screw Movement | Beam Movement |
|---|---|---|
| A | turn to left | up |
| A | turn to right | down |
| B | turn to left | right |
| B | turn to right | left |

**Fig. 33.** Adjusting screws for aiming headlights (1966 cars) are shown here. Screw A controls vertical movement, screw B lateral movement.

## 6.3 Aiming the Headlights

While the following instructions for aiming headlights will be found to conform in most cases to the law, highway regulations of the individual states will, of course, be the final authority. Check the requirements of the state in which car is registered.

1. Lights are to be adjusted while car is standing on level surface 25 feet (7.62 m) from vertical wall.
2. Tire pressure must be correct for the car.
3. Driver's seat is to be loaded with one person or a weight of 154 pounds (70 kg).
4. Vehicle is to be rolled back and forth a few yards to settle suspension.
5. Headlights are to be adjusted separately. Light not being adjusted is to be covered.
6. Aiming surface is to be target with dimensions given in Fig. 34.
7. Headlights are to be adjusted on low beam. High beam will then be in correct adjustment.
8. A correctly-aimed beam has upper edge of its high intensity zone on horizontal line H and left edge 2 inches to right of vertical line V (Fig. 34).

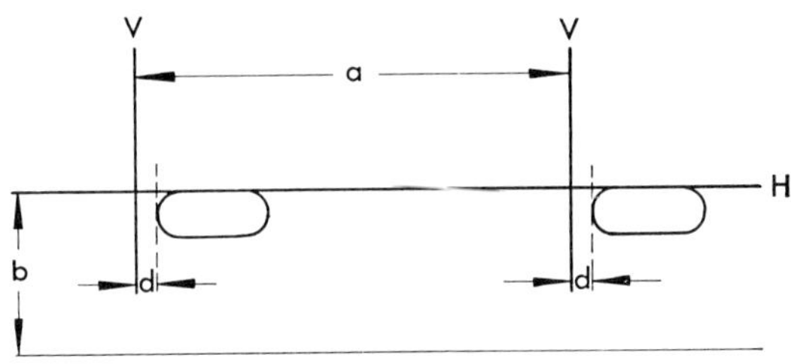




**Fig. 34.** Target for adjustment of headlights has vertical lines (V) and horizontal line (H) intersecting at centers of the two headlights. Distance (b) is height of headlight center from ground. Other distances are: (a), 41.1 inches (1044 mm) or 39.53 inches (1004 mm), depending on car model; (d), 2.0 inches (50.8 mm). Ovals touching line (H) represent areas of high intensity in the low beam light pattern. The distance (d) is greater on cars with the modified fender and headlights, from 1967 models on. See text.

## 6.4 Removing and Installing Front Turn Signal

**To remove:**

1. Remove screw that fastens lens to bulb holder (see Fig. 35).

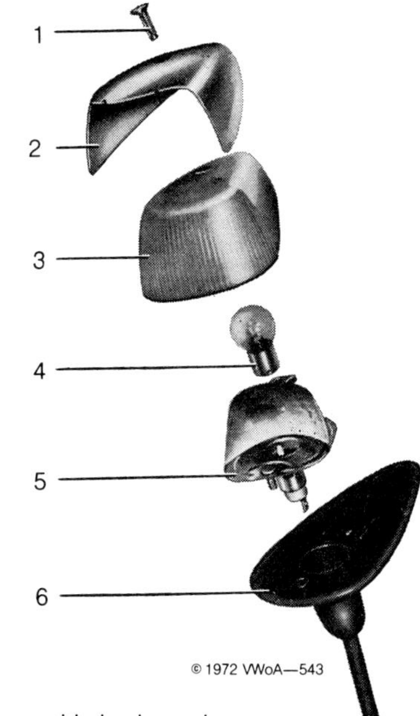


1. Screw
2. Cover
3. Lens
4. Bulb
5. Bulb holder
6. Packing



**Fig. 35.** Front turn signal assembly is shown here.

2. Take off lens.
3. Screw off both attaching nuts for bulb holder. You will find them under fender (see Fig. 36).
4. Pull up the holder with bulb and disconnect cable.
5. Pull out cable.
6. Loosen cable sleeve from side panel. Pull up packing and take it out.

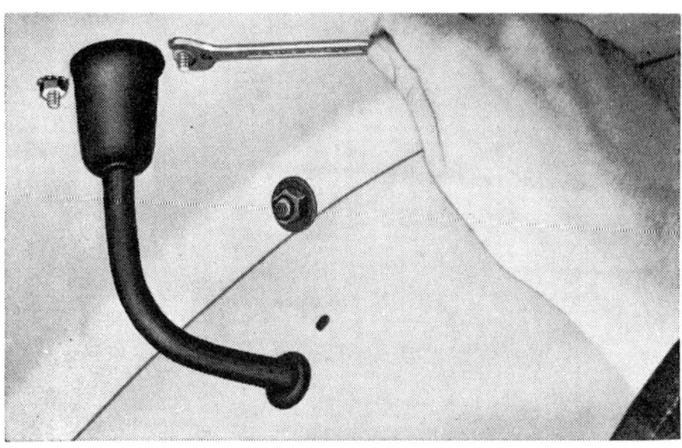



**Fig. 36.** Cable and attaching nuts for front turn signal are under fender.

**To install:** The procedure is the reverse of the removal procedure with these precautions to be taken:

1. Be careful not to damage the cable sleeve when pushing it into side panel.
2. Do not use excessive force when tightening attaching nuts for the bulb holder.

## 6.5 Replacing License Plate Light

The housing for the license plate light is attached to the rear hood of the car, and for easy access to the light the hood must be opened.

**To replace bulb:**

***CAUTION*** —
*Make sure light is switched off.*

1. Open rear hood.
2. Loosen both screws on light housing and remove lens, as shown in Fig. 37.

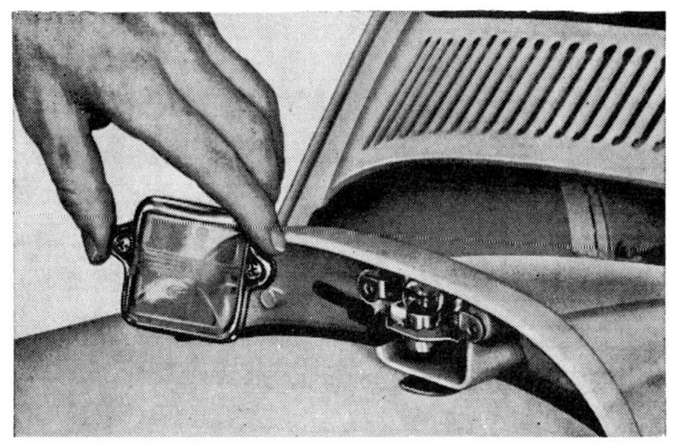



**Fig. 37.** License plate light has lens removed.

3. Put in new bulb (see table below).

The bulb should seat snugly and make good contact. Check tension of the contact springs and clean them if necessary. Check the housing gasket and replace it if it is damaged.

| License Plate Bulb | Standard Replacement | VW Part Number |
|---|---|---|
| 6-volt | 81 | N 17 719 1 |
| 12-volt | 89 | N 17 719 2 |

## 6.6 Rear Lights

On the earlier sedans and convertibles of the years covered in this Manual, a brake/tail light and a turn signal light are mounted together in a housing on each of the rear fenders, as shown in Figs. 38 and 39. This arrangement was modified in the 1968 models (and thereafter) to include a back-up light.

Another change was made, from the 1967 model on, to prevent incorrect installation of the brake/tail light bulb. The new bulb holders incorporating this modification can be identified by their markings.

**On the turn signal bulb holder:**
6 volt 18 watt; 12-volt 21 watt and 32 candle power (cp)

**On the brake/tail light bulb holder:**
6 volt 18/5 watt; 12 volt 21/5 watt and 32/4 cp

The following table gives the correct bulbs for the different lights in the rear fender assemblies. The letters A and B refer to the designations on Figs. 38 and 39.

| | Standard Replacement | VW Part Number |
|---|---|---|
| **(A) Turn Signal Bulb (single filament)** | | |
| 6-volt | 1129 | N 17 731 1 |
| 12-volt | 1073 | N 17 732 2 |
| **(B) Brake/tail Bulb (double filament)** | | |
| 6-volt | 1154 | N 17 737 1 |
| 12-volt | 1034 | N 17 738 2 |

**To replace:**

1. Remove two screws and take off lens.
2. Remove bulb by pressing down lightly and turning it to left.
3. When inserting the twin-filament bulb, be sure to have retaining pin nearest the glass pointing down.

**NOTE —**
Repairs to the lighting system must conform to motor vehicle laws. Lights from different manufacturers may be used if they carry the official stamp of approval for the vehicle on which they are to be installed.

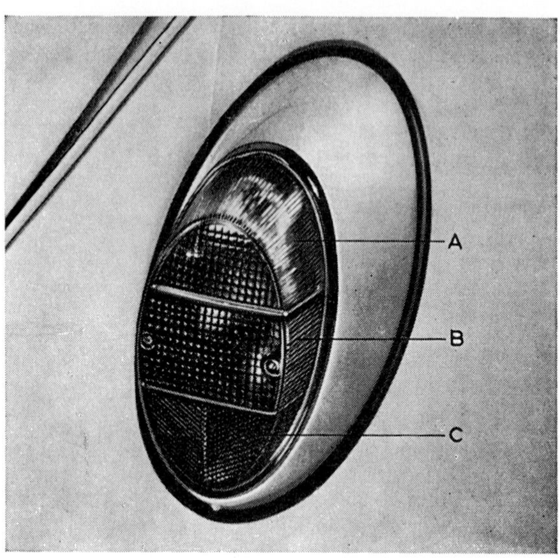




**Fig. 38.** Rear light assembly consists of turn signal (A); brake/tail light (B), and reflector (C).

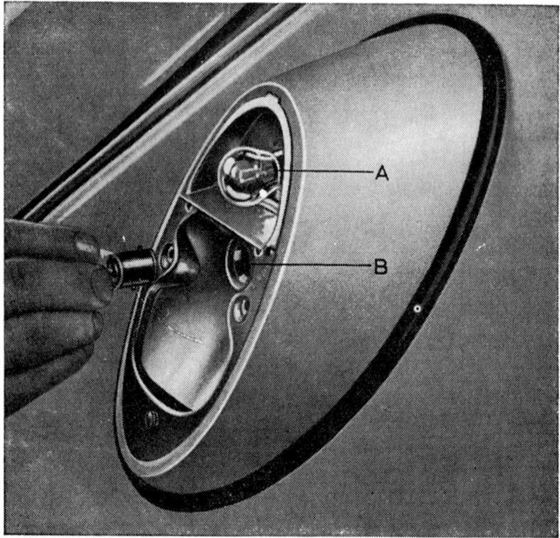




**Fig. 39.** Bulb locations in tail light housing are shown here: turn signal (A); brake/tail light (B).

The 1968 changes in the rear lights, as seen in Fig. 40, included modifications of the housing, bulb-holder and lens as well as addition of a back-up light. The new lens incorporates an integral reflector.

***CAUTION —***
*To avoid short circuit when working with lights, disconnect battery ground strap.*

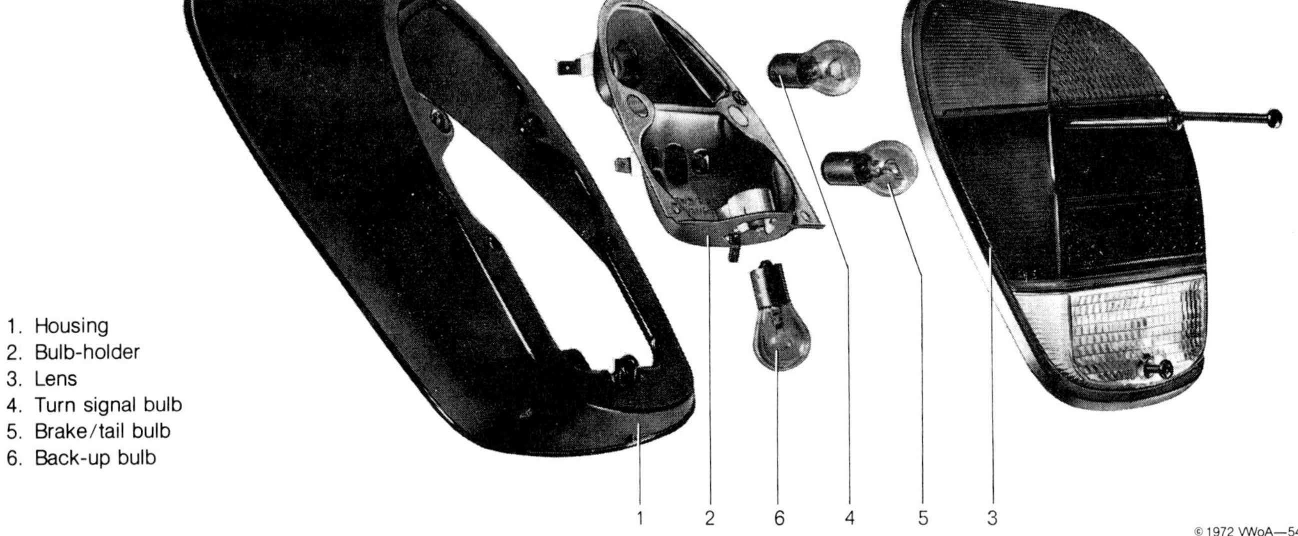


**Fig. 40.** Modified tail light for 1968 and later cars is shown here in exploded view.

## 6.7 Interior Light

The interior light, which is in the left-hand roof member over the door pillar, has a tumbler switch in the housing by which the light can be turned on or off when the doors are either open or closed.

**To replace interior light:**

1. Grip light housing at both ends and pull it out of the opening in roof. Remove bulb as in Fig. 41.
2. Put in new bulb (see table at right); make sure bulb seats properly with good contact.

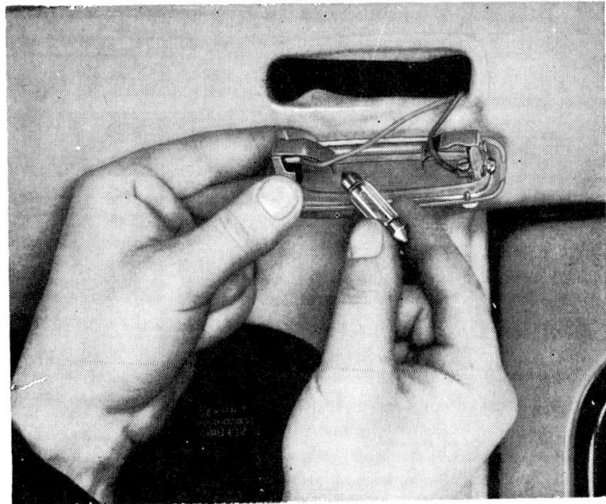


**Fig. 41.** Interior light with bulb removed is shown here pulled from its seat in the roof member.

| Interior Light Bulb | VW Part Number |
|---|---|
| 6-volt | N 17 723 1 |
| 12-volt | N 17 723 2 |

Contact switches in the door posts on both sides of the car turn on the interior light automatically when the doors are opened.

**To remove and install contact switch:**

1. Remove screw below switch push button, as shown in Fig. 42. Pull out switch and disconnect cable.
2. When installing make sure switch is grounded properly.

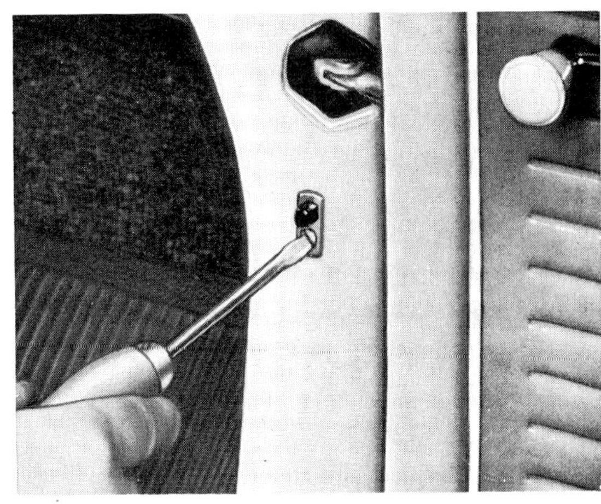


**Fig. 42.** Contact switch for interior light comes out of door post when single screw has been removed.

## 6.8 Replacing Bulbs for Warning and Instrument Lights

All instrument panel lights are accessible from the front luggage compartment, as shown in Fig. 43. Included are the fuel gauge and speedometer lights, the warning lights for oil pressure and generator operation and the turn indicator and headlight high beam signals. They are reached by lifting the front hood and removing the cover at the back of the instrument panel.

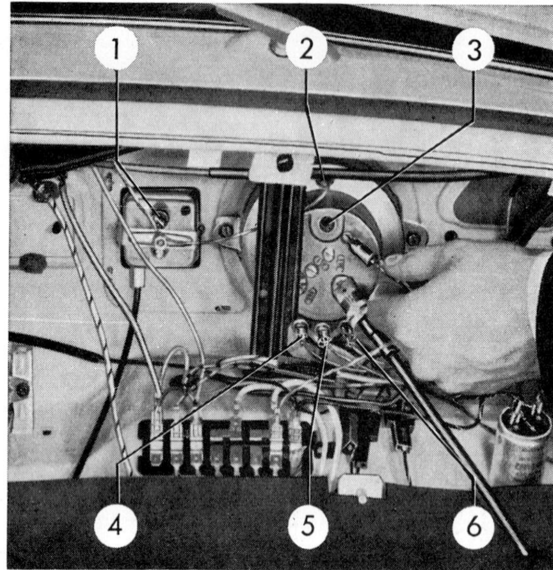




1. Fuel gauge light
2. Speedometer light
3. Head lights
4. Oil pressure signal
5. Turn signal
6. Generator warning light

**Fig. 43.** Electrical connections for the instrument panel, 1966 and 1967 models, are shown here. Connections are behind cover in front luggage compartment.

## 6.9 Turn Signal System

The front turn signal lights are on the front fenders above the headlights. The rear turn signals are in the housings for the combined brake and tail lights units. A self-cancelling switch below the steering wheel operates these turn indicators. A flasher unit controls the emergency flashing signal. The table below specifies bulbs for these lights:

| Front and Rear Bulbs | Standard Replacement | VW Part Number |
|---|---|---|
| 6-volt | 1129 | N 17 731 1 |
| **Front Bulb** | | |
| 12-volt | 1034 | N 17 738 2 |
| **Rear Bulb** | | |
| 12-volt | 1073 | N 17 732 2 |

**To replace bulb (front):**

1. Remove screw that fastens lens to bulb holder (see Fig. 44).

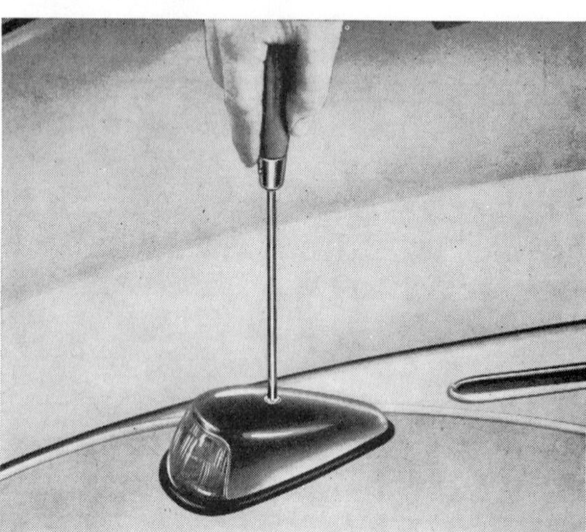



**Fig. 44.** Front turn signal on fender has lens held by a single screw.

2. Lift off lens.
3. Take out old bulb and put in new one, seating it firmly and with good contact (see Fig. 45).

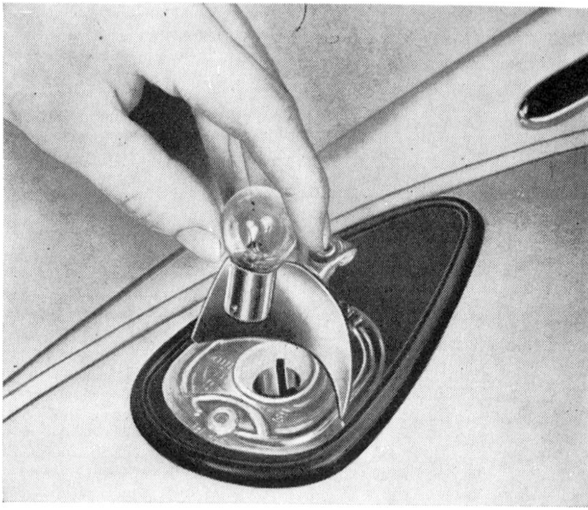



**Fig. 45.** Bulb holder for front turn signal is shown with lens removed.

4. Inspect rubber seal between the bulb holder and fender and replace it if worn or damaged.
5. Install lens, being careful to seat it in the channel in packing.

Instructions for replacing bulb in the rear turn signal are given for the sedan in **6.6 Rear Lights** and for the Karmann Ghia models in **7.2 Rear Lights.**

## 6.10 Emergency Flasher System

On VW cars all four turn signal lights flash in unison when you actuate the emergency flasher system. You pull the red knob labeled "EMERGENCY" to put the system in operation. An indicator light in the switch knob flashes with the emergency lights.

**Fig. 46.** Emergency flasher system on 1966 and 1967 cars is pictured schematically here in this wiring diagram.

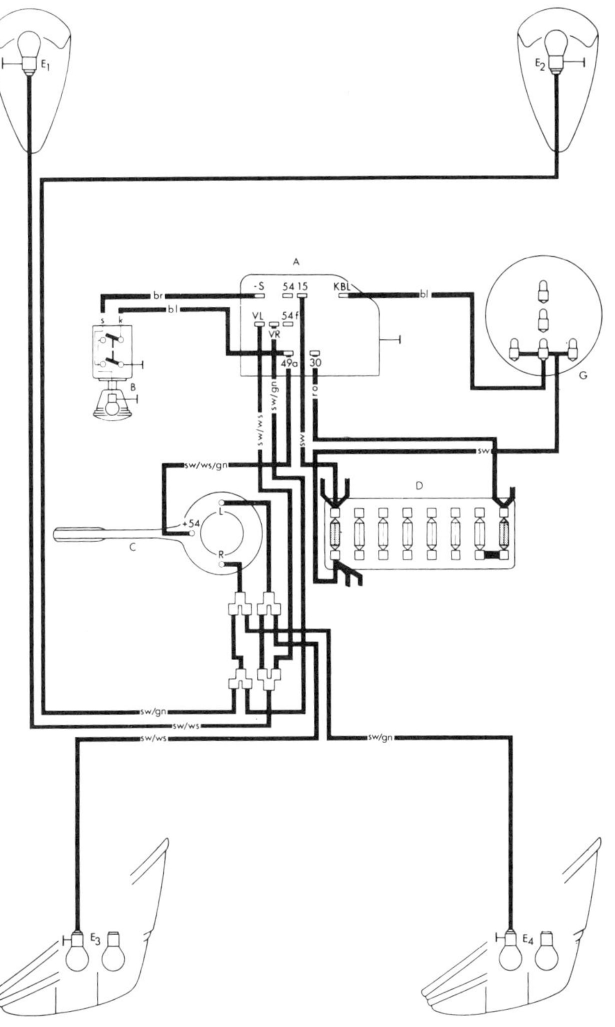


As introduced in August 1966, the system consisted basically of a switch and relay connected with the turn signal lights. Fig. 46 is the wiring diagram for the system. In January 1968 a change was made to incorporate some of the relay functions in the switch. The wiring diagram for this arrangement is shown in Fig. 47. To see where these circuits fit in the entire electrical system study these two diagrams with reference to the wiring diagrams (Figs. 1-4) which appear after the contents pages of this section.

The procedures for testing the relay and the flasher switch apply to both the old and new flasher systems. They should be followed in the sequence given.

**Fig. 47.** Emergency flasher system for 1968 models and later cars is pictured schematically in this wiring diagram.

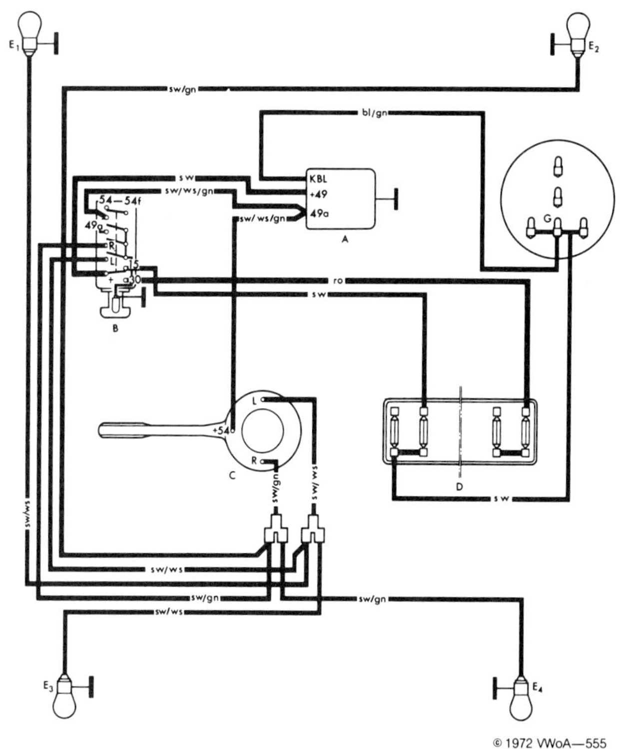


**Color Codes**

bl. blue
li. lilac
br. brown
ro. red
ge. yellow
sw. black
gn. green
ws. white
gr. gray

**For example: sw/ws/gn = black-white-green**

A. Flasher and turn signal relay
B. Emergency flasher switch
C. Turn signal switch
D. Fuse box
$E_1$. Turn signal light
$E_1$. Turn signal light
$E_2$. Turn signal light
$E_3$. Turn signal light
$E_4$. Turn signal light
F. Turn signal indicator light

**10**

**To test relay:**

1. With ignition off, connect terminal + or 49 (depending on manufacturer's designation) of the relay (see Fig. 48) to terminal 30 of the fuse box.

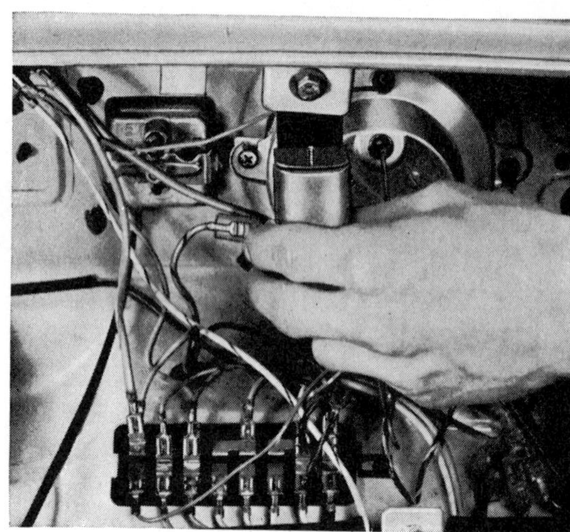



**Fig. 48.** Flasher relay, in mechanic's hand, is mounted at back of instrument panel.

2. Operate turn signal in both directions.
3. If both signals are in working order, the relay and switch are not defective.

**To test flasher switch:**

> ***CAUTION —***
> *Disconnect battery at ground strap.*

1. Remove steering wheel (see **FRONT AXLE).**
2. Remove flasher switch and turn it on.
3. Connect ohmmeter across terminals 30 and + to test for continuity. (If ohmmeter gives reading of resistance, the circuit is continuous.)
4. Test terminals 49a, R and L on switch for continuity of circuit.
5. If any resistance is measured, replace flasher switch.

> **NOTE —**
> Make sure that all contacts on turn signal bulbs are connected properly and that bulb holders are free of corrosion. Faults here will show up as malfunction of flasher or switch.

## 6.11 Replacing Turn Signal Flasher Relay

> ***CAUTION —***
> *Before beginning work, disconnect battery ground strap to avoid short circuits.*

The flasher relay is mounted above the fuse box at the back of the instrument panel as shown in Fig. 48. To get at it, remove instrument panel cover.

1. Disconnect the three cables on the relay.
2. Screw relay out of retainer (see Fig. 48).
3. Screw in replacement relay and connect cables.
4. Check to make sure that cable connections are correct.

> **NOTE —**
> When making any repair on the turn signal system, check the ground connection between flasher relay and car body. A poor connection here can put the entire turn signal system out of operation. Often a flasher relay in perfect working order is replaced when in fact the only fault is in the ground connection.

The flasher frequency depends on the voltage available. The voltage, of course, has a wide range depending on engine speed. It is entirely normal for the flasher to work more slowly at engine idle than at high rpm when generator output is maximum. A good relay will give a flasher frequency of 60 to 120 impulses a minute.

**To remove emergency flasher switch:**

1. Disconnect battery ground strap.
2. Remove instrument panel cover at back of luggage compartment. On 1968 and 1969 models take out the fresh air box also.
3. Disconnect leads from switch.
4. Pull switch knob out and unscrew knob.
5. With special wrench remove escutcheon.
6. Take switch out of panel.

The installation procedure is the reverse of removal.

## 6.12 Brake Light Switch

All cars from the 1967 model on have the dual circuit brake system and consequently have two brake light switches, which are screwed into the two circuits of the master cylinder. Earlier cars have one switch (see Fig. 49). No brake light switch can be adjusted.

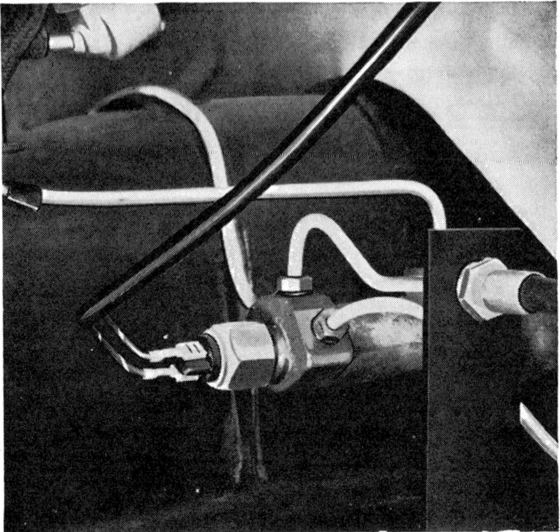

© 1972 VWoA—557

**Fig. 49.** Brake light switch screws into master cylinder. Single-circuit switch is shown here.

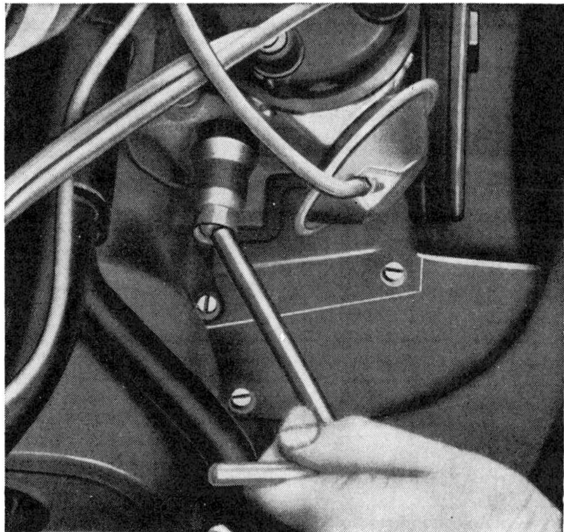

© 1972 VWoA—558

**Fig. 50.** Oil pressure switch screws into line between oil pump and oil cooler.

**To remove switch:**

1. Raise front of car.
2. Take off left front wheel.
3. Pull cables off switch.
4. Place container to catch brake fluid.
5. Screw out switch.

***WARNING*** —
*Whenever a new brake light switch is installed, the brake system must be bled.*

Installation of the brake light switch is the reverse of removal procedure.

## 6.13 Oil Pressure Switch

The oil pressure switch (see Fig. 50) is screwed into the oil pressure line between the oil pump and oil cooler and is connected to a warning light on the speedometer face. Depending on car model, this light is green or red.

The switch is a set of contact points which are held closed by a spring until oil pressure against a diaphragm overcomes the spring force and opens the points. When the engine is not running, the switch is closed. When ignition is on, battery current flows through circuit including terminal 15 of the ignition, the warning light and the closed switch. The warning light comes on. But as soon as the running engine builds up enough pressure in the oil passage to move the diaphragm in the oil pressure switch, the contact points open to break the circuit. The warning light goes off.

The oil pressure switch can be tested for proper functioning, but it cannot be repaired. A defective switch must be replaced.

***CAUTION*** —
*Disconnect battery ground strap before beginning work.*

**To remove switch:**

1. Disconnect cable at oil pressure switch.
2. Screw out switch (see Fig. 50).

**To install:**

1. Follow procedure for removal but in reverse order, taking care not to damage the tapered thread by using too much force to screw in the switch. The thread acts as a seal.
2. Check to be sure that switch is operating the warning light in the speedometer.

**10**

### Testing Oil Pressure Switch

There is a simple device for testing the oil pressure switch. It consists of a gauge and a test light.

1. Bring engine to operating temperature.
2. Screw switch into testing device.
3. Screw testing device into seat for the switch on the oil line, as shown in Fig. 51.

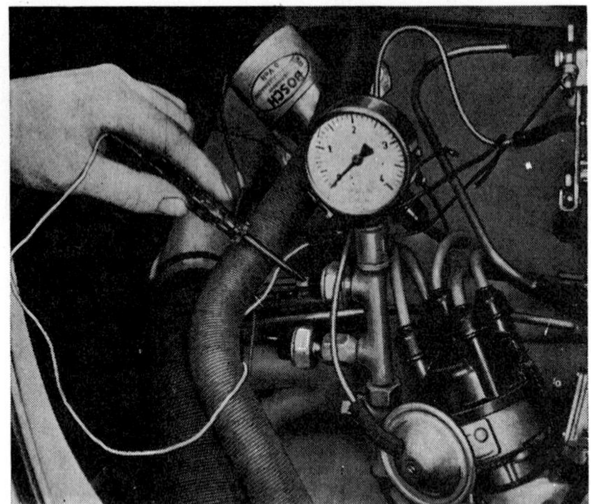



**Fig. 51.** Testing device for oil pressure switch consists of gauge and light. See text for procedure.

4. Connect one lead of test light to the oil pressure switch and other lead to terminal 15 at the ignition coil. The test light should turn on. If it does not, the switch is defective.

***CAUTION —***
*If the oil pressure warning light stays on continuously when car is in operation, the chances are that something has happened to stop circulation of oil. The engine has ceased to receive lubrication. Check oil level and look for leaks if it is low. If the cause appears to be somewhere else, do not drive but get in touch with your nearest Authorized VW Dealer. Occasional lighting of the warning signal at idle does not indicate trouble if the light goes out again as soon as engine speed increases.*

5. Start engine. The test device gauge will register pressure in the oil line. Above some point in the range 2.1 to 6.4 psi (0.15 to 0.45 kg/cm$^2$) the light should go out. At lower pressure the contact points should be closed and the warning light on.
6. Stop engine but leave ignition switch on. Disconnect primary coil wire. Since oil pressure decreases slowly, there may be a slight delay before the light comes on.

## 7. LIGHTING SYSTEM
(Karmann Ghia models)

The main differences in the lighting system of the Karmann Ghia models are found in the adjustments of the sealed beam headlights, the arrangement of the rear lights and the location of the interior lights.

### 7.1 Sealed Beam Headlights

The Karmann Ghia headlights, like those on the sedan and convertible, have adjusting screws (Fig. 52) for vertical and horizontal (lateral) aim of the beams, but the controlling movements are in the opposite directions on the Karmann Ghia, as shown in following table.

| | Adjustments | |
|---|---|---|
| **Screw** | **Screw Movement** | **Beam Movement** |
| A | turn to right | up |
| A | turn to left | down |
| B | turn to right | right |
| B | turn to left | left |

The correct bulbs for the Karmann Ghia sealed beam headlights are:

| Sealed Beam Headlights (Karmann Ghia) | Standard Replacement | VW Part Number |
|---|---|---|
| 6-volt | 6006 | 111 941 161 A |
| 12-volt | 6012 | 111 941 261 A |

**Fig. 52.** Karmann Ghia headlight has adjusting screws in different locations. Screw (a) controls vertical aim, screw (b) lateral aim. This is a sealed beam headlight.

The sealed beam unit on the Karmann Ghia can be replaced after the trim ring has been removed and the headlight unit taken out of its housing.

The parking light is combined with the turn signal light on the Karmann Ghia, a twin-filament bulb serving for both. The correct bulbs are:

| Parking/Turn Signal Bulb (Karmann Ghia) | Standard Replacement | VW Part Number |
|---|---|---|
| 6-volt | 1129 | N 17 731 1 |
| 12-volt | 1073 | N 17 732 2 |

## 7.2 Rear Lights

A brake light, turn signal and tail light with reflector are mounted in each rear fender, as shown in Fig. 53. The correct bulbs are:

| | Standard Replacement | VW Part Number |
|---|---|---|
| **Turn Signal Bulb** | | |
| 6-volt | 1129 | N 17 731 1 |
| 12-volt | 1073 | N 17 732 2 |
| **Brake Light Bulb** | | |
| 6-volt | 1129 | N 17 731 1 |
| 12-volt | 1073 | N 17 732 2 |
| **Tail Light Bulb** | | |
| 6-volt | 81 | N 17 719 1 |
| 12-volt | 67 | N 17 718 2 |

© 1972 VWoA—561

1. Turn signal
2. Brake light
3. Tail light

**Fig. 53.** Karmann Ghia tail light assembly is shown here.

**To replace bulb:**

1. Remove two Phillips screws and take off chrome rim with lenses (Fig. 53).
2. Put in new bulbs, making sure to seat them properly with good contact.
3. Replace with chrome frame, being careful of the seating.

**To replace rear light housing:**

1. Remove two Phillips screws and take off chrome rim with lenses, as in previous procedure.
2. Take out engine compartment insulation on the side of light you are working on. Bend down clips securing the insulation and then remove the air cleaner insert and battery.
3. Disconnect cables to the light assembly.
4. Loosen the two wing screws.
5. Lift out housing with gasket, as in Fig. 54. When reinstalling housing make sure that gaskets are properly seated.

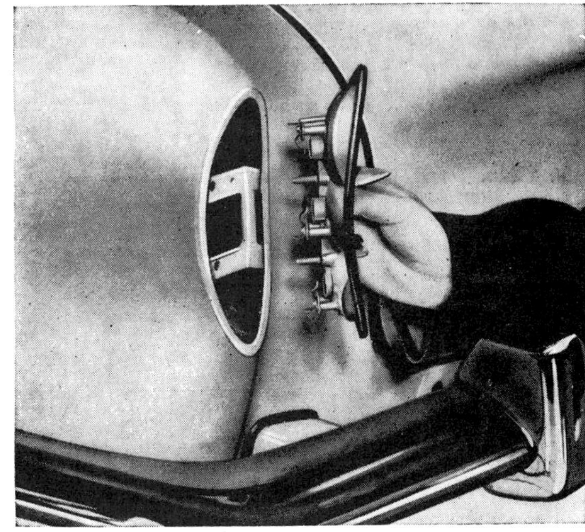

© 1972 VWoA—562

**Fig. 54.** Tail light unit on Karmann Ghia is shown here removed from housing in fender.

## 7.3 License Plate Lights

The Karmann Ghia models have two license plate lights in the handle of the rear hood. The following table specifies correct bulbs:

| License Plate Bulb | Standard Replacement | VW Part Number |
|---|---|---|
| 6-volt | 81 | N 17 719 1 |
| 12-volt | 67 | N 17 718 2 |

**10**

**To replace bulbs:**

1. Open rear hood.
2. Remove two screws and glass insert (see Fig. 55).

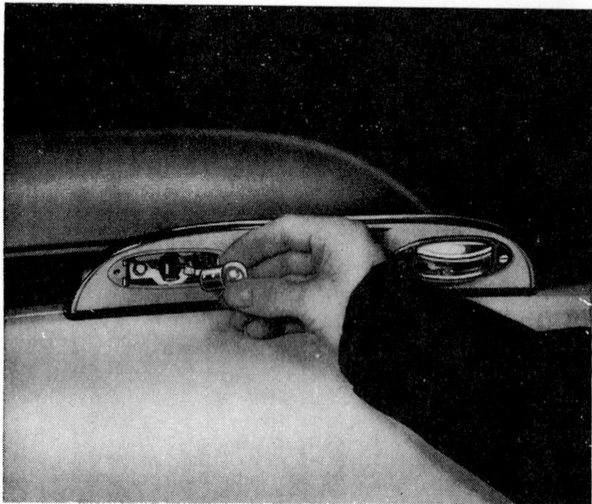



**Fig. 55.** License plate lights on Karmann Ghia are in rear hood handle.

3. Put in new bulbs. Check that groove in glass fits over lug in housing.

**To remove housing:**

1. Open rear hood and bend up cable clips.
2. Remove four screws holding handle and take off handle with gasket. Location of screws is shown in Fig. 56.

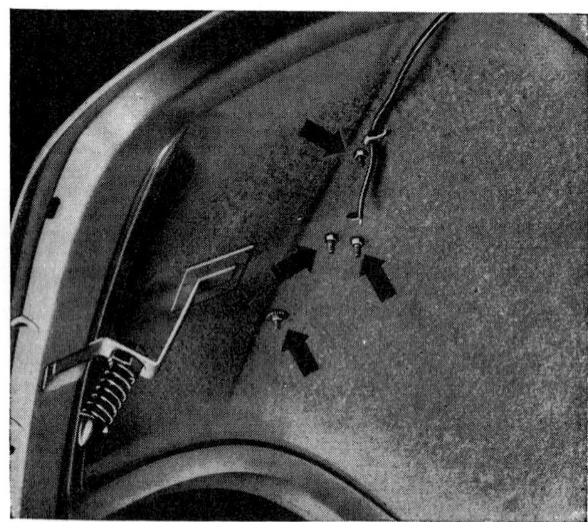



**Fig. 56.** Rear hood handle on Karmann Ghia has four small screws (black arrows).

3. Disconnect cable.
4. Unscrew glass insert and remove lamp housing.
5. Unsolder cable from old housing.

**To install:**

1. Follow the five steps of removal procedure but in reverse order.

## 7.4 Interior Light

Opening or closing either door automatically operates the interior light. A three-position switch in the fitting allows manual control of light independent of door position. Correct bulbs are:

| Interior Light Bulb | Standard Replacement | VW Part Number |
|---|---|---|
| 6-volt | Not available | N 17 717 1 |
| 12-volt | Not available | N 17 717 2 |

**To replace bulb:**

1. Grip rim of light fitting with both hands and pull out of roof opening (see Fig. 57).
2. Replace bulb.

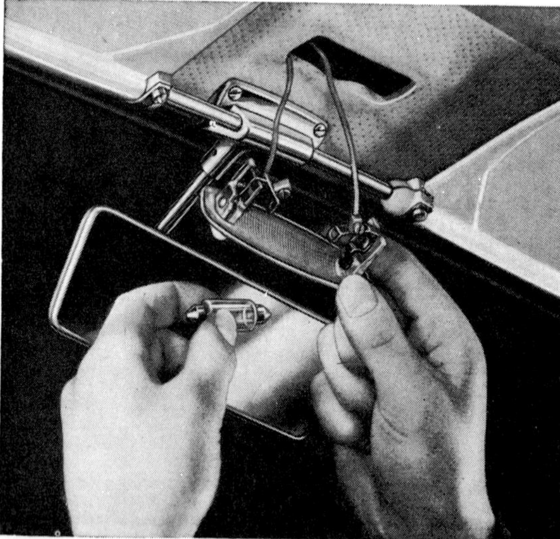



**Fig. 57.** Interior light on Karmann Ghia is in roof member housing above rear view mirror.

**To remove fitting:**

1. Pull out light and disconnect the two cables.
2. When reinstalling, make sure cable connections are correct.

**To remove door contact switch:**

1. Pull contact switch out of door hinge pillar, as shown in Fig. 58.
2. Disconnect cable.

**Fig. 58.** Contact switch for Karmann Ghia interior light is in door post.

## 8. WINDSHIELD WIPERS

A metal frame behind the instrument panel holds the windshield wiper motor and the mechanical linkage for the wipers. To get at the assembly, you raise the front hood and take off the instrument panel cover at the back of the luggage compartment. You turn the motor on or off with a rotary switch on the instrument panel. There is a push-button in the switch knob to actuate the water jet for washing the windshield.

### 8.1 Wiper Motor

On the early cars covered in this Manual (6-volt system) the windshield wiper motor is single-speed. From the 1967 model on (12-volt system) a two-speed motor is installed in conjunction with a three-position switch as standard equipment. The switch positions are: left, "OFF"; center, "SLOW"; right, "FAST."

When the windshield wiper switch is turned off, the wiper blades park automatically at the left ends of their arcs of travel. An eccentric plate turning on the wiper shaft and a double contact in the circuit (see Figs. 59 and 60) are the key to the parking movement.

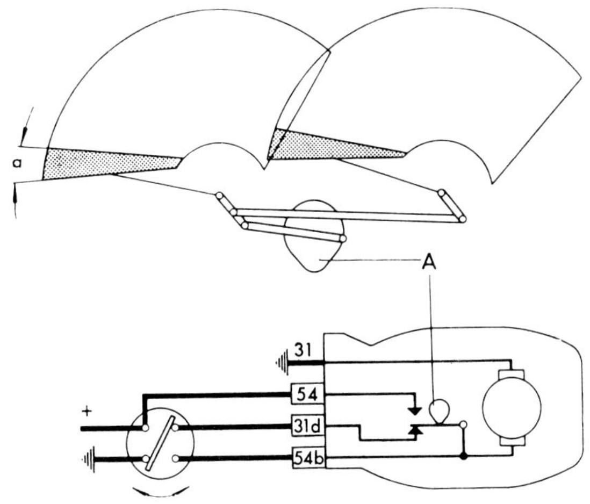




A. Eccentric plate
a. End position

**Fig. 59.** Automatic parking of windshield wiper depends on mechanical linkage and electric circuit shown schematically here and in Fig. 60. For the parking arrangement to work, blades must be in shaded areas (a) of upper diagram when eccentric plate (A) breaks circuit at one contact of a double contact in the wiper motor and then grounds it at other contact. In lower diagram wiper switch is at left and motor at right. The motor has been switched off and the eccentric plate has grounded circuit. See text.

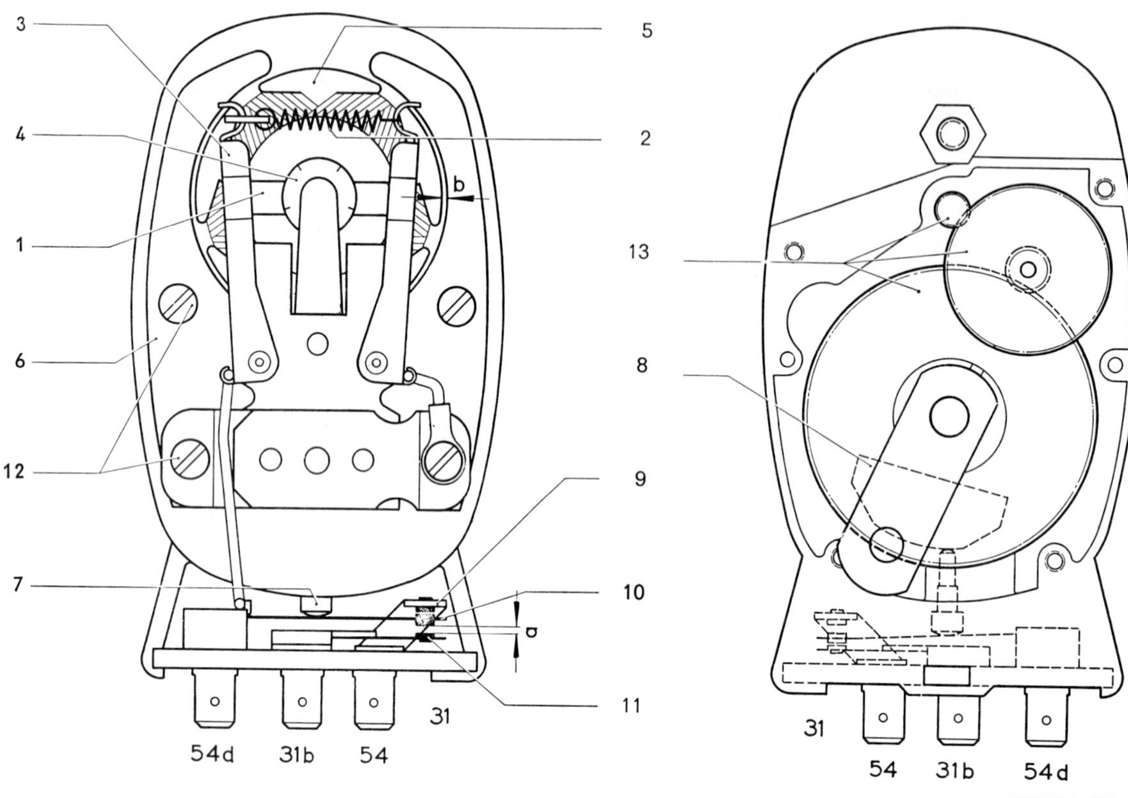


**Fig. 60.** Windshield wiper motor is shown schematically in these two views. The diagram at the right is reverse of left view.

1. Brush
2. Spring
3. Brush holder
4. Commutator
5. Armature
6. Pole shoe
7. Cylinder bolt
8. Eccentric plate
9. Contact
10. Contact spring
11. Contact
12. Attaching screws
13. Gears

a. .031″ (0.8 mm)
b. Clearance

After the switch has been turned off, current continues to flow to the motor until the camming action of the eccentric breaks the circuit at one contact and short circuits the current at the other. Because the turning of the eccentric and the movement of the wiper arm linkage are synchronized, the blades stop in the end position. To move them again from this parked position, the switch must be operated.

***CAUTION —***
*For the automatic parking arrangement to work correctly, the movement of the wiper arms must be unrestricted. If some obstruction should hold the blades outside the shaded sectors marked (a) and (b) in Fig. 59, the motor would be damaged and probably ruined. Even with the wiper switch at off, the current supply to the motor would continue. In a short time the armature windings would burn out.*

## 8.2 Precautions

To prevent damage to the wiper motor, observe the following precautions:

1. Before switching wiper on in cold weather, make sure that blades are not frozen to the windshield. If blades are not free to travel, they may start to move but stick again. Current then will continue to flow to the motor even if switch is turned to "Off."
2. In a snowstorm be sure that a buildup of snow at edges of cleared areas on the windshield will not keep blades from reaching park positions.
3. When voltage is low (battery almost dead), blades may stick in the middle of their arcs on a dry windshield. Move them to end positions.
4. If a blade sticks on windshield and you are unable to move it, take out fuse for the circuit.

### 8.3 Makes of Motor

The wiper motor on your VW may be of either SWF or Bosch manufacture. The trademark identifies the Bosch, as does the screw that fastens the cover to the housing. The SWF motor has a clip instead of the screw. The terminals for cable connections are the same on both motors. The motors are interchangeable.

## 8.4 Troubleshooting and Maintenance

A troubleshooting chart for windshield wiper motor malfunctions is given in **Table h.**

When the windshield wiper system is undergoing repair of any kind, the linkage, the spindles and the wiper arm joints should be oiled. At each maintenance inspection blade contact, uniformity of blade stroke and blade parking operation should be checked.

### 8.5 Removing and Installing Wiper Motor and Linkage Assembly

**To remove:**

1. Disconnect battery ground strap.
2. Loosen clamp screws in wiper arm brackets and remove arms.

**Table h. Windshield Wiper Motor Troubleshooting**

| Symptom | Cause | Remedy |
|---|---|---|
| 1. Windshield wiper motor does not work, operates too slowly, cuts out or comes to a standstill | a. Brushes worn | a. Replace brushes. |
| | b. Brush tension spring too weak | b. Replace tension spring. |
| | c. Brush levers not free on their pivots | c. Free brush levers. |
| | d. Commutator dirty | d. Clean commutator.* |
| | e. Moving joints of windshield wiper linkages dry or jammed | e. Thoroughly lubricate all moving joints with universal grease, eliminate jamming. |
| | f. Battery voltage too low | f. Charge battery; check cables and connections. |
| | g. Armature burned by short circuits | g. Replace motor or armature.* |
| | h. "On" position of switch not correct. No connection between terminal 1 and 2. Faulty connection from terminal 1 to terminal 54 of motor | h. Replace switch; repair faulty connection (loose contacts). |
| 2. Windshield wiper motor continues to run or fails to return blades to parking position after manual switch is turned off | a. Contacts in housing damaged | a. Replace contacts.* |
| | b. Contact spring bent | b. Replace contacts.* |
| | c. Contact bracket (insulation plate) broken | c. Replace contacts.* |
| | d. Spring contact terminal 31b does not make contact with spring contact terminal 54d. | d. Adjust contact gap to 0.031 inch (0.8 mm) or replace contacts. |
| | e. Contacts dirty | e. Clean contacts. |
| | f. Windshield wiper motor cannot be switched off | f. Screw button back slightly and bend contacts. |
| | g. Poor connection from terminal 31b via wiper switch to ground | g. Check connection and replace parts if necessary. |
| 3. Wiper linkage squeaks. Motor operates slowly. Armature is burned | a. Moving joints of windshield wiper linkages need grease | a. Thoroughly grease all moving joints with universal grease. |
| | b. Point of armature spindle rests against stop of brush holder | b. Bend stop into shape.* |
| | c. Motor cover not correctly positioned on housing | c. Seal cover properly. |

***Authorized VW repair shop or specialty shop should make this repair.**

3. Remove both wiper bearing nuts with washers and outer bearing seals (see Fig. 61).
4. Remove instrument panel cover (front luggage compartment).
5. Disconnect cables from wiper motor.
6. Remove glove box.
7. Remove screw that secures wiper frame. Take off frame with motor and linkage. See Fig. 61.

© 1972 VWoA—569

**Fig. 61.** Metal frame holding windshield wiper motor and linkage comes out as unit after bolt is removed.

**To install:** The procedure is the reverse of the removal procedures but with these additional steps.

1. When installing wiper frame make sure wiper spindles are at right angles to windshield. Move frame about in opening until spindle position is correct.
2. Double-check the order of installation of seals and washers (Fig. 62).

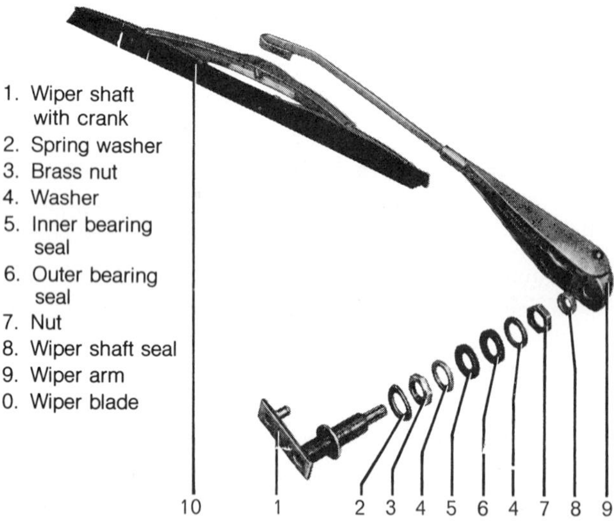


© 1972 VWoA—570

**Fig. 62.** Blade and arm of windshield wiper are seen here in exploded view.

3. Make sure that ground strap is making good contact at windshield frame securing screw.

## 8.6 Removing and Installing Motor

**To remove:**

1. Remove frame with motor and linkage (see **8.5 Removing and Installing Wiper Motor and Linkage Assembly**).
2. Remove lock washer and spring washer from drive shaft and disconnect driving link, as in Fig. 63.
3. Loosen wiper shaft securing nut, remove one motor securing nut and disengage motor from frame.

Installation is the same procedure in reverse.

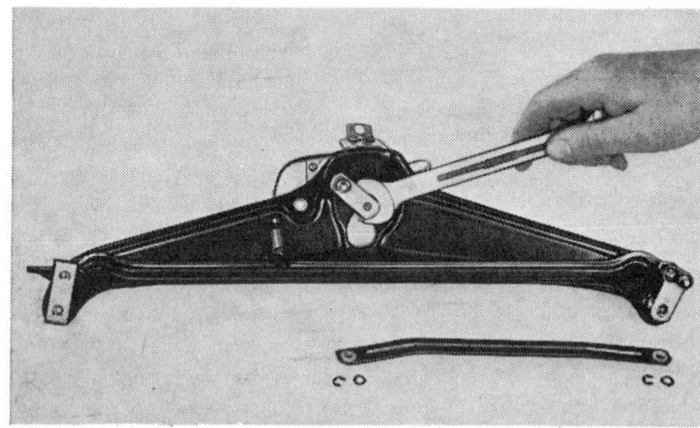

© 1972 VWoA—571

**Fig. 63.** Driving link (metal piece in foreground) comes off the windshield wiper frame when the unit is disassembled.

## 8.7 Replacing Wiper Shafts

**To remove old shaft:**

1. Remove frame with motor (see **8.5 Removing and Installing Wiper Motor and Linkage Assembly**).
2. Unhook spring between frame and connecting rod.
3. Remove lock and spring washers at the bearings. Take off driving link and connecting rod.
4. Remove inner seal and washer.
5. Unscrew retaining nut and take out shaft assembly.

**To install new shaft:** Installation is the reverse of removal with these additional steps:

1. Make sure that pressed lug on wiper frame engages in groove in wiper bearing.
2. Check plastic bushings in the linkage for wear. If necessary, replace links.
3. Hollow side of links must be toward frame and angled end of driving link toward right wiper bearing.
4. Position inner bearing seal with shoulder of rubber molding toward the wiper arm.
5. Tighten arm nut with torque wrench: 2.5 to 2.9 foot-pounds on the sedan, 3 to 4.4 foot-pounds on the Karmann Ghia.

## 8.8 Replacing Carbon Brushes

**To remove old brushes:**

1. Take out windshield frame with motor (see **8.5 Removing and Installing Wiper Motor and Linkage Assembly**).
2. Take motor off frame.
3. Take off cover after removing screw (Bosch) or clip (SWF).
4. Unhook brush holder spring (see Fig. 64).

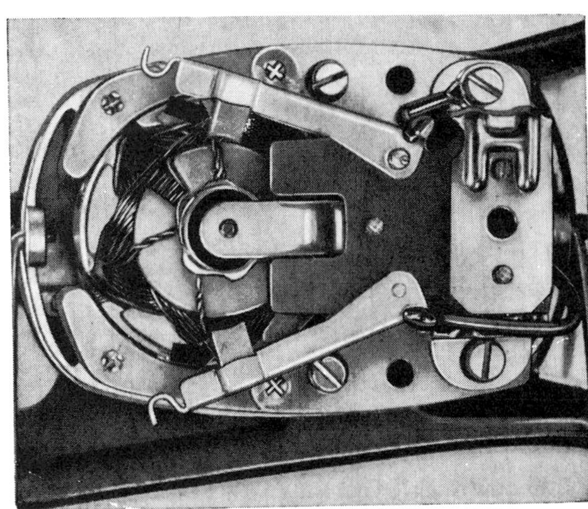



**Fig. 64.** Brush holders of wiper motor are seen here with connecting spring removed. View is same as left diagram in Fig. 60.

5. Swing brush holders outward.
6. With needle nose pliers pull out old brushes.
7. Insert new brushes. Make sure that they are tight in holders and properly seated.

**NOTE —**
When you replace carbon brushes, inspect and clean the commutator. Clear slots between segments of carbon of carbon dust. Wipe away oil or grease on brush surfaces. Use a clean cloth moistened with solvent for cleaning commutator. You may use a polishing cloth (fine grade) on burned spots.

8. Replace brush holder, spring and cover. Do not overtighten screw on cover of Bosch motor. The cover should not be indented around screw head.

If more extensive repair seems to be needed, the wiper motor should be replaced.

## 8.9 Removing and Installing Wiper Switch

**NOTE —**
The push-pull wiper switch is no longer available. The rotary switch with modification must be used for replacement.

**To remove:**

1. Disconnect battery ground strap.
2. Bleed windshield washer fluid container.
3. Unscrew switch knob and take out push-button for windshield washer.
4. Unscrew switch retaining ring (escutcheon). Special wrench should be used.
5. Remove instrument panel cover (rear of luggage compartment).
6. Remove the two hoses running from the fresh air control box to the fresh air outlets (if this step is applicable to your model).
7. Pull out switch. Disconnect wires, water hoses.

**To install:**

1. If wiper motor is single-speed (1966 model car), connect terminal 53 to terminal 53b before installing new switch. On models 1967 through 1969 install switch without modification.
2. Connect terminals according to wiring diagrams. Connect water hoses.
3. For the remainder of installation procedure follow, but in reverse order, steps for removing switch.
4. Wet windshield. Operate wipers to test.

## 8.10 Wiper Blades

Over a spell of dry weather dead insects and splashes of oil and tar from the road clog windshield wiper blades.

Windshield wiper blades need fairly frequent, thor-

ough cleaning if they are to continue to give you a clear view of the road, day or night, in bad weather. Take blades off arms and wash them in alcohol or in a strong detergent solution, scrubbing with a hard nylon brush. Be careful not to damage blades but be thorough.

It is a good idea to examine the blades from time to time under an ordinary magnifying glass. If any cracks or other signs of deterioration can be seen or if the blade edges are no longer sharp, blades should be replaced.

The windshield too may need special cleaning beyond the ordinary scrubbing. Silicones, which are an ingredient of many polishes for paint and chrome, are often transferred to the windshield from sponges, chamois and rags. The slightest trace of silicones will cause streaking and clouding of the glass in rain. The following procedures will remove silicones from the glass:

1. Make a paste of French chalk (talc) and water. Add a few drops of liquid ammonia. Rub paste on windshield and allow to dry. Wipe off. Be careful to keep paste away from paintwork.
2. Wash windshield with commercial window cleaner. Apply a solution of one part muriatic acid and nine parts water. Rinse thoroughly with clean water.

## 8.11 Removing and Installing Wiper Blades

A small stop in the joint between blade and arm keeps blade from swinging free when the arm folds on the windshield.

**To remove:**

1. Holding arm, not blade, pull away from windshield (see Fig. 65).

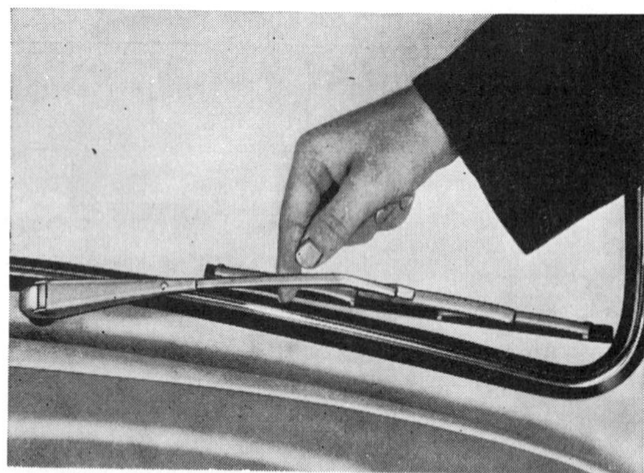



**Fig. 65.** Wiper arm is pulled away from windshield for removal of blade.

**NOTE** —
If it is necessary to take off wiper arm, merely loosen the exposed lock screw on the shaft and remove. Be sure to note angle of arm and maintain it when re-installing.

2. Pivot blade about 30 degrees to expose underside of blade bracket (see Fig. 66).

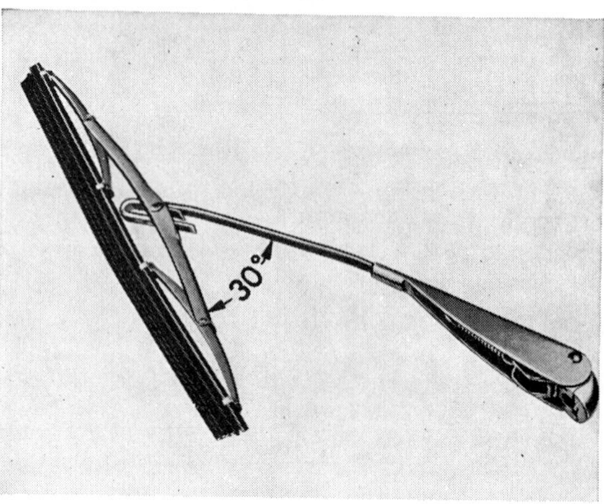




**Fig. 66.** Wiper blade is pivoted about 30 degrees from arm before it can slide through spring clip. See text.

3. Look inside hook on end of the arm for a contoured spring retaining clip. If necessary, press the clip ends together enough to disengage clip and let you push the blade through it and down arm. When blade is free, take it off the arm.

**To install:**

1. The arm hooks over rivet in opening in the wiper blade bracket. The rivet divides opening into a large opening and a small opening. Make sure that you put arm through the smaller of these two openings when you hook it over rivet. The spring clip then should snap in place.
2. If clip ends have spread, pinch them together against hook of arm.
3. To adjust wiping range, pull arm away from windshield. Loosen clamping screw. Adjust clamp and test wiper action on wet windshield until blade wipes a uniform area. Blade must not strike frame.

## 8.12 Troubleshooting Windshield Wiper System

Windshield wiping problems are described and illustrated in **Table I.** Probable causes and suggested remedies are given.

## Table i. Windshield Wiping System Troubleshooting Chart

| Symptom | Cause | Remedy |
|---|---|---|
|  © 1972 VWoA—762<br>1. Smearing | a. Blade dirty<br>b. Frayed blade lips; rubber damaged or worn out.<br>c. Blades old, surface cracked | a. Clean blade with hard nylon brush and soap solution or alcohol.<br>b. Install new blades.<br>c. Install new blades. |
|  © 1972 VWoA—763<br>2. Traces of water on windshield form small beads | Window soiled by paint, polish, oil or diesel exhaust deposits | Clean windshield with clean cloth and grease/oil silicone remover. |
| 3. Blade misses parts of windshield | a. Blade torn out of retainer<br>b. Blade not in uniform contact with glass; spring or retainer distorted<br>c. Pressure exerted by wiper insufficient | a. Re-install blade carefully.<br>b. Improper fit of blade often causes this defect. Install new blade.<br>c. Lubricate arm linkage and spring lightly or install new arm. |
|  © 1972 VWoA—764<br>4. Blade wipes well on one side but badly on other, shudders. | a. Blade distorted, no longer "flips"<br>b. Wiper arm distorted; blade not vertical on the windshield | a. Clean blade with hard nylon brush and soap solution or alcohol or install new blade.<br>b. Twist arm carefully until it is vertical. |

**The illustrations are of a windshield wiper on a Type 3 car, but they apply to your car also.**

## 8.13 Replacing Blade Fillers

Rubber fillers in the windshield wiper blades do the actual work of wiping the windshield. In ordinary use these fillers wear enough to require replacement at intervals of not more than twelve months. Formerly the entire assembly had to be replaced, but now the fillers alone are supplied as replacement parts.

The rubber filler is roughly in the form of a triangular prism. On each side of the prism there is a groove to hold a strengthening metal strip. Metal clips at the ends of the wiper bracket hold the rubber filler and the metal strips. The fingers of each clip, reaching around the metal strips, clamp into recesses in the filler below the grooves for the strips. The clip has a grip on both filler and metal strip. In the wiping action across the windshield pressure on the thin edge of the filler forces the metal strips outward against the fingers of the clips. Thus the bracket holds the filler securely.

Note that the grooves for the metal reinforcing strips are longer at one end of the filler. This is the end that should be down when the blades are in place on the windshield. When removing a filler from the bracket, you begin the work at the short end, as shown in Fig. 67.

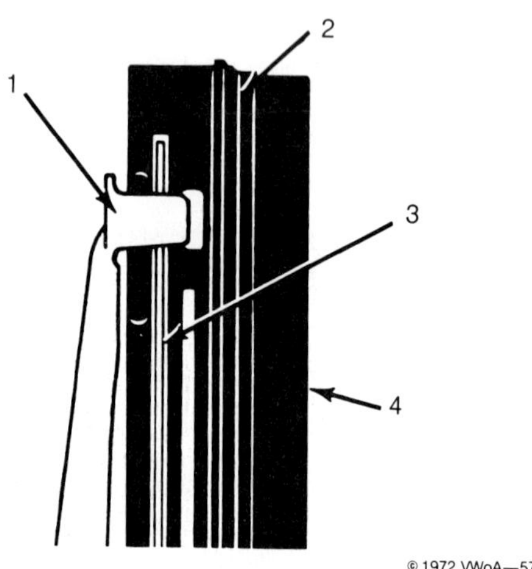


1. Retaining clip
2. Short end of filler
3. Steel strip
4. Filler

**Fig. 67.** Rubber filler assembly for windshield wiper blade consists of parts shown here. Note that retaining clip rests snugly in short end of filler.

**To remove rubber filler:**

1. Take off rubber blade (see **8.11 Removing and Installing Wiper Blades**).
2. Squeezing end of filler between thumb and finger, twist filler loose from one finger of retaining clip. Let that finger rest in the groove for the metal strip.
3. Twist filler loose from opposite finger of retaining clip, freeing end of filler.
4. As shown in Fig. 68, now slide filler down through loosened retaining clip and pull out metal strips.
5. Slide filler out of other retaining clip.

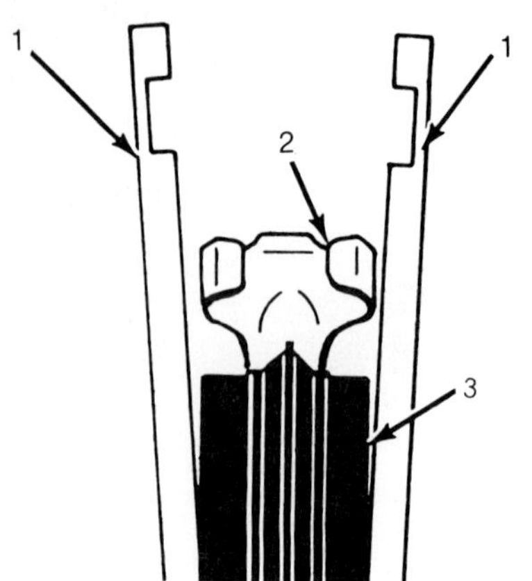


1. Steel strip
2. Retaining clip
3. Filler

**Fig. 68.** Retaining clip is loosened before steel strips are removed from rubber filler.

**To install:**

1. Insert metal strips in grooves of new filler, with strip notches inward as shown in Fig. 69.
2. Holding filler in a way to keep strips in their grooves, slide filler carefully into retaining clips, long end first.

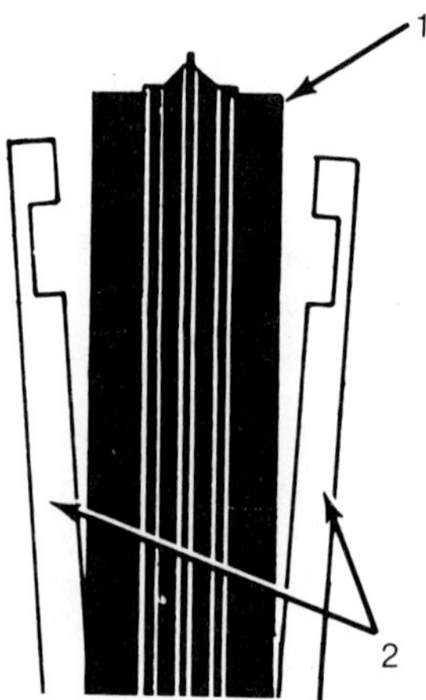


1. Filler
2. Steel strip

**Fig. 69.** Metal strips are inserted into rubber filler with notches inward, as shown here.

3. As short end of filler and retaining clip come together, apply firm but careful pressure on filler to let fingers of retaining clip ride over ridge and into recess. Fig. 70 shows correct installation.

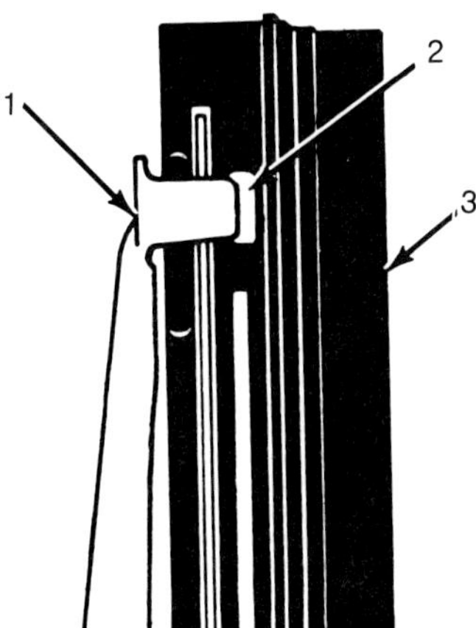


© 1972 VWoA—578

1. Retaining clip 2. Recess 3. Filler

**Fig. 70.** Recess in rubber filler must receive fingers of retaining clip for correct installation.

4. Re-install wiper blade (see **8.11 Removing and Installing Wiper Blades**) and test wiping action of new filler on the windshield.

## 8.14 Windshield Washing System

Pressing the push-button on the windshield wiper switch knob opens a valve to spray the windshield with water or other cleaning fluid. The spray from twin jets on the cowl just ahead of the windshield continues as long as the push-button is depressed or until the supply of cleaning fluid is exhausted.

The fluid is kept under pressure in a plastic container in the front luggage compartment, behind the spare wheel. The container has a capacity of about 1 quart (1 liter) in the 1966 and 1967 models (see Fig. 71). Equipped with a valve like the valve on a tire, the container can take enough compressed air to spray the entire contents on the windshield. On cars to July 1967 the pressure must not exceed 35 pounds per square inch (psi) or 2.5 kg/cm$^2$, but that pressure is sufficient to empty the container. The 1968 and 1969 models require 43 psi. There is an accessory high pressure hose available to connect the container to the spare tire.

**NOTE —**
Cars after August 1967 have a modified container. It is attached to the spare wheel through the bolt holes. Two plastic pegs hold it in place.

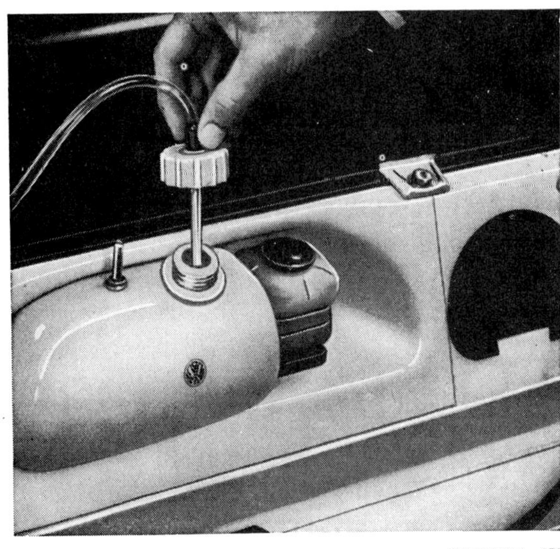

© 1972 VWoA—579

**Fig. 71.** Windshield washer has line leading from cap of container in luggage compartment to spray jet on cowl.

The accessory hose, which is colored black, has a valve, shown in Fig. 72. Use of this attachment has the following advantages:

1. The greater volume of air keeps pressure up.

© 1972 VWoA—580

**Fig. 72.** Modified washer system for windshield has pressure line connection to spare tire. Container and tire are pressurized together through valve insert (1). Valve (2) closes when pressure falls below 18 psi. Small valve (3) is closed for filling container. The 1968 and 1969 containers are attached to wheel.

10

The container can be filled with water or cleaning fluid several times before it is necessary to check air pressure.

2. Valve insert (1) in pressure hose (Fig. 72) is easy to get at for filling container and tire with air.
3. Spring-loaded valve (2) in hose closes connection between tire and container when tire pressure falls below 18 psi (1.3 kg/cm²).

When you are removing or attaching the pressure hose or refilling the container, close the small valve (3). The end of the hose marked "RES. RAD" is the one to attach to the tire valve. Make sure that spare tire is kept at 35 or 43 psi, depending on model of your car. If you do not use the accessory hose, have container pressure checked regularly. To leave room for an air cushion, fill container only to lower end of the small tube.

A mixture of VW windshield washer fluid and water in proportions recommended on label makes a better cleaning fluid than plain water. The alcohol solution removes insects from the windshield better and in winter resists freezing down to 10 degrees Fahrenheit.

**To remove and install spray jet:**

1. Remove instrument panel cover at back of luggage compartment.
2. Press jet with rubber seal upward out of cowl.
3. When installing make sure that rubber seal is properly seated.
4. Insert hardened needle in jet for a lever to turn jet. Adjust jet to spray symmetrical pattern of water on windshield.

## 9. HORN

When you press the horn half-ring on the steering wheel hub of your car, you are mechanically closing an electric circuit that connects the battery with a breaker mechanism and an electromagnet to produce vibration of a metal diaphragm. It is the frequency of this vibration that gives the horn its characteristic tone.

The breaker mechanism feeds current intermittently to the electromagnet, and the on/off action of the magnet vibrates the diaphragm by alternately flexing and relaxing the metal. The VW horn has a condenser or short circuit ring across the points of the breaker mechanism to reduce arcing and prolong the life of the points.

### Maintenance

If the horn is not working, look for worn or dirty points in the breaker mechanism or for a defective condenser. Water in the horn could also be the cause. Care should be taken to prevent damage to the bracket that holds the horn (see Fig. 73). The horn should not touch the car body. Contact will affect the vibration.

**To remove and install horn:**

1. Remove bolt (Fig. 73) holding the horn bracket under left front fender.

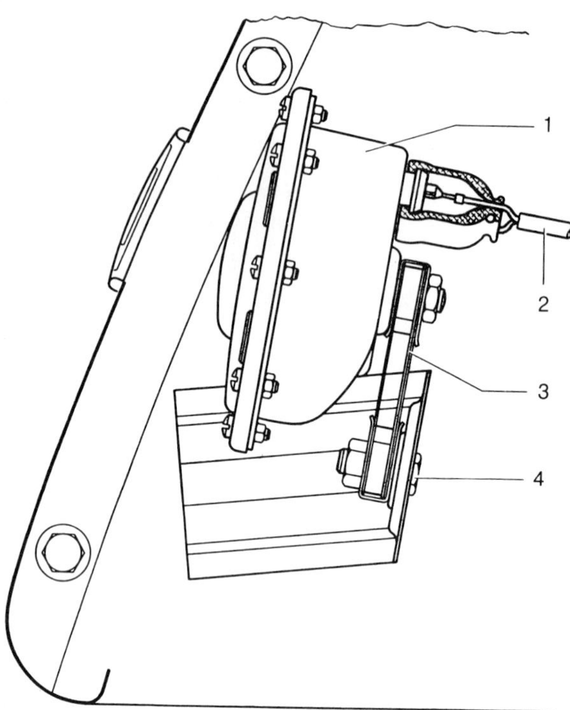


**Fig. 73.** Beetle horn and mounting are shown schematically here. Horn is at (1), cable at (2), bracket (3) and bolt (4).

2. Disconnect cable and remove horn.
3. When installing horn, make sure it does not touch the body at any point. Do not turn adjustment screw on the horn. A wrong adjustment here will seriously damage contact points of breaker mechanism.

If the horn gives trouble, look first for defects in the black-yellow cable running to the horn from the first fuse from the left in the fuse box. Then look at the cable running to ground by way of the horn lever (steering wheel half ring). Loose or corroded connections are often the cause of troubles in the horn system. The ground cable runs through the hollow steering column to the steering gear box at a terminal on the coupling disk. Another cable, colored brown, runs from horn to steering column.

Fig. 74 shows an exploded view of the horn ring.

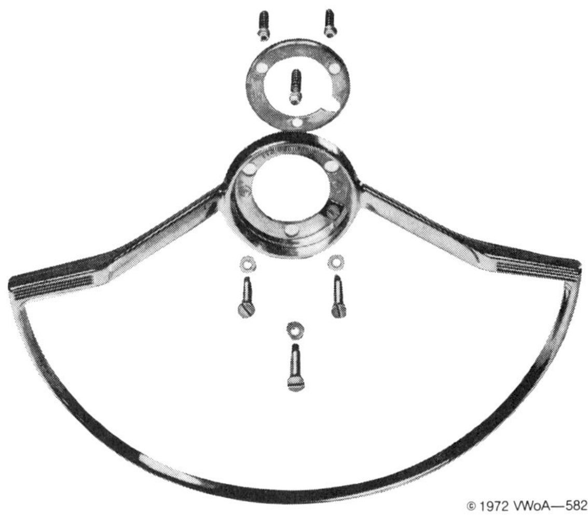



**Fig. 74.** Ring assembly is shown in exploded view.

**To remove and install ring:**

1. Remove horn fuse.
2. Remove horn ring cap.
3. Remove three screws and take off lever (Fig. 75).

Installation takes place in reverse order. Make sure that insulation, springs and contact plate are in correct positions.

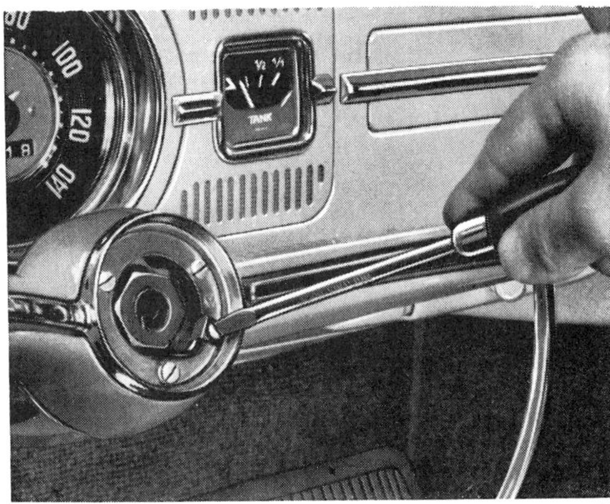




**Fig. 75.** Horn lever ring is held with three screws which are exposed by removing ring cap.

## 10. REPLACING FUSES

The fuse box, which has a transparent cover, is under the instrument panel near the steering column. From 1967 on, the cars covered in this Manual have been equipped with boxes holding 10 fuses, as in Fig. 76. The fuse box for the 1966 model has 8. (The 1968 cars also have 2 fuses on the fan housing in the engine compartment.) Symbols to help in identification of the various circuits are embossed on the box cover.

When a fuse burns out, it is not enough merely to replace it with a new one. The cause of the short circuit or overload must be found and corrected. Putting in a replacement then becomes the simple matter of taking off the fuse box cover, removing the old fuse and putting in a new one. It is advisable to keep a few spares (8 and 16 Amp) in the car.

***CAUTION*** —
*Do not patch up burned fuses with tin foil or wire. A current through such a connection can cause serious damage elsewhere in the electrical circuits.*

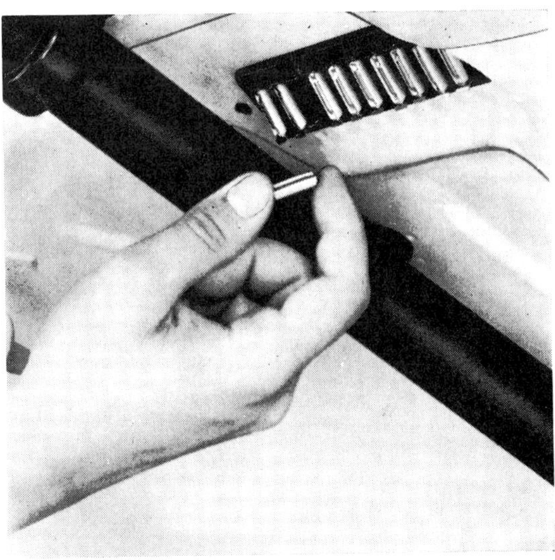



**Fig. 76.** Fuse box is shown with transparent cover off.

## 11. REAR WINDOW DEFOGGER

The 1969 sedan is equipped with a circuit for defogging the rear window. Wires bonded to the glass are the heating elements. A toggle switch under the instrument panel to the left of the ashtray actuates the defogger, and a green light in the speedometer signals that it is in operation. The defogger system should be kept on only long enough to clear the rear window.

**To remove defogger switch:**

1. Disconnect battery ground strap.

2. Remove instrument panel cover in luggage compartment.
3. Unscrew escutcheon, remove switch and disconnect wire.

The installation procedure is the reverse.

The relay for closing the rear window defogger circuit is under the rear seat.

**To remove relay:**

1. Disconnect battery ground strap.
2. Disconnect wires and take out relay.

When replacing the relay, check against the wiring diagram for the correct wiring connections and make sure that there is a good ground connection to the body.

**To remove heated rear window:**

1. Disconnect positive wire at its terminal, which is at left edge of window as you look toward rear of car. This wire is connected to relay under rear seat.
2. Disconnect ground wire at terminal at the right side of window (looking toward rear of the car) as shown in Fig. 77. This wire grounds at a sheet metal screw in side panel behind trim panel.

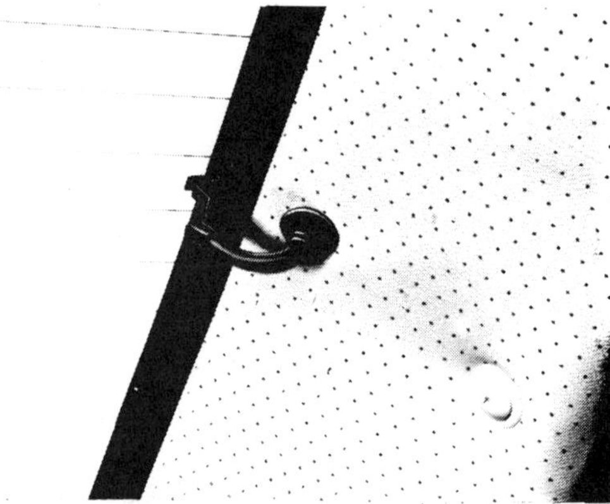



**Fig. 77.** Heated rear window has cable connections at either side. Terminal for ground, shown here, is at right when facing toward rear of car.

3. Take out window. While this operation is the same as removing an unheated window, it is not recommended for the do-it-yourselfer. Without special tools and previous experience, the risk of breaking the window is high.

Installation of the heated window is the reverse of the removal procedure.

## 12. IGNITION/STARTER SWITCH

The ignition/starter switch on the older cars covered in this Manual is on the instrument panel. Beginning with the 1968 model, the switch is incorporated into the housing for the steering wheel lock.

The switch has a mechanical non-repeat lock which prevents the starter pinion from making contact with the flywheel ring gear (see **2.3 Starter Motor**) when the engine is running. Once engine has started, operation of the starter cannot be repeated until the ignition has been switched first to "OFF" and then to "ON" again.

**To replace ignition/starter switch** (early version):

1. Disconnect battery ground strap.
2. Remove instrument panel cover in luggage compartment.
3. Disconnect cables at switch terminals.
4. Remove screw holding switch bracket.

Reverse order of procedure to install new switch.

**To replace new version:**

1. Disconnect battery ground strap.
2. Remove steering wheel, circlip and plastic bushing.
3. Loosen turn signal switch and remove two screws holding retainer plate (see arrow A in Fig. 78).
4. Insert ignition key in lock and turn slightly. Pull lock cylinder out until retaining spring shows through opening at arrow B, Fig. 78. Depress retaining spring with a piece of steel wire and, at the same time, pull lock cylinder out of its housing.

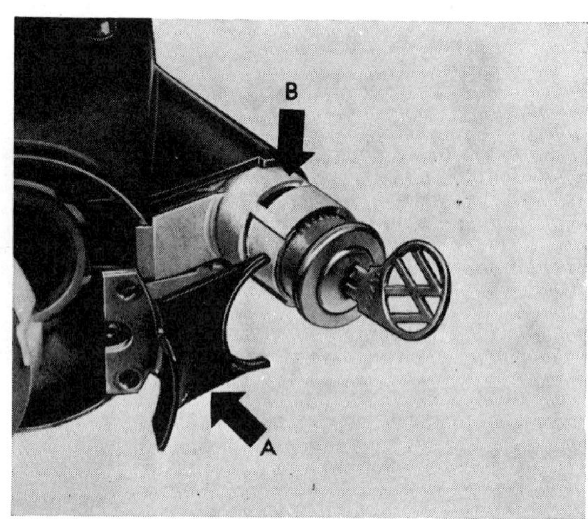




**Fig. 78.** Ignition/starter switch is removed after retainer plate (A) is freed and retainer spring is depressed through opening (B). See text.

When installing switch, be sure to push the lock cylinder in far enough for insertion of the retainer plate.

## 13. KARMANN GHIA ACCESSORIES

The horn and front turn signals on the Karmann Ghia models differ from those on the sedan and convertible. Other accessories may also show minor differences.

### 13.1 Horns

The Karmann Ghia models have a pair of matched horns in a recess in the spare wheel compartment. A rubber boot encloses the assembly and provides a seal. As in the other VW cars, the half ring on the steering wheel operates the horns by way of a relay.

#### Maintenance

Flexible mounting parts and rubber boot must be in good condition. Check from time to time for damage.

#### Removal and Installation

**To remove:**

1. Remove horn fuse (first from left) from fuse box.
2. Disconnect cable from terminal 87 at relay.
3. Loosen rubber boot in front panel.
4. Lift out spare wheel and disconnect cable at horns.
5. Remove securing bolts (see Fig. 79) and lift out horns with boot.

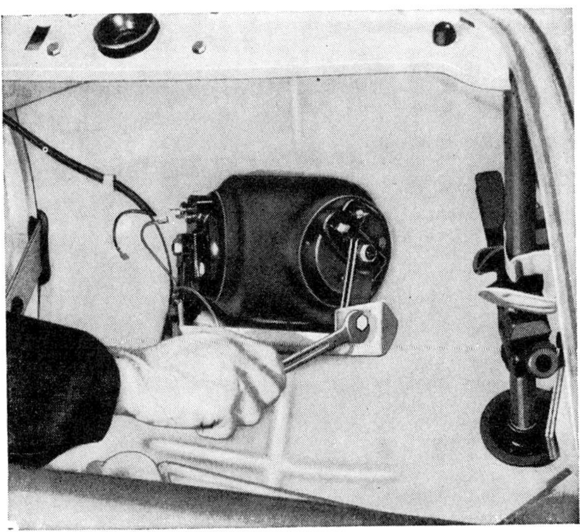

© 1972 VWoA—587

**Fig. 79.** Karmann Ghia horns are behind rubber boot in recess at front of spare wheel compartment.

6. Take horn out of boot.

When installing horns, make sure that ground connection is good, that rubber boot is correctly positioned and that horns are not in contact with the car body.

**To replace horn relay:**

1. Remove fuse from fuse box (first from left).
2. Disconnect the four cables from relay (see Fig. 80).

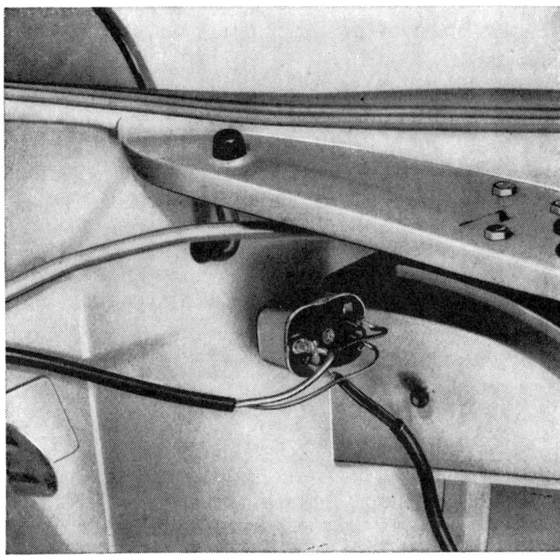

© 1972 VWoA—588

**Fig. 80.** Relay for horn in Karmann Ghia has four cable connections.

3. Lift relay from side panel mounting, as in Fig. 81.

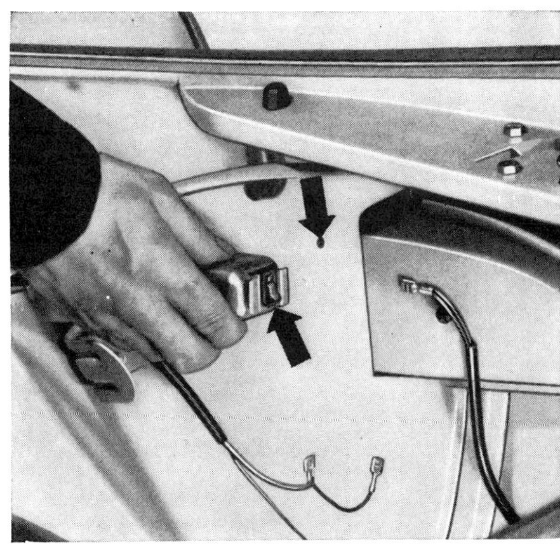

© 1972 VWoA—589

**Fig. 81.** Mounting stud on back of Karmann Ghia horn relay is indicated by lower black arrow. Upper arrow points to hole in side panel for the stud.

When installing, check cable connections against wiring diagram.

## 13.2 Turn Signal System

The front turn signal lights are mounted on the fenders below the headlights. The rear signals are in housing with brake and tail lights.

The correct bulbs are:

| | Standard Replacement | VW Part Number |
|---|---|---|
| **Front and Rear Bulbs** 6-volt | 1129 | N 17 731 1 |
| **Front Bulb** 12-volt | 1034 | N 17 738 2 |
| **Rear Bulb** 12-volt | 1073 | N 17 732 2 |

**To replace front bulb:**

1. Remove two securing screws visible in Fig. 82.

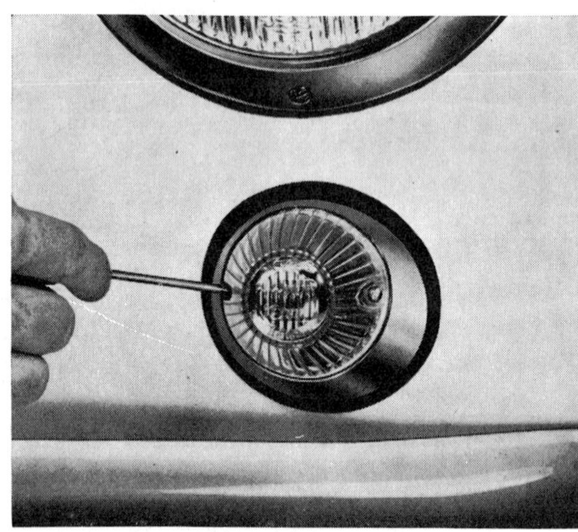



**Fig. 82.** Turn signal on Karmann Ghia is mounted below headlight. Two screws hold chrome ring and lens.

2. Take off chrome ring (bezel) and lens.
3. Put in new bulb.

Installation is the reverse of removal. Check seating of gasket between bezel and lens and gasket between lens and bulb holder.

**To replace bulb holder:**

1. Remove two screws and take off bezel with lens.
2. Take off two nuts under fender and remove bulb holder (see Fig. 83).

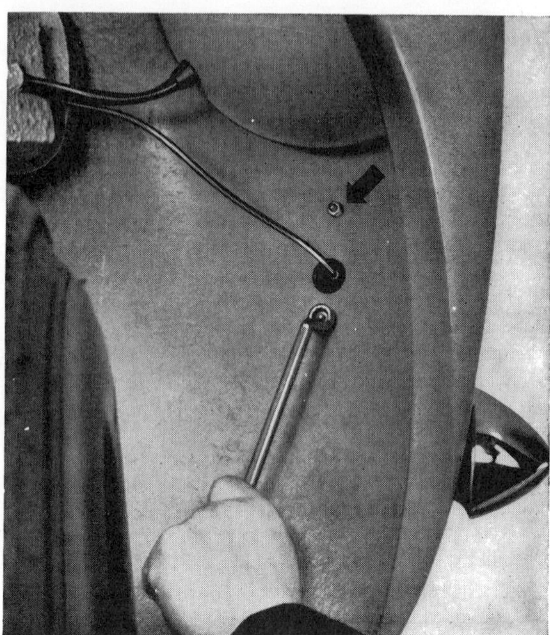



**Fig. 83.** Securing nuts for turn signal bulb holder on Karmann Ghia are under front fender.

When installing, check gasket between bulb holder and fender seal (see Fig. 84).

**Fig. 84.** Bulb holder of Karmann Ghia front turn signal pulls out of housing in fender.

## 14. INSTRUMENTS
(sedan and convertible)

Only new instruments with modifications or revisions will be available as replacement parts. Though the means of attachment may differ in these new instruments, the procedures for installation will be the same as for the original instruments on the various car models.

### 14.1 Speedometer

A flexible cable from the left front wheel drives the speedometer and odometer (mileage recorder).

The speedometer incorporates the components shown in Fig. 85 and works on magnetic induction (see **5. Generator**). The cable drive shaft, which is turning at a rotational speed proportional to car road speed, spins

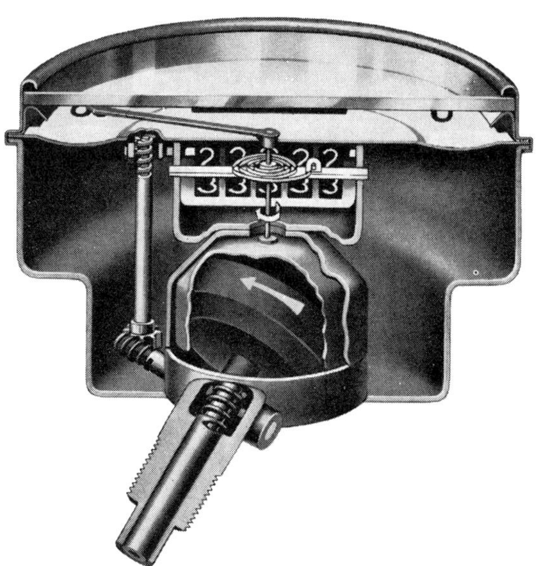

© 1972 VWoA—593

**Fig. 85.** Cutaway view of speedometer shows permanent magnet on flexible cable, freely rotating aluminum cup, braking hairspring and pointer arm. Arrow shows direction of magnet spin. See text.

the permanent magnet. Lines of force in the magnetic field of the spinning permanent magnet induce electric currents in the freely rotating aluminum cup. Interaction of those currents and the field sets up a torque (called "magnetic drag") that turns the cup in the same direction as the magnet.

A shaft attached to the aluminum cup turns with the cup against the braking force of a control hairspring. This shaft carries the speedometer needle. When the shaft on the cup turns, the needle deflects and points to a speed reading on the speedometer dial. The faster the magnet rotates, the greater the torque, which translates into greater deflection of the needle. Since the field of the magnet, which is a permanent magnet, is of unchanging strength, any change in torque on the aluminum cup must be a change caused by car speed alone. Calibration of the rpm of the flexible cable and of the braking action of the hairspring on the aluminum cup produces an accurate gauge of the road speed of the car.

The hairspring helps to return the speed indicator to zero when the car is stopped. The cable shaft, besides spinning the magnet, also operates a triple worm mechanism which turns the five numeral wheels registering car mileage.

#### Removing and Installing Speedometer

***CAUTION—***
*Disconnect battery ground strap.*

**To remove:**

1. Remove instrument panel cover in luggage compartment.
2. Remove warning bulbs and instrument light.
3. Release knurled nut and pull off cable.
4. Remove the two slotted screws that attach speedometer to instrument panel (see Fig. 86).
5. Remove speedometer from instrument panel.

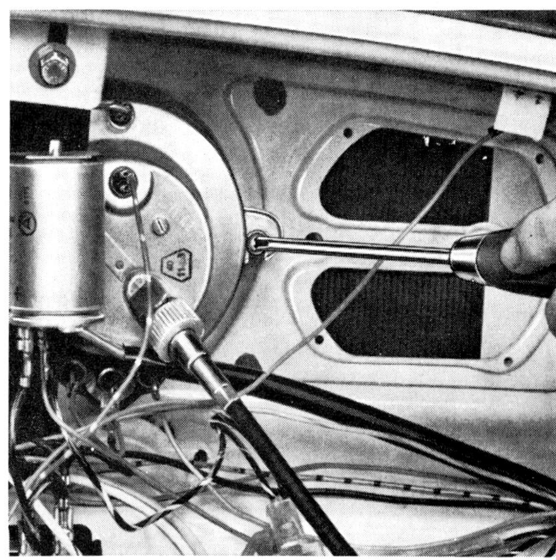

© 1972 VWoA 594

**Fig. 86.** Speedometer installation is shown here. Before screws are tightened, position of speedometer should be checked from driver's seat.

**To install:** Follow removal procedure in reverse order. Before tightening slotted screws, adjust position of speedometer to bring figures on the face upright.

10

## Speedometer with Fuel Gauge

Sedans and convertibles from the 1968 models on have a speedometer with built-in fuel gauge (see Fig. 87). A speedometer with an additional warning light is available for cars with Automatic Stick Shift transmission. (The warning light signals overheating of torque converter fluid.) This modification applies also to Karmann Ghia models with Automatic Stick Shift.

**Fig. 87.** Electric fuel gauge has dial on speedometer face.

***CAUTION*** —
*Disconnect battery ground strap to prevent short circuit.*

**To remove and install new speedometer:**

1. Remove instrument panel cover in luggage compartment.
2. Detach headlight dimmer relay for easier access to warning light connections.
3. Disconnect warning light connections.
4. Remove left fresh air hose.
5. Remove the securing screws and take out the speedometer.

Installation is the reverse procedure.

## Operation of Electric Fuel Gauge

A bimetal vibrator (voltage regulator) holds the gauge under continuous even voltage while ignition is on. The sending unit for the gauge is a rheostat operated by the fuel tank float. As the fuel level in the tank rises or falls, the rheostat varies the resistance in the gauge circuit. Since the voltage remains constant, variation of resistance varies the amount of current flowing through a resistance coil wound around a bimetal arm coupled to the gauge needle. As the arm bends under the varying heat from the varying current, it moves the needle across the gauge dial against the braking action of a spring. Thus, needle movement on the fuel gauge depends on current in the coil, which depends on the level of fuel in the tank.

## Testing Electric Fuel Gauge

All tests of fuel gauge functioning can be carried out with gauge in place.

**NOTE** —
For removal and replacement of electrical sending unit, see **14.2 Mechanical Fuel Gauge.**

**To check vibrator:**

1. Switch on ignition.
2. Connect voltmeter as shown in Fig. 88. If vibrator is not defective, voltmeter will give reading of pulsating voltage. If it does not, replace vibrator.

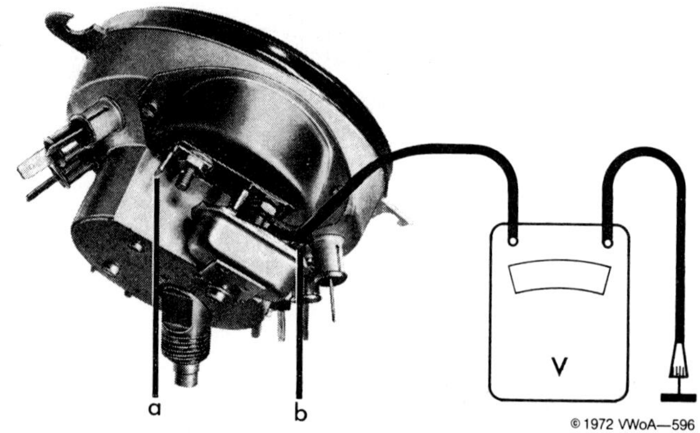




**Fig. 88.** Fuel gauge vibrator is tested with this hook-up. Cable from sending unit in fuel tank is connected at (a). Terminal 15 is at (b). Other lead from voltmeter is to ground. See text.

**To check gauge:**

1. Check vibrator (see above) for functioning and then proceed with this test.
2. Switch on ignition.
3. Detach sending unit cable from gauge.
4. Connect the gauge terminal briefly with ground.

If gauge gives no reading when grounded, it is defective and must be replaced. If the needle does move when gauge is grounded, any defect in the system must be in the cable from the sending unit or in the sending unit itself.

The gauge and vibrator can be replaced after speedometer has been removed from the instrument panel.

### Removing and Installing Speedometer Cable

**To remove:**

1. Loosen knurled nut at speedometer.
2. Remove hub cap from left front wheel.
3. Remove cotter pin or circlip in square end of cable at the dust cap (see Fig. 89).

© 1972 VWoA—597

**Fig. 89.** Speedometer cable is attached at stub axle of left front wheel and held with cotter pin at dust cap.

4. Pull cable out of stub axle.
5. Pull cable out of the guide channel and grommet on car body.

**To install:**

1. Be careful not to kink cable or strain it.
2. Pull cable through grommet in front panel, being careful to seat grommet properly.
3. Attach cable with clips.
4. Insert square drive piece correctly in the speedometer head.
5. Put new rubber sleeve in steering knuckle.
6. Insert new cotter pin at dust cap.
7. Seal end of cable with sealing compound.

**_CAUTION_ —**
*Care must be exercised to route the cable correctly.*

For silent operation free of oscillations, the cable must be routed to eliminate sharp bends of radius less than 6 inches (150 mm). When car wheels are in straight-ahead position, the cable should hang in a smooth curve. It should not kink or pull in any wheel position.

Crushing of the metal casing of the cable will cause needle flicker. A kink anywhere will lead quickly to breakage. Proper seating of the rubber seal in the steering knuckle (see Fig. 90) is important because water in the knuckle would lead to damage of bearings and freezing of the cable in winter. Use only cold-resistant, water-repellant oil and grease to lubricate cable.

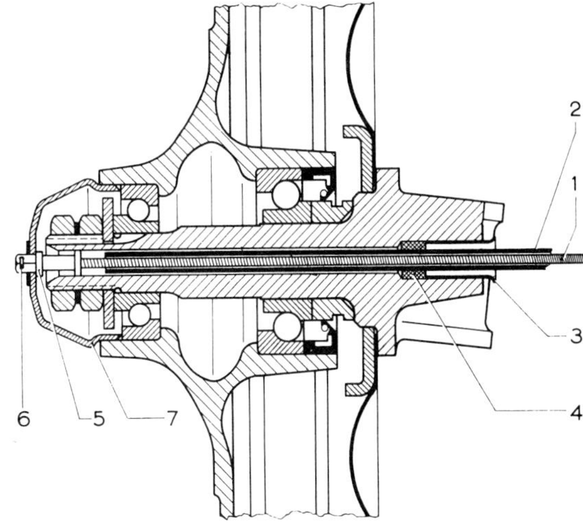


© 1972 VWoA—598

1. Cable
2. Plastic sheath
3. Metal sleeve
4. Rubber sleeve
5. Square drive end
6. Cotter pin
7. Dust cap with square hole

**Fig. 90.** Flexible cable attachment at left front wheel is shown in cross-section.

## 14.2 Mechanical Fuel Gauge (VW 1300 only)

By means of a mechanical linkage and cable, the sending unit transmits movement of the fuel tank float to the gauge in the instrument panel to show the amount of fuel in the tank. When the needle of the gauge is on "R" (reserve), about 1.3 U.S. gallons (5 liters) remain in the tank.

## Removing and Installing Sending Unit

The tank components (including sending unit) of the mechanical fuel gauge are illustrated in Fig. 91.

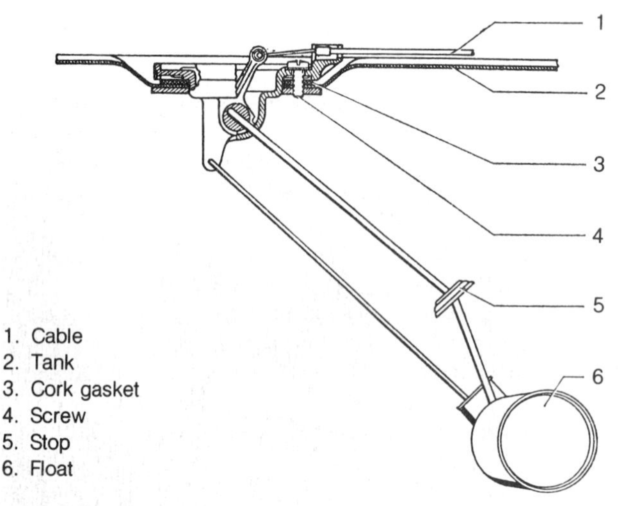


**Fig. 91.** Mechanical fuel gauge operates by linkage shown in this diagram. Movement of float (6) operates lever that pulls on cable (1).

**To remove sending unit:**

1. To avoid spilling fuel when sending unit is removed, make sure that tank is not full to filler neck.
2. Take spare wheel, jack and tools out of front luggage compartment. Remove compartment lining.

> ***WARNING —***
> *Disconnect battery against danger of sparking from a short circuit. Keep fire extinguisher handy. When using a screwdriver or any steel tool, be careful not to strike a spark.*

3. Take off cover of sending unit (see Fig. 92).
4. Disconnect cable or wire running to fuel gauge.
5. Remove securing screws and take out the sending unit and gasket.

**To install:**

1. Replace old washers that were under securing screws and the old gasket that was between sending unit and fuel tank.
2. Install sending unit by following steps of removal procedure in reverse order.
3. Adjust gauge.

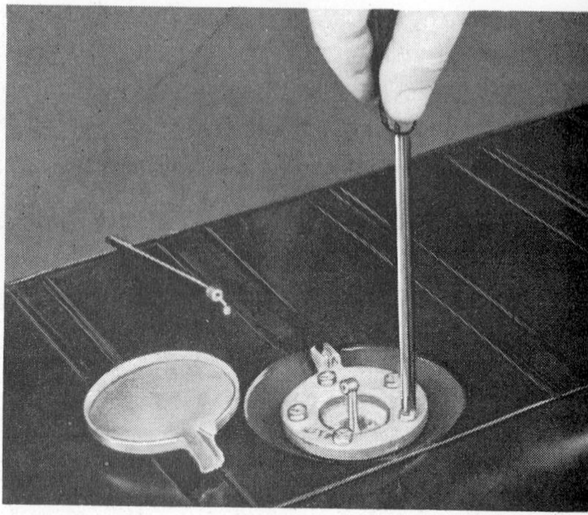


**Fig. 92.** Operating lever of mechanical fuel gauge is shown here with sending unit cover removed.

## Removing, Installing and Adjusting Mechanical Fuel Gauge

**To remove:**

1. Take out luggage compartment lining.
2. Remove cover of sending unit.
3. Disconnect cable to gauge.
4. Pull cable from under the felt pad on floor of luggage compartment.
5. Take light bulb out of gauge.
6. Remove knurled nut and take off gauge bracket.
7. From driver's seat, take gauge out of instrument panel.

**To install:**

1. Follow removal procedure in reverse, routing cable under felt pad in luggage compartment.

**To adjust:**

1. Take off cover of sending unit to expose lever to which gauge cable is attached.
2. Press lever to rear to force fuel tank float to its lowest position.
3. Keeping lever depressed, adjust gauge by turning knurled screw on gauge (Fig. 93) in clockwise direction (indicated by arrow in Fig. 94) until gauge needle is on stop at low end of its scale.
4. Press sending unit cover back in place.

Further calibration is unnecessary. By this adjustment at least 1.3 U.S. gallons (5 liters) will be in the tank when needle points to reserve mark. Slight inaccuracy in the upper range of gauge is not important.

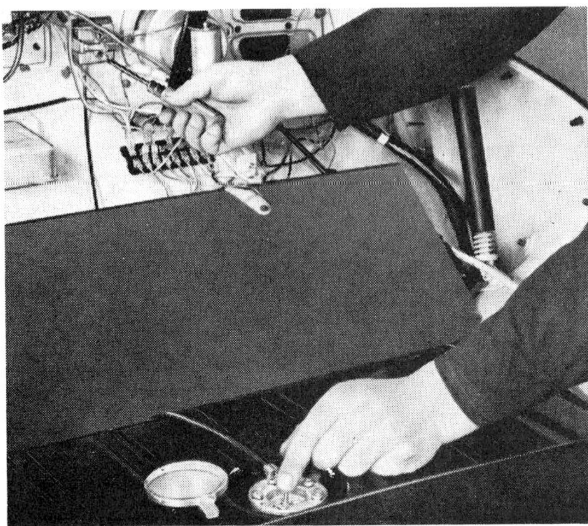

© 1972 VWoA—601

**Fig. 93.** Sending unit lever (at forefinger of left hand) is depressed to rear while screwdriver turns knurled screw for gauge adjustment.

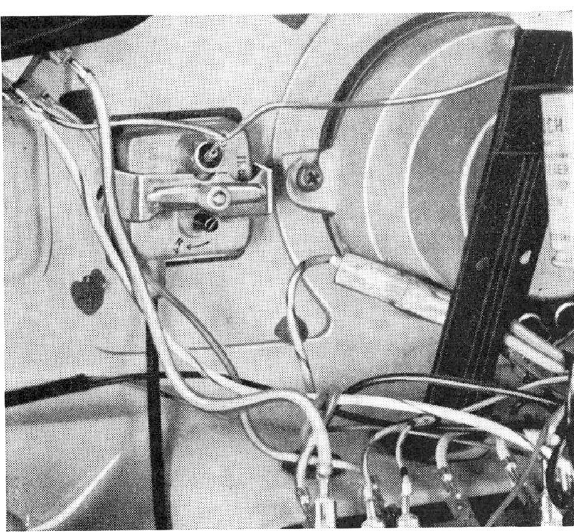

© 1972 VWoA—602

**Fig. 94.** Knurled screw is turned in direction indicated by the small arrow for adjustment of the mechanical fuel gauge.

## 14.3 Karmann Ghia Instruments

The Karmann Ghia models have a speedometer and electric fuel gauge that are somewhat different from the sedan instruments. Karmann Ghias also have a clock.

### Clock

The electrically-driven clock is on the instrument panel at right of speedometer. The clock is set by pushing in the knob at center of dial and turning it to correct time. The clock light comes on automatically when car lights are switched on.

**To remove:**

1. Remove instrument panel cover (rear of the front luggage compartment).
2. Pull out the two bulbs and disconnect supply cable.
3. Remove the two attaching screws (see Fig. 95).

© 1972 VWoA—603

**Fig. 95.** Karmann Ghia clock has cable connections shown here. Black arrows point to fastening screws.

4. Take clock out of instrument panel.

**To install:**

1. Insert clock in opening in back of instrument panel. Before tightening attaching screws, make sure clock is in correct position.
2. In reverse order, follow the remaining steps of removal procedure.

### Speedometer

From the 1967 model on, Karmann Ghias have a modified speedometer light and smaller warning lights, (Fig. 96) which are held in a plastic retainer in the speedometer.

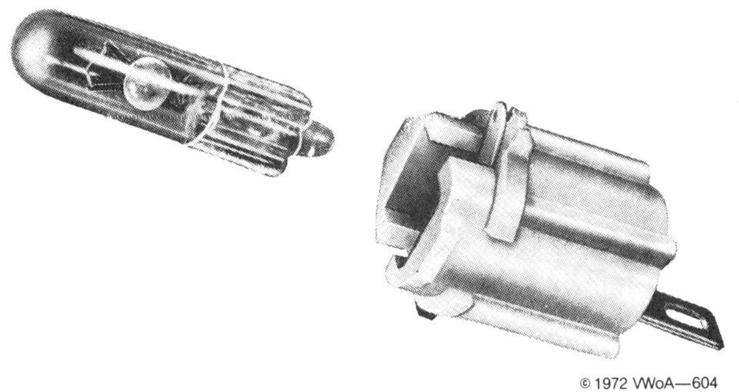

© 1972 VWoA—604

**Fig. 96.** Warning light retainer in post-1967 Karmann Ghia speedometer is shown here with light bulb.

10

Cable shoes 0.110 inch (2.8 mm) wide connect cables to tabs on the warning light retainers (see Fig. 97). These shoes, which can be installed with AMP pliers, are available as replacement part 141 971 945.

**Fig. 97.** Warning light connections on back of post-1967 Karmann Ghia speedometer are made with cable shoes shown here.

**To assemble speedometer:**

1. Steering wheel must be removed and turn signal switch detached before speedometer is removed.
2. To remove warning lights, turn retainer 90 degrees to the left and take it off, using needle pliers if required. Then pull out warning light. Reverse sequence for installation.

## 15. ELECTRICAL SYSTEM TECHNICAL DATA

### I. General data

| | |
|---|---|
| Generator | Technical data and test figures given in text |
| Starter | |
| Distributor | Details of distributor interchangeability given in **Engine** section |
| Dwell angle | Battery ignition 44-50° |
| Firing order | 1—4—3—2 |

**Spark plugs**

| Type | Heat value | Thread | Electrode gap battery |
|---|---|---|---|
| Bosch W 145 T1<br>Beru 145/14 | 145 | 14 mm | 0.7<br>(.028) |

### II. Batteries

**a-Standard equipment**

| Type | 1 |
|---|---|
| from Chassis No. 116 000 001 | 6 v/66 Ah |
| from Chassis No. 117 000 001 | 12 v/36 Ah |

**b- Checking battery**

Level of electrolyte over the plates and separators 5 mm

If electrolyte level indicators are installed, top acid up to level shown.

Cell voltage (measured with a cell tester):
Charged: 2.0 volts
Discharged: 1.6 volts
or total voltage measured under load:
Cell voltage x number cells

The difference in voltage between the cells must not exceed 0.2 volts

| State of charge | Normal Specific gravity | Acid freezes at | Tropical Specific gravity |
|---|---|---|---|
| Discharged | 1.12 | -11°C/12.2°F | 1.08 |
| Half charged | 1.20 | -27°C/-16.6°F | 1.16 |
| Fully charged | 1.285 | -68°C/-90.0°F | 1.23 |

| | Sedan and Convertible | Karmann Ghia Models |
|---|---|---|
| Ratio, crankshaft-generator | approx. 1:18 | approx. 1:1.8 |

| | All models |
|---|---|
| Turn indicator | Flashing type. Self-cancelling lever on the steering column |
| Instrument lights | Rheostat-controlled |
| Windshield wipers | Electric, with two arms and self-parking |
| Windshield washer | Pneumatically-operated by button in windshield wiper switch. Transparent water container under the front hood |
| Capacity | Approximately 1 quart |
| Pressure | Max. 35 psi (2.5 kg/cm²) |
| Fuses | 8 point fuse box below the instrument panel to the right of the steering column |